National

Road Maps & Town Plans- Great Britain

George Philip & Son Limited

Contents

Key Map   **1**

Sectional Maps of Great Britain   **2-64**
General Scale 5 miles = 1 inch

Sectional Maps of Approaches to London   **65-72**
Scale ¾ inch = 1 mile

Sectional Maps of London   **73-80**
Scale 2 inches = 1 mile

Sectional Maps of Central London   **81-88**
Scale 5 inches = 1 mile

Town Plans   **89-120**
See Contents List on page 89

Index to Sectional Maps of Great Britain   **1-48**

**Index to Sectional Maps of London
and Approaches to London**   **49-72**

ISBN O 540 05277 9

© 1975 George Philip & Son Ltd.

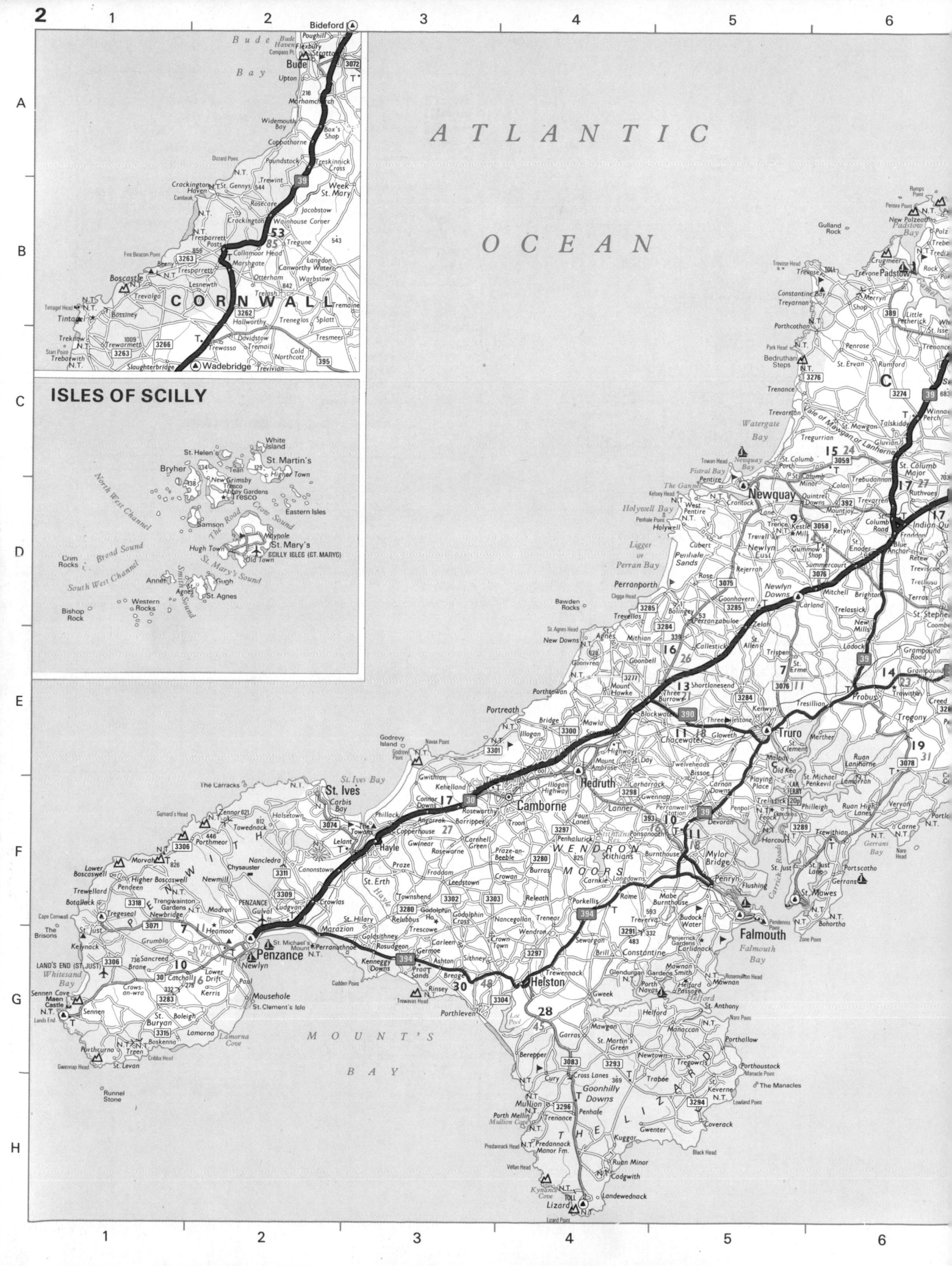

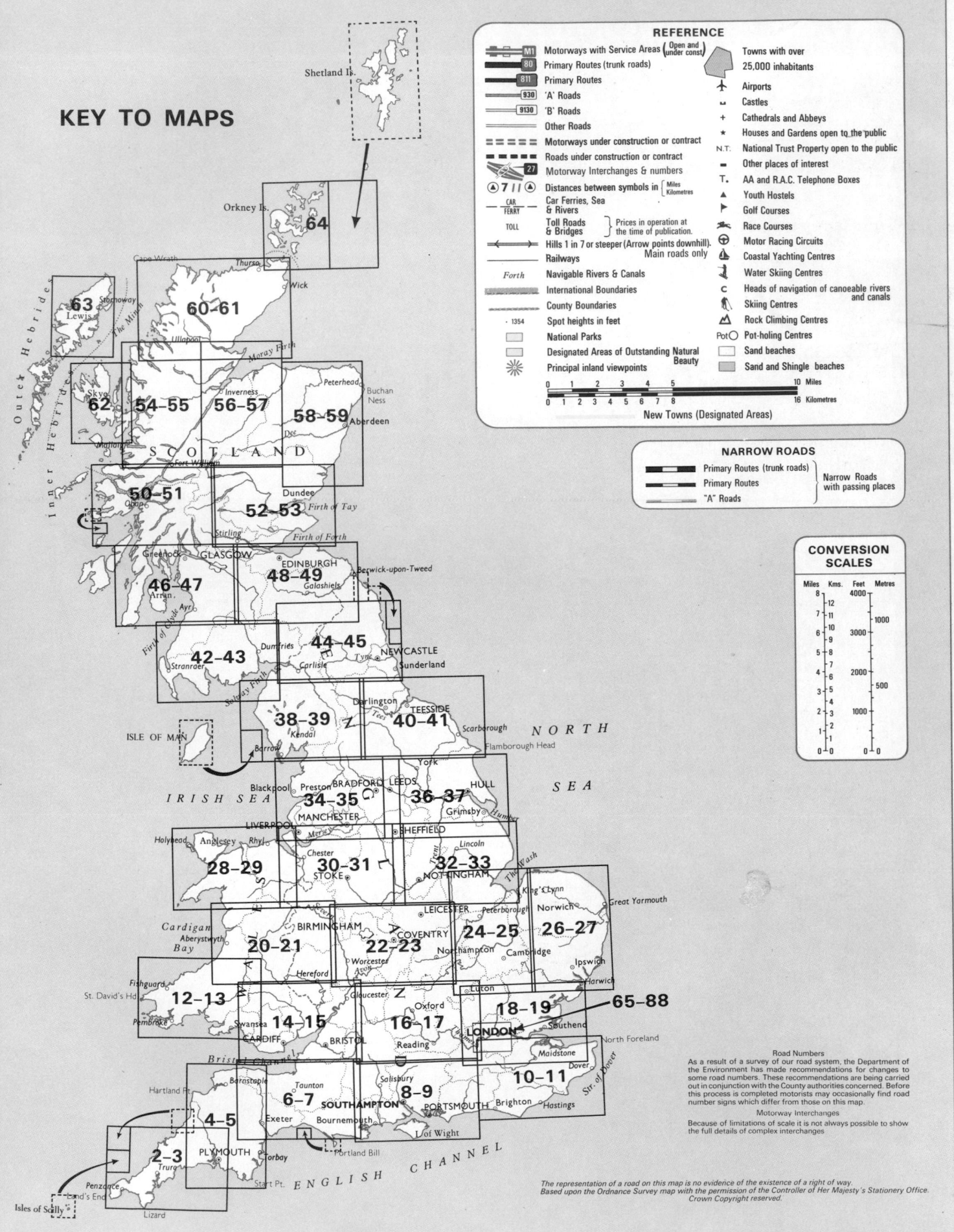

1

KEY TO MAPS

Shetland Is.

Orkney Is. **64**

Cape Wrath
Thurso
Wick

63
Stornoway
Lewis

60-61

Ullapool

62
Skye
Inverness

54-55   **56-57**

Peterhead
Buchan
Ness

58-59
Aberdeen

Dee

S C O T L A N D

Fort William

Moray Firth

50-51
Oban

Dundee

52-53
Firth of Tay

Stirling
Firth of Forth

GLASGOW
Greenock
EDINBURGH
Berwick-upon-Tweed

46-47
Arran
Ayr

48-49
Galashiels

Firth of Clyde

42-43
Stranraer

Dumfries

44-45
Carlisle

NEWCASTLE
Tyne
Sunderland

ISLE OF MAN

Barrow

Darlington
Tees

38-39
Kendal

40-41
TEESSIDE

Scarborough
N O R T H
Flamborough Head

York

I R I S H   S E A

Blackpool Preston BRADFORD LEEDS HULL
Grimsby Humber

34-35
MANCHESTER

36-37

S E A

LIVERPOOL
Mersey
SHEFFIELD

Holyhead Anglesey Rhyl
Chester
Lincoln

28-29

30-31
STOKE

Trent

32-33
NOTTINGHAM

The Wash
King's Lynn

Great Yarmouth

Cardigan
Bay
Aberystwyth

BIRMINGHAM

LEICESTER Peterborough Norwich

COVENTRY

20-21

22-23

24-25

26-27

Northampton
Cambridge
Ipswich

Worcester
Avon
Hereford

Fishguard
St. David's Hd

12-13

Luton

Harwich

Gloucester

Oxford

18-19

65-88

Pembroke

Swansea

14-15

16-17

LONDON
Southend

CARDIFF
BRISTOL
Reading

Maidstone

North Foreland

Bristol Channel

Salisbury

10-11
Brighton
Dover
Str. of Dover

Barnstaple

8-9
PORTSMOUTH

Hartland Pt

Taunton

6-7
SOUTHAMPTON

Hastings

Exeter
Bournemouth

I. of Wight

4-5

Portland Bill

2-3
PLYMOUTH
Truro
Torbay

Start Pt.

Penzance

E N G L I S H   C H A N N E L

Land's End

Isles of Scilly

Lizard

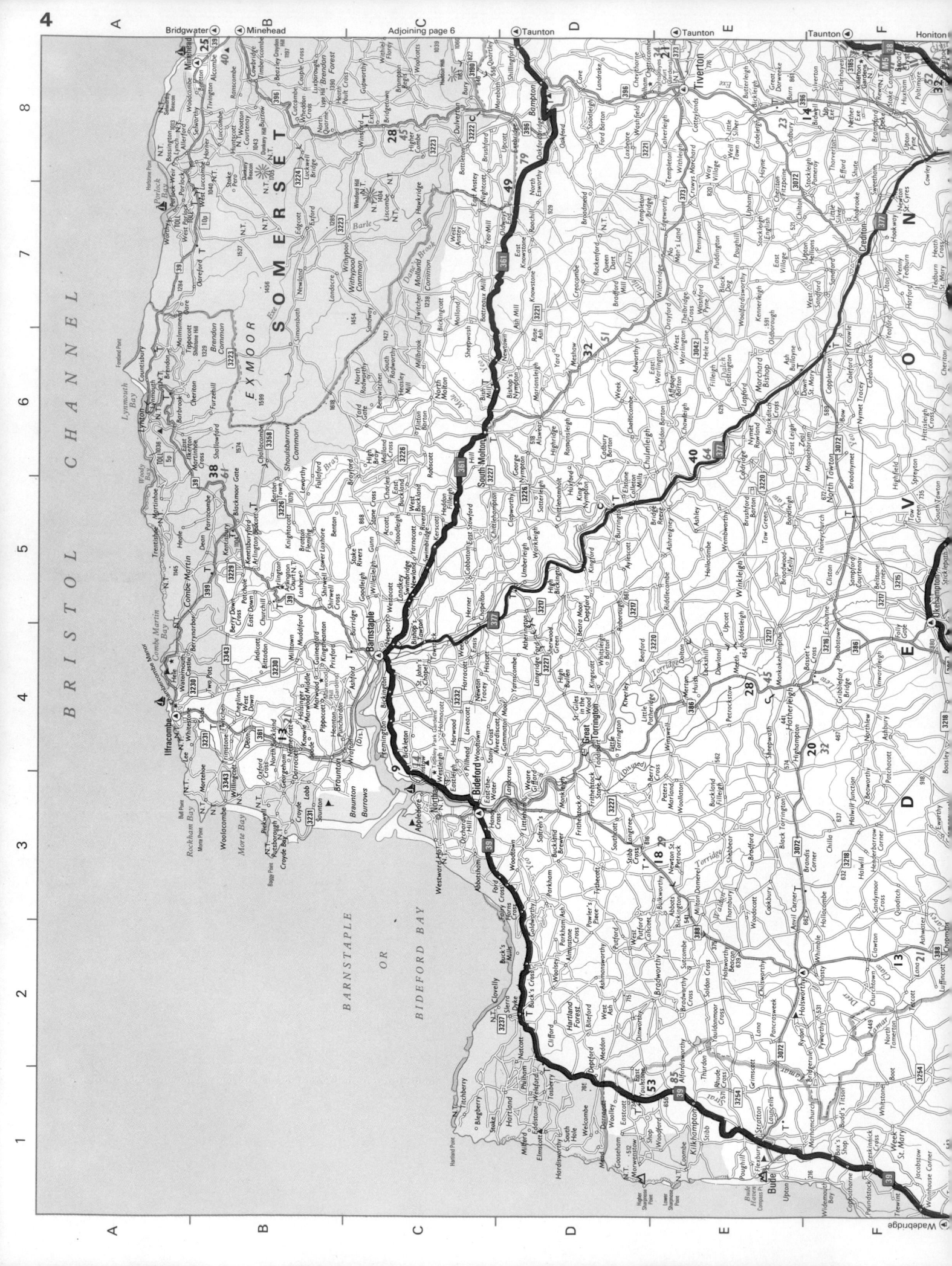

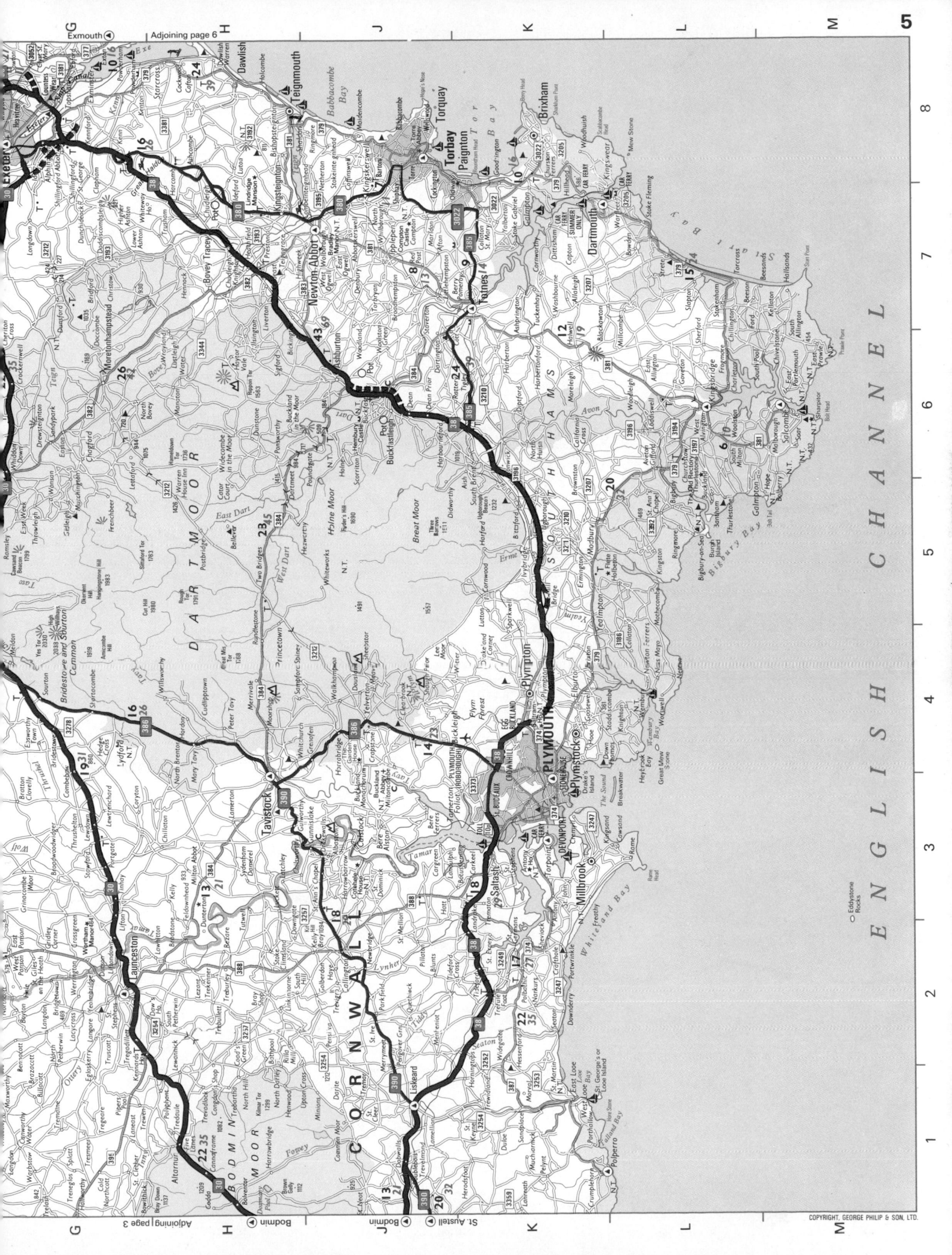

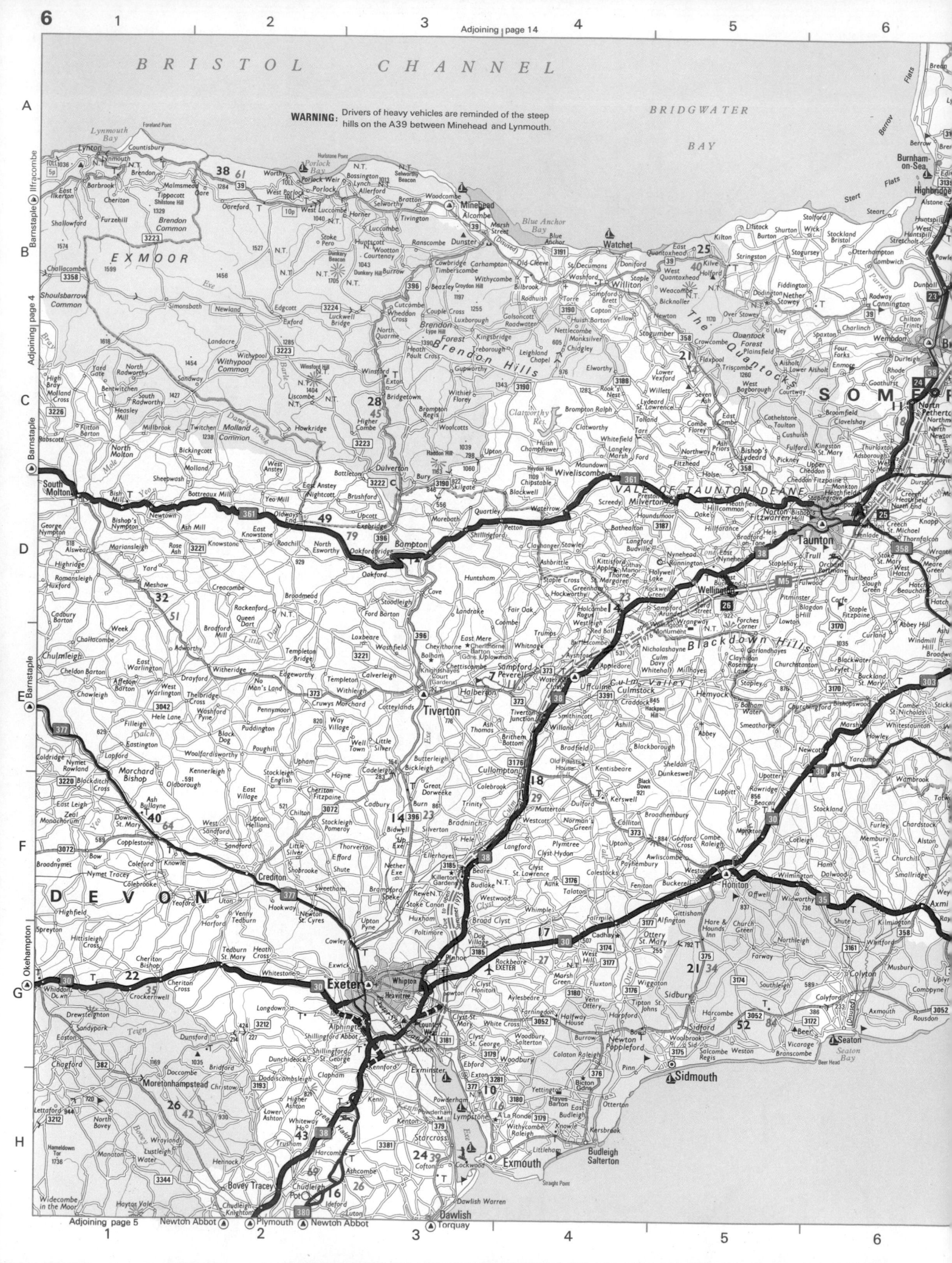

6

WARNING: Drivers of heavy vehicles are reminded of the steep
hills on the A39 between Minehead and Lynmouth.

BRISTOL CHANNEL

BRIDGWATER
BAY

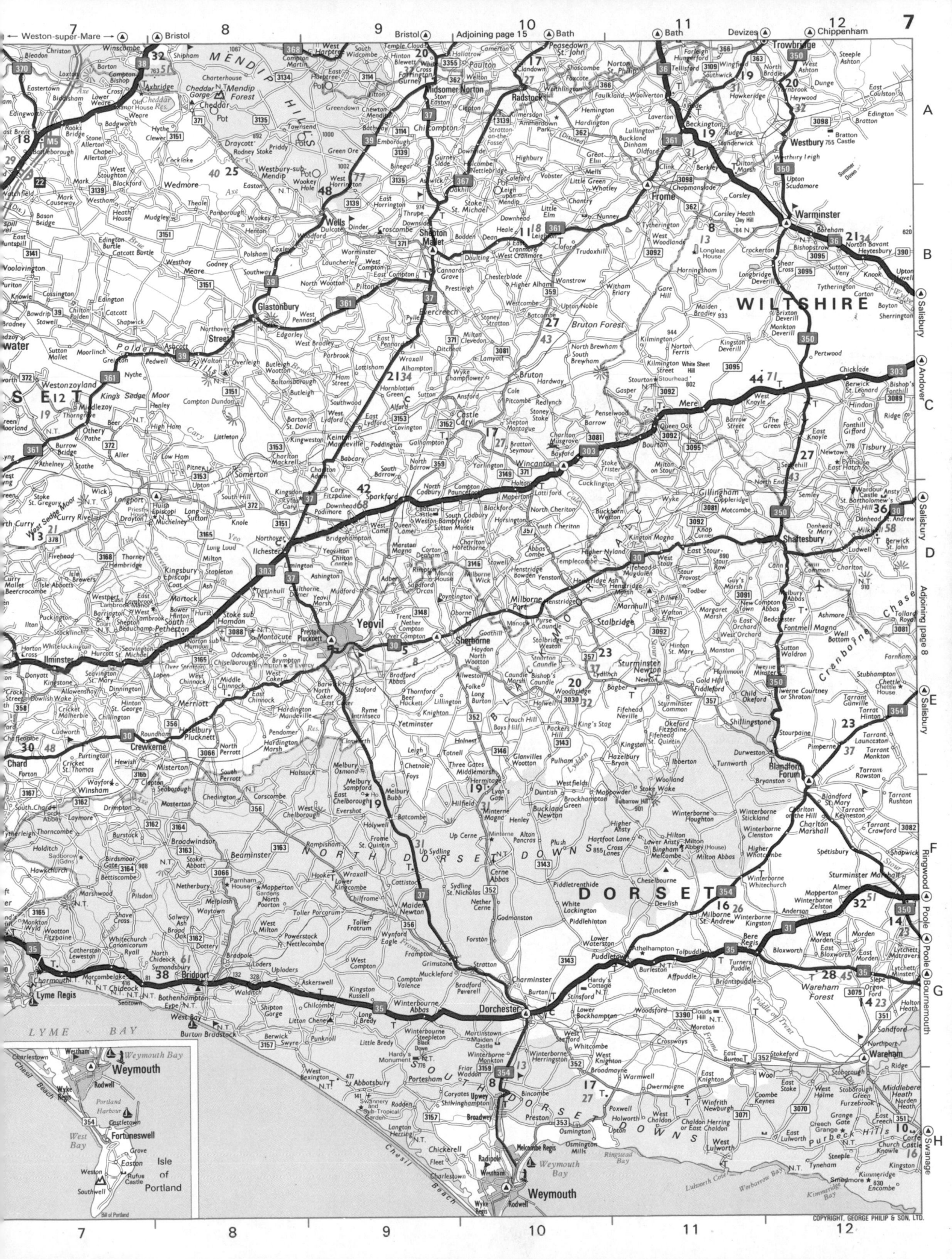

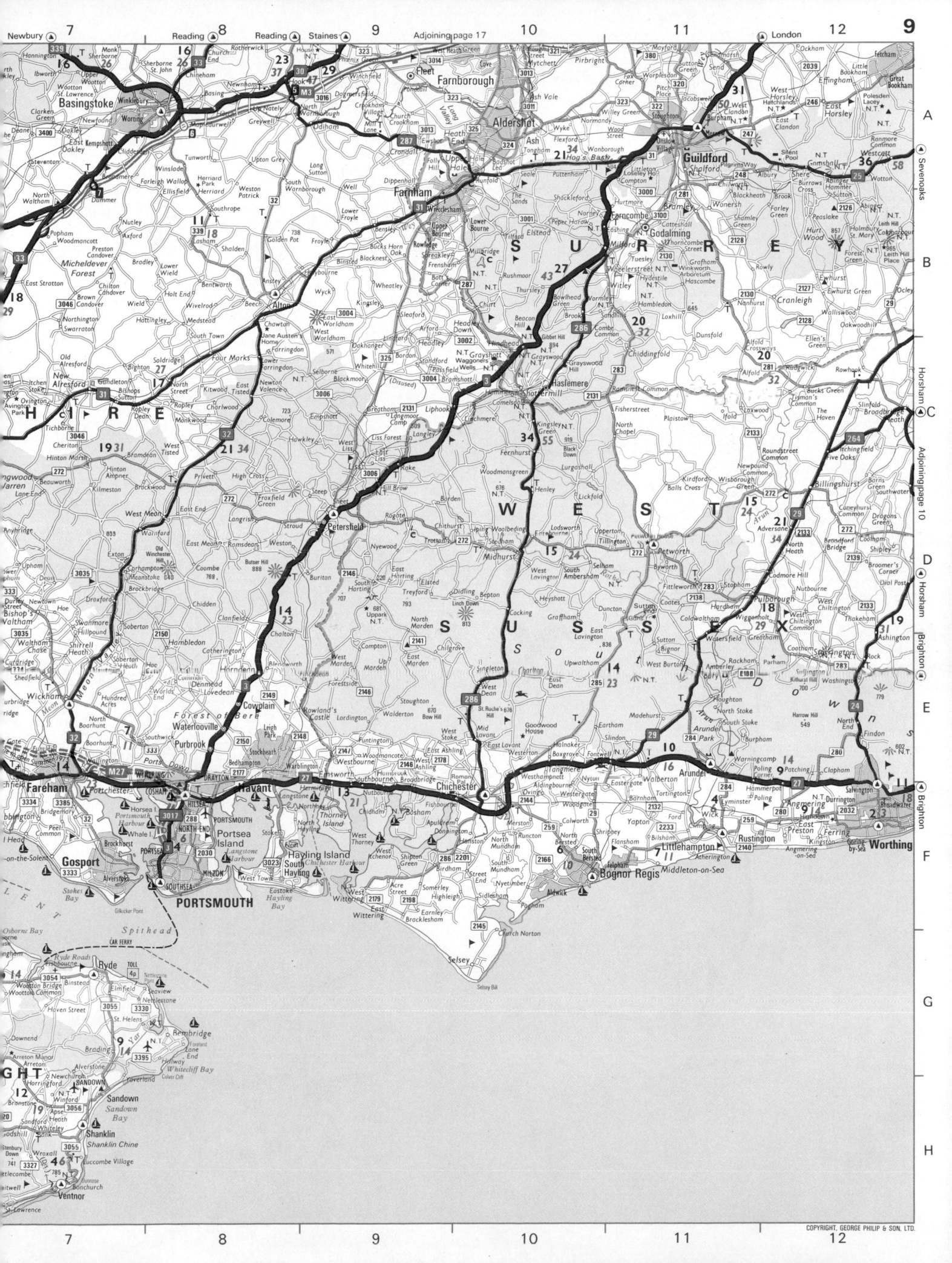

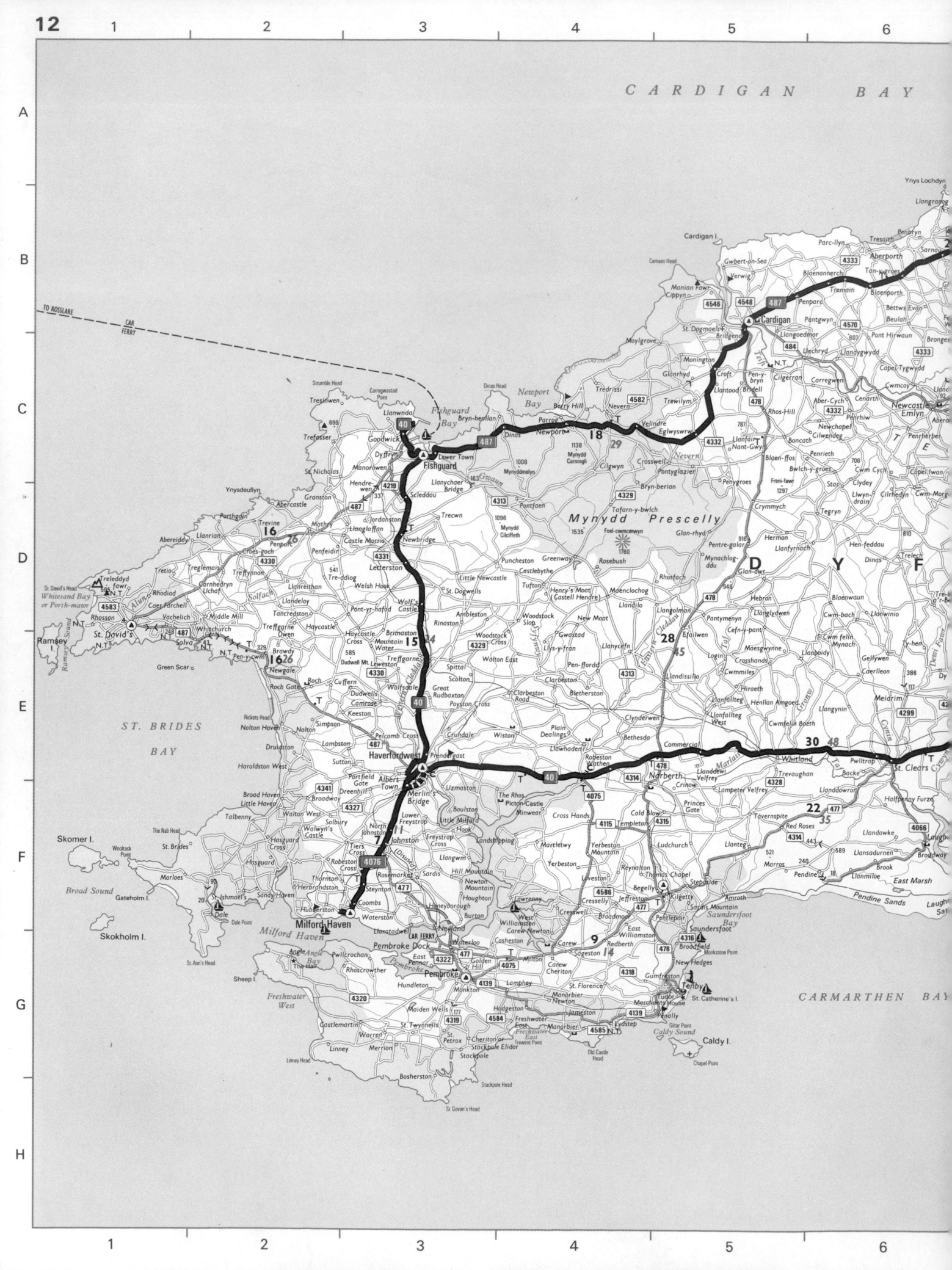

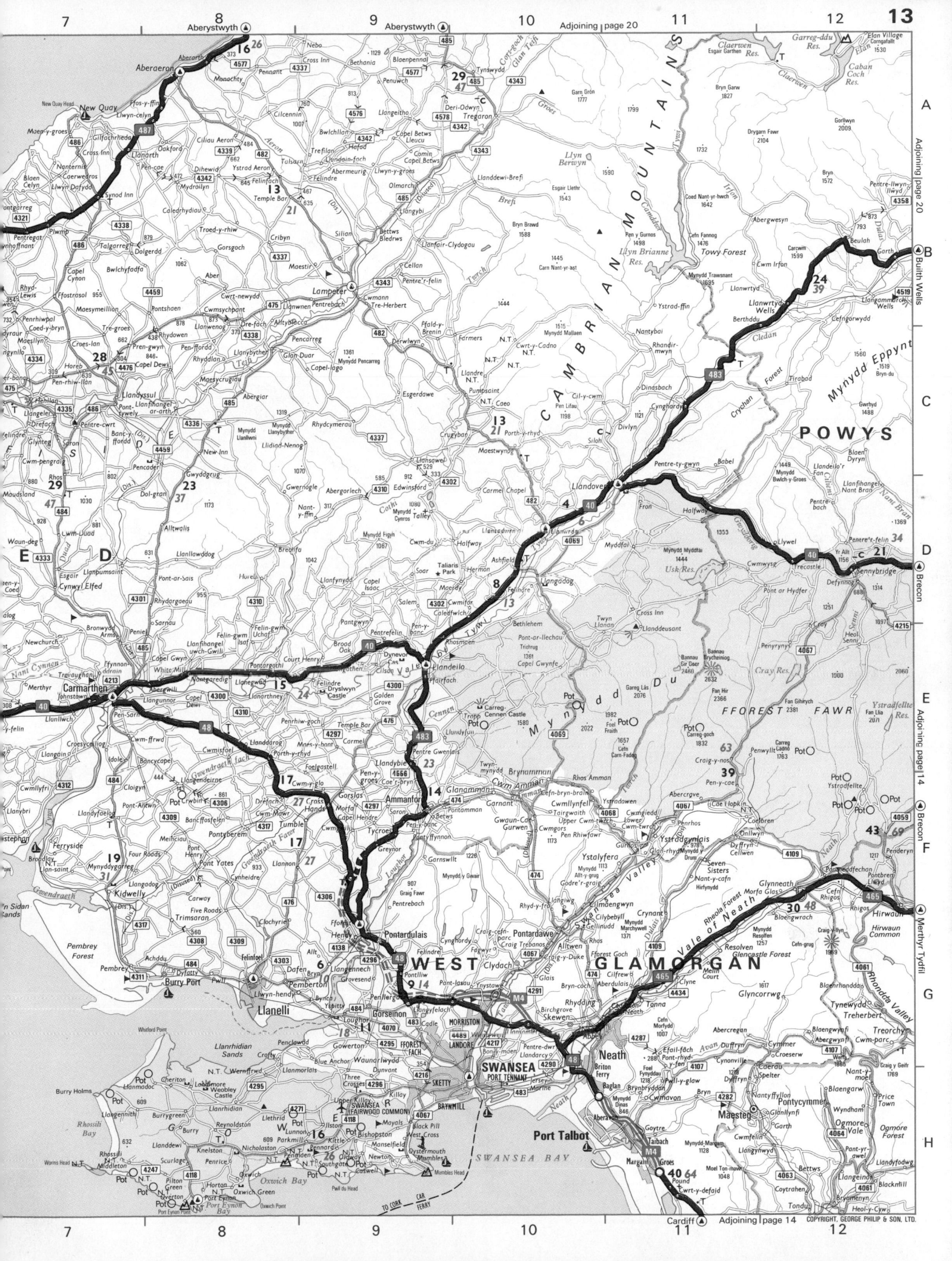

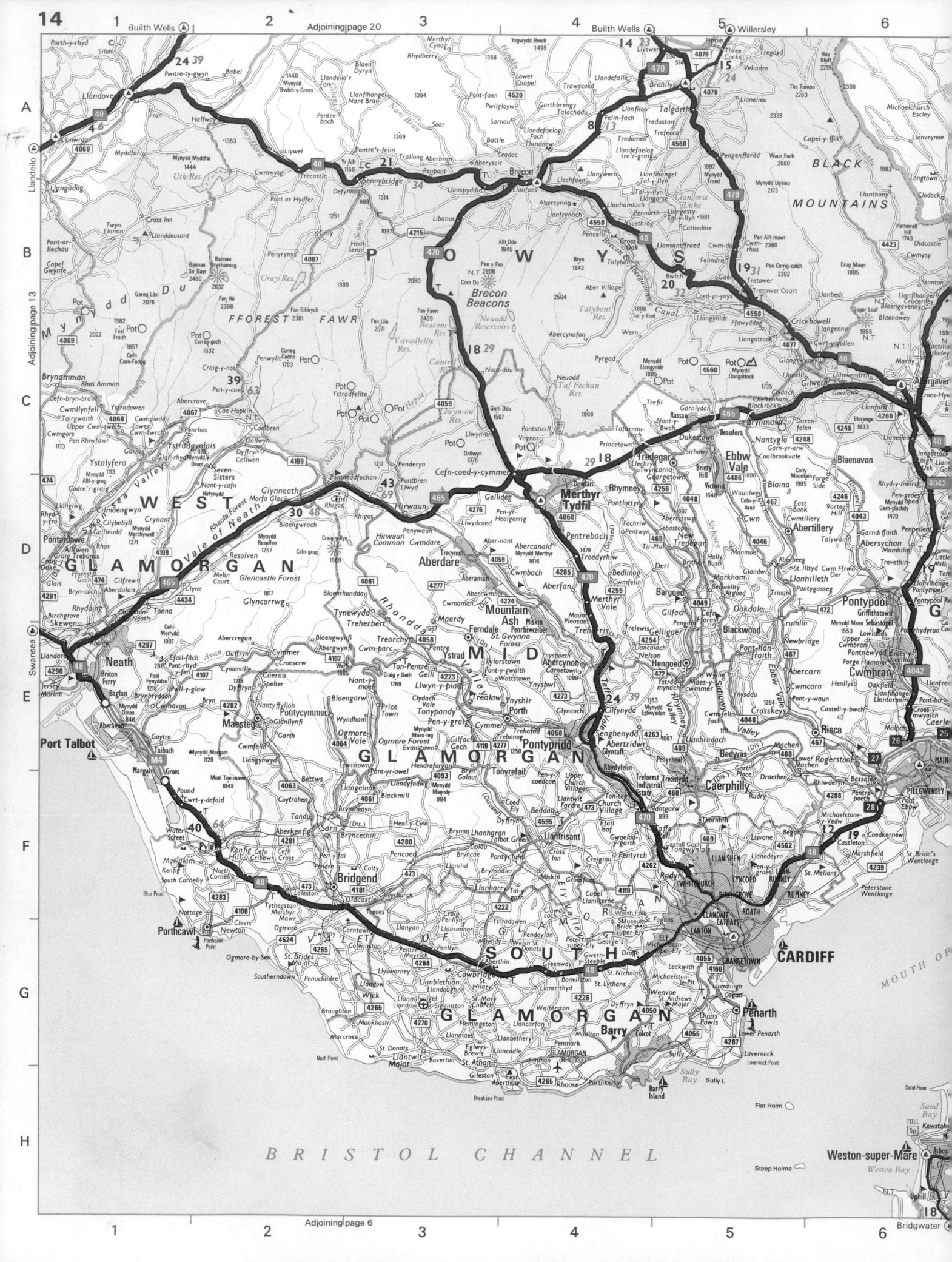

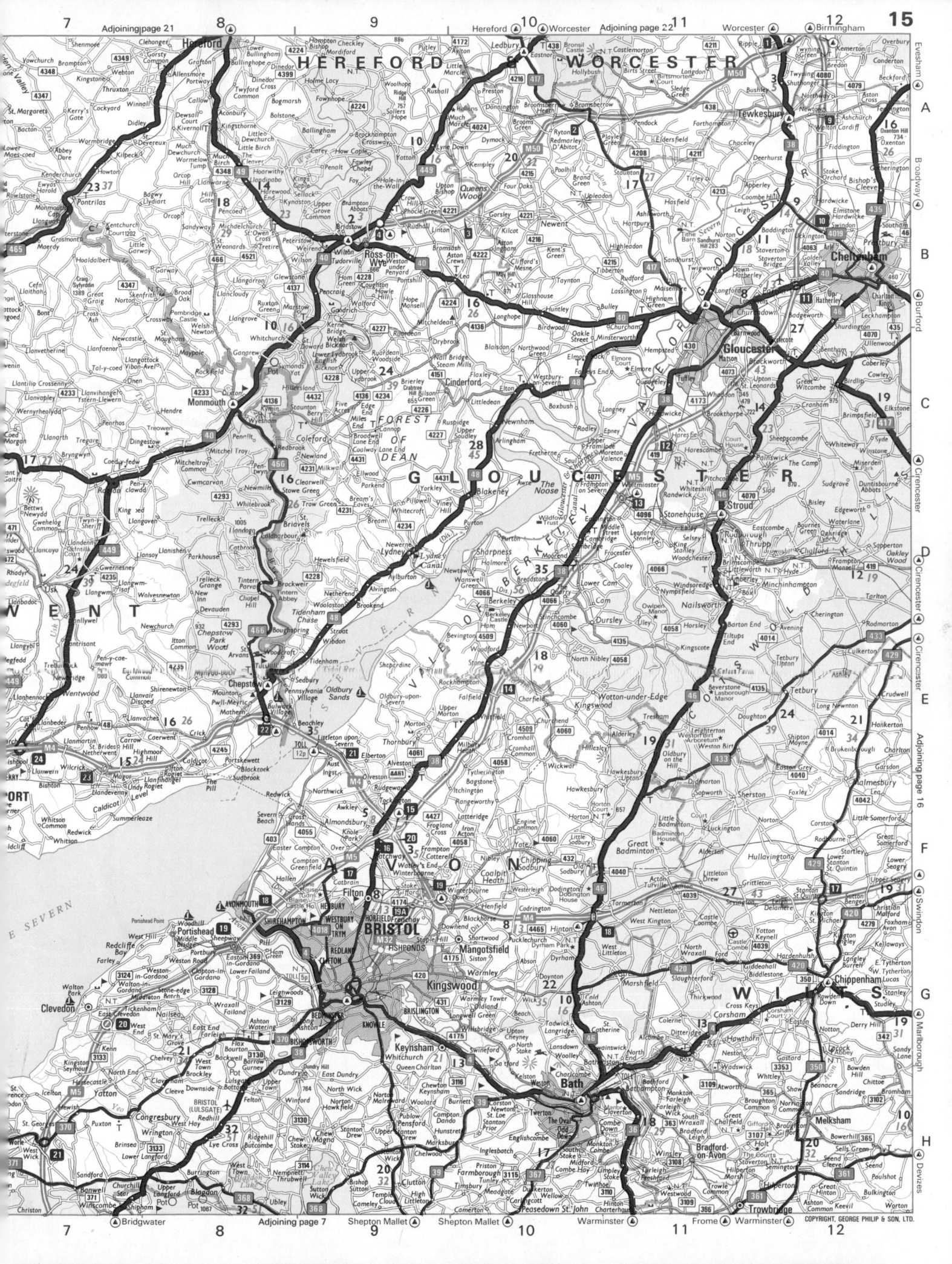

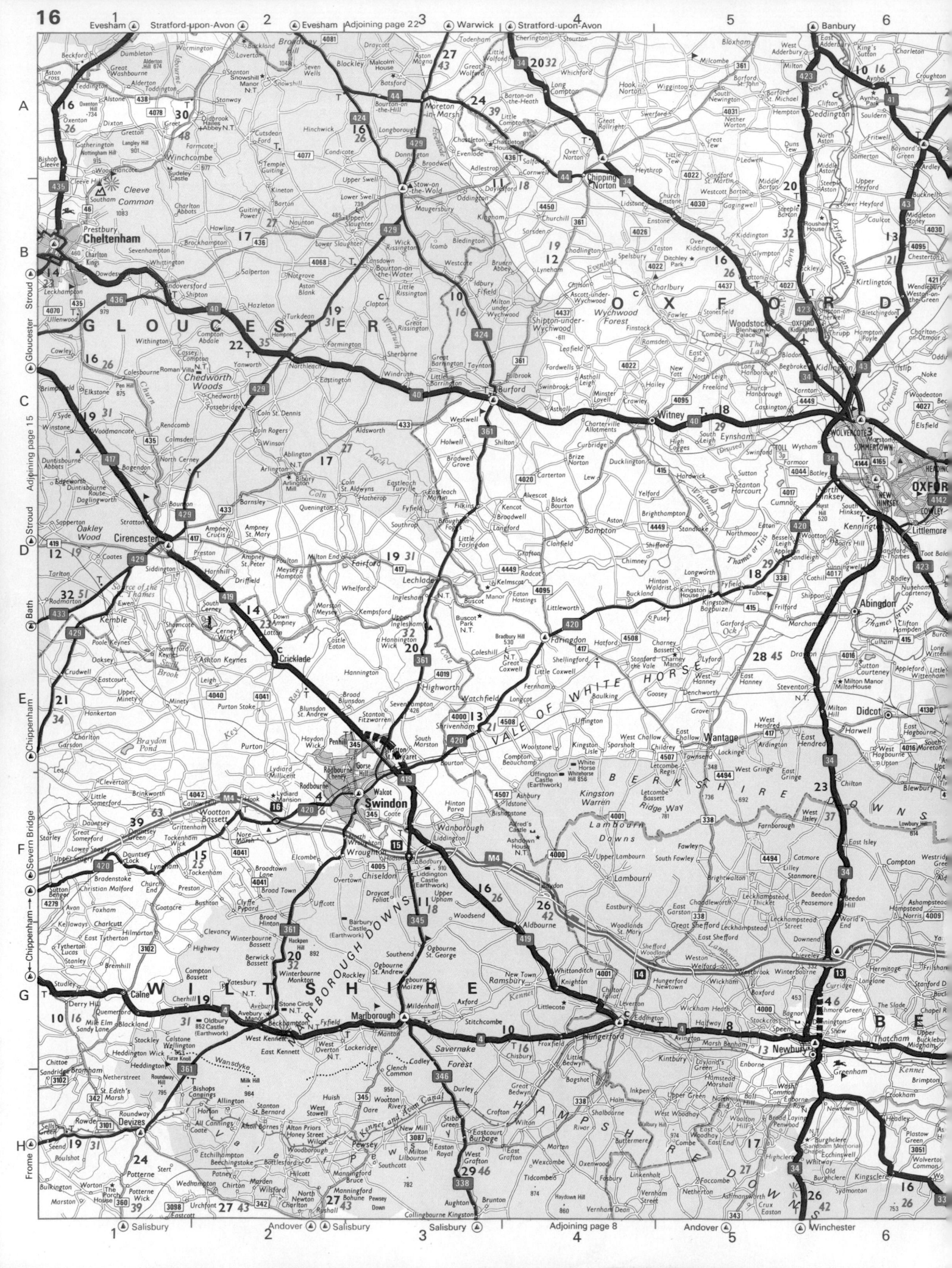

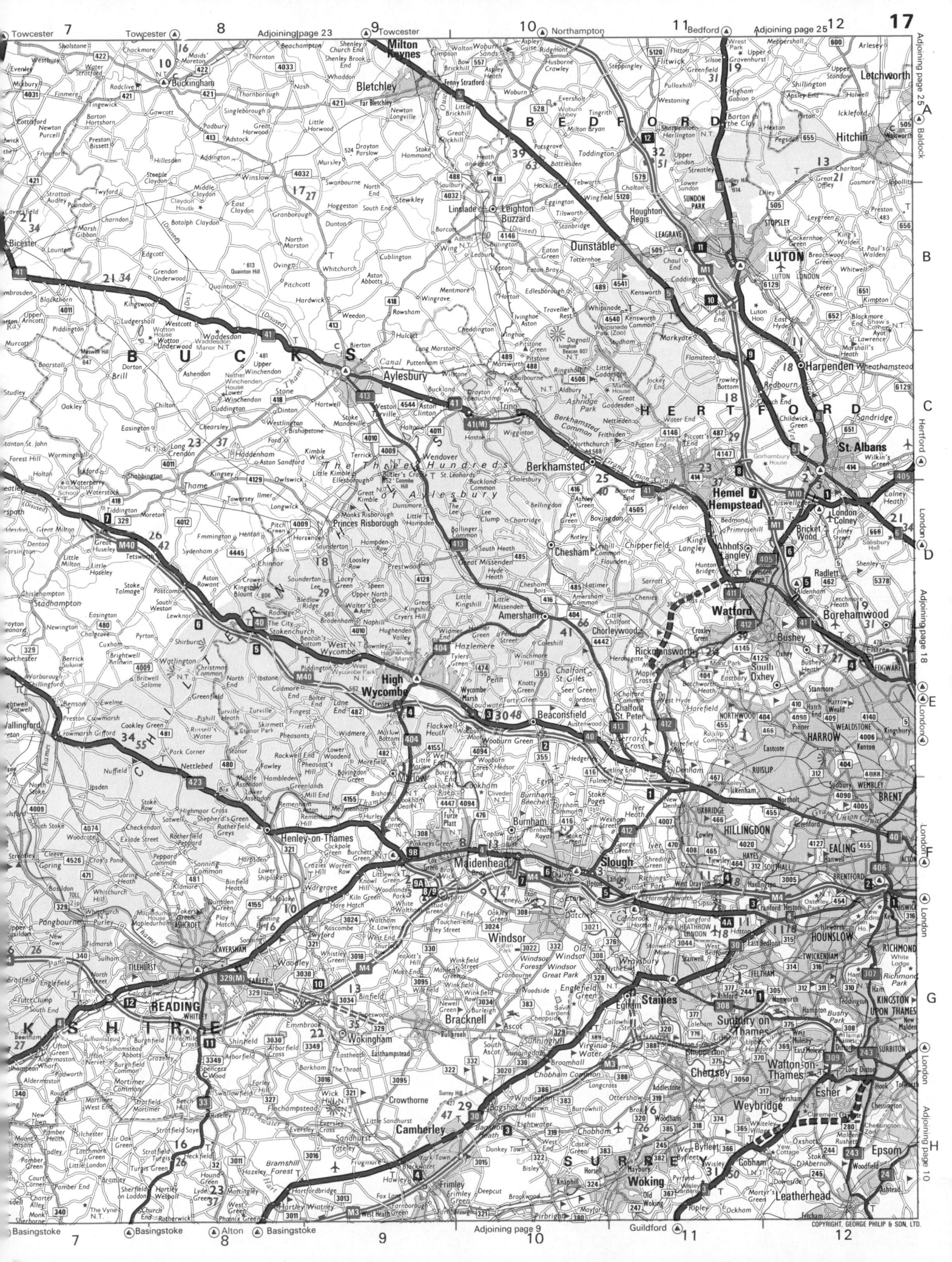

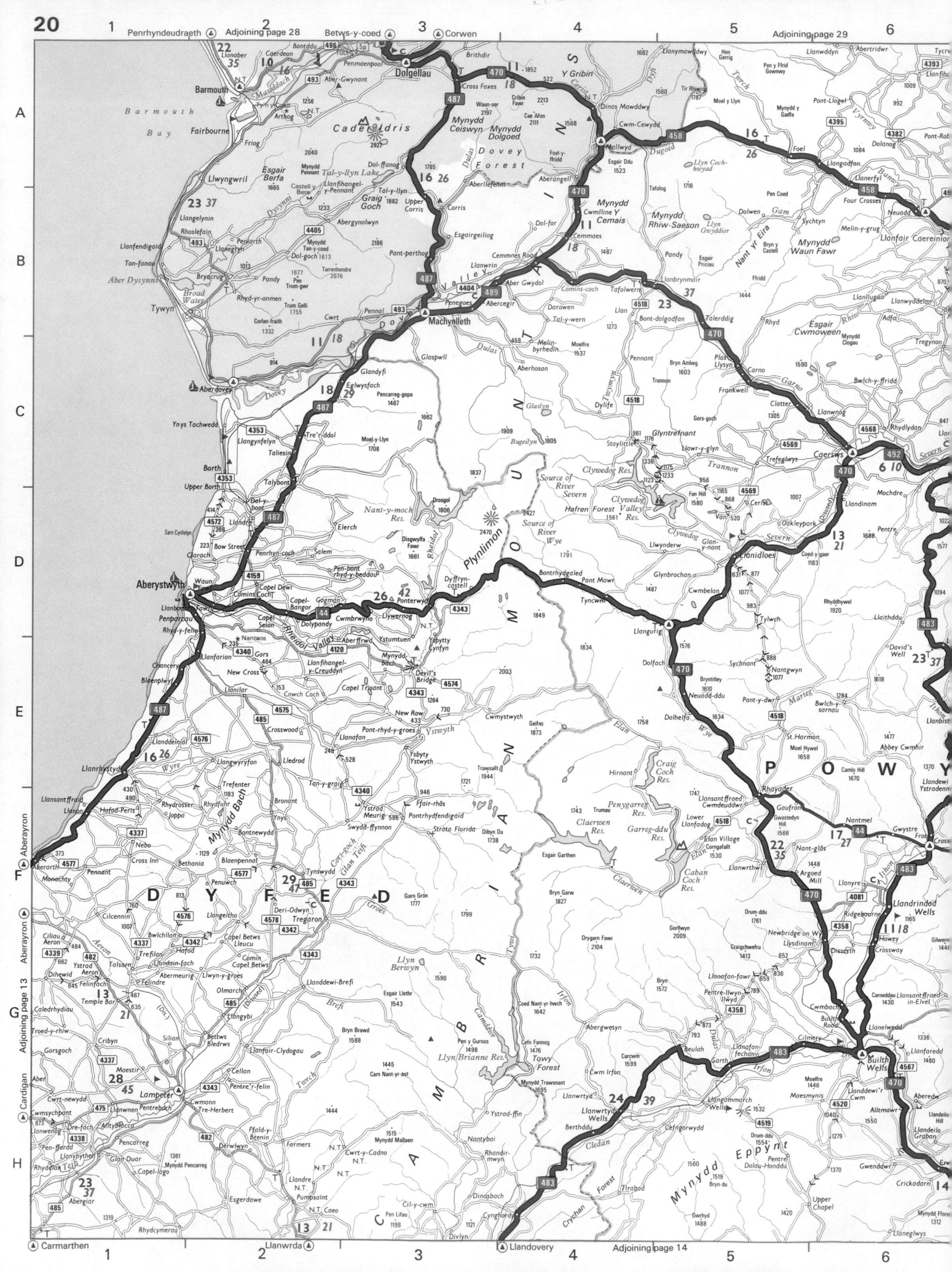

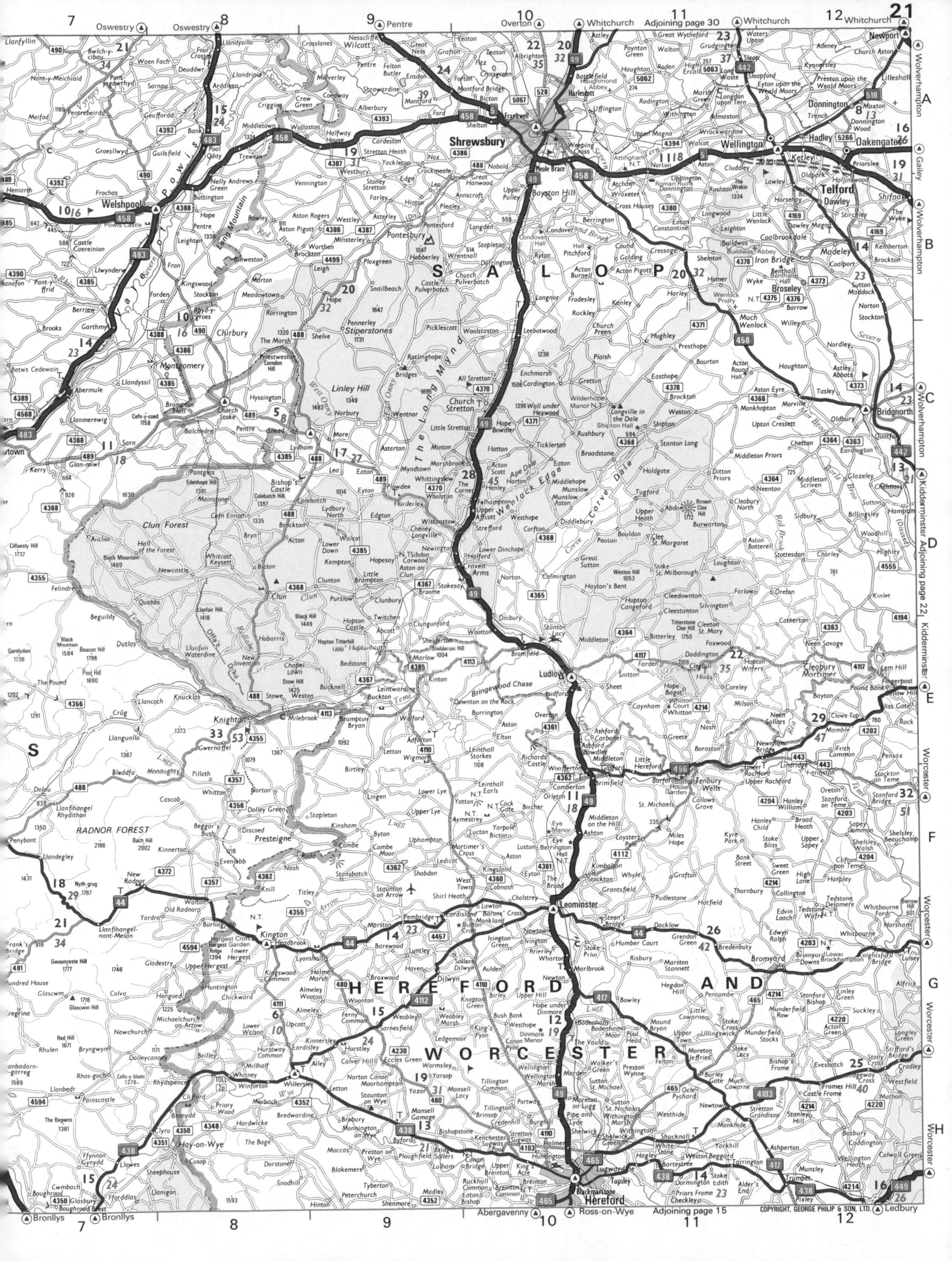

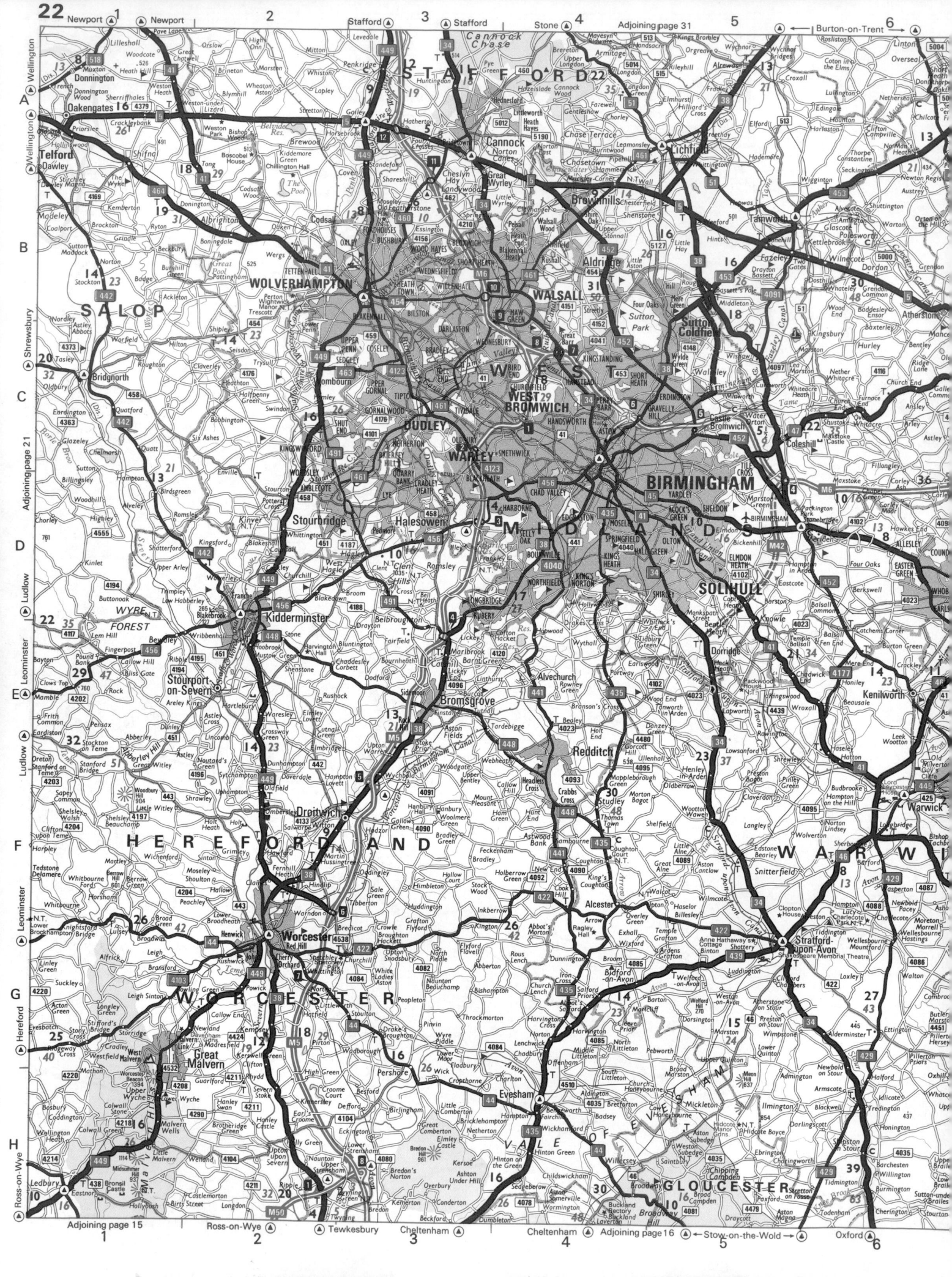

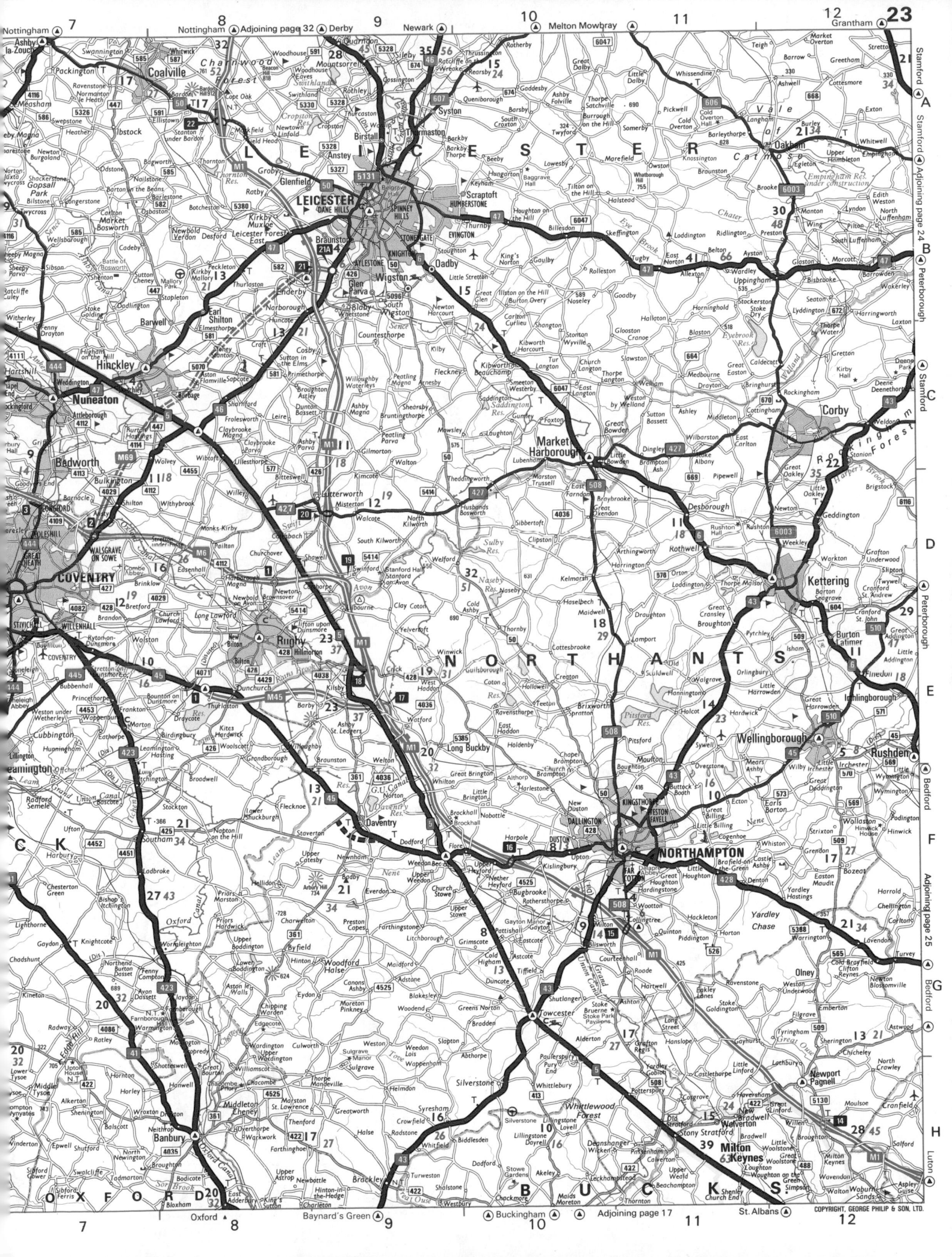

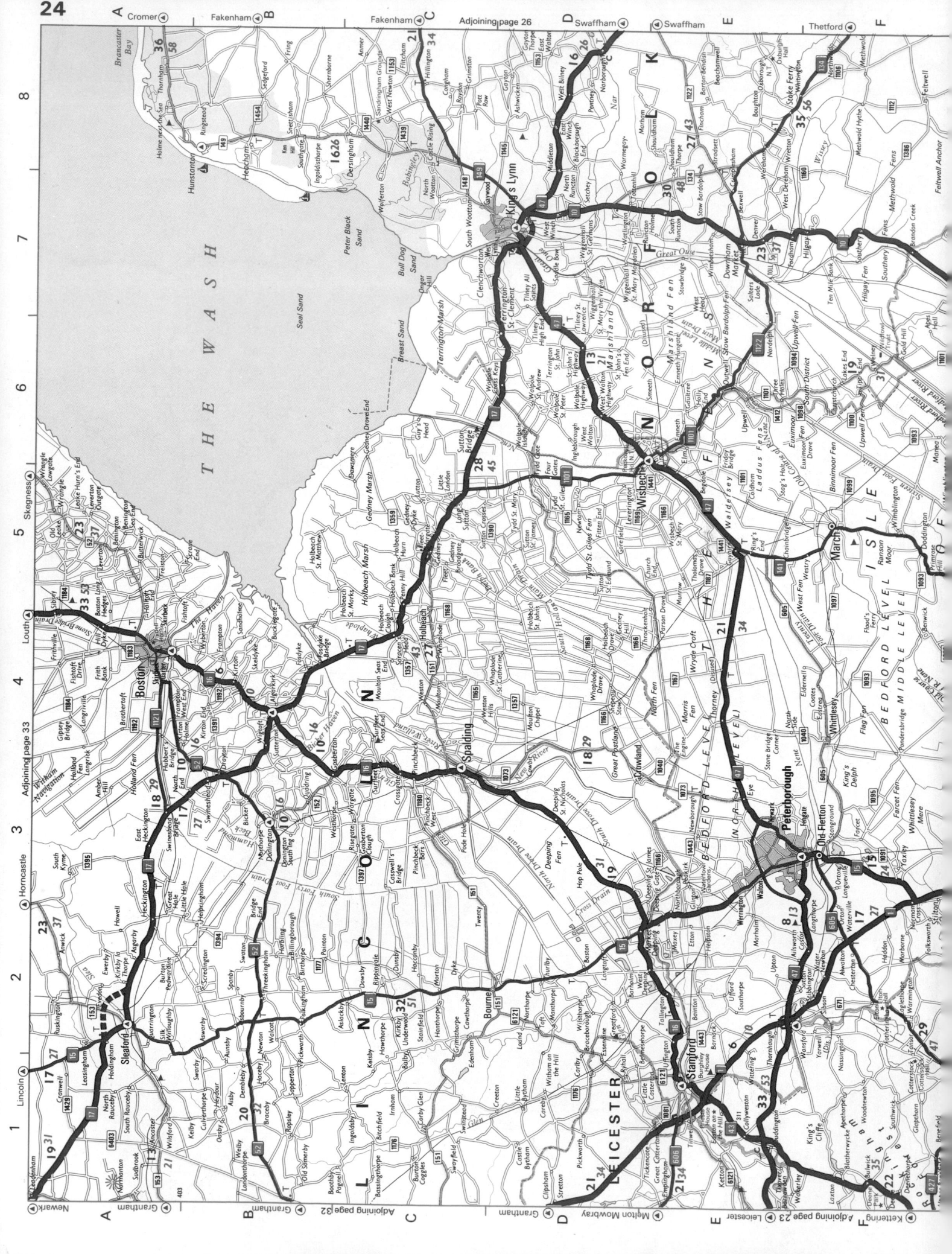

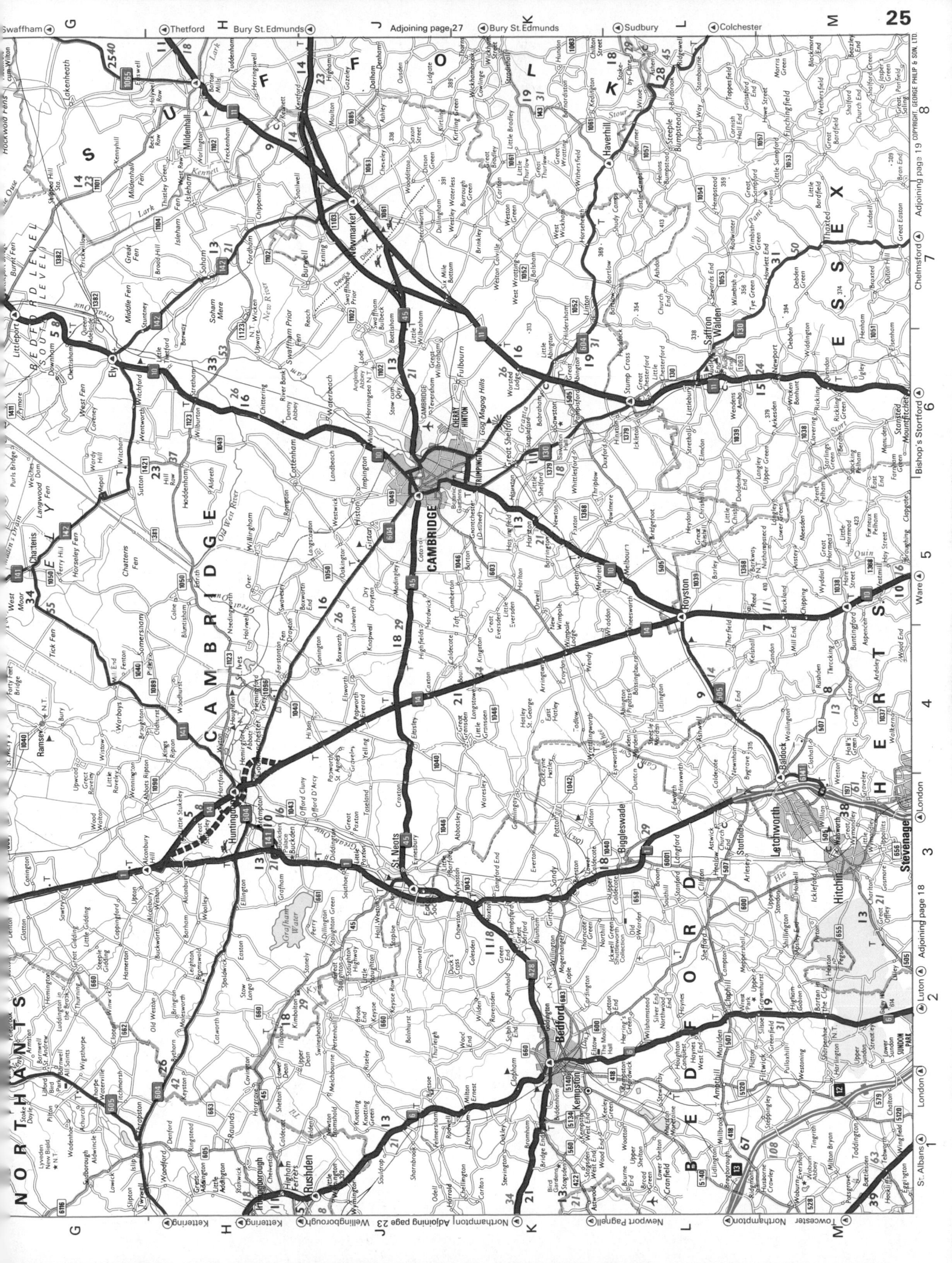

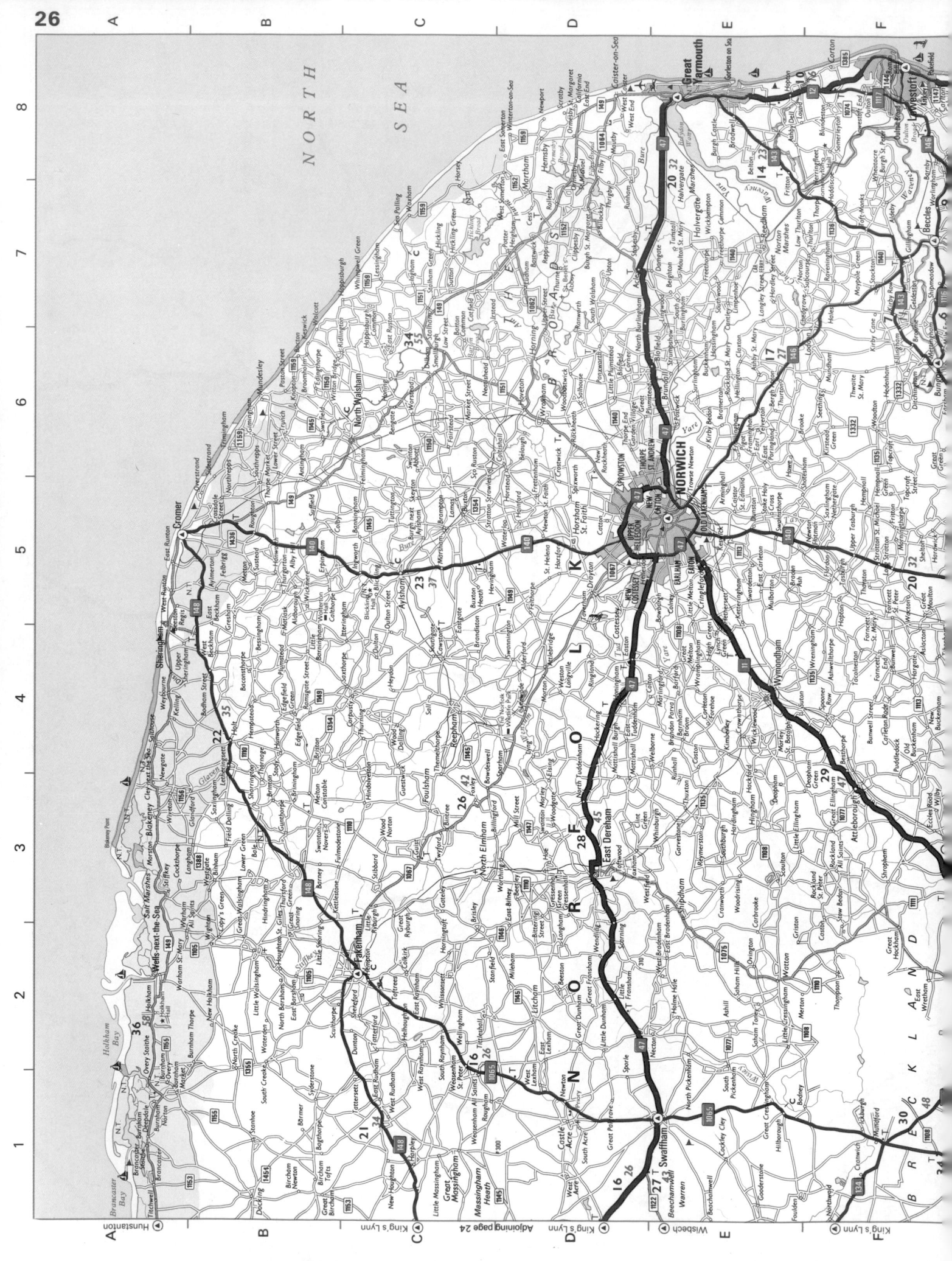

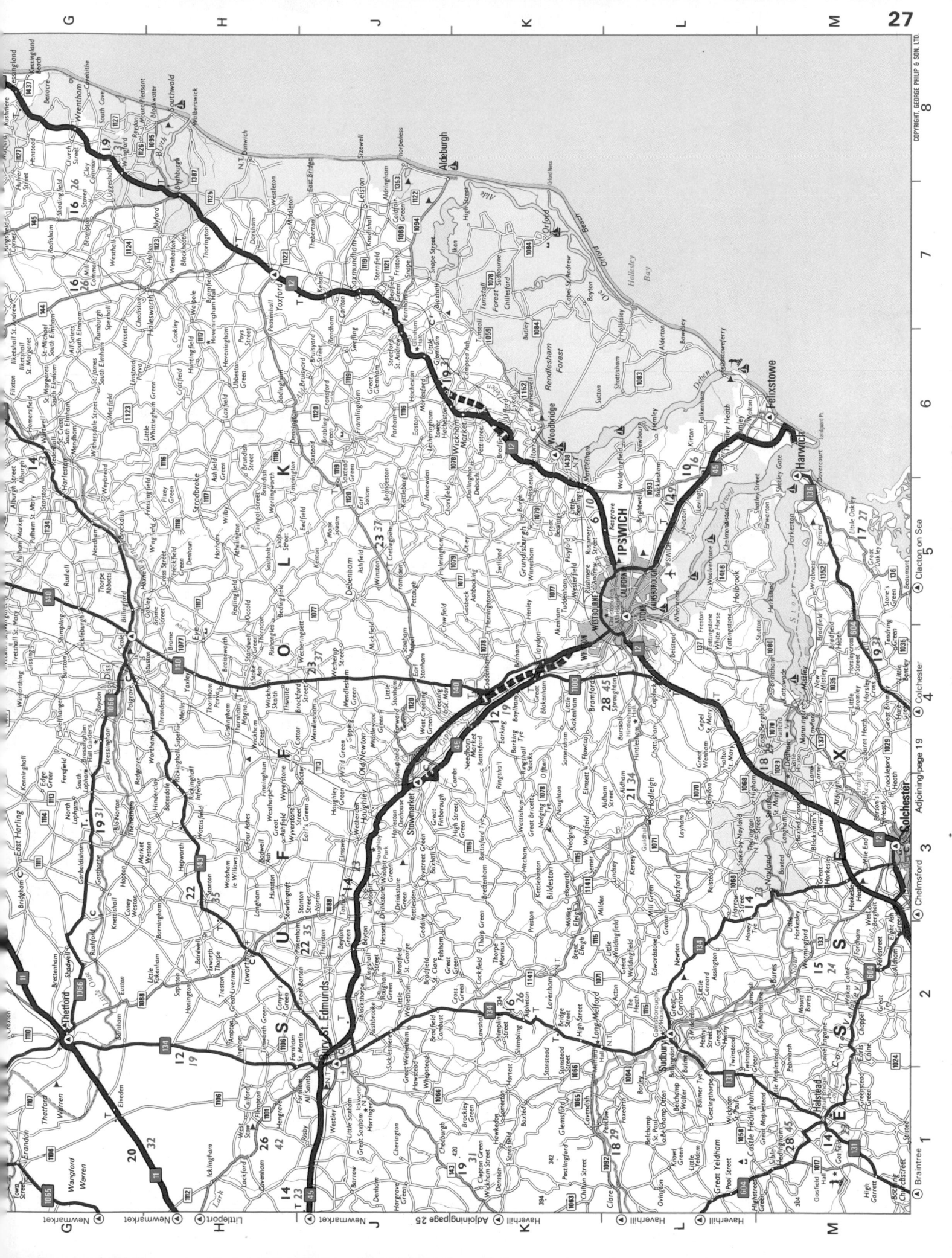

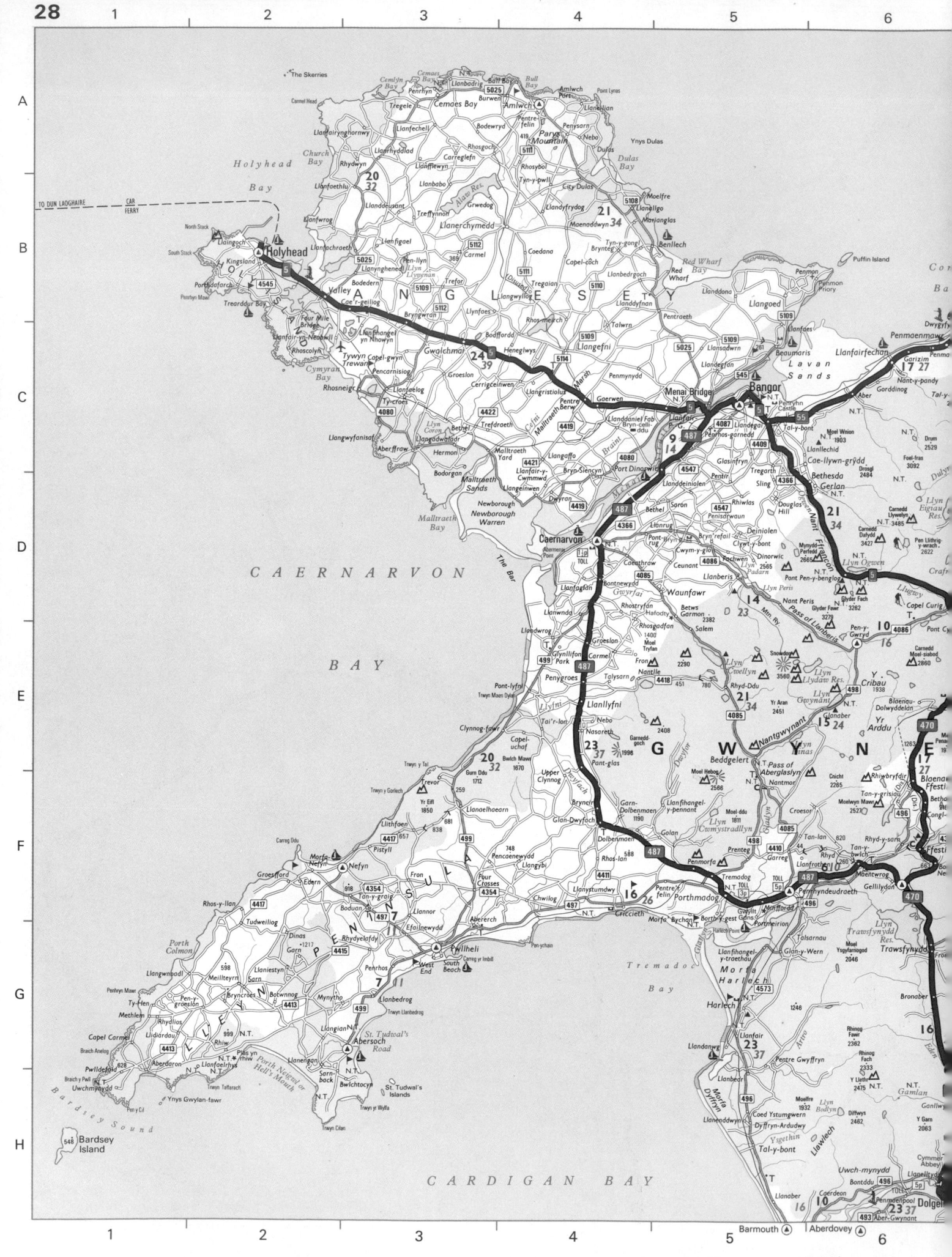

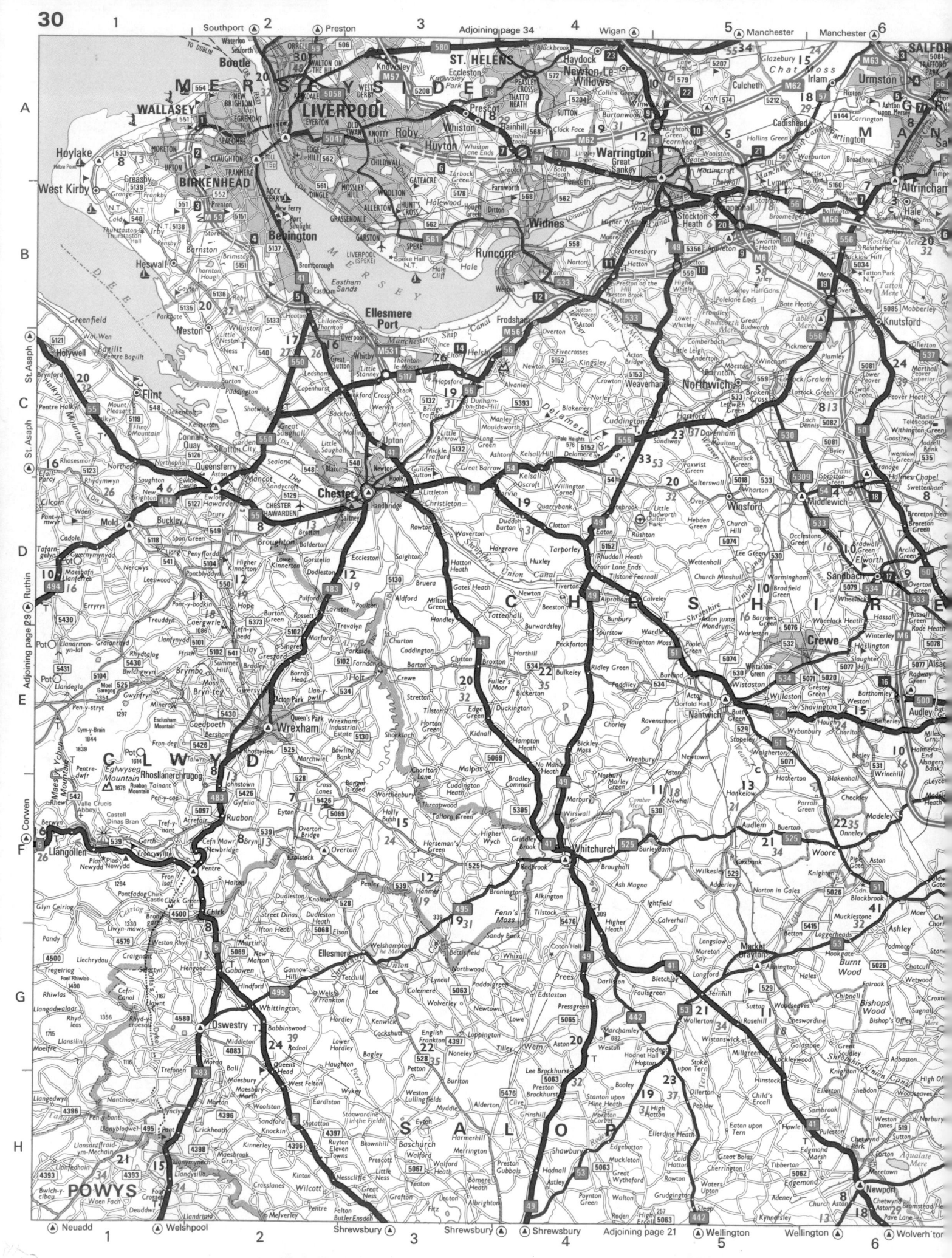

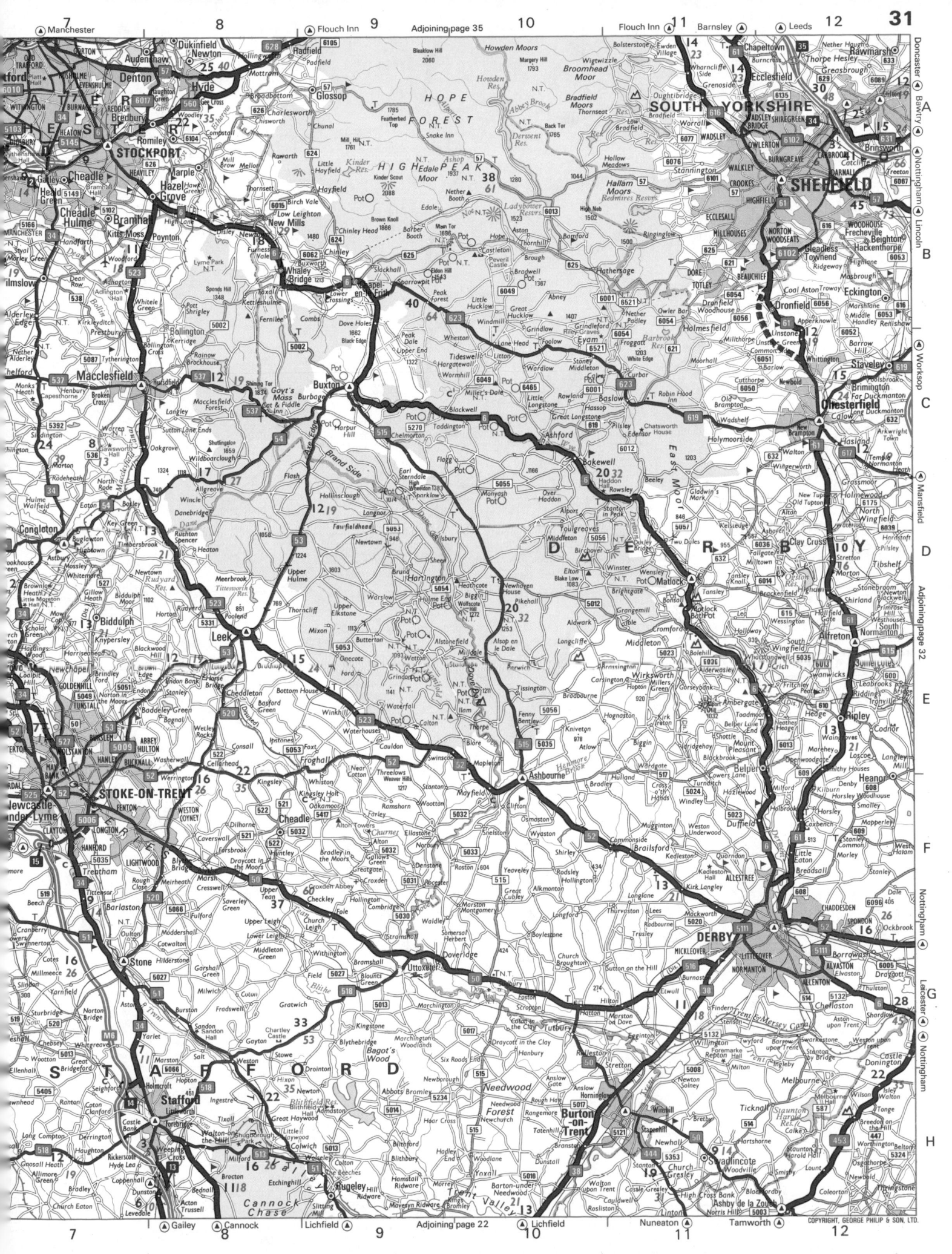

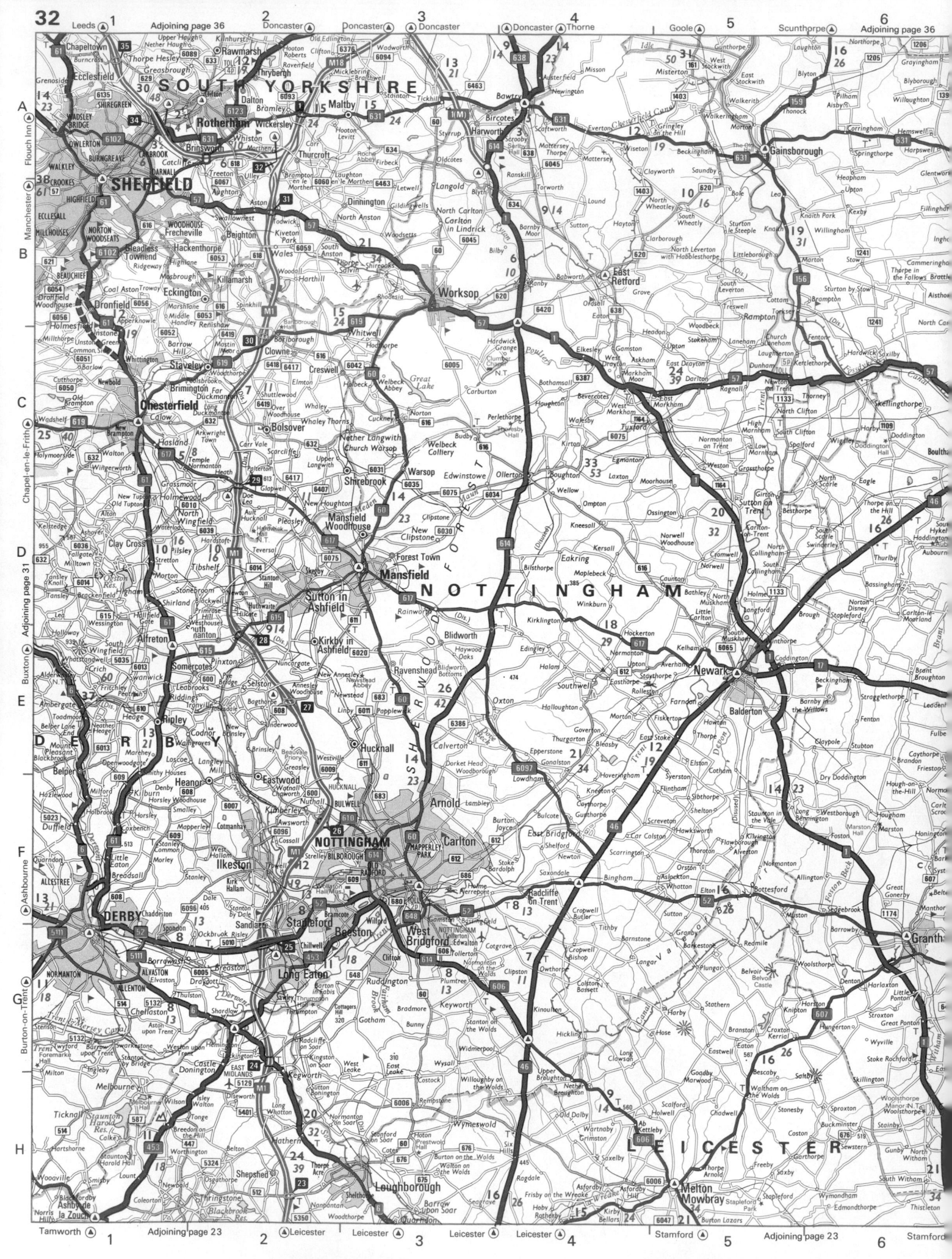

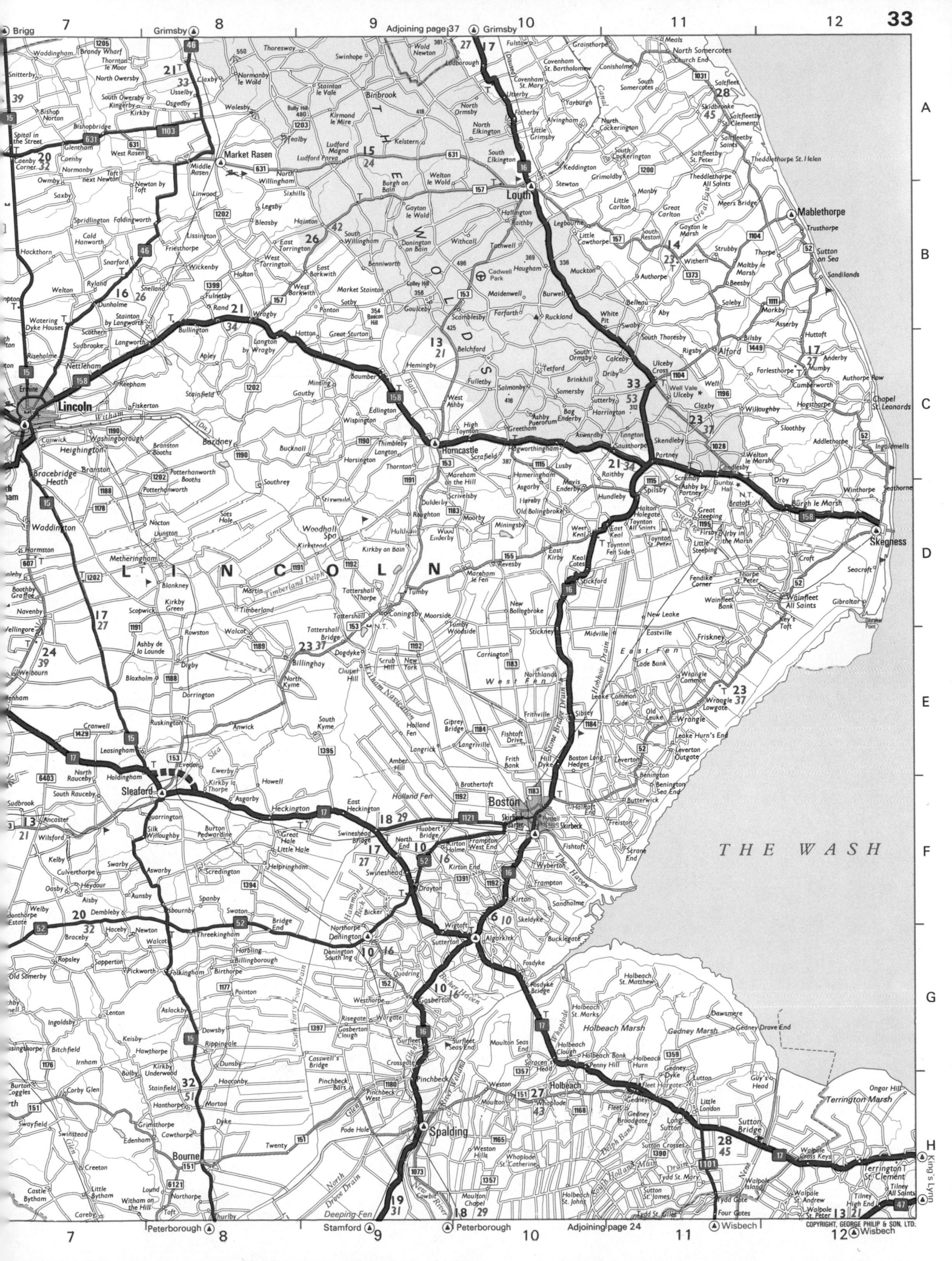

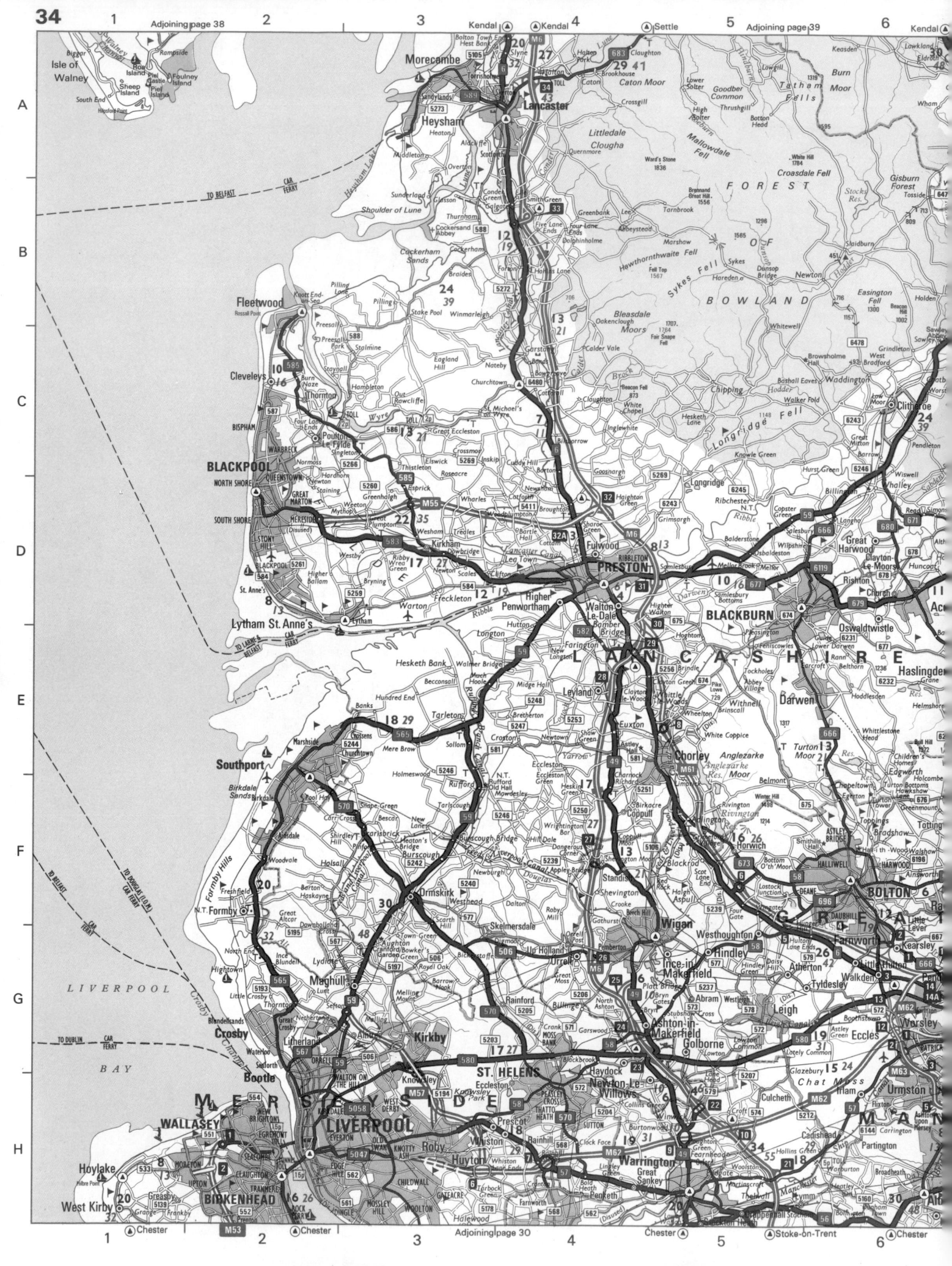

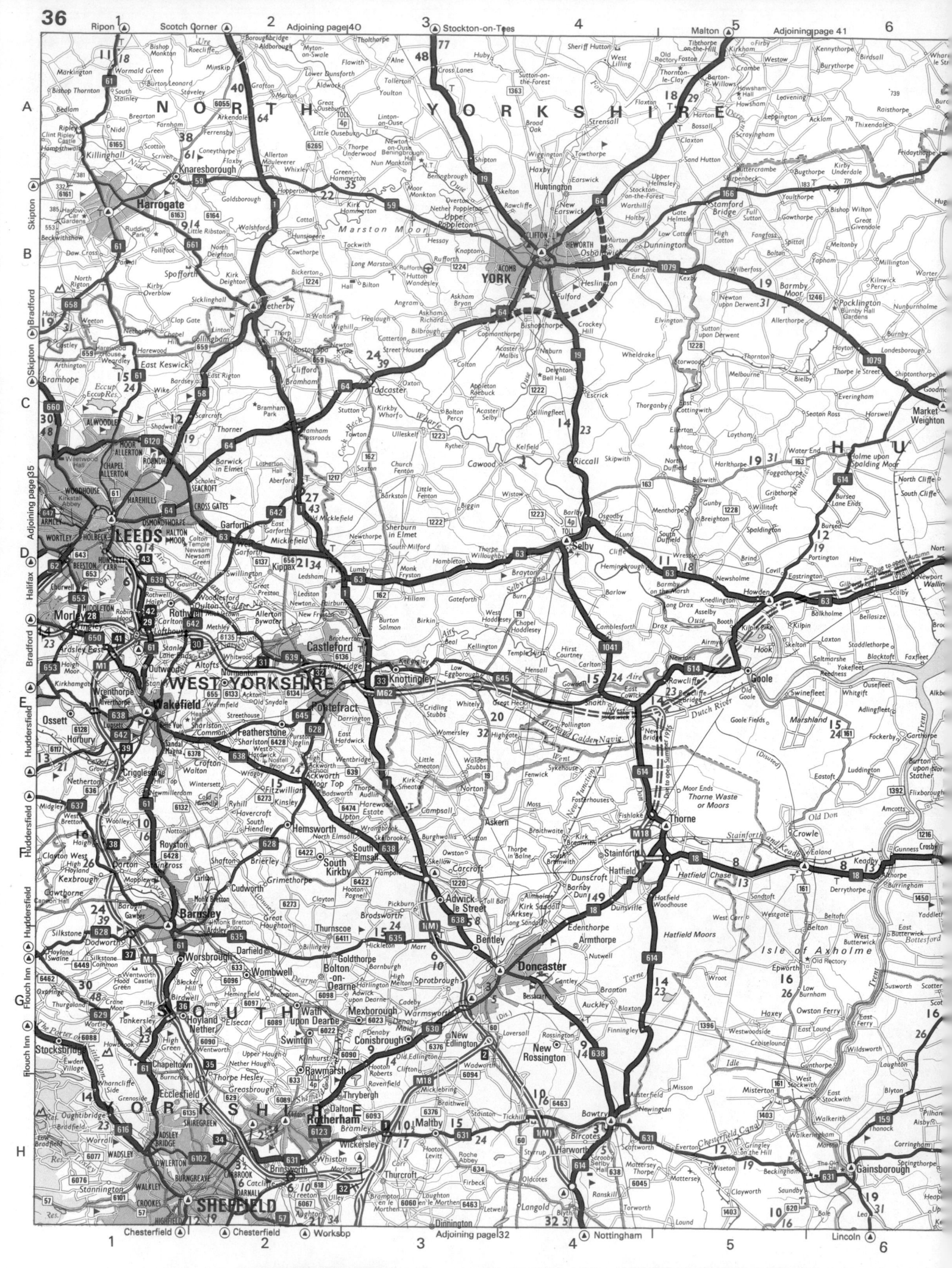

NORTH SEA

Bridlington Bay

KINGSTON UPON HULL

Scarborough

Bridlington

Hornsea

Withernsea

MOUTH OF THE HUMBER

Grimsby

Cleethorpes

Scunthorpe

Brigg

Market Rasen

Louth

Boston

YORKSHIRE WOLDS

EAST RIDING

HOLDERNESS

LINCOLN

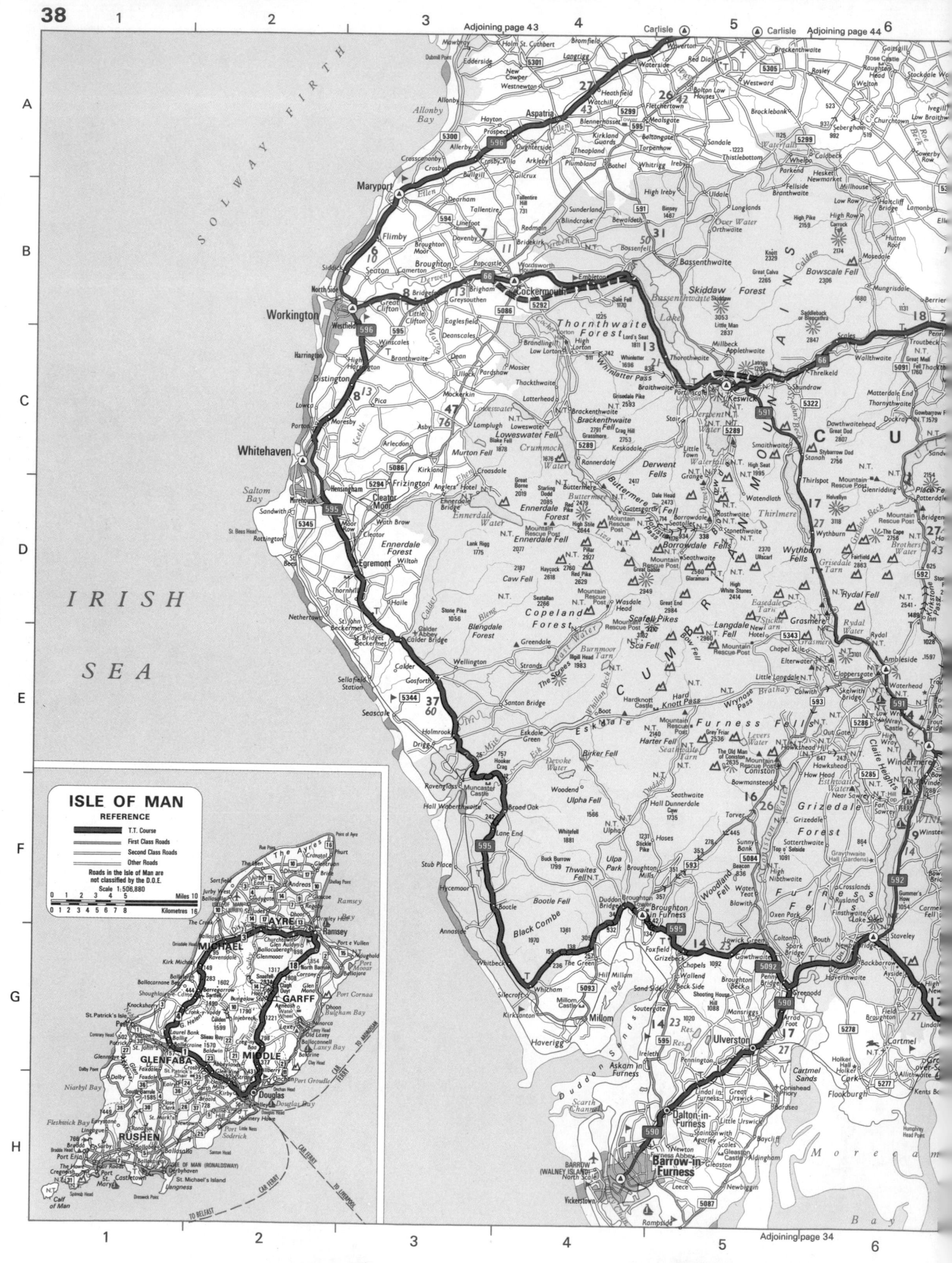

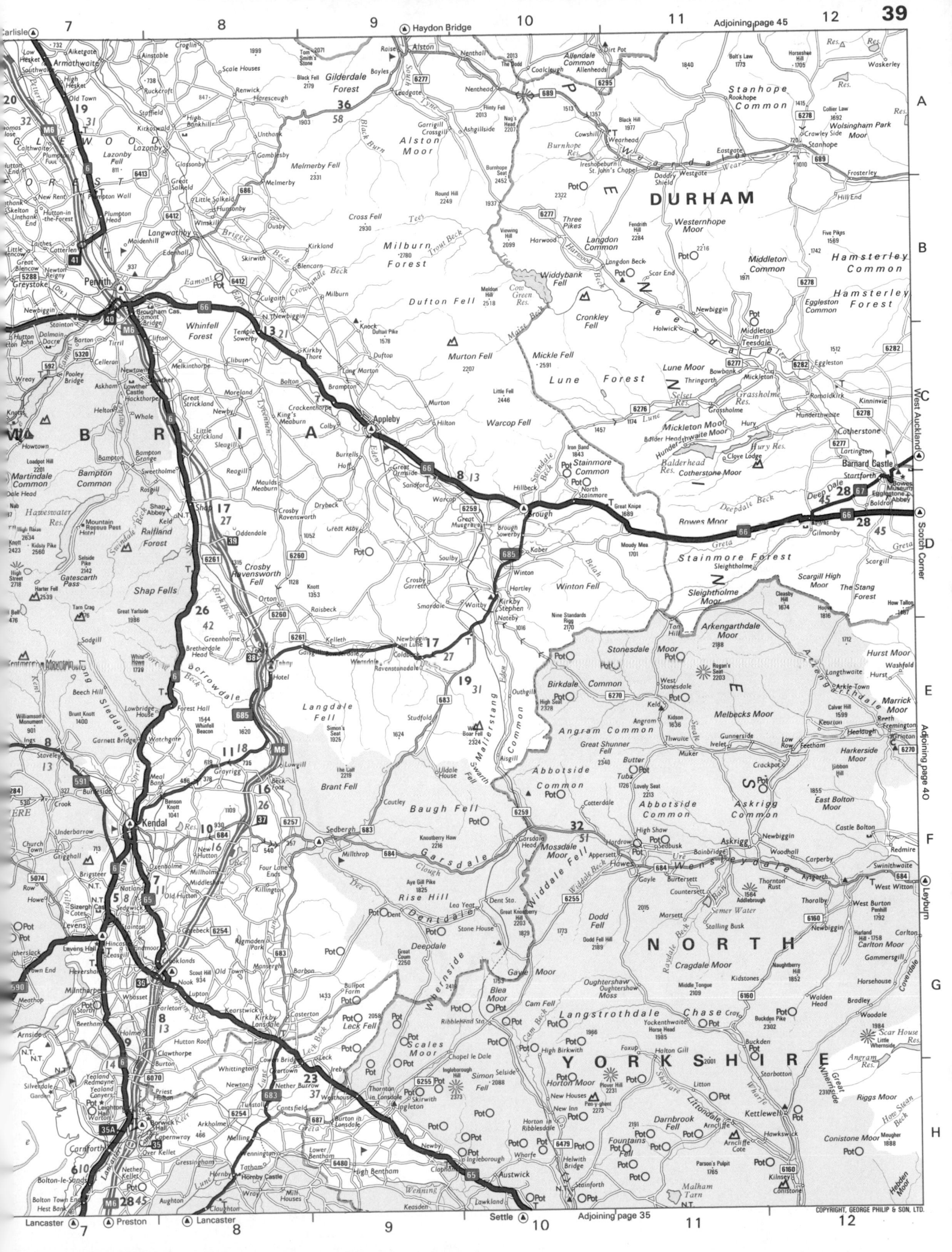

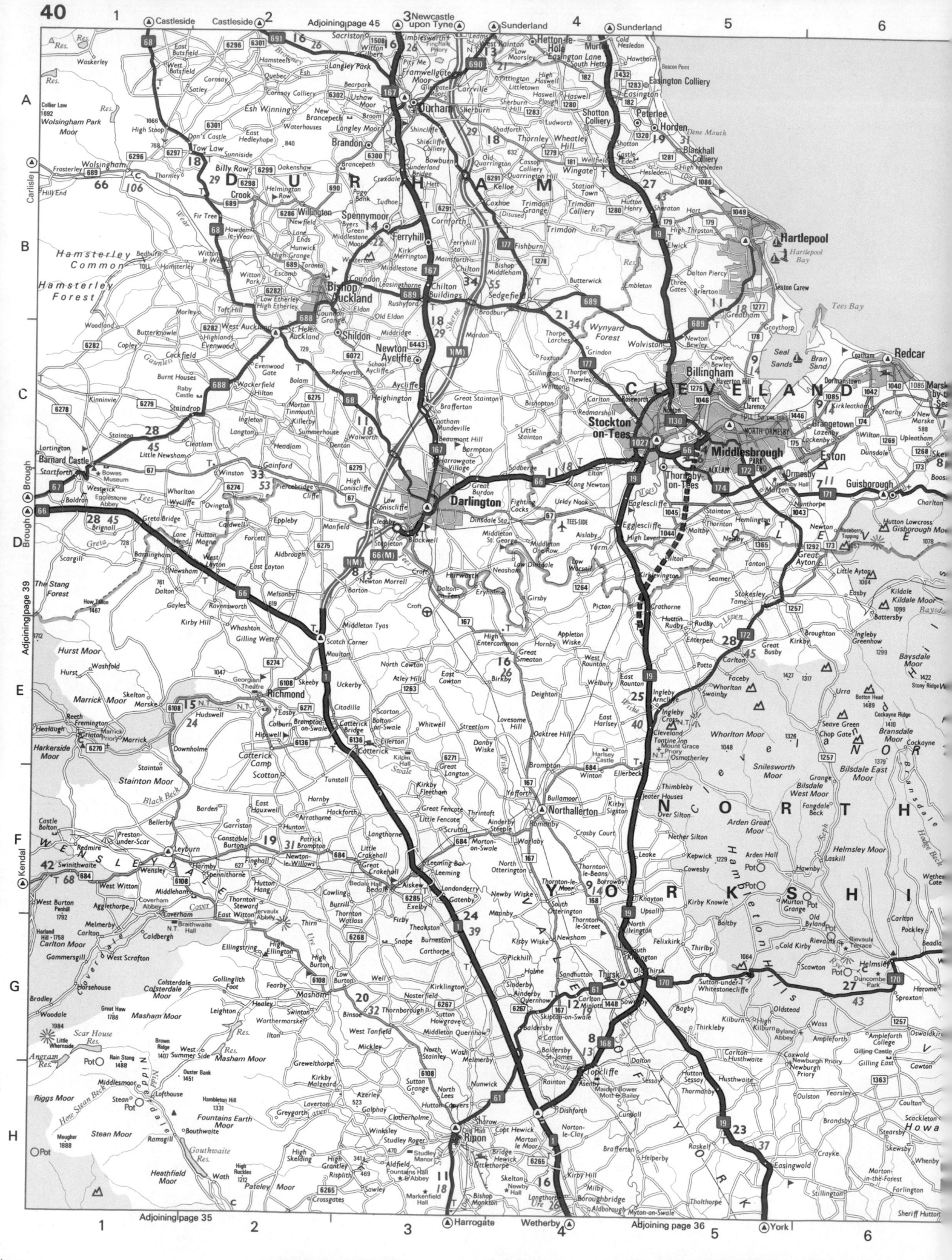

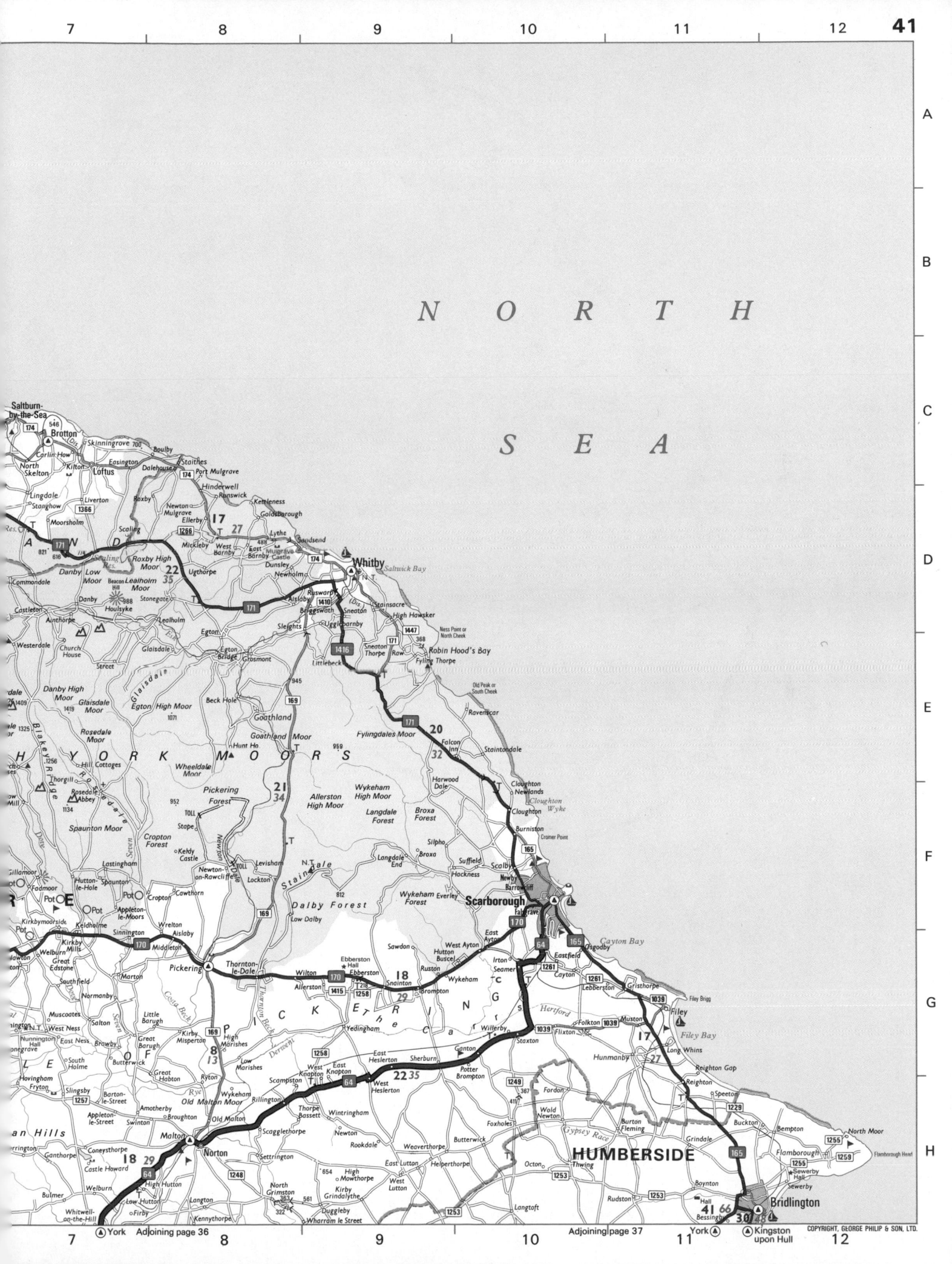

N O R T H

S E A

Saltburn-by-the-Sea
174
Brotton
546
Skinningrove
Carlin How
700
Boulby
Kilton
Easington
Staithes
North
Skelton
Loftus
174
Hinderwell
Port Mulgrave
Dalehouse
Runswick
Lingdale
Liverton
Roxby
Newton
Goldsborough
Kettleness
Stanghow
1366
Moorsholm
1266
Mulgrave
Ellerby
Lythe
Sandsend
171
821
616
Scaling
West
Barnby
Mulgrave
Castle
T 27
East
Barnby
17
Whitby
Saltwick Bay
Danby Low
Moor
Mickleby
Dunsley
Newholm
N.T.
22
Roxby High
Moor
Ugthorpe
35
Ruswarp
Commondale
Danby
Beacon Hill
988
Stonegate
Lealholm
Moor
Aislaby
Briggswath
1410
Sneaton
Stainsacre
High Hawsker
Castleton
Ainthorpe
Houlsyke
Lealholm
171
Sleights
Ugglebarnby
T
1447
Ness Point or
North Cheek
Westerdale
Church
House
Egton
Egton
Bridge
Grosmont
1416
Sneaton
Thorpe
Raw
388
Littlebeck
Robin Hood's Bay
Fyling Thorpe
Glaisdale
945
Street
Danby High
Moor
Egton High Moor
Beck Hole
169
Old Peak or
South Cheek
1419
Glaisdale
Moor
1071
Goathland
171
Fylingdales Moor
20
Falcon
Inn
Ravenscar
1325
1256
Hill
Cottages
Goathland Moor
959
32
Staintondale
Rosedale
Moor
Hunt Ho.
Y O R K   M O O R S
Rosedale
Abbey
1134
Wheeldale
Moor
Pickering
Forest
21
34
Wykeham
High Moor
Harwood
Dale
Cloughton
Newlands
Cloughton
Wyke
Thorgill
952
Allerston
High Moor
Langdale
Forest
Cloughton
Burniston
Cramer Point
Spaunton Moor
Cropton
Forest
TOLL
Stape
Keldy Castle
TOLL
Levisham
Staindale
N.T.
Silpho
Broxa
Forest
165
Suffield
Hackness
Scalby
Lastingham
Newton-
on-Rawcliffe
Lockton
Langdale
End
Broxa
Newby
Barrowcliff
Gillamoor
Hutton-
le-Hole
Spaunton
Cawthorn
Dalby Forest
Wykeham
Forest
Everley
Scarborough
Fadmoor
Pot
E
Cropton
Low Dalby
812
Falsgrave
Kirkbymoorside
Keldholme
Appleton-
le-Moors
169
170
Pot
Pot
Middleton
170
Sawdon
West Ayton
East
Ayton
165
Cayton Bay
Welburn
Kirkby
Mills
Sinnington
Thornton-
le-Dale
Wilton
Hutton
Buscel
Ruston
64
Osgodby
Eastfield
Great
Edstone
Marton
Pickering
170
Allerston
1415
Snainton
Wykeham
Irton
Seamer
1261
Cayton
Southfield
1258
Brompton
T
C
165
Normanby
29
S
1261
Lebberston
Gristhorpe
Muscoates
West Ness
Salton
Little
Barugh
Kirby
Misperton
P I C K E R I N G
Yedingham
Wykeham
Willerby
1039
Hertford
Folkton
1039
Muston
1039
Filey
Filey Brigg
West Ness
8
High
Marishes
Sherburn
Ganton
Staxton
Flixton
17
Filey Bay
South
Holme
Brawby
Great
Habton
13
Low
Marishes
East
Heslerton
Potter
Brompton
1249
Hunmanby
27
Hovingham
N.T.
East Ness
Ryton
1258
East
Knapton
West
Heslerton
22 35
367
Fordon
Long Whins
Fryton
Slingsby
Barton-
le-Street
Old Malton Moor
Rillington
64
Reighton Gap
Appleton-
le-Street
Amotherby
Swinton
Old Malton
Thorpe
Bassett
Wintringham
Newton
Foxholes
Wold
Newton
Reighton
T
Speeton
1257
Broughton
Scagglethorpe
Rookdale
Butterwick
Weaverthorpe
Burton
Fleming
1229
an Hills
Malton
18 29
Coneysthorpe
Castle Howard
High Hutton
Settrington
H U M B E R S I D E
Grindale
165
Flamborough
1255
North Moor
Norton
1248
East Lutton
High
Mowthorpe
Helperthorpe
Thwing
1255
Sewerby
Hall
Bulmer
Welburn
Langton
North
Grimston
561
West
Lutton
Kirby
Grindalythe
654
363
Octon
1253
Boynton
41 66
Bridlington
64
Low Hutton
Firby
Kennythorpe
322
Duggleby
Langtoft
Rudston
1253
30 48
Whitwell-
on-the-Hill
Wharram le Street
1253

COPYRIGHT, GEORGE PHILIP & SON, LTD.

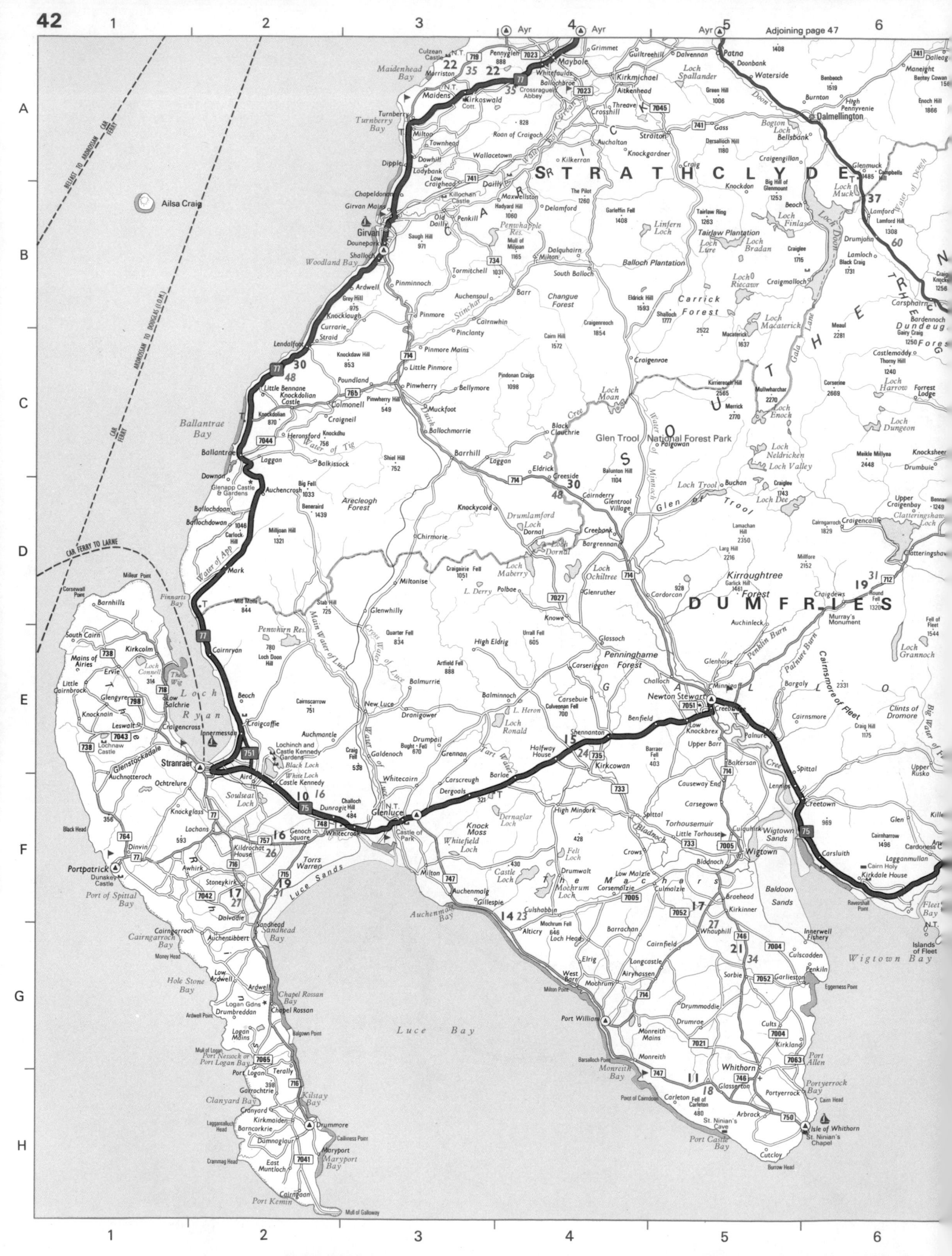

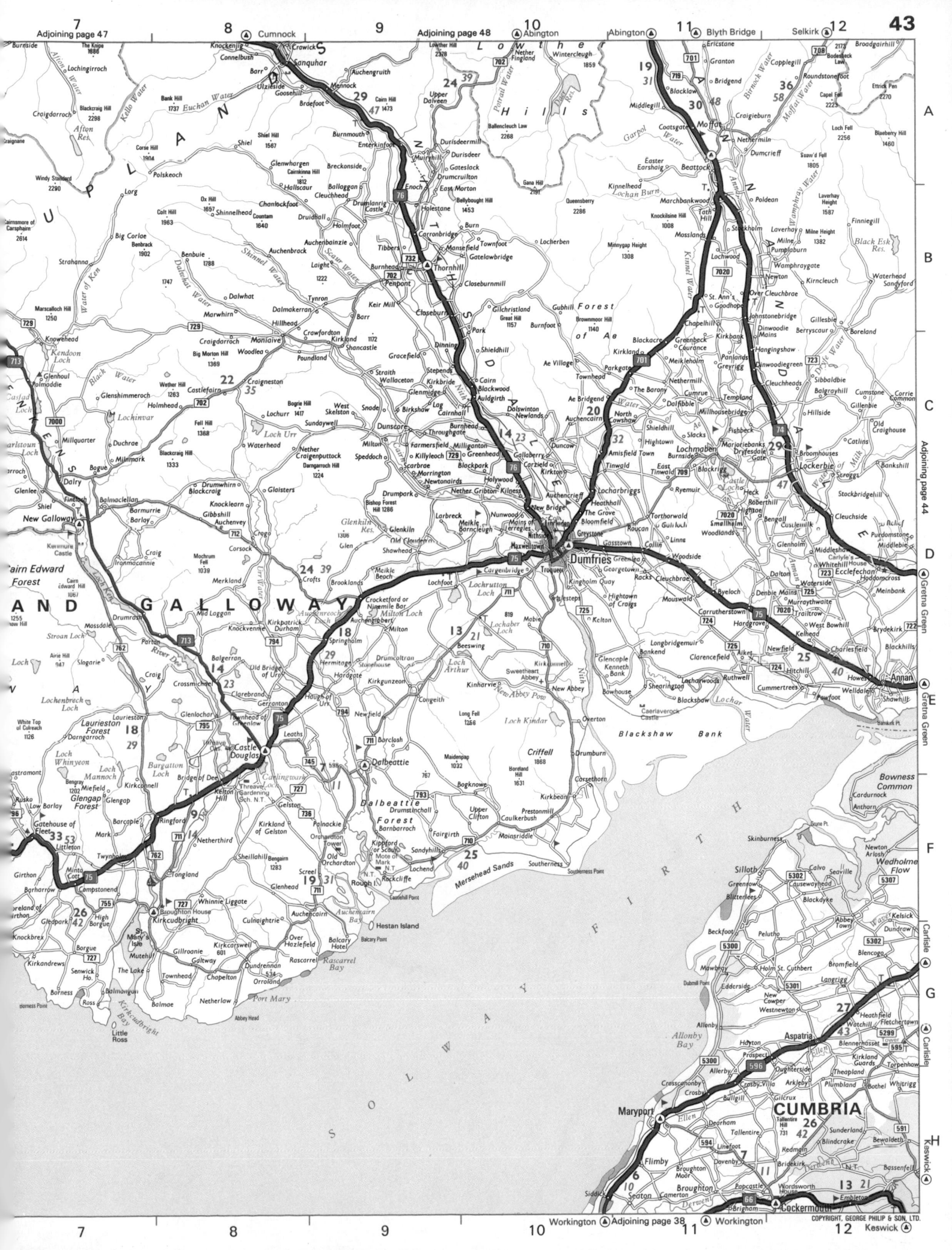

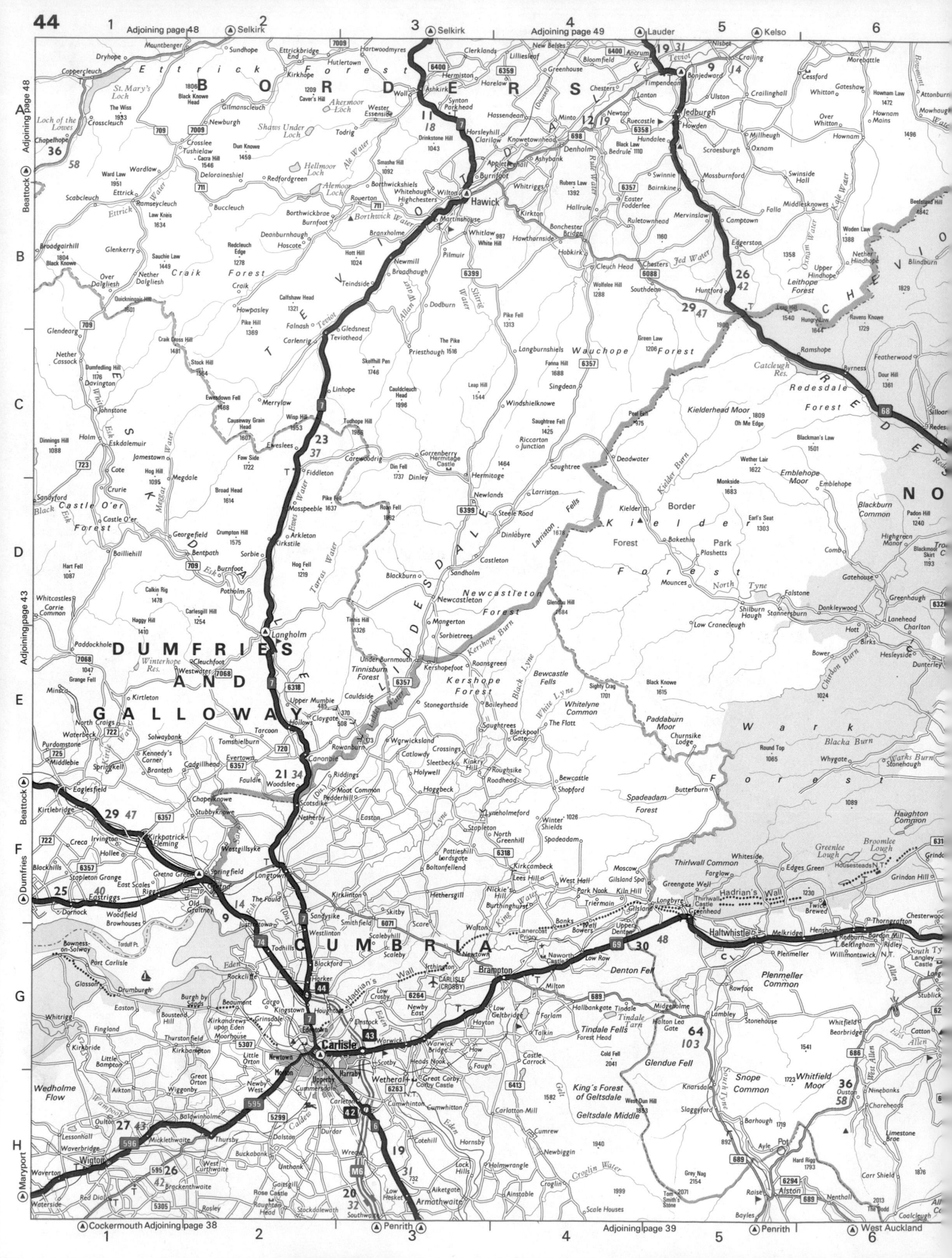

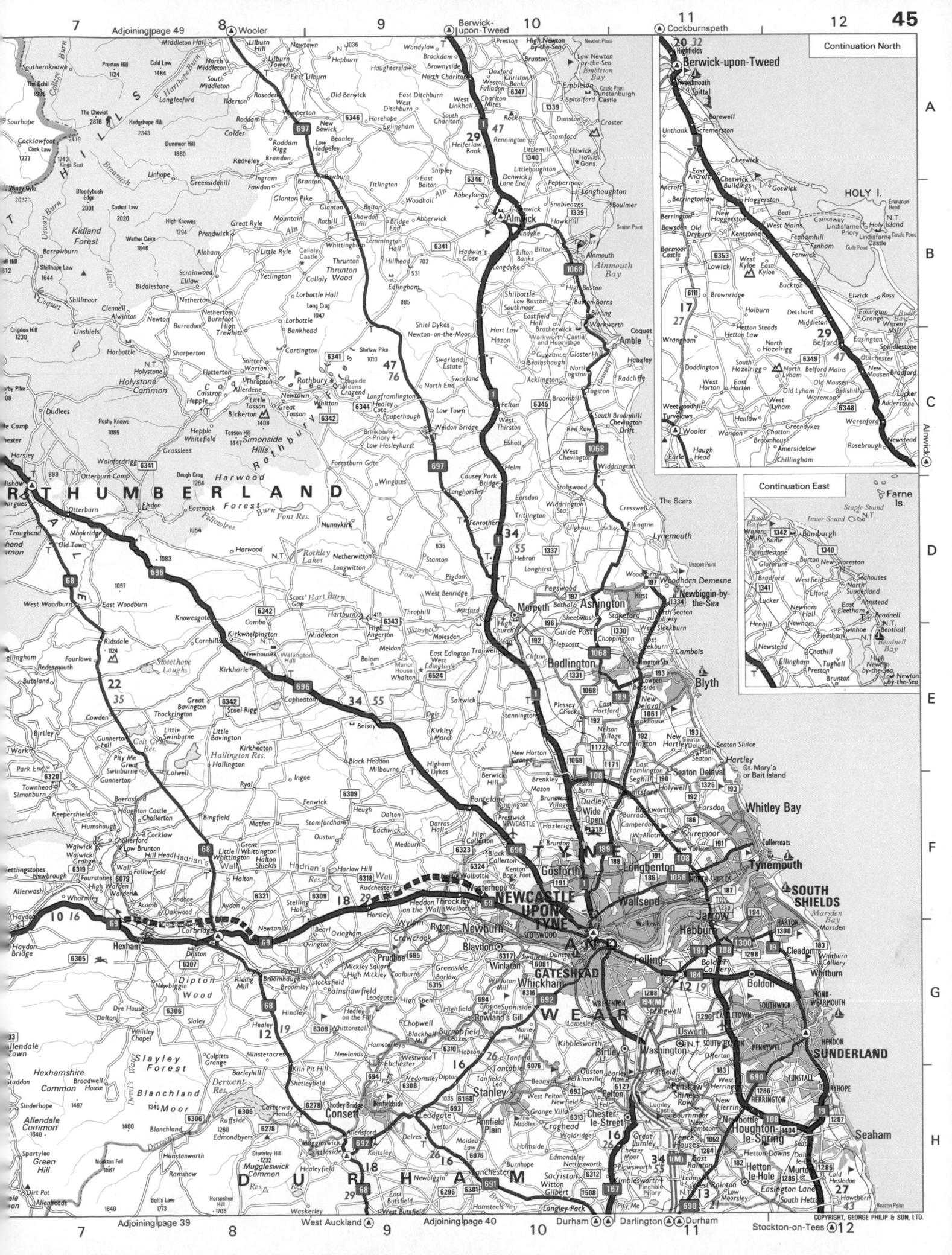

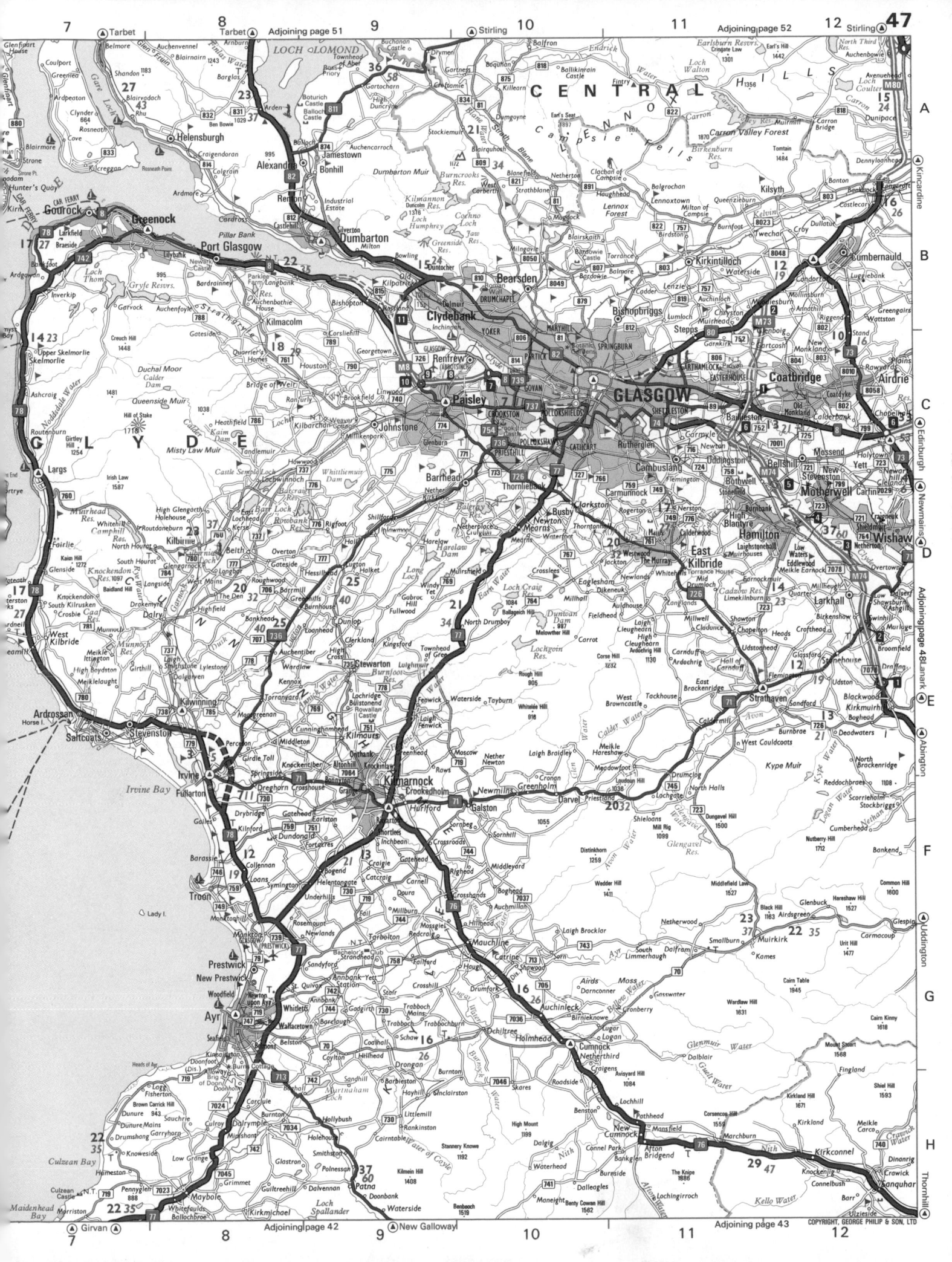

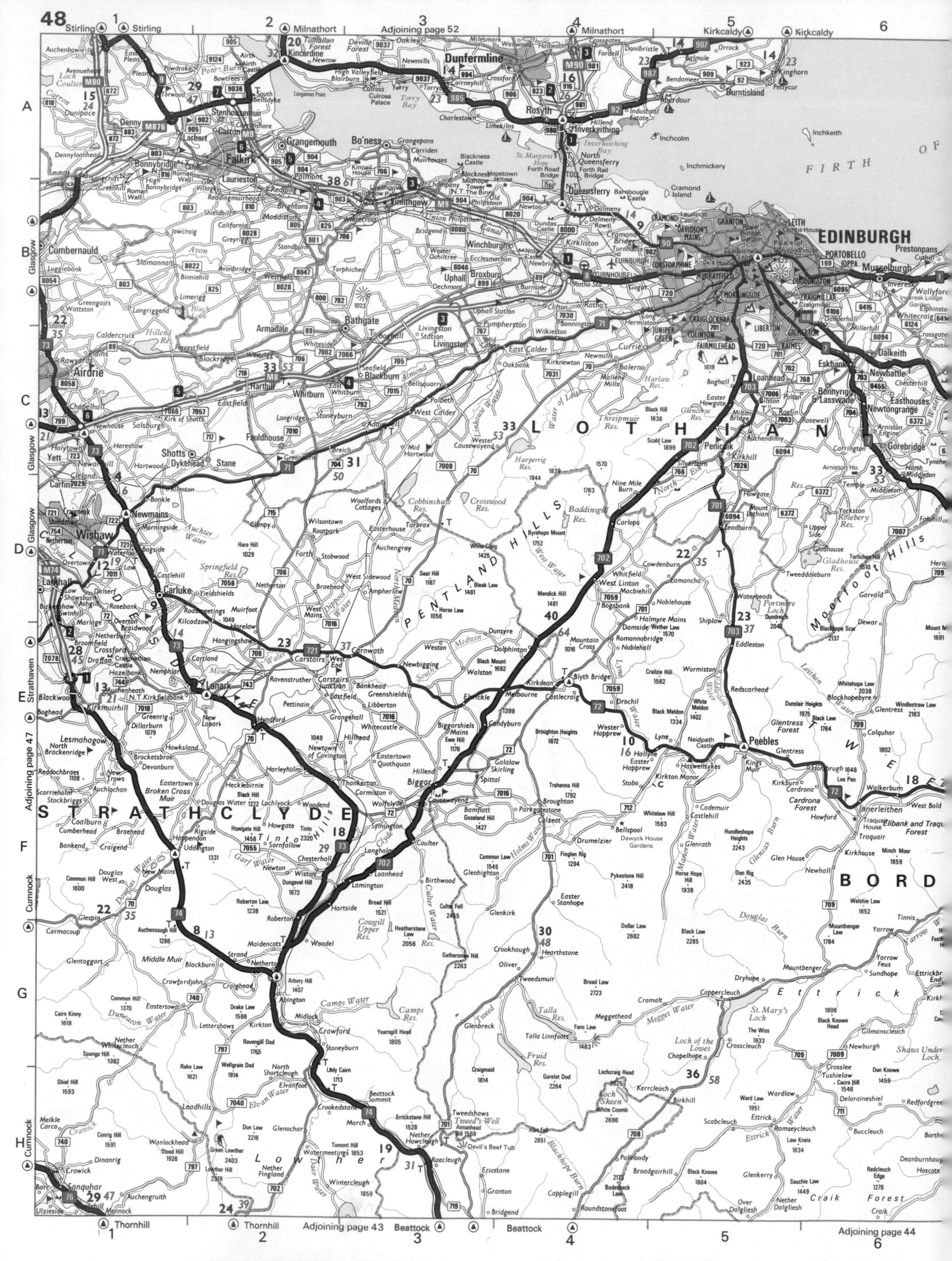

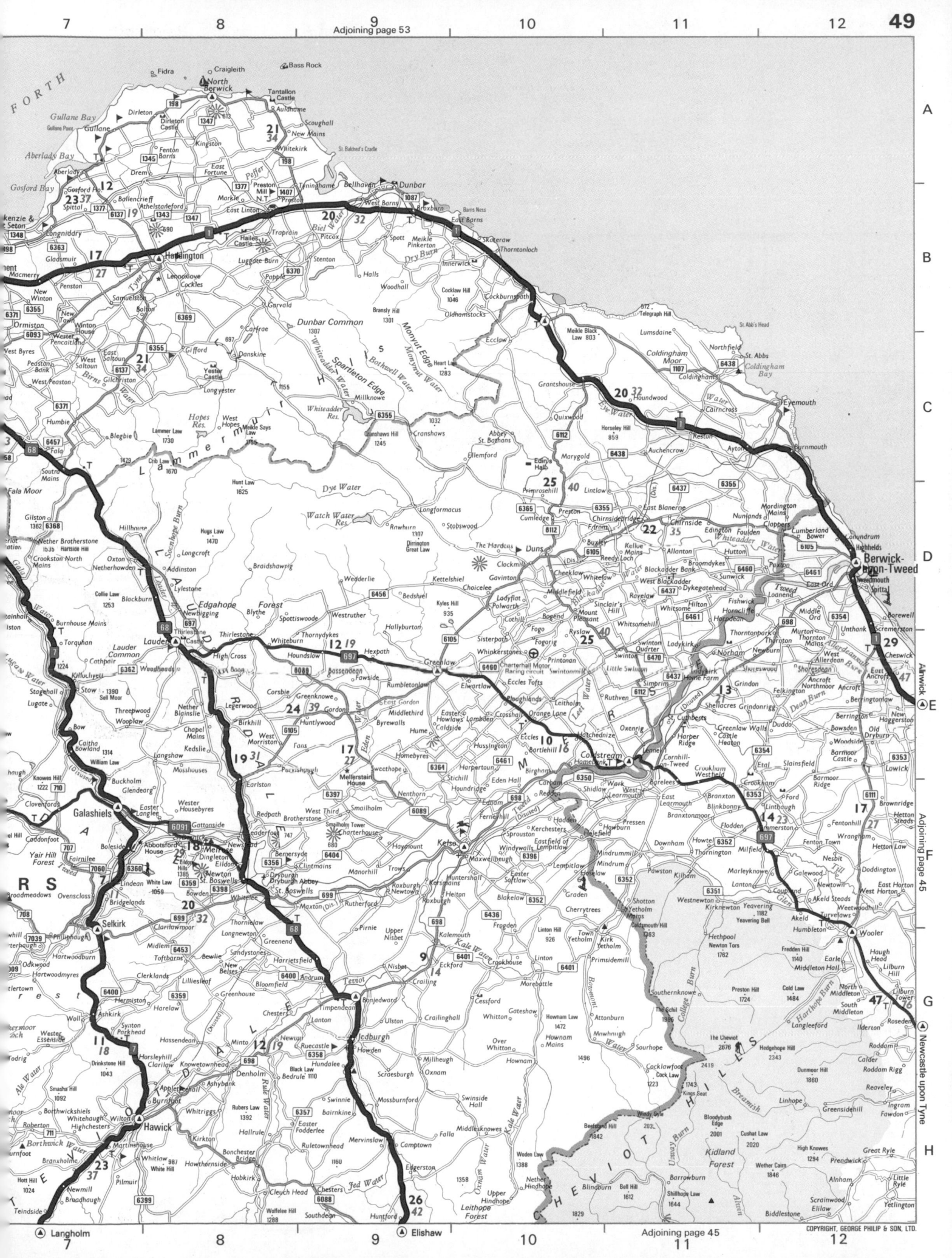

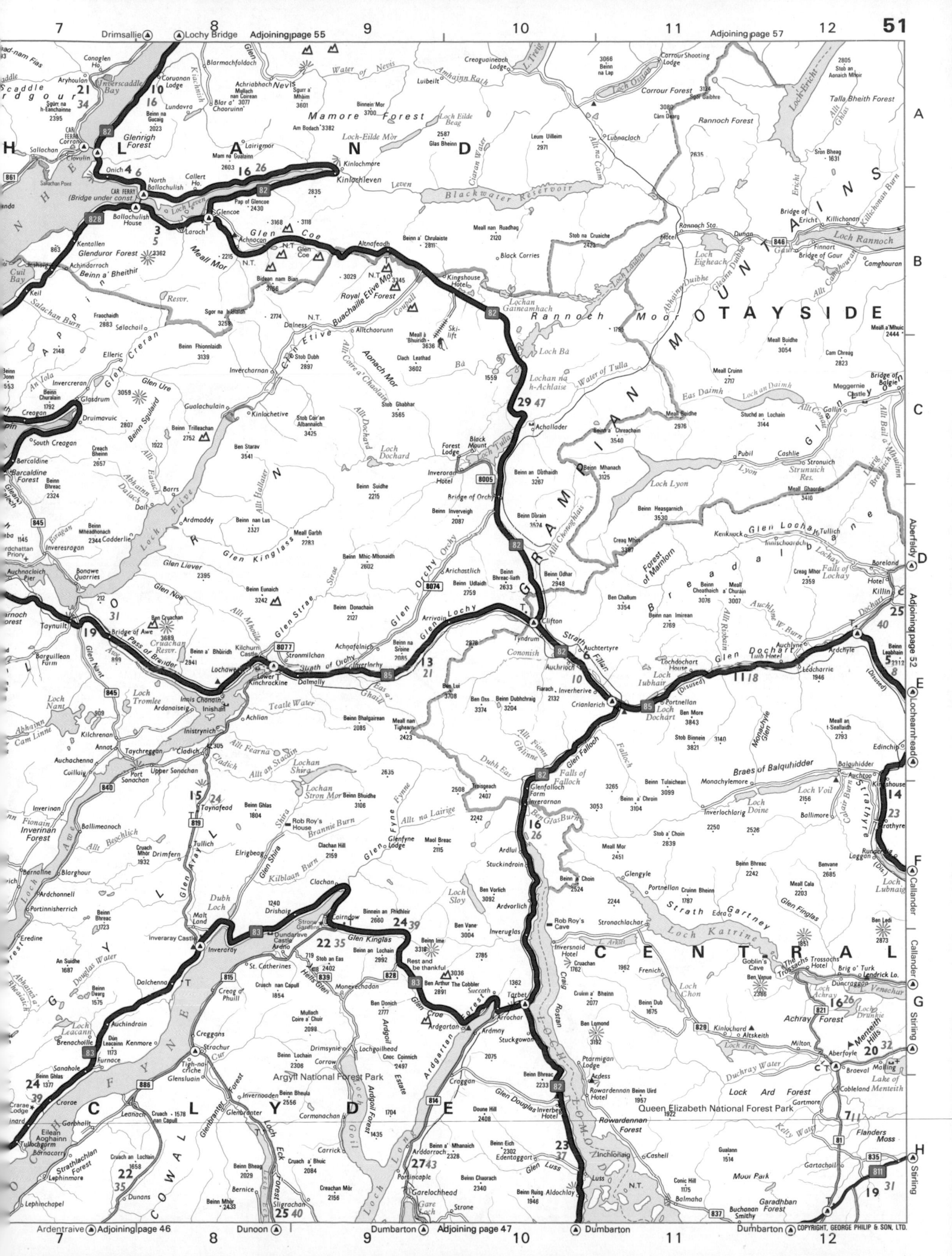

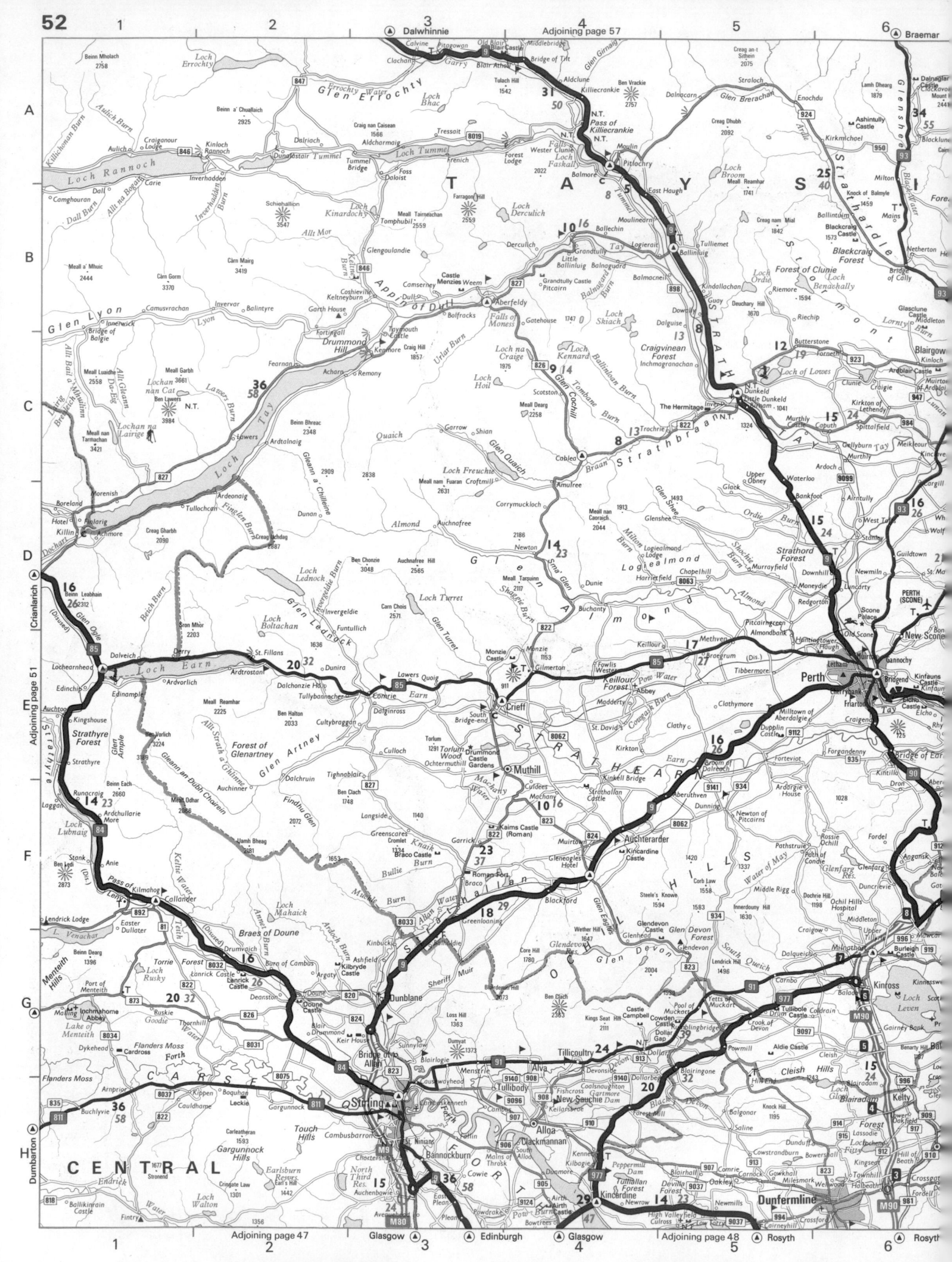

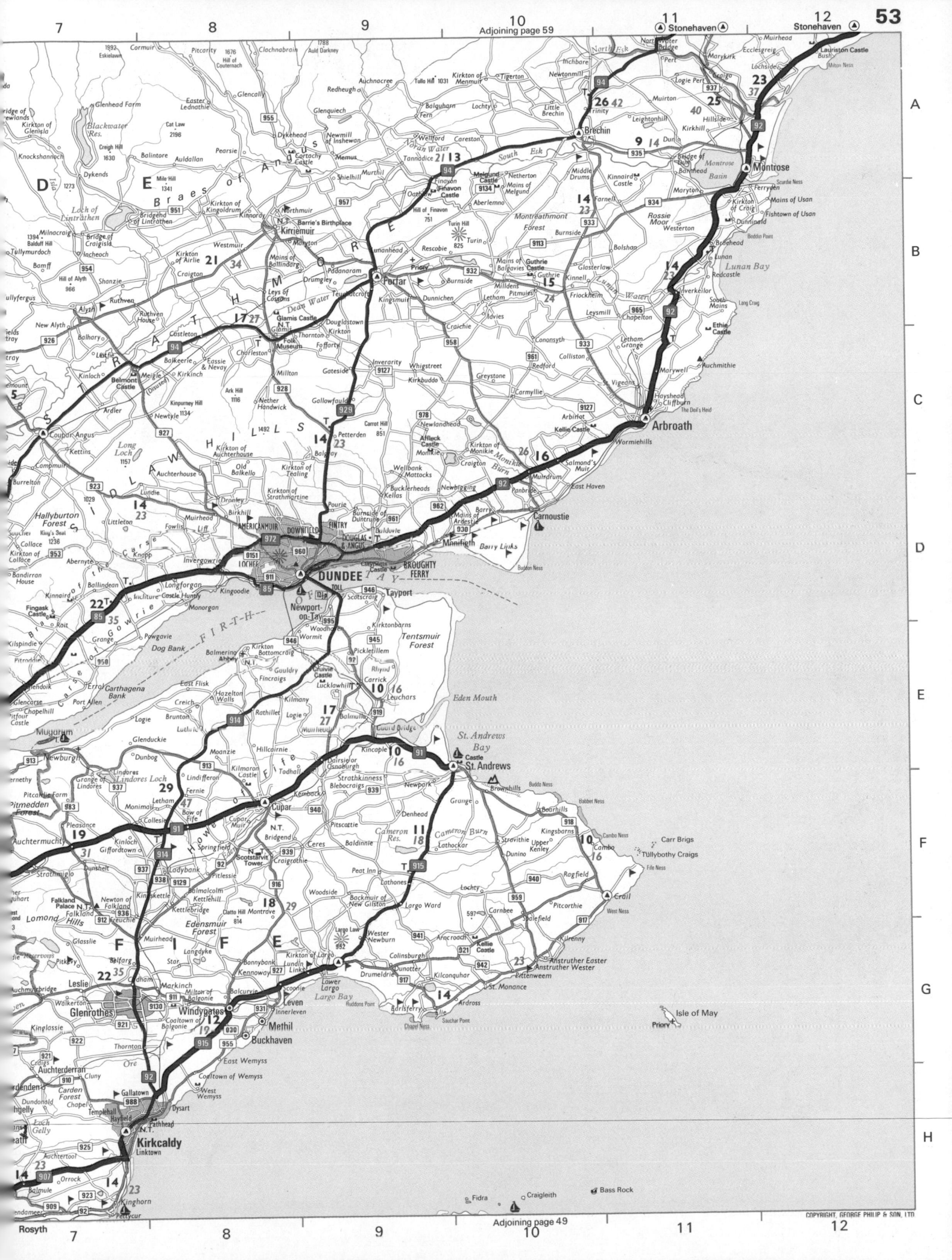

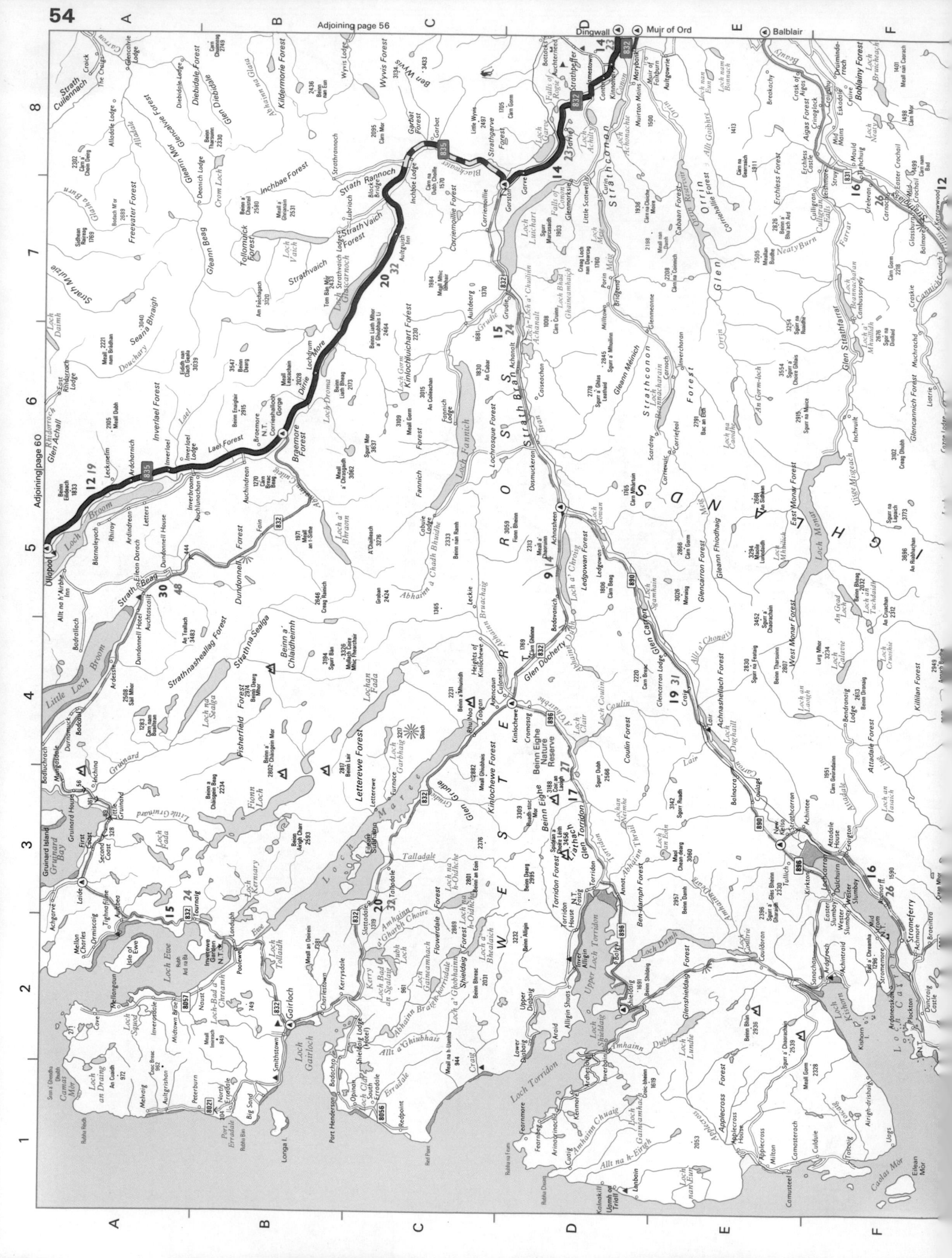

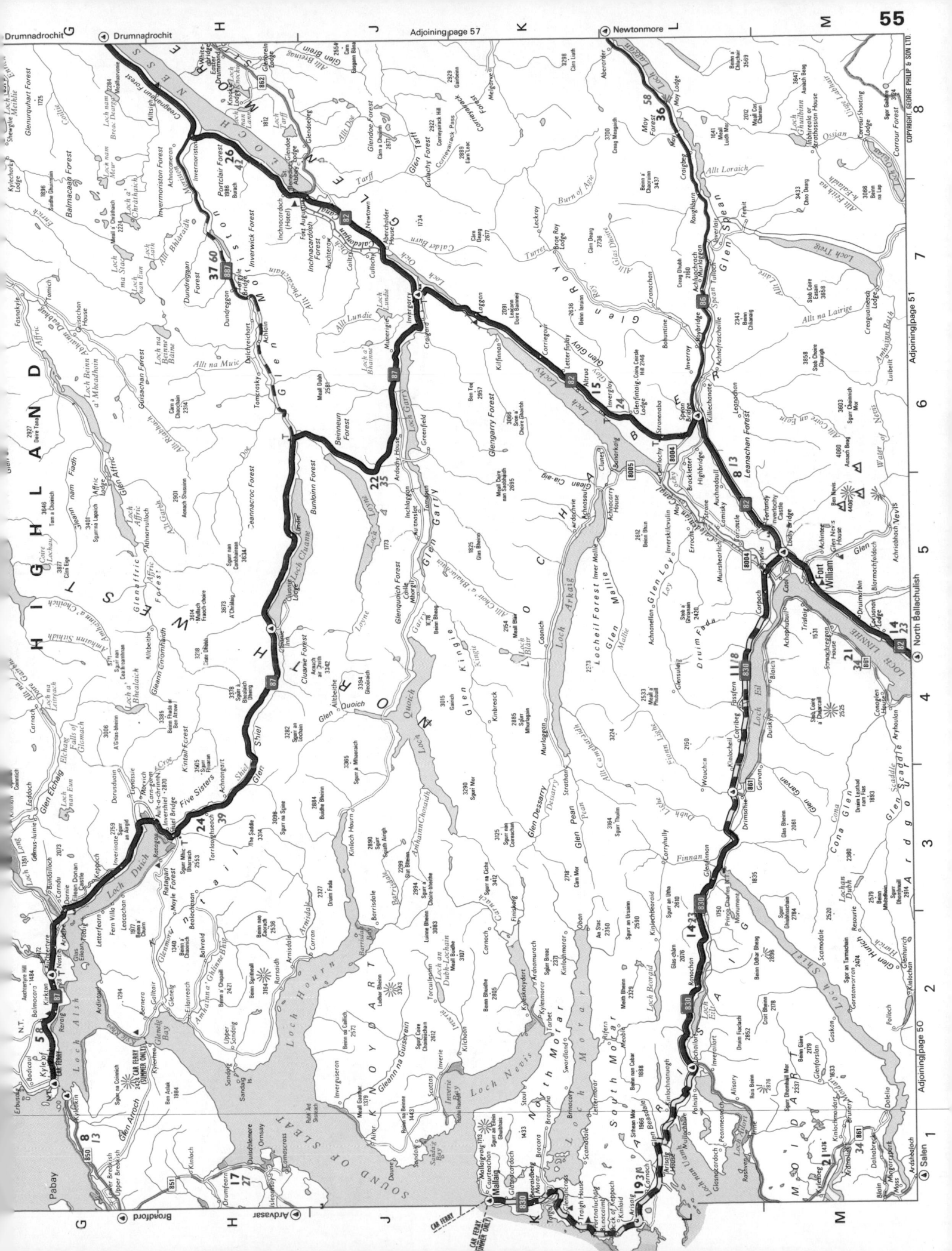

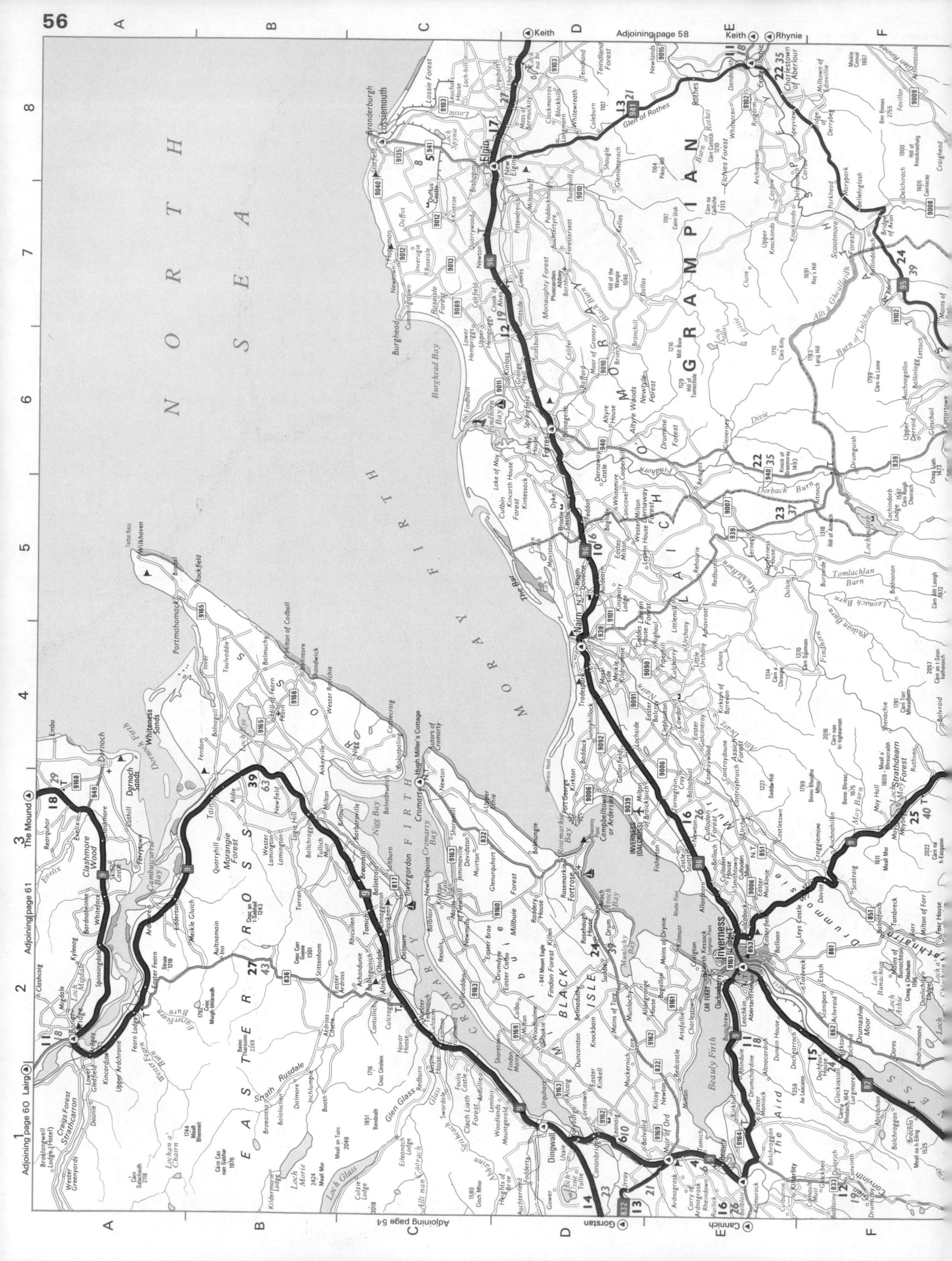

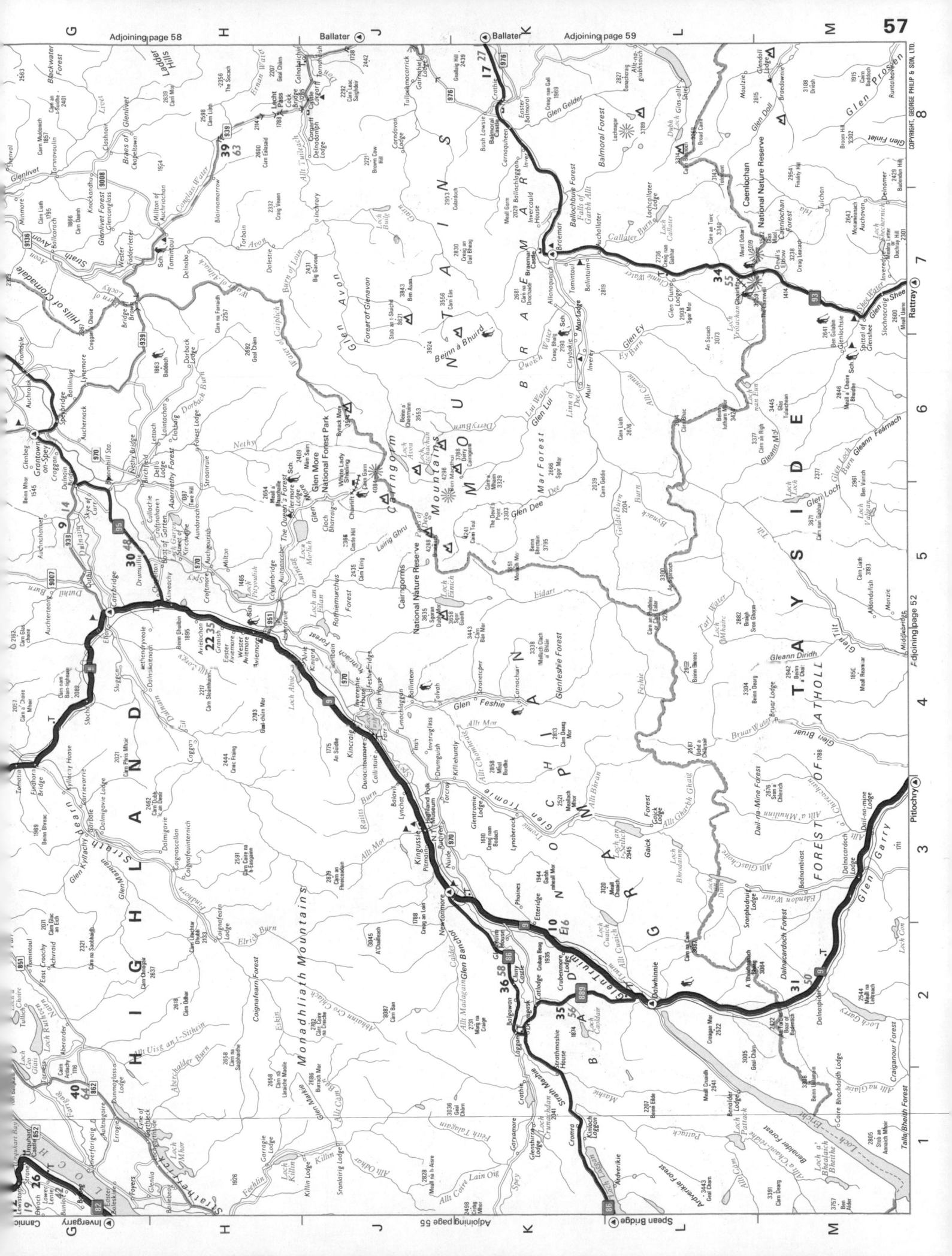

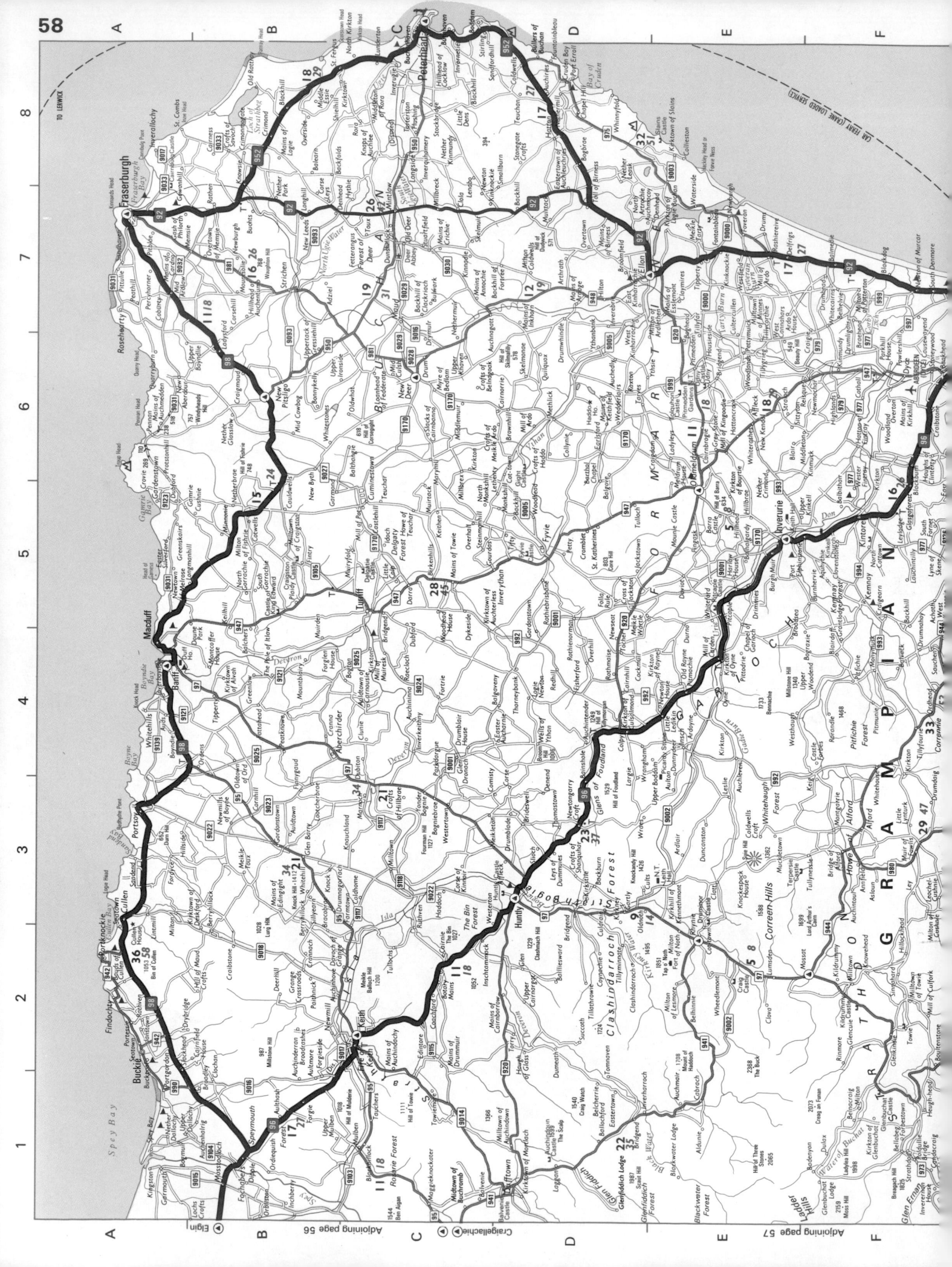

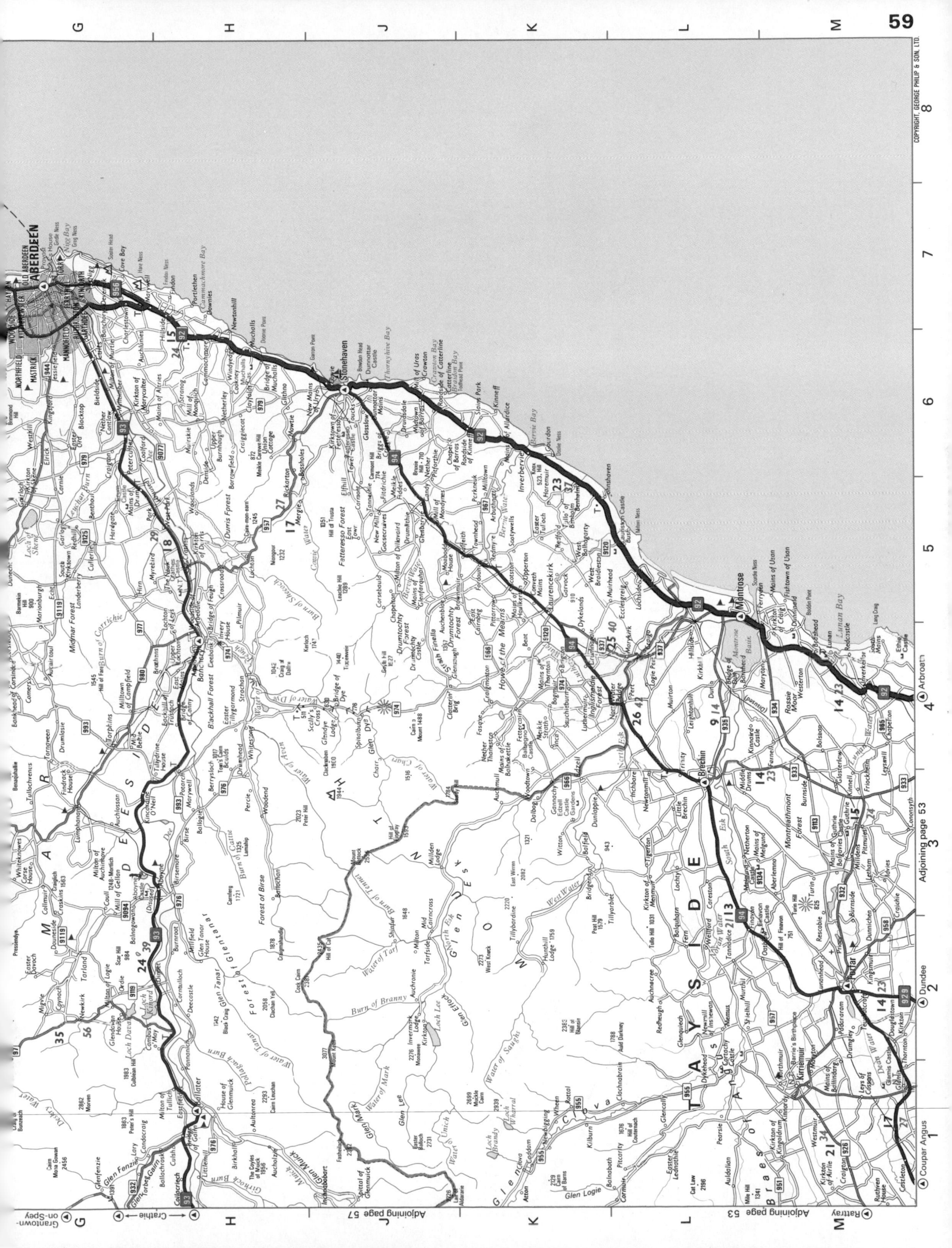

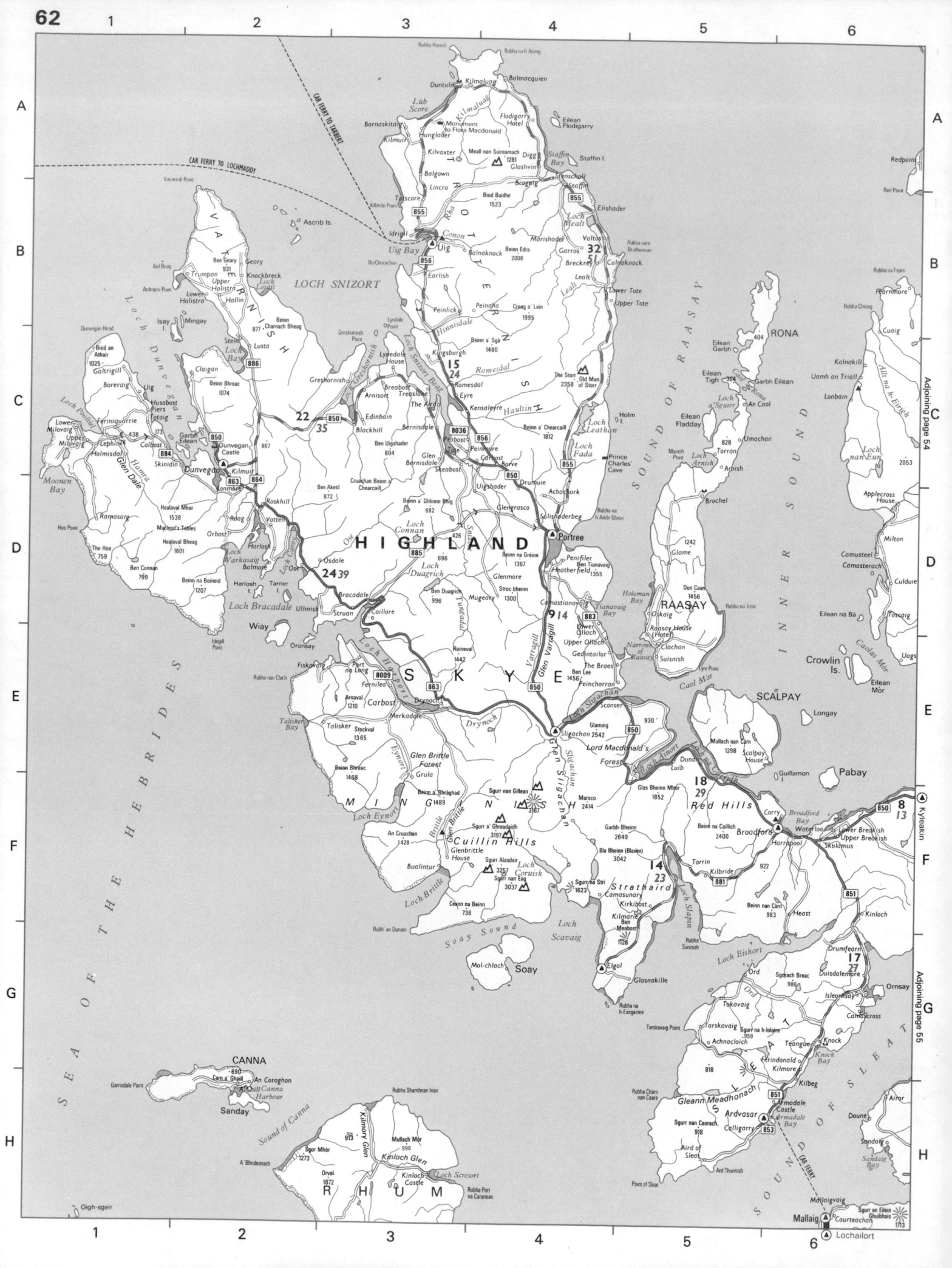

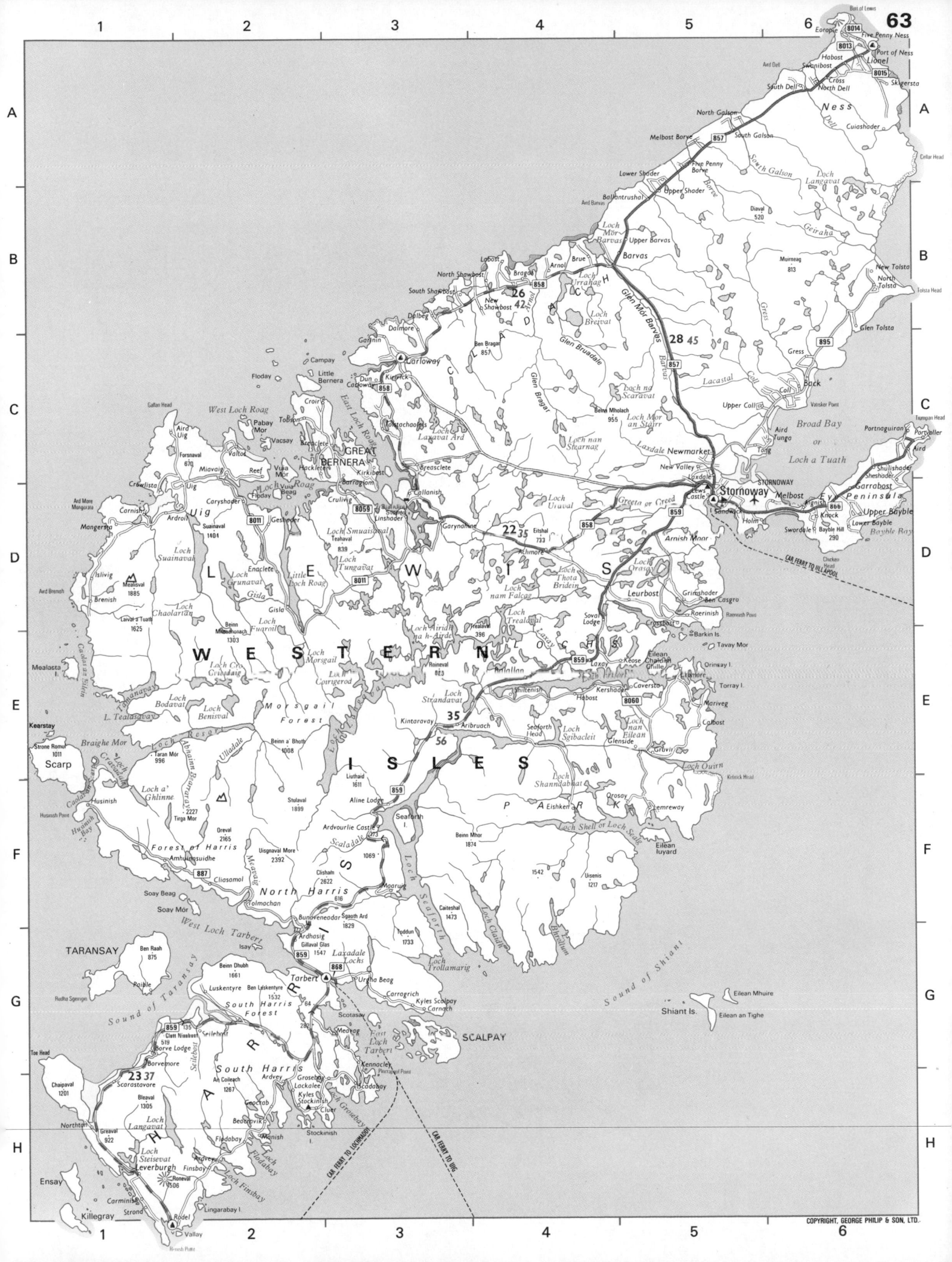

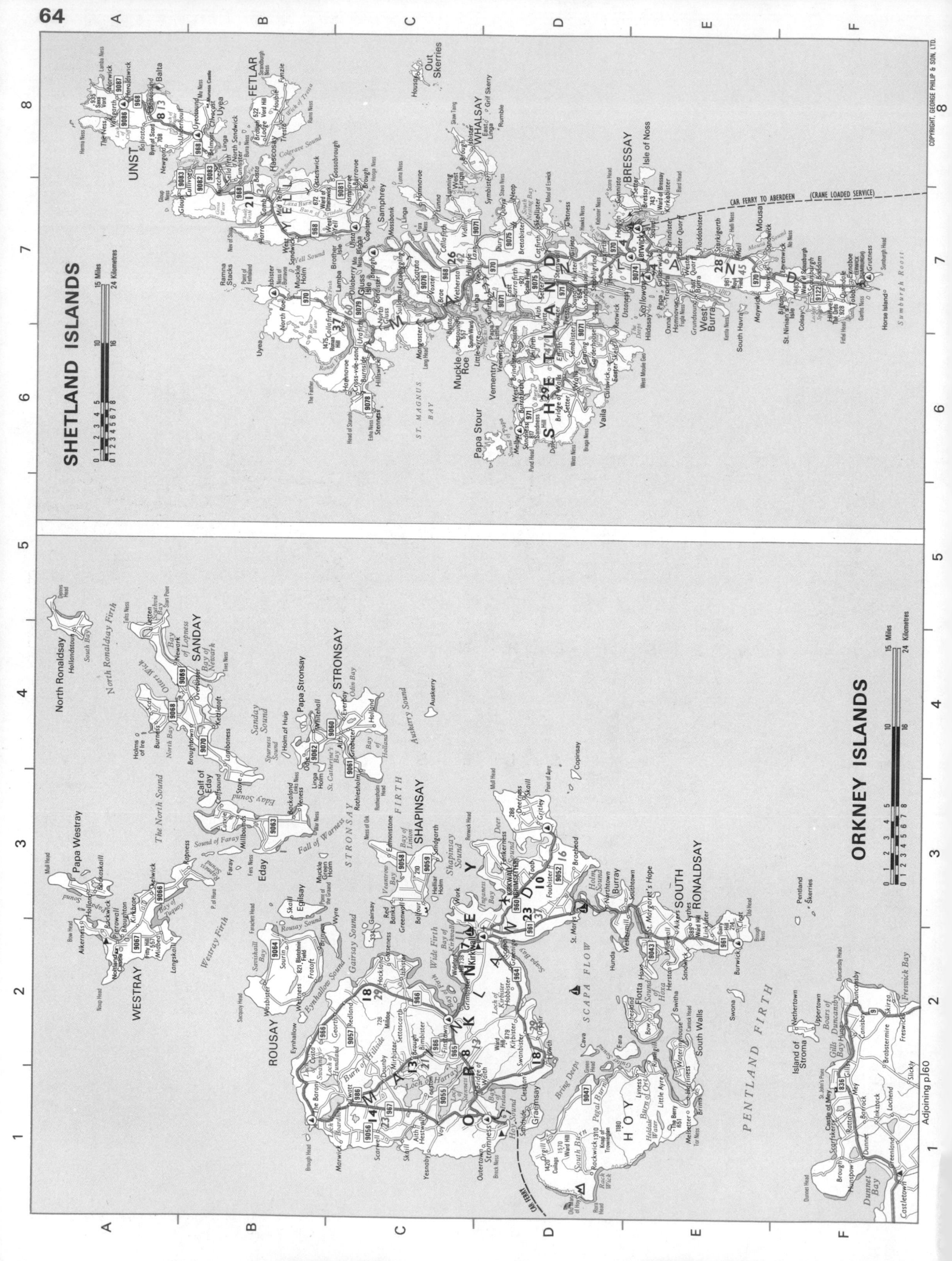

SHETLAND ISLANDS

ORKNEY ISLANDS

CAR FERRY TO ABERDEEN (CRANE LOADED SERVICE)

FETLAR

UNST

YELL

SHETLAND

BRESSAY

WHALSAY

Out Skerries

Isle of Noss

Muckle Roe

Papa Stour

St. Magnus Bay

NORTH RONALDSAY

SANDAY

WESTRAY

PAPA WESTRAY

ROUSAY

STRONSAY

SHAPINSAY

EDAY

O R K N E Y

HOY

SOUTH RONALDSAY

SCAPA FLOW

PENTLAND FIRTH

Pentland Skerries

Island of Stroma

Dunnet Bay

Adjoining p.60

Miles

Kilometres

0 1 2 3 4 5 6 7 8

10

15 Miles

16

24 Kilometres

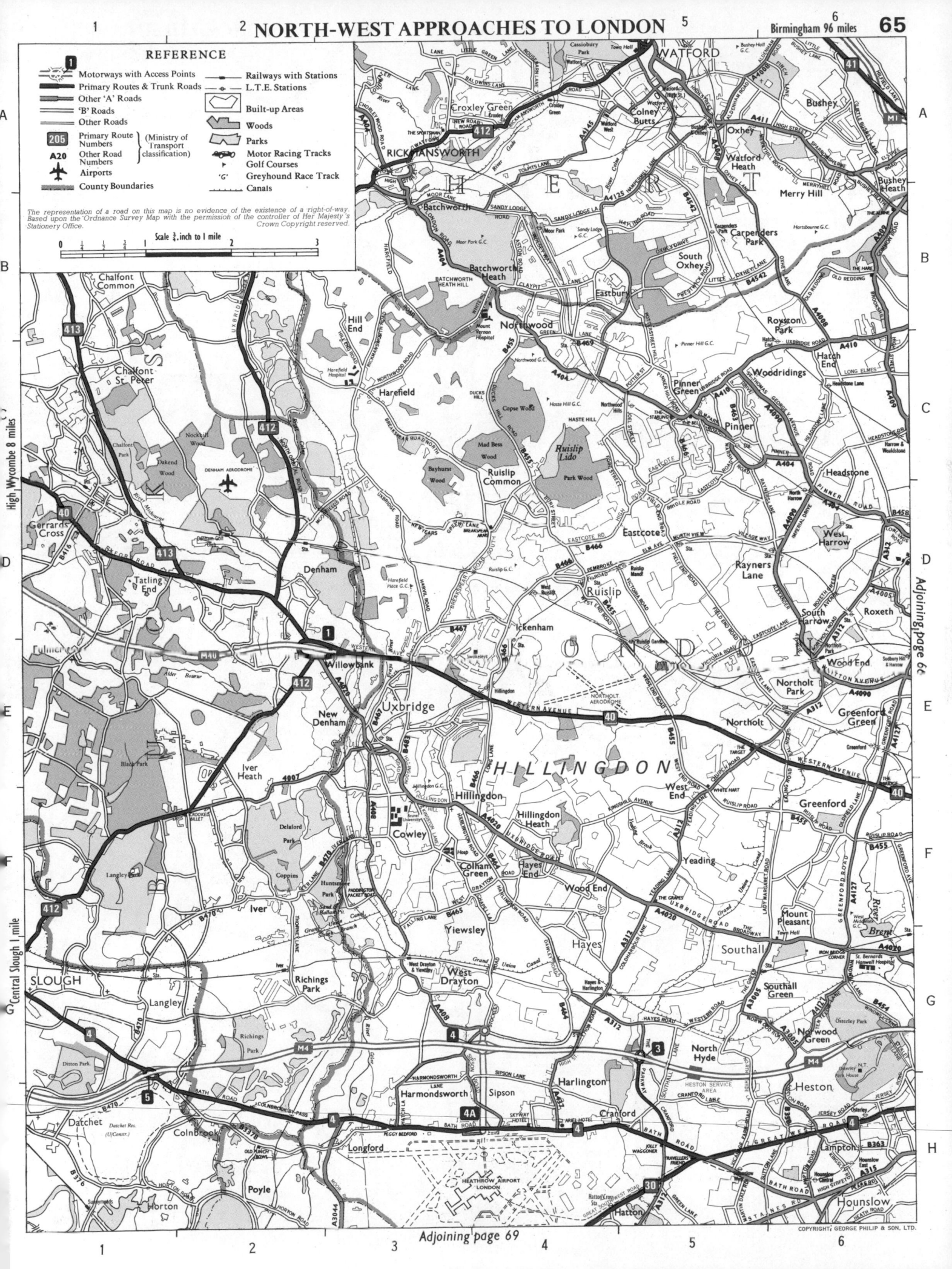

Adjoining page 65

Adjoining page 69

Adjoining page 70

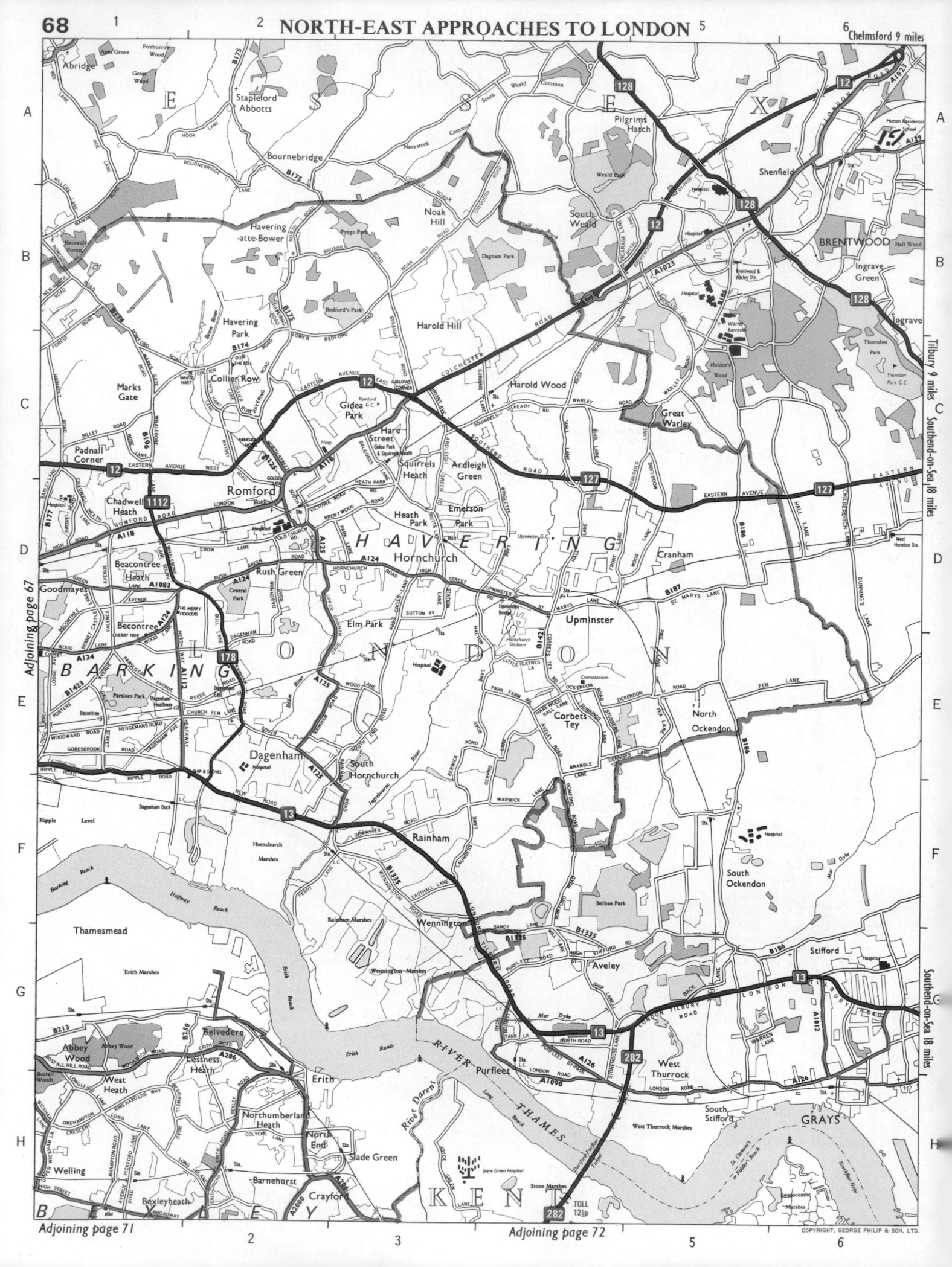

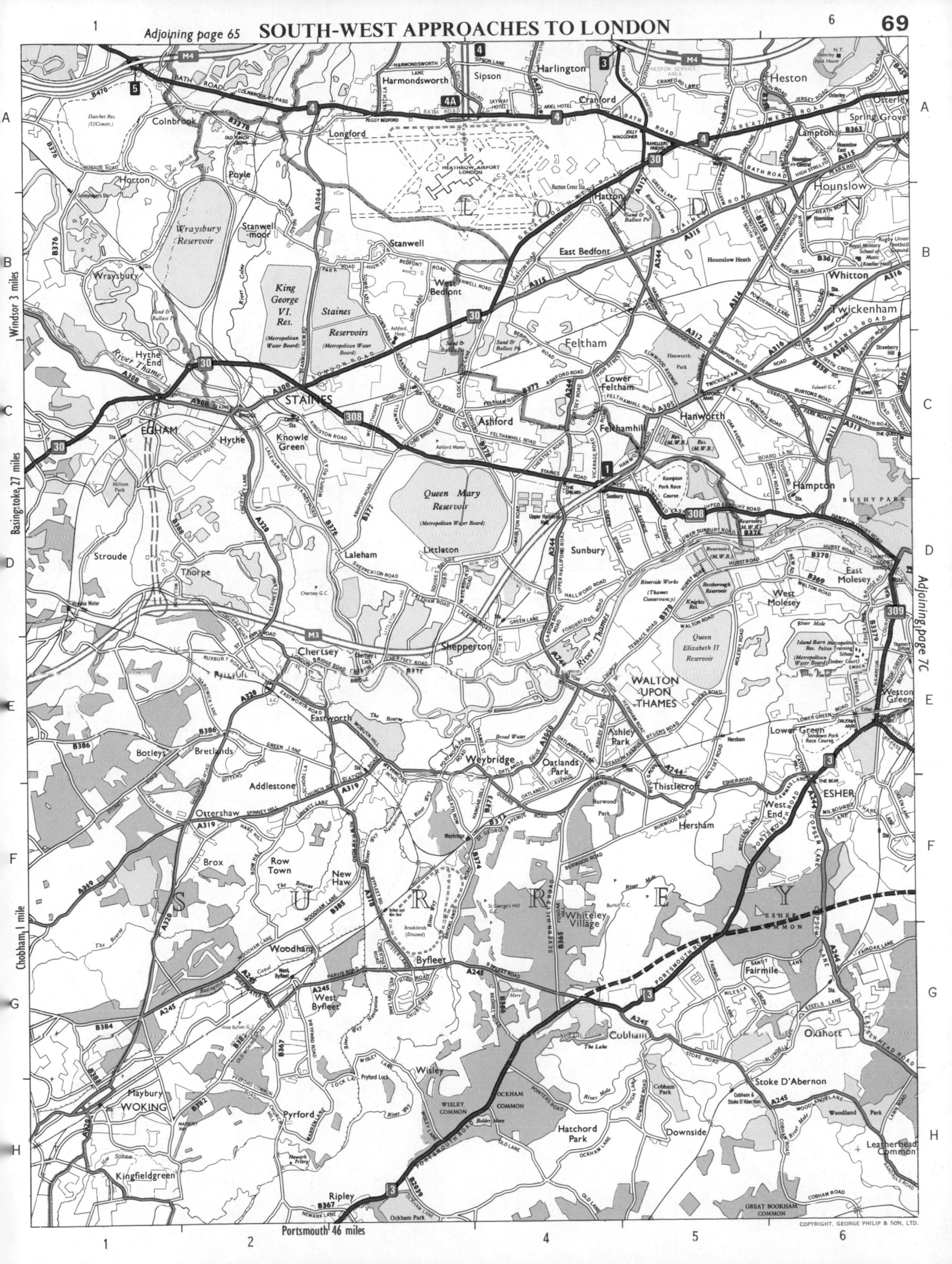

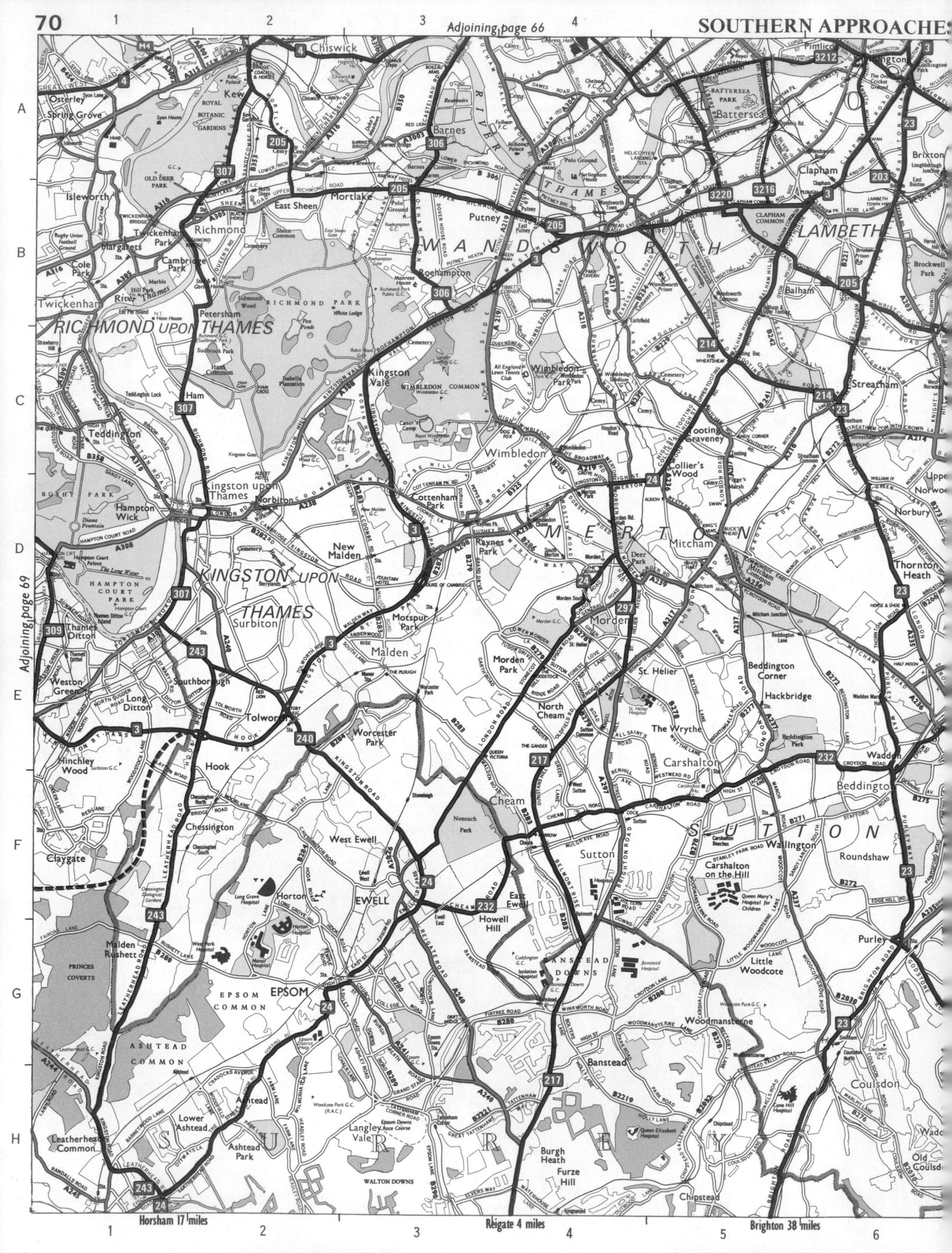

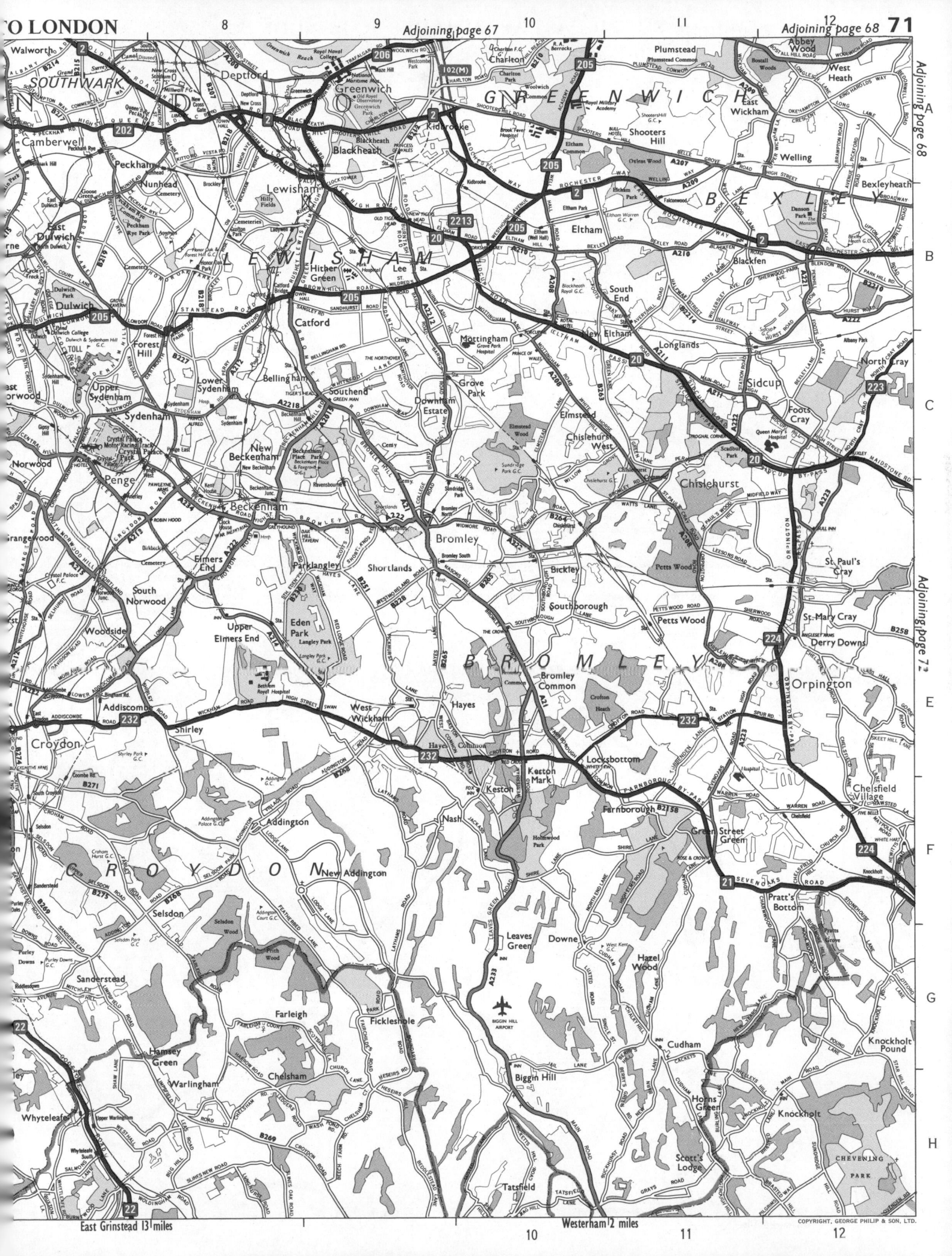

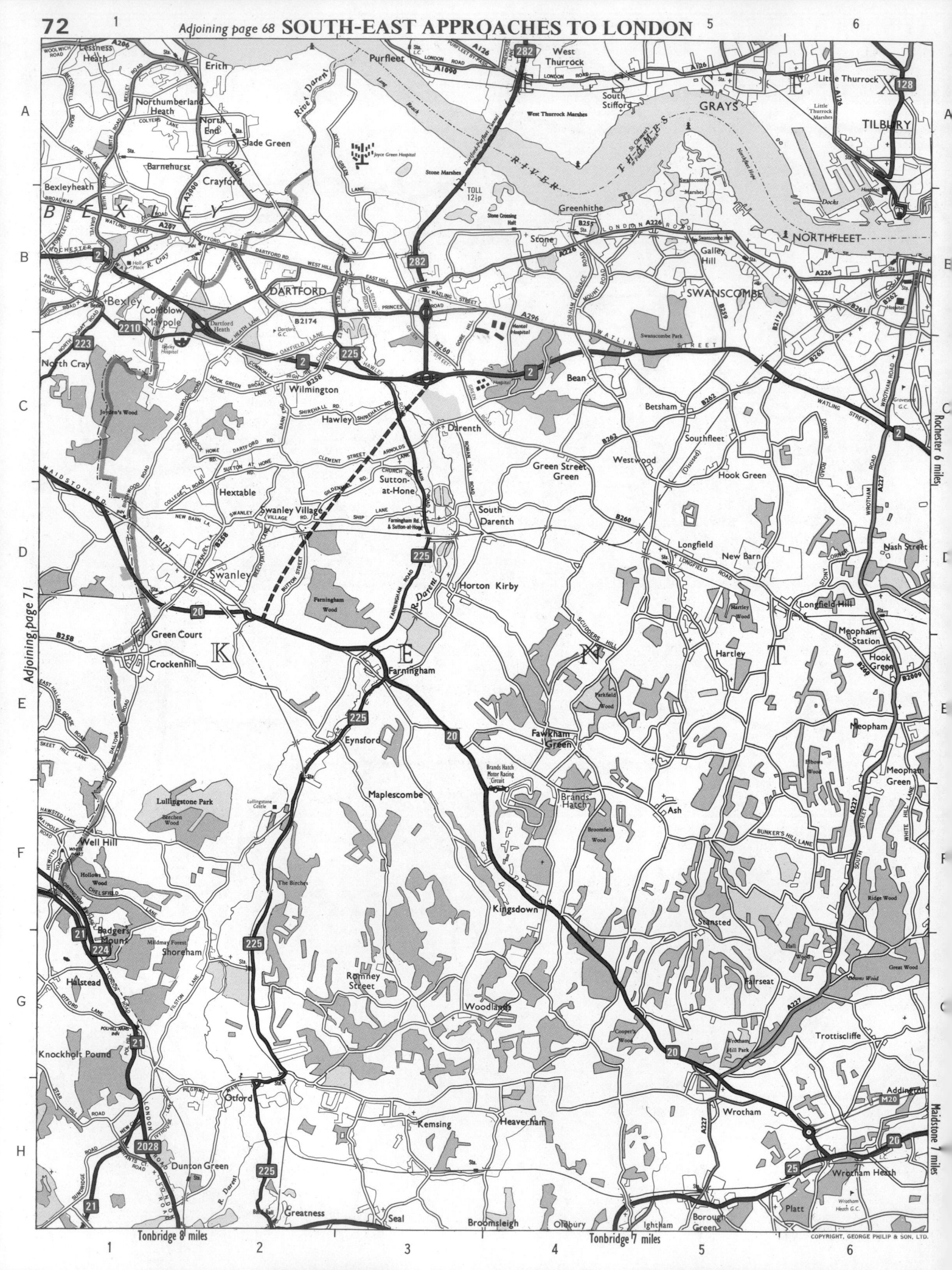

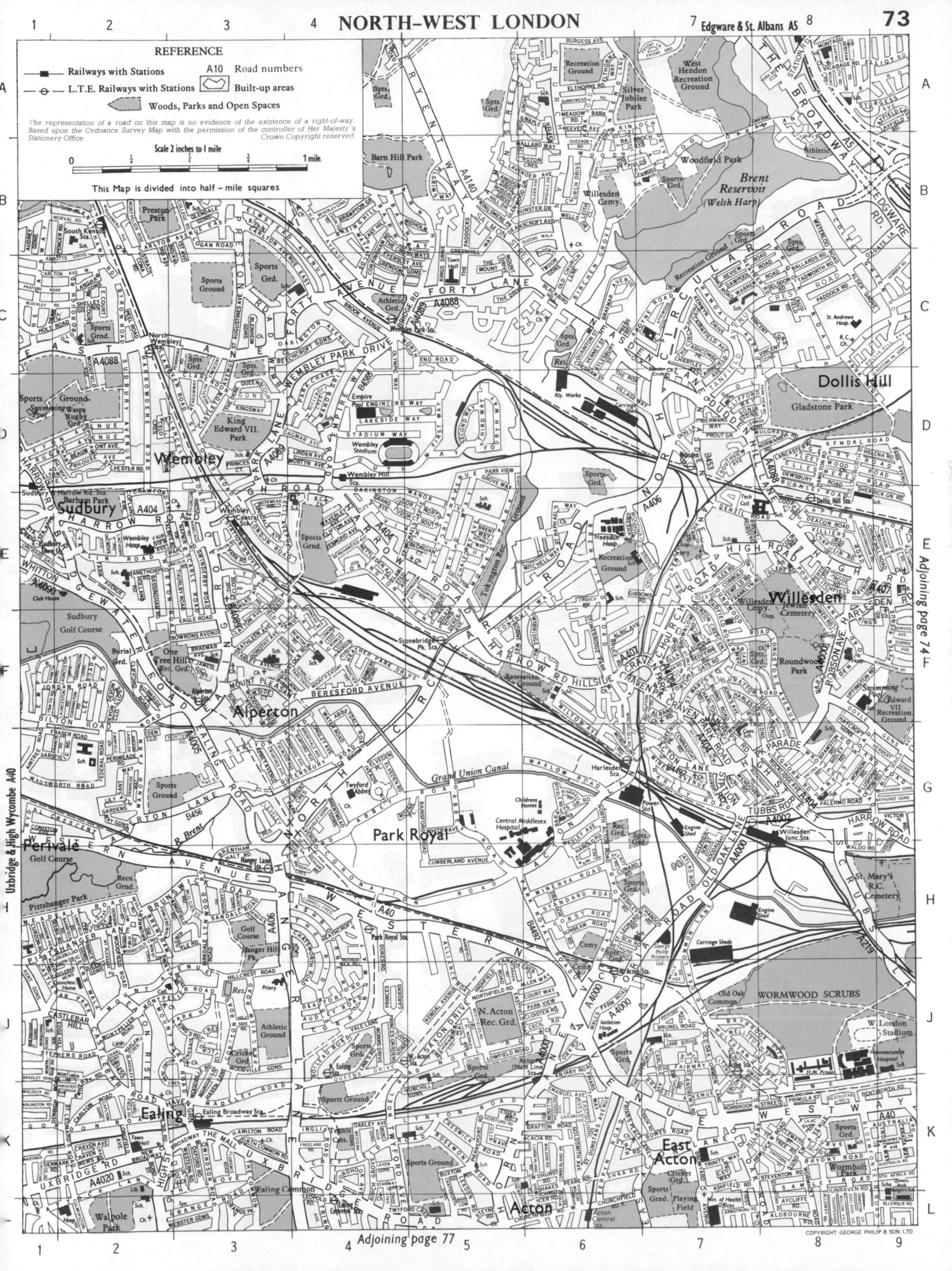

COPYRIGHT. GEORGE PHILIP & SON. LTD.

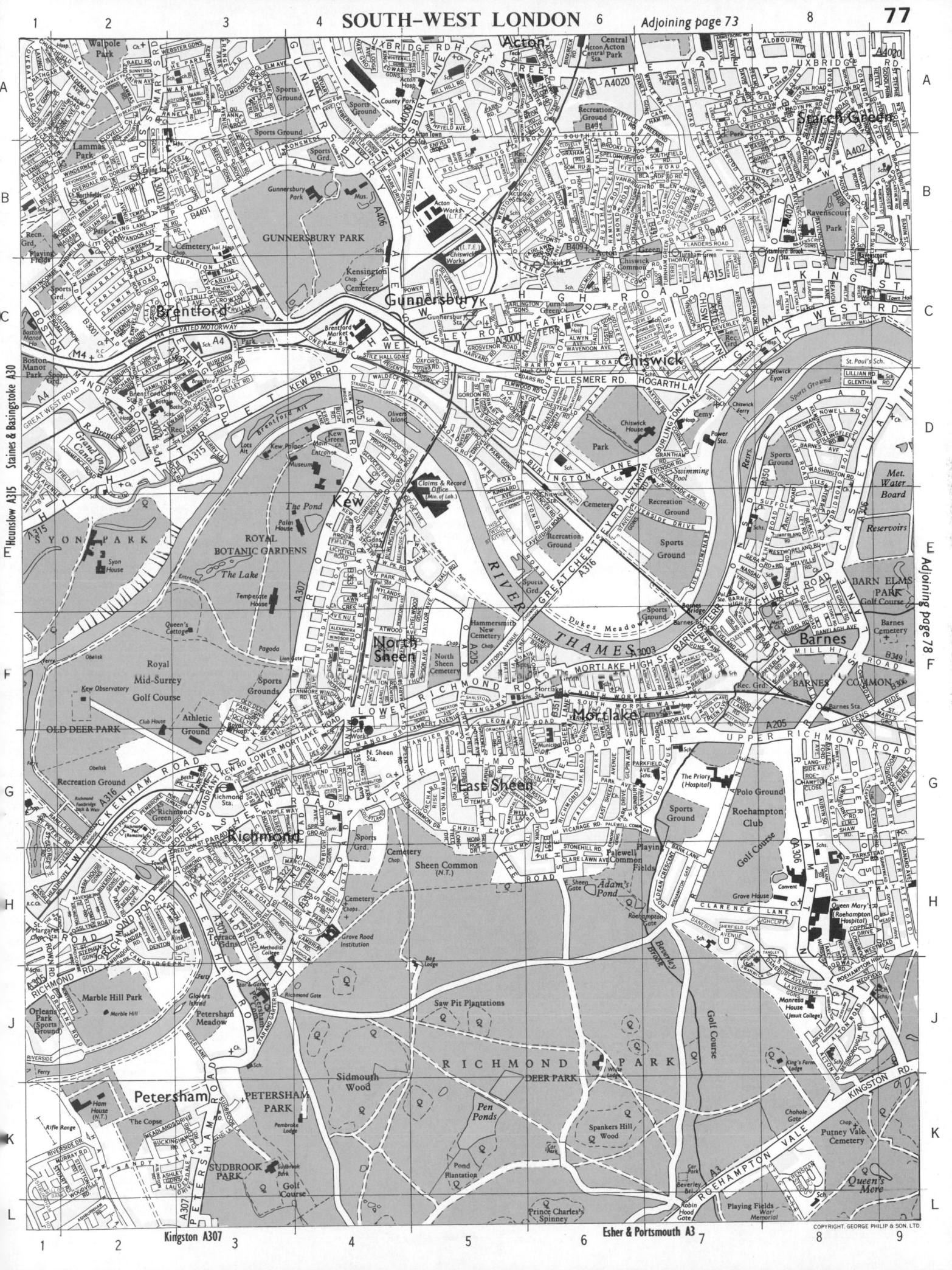

Adjoining page 75

Adjoining page 80

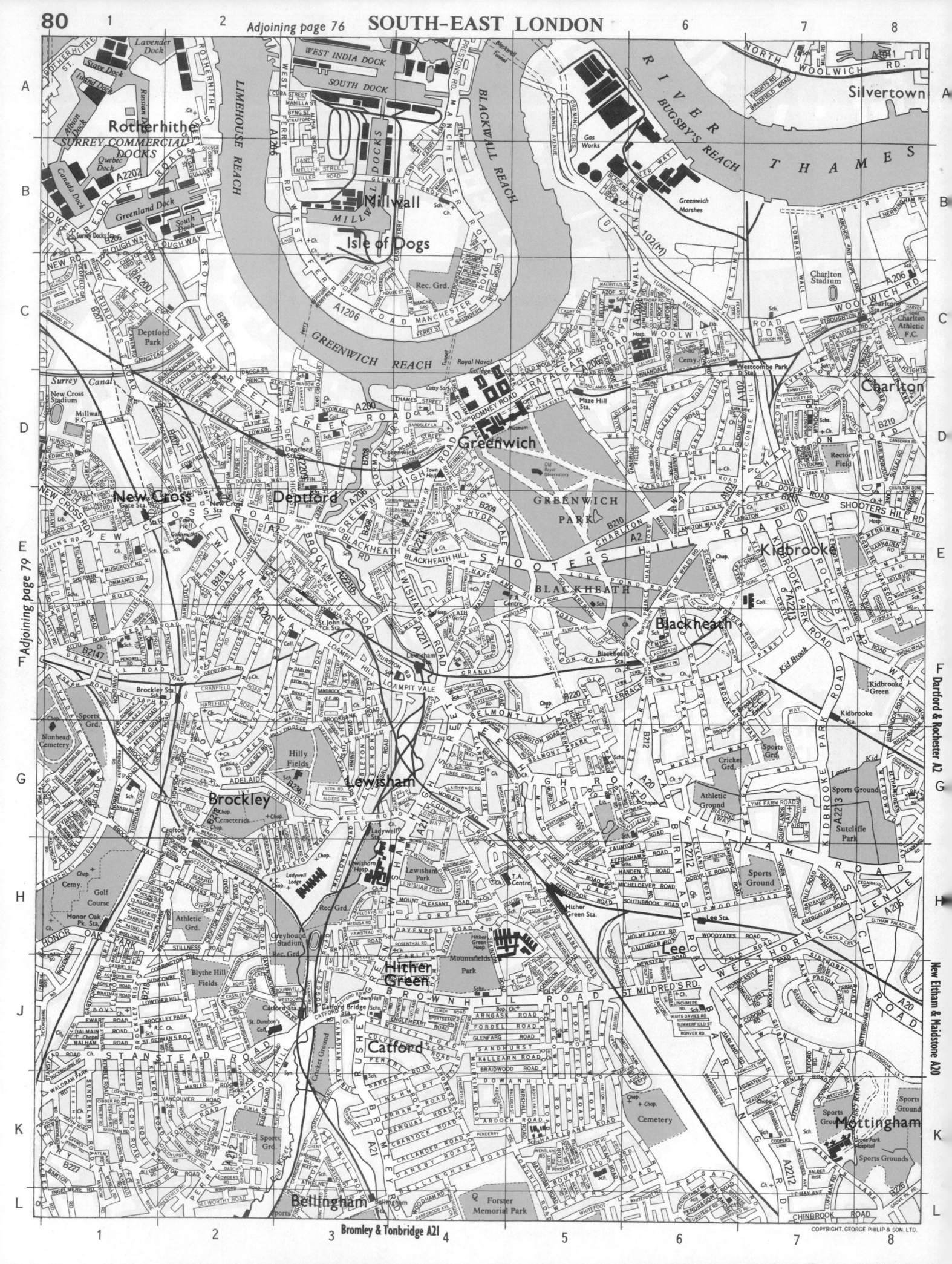

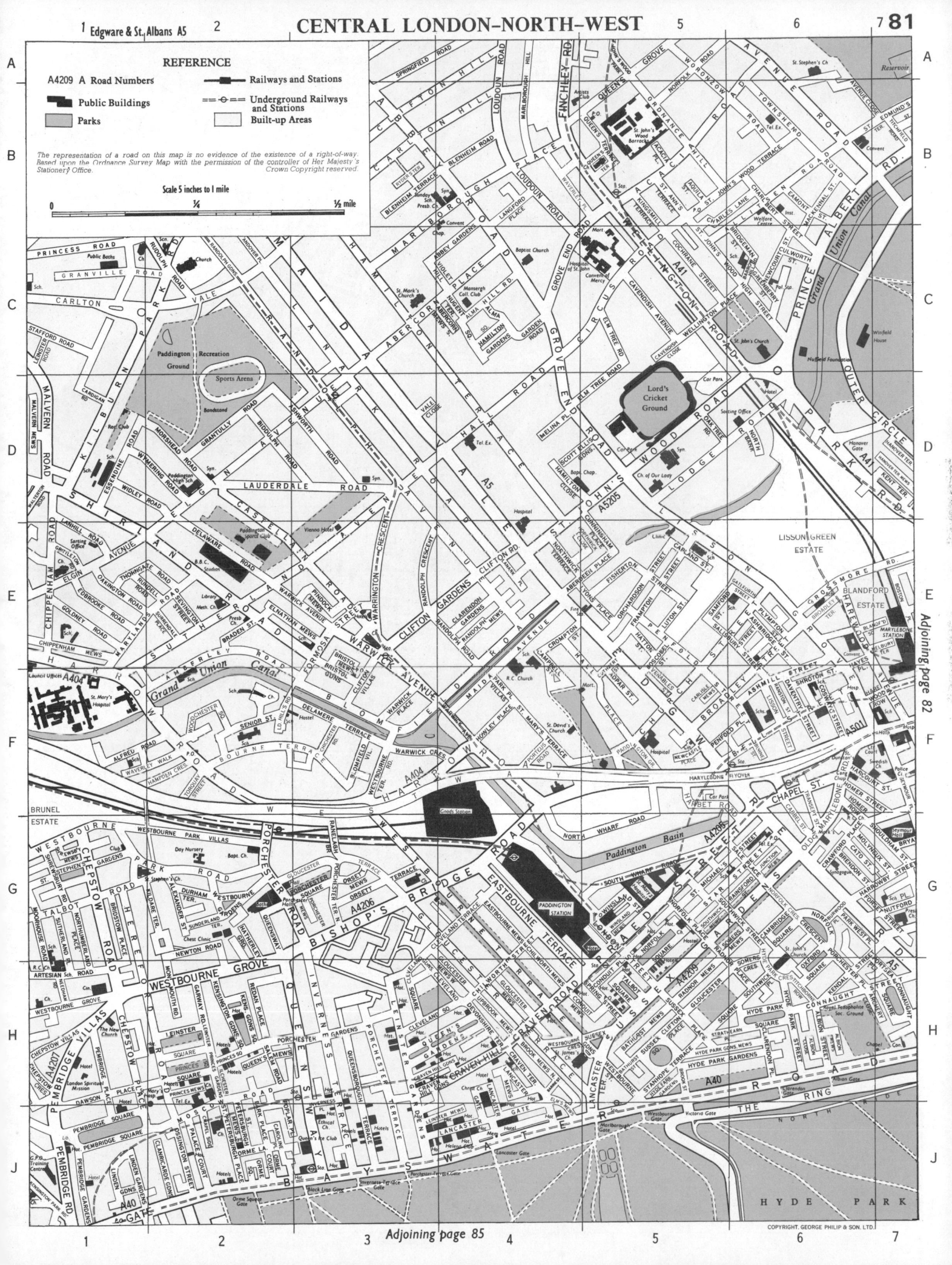

REFERENCE

A4209 A Road Numbers

Public Buildings

Parks

Railways and Stations

Underground Railways and Stations

Built-up Areas

The representation of a road on this map is no evidence of the existence of a right-of-way. Based upon the Ordnance Survey Map with the permission of the controller of Her Majesty's Stationery Office.   Crown Copyright reserved.

Scale 5 inches to 1 mile

0   ¼   ½ mile

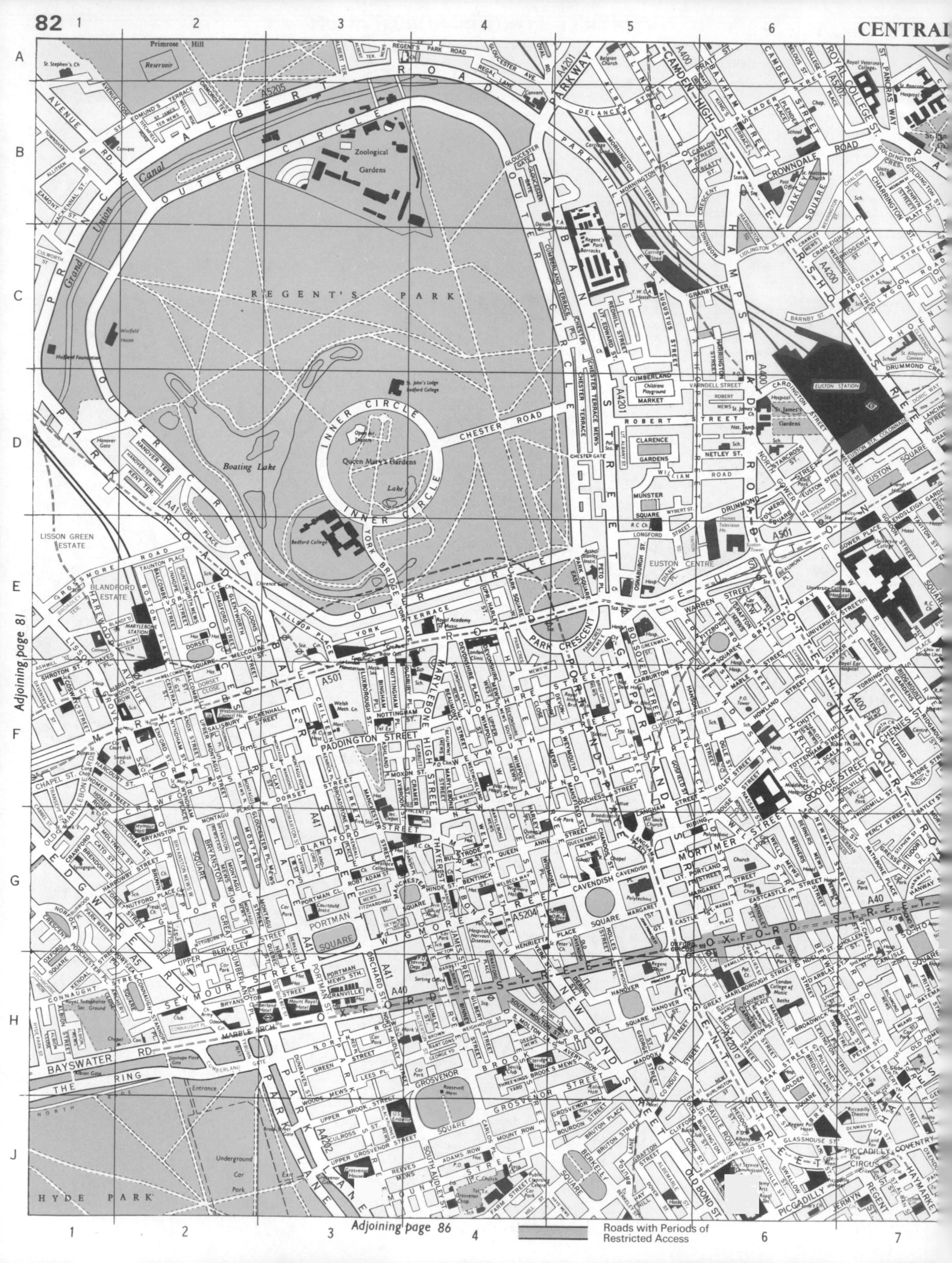

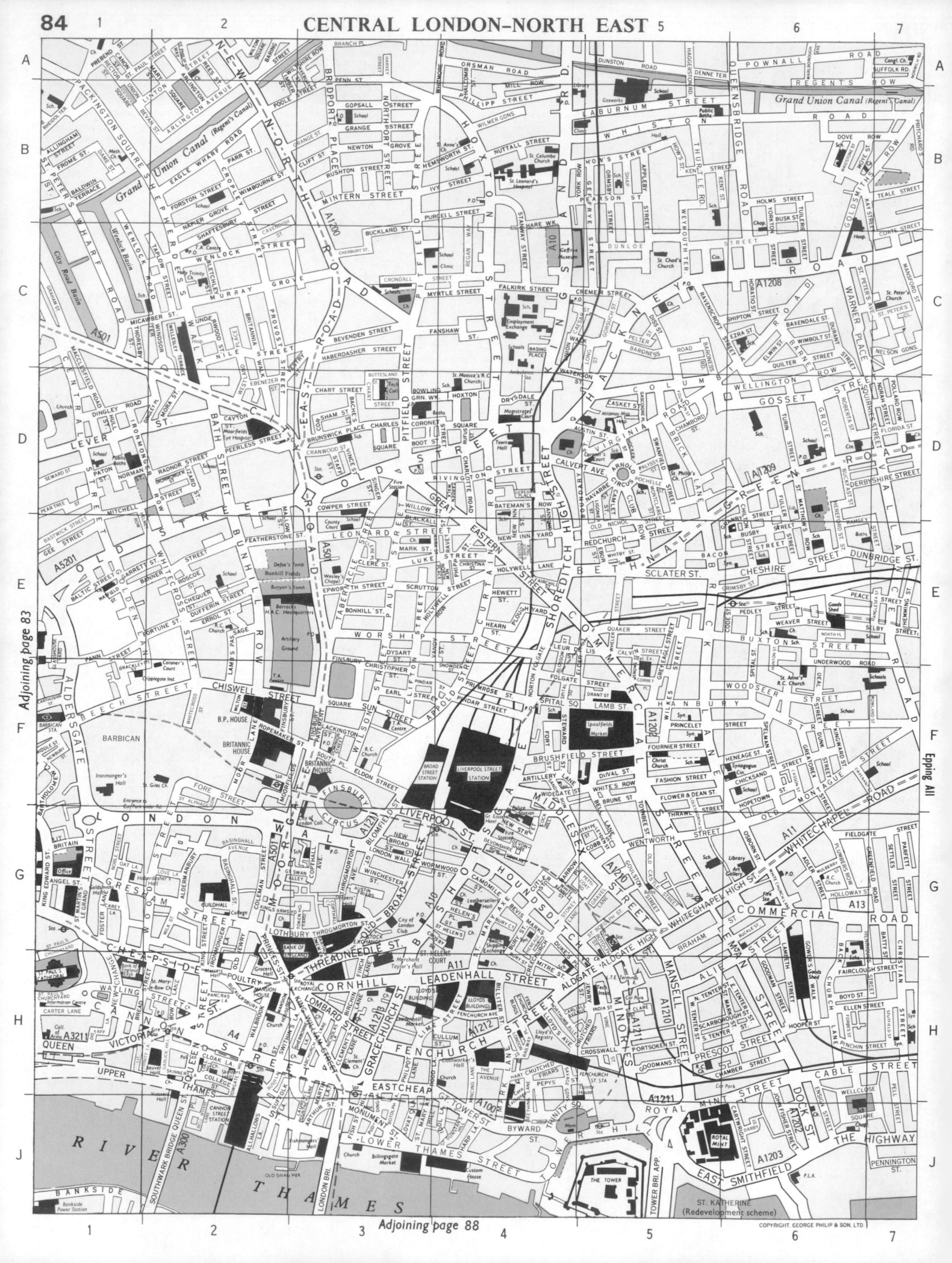

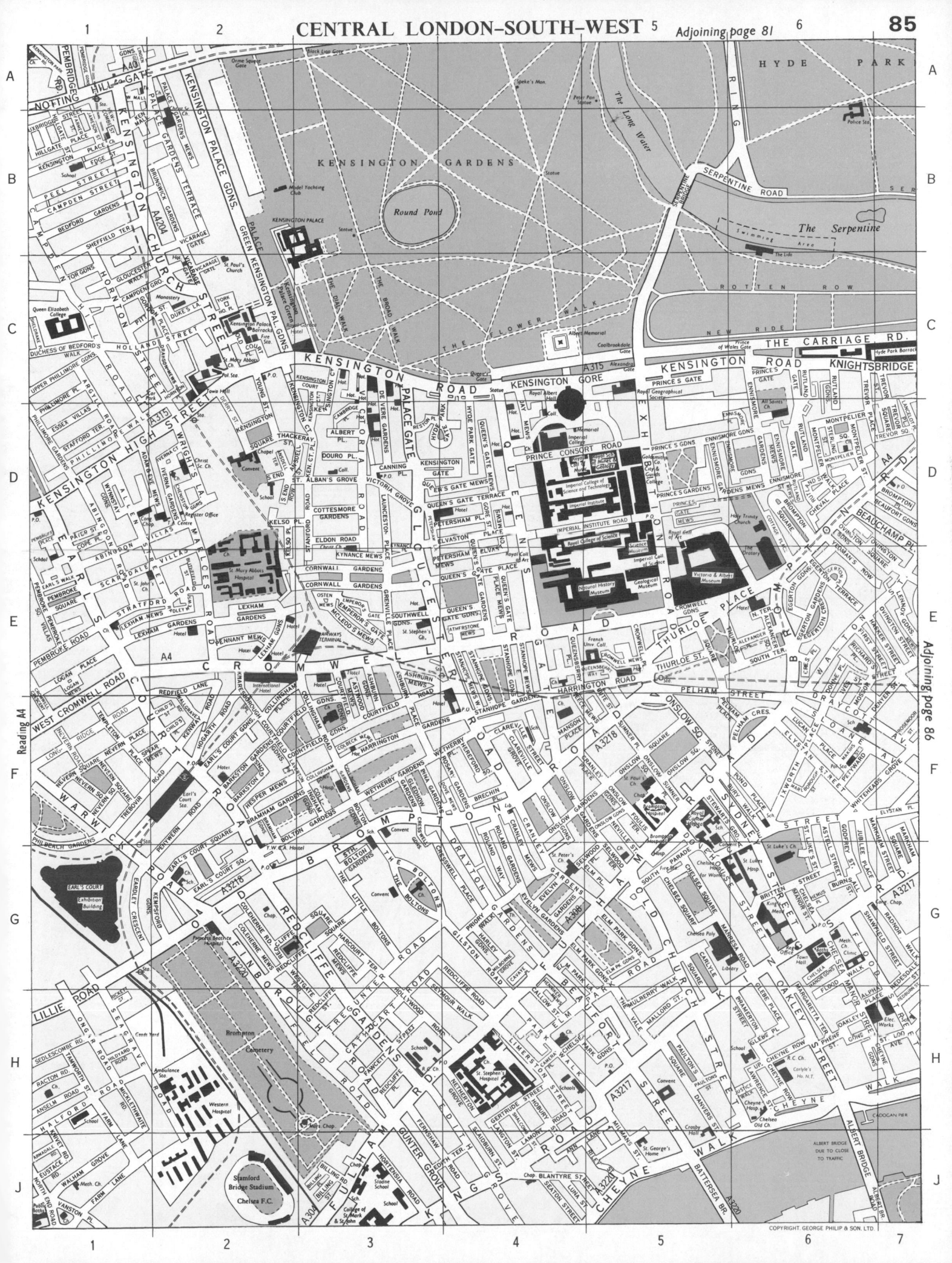

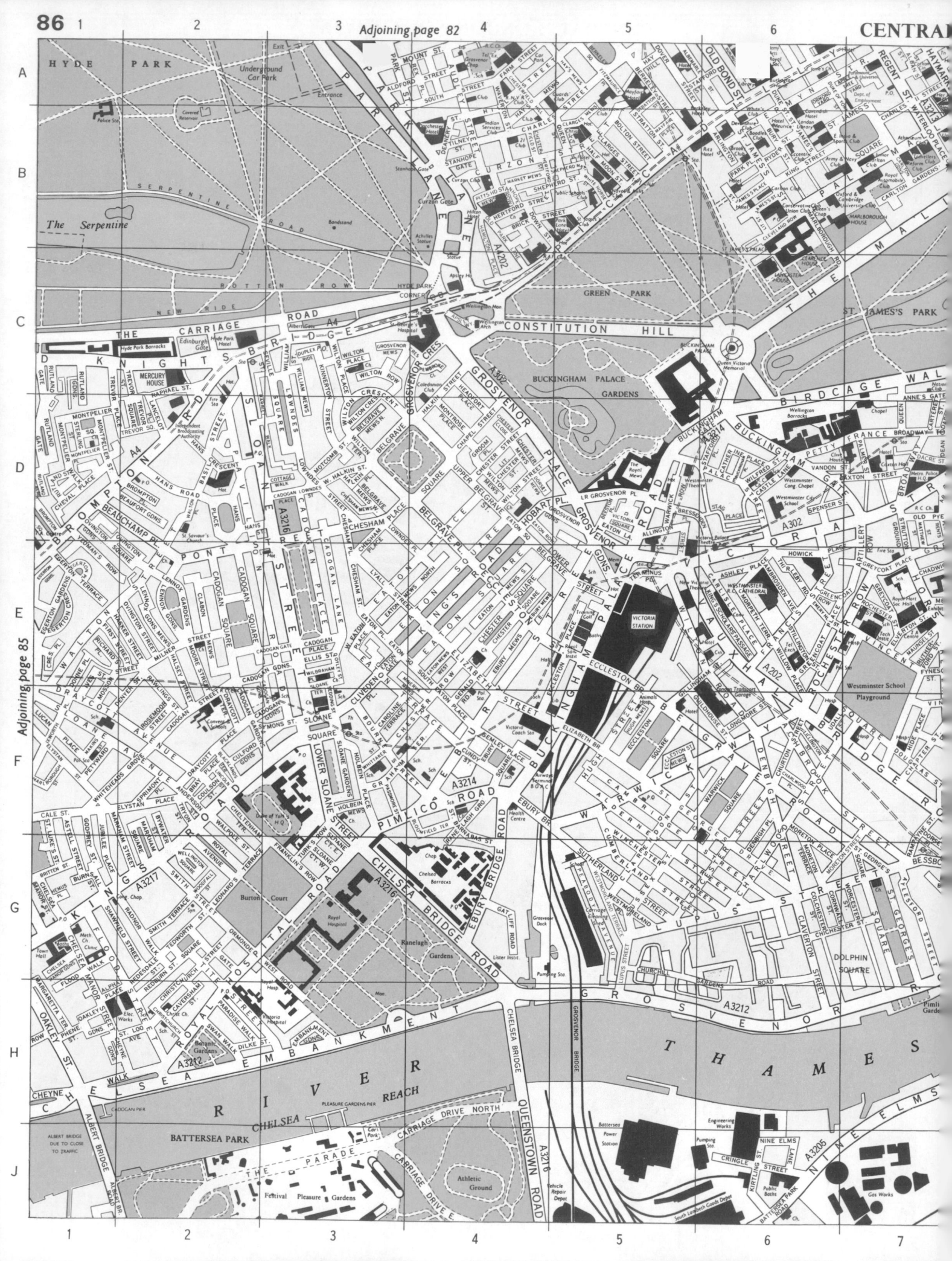

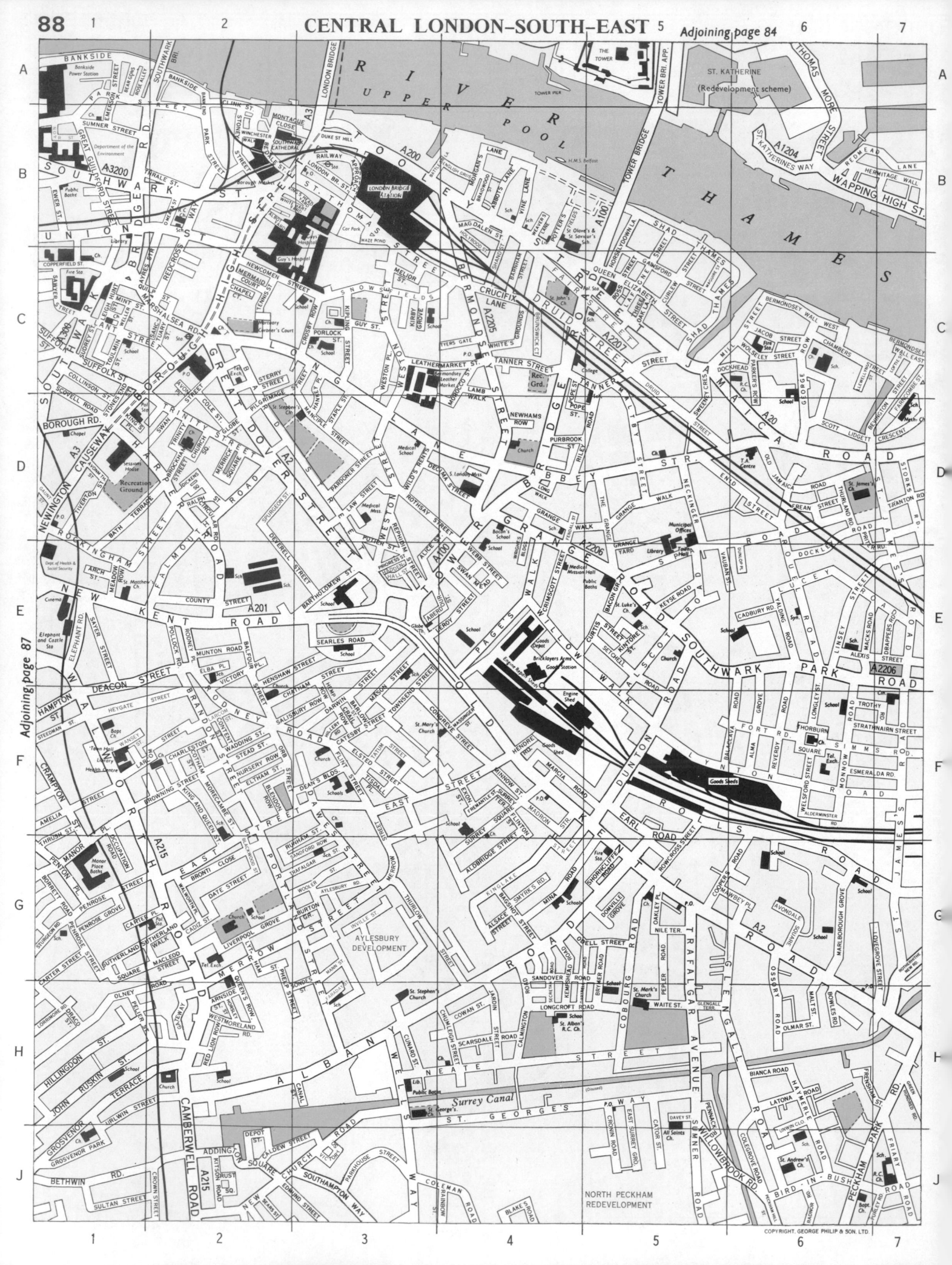

Town Plan Section

Contents

Aberdeen, 1½ inches =1 mile   page 91
Bath 1½ inches =1 mile 118
Birmingham 1½ inches =1 mile 108
Birmingham City Centre 3 inches =1 mile 109
Blackburn, 1½ inches =1 mile 99
Blackpool, 1½ inches =1 mile 99
Bolton, 1½ inches =1 mile 103
Bournemouth 1½ inches =1 mile 119
Bradford, 1½ inches =1 mile 98
Brighton 1½ inches =1 mile 120
Bristol 1½ inches =1 mile 116
Bristol City Centre 3 inches =1 mile 117
Burnley, 1½ inches =1 mile 99
Cambridge 1½ inches =1 mile 112
Cambridge City Centre 3 inches =1 mile 112
Canterbury 1½ inches =1 mile 120
Cardiff 1½ inches =1 mile 115
Cardiff City Centre 3 inches =1 mile 115
Coventry 1½ inches =1 mile 111
Coventry City Centre 3 inches =1 mile 111

Derby 1½ inches =1 mile 107
Doncaster, 1½ inches =1 mile 105
Dundee, 1½ inches =1 mile 93
Edinburgh, 1½ inches =1 mile 92
Edinburgh, City Centre 3 inches =1 mile 93
Exeter, 1½ inches =1 mile 118
Gateshead, 1½ inches =1 mile 95
Glasgow, 1½ inches =1 mile 90
Glasgow, City Centre 3 inches =1 mile 91
Gloucester 1½ inches =1 mile 117
Halifax, 1½ inches =1 mile 97
Harrogate, 1½ inches =1 mile 99
Huddersfield, 1½ inches =1 mile 97
Hull, 1½ inches =1 mile 98
Hull, City Centre 3 inches =1 mile 99
Ipswich 1½ inches =1 mile 113
Jarrow & S. Shields, 1½ inches =1 mile 94
Leeds, 1½ inches =1 mile 96
Leeds, City Centre 3 inches =1 mile 96
Leicester 1½ inches =1 mile 110

Leicester City Centre 3 inches =1 mile 110
Liverpool, 1½ inches =1 mile 100
Liverpool, City Centre 3 inches =1 mile 101
Manchester, 1½ inches =1 mile 102
Manchester, City Centre 3 inches =1 mile 103
Middlesbrough, 1½ inches =1 mile 95
Newcastle, 1½ inches =1 mile 94
Newcastle, City Centre 3 inches =1 mile 94
Newport (Mon.) 1½ inches =1 mile 114
Northampton 1½ inches =1 mile 110
Norwich 1½ inches =1 mile 113
Nottingham 1½ inches =1 mile 107
Nottingham City Centre 3 inches =1 mile 107
Oldham, 1½ inches =1 mile 103
Oxford 1½ inches =1 mile 112
Oxford City Centre 3 inches =1 mile 112
Perth, 1½ inches =1 mile 91
Plymouth 1½ inches =1 mile 117
Portsmouth 1½ inches =1 mile 120
Preston, 1½ inches =1 mile 99

Rotherham, 1½ inches =1 mile 105
Sheffield, 1½ inches =1 mile 104
Sheffield, City Centre 3 inches =1 mile 105
Southampton 1½ inches =1 mile 119
Southend 1½ inches =1 mile 113
St. Helens, 1½ inches =1 mile 101
Stoke-on-Trent 1½ inches =1 mile 106
Stoke-on-Trent (Hanley) City Centre 3 inches =1 mile 106
Stratford-upon-Avon 1½ inches =1 mile 111
Sunderland, 1½ inches =1 mile 95
Swansea 1½ inches =1 mile 114
Swansea City Centre 3 inches =1 mile 114
Taunton 1½ inches =1 mile 118
Torquay 1½ inches =1 mile 118
Wallasey & Birkenhead, 1½ inches =1 mile 101
Warrington, 1½ inches =1 mile 101
Wolverhampton 1½ inches =1 mile 109
York, 1½ inches =1 mile 97

Reference

Town Plans

Scale: 1½ inches =1 mile

0   ¼   ½   1

Motorways
Main Through Roads
Other Main Roads
Second Class Roads
Other Roads
Public Parks & Open Spaces
Areas not built over
Railways
Railway Stations

Road Numbers
As a result of a survey of our road system, the Department of the Environment has made recommendations for changes to some road numbers. These recommendations are being carried out in conjunction with the County authorities concerned. Before this process is completed motorists may occasionally find road number signs which differ from those on this map.

D.O.E. Road Numbers

M1 — Motorways
A64(T) 57 — Primary Routes
A61 61 — Other 'A' Roads
B901 — 'B' Roads
43 — Motorway Access Point Numbers
P — Car Parks
+ — Churches of Interest
— Canals
Mus. Hosp. Sch. — Public Buildings of Interest

City Centre Plans

Scale: 3 inches =1 mile

0   ¼   ½

Motorways
Main Through Roads
Other Main Roads
Second Class Roads
Other Roads
Public Parks & Open Spaces
Areas not built over
Railways
Railway Stations

D.O.E. Road Numbers

M1 — Motorways
A64(T) 57 — Primary Routes
A61 61 — Other 'A' Roads
B901 — 'B' Roads
→ → → — One Way Streets
P — Car Parks
Ch. ■ / Sch. ■ — Public Buildings of Interest
— Roads of Limited Access

Locator Maps

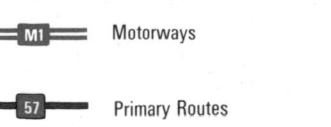

M1 — Motorways
57 — Primary Routes
621 — Other 'A' Roads

— Towns with Town Plans
— Other Towns

Abbreviations in Text

Cent.	Century	Ho.	House
Ch.	Church	M.D.	
Coll.	College	Mls. m.	Miles
Dec.	Decorated	Perp.	Perpendicular
E.C.	Early Closing Day	Pop.	Population
Ed.	Educated	R.C.	Roman Catholic
E.E.	Early English	Sch.	School

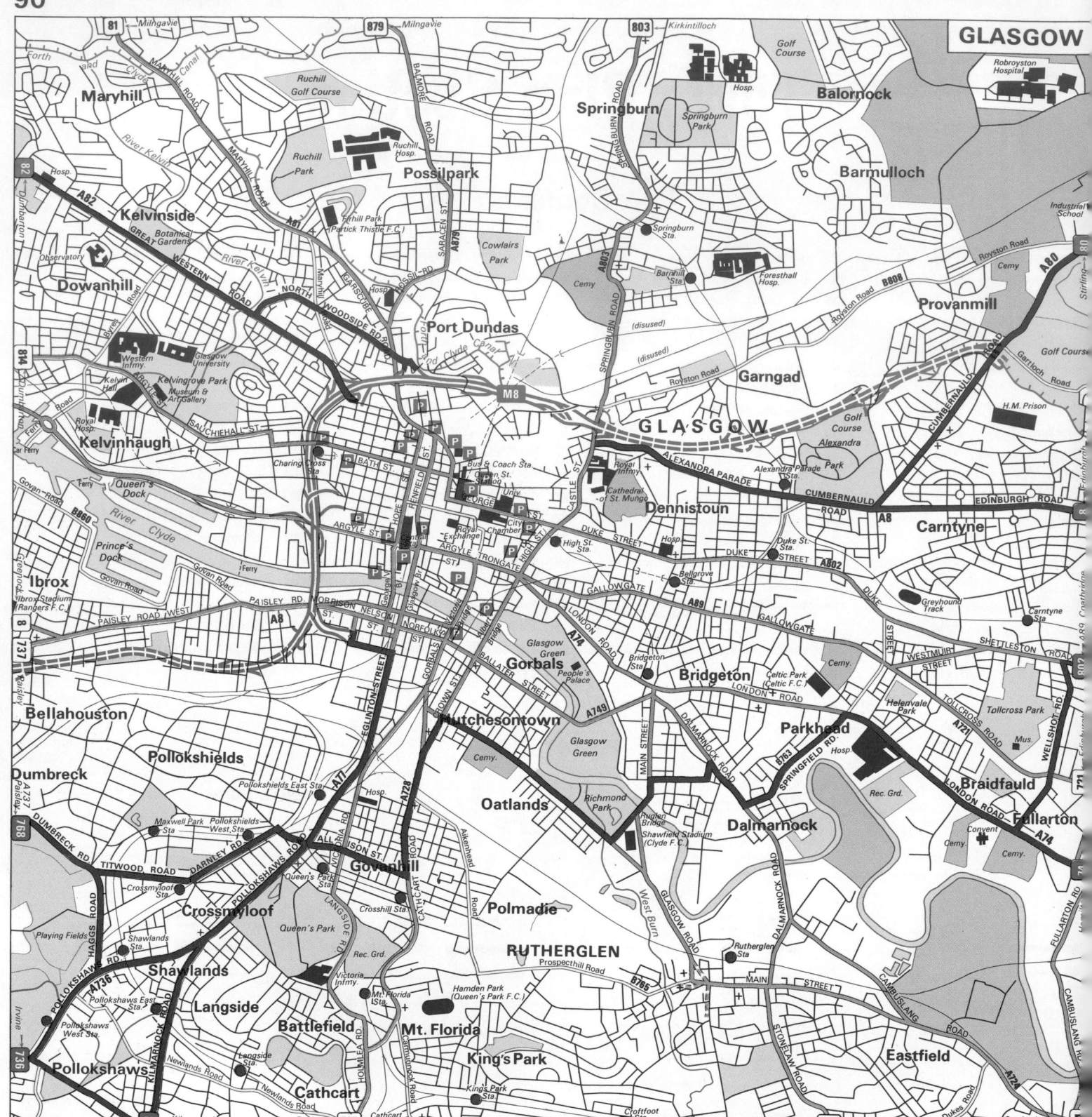

GLASGOW

Population:896,958.E.C. Tuesday; M.D. Wednesday.

London 399 miles; Edinburgh 44 miles; Manchester 212 miles.

Large port, shipbuilding and industrial centre. The Cathedral is built on the site of an earlier church erected by St. Mungo; early English Gothic choir; Rood Screen. In the S.E. Chapel is St. Mungo's Well and the tomb of Bishop Wishart. People's Palace, museum devoted to the history of Glasgow. James Watt's workshop in Trongate. Art Gallery and Museum in Kelvingrove Park. The University established 1450, is housed, in Kelvingrove Park, in buildings designed by Sir George Gilbert Scott. University Library; Hunterian Museum and Library. Golf.

ABERDEEN

Population:182,006.
E.C. Wed. and Sat.
M.D. Friday.
London 501 miles,
Glasgow 150 miles,
Edinburgh 123 miles.
University city, resort
and fishing port.
Exporter of cattle
and granite. Old
Aberdeen; St.
Machar's Cathedral,
15th Cent.; King's
College 1495.
New Aberdeen 'the
Granite City'. Ancient
Market Cross, 1686.
Art Gallery and
Museum; Marischal
College; Town House,
1866, incorporating
tower of 14th Cent.
Tolbooth. E. Church
rebuilt 1837. W.
Church rebuilt 1763.
14th Cent. Bridge of
Balgownie.
Angling, golf.

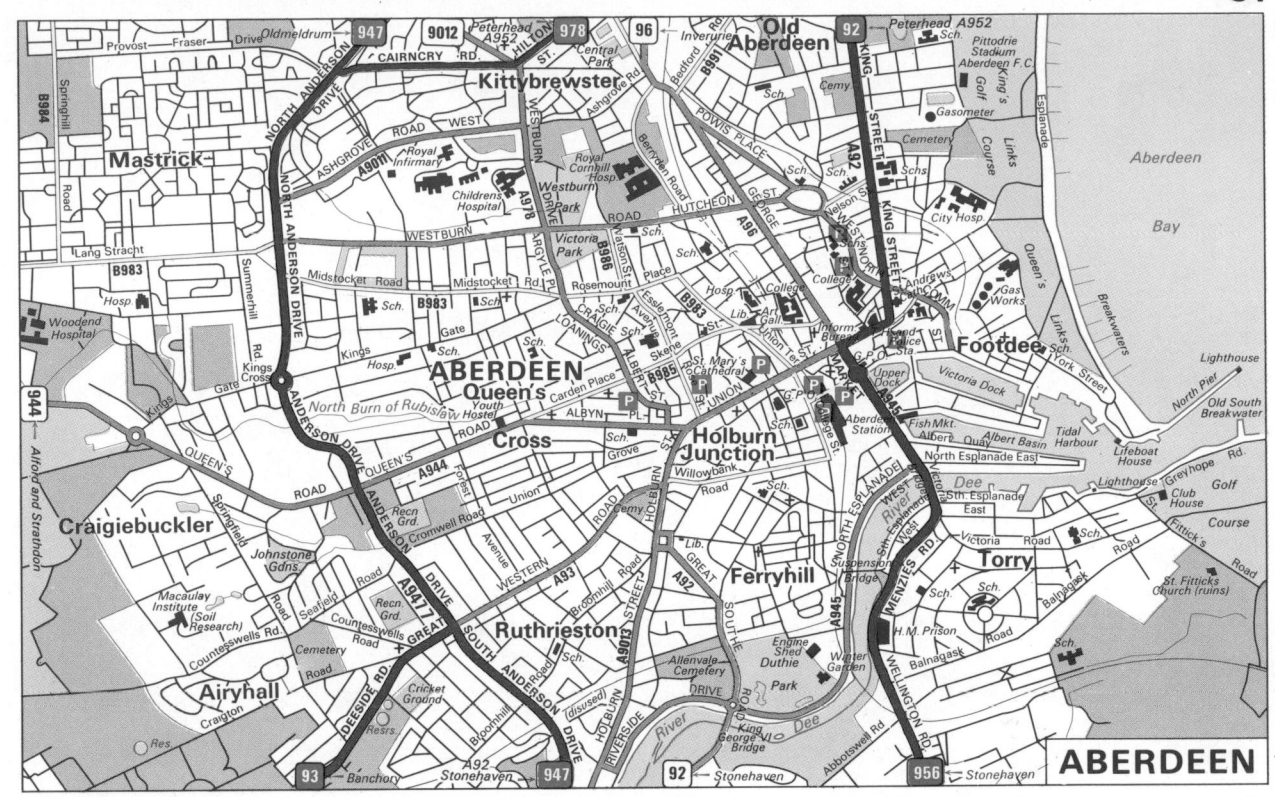

PERTH

Population:43,051. E.C. Wed. M.D. Fri.
London 415 miles, Glasgow 61 miles,
Edinburgh 42 miles. Motorail Terminal.
Capital of Scotland until 1452. St. John's
Church; square central tower surmounted by
15th Cent. steeple. South Inch, once used
for witch burnings and archery. North Inch,
scene of judicial combat in 1396. Art
Gallery and Museum; St. Ninian's Cathedral;
Fair Maid of Perth's House; ruins of Elcho
Castle 16th Cent. Angling, golf.

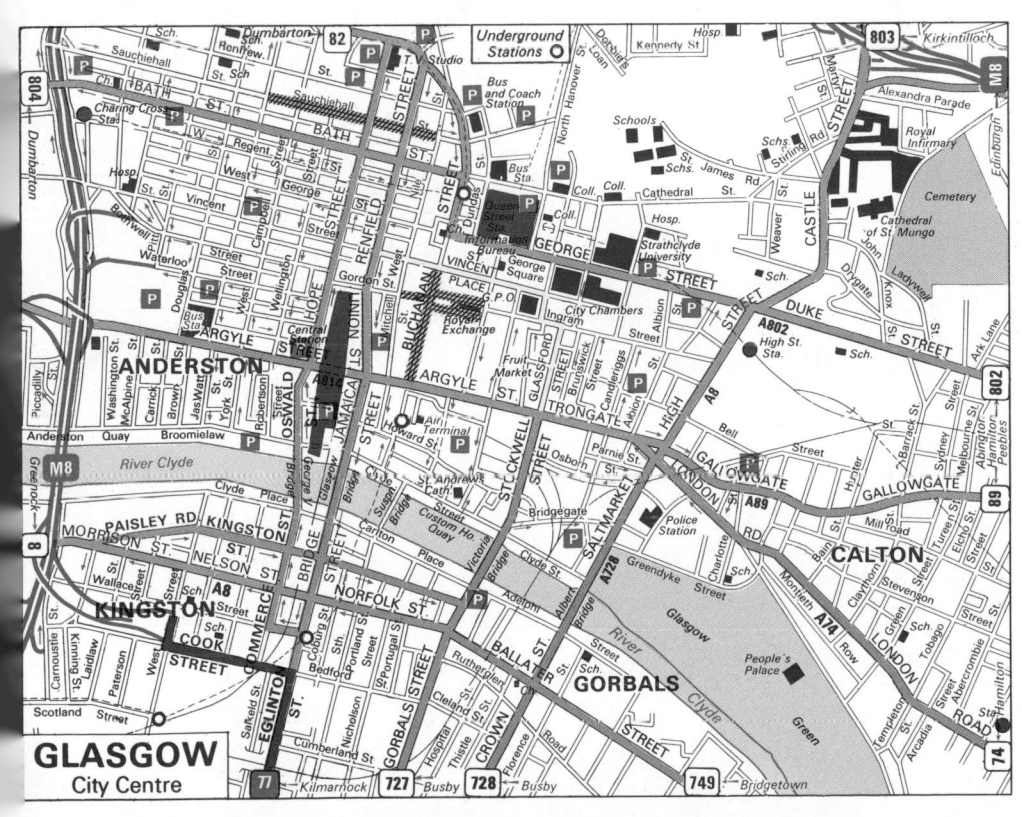

EDINBURGH

Population: 453,422. E.C. Tuesday, Wednesday or Saturday.

M.D. Tuesday and Wednesday.

London 377 miles; Glasgow 44 miles.

Capital of Scotland and University City with an outport at Leith. Princes Street with Scott Monument and Royal Scottish Academy. Castle; St. Margarets Chapel; and Scottish National War Memorial; National Gallery and Parliament Hall; St. Giles Cathedral; St. Mary's Cathedral; National Library of Scotland; John Knox's House; Holyrood Palace and Abbey. Greyfriars Church where National Covenant was signed in the churchyard. Angling, golf.

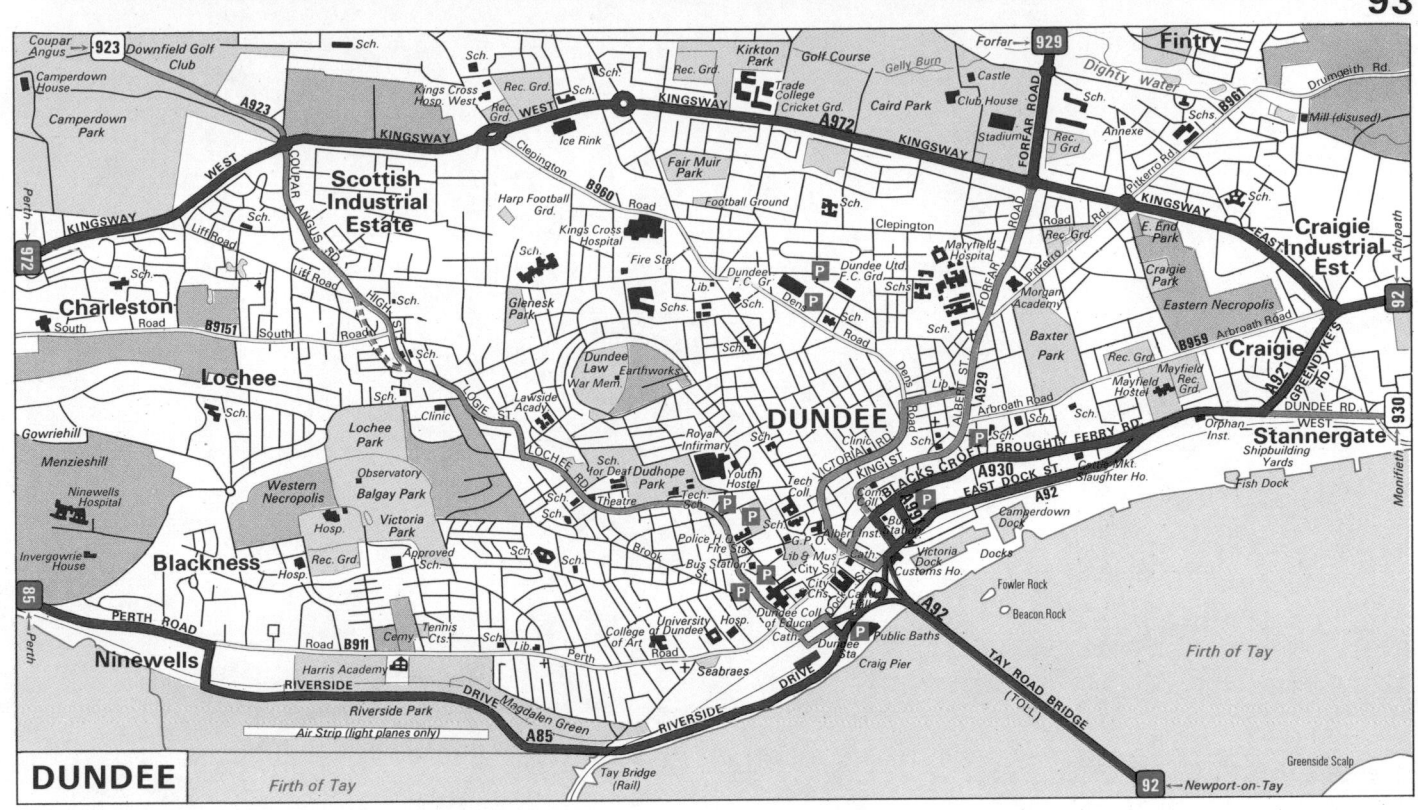

DUNDEE
Population:182,084
E.C. Wednesday. M.D. Tuesday and Friday.
London 426 miles, Edinburgh 54 miles,
Glasgow 74 miles.
Port and industrial town. University; Albert Institute
and Library; Museum and Art Galleries; Caird Hall
(City Offices). Dundee Law 572 ft. Road and rail Tay
Bridges. Golf.

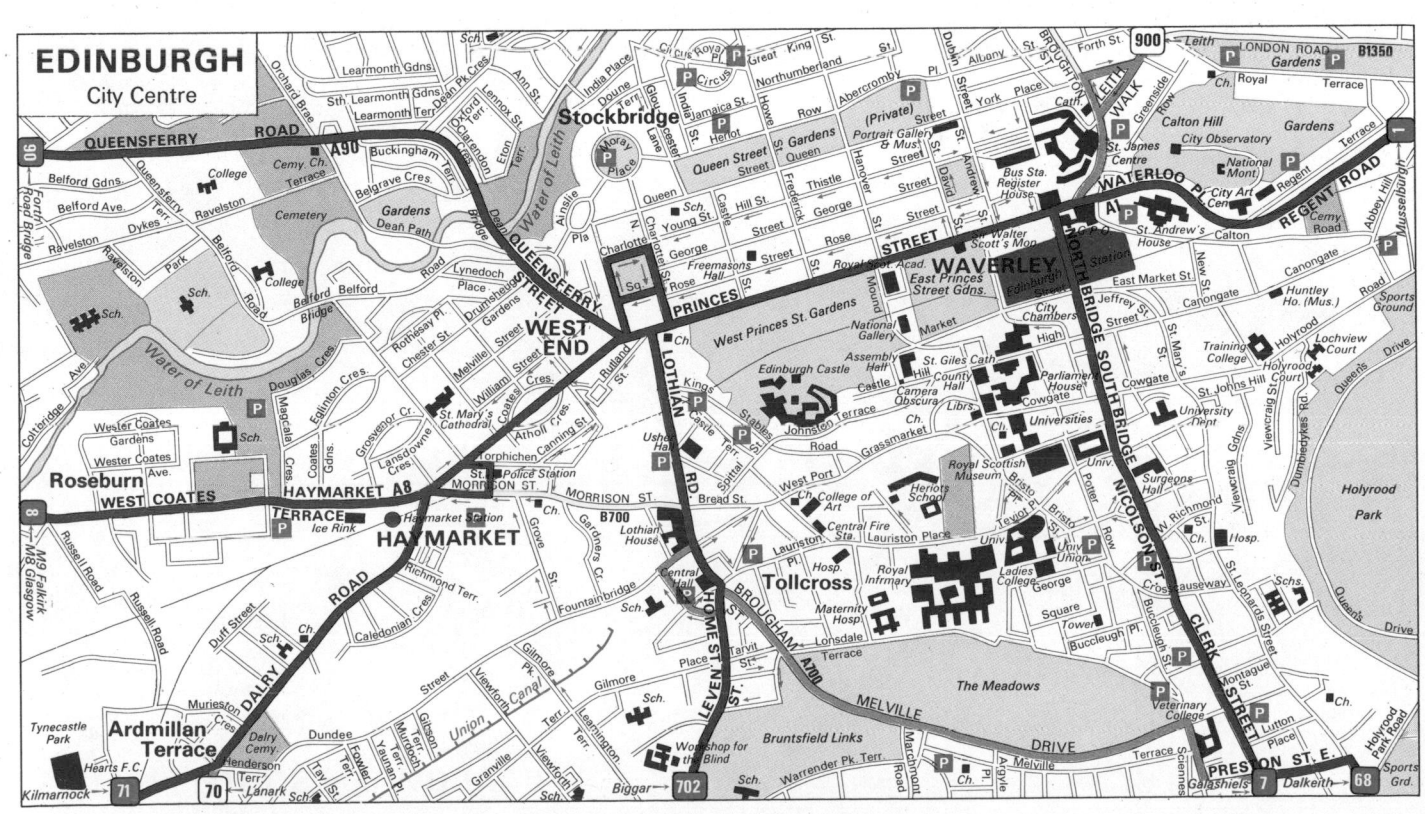

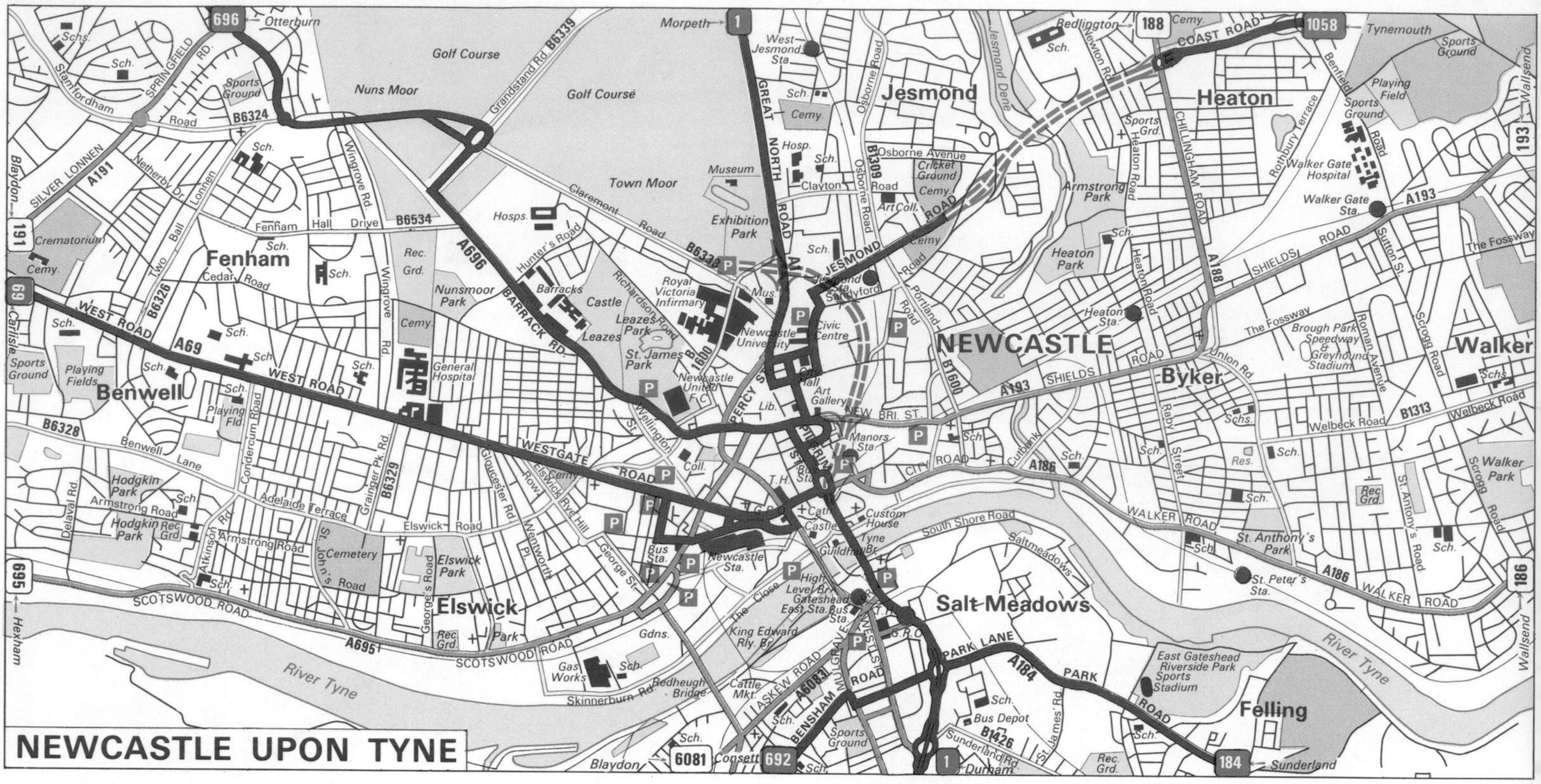

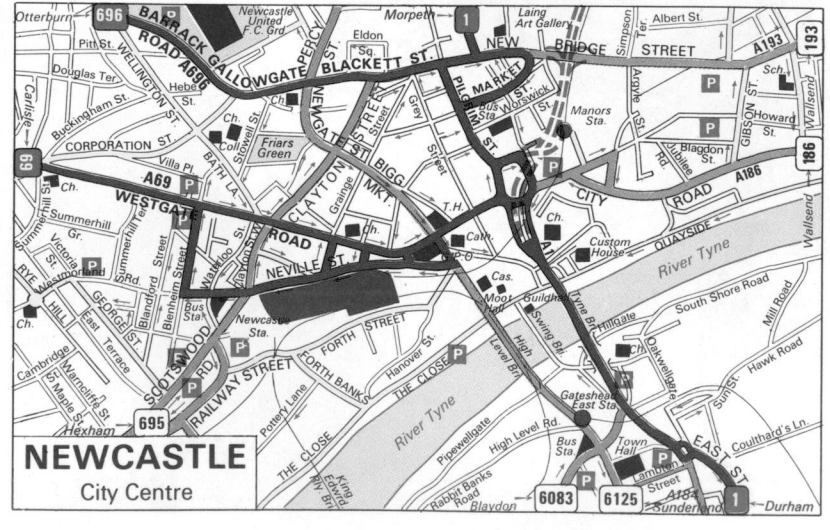

NEWCASTLE UPON TYNE

NEWCASTLE UPON TYNE
Population: 222,153
E.C. Wednesday or Saturday.
M.D. Tuesday and Saturday.
London 271 miles, Edinburgh 107 miles, Manchester 132 miles.
Formerly the Roman Station of Pons Ælius but now the industrial capital of North East England. The Cathedral was formerly one of the largest parish churches in England with fine spire and ancient font cover. Remains of 12th Cent. Castle, Keep restored. The original entrance to the castle is the Black Gate, the upper part of which contains a collection of Roman antiquities. Remains of 14th Cent. Town Walls. Guildhall 1658; Trinity Hall, early 18th Cent. chapel and hall. All Saints' Church rebuilt 1789 with 15th Cent. German Brass. Museums and Laing Art Galleries. Angling, golf.

JARROW
Population: 28,779 E.C. Wed. Newcastle 7 miles. Monastery where Venerable Bede lived and worked. St. Paul's Church original burial place of Bede. Norman Tower and Saxon Chancel. First English glass made at Monastery.

SOUTH SHIELDS
Population: 100,513 E.C. Wed. Newcastle 10 miles. Seaport and resort built on site of Roman Camp. Remains of Roman Fort. Lifeboat Memorial commemorates first standard lifeboat.

NEWCASTLE
City Centre

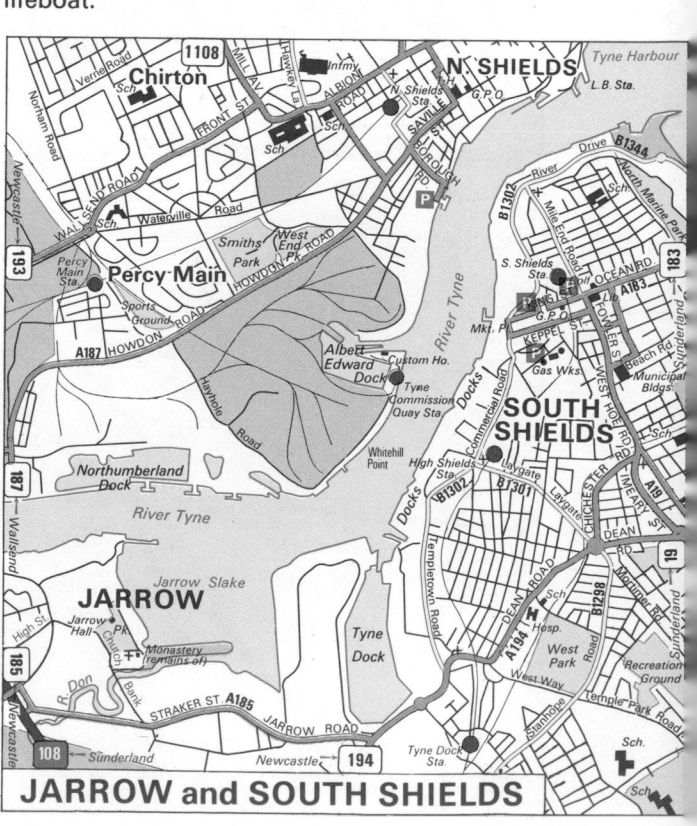

JARROW and SOUTH SHIELDS

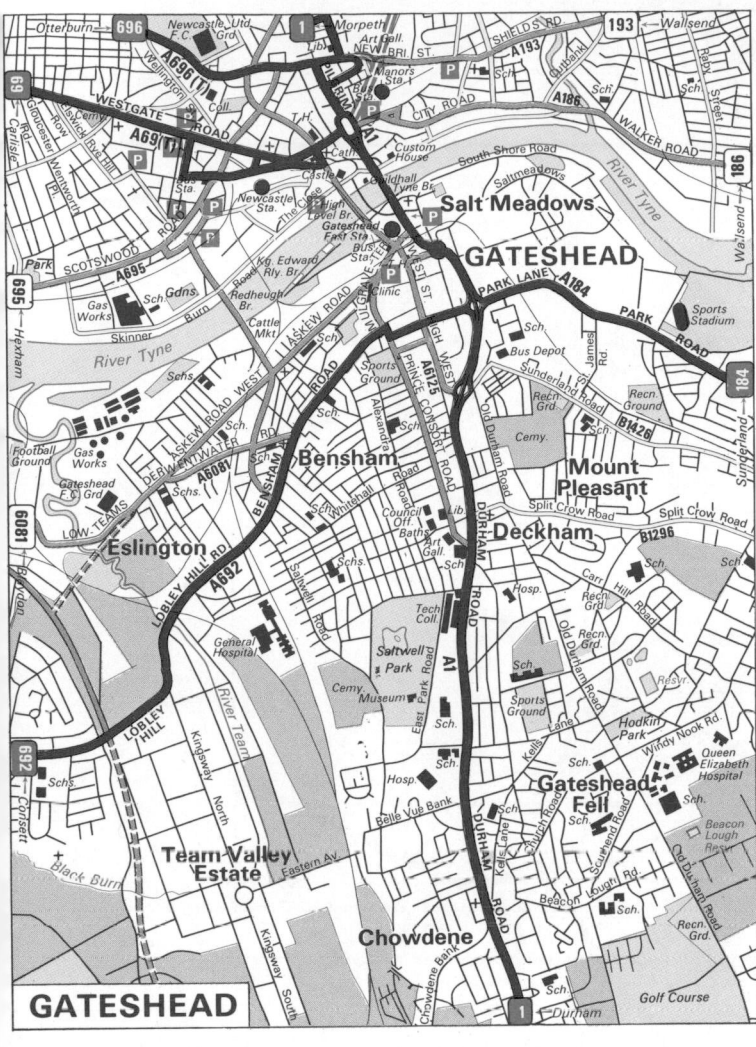

GATESHEAD

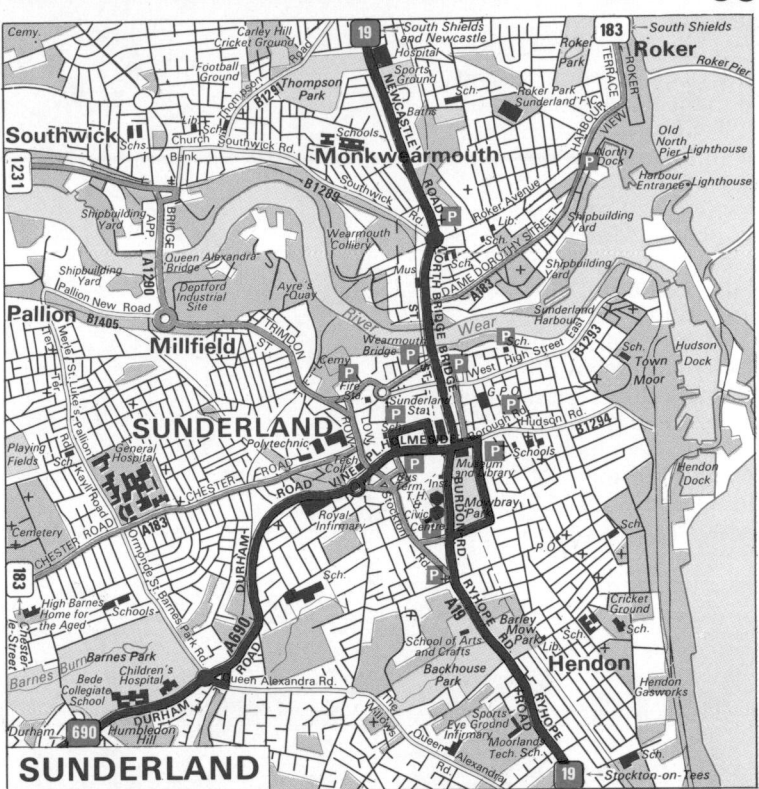

SUNDERLAND

SUNDERLAND

Population: 216,892. E.C. Wed. London 269 miles, Newcastle 12 miles. Important port with shipbuilding and marine engineering. Saxon Monastery at Monkwearmouth also St. Peter's Church. Museum, Art Gallery. Angling, bathing, golf.

GATESHEAD

Population: 94,457. E.C. Wed. Newcastle 1 mile.
Industrial town on south bank of Tyne opposite Newcastle. Connected with Newcastle by five bridges. High Level Bridge 1850 by R. Stephenson. 14th Cent. St. Mary's Church with Norman Doorway and Jacobean Woodwork. Holy Trinity Church. Industrial Museum in Saltwell Park. Shipley Art Gallery. Golf.

MIDDLESBROUGH

Population: 154,580. E.C. Wednesday. M.D. Saturday.
London 246 miles, Newcastle 37 miles.
Important port, industrial and shopping centre on River Tees. Entirely developed since 1800. Dorman Museum; R.C. Cathedral; Marton, birthplace of Capt. Cook 3 miles. Interesting transporter bridge over Tees. Golf, angling.

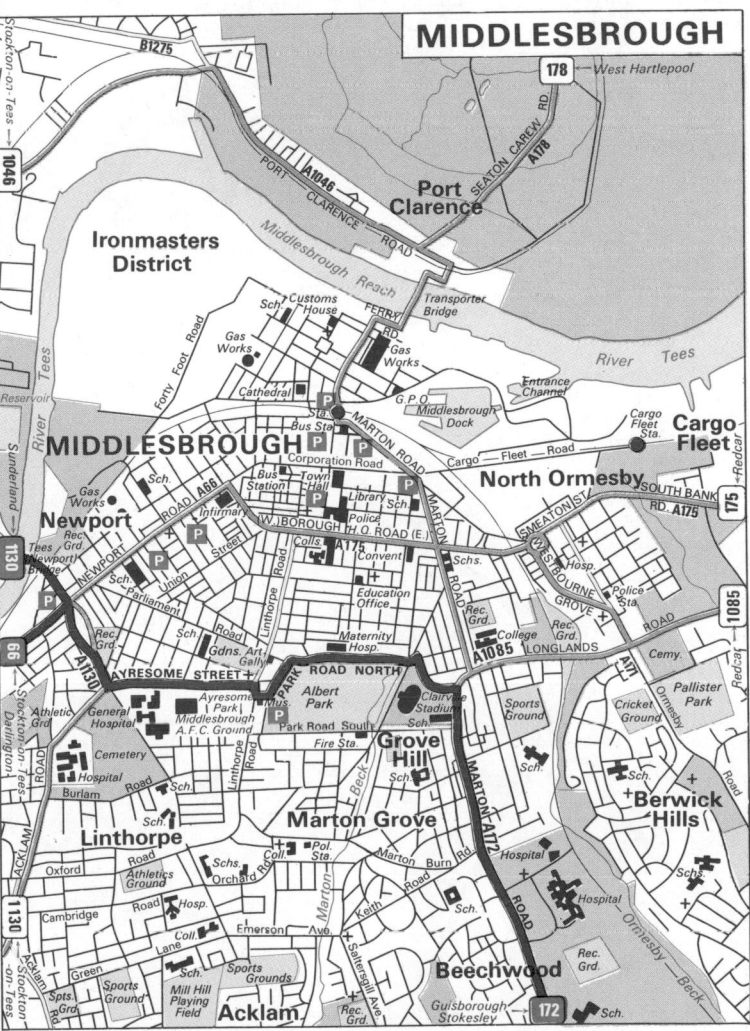

MIDDLESBROUGH

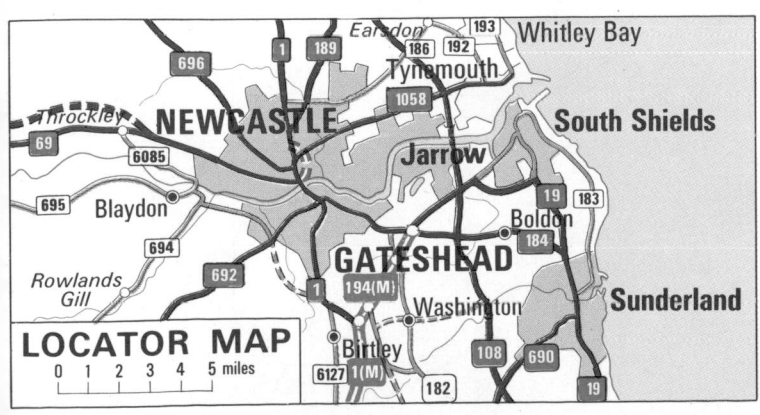

LOCATOR MAP

0 1 2 3 4 5 miles

LEEDS

Pop.494,971 E.C. Wed.
M.D. Tue. London 190 mls.
Manchester 40 mls. Centre
19th Cent. development
of cloth industry. City Art
Gallery and Museum; St.
Ann's R.C. Cathedral;
St. John's Church 1634
Renaissance woodwork; St.
Peter's Church 10th Cent.
cross. University founded
1877. Kirkstall Abbey (3½ m.
N.W.) Cistercian ruins with
chapter house, church and
tower. Lord Darnley born at
Temple Newsham now a
Museum (4 miles N.).
Harewood House 18th
Cent. Angling, golf.

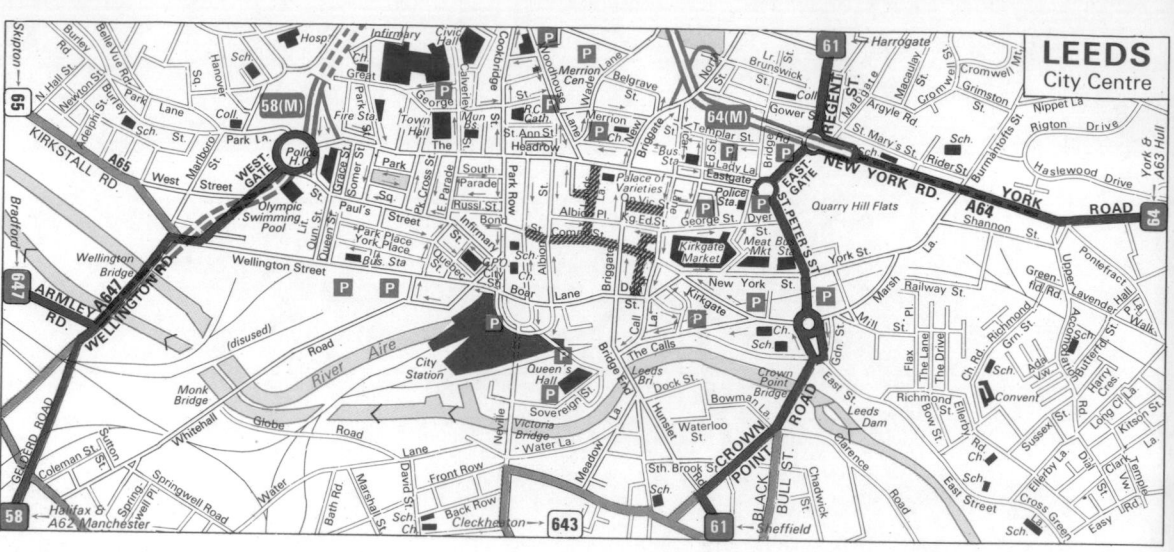

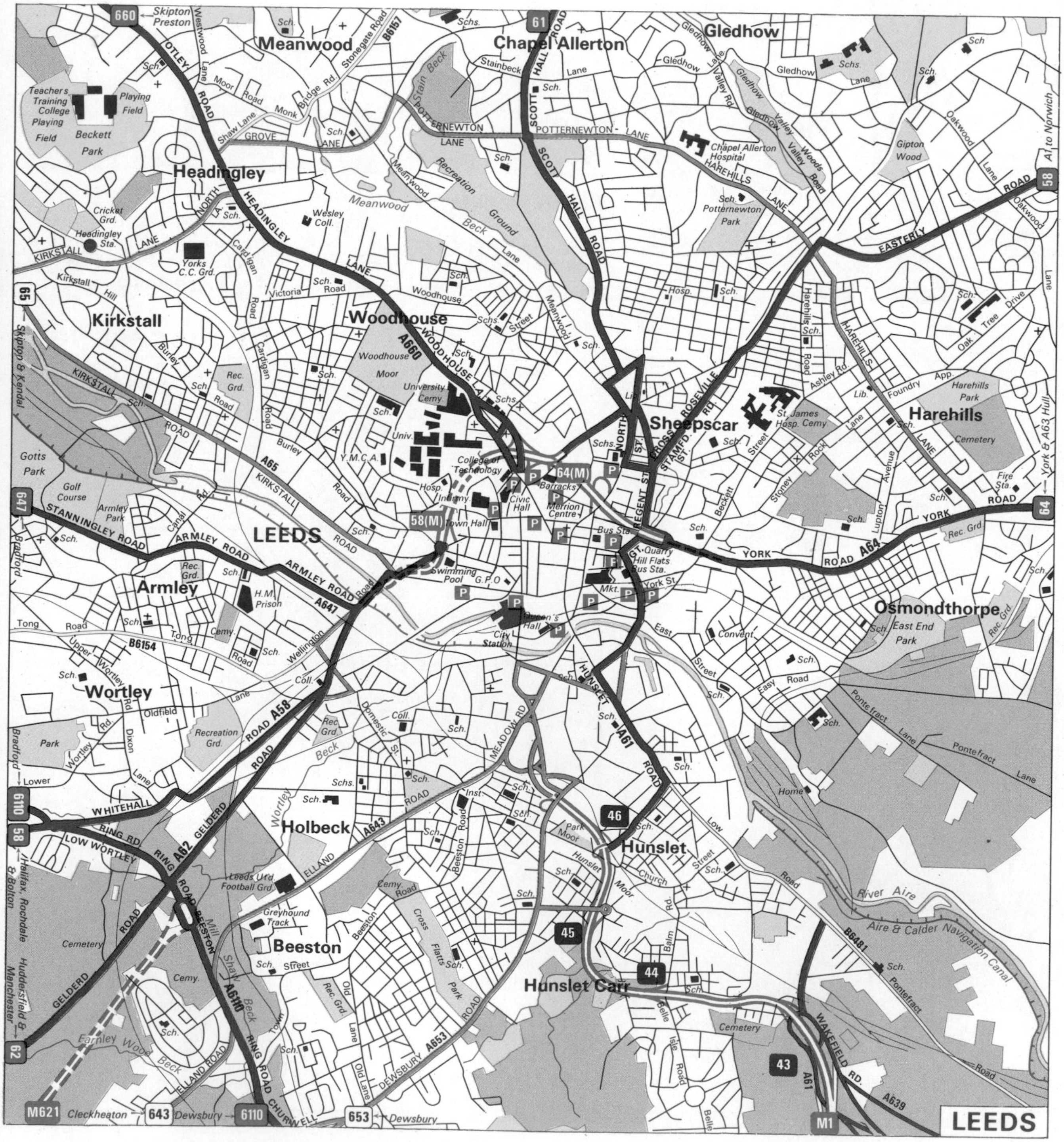

LEEDS
City Centre

LEEDS

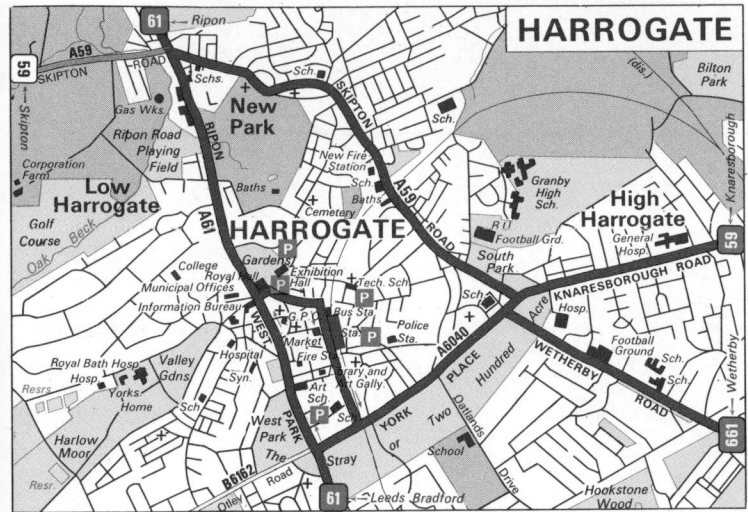

HARROGATE

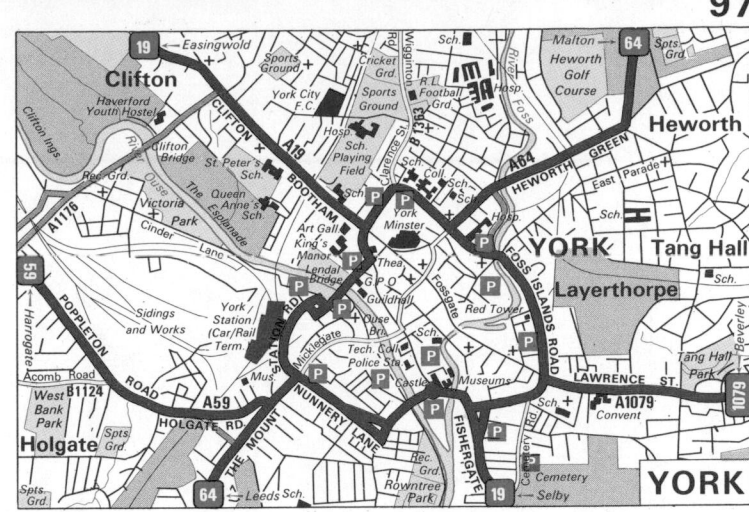

YORK

HARROGATE Population:64,280 E.C. Wed. London 207 miles, Leeds 16 miles. Popular spa and touring centre for the Dales. Grand buildings round 'The Stray'. Beautiful gardens; Baths; Pump Room; Royal Hall and Concert Room; Museum and Art Gallery. Nearby are Ripley Castle (3 m. N.W.) and Harewood House (7 m. S.). Angling, golf, riding, swimming.

YORK Population:104,513 E.C. Wed. M.D. Sat. London 196 miles, Manchester 64 miles. Roman Eboracum. Medieval walls and gates well preserved. York Minster. E.E., Dec. and Perp. begun in 11th Cent. St. Williams Coll. Jacobean. Treasurers Ho. 17th Cent. St. Mary's Abbey ruins. Shambles. St. Peter's Sch. Merchant Adventurer's Hall, St. Margaret's Church.

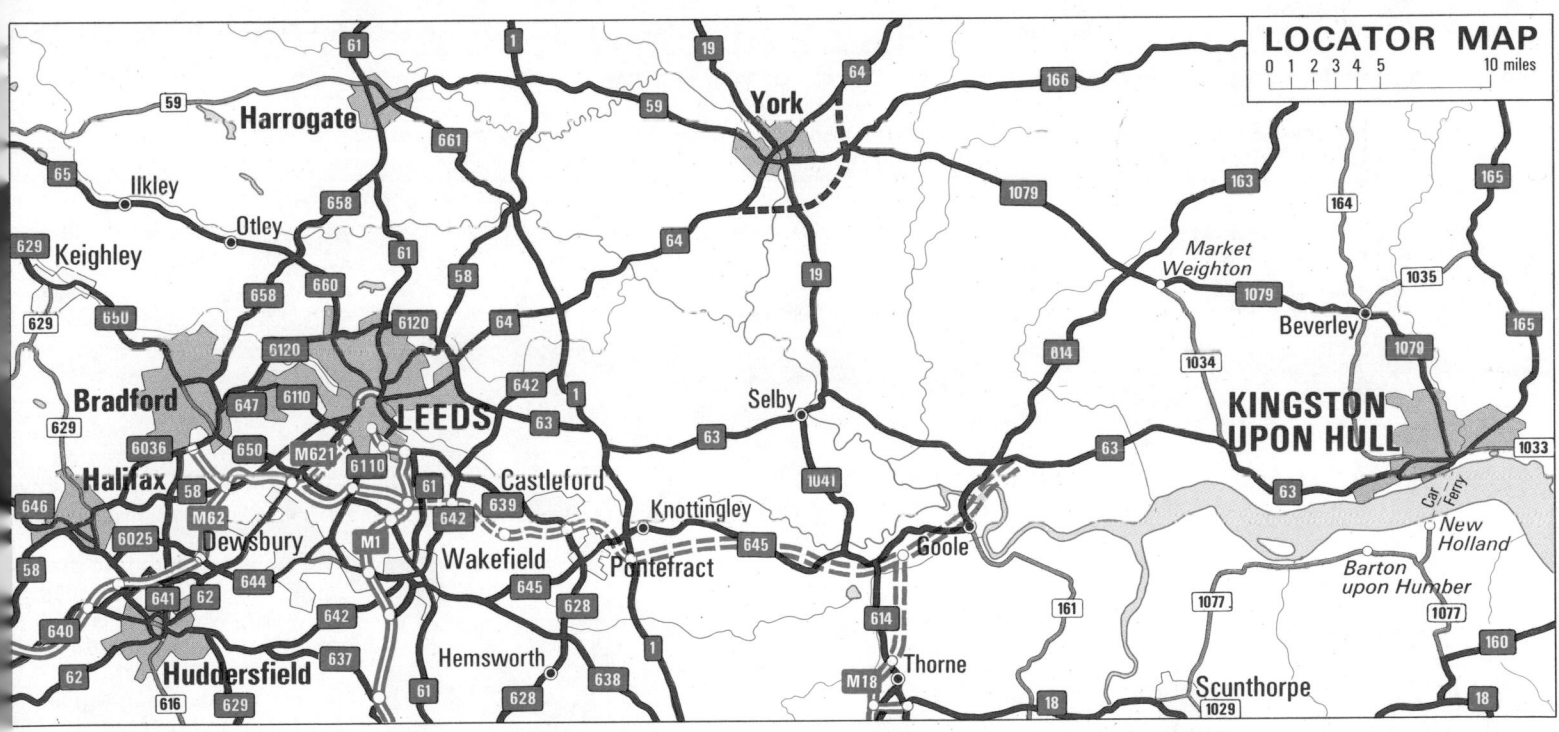

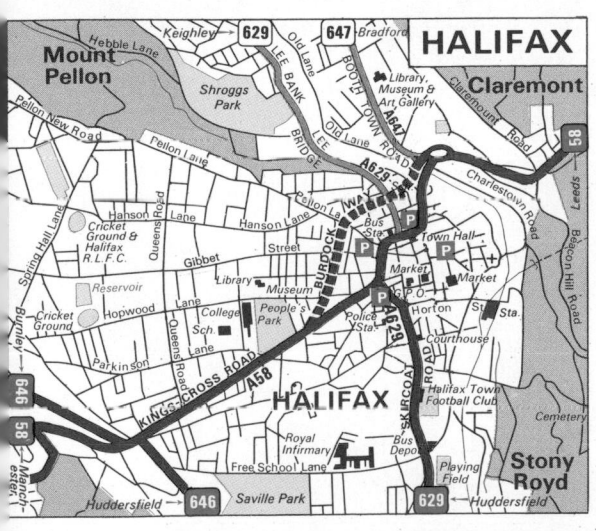

HALIFAX

HALIFAX Pop.91,171 E.C. Thur. M.D. Daily. London 193 miles, Bradford 8 miles. Woollen town. St. John's Ch. Old Piece Hall, Shibden Park & Hall; Folk Museum. Bankfield Art Gallery and Museum.

HUDDERS-FIELD Pop.131,190 E.C. Wed. M.D. Mon. London 184 mls. Bradford 11 miles. Woollens, chemicals, engineering. Town Hall; Art Gallery; Museum; Old Cloth Hall; Almondbury Ch. Roman remains.

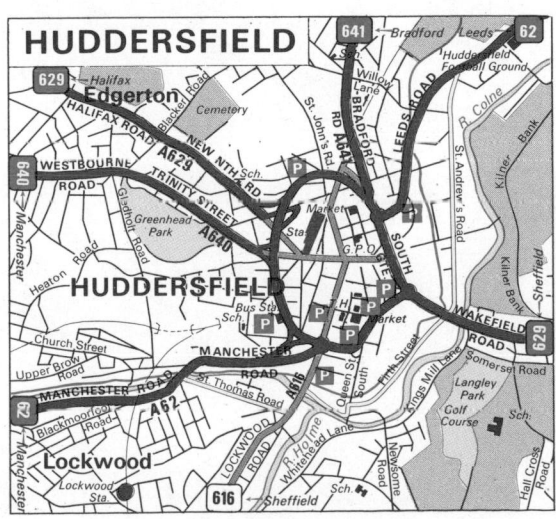

HUDDERSFIELD

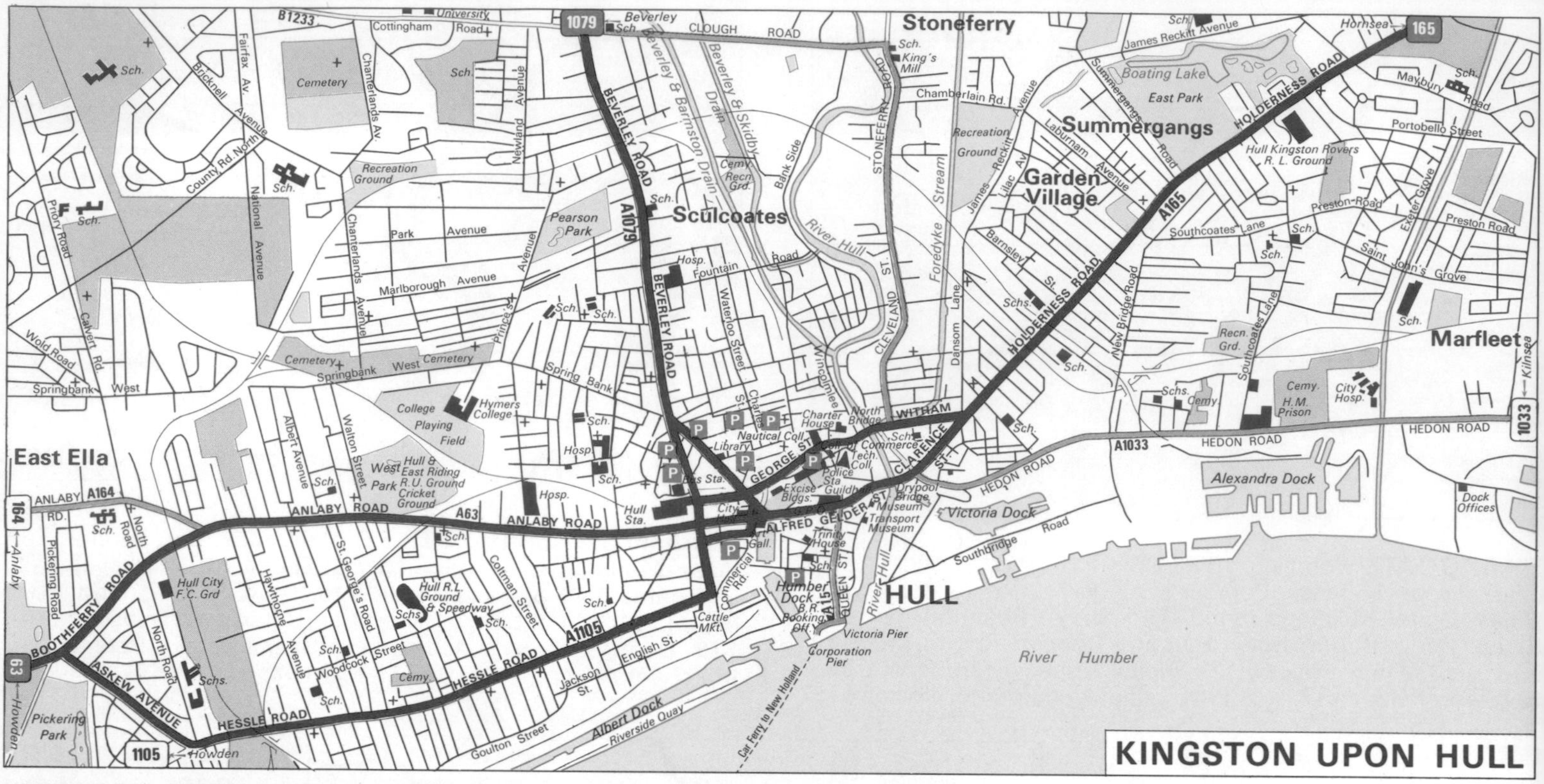

KINGSTON UPON HULL

KINGSTON UPON HULL Population:285,472. E.C. Thur. M.D. Tue. and Sat. London 168 miles, Manchester 94 miles. Seaport laid out by Edward I. Holy Trinity Church Dec. and Perp. Wm. Wilberforce and Andrew Marvel ed. Grammar Sch. rebuilt 1583. Wilberforce Mus. in Tudor House birthplace. St. Mary's Ch. Law Cts., University; Ferens Art Gallery.

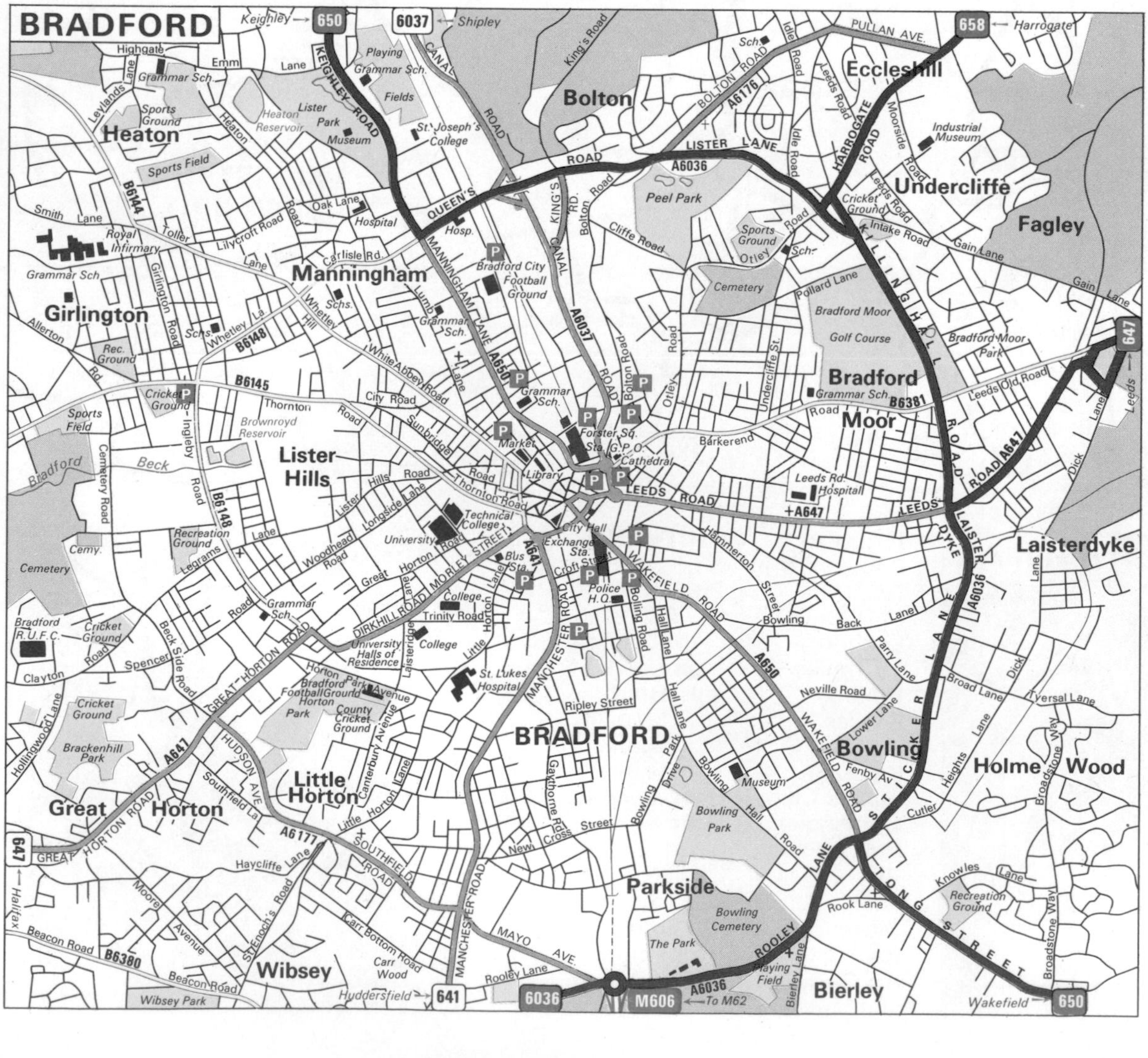

BRADFORD

BRADFORD
Population: 293,756.
E.C. Wednesday.
M.D. Monday and Thursday.
London 200 miles,
Manchester 34 miles,
Leeds 9 miles.
Centre of worsted trade with numerous mills and warehouses. It is a stone-built city with a Town Hall dating from 1873. St. Peter's Church 15th Cent. has become the Cathedral of a new diocese. Cartwright Memorial Hall honours the inventor of the power loom. Natural History and Archaeological Museum; Bolling Hall 14th Cent. Delius was born here in 1863. Emily, Charlotte, Anne and Branwell Brontë born at Thornton. An Industrial Museum to be opened in Moorside Road, Eccleshill.
Golf.

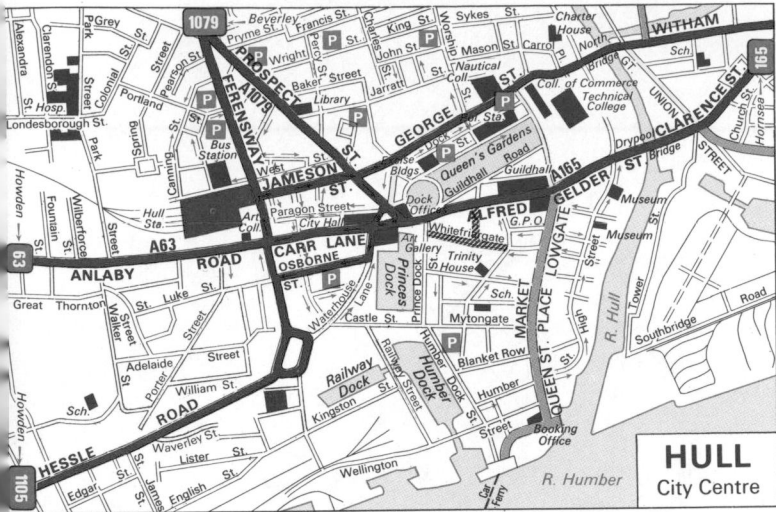

HULL
City Centre

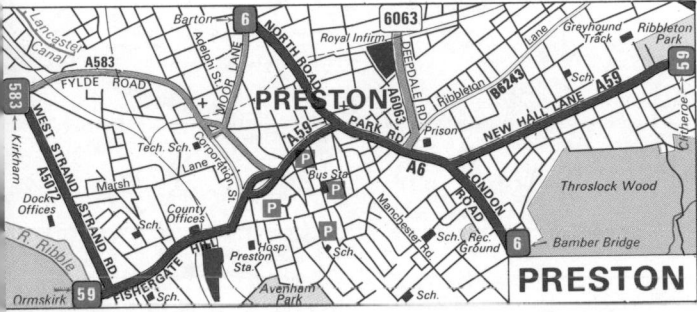

PRESTON

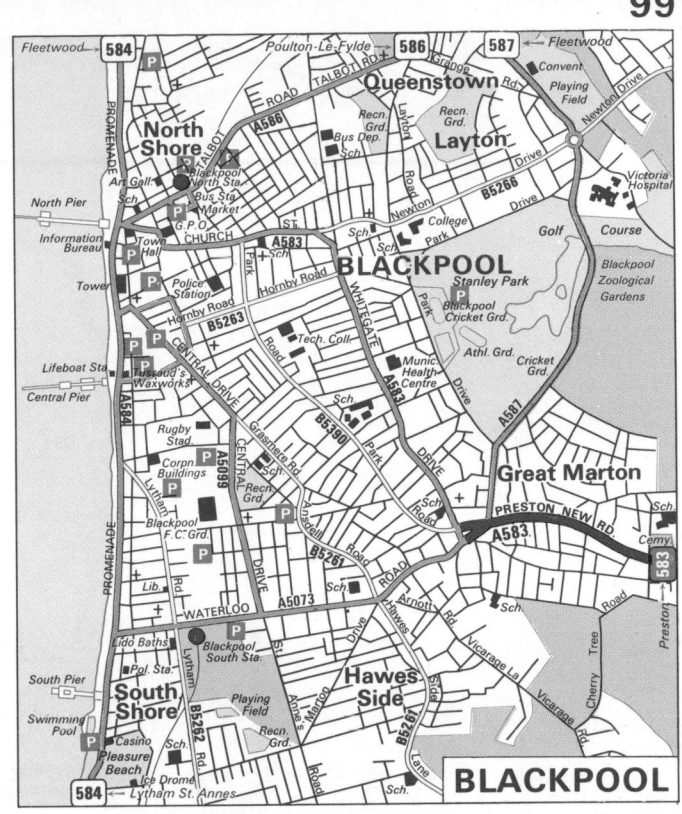

BLACKPOOL

PRESTON

Population: 97,365 E.C. Thur. M.D. Mon., Wed. and Sat. London 213 miles, Manchester 29 miles. Important cotton spinning and weaving centre, also docks and engineering. Sir Richard Arkwright, inventor, born here 1732. Parish Church has 15th and 17th Cent. silver crosses. Harris Public Library and Museum. Avenham Park scene of egg-rolling carnival Easter Monday. Golf.

BLACKPOOL

Population: 151,311 E.C. Wednesday. London 227 miles, Manchester 45 miles. Popular holiday resort on Lancashire coast with 7 mile promenade, splendid sands, five ballrooms and three piers. Views from 520 ft. Blackpool Tower with ballroom, aquarium, aviary, zoo, roof gardens and circus on same site. Grundy Art Gallery. R.C. Church by Pugin. Stanley Park with rose and Italian gardens. Angling, boating, bathing, cricket and golf.

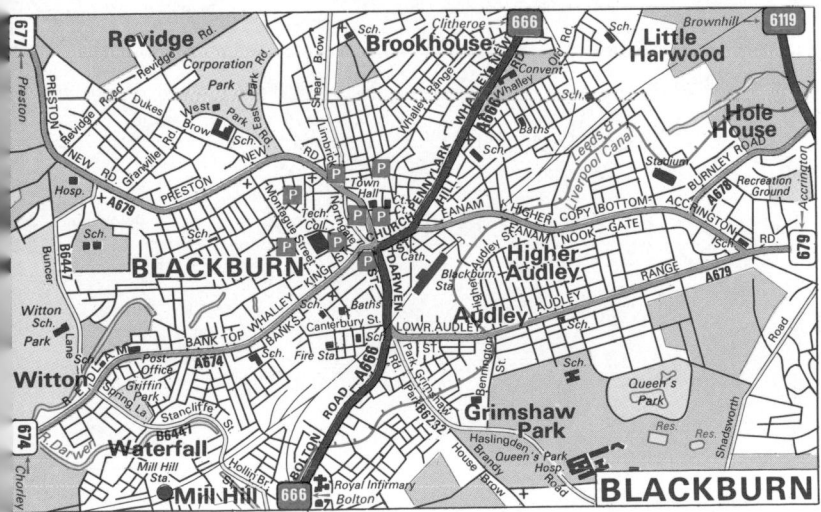

BLACKBURN

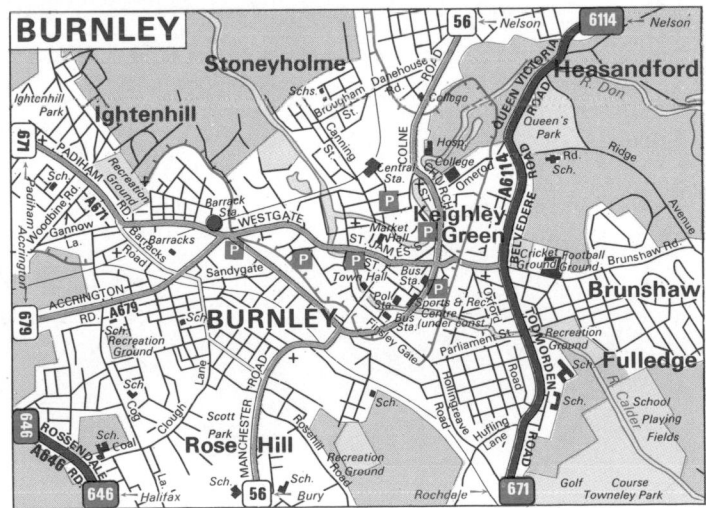

BURNLEY

BLACKBURN

Population: 101,672 E.C. Thursday. London 213 miles, Manchester 24 miles. Industrial and marketing centre and one of the world's greatest cotton manufacturing centres. 19th Cent. Cathedral; 19th Cent. Town Hall; Market Hall; Leur's Textile Museum and Museum and Art Gallery. St. Gabriel's Church built in the modern idiom. Corporation Park. Golf.

BURNLEY

Population: 76,483 E.C. Tuesday. London 206 miles, Manchester 24 miles. Set amid moorland country it is an engineering centre. Partly 15th Century Parish Church, St. Mary's R.C. Church by Pugin. Paulinas Cross and Bank Hall. Towneley Park with Towneley Hall Museum and Art Gallery. Golf.

LIVERPOOL

LIVERPOOL

Population:606,834 E.C. Wednesday or Saturday. M.D. Daily.
London 205 miles, Birmingham 94 miles, Manchester 34 miles.
City and port on the Mersey with a dock frontage exceeding 7 miles. Royal Liver Building, 17 storeys with two towers surmounted by figures of the 'Liver', a mythical bird. Town Hall, the oldest public building, 1754. Public museums and Library; Walker Art Gallery; St. George's Hall; Cathedral, begun 1904, worthy of note are stained glass and great organ. R.C. Cathedral, designed by Sir Edwin Lutyens, begun 1933 and consecrated 1967. Mersey Tunnel, opened 1934. University founded in 1881. Birthplace of Gladstone. Golf, horse racing.

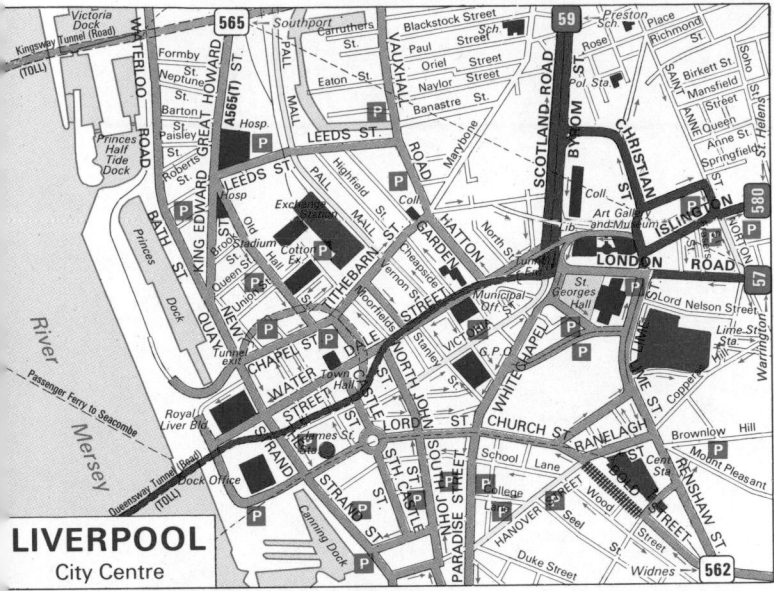

LIVERPOOL
City Centre

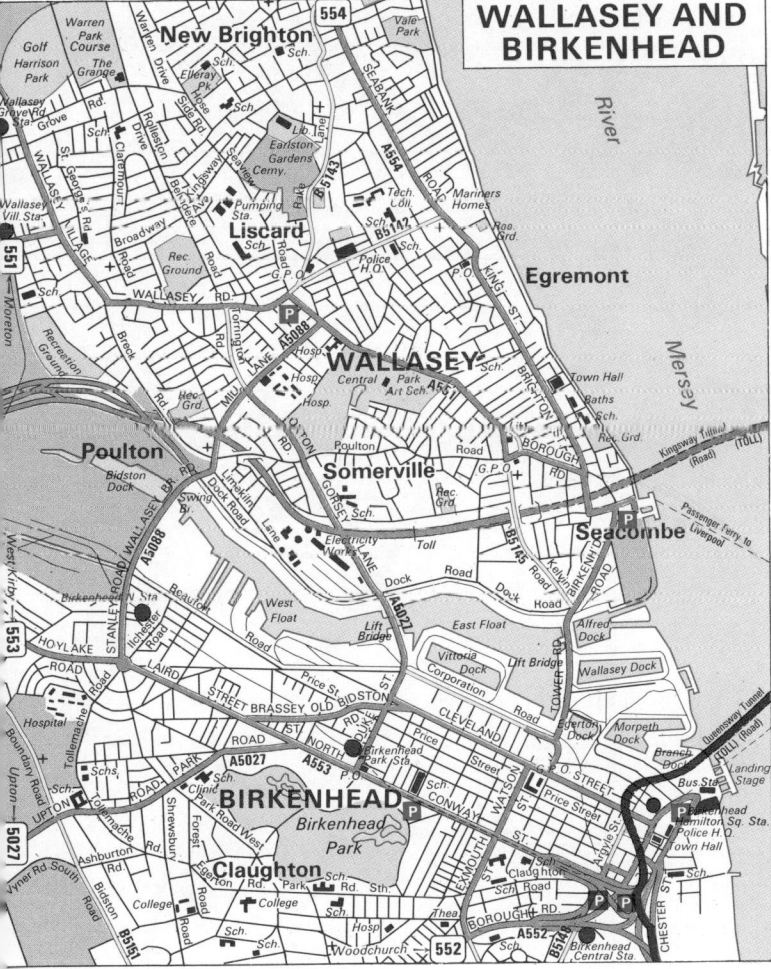

WALLASEY AND BIRKENHEAD

WARRINGTON

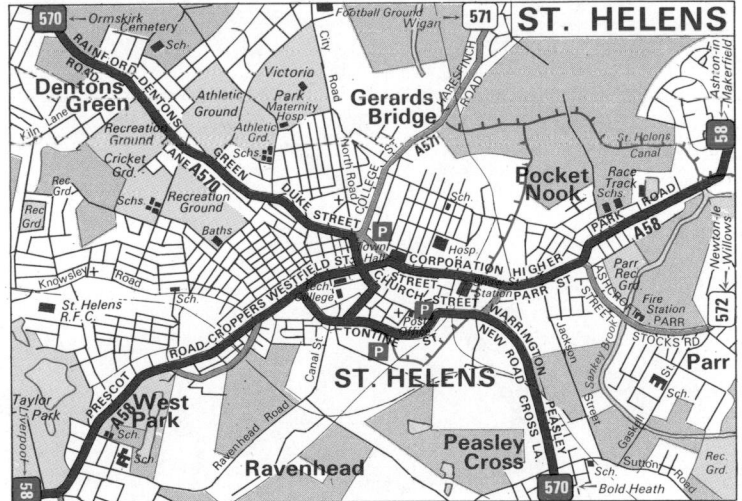

ST. HELENS

Pop:104,173. E.C. Thur.
London192 miles,
Manchester 22 miles.
Famous for glass making.
St. Mary's R.C. Church. The
ruined 15th Cent. Chantry
Chapel of Windlesham Abbey;
17th Cent. cottage, birthplace
of R. J. Seddon, Prime
Minister of New Zealand
from 1893-1906.
A largely engineering and
heavy industry town.
Angling, boating, golf.

WARRINGTON

Pop:68,262. E.C. Thur.
London 183 miles,
Manchester 17 miles.
Ancient borough on banks of
River Mersey. Rebuilt church
of St. Elphin with spire 281 ft.
high. Holy Trinity Church;
St. Mary's R.C. Church
designed by A. W. N. Pugin;
Barley Mow Inn;
Cromwell Statue; Museum;
The Old Academy, 18th Cent.
Town Hall and Wilderspool,
site of Roman Veratinum.
Boating, golf.

WALLASEY AND BIRKENHEAD

Population:234,799. E.C. Wallasey Wednesday.
Birkenhead Thursday.
London 199 miles, Birmingham 96 miles.
Birkenhead is a large port and industrial town, with
shipbuilding industry on West bank of Mersey.
Priory ruins with Chapter House and vaulted
crypts, Williamson Art Gallery and Museum.
Birkenhead and Arrowe Parks. Hamilton Square,
one of largest and finest in England. Wallasey is
large residential and holiday resort north of
Birkenhead with fine sands and fun fair. Bathing,
boating, golf.

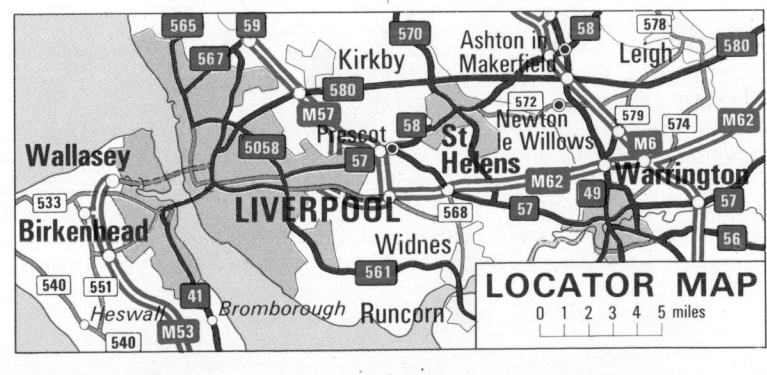

LOCATOR MAP
0 1 2 3 4 5 miles

MANCHESTER

MANCHESTER
Population: 541,468
E.C. Wednesday and Saturday. M.D. Tuesday and Friday.
London 189 miles, Birmingham 80 miles.
Centre of the cotton manufacturing area and it is linked to the sea by the Ship Canal, opened 1894. Also has fine modern docks. Central Library; Town Hall; Royal Exchange. Cath. 15th Cent., mainly Perpendicular, formerly parish church, tower, choir and stalls. Chetham's Hospital, 15th Cent., with what is claimed to be the first public library in Europe; now a school. John Ryland's Library; City Art Gallery; University, founded 1880. Museum; Whitworth Art Gallery; Three halls at Platt, Heaton and Wythenshawe, now house museums. Golf.

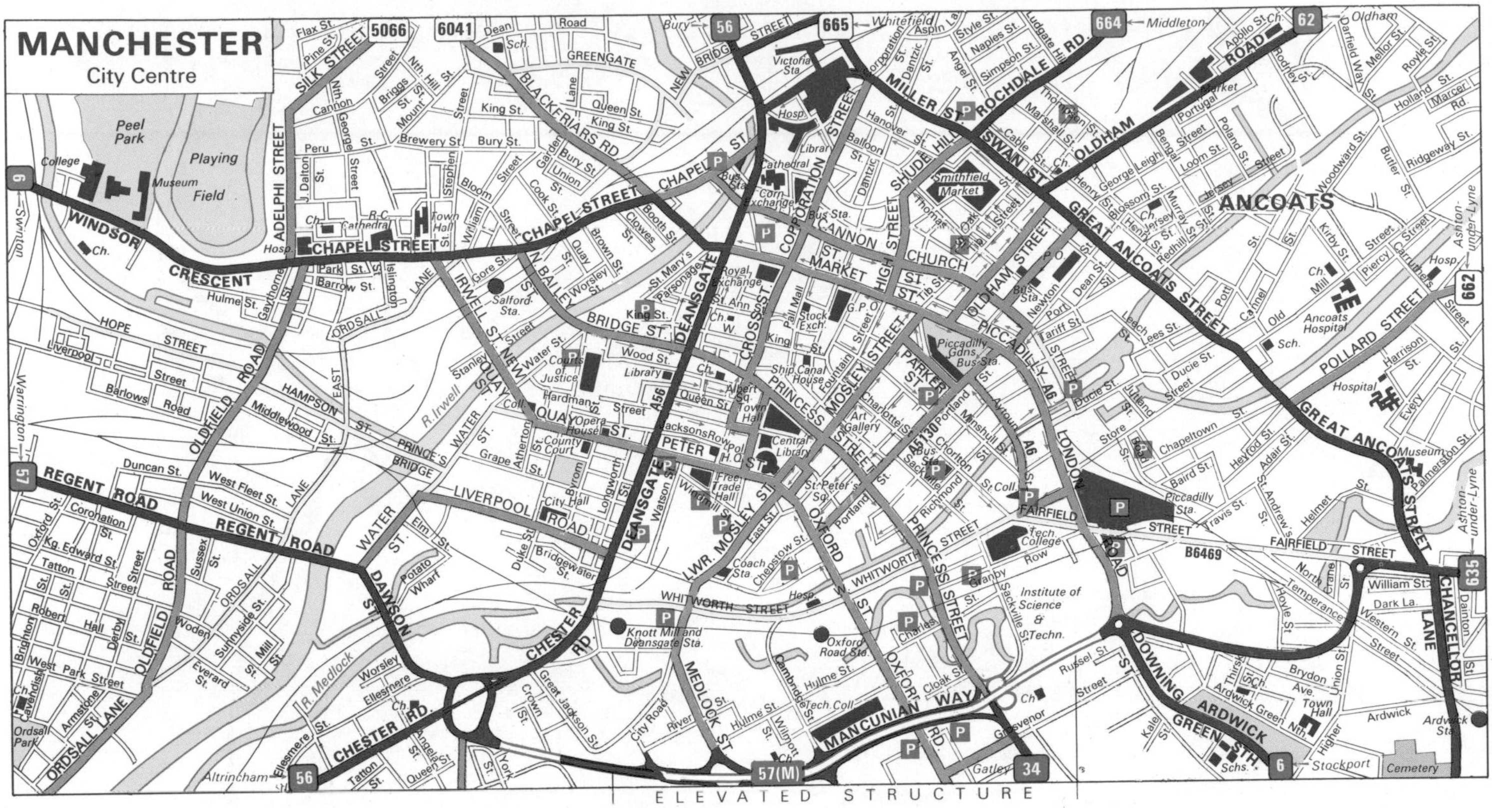

MANCHESTER
City Centre

BOLTON

Population: 154,360. E.C. Wednesday.
London 195 miles, Manchester 12 miles.
Bolton is one of the 'cotton towns' of Lancashire and is the centre of fine spinning and weaving industries. Richard Arkwright and Samuel Crompton were the inventors of spinning machinery and are especially associated with the town. St. Mary's Church Decorated and Perpendicular, modern Parish Church. Man and Scythe Inn, 17th Cent. Town Hall, 19th Cent: Art Gallery, Library and Museum. Golf.

OLDHAM

Population: 105,705.
E.C. Tuesday.
London 186 miles,
Manchester 7 miles.
Oldham is one of the 'cotton towns' and is a great textile and engineering centre. Art Gallery, Museum and Library, Town Hall. Golf.

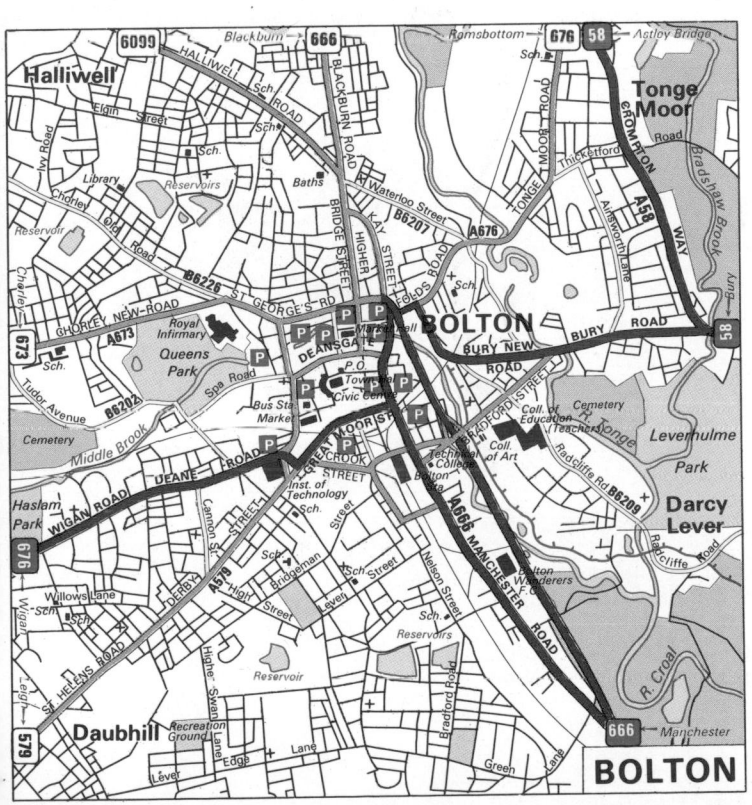

BOLTON

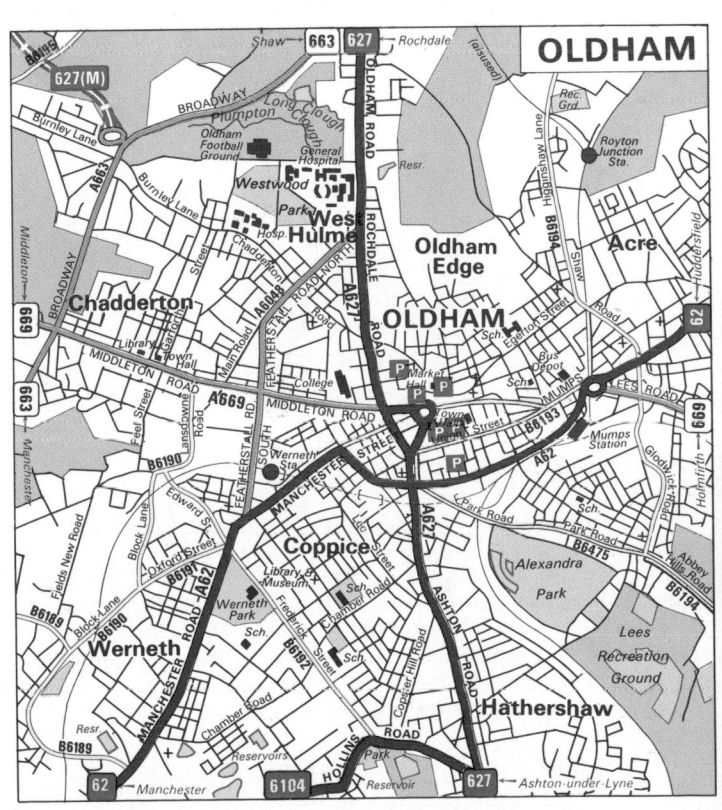

OLDHAM

SHEFFIELD

Population: 520,325

E.C. Thursday. M.D. Tuesday, Wednesday and Saturday.

London 162 miles, Manchester 38 miles.

Industrial and university city long famous for the manufacture of cutlery, silverware and plate. Cathedral, formerly Parish Church, with monuments in the Shrewsbury Chapel. Cutler's Hall, 1832. Town Hall, tower 210 ft., surmounted by a 7 ft. statue of Vulcan. City Hall; Central Library and Graves Art Gallery; City Museum, Manor Lodge, 16th Cent., occupied occasionally by Queen Mary when in captivity. Ruskin Museum; Beauchief Abbey ruins, partly restored, now a church. Golf.

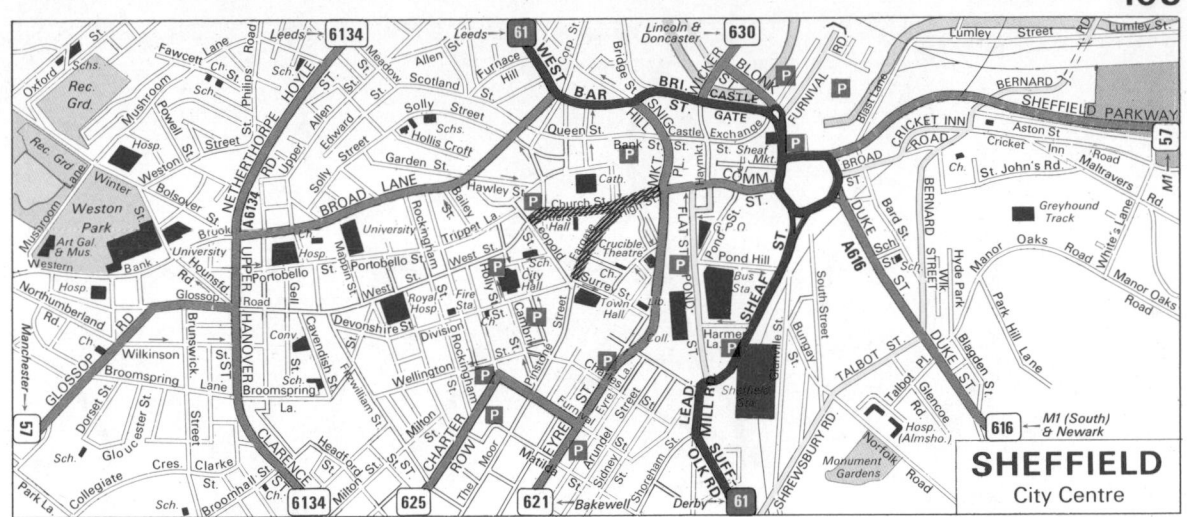

SHEFFIELD
City Centre

ROTHERHAM

Population: 84,646
E.C. Thur.
M.D. Mon. and Sat.
London 165 miles,
Sheffield 6 miles.
Industrial town on the
banks of the River
Rother. Five-arched
Chantry Bridge with 15th
Cent. Chapel in centre.
All Saints Church 15th
Cent., with crocketed spire.
Museum and Art Gallery
in Clifton Park. Nearby
are Wentworth
Woodhouse and Roche
Abbey ruins. Golf.

LOCATOR MAP

0 1 2 3 4 5 miles

DONCASTER

Pop: 82,505.
E.C. Thur. M.D. Tue. & Sat.
London 158 miles,
Sheffield 18 miles.
Old borough dating from
1194. Mansion House,
1748, houses Council
Chamber and Mayor's
Parlour. Corn Exchange
and Market Hall used for
concerts, etc. Grammar
School founded 13th Cent.
Parish Church of
St. George built 1858 to
replace earlier one burnt
down. New Museum and
Art Gallery. Many parks
including Hexthorpe Flatts.
Race course home of the
classic St. Leger race.

ROTHERHAM

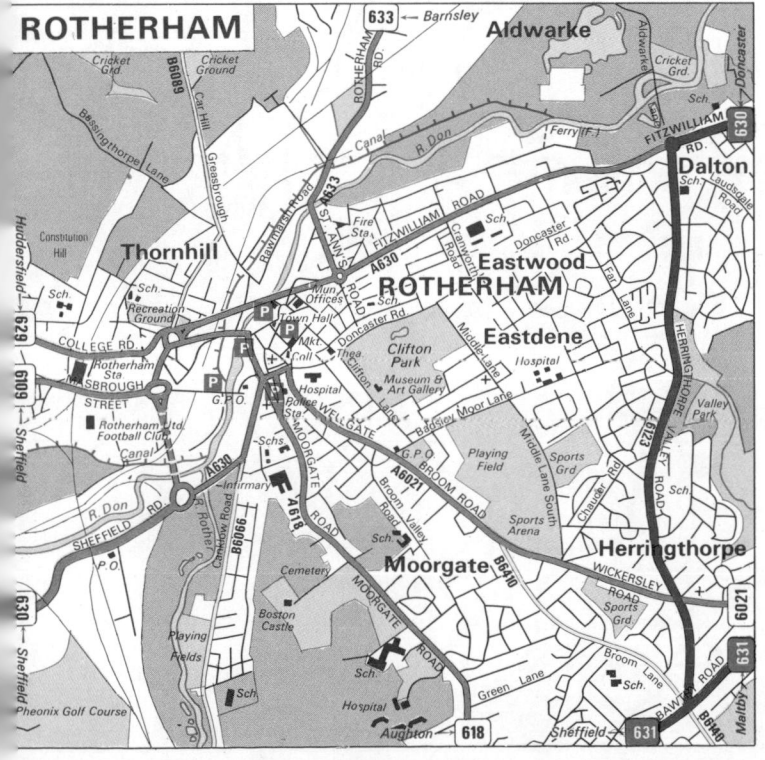

DONCASTER

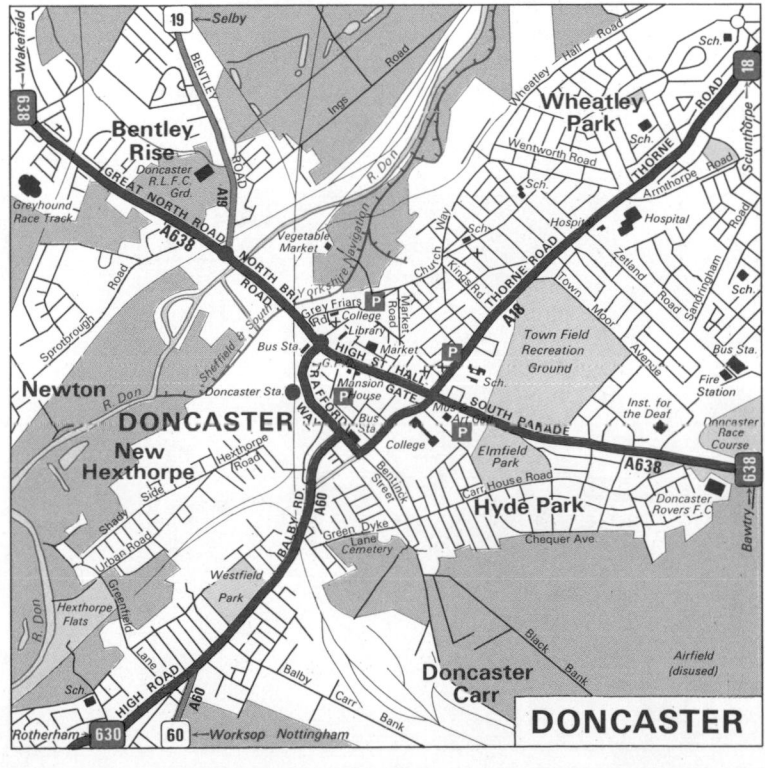

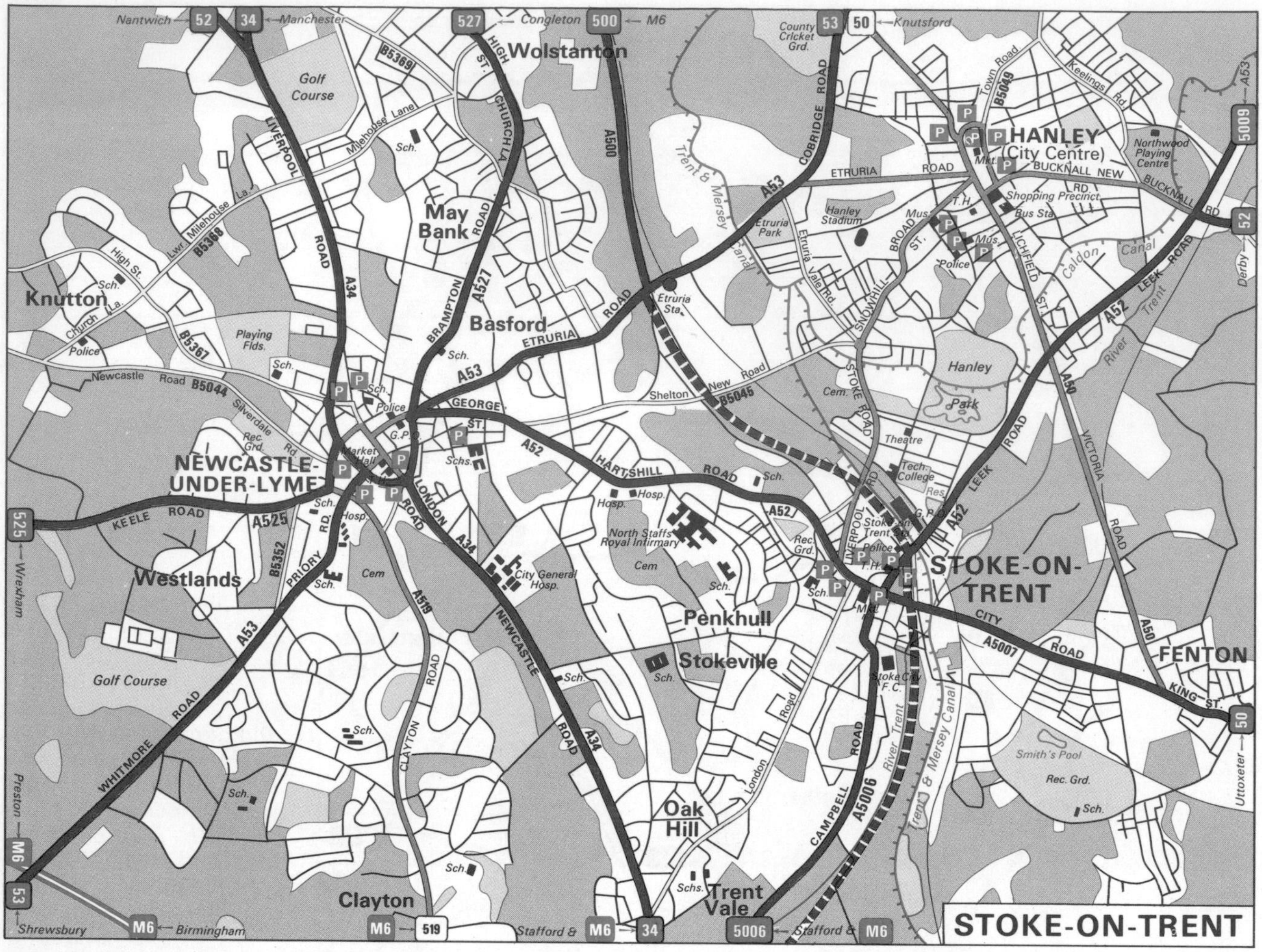

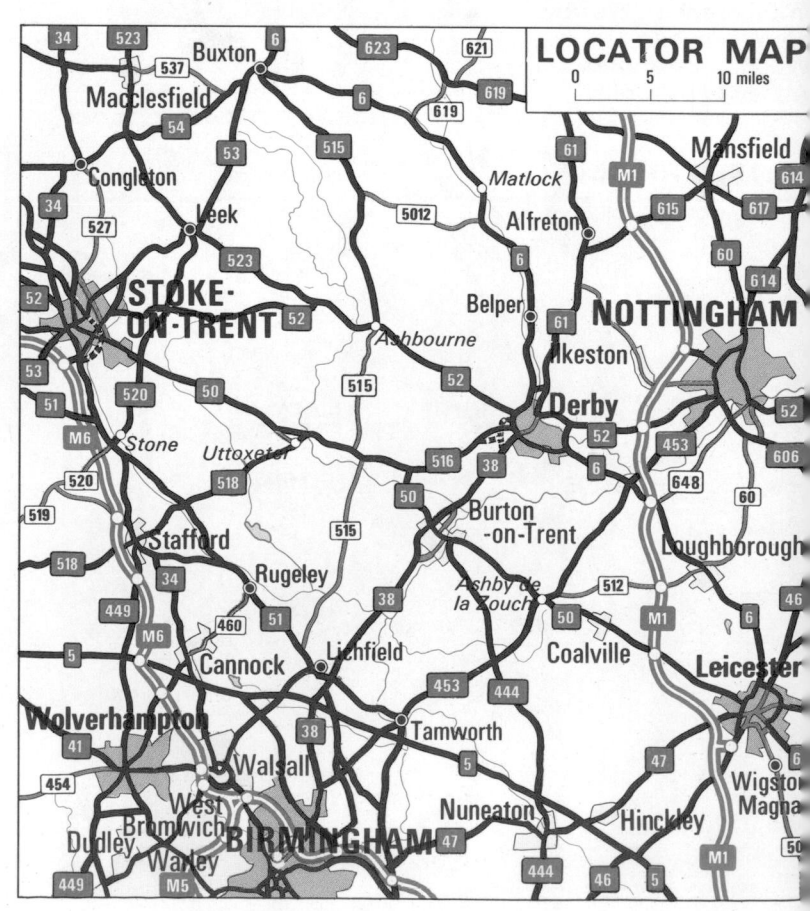

STOKE-ON-TRENT

Population: 265,153 E.C. Thursday. M.D. Saturday.
London 152 miles, Birmingham 43 miles.
The railway centre of the Potteries and the 'Kaype'
of Arnold Bennett (born at Hanley 1867). St. Peter's
Church 1839, contains memorials to Josiah Wedge-
wood, the two Josiah Spodes and a window to
Thomas Minton. Etruria, founded 1769 by Wedgewood,
pottery works still carried on by his descendants.
Etruria Hall, his residence, now used as offices,
museum and for exhibitions of pottery. Ford Green
Hall Folk Museum. Golf.

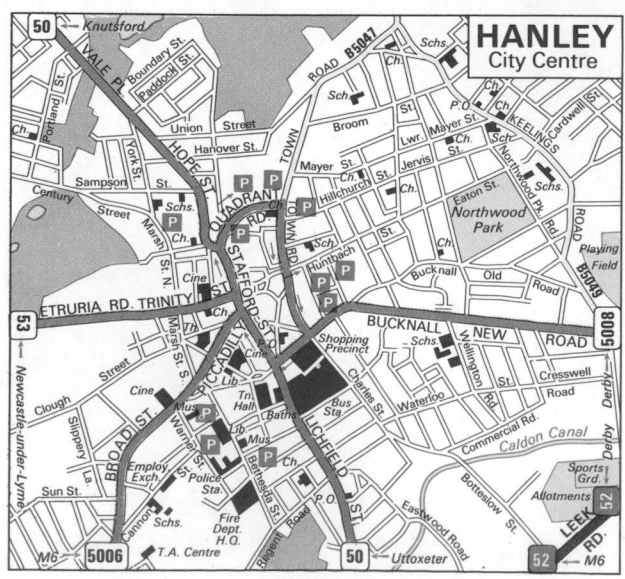

NOTTINGHAM

NOTTINGHAM
Population:299,758.E.C. Thur. M.D. Wednesday and Saturday.
London 123 miles, Birmingham 51 miles.
Industrial and university city on River Trent. 17th Cent. Castle on site of Norman Castle, now a museum and art gallery. Castle Rock pierced by passages and caves. St. Mary's Church is Perpendicular and has a fine nave and tower. Newdigate House, where Marshall Tallard resided. St. Peter's Church. R.C. Cathedral designed by Pugin. Golf, angling.

DERBY
Population:219,580
E.C. Wednesday. M.D. Tues., Thurs., Fri., Sat.
London 126 miles, Birmingham 40 miles.
Historic county town and industrial centre. Cathedral rebuilt 1725 with 16th Cent. Perpendicular tower, 210 ft. St. Werburgh's partly rebuilt, where Dr. Johnson was married. St. Peter's Church 14th-15th Cent. Chapel of Our Lady of the Brigg (c. 1330) beside St. Mary's Bridge. Royal Crown Derby Works. Eagle Centre (Shopping) & Civic Hall. Roman Well at Chester Green. Art Gallery and Museums.

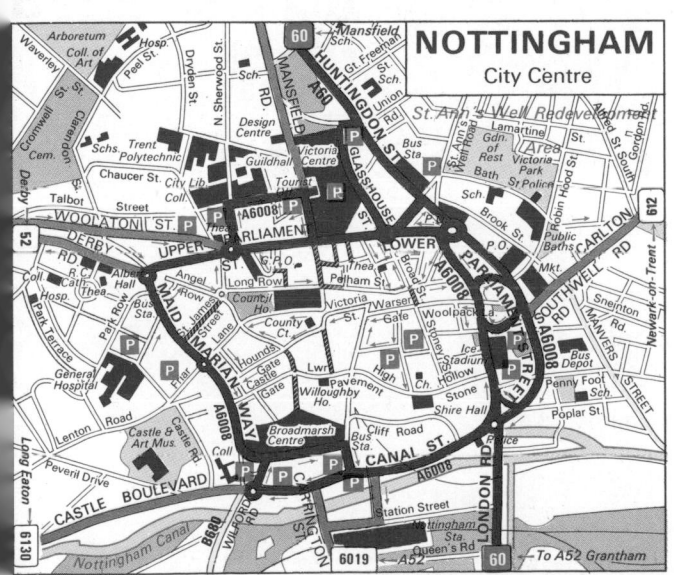

NOTTINGHAM
City Centre

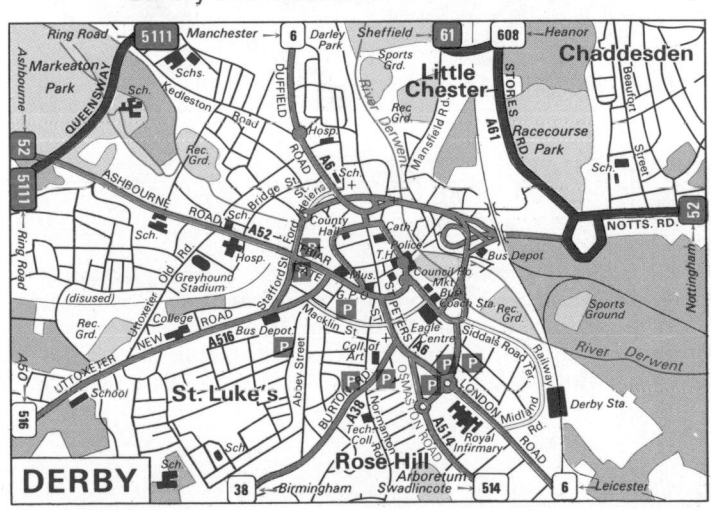

DERBY

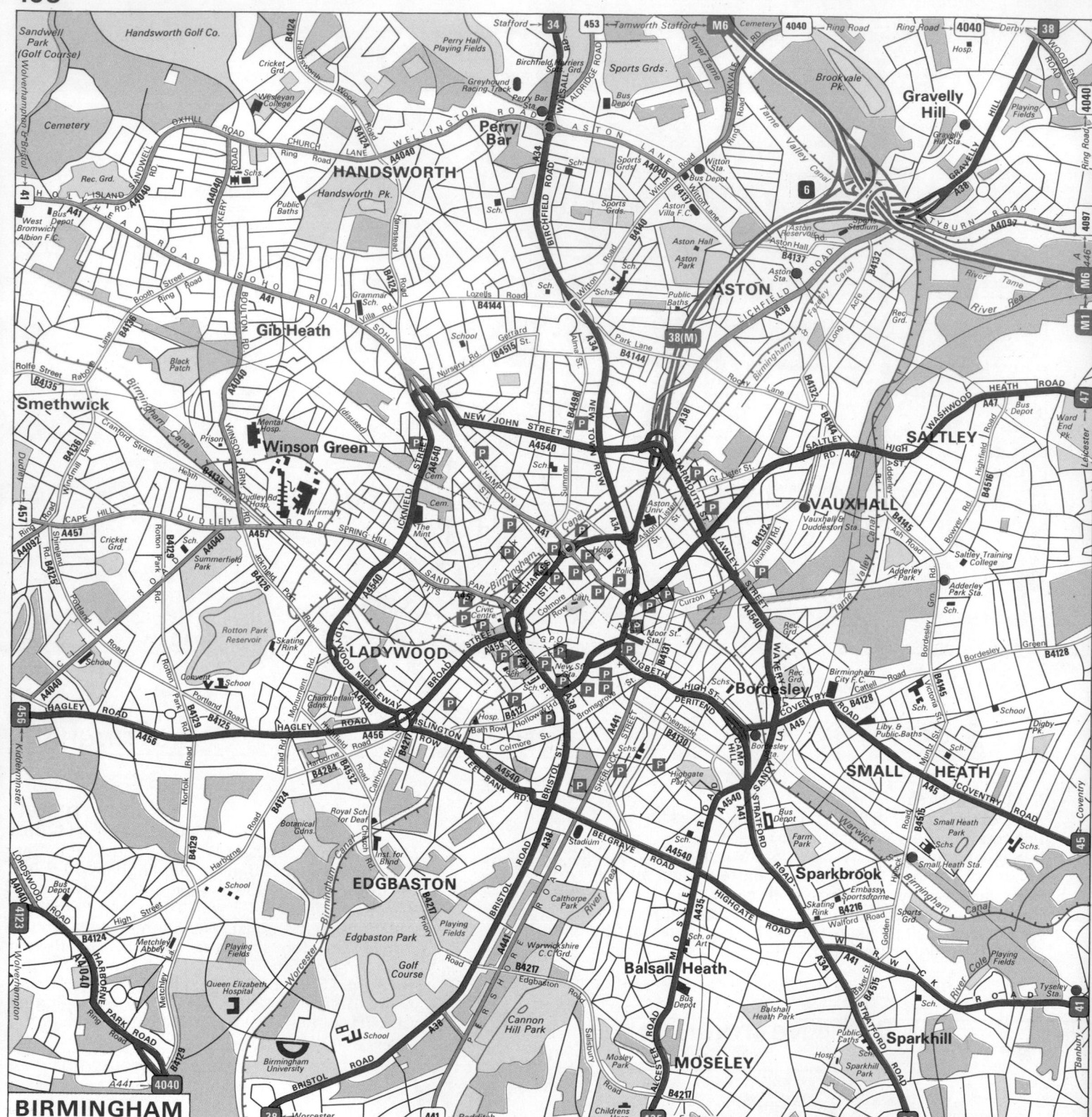

BIRMINGHAM

Population: 1,013,366

E.C. Wednesday and Saturday. M.D. Tuesday.

London 110 miles, Manchester 80 miles.

Great industrial centre, university city. Feeney Galleries in Council House, 1880. Town Hall, 1850, contains fine organ. Hall of Memory; Joseph Chamberlain Museum; Boulton and Watt Museum. St. Philip Cathedral, beautiful windows by Burne-Jones. R.C. Cathedral by Pugin. Barber Institute of Fine Arts. Aston Hall, 17th Cent. mansion, now a museum and art gallery. Rotunda. Bull Ring Shopping Centre. Botanical Gardens. Golf.

BIRMINGHAM
City Centre

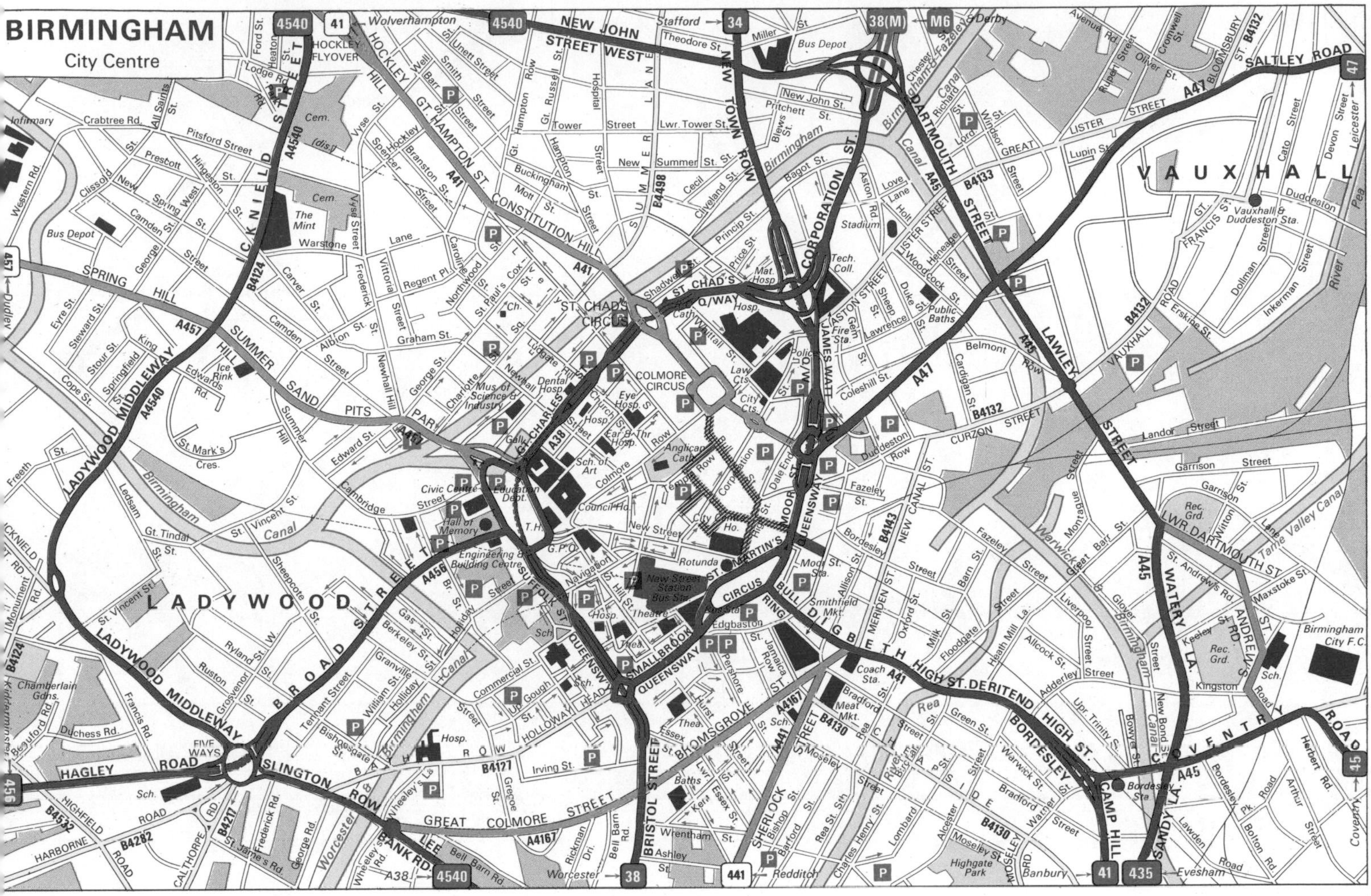

WOLVERHAMPTON

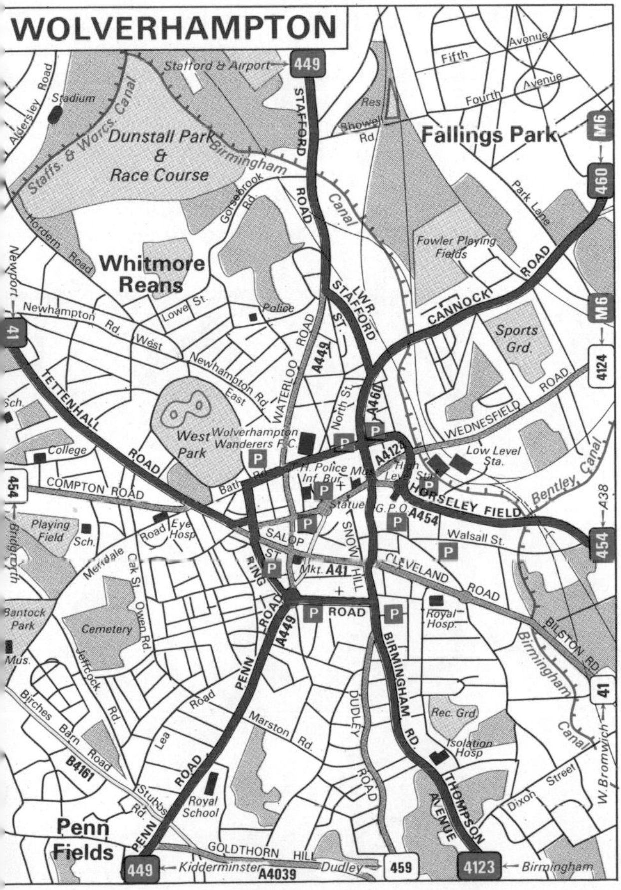

WOLVERHAMPTON
Population: 268,847
E.C. Thursday.
London 125 miles, Birmingham 15 miles.
Industrial town on the western fringe of the Black Country. 18th Cent. St. John's Church in Grecian Style. 10th Cent. St. Peter's Church with some excellent Perpendicular design. Queen Square with statue of Prince Consort. Municipal Art Gallery and Museum, Public Library and 19th Cent. Town Hall. Golf.

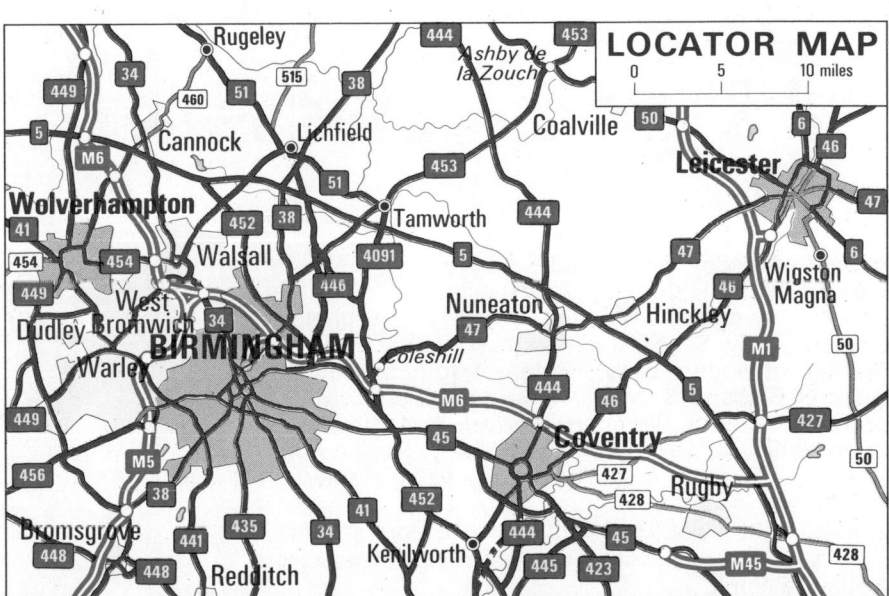

LOCATOR MAP

0   5   10 miles

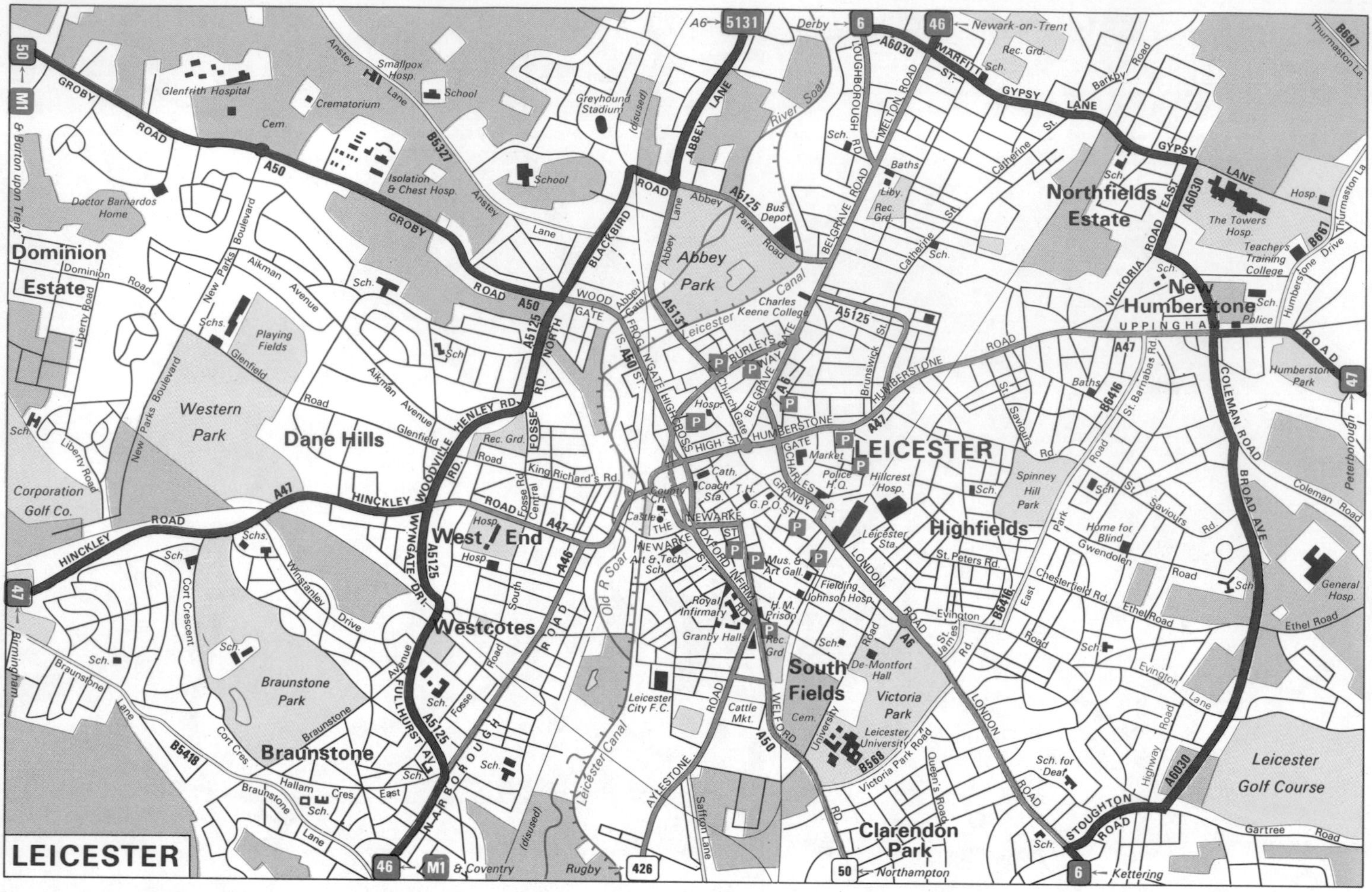

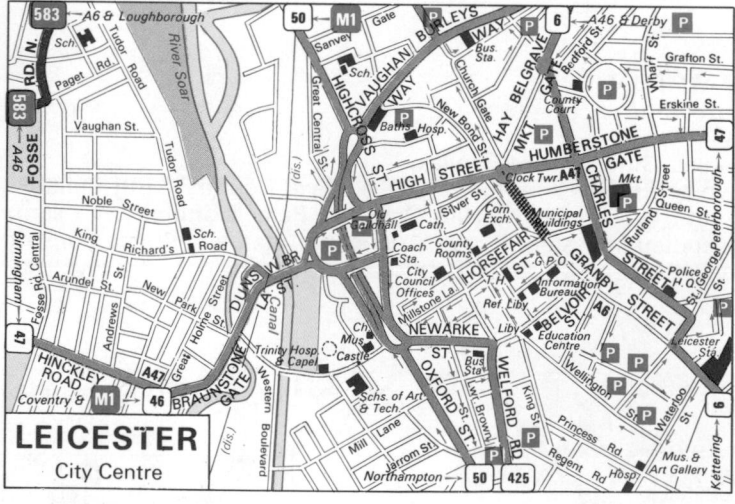

LEICESTER

LEICESTER
Population: 283,549
E.C. Thursday.
M.D. Wednesday, Friday and Saturday.
London 99 miles, Birmingham 40 miles.
County town and industrial centre. St. Nicholas Church partly Saxon and Norman. Jewry wall of Roman Masonry. Bow Bridge, traditional burial place of Richard III. Norman Castle, ruins. St. Mary de Castro Church, Norman chancel, roof. Newarke Chantry House, 1512 (damaged 1940). Skeffington House, museum of local history. Newarke Gateway 1322, St. Martin's Church, Cathedral of new diocese. 16th Cent. Guildhall. City Museum and Art Gallery; Roman pavements; University; Leicester Abbey, remains.

NORTHAMPTON
Population: 126,608 E.C. Thur. M.D. Wed. and Sat.
London 65 miles, Birmingham 49 miles.
County town and centre of footwear industry. St. Peter's Church, a fine example of the Norman Period. Hazelrigge Mansion which survived the fire of 1675. Town Hall and Guildhall. Lawrence Washington was mayor in 1532 and 1545. Museum. St. Giles's Church, Perpendicular with some Norman. St. Sepulchre's, one of four round churches in England. R.C. Cathedral by Pugin, 1864. Eleanor Cross 1291 erected by Edward I.

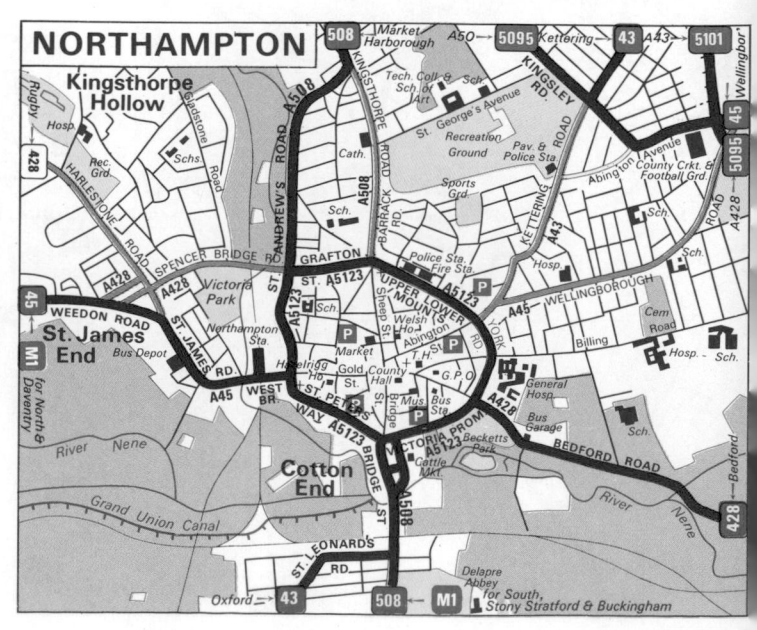

NORTHAMPTON

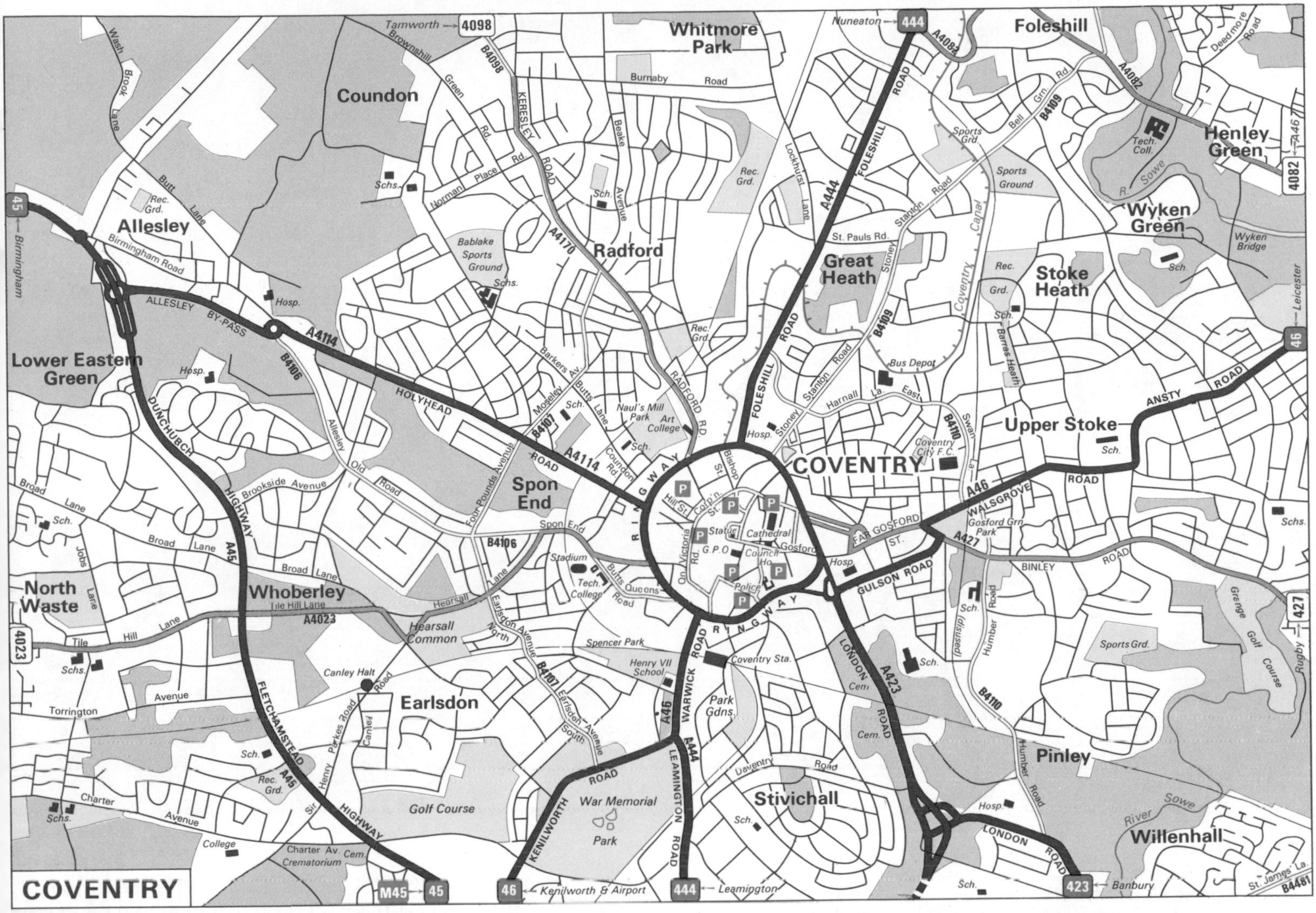

COVENTRY

COVENTRY. Pop: 334,839. E.C. Wed. M.D. Tue. & Sat. London 89 miles, Birmingham 17 miles. Industrial City associated with the motor industry. Remains of 14th Cent. cathedral include outer walls, tower and spire, 303 ft. Adjoining is new Cathedral designed by Basil Spence. St. Mary's Hall founded 13th Cent. for local trade guilds. Ford's almshouses badly damaged 1940. Bablake School & Bond's Almshouses, 16th Cent. Holy Trinity Ch., Perp. with spire 237 ft. Remains of medieval town walls & gates. Godiva statue Ellen Terry born here. The Precinct shopping centre. Golf.

STRATFORD-UPON-AVON. Pop:19,449. E.C. Thur. M.D. Tue. & Fri. London 91 miles, Birmingham 24 miles. Market town. Shakespeare's birthplace and Museum. Shakespeare Memorial Theatre. Collegiate Church, Shakespeare's burial place. Grammar School, Guildhall and Chapel. Harvard House; Town Hall and 15th Cent. Clopton Bridge over River Avon; Anne Hathaway's Cottage, Shottery, and nearby Charlecote Hall. Angling, boating, golf.

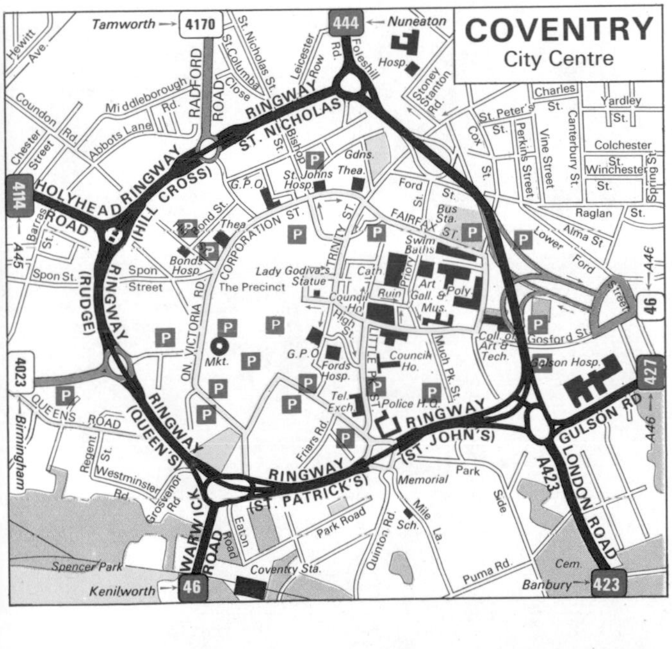

COVENTRY City Centre

STRATFORD-UPON-AVON

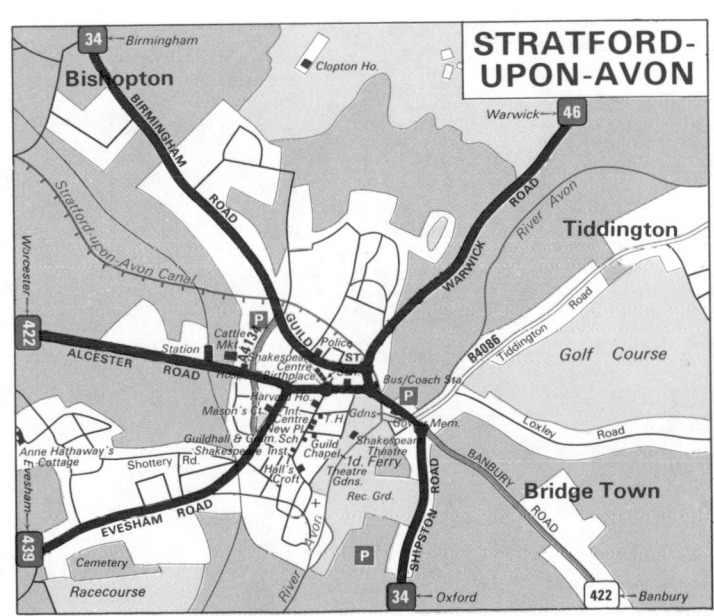

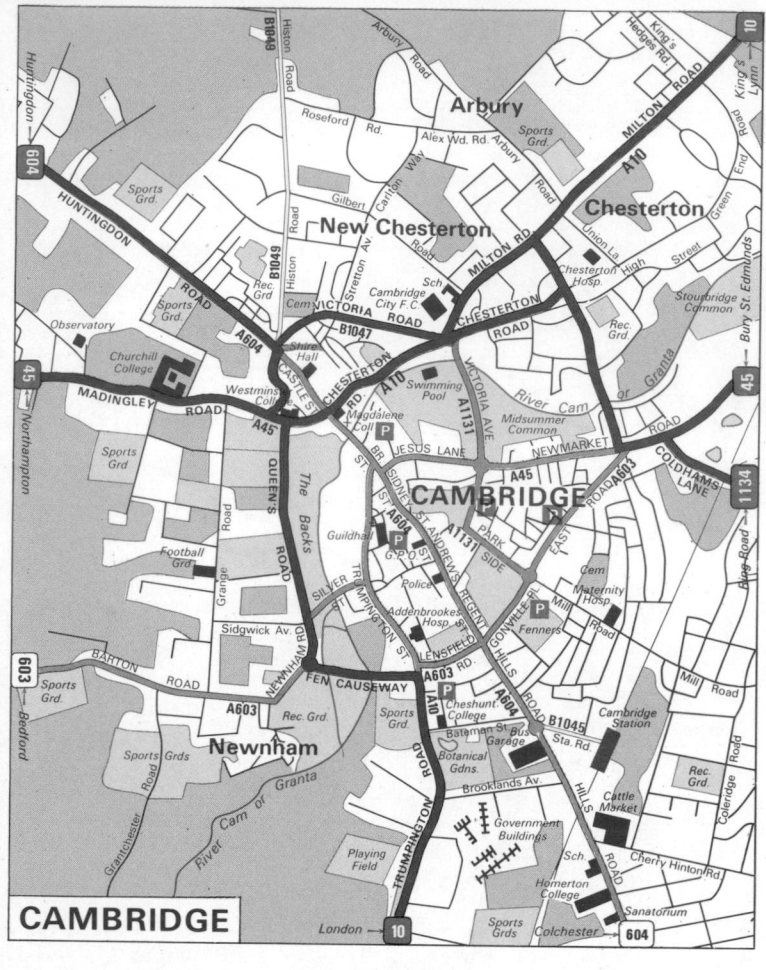

CAMBRIDGE

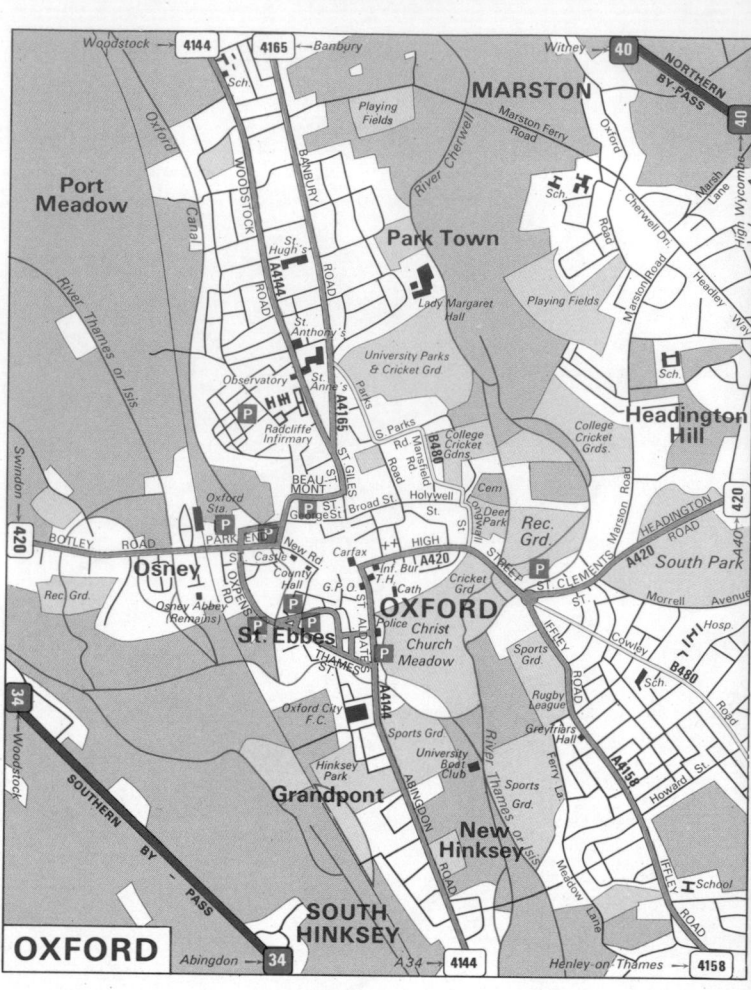

OXFORD

CAMBRIDGE
Population: 98,519
E.C. Thursday. M.D. Monday, Wednesday and Saturday.
London 53 miles, Birmingham 99 miles.
County town and university city. Of architectural note; gateways of St. John's, Queens', Trinity College Hall; interior of King's College Chapel (late Perpendicular), Combination Room of St. John's. Gardens of Christ's, 'The Backs'. St. Mary's the Great; St. Sepulchre oldest of four round churches in England. Fitzwilliam Museum and Art Gallery. University Library. Botanical Gardens. Golf.

OXFORD
Population: 108,564 E.C. Thursday. M.D. Wednesday.
London 56 miles, Birmingham 64 miles.
County town and university city. Noteworthy colleges are: Christchurch whose chapel is now the Cathedral, mainly 12th Cent.; Merton, medieval library, the oldest college; Magdalen, Perpendicular, water walks; New College, founded 1379; Wadham College, hall and gardens. Bodleian Library. Ashmolean Museum. High Street. St. Mary's Church, Perpendicular with Decorated spire, 188 ft. Radcliffe Camera, viewpoint. University Museum, St. Peter-in-the-East Church, Norman crypt. Castle remains. Angling, boating, golf.

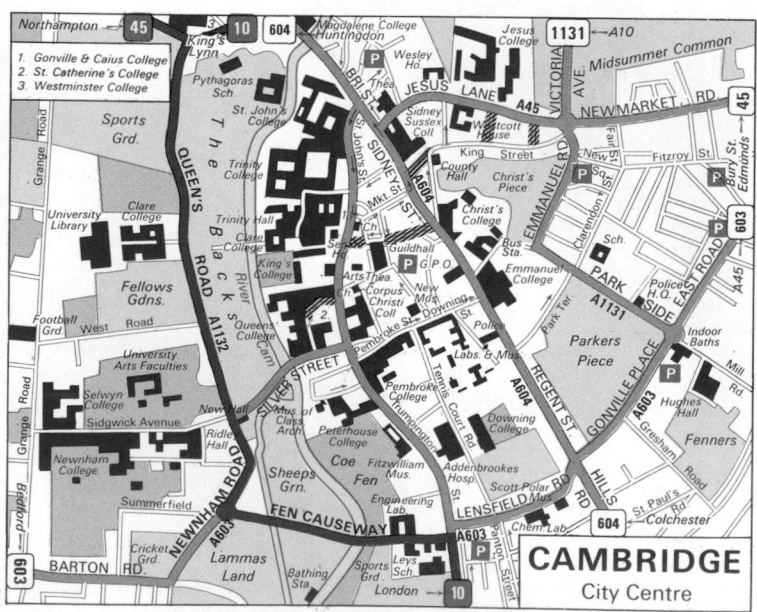

CAMBRIDGE
City Centre

1. Gonville & Caius College
2. St. Catherine's College
3. Westminster College

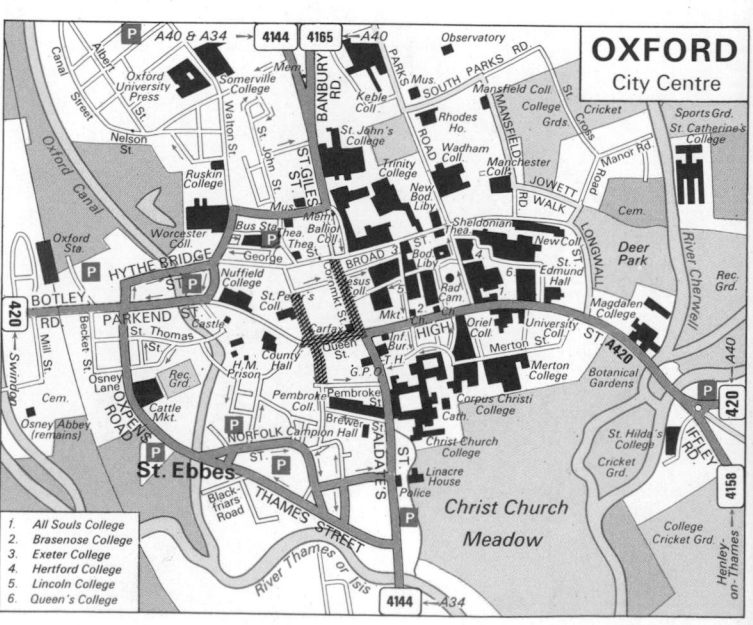

OXFORD
City Centre

1. All Souls College
2. Brasenose College
3. Exeter College
4. Hertford College
5. Lincoln College
6. Queen's College

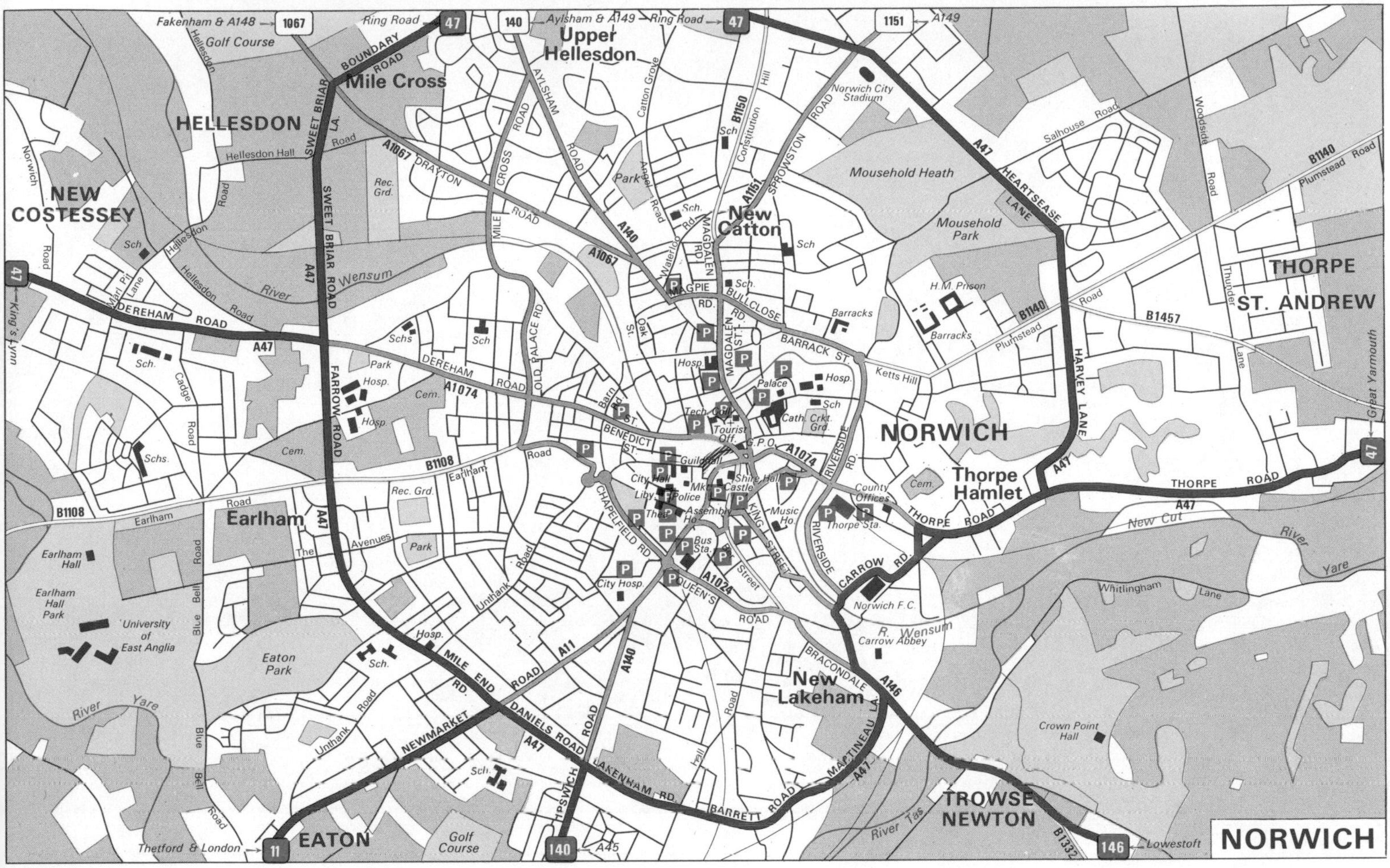

NORWICH

NORWICH. Population:121,688 E.C. Thur. M.D. Wed. & Sat. London 110 miles, Birmingham155 miles. County town. Castle *c*. 1130, now a museum. Cathedral mainly Norman with Decorated spire 315 ft. Guildhall. Bishop's Bridge, 13th Cent. Angling, golf, yachting.

IPSWICH. Population:123,312 E.C. Wed. and Sat. M.D. Tue. London 70 miles, Birmingham 152 miles. Angling, boating, golf.

SOUTHEND ON SEA. Pop:162,770 E.C. Wed. London 40 miles. Pier, 1⅓ miles long. Angling, bathing, boating, golf, sailing.

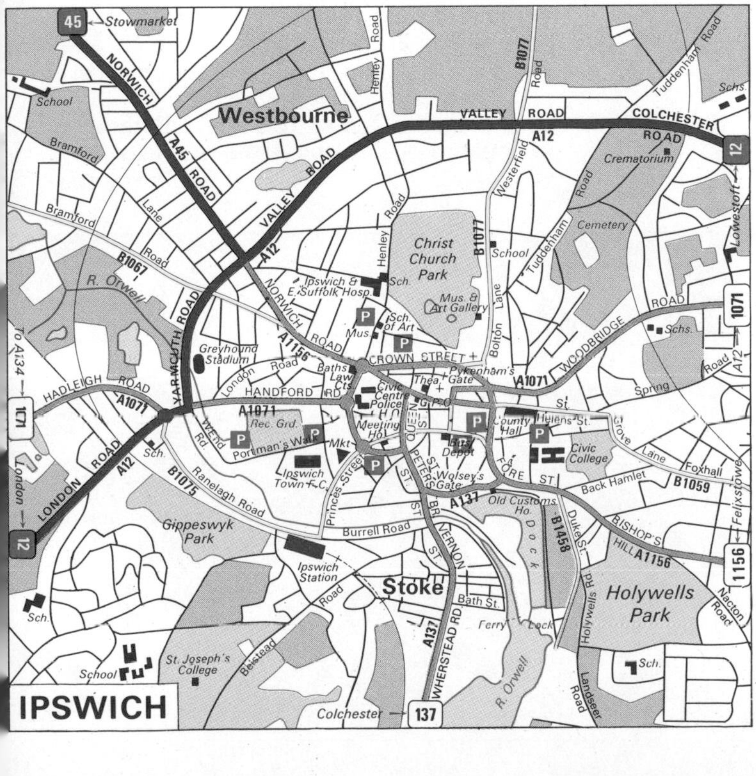

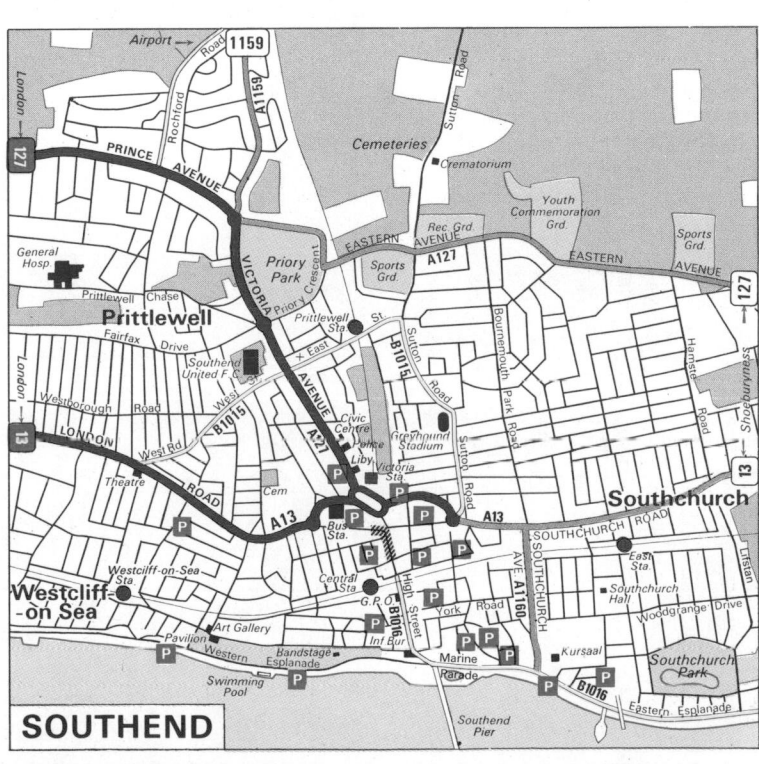

IPSWICH

SOUTHEND

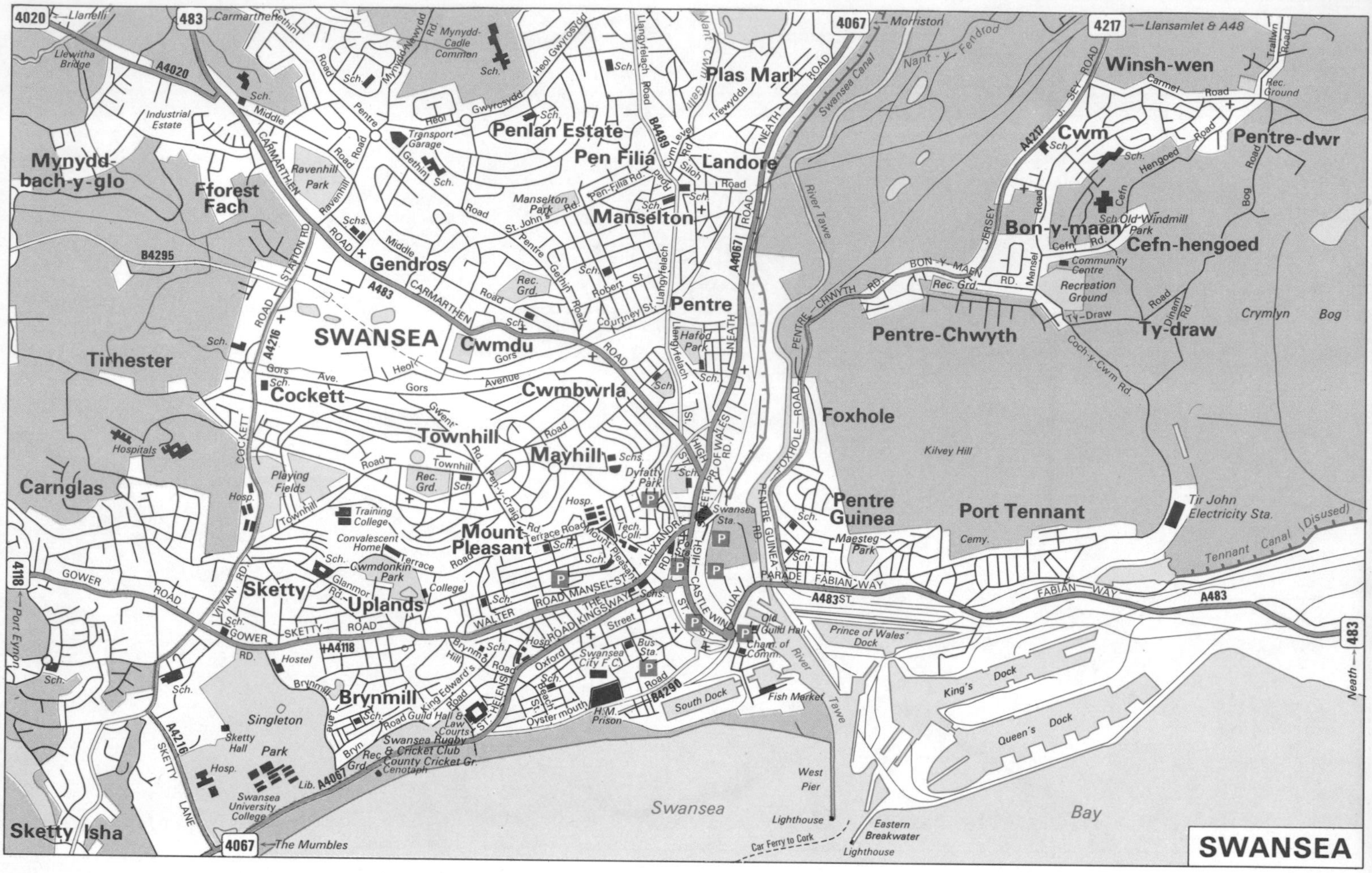

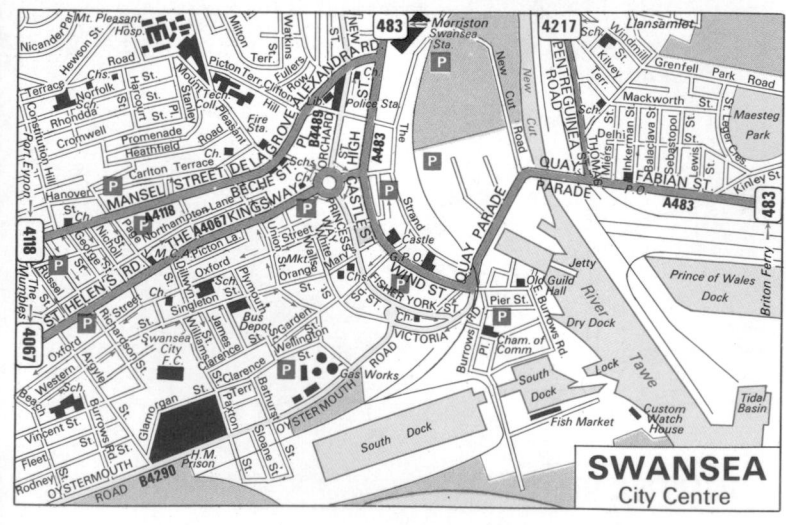

SWANSEA

Population: 172,566.
E.C. Thur. M.D. Wed. and Sat.
London 192 miles, Birmingham 126 miles.
Industrial centre and university town. Port and docks. Remains of 14th Cent. Castle. St. Mary's Church – remains. Civic Centre. Guildhall notable as containing Brangwyn panels. Deffett Francis Gallery; Glynn Vivian Art Gallery; and others. Nash House, birthplace of 'Beau' Nash, leader of fashion in Georgian society. Market, largest in Wales. University College and Singleton Park. Oystermouth Castle, remains of hall, gatehouse and keep. Gower Peninsula.
Bathing, boating, caving, golf.

NEWPORT

Population: 112,048.
E.C. Thursday.
London 141 miles, Birmingham 90 miles.
Once a walled town situated beside the River Usk, it is now an important industrial centre with extensive and modern docks. Remains of Norman Castle on the bank of the river. Cathedral Church of St. Woolo's, retaining Perpendicular tower, fine Norman arch and nave, early English chapel. Museum and Art Gallery containing Roman relics from Caerwent and Caerleon. Murenger House 16th Cent. Civic Centre. One of two Transporter Bridges in England, 177 ft. above the waters of the Usk.
Fishing, golf.

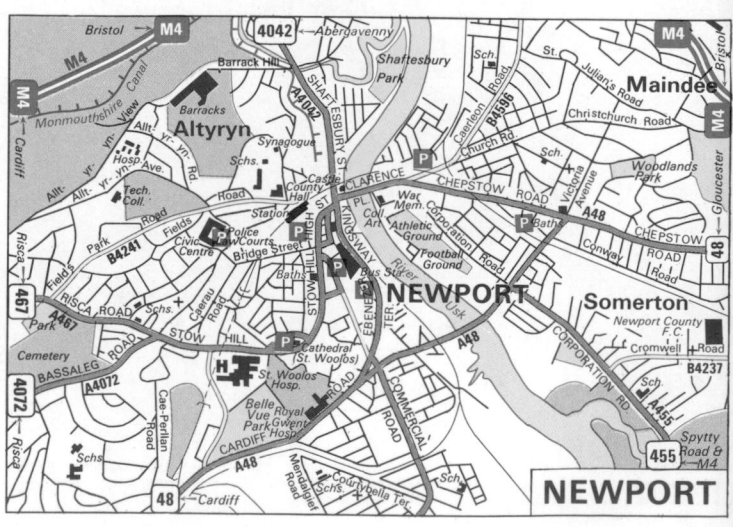

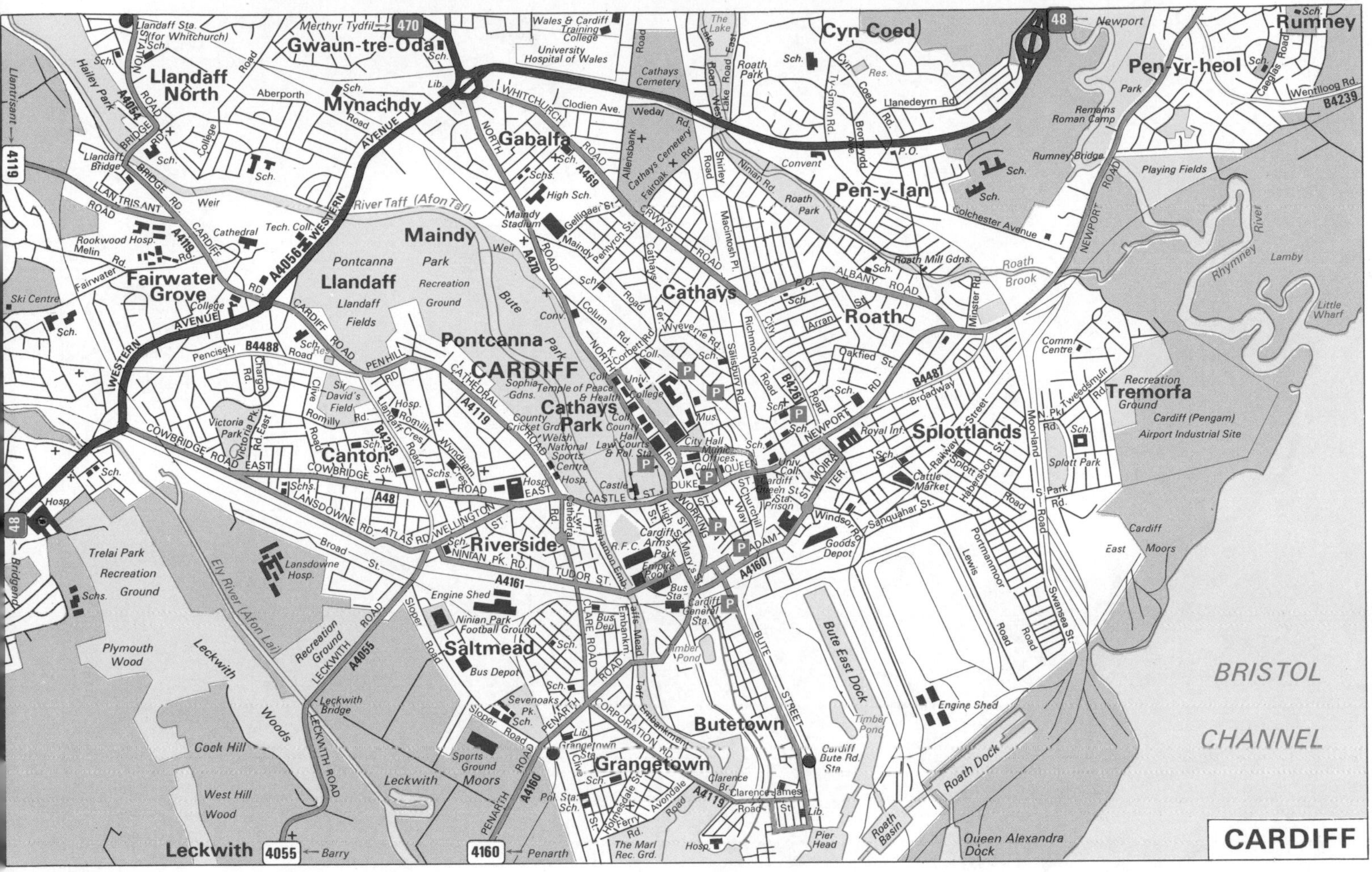

CARDIFF

Population: 278,221
E.C. Wednesday.
M.D. Thursday and Saturday.
London 154 miles,
Birmingham 101 miles,
Bristol 42 miles.
Seaport and university city.
Castle, begun 1090, on site of
Roman Castrum, Gateway
recently rebuilt, 'Black Tower',
13th Cent. In Cathays Park are
the municipal buildings,
including City and County Halls.
University College, National
Museum of Wales, Law Courts,
Welsh National War Memorial.
Llandaff Cathedral, Norman and
Early English, restored after
war damage; famous statue by
Epstein, Reredos by Rossetti,
Chapter House, Bishop's Palace
gatehouse 1300. Golf.

CARDIFF

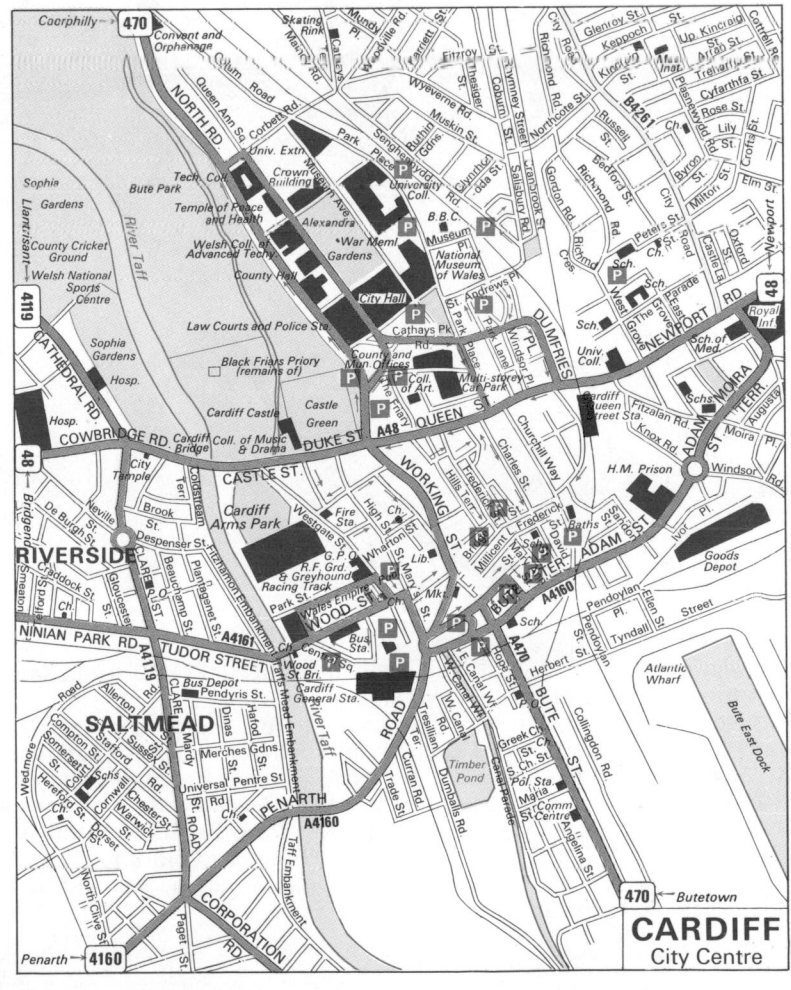

CARDIFF
City Centre

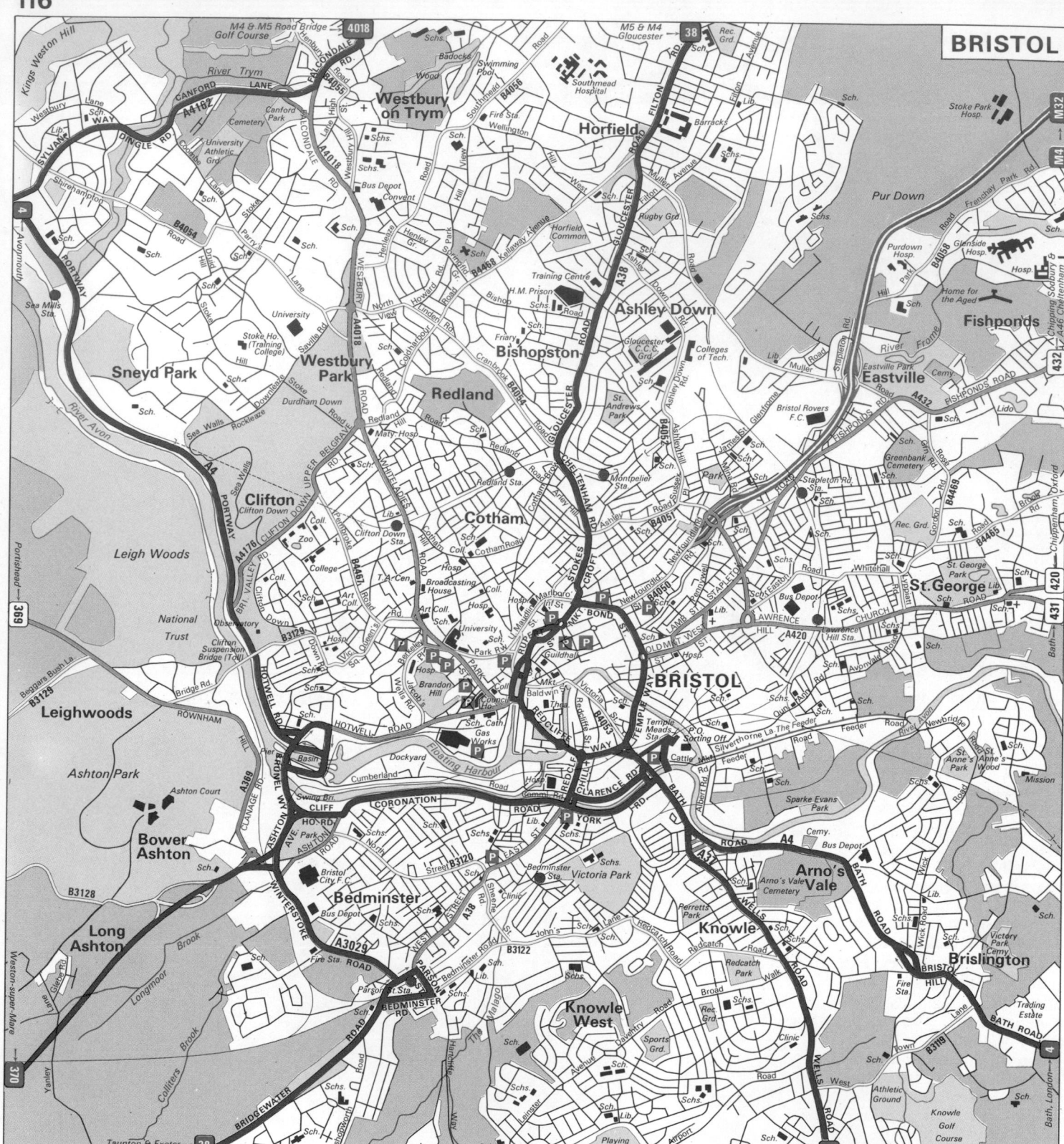

BRISTOL

BRISTOL
Population:425,203.E.C. Wednesday and Saturday. M.D. Thursday.
London 117 miles, Birmingham 85 miles.
Industrial and university city. Docks at Bristol, Avonmouth and Portishead. Cathedral, Norman chapter house; Lady Chapel, Early English. Lord Mayor's Chapel, originally founded in 1225, it is the only civic chapel in England. Norman Abbey Gateway; St. Mary Redcliff Church, Perpendicular. Theatre Royal, oldest in England. Art Gallery and Museum. Red Lodge and Georgian House. Folk Museum at Blaise Castle Estate. Many old inns and houses. Clifton Suspension Bridge spanning the impressive Avon Gorge. Cabot Tower; he sailed west from Bristol to discover Newfoundland. Bristol Grammar School, 16th Cent. Corn-market with the famous 'nails' outside. Numerous old churches in the 'City' including John Wesley's Chapel in Broadmead. Part of Temple Meads station is the original terminus designed by I. K. Brunel for the London and Bristol Railway. Downs and Zoological Gardens at Clifton. Golf.

BRISTOL
City Centre

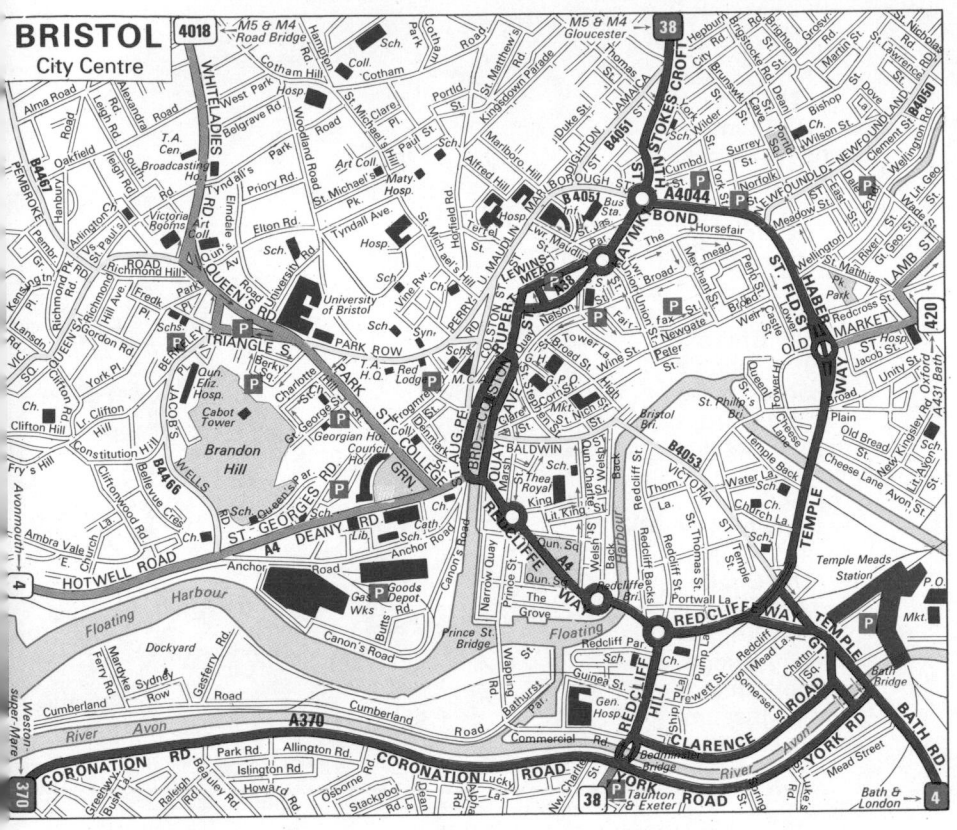

GLOUCESTER

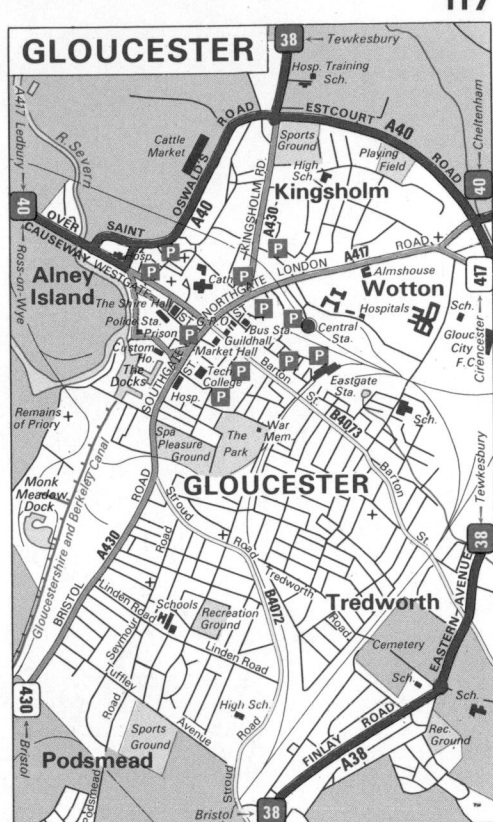

PLYMOUTH

Population: 239,314 E.C. Wed. M.D. Tue., Thur. and Sat.
London 214 miles, Birmingham 210 miles.
Important port and naval dock. Drake, Cook, Hawkins and Chichester started voyages from here. Last port of call of Pilgrim Fathers. The Hoe, where Drake is said to have been playing bowls while the Spanish Armada approached. Smeaton's Tower, a re-erected part of the third Eddystone Lighthouse, Barbican Fish Market. Remains of 14th Cent. Castle Gatehouse. St. Andrew's Church, 15th Cent., Pysten House 15th Cent. monastic house. Art Gallery and Museum. Stonehouse in which is the Royal William Victualling Yard. Recently rebuilt Civic Centre and town centre. Angling, bathing, boating, golf.

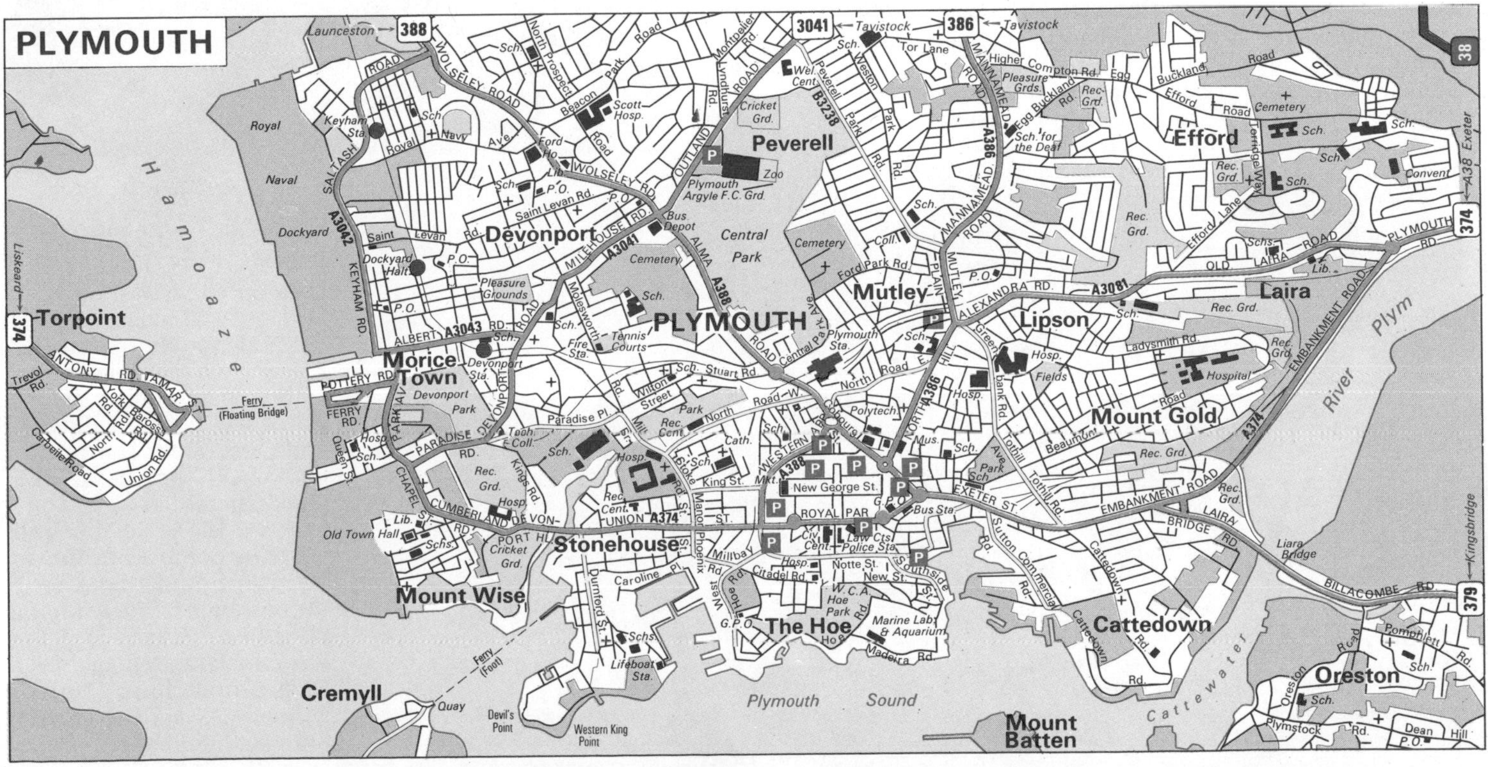

GLOUCESTER

Population:90,590 E.C. Thur. M.D. Mon. & Sat.
London 103 miles, Birmingham 51 miles.
Inland port and county town. Fine Cathedral, once the Benedictine Abbey church, Norman vaulting in nave, East Window, 1352; tomb of Edward II; 14th Cent. stalls, Lady Chapel, 1498. Norman Crypt, Cloisters, fan tracery vaulting. Chapter House, Norman; Library including copy of Coverdale's Bible, Abbot's House. Folk Museum. St. Nicholas Church. New Inn, 1450. Norman Church of St. Mary de Lode, on site of Roman Temple.

PLYMOUTH

![Map of Plymouth showing Torpoint, Cremyll, Devonport, Stonehouse, Mount Wise, The Hoe, Mount Batten, Peverell, Mutley, Lipson, Laira, Efford, Mount Gold, Cattedown, Oreston, and surrounding areas with Plymouth Sound and River Plym.]

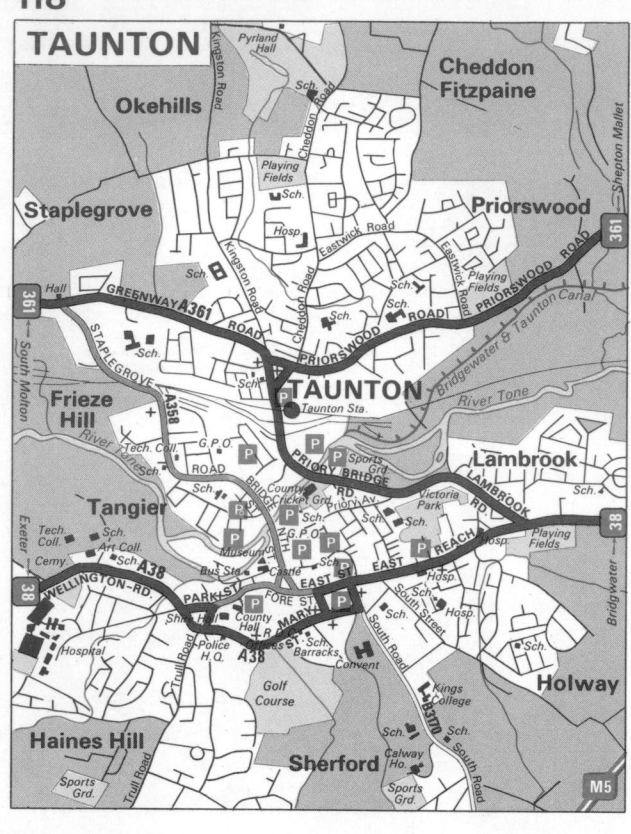

TAUNTON

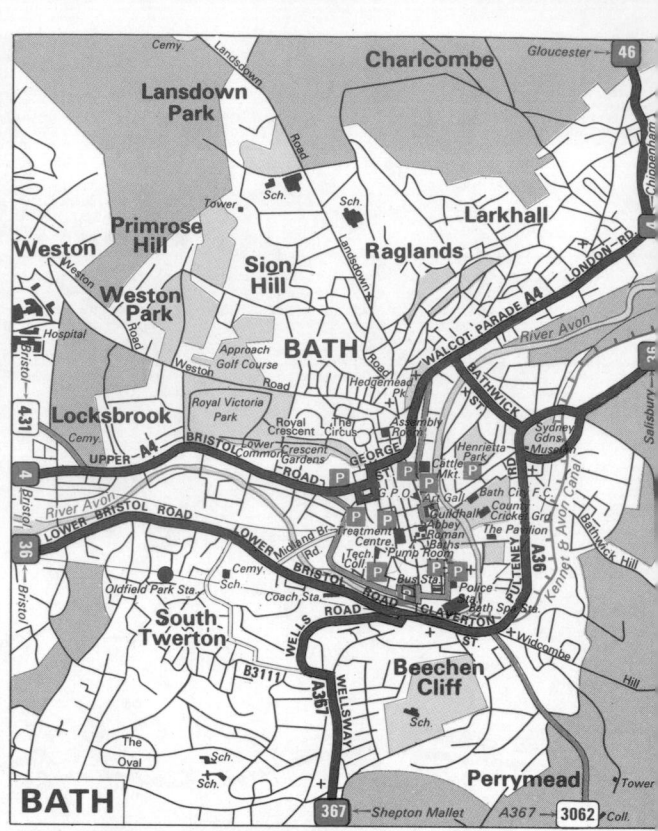

BATH
Population:84,545.
E.C. Thur. & Sat.
M.D. Wed.
London 108 miles,
Birm'ham 88 miles.
Spa and residential
town since Roman
occupation.
Roman Bath;
Grand
Pump Room.
Abbey Church,
from 1499; 'Jacob's
Ladder' flanks
West Front
window. Retains
some fine houses
of the 18th Cent.,
notably 'The
Royal Crescent'
and 'The Circus'.
Art Gallery.
Robert Adam's
Pulteney Bridge.
Holburne of
Menstrie Museum,
Sydney Gardens.

TAUNTON
Population:37,373. E.C. Thursday. M.D. Saturday.
London 145 mls., Birmingham 131 mls., Bristol 43 mls.
County town of Somerset. St. Mary Magdalen's Ch.,
Perpendicular, sculptured tower (reconstructed 1862);
St. James's Church (rebuilt); Priory Barn, 12th Cent.
Taunton Castle, Norman, now museum; Hall was
scene of the 'Bloody Assize', 1685. White Hart has
historic associations. Market Ho., Guildhall. Golf.

TORQUAY   (Torbay Population: 108,888)
Population: 52,300. E.C. Wednesday and Saturday.
London 191 miles, Birmingham 188 miles.
Large seaside resort. Ruins of Torre Abbey with
'Spanish Barn' and Art Gallery. Torquay Natural
History Museum where prehistoric remains from
Kent's Cavern are arranged. The 12th Cent. St.
Michael's Chapel. The coastline is of much geological
interest. Angling, bathing, boating, golf, sailing.

EXETER

EXETER
Population:95,729
E.C. Wed. M.D. Fri.
London 169 miles,
Plymouth 42 miles.
Formerly the Roman city Isca,
Exeter is now an historic,
cathedral and university city.
Cathedral, mainly Early English
and Decorated; Norman towers
built over transepts; West Front.
Guildhall rebuilt 1330 and
restored 1464. Rougemont
Gardens contain remains of
Norman Rougemont Castle and
the entrance to the subterranean
passages. Tucker's Hall, fine
oak panelling, guild relics.
Mols Coffee House, 16th Cent.
Numerous Georgian and Regency
houses. Angling, boating, golf.

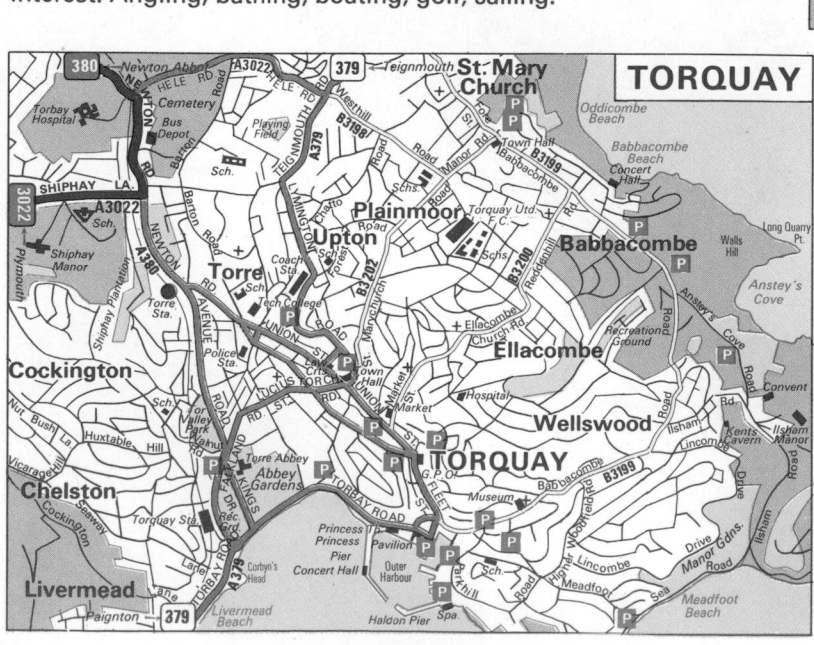

TORQUAY

BOURNEMOUTH

Pop:153,425.
E.C. Wed.
London
103 miles,
Birmingham
146 miles.
Renowned for
cliff walks,
sands, gardens
and chines,
Alum, Durley,
Middle and
Boscombe.
19th Cent. Holy
Trinity Church
with reredos by
John Byam
Shaw. Natural
Science
Museum,
Russell Cotes Art
Gallery and
Museum. Over-
cliff Drives, Pier
and Winter
Gardens. Golf.

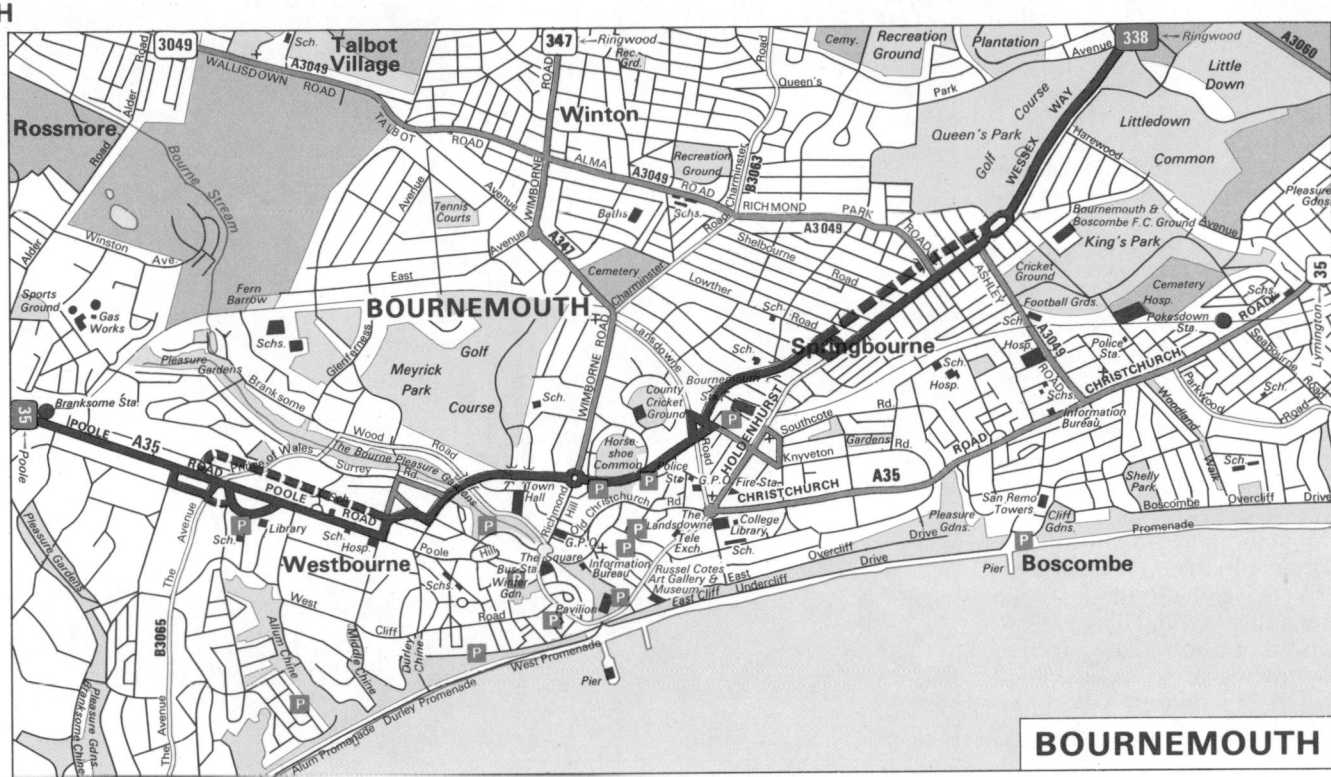

BOURNEMOUTH

SOUTHAMPTON

Pop:214,826.
E.C. Wed.
London 76 miles,
Birmingham
124 miles.
Britain's chief
passenger port,
Extensive
docks. God's
House Gate,
part of Town
Wall. Canute's
House, medieval.
West Quay,
whence the
Pilgrim Fathers'
Mayflower
sailed. Garden of
Remembrance.
St. Michael's
Church 1100,
restored. Tudor
House museum.
Three town
gates remain,
Bargate and two
posterns. Civic
Centre.
University and
Sims Library.
The ruins of
Netley Abbey.
Angling, boating
golf.

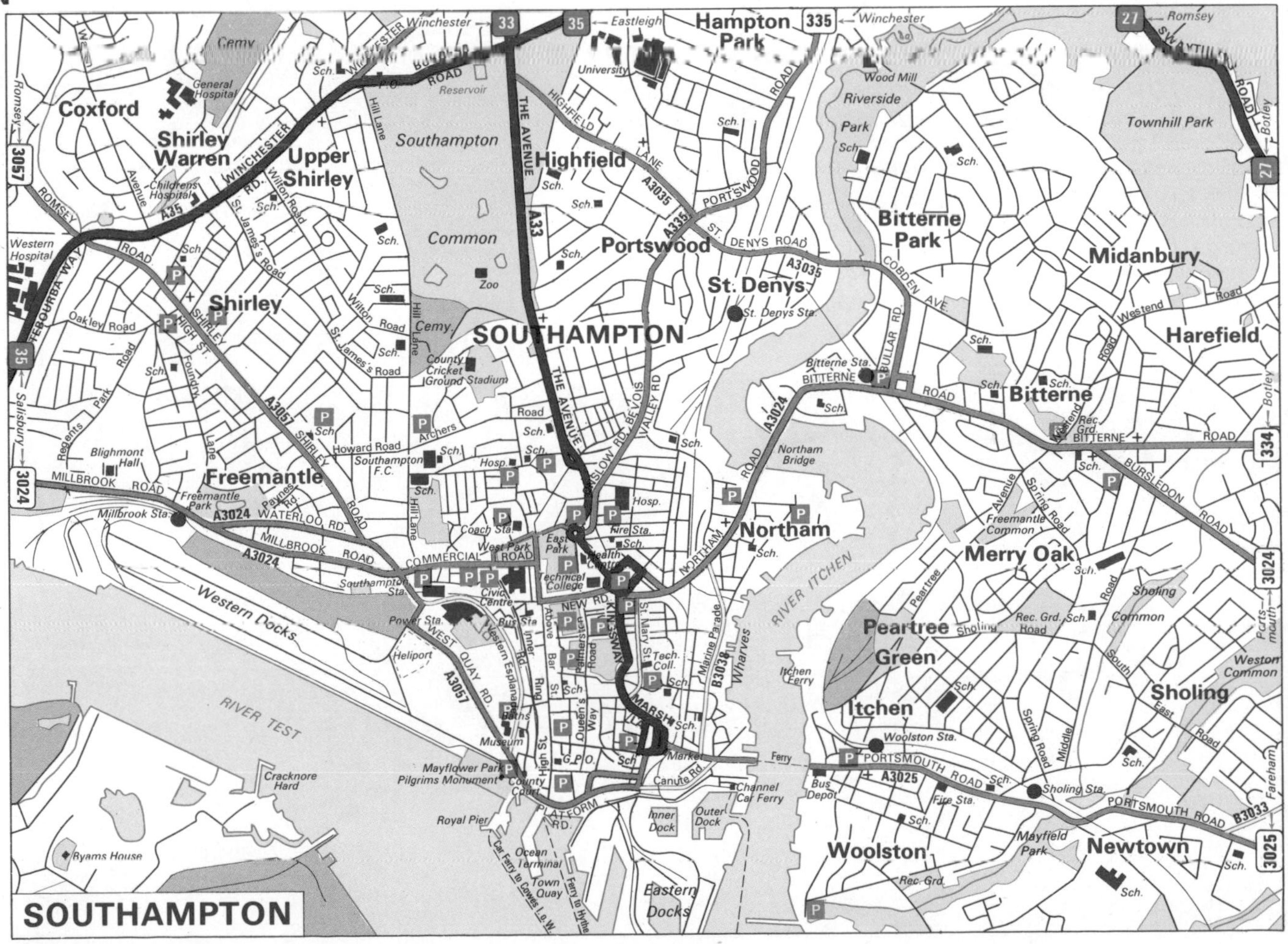

SOUTHAMPTON

120

PORTSMOUTH
Population:196,973
E.C. Wed.
M.D. Tue., Thur. and Sat.
London 70 miles.
Birmingham 137 miles.
Portsmouth, a base of the Royal Navy, and the seaside resort Southsea are built on an island alongside a fine land-locked harbour. The Cathedral Church of St. Thomas of Canterbury, 12th Cent. and partly rebuilt in the 17th Cent. R.C., 19th Cent. Cathedral of St. John with an imposing Rose Window. Dickens birthplace,now a museum. H.M.S. Victory in the Dockyard also Victory Museum and Naval College. Great Smithy, Old Sally Port where Nelson and Blake sailed from. King James Gate and Landport Gate, former gateways of the old walled town. Angling, bathing, boating, golf.

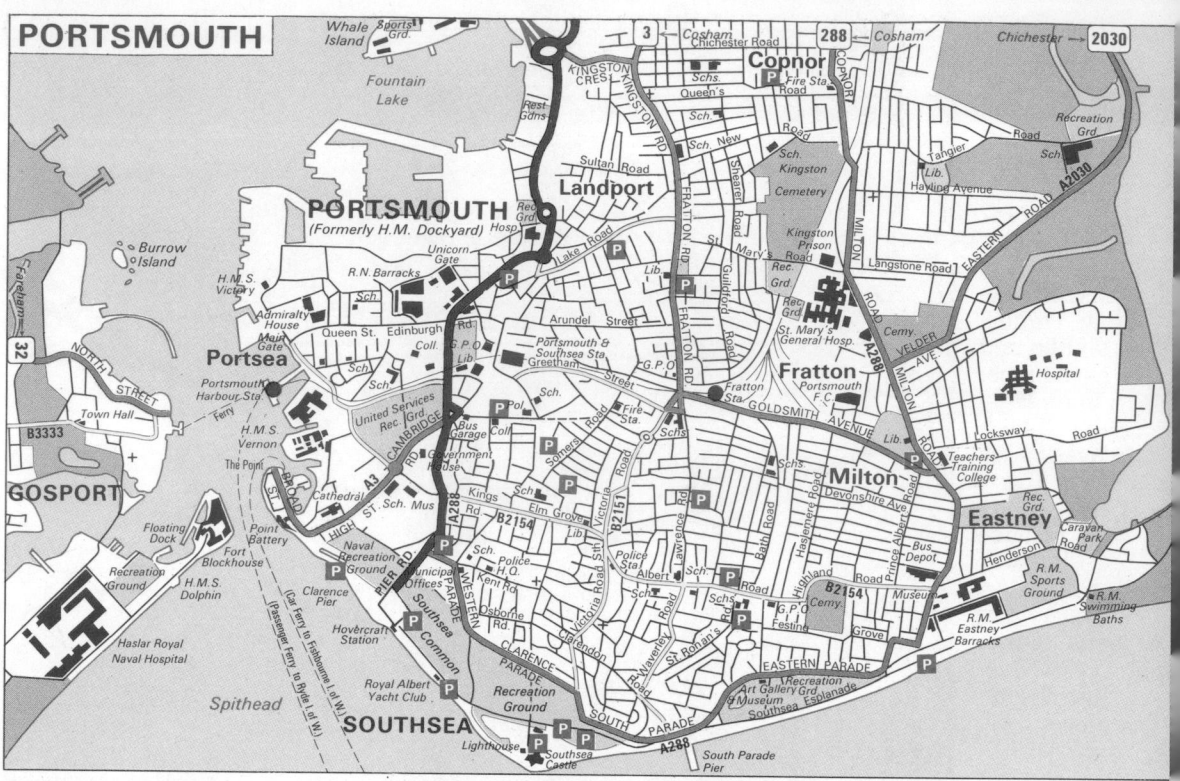

CANTERBURY Population:33,157
E.C. Thur. M.D. Mon. and Sat.(General M.D. Wed.)
London 58 miles, Birmingham 172 miles.
Ecclesiastical centre. West Gate. St. Peter's Church 13th Cent. St. Thomas's Hospital founded 12th Cent. 'Weavers' Houses'. St. John's Hospital founded by Lanfranc. Cathedral, 11th to 15th Cent.; 'Bell Harry' central tower; N.W. transept scene of Thomas à Becket's murder, 1170; Shrine in Trinity Chapel; Tomb of Black Prince. King's School – Norman staircase.
Angling, boating, golf.

BRIGHTON Population:166,081
E.C. Wed., Thur. and Sat. M.D. Tue., Thur. and Sat.
London 52 miles, Birmingham 162 miles.
Seaside resort made famous by George IV. Royal Pavilion, 1784, built for George, Prince of Wales (who later became George IV), rebuilt 1817, in oriental style by Nash. Mrs. Fitzherbert, wife of George IV, is buried here. St. Nicholas Church, Norman font; Museums and Art Galleries; Whitehawk Camp (neolithic earthworks); Devil's Dyke, beauty spot, ringed by prehistoric entrenchment. Angling, bathing, boating, golf.

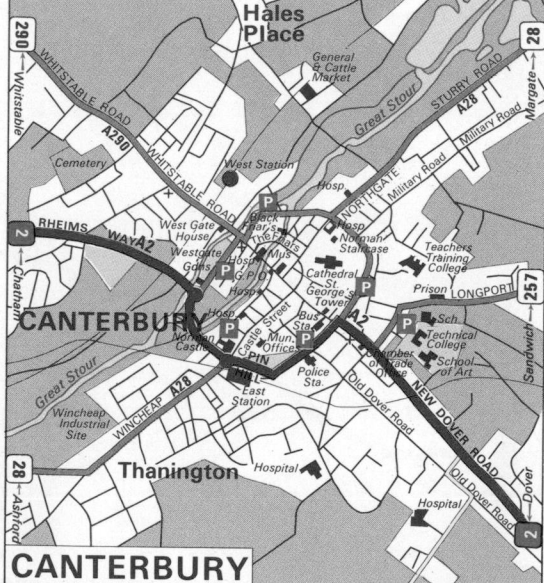

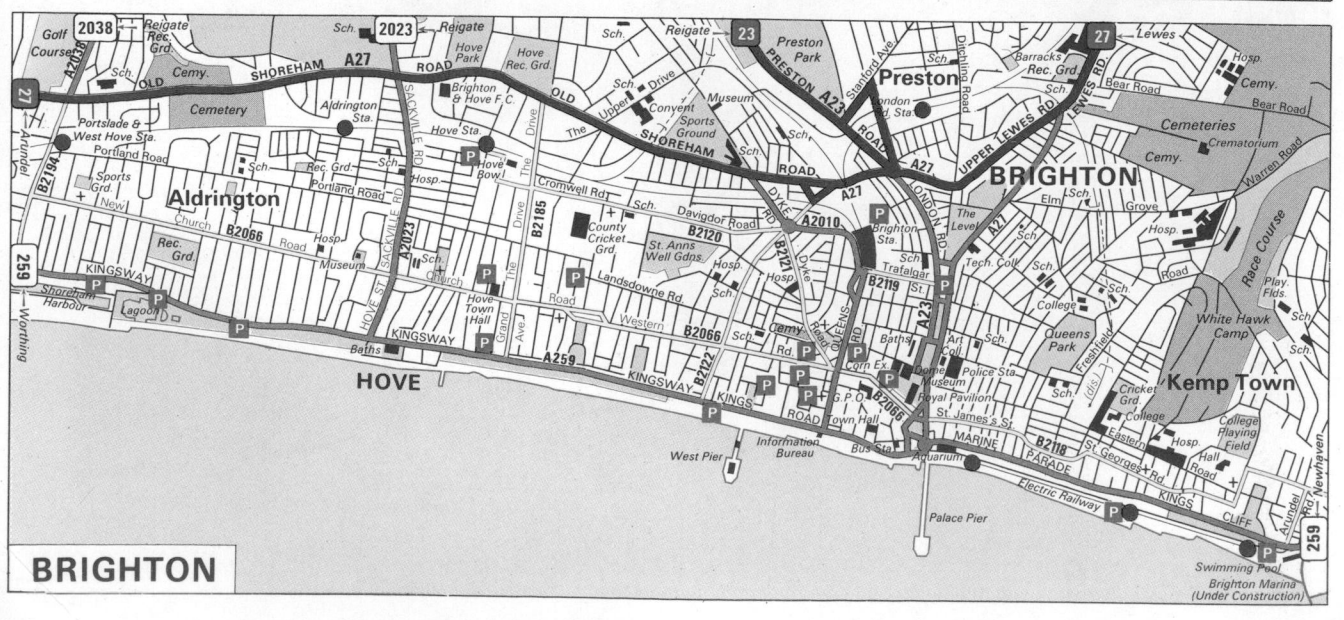

INDEX TO SECTIONAL MAP OF GREAT BRITAIN

ABBREVIATIONS

Aber. – *Aberdeen*
Angl. – *Anglesey*
Arg. – *Argyll*
Beds. – *Bedfordshire*
Berks. – *Berkshire*
Ber. – *Berwick*
Bldgs. – *Buildings*
Brec. – *Breconshire*
Bri. – *Bridge*
Bucks. – *Buckinghamshire*
Caer. – *Caernarvonshire*
Caith. – *Caithness*
Cambs. – *Cambridgeshire and Isle of Ely*
Cards. – *Cardiganshire*
Carm. – *Carmarthenshire*
Cas. – *Castle*
Ches. – *Cheshire*
Clack. – *Clackmannan*
Cnr. – *Corner*
Co. – *County*
Com. – *Common*
Corn. – *Cornwall*
Cumb. – *Cumberland*
Denb. – *Denbighshire*
Derby. – *Derbyshire*
Dumf. – *Dumfries*
Dunb. – *Dunbarton*
Dur. – *Durham*
E. Loth. – *East Lothian*
E. & W. Suff. – *East & West Suffolk*
E. & W. Sussex – *East & West Sussex*
E. Riding – *East Riding*
Flint – *Flintshire*
For. – *Forest*
Glam. – *Glamorgan*
Glos. – *Gloucestershire*
Grn. – *Green*
Gt. – *Great*
Hants. – *Hampshire*
Herefs. – *Herefordshire*
Herts. – *Hertfordshire*
Ho. – *House*
Holl. – *Holland*
Hth. – *Heath*
Hunts. – *Huntingdon and Peterborough*
Inver. – *Inverness*
I. – *Island*
I.o.M. – *Isle of Man*
I.o.W. – *Isle of Wight*
Junc. – *Junction*
Kest. – *Kesteven*
Kinc. – *Kincardine*
Kinr. – *Kinross*
Kirk. – *Kirkcudbright*
L. – *Lake*
Lan. – *Lanark*
Lancs. – *Lancashire*
Leics. – *Leicestershire*
Lincs. – *Lincolnshire*
Lind. – *Lindsey*
Lo. – *Lodge*
London – *Greater London*
Mer. – *Merionethshire*
Midloth. – *Midlothian*
Mon. – *Monmouthshire*
Mont. – *Montgomeryshire*
Norf. – *Norfolk*
Northants. – *Northamptonshire*
N. Riding – *North Riding*
Northumb. – *Northumberland*
Notts. – *Nottinghamshire*
Oxon. – *Oxfordshire*
Peeb. – *Peebles*
Pemb. – *Pembrokeshire*
Rad. – *Radnorshire*
Ren. – *Renfrew*
Ross & Crom. – *Ross & Cromarty*
Rox. – *Roxburgh*
Rut. – *Rutland*
Sel. – *Selkirk*
Salop. – *Shropshire*
Som. – *Somerset*
Staffs. – *Staffordshire*
Sta. – *Station*
Stir. – *Stirling*
Suff. – *Suffolk*
Suther. – *Sutherland*
Vill. – *Village*
War. – *Warwickshire*
Wig. – *Wigtown*
Wilts. – *Wiltshire*
W. Loth. – *West Lothian*
W. Riding – *West Riding*
Westmor. – *Westmorland*
Worcs. – *Worcestershire*
Yorks. – *Yorkshire*

The county names used to distinguish two or more places with the same name in this index are those in use prior to 1st April 1974.

MAP
32 Ab Kettleby H 4
7 Abbas Combe D 10
22 Abberley E 1
19 Abberton, Essex B 10
22 Abberton, Worcs. G 3
45 Abberwick B 9
18 Abbess Roding C 6
6 Abbey E 5
20 Abbey Cwmhir E 6
15 Abbey Dore A 7
6 Abbey Hill D 6
31 Abbey Hulton E 7
49 Abbey St. Bathans C 10
32 Abbey Town F 12
34 Abbey Village E 5
38 Abbeylands, I.o.M. G 2
45 Abbeylands, Northumb. B 10
34 Abbeystead B 4
4 Abbots Bickington E 3
31 Abbots Bromley H 9
17 Abbots Langley D 11
22 Abbot's Morton G 4
25 Abbots Ripton G 3
22 Abbot's Salford G 4
7 Abbotsbury H 9
4 Abbotsham C 3
5 Abbotskerswell J 7
25 Abbotsley K 3
8 Abbotswood D 5
8 Abbotts Ann B 5
21 Abcott E 9
21 Abdon D 11
28 Aber, Caer. C 6
13 Aber, Cards. B 8
13 Aberarth A 8
12 Aber-Cych C 6
20 Aber Gwydol B 3
28 Aber-Gwynant H 6
14 Aber Village B 4
13 Aberaeron A 8
14 Aberaman D 3
20 Aberangell A 4
12 Aberarad C 6
57 Aberarder, Inver. G 2
55 Aberarder, Inver. L 8
52 Aberargie F 6
13 Aberavon H 11
13 Aber-banc C 7
14 Aberbeeg D 5
14 Aberbran A 3
14 Abercanaid D 4
14 Abercarn E 5
12 Abercastle D 2
20 Abercegir B 4
55 Aberchalder House J 7
58 Aberchirder B 4
14 Abercrave C 2
14 Abercregan E 2
14 Abercwmboi D 3
14 Abercynafon C 4
14 Abercynon E 4
14 Aberdare D 3
28 Aberdaron H 1
59 Aberdeen G 7
58 Aberdeen, Co. F 4
48 Aberdour A 5
20 Aberdovey C 2
13 Aberdulais G 11
20 Aberedw H 6
12 Abereiddy D 2
28 Abererch G 3
14 Aberfan D 4
52 Aberfeldy B 3
28 Aberffraw C 3
20 Aberffrwd E 2

MAP
36 Aberford C 2
51 Aberfoyle G 12
14 Abergavenny C 6
29 Abergele B 9
13 Abergiar C 8
13 Abergorlech D 9
20 Abergwesyn G 4
13 Abergwili E 8
14 Abergwynfi E 2
20 Abergynolwyn B 2
20 Aberhosan C 4
14 Aberkenfig F 2
49 Aberlady A 7
53 Aberlemno B 10
20 Aberllefenni A 3
20 Abermeurig G 1
21 Abermule C 7
13 Abernant, Carm. E 7
14 Aber-nant, Glam. D 3
53 Abernethy E 7
53 Abernyte D 7
12 Aberporth B 6
28 Abersoch G 3
14 Abersychan D 6
14 Aberthin G 3
14 Abertillery D 5
14 Abertridwr, Glam. E 4
29 Abertridwr, Mont. H 9
14 Abertysswg D 5
52 Aberuthven F 5
14 Aberyscir A 3
20 Aberystwyth D 2
16 Abingdon D 6
9 Abinger B 12
9 Abinger Hammer A 12
48 Abington G 2
25 Abington Pigotts L 4
16 Ablington, Glos. C 2
8 Ablington, Wilts. A 3
31 Abney B 10
59 Aboyne H 3
34 Abram G 5
56 Abriachan F 1
18 Abridge D 5
15 Abson G 10
23 Abthorpe G 10
33 Aby B 11
36 Acaster Malbis C 4
36 Acaster Selby C 3
4 Accott C 5
34 Accrington D 6
62 Achachork D 4
50 Achadun D 5
50 Achafolla F 5
46 Achahoish B 3
51 Achallader C 10
46 Achamore Farm E 1
54 Achanalt D 6
46 Achanamara A 3
56 Achandunie C 2
60 Achany F 6
55 Achaphubuil M 5
50 Acharacle A 4
50 Acharn, Argyll C 4
52 Acharn, Perth C 2
61 Acharole C 11
46 Acharosson B 4
50 Achateny A 3
58 Achath F 5
61 Achavanich C 11
56 Achavraat E 5
60 Achavraie F 2
13 Achddu G 8
61 Achentoul D 8
60 Achfary C 4
60 Achgarve G 1

MAP
60 Achiemore, Kyle of Durness, Suther. A 4
61 Achiemore, Suther. B 9
62 A'Chill H 2
60 Achiltibuie F 2
61 Achina B 7
51 Achindarroch B 7
55 Achintee, Inver. M 5
54 Achintee, Ross and Cromarty F 3
54 Achintraid F 2
55 Achlain H 6
50 Achleck C 1
46 A'Chleit E 2
51 Achlian E 8
55 Achluachrach L 7
60 Achlyness B 4
60 Achmelvich E 2
63 Achmore, Lewis, Ross and Cromarty D 4
52 Achmore, Perth D 1
54 Achmore, Ross and Cromarty F 2
51 Achnaba, Arg. D 7
46 Achnaba, Arg. A 4
57 Achnabat G 2
60 Achnacarnin D 2
55 Achnacarry Ho. L 5
62 Achnacloich G 5
61 Achnaclyth D 10
51 Achnacon B 8
55 Achnaconeran H 8
50 Achnacraig C 2
50 Achnacroish C 6
50 Achnadrish B 2
51 Achnafalnich E 9
55 Achnafraschoille L 6
56 Achnaggaron C 2
50 Achnaha A 2
50 Achnahanat G 6
50 Achnalea A 6
61 Achnaluachrach F 7
55 Achnanellan L 5
60 Achnanerain F 6
55 Achnangart H 3
55 Achnasaul K 5
54 Achnasheen D 5
56 Achnastank F 8
50 Achosnich A 2
50 Achranich C 4
61 Achreamie A 9
51 Achriabhach A 8
60 Achriesgill B 4
61 Achrimsdale F 9
61 Achtoty B 7
25 Achurch G 1
60 Achuvoldrach B 6
61 Achvaich G 7
57 Achvraid, Inver. G 2
56 Achvraid, Inver. F 2
61 Ackergill B 12
36 Acklam, East Riding A 5
40 Acklam, North Riding C 5
22 Ackleton B 1
45 Acklington C 10
36 Ackton E 2
36 Ackworth Moor Top F 2
26 Acle D 7
22 Acock's Green D 5
11 Acol A 11
45 Acomb, Northumb. F 7
36 Acomb, Yorks. B 4
15 Aconbury A 8

MAP
34 Acre E 6
9 Acre Street F 9
29 Acrefair F 12
30 Acton, Cheshire E 5
8 Acton, Dorset H 1
18 Acton, London F 2
21 Acton, Salop. D 8
27 Acton, Suffolk L 2
30 Acton Bridge C 4
21 Acton Burnell B 10
21 Acton Green G 12
30 Acton Park E 2
21 Acton Pigott B 11
21 Acton Round C 11
21 Acton Scott C 10
31 Acton Trussell H 8
15 Acton Turville F 11
30 Adbaston G 6
7 Adber D 9
30 Adderley F 5
45 Adderstone C 12
48 Addiewell C 3
35 Addingham B 9
17 Addington, Bucks A 8
10 Addington, Kent B 5
18 Addington, London G 4
49 Addinston D 8
17 Addlestone H 11
33 Addlethorpe C 12
30 Adeney H 5
20 Adfa B 6
21 Adforton E 9
11 Adisham C 11
16 Adlestrop A 3
36 Adlingfleet E 6
31 Adlington, Ches. B 7
34 Adlington, Lancs. F 5
21 Admaston, Salop. A 11
31 Admaston, Staffs. H 9
22 Admington G 5
17 Adstock A 8
23 Adstone G 9
9 Adversane D 12
56 Advie F 7
36 Adwick le Street F 3
36 Adwick upon Dearne G 3
4 Adworthy D 6
58 Adziel B 7
43 Ae Bridgend C 10
43 Ae Village C 10
4 Affeton Barton E 6
58 Affleck, Aber. D 3
58 Affleck, Aber. E 6
7 Affpuddle G 11
55 Affric Lodge G 5
29 Afon-wen C 10
5 Afton, Devon J 7
8 Afton, I.o.W. G 5
47 Afton Bridgend H 11
40 Agglethorpe F 1
38 Agneash G 2
63 Aignish D 6
37 Aike C 8
64 Aikerness A 2
64 Aikers E 2
43 Aiket E 11
39 Aiketgate A 7
44 Aikton H 1
21 Ailey G 9
24 Ailsworth F 2
40 Ainderby Steeple F 4
19 Aingers Green B 11
34 Ainsdale F 2
39 Ainstable A 7

MAP
34 Ainsworth F 6
41 Ainthorpe D 7
34 Aintree G 3
50 Aird, Arg. G 5
63 Aird, Ross & Crom. C 6
42 Aird, Wig. F 2
62 Aird of Sleat H 5
63 Aird Tunga C 6
63 Aird Uig C 2
60 Airdachuilinn C 4
47 Airdrie C 12
47 Airdsgreen F 12
54 Airigh-drishaig F 1
36 Airmyn E 5
52 Airntully D 6
55 Airor J 1
52 Airth H 4
35 Airton A 7
42 Airyhassen G 4
33 Aisby, Kest. F 7
32 Aisby, Lind. A 6
39 Aisgill E 10
5 Aish K 6
6 Aisholt C 5
40 Aiskew F 3
40 Aislaby, Dur. D 4
41 Aislaby, N. Riding G 8
41 Aislaby, N. Riding D 8
32 Aisthorpe B 6
64 Aith, Orkney Is. C 4
64 Aith, Shetland Is. D 7
64 Aith Hestwall C 1
42 Aitkenhead A 4
56 Aitnoch F 5
49 Akeld F 12
49 Akeld Steads F 12
23 Akeley H 10
27 Akenham K 5
3 Albaston C 11
21 Alberbury A 9
12 Albert Town E 3
10 Albourn F 1
22 Albrighton, Salop. B 2
30 Albrighton, Salop. H 4
27 Alburgh G 6
27 Alburgh Street G 5
18 Albury, Herts. B 4
9 Albury, Surrey A 12
26 Alby Hill B 5
56 Alcaig D 1
22 Alcester F 4
10 Alciston G 4
6 Alcombe, Som. B 3
15 Alcombe, Wilts. G 11
25 Alconbury H 3
25 Alconbury Hill G 3
25 Alconbury Weston H 3
47 Aldandulish M 5
26 Aldborough, Norf. B 5
40 Aldborough, Yorkshire H 4
16 Aldbourne G 4
37 Aldbrough, E. Riding, C 10
40 Aldbrough, N. Riding, D 2
17 Aldbury C 10
52 Aldcharmaig A 3
34 Aldcliffe A 3
52 Aldclune A 4
27 Aldeburgh J 8
26 Aldeby F 7
18 Aldenham D 1

MAP
8 Alderbury C 3
26 Alderford D 4
15 Alderley E 11
31 Alderley Edge B 7
17 Aldermaston H 7
17 Aldermaston Wharf G 7
22 Alderminster G 6
21 Alder's End H 11
8 Aldershot, Dorset E 3
9 Aldershot, Hants. A 10
16 Alderton, Glos. A 1
23 Alderton, Northants. G 10
30 Alderton, Salop. H 4
27 Alderton, Suffolk L 6
15 Alderton, Wilts. F 11
31 Alderwasley E 11
40 Aldfield H 3
30 Aldford D 3
19 Aldham, Essex A 9
27 Aldham, Suffolk L 3
27 Aldham Street L 3
56 Aldie B 3
9 Aldingbourne F 10
38 Aldingham H 5
22 Aldington H 4
11 Aldington Corner D 9
51 Aldochlay H 10
25 Aldreth H 5
22 Aldridge B 4
27 Aldringham J 7
16 Aldsworth C 3
58 Aldunie E 1
31 Aldwark, Derby D 10
36 Aldwark, Yorks. A 2
9 Aldwick F 10
25 Aldwincle G 1
16 Aldworth F 6
47 Alexandria A 9
6 Aley B 5
4 Alfardisworthy E 2
6 Alfington F 5
9 Alfold C 11
9 Alfold Crossways C 11
58 Alford, Aberdeen. F 3
33 Alford, Lincs. C 11
7 Alford, Somerset C 9
32 Alfreton E 1
22 Alfrick G 1
10 Alfriston H 4
24 Algarkirk B 4
7 Alhampton C 9
63 Aline Lodge F 3
55 Alisary L 1
36 Alkborough E 6
23 Alkerton H 7
11 Alkham D 11
30 Alkington F 4
31 Alkmonton F 10
27 All Saints, South Elmham G 6
21 All Stretton C 10
60 Alladale Lodge G 5
5 Allaleigh K 7
57 Allanaquoich K 7
56 Allanfearn E 3
56 Allangrange Ho. E 2
49 Allanton D 11
8 Allbrook D 6
16 All Cannings H 2
45 Allendale Town G 7
39 Allenheads A 10
18 Allen's Green B 4
45 Allensford H 9
15 Allensmore A 8

MAP
31 Allenton, Derby .G 12
48 Allenton, Lan....B 10
7 Aller..........C 7
43 Allerby.........H 11
45 Allerdene........C 8
6 Allerford........B 3
41 Allerston........G 9
36 Allerthorpe......B 5
30 Allerton, Lancs..B 3
35 Allerton, Yorks. .D 10
36 Allerton Bywater .D 2
36 Allerton Mauleverer
   A 2
45 Allerwash........F 7
22 Allesley.........D 6
31 Allestree........F 11
23 Allexton........B 11
31 Allgreave........D 8
19 Allhallows.......F 8
54 Alligin Shuas....D 2
31 Allimore Green...H 7
32 Allington, Lincs. F 6
8 Allington, Wilts. B 4
16 Allington, Wilts. H 2
38 Allithwaite......G 6
52 Alloa...........H 4
43 Allonby.........G 11
47 Alloway.........H 8
7 Allowenshay......E 7
13 Allt............G 9
55 Alltbeithe, Inver...G 4
55 Alltbeithe, Inver...J 4
51 Alltchaorunn.....B 9
20 Alltmawr........H 6
60 Alltnacaillich....C 5
57 Allt-na-giubhsaich .L 8
60 Allt na h'Airbhe .G 3
60 Allton Dubh......F 2
55 Alltsigh........H 8
13 Alltwalis........D 8
13 Alltwen.........G 10
13 Alltyblacca......B 8
7 Allweston.......E 10
32 Alma Park Estate .G 9
21 Almeley.........G 9
21 Almeley Wooton. .G 9
7 Almer...........F 12
31 Almholme........F 4
30 Almington.......G 5
4 Alminstone Cross .D 2
52 Almondbank......E 5
35 Almondbury......F 10
15 Almondsbury.....F 9
45 Alndyke.........B 10
36 Alne...........A 3
56 Alness..........C 2
45 Alnham.........B 8
45 Alnmouth........B 10
45 Alnwick.........B 10
27 Alphamstone.....M 2
27 Alpheton........K 2
5 Alphington......G 8
31 Alport..........D 10
30 Alpraham........D 4
19 Alresford.......B 10
   E 12
22 Alrewas........A 5
30 Alsager.........E 6
30 Alsagers Bank....E 6
31 Alsop en le Dale .E 10
44 Alston, Cumb....H 5
6 Alston, Devon...F 6
16 Alstone, Glos...A 1
6 Alstone, Som.....B 6
31 Alstonefield.....E 9
4 Alswear.........D 6
61 Altanduin.......E 8
3 Altarnun........B 9
60 Altassmore......G 6
46 Altgaltraig......B 5
34 Altham.........D 6
19 Althorne........D 9
36 Althorpe........F 6
42 Alticry.........G 4
61 Altnabea........E 10
61 Altnabreac Sta....C 9
56 Altnacardich.....D 1
60 Altnacealgach Hot. F 4
50 Altnacraig......E 6
51 Altnafeadh......B 9
60 Altnaharra......D 6
35 Altofts.........E 12
32 Alton, Derby....D 1
9 Alton, Hants....B 8
31 Alton, Staffs....F 9
16 Alton Barnes....H 2
7 Alton Pancras...F 10
16 Alton Priors....H 2
47 Altonhill.......E 9
30 Altrincham......A 6
55 Altrua..........K 6
51 Altskeith.......G 11
56 Alltyre House....D 6
52 Alva...........G 4

MAP
30 Alvanley........C 4
31 Alvaston........G 12
22 Alvechurch......E 4
22 Alvecote........B 6
8 Alvediston......D 1
22 Alveley.........D 1
9 Alverdiscott.....C 4
9 Alverstoke......F 7
35 Alverthorpe.....E 11
32 Alverton........F 5
16 Alvescot........D 4
22 Alveston, Glos...E 9
22 Alveston, War....F 6
22 Alverstone......F 5
8 Alvaston........C 1
57 Alvie...........J 4
33 Alvingham......A 10
15 Alvington.......D 9
24 Alwalton........F 2
45 Alwinton........B 5
35 Alwoodley......C 11
53 Alyth..........B 7
33 Amber Hill......D 9
9 Amberley, Glos. .D 11
9 Amberley, Sussex E 11
31 Ambergate......E 11
22 Amble..........C 11
22 Amblecote......D 2
35 Ambler Thorn....D 9
38 Ambleside.......E 6
12 Ambleston.......D 3
17 Ambrosden......B 7
38 Amcotts........F 6
53 Americanmuir....D 8
17 Amersham......D 10
17 Amersham Com...D 10
45 Amersidelaw.....C 12
8 Amesbury.......B 3
63 Amhuinnsuidhe..F 2
22 Amington.......B 6
43 Amisfield Town...C 11
28 Amlwch.........A 4
28 Amlwch Port.....A 4
13 Ammanford......F 9
41 Amotherby......H 7
17 Ampfield.......D 5
48 Ampherlaw......D 3
40 Ampleforth......G 6
40 Ampleforth Coll..G 6
16 Ampney Crucis...D 2
16 Ampney St. Mary .D 2
16 Ampney St. Peter .D 2
8 Amport........B 4
8 Ampthill........L 1
27 Ampton.........H 2
12 Amroth.........F 5
52 Amulree........C 4
62 An Caol........C 5
62 An Coroghon....H 2
50 Anaheilt........A 5
54 Anancaun.......C 4
33 Ancaster........F 7
21 Anchor.........D 7
49 Ancroft.........E 12
49 Ancroft Northmoor
   E 12
49 Ancrum.........G 9
33 Anderby........C 12
21 Anderson.......F 12
30 Anderton.......C 5
8 Andover........B 5
8 Andover Down....B 5
16 Andoversford....B 1
38 Andreas........F 2
52 Angask.........F 6
2 Angarrack.......F 3
12 Angle..........G 2
38 Anglers' Hotel...D 3
28 Anglesey........C 4
9 Angmering......F 12
9 Angmering-on-SeaF 12
39 Angram, N. Riding
   E 11
36 Angram, W. Riding
   B 3
53 Angus, County...B 9
51 Anie...........F 1
56 Ankerville......B 4
37 Anlaby.........D 8
58 Annfield........G 1
58 Annfield Plain....H 10
45 Annitsford......F 11

MAP
21 Annscroft.......B 10
45 Annstead.......D 12
7 Ansford........C 10
22 Ansley.........C 6
31 Anslow.........H 10
31 Anslow Gate.....H 10
9 Anstey, Hants....B 8
25 Anstey, Herts....M 5
23 Anstey, Leics....A 9
53 Anstruther EasterG 10
53 Anstruther WesterG 10
10 Ansty, Sussex...F 2
23 Ansty, War......D 7
8 Ansty, Wilts....C 1
9 Anthill Common..E 8
43 Anthorn........F 12
26 Antingham......B 6
3 Antony.........D 11
2 Anvil Corner....E 2
33 Anwick.........E 8
42 Anwoth.........F 6
42 Apes Hall.......F 6
24 Apethorpe......F 1
33 Apley..........C 8
32 Apperknowle....B 1
15 Apperley.......B 11
39 Appersett.......F 10
50 Appin House....C 6
37 Appleby, Lincs...F 7
39 Appleby, Westmor.C 9
22 Appleby Magna...A 6
22 Appleby Parva...A 6
18 Appleby Street...D 3
54 Applecross......E 1
54 Applecross House .E 1
4 Appledore, Devon.C 3
6 Appledore, Devon.E 4
11 Appledore, Kent..E 8
11 Appledore Heath..E 8
16 Appleford.......E 6
9 Appleshaw......A 4
38 Applethwaite....C 5
16 Appleton, Berks...D 5
30 Appleton, Ches...B 5
40 Appleton, Yorks...E 4
36 Appleton Roebuck C 3
41 Appleton-le-Moors F 7
41 Appleton-le-Street.H 7
49 Appletreehall....H 8
35 Appletreewick....A 9
6 Appley.........D 4
34 Appley Bridge....F 4
6 Apse Heath......H 7
18 Apsley End......A 1
9 Apuldram.......F 9
58 Aquhythie......F 5
54 Araid..........D 2
54 Aranarff........F 3
59 Arbeadie.......H 4
53 Arbirlot........C 10
17 Arborfield......G 8
17 Arborfield Cross .G 8
42 Arbrack.........H 5
53 Arbroath........C 11
59 Arbuthnott......K 5
56 Archiestown.....E 8
30 Arclid Green.....D 6
60 Ardachadail.....G 3
46 Ardachearanbeg..A 5
50 Ardachoil.......D 4
46 Ardachuple.....A 5
55 Ardachvie.......K 5
50 Ardalanish......F 1
51 Ardanaiseig......E 8
54 Ardaneaskan....F 2
50 Ardanstur......F 5
52 Ardargie House...F 5
50 Ardarie.........A 5
54 Ardarroch.......F 2
46 Ardbeg.........C 6
60 Ardcharnich.....G 3
50 Ardchiavaig.....F 1
51 Ardchonnell.....F 7
50 Ardchrishnish....E 2
52 Ardchullarie More.F 1
51 Ardchyle........E 12
53 Ardcross........G 10
51 Arddarroch......H 9
21 Arddleen.......A 8
18 Ardeley.........A 3
55 Ardelve.........G 2
47 Arden..........A 4
40 Arden Hall......F 5
50 Ardencaple Ho....F 5
22 Ardens Grafton..G 5
50 Ardentallan Ho....E 5
46 Ardentraive.....B 5
52 Ardeonaig......D 2
51 Ardess.........H 10
60 Ardessie........G 2
50 Ardfern........G 5
51 Ardgartan.......G 10
60 Ardgay.........G 6

MAP
47 Ardgowan.......B 7
63 Ardhasig........G 2
54 Ardheslaig......D 2
50 Ardinamar......F 5
60 Ardindrean......G 3
10 Ardingly........E 2
16 Ardington......E 5
58 Ardintoul.......G 2
58 Ardlair.........E 3
46 Ardlamont House .C 5
46 Ardlarach.......F 5
27 Ardleigh........M 3
53 Ardler..........C 7
16 Ardley.........A 6
51 Ardlui.........F 10
46 Ardlussa........A 2
60 Ardmair........G 3
46 Ardmaleish......C 6
51 Ardmay.........G 10
46 Ardminish.......E 2
62 Ardmolich......M 1
61 Ardmore,
   Ross & Crom..H 7
50 Ardmore, Argyll. .E 5
47 Ardmore, Dunb. .B 8
50 Ardnacross......C 3
54 Ardnadam.......A 7
39 Ardnagrask......E 1
55 Ardnamurach....K 2
47 Ardneil.........D 7
51 Ardno..........G 8
61 Ardochu........F 7
47 Ardochry........E 11
47 Ardochy House...J 6
50 Ardow..........B 2
38 Ardoyne........E 4
46 Ardpatrick......C 3
46 Ardpatrick House .C 3
47 Ardpeaton......A 7
46 Ardrishaig......A 3
63 Ardroil.........D 1
44 Ardross Castle....B 2
47 Ardrossan.......E 7
50 Ardshealach.....A 4
35 Ardsley.........G 12
35 Ardsley East.....E 11
50 Ardslignish......A 3
52 Ardtalnaig.......C 2
52 Ardtaraig.......A 5
50 Ardtoe.........A 4
52 Ardtrostan......E 2
50 Arduaine.......F 5
56 Ardullie........C 1
50 Ardura.........E 4
62 Ardvasar.......H 5
50 Ardvergnish.....E 3
57 Ardverikie......L 1
63 Ardvey,
   Loch Finsbay..H 2
63 Ardvey,
   Loch Stockinish.H 2
51 Ardvorlich, Dunb.F 10
52 Ardvorlich, Perth..E 1
63 Ardvourlie Castle..F 3
42 Ardwell, Ayr.....B 3
52 Ardwell, Wig....G 2
22 Areley Kings.....E 2
9 Arford.........B 9
52 Argaty.........G 2
4 Argoed.........D 5
20 Argoed Mill.....F 5
51 Argyll, Co......E 8
63 Aribruach.......H 2
51 Arichastlich.....D 10
50 Aridhglas.......F 1
50 Arinacrinachd...D 1
50 Ariogan........E 6
55 Arisaig.........L 1
55 Arisaig House....L 1
36 Arkendale......A 2
25 Arkesden.......M 6
39 Arkholme.......H 8
39 Arkle Town.....E 12
44 Arkleby........H 12
44 Arkleton.......D 2
18 Arksey.........D 2
36 Arksey.........F 4
32 Arkwright Town ..C 2
15 Arle..........B 12
25 Arlecdon.......C 3
25 Arlesey........L 3
21 Arleston.......A 12
22 Arley, Cheshire...B 5
22 Arley, War......C 6
15 Arlingham......C 10
4 Arlington, Devon .B 5
16 Arlington, Glos...C 2
10 Arlington, Sussex .G 4

MAP
4 Arlington Beccott .B 5
61 Armadale, Suther..B 8
48 Armadale, W. Loth.
   C 2
62 Armadale Castle ..H 6
39 Armathwaite.....A 7
26 Arminghall......E 5
22 Armitage........E 3
35 Armley.........D 11
22 Armscote.......H 6
25 Armston........G 2
36 Armthorpe......G 4
47 Arnburn........A 8
39 Arncliffe.......H 11
39 Arncliffe Cote...H 11
53 Arncroach.......G 10
8 Arne...........G 1
23 Arnesby........C 9
46 Arnicle.........F 2
55 Arnisdale.......H 2
62 Arnish.........C 5
62 Arnisort........C 3
48 Arniston Engine..C 6
63 Arnol..........B 4
32 Arnold, Notts....F 3
37 Arnold, Yorks....C 9
52 Arnprior........H 1
39 Arnside........G 7
50 Aros Mains......C 3
38 Arrad Foot......G 5
37 Arram..........C 8
40 Arrathorne......F 2
9 Arreton........G 7
25 Arrington......K 4
51 Arrivain........D 10
51 Arrochar........G 10
22 Arrow..........F 4
56 Artafallie.......E 2
35 Arthington......C 11
23 Arthingworth....D 11
20 Arthog.........A 2
58 Arthrath........D 7
9 Arundel........E 11
21 Aryhoulan......A 7
38 Asby..........C 3
37 Asby cum Fenby.G 10
46 Ascog.........C 6
17 Ascot.........G 10
16 Ascott-under-
   Wychwood....B 4
40 Asenby.........H 4
32 Asfordby........H 4
32 Asfordby Hill.....H 4
33 Asgarby........D 10
24 Asgarby........A 2
11 Ash, Kent.......B 11
10 Ash, Kent.......B 5
7 Ash, Somerset...D 8
9 Ash, Surrey.....A 10
4 Ash Bullayne....E 6
23 Ash Green......D 7
30 Ash Magna......F 4
4 Ash Mill........D 6
6 Ash Priors......C 5
6 Ash Thomas.....E 3
9 Ash Vale.......A 10
16 Ashampstead....F 6
27 Ashbacking.....K 5
31 Ashbourne......F 10
6 Ashbrittle......D 4
5 Ashburton......J 6
4 Ashbury, Devon .F 4
16 Ashbury, Berks..F 4
37 Ashby..........F 7
33 Ashby by Partney D 11
33 Ashby de la Launde E 7
31 Ashby de la Zouch
   H 12
26 Ashby Dell......E 8
23 Ashby Folville...A 10
23 Ashby Magna....C 9
23 Ashby Parva.....C 9
33 Ashby Puerorum .C 10
23 Ashby St. Ledgers .E 9
26 Ashby St. Mary ..E 6
15 Ashchurch......A 12
14 Ashcombe, Som..H 6
6 Ashcombe, Devon H 3
7 Ashcott.........B 3
47 Ashcraig........C 7
17 Ashcroft........F 8
25 Ashdon.........L 7
9 Ashe..........A 7
19 Asheldham......D 9
25 Ashen..........L 8
17 Ashendon......C 8
13 Ashfield, Carm..G 10
27 Ashfield, E. Suffolk J 5
52 Ashfield, Perth...G 3
27 Ashfield Green...H 6

MAP
11 Ashford, Kent....D 9
17 Ashford, Surrey...H 10
21 Ashford Bowdler .E 10
21 Ashford Carbonel E 10
47 Ashford Hill.....H 6
47 Ashgill.........D 12
39 Ashgillside......A 10
6 Ashill, Devon....E 4
26 Ashill, Norfolk....E 2
6 Ashill, Somerset..D 6
25 Ashington, Essex .E 8
45 Ashington,
   Northumb....D 10
7 Ashington, Som...D 9
9 Ashington, Sussex E 12
49 Ashkirk........G 7
8 Ashlett.........F 6
15 Ashleworth.....B 11
25 Ashley, Cambs...J 8
30 Ashley, Cheshire .B 6
4 Ashley, Devon....E 5
15 Ashley, Glos.....E 12
8 Ashley, Hants....C 5
8 Ashley, Hants....G 4
11 Ashley, Kent....C 11
23 Ashley, Northants C 11
30 Ashley, Staffs....F 6
17 Ashley Green....D 10
8 Ashley Heath....F 3
16 Ashmansworth...H 5
4 Ashmansworthy..D 2
7 Ashmore........D 12
16 Ashmore Green..G 6
22 Ashorne........F 6
32 Ashover........D 1
22 Ashow..........E 6
21 Ashperton......H 11
7 Ashprington....K 7
4 Ashreigney......E 5
16 Ashtead........B 1
30 Ashton, Cheshire .C 4
2 Ashton, Cornwall .G 3
21 Ashton, Herefs...F 10
23 Ashton, Northants.
   G 11
25 Ashton, Northants. G 2
15 Ashton Common H 12
16 Ashton Keynes...E 2
34 Ashton-in-Makerfield
   G 5
22 Ashton under Hill H 3
35 Ashton under Lyne G 8
34 Ashton-upon-
   Mersey.......H 6
9 Ashurst, Hants...E 5
10 Ashurst, Kent...D 4
10 Ashurst, Sussex..F 1
10 Ashurstwood....D 3
4 Ashwater.......F 3
25 Ashwell, Herts...L 4
8 Ashwell, Rutland A 12
26 Ashwellthorpe...F 4
7 Ashwick........A 9
26 Ashwicken......D 8
49 Ashybank.......H 8
38 Askam in Furness.G 4
36 Askern.........F 3
7 Askerswell......G 9
39 Askham........C 7
36 Askham Bryan...B 3
36 Askham Richard..B 3
50 Asknish........H 6
39 Askrigg........F 11
35 Askwith........B 10
24 Aslackby.......C 2
26 Aslacton.......F 4
32 Aslockton......F 5
58 Asloun.........F 3
43 Aspatria.......G 12
18 Aspenden......A 4
25 Aspley Guise....H 12
17 Aspley Heath...A 10
34 Aspull.........F 5
36 Asselby........D 5
33 Asserby........B 12
27 Assington......L 2
56 Assynt House....C 2
13 Astbury........D 7
23 Astcote........G 10
21 Asterley........B 9
21 Asterton.......C 9
16 Asthall........C 4
16 Asthall Leigh....C 4
21 Astley, Salop....H 4
22 Astley, War......C 6
22 Astley, Worcs....E 1
21 Astley Abbots...C 12
34 Astley Bridge....F 6
22 Astley Cross....E 2
34 Astley Green....G 6
17 Aston, Berks....F 9
30 Aston, Cheshire...E 5

MAP
30 Aston, Cheshire ... B 4
31 Aston, Derby ... B 10
29 Aston, Flintshire ... C 12
21 Aston, Herefs. ... E 10
21 Aston, Herefs. ... F 10
18 Aston, Herts. ... B 3
16 Aston, Oxon. ... D 4
30 Aston, Salop ... G 4
21 Aston, Salop ... A 11
30 Aston, Staffs. ... F 6
31 Aston, Staffs. ... G 7
22 Aston, War. ... C 4
32 Aston, Yorks. ... B 2
17 Aston Abbotts ... B 9
16 Aston Blank ... B 2
21 Aston Botterell ... D 11
22 Aston Cantlow ... F 5
17 Aston Clinton ... C 9
15 Aston Crews ... B 10
15 Aston Cross ... A 12
18 Aston End ... B 3
21 Aston Eyre ... C 12
22 Aston Fields ... E 3
23 Aston Flamville ... C 8
15 Aston Ingham ... B 10
30 Aston juxta Mondrum ... D 5
23 Aston le Walls ... G 8
16 Aston Magna ... A 3
21 Aston on Clun ... D 9
21 Aston Pigott ... B 9
21 Aston Rogers ... B 9
17 Aston Rowant ... D 8
17 Aston Sandford ... C 8
22 Aston Somerville ... H 4
22 Aston Subedge ... H 5
16 Aston Tirrold ... F 6
31 Aston upon Trent ... G 12
16 Aston Upthorpe ... E 6
25 Astwick ... L 3
25 Astwood ... K 1
22 Astwood Bank ... F 4
24 Aswarby ... B 2
33 Aswardby ... C 10
21 Atcham ... B 11
27 Athelington ... H 5
7 Athelney ... C 7
49 Athelstaneford ... B 8
4 Atherington, Devon ... D 5
9 Atherington, Sussex ... F 11
22 Atherstone ... B 6
22 Atherstone on Stour ... G 5
34 Atherton ... G 5
55 Athnamulloch ... G 5
40 Atley Hill ... E 3
31 Atlow ... E 10
54 Attadale House ... F 3
26 Attleborough, Norf. ... F 3
23 Attleborough, Warwickshire ... C 7
26 Attlebridge ... D 4
59 Atton ... K 1
49 Attonburn ... G 10
37 Atwick ... B 9
15 Atworth ... H 11
32 Aubourn ... D 6
51 Auchachenna ... E 7
46 Auchagallon ... F 4
57 Auchallater ... K 7
42 Auchalton ... A 4
57 Auchavan ... M 7
46 Auchbroad ... A 3
58 Auchedly ... D 6
43 Auchenbainzie ... B 9
59 Auchenblae ... J 5
47 Auchenbothie Ho. ... B 8
52 Auchenbowie ... H 3
43 Auchenbrack ... B 8
46 Auchenbreck ... A 5
43 Auchencairn, Dumfries ... C 10
43 Auchencairn, Kirkcudbright ... F 9
47 Auchencarroch ... A 9
47 Auchencrieff ... D 10
42 Auchencrosh ... D 2
49 Auchencrow ... C 11
48 Auchendinny ... C 5
47 Auchenfoyle ... B 8
43 Auchengibbert ... D 9
48 Auchengray ... D 3
43 Auchengruith ... A 9
58 Auchenhairig ... B 1
48 Auchenheath ... E 1
42 Auchenmalg ... F 3
42 Auchensoul ... B 3
42 Auchentibbert ... G 2
47 Auchentiber ... E 8
47 Auchenvennel ... A 8
43 Auchenvey ... D 8

MAP
57 Auchernack ... G 6
57 Auchgourish ... H 5
46 Auchinadrian ... D 2
58 Auchinderran ... B 2
51 Auchindrain ... G 6
54 Auchindrean ... B 6
58 Auchinhove ... B 2
58 Auchininna ... C 4
47 Auchinleck, Ayr. ... G 10
42 Auchinleck, Kirk. ... D 5
47 Auchinloch ... B 11
52 Auchinner ... F 2
58 Auchintender ... D 4
59 Auchintoul, Aber. ... G 4
58 Auchintoul, Aber. ... F 3
58 Auchiries ... D 8
58 Auchleven ... E 4
48 Auchlochan ... F 1
59 Auchlossan ... G 3
60 Auchlunachan ... H 3
59 Auchlunies ... G 6
51 Auchlyne ... E 12
58 Auchmacoy ... D 7
42 Auchmantle ... E 2
47 Auchmillan ... F 10
53 Auchmithie ... C 11
53 Auchmuirbridge ... G 7
59 Auchmull ... K 3
51 Auchnacloich Pier ... D 7
50 Auchnacraig ... D 4
59 Auchnacree ... L 2
55 Auchnadaull ... L 5
52 Auchnafree ... D 3
56 Auchnagallin ... F 6
58 Auchnagatt ... C 7
46 Auchnaha ... A 4
57 Auchnahannet ... G 5
56 Auchnahillin ... F 3
42 Auchnotteroch ... F 1
59 Aucholzie ... H 1
51 Auchrioch ... E 10
57 Auchroisk ... G 6
59 Auchronie ... J 2
60 Auchtascailt ... H 3
52 Auchterarder ... F 4
55 Auchteraw ... J 7
53 Auchterderran ... H 7
53 Auchterhouse ... C 8
53 Auchtermuchty ... F 7
54 Auchterneed ... D 8
57 Auchterteang ... G 5
53 Auchtertool ... H 7
56 Auchtertyre, Moray ... D 7
51 Auchtertyre, Perth ... E 10
55 Auchtertyre, Ross & Crom. ... G 2
52 Auchtoo ... E 1
61 Auckingill ... B 12
36 Auckley ... G 4
58 Auckmair ... E 1
35 Audenshaw ... G 8
30 Audlem ... F 5
30 Audley ... E 6
25 Audley End ... L 6
58 Auds ... A 4
36 Aughton, E. Riding ... C 5
34 Aughton, Lancs. ... G 3
39 Aughton, Lancs. ... H 8
32 Aughton, W. Rid. ... B 2
16 Aughton, Wilts. ... H 3
53 Auldallan ... A 8
56 Auldearn ... D 5
21 Aulden ... G 10
43 Auldgirth ... C 10
49 Auldhame ... A 8
47 Auldhouse ... D 11
58 Auldtown ... B 3
58 Auldtown of Carnousie ... C 4
52 Aulich ... A 1
32 Ault Hucknall ... D 2
55 Ault-a-chrinn ... H 3
60 Aultanrynie ... D 4
60 Aultbea ... G 1
54 Aultdearg ... C 7
56 Aultfearn ... E 1
54 Aultgowrie ... E 8
54 Aultgrishan ... A 1
54 Aultguish Inn ... C 7
58 Aulthash ... B 1
61 Aultiphurst ... A 8
58 Aultmore ... B 1
57 Aultnagoire ... G 1
56 Aultnamain Inn ... B 2
57 Aultnancaber ... H 5
55 Aultnaslat ... J 5
58 Aulton ... E 3
59 Aultonrea ... H 1
57 Aundorach ... H 5
6 Aunk ... F 4
24 Aunsby ... B 1

MAP
15 Aust ... E 9
17 Austenwood ... E 10
36 Austerfield ... H 4
35 Austonley ... F 9
22 Austrey ... B 6
39 Austwick ... H 10
33 Authorpe ... B 11
33 Authorpe Row ... C 12
16 Avebury ... G 2
18 Aveley ... F 6
15 Avening ... E 12
52 Avenuehead ... H 3
32 Averham ... E 5
5 Aveton Gifford ... L 6
57 Avielochan ... H 5
57 Aviemore ... H 4
46 Avinagillan ... C 3
16 Avington, Berks. ... G 5
9 Avington, Hants. ... C 7
56 Avoch ... D 3
16 Avon ... F 1
15 Avon, Co. ... F 9
23 Avon Dassett ... G 7
48 Avonbridge ... B 2
15 Avonmouth ... F 8
5 Avonwick ... K 6
8 Awbridge ... D 5
42 Awhirk ... F 2
15 Awkley ... F 9
6 Awliscombe ... F 5
15 Awre ... D 10
32 Awsworth ... F 2
7 Axbridge ... A 8
9 Axford, Hants. ... B 7
16 Axford, Wilts. ... G 3
6 Axminster ... F 6
6 Axmouth ... G 6
40 Aycliffe ... C 3
45 Aydon ... F 8
15 Aylburton ... D 9
44 Ayle ... H 5
6 Aylesbeare ... G 4
17 Aylesbury ... C 9
37 Aylesby ... F 9
4 Aylescott ... D 5
10 Aylesford ... B 6
11 Aylesham ... C 11
23 Aylestone ... B 9
26 Aylmerton ... B 5
26 Aylsham ... C 5
15 Aylton ... A 9
21 Aymestrey ... F 9
16 Aynho ... A 6
18 Ayot St. Lawrence ... B 2
18 Ayot St. Peter ... B 2
47 Ayr ... G 8
47 Ayr, County ... F 9
39 Aysgarth ... F 12
6 Ayshford ... E 4
38 Ayside ... G 6
23 Ayston ... B 12
18 Aythorpe Roding ... B 6
49 Ayton ... C 11
40 Azerley ... H 3
5 Babbacombe ... J 8
30 Babbinswood ... G 2
7 Babcary ... C 9
13 Babel ... C 11
29 Babell ... C 11
7 Babington ... A 10
25 Babraham ... K 6
32 Babworth ... B 4
63 Back ... C 6
55 Back of Keppoch ... L 1
64 Backaland ... B 3
64 Backaskaill ... A 3
38 Backbarrow ... G 6
58 Backburn ... D 3
12 Backe ... E 6
58 Backfolds ... B 8
30 Backford ... C 3
30 Backford Cross ... C 3
58 Backhill, Aber. ... D 5
58 Backhill, Aber. ... F 5
58 Backhill, Aber. ... D 7
58 Backhill of Clackriach ... C 7
58 Backhill of Fortree ... D 7
59 Backhill of Trustach ... H 4
61 Backies ... F 8
53 Backmuir of New Gilston ... F 9
15 Backwell ... G 8
45 Backworth ... F 11
18 Bacon End ... B 6
58 Baconsthorpe ... B 4
15 Bacton, Herefs. ... A 7
26 Bacton, Norfolk ... B 6
27 Bacton, Suffolk ... J 3
35 Bacup ... E 7
54 Badachro ... B 2
60 Badagyle ... F 2

MAP
61 Badanloch Lodge ... D 8
54 Badavanich ... D 5
16 Badbury ... F 3
23 Badby ... F 9
60 Badcall, Ross & Crom. ... G 2
60 Badcall, Suther. ... C 3
60 Badcall, Loch Inchard, Sutherland ... B 4
31 Baddeley Green ... E 8
22 Baddesley Ensor ... B 6
60 Baddidarach ... E 2
15 Baddington ... B 12
56 Baddock ... D 4
58 Badenyon ... F 1
7 Badford Peverell ... G 10
22 Badge ... B 1
10 Badger's Mount ... B 4
15 Badgeworth ... B 12
7 Badgworth ... A 7
55 Badicaul ... G 1
27 Badingham ... H 6
60 Badintagairt ... F 5
11 Badlesmere ... C 9
60 Badluchrach ... G 2
60 Badnabay ... C 3
57 Badnambiast ... M 3
56 Badnonan ... F 5
60 Badrallach ... G 2
22 Badsey ... H 4
9 Badshot Lea ... A 10
36 Badsworth ... F 2
27 Badwell Ash ... H 3
33 Bag Enderby ... C 10
7 Bagber ... E 11
40 Bagby ... G 5
16 Bagendon ... C 1
29 Bagillt ... C 11
23 Baginton ... E 7
13 Baglan ... H 10
30 Bagley ... G 3
31 Bagnal ... E 8
16 Bagnor ... G 5
17 Bagshot, Surrey ... H 10
16 Bagshot, Wilts. ... H 4
15 Bagstone ... F 10
26 Bagthorpe, Norf. ... B 1
32 Bagthorpe, Notts. ... E 2
23 Bagworth ... A 8
15 Bagwy Llydiart ... B 8
35 Baildon ... C 10
46 Baile Boidheach ... B 2
50 Baile Mor ... F 1
57 Baileneag ... H 1
58 Baileyhead ... E 3
44 Bailliehill ... D 1
47 Baillieston ... C 11
58 Bailliesward ... D 2
39 Bainbridge ... F 11
58 Bainshole ... D 4
24 Bainton, Hunts. ... E 2
37 Bainton, Yorks. ... B 7
44 Bairnkine ... B 5
18 Baker Street ... F 6
18 Baker's End ... B 4
44 Bakethin ... D 4
31 Bakewell ... C 10
29 Bala ... G 8
52 Balado ... G 6
63 Balallan ... E 4
56 Balalochan ... B 1
50 Balarumindubh ... H 1
57 Balavil ... J 3
57 Balbeg ... G 1
52 Balbeggie ... D 6
58 Balbithan ... F 5
56 Balblair, Inverness ... E 1
56 Balblair, Ross & Crom. ... C 3
43 Balcary ... G 9
21 Balchedre ... C 8
58 Balchers ... B 4
60 Balchladich ... D 2
56 Balchraggan, Inver. ... F 1
56 Balchraggan, Inver. ... E 1
60 Balchreick ... B 3
10 Balcombe ... E 2
53 Balcurvie ... G 8
39 Balder Head ... C 11
40 Baldersby ... G 4
40 Baldersby St. James ... G 4
34 Balderstone ... D 5
30 Balderton ... D 2
53 Baldinnie ... F 9
25 Baldock ... M 3
53 Baldovie ... D 9
38 Baldrine ... G 2
11 Baldslow ... G 7
38 Baldwin ... G 2
44 Baldwinholme ... H 2
30 Baldwins Gate ... F 6
26 Bale ... B 3
58 Balearn ... B 8

MAP
48 Balerno ... C 4
59 Balfeith ... K 5
59 Balfield ... K 3
64 Balfour ... C 3
47 Balfron ... A 10
58 Balgaveny ... D 4
43 Balgerran ... E 8
52 Balgonar ... H 5
58 Balgove ... D 6
57 Balgowan ... K 2
62 Balgown ... A 3
53 Balgray ... C 9
43 Balgrayhill ... C 12
47 Balgrochan ... B 11
54 Balgy ... D 2
52 Balhaldie ... G 3
58 Balhalgardy ... E 5
18 Balham ... G 3
53 Balharry ... C 7
64 Baliasta ... A 8
61 Baligill ... A 8
56 Balintore ... B 4
53 Balintore ... A 7
56 Balintraid ... C 3
57 Balintuim ... K 7
52 Balintyre ... B 2
53 Balkeerie ... C 8
36 Balkholme ... D 6
42 Balkissock ... C 2
30 Ball ... G 2
16 Ball Hill ... H 5
38 Ballabeg ... H 1
38 Ballacannell ... G 2
38 Ballacarnane Beg. ... G 1
57 Ballachlaggan ... K 8
59 Ballachrosk ... H 1
51 Ballachulish Ho. ... B 7
38 Ballacraine ... G 1
38 Ballacuberagh ... G 2
43 Ballaggan ... B 9
38 Ballajora ... G 3
38 Ballakaigan ... H 1
38 Ballaleigh ... G 1
42 Ballantrae ... C 2
63 Ballantrushal ... B 5
19 Ballards Gore ... E 9
38 Ballasalla, I.o.M. ... F 2
38 Ballasalla, I.o.M. ... H 1
59 Ballater ... H 1
38 Ballaugh ... G 2
56 Ballchraggan ... B 3
57 Ballcorah ... G 7
52 Ballechin ... B 4
49 Ballencrieff ... B 7
46 Ballianlay ... C 5
50 Balliemore ... E 5
38 Ballig ... G 1
52 Balikinrain Castle ... H 1
51 Ballimeanoch ... F 7
51 Ballimore ... F 12
56 Ballindalloch ... F 7
53 Ballindean ... D 7
27 Ballingdon ... L 2
17 Ballinger Com. ... D 10
15 Ballingham ... A 9
52 Ballingry ... G 6
56 Ballinlagg ... F 6
57 Ballinluig, Inver. ... G 6
52 Ballinluig, Perth ... B 5
57 Ballintean ... J 4
52 Ballintuim ... B 6
42 Ballminnoch ... E 4
56 Balloan ... E 2
56 Balloch, Inverness ... E 3
47 Balloch, Dunb. ... A 9
59 Ballochan ... H 3
42 Ballochbroe ... A 4
42 Ballochdoan ... D 2
42 Ballochdowan ... D 2
58 Ballochford ... D 1
46 Ballochgoy ... C 6
42 Ballochmorrie ... C 3
46 Ballochroy ... D 2
59 Ballogie ... H 3
9 Balls Cross ... D 11
10 Ball's Green ... D 4
50 Ballygown ... C 2
50 Ballymeanoch ... H 5
55 Balmacara ... G 2
43 Balmaclellan ... D 7
52 Balmacneil ... B 5
53 Balmacolm ... F 8
62 Balmacquien ... A 4
43 Balmae ... G 7
51 Balmaha ... H 11
50 Balmaneach ... D 2
43 Balmangan ... G 7
58 Balmedie ... F 7
53 Balmerino ... E 8
8 Balmerlawn ... F 5
54 Balmore, Inver. ... F 7
62 Balmore, Skye, Inver. ... D 2

MAP
52 Balmore, Perth ... A 4
47 Balmore, Stirling ... B 11
56 Balmuchy ... B 4
53 Balmule ... H 7
53 Balmullo ... E 9
56 Balmungie ... D 3
42 Balmurrie ... E 3
59 Balnaboth ... K 1
56 Balnabruaich ... C 3
56 Balnabual ... E 3
61 Balnacoil Lodge ... F 8
54 Balnacra ... E 3
56 Balnacraig ... F 1
56 Balnafoich ... F 2
56 Balnagall ... B 4
56 Balnageith ... D 6
59 Balnagowan ... G 2
52 Balnaguard ... B 4
56 Balnaguisich ... C 2
55 Balnain ... G 8
60 Balnakeil ... A 5
62 Balnaknock ... B 3
56 Balnapaling ... C 4
59 Balquharn ... L 2
51 Balquhidder ... E 12
22 Balsall ... E 6
22 Balsall Common ... D 6
23 Balscott ... H 7
25 Balsham ... K 7
64 Baltasound ... A 8
30 Balterley ... E 6
42 Baltersan ... E 5
32 Balterton ... E 5
58 Balthangie ... C 6
7 Baltonsborough ... C 8
50 Balure ... C 6
58 Balvack ... F 4
56 Balvaird ... D 1
58 Balvenie ... C 1
50 Balvicar ... F 5
55 Balvraid, Inver. ... H 2
56 Balvraid, Inver. ... F 4
34 Bamber Bridge ... E 4
18 Bamber's Green ... B 6
45 Bamburgh ... D 12
53 Bamff ... B 7
48 Bamflatt ... F 3
31 Bamford ... B 10
6 Bampton, Devon ... D 3
16 Bampton, Oxon. ... D 4
39 Bampton, Westmorland ... C 7
39 Bampton Grange ... C 7
33 Banavie ... M 3
23 Banbury ... H 8
13 Bancffosfelen ... F 8
59 Banchory, Kinc. ... G 7
59 Banchory, Kinc. ... H 4
13 Bancycapel ... E 7
12 Banc-y-felin ... E 6
13 Banc-y-ffordd ... C 7
53 Bandirran House ... D 7
58 Banff ... A 4
28 Bangor ... C 5
30 Bangor-Is-coed ... F 3
27 Banham ... G 4
8 Bank, Hants. ... E 4
21 Bank, Mont. ... A 8
35 Bank Newton ... B 8
21 Bank Street ... F 11
43 Bankend, Dumf. ... E 11
48 Bankend, Lanark ... F 1
52 Bankfoot, Perth ... D 5
47 Bankfoot, Renfrew ... B 7
47 Bankglen ... H 11
58 Bankhead, Aber. ... F 6
59 Bankhead, Aber. ... G 4
47 Bankhead, Ayr. ... D 8
48 Bankhead, Lanark ... E 3
45 Bankhead, Northumberland ... B 8
47 Banknock ... B 12
44 Banks, Cumb. ... F 4
34 Banks, Lancs. ... E 3
43 Bankshill ... C 12
26 Banningham ... C 5
19 Bannister Green ... B 7
52 Bannockburn ... H 3
10 Banstead ... B 1
5 Bantham ... L 5
47 Banton ... B 12
15 Banwell ... H 7
11 Bapchild ... B 8
50 Barachandroman ... E 4
47 Barassie ... F 8
50 Baravullin ... D 6
56 Barbaraville ... C 3
31 Barber Booth ... B 9
47 Barbieston ... H 9
39 Barbon ... G 8
50 Barbreck House ... G 5
4 Barbrook ... A 6
23 Barby ... E 9

MAP

51 Barcaldine........C 7
43 Barcaple.........F 7
22 Barchesten.......H 6
47 Barclaugh........G 9
43 Barclosh.........E 9
10 Barcombe.........G 3
10 Barcombe Cross...F 3
40 Barden...........F 2
35 Barden Scale.....A 9
42 Bardennoch.......B 6
64 Bardister........C 7
61 Bardnabeinne.....G 7
33 Bardney..........C 8
23 Bardon...........A 8
44 Bardon Mill......G 6
47 Bardowie.........B 10
47 Bardrainney......B 8
38 Bardsea..........H 5
35 Bardsey..........C 12
27 Bardwell.........H 2
49 Barelees.........F 11
21 Barewood.........G 9
46 Barfad...........B 4
26 Barford, Norfolk..E 4
22 Barford, War.....F 6
16 Barford St. John..A 5
8 Barford St. Martin C 2
16 Barford St. Michael A 5
11 Barfreston.......C 11
42 Bargaly..........E 5
47 Barglas..........A 8
14 Bargoed..........D 5
42 Bargrennan.......D 4
51 Barguillean Farm..E 7
25 Barham, Hunts....H 5
11 Barham, Kent....C 10
27 Barham, Suffolk..K 4
43 Barharrow........F 7
24 Barholm..........D 2
44 Barhough.........H 5
23 Barkby...........A 9
23 Barkby Thorpe....A 9
32 Barkestone.......G 5
17 Barkham..........G 9
18 Barking, Essex...E 5
27 Barking, Suffolk..K 4
27 Barking Tye......K 4
35 Barkisland.......E 9
32 Barkston, Lincs..F 6
36 Barkston, Yorks..D 3
25 Barkway..........M 5
42 Barlae...........F 4
31 Barlaston........F 7
43 Barlay...........D 7
32 Barlborough.....C 2
36 Barlby...........D 4
23 Barlestone.......B 8
25 Barley, Herts....L 5
35 Barley, Lancs....D 7
45 Barley Mow.....H 11
45 Barleyhill.......H 8
23 Barleythorpe....A 11
19 Barling..........E 9
32 Barlow, Derby....C 1
45 Barlow, Durham..G 9
36 Barlow, Yorks....D 4
36 Barmby Moor......B 5
36 Barmby on the Marsh
..................D 5
26 Barmer...........B 1
49 Barmoor Castle...F 12
49 Barmoor Ridge...E 12
20 Barmouth.........A 2
40 Barmpton.........C 3
37 Barmston.........A 9
43 Barmurrie........D 7
51 Barnacarry.......H 7
24 Barnack..........E 2
23 Barnacle.........D 7
51 Barnaline........F 7
39 Barnard Castle...C 12
25 Barnardiston.....K 8
43 Barnbarroch......F 9
36 Barnburgh.......G 3
26 Barnby...........F 8
36 Barnby Dun.......D 4
32 Barnby in the Willows
..................E 6
32 Barnby Moor.....B 4
42 Barncorkrie......H 2
18 Barnes...........F 2
10 Barness Street...C 5
18 Barnet...........D 3
37 Barnetby le Wold..F 8
26 Barney...........B 3
27 Barnham, Suffolk.G 2
9 Barnham, Sussex..F 11
26 Barnham Broom...E 4
59 Barnhead.........L 4
56 Barnhill.........D 7
42 Barnhills........D 7
27 Barningham, Suff..H 3
40 Barningham,Yorks.D 1

37 Barnoldby le Beck
..................G 10
35 Barnoldswick.....C 7
9 Barns Green.....C 12
16 Barnsley, Glos...D 2
35 Barnsley, Yorks..F 12
4 Barnstaple......C 4
30 Barnston, Cheshire B 1
18 Barnston, Essex..B 6
32 Barnstone........G 4
22 Barnt Green......E 4
30 Barnton..........C 5
25 Barnwell All Saints G 2
25 Barnwell St. Andrew
..................G 2
15 Barnwood.........C 11
21 Barons' Cross...G 10
47 Barr, Ayr.......H 12
42 Barr, Ayr........B 4
43 Barr, Dumfries...B 9
58 Barra Castle.....E 5
42 Barrachan........G 4
50 Barrachrail......E 5
63 Barraglom........D 3
45 Barrasford.......F 7
50 Barravullin......G 5
38 Barregarrow......G 2
47 Barrhead.........D 10
42 Barrhill.........C 3
25 Barrington, Cambs.K 5
7 Barrington, Som..D 7
2 Barripper........F 3
55 Barrisdale.......J 3
47 Barrmill.........D 8
61 Barrock.........A 11
34 Barrow, Lancs....C 6
23 Barrow, Rutland .A 12
21 Barrow, Salop...B 12
7 Barrow, Som.....C 10
27 Barrow, Suffolk ...J 1
15 Barrow Gurney...G 8
37 Barrow Haven.....E 8
32 Barrow Hill......C 1
38 Barrow-in-Furness H 5
34 Barrow Nook......G 3
7 Barrow Street...C 11
37 Barrow-upon-Humber
..................E 8
32 Barrow-upon-Soar H 3
32 Barrow-upon-Trent
..................G 12
45 Barrowburn......B 7
32 Barrowby.........G 6
41 Barrowcliff.....F 10
23 Barrowden......B 12
35 Barrowford.......C 7
30 Barrows Green....D 5
51 Barrs............D 8
53 Barry, Angus...D 10
14 Barry, Glam.....G 4
23 Barsby..........A 10
26 Barsham..........F 7
22 Barston..........D 5
21 Bartestree......H 11
58 Barthol Chapel...D 6
30 Barthomley.......E 6
34 Bartle Hall......D 4
49 Bartlehill......E 10
8 Bartley..........E 4
25 Bartlow..........L 7
25 Barton, Cambs....K 5
30 Barton, Cheshire.E 3
5 Barton, Devon...J 8
16 Barton, Glos....B 2
34 Barton, Lancs....C 4
34 Barton, Lancs....F 2
7 Barton, Somerset..A 7
22 Barton, War.....G 4
39 Barton, Westmor..C 7
40 Barton, Yorks....D 3
24 Barton Bendish...E 8
26 Barton Common...C 7
15 Barton End......E 11
17 Barton Hartshorn .A 7
32 Barton in Fabis...G 2
23 Barton-in-the-Beans
..................B 7
25 Barton-in-the-Clay M 2
25 Barton Mills.....H 8
8 Barton-on-Sea...G 4
16 Barton-on-the-Heath
..................A 4
7 Barton St. David..C 8
23 Barton Seagrave .D 12
8 Barton Stacey....B 6
4 Barton Town.....B 5
37 Barton Waterside..E 8
41 Barton-le-Street..H 1
36 Barton-le-Willows.A 5
31 Barton-under-
Needwood.....H 8
37 Barton-upon-Humber
..................E 8

35 Barugh..........F 11
63 Barvas..........B 5
25 Barway..........H 6
23 Barwell.........B 8
7 Barwick.........E 9
36 Barwick in Elmet..C 2
30 Baschurch.......H 3
23 Bascote.........F 7
31 Basford Green....E 8
34 Bashall Eaves...C 6
8 Bashley.........F 4
17 Basildon, Berks..F 7
19 Basildon, Essex..E 7
9 Basing..........A 8
9 Basingstoke.....A 7
31 Baslow..........C 11
7 Bason Bridge....B 7
14 Bassaleg........F 6
49 Bassendean......E 9
38 Bassenfell......B 4
38 Bassenthwaite...B 5
38 Bassenthwaite Lake
Station.......B 4
4 Basset's Cross...F 4
3 Bassett.........D 5
22 Bassett's Pole....B 5
25 Bassingbourn....L 4
32 Bassingfield.....F 3
32 Bassingham......D 6
33 Bassingthorpe...G 7
64 Basta...........B 7
26 Bastwick........D 7
18 Batchworth Heath.E 1
7 Batcombe, Dorset .F 8
7 Batcombe, Som...B 10
30 Bate Heath......B 5
15 Bath............H 10
15 Bathampton.....H 11
15 Bathealton......D 4
15 Batheaston......G 11
15 Bathford........H 11
48 Bathgate........B 3
32 Bathley.........D 5
10 Bathpool, Corn..B 10
6 Bathpool, Som...D 6
15 Bathway.........A 9
35 Batley..........E 11
16 Batsford........A 3
40 Battersby.......D 6
18 Battersea.......F 3
27 Battisford......K 4
27 Battisford Tye...K 3
10 Battle, Sussex...F 6
14 Battle, Brec.....A 3
21 Battlefield.....A 10
19 Battlesbridge...D 8
25 Battlesden.....A 10
6 Battleton.......C 3
8 Battramsley.....F 5
9 Batt's Corner...B 9
58 Bauds of Cullen..A 2
17 Baughurst.......H 7
59 Baulds..........H 4
16 Baulking........E 4
33 Baumber.........C 9
26 Bawburgh........E 5
34 Bawdeswell......C 3
7 Bawdrip.........B 7
27 Bawdsey.........L 6
32 Bawtry..........A 4
34 Baxenden........E 6
22 Baxterley.......B 6
7 Baybridge.......D 7
38 Baycliff........H 5
16 Baydon..........F 4
16 Bayford, Herts...C 3
7 Bayford, Som...C 10
39 Bayles..........A 9
8 Baylham.........K 4
16 Baynards' Green..A 6
21 Bayston Hill.....B 10
21 Bayton..........E 12
50 Beach, Argyll...B 5
15 Beach, Glos.....G 10
23 Beachampton....H 11
24 Beachamwell....E 8
15 Beachley........E 9
19 Beacon End......A 9
8 Beacon Hill, Dor..G 1
9 Beacon Hill, Surrey
..................B 10
17 Beacon's Bottom..E 9
17 Beaconsfield....E 10
63 Beacravik.......H 2
40 Beadlam.........G 6
45 Beadnell........D 12
4 Beaford.........D 4
45 Beal, Northumb..B 12
36 Beal, Yorks.....E 3

55 Bealachasan......H 3
7 Beaminster.......F 8
45 Beamish.........H 10
35 Beamsley.........B 9
10 Bean............A 5
15 Beanacre........H 12
45 Beanley..........A 9
4 Beara Moor......D 4
44 Bearbridge......G 6
6 Beare...........F 3
10 Beare Green......D 1
45 Bearl............G 9
22 Bearley..........F 5
50 Bearnus.........C 1
40 Bearpark........A 3
47 Bearsden.........B 10
11 Bearsted........C 7
8 Bearwood........F 2
43 Beattock........A 11
48 Beattock Summit .H 3
18 Beauchamp Roding C 6
32 Beauchief.......B 1
14 Beaufort........C 5
8 Beaulieu........F 5
56 Beauly..........E 1
28 Beaumaris.......C 5
44 Beaumont, Cumb..G 2
19 Beaumont, Essex.A 11
40 Beaumont Hill...C 3
22 Beausale........E 6
9 Beauworth.......C 7
6 Beaworthy.......F 3
6 Beazley.........B 3
19 Beazley End.....A 7
30 Bebington.......B 2
45 Bebside.........E 11
26 Beccles.........F 7
34 Becconsall......E 3
39 Beck Foot.......F 8
41 Beck Hole.......E 8
25 Beck Row........H 8
38 Beck Side.......G 5
22 Beckbury........B 1
18 Beckenham.......G 4
43 Beckfoot........G 11
16 Beckford........A 1
16 Beckhampton....G 2
32 Beckingham, Lincs E 6
32 Beckingham, Notts.A 5
7 Beckington.....A 11
8 Beckley, Hants...F 4
16 Beckley, Oxon...C 6
11 Beckley, Sussex..F 7
35 Beckwithshaw...B 11
18 Becontree.......E 5
40 Bedale..........F 3
40 Bedburn.........B 1
7 Bedchester.....D 12
25 Bedford.........K 2
25 Bedfordshire, Co..K 2
9 Bedhampton.....E 8
27 Bedingfield.....H 5
35 Bedlam..........A 11
45 Bedlington.....E 10
14 Bedlinog........D 4
15 Bedminster......G 9
17 Bedmond........D 11
31 Bednall.........H 8
49 Bedrule.........H 8
49 Bedshiel........D 9
21 Bedstone.......E 9
23 Bedworth.......C 7
14 Bedwas..........E 5
14 Bedwellty.......D 5
16 Beechingstoke...H 2
16 Beedon..........F 6
16 Beedon Hill.....F 6
37 Beeford.........B 9
31 Beeley..........C 11
37 Beelsby.........G 9
17 Beenham.........G 7
2 Beeny...........B 1
7 Beer, Devon.....G 6
7 Beer, Somerset...C 7
7 Beer Hackett....E 9
7 Beercrocombe....D 7
5 Beesands........M 7
33 Beesby..........B 11
7 Beeson..........L 7
25 Beeston, Beds...K 3
30 Beeston, Cheshire .D 4

26 Beeston, Norfolk..D 2
32 Beeston, Notts...G 3
35 Beeston, Yorks...D 11
26 Beeston Regis....A 5
10 Beeswing........E 10
39 Beetham.........G 7
26 Beetley.........D 3
14 Began...........F 5
26 Begbroke........C 5
24 Begdale.........E 6
21 Begelly.........F 5
21 Beggar's Bush...F 8
21 Beguildy........D 7
22 Beighton, Norf...E 7
32 Beighton, Yorks..B 2
47 Beith...........D 8
11 Bekesbourne....C 10
26 Belaugh.........D 6
22 Belbroughton....D 3
27 Belchamp Otten..L 1
27 Belchamp St. Paul.L 1
27 Belchamp Walter..L 1
58 Belcherrie......D 1
33 Belchford......C 10
18 Bell Bar........C 3
35 Bell Busk.......B 7
58 Bell Heath......D 3
58 Bellabeg........F 1
50 Bellanoch.......H 5
33 Belleau.........B 11
56 Bellehiglash....F 7
40 Bellerby........F 1
5 Bellever........H 5
49 Bellhaven.......B 9
17 Bellingdon......D 10
45 Bellingham......E 7
55 Belloch.........F 2
46 Bellochantuy....F 2
10 Bells Yew Green..D 5
45 Bellsbank.......A 5
47 Bellshill, Lanark .C 12
45 Bellshill,
Northumb.....C 12
48 Bellspool.......C 4
48 Bellsquarry.....C 3
42 Bellymore.......C 3
56 Belmaduthy......D 2
24 Belmesthorpe....D 1
47 Belmont, Ayr....G 8
34 Belmont, Lancs...F 5
64 Belmont, Shetland Is.
..................B 8
47 Belmore.........A 7
58 Belnacraig......F 1
31 Belowda.........D 7
31 Belper..........E 11
31 Belper Lane End .E 11
27 Belsay..........E 9
27 Belstead........L 4
47 Belston.........G 9
4 Belstone........F 5
4 Belstone Corner..F 5
34 Belthorn........E 6
45 Beltinge........A 10
44 Beltingham......G 6
36 Beltoft.........F 6
32 Belton, Leics...H 2
32 Belton, Kesteven .F 6
36 Belton, Lindsey..F 6
26 Belton, Norfolk..E 8
23 Belton, Rutland .B 11
32 Belvoir.........G 5
49 Bemersyde.......F 8
8 Bemerton.......C 3
21 Bempton.......H 12
61 Ben Armine Lodge E 7
63 Ben Casgro......D 5
57 Benalder Lodge..L 1
43 Benbruie........B 8
54 Bendronaig Lodge F 4
24 Benefield.......F 1
11 Benenden........E 7
42 Benfield........E 5
27 Benfield Green...J 7
45 Benfieldside....F 4
43 Bengall.........D 12
26 Bengate.........C 6
14 Bengeworth......H 4
59 Benholm........K 5
36 Beningbrough....A 3
18 Benington, Herts..B 3
32 Benington, Lincs.E 11
33 Benington Sea End F 11

28 Benllech........B 4
46 Benmore.........A 6
60 Benmore Lodge...F 4
5 Bennacott.......G 2
46 Bennecarrigan ...G 4
33 Benniworth......B 9
10 Benover.........C 6
17 Benson..........E 7
47 Benston........H 10
59 Bent............K 4
45 Benthall,
Northumb.....D 12
21 Benthall, Salop..B 12
15 Bentham........C 12
59 Benthoul........G 5
9 Bentley, Hants...B 9
22 Bentley, War....C 6
37 Bentley, E. Riding D 8
36 Bentley, W. Riding G 3
22 Bentley Heath...D 5
4 Benton..........B 5
46 Benton Polliwilline H 2
44 Bentpath........D 2
24 Bentwick........F 4
4 Bentwitchen.....C 6
9 Bentworth.......B 8
42 Beoch, Ayr......B 6
42 Beoch, Wigtown..E 2
42 Beoley..........E 4
55 Beoraidberg.....K 1
9 Bepton..........D 10
18 Berden..........A 5
5 Bere Alston.....J 3
5 Bere Ferrers....J 3
7 Bere Regis......G 11
2 Berepper........G 4
26 Bergh Apton.....E 6
9 Berkeley........D 10
17 Berkhamsted....C 10
7 Berkley........A 11
16 Berkshire, Co...F 5
22 Berkswell.......D 6
18 Bermondsey......F 3
55 Bernera........G 2
62 Bernisdale......C 3
17 Berrick Salome...E 7
61 Berriedale......E 10
38 Berrier.........B 6
21 Berriew.........B 7
49 Berrington, Northumb.
..................E 12
21 Berrington, Salop.B 10
49 Berringtonlaw...E 12
6 Berrow..........A 6
22 Berrow Green....F 1
4 Berry Cross.....D 3
4 Berry Down Cross .B 4
15 Berry Hill, Glos...C 9
12 Berry Hill, Pem...C 4
5 Berry Pomeroy...K 7
58 Berryhillock, Banff B 2
4 Berrynarbor.....A 4
18 Berry's Green....H 4
43 Berryscaur......B 12
59 Berrysloch......H 3
29 Bersham........E 12
20 Berthddu........H 4
49 Berwick, Co.....D 9
7 Berwick, Dorset..F 3
10 Berwick, Sussex..H 4
16 Berwick Bassett..B 2
45 Berwick Hill....F 10
8 Berwick St. James .B 2
8 Berwick St. John..D 1
7 Berwick St. Leonard
..................C 12
49 Berwick-upon-Tweed
..................D 12
29 Berwyn.........F 11
32 Bescaby........G 5
34 Bescar.........F 3
22 Besford........H 3
36 Bessacarr......G 4
10 Bessels Green...C 4
16 Bessels Leigh...D 5
37 Bessingby.......A 9
26 Bessingham.....B 4
10 Best Beech Hill..E 5
26 Besthorpe, Norf..F 4
32 Besthorpe, Notts.D 5
37 Beswick.........B 8
10 Betchworth......C 1
28 Bethania, Caer..E 5
20 Bethania, Cards..F 1
28 Bethel, Anglesey..C 2
28 Bethel, Caer....D 5
29 Bethel, Mer.....F 9
11 Bethersden......D 8
28 Bethesda, Caer..D 5
12 Bethesda, Pem...E 4
13 Bethlehem.......D 10
18 Bethnal Green...E 7
30 Betley..........E 5

MAP

10 Betsham..........A 5
11 Betteshanger.....C 11
7 Bettiscombe......F 7
30 Bettisfield.......G 3
30 Betton..........G 5
14 Bettws..........F 2
20 Bettws Bledrws...G 2
12 Bettws Evan....B 6
15 Bettws Newydd...D 7
61 Bettyhill.........B 7
13 Betws...........F 9
21 Betws Cedewain..C 7
28 Betws Garmon...D 5
29 Betws Gwerful Goch
   F 9
29 Betws-y-coed....E 7
29 Betws-yn-Rhos...C 8
20 Beulah, Brec.....G 5
12 Beulah, Cards....B 6
32 Bevercotes......C 4
37 Beverley........C 8
15 Beverstone.......E 11
15 Bevington......E 10
38 Bewaldeth........B 4
44 Bewcastle.........F 4
22 Bewdley.........E 1
35 Bewerley.......A 10
37 Bewholme.......B 9
49 Bewlie.........G 8
10 Bexhill.........G 6
18 Bexley.........F 5
18 Bexleyheath.....F 5
24 Bexwell.........E 7
27 Beyton..........J 2
27 Beyton Green....J 2
16 Bibury..........C 2
17 Bicester........B 7
22 Bickenhill......D 5
24 Bicker.........B 3
34 Bickerstaffe.....G 3
30 Bickerton, Ches...E 4
45 Bickerton, Northumb.
   C 8
36 Bickerton, Yorks. B 2
4 Bickingcott....C 6
4 Bickington, Devon C 4
5 Bickington, Devon H 7
6 Bickleigh, Devon.E 3
5 Bickleigh, Devon..J 4
4 Bickleton......C 4
30 Bickley Moss.....E 4
19 Bicknacre........D 8
6 Bicknoller.......B 5
11 Bicknor........B 7
8 Bickton, Hants...E 3
21 Bicton, Herefs...F 10
21 Bicton, Salop.....D 8
21 Bicton, Salop...A 10
11 Biddenden........D 7
11 Biddenden Green .D 7
25 Biddenham.....K 1
7 Biddisham......A 7
23 Biddlesden.....H 9
45 Biddlestone,
   Northumb.....B 8
15 Biddlestone, Wilts.
   G 11
31 Biddulph.......D 7
31 Biddulph Moor...D 7
4 Bideford........C 3
22 Bidford-on-Avon..G 4
10 Bidorough......D 4
6 Bidwell.........F 3
36 Bielby.........C 5
59 Bieldside.......G 6
8 Bierley, Hants....H 6
35 Bierley, Yorks...D 10
17 Bierton........C 9
43 Big Corlae......B 7
54 Big Sand.......B 1
5 Bigbury.........L 5
5 Bigbury-on-Sea...L 5
37 Bigby..........F 8
48 Biggar, Lanark....F 3
34 Biggar, Lancs...A 1
48 Biggarshiels Mains E 3
31 Biggin, Derby....E 11
31 Biggin, Derby....D 10
36 Biggin, Yorks...D 3
18 Biggin Hill......H 4
25 Biggleswade....L 3
9 Bighton........C 7
9 Bignor.........E 11
64 Bigton.........D 7
3 Bilberry........D 7
32 Bilborough......F 3
6 Bilbrook.......B 4
36 Bilbrough.......C 3
32 Bilby..........B 4
27 Bildeston......K 3
3 Billacott......A 9
19 Billericay......D 7
32 Billesdon.......B 10

22 Billesley.........F 5
24 Billingborough......B 2
34 Billinge.........G 4
27 Billingford.....G 5
26 Billingford......C 3
40 Billingham......C 5
33 Billinghay......E 8
36 Billingley......G 2
9 Billinghurst....C 12
21 Billingsley.....D 12
17 Billington, Beds..B 10
34 Billington, Lancs. .D 6
26 Billockby........D 7
40 Billy Row.......A 2
34 Bilsborrow......C 4
33 Bilsby..........C 11
9 Bilsham.......F 11
11 Bilsington.......E 9
32 Bilson Green....C 9
32 Bilsthorpe......D 4
48 Bilston, Midloth...C 5
22 Bilston, Staffs...B 3
23 Bilstone........B 7
11 Bilting.........C 9
45 Bilton, Northumb.
   B 10
37 Bilton, E. Riding..D 9
31 Bilton, W. Riding .B 3
23 Bilton, War......E 8
45 Bilton Banks.....B 10
64 Bimbister........C 2
37 Binbrook........H 10
7 Bincombe......H 10
61 Bindal..........H 9
2 Binegar........A 9
17 Binfield........G 9
17 Binfield Heath....F 8
45 Bingfield.......F 8
32 Bingham.......F 4
7 Bingham's Melcombe
   F 11
35 Bingley........C 10
26 Binham.........B 3
8 Binley.........A 6
48 Binniehill......B 1
40 Binsoe.........G 3
9 Binstead........G 7
9 Binsted.......B 9
26 Binton.........G 5
26 Bintree........C 3
21 Binweston......B 8
9 Birch, Essex....B 9
35 Birch, Lancs....F 7
19 Birch Green.....B 9
31 Birch Vale......B 8
26 Bircham Newton..B 1
26 Bircham Tofts....B 1
18 Birchanger......E 7
21 Bircher........F 10
57 Birchfield......G 5
14 Birchgrove, Cardiff,
   Glamorgan....F 5
13 Birchgrove, Glam.G 10
11 Birchington......A 11
31 Birchover......D 10
32 Bircotes........A 3
22 Bird End........C 4
25 Birdbrook......L 8
9 Birdham........F 9
23 Birdingbury.....E 8
15 Birdlip........C 12
36 Birdsall........A 6
22 Birdsgreen......D 1
7 Birdsmoor Gate...F 7
47 Birdston........B 11
35 Birdwell.......G 12
15 Birdwood......B 10
49 Birgham........E 10
34 Birkacre........F 4
40 Birkby.........E 3
34 Birkdale........F 2
30 Birkenhead......A 2
58 Birkenhills.....C 5
47 Birkenshaw, Lanark
   D 12
35 Birkenshaw, Yorks.
   D 10
59 Birkhall........H 1
53 Birkhill, Angus..D 8
49 Birkhill, Berwick. .E 8
48 Birkhill, Dumfries .H 5
36 Birkin.........D 3
44 Birks..........E 6
43 Birkshaw.......E 4
21 Birley.........G 10
10 Birling, Kent....B 5
45 Birling, Northumb. B10
22 Birlingham......H 3
22 Birmingham.....D 5
52 Birnam.........C 5
47 Birnieknowe.....G 10
59 Birse..........H 3
59 Birsemore......H 3

23 Birstall, Leics......A 9
35 Birstall, Yorks....E 11
35 Birstwith......A 11
24 Birthorpe.......B 2
48 Birthwood......F 3
45 Birtley, Durham..G 11
21 Birtley, Herefs...E 9
45 Birtley, Northumb. E 7
15 Birts Street.....A 11
23 Bisbrooke......B 12
4 Bish Mill......C 6
17 Bisham........F 9
22 Bishampton.....G 3
40 Bishop Auckland..B 2
37 Bishop Burton....C 7
40 Bishop Middleham B 3
40 Bishop Monkton..H 3
33 Bishop Norton...A 7
15 Bishop Sutton...H 9
35 Bishop Thornton.A 10
36 Bishop Wilton....B 7
33 Bishopbridge.....A 7
47 Bishopbriggs.....B 11
56 Bishopmill......C 8
16 Bishops Cannings.H 2
21 Bishop's Castle....D 8
7 Bishop's Caundle.E 10
15 Bishop's Cleeve..B 12
8 Bishop's Fonthill..C 1
21 Bishop's Frome..G 12
18 Bishop's Green...B 6
6 Bishop's Hull.....D 5
23 Bishop's Itchington F 7
6 Bishop's Lydeard..C 5
4 Bishop's Nympton D 6
30 Bishop's Offley...G 6
18 Bishop's Stortford.B 5
9 Bishop's Sutton...C 7
22 Bishop's Tachbrook F 6
4 Bishop's Tawton..C 4
9 Bishop's Waltham.D 7
22 Bishop's Wood...A 2
11 Bishopsbourne...C 10
5 Bishopsteignton...H 8
8 Bishopstoke.....D 6
13 Bishopstone.....H 9
17 Bishopstone, Bucks.
   C 9
21 Bishopstone, Herefs.
   H 9
10 Bishopstone, Sussex
   H 4
8 Bishopstone, Wilts.C 2
16 Bishopstone, Wilts .F 3
7 Bishopstrow....B 11
6 Bishopswood....E 6
15 Bishopsworth...G 9
36 Bishopthorpe....B 4
40 Bishopton, Dur...C 4
47 Bishopton, Ren...B 9
13 Bishpool.......E 7
15 Bishton.......F 7
15 Bisley, Glos.....D 12
17 Bisley, Surrey...H 10
34 Bispham........C 2
2 Bissoe.........E 5
33 Bisterne Close....F 4
33 Bitchfield......G 7
4 Biteford........D 2
4 Bittadon.......B 4
5 Bittaford.......K 5
26 Bittering Street...D 2
21 Bitterley........E 11
8 Bitterne........E 6
23 Bitteswell......D 8
8 Bix...........F 8
64 Bixter.........D 7
23 Blaby..........B 9
16 Black Bourton...D 4
54 Black Bridge....C 7
45 Black Callerton ..F 10
42 Black Clauchrie...C 4
51 Black Corries....B 10
50 Black Croft......D 6
4 Black Dog......E 7
45 Black Heddon...E 9
51 Black Mount....C 10
19 Black Notley....B 7
13 Black Pill......H 9
4 Black Torrington..E 3
43 Blackacre......C 11
49 Blackadder Bank .D 11
5 Blackawton.....L 7
6 Blackborough....E 4
24 Blackborough End D 8
10 Blackboys.....F 4
31 Blackbrook, Derby
   E 11
34 Blackbrook, Lancs.G 4
30 Blackbrook, Staffs. F 6
58 Blackburn, Aber..F 6
48 Blackburn, Lanark G 2
34 Blackburn, Lancs. .D 5

49 Blackburn,
   Midlothian....D 8
44 Blackburn, Rox. .D 3
48 Blackburn,
   W. Lothian....C 3
43 Blackcraig......D 8
4 Blackditch Cross..E 6
58 Blackdog........F 7
43 Blackdyke......F 12
35 Blacker Hill.....G 12
8 Blackfield......F 6
44 Blackford, Cumb..G 2
52 Blackford, Perth...F 4
7 Blackford, Som...A 7
7 Blackford, Som...D 10
31 Blackfordby.....H 11
8 Blackgang......H 6
40 Blackhall Colliery .A 5
43 Blackhall Mill....G 9
10 Blackham.......D 4
49 Blackhaugh......E 7
19 Blackheath, Essex B 10
27 Blackheath, Suff...H 7
9 Blackheath, Surrey
   B 11
22 Blackheath,Worcs. D 3
58 Blackhill, Aber....B 8
58 Blackhill, Aber....C 8
62 Blackhill, Inver...C 3
58 Blackhillock......C 1
56 Blackhills, Moray.D 8
44 Blackhills, Dumfries
   F 1
15 Blackhorse......F 10
48 Blackhopebyre....E 6
16 Blackland......G 1
43 Blacklaw......A 11
35 Blackley........G 7
52 Blacklunans......A 6
21 Blackmarstone...H 10
14 Blackmill.......F 3
9 Blackmoor......C 9
4 Blackmoor Gate..B 5
18 Blackmore......D 6
25 Blackmore End,
   Essex......M 8
18 Blackmore End,
   Hertfordshire...B 2
48 Blackness.......A 3
9 Blacknest.......B 9
35 Blacko.........C 7
43 Blackpark......C 10
34 Blackpool......C 2
44 Blackpool Gate...E 4
48 Blackridge......C 2
43 Blackrigg......C 11
14 Blackrock, Brec...C 5
15 Blackrock, Mon...E 8
34 Blackrod.......F 5
43 Blackshaw......E 11
35 Blackshaw Head..D 8
27 Blacksmith's Cnr..M 3
10 Blackstone......F 1
17 Blackthorn......B 7
27 Blackthorpe.....J 2
36 Blacktoft.......E 6
59 Blacktop.......G 6
2 Blackwater, Corn..E 4
17 Blackwater, Hants.H 9
8 Blackwater, I.o.W.G 6
6 Blackwater, Som...E 6
27 Blackwater, Suff...H 8
58 Blackwater Lodge .E 1
46 Blackwaterfoot....G 4
31 Blackwell, Derby .C 10
32 Blackwell, Derby..B 2
40 Blackwell, Durham D 3
6 Blackwell, Som...D 4
22 Blackwell, War...H 6
43 Blackwood,
   Dumfries......C 10
47 Blackwood,
   Lanark......E 12
14 Blackwood, Mon. .E 5
31 Blackwood Hill ..E 8
30 Blacon........C 2
42 Bladnoch......F 5
16 Bladon........C 5
13 Blaen Celyn.....B 7
14 Blaen Dyryn.....A 3
12 Blaenannerch.....B 6
28 Blaenau-Dolwyddelan.
   E 6
28 Blaenau Ffestiniog.F 6
14 Blaenavon......C 6
14 Blaenawey......B 6
12 Blaen-ffos......C 5
14 Blaengarw......E 2
14 Blaengavenny....B 6
14 Blaengwrach....D 2
14 Blaengwynfi....E 2
20 Blaenpennal.....F 2
20 Blaenplwyf.....E 1

12 Blaenporth......B 6
12 Blaenwaun......D 6
13 Blaen-y-Coed....D 7
14 Blaerhondda....D 3
6 Blagdon Hill....D 5
15 Blagdon........H 8
55 Blaich........M 4
50 Blain.........A 4
14 Blaina.........D 5
58 Blair.........E 6
52 Blair Atholl......A 4
52 Blair Drummond..G 2
48 Blairburn......A 3
58 Blairdaff........F 4
52 Blairgowrie.....C 6
52 Blairingone.....G 5
52 Blairhall.......H 5
52 Blairlogie.......G 3
47 Blairmore, Argyll .A 7
60 Blairmore, Suther..B 3
47 Blairnairn......A 8
57 Blairnamarrow....H 8
47 Blairquhosh.....A 10
46 Blair's Ferry.....B 5
47 Blairskaith......B 10
47 Blairvadach.....A 7
15 Blaisdon.......C 10
22 Blakebrook......D 2
22 Blakedown......D 2
49 Blakelaw......F 10
30 Blakemere, Ches..C 4
21 Blakemere, Herefs. H 9
26 Blakeney, Norfolk.A 3
15 Blakeney, Glos...D 10
30 Blakenhall, Ches...E 6
22 Blakenhall, Staffs. B 3
22 Blakenhall Heath..B 4
23 Blakesley.......G 9
45 Blanchland......H 8
35 Bland Hill.......B 10
7 Blandford Forum E 12
7 Blandford St.Mary F 12
47 Blanefield......A 10
33 Blankney.......D 8
51 Blar a' Chaoruinn .A 8
50 Blaran.........F 6
51 Blarghour......F 7
55 Blarmachfoldach,
   Inverness.....M 5
51 Blarmachfoldach,
   Inverness.....A 8
60 Blarnaleyoch....G 3
8 Blashford......E 3
23 Blaston........C 11
24 Blatherwycke....F 1
38 Blawith.......F 5
27 Blaxhall.......J 7
36 Blaxton........G 4
45 Blaydon......G 10
7 Bleadon.......A 7
11 Blean.........B 10
33 Bleasby, Lincs...B 8
32 Bleasby, Notts...E 4
53 Blebocraigs.....F 9
21 Bleddfa.......F 7
16 Bledington......B 3
17 Bledlow.......D 8
17 Bledlow Ridge...D 9
4 Blegberry......C 1
49 Blegbie.......C 7
39 Blencarn......B 9
43 Blencogo......G 12
9 Blendworth.....E 8
43 Blennerhasset...G 12
16 Bletchingdon...B 6
10 Bletchingley....C 2
17 Bletchley, Bucks..A 9
30 Bletchley, Salop..G 5
12 Bletherston.....E 4
25 Bletsoe........J 1
16 Blewbury......F 6
26 Blickling......C 5
32 Blidworth......E 3
32 Blidworth Bottoms E 3
44 Blindburn......B 6
38 Blindcrake......B 4
10 Blindley Heath...C 2
49 Blinkbonny.....F 11
3 Blisland.......B 8
22 Bliss Gate......E 1
8 Blissford.......D 3
23 Blisworth......G 10
31 Blithbury......H 9
31 Blithford......H 9
43 Blitterlees......F 11
27 Blo Norton......G 3
16 Blockley.......A 3
26 Blofield.......E 6
26 Blofield Corner...D 6
43 Bloomfield,
   Dumfries.....D 10

49 Bloomfield, Rox...G 8
31 Blore..........E 10
31 Blounts Green...G 9
16 Bloxham......A 5
33 Bloxholm.......E 8
22 Bloxwich.......C 5
7 Bloxworth......G 12
35 Blubberhouses...B 10
26 Blundeston.....F 8
25 Blunham......K 3
16 Blunsdon St. Andrew
   E 2
22 Bluntington.....E 2
25 Bluntisham.....H 5
3 Blunts........C 10
37 Blyborough.....H 7
27 Blyford........H 7
22 Blymhill......A 2
45 Blyth, Northumb. E 11
32 Blyth, Notts.....B 3
48 Blyth Bridge....E 4
27 Blythburgh.....H 7
49 Blythe........D 8
31 Blythe Bridge...E 4
31 Blythe Marsh...F 8
31 Blythebridge...G 9
36 Blyton........H 6
53 Boarhills......F 10
9 Boarhunt.......E 7
16 Boars Hill......D 6
10 Boarshead......E 4
17 Boarstall......C 7
4 Boasley Cross...F 4
57 Boat of Garten ..H 5
56 Boath.........B 1
11 Bobbing......B 7
22 Bobbington.....C 2
18 Bobbingworth...C 5
56 Bublainy......F 1
19 Bocking.......B 7
19 Bocking Churchstreet
   A 7
3 Boconnoc......D 8
58 Boddam, Aber...C 8
64 Boddam, Shetland Is.
   F 7
7 Bodden.......B 10
28 Bodedern......B 3
29 Bodelwyddan....C 9
21 Bodenham, Herefs.
   G 10
8 Bodenham, Wilts. D 3
21 Bodenham Moor.G 10
28 Bodewryd......A 3
29 Bodfari........C 10
28 Bodffordd......C 4
26 Bodham Street...B 4
10 Bodiam........E 6
23 Bodicote.......H 8
3 Bodieve.......B 7
3 Bodinnick......D 8
10 Bode Street Grn..G 5
3 Bodmin........C 8
29 Bodnant.......C 7
26 Bodney........E 1
28 Bodorgan......C 3
11 Bodsham Green...D 9
28 Boduan........F 3
3 Bodwen.......D 7
56 Bogallan.......E 2
58 Bogbrae.......D 8
47 Bogend, Ayr....F 9
49 Bogend, Berwick .D 10
47 Boghall, Ayr....H 9
48 Boghall, Midloth..C 5
48 Boghall, W. Loth..C 3
58 Boghead, Aber....C 5
47 Boghead, Ayr....F 10
47 Boghead, Lanark.E 12
56 Boghole......D 5
43 Bogknowe......F 10
15 Bogmarsh......A 8
59 Bogmuir, Kinc...K 4
58 Bogmuir, Moray..A 1
58 Bogniebrae.....C 3
9 Bognor Regis...F 11
58 Bograxie.......F 4
48 Bogsbank......D 4
48 Bogside........D 1
58 Bogton........C 4
43 Bogue.........C 7
2 Bohortha......F 6
55 Bohuntine......L 7
3 Bokiddick......C 7
40 Bolam, Durham..C 2
45 Bolam, Northumb. E 9

MAP

5 Bolberry........M 6
30 Bold Heath........A 4
45 Boldon Colliery..G 11
8 Boldre........F 5
40 Boldron........D 1
32 Bole........B 5
31 Bolehill........E 11
2 Boleigh........G 2
49 Boleside........F 7
52 Bolfracks........B 3
6 Bolham........E 3
6 Bolham Water....E 5
2 Bolingey........D 5
31 Bollington, Ches. B 8
30 Bollington, Ches. B 6
31 Bollington Cross ..C 8
10 Bolney........F 1
25 Bolnhurst........J 2
53 Bolshan........B 11
32 Bolsover........C 2
32 Bolsterstone....G 11
15 Bolstone........A 8
40 Boltby........F 5
17 Bolter End........E 9
49 Bolton, E. Lothian B 7
34 Bolton, Lancs...A 6
45 Bolton, Northumb. B 9
39 Bolton, Westmor. .C 8
36 Bolton, Yorks....B 5
35 Bolton Abbey....B 9
35 Bolton Bridge....B 9
34 Bolton by Bowland B 6
39 Bolton-le-Sands..H 7
38 Bolton Low Houses A 5
36 Bolton-on-Dearne .G 2
40 Bolton-on-Swale..E 3
36 Bolton Percy....C 3
39 Bolton Town End .H 7
44 Boltonfellend....F 3
3 Bolventor........B 9
30 Bomere Heath....H 3
60 Bonar Bridge....G 6
51 Bonawe Quarries ..D 7
37 Bonby........F 8
12 Boncath........C 5
44 Bonchester Bridge .B 4
9 Bonchurch........H 7
4 Bondleigh........E 5
34 Bonds........C 4
22 Bonehill........B 5
48 Bo'ness........A 3
52 Bonhard........D 6
47 Bonhill........A 9
22 Boningale........B 2
49 Bonjedward....G 9
48 Bonkle........D 1
48 Bonnington....B 4
53 Bopnybank....G 8
48 Bonnybridge....A 1
58 Bonnykelly....B 6
48 Bonnyrigg and
   Lasswade....C 6
47 Bonnyton........F 9
31 Bonsall........D 11
15 Bont........B 7
28 Bont Newydd....F 6
28 Bontddu........H 6
20 Bont-dolgadfan..B 4
28 Bont-newydd, Caer D 4
20 Bontnewydd,
   Cardiganshire....F 2
20 Bontrhydgaled....D 9
29 Bontuchel........D 10
14 Bonvilston........G 4
13 Bon-y-maen....G 10
4 Boode........B 4
30 Booley........H 4
49 Boon........E 8
41 Boosbeck........C 7
4 Boot........F 1
36 Booth........D 5
35 Booth Wood.....E 9
33 Boothby Graffoe .D 7
33 Boothby Pagnell .G 7
34 Boothtown........G 6
38 Bootle, Furness,
   Lancashire....F 4
34 Bootle, Lancs....H 2
52 Boquhan, Stirling .H 2
47 Boquhan, Stirling A 10
21 Boraston........E 11
9 Borden........D 9
35 Bordley........A 8
9 Bordon, Essex....C 9
19 Boreham, Essex...B 7
10 Boreham Street ..G 5
18 Borehamwood....D 2
43 Boreland, Dumf. .B 12
52 Boreland, Perth ..D 1
43 Boreland of Girthon F 7
62 Boreraig........C 1
49 Borewell........D 12

61 Borgie House....B 7
61 Borgue, Caith...E 10
27 Borgue, Kirk....G 7
27 Borley........L 1
62 Bornaskitaig....A 3
43 Borness........G 7
10 Borough Green..B 5
40 Boroughbridge...H 4
30 Borras Head....E 2
61 Borrobol Lodge ..E 8
32 Borrowash......G 1
40 Borrowby........F 4
38 Borrowdale......D 5
59 Borrowfield......H 6
20 Borth........C 2
44 Borthwickbrae...B 2
44 Borthwickshiels...B 3
Borth-y-gest.....F 5
62 Borve........C 4
63 Borve Lodge......G 1
63 Borvemore......G 1
39 Borwick........H 7
21 Bosbury........H 12
3 Boscastle........A 8
8 Boscombe, Hants..G 3
8 Boscombe, Wilts..B 3
3 Boscoppa........D 7
9 Bosham........F 9
12 Bosherston......G 3
2 Boskenna........G 1
31 Bosley........D 7
36 Bossall........A 5
59 Bossholes........H 6
3 Bossiney........A 8
11 Bossingham......C 10
6 Bossington......A 3
30 Bostock Green ..C 5
24 Boston........A 4
33 Boston Long Hedges E 10
36 Boston Spa......C 2
3 Boswinger........F 7
2 Botallack........F 1
18 Botany Bay......D 3
58 Botarie Mains....B 11
23 Botcheston......B 8
27 Botesdale......H 3
45 Bothal........D 10
32 Bothamsall......C 4
43 Bothel........H 12
7 Bothenhampton...B 8
47 Bothwell........D 12
17 Botley, Bucks....D 10
8 Botley, Hants....E 6
16 Botley, Berks....C 6
17 Botolph Claydon..B 8
10 Botolphs........G 1
54 Bottacks........D 8
32 Bottesford, Leics..F 5
37 Bottesford, Lincs..F 7
25 Bottisham......J 6
16 Bottlesford......H 2
31 Bottom House....E 9
34 Bottom O'th'Moor F 5
53 Bottomcraig......E 8
35 Bottoms........E 8
34 Botton Head....A 5
38 Bottongate......A 5
4 Botreaux Mill....C 7
3 Botusfleming....D 11
28 Botwnnog........G 2
10 Bough Beech....C 4
21 Boughrood........H 7
21 Boughrood Brest..H 7
15 Boughspring......E 9
24 Boughton, Norfolk E 8
32 Boughton, Notts..C 4
11 Boughton Aluph..C 9
23 Boughton........E 11
11 Boughton Lees....C 9
11 Boughton Malherbe C 7
10 Boughton
   Monchelsea ....C 6.
11 Boughton Street..B 9
41 Boulby........C 8
21 Bouldon........D 11
45 Boulmer........B 11
12 Boulston........F 3
58 Boultenstone......F 2
32 Boultham........C 6
23 Bounton on Dunsmore
   E 8
25 Bourn:........K 4
24 Bourne........D 2
25 Bourne End, Beds..L 1
17 Bourne End,
   Bucks.....E 10
17 Bourne End,
   Hertfordshire..D 11
18 Bournebridge....D 5
8 Bournemouth.....G 3
19 Bournes Green,
   Essex....E 9

15 Bournes Green,
   Gloucestershire D 12
22 Bournheath......E 3
45 Bournmoor......H 11
22 Bournville......D 4
16 Bourton, Berks...E 3
7 Bourton, Dorset .C 11
21 Bourton, Salop...C 11
16 Bourton-on-the-Hill
   A 3
16 Bourton-on-the-Water
   B 3
44 Boustead Hill....G 1
38 Bouth........G 6
40 Bouthwaite......H 2
17 Boveney........F 10
14 Boverton........G 3
4 Bovey Tracey....H 7
17 Bovingdon........D 11
17 Bovingdon Green .E 9
18 Bovinger........C 5
4 Bow, Devon....F 6
49 Bow, Midlothian ..E 7
64 Bow, Orkney Is...E 2
17 Bow Brickhill....A 10
53 Bow of Fife......F 8
20 Bow Street......D 2
39 Bowbank........C 11
40 Bowburn........A 3
8 Bowcombe........G 6
6 Bowd........G 4
5 Bowden, Devon...L 7
49 Bowden, Roxburgh F 8
15 Bowden Hill......H 12
39 Bowderdale......E 9
30 Bowdon........B 6
44 Bower........E 6
7 Bower Hinton....D 8
8 Bowerchalke.....D 2
15 Bowerhill......H 12
61 Bowermadden....B 11
31 Bowers........G 7
19 Bowers Gifford....E 7
52 Bowershall......H 6
61 Bowertower......B 11
39 Bowers........D 12
34 Bowgreave......C 4
49 Bowhill........G 7
49 Bowhouse........E 11
3 Bowithick........A 9
34 Bowker's Green...G 3
38 Bowland Bridge ..F 6
21 Bowley........G 11
9 Bowlhead Green .B 10
16 Bowling........B 9
22 Bowling Green....G 2
22 Bowmanstead....D 5
44 Bowness-on-Solway G1
38 Bowness-on-
   Windermere....E 6
49 Bowsden........E 12
61 Bowside Lodge....B 8
15 Bowtrees........A 2
15 Box, Glos........D 11
15 Box, Wilts......G 11
15 Boxbush........C 10
16 Boxford, Berks...G 5
27 Boxford, Suffolk ..L 3
9 Boxgrove........E 10
10 Boxley........B 6
4 Box's Shop......F 1
27 Boxted, Essex....M 3
27 Boxted, Suffolk ..K 1
27 Boxted Cross....M 3
25 Boxworth........J 4
24 Boxworth End....H 5
11 Boyden Gate....B 11
32 Boylestone......G 10
58 Boyndie........A 4
41 Boynton........H 11
7 Boys Hill........B 11
10 Boyton, Cornwall .G 2
27 Boyton, Suffolk ..K 7
8 Boyton, Wilts....B 1
18 Boyton Cross....C 6
23 Bozeat........F 12
32 Brackenfield....D 1
38 Brackenthwaite,
   Cumberland....C 4
44 Brackenthwaite,
   Cumberland....H 1

9 Bracklesham....F 9
55 Brackletter......L 6
46 Brackley, Argyll..E 3
23 Brackley, Northants.
   H 9
60 Brackloch........E 3
27 Bracknell........G 9
52 Braco........F 3
26 Bracobrae......B 3
26 Bracon Ash......E 5
55 Bracora........K 1
32 Bracorina......K 1
31 Bradbourne......E 10
40 Bradbury........B 3
18 Bradda........H 1
23 Bradden........G 10
17 Bradenham......D 9
17 Bradenstoke......F 1
6 Bradfield, Devon .E 4
7 Bradfield, Essex ..M 4
35 Bradfield, Yorks. H 11
27 Bradfield Combust.J 2
30 Bradfield Green...D 5
32 Bradfield Heath ..M 4
27 Bradfield St. Clair .J 2
27 BradfieldSt.George J 2
4 Bradford, Devon .E 3
45 Bradford, Northumb.
   D 11
35 Bradford, Yorks. D 10
7 Bradford Abbas .E 9
15 Bradford Leigh ..H 11
4 Bradford Mill....D 7
15 Bradford-on-Avon
   H 11
9 Brading........G 7
30 Bradley, Denb....E 2
31 Bradley, Derby...F 10
9 Bradley, Hants...B 7
37 Bradley, Lincs...F 10
22 Bradley, Staffs...C 3
31 Bradley, Staffs...H 7
22 Bradley, Worcs...F 3
39 Bradley, Yorks...G 12
30 Bradley Common .F 4
22 Bradley Green....F 3
31 Bradley in the Moors
   F 9
32 Bradmore........G 3
7 Bradney........B 7
6 Bradninch........F 3
31 Bradnop........E 8
7 Bradpole........G 8
34 Bradshaw........F 6
5 Bradstone......H 3
30 Bradwall Green...D 6
31 Bradwell, Derby .B 10
19 Bradwell, Essex ..B 8
26 Bradwell, Suffolk. E 8
23 Bradwell, Bucks..H 11
16 Bradwell Grove ..C 3
19 Bradwell-on-Sea .C 10
19 Bradwell Waterside
   C 10
4 Bradworthy......E 2
4 Bradworthy Cross. E 2
64 Brae........C 7
60 Brae Doune......G 5
60 Brae of Achnahaird
   E 2
55 Brae Roy Lodge .K 7
56 Braeantra......A 1
57 Braedownie......M 8
43 Braefoot........A 9
52 Braegrum........E 5
58 Braehead, Aber...F 7
53 Braehead, Angus .B 11
48 Braehead, Lanark .D 2
48 Braehead, Lanark .F 1
64 Braehead, Orkney Is.
   D 3
42 Braehead,Wigtown F 5
61 Braehungie......D 11
54 Braeintra........F 2
60 Braelangwell Lodge
   (Hotel)........G 6
57 Braemar........K 7
61 Braemore, Caith..D 10
54 Braemore, Ross &
   Cromarty......B 6
47 Braeside........B 7
51 Braeval........G 12
40 Brafferton, Dur...C 3
40 Brafferton, Yorks. H 4
40 Brafferton,
   Yorkshire.....H 4
23 Bradfield-on-the-Green
   F 11
63 Bragar........B 4
18 Bragbury End....B 3
50 Braglenbeg......E 6
34 Braides........B 3

49 Braidshawrig....D 8
48 Braidwood......E 1
31 Brailsford......F 11
45 Brainshaugh....C 10
19 Braintree........B 7
27 Braiseworth......H 4
8 Braishfield........E 5
38 Braithwaite, Cumb.C 5
36 Braithwaite, Yorks. F 4
32 Braithwell......A 3
10 Bramber........G 1
32 Bramcote........F 2
9 Bramdean........C 7
26 Bramerton......E 6
18 Bramfield, Herts..B 7
27 Bramfield, Suffolk.H 7
27 Bramford........K 4
31 Bramhall........B 7
36 Bramham........C 2
36 Bramham Crossroads
   C 2
35 Bramhope........C 11
17 Bramley, Hants...H 7
9 Bramley, Surrey..B 11
32 Bramley, Yorks...A 2
44 Brampton, Cumb..G 4
15 Brampton, Herefs..A 7
25 Brampton, Hunts. H 3
32 Brampton, Lincs..B 6
26 Brampton, Norf...C 5
27 Brampton, Suffolk G 7
39 Brampton, Westmor.
   C 9
36 Brampton, Yorks..G 2
15 Brampton Abbots .B 9
23 Brampton Ash....C 11
21 Brampton Bryan ..E 9
32 Brampton en le
   Morthen........A 2
31 Bramshall......G 9
8 Bramshaw........E 4
9 Bramshott........C 9
18 Bran End........A 6
50 Branault........A 3
26 Brancaster......A 1
26 Brancaster Staithe A 1
40 Brancepeth......A 2
56 Branchill........D 6
15 Brand Green....B 10
56 Branderburgh....C 8
37 Brandesburton ..B 9
27 Brandeston......J 5
4 Brandis Corner ..E 3
26 Brandiston......C 4
38 Brandlingill......C 4
40 Brandon, Durham A 3
32 Brandon, Lincs...C 7
45 Brandon, Northumb.
   A 8
27 Brandon, Suffolk .G 1
23 Brandon, War....D 7
24 Brandon Creek....F 7
26 Brandon Parva....E 4
40 Brandsby........H 6
37 Brandy Wharf....G 8
2 Brane........G 1
8 Branksome......G 2
8 Branksome Park ..G 2
8 Bransbury........B 6
6 Branscombe......G 5
22 Bransford........G 1
8 Bransgore........F 3
32 Branston, Leics...G 5
33 Branston, Lincs...C 7
31 Branston, Staffs. .H 10
33 Branston Booths ..C 8
9 Branstone........H 7
32 Brant Broughton .E 6
44 Branteth........E 1
27 Brantham........C 5
38 Branthwaite,Cumb. C 3
38 Branthwaite,Cumb. B 5
37 Brantingham......D 7
45 Branton, Northumb.
   A 8
36 Branton, Yorks...G 4
44 Branxholme......B 3
49 Branxton........F 11
49 Branxtonmoor....F 11
31 Brassington......E 11
10 Brasted........C 3
10 Brasted Chart....C 3
59 Brathens........H 4
33 Bratoft........D 11
33 Brattleby........B 7
6 Bratton, Somerset .B 3
8 Bratton, Wilts....A 1
5 Bratton Clovelly ..G 3
4 Bratton Fleming ..B 5
7 Bratton Seymour .C 10
18 Braughing........A 4

23 Braunston,
   Northants......E 9
23 Braunston, Rut...A 11
23 Braunstone......B 9
4 Braunton........B 4
41 Brawby, Yorks...G 7
12 Brawdy, Pemb....E 2
61 Brawlbin........B 10
17 Bray........F 10
3 Bray Shop......B 10
17 Bray Wick......F 9
23 Braybrooke......D 11
4 Brayford........C 6
36 Brayton........D 4
3 Brazacott........A 9
62 Breabost........C 3
11 Breach........B 7
2 Breachwood Green B 2
63 Breaclete......C 3
31 Breadsall......F 12
5 Breadstone......D 10
54 Breafield........F 8
2 Breage........G 3
54 Breakachy......E 8
15 Bream........D 9
8 Breamore........D 3
15 Bream's Eaves...D 9
4 Brean........A 6
35 Brearton......A 11
63 Breasclete......C 3
32 Breaston......G 2
13 Brechfa........D 8
59 Brechin........L 4
43 Breckonside....A 9
62 Breckrey........B 4
14 Brecon........A 4
35 Bredbury........H 8
11 Brede........F 7
21 Bredenbury......G 11
27 Bredfield........K 6
11 Bredger........B 7
11 Bredhurst......B 7
22 Bredicot........G 3
15 Bredon........A 12
22 Bredon's Norton .H 3
21 Bredwardine......H 9
32 Breedon on the Hill
   H 1
48 Breich........C 1
36 Breighton......D 5
21 Breinton......H 10
21 Breinton Com...H 10
16 Bremhill........G 1
51 Brenachoille....G 7
10 Brenchley......D 5
4 Brendon........A 6
46 Brenfield......A 3
63 Brenish........D 1
45 Brenkley........F 10
27 Brent........E 2
27 Brent Eleigh....K 2
6 Brent Knoll....A 6
25 Brent Pelham....M 5
18 Brentford........F 2
18 Brentwood......E 6
11 Brenzett........E 8
22 Brereton........A 4
30 Brereton Green ..D 6
30 Brereton Heath ..D 6
64 Bressay........E 7
27 Bressingham....G 4
64 Bretabister......D 7
31 Bretby........H 11
23 Bretford........D 7
22 Bretforton......H 4
39 Bretherdale Head .E 8
34 Bretherton......E 4
6 Brett........B 4
27 Brettenham, Suff. K 3
27 Brettenham, Norf. G 2
30 Bretton........D 2
10 Brewer Street....C 2
22 Brewood........A 2
56 Briach........D 6
7 Briantspuddle....G 11
18 Bricket Wood....D 1
22 Bricklehampton ..H 3
38 Bride........F 2
38 Bridekirk......B 4
12 Bridell........C 5
5 Bridestowe......G 7
58 Brideswell......D 3
5 Bridford........G 7
11 Bridge, Kent....C 10
2 Bridge, Cornwall .E 4
25 Bridge End,
   Bedfordshire....K 1
24 Bridge End, Lincs..B 2
45 Bridge End,
   Northumb......B 9
40 Bridge Hewick...H 4
58 Bridge of Alford .F 3
52 Bridge of Allan ..G 3

MAP

56 Bridge of Avon....F 7
51 Bridge of Awe....E 7
51 Bridge of Balgie, Perth..C 12
53 Bridge of Brewlands A 7
57 Bridge of Brown..G 7
52 Bridge of Cally..B 6
59 Bridge of Canny..H 4
53 Bridge of Craigisla.B 7
43 Bridge of Dee.....F 8
56 Bridge of Derrybeg.F 8
58 Bridge of Don....F 7
59 Bridge of Dun....L 4
59 Bridge of Dye....J 4
52 Bridge of Earn...E 6
51 Bridge of Ericht..B 12
59 Bridge of Feugh..H 4
61 Bridge of Forss..A 10
59 Bridge of Gairn..H 1
59 Bridge of Gaur...B 12
53 Bridge of Lintrathen B 7
59 Bridge of Murchalls H 6
51 Bridge of Orchy.D 10
52 Bridge of Tilt.....A 4
64 Bridge of Waith..D 1
64 Bridge of Walls..D 6
47 Bridge of Weir....C 9
4 Bridge Reeve.....E 5
21 Bridge Sollars..H 9
27 Bridge Street.....K 2
30 Bridge Trafford..C 3
25 Bridgefoot, Cambs.L 5
38 Bridgefoot, Cumb..B 3
7 Bridgehampton..D 9
49 Bridgelands......F 7
9 Bridgemary......F 7
58 Bridgend, Aber...C 5
58 Bridgend, Aber...D 3
58 Bridgend, Aber...E 6
59 Bridgend, Angus..K 3
50 Bridgend, Argyll..H 6
58 Bridgend, Banff...D 1
12 Bridgend, Cards...B 5
3 Bridgend, Corn...D 8
43 Bridgend, Dumf..A 11
53 Bridgend, Fife....F 8
14 Bridgend, Glam...F 2
52 Bridgend, Perth...E 6
54 Bridgend, Ross & Cromarty....D 7
38 Bridgend, Westmor. D 6
48 Bridgend, W. Lothian B 3
4 Bridgerule.......F 1
21 Bridges.........C 9
3 Bridgetown, Corn. A 10
6 Bridgetown, Som...C 3
22 Bridgetown, Staffs. A 3
27 Bridgham.......G 3
21 Bridgnorth......C 12
7 Bridgwater......B 6
41 Bridlington.....H 12
7 Bridport........G 8
15 Bridstow.......B 9
35 Brierfield........D 7
5 Brierley, Herefs..G 10
36 Brierley, Yorks...F 2
22 Brierley Hill.....C 3
40 Brierton........B 5
14 Briery Hill......C 5
51 Brig o' Turk....G 12
37 Brigg.........F 8
59 Briggs of Criggie..J 6
41 Briggswath......D 9
38 Brigham, Cumb..B 3
37 Brigham, Yorks..B 8
35 Brighouse.......E 10
8 Brighstone......H 6
16 Brighthampton...D 5
31 Brightgate......D 11
10 Brightling......F 5
19 Brightlingsea....B 10
2 Brighton, Corn..D 6
10 Brighton, Sussex..H 2
48 Brightons........B 2
16 Brightwalton.....F 5
17 Brightwell, Oxon..E 7
27 Brightwell, Suffolk.L 5
17 Brightwell Baldwin E 7
40 Brignall........D 1
37 Brigsley........G 10
39 Brigsteer.......F 8
23 Brigstock.......D 12
17 Brill, Bucks....C 7
2 Brill, Cornwall..G 4
21 Brilley.........G 8
12 Brimaston.......D 3
21 Brimfield.......F 10

32 Brimington......C 1
15 Brimpsfield.....C 12
16 Brimpton........H 6
64 Brims..........E 1
15 Brimscombe.....D 11
30 Brimstage.......B 2
57 Brin...........G 2
55 Brinacory.......K 1
36 Brind..........D 5
64 Brindister, Shetland Is. D 6
64 Brindister, Shetland Is. E 7
34 Brindle.........E 5
31 Brindley Ford....E 7
22 Brineton........A 2
23 Bringhurst......C 11
25 Brington........H 2
26 Briningham......B 3
33 Brinkhill........C 10
25 Brinkley........K 7
23 Brinklow........D 8
16 Brinkworth......F 1
34 Brinscall.......E 5
15 Brinsea.........H 7
32 Brinsley........E 2
21 Brinsop........H 10
32 Brinsworth......A 1
26 Brinton.........B 3
64 Brinyan........B 2
26 Brisley.........C 3
15 Brislington......G 9
11 Brissenden Green .D 8
15 Bristol.........G 9
26 Briston.........B 4
35 Britannia.......E 7
8 Britford........C 3
14 Brithdir, Glam..D 5
29 Brithdir, Mer....H 7
10 British Legion Village B 6
13 Briton Ferry....G 10
17 Britwell Salome...E 7
5 Brixham........K 8
5 Brixton.........K 4
7 Brixton Deverill..B 11
23 Brixworth.......E 10
16 Brize Norton....C 4
16 Broad Blunsdon..E 2
22 Broad Campden..H 5
8 Broad Chalke.....C 2
6 Broad Clyst......D 7
25 Broad Green, Beds. L 1
19 Broad Green, Essex B 8
22 Broad Green, Worcs. F 1
12 Broad Haven....F 1
21 Broad Heath....F 12
25 Broad Hill......H 7
16 Broad Hinton....F 2
16 Broad Laying....H 5
22 Broad Marston...G 5
13 Broad Oak, Carm..E 9
38 Broad Oak, Cumb. F 4
7 Broad Oak, Dorset G 8
15 Broad Oak, Herefs. B 8
11 Broad Oak, Sussex F 7
36 Broad Oak, Yorks. A 4
11 Broad Street.....B 7
19 Broad Street Green C 8
16 Broad Town.....F 2
35 Broadbottom....H 8
9 Broadbridge.....E 9
9 Broadbridge Hth. C 12
12 Broadfield......G 5
62 Broadford......F 5
9 Broadford Bri...D 12
48 Broadgairhill....H 5
44 Broadhaugh.....B 3
61 Broadhaven.....C 12
30 Broadheath......A 6
7 Broadhembury...F 5
5 Broadhempston...J 7
11 Broadland Row...F 7
13 Broadlay........F 7
58 Broadley.......B 1
18 Broadley Com....C 4
4 Broadmead......D 7
49 Broadmeadows...F 7
9 Broadmere......A 7
12 Broadmoor......F 4
4 Broadnymet.....F 6
11 Broadoak, Kent..B 10
10 Broadoak, Sussex. F 5
58 Broadrashes.....B 2
58 Broadsea........B 1
11 Broadstairs.....A 12
8 Broadstone, Dorset F 2
21 Broadstone, Salop C 11
16 Broadtown Lane .F 2
22 Broadwas.......G 1
18 Broadwater, Herts. B 2

9 Broadwater, Sussex F 12
12 Broadway, Carm..F 6
12 Broadway, Pemb..F 7
6 Broadway, Som...E 6
22 Broadway, Worcs. H 4
16 Broadwell, Glos...A 3
16 Broadwell, Oxon..D 3
23 Broadwell, War...F 8
45 Broadwell House..H 7
15 Broadwell Lane End C 9
7 Broadwey.......H 10
7 Broadwindsor....F 8
4 Broadwood-Kelly .E 5
5 Broadwoodwidger.G 3
21 Brobury.........H 9
62 Brochel.........D 5
45 Brockbridge.....D 7
45 Brockdam.......A 9
27 Brockdish.......G 5
45 Brockenhurst....F 4
48 Brocketsbrae....E 1
27 Brockford Street..J 4
23 Brockhall.......F 9
16 Brockham.......C 1
16 Brockhampton, Glos. B 1
15 Brockhampton, Herefordshire...A 9
7 Brockhampton Green F 10
35 Brockholes......F 10
31 Brockhouse......C 8
9 Brockhurst......F 7
38 Brocklebank.....A 5
37 Brocklesby......F 9
15 Brockley........H 8
27 Brockley Green...K 1
22 Brockton, Salop...B 1
21 Brockton, Salop..B 8
21 Brockton, Salop .C 11
15 Brockweir.......D 8
9 Brockwood......D 7
15 Brockworth......C 12
31 Brocton........H 8
46 Brodick.........F 5
36 Brodsworth......F 3
62 Brogaig........A 4
25 Brogborough....L 1
30 Broken Cross, Cheshire.....C 6
31 Broken Cross, Cheshire......C 7
15 Brokenborough ..E 12
30 Bromborough....B 2
27 Brome..........H 4
27 Brome Street....H 5
27 Bromeswell.....K 6
43 Bromfield, Cumb. G 12
21 Bromfield, Salop .E 10
25 Bromham, Beds...K 1
16 Bromham, Wilts...H 1
18 Bromley.........G 4
11 Bromley Green...D 8
10 Brompton, Kent ..A 6
41 Brompton, N. Riding G 9
40 Brompton, N. Riding E 4
21 Brompton Hall...C 8
40 Brompton-on-Swale E 2
6 Brompton Ralph..C 4
6 Brompton Regis...C 3
15 Bromsash.......B 9
15 Bromsberrow....A 10
22 Bromsgrove.....E 3
30 Bromstead Heath .H 6
21 Bromyard.......G 12
21 Bromyard Downs G 12
28 Bronaber........G 6
20 Bronant.........F 2
12 Brongest........C 6
30 Bronington......F 4
14 Bronllys........A 5
13 Bronwydd Arms..E 7
21 Bronydd........H 8
14 Bronydd Com....C 4
8 Brook, Carm....F 6
8 Brook, Hants....C 5
8 Brook, Hants....E 4
8 Brook, I.o.W....H 5
11 Brook, Kent.....D 9
9 Brook, Surrey...B 12
9 Brook, Surrey...B 10
25 Brook End......J 2
8 Brook Hill......F 5
18 Brook Street, Essex E 6
10 Brook Street, Sussex E 2
26 Brooke, Norfolk..E 6
23 Brooke, Rutland .B 12
15 Brookend.......D 9

47 Brookfield.......C 9
34 Brookhouse......A 4
31 Brookhouse Green D 7
11 Brookland.......E 8
43 Brooklands......D 9
18 Brookmans Park ..D 2
21 Brooks..........C 11
15 Brookthorpe.....C 11
17 Brookwood......H 10
25 Broom, Beds.....L 1
40 Broom, Durham ..A 3
22 Broom, War.....G 4
22 Broom, Worcs....D 3
8 Broom Hill......F 2
52 Broom of Dalreoch E 5
49 Broomdykes.....D 11
26 Broome, Norfolk .F 6
21 Broome, Salop...D 9
10 Broome Park.....C 1
30 Broomedge......B 5
9 Broomer's Crn...D 12
58 Broomfield, Aber..D 7
19 Broomfield, Essex .C 7
11 Broomfield, Kent A 10
11 Broomfield, Kent..C 7
48 Broomfield, Lan...E 1
6 Broomfield, Som. .C 6
36 Broomfleet......D 6
17 Broomhall......G 10
45 Broomhaugh.....G 8
45 Broomhill, Northumb. C 10
56 Broomhill, Ross & Cromarty.....C 3
57 Broomhill Station .G 6
26 Broomholm......B 6
45 Broomhouse.....C 11
43 Broomhouses....C 12
45 Broomley........G 8
15 Brooms Green ...A 10
15 Broomsberrow Heath A 10
61 Brora..........F 9
21 Broseley........B 12
22 Brotheridge Green.H 2
49 Brotherstone....F 9
33 Brothertoft......F 10
36 Brotherton......E 3
45 Brotherwick.....C 10
41 Brotton........C 7
61 Broubster.......B 10
61 Brough.........A 11
31 Brough, Derby...B 10
32 Brough, Notts.....D 5
64 Brough, Orkney Is. C 2
64 Brough, Whalsay, Shetland Is......C 8
64 Brough, Yell, Shetland Is....C 7
39 Brough, Westmor. D 10
37 Brough, Yorks...D 7
64 Brough Lodge....B 8
39 Brough Sowerby .D 10
30 Broughall.......F 4
23 Broughton, Bucks. H 12
38 Broughton, Cumb. B 3
30 Broughton, Flint..D 2
14 Broughton, Glam..G 2
8 Broughton, Hants..C 4
25 Broughton, Hunts..G 4
34 Broughton, Lancs. D 4
37 Broughton, Lincs. .F 7
23 Broughton, Northants. E 11
64 Broughton, Orkney Is. A 2
23 Broughton, Oxon .H 7
48 Broughton, Peebles F 4
40 Broughton, N. Riding E 6
41 Broughton, N. Riding H 8
35 Broughton, W. Riding B 8
23 Broughton Astley .C 8
38 Broughton Beck. G 5
15 Broughton Com..H 12
16 Broughton Foggs .D 3
15 Broughton Gifford H 12
22 Broughton Hackett G 3
38 Broughton in Furness F 5
38 Broughton Mills. F 4
38 Broughton Moor..B 3
64 Broughtown.....D 2
53 Broughty Ferry..D 9
44 Browhouses.....G 1
9 Brown Candover..B 7

31 Brown Edge......E 7
58 Brownhill, Aber...D 6
30 Brownhill, Salop. .H 3
53 Brownhills, Fife..F 8
22 Brownhills, Staffs. B 4
31 Brownlow Heath..D 7
59 Brownmuir......K 5
15 Brownridge......B 11
15 Brown's Hill.....D 12
23 Brownsover......D 8
5 Brownston......K 6
45 Brownyside......A 9
17 Brox...........H 11
18 Broxa..........F 9
18 Broxbourne......C 4
49 Broxburn, E. Lothian B 9
48 Broxburn, W. Lothian B 4
18 Broxted.........A 6
30 Broxton........E 3
7 Broxwood.......G 9
10 Broyle Side......G 3
61 Bruan.........C 21
57 Bruar Lodge.....M 4
63 Brue...........B 4
30 Bruera.........D 3
16 Bruern Abbey....B 4
27 Bruisyard.......J 6
27 Bruisyard Street..J 6
36 Brumby.........F 6
31 Brund..........D 9
26 Brundall........E 6
27 Brundish.......H 5
27 Brundish Street..H 6
55 Brunery........M 1
45 Brunswick Village F 10
23 Bruntingthorpe...C 9
53 Brunton, Fife....E 8
45 Brunton, Northumb. A 10
16 Brunton, Wilts...H 3
6 Brushford.......D 3
4 Brushford Barton .E 5
7 Bruton.........C 10
21 Bryanston.......F 12
43 Brydekirk.......E 12
29 Brymbo........E 12
7 Brympton.......E 8
29 Bryn, Carm.....G 9
29 Bryn, Denbigh...F 12
13 Bryn, Glam.....H 11
34 Bryn, Lancs.....G 4
21 Bryn, Salop.....D 8
34 Bryn Gates.....G 5
14 Bryn Golau.....E 3
28 Bryn-Siencyn....D 4
13 Brynamman.....F 10
12 Bryn-berian.....C 4
13 Brynbryddan....H 11
14 Bryncethin......F 2
29 Bryncir.........F 4
13 Bryn-coch......G 10
28 Bryncroes......G 2
13 Bryncrug.......B 2
29 Bryneglwys.....E 10
29 Brynford.......C 11
28 Bryngwran......B 3
15 Bryngwyn, Mon...C 7
21 Bryngwyn, Rad...G 7
12 Bryn-henllan....C 4
13 Brynhoffnant....B 7
34 Bryning........D 3
14 Brynmawr......C 5
14 Brynmenyn.....F 2
13 Brynmill........H 10
28 Bryn'refail......D 5
14 Brynsadler......F 3
29 Bryn-teg.......E 12
14 Bryn-y-Cae.....F 3
14 Bryn-y-gwenin...C 6
29 Bryn-y-maen....C 7
62 Bualintur.......F 3
23 Bubbenhall.....E 7
36 Bubwith.......C 5
48 Buccleuch......H 6
42 Buchan.........D 5
47 Buchanan Castle .A 9
51 Buchanan Smithy H 11
58 Buchanhaven....C 8
52 Buchanty.......D 4
52 Buchlyvie.......H 1
58 Buchts.........B 7
44 Buckabank......H 2
25 Buckden, Hunts..H 3
39 Buckden, Yorks..G 11
26 Buckenham......E 6
6 Buckerell.......F 5
5 Buckfast........J 6
5 Buckfastleigh....J 6
53 Buckhaven......G 8
49 Buckholm.......E 7
18 Buckhurst Hill...E 4

58 Buckie.........A 2
17 Buckingham.....A 8
17 Buckinghamshire, Co. C 8
16 Buckland, Berks..D 4
17 Buckland, Bucks..C 9
5 Buckland, Devon..L 5
16 Buckland, Glos...A 2
25 Buckland, Herts..M 5
11 Buckland, Kent..D 11
10 Buckland, Surrey..C 1
4 Buckland Brewer..D 3
17 Buckland Com...C 10
7 Buckland Dinham A 11
4 Buckland Filleigh .E 3
5 Buckland in the Moor H 6
5 Buckland Monachorum ..J 4
7 Buckland Newton F 10
6 Buckland St. Mary E 6
24 Bucklegate......B 4
53 Bucklerheads....D 9
8 Bucklers Hard....F 5
27 Bucklesham.....L 5
29 Buckley........D 12
30 Bucklow Hill.....B 6
32 Buckminster.....H 6
33 Bucknall, Lincs...C 9
16 Bucknall, Oxon...B 6
21 Bucknell, Salop...E 9
31 Bucknall, Staffs...E 7
58 Buckpool.......A 2
4 Buck's Cross.....D 2
9 Bucks Green.....C 12
9 Bucks Horn Oak..B 9
4 Buck's Mills.....D 2
7 Buckthorn Weston D 10
21 Buckton, Herefs...E 9
45 Buckton, Northumb. B 12
41 Buckton, Yorks. .H 11
25 Buckworth......H 2
16 Buclebury......G 6
22 Budbrooke......F 6
32 Budby..........C 3
4 Budd's Titson...F 1
4 Bude...........E 1
6 Budlake........F 3
45 Budle..........D 12
6 Budleigh Salterton H 4
2 Budock Water....F 5
30 Buerton........D 7
23 Bugbrooke......F 10
31 Buglawton......D 7
7 Bugle..........D 7
36 Bugthorpe......A 5
21 Buildwas.......B 11
47 Builstonend.....E 9
20 Builth Road.....G 6
20 Builth Wells.....G 6
17 Bulbourne......C 10
24 Bulby..........C 2
32 Bulcote.........F 4
6 Bulford........B 3
30 Bulkeley.......E 4
23 Bulkington, War..D 7
15 Bulkington, Wilts H 12
4 Bulkworthy.....E 3
28 Bull Bay........A 4
8 Bull Hill........F 5
40 Bullamoor.......F 4
17 Bullbrook.......G 9
58 Bullers of Buchan D 8
15 Bulley.........B 11
43 Bullgill........H 11
15 Bullinghope.....A 8
8 Bullington, Hants..B 6
33 Bullington, Lincs. .B 8
39 Bullpot Farm....G 9
46 Bullwood.......B 6
27 Bulmer, Essex...L 2
41 Bulmer, Yorks...H 7
27 Bulmer Tye.....L 1
18 Bulphan........E 6
10 Bulverhythe.....G 6
58 Bulwark........C 7
15 Bulwark Village..E 8
32 Bulwell........F 3
24 Bulwick........F 1
18 Bumble's Green..C 4
55 Bunacaimb......K 1
55 Bunarkaig......L 6
63 Bunaveneadar...F 2
30 Bunbury........D 4
56 Bunchrew......E 2
55 Bundalloch......G 3
50 Bunessan......E 1
38 Bungalow Station G 2
26 Bungay.........F 6
57 Bunloit.........G 1

MAP
32 Bunny.........G 3
54 Buntait.........F 8
18 Buntingford....A 4
26 Bunwell........F 4
26 Bunwell Street....F 4
31 Burbage, Derby..C 9
23 Burbage, Leics..C 8
16 Burbage, Wilts...H 3
17 Burchett's Green..F 9
8 Burcombe........C 2
16 Burcot, Oxon....E 6
22 Burcot, Worcs...E 3
17 Burcott........B 9
36 Burdale........A 6
27 Bures..........M 2
26 Burford, Oxon....C 4
21 Burford, Salop..F 11
50 Burg...........C 1
10 Burgess Hill....F 2
27 Burgh..........K 5
44 Burgh by Sands...G 2
26 Burgh Castle....E 8
10 Burgh Heath.....B 1
33 Burgh le Marsh..D 12
58 Burgh Muir......E 5
26 Burgh next Aylsham
C 5
33 Burgh on Bain...B 9
26 Burgh St.Margaret D 7
26 Burgh St. Peter..F 8
16 Burghclere......H 6
56 Burghead.......C 7
17 Burghfield......G 7
17 Burghfield Com...G 7
21 Burghill.......H 10
36 Burghwallis.....F 3
10 Burham........B 6
9 Buriton........D 9
30 Burland........E 5
3 Burlawn........C 7
17 Burleigh.......G 10
6 Burlescombe....E 4
7 Burleston......G 11
8 Burley, Hants....F 3
23 Burley, Rutland..A 12
21 Burley Gate....H 11
35 Burley in Wharfdale
C 10
8 Burley Lodge....E 4
8 Burley Street....F 3
30 Burleydam......F 5
21 Burlingjobb....G 8
10 Burlow........F 4
30 Burlton........H 3
11 Burmarsh.......E 9
22 Burmington.....H 6
6 Burn, Devon....F 3
43 Burn, Dumfries..B 10
36 Burn, Yorks.....D 4
34 Burn Naze......C 2
52 Burn of Cambus..G 2
35 Burnage........H 7
31 Burnaston......G 11
47 Burnbank.......D 11
47 Burnbrae.......E 12
36 Burnby........C 6
35 Burncross......G 12
39 Burneside......F 7
64 Burness........A 4
40 Burneston......G 3
15 Burnett........H 10
43 Burnfoot, Dumf..B 10
44 Burnfoot, Dumf...D 2
45 Burnfoot, Northumb.
B 8
44 Burnfoot, Rox...A 3
44 Burnfoot, Rox...B 2
47 Burnfoot, Stirling B 11
32 Burngreave.....A 1
17 Burnham, Bucks..F 10
37 Burnham, Lincs...E 8
17 Burnham Beeches F 10
26 Burnham Deepdale A 1
18 Burnham Green...B 3
26 Burnham Market..A 1
26 Burnham Norton..A 1
26 Burnham Overy...A 1
26 Burnham Thorpe..B 2
6 Burnham-on-Sea..A 6
19 Burnham-on-Crouch
D 9
58 Burnhaven......C 8
43 Burnhead, Dumf..C 10
43 Burnhead, Dumf...B 9
58 Burnhervie.....F 5
22 Burnhill Green...B 1
45 Burnhope......H 10
47 Burnhouse......D 8
49 Burnhouse Mains .D 7
41 Burniston......F 10
35 Burnley........D 7
49 Burnmouth, Ber..C 12
43 Burnmouth, Dumf. A 9

45 Burnopfield......G 10
59 Burnroot........H 2
35 Burnsall........A 9
53 Burnside, Angus..B 9
47 Burnside, Ayr....H 10
45 Burnside, Dumf...C 11
32 Burnside, Fife....F 6
56 Burnside, Nairn...F 5
64 Burnside, Shetland Is.
C 6
48 Burnside, W. Lothian
B 4
53 Burnside of Duntrune
D 9
19 Burnt Heath.....A 10
40 Burnt Houses....C 2
35 Burnt Yates.....A 11
2 Burnthouse......F 5
48 Burntisland......A 5
47 Burnton, Ayr.....H 8
47 Burnton, Ayr.....A 4
47 Burnton, Ayr.....H 10
22 Burntwood......A 4
9 Burpham, Surrey..A 1
9 Burpham, Sussex.E 11
45 Burradon, Northumb.
B 8
45 Burradon, Northumb.
F 11
2 Burras.........F 4
39 Burrells........C 9
53 Burrelton......C 7
4 Burridge, Devon..C 4
9 Burridge, Hants...E 7
40 Burrill.........F 3
36 Burringham.....F 6
4 Burrington, Devon D 5
21 Burrington, Herefs.
E 10
15 Burrington, Som..H 8
25 Burrough Green...H 7
23 Burrough on the Hill
A 10
6 Burrow, Devon...G 4
6 Burrow, Somerset..B 3
7 Burrow Bridge....C 7
17 Burrowhill......H 10
9 Burrows Cross...A 12
13 Burry..........H 8
13 Burry Port.......G 8
13 Burrygreen......H 8
34 Burscough......F 3
34 Burscough Bridge.F 3
36 Bursea.........D 6
36 Bursea Lane Ends.D 6
37 Burshill........B 8
8 Bursledon......E 6
31 Burslem........E 7
27 Burstall........L 4
7 Burstock.......F 7
27 Burston, Norfolk..G 4
31 Burston, Staffs...G 8
10 Burstow........D 2
37 Burstwick......D 10
39 Burtersett......F 11
44 Burthinghurst....F 4
30 Burton, Cheshire..C 2
30 Burton, Cheshire..D 4
7 Burton, Dorset...G 10
8 Burton, Hants....G 3
33 Burton, Lincs....C 7
45 Burton, Northumb.
D 12
12 Burton, Pemb....F 3
6 Burton, Somerset..B 5
39 Burton, Westmor..G 8
39 Burton, Westmor..G 8
16 Burton, Wilts....F 11
37 Burton Agnes....A 9
7 Burton Bradstock .G 8
33 Burton Coggles ...H 7
37 Burton Constable .C 9
23 Burton Dassett...G 7
41 Burton Fleming .H 11
30 Burton Green, Denb.
D 2
22 Burton Green, War.
E 6
23 Burton Hastings ..C 7
39 Burton in Lonsdale
H 9
37 Burton Joyce....F 4
23 Burton Latimer .E 12
32 Burton Lazars...H 5
35 Burton Leonard .A 12
32 Burton on the Wolds
H 3
31 Burton-on-Trent .H 10
23 Burton Overy....B 10
24 Burton Pedwardine
A 2
37 Burton Pidsea ...D 10

36 Burton Salmon....D 3
36 Burton upon Stather
E 6
34 Burtonwood......H 4
30 Burwardsley.....D 4
21 Burwarton......D 11
10 Burwash.........F 5
10 Burwash Common.F 5
10 Burwash Weald....F 5
25 Burwell, Cambs...J 7
33 Burwell, Lincs....B 10
28 Burwen.........A 4
64 Burwick........E 2
25 Bury, Hunts......G 4
35 Bury, Lancs......F 7
6 Bury, Somerset....C 3
9 Bury, Sussex.....E 11
18 Bury Green......B 4
27 Bury St. Edmunds .J 2
36 Burythorpe......A 6
47 Busby..........D 10
41 Buscel.........G 9
16 Buscot.........D 3
59 Bush...........L 5
21 Bush Bank......G 10
27 Bush Green......G 5
57 Bush Lawsie......K 8
22 Bushbury.......B 3
18 Bushey.........D 1
18 Bushey Heath....E 2
15 Bushley........A 11
16 Bushton........F 2
64 Busta..........C 7
45 Buston Barns....B 10
18 Butcher's Pasture ..B 6
15 Butcombe......H 8
45 Buteland.......E 7
7 Butleigh........C 8
7 Butleigh Wootton .C 8
17 Butler's Cross....C 9
22 Butlers Marston...G 6
27 Butley.........K 7
30 Butt Green......E 5
44 Butterburn......F 5
36 Buttercrambe....A 5
40 Butterknowle....C 1
6 Butterleigh......E 3
38 Buttermere, Cumb.D 4
16 Buttermere, Wilts. H 4
30 Butters Green....E 6
35 Buttershaw.....D 10
52 Butterstone.....C 5
31 Butterton......E 9
40 Butterwick, Dur...B 4
41 Butterwick, E. Riding
H 10
24 Butterwick, Lincs..A 5
41 Butterwick, N. Riding
G 7
21 Buttington......B 8
23 Buttock's Booth ..F 11
22 Buttonoak......D 1
8 Butt's Green......C 4
8 Buttsash........E 6
27 Buxhall.........J 3
49 Buxley.........D 10
10 Buxted.........F 4
31 Buxton, Derby...C 9
26 Buxton, Norfolk..C 5
26 Buxton Heath....C 5
14 Bwlch.........B 5
29 Bwlchgwyn.....E 11
20 Bwlchllan......F 1
29 Bwlchtocyn.....H 3
29 Bwlch-y-cibau ..H 11
29 Bwlch-y-ddâr ...H 11
13 Bwlchyfadfa....B 8
20 Bwlch-y-ffridd...C 6
12 Bwlch-y-groes....C 6
20 Bwlch-y-sarnau..E 6
43 Byeloch.......D 11
40 Byers Green.....B 2
23 Byfield........G 8
17 Byfleet........H 11
21 Byford........H 9
25 Bygrave.......L 4
61 Bylbster.......B 11
29 Bylchau........D 9
30 Byley.........C 6
13 Bynea.........G 9
23 Byrewalls......C 6
44 Byrness........C 6
25 Bythorn.......H 2
21 Byton.........F 9
21 Bywell........G 8
9 Byworth.......D 11
52 Cablea.........C 4
37 Cabourne......C 9
58 Cabrach.......E 1
54 Cabuie Lodge...C 5
6 Cadbury........F 3
4 Cadbury Barton..D 6
59 Caddam.......K 1

47 Cadder.........B 11
51 Cadderlie......D 7
17 Caddington.....B 11
23 Cadeby, Leics...B 7
36 Cadeby, Yorks...G 3
6 Cadeleigh......E 3
48 Cademuir......F 5
44 Cadgillhead.....F 4
53 Cadham.........G 7
34 Cadishead......H 6
13 Cadle.........G 9
16 Cadley, Wilts...G 3
16 Cadley, Wilts...A 4
37 Cadney........G 8
29 Cadole........D 11
13 Cadoxton-Juxta-Neath
G 11
60 Cadubh........G 3
14 Cae Hopkin....C 2
28 Caeathraw.....D 4
28 Cae-lwyn-grydd ...C 5
33 Caenby........A 7
33 Caenby Corner...A 7
13 Caeo.........C 10
13 Caer Farchell....D 1
14 Caerau........E 2
13 Cae'r-bryn.....F 9
28 Caerdeon......H 6
28 Cae'r-geiliog...B 3
14 Caerhun.......C 7
12 Caerleon......E 6
14 Caerlleon......E 6
28 Caernarvon.....D 4
14 Caerphilly.....F 5
20 Caersws......C 6
13 Caerwedros.....A 7
15 Caerwent......E 8
29 Caerwys......C 10
57 Caggan........H 4
43 Cairn..........C 10
50 Cairnbaan.....H 5
42 Cairnbrogie.....E 6
49 Cairncross.....C 11
42 Cairnderry.....D 4
51 Cairndow......F 9
58 Cairness.......B 8
48 Cairneyhill.....A 3
42 Cairnfield......G 5
58 Cairnfield House ..B 2
42 Cairngaan......H 2
42 Cairngarroch....G 1
43 Cairnhall......C 10
58 Cairnhill......D 4
58 Cairnie, Aber...C 2
59 Cairnie, Aber...B 9
58 Cairnorrie.....D 6
42 Cairnryan......E 2
42 Cairnsmore.....E 5
47 Cairntable.....H 9
42 Cairnwhin......B 3
54 Caiseachan.....D 6
45 Caister-on-Sea ..D 8
37 Caistor.......G 9
26 Caistor St.Edmund E 5
45 Caistron......C 8
49 Caitha Bowland...E 7
61 Caithness, Co....C 10
63 Calbost........E 5
8 Calbourne......G 6
33 Calceby........C 11
22 Calchems Corner..E 6
15 Calcot Farm....E 11
17 Calcot Row.....G 7
56 Calcots Station...C 8
11 Calcott........B 10
38 Caldbeck......A 6
40 Caldbergh......G 1
25 Caldecote,
Bedfordshire..L 3
25 Caldecote,
Cambridgeshire K 4
24 Caldecott, Hunts..H 1
23 Caldecott, Rut...C 12
38 Calder, Cumb...E 3
49 Calder, Northumb.
G 12
38 Calder Bridge...D 4
35 Calder Grove...E 11
61 Calder Mains...B 10
34 Calder Vale....C 4
47 Calderbank.....C 12
35 Calderbrook....E 8
48 Caldercruix....C 1
47 Caldermill.....E 11
47 Calderwood....D 11
15 Caldicot......E 8

49 Caldside........E 9
40 Caldwell.......D 2
30 Caldy.........B 1
13 Caledfwlch.....D 10
13 Caledrhydiau...B 8
64 Calfsound......B 3
50 Calgary.......B 1
56 Califer........D 6
26 California, Norf..D 8
48 California, Stir...B 2
27 California, Suff...L 5
5 California Cross..K 6
31 Calke.........H 12
45 Callaly........B 9
52 Callander......F 1
63 Callanish......D 3
51 Callert House....A 8
2 Callestick......E 5
62 Calligarry.....H 5
3 Callington......C 10
15 Callow.........A 8
22 Callow End.....G 2
22 Callow Hill, Worcs.
E 1
22 Callow Hill, Worcs.
F 4
16 Callow Hill......F 1
17 Callowhill......G 11
21 Callows Grave...F 11
8 Calmore.......E 5
16 Calmsden......C 1
16 Calne.........G 1
32 Calow.........C 1
8 Calshot........F 6
3 Calstock......C 11
16 Calstone Wellington
G 1
26 Calthorpe......B 5
39 Calthwaite.....A 7
35 Calton, Yorks....A 8
31 Calton, Staffs...E 9
30 Calveley......D 4
31 Calver........C 11
21 Calver Hill....G 9
30 Calverhall....F 5
6 Calverleigh....E 3
35 Calverley......C 10
23 Calverton, Bucks.H 11
32 Calverton, Notts..E 3
52 Calvine......A 3
43 Calvo........F 12
48 Calzeat.......F 4
15 Cam..........D 10
62 Camascross....G 6
50 Camasine......A 5
50 Camasnacroise..B 6
54 Camasterach....E 1
62 Camastianavaig ..D 4
54 Camasunary....F 4
56 Camault Muir....F 1
64 Camb.........B 7
11 Camber........F 8
17 Camberley.....H 9
18 Camberwell.....F 3
36 Camblesforth....D 4
53 Cambo, Fife....F 10
45 Cambo, Northumb.
D 8
45 Cambois......E 11
2 Camborne......F 4
25 Cambridge, Cambs.J 5
15 Cambridge, Glos. D 10
25 Cambridgeshire and
Isle of Ely, Co. .K 5
52 Cambus........H 3
59 Cambus o'May ..G 2
52 Cambusbarron...H 3
52 Cambuskenneth..H 3
47 Cambuslang....C 11
61 Cambusmore Lo. .G 8
54 Cambussorray...F 7
18 Camden........E 3
15 Cameley.......H 9
3 Camelford.....A 8
48 Camelon......A 2
9 Camelsdale....C 10
56 Camerory......F 6
38 Camerton, Cumb..E 4
7 Camerton, Som. .A 10
52 Camghouran....B 1
55 Camisky......L 5
59 Cammachmore..H 6
32 Cammeringham..B 6
56 Campbeltown or
Ardersier...D 3
46 Campbeltown....G 2
45 Camperdown....F 11
53 Campmuir......C 7
25 Camps Green...L 7
36 Campsall.......F 3
27 Campsey Ash....K 6
25 Campton......L 2
44 Camptown......B 5

12 Camrose.......E 3
52 Camserney.....B 3
61 Camster.......C 11
54 Camus-luinie...G 3
54 Camusteel.....E 1
52 Camusvrachan..B 1
8 Canada.......D 4
59 Candacraig....G 1
58 Candacraig House .F 1
33 Candlesby......C 11
59 Candy.........J 5
48 Candyburn.....E 3
17 Cane End......F 8
19 Canewdon.....D 9
18 Canfield End...B 6
8 Canford Bottom..F 2
8 Canford Magna..F 2
61 Canisbay......A 12
7 Cann.........D 12
7 Cann Common ..D 12
3 Cannaframe....B 9
7 Cannards Grave..B 9
54 Cannich.......F 7
6 Cannington....B 6
22 Cannock......A 3
22 Cannock Wood..A 4
15 Cannop.......C 9
21 Canon Bridge...H 10
21 Canon Pyon....G 10
44 Canonbie......E 2
23 Canons Ashby...G 9
2 Canonstown....F 2
11 Canterbury....B 10
26 Cantley, Norfolk .E 7
36 Cantley, Yorks...G 4
14 Canton........G 5
56 Cantraybruich...E 3
56 Cantraydoune...E 3
56 Cantraywood,
E 3
39 Cantsfield.....H 8
19 Canvey........F 8
33 Canwick......C 7
2 Canworthy Water .B 2
55 Caol.........M 5
55 Caonich......K 4
10 Capel.........D 1
20 Capel-Bangor....D 2
20 Capel Betws Lleucu
G 2
28 Capel Carmel....G 1
28 Capel Curig....D 6
13 Capel Cynon....B 7
13 Capel Dewi, Carm. E 8
20 Capel Dewi, Cards.
D 2
13 Capel Dewi, Cards.
C 8
13 Capel Garmon...E 7
13 Capel Gwyn....E 8
13 Capel Gwynfe...E 10
13 Capel Hendre...F 9
13 Capel Isaac....D 9
12 Capel Iwan....C 6
11 Capel le Ferne ..D 11
14 Capel Llanilterne .F 4
27 Capel St. Andrew .K 7
27 Capel St. Mary...L 4
20 Capel Seion....D 2
20 Capel Trisant...E 3
14 Capel Tygwydd..C 6
28 Capel-côch....B 4
28 Capel-gwyn....C 3
13 Capel-lago....C 9
28 Capel-uchaf....E 4
29 Capelulo......C 7
14 Capel-y-ffin....A 6
30 Capenhurst....C 2
39 Capernwray....H 8
45 Capheaton....E 8
48 Cappercleuch...G 5
48 Capplegill.....H 4
5 Capton, Devon ..K 7
6 Capton, Somerset .B 4
52 Caputh........C 6
32 Car Colston....F 4
2 Carbis Bay.....F 2
62 Carbost, Skye....E 3
62 Carbost, Skye....C 4
60 Carbreck......B 4
32 Carbrook......A 1
26 Carbrooke.....E 3
32 Carburton......C 3
3 Carclaze.......D 7
47 Carcluie......H 8
36 Carcroft......F 3
53 Cardenden....H 7
21 Cardeston....A 9
14 Cardiff.......G 5
12 Cardigan.....B 5
25 Cardington,
Bedfordshire....K 2
21 Cardington, Salop.
C 10

MAP

3 Cardinham......C 8
42 Cardorcan.....D 5
56 Cardow........E 7
48 Cardrona......F 6
47 Cardross......B 8
43 Cardurnock.....F 12
24 Careby.........D 1
59 Careston.......L 3
12 Carew..........G 4
12 Carew Cheriton..G 4
12 Carew Newton...F 4
44 Carewoodrig....C 3
15 Carey..........A 9
47 Carfin.........D 12
49 Carfrae........B 8
43 Cargenbridge...D 10
52 Cargill........C 6
44 Cargo..........G 2
3 Cargreen.......C 11
49 Carham.........F 10
6 Carhampton.....B 3
2 Carharrack.....F 4
52 Carie..........A 1
8 Carisbrooke....G 6
38 Cark...........G 6
3 Carkeel........D 11
2 Carland........D 5
44 Carlatton Mill...H 4
24 Carlby.........D 2
35 Carlecotes.....G 10
2 Carleen........G 3
44 Carlenrig......C 2
44 Carleton, Cumb..H 3
42 Carleton, Wig...H 5
35 Carleton, Yorks..B 8
26 Carleton Forehoe .E 4
26 Carleton Rode...F 4
2 Carlidnack.....G 5
41 Carlin How.....C 7
15 Carlingcott......H 10
44 Carlisle.......G 2
48 Carlops........D 4
63 Carloway.......C 3
25 Carlton, Beds...K 1
25 Carlton, Cambs..K 7
40 Carlton, Durham..C 4
23 Carlton, Leics...B 8
40 Carlton, N. Riding E 5
40 Carlton, N. Riding F 6
40 Carlton, N. Riding G 1
32 Carlton, Notts...F 3
27 Carlton, Suffolk..J 7
36 Carlton, W. Riding E 4
33 Carlton, W. Riding D 1
35 Carlton, W. Riding
        F 12
26 Carlton Colville..F 8
23 Carlton Curlieu ..B 10
40 Carlton Husthwaite
        G 5
32 Carlton in Lindrick B 3
40 Carlton Miniott..G 4
32 Carlton Scroop...F 6
32 Carlton-le-Moorland
        D 6
32 Carlton-on-Trent..D 5
48 Carluke........D 1
3 Carlyon Bay....D 7
48 Carmacoup......G 1
13 Carmarthen.....E 7
13 Carmel, Carm....E 9
28 Carmel, Caer....E 4
28 Carmel, Anglesey..B 3
29 Carmel, Flintshire
        C 11
13 Carmel Chapel...D 10
38 Carmel Fell....F 6
63 Carminish......H 1
59 Carmont........J 5
47 Carmunnock.....D 11
47 Carmyle........C 11
53 Carmyllie......C 10
37 Carnaby........A 9
63 Carnach, Harris..G 3
55 Carnach, Inver...L 1
55 Carnach, Ross &
    Cromarty......G 4
57 Carnachuin.....K 4
57 Carnaqueen.....K 8
53 Carnbee........F 10
52 Carnbo ....G 5
55 Carnoch........G 3
47 Carnduff.......E 11
2 Carne..........F 6
47 Carnell........D 11
14 Carnetown......E 4
39 Carnforth......H 7
55 Carn-gorm......G 3
12 Carnhedryn Uchaf D 2
2 Carnhell Green....F 3
63 Carnish........D 1
2 Carnkie........F 4
20 Carno..........C 5

55 Carnoch, Inver....K 2
54 Carnoch, Inver....F 7
54 Carnoch, Ross &
    Cromarty......E 6
52 Carnock........H 5
2 Carnon Downs....F 5
53 Carnoustie.....D 10
48 Carnwath.......E 3
29 Carog..........E 7
39 Carperby.......F 12
32 Carr...........A 2
34 Carr Cross.....F 3
44 Carr Shield......H 6
32 Carr Vale......C 2
46 Carradale......E 3
63 Carragrich.....G 3
57 Carrbridge.....G 5
35 Carrbrook......G 8
28 Carreglefn.....A 3
12 Carregwen......C 6
51 Carrick, Argyll..H 9
53 Carrick, Fife...E 9
46 Carriden.......A 3
34 Carrington, Ches..H 6
33 Carrington, Lincs.
        E 10
48 Carrington, Midloth.
        C 6
29 Carrog.........F 10
56 Carron, Moray...E 8
48 Carron, Stirling..A 2
47 Carron Bridge ..A 12
48 Carronbridge...B 9
48 Carronshore....A 2
47 Carrot.........E 10
15 Carrow Hill......E 7
43 Carrutherstown..D 11
46 Carrville......A 3
46 Carsaig, Argyll..A 2
50 Carsaig, Argyll...E 3
42 Carscreugh.....F 3
46 Carse House......C 2
42 Carsebuie......E 4
42 Carsegown......F 5
42 Carseriggan....E 4
43 Carsethorn......F 10
31 Carsington.....E 11
46 Carskiey.......H 2
42 Carsluith......F 6
42 Carsphairn.....B 6
48 Carstairs......E 2
48 Carstairs Junction .E 2
49 Carterhaugh....G 7
8 Carter's Clay...D 4
16 Carterton......C 4
45 Carterway Heads..H 8
3 Carthew........D 7
45 Carthorpe......G 3
48 Cartland.......E 1
38 Cartmel........G 6
13 Carway.........F 8
7 Cary Fitzpaine..D 9
63 Caryshader.....D 2
43 Carzield.......C 10
21 Cascob.........F 8
51 Cashell........H 11
51 Cashlie........C 12
8 Cashmoor.......E 1
16 Cassey Compton..C 1
16 Cassington, Oxon C 5
7 Cassington, Som..B 7
24 Cassop Colliery ..A 4
14 Castell-y-bwch...E 6
39 Casterton......G 8
26 Castle Acre......D 1
23 Castle Ashby...F 11
31 Castle Bank....H 7
39 Castle Bolton..F 12
22 Castle Bromwich..C 5
24 Castle Bytham..D 1
21 Castle Caereinion .B 7
25 Castle Camps...L 7
44 Castle Carrock..G 4
7 Castle Cary....C 10
15 Castle Coombe..F 11
22 Castle Donington .G 2
43 Castle Douglas..E 8
16 Castle Eaton...E 2
40 Castle Eden....A 4
58 Castle Forbes..F 4
21 Castle Frome...H 12
17 Castle Green...F 10
31 Castle Gresley..H 11
49 Castle Heaton..E 11
10 Castle Hill....D 6
41 Castle Howard..H 7
53 Castle Huntly..D 8
42 Castle Kennedy..F 2
12 Castle Morris..D 3

44 Castle O'er.....D 1
21 Castle Pulverbatch.B 9
24 Castle Rising...C 8
56 Castle Stuart......E 3
12 Castlebythe....D 4
47 Castlecary.....B 12
48 Castlecraig, Peeb. .E 4
56 Castlecraig, Ross &
    Cromarty......C 4
43 Castlefairn....C 8
36 Castleford.....E 2
58 Castlehill, Aber...C 5
47 Castlehill, Dunb..B 9
48 Castlehill, Lanark .D 1
48 Castlehill, Peeb..F 5
42 Castlemaddy....C 6
12 Castlemartin...G 3
43 Castlemilk.....D 12
15 Castlemorton...A 11
45 Castleside.....H 9
23 Castlethorpe...H 11
53 Castleton, Angus..C 8
46 Castleton, Argyll..A 4
31 Castleton, Derby.B 10
35 Castleton, Lancs...F 7
14 Castleton, Mon....F 6
44 Castleton, Rox....D 3
41 Castleton, Yorks. .D 7
61 Castletown, Caith.
        A 11
7 Castletown, Dorset H 7
45 Castletown, Dur..G 11
56 Castletown, Inver. E 3
38 Castletown, I.o.M. H 1
35 Castley.........C 11
26 Caston, Norfolk..F 2
24 Castor, Hunts....F 2
43 Castramont.....E 7
13 Caswell........H 9
31 Cat and Fiddle Inn C 8
46 Catacol........D 4
15 Catbrain.......F 9
15 Catbrook.......D 8
2 Catchall.......G 2
32 Catcliffe......A 2
7 Catcott........B 7
7 Catcott Burtle..B 7
47 Catcraig.......F 9
10 Caterham.......C 2
26 Catfield.......C 7
64 Catfirth.......D 7
18 Catford........G 4
34 Catforth.......D 4
14 Cathays........F 5
47 Cathcart.......C 10
14 Cathedine......B 5
9 Catherington...E 8
7 Catherston Leweston
        G 7
21 Catherton......E 12
49 Cathpair.......E 7
43 Catlins........C 12
57 Catlodge.......K 2
44 Catlowdy.......E 3
16 Catmore........F 5
34 Caton..........A 4
5 Cator Court....H 5
10 Catsfield......G 6
22 Catshill.......E 3
36 Cattal.........B 2
27 Cattawade......M 4
34 Catterall......C 4
40 Catterick......E 3
40 Catterick Bridge..E 3
40 Catterick Camp..E 3
39 Catterlen......B 7
59 Catterline.....J 6
40 Catterton......C 3
9 Catteshall.....B 11
23 Catthorpe......D 9
7 Cattistock.....E 10
26 Catton, Norfolk..D 5
44 Catton, Northumb.G 6
40 Catton, Yorks....G 4
37 Catwick........C 9
25 Catworth.......H 2
16 Caulcot........H 2
52 Cauldhame......H 1
31 Cauldon........E 9
44 Cauldside......E 3
31 Cauldwell......H 11
58 Cauldwells.....B 5
43 Caulkerbush....F 10
7 Caundle Marsh ..E 10
22 Caunsall.......D 2
32 Caunton........D 5
42 Causeway End...F 5
58 Causewayend, Aber.
        F 7
48 Causewayend, Lanark
        F 3

43 Causewayhead, Cumb.
        F 12
52 Causewayhead, Stir.
        H 3
45 Causey Park Bri..D 10
39 Cautley.........F 9
27 Cavendish......K 1
27 Cavenham.......H 1
17 Caversfield....B 7
17 Caversham......G 8
36 Caverswall.....F 8
3 Cawsand........E 11
26 Cawston........C 4
35 Cawthorne......F 11
24 Cawthorpe......C 2
36 Cawood.........C 3
40 Cawton.........G 6
21 Caynham.......E 11
32 Caythorpe, Lincs..E 6
32 Caythorpe, Notts..F 4
21 Cayton.........G 10
61 Ceann-na-coille..C 7
29 Cefn-Berain....C 9
29 Cefn Coch, Mer..G 10
29 Cefn Coch, Mont. H 10
14 Cefn Cribbwr...F 2
14 Cefn Cross.....F 2
21 Cefn Einion....D 8
14 Cefn Fforest...D 5
15 Cefn Llaithan..B 7
29 Cefn Mawr......F 12
29 Cefn Rhigos....D 2
29 Cefn-brith.....E 8
13 Cefn-bryn-brain..F 10
14 Cefn-coed-y-cymmer
        C 3
29 Cefn-ddwysarn   F 9
29 Cefngorwydd....F 9
29 Cefn-y-bedd....E 12
12 Cefn-y-pant....D 5
9 Cellan.........B 9
31 Cellarhead.....E 8
39 Celleron.......C 7
28 Cemaes Bay.....A 3
20 Cemmaes.......B 4
20 Cemmaes Road...B 4
12 Cenarth........C 6
53 Ceres..........F 9
20 Cerist.........D 5
7 Cerne Abbas....F 10
16 Cerney Wick....E 2
28 Cerrigceinwen..C 4
29 Cerrigydrudion..E 9
26 Cess...........D 7
49 Cessford.......G 10
20 Ceunant........N 8
15 Chaceley.......A 11
2 Chacewater.....E 5
22 Chackmore.....A 8
23 Chacombe.......H 8
22 Chad Valley....D 4
22 Chadbury.......G 4
35 Chadderton.....G 7
31 Chaddesden.....F 12
22 Chaddesley Corbett
        E 2
16 Chaddleworth...F 5
14 Chadlington....B 4
23 Chadshunt......G 7
32 Chadwell.......H 5
18 Chadwell St. Mary F 6
22 Chadwick End...E 5
7 Chaffcombe.....E 7
5 Chagford.......G 6
10 Chailey........F 3
24 Chainbridge....E 5
10 Chainhurst.....C 6
8 Chalbury.......E 2
8 Chalbury Com...E 2
10 Chaldon........C 2
7 Chaldon Herring or
    East Chaldon..H 11
8 Chale..........H 6
8 Chale Green....H 6
17 Chalfont St. Giles E 10
17 Chalfont St. Peter E 11
15 Chalford.......D 12
17 Chalford Com...E 11
17 Chalgrove......D 7
10 Chalk..........A 5
4 Challacombe, Devon
        B 6
4 Challacombe, Devon
        D 6
42 Challoch.......G 7
11 Challock Lees..C 8
17 Chalton, Beds...B 11

9 Chalton, Hants....E 8
17 Chalvey........F 10
10 Chalvington....G 4
48 Champany.......B 3
20 Chancery.......E 1
17 Chandler's Cross.D 11
8 Chandler's Ford ..D 6
43 Chanlockfoot...B 8
7 Chantry........B 10
53 Chapel.........H 7
7 Chapel Allerton..A 7
35 Chapel Allerton..C 11
3 Chapel Amble...B 7
23 Chapel Brampton.E 10
30 Chapel Chorlton ..F 6
23 Chapel End.....C 7
22 Chapel Green...D 6
36 Chapel Haddlesey .D 4
58 Chapel Hill, Aber. D 8
33 Chapel Hill, Lincs..E 9
15 Chapel Hill, Mon. D 8
35 Chapel Hill, Yorks.
        C 12
21 Chapel Lawn.....E 8
39 Chapel le Dale....G 9
49 Chapel Mains...E 8
59 Chapel of Barras .J 6
58 Chapel of Garioch E 5
42 Chapel Rossan...G 2
16 Chapel Row, Berks.
        G 6
10 Chapel Row, Sussex
        G 5
33 Chapel St. Leonards
        C 12
38 Chapel Stile...E 5
25 Chapeland Way ...L 8
42 Chapeldonan....B 3
31 Chapel-en-le-Frith .B 9
47 Chapelhall.....C 12
43 Chapelhill, Dumf. B 11
53 Chapelhill, Perth .E 7
52 Chapelhill, Perth D 5
48 Chapelhope.....G 5
44 Chapelknowe....F 2
38 Chapels........G 5
53 Chapelton, Angus B 11
4 Chapelton, Devon .C 5
59 Chapelton, Kinc..J 5
43 Chapelton, Kirk..G 8
47 Chapelton, Lan...E 11
57 Chapelton, Inver. .H 5
57 Chapelton, Banff G 8
34 Chapeltown, Lancs.F 6
35 Chapeltown, Yorks.
        G 12
5 Chapmans Well..G 2
7 Chapmanslade...B 11
18 Chapmore End...B 3
19 Chappel........A 9
7 Chard..........E 7
6 Chardstock.....F 6
44 Chareheads.....H 6
15 Charfield......E 10
11 Charing........C 8
11 Charing Cross..E 3
11 Charing Heath..C 8
22 Charingworth...H 5
16 Charlbury......B 5
15 Charlcombe.....H 10
16 Charlcutt......G 1
22 Charlecote.....F 6
4 Charles........C 6
43 Charlesfield...E 12
53 Charleston.....C 8
59 Charlestown, Aber.G 7
3 Charlestown, Corn.E 7
7 Charlestown, Dorset
        H 9
48 Charlestown, Fife .A 3
54 Charlestown, Ross &
    Cromarty......B 2
56 Charlestown, Ross &
    Cromarty......E 2
35 Charlestown, Yorks.
        D 8
56 Charlestown of
    Aberlour......E 8
35 Charlesworth...H 9
5 Charleton, Devon .L 6
16 Charlton, Oxon...A 6
6 Charlinch......B 6
18 Charlton, Herts..A 2
44 Charlton, Northumb.
        D 6
9 Charlton, Sussex .E 10
8 Charlton, Wilts...A 3
8 Charlton, Wilts...D 3
16 Charlton, Wilts...H 2
7 Charlton, Wilts...D 12
16 Charlton, Wilts...E 1
22 Charlton, Worcs...H 4
40 Charlton, Yorks...D 6

16 Charlton Abbots ..B 1
7 Charlton Adam...C 9
7 Charlton Horethorne
        D 10
16 Charlton Kings...B 1
7 Charlton Mackrell C 8
7 Charlton Marshall
        F 12
45 Charlton Mires ..A 10
7 Charlton Musgrove
        C 10
16 Charlton-on-Otmoor
        C 6
7 Charlton-on-the-Hill
        F 12
9 Charlwood, Hants. C 8
10 Charlwood, Surrey D 1
7 Charminster....G 10
7 Charmouth......G 7
16 Charndon.......B 7
16 Charney Bassett...E 5
34 Charnock Richard. F 4
27 Charsfield.....J 5
11 Chart Sutton...C 7
17 Charter Alley...H 7
49 Charterhouse,
    Roxburgh......F 9
7 Charterhouse, Som.
        A 8
52 Chartershall......H 3
16 Charterville
    Allotments....C 4
11 Chartham.......C 9
11 Chartham Hatch ..B 9
8 Charton........A 5
17 Chartridge.....D 10
23 Charwelton.....G 8
4 Chase Terrace...A 4
22 Chasetown......A 4
16 Chastleton.....A 3
4 Chasty.........F 2
34 Chatburn.......C 6
30 Chatcull.......G 6
10 Chatham........B 6
45 Chathill.......E 12
10 Chattenden.....A 6
25 Chatteris......G 5
27 Chattisham.....L 4
45 Chatton........C 12
17 Chaul End......B 11
4 Chawleigh......E 6
25 Chawston.......K 3
9 Chawton........B 8
31 Cheadle, Cheshire A 7
31 Cheadle, Staffs....F 8
31 Cheadle Hulme....B 7
18 Cheam..........G 2
17 Cheapside......G 10
17 Chearsley......C 8
31 Chebsey........G 7
17 Checkendon.....F 7
30 Checkley, Cheshire F 6
21 Checkley, Herefs. H 11
31 Checkley, Staffs...F 9
27 Chedburgh......J 1
7 Cheddar........A 8
17 Cheddington...B 10
31 Cheddleton.....E 8
6 Cheddon Fitzpaine C 6
26 Chedgrave......E 7
7 Chedington.....F 8
27 Chediston......G 7
16 Chedworth.....C 2
17 Chedzoy........B 7
49 Cheeklaw.......D 10
35 Cheetham Hill ...G 7
4 Cheglinch......B 4
4 Cheldon Barton..E 6
31 Chelford.......C 7
31 Chellaston.....G 12
25 Chellington....K 1
22 Chelmarsh.....C 1
27 Chelmondiston..L 5
31 Chelmorton.....C 9
19 Chelmsford.....C 7
18 Chelsea........F 3
18 Chelsfield Village..G 5
27 Chelsworth.....K 3
14 Cheltenham, Brec..C 5
16 Cheltenham, Glos.
        B 12
25 Chelveston.....H 1
15 Chelvey........G 8
15 Chelwood.......H 9
10 Chelwood Com...E 3
10 Chelwood Gate ...E 3
21 Cheney Longville .D 9
17 Chenies........D 11
15 Chepstow.......E 8
16 Cherhill.......G 1
15 Cherington, Glos. D 3
22 Cherington, War. .H 6
13 Cheriton, Glam..H 8

MAP
9 Cheriton, Hants...C 7
11 Cheriton, Kent...D 11
4 Cheriton, Som....A 6
4 Cheriton Bishop...F 6
5 Cheriton Cross...G 6
6 Cheriton Fitzpaine F 2
12 Cheriton or Stackpole Elidor...G 3
30 Cherrington...H 5
37 Cherry Burton...C 7
25 Cherry Hinton...K 6
22 Cherry Orchard...G 2
52 Cherrybank...E 6
49 Cherrytrees...F 10
17 Chertsey...G 11
7 Cheselbourne...F 11
17 Chesham...D 10
17 Chesham Bois...D 10
30 Cheshire, Co....D 5
18 Cheshunt...D 4
22 Cheslyn Hay...A 3
18 Chessington...H 2
30 Chester...D 3
45 Chester Moor...H 11
7 Chesterblade...B 10
32 Chesterfield...C 1
22 Chesterfield...B 4
48 Chesterhall...F 2
48 Chesterhill...C 6
45 Chester-le-Street H 11
44 Chesters, Rox...B 5
49 Chesters, Rox...G 8
24 Chesterton, Hunts. F 2
16 Chesterton, Oxon B 6
31 Chesterton, Staffs...E 7
23 Chesterton Green...F 7
44 Chesterwood...F 6
11 Chestfield...B 10
30 Cheswardine...G 6
45 Cheswick...A 11
45 Cheswick Bldgs...A 11
7 Chetnole...E 9
6 Chettiscombe...E 3
25 Chettisham...G 6
8 Chettle...E 1
21 Chetton...C 12
30 Chetwynd Aston...H 6
30 Chetwynd Park...H 6
25 Cheveley...J 8
10 Chevening...B 4
27 Chevington...J 1
45 Chevington Drift C 11
6 Chevithorne...E 3
15 Chew Magna...H 9
15 Chew Stoke...H 9
15 Chewton Keynsham H 9
7 Chewton Mendip...A 9
23 Chicheley...G 12
9 Chichester...F 10
7 Chickerell...H 9
7 Chicklade...C 12
21 Chickward...G 8
9 Chidden...D 8
9 Chiddingfold...C 11
10 Chiddingly...G 4
10 Chiddingstone...D 4
10 Chiddingstone Causeway...C 4
10 Chiddingstone Hoath D 4
7 Chideock...G 7
6 Chidgley...C 4
9 Chidham...F 9
16 Chieveley...G 5
18 Chignall St. James C 6
18 Chignall Smealy...C 6
18 Chigwell...E 4
18 Chigwell Row...E 5
8 Chilbolton...B 5
8 Chilcomb...C 6
7 Chilcombe...G 9
7 Chilcompton...A 9
22 Chilcote...A 6
7 Child Okeford...E 11
30 Childer Thornton B 2
34 Children's Homes E 6
16 Childrey...E 5
30 Child's Ercall...H 5
22 Childswickham...H 4
30 Childwall...A 3
18 Childwick Green...C 1
7 Chilfrome...F 9
9 Chilgrove...E 9
11 Chilham...C 9
8 Chilhampton...C 3
4 Chilla...F 3
5 Chillaton...H 3
11 Chillenden...C 11
8 Chillerton...H 6
27 Chillesford...K 7
45 Chillingham...C 12
5 Chillington, Devon L 7
7 Chillington, Somerset...E 7
32 Chillwell...G 2
8 Chilmark...C 1
16 Chilson...B 4
3 Chilsworthy, Cornwall B 11
4 Chilsworthy, Devon E 2
7 Chilthorne Domer D 8
16 Chilton, Berks...F 6
17 Chilton, Bucks...C 8
4 Chilton, Devon...E 7
40 Chilton, Durham...B 3
40 Chilton Buildings...B 3
9 Chilton Candover B 7
7 Chilton Cantelo...D 9
16 Chilton Foliat...G 4
7 Chilton Polden...B 7
27 Chilton Street...K 1
6 Chilton Trinity...B 6
8 Chilworth, Hampshire...D 5
9 Chilworth, Surrey A 11
16 Chimney...D 4
9 Chineham...A 8
18 Chingford...E 4
31 Chinley...B 9
31 Chinley Head...B 9
17 Chinnor...D 8
30 Chipnall...G 6
25 Chippenham, Oxon H 8
15 Chippenham, Wilts. G 12
17 Chipperfield...D 11
25 Chipping, Herts...M 5
34 Chipping, Lancs...C 5
22 Chipping Campden H 5
16 Chipping Norton...B 4
15 Chipping Sodbury F 10
23 Chipping Warden G 8
6 Chipstable...D 4
10 Chipstead, Kent...B 4
10 Chipstead, Surrey D 2
21 Chirbury...C 8
29 Chirk...F 12
29 Chirk Green...F 12
42 Chirmorie...D 3
49 Chirnside...D 11
49 Chirnsidebridge...D 11
16 Chirton...H 2
16 Chisbury...G 4
7 Chiselborough...E 8
16 Chiseldon...F 3
17 Chislehampton...D 7
18 Chislehurst...G 4
11 Chislet...B 11
35 Chisley...D 9
18 Chiswell Green...C 1
18 Chiswick...F 2
35 Chisworth...H 8
11 Chitcombe...F 7
9 Chithurst...D 9
25 Chittering...H 6
8 Chitterne...B 2
4 Chittlehamholt...D 5
4 Chittlehampton...C 5
15 Chittoe...H 12
5 Chivelstone...M 6
17 Chobham...H 10
49 Choicelee...D 10
8 Cholderton...B 4
17 Cholesbury...C 10
45 Chollerford...F 7
45 Chollerton...F 7
17 Cholsey...E 7
21 Cholstrey...F 10
40 Chop Gate...E 6
45 Choppington...E 10
45 Chopwell...G 9
30 Chorley, Cheshire E 4
34 Chorley, Lancs...E 5
21 Chorley, Salop...D 12
22 Chorley, Staffs...A 4
17 Chorleywood...E 11
30 Chorlton...E 6
35 Chorlton cum Hardy H 7
30 Chorlton Lane...E 3
25 Chrishall...L 5
24 Christchurch, Cambs. F 6
8 Christchurch, Hants. G 3
15 Christchurch, Mon. E 7
16 Christian Malford F 1
30 Christleton...D 3
17 Christmas Com...E 8
7 Christon...A 7
45 Christon Bank...A 10
5 Christow...G 7
9 Christ's Hospital C 12
47 Chryston...B 11
5 Chudleigh...H 7
5 Chudleigh Knighton H 7
4 Chulmleigh...E 6
35 Chunal...H 9
34 Church...D 6
30 Church Aston...H 6
23 Church Brampton E 10
31 Church Broughton G 10
9 Church Crookham A 9
31 Church Eaton...H 7
25 Church End, Beds. L 3
19 Church End, Essex A 7
25 Church End, Essex L 7
17 Church End, Hampshire...H 7
17 Church End, Hertfordshire...C 12
37 Church End, Kent...G 12
18 Church End, London...E 3
24 Church End, Norf. E 5
22 Church End, War. C 6
16 Church End, Wilts. F 1
16 Church Enstone...B 5
36 Church Fenton...C 3
6 Church Green...G 5
31 Church Gresley...H 11
16 Church Hanborough C 5
30 Church Hill...D 5
22 Church Honeybourne H 5
41 Church House...E 7
41 Church Houses...E 7
8 Church Knowle...H 1
32 Church Laneham...C 5
23 Church Langton C 10
23 Church Lawford...D 8
31 Church Lawton...E 7
31 Church Leigh...G 9
22 Church Lench...G 4
30 Church Minshull...D 5
21 Church Preen...C 11
21 Church Pulverbatch B 9
21 Church Stoke...C 8
23 Church Stowe...F 9
10 Church Street, Kent A 6
27 Church Street, Suffolk G 8
21 Church Stretton...C 10
39 Church Town...F 7
14 Church Village...F 4
32 Church Warsop...C 3
15 Churcham...B 11
15 Churchdown...B 12
18 Churchend, Essex B 6
19 Churchend, Essex E 10
15 Churchend, Glos. E 10
22 Churchfield...C 4
4 Churchill, Devon...B 5
6 Churchill, Devon...F 6
22 Churchill, Salop...D 2
16 Churchill, Oxon...B 4
15 Churchill, Som...H 7
22 Churchill, Worcs. G 3
6 Churchingford...E 5
23 Churchover...D 8
6 Churchstanton...E 5
5 Churchstow...L 6
38 Churchtown, Cumb. A 6
4 Churchtown, Dev. F 2
38 Churchtown, I.o.M. G 2
34 Churchtown, Lancs. C 4
34 Churchtown, Lancs. E 3
44 Churnsike Lodge...E 5
5 Churston Ferrers...K 8
9 Churt...B 10
30 Churton...E 3
35 Churwell...D 11
8 Chute Standen...A 5
28 Chwilog...F 4
29 Cilcain...D 11
13 Cilcennin...A 8
13 Cilfrew...G 11
14 Ciffynydd...E 4
12 Cilgerran...C 5
12 Cilgwyn...C 4
13 Ciliau Aeron...A 8
13 Cilmaengwyn...F 10
50 Cilmalieu...B 6
20 Cilmery...G 5
12 Cilrhedyn...D 6
13 Cilsan...E 9
29 Ciltalgarth...F 8
12 Cilwendeg...C 6
13 Cilybebyll...F 10
13 Cil-y-cwm...C 11
15 Cinderford...C 10
12 Cippyn...B 5
16 Cirencester...D 1
40 Citadilla...E 2
28 City Dulas...B 4
57 Clach Bharraig...J 5
46 Clachaig, Argyll...A 6
57 Clachaig, Inver...H 6
50 Clachan, Argyll...C 6
50 Clachan, Argyll...F 5
51 Clachan, Argyll...F 9
46 Clachan, Argyll...D 3
62 Clachan, Inver...E 5
52 Clachan, Perth...A 3
47 Clachan of Campsie A 11
46 Clachan of Glendaruel A 5
50 Clachan-Seil...F 5
46 Clachbreck...B 3
59 Clachnabrain...L 1
60 Clachtoll...D 2
52 Clackavoid...A 6
52 Clackmannan...H 4
52 Clackmannan, Co. G 4
56 Clackmarras...D 8
19 Clacton on Sea...B 11
47 Cladance...E 11
51 Cladich...E 8
50 Claggan...C 4
62 Claigan...C 2
22 Claines...F 2
60 Clais Charnach...A 4
60 Claisfearn...C 3
7 Clandown...A 10
9 Clanfield, Hants...D 8
16 Clanfield, Oxon...D 4
8 Clanville...A 5
46 Claonaig...D 4
35 Clap Gate...B 12
11 Clap Hill...D 9
8 Clapgate, Dorset...F 2
13 Clapgate, Herts...A 4
25 Clapham, Beds...K 1
6 Clapham, Devon...H 2
18 Clapham, London F 3
9 Clapham, Sussex E 12
39 Clapham, Yorks...H 9
49 Clappers...D 12
38 Clappersgate...E 6
16 Clapton, Glos...B 3
7 Clapton, Somerset F 7
7 Clapton, Som...A 10
15 Clapton-in-Gordano G 8
4 Clapworthy...D 5
20 Clarach...D 2
12 Clarbeston...E 4
12 Clarbeston Road...E 4
32 Clarborough...B 4
27 Clare...L 1
43 Clarebrand...E 8
43 Clarencefield...E 11
49 Clarilaw...G 8
49 Clarilawmoor...F 8
9 Clarken Green...A 7
47 Clarkston...D 10
61 Clashcoig...G 7
58 Clashindarroch...D 2
58 Clashmore...G 7
60 Clashnessie...D 2
57 Clashnoir...G 8
52 Clathy...E 5
52 Clathymore...E 5
58 Clatt...E 3
20 Clatter...C 5
8 Clatterford...G 6
59 Clattering Bridge...J 4
42 Clatteringshawes...D 6
6 Clatworthy...C 4
30 Claughton, Ches...A 2
34 Claughton, Lancs...A 4
34 Claughton, Lancs...C 4
6 Clavelshay...C 6
22 Claverdon...F 5
15 Claverham...H 8
25 Clavering...M 6
22 Claverley...C 2
15 Claverton...H 11
14 Clawdd-coch...F 4
29 Clawddnewydd...E 10
39 Clawthorpe...G 8
4 Clawton...F 2
37 Claxby, Lincs...H 9
33 Claxby, Lincs...C 11
26 Claxton, Norfolk...E 6
36 Claxton, Yorks...A 5
23 Clay...D 9
27 Clay Common...G 8
32 Clay Cross...D 1
57 Claybokie...K 6
23 Claybrooke Magna C 8
23 Claybrooke Parva C 8
23 Claydon, Oxon...G 8
27 Claydon, Suffolk K 4
59 Clayfolds...H 6
44 Claygate, Dumf...E 2
10 Claygate, Kent...D 6
17 Claygate, Surrey H 12
6 Clayhanger, Devon D 4
22 Clayhanger, War...B 4
6 Clayhidon...E 5
8 Clayhill, Hants...E 5
11 Clayhill, Sussex...F 7
58 Claymires...E 7
32 Claypole...E 6
31 Clayton, Staffs...F 7
10 Clayton, Sussex...G 2
35 Clayton, Yorks...D 10
36 Clayton, Yorks...F 2
34 Clayton Green...E 5
35 Clayton West...F 11
34 Clayton-le-Moors D 6
34 Clayton-le-Woods E 4
32 Clayworth...A 4
45 Cleadon...G 12
5 Clearbrook...J 4
15 Clearwell...D 9
40 Cleasby...D 3
64 Cleat...E 2
40 Cleatlam...C 1
38 Cleator...D 3
38 Cleator Moor...D 3
35 Cleckheaton...E 10
21 Clee St. Margaret D 11
21 Cleedownton...D 11
21 Cleehill...E 11
21 Cleestanton...D 11
37 Cleethorpes...F 10
21 Cleeton St. Mary E 11
17 Cleeve, Berks...F 7
15 Cleeve, Somerset...H 8
16 Cleeve Hill...A 1
22 Cleeve Prior...G 4
15 Clehonger...A 8
50 Cleigh...E 6
52 Cleish...G 6
48 Cleland...D 1
50 Clenamacrie...E 6
16 Clench Common...H 3
24 Clenchwarton...C 7
45 Clennell...B 7
22 Clent...D 3
21 Cleobury Mortimer E 12
21 Cleobury North...D 11
56 Clephanton...E 4
47 Clerkland...E 9
49 Clerklands...G 7
64 Clestran...D 1
44 Cleuch Head...B 4
43 Cleuchbrae...D 11
44 Cleuchfoot...E 2
43 Cleuchhead...B 9
43 Cleuchheads...C 12
43 Cleuchside...D 12
16 Clevancy...G 2
15 Clevedon...G 7
40 Cleveland, Co...C 5
40 Cleveland Tontine Inn E 5
34 Cleveleys...C 2
16 Cleverton...F 1
14 Clevis...G 2
7 Clewer...A 8
26 Cley-next-the-Sea A 3
63 Cliasamol...F 2
39 Cliburn...C 8
9 Cliddesden...A 7
50 Cliff...A 4
11 Cliff End...G 7
10 Cliff Woods...A 6
53 Cliffburn...C 11
11 Cliffe, Kent...F 7
36 Cliffe, Yorks...D 4
40 Cliffe, Yorks...D 2
4 Clifford, Devon...D 2
21 Clifford, Herefs...H 8
36 Clifford, Yorks...C 2
22 Clifford Chambers G 5
15 Glifford's Mesne B 10
11 Cliffsend...B 12
25 Clifton, Beds...L 3
31 Clifton, Derby...F 10
15 Clifton, Glos...G 9
34 Clifton, Lancs...D 4
48 Clifton, Midloth...B 4
45 Clifton, Northumb. E 10
32 Clifton, Notts...G 3
16 Clifton, Oxon...A 6
51 Clifton, Perth...D 10
35 Clifton, W. Riding B 10
36 Clifton, W. Riding G 3
39 Clifton, Westmor...C 8
22 Clifton, Worcs...G 2
36 Clifton, Yorks...B 4
22 Clifton Campville A 6
16 Clifton Hampden...E 6
23 Clifton Reynes...G 12
23 Clifton upon Dunsmore...D 8
21 Clifton upon Teme F 12
11 Cliftonville...A 12
9 Climping...F 11
48 Climpy...D 2
7 Clink...A 11
35 Clint...A 11
26 Clint Green...D 3
49 Clintmains...F 8
26 Clippesby...D 7
24 Clipsham...D 1
4 Clipston, Devon...F 5
23 Clipston, N'thants D 10
32 Clipston, Notts...G 4
32 Clipstone...D 3
34 Clitheroe...C 6
30 Clive...H 4
64 Clivocast...B 8
37 Clixby...G 8
29 Clocaenog...E 10
58 Clochan...B 1
13 Clochyrie...F 8
30 Clock Face...A 4
49 Clockmill...D 10
14 Clodock...B 6
7 Cloford...B 10
13 Cloigyn...F 8
58 Clola...C 7
25 Clophill...L 2
25 Clopton...G 2
27 Clopton Green...K 1
38 Close Clark...H 1
43 Closeburn...B 9
43 Closeburnmill...B 10
7 Closworth...E 9
25 Clothall...M 4
40 Clotherholme...H 3
30 Clotton...D 4
35 Clough...F 9
35 Clough Foot...E 8
41 Cloughton...F 10
41 Cloughton Newlands F 10
64 Clousta...D 6
58 Clova, Aberdeen...E 2
59 Clova, Angus...K 1
39 Clove Lodge...C 11
4 Clovelly...D 2
49 Clovenfords...F 7
58 Clovenstone...F 5
56 Cloves...D 7
51 Clovulin...A 7
35 Clow Bridge...D 7
32 Clowne...C 2
25 Clows Top...E 12
55 Cluanie Inn...H 4
55 Cluanie Lodge...H 5
21 Cluddley...A 11
63 Cluer...H 2
21 Clun...D 8
56 Clunas...E 4
21 Clunbury...D 9
56 Clune...E 7
55 Clunes...K 6
21 Clungunford...E 9
58 Clunie, Banff...C 4
52 Clunie, Perth...C 6
21 Clunton...D 9
53 Cluny...H 7
57 Cluny Castle...K 2
30 Clutton, Cheshire E 3
15 Clutton, Som...H 9
29 Clwyd, Co...E 10
14 Clydach, Brec...C 5
13 Clydach, Glam...G 10
14 Clydach Vale...E 3
47 Clydebank...B 10
12 Clydey...C 6
16 Clyffe Pypard...F 2
47 Clynder...A 7
12 Clynderwen...E 5
13 Clyne...G 11
61 Clynekirkton...F 8
61 Clynelish...F 8
28 Clynnog-fawr...E 4
21 Clyro...H 7
6 Clyst Honiton...G 3
6 Clyst Hydon...F 4
6 Clyst St. George G 3
6 Clyst St. Lawrence F 4
6 Clyst St. Mary...G 3

MAP

28 Clywt-y-bont....D 5
20 Cnwch Coch......E 2
58 Coachford........C 2
3 Coad's Green....B 10
32 Coal Aston........B 1
21 Coalbrookdale....B 12
14 Coalbrookvale....C 5
48 Coalburn..........F 1
45 Coalburns........G 9
39 Coalcleugh......A 10
15 Coaley..........D 11
59 Coalford........G 6
47 Coalhall........G 9
19 Coalhill..........D 7
15 Coalpit Heath...F 10
31 Coalpit Hill......E 7
21 Coalport........B 12
52 Coalsnaughton....H 4
53 Coaltown of Balgonie
            G 8
53 Coaltown of Wemyss
            H 8
23 Coalville........A 8
15 Coalway Lane End C 9
7 Coat............D 8
47 Coatbridge......C 12
47 Coatdyke........C 12
16 Coate, Wilts....H 2
16 Coate, Wilts....F 3
16 Coates, Glos....D 1
24 Coates, Hunts....F 4
9 Coates, Sussex...D 11
40 Coatham........C 6
40 Coatham Mundeville
            C 3
43 Coatsgate......A 11
4 Cobbaton........C 5
15 Coberley......C 12
10 Cobham, Kent....A 5
17 Cobham, Surrey .H 11
51 Cobleland......H 12
21 Cobnash........F 10
58 Coburty..........A 7
57 Cock Bridge....H 8
19 Cock Clarks......D 8
21 Cock Gate......F 10
40 Cockayne........E 6
25 Cockayne Hatley..K 4
49 Cockburnspath...B 10
49 Cockenzie and
    Port Seton....B 7
34 Cockerham......B 3
38 Cockermouth....B 4
18 Cockernhoe Green B 1
40 Cockfield, Durham C 2
27 Cockfield, Suffolk .K 2
9 Cocking........D 10
5 Cockington......J 8
7 Cocklake........A 8
45 Cocklaw........F 7
49 Cocklawfoot....G 11
49 Cockles..........B 8
26 Cockley Cley....E 1
58 Cockmuir........D 4
17 Cockpole Green...F 9
30 Cockshutt........G 3
26 Cockthorpe......A 3
6 Cockwood......H 3
15 Cockyard........A 7
3 Codda..........B 9
27 Coddenham......K 4
30 Coddington, Ches..E 3
21 Coddington, Her. H 12
32 Coddington, Notts.E 5
8 Codford St. Mary .B 1
8 Codford St. Peter .B 1
18 Codicote........B 2
9 Codmore Hill....D 12
32 Codnor..........E 1
15 Codrington......F 10
22 Codsall..........B 2
22 Codsall Wood....B 2
14 Coed Ely........F 4
15 Coed Morgan....C 7
28 Coed Ystumgwern H 5
26 Coedana........B 4
14 Coedkernew......F 6
29 Coedpoeth......E 12
21 Coedway........A 9
13 Coed-y-bryn....C 7
15 Coed-y-fedw....C 7
14 Coed-yr-ynys....B 5
14 Coelbren........C 2
5 Coffinswell......J 8
6 Cofton..........H 4
22 Cofton Hacket...E 3
14 Cogan..........G 5
23 Cogenhoe......F 11
19 Coggeshall......B 8
19 Coggeshall Hamlet B 8
57 Coignafearn Lo...F 2
57 Coignafeuinternich H 3
57 Coignascallan....H 3

59 Coilacriech......H 1
57 Coilintuie......J 4
51 Coillaig........E 7
55 Coille Mhorgil....J 5
62 Coillore........D 3
55 Coiltry........J 7
57 Coire Bhachdaidh
    Lodge........M 1
14 Coity..........F 3
60 Colaboll........F 6
2 Colan..........D 6
6 Colaton Raleigh .G 4
62 Colbost........C 1
40 Colburn........E 2
8 Colbury........E 5
14 Colby, I.o.M.....H 1
26 Colby, Norfolk...B 5
39 Colby, Westmor...C 9
14 Colcot..........G 4
16 Cold Ash........G 6
23 Cold Ashby....D 10
16 Cold Ashton....G 10
12 Cold Blow......F 5
23 Cold Brayfield...G 12
33 Cold Hanworth...B 7
30 Cold Hatton....H 5
45 Cold Hesleden...H 12
35 Cold Hiendly....F 12
23 Cold Higham....G 10
40 Cold Kirby......G 5
3 Cold Northcott...A 9
19 Cold Norton....D 8
23 Cold Overton....A 11
39 Coldbeck........E 9
60 Coldbackie......B 6
10 Coldean........G 2
5 Coldeast........H 7
16 Colden Common. D 6
27 Coldfair Green...J 7
24 Coldham........E 5
15 Coldharbour, Glos. D 8
10 Coldharbour, Kent C 4
58 Coldhome......C 3
49 Coldingham ....C 11
52 Coldrain........G 6
11 Coldred........C 11
4 Coldridge......E 6
49 Coldstream....E 11
9 Coldwaltham....D 11
58 Coldwells......D 8
58 Coldwells Croft..E 3
9 Cole..........C 10
18 Cole Green......C 3
8 Cole Henley....A 6
21 Colebatch......D 8
4 Colebrook......F 3
4 Colebrooke......F 6
56 Coleburn......D 8
37 Coleby, Lincs....E 6
33 Coleby, Lincs....D 7
4 Coleford, Devon .F 6
15 Coleford, Glos...C 9
7 Coleford, Som. .A 10
2 Colehill........F 2
10 Coleman's Hatch .E 3
30 Colemere........G 3
9 Colemore........C 8
32 Coleorton......H 1
15 Colerne........G 11
16 Colesbourne....C 1
25 Colesden........K 2
16 Coleshill, Berks..E 3
17 Coleshill, Bucks..E 10
22 Coleshill, War....C 5
6 Colestocks......F 4
10 Colgate........E 1
47 Colgrain........A 8
53 Colinsburgh....G 9
48 Colinton......C 5
46 Colintraive......B 5
26 Colkirk........C 2
63 Coll............C 6
53 Collace........D 7
64 Collafirth......C 7
2 Collamoor Head ..B 2
5 Collaton........L 4
5 Collaton St. Mary .K 7
47 Collenan........F 8
53 Collesie........F 7
4 Colleton Mills ...D 5
18 Collier Row......E 5
10 Collier Street....C 6
18 Collier's End....B 4
58 Collieston......E 8
43 Collin..........D 11
8 Collingbourne Ducis
            A 4
8 Collingbourne
    Kingston......A 4
35 Collingham....C 12
21 Collington......F 12
23 Collingtree......G 11

34 Collins Green....H 4
53 Colliston........C 10
6 Colliton........F 4
59 Collmuir........G 3
58 Collynie........D 6
24 Collyweston....E 1
42 Colmonell......C 3
25 Colmworth......J 2
16 Coln Rogers......C 2
16 Coln St. Aldwyn .D 2
16 Coln St. Dennis..C 2
57 Colnabaichin....H 8
17 Colnbrook......F 11
25 Colne, Hunts....H 5
35 Colne, Lancs.....C 7
27 Colne Engaine...M 2
26 Colney..........E 5
18 Colney Heath....C 2
18 Colney Street....D 2
45 Colpitts Grange..G 8
58 Colpy..........D 4
48 Colquhar........E 6
4 Colscott........D 2
40 Colsterdale......G 2
32 Colsterworth....H 6
32 Colston Bassett..G 4
56 Coltfield........C 7
26 Coltishall......D 6
38 Colton, Lancs....G 5
26 Colton, Norfolk...D 4
31 Colton, Staffs....H 9
36 Colton, W. Riding C 3
35 Colton, W. Riding D 12
21 Colva..........G 7
22 Colwall Green...H 1
22 Colwall Stone...H 1
45 Colwell..........E 8
31 Colwich........H 8
14 Colwinston......G 3
38 Colwith........E 5
9 Colworth......F 10
29 Colwyn Bay......B 8
6 Colyford........G 6
6 Colyton........G 6
44 Comb..........D 6
16 Combe, Berks....H 5
21 Combe, Herefs....F 9
16 Combe, Oxon....C 5
9 Combe Common. B 10
21 Combe Moor....F 9
6 Combe Florey....C 5
4 Combe Martin...A 5
6 Combe Raleigh...F 5
6 Combe St, Nicholas E 6
5 Combebow......G 4
5 Combeinteignhead .J 8
30 Comberbach....C 5
25 Comberton, Cambs.K 5
21 Comberton, Herefs.
            F 10
6 Combpyne......G 6
31 Combridge......F 9
22 Combrook......G 6
31 Combs, Derby....B 9
27 Combs, Suffolk...K 3
6 Combwich......B 6
59 Comers........A 2
20 Comin Capel BetwsG 2
20 Comins-coch....D 2
20 Comins-coch....B 4
58 Comisty........C 3
12 Commercial......E 5
14 Common Coed-y-paen
            D 6
32 Common Side....D 1
41 Commondale....D 7
3 Common Moor...C 9
31 Commonside....F 11
31 Compstall......A 8
43 Compstonend....F 7
16 Compton, Berks..F 6
5 Compton, Devon .J 7
8 Compton, Hants..C 6
9 Compton, Surrey .A 11
9 Compton, Sussex. E 9
16 Compton, Wilts..A 3
7 Compton Abbas .D 12
16 Compton Abdale..C 2
16 Compton Bassett..G 1
16 Compton Beauchamp
            E 4
7 Compton Bishop .A 7
8 Compton
    Chamberlayne ..C 2
15 Compton Dando..H 9
7 Compton Dundon. C 8
15 Compton Greenfield
            F 9
7 Compton Martin .A 8
7 Compton Pauncefoot
            D 10
7 Compton Valence .G 9
52 Comrie, Fife.....H 5

52 Comrie, Perth....E 3
52 Conaglen House ..A 7
46 Conchra........A 5
16 Condicote......A 3
47 Condorrat......B 12
21 Condover......B 10
27 Coney Weston...G 3
9 Coneyhurst Com. D 12
41 Coneysthorpe....H 7
35 Coneythorpe....A 12
58 Confunderland...F 3
3 Congdon's Shop .B 10
43 Congeith........E 9
23 Congerstone....B 7
31 Congham........D 2
30 Congleton......D 7
28 Congl-y-wal....F 6
56 Conicavel........D 5
33 Coningsby......D 9
25 Conington, Cambs. J 4
25 Conington, Hunts. G 3
36 Conisbrough....G 3
33 Conisholme....H 11
37 Coniston, Yorks..D 9
38 Coniston, Lancs...E 5
33 Coniston Cold...B 7
39 Conistone......H 12
29 Connah's Quay ..C 12
50 Connel..........D 6
47 Connel Park....H 11
47 Connelbush....H 12
3 Connor Downs...F 3
56 Cononbridge....D 1
35 Cononley........B 8
31 Consall........E 8
45 Consett........H 9
40 Constable Burton..F 2
2 Constantine....G 4
2 Constantine Bay..B 6
54 Contin..........D 8
56 Contullich......C 2
49 Conundrum.....D 12
59 Conveth Mains...K 5
56 Convinth......F 1
29 Conwy..........B 7
11 Conyer..........B 8
11 Conyer's Green...H 2
10 Cooden........G 6
12 Coombs........F 4
56 Cooperhill......D 6
10 Cooper's Corner..C 4
10 Cooper's Green...F 4
18 Coopersale Com...D 5
9 Cootham......E 12
27 Copdock......L 4
19 Copford Green...B 9
64 Copister........C 7
25 Cople..........K 2
40 Copley..........C 1
36 Copmanthorpe....B 3
2 Coppathorne....A 2
31 Coppenhall......H 7
2 Copperhouse....F 3
25 Coppingford....G 3
7 Coppleridge....D 11
25 Copplestone....K 2
34 Coppull........F 4
34 Coppull Moor....F 4
10 Copsale........F 1
34 Copster Green...D 5
22 Copt Heath....D 5
40 Copt Hewick....H 4
23 Copt Oak......A 8
10 Copthorne......D 2
7 Copyside......F 8
6 Copy's Green....B 2

8 Copythorne......E 5
45 Corbridge......G 8
23 Corby..........C 12
33 Corby Glen......H 7
21 Coreley........E 11
17 Cores End......E 10
6 Corfe..........D 6
8 Corfe Castle....H 1
8 Corfe Mullen....F 1
21 Corfton........D 10
57 Corgariff........J 8
9 Corhampton....D 7
10 Cork's Pond....D 5
22 Corley..........D 6
22 Corley Ash......C 6
22 Corley Moor....D 6
48 Cormiston......F 3
51 Cormonachan...H 9
53 Cormuir........A 8
57 Corndavon Lodge .J 8
40 Cornforth......B 3
58 Cornhill........B 3
49 Cornhill-on-TweedE 11
45 Cornhills......E 8
35 Cornholme......D 8
25 Cornish Hall End..L 8
40 Cornsay........A 2
40 Cornsay Colliery ..A 2
14 Corntown, Glam. .G 3
56 Corntown, Ross &
    Cromarty....D 1
59 Corntulloch......H 2
3 Cornwall, County .C 8
16 Cornwell........A 4
5 Cornwood......K 5
5 Cornworthy....K 7
55 Corpach........M 5
26 Corpusty......C 4
51 Corran, Argyll...A 7
55 Corran, Inver....J 2
46 Corranbuie......C 3
38 Corrany........G 2
55 Corribeg........L 4
46 Currie..........E 5
43 Corrie Common .C 12
46 Corriecravie....G 4
54 Corriefeol......E 6
55 Corriegour......K 6
54 Corriemoillie....C 7
60 Corriemulzie Lo..G 4
57 Corrievorrie....G 3
54 Corrievuic......E 6
55 Corrimony......G 7
19 Corringham, Essex F 7
32 Corringham, Lincs.A 6
20 Corris..........B 3
51 Corrour Shooting
    Lodge........A 11
51 Corrow........G 9
62 Corry..........F 6
56 Corry of Ardnagrask
            E 1
46 Corrygills......F 5
55 Corryhully......L 3
60 Corrykinloch....E 5
52 Corrymuckloch...D 4
50 Corrynachenchy..C 4
49 Corsbie........E 8
7 Corscombe......F 8
58 Corse, Aberdeen .D 3
58 Corse, Aberdeen .B 7
59 Corse House....G 3
58 Corse of Kinnoir..C 3
59 Corsebauld......J 5
58 Corsehill........B 7
42 Corsemalzie....F 4
15 Corsham......G 11
59 Corsindae......G 4
7 Corsley........B 11
7 Corsley Heath...B 11
47 Corsliehill......C 9
43 Corsock........D 8
15 Corston, Glos...F 12
15 Corston, Som...H 10
48 Corstorphine....B 5
59 Cortachy Castle ..L 1
26 Corton, Suffolk...F 8
8 Corton, Wilts....B 11
7 Corton Denham ..D 9
51 Coruanan Lodge ..A 8
29 Corwen........F 10
7 Coryates......H 9
5 Coryton, Devon..G 3
19 Coryton, Essex...F 7
23 Cosby..........C 9
22 Coseley........C 3
17 Cosgrove......H 11
9 Cosham........F 8
12 Coshaston......G 3
52 Coshieville....B 3
32 Cossall........F 2
23 Cossington....A 9
64 Costa..........B 2

26 Costessey........D 5
32 Costock........H 3
32 Coston, Leics....H 6
26 Coston, Norfolk...E 4
44 Cote............C 1
30 Cotebrook......D 4
14 Cotehill........H 3
31 Cotes, Staffs.....G 7
39 Cotes, Westmor...F 7
23 Cotesbach......D 8
32 Cotgrave........G 3
58 Cothall........F 6
32 Cotham........E 5
6 Cothelstone....C 5
39 Cotherstone....C 12
16 Cothill, Berks...D 6
49 Cothill, Berwick .D 10
6 Cotleigh........F 5
32 Cotmanhay......F 2
25 Coton, Cambs....J 5
23 Coton, Northants.E 10
31 Coton, Staffs.....H 7
31 Coton, Staffs.....G 8
31 Coton Clanford .H 7
22 Coton in the Elms. A 6
31 Coton in the Clay G 10
5 Cott............K 6
34 Cottam, Lancs...D 4
32 Cottam, Notts....B 5
56 Cottartown......F 6
25 Cottenham......H 5
39 Cotterdale......F 10
18 Cottered........A 3
24 Cotterstock......F 1
23 Cottesbrooke...E 10
23 Cottesmore....A 12
6 Cotteylands....E 3
23 Cottingham,
    Northants....C 11
37 Cottingham, Yks. .D 8
35 Cottingley......C 9
17 Cottisford......A 7
2 Cotton........J 4
25 Cotton End....L 2
58 Cot-town, Aber...E 2
58 Cot-town, Aber. .D 6
31 Cotwalton......G 8
58 Cotwells........B 5
3 Couchsmill......D 8
15 Coughton, Herefs..B 9
22 Coughton, War...F 4
46 Coulaghailtro...C 2
54 Coulags........E 3
54 Coulderan......E 2
54 Coulin Lodge ...D 4
59 Coull..........G 3
47 Coulport........A 7
18 Coulsdon......H 3
8 Coulston......A 1
48 Coulter........F 3
40 Coulton........H 6
21 Cound..........B 11
40 Coundon, Durham B 3
22 Coundon, War...D 6
40 Coundon Grange..B 2
39 Countersett......F 11
23 Countesthorpe...C 9
6 Countess......B 3
6 Countess Wear..G 3
4 Countisbury....A 6
53 Coupar Angus...C 7
49 Coupland......F 12
6 Couple Cross....B 3
46 Cour..........E 3
43 Courance......C 11
17 Court Corner....H 7
13 Court Henry....E 9
55 Courteachan....K 1
23 Courteenhall...G 11
19 Courtsend......E 10
6 Courtway......C 5
48 Cousland......C 6
10 Cousleywood....E 5
46 Coustonn......B 6
6 Cove, Devon....D 3
47 Cove, Dunbarton .A 7
9 Cove, Hampshire A 10
54 Cove, Ross & Crom.
            A 2
59 Cove Bay......G 7
27 Covehithe......G 8
22 Coven..........A 3
25 Coveney......G 6
37 Covenham St.
    Bartholomew..H 11
37 Covenham St. Mary
            H 11
23 Coventry......D 7
2 Coverack......H 5
40 Coverham......F 1
25 Covington......H 2
22 Cow Honeybourne H 5
39 Cowan Bridge ..G 8

11

MAP
10 Cowbeech......G 5
24 Cowbit......D 4
14 Cowbridge, Glam..G 3
6 Cowbridge, Som..B 3
10 Cowden, Kent....D 3
45 Cowden, Northumb. E 7
52 Cowdenbeath......H 6
48 Cowdenburn......D 5
8 Cowes......F 6
40 Cowesby......F 5
10 Cowfold......F 1
59 Cowie, Kinc....J 6
52 Cowie, Stirling....H 3
45 Cowpen......E 11
40 Cowpen Bewley....C 5
31 Cowers Lane....E 11
6 Cowley, Devon...G 3
15 Cowley, Glos....C 12
18 Cowley, London..F 1
16 Cowley, Oxon....D 6
40 Cowling, N. Riding F 3
35 Cowling, W. Riding C 8
25 Cowlinge....K 8
9 Cowplain......E 8
39 Cowshill......A 10
52 Cowstrandburn..H 5
36 Cowthorpe......B 2
17 Cox Green......F 9
30 Coxbank......F 5
31 Coxbench......F 12
10 Coxheath......C 6
11 Coxhill......C 11
40 Coxhoe......B 3
7 Coxley......B 8
18 Coxtie Green....D 5
40 Coxwold......G 5
14 Coychurch......F 3
47 Coylton......G 9
57 Coylumbridge....H 5
59 Coynach......G 2
58 Coynachie......D 2
14 Coytrahen......F 2
54 Cozae Lodge....F 6
22 Crabbs Cross....F 4
10 Crabtree......F 1
61 Crackaig......F 9
39 Crackenthorpe..C 9
2 Crackington......B 2
2 Crackington Haven B 2
22 Crackley......E 6
22 Crackley bank....A 1
39 Crackpot......E 12
35 Cracoe......A 8
6 Craddock......E 4
22 Cradley......G 1
22 Cradley Heath....D 3
14 Cradoc......A 3
3 Crafthole......D 10
45 Cragend......C 9
35 Cragg......E 8
51 Craggan, Dunb..H 10
57 Craggan, Moray..G 6
60 Craggan, Ross & Cromarty......G 4
56 Craggiemore......F 3
45 Craghead......H 10
58 Craibstone, Aber..F 6
58 Craibstone, Banff..B 2
53 Craichie......B 10
42 Craig, Ayr......A 5
43 Craig, Kirk......D 7
43 Craig, Kirk......E 8
54 Craig, Ross & Crom. E 4
46 Craig Lodge......B 5
14 Craig Penllyn....F 3
13 Craig Trebanos..G 10
52 Craiganour Lodge.A 1
55 Craigard......J 7
55 Craigbeg......L 8
42 Craigcaffie......E 2
13 Craig-cefn-parc..G 10
58 Craigdam......E 6
43 Craigdarroch,Dumf C8
43 Craigdarroch, Ayr.A 7
42 Craigdews......D 6
54 Craigdhu......F 8
58 Craigearn......F 5
56 Craigellachie......E 8
42 Craigencallie......D 6
42 Craigencross......E 1
48 Craigend, Lanark..F 1
52 Craigend, Perth...E 6
47 Craigendoran......A 8
42 Craigengillan......A 5
42 Craigenrae......C 4
47 Craigens......G 10
59 Craiggiecat......H 6
56 Craighead, Banff..F 8
48 Craighead, Lanark G 2
58 Craigie, Aberdeen..F 6

47 Craigie, Ayr......F 9
52 Craigie, Perth.....C 6
43 Craigieburn......A 11
48 Craiglockhart......B 4
42 Craimalloch......B 5
58 Craigmaud......B 6
46 Craigmore......C 6
59 Craigmoston......K 4
30 Craignant......G 1
42 Craigneil......C 2
43 Craigneston......C 8
47 Craigneuk......D 12
50 Craignure......D 4
59 Craigo......L 4
52 Craigow......F 6
53 Craigrothie......F 8
53 Craigs......G 7
59 Craigton, Aber...G 6
53 Craigton, Angus..C 10
53 Craigton, Angus...B 8
47 Craigton, Lanark D 10
54 Craigton, Ross & Cromarty......F 3
56 Craigton, Ross & Cromarty......E 2
61 Craigtown......B 9
13 Craig-y-Duke...G 10
14 Craig-y-nos......C 2
44 Craik......B 2
53 Crail......F 11
49 Crailing......G 9
49 Crailinghall......G 9
36 Craiselound......G 5
48 Cramalt......G 5
36 Crambe......A 5
45 Cramlington......E 11
48 Cramond......B 5
48 Cramond Bridge..B 4
55 Cranachan......L 7
30 Cranage......C 6
31 Cranberry......G 7
58 Cranbog......F 7
8 Cranborne......E 2
17 Cranbourne......G 10
10 Cranbrook......D 6
10 Cranbrook Com..D 6
35 Crane Moor......G 11
25 Cranfield......L 1
18 Cranford......F 1
23 Cranford St. Andrew D 12
23 Cranford St. John D 12
15 Cranham, Glos...C 12
18 Cranham, London.E 6
34 Crank......G 4
9 Cranleigh......B 12
8 Cranmore......G 5
58 Cranna......B 4
58 Crannach......B 2
50 Crannich......C 2
23 Cranoe......C 11
27 Cransford......J 6
49 Cranshaws......C 9
38 Cranstal......F 2
37 Cranswick......B 8
2 Crantock......D 5
33 Cranwell......E 7
26 Cranwich......F 1
26 Cranworth......E 3
42 Cranyard......H 2
5 Crapstone......J 4
51 Crarae......H 7
60 Crask Inn......E 6
54 Crask of Aigas...E 8
54 Craskie......F 7
59 Craskins......G 3
45 Craster......A 10
27 Cratfield......H 6
59 Crathes......H 5
57 Crathie......K 1
40 Crathorne......D 5
21 Craven Arms....D 10
45 Crawcrook......G 9
48 Crawford......G 2
48 Crawfordjohn......G 2
43 Crawfordton......B 9
47 Crawick......H 12
8 Crawley, Hants...C 6
16 Crawley, Oxon....C 4
10 Crawley, Sussex...D 1
10 Crawley Down....D 2
39 Crawley Side....A 12
35 Crawshaw Booth..E 7
59 Crawton......J 6
14 Cray, Brec......B 2
39 Cray, Yorks......G 11
18 Crayford......F 5
40 Crayke......H 6
19 Crays Hill......E 7
17 Crazies Hill......F 9
50 Creach Bheinn Lodge E 4

4 Creacombe......D 7
51 Creag a' Phuill...G 8
51 Creagan......C 7
46 Creagan Beag.....A 3
51 Creaguaineach Lodge A 10
23 Creaton......E 10
44 Creca......F 1
21 Credenhill......H 10
21 Crediton......F 7
42 Creebank......D 4
42 Creebridge......E 5
6 Creech Heathfield.D 6
6 Creech St. Michael D 6
2 Creed......E 6
42 Creekmouth......F 5
42 Creeside......C 4
27 Creeting St. Mary.J 4
24 Creeton......D 1
42 Creetown......F 6
51 Cregerina......G 7
51 Creggans......G 8
38 Cregneish......H 1
38 Creg-ny-Baa......G 2
53 Creich......E 8
14 Creigiau......F 4
54 Crelevan......F 7
5 Cremyll......D 11
21 Cressage......B 11
17 Cresselly......F 4
17 Cressex......E 9
19 Cressing......B 8
45 Cresswell, Northumb. D 11
12 Cresswell, Pemb..F 4
31 Cresswell, Staffs..F 8
32 Creswell......C 2
27 Cretingham......J 5
46 Cretshengan......C 2
30 Crew Green......A 8
30 Crewe, Cheshire..E 3
30 Crewe, Cheshire..E 6
8 Crewkerne......E 7
51 Crianlarich......E 11
13 Cribyn......B 8
28 Criccieth......F 4
31 Crich, Derby......E 12
15 Crick, Mon......E 8
23 Crick, Northants..E 9
20 Crickadarn......H 6
7 Cricket Malherbie.E 7
7 Cricket St. Thomas E 7
30 Crickheath......H 2
14 Crickhowell......B 5
16 Cricklade......E 2
18 Cricklewood......E 3
36 Cridling Stubbs...E 3
52 Crieff......E 3
21 Criggian......A 8
35 Crigglestone......E 11
58 Crimond......B 8
58 Crimonmogate......B 8
24 Crimplesham......E 7
54 Crinaglack......F 8
50 Crinan......H 5
26 Cringleford......E 5
12 Crinow......F 5
6 Cripplestyle......E 3
10 Cripp's Corner....F 6
38 Croasdale......C 3
4 Crock Street......E 7
10 Crockenhill......A 4
5 Crockernwell......G 6
5 Crockerton......B 11
43 Crocket or Ninemile Bar......D 9
36 Crockey Hill......B 4
10 Crockham Hill....C 3
10 Crockhurst Street .D 5
19 Crockleford Hth..A 10
21 Crockmeole......A 9
14 Croes-Hywel......C 6
14 Croeserw......B 3
12 Croes-goch......D 2
13 Croes-lan......C 7
28 Croesor......F 6
14 Croes-y-ceiliog...E 6
14 Croesyceiliog......E 7
14 Croes-y-mwyalch.E 6
12 Croft, Cards......C 5
34 Croft, Lancs......H 5
23 Croft, Leics......C 8
33 Croft, Lincs......D 12
40 Croft, Yorks......D 3
47 Croftamie......A 9
47 Crofthead......E 12
52 Croftmill......C 3
57 Croftmore......H 5
57 Croftnahaven......H 5
35 Crofton, Wilts...H 4
35 Crofton, Yorkshire E 12
43 Crofts......D 8
58 Crofts of Belnagoak C 6

58 Crofts of Haddo..D 6
58 Crofts of Hillbrae .C 3
58 Crofts of Meikle Ardo D 6
38 Crofts of Savoch..B 8
58 Crofts of Shanquhar D 3
13 Crofty......G 8
50 Croggan......E 4
44 Croglin......H 4
43 Crogo......D 8
60 Croick......G 5
56 Cromarty......C 3
58 Cromasag......D 4
58 Cromblet......D 5
57 Cromdale......G 6
18 Cromer, Herts....A 3
26 Cromer, Norfolk..A 5
31 Cromford......E 11
15 Cromhall......E 10
15 Cromhall Com...E 10
63 Cromore......E 5
57 Cromra......K 1
32 Cromwell......C 2
47 Cronan......E 10
47 Cronberry......G 11
9 Crondall......A 9
38 Cronk-y-Voddy...G 2
10 Cronton......A 4
40 Crook, Durham...B 2
39 Crook, Westmor...F 7
56 Crook of Alves...D 7
52 Crook of Devon ..G 5
34 Crooke......F 4
47 Crookedholm......F 9
48 Crookedstane......H 1
32 Crookes......B 1
16 Crookham, Berks.H 6
49 Crookham, Northumb. F 11
9 Crookham Village.A 9
49 Crookham Westfield F 11
48 Crookhaugh......G 4
49 Crookhouse......G 10
39 Crooklands......G 8
47 Crookston......C 10
49 Crookston North Mains......D 7
22 Croome Court....H 2
23 Cropredy......G 8
23 Cropston......A 9
22 Cropthorne......H 3
41 Cropton......F 8
32 Cropwell Bishop .G 4
32 Cropwell Butler...F 4
47 Crosbie......D 7
43 Crosby, Cumb....H 11
38 Crosby, I.o.M....G 2
34 Crosby, Lancs....G 2
36 Crosby, Lincs....F 6
40 Crosby Court....F 4
39 Crosby Garrett...D 9
39 Crosby Ravensworth D 8
43 Crosby Villa......H 11
7 Croscombe......B 9
7 Cross......A 7
15 Cross Ash......B 7
10 Cross-at-Hand....C 6
20 Cross Foxes......A 3
35 Cross Gates......D 12
27 Cross Green......K 2
13 Cross Hands, Carm. F 9
15 Cross Hands, Glos. F 9
12 Cross Hands, Pemb. F 4
35 Cross Hills......C 9
21 Cross Houses....B 11
10 Cross in Hand....F 4
13 Cross Inn, Cards..A 7
13 Cross Inn, Cards..A 9
13 Cross Inn, Carm..D 11
14 Cross Inn, Glam..F 4
10 Cross Keys, Kent .C 4
15 Cross Keys, Wilts.G 11
2 Cross Lanes, Corn. G 4
30 Cross Lanes, Denb. F 2
7 Cross Lanes, Dorset F 11
36 Cross Lanes, Yorks. A 3
63 Cross North Dell..A 6
14 Cross Oak......B 4
58 Cross of Jackson..D 5
31 Cross o'th Hands .F 11
27 Cross Street......H 5
46 Crossaig......D 5
63 Crossbost......D 5
43 Crosscanonby....H 11
48 Crosscleuch......G 5

26 Crossdale Street...B 5
34 Crossens......E 3
48 Crossford, Fife....A 3
48 Crossford, Lanark E 1
24 Crossgate......C 3
48 Crossgatehall......C 6
52 Crossgates, Fife...H 6
20 Crossgates, Rad...F 6
40 Crossgates, Yorks. H 2
39 Crossgill, Cumb...A 9
34 Crossgill, Lancs...A 4
42 Crosshill, Ayr....E 5
47 Crosshill, Ayr....G 9
52 Crosshill, Fife....G 6
47 Crosshouse......F 9
44 Crossings......E 3
14 Crosskeys......E 5
61 Crosskirk......A 10
38 Crosslands......F 6
30 Crosslanes......H 2
48 Crosslee......G 6
47 Crosslees......D 10
43 Crossmichael......E 8
34 Crossmor......C 3
10 Crosspost......F 1
47 Crossroads, Ayr...F 9
59 Crossroads, Kinc..H 5
35 Crossroads, Yorks.C 9
64 Cross-voe-sand....C 6
56 Crossway, Herefs..A 9
15 Crossway, Mon...B 8
20 Crossway, Rad....G 6
22 Crossway Green...E 2
7 Crossways......G 11
12 Crosswell......C 5
20 Crosswood......E 2
34 Croston......E 4
26 Crostwick......D 6
7 Crouch......C 5
7 Crouch Hill......E 10
8 Croucheston......D 2
16 Croughton......A 6
58 Crovie......A 5
8 Crow......F 3
35 Crow Edge......G 10
15 Crow Hill......B 9
2 Crowan......F 4
10 Crowborough......E 4
10 Crowborough Town E 4
6 Crowcombe......C 5
35 Crowden......G 9
17 Crowell......F 3
23 Crowfield, Northants. H 9
27 Crowfield, Suffolk .J 5
10 Crowhurst, Surrey .C 3
10 Crowhurst, Sussex.G 6
10 Crowhurst Lane End C 3
24 Crowland......D 3
2 Crowlas......F 2
36 Crowle, Lincs....F 5
22 Crowle, Worcs....G 3
17 Crowmarsh Gifford E 7
2 Crown Town......G 3
5 Crownhill......K 4
26 Crownthorpe......E 4
42 Crows......F 4
2 Crows-an-wra....G 1
17 Crowthorne......H 9
16 Crowton......C 4
22 Croxall......A 5
37 Croxby......G 9
34 Croxdale......B 3
31 Croxden......F 9
17 Croxley Green....E 11
23 Croxton, Hunts....J 3
37 Croxton, Lincs....F 8
27 Croxton, Norfolk .G 2
30 Croxton, Staffs....G 6
32 Croxton Kerrial...G 5
47 Croy, Dunb......B 12
54 Croy, Inver......E 4
4 Croyde......B 3
4 Croyde Bay......B 3
23 Croydon, Cambs..K 4
18 Croydon, London .G 3
57 Crubenmore Lo...K 2
58 Cruden Bay......D 8
16 Crudwell......E 1
21 Crug......E 1
2 Crugmeer......B 6
13 Crugybar......C 10
54 Cruive......F 8
63 Crulivig......D 3

14 Crumlin......D 5
3 Crumplehorn......E 9
11 Crundale, Kent ...C 9
11 Crundale, Pemb...E 3
44 Crurie......D 1
6 Cruwys Morchard .E 2
16 Crux Easton......H 5
13 Crwbin......F 8
17 Cryers Hill......D 9
12 Crymmych......D 5
13 Crynant......F 11
54 Cuaig......D 1
23 Cubbington......E 7
2 Cubert......D 5
17 Cublington......B 9
10 Cuckfield......F 2
7 Cucklington......D 10
32 Cuckney......C 3
17 Cuddesdon......D 7
17 Cuddington, Bucks. C 8
30 Cuddington, Ches..C 4
30 Cuddington Heath.F 3
34 Cuddy Hill......C 4
18 Cudham......H 4
5 Cudlipptown......H 4
7 Cudworth, Som...E 7
36 Cudworth, Yorks..F 2
12 Cuffern......E 2
18 Cuffley......D 3
63 Cuiashader......A 6
54 Culaneilan......D 4
56 Culbo......D 2
56 Culbokie......D 2
56 Culburnie......E 1
56 Culcabock......E 2
56 Culcairn......C 2
56 Culcharry......E 4
34 Culcheth......H 5
56 Culcraggie......C 2
52 Culdees......F 4
58 Culdrain......D 3
54 Culduie......F 1
27 Culford......H 1
39 Culgaith......B 8
16 Culham......E 6
46 Culinlongart......H 2
60 Culkien......D 2
60 Culkein Drumbeg .D 3
15 Culkerton......E 12
57 Cullachie......G 5
58 Cullen......A 3
45 Cullercoats......F 12
59 Cullerlie......G 5
56 Cullicudden......C 2
54 Culligran......F 7
35 Cullingworth......D 9
50 Cullipool......F 5
64 Cullivoe......B 8
52 Culloch......E 3
55 Cullochy......J 7
56 Culloden House...E 3
6 Cullompton......E 4
5 Culm Davy......E 5
61 Culmaily......G 8
42 Culmalzie......F 5
21 Culmington......D 10
6 Culmstock......E 5
60 Culnacraig......F 2
43 Culnaightrie......F 8
62 Culnaknock......B 4
42 Culquhirk......F 5
60 Culrain......G 6
48 Culross......A 3
47 Culroy......H 8
42 Culscadden......G 5
59 Culsh......H 1
42 Culshabbin......F 4
64 Culswick......D 6
58 Cultercullen......E 7
58 Cults, Aberdeen...D 3
59 Cults, Aberdeen...G 6
42 Cults, Wigtown...F 5
52 Cultybraggan......E 3
10 Culverstone Green.B 5
33 Culverthorpe......F 7
23 Culworth......G 9
56 Culzie Lodge......C 1
47 Cumberhead......F 12
49 Cumberland Bower D 12
47 Cumbernauld......B 12
33 Cumberworth......C 12
38 Cumbria, Co.....C 5
58 Cuminestown......C 5
49 Cumledge......D 10
44 Cummersdale......H 2
43 Cummertrees......E 12
56 Cummingstown...C 7
47 Cumnock......G 10
16 Cumnor......D 5
44 Cumrew......H 4
43 Cumrue......C 11

MAP
43 Cumstone C 12
44 Cumwhinton H 3
44 Cumwhitton H 3
40 Cundall H 4
47 Cunninghamhead E 8
64 Cunnister B 7
53 Cupar F 8
53 Cupar Muir F 8
8 Cupernnam D 5
31 Curbar C 11
16 Curbridge, Oxon C 4
9 Curdbridge, Hants. E 7
22 Curdworth C 5
54 Curin D 7
6 Curland E 6
42 Currarie B 2
16 Curridge G 6
48 Currie C 4
7 Curry Mallet D 7
7 Curry Rivel D 7
10 Curtisden Green D 6
2 Cury G 4
58 Cushnie B 5
6 Cushuish C 5
21 Cusop H 8
64 Cusvie B 3
42 Cutcloy H 5
6 Cutcombe B 3
48 Cuthill, Midloth. B 6
61 Cuthill, Suther. H 8
22 Cutnall Green E 2
16 Cutsdean A 2
31 Cutthorpe C 11
17 Cuxham E 7
10 Cuxton A 6
37 Cuxwold G 9
29 Cwm, Flint C 10
14 Cwm, Mon. D 5
20 Cwm-Cewydd A 4
12 Cwm Cych C 6
13 Cwm-Duad D 7
14 Cwm Ffrwd Oer D 6
20 Cwm Irfon G 4
13 Cwm-Mawr F 8
12 Cwm Morgan D 6
29 Cwm-Penmachno E 7
14 Cwmaman D 3
14 Cwmann B 9
13 Cwmavon H 11
12 Cwm-bach, Carm. D 6
12 Cwm-bach, Glam. D 4
20 Cwm-bach, Rad. G 6
21 Cwm-bach, Rad. H 7
20 Cwmbelan D 5
14 Cwmbran E 6
20 Cwmbrwyno D 3
14 Cwmcarn E 5
15 Cwmcarvan D 8
12 Cwmcoy C 6
14 Cwmdare D 3
14 Cwm-du, Brec. B 5
13 Cwm-du, Carm. D 9
14 Cwmfelin, Glam. D 4
14 Cwmfelin, Glam. E 2
12 Cwmfelin Boeth E 5
14 Cwmfelin-fach E 5
12 Cwmfelin-Mynach E 6
13 Cwm-ffrwd E 7
14 Cwmgiedd C 1
13 Cwmgors F 10
13 Cwmgwili F 9
14 Cwmifor D 10
13 Cwmisfael E 8
20 Cwmlline B 4
13 Cwmllyfri F 7
13 Cwmllynfell F 10
12 Cwmmiles E 5
14 Cwm-parc E 3
13 Cwm-pengraig C 7
14 Cwm-rhos B 5
14 Cwmsychpant B 8
14 Cwmtillery D 5
14 Cwmwysg A 2
14 Cwm-y-glo F 9
14 Cwmyoy B 6
20 Cwmystwyth E 3
20 Cwrt B 2
14 Cwrt-newydd B 8
13 Cwrt-y-Cadno C 10
14 Cwrt-y-defaid F 1
14 Cwrt-y-gollen C 6
28 Cwym-y-glo D 5
14 Cymmer, Glam. E 3
14 Cymmer, Glam. E 2
14 Cyncoed F 5
13 Cynghordy, Glam. G 10
13 Cynghordy, Carm. C 11
13 Cynheidre F 8
14 Cynonville E 2
29 Cynwyd F 10
13 Cynwyl Elfed D 7
35 Dacre Banks A 10

MAP
23 Dadford H 10
23 Dadlington B 7
13 Dafen G 8
18 Dagenham F 5
16 Daglingworth D 1
17 Dagnall C 10
51 Dail D 8
42 Dailly B 3
57 Dail-na-mine Lo. M 3
53 Dairsie or Osnaburgh E 9
34 Daisy Hill G 5
51 Dalavich F 7
43 Dalbeattie E 9
63 Dalbeg B 3
47 Dalblair G 11
59 Dalbog K 3
38 Dalby H 1
61 Dalchalm F 9
51 Dalchenna G 8
52 Dalchonzie Ho. E 2
60 Dalchork F 6
55 Dalchreichart H 7
52 Dalchruin E 2
54 Dalchuirn F 3
56 Dalcross Station E 3
33 Dalderby D 9
32 Dale, Derby F 2
12 Dale, Pembroke F 2
64 Dale, Shetland Is. D 6
39 Dale Head D 7
41 Dalehouse C 8
50 Dalelia A 5
57 Dalestie H 7
43 Dalfibble C 11
47 Dalfram G 11
47 Dalgarven E 8
47 Dalgig H 10
52 Dalginross E 3
48 Dalguise B 5
61 Dalhalvaig B 9
25 Dalham J 8
46 Dalinlongart A 6
48 Dalkeith C 6
52 Dall B 1
56 Dallas D 7
47 Dalleagles H 10
27 Dallinghoo K 5
10 Dallington, Sussex F 5
23 Dallington, Northants. F 10
39 Dalmain Dacre C 7
43 Dalmakerran B 8
51 Dalmally E 9
42 Dalmellington A 6
48 Dalmeny B 4
48 Dalmeny Rows B 4
60 Dalmichy F 6
57 Dalmigavie H 3
57 Dalmigavie Lodge G 3
63 Dalmore, Lewis B 3
56 Dalmore, Ross & Cromarty C 2
56 Dalmore, Ross & Cromarty B 1
47 Dalmuir B 10
56 Dalmunach E 8
50 Dalnabreck A 4
57 Dalnacardoch Lo. M 3
52 Dalnacarn A 5
57 Dalnahaitnach H 4
61 Dalnamain G 7
57 Dalnaspidal M 2
61 Dalnawillan Lo. C 10
51 Dalness B 9
61 Dalnessie E 7
52 Daloist A 3
52 Dalqueich G 6
42 Dalquhairn B 4
61 Dalreavoch F 7
52 Dalriach A 2
47 Dalry, Ayr D 8
43 Dalry, Kirk. C 7
47 Dalrymple H 8
48 Dalserf D 1
44 Dalston H 2
43 Dalswinton C 10
43 Dalton, Dumf. D 12
34 Dalton, Lancs. F 4
41 Dalton, Northumb. F 9
45 Dalton, Northumb. G 7
40 Dalton, N. Riding G 4
40 Dalton, N. Riding D 1
32 Dalton, W. Riding A 2
40 Dalton Piercy B 5
38 Dalton-in-Furness H 5
45 Dalton-le-Dale H 12
40 Dalton-on-Tees D 3
46 Daltot A 3
42 Dalvadie F 2
52 Dalveich E 1
47 Dalvennan H 9
61 Dalvina Lodge C 7

MAP
43 Dalwhat B 8
57 Dalwhinnie L 2
6 Dalwood F 6
8 Damerham D 3
26 Damgate E 7
42 Damnaglaur H 2
48 Damside D 4
11 Danaway Borden B 7
19 Danbury C 8
41 Danby D 7
40 Danby Wiske E 3
56 Dandaleith E 8
48 Danderhall B 6
18 Dane End B 3
23 Dane Hills B 9
31 Danebridge D 8
10 Danehill E 3
34 Dangerous Corner F 4
40 Dan's Corner A 1
49 Danskine C 8
22 Danzey Green E 5
14 Daren-felen C 5
10 Darenth A 4
30 Daresbury B 4
36 Darfield G 2
11 Dargate B 9
45 Dargues D 7
3 Darite C 9
22 Darlaston C 3
35 Darley A 10
31 Darley Bridge D 11
22 Darlingscott H 6
40 Darlington D 3
30 Darliston G 4
32 Darlton C 5
32 Darnall A 1
56 Darnaway Castle D 5
47 Darnconner G 10
43 Darngarroch E 7
49 Darnick F 8
20 Darowen B 4
58 Darra C 5
4 Darracott, Corn. D 1
4 Darracott, Devon B 3
45 Darras Hall F 9
36 Darrington E 3
27 Darsham H 7
10 Dartford A 4
5 Dartington J 6
5 Dartmeet H 5
5 Dartmouth K 7
35 Darton F 11
47 Darvel F 10
34 Darwen E 6
17 Datchet F 10
18 Datchworth B 3
18 Datchworth Green B 3
34 Daubhill F 6
16 Dauntsey F 1
16 Dauntsey Green F 1
16 Dauntsey Lock F 1
30 Davenham C 5
23 Daventry F 9
20 David's Well E 6
48 Davidson's Mains B 5
56 Davidston C 3
3 Davidstow A 8
44 Davington C 1
58 Daviot, Aberdeen E 5
56 Daviot, Inverness F 3
17 Davis Street G 9
58 Davoch of Grange C 2
35 Daw Cross B 11
10 Dawesgreen C 1
30 Dawley B 12
21 Dawley Bank B 12
21 Dawley Magna B 12
5 Dawlish H 8
7 Dawlish Wake E 7
6 Dawlish Warren H 3
29 Dawn C 8
19 Daws Heath E 8
3 Daw's House A 10
24 Dawsmere C 5
38 Dawthwaitehead C 6
16 Daylesford B 3
44 Deadwater C 4
47 Deadwaters E 12
11 Deal C 12
38 Dean, Cumb. C 3
4 Dean, Devon B 4
4 Dean, Devon B 5
5 Dean, Devon J 6
8 Dean, Dorset D 1
9 Dean, Hants. D 7
7 Dean, Somerset B 10
5 Dean Prior J 6
31 Dean Row B 7
10 Dean Street C 6
44 Deanburnhaugh B 2
9 Deane A 7
60 Deanich Lodge H 5
8 Deanland D 2

MAP
38 Deanscales C 3
23 Deanshanger Hill H 11
52 Deanston G 2
38 Dearham B 3
27 Debach K 5
25 Debden, Essex M 7
18 Debden Estate D 4
25 Debden Green M 7
27 Debenham J 5
48 Dechmont B 3
16 Deddington A 6
27 Dedham M 4
59 Deebank H 4
59 Deecastle H 2
23 Deene C 12
24 Deenethorpe F 1
17 Deepcut H 10
24 Deeping Gate E 3
24 Deeping St. James E 3
24 Deeping St. Nicholas D 3
58 Deerhill B 2
15 Deerhurst A 11
64 Deerness D 3
22 Defford H 3
14 Defynnog B 2
29 Deganwy B 7
40 Deighton, N. Riding E 4
35 Deighton, W. Riding E 10
36 Deighton C 4
28 Deiniolen D 5
3 Delabole A 8
30 Delamere C 4
42 Delamford B 4
56 Delchirach F 7
58 Delfrigs E 7
57 Dell Lodge H 6
56 Delliefure F 6
57 Delnabo H 7
57 Delnadamph Lo. J 8
57 Delnamer M 7
48 Deloraineshiel H 6
35 Delph F 8
45 Delves H 9
24 Dembleby B 1
36 Denaby G 3
36 Denaby Main G 3
43 Denbie Mains D 11
29 Denbigh D 10
5 Denbury J 7
32 Denby F 1
35 Denby Dale F 11
16 Denchworth E 5
58 Denend D 3
25 Denford H 1
19 Dengie D 9
17 Denham, Bucks. E 11
27 Denham, Suffolk H 5
27 Denham, Suffolk J 1
58 Denhead, Aber. B 7
58 Denhead, Aber. E 7
53 Denhead, Fife F 9
49 Denholm G 8
35 Denholme D 9
9 Denmead E 8
27 Dennington H 6
48 Denny A 1
10 Denny Bottom D 4
8 Denny Lodge E 5
48 Dennyloanhead A 1
35 Denshaw F 8
59 Denside H 5
27 Denston K 1
31 Denstone F 9
39 Dent F 9
39 Dent Station F 10
25 Denton, Hunts. G 2
11 Denton, Kent C 11
35 Denton, Lancs. H 8
32 Denton, Lincs. G 6
27 Denton, Norfolk G 6
23 Denton, Northants. F 11
17 Denton, Oxon D 7
10 Denton, Sussex H 3
40 Denton, N. Riding C 2
35 Denton, W. Riding B 10
24 Denver E 7
45 Denwick B 10
45 Denwick Lane End A 10
26 Deopham E 3
26 Deopham Green F 3
4 Deptford, Devon D 5
4 Deptford, Devon D 1
18 Deptford, London F 4
8 Deptford, Wilts. B 2
31 Derby G 11
38 Derbyhaven H 1
32 Derbyshire, Co. D 11
52 Derculich B 4

MAP
42 Dergoals F 3
14 Deri D 5
20 Deri-Odwyn F 2
52 Derry E 1
15 Derry Hill G 12
50 Derryguaig D 2
11 Derringstone C 10
31 Derrington H 7
36 Derrythorpe F 6
24 Dersingham C 8
50 Dervaig B 2
29 Derwen E 10
13 Derwlwyn C 9
23 Desborough D 11
23 Desford B 8
45 Detchant B 12
11 Detling B 7
29 Deuddwr H 11
15 Devauden D 8
59 Devenick G 7
20 Devil's Bridge E 3
16 Devizes H 1
4 Devon, County F 5
48 Devonburn E 1
3 Devonport D 11
52 Devonside G 4
2 Devoran F 5
48 Dewar D 6
7 Dewlish F 11
15 Dewsall Court A 8
35 Dewsbury E 11
38 Dhoon G 2
38 Dhoor F 2
38 Dhowin F 2
9 Dial Post D 12
8 Dibden E 5
8 Dibden Purlieu E 5
27 Dickleburgh G 4
16 Didbrook A 2
16 Didcot E 6
25 Diddington J 3
21 Diddlebury D 10
15 Didley A 7
9 Didling D 10
15 Didmarton F 11
35 Didsbury H 7
5 Didworthy J 5
60 Diebidale Lodge H 5
33 Digby E 8
62 Digg A 4
35 Diggle F 9
34 Digmoor G 4
18 Digswell Water B 3
13 Dihewid A 8
47 Dikeneuk D 11
26 Dilham C 6
31 Dilhorne F 8
48 Dillarburn E 1
25 Dillington J 2
45 Dilston G 8
7 Dilton Marsh A 11
21 Dilwyn G 9
48 Dinanrig H 1
28 Dinas, Caer. G 3
12 Dinas, Carm. D 6
12 Dinas, Pemb. C 4
20 Dinas Mawddwy A 4
14 Dinas Powis G 5
13 Dinasbach C 11
7 Dinder B 9
15 Dinedor A 8
15 Dinedor Cross A 8
15 Dingestow C 7
30 Dingle B 2
49 Dingleton F 8
23 Dingley C 11
56 Dingwall D 1
44 Dinlabyre D 4
44 Dinley C 3
59 Dinnet H 2
43 Dinning C 9
45 Dinnington, Northumb. F 10
7 Dinnington, Som. E 7
28 Dinorwic D 5
40 Dinsdale Station D 4
17 Dinton, Bucks. C 8
8 Dinton, Wilts. C 2
42 Dinvin F 1
43 Dinwoodie Mains C 11
43 Dinwoodiegreen C 11
4 Dinworthy D 2
46 Dippen F 3
9 Dippenhall A 9
46 Dippin G 5
42 Dipple, Ayr A 3
58 Dipple, Moray B 1
5 Diptford K 6
45 Dipton H 9
49 Dirleton A 8
21 Discoed F 8
32 Diseworth H 2
40 Dishforth H 4

MAP
31 Disley B 8
27 Diss G 4
20 Disserth G 6
38 Distington C 2
8 Ditchampton C 2
7 Ditcheat C 9
26 Ditchingham F 6
10 Ditchling F 2
15 Ditteridge G 11
5 Dittisham K 7
10 Ditton, Kent B 6
30 Ditton, Lancs. B 3
25 Ditton Green J 8
21 Ditton Priors D 11
57 Divach G 1
13 Divlyn C 11
16 Dixton, Glos. A 1
15 Dixton, Mon. C 8
35 Dobcross F 8
3 Dobwalls C 9
5 Doccombe G 6
56 Dochfour House F 2
56 Dochgarroch F 2
26 Docking B 1
21 Docklow G 11
38 Dockray C 6
44 Dodburn B 3
18 Doddinghurst D 6
24 Doddington, Cambs. F 5
11 Doddington, Kent B 8
32 Doddington, Lincolnshire C 6
49 Doddington, Northumb. F 12
21 Doddington, Salop. E 11
6 Doddiscombsleigh H 2
23 Dodford, Northants. F 9
22 Dodford, Worcs. E 3
15 Dodington, Glos. F 10
6 Dodington, Som. B 5
30 Dodleston D 2
35 Dodworth G 11
32 Doe Lea D 2
6 Dog Village G 3
33 Dogdyke E 9
9 Dogmersfield A 9
20 Dolanog A 6
14 Dolau, Glam. F 3
21 Dolau, Rad F 7
28 Dolbenmaen F 4
20 Dolfach E 5
20 Dol-ffanog A 3
20 Dol-for, Mont. B 4
20 Dol-for, Mont. D 6
29 Dolgarrog C 7
28 Dolgellau H 6
13 Dolgerdd B 7
20 Dol-goch B 2
13 Dol-gran D 8
20 Dolhelfa E 5
61 Doll F 8
52 Dollar G 4
52 Dollarbeg G 4
20 Dolley Green F 8
21 Dolleycanney G 7
34 Dolphinholme B 4
48 Dolphinton E 4
4 Dolton E 4
29 Dolwen, Denb. C 8
20 Dolwen, Mont. B 5
20 Dolwyd B 7
29 Dolwyddelan E 7
20 Dol-y-bont D 2
20 Dolypandy D 2
36 Doncaster G 4
8 Donhead St. Andrew D 1
7 Donhead St. Mary D 12
52 Donibristle H 6
6 Doniford B 4
24 Donington, Lincs. B 3
22 Donington, Salop. B 2
33 Donington on Bain B 9
24 Donington South Ing B 3
22 Donisthorpe A 6
17 Donkey Town H 10
44 Donkleywood D 6
16 Donnington, Berks. G 6
16 Donnington, Glos. A 3
21 Donnington, Salop. B 11
21 Donnington, Salop. A 12
9 Donnington, Sussex F 10
15 Donnington, Worcs. A 10

MAP

21 Donnington Wood A 12
7 Donyatt E 7
47 Doonbank H 9
47 Doonfoot G 8
47 Doonholm H 8
57 Dorback Lodge H 6
7 Dorchester, Dorset G 10
17 Dorchester, Oxon E 7
22 Dordon B 6
31 Dore B 11
56 Dores F 2
32 Dorket Head E 3
10 Dorking C 1
10 Dormans Land D 3
40 Dormanston C 6
21 Dormington H 11
17 Dorney F 10
55 Dornie G 3
61 Dornoch G 8
44 Dornock F 1
61 Dorrery B 10
22 Dorridge E 5
33 Dorrington, Lincs. E 8
21 Dorrington, Salop. B 10
7 Dorset, County F 10
22 Dorsington G 5
21 Dorstone H 8
17 Dorton C 7
55 Dorusduain G 3
54 Dosmuckeran D 6
22 Dosthill B 6
7 Dottery G 8
3 Doublebois C 9
15 Doughton E 12
38 Douglas, I.o.M. H 2
48 Douglas, Lanark F 1
53 Douglas & Angus D 9
28 Douglas Hill D 5
48 Douglas Water F 2
48 Douglas West F 1
53 Douglastown B 9
46 Dougrie F 4
7 Doulting B 10
64 Dounby C 1
55 Doune, Inverness J 1
52 Doune, Perth G 2
42 Dounepark B 3
59 Douneside G 2
60 Dounie G 6
58 Dounie Park B 4
47 Doura F 9
5 Dousland J 4
31 Dove Holes B 9
38 Dovenby B 3
11 Dover D 12
27 Dovercourt M 6
22 Doverdale F 2
31 Doveridge G 9
52 Dowally B 5
34 Dowbridge D 3
16 Dowdeswell B 1
42 Dowhill A 3
14 Dowlais D 4
4 Dowland E 4
16 Down Ampney D 2
15 Down Hatherley B 11
4 Down St. Mary E 6
5 Down Thomas L 4
42 Downan, Ayr C 2
56 Downan, Banff F 7
3 Downderry D 10
18 Downe H 4
16 Downend, Berks. G 6
15 Downend, Glos. A 8
9 Downend, I.o.W. G 7
53 Downfield D 8
3 Downgate B 9
25 Downham, Cambs. G 6
19 Downham, Essex D 7
34 Downham, Lancs. C 6
49 Downham, Northumb. F 11
24 Downham Market E 7
7 Downhead, Som. D 9
7 Downhead, Som. B 10
52 Downhill D 6
34 Downholland Cross F 2
40 Downholme E 1
59 Downies H 7
17 Downley C 9
7 Downside, Som. A 10
7 Downside, Som. B 9
15 Downside, Som. H 8
17 Downside, Surrey H 12
8 Downton, Hants. G 4
8 Downton, Wilts. D 3
21 Downton on the Rock E 9
24 Dowsby C 2

45 Doxford A 10
15 Doynton G 10
14 Draethen F 5
48 Draffan E 1
9 Dragons Green D 12
5 Drakeland Corner K 4
47 Drakemyre D 8
22 Drake's Broughton G 4
22 Drakes Cross D 4
3 Drakewalls C 11
23 Draughton, Northants. D 11
35 Draughton, Yorks. B 9
36 Drax D 5
16 Draycot Foliat F 3
23 Draycote E 8
32 Draycott, Derby G 2
16 Draycott, Glos. A 3
7 Draycott, Som. A 8
31 Draycott in the Clay G 10
31 Draycott in the Moors F 8
4 Drayford E 6
16 Drayton, Berks. E 6
9 Drayton, Hants. E 8
23 Drayton, Leics. C 11
24 Drayton, Lincs. B 4
26 Drayton, Norfolk D 5
23 Drayton, Oxon H 8
23 Drayton, Salop. E 3
7 Drayton, Som. D 7
22 Drayton Bassett B 5
17 Drayton Beauchamp C 10
17 Drayton Parslow A 9
17 Drayton St. Leonard D 7
35 Drebley A 9
13 Dreenhill F 3
13 Dre-fach, Cards. B 8
13 Drefach, Carm. C 7
13 Drefach, Carm. F 8
47 Dreghorn F 8
11 Drellingore N 11
49 Drem A 8
5 Drewsteignton G 6
33 Driby C 11
16 Driffield, Glos. D 2
37 Driffield, Yorks. A 8
38 Drigg E 3
29 Drighlington D 11
51 Drimfern F 8
58 Drimmies E 5
50 Drimnin B 3
50 Drimnin House B 3
7 Drimpton F 7
51 Drimsallie L 3
51 Drimsynie G 9
27 Drinkstone J 3
27 Drinkstone Green J 3
51 Drishaig F 8
48 Drochil E 4
31 Drointon G 9
22 Droitwich F 2
52 Dron F 6
32 Dronfield B 1
31 Dronfield Woodhouse B 11
47 Drongan G 9
53 Dronley D 8
14 Drope G 4
5 Droxford D 7
29 Druid F 9
43 Druidhall B 9
13 Druidsdale J 6
12 Druidston E 2
46 Druim A 2
55 Druimarbin M 5
51 Druimavuic C 7
54 Druimdhu D 5
46 Druimdrishaig B 2
54 Druimindarroch F 8
46 Druimyeon More D 2
52 Drum, Aberdeen E 5
46 Drum, Argyll B 4
52 Drum, Kinc. G 5
56 Drum, Ross & Cromarty D 2
60 Drumbeg D 3
58 Drumblade D 3
58 Drumblair House C 4
42 Drumbreddan G 2
55 Drumbuie, Ross & Cromarty G 2
42 Drumbuie, Kirk. C 6
44 Drumburgh G 1
43 Drumburn E 10
47 Drumchapel B 10
56 Drumchardine E 1
48 Drumclog E 11
43 Drumcoltran E 9

56 Drumcroy F 1
43 Drumcruilton A 9
58 Drumdaig F 3
56 Drumdyre D 2
53 Drumeldrie G 9
48 Drumelzier F 4
62 Drumfearn G 6
47 Drumfork G 10
57 Drumgask K 2
53 Drumgley B 9
57 Drumguish, Inver. J 4
56 Drumguish, Moray F 6
58 Drumhead, Aber. F 7
59 Drumhead, Aber. H 4
42 Drumjohn B 6
43 Drumlanrig Castle B 9
59 Drumlasie G 4
46 Drumlemble B 6
58 Drumligair F 6
59 Drumlithie J 5
42 Drummoddie G 5
56 Drummond C 2
42 Drummore H 2
57 Drumnadrochit G 1
59 Drumnagair K 4
58 Drumnagorrach B 3
58 Drumnahoy F 4
42 Drumpail E 3
42 Drumpark D 9
42 Drumrae G 5
43 Drumrash D 7
60 Drumrunie Lodge F 3
58 Drums E 7
47 Drumshang H 7
43 Drumstinchall G 8
59 Drumtochty Castle J 4
62 Drumuie D 4
57 Drumuillie G 5
52 Drumvaich G 2
42 Drumwalt F 4
42 Drumwhindle D 7
43 Drumwhirn D 8
29 Drury D 12
32 Dry Doddington F 6
25 Dry Drayton J 5
19 Dry Street E 7
39 Drybeck D 9
47 Drybridge F 8
58 Drybridge A 2
15 Drybrook C 9
49 Dryburgh F 8
43 Dryfesdale Gate C 11
48 Dryhope G 5
47 Drymen A 9
58 Drymuir C 6
62 Drynoch E 3
60 Duag Bridge G 4
58 Dubford, Aber. C 5
58 Dubford, Banff A 5
58 Dubiton C 4
60 Duchally E 5
43 Duchrae C 7
8 Duck Street A 5
30 Duckington E 4
16 Ducklington C 4
25 Duck's Cross K 2
25 Duddenhoe End L 6
48 Duddingston B 6
24 Duddington E 1
10 Duddleswell E 3
49 Duddo E 12
30 Duddon D 4
38 Duddon Bridge F 4
45 Dudlees C 21
30 Dudleston F 2
30 Dudleston Heath F 2
45 Dudley, Northants. F 10
22 Dudley, Staffs. C 3
12 Dudwells E 3
31 Duffield F 11
14 Duffryn E 2
58 Dufftown D 1
56 Duffus C 7
39 Dufton C 9
41 Duggleby H 9
62 Duisdalemore G 6
55 Duisky M 4
14 Dukestown C 5
35 Dukinfield G 8
56 Dularich F 1
28 Dulas A 4
58 Dulax F 1
7 Dulcote B 9
6 Dulford F 8
52 Dull B 3
47 Dullatur B 12
25 Dullingham F 6
57 Dulnain Bridge G 5
3 Duloe, Cornwall D 9
25 Duloe, Hunts. J 3
56 Dulsie E 5
6 Dulverton C 3

18 Dulwich G 3
47 Dumbarton B 9
16 Dumbleton A 1
43 Dumcrieff A 11
58 Dumeath D 2
43 Dumfries D 10
47 Dumgoyne A 10
9 Dummer B 7
59 Dun L 4
63 Dun Carloway C 3
57 Dunachtonmore J 4
56 Dunain House E 2
52 Dunalastair A 2
52 Dunan, Perth D 2
51 Dunan, Perth B 11
46 Dunan, Ross & Cromarty B 6
62 Dunan, Skye E 5
51 Dunans H 7
49 Dunbar H 2
52 Dunbeath D 11
52 Dunblane G 3
53 Dunbog E 7
6 Dunboll B 6
8 Dunbridge C 5
61 Duncansby A 12
58 Duncanston, Aber. E 3
56 Duncanston, Ross & Cromarty D 2
6 Dunchideock G 2
23 Dunchurch E 8
23 Duncote G 10
9 Duncow C 10
51 Duncraggan G 12
54 Duncraig Castle F 2
56 Duncrievie F 6
9 Duncton D 11
7 Dundon C 8
47 Dundonald, Ayr. F 8
53 Dundonald, Fife H 7
60 Dundonnell Hotel H 2
60 Dundonnell House H 3
43 Dundraw G 12
43 Dundreggan H 7
43 Dundrennan G 8
15 Dundry H 8
59 Dunecht G 5
48 Dunfermline A 1
35 Dunford Bridge G 10
7 Dunge A 12
52 Dunham C 5
30 Dunham Town B 6
30 Dunham-on-the-Hill C 3
22 Dunhampton E 2
33 Dunholme B 7
52 Dunie C 4
53 Dunino F 10
48 Dunipace A 1
52 Dunira E 2
15 Dunkerton H 10
6 Dunkeswell E 5
11 Dunkirk B 9
10 Dunk's Green C 5
59 Dunlappie K 3
52 Dunley E 1
56 Dunlichity Lodge F 2
47 Dunlop D 7
30 Dunmaglass Lodge G 2
3 Dunmere C 7
52 Dunmore, Stirling H 4
46 Dunmore, Argyll C 3
11 Dunn Street B 7
61 Dunnet A 11
58 Dunnichen B 10
53 Dunninald B 11
52 Dunning E 4
22 Dunnington, War. G 4
37 Dunnington, E. Riding B 9
36 Dunnington, E. Riding B 4
35 Dunnockshaw D 7
59 Dunnottar Mains J 6
58 Dunnydeer E 4
50 Dunollie D 6
58 Dunoon B 6
53 Dunotter G 9
42 Dunragit F 2
58 Dunrostan A 2
49 Duns D 10
16 Duns Tew A 5
24 Dunsby C 2
43 Dunscore C 9
40 Dunscroft F 4
40 Dunsdale C 6
17 Dunsden Green F 8
9 Dunsfold B 11
5 Dunsford G 7
53 Dunshelt F 7

58 Dunshillock C 7
41 Dunsley D 8
17 Dunsmore D 9
34 Dunsop Bridge B 5
50 Dunstaffnage Farm D 6
31 Dunstall H 10
6 Dunster D 2
45 Dunston, Dur. G 10
33 Dunston, Lincs. D 8
26 Dunston, Norfolk E 5
45 Dunston, Northumb. A 10
31 Dunston, Staffs. H 8
5 Dunstone H 6
36 Dunsville F 4
37 Dunswell D 8
48 Dunsyre E 3
44 Dunterley E 6
5 Dunterton D 4
16 Duntisbourne Abbots C 1
16 Duntisbourne Rouse D 1
7 Duntish F 10
47 Duntocher B 9
17 Dunton, Bucks. B 9
26 Dunton, Norfolk C 2
25 Dunton, Oxon L 3
23 Dunton Bassett C 9
10 Dunton Green B 4
18 Dunton Wayletts E 6
62 Duntulm A 3
47 Dunure H 7
47 Dunure Mains H 7
13 Dunvant H 9
62 Dunvegan C 2
9 Dunwich H 8
52 Dupplin Castle E 5
44 Durdar H 2
40 Durham A 3
43 Durisdeer A 10
43 Durisdeermill A 9
6 Durleigh C 6
16 Durley, Wilts. H 3
8 Durley, Hants. D 6
9 Durley Street D 7
60 Durnamuck G 2
60 Durness A 5
58 Durno E 5
9 Durrington, Sussex F 12
8 Durrington, Wilts. B 3
15 Dursley D 10
6 Durston C 6
7 Durweston E 11
64 Dury D 7
23 Duston F 10
57 Duthil G 5
21 Dutlas E 7
18 Duton Hill A 6
3 Dutson A 10
30 Dutton B 4
25 Duxford L 6
53 Dwygyfylchi C 7
28 Dwyran D 4
58 Dyce F 6
45 Dye House G 7
13 Dyfatty G 8
12 Dyfed, Co. D 6
14 Dyffryn, Carm. E 6
14 Dyffryn, Glam. F 4
14 Dyffryn, Glam. E 2
14 Dyffryn, Glam. G 4
12 Dyffryn, Pemb. C 3
28 Dyffryn-Arduddwy H 5
14 Dyffryn Cellwen C 2
20 Dyffryn-castell D 3
4 Dyke, Devon D 2
24 Dyke, Lincs. C 2
56 Dyke, Moray D 5
49 Dykegatehead D 11
59 Dykehead, Angus L 1
48 Dykehead, Lanark C 2
52 Dykehead, Perth G 1
59 Dykelands K 5
53 Dykends A 7
58 Dykeside C 5
20 Dylife C 4
11 Dymchurch E 9
15 Dymock A 10
43 Dyrham G 10
53 Dysart H 8
29 Dyserth B 10
45 Eachwick F 9
34 Eagland Hill C 3
32 Eagle D 6
40 Eaglescliffe Junc. D 4
38 Eaglesfield, Cumb. B 3
44 Eaglesfield, Dumf. F 1
47 Eaglesham D 10
24 Eaglethorpe F 2
38 Eairy H 1

23 Eakley Lanes G 11
32 Eakring D 4
36 Ealand F 6
18 Ealing F 2
39 Eamont Bridge B 7
35 Earby C 8
34 Earcroft E 6
21 Eardington C 12
21 Eardisland F 9
21 Eardisley G 8
21 Eardiston, Worcs. F 12
30 Eardiston, Salop. H 2
25 Earith H 5
23 Earl Shilton B 8
27 Earl Soham J 5
31 Earl Sterndale C 9
27 Earl Stonham J 4
49 Earle G 12
17 Earley G 8
62 Earlish B 3
23 Earls Barton F 12
19 Earls Colne A 8
22 Earl's Croome H 2
27 Earl's Green J 3
22 Earlsdon D 6
53 Earlsferry G 9
58 Earlsford D 6
47 Earlston, Ayr. F 9
49 Earlston, Berwick F 8
22 Earlswood E 5
15 Earlswood Com. E 8
9 Earnley F 9
47 Earnockmuir D 11
45 Earsdon, Northumb. D 10
45 Earsdon, Northumb. F 11
26 Earsham F 6
36 Earswick A 4
9 Earystane H 1
40 Easby, Yorks. D 6
40 Easby, Yorks. E 2
50 Easdale F 5
9 Easebourne D 10
23 Easenhall D 8
9 Eashing B 11
17 Easington, Bucks. C 8
40 Easington, Dur. A 4
45 Easington, Northumb. C 12
17 Easington, Oxon. D 7
37 Easington, Yorks. E 11
41 Easington, Yorks. C 7
40 Easington Colliery A 4
45 Easington Grange B 12
45 Easington Lane H 12
40 Easingwold H 5
11 Easole Street C 11
53 Eassie & Nevay C 8
14 East Aberthaw H 4
16 East Adderbury A 6
5 East Allington L 6
45 East Ancroft A 11
4 East Anstey C 7
9 East Ashling E 9
58 East Auchronie F 6
41 East Ayton G 10
14 East Bank D 5
33 East Barkwith B 9
10 East Barming C 6
41 East Barnby D 8
18 East Barnet D 3
49 East Barns B 9
26 East Barsham B 2
26 East Beckham B 5
18 East Bedfont F 1
27 East Bergholt M 4
26 East Bilney D 3
49 East Blanerne D 11
10 East Blatchington H 4
7 East Bloxworth G 12
45 East Boldon G 11
8 East Boldre F 5
45 East Bolton A 11
47 East Brackenridge E 11
26 East Bradenham E 2
7 East Brent A 7
27 East Bridge J 7
32 East Bridgford F 4
45 East Brunton F 10
4 East Buckland C 5
6 East Budleigh H 4
64 East Burra E 7
7 East Burton G 11
40 East Butsfield A 1
36 East Butterwick G 6
59 East Cairnbeg K 5
48 East Calder C 4
26 East Carleton E 5
23 East Carlton C 11

MAP
16 East Challow.....E 5
7 East Chelborough..F 9
10 East Chiltington...G 3
7 East Chinnock....E 8
8 East Chisenbury....A 3
9 East Clandon....A 12
17 East Claydon....B 8
15 East Clevedon....G 7
7 East Coker......E 9
6 East Combe......C 5
7 East Compton....B 9
36 East Cottingwith..C 5
8 East Cowes.......F 6
36 East Cowick......E 4
40 East Cowton......E 3
45 East Cramlington E 11
7 East Cranmore....B 10
8 East Creech......H 1
57 East Croachy......G 2
46 East Darlochan...G 2
8 East Dean, Hants..C 4
9 East Dean, Sussex E 10
26 East Dereham.....D 3
45 East Ditchburn....A 9
4 East Down.......B 5
32 East Drayton.....C 5
15 East Dundry......H 9
45 East Edington....E 10
8 East End, Dorset..F 2
16 East End, Hants..H 5
9 East End, Hants...D 8
8 East End, Hants..F 5
18 East End, Herts...A 4
11 East End, Kent....H 5
26 East End, Norfolk D 8
16 East End, Oxon...C 5
15 East End, Som....G 8
37 East End, Yorks. D 10
8 East Erlestoke....A 1
10 East Farleigh....C 6
23 East Farndon....D 10
36 East Ferry......G 6
45 East Fleetham...D 12
53 East Flisk......E 8
49 East Fortune......A 8
36 East Garforth....D 2
16 East Garston.....F 5
49 East Gordon.....E 9
16 East Grafton.....H 4
8 East Grimstead...C 4
16 East Gringe......E 5
10 East Grinstead...D 3
11 East Guldeford...F 8
23 East Haddon.....E 10
16 East Hagbourne..E 6
37 East Halton......E 9
37 East Halton Skitter E 9
18 East Ham.......F 4
16 East Hanney......E 5
19 East Hanningfield.D 7
36 East Hardwick....E 2
27 East Harling.....G 3
40 East Harlsey......E 4
8 East Harnham....C 3
7 East Harptree....A 9
45 East Hartford....E 11
9 East Harting......D 9
7 East Hatch......C 12
25 East Hatley......K 4
52 East Haugh......B 4
40 East Hauxwell....F 2
53 East Haven......D 10
24 East Heckington..A 3
40 East Hedleyhope..A 2
16 East Hendred.....E 5
41 East Heslerton....G 9
10 East Hoathly.....F 4
7 East Horrington...B 9
9 East Horsley......A 12
45 East Horton......C 11
7 East Huntspill....B 7
17 East Hyde......B 12
4 East Ilkerton.....A 6
16 East Ilsley......F 6
33 East Keal......D 11
16 East Kennett.....G 2
35 East Keswick....C 12
47 East Kilbride...D 11
58 East Kinharrachie.D 7
33 East Kirby......D 10
41 East Knapton.....H 9
7 East Knighton....H 11
4 East Knowstone..D 7
7 East Knoyle......C 4
45 East Kyloe......B 12
7 East Lambrook...D 7
11 East Langdon...C 12
23 East Langton....C 10
61 East Langwell.....F 7
9 East Lavant......E 10
40 East Layton.....D 2
32 East Leake......H 3
4 East Leigh......E 6

49 East Learmouth..F 11
26 East Lexham.....D 2
45 East Lilburn......A 8
49 East Linton......B 8
9 East Liss......C 9
47 East Lockhead....D 8
3 East Looe.......D 9
49 East Lothian, Co..B 8
36 East Lound......G 6
9 East Lovington ...E 10
7 East Lulworth....H 12
41 East Lutton......H 9
7 East Lydford.....C 9
59 East Mains......H 4
10 East Malling.....B 6
9 East Marden......E 9
32 East Markham....C 5
35 East Marton......B 8
9 East Meon......D 8
6 East Mere......E 3
19 East Mersea.....C 10
17 East Molesey....G 12
7 East Mordon....G 12
43 East Morton, Dumf.

35 East Morton, Yorks.
C 9
42 East Muntloch...H 2
41 East Ness......G 7
23 East Norton......B 11
6 East Nynehead....D 5
9 East Oakley.....A 7
5 East Ogwell......J 7
7 East Orchard....D 11
49 East Ord......D 12
5 East Panson.....G 2
10 East Peckham....C 5
12 East Pennar......G 3
7 East Pennard....C 9
52 East Plean......H 3
26 East Poringland....E 6
5 East Portlemouth .M 6
5 East Prawle......M 6
9 East Preston.....F 12
6 East Quantoxhead.B 5
45 East Rainton.....H 11
37 East Ravendale...G 10
26 East Raynham ...C 2
32 East Retford......B 4
37 East Riding, Co...C 8
35 East Rigton......C 12
40 East Rounton.....E 4
26 East Rudham.....C 1
26 East Runton......A 5
26 East Ruston......C 6
49 East Saltoun.....C 7
44 East Scales......F 1
16 East Shefford....G 5
45 East Sleekburn....E 11
26 East Somerton....D 8
36 East Stockwith...H 6
7 East Stoke, Dorset
H 12
32 East Stoke, Notts..E 5
7 East Stour......D 11
11 East Stourmouth .B 11
4 East Stowford....C 5
9 East Stratton.....B 7
11 East Studdal....C 11
10 East Sussex, Co...F 5
3 East Taphouse...C 9
19 East Tilbury......F 7
43 East Tinwald...C 11
9 East Tistead......C 8
33 East Torrington ..B 8
59 East Town......J 5
26 East Tuddenham..D 4
8 'East Tytherley....C 4
16 East Tytherton...G 1
4 East Village......E 7
24 East Walton......D 8
4 East Warlington..E 6
5 East Week......G 5
8 East Wellow......D 5
53 East Wemyss.....G 8
48 East Whitburn....C 2
19 East Wick......D 10
12 East Williamston..F 4
24 East Winch......D 8
9 East Wittering.....F 9
40 East Witton......G 2
45 East Woodburn...D 7
16 East Woodhay....H 5
9 East Worldham....B 9
26 East Wretham.....F 2
4 East Youlstone....D 1
10 Eastbourne......H 5
11 Eastbury, Berks...F 4
37 Eastburn......B 7
18 Eastbury, Herts...E 1
16 Eastbury, Berks...F 4
37 Eastchurch......A 8
15 Eastcombe......D 12
18 Eastcote, London .E 1

23 Eastcote, Northants.
G 10
22 Eastcote, War.....D 5
4 Eastcott, Devon..D 1
8 Eastcott, Wilts...A 2
16 Eastcourt, Wilts..H 3
16 Eastcourt, Wilts..E 1
10 Eastdean......H 4
19 Eastend......E 9
56 Easter Ardross....B 2
58 Easter Aucharnie..D 4
57 Easter Aviemore .H 4
56 Easter Balcroy....H 4
57 Easter Balmoral...K 8
57 Easter Boleskine..G 1
56 Easter Brae......C 2
15 Easter Compton..F 9
54 Easter Crochail....F 8
56 Easter Culbo......D 2
59 Easter Davoch...G 2
55 Easter Drummond H 8
52 Easter Dullater....F 1
43 Easter Earshaig ..A 11
61 Easter Fearn......H 7
44 Easter Fodderance..B 4
56 Easter Galcantray.E 4
22 Easter Green.....D 6
48 Easter Happrew....E 4
48 Easter Howgate...C 5
49 Easter Howlaws..E 10
56 Easter Kinkell....D 1
49 Easter Langlee....F 8
53 Easter Lednathie..A 8
56 Easter Milton......D 5
56 Easter Moniack...E 1
56 Easter Muckovie..E 3
59 Easter Ord......G 6
64 Easter Quarff.....E 7
58 Easter Silverford ..A 5
64 Easter Skeld......D 6
54 Easter Slumbay....F 3
49 Easter Softlaw ...F 10
48 Easter Stanhope..F 4
59 Easter Tillygarmond
H 4
59 Easter Tulloch ...K 5
56 Easterfield......E 3
9 Eastergate......F 11
47 Easterhouse, Lan. C 11
48 Easterhouse, Peeb..D 3
8 Easterton......A 2
58 Eastertown, Banff. D 1
48 Eastertown, Lan...F 2
48 Eastertown, Lan...E 3
48 Eastertown, Lan...G 1
7 Eastertown, Som..A 7
58 Eastertown of
Auchleuchries ..D 8
59 Eastfield, Aber...H 1
48 Eastfield, Lanark..C 2
48 Eastfield, Lanark..E 3
41 Eastfield, Yorks..G 10
45 Eastfield Hall ...B 10
49 Eastfield of Lempitlaw
F 10
39 Eastgate, Dur....A 11
26 Eastgate, Norfolk .C 4
30 Eastham......B 2
17 Easthampstead....G 9
17 Eastheath......G 9
4 East-the-Water....C 3
21 Easthope......C 11
19 Easthorpe, Essex..B 9
32 Easthorpe, Notts..E 4
48 Easthouses......C 6
16 Eastington, Devon.E 6
15 Eastington, Glos..D 11
16 Eastington, Glos...C 2
16 Eastleach Martin..D 3
16 Eastleach Turville D 3
4 Eastleigh, Devon..C 4
8 Eastleigh, Hants..D 6
11 Eastling......B 1
45 Eastnook......D 8
15 Eastnor......A 10
36 Eastoft......E 6
9 Eastoke......F 8
44 Easton, Cumb.....G 1
44 Easton, Cumb.....F 3
5 Easton, Devon....G 6
7 Easton, Dorset...H 7
8 Easton, Hants....C 6
25 Easton, Hunts...H 2
8 Easton, I.o.W.....G 5
32 Easton, Leics....G 6
26 Easton, Norfolk...D 4
7 Easton, Somerset..A 7
27 Easton, Suffolk...J 6
15 Easton, Wilts....G 12
15 Easton Grey......D 4
15 Easton-in-GordanoG 8
23 Easton Maudit...F 12
24 Easton-on-the-Hill.E 1

16 Easton Royal....H 3
24 Eastrea......F 4
44 Eastriggs......F 1
36 Eastrington......D 5
11 Eastry......C 11
33 Eastville......E 11
32 Eastwell......G 5
18 Eastwick......C 4
19 Eastwood, Essex ..E 8
32 Eastwood, Notts..F 2
23 Eathorpe......E 7
16 Eaton, Berks....D 5
30 Eaton, Cheshire..D 4
31 Eaton, Cheshire..D 7
32 Eaton, Leics....B 4
32 Eaton, Leics....G 5
26 Eaton, Norfolk...E 5
21 Eaton, Salop.....C 9
21 Eaton, Salop....C 10
21 Eaton Bishop...H 10
17 Eaton Bray......B 10
21 Eaton Constantine
B 11
17 Eaton Green...B 10
16 Eaton Hastings...D 4
25 Eaton Socon....J 3
30 Eaton upon Tern .H 5
41 Ebberston......G 9
8 Ebbesbourne Wake
D 2
14 Ebbw Vale......C 5
45 Ebchester......G 9
15 Ebdon......H 7
6 Ebford......G 3
15 Ebley......D 11
22 Ebrington......H 5
5 Ebsworthy Town..G 4
16 Ecchinswell......H 6
49 Ecclaw......C 10
43 Ecclefechan......D 12
49 Eccles, Berwick .E 10
10 Eccles, Kent....B 6
34 Eccles, Lancs....G 6
21 Eccles Green......H 9
26 Eccles Road.....F 3
49 Eccles Tofts......E 10
32 Ecclesall......B 1
35 Ecclesfield......H 12
59 Ecclesgreig......L 5
31 Eccleshall......G 7
35 Eccleshill......D 10
48 Ecclesmachan.....B 3
30 Eccleston, Ches...D 3
34 Eccleston, Lancs..H 4
34 Eccleston, Lancs..E 4
34 Eccleston Green...E 4
35 Eccup......C 11
59 Echt......G 5
49 Eckford......G 9
22 Eckington ......H 3
23 Ecton......F 11
31 Edale......B 9
10 Edburton......G 1
43 Edderside......G 11
61 Edderton......H 7
16 Eddington, Berks..G 4
11 Eddington, Kent .A 10
4 Eddistone......D 1
48 Eddleston......E 5
47 Eddlewood......D 12
49 Eden Hall......F 10
10 Edenbridge......C 3
35 Edenfield......E 7
39 Edenhall......B 8
24 Edenham......C 2
31 Edensor......C 11
51 Edentaggart.....H 10
36 Edenthorpe......F 4
44 Edentown......G 2
28 Edern......F 2
7 Edgarley......C 8
22 Edgbaston......D 4
17 Edgcott, Bucks...B 8
6 Edgcott, Som....B 2
15 Edge End......C 9
30 Edge Green, Ches.E 3
27 Edge Green, Norf..G 3
30 Edge Hill......A 2
30 Edgebottom......H 4
26 Edgefield......B 4
26 Edgefield Green...B 6
30 Edgemond......H 6
26 Edgerston......B 5
44 Edges Green......F 5
35 Edgeside......E 7
15 Edgeworth......D 12
4 Edgeworthy......E 7
30 Edgmond Marsh..H 6
21 Edgton......D 9
18 Edgware......E 2
34 Edgworth......E 6
52 Edinample......E 1

62 Edinbain......C 3
48 Edinburgh......B 5
52 Edinchip......E 1
22 Edingale......A 6
32 Edingley......E 4
26 Edingthorpe......B 6
49 Edington, Ber...D 11
7 Edington, Som...B 7
8 Edington, Wilts...A 1
7 Edington Burtle...B 7
7 Edingworth......A 7
58 Edintore......C 2
23 Edith Weston...B 12
6 Edithmead......A 6
17 Edlesborough...B 10
45 Edlingham, Northumb.
B 9
33 Edlington, Lind...C 9
45 Edmondbyers.....H 8
8 Edmondsham......E 2
45 Edmondsley.....H 10
32 Edmondthorpe...H 6
64 Edmonstone......C 3
18 Edmonton......E 3
26 Ednam......F 10
51 Edra......F 11
49 Edrom......D 11
30 Edstaston......G 4
22 Edstone......F 5
21 Edvin Loach.....G 12
32 Edwalton......D 3
27 Edwardstone......L 2
13 Edwinsford......D 9
32 Edwinstowe......D 3
25 Edworth......L 3
21 Edwyn Ralph...G 12
59 Edzell......K 3
14 Efail Isaf......F 4
29 Efail-Parcy......C 11
13 Efail-fâch......G 11
28 Efailnewydd......G 3
29 Efail rhyd......H 11
12 Efailwen......D 5
29 Efenechtyd......E 10
9 Effingham......A 12
5 Efford......F 8
11 Egerton, Kent....C 8
34 Egerton, Lancs...F 6
5 Egg Buckland....K 4
17 Eggington......B 10
40 Egglescliffe......D 4
39 Eggleston......C 12
17 Egham......G 11
23 Egleton......A 12
45 Eglingham......A 9
3 Egloshayle......C 7
3 Egloskerry......A 9
14 Eglwys-Brewis....G 3
29 Eglwysbach......C 7
20 Eglwysfach......C 3
12 Eglwyswrw......C 5
32 Egmanton......C 4
38 Egremont, Cumb..D 3
30 Egremont, Lancs. .A 2
41 Egton......D 8
41 Egton Bridge......E 8
17 Egypt......F 10
19 Eight Ash Green..A 9
50 Eignaig......C 5
57 Eil......H 4
55 Eilanreach......H 2
49 Eildon......F 8
60 Eilean Darach...H 3
56 Eileanach Lodge ..C 1
63 Eishken......F 4
20 Elan Village......F 5
15 Elberton......E 9
5 Elburton......K 4
52 Elcho......E 6
16 Elcombe......F 2
24 Eldernell......F 4
15 Eldersfield......A 11
40 Eldon......B 3
42 Eldrick......C 4
34 Eldroth......A 6
35 Eldwick......C 10
20 Elerch......D 2
59 Elfhill......J 5
45 Elford, Northumb.
D 12
22 Elford, Staffs....A 5
56 Elgin......C 8
62 Elgol......G 4
11 Elham......D 10
53 Elie......G 9
45 Elilaw......B 8
8 Eling......E 5
62 Elishader......B 4
45 Elishaw......D 7
32 Elkesley......C 4
16 Elkstone......C 1
57 Ellan......G 5

35 Elland......E 10
46 Ellary......B 2
31 Ellastone......F 9
34 Ellel......B 4
49 Ellemford......C 10
31 Ellenhall......G 7
9 Ellen's Green....C 12
40 Ellerbeck......E 4
41 Ellerby......D 8
30 Ellerdine Heath...H 5
6 Ellerhayes......F 3
51 Elleric......C 7
37 Ellerker......D 7
30 Ellerton, Salop...H 6
40 Ellerton, N. Riding E 3
36 Ellerton, E. Riding C 5
17 Ellesborough......C 9
30 Ellesmere......G 2
30 Ellesmere Port ...C 3
8 Ellingham, Hants...E 3
26 Ellingham, Norf...F 6
45 Ellingham, Northumb.
E 12
40 Ellingstring......G 2
25 Ellington, Hunts..H 3
45 Ellington, Northumb.
D 11
9 Ellisfield......B 8
23 Ellistown......A 8
58 Ellon......D 7
38 Ellonby......B 6
37 Elloughton......D 7
15 Ellwood......C 9
24 Elm......E 6
7 Elm......D 11
18 Elm Park......E 5
22 Elmbridge......E 2
25 Elmdon, Essex....L 6
22 Elmdon, War....D 5
22 Elmdon Heath....D 5
18 Elmers End......G 4
23 Elmesthorpe......C 8
22 Elmhurst......A 5
22 Elmley Castle....H 3
22 Elmley Lovett....E 2
15 Elmore......C 11
15 Elmore Back.....C 10
4 Elmscott......D 1
27 Elmsett......K 3
19 Elmstead Market .B 10
11 Elmstone......B 11
15 Elmstone Hardwicke
B 12
27 Elmswell, Suffolk .J 3
37 Elmswell, Yorks...A 7
32 Elmton......C 2
60 Elphin......F 3
48 Elphinstone......B 6
59 Elrick......G 6
42 Elrig......G 4
51 Elrigbeag......F 8
45 Elsdon......D 7
35 Elsecar......G 12
18 Elsenham......A 5
16 Elsfield......C 6
37 Elsham......F 8
26 Elsing......D 4
35 Elslack......B 8
30 Elson......G 2
48 Elsrickle......E 3
9 Elstead, Surrey...B 10
9 Elsted, Sussex....D 9
32 Elston, Notts....E 5
8 Elston, Wilts....B 2
4 Elstone......D 5
37 Elstonwick......D 10
25 Elstow......K 2
18 Elstree......D 2
34 Elswick......C 3
25 Elsworth......J 4
38 Elterwater......E 5
11 Eltham......F 4
25 Eltisley......J 4
30 Elton, Cheshire...C 3
31 Elton, Derby....D 10
40 Elton, Durham...C 4
15 Elton, Glos....C 10
21 Elton, Herefs....E 10
24 Elton, Hunts....F 2
32 Elton, Notts....F 5
48 Elvanfoot......H 2
31 Elvaston......G 12
27 Eveden......G 1
11 Elvington, Kent..C 11
36 Elvington, Yorks..B 5
49 Elwartlaw......E 10
8 Elwick, Durham..B 5
45 Elwick, Northumb.
B 12
30 Elworth......D 6
6 Elworthy......C 4
25 Ely, Cambs.....G 6

MAP		
14	Ely, Glam.	G 5
23	Emberton	G 12
44	Emblehope	D 6
38	Embleton, Cumb.	B 4
40	Embleton, Dur.	B 4
45	Embleton, Northumb.	A 10
61	Embo	G 8
35	Embsay	B 8
8	Emery Down	E 4
35	Emley	F 11
35	Emley Moor	F 11
17	Emmbrook	G 8
17	Emmington	D 8
24	Emneth	E 6
24	Emneth Hungate	E 6
23	Empingham	A 12
9	Empshott	C 9
9	Emsworth	E 9
63	Enaclete	D 2
16	Enborne	G 5
16	Enborne Row	H 5
21	Enchmarsh	C 10
7	Encombe	H 12
23	Enderby	B 8
39	Endmoor	G 7
31	Endon	E 7
31	Endon Bank	E 8
18	Enfield	D 3
8	Enford	A 3
15	Engine Common	F 10
17	Englefield	G 7
17	Englefield Green	G 10
15	English Bicknor	C 9
30	English Frankton	G 3
15	Englishcombe	H 10
8	Enham Alamein	A 5
6	Enmore	C 6
38	Ennerdale Bridge	D 3
43	Enoch	B 9
52	Enochdu	A 5
50	Ensay	C 1
8	Ensbury	F 2
21	Ensdon	A 9
4	Ensis	C 4
16	Enstone	B 5
43	Enterkinfoot	A 9
40	Enterpen	E 5
22	Enville	C 2
50	Eorabus	E 1
63	Eoropie	A 6
15	Epney	C 11
32	Epperstone	E 4
18	Epping	D 4
18	Epping Green	C 3
18	Epping Green	C 4
18	Epping Upland	C 4
40	Eppleby	D 2
8	Epsom	B 1
23	Epwell	H 7
36	Epworth	G 5
29	Erbistock	F 12
55	Erbusaig	G 1
54	Ercnless Castle	E 8
22	Erdington	C 5
51	Eredine	G 7
60	Eriboll	B 5
48	Ericstane	H 3
10	Eridge Green	E 4
46	Erines	B 4
25	Eriswell	G 8
18	Erith	F 5
33	Ermine	C 7
5	Ermington	K 5
26	Erpingham	B 5
55	Errocht	L 5
57	Errogie	G 1
53	Errol	E 7
29	Erryrys	D 11
42	Ervie	E 1
27	Erwarton	M 5
20	Erwood	H 6
40	Eryholme	D 3
46	Escart	C 3
40	Escomb	B 2
36	Escrick	C 4
13	Esgair	D 7
20	Esgairgeiliog	B 3
13	Esgerdawe	C 9
40	Esh	A 2
40	Esh Winning	A 2
17	Esher	H 12
45	Eshott	C 10
35	Eshton	B 8
54	Eskadale	F 8
48	Eskbank	C 6
38	Eskdale Green	E 4
44	Eskdalemuir	C 1
37	Eskham	G 11
34	Esprick	D 3
24	Essendine	D 1
18	Essendon	C 3
19	Essex, Co.	C 7
56	Essich	F 2
22	Essington	B 3
40	Eston	C 6
18	Etal	E 11
16	Etchilhampton	H 2
10	Etchingham	E 6
11	Etchinghill, Kent	D 10
31	Etchinghill, Staffs.	H 8
17	Eton	F 10
17	Eton Wick	F 10
57	Etteridge	K 3
22	Ettington	G 6
24	Etton, Hunts.	E 2
37	Etton, Yorks.	C 7
48	Ettrick	H 5
48	Ettrickbridge End	G 5
31	Etwall	G 11
27	Euston	G 2
40	Euximoor Drove	F 6
34	Euxton	E 4
14	Evanstown	E 3
36	Evanton	C 2
33	Evedon	E 8
61	Evelix	G 7
21	Evenjobb	E 9
17	Evenley	A 7
16	Evenlode	A 3
40	Evenwood	C 2
40	Evenwood Gate	C 2
64	Everbay	C 4
6	Evercreech	B 9
23	Everdon	F 9
36	Everingham	C 6
8	Everleigh	A 3
41	Everley	F 10
25	Eversholt	M 1
7	Evershot	F 9
17	Eversley	H 8
17	Eversley Cross	H 9
37	Everthorpe	D 7
25	Everton, Beds.	K 3
8	Everton, Hants.	G 4
30	Everton, Lancs.	A 2
32	Everton, Notts.	A 4
44	Evertown	E 2
21	Evesbatch	H 12
22	Evesham	H 4
23	Evington	B 10
35	Ewden Village	G 11
10	Ewell	B 1
11	Ewell Minnis	D 11
16	Ewelme	E 7
16	Ewen	D 1
14	Ewenny	G 2
33	Ewerby	E 8
44	Eweslees	C 2
9	Ewhurst, Surrey	B 12
11	Ewhurst, Sussex	F 7
9	Ewhurst Green	B 12
29	Ewloe	D 12
4	Eworthy	F 3
9	Ewshot	A 9
15	Ewyas Harold	B 7
4	Exbourne	F 5
8	Exbury	F 6
6	Exebridge	D 3
6	Exelby	F 5
6	Exeter	G 3
6	Exford	B 2
22	Exhall	G 4
17	Exlade Street	F 7
6	Exminster	G 3
6	Exmouth	H 4
64	Exnaboe	F 7
25	Exning	J 7
6	Exton, Devon	H 3
6	Exton, Hants.	D 7
23	Exton, Rutland	A 12
6	Exton, Somerset	C 3
6	Exwick	G 3
31	Eyam	C 10
23	Eydon	G 9
21	Eye, Herefs.	F 10
24	Eye, Hunts.	E 3
27	Eye, Suffolk	H 4
49	Eyemouth	C 12
25	Eyeworth	L 4
11	Eyhorne Street	J 7
27	Eyke	K 6
25	Eynesbury	J 3
16	Eynsford	B 4
16	Eynsham	C 5
7	Eype	G 8
62	Eyre	G 3
11	Eythorne	C 11
29	Eyton, Denbigh	F 12
21	Eyton, Herefs.	F 10
21	Eyton, Salop	D 9
30	Eyton, Salop	H 3
21	Eyton upon the Weald Moors	A 12
16	Faccombe	H 5
40	Faceby	E 5
28	Fachwen	D 5
35	Facit	E 9
30	Faddiley	E 4
55	Faddoch	G 3
41	Fadmoor	F 7
31	Fagginton	G 11
13	Fagwyr	G 10
47	Fail	F 9
15	Failand	G 8
47	Failford	G 9
35	Failsworth	G 8
54	Fain	B 5
6	Fair Oak	D 4
8	Fair Oak	D 6
17	Fair Oak Green	H 7
20	Fairbourne	A 2
36	Fairburn	D 2
22	Fairchild	H 4
22	Fairfield	E 3
16	Fairford	D 3
43	Fairgirth	F 9
47	Fairlie	D 7
11	Fairlight	G 7
11	Fairlight Cove	G 7
6	Fairmile	F 4
48	Fairmilehead	C 5
49	Fairnilee	F 7
30	Fairoak	G 6
10	Fairseat	B 5
26	Fairstead, Norfolk	C 6
19	Fairstead, Sussex	B 7
10	Fairwarp	E 3
4	Fairy Cross	D 3
26	Fakenham	C 2
49	Fala	C 7
48	Falahill	D 6
41	Falcon Inn	E 10
33	Faldingworth	B 8
15	Falfield	E 10
27	Falkenham	L 6
48	Falkirk	A 2
44	Falla	B 5
32	Fallgate	D 1
52	Fallin	H 3
45	Fallowfield	F 7
10	Falmer	G 2
2	Falmouth	F 5
44	Falnash	B 2
41	Falsgrave	F 10
44	Falstone	D 5
60	Fanagmore	C 3
40	Fangdale Beck	F 6
36	Fangfoss	B 5
50	Fanmore	C 2
54	Fannich Lodge	C 6
49	Fans	E 9
17	Far Bletchley	A 9
23	Far Cotton	F 11
32	Far Duckmanton	C 2
38	Far Sawrey	F 6
24	Farcet	F 3
21	Farden	E 11
9	Fareham	F 7
22	Farewell	A 4
33	Farforth	B 10
44	Farglow	F 5
16	Faringdon	E 4
34	Farington	E 4
44	Farlam	G 4
15	Farleigh, Som.	G 8
10	Farleigh, Surrey	B 3
7	Farleigh Hungerford	A 11
9	Farleigh Wallop	A 8
15	Farleigh Wick	H 11
33	Farlesthorpe	C 11
39	Farleton	G 8
31	Farley, Cheshire	F 9
21	Farley, Salop	B 9
15	Farley, Somerset	G 7
8	Farley, Wiltshire	C 4
9	Farley Green	B 12
17	Farley Hill	H 8
11	Farleys End	C 11
40	Farlington	H 6
21	Farlow	D 11
29	Farm Yard	D 7
15	Farmborough	H 10
16	Farmcote	A 2
13	Farmers	C 10
43	Farmersfield	C 9
16	Farmington	C 2
16	Farmoor	C 5
58	Farmtown	C 3
16	Farnborough, Berks.	F 5
9	Farnborough, Hants.	A 10
23	Farnborough, War.	G 8
17	Farnborough Grn.	H 9
9	Farncombe	H 9
30	Farndon, Denbigh.	E 3
32	Farndon, Notts.	E 5
53	Farnell	B 11
8	Farnham, Dorset	E 1
18	Farnham, Essex	A 5
9	Farnham, Surrey	B 9
35	Farnham, Yorks.	A 12
22	Farnham Com.	F 10
18	Farnham Green	A 5
17	Farnham Royal	F 10
35	Farnhill	C 9
6	Farningham	G 4
10	Farningham	A 4
35	Farnley, Yorks.	B 11
35	Farnley, Yorks.	D 11
35	Farnley Tyas	F 10
30	Farnworth, Lancs.	B 4
34	Farnworth, Yorks.	G 6
30	Farr, Inverness	F 2
57	Farr, Inverness	J 4
61	Farr, Sutherland	B 7
56	Farr House	F 2
9	Farringdon	C 8
7	Farrington Gurney	A 9
35	Farsley	D 10
23	Farthinghoe	H 8
11	Farthingloe	D 11
23	Farthingstone	G 9
35	Fartown	E 10
6	Farway	G 5
3	Fasag	D 3
50	Faskadale	A 2
55	Fasnakyle	G 7
55	Fassfern	L 4
45	Fatfield	H 11
44	Fattahead	B 4
44	Faugh	G 3
48	Fauldhouse	C 2
6	Fauldie	F 2
19	Faulkbourne	B 8
7	Faulkland	A 10
30	Faulsgreen	G 4
11	Faversham	B 9
56	Favillar	F 8
22	Fawdon	B 8
31	Fawfieldhead	D 9
10	Fawkham Green	B 5
16	Fawler, Berks.	F 5
17	Fawler, Bucks.	E 8
8	Fawley, Hants.	F 6
15	Fawley Chapel	A 9
49	Fawside	E 9
22	Fazeley	B 5
56	Fearby	G 2
56	Fearn	B 4
60	Fearn Lodge	H 6
44	Fearnan	C 2
54	Fearnbeg	D 1
30	Fearnhead	A 5
54	Fearnmore	D 1
22	Featherstone, War.	B 3
36	Featherstone, Yorks.	E 2
44	Featherwood	C 6
22	Feckenham	F 4
56	Feddan	D 5
19	Feering	B 8
39	Feetham	E 12
22	Felbridge	D 3
26	Felbrigg	B 5
10	Felcourt	D 3
17	Felden	D 11
7	Feldownhead	H 2
21	Felhampton	D 10
13	Felin-Wnda	B 6
20	Felindre, Brec.	B 5
13	Felindre, Cards.	G 1
13	Felindre, Carm.	D 10
13	Felindre, Carm.	C 9
13	Felindre, Glam.	E 9
13	Felindre, Radnor.	D 7
14	Felin-fach, Brec.	A 4
13	Felinfach, Cards.	A 8
13	Felinfoel	G 8
13	Felin-gwm Isaf	E 8
13	Felin-gwm Uchaf	E 8
40	Felixkirk	G 5
27	Felixstowe	M 6
27	Felixstoweferry	L 6
49	Felkington	E 12
45	Felling	G 11
38	Fellside	B 5
25	Felmersham	J 1
26	Felmingham	C 6
9	Felpham	F 11
27	Felsham	J 2
19	Felstead	B 7
18	Feltham	G 1
26	Felthorpe	D 5
21	Felton, Herefs.	G 11
45	Felton, Northumb.	C 10
15	Felton, Somerset	H 8
21	Felton Butler	A 9
24	Feltwell	F 8
25	Fen Drayton	H 4
22	Fen End	E 6
35	Fenay Bridge	F 10
35	Fence	C 7
45	Fence Houses	H 11
33	Fendike Corner	D 11
56	Fendom	B 4
24	Fengate	F 3
45	Fenham	B 12
45	Fenhamhill	B 12
34	Feniscowles	E 5
6	Feniton	F 4
31	Fenny Bentley	E 10
23	Fenny Compton	G 7
23	Fenny Drayton	B 7
17	Fenny Stratford	A 10
45	Fenrother	D 10
25	Fenstanton	H 4
32	Fenton, Lincs.	C 6
32	Fenton, Notts.	E 6
31	Fenton, Staffs.	F 7
49	Fenton Barns	A 8
49	Fenton Town	F 12
49	Fentonhill	F 12
47	Fenwick, Ayr	E 9
45	Fenwick, Northumb.	F 9
45	Fenwick, Northumb.	B 12
36	Fenwick, Yorks.	E 4
46	Feochaig	H 3
2	Feock	F 5
62	Ferindonald	G 6
62	Feriniquarrie	C 1
50	Ferlochan	D 6
59	Fern	L 2
55	Fern Villa	G 3
14	Ferndale	E 3
8	Ferndown	F 2
49	Ferneyhill	F 10
16	Fernham	E 4
10	Fernhill	D 2
22	Fernhill Heath	F 2
9	Fernhurst	C 10
53	Fernie	F 8
62	Fernilea	E 3
31	Fernilee	B 8
21	Ferny Common	G 9
35	Ferrensby	A 12
9	Ferring	F 12
25	Ferry Hill	G 5
36	Ferrybridge	E 3
53	Ferryden	B 12
59	Ferryhill, Aber.	G 7
40	Ferryhill, Durham.	B 3
40	Ferryhill Station	B 3
13	Ferryside	F 7
61	Ferrytown	H 7
27	Fersfield	G 4
53	Fersit	L 7
57	Feshiebridge	J 4
58	Fetterangus	C 7
59	Fettercairn	K 4
35	Fewston	B 10
13	Ffairfach	E 9
20	Ffair-rhôs	F 3
13	Ffald-y-Brenin	C 9
14	Ffawyddog	B 5
28	Ffestiniog	F 6
29	Ffordd-las, Denb.	C 7
21	Fforddlas, Rad.	H 7
13	Fforest	G 9
13	Fforest fach	G 9
13	Fforest Goch	G 10
13	Ffostrasol	B 7
13	Ffos-y-ffin	A 8
29	Ffrith	E 12
21	Ffynnon Gynydd	H 7
13	Ffynnon-ddrain	E 7
29	Ffynnongroew	B 10
60	Fiag Bridge	E 5
60	Fiag Lodge	D 5
13	Fiddington, Glos.	A 12
6	Fiddington, Som.	B 5
7	Fiddleford	E 11
18	Fiddlers Hamlet	E 5
44	Fiddleton	C 2
31	Field	G 9
38	Field Broughton	G 6
26	Field Dalling	B 3
23	Field Head	A 8
47	Fieldhead	D 11
53	Fife, County	G 7
58	Fife of Keith	C 2
7	Fifehead Magdalen	D 11
7	Fifehead Neville	E 11
7	Fifehead St. Quintin	E 11
17	Fifield, Berks.	F 10
16	Fifield, Glos.	B 3
8	Fifield, Wilts.	A 3
8	Fifield Bavant	D 2
13	Fighelden	A 3
40	Fighting Cocks	D 4
26	Filby	D 8
41	Filey	G 11
16	Filgrave	G 12
16	Filkins	D 3
4	Filleigh, Devon	E 6
4	Filleigh, Devon	C 5
32	Fillingham	B 6
22	Fillongley	C 6
15	Filton	F 9
37	Fimber	A 7
59	Finavon	L 2
24	Fincham	E 8
17	Finchampstead	H 9
50	Fincharn	G 6
9	Finchdean	E 9
25	Finchingfield	M 8
18	Finchley	E 3
57	Fincraigs	E 8
31	Findern	G 11
56	Findhorn	C 6
57	Findhorn Bridge	G 4
58	Findochty	A 2
59	Findon, Kinc.	H 7
9	Findon, Sussex	E 12
56	Findon Mains	D 2
59	Findrack House	G 3
26	Finedon	E 12
27	Fingal Street	H 5
58	Fingask, Aber.	E 5
52	Fingask, Perth	E 6
22	Fingerpost	E 1
27	Fingest	E 8
40	Finghall	F 2
44	Fingland, Cumb.	G 1
47	Fingland, Dumf.	H 12
11	Finglesham	C 12
19	Fingringhoe	B 10
55	Finiskaig	K 2
52	Finlarig	D 1
17	Finmere	A 7
55	Finnart	B 12
43	Finniegill	B 12
27	Finningham	H 3
36	Finningley	G 4
58	Finnygaud	B 3
63	Finsbay	H 2
18	Finsbury	F 3
22	Finstall	E 3
38	Finsthwaite	F 6
16	Finstock	C 4
64	Finstown	D 7
43	Fintloch	D 7
58	Fintry, Aberdeen	B 5
59	Fintry, Angus	D 8
47	Fintry, Stirling	A 11
50	Fionnphort	F 1
40	Fir Tree	B 2
32	Firbeck	A 3
41	Firby, E. Riding	H 7
40	Firby, N. Riding	F 2
33	Firsby	D 11
60	First Coast	G 1
34	Fishlake	F 4
43	Fishbeck	C 11
9	Fishbourne, Hants	G 7
9	Fishbourne, Sussex	F 10
40	Fishburn	B 4
52	Fishcross	H 4
58	Fisherford	D 4
6	Fisher's Pond	D 6
9	Fisherstreet	C 11
47	Fisherton, Ayr	H 7
56	Fisherton, Inver.	E 3
8	Fisherton de la Mere	B 2
12	Fishguard	C 3
15	Fishponds	G 9
35	Fishpool, Lancs.	F 7
32	Fishpool, Notts.	E 3
24	Fishtoft	A 5
33	Fishtoft Drive	E 4
53	Fishtown of Usan	B 12
49	Fishwick	D 11
62	Fiskavaig	E 2
32	Fiskerton, Lincs.	C 7
32	Fiskerton, Notts.	E 4
37	Fitling	D 10

MAP
24 Fitten End D 5
8 Fittleton A 3
9 Fittleworth D 11
30 Fitz H 3
6 Fitzhead C 5
36 Fitzwilliam F 2
50 Fiunary C 3
15 Five Acres C 9
10 Five Ashes F 4
34 Five Lane Ends B 4
3 Five Lanes B 9
10 Five Oak Green D 5
9 Five Oaks C 12
63 Five Penny Borve A 5
63 Five Penny Ness A 6
13 Five Roads F 8
30 Fivecrosses C 4
7 Fivehead D 7
19 Flack's Green B 7
17 Flackwell Heath E 9
22 Fladbury G 3
64 Fladdabister E 7
31 Flagg C 10
41 Flamborough H 2
17 Flamstead C 11
9 Flansham F 11
35 Flappit Spring C 9
35 Flasby B 8
31 Flash C 8
17 Flaunden D 11
32 Flawborough F 5
36 Flawith A 3
15 Flax Bourton G 8
35 Flaxby A 12
15 Flaxley C 10
6 Flaxpool C 5
36 Flaxton A 4
23 Fleckney C 10
23 Flecknoe F 8
7 Fleet, Dorset H 9
9 Fleet, Hants A 9
9 Fleet, Hants F 8
24 Fleet, Lincs C 5
33 Fleet Hargate H 11
45 Fleetham E 12
34 Fleetwood B 2
14 Flemingston G 3
47 Flemington, Lan. C 11
47 Flemington, Lan. E 12
27 Flempton H 1
38 Fletchertown A 4
10 Fletching F 3
4 Flexbury E 1
9 Flexford A 10
38 Flimby B 3
10 Flimwell E 6
29 Flint C 11
29 Flint Mountain C 11
32 Flintham F 5
37 Flinton D 10
24 Flitcham C 8
25 Flitton L 2
4 Flitton Barton C 6
25 Flitwick M 1
36 Flixborough F 6
34 Flixton, Lancs H 6
27 Flixton, Suffolk G 4
41 Flixton, Yorks G 10
35 Flockton F 11
35 Flockton Green F 11
49 Flodden F 11
63 Flodabay H 2
62 Flodigarry Hotel A 4
24 Flood's Ferry F 5
38 Flookburgh H 6
26 Flordon F 5
23 Flore F 9
45 Flotterton C 8
35 Flouch Inn G 10
27 Flowton K 4
58 Flushing, Aber C 8
2 Flushing, Cornwall F 5
6 Fluxton G 4
22 Flyford Flavell G 3
19 Fobbing E 7
58 Fochabers B 1
14 Fochriw D 4
36 Fockerby E 6
56 Fodderty D 1
7 Foddington C 9
20 Foel A 5
13 Foelgastell E 9
53 Foffarty C 9
36 Foggathorpe C 5
49 Fogo D 10
49 Fogorig E 10
60 Foindle C 3
53 Folda A 7
31 Fole F 9
23 Foleshill D 7
7 Folke E 10
11 Folkestone E 11
24 Folkingham B 2

MAP
10 Folkington H 4
24 Folksworth F 2
41 Folkton G 10
58 Folla Rule D 5
35 Follifoot B 12
4 Folly Gate F 4
9 Folly Hill A 9
14 Fonmon G 4
7 Fonthill Gifford C 12
7 Fontmell Magna E 12
9 Fontwell E 10
31 Foolow C 10
18 Foots Cray G 5
58 Forbestown F 1
6 Forches Corner D 5
50 Ford, Argyll G 6
17 Ford, Bucks C 8
5 Ford, Devon L 7
4 Ford, Devon D 3
16 Ford, Glos A 2
49 Ford, Northumb. F 12
21 Ford, Salop A 9
6 Ford, Somerset C 4
31 Ford, Staffs E 9
9 Ford, Sussex F 11
15 Ford, Wilts G 11
6 Ford Barton D 3
19 Ford End B 7
6 Ford Street D 5
10 Fordcombe D 4
52 Fordel F 6
52 Fordell H 6
21 Forden B 8
25 Fordham, Cambridgeshire H 7
19 Fordham, Essex A 9
24 Fordham, Norfolk E 7
22 Fordhouses B 3
8 Fordingbridge E 3
41 Fordon H 10
59 Fordoun K 5
19 Fordstreet A 9
16 Fordwells C 4
11 Fordwich B 10
58 Fordyce A 3
31 Forebridge H 8
9 Forest Green B 12
39 Forest Hall E 8
44 Forest Head G 4
17 Forest Hill C 7
51 Forest Lo., Argyll C 10
56 Forest Lo., Inver. H 6
57 Forest Lo., Kirk. C 10
52 Forest Lo., Perth A 4
52 Forest Mill H 4
10 Forest Row D 3
32 Forest Town D 3
45 Forestburn Gate C 9
56 Foresterseat D 7
9 Forestside E 9
53 Forfar B 9
52 Forgandenny E 6
14 Forge Hammer E 6
14 Forge Side D 6
58 Forgie B 1
58 Forgieside B 1
58 Forglen House B 4
34 Formby F 2
26 Forncett End F 4
26 Forncett St. Mary F 4
26 Forncett St. Peter F 5
52 Forneth C 6
27 Fornham All Saints J 1
27 Fornham St. Martin H 2
56 Forres D 6
48 Forrestfield C 1
31 Forsbrook F 8
61 Forse D 11
61 Forse House D 11
61 Forsinain C 9
61 Forsinard C 9
61 Forsinard Station C 8
7 Forston G 10
55 Fort Augustus J 7
56 Fort George D 3
55 Fort William M 5
47 Fortacres F 9
52 Forteviot E 5
48 Forth D 2
15 Forthampton A 11
52 Fortingall B 2
8 Forton, Hants B 6
34 Forton, Lancs B 4
21 Forton, Salop A 9
7 Forton, Somerset E 7
30 Forton, Staffs H 6
58 Fortrie C 4
56 Fortrose D 3
7 Fortuneswell H 7
17 Forty Green E 10
25 Forty Feet Bridge G 4
27 Forward Green J 4

MAP
16 Fosbury H 4
24 Fosdyke B 4
24 Fosdyke Bridge B 4
52 Foss A 3
16 Fossebridge C 2
18 Foster Street C 5
36 Fosterhouses F 4
31 Foston, Derby G 10
32 Foston, Lincs F 6
36 Foston, Yorks A 5
37 Foston on the Wolds B 8
33 Fotherby A 10
24 Fotheringhay F 2
64 Foubister D 3
10 Foul Mile F 5
49 Foulden, Berwick D 11
26 Foulden, Norfolk E 1
56 Foulis Castle C 1
35 Foulridge C 7
26 Foulsham C 3
58 Fountainbleau, Aber. D 8
58 Fountainbleau, Aber. E 7
49 Fountainhall D 7
27 Four Ashes H 3
28 Four Crosses, Caer. F 3
29 Four Crosses, Mont. H 12
20 Four Crosses, Mont. B 6
22 Four Crosses, Staffs. A 3
10 Four Elms C 3
6 Four Forks C 6
34 Four Gate F 5
24 Four Gotes D 5
30 Four Lane Ends, Ches. D 4
34 Four Lane Ends, Lancashire B 4
34 Four Lane Ends, Lancashire C 2
36 Four Lane Ends, Yorkshire B 4
39 Four Lane Ends, Yorkshire F 8
2 Four Lanes F 4
9 Four Marks C 8
28 Four Mile Bridge B 2
15 Four Oaks, Glos. B 10
11 Four Oaks, Sussex F 7
22 Four Oaks, War. D 6
22 Four Oaks, War. B 4
13 Four Roads, Carm. F 8
38 Four Roads, I.o.M. H 1
10 Four Throws E 6
30 Fourlanes End D 6
45 Fourlaws E 7
45 Fourstones F 7
8 Fovant C 2
58 Foveran E 7
3 Fowey D 8
58 Fowlershill F 7
10 Fowlhall C 6
53 Fowlis D 8
52 Fowlis Wester E 4
25 Fowlmere L 5
15 Fownhope A 9
9 Fox Corner A 11
17 Fox Lane H 9
7 Foxcote A 10
38 Foxdale H 1
27 Foxearth L 1
38 Foxfield G 5
16 Foxham F 1
3 Foxhole D 7
41 Foxholes H 10
10 Foxhunt Green F 4
26 Foxley, Norfolk C 3
15 Foxley, Wilts F 12
31 Foxt E 9
25 Foxton, Cambs K 5
40 Foxton, Durham C 4
23 Foxton, Leics C 10
39 Foxup G 11
30 Foxwist Green C 5
21 Foxwood E 11
15 Foy A 9
57 Foyers G 1
7 Foys E 9
2 Fraddam F 3
2 Fraddon D 6
22 Fradley A 5
31 Fradswell G 8
37 Fraisthorpe A 9
10 Framfield F 4
26 Framingham Earl E 6
26 Framingham Pigot E 6
27 Framlingham J 6
7 Frampton, Dorset G 9
24 Frampton, Lincs B 4

MAP
15 Frampton Cotterell F 9
15 Frampton Mansell D 12
15 Frampton on Severn D 10
24 Frampton West End B 4
27 Framsden J 5
40 Framwellgate Moor A 3
22 Franche D 2
30 Frandley B 5
30 Frankby B 1
22 Frankley D 3
21 Frank's Bridge G 7
23 Frankton E 7
20 Frankwell, Mont. C 5
21 Frankwell, Salop. A 10
10 Frant E 5
58 Fraserburgh A 7
19 Frating B 10
19 Frating Green B 10
3 Freathy D 11
32 Frecheville B 1
25 Freckenham H 8
34 Freckleton D 3
32 Freeby H 5
16 Freeland C 5
26 Freethorpe E 7
26 Freethorpe Com. E 7
24 Freiston A 5
4 Fremington, Devon C 4
40 Fremington, Yorks. E 1
15 Frenchay F 9
5 Frenchbeer G 5
51 Frenich, Perth G 11
52 Frenich, Perth A 3
9 Frensham B 9
61 Fresgoe A 9
34 Freshfield F 2
8 Freshwater G 5
12 Freshwater East G 4
27 Fressingfield H 5
61 Freswick A 12
15 Fretherne C 10
26 Frettenham D 5
53 Freuchie F 7
12 Freystrop Cross F 3
7 Friar Waddon H 10
52 Friarton E 6
24 Friday Bridge E 6
10 Friday Street H 5
36 Fridaythorpe A 6
18 Friern Barnet E 3
33 Friesthorpe B 8
32 Frieston E 6
17 Frieth E 9
16 Frilford D 5
16 Frilsham G 6
17 Frimley H 9
17 Frimley Green H 10
10 Frindsbury A 6
24 Fring B 8
17 Fringford A 7
11 Frinsted B 7
19 Frinton B 12
53 Friockheim B 10
20 Friog A 2
32 Frisby on the Wreake H 4
33 Friskney E 11
27 Friston, Suffolk J 7
10 Friston, Sussex H 4
32 Fritchley E 1
33 Frith Bank E 10
21 Frith Common E 12
8 Fritham E 4
4 Frithelstock D 3
4 Frithelstock Stone D 3
17 Frithsden C 11
33 Frithville E 10
11 Frittenden D 7
26 Fritton, Norfolk F 5
26 Fritton, Norfolk E 7
16 Fritwell A 6
38 Frizington D 3
15 Frocester D 11
21 Frochas B 7
21 Frodesley B 10
37 Frodingham F 7
30 Frodsham B 4
49 Frogden G 10
31 Froggatt C 11
31 Froghall E 9
15 Frogland Cross F 9
5 Frogmore, Devon L 6
17 Frogmore, Hants H 9
23 Frolesworth C 8
7 Frome B 11
7 Frome St. Quintin F 9
21 Fromes Hill H 12
28 Fron, Caer E 4
28 Fron, Caer F 3

MAP
13 Fron, Carm. D 11
21 Fron, Mont B 8
20 Fron, Rad F 6
29 Fron Isaf F 12
29 Froncysyllte F 12
29 Fron-deg E 12
29 Frongoch F 8
28 Fron-oleu G 6
39 Frosterley A 12
64 Frotoft B 2
16 Froxfield G 4
9 Froxfield Green D 8
9 Froyle B 9
18 Fryerning D 6
41 Fryton H 7
32 Fulbeck E 6
25 Fulbourn K 6
16 Fulbrook C 4
6 Fulford, Somerset C 5
31 Fulford, Staffs F 8
36 Fulford, Yorks B 4
18 Fulham F 2
10 Fulking G 1
36 Full Sutton B 5
4 Fullaford B 6
47 Fullarton F 8
19 Fuller Street B 7
30 Fuller's Moor E 4
8 Fullerton B 5
33 Fulletby C 10
47 Fullwood D 9
17 Fulmer F 10
26 Fulmodestone B 3
33 Fulnetby B 8
37 Fulstow G 11
34 Fulwood, Lancs D 4
6 Fulwood, Som D 5
9 Funtington E 9
9 Funtley E 7
52 Funtullich D 2
64 Funzie B 8
6 Furley F 6
51 Furnace, Argyll G 7
54 Furnace, Ross & Cromarty C 3
22 Furnace End C 6
10 Furner's Green E 3
36 Furness E 5
31 Furness Vale B 8
18 Furneux Pelham A 4
17 Furze Platt F 9
7 Furzebrook H 12
4 Furzehill B 6
6 Fyfet E 6
16 Fyfield, Berks D 5
18 Fyfield, Essex C 6
16 Fyfield, Glos D 3
8 Fyfield, Hants A 4
16 Fyfield, Wilts G 2
41 Fyling Thorpe E 9
58 Fyvie D 5
47 Gabroc Hill D 9
23 Gaddesby A 10
47 Gadgirth G 9
14 Gaer B 5
28 Gaerwen C 4
16 Gagingwell B 5
57 Gaick Lodge L 3
47 Gailes F 8
22 Gailey A 3
40 Gainford C 2
32 Gainsborough, Lincs. A 5
27 Gainsborough, Suffolk L 5
25 Gainsford End L 8
59 Gairloch, Aber C 5
43 Gairloch, Dumf. D 11
54 Gairloch, Ross & Cromarty B 2
55 Gairlochy L 6
52 Gairney Bank G 6
57 Gairnshiel Lodge J 8
39 Gaisgill E 8
44 Gaitsgill H 2
48 Galalaw E 3
49 Galashiels F 7
42 Galdenoch E 3
49 Galewood F 12
34 Galgate B 4
7 Galhampton C 9
43 Gallaberry C 10
50 Gallanach E 5
50 Gallanachmore E 5
53 Gallatown H 7
50 Gallchoille H 5
22 Galley Common C 6
19 Galleyend D 7
19 Galleywood D 7
51 Gallin C 12
53 Gallowfauld C 9
22 Gallows Green F 3
31 Gallows Green F 9

MAP
55 Galltair G 2
5 Galmpton, Devon K 7
5 Galmpton, Devon M 6
40 Galphay H 3
47 Galston F 10
62 Galtrigill C 1
43 Galtway G 8
39 Gamblesby A 8
25 Gamlingay K 3
4 Gammaton Moor D 4
40 Gammersgill G 1
58 Gamrie A 5
32 Gamston, Notts. C 4
32 Gamston, Notts. F 3
15 Ganarew C 8
50 Ganavan D 6
28 Ganllwyd H 6
59 Gannachy K 3
52 Gannochy E 6
30 Gannow Hill G 2
37 Ganstead D 9
41 Ganthorpe H 7
41 Ganton G 10
50 Gaodhail D 3
54 Garbat C 8
51 Garbhallt H 7
27 Garboldisham G 3
57 Garbole G 3
29 Garden City C 12
58 Gardenstown A 5
64 Garderhouse D 6
37 Gardham C 7
7 Gare Hill B 11
51 Garelochhead H 9
16 Garford E 5
36 Garforth D 2
35 Gargrave B 8
52 Gargunnock H 2
63 Garinin C 3
28 Garizim C 6
42 Garlieston G 5
11 Garlinge Green C 9
59 Garlogie G 5
58 Garmond B 5
50 Garmony D 4
58 Garmouth A 1
28 Garn G 2
28 Garn-Dolbenmaen F 4
13 Garnant F 10
14 Garndiffaith D 6
39 Garnett Bridge E 7
47 Garnkirk C 11
14 Garnlydan C 5
13 Garnswllt F 9
14 Garn-yr-erw C 5
63 Garrabost D 6
57 Garragie H 1
2 Garras G 4
28 Garreg F 5
52 Garrick F 3
39 Garrigill A 9
40 Garriston F 2
43 Garroch C 7
42 Garrochtrie H 2
62 Garros B 4
52 Garrow C 3
47 Garryhorn H 8
39 Garsdale Head F 10
16 Garsdon E 1
31 Garshall Green G 8
17 Garsington D 7
34 Garstang C 4
30 Garston B 3
34 Garswood G 4
51 Gartachoil H 12
47 Gartcosh C 11
20 Garth, Brec G 5
29 Garth, Denb F 11
14 Garth, Glam E 2
38 Garth, I.o.M H 2
52 Garth House B 2
14 Garth Place E 5
47 Garthamlock C 11
14 Garthbrengy A 4
59 Garthdee G 7
21 Garthmyl C 7
32 Garthorpe, Leics. H 5
36 Garthorpe, Lincs. E 6
58 Gartly D 3
51 Gartmore H 12
46 Gartnagrenach C 3
47 Gartness A 10
47 Gartocharn A 9
37 Garton D 10
37 Garton-on-the-Wolds A 7
61 Gartymore E 9
49 Garvald, E. Loth. B 8
48 Garvald, Midloth. D 6
57 Garvamore K 1
55 Garvan M 3
50 Garvard H 1
54 Garve D 8

MAP

26 Garvestone......E 3
59 Garvock, Kinc...K 5
47 Garvock, Renfrew.B 7
15 Garway.........B 8
63 Garynahine ......D 3
58 Gash of Philorth..A 7
55 Gaskan.........M 2
7 Gaspar.........C 11
42 Gass...........A 5
43 Gasstown......D 10
47 Gasswater......G 11
15 Gastard........G 12
27 Gasthorpe......G 3
8 Gatcombe......H 6
36 Gate Helmsley..B 5
30 Gateacre.......A 3
39 Gatebeck......G 8
36 Gateforth......D 3
47 Gatehead, Ayr..F 9
44 Gatehouse, Northumb.
               D 6
52 Gatehouse, Perth..B 4
43 Gatehouse of Fleet F 7
43 Gatelawbridge...B 10
26 Gateley........C 3
40 Gatenby........F 3
30 Gates Heath...D 3
38 Gatesgarth.....D 4
49 Gateshaw......G 10
45 Gateshead.....G 10
53 Gateside, Angus..C 9
47 Gateside, Ayr....D 8
52 Gateside, Fife...F 6
56 Gateside, Moray..D 7
47 Gateside, Renfrew.B 8
43 Gateslack......A 10
34 Gathurst.......F 4
31 Gatley.........A 7
10 Gatton.........C 3
49 Gattonside.....F 8
20 Gaufron........F 5
23 Gaulby.........B 10
53 Gauldry........E 8
24 Gaultree........A 7
8 Gaunt's Common..F 2
33 Gautby........C 9
49 Gavinton.......D 10
58 Gawanhill......A 8
35 Gawber........F 11
17 Gawcott........A 8
38 Gawthwaite....G 5
23 Gaydon........G 7
23 Gayhurst.......G 11
39 Gayle..........F 11
40 Gayles.........D 1
30 Gayton, Cheshire..B 1
24 Gayton, Norfolk..D 8
23 Gayton, Northants.
               G 10
31 Gayton, Staffs...G 8
33 Gayton le Marsh.B 11
33 Gayton le Wold...B 9
24 Gayton Thorpe...D 8
24 Gaywood.......C 7
25 Gazeley........J 8
62 Geary..........B 2
56 Geddes House...D 4
27 Gedding........J 2
23 Geddington....D 12
62 Gedintailor.....E 4
24 Gedney.........C 5
24 Gedney Broadgate.C 5
24 Gedney Drove End
               C 6
24 Gedney Dyke....C 5
24 Gedney Hill.....D 4
35 Gee Cross......H 8
60 Geisgeil.......C 3
26 Geldeston......F 7
29 Gell...........C 8
14 Gelli..........E 3
14 Gellideg.......D 3
14 Gelligaer.......E 5
28 Gellilydan.....F 6
13 Gellinudd......G 10
29 Gellioedd......F 8
52 Gellyburn......C 6
43 Gelston........F 8
37 Gembling......A 9
42 Genoch Square...F 2
22 Gentleshaw......A 4
63 Geocrab........H 2
17 George Green...F 11
4 George Nympton.D 6
44 Georgefield....D 1
4 Georgeham......B 3
43 Georgetown, Dumf.
               D 10
14 Georgetown, Mon.C 5
47 Georgetown, Ren..C 9
61 Georgmas Junction
    Station.......B 11
64 Georth.........C 2

28 Gerlan.........C 6
4 Germansweek....F 3
2 Germoe........G 3
2 Gerrans........F 6
43 Gerranton......E 8
17 Gerrards Cross..E 11
63 Geshader.......D 2
27 Gestingthorpe...L 1
21 Geuffordd......A 7
43 Gibbshill......D 8
33 Gibraltar......D 12
15 Giddeahall....G 11
18 Gidea Park.....E 5
5 Gidleigh.......G 5
49 Gifford........C 8
53 Giffordtown....F 7
35 Giggleswick....A 7
36 Gilberdyke.....D 6
43 Gilchristland....B 10
49 Gilchriston.....C 7
43 Gilcrux........H 12
35 Gildersome.....D 11
32 Gildingwells....B 3
40 Gilesgate Moor..A 3
14 Gileston.......H 3
14 Gilfach........D 5
14 Gilfach Goch...E 3
13 Gilfachrheda....A 7
41 Gillamoor......F 7
43 Gillenbie......C 12
43 Gillesbie......B 12
42 Gillespie......F 3
40 Gilling East....G 6
40 Gilling West....E 2
7 Gillingham, Dorset
               D 11
11 Gillingham, Kent .A 7
26 Gillingham,
    Norfolk......F 7
61 Gillock........B 11
31 Gillow Heath...D 7
18 Gillroanie.....G 8
61 Gills..........A 12
10 Gill's Green....E 6
43 Gilmanscleuch..G 6
48 Gilmerton, Midloth.
               C 5
52 Gilmerton, Perth..E 4
39 Gilmonby......D 12
23 Gilmorton.....C 9
44 Gilsland.......F 5
44 Gilsland Spa....F 5
49 Gilston........D 7
14 Gilwern........C 6
26 Gimingham.....B 6
27 Gipping.......J 4
47 Gipsey Bridge...E 10
47 Girdle Toll.....E 8
64 Girlsta........D 7
40 Girsby........D 4
25 Girtford......K 3
47 Girthill.......E 7
47 Girthon........F 7
25 Girton, Cambs...J 5
32 Girton, Notts...D 5
42 Girvan.........B 3
42 Girvan Mains...B 3
35 Gisburn.......B 7
63 Gisla..........D 2
26 Gisleham......F 8
27 Gislingham.....H 4
27 Gissing........G 4
6 Gittisham.......F 5
10 Givons Grove...C 1
52 Glack..........D 5
56 Glackbea.......F 1
56 Glackossian....F 2
11 Gladdish.......C 7
21 Gladestry......G 8
48 Gladhouse......D 6
49 Gladsmuir.....B 7
31 Gladwin's Mark .D 11
13 Glais..........G 10
48 Glaisdale......E 8
43 Glaisters......D 8
53 Glamis.........B 8
13 Glan Duar......C 8
28 Glan-Dwyfach...F 4
28 Glanaber......E 6
13 Glanamman.....F 10
26 Glandford......B 3
29 Glandwr.......D 5
12 Glan-dwr.......D 5
20 Glandyfi.......C 3
14 Glangrwyney...C 5
14 Glanllynfi.....E 2
21 Glan-miwl......C 7
14 Glanryd.......C 5
14 Glan-ryd, Brec...C 1
12 Glan-ryd, Pemb...D 5
45 Glanton.......B 9
45 Glanton Pike...B 9
7 Glanvilles WoottonE10

29 Glan-y-don.....B 11
20 Glan-y-nant.....D 5
29 Glanyrafon......F 9
28 Glan-y-Wern....G 5
24 Glapthorn......F 1
32 Glapwell.......D 2
57 Glas-allt Shiel...L 8
21 Glasbury.......H 7
56 Glaschoil.......A 7
38 Glascoe........F 2
58 Glascoforest....F 5
22 Glascote.......B 6
21 Glascwm.......G 7
51 Glasdrum.......C 7
29 Glasfryn.......E 8
47 Glasgow......C 10
62 Glashvin.......A 4
28 Glasinfryn.....C 5
59 Glaslaw........J 6
55 Glasnacardoch, Inver.
               L 1
55 Glasnacardoch, Inver.
               K 1
62 Glasnakille.....G 5
20 Glaspwll.......C 3
54 Glassburn......F 7
42 Glasserton.....H 5
47 Glassford......E 12
15 Glasshouse Hill..B 10
35 Glasshouses....A 10
53 Glasslie.......G 7
42 Glassoch.......E 4
44 Glasson, Cumb...G 1
34 Glasson, Lancs...B 3
39 Glassonby......A 8
53 Glasterlaw.....B 10
23 Glaston........B 12
7 Glastonbury.....B 8
47 Glastron.......H 8
25 Glatton........G 2
34 Glazebury......G 5
21 Glazely........D 12
32 Gleadless Townend
               B 1
38 Gleaston......H 5
46 Glecknabae.....C 5
43 Gledpark.......F 7
44 Gledsnest......B 3
46 Glemanuilt.....H 1
27 Glemsford......K 1
58 Glen, Banff....D 2
42 Glen, Kirk.....F 6
43 Glen, Kirk.....D 9
52 Glen, Perth....E 6
38 Glen Auldyn....G 2
58 Glen Barry......B 3
62 Glen Bernisdale..C 3
50 Glen Borrodale..A 3
57 Glen Clunie Lodge L 7
58 Glen Dronoch...C 4
48 Glen House.....F 6
38 Glen Mona.....G 2
55 Glen Nevis House.M 5
23 Glen Parva......B 9
59 Glen Tanar House H 2
63 Glen Tolsta....B 6
48 Glen Village....B 2
38 Glen Vine......G 2
55 Glenancross....K 1
50 Glenaros House..C 3
46 Glenbarr......F 2
50 Glenbeg, Argyll..A 3
57 Glenbeg, Moray.G 6
59 Glenbervie......J 5
47 Glenboig......C 12
51 Glenbranter....H 8
48 Glenbreck......G 3
55 Glenbrein Lodge .H 8
62 Glenbrittle House .F 3
58 Glenbuchat Lodge.F 1
47 Glenbuck......F 12
47 Glenburn......C 9
59 Glencally......L 1
60 Glencalvie Lodge .G 5
60 Glencanisp Lodge.E 3
43 Glencaple......E 10
54 Glencarron Lodge.E 4
53 Glencarse......E 7
60 Glencassley Castle.F 5
46 Glencloy.......F 5
51 Glencoe.......B 8
57 Glenconglass...G 7
52 Glencraig......H 6
50 Glencripesdale...B 4
58 Glencuie......C 1
59 Glendavan House.G 2
44 Glendearg, Dumf..C 1
49 Glendearg, Selkirk.F 8
52 Glendevon.....C 8
55 Glendoe Lodge .H 8
55 Glendoebeg....J 8
53 Glendoick......E 7
57 Glendoll Lodge...M 8

53 Glenduckie......E 7
59 Glendye Lodge...J 4
52 Gleneagles Hotel . F 4
55 Gleneig.......H 2
56 Glenerney......E 6
51 Glenfalloch Farm F 10
52 Glenfarg........F 6
59 Glenfenzie......G 1
56 Glenferness House.E 5
58 Glenfiddich Lodge D 1
23 Glenfield........B 9
47 Glenfinart House..A 7
55 Glenfinnan......L 3
55 Glenfintaig Lodge .L 6
52 Glenfoot.......F 6
55 Glenforslan......M 1
51 Glenfyne Lodge..F 9
47 Glengarnock....D 8
52 Glengoulandie...B 3
62 Glengrasco......D 4
51 Glengyle.......F 11
42 Glengyre.......E 1
43 Glenhead, Kirk..F 8
52 Glenhead, Perth ..G 4
53 Glenhead Farm...A 7
48 Glenhighton....F 4
22 Glenhoise......E 5
43 Glenholm......D 12
43 Glenhoul.......C 7
50 Glenhurich......A 5
48 Glenkerry......H 5
43 Glenkiln.......D 9
58 Glenkindie......F 2
48 Glenkirk.......F 3
56 Glenlatterach...D 7
43 Glenlee........D 7
57 Glenlia........H 1
43 Glenlochar.....E 8
57 Glenlochsie.....M 6
46 Glenloig.......F 4
42 Glenluce.......F 3
54 Glenmarksie....D 7
46 Glenmassan.....A 6
38 Glenmaye......G 1
54 Glenmeanne....D 7
43 Glenmidge......C 9
38 Glenmooar.....G 2
50 Glenmore, Argyll.F 6
50 Glenmore, Argyll .A 3
62 Glenmore, Inver..D 4
57 Glenmore Lodge..H 5
50 Glenmorven Cott..B 3
42 Glenmuck......A 6
48 Glenochar......H 2
59 Glenquiech......L 2
48 Glenrath.......F 5
38 Glenridding.....D 6
46 Glenrisdell.....D 4
60 Glenrossal......F 5
53 Glenrothes......G 7
42 Glenruther......D 4
50 Glensanda......C 5
59 Glensaugh......J 4
52 Glenshee......D 5
43 Glenshimmeroch..C 7
57 Glenshirra Lodge .K 1
47 Glenside, Ayr....D 7
63 Glenside, Ross &
    Cromarty......E 5
51 Glensluain .....H 8
46 Glenstriven....B 6
55 Glensulaig......L 4
48 Glentaggart.....G 1
33 Glentham......A 7
48 Glentress, Peebles .E 5
48 Glentress, Peebles .E 6
57 Glentromie Lodge.K 3
43 Glentrool Village .D 4
38 Glentruan......F 2
57 Glentruim House..K 2
47 Glentworth......A 6
56 Glenurquhart...C 3
43 Glenwhargen...A 8
43 Glenwhilly.....D 3
48 Glespin........G 1
43 Gletness.......D 7
15 Glewstone.....B 9
24 Glinton........E 3
59 Glithno........H 6
23 Glooston.......C 11
35 Glossop........H 9
15 Gloster Hill....C 10
15 Gloucester.....C 11
15 Gloucestershire, Co.
               D 10
64 Gloup.........A 7
2 Gloweth.......E 5
35 Glusburn......C 8
61 Glutt Lodge....D 9
2 Gluvian.......C 6
2 Glympton......B 5
29 Glyn..........D 7

12 Glyn-Arthen....B 6
29 Glyn Ceiriog....F 11
29 Glynbrochan....D 5
14 Glyncoch......E 4
14 Glyncorrwg....D 2
10 Glynde........G 3
29 Glyndyfrdwy....F 10
28 Glynllifon Park ...E 4
14 Glynneath......D 2
14 Glyntaff.......E 4
14 Glynteg.......C 7
31 Gnosall.......H 7
31 Gnosall Heath ...H 7
23 Goadby.......B 11
32 Goadby Marwood.H 5
11 Goat Lees......C 9
16 Goatacre......F 1
7 Goathill.......E 10
41 Goathland.....E 8
62 Goathurst......C 6
10 Goathurst Com...C 4
60 Gobernuisgach Lodge
               C 5
30 Gobowen......G 2
9 Godalming.....B 11
11 Goddard's Green..E 7
10 Godden Green...C 4
6 Godford Cross....F 5
25 Godmanchester..H 3
7 Godmanston....F 10
11 Godmersham....C 9
7 Godney........B 8
2 Godolphin Cross..F 3
13 Godre'r-graig....F 11
8 Godshill, Hants...E 3
9 Godshill, I.o.W...H 7
10 Godstone......C 2
8 Godwinscroft...F 3
14 Goetre.........D 6
18 Goff's Oak......D 3
48 Gogar.........B 4
20 Gogfnan.......D 2
28 Golan..........F 5
3 Golant.........D 8
3 Golberdon......C 10
34 Golborne......G 5
35 Golcar........E 9
24 Gold Hill, Cambs..F 6
7 Gold Hill, Dorset E 11
15 Goldcliff......F 7
16 Golden Balls....D 6
10 Golden Cross...G 4
10 Golden Green...C 5
13 Golden Grove...E 9
8 Golden Hill, Hants.F 4
12 Golden Hill, Pem..G 3
9 Golden Pot.....B 8
15 Golden Valley ..B 12
31 Goldenhill......E 7
18 Golders Green...E 3
19 Goldhanger....C 9
21 Golding.......B 11
25 Goldington....K 2
41 Goldsborough,
    N. Riding......D 8
36 Goldsborough,
    W. Riding.....B 2
2 Goldsithney....G 3
30 Goldstone......G 6
36 Goldthorpe.....G 3
56 Gollanfield.....D 4
40 Gollinglith Foot ..G 2
11 Golsoncott......B 4
61 Golspie.......G 8
61 Golval.........B 9
8 Gomeldon......C 3
35 Gomersal......E 10
50 Gometra House...C 1
9 Gomshall......A 12
32 Gonalston......E 4
64 Gonfirth ....D 7
18 Good Easter....C 6
26 Gooderstone....E 1
43 Goodhope......B 11
4 Goodleigh.....C 5
36 Goodmanham...C 6
11 Goodnestone, Kent
               C 11
11 Goodnestone, KentB 9
15 Goodrich......B 9
5 Goodrington....K 8
12 Goodwick......C 3
8 Goodworth Clatford
               B 5
23 Goodyers End...D 7
36 Goole.........E 5
36 Goole Fields....E 5
2 Goonbell......E 4
2 Goonhavern....D 5
10 Goose Green...C 5
59 Goosecruives....J 5

4 Gooseham......D 1
43 Goosehill......A 8
5 Goosewell......K 4
16 Goosey........E 4
34 Goosnargh.....C 4
30 Goostrey......C 6
22 Gorcott Hill....E 4
28 Gorddinog......C 6
49 Gordon........E 9
61 Gordonbush....F 8
58 Gordonstown,
    Aberdeen.....D 5
58 Gordonstown, Banff
               B 3
48 Gorebridge.....C 6
24 Gorefield......D 5
17 Goring........F 7
9 Goring-by-Sea ...F 12
17 Goring Heath...F 7
26 Gorleston on Sea..E 8
22 Gornalwood....D 4
3 Gorran Churchtown
               E 7
3 Gorran Haven...E 7
44 Gorrenberry....C 3
20 Gors..........E 2
16 Gorse Hill.....E 3
29 Gorsedd.......C 10
13 Gorseinon......G 9
64 Gorseness......C 2
31 Gorseybank....E 11
13 Gorsgoch......B 8
13 Gorslas........F 9
15 Gorsley.......B 10
54 Gorstan.......D 7
55 Gorstanvorran...M 2
30 Gorstella......D 2
15 Gorsty Common..A 8
35 Gorton........G 7
27 Gosbeck.......K 5
24 Gosberton......B 3
24 Gosberton Clough..C 3
27 Gosfield.......M 1
21 Gosford.......F 10
49 Gosford House...B 7
38 Gosforth, Cumb..E 3
45 Gosforth, Northumb.
               F 10
18 Gosmore......A 2
9 Gosport.......F 7
64 Gossabrough....C 8
45 Goswick.......B 12
32 Gotham.......G 3
16 Gotherington...A 1
10 Goudhurst.....D 6
33 Goulceby......B 9
47 Gourock......B 7
58 Gourdas......C 5
59 Gourdon......K 6
47 Govan.........C 10
32 Goverton......E 4
5 Goveton.......L 6
14 Govilon.......C 6
36 Gowdall......E 4
56 Gower.........D 1
13 Gowerton......G 9
52 Gowkhall......H 5
36 Gowthorpe.....B 5
37 Goxhill, Lincs...E 9
37 Goxhill, Yorks...C 9
37 Goxhill Haven...E 9
13 Goytre........H 11
43 Gracefield......C 9
49 Graden.......F 10
9 Graffham......D 10
25 Grafham, Hunts..H 3
9 Grafham, Surrey.B 11
15 Grafton, Herefs...A 8
16 Grafton, Oxon...D 4
30 Grafton, Salop...H 3
21 Grafton, Worcs..F 11
36 Grafton, Yorks...A 2
22 Grafton Flyford...G 3
23 Grafton Regis...G 11
23 Grafton Underwood
               D 12
11 Grafty Green....C 7
29 Graianrhyd.....E 11
29 Graig..........C 7
29 Graig-fechan....E 10
48 Graigmillar.....B 6
19 Grain.........F 9
37 Grainsby......G 10
37 Grainthorpe....G 11
2 Grampound.....E 6
2 Grampound Road.E 6
17 Granborough....B 8
32 Granby........G 5
23 Grandborough...E 8
52 Grandtully.....B 4
34 Grane.........E 6
47 Grange, Ayr....F 9
30 Grange, Cheshire.B 1

MAP		MAP		MAP		MAP		MAP		MAP	
38	Grange, Cumb....C 5	22	Great Chatwell....A 1	18	Great Parndon....C 4	11	Greenhill, Kent..A 10	30	Grindley Brook ...F 4	8	Gurnard.........F 6
53	Grange, Fife.....F 10	25	Great Chesterford.L 6	25	Great Paxton......J 3	48	Greenhill, Stirling .B 1	31	Grindlow........B 10	7	Gurney Slade.....A 9
53	Grange, Perth....E 7	8	Great Cheverell...A 1	34	Great Plumpton ..D 3	47	Greenhills.......D 8	40	Grindon, Durham...C 4	14	Gurnos.........C 1
40	Grange, Yorks....F 6	25	Great Chishill....L 5	26	Great Plumstead ..D 6	10	Greenhithe......A 5	44	Grindon, Northumb.	8	Gussage All Saints E 2
58	Grange Crossroads B 2	19	Great Clacton....B 11	32	Great Ponton.....G 6	47	Greenholm......F 10		F 6	8	Gussage St.AndrewE 1
7	Grange Gate....H 12	38	Great Clifton.....B 3	36	Great Preston.....D 2	39	Greenholme.....E 8	49	Grindon, Northumb.	8	Gussage St.MichaelE 1
56	Grange Hall......D 6	37	Great Coate.....F 10	25	Great Raveley.....G 4	49	Greenhouse......G 8		E 11	11	Guston.........D 11
35	Grange Moor.....E 11	22	Great Comberton .H 3	16	Great Rissington..B 3	35	Greenhow Hill ....A 9	31	Grindon, Staffs....E 9	64	Gutcher.........B 8
53	Grange of Lindores E 7	44	Great Corby .....H 3	16	Great Rollright...A 4	64	Greenigo.......D 2	49	Grindon Hill......F 6	53	Guthrie.........B 10
45	Grange Villa......H 10	27	Great Cornard....L 2	12	Great Rudbaxton .E 3	49	Greenknowe.....E 9	49	Grindonrigg......E 11	24	Guy's Head.......C 6
48	Grangehall......E 2	37	Great Cowden ...C 10	26	Great Ryburgh ...C 3	61	Greenland.......A 11	32	Gringley on the Hill	7	Guy's Marsh....D 11
31	Grangemill......D 11	16	Great Coxwell....E 4	45	Great Ryle.......B 8	17	Greenlands......F 8		A 4	24	Guyhirn........E 5
48	Grangemouth.....A 2	40	Great Crakehall ..F 3	19	Great Saling.....A 7	58	Greenlaw, Banff..B 4	44	Grinsdale........G 2	45	Guyzance.....C 10
38	Grange-over-Sands	23	Great Cransley ..D 11	39	Great Salkeld.....B 8	49	Greenlaw, Berwick E 9	30	Grinshill ....H 4	14	Gwaelod-y-garth...F 4
	G 6	26	Great Cressingham E 2	25	Great Sampford...L 7	49	Greenlaw Walls..E 12	40	Grinton........E 1	29	Gwaenysgor.....B 10
48	Grangepans......A 3	34	Great Crosby......G 2	30	Great Sankey.....A 4	43	Greenlea, Dumf..D 11	64	Gristhorpe......G 11	28	Gwalchmai.......C 3
14	Grangetown, Glam.	31	Great Cubley....F 10	30	Great Saughall....C 2	47	Greenlea, Dunb...A 7	26	Griston........E 2	12	Gwastad.........D 4
	G 5	23	Great Dalby......A 10	27	Great Saxham.....J 1	52	Greenloaning.....F 3	64	Gritley.........D 3	13	Gwaun-cae-Gurwen
40	Grangetown, Yks..C 6	23	Gt. Doddington ..F 12	16	Great Shefford...G 5	34	Greenmount......F 6	16	Grittenham......F 1		F 10
57	Granish..........H 5	6	Great Dorweeke...F 3	25	Great Shelford....K 6	47	Greenock........B 8	15	Grittleton......F 11	12	Gwbert-on-Sea....B 5
37	Gransmoor......A 9	15	Great Doward....C 9	40	Great Smeaton....E 4	38	Greenodd........G 5	38	Grizebeck........G 5	2	Gweek..........G 4
12	Granston.......D 2	26	Great Dunham ...D 2	26	Great Snoring.....B 2	48	Greenrig.........E 1	38	Grizedale........F 6	15	Gwehelog Com...D 7
25	Grantchester......K 5	18	Great Dunmow....B 6	16	Great Somerford ..F 1	43	Greenrow........F 11	64	Grobister......C 4	20	Gwenddwr......H 6
32	Grantham........G 6	8	Great Durnford ...F 2	30	Great Soudley.....G 6	23	Greens Norton ..G 10	23	Groby..........A 8	2	Gwennap........F 4
58	Grantlodge......F 5	18	Great Easton, Essex	40	Great Stainton....C 3	52	Greenscares......F 3	29	Groes, Denb.....D 9	14	Gwent, Co.......D 6
48	Granton, Dumf...H 3		A 6	19	Great Stambridge .E 9	48	Greenshields......E 3	13	Groes, Glam...H 11	2	Gwenter.........H 4
48	Granton, Midloth..B 5	23	Great Easton, Leics.	25	Great Staughton...J 2	45	Greenside........G 9	14	Groesfaen.......F 4	21	Gwernaffel......E 8
57	Grantown-on-Spey G 6		C 11	33	Great Steeping...D 11	45	Greensidehill ....A 8	28	Groesffordd......F 2	15	Gwernesney......D 7
21	Grantsfield......F 10	34	Great Eccleston ...C 3	11	Great Stonar....B 12	58	Greenskairs......A 5	29	Groesffordd......C 7	13	Gwernogle......D 8
49	Grantshouse......C 10	41	Great Edstone....G 7	39	Great Strickland ..C 8	19	Greenstead Green.A 8	21	Groesllwyd......A 7	29	Gwernymynydd..D 11
30	Grappenhall......B 5	26	Great Ellingham ..F 3	25	Great Stukeley....H 3	18	Greensted Green..D 5	28	Groeslon, Angl...C 3	14	Gwern-y-Steeple..G 4
37	Grasby..........G 8	7	Great Elm........A 10	33	Great Sturton.....C 9	64	Greenwall.......C 3	28	Groeslon, Caer...E 4	30	Gwersyllt.......E 2
38	Grasmere........D 6	25	Great Eversden ...K 5	30	Gt. Sutton, Ches...C 2	14	Greenway, Glam..G 4	46	Grogport........E 3	29	Gwespyr........B 10
35	Grasscroft......G 8	40	Great Fencote....F 3	21	Gt. Sutton, Salop. D 10	12	Greenway, Pem...D 4	29	Gronant........B 10	2	Gwinear.........F 3
30	Grassendale......B 3	27	Great Finborough .J 3	45	Great Swinburne ..E 7	18	Greenwich.......F 4	10	Groombridge....D 4	2	Gwithian.........F 3
39	Grassholme......C 11	26	Great Fransham ..D 2	19	Great Tarpots.....E 7	16	Greet..........A 1	63	Grosebay........H 2	29	Gwyddelwern....F 10
35	Grassington......A 9	17	Great Gaddesden .C 11	16	Great Tew.......A 5	21	Greete.........E 11	15	Grosmont, Mon...B 7	13	Gwyddgrug......C 8
45	Grasslees........C 8	25	Great Gidding....G 2	19	Great Tey.......A 9	33	Greetham, Lincs..C 10	41	Grosmont, Yorks..E 8	29	Gwynfryn.......E 11
32	Grassmoor......D 1	36	Great Givendale ..B 6	25	Great Thurlow....K 8	23	Greetham, Rut..A 12	27	Groton.........L 2	29	Gwynedd, Co....E 5
32	Grassthorpe......C 5	27	Great Glemham ..J 6	4	Great Torrington .D 4	35	Greetland.......E 9	16	Grove, Berks....E 5	20	Gwystre........F 6
8	Grateley........B 4	23	Great Glen......B 10	45	Great Tosson ....C 8	7	Greinton.......C 7	7	Grove, Dorset...H 7	29	Gwytherin......D 8
31	Gratwich........G 9	32	Great Gonerby....F 6	19	Great Totham ....C 8	23	Grendon,N'thants F 12	32	Grove, Notts.....B 4	29	Gyfelia........F 12
18	Graveley, Herts. ..A 2	15	Great Graig......B 7	38	Great Urswick ...H 5	22	Grendon, War....B 6	13	Grovesend......G 9	29	Gyffin..........C 7
25	Graveley, Hunts..J 4	25	Great Gransden ..K 4	19	Great Wakering...F 9	22	Grendon Common B 6	30	Grudgington ....H 5	29	Gyffylliog......D 10
22	Gravelly Hill.....C 5	26	Great Green, Norf.F 6	27	Great Waldingfield L 2	11	Grendon Green...B 8	54	Grudie.........D 7	21	Habberley......B 9
11	Graveney........B 9	27	Great Green, Suff..K 2	26	Great Walsingham B 2	17	Grendon Underwood	60	Gruids.........F 6	63	Habost, Lewis...E 4
10	Gravesend......A 5	41	Great Habton.....G 8	19	Great Waltham ...C 7		B 8	60	Gruinard House ..G 1	63	Habost, Lewis...A 6
63	Gravir..........E 5	24	Great Hale......A 2	18	Great Warley.....E 3	42	Grennan........E 3	62	Grula..........E 3	37	Habrough.......F 9
37	Grayingham......G 7	18	Great Hallingbury .B 5	16	Great Washbourne A 1	5	Grenofen.......J 4	50	Gruline House....D 3	24	Hacconby......C 2
39	Grayrigg........E 8	21	Great Hanwood .B 10	27	Great Welnetham..J 2	35	Grenoside.......H 11	2	Grumbla........G 1	24	Haceby........B 1
18	Grays..........F 6	23	Great Harrowden.E 12	27	Great Wenham....L 4	30	Gresford........E 2	27	Grundisburgh....K 5	31	Hacheston......J 6
9	Grayshott......C 10	34	Great Harwood...D 6	45	Great Whittington.F 8	26	Gresham........B 5	64	Grundsound.....E 7	32	Hackenthorpe...B 1
9	Grayswood......C 10	17	Great Haseley....D 7	19	Great Wigborough B 9	62	Greshornish.....C 3	64	Gruting.........D 6	18	Hacketts........C 3
40	Graythorp......B 5	37	Great Hatfield....C 9	25	Great Wilbraham .K 5	63	Gress..........C 6	64	Grutness........F 7	26	Hackford.......E 3
17	Grazeley........G 8	31	Great Haywood...H 8	8	Great Wishford...C 2	26	Gressenhall ....D 3	28	Grwedog........B 3	40	Hackforth......E 3
36	Greasbrough.....H 2	23	Great Heath......D 7	15	Great Witcombe .C 12	26	Gressenhall Grn...D 3	51	Gualachulain.....C 8	64	Hackland.......C 2
30	Greasby........B 1	36	Great Heck......E 4	22	Great Witley.....E 1	39	Gressingham....H 8	60	Gualin House....B 4	25	Hacklete.......C 2
32	Greasley........E 2	27	Great Henny.....L 2	16	Great Wolford...A 3	30	Grestey Green....E 6	53	Guard Bridge....E 9	23	Hackleton......G 11
25	Great Abington...K 6	15	Great Hinton ...H 12	25	Great Wratting...K 8	44	Gretna.........F 2	22	Guarlford.......H 2	41	Hackness......F 10
25	Great Addington..H 1	26	Great Hockham...F 2	18	Great Wymondley.A 2	40	Greta Bridge....D 1	52	Guay...........B 5	18	Hackney........E 4
22	Great Alne.......F 5	19	Great Holland ..B 12	22	Great Wyrley.....A 3	44	Gretna Green....F 1	43	Gubhill.........B 10	33	Hackthorn......B 7
34	Great Altcar......F 2	27	Great Horkesley...M 3	30	Great Wytheford..H 4	16	Gretton, Glos....A 1	11	Guestling Green ..G 7	39	Hackthorpe.....C 7
18	Great Amwell....C 4	25	Great Hormead ..M 5	26	Great Yarmouth...E 8	23	Gretton, N'thants C 12	11	Guestling Icklesham	45	Hadden........F 10
39	Great Asby......D 9	35	Great Horton ...D 10	27	Great Yeldam....L 1	21	Gretton, Salop...C 10		F 7	17	Haddenham, Bucks. C8
27	Great Ashfield....H 3	17	Great Horwood...A 8	18	Greater London, Co. F3	40	Grewelthorpe....G 2	26	Guestwick.......C 3	25	Haddenham, Cambs.
40	Great Ayton.....D 6	23	Great Houghton,	35	Greater Manchester,	58	Grey Stone......E 6	34	Guide..........E 6		H 6
19	Great Baddow....C 7		Northants......F 11		Co.............G 7	40	Greygarth.......H 2	45	Guide Post.....E 10	49	Haddington, E. Loth.
15	Great Badminton.F 11	36	Great Houghton,	24	Greatford......D 2	13	Greynor........F 9	25	Guilden Morden ..L 4		B 8
25	Great Bardfield...M 8		Yorkshire......F 2	31	Greatgate......F 9	25	Greyrigg, Dumf..C 11	30	Guilden Sutton ..C 3	32	Haddington, Lincs. D 6
25	Great Barford....K 2	31	Great Hucklow ..B 10	40	Greatham, Dur...B 5	48	Greyrigg, Stirling .B 2	9	Guildford......A 11	26	Haddiscoe......F 7
22	Great Barr......C 4	37	Great Kelk.......A 8	9	Greatham, Hants..C 8	38	Greysouthen.....B 3	52	Guildtown......D 6	58	Haddoch.......C 3
16	Great Barrington..C 3	17	Great Kimble ....D 9	9	Greatham, Sussex E 11	52	Greystoke, Angus C 10	23	Guilsborough...E 10	23	Haddon........F 2
30	Great Barrow....C 3	17	Great Kingshill ...D 9	11	Greatstone-on-Sea. F 9	39	Greystoke, Cumb..B 7	21	Guilsfield......A 8	35	Hade Edge......G 10
27	Great Barton....J 2	40	Great Langton ...F 3	23	Greatworth......H 9	43	Greystone.......D 10	11	Guilton........B 11	35	Hademore......A 5
41	Great Barugh....G 7	19	Great Leighs.....B 7	9	Greywell........A 8	9	Gribbleford Bridge F 4	47	Guiltreehill.....H 8	35	Hadfield.......G 9
45	Great Bavington..E 8	37	Great Limber ...F 9	25	Green End......K 2	36	Gribthorpe......D 5	4	Guineaford......B 4	18	Hadham Cross...B 4
27	Great Bealings...K 5	23	Great Linford ...H 12	36	Green Hammerton A 2	50	Gribun.........D 2	55	Guisachan House .G 7	18	Hadham Ford....B 4
16	Great Bedwyn...H 4	25	Great Livermere .H 2	7	Green Ore.......B 9	5	Gridley Corner....G 2	40	Guisborough....D 6	19	Hadleigh, Essex...E 8
19	Great Bentley....B 11	31	Great Longstone .C 10	10	Green Street Green A 5	23	Griff...........C 7	35	Guiseley......C 10	27	Hadleigh, Suffolk..L 3
23	Great Billing.....F 11	45	Great Lumley....H 11	18	Green Tye.......B 4	16	Guiting Power...B 2	26	Guist.........C 3	31	Hadley........A 12
26	Great Bircham...B 1	22	Great Malvern ...G 1	34	Greenbank......B 4	16	Griffithstown....D 6	16	Guiting Power...B 2	31	Hadley End.....H 10
27	Great Blakenham .K 4	27	Great Maplestead.M 1	43	Greenbeck.......C 11	39	Grigghall.......F 7	64	Gulberwick.....E 7	18	Hadley Wood....D 3
39	Great Blencow...B 7	34	Great Marton ...D 2	48	Greenburn.......C 2	64	Grimbister......C 2	49	Gullane........A 7	10	Hadlow.........C 5
30	Great Bolas.....H 5	26	Great Massingham C 1	38	Greencastle......E 4	36	Grimethorpe.....F 2	2	Gulval.........G 2	10	Hadlow Down....F 4
9	Great Bookham..A 12	26	Great Melton.....E 4	7	Greendown......A 9	22	Grimley........F 2	5	Gulworthy.......H 3	30	Hadnall........H 4
23	Great Bourton ...H 8	17	Great Milton ....D 7	45	Greendykes......C 12	24	Grimmet.......H 8	23	Gumley........C 10	25	Hadstock.......L 7
23	Great Bowden....C 11	17	Great Missenden D 10	49	Greenend........G 8	33	Grimoldby......A 11	2	Gummow's Shop .D 6	45	Hadwin's Close...B 10
25	Great Bradley....K 8	34	Great Mitton ....C 6	25	Greenfield, Beds..M 2	34	Grimsargh......D 5	32	Gunby, Lincs....H 6	22	Hadzor.........F 3
19	Great Braxted....C 8	11	Great Mongeham C 12	29	Greenfield, Ches..B 11	37	Grimsby........F 10	36	Gunby, Yorks....D 5	11	Haffenden Quarter D 7
27	Great Bricett....K 3	34	Great Moss.....C 6	55	Greenfield, Inver..J 6	23	Grimscote......G 10	9	Gundleton......C 7	20	Hafod.........G 1
17	Great Brickhill...A 10	39	Great Musgrave .D 10	17	Greenfield, Oxon..E 8	4	Grimscott......E 1	4	Gunn...........C 5	29	Hafod-Dinbych...E 8
31	Great Bridgeford..G 7	30	Great Ness ......H 3	35	Greenfield, Yorks..G 8	22	Grimshader.....D 5	39	Gunnerside......E 11	20	Hafod-Peris.....F 1
23	Great Brington...F 10	19	Great Oakley, Essex	18	Greenford......F 1	24	Grimsthorpe....C 2	45	Gunnerton.......F 7	35	Haggate.........D 7
19	Great Bromley...A 10		A 11	48	Greengairs......B 1	32	Grimston, Leics..H 4	45	Gunnerton Fell...E 7	44	Haggbeck.......F 3
30	Great Budworth...B 5	23	Great Oakley,	44	Greengate Well....F 5	24	Grimston, Norfolk C 8	36	Gunnersmere....F 6	49	Haggerston......B 11
40	Great Burdon....D 3		Northants.....D 12	34	Greenhalgh......D 5	37	Grimston, Yorks. D 10	3	Gunnislake.....C 11	21	Hagley, Herefs. .H 11
19	Great Burstead...E 7	18	Great Offley.....A 1	16	Greenham, Berks..H 6	7	Grimstone......G 9	64	Gunnista.......D 7	22	Hagley, Worcs...D 3
40	Great Busby.....E 5	39	Great Ormside....C 9	6	Greenham, Som...D 4	9	Grinacombe Moor G 3	36	Gunthorpe, Lincs..G 8	31	Hagworthingham C 10
18	Great Canfield....B 6	44	Great Orton......H 2	44	Greenhead......E 9	41	Grindale.......H 11	26	Gunthorpe, Norf..B 3	34	Haigh, Lancs....F 5
33	Great Carlton....B 11	36	Great Ouseburn ..A 2	47	Greenhead, Ayr..E 9	22	Grindle........B 1	32	Gunthorpe, Notts..F 4	35	Haigh, Yorks.....F 11
24	Great Casterton..E 1	23	Great Oxendon ..D 10	43	Greenhead, Dumf.C 10	31	Grindleford......B 11	8	Gunville........G 6	35	Haigh Moor.....E 11
15	Great Chalfield ..H 11	18	Great Oxney Grn..C 6	44	Greenhead,	34	Grindleton......C 6	34	Gupworthy......C 3	34	Haighton Green...D 4
11	Great Chart......D 8	26	Great Palgrave ..D 1		Northumb.....F 5						

MAP

25 Hail Weston......J 3
38 Haile..........D 3
18 Hailey, Herts....C 4
16 Hailey, Oxon....C 4
10 Hailsham.......G 5
18 Hainault........E 4
26 Hainford.......D 5
33 Hainton........B 9
37 Haisthorpe......A 9
32 Halam.........E 4
52 Halbeath.......H 6
6 Halberton......E 3
61 Halcro.........B 11
30 Hale, Cheshire...B 6
8 Hale, Hants.....D 3
30 Hale, Lancs......B 3
9 Hale, Surrey.....A 10
30 Hale Cliff.......B 3
10 Hale Street......C 5
30 Halebarns.......B 6
26 Hales, Norfolk...F 7
30 Hales, Staffs.....G 6
22 Halesowen......D 3
27 Halesworth......H 7
30 Halewood.......B 3
22 Halford, War.....H 6
21 Halford, Salop...D 10
12 Halfpenny Furze..F 6
22 Halfpenny Green..C 2
16 Halfway, Berks...G 5
13 Halfway, Carm...D 11
13 Halfway, Carm...D 10
3 Halfway House,
   Cornwall.......C 8
6 Halfway House,
   Devon........G 4
21 Halfway House,
   Salop.........A 9
42 Halfway House,
   Wigtown.......E 4
11 Halfway Houses..A 8
35 Halifax.........E 9
47 Halket ....D 9
61 Halkirk........B 10
29 Halkyn.........C 11
47 Hall..........D 9
38 Hall Dunnerdale..F 5
22 Hall Green......D 5
47 Hall of Carnduff .E 11
21 Hall of the Forest .D 7
38 Hall Waberthwaite F 3
10 Halland........F 4
23 Hallaton.......B 11
7 Hallatrow......A 10
44 Hallbankgate.....G 4
15 Hallen.........F 8
32 Hallfield Gate....D 1
62 Hallin.........B 2
10 Halling........B 6
33 Hallington,
   Lincs.........B 10
45 Hallington,
   Northumb......E 8
34 Halliwell.......F 6
32 Halloughton.....E 4
22 Hallow.........F 2
44 Hallrule.......B 4
49 Halls.........B 9
18 Hall's Green.....A 3
5 Hallsands......M 7
43 Hallscaur......B 8
24 Halltoft End.....A 5
49 Halltree.......D 7
3 Hallworthy.....A 9
49 Hallyburton.....D 9
48 Hallyne........E 5
30 Halmer End.....E 6
15 Halmore.......D 10
48 Halmyre Mains...D 4
9 Halnaker.......E 10
34 Halsall........F 2
23 Halse, Northants.H 9
6 Halse, Somerset...C 5
2 Halsetown......F 7
37 Halsham........D 10
4 Halsinger......B 4
27 Halstead, Essex..M 1
10 Halstead, Kent...B 4
23 Halstead, Leics...B 11
7 Halstock......E 8
38 Haltcliff Bridge..B 6
33 Haltham.......D 9
17 Halton, Bucks...C 9
30 Halton, Cheshire..B 4
29 Halton, Denb...F 12
34 Halton, Lancs...A 4
45 Halton, Northumb. F 8
35 Halton East..G 5
39 Halton Gill....G 11
33 Halton Holegate .D 11
44 Halton Lea Gate..G 5
35 Halton Moor...D 12
34 Halton Park......A 4

45 Halton Shields....F 8
35 Halton West......B 7
44 Haltwhistle.....G 5
26 Halvergate.......E 7
5 Halwell.........K 6
4 Halwill.........F 3
4 Halwill Junction..F 3
6 Ham, Devon....F 6
15 Ham, Glos......D 10
11 Ham, Kent.....C 12
18 Ham, London...G 2
16 Ham, Wilts.....F 4
11 Ham Green, Kent.A 7
15 Ham Green, Som. G 8
22 Ham Green, Worcs.
         F 4
10 Ham Hill......B 6
11 Ham Street, Kent .E 8
7 Ham Street, Som. .C 9
8 Hamble........E 6
17 Hambleden......E 8
9 Hambledon, Hants.E 8
9 Hambledon, Surrey
         B 11
34 Hambleton, Lancs. C 3
36 Hambleton, Yorks.D 3
7 Hambridge......D 7
9 Hambrook......E 9
33 Hameringham....C 10
25 Hamerton......G 2
47 Hamilton.......D 12
9 Hammer.......C 10
9 Hammerpot.....F 11
18 Hammersmith....F 2
22 Hammerwich....A 4
7 Hammoon......E 11
64 Hamnavoe, W. Burra
         E 7
64 Hamnavoe, Yell...C 7
64 Hamnavoe, Zet...C 7
64 Hamnavoe, Zet...C 7
10 Hampden.......H 5
17 Hampden Row...D 9
16 Hampnett......C 2
36 Hampole.......F 3
8 Hampreston.....F 2
8 Hampshire, Co....C 6
18 Hampstead......E 3
16 Hampstead Norris.F 6
35 Hampsthwaite ...A 11
18 Hampton, London G 1
22 Hampton, Salop. .D 1
22 Hampton, Worcs. H 4
15 Hampton Bishop..A 9
30 Hampton Heath..E 4
22 Hampton in Arden D 5
22 Hampton Lovett..F 2
22 Hampton Lucy...F 6
22 Hampton on the Hill
         F 6
16 Hampton Poyle...C 6
31 Hamstall Ridware.H 9
8 Hamstead, Hants..G 5
22 Hamstead, War...C 4
16 Hamstead Marshall
         H 5
40 Hamsteels........A 2
40 Hamsterley, Dur..B 1
45 Hamsterley, Dur. .G 9
8 Hamworthy.....G 1
31 Hanbury, Staffs. .G 10
22 Hanbury, Worcs...F 3
30 Handbridge.....D 3
10 Handcross......E 2
31 Handforth......D 2
30 Handley, Cheshire D 3
8 Handley, Dorset..D 2
22 Handsacre......A 4
22 Handsworth......C 4
17 Handy Cross, Bucks.
         E 9
4 Handy Cross, Devon
         C 3
31 Hanford.......F 7
8 Hanging Langford.B 2
43 Hangingshaw, Dumf.
         C 11
48 Hangingshaw, Lan. E 2
30 Hankelow.......F 5
16 Hankerton......E 1
10 Hankham......G 5
31 Hanley.........E 7
31 Hanley Castle...H 2
21 Hanley Child....F 12
22 Hanley Swan....H 2
21 Hanley William. F 12
35 Hanlith........A 8
30 Hanmer........F 3
9 Hannington, Hants.
         A 7
23 Hannington,
   Northants......E 11
16 Hannington, Wilts. E 3

16 Hannington Wick .E 3
23 Hanslope......G 11
24 Hanthorpe......C 2
18 Hanwell, London..F 2
23 Hanwell, Oxon...H 8
18 Hanworth, Lond. .G 1
26 Hanworth, Norf...B 5
48 Happendon......F 1
26 Happisburgh.....B 7
26 Happisburgh Com. C 7
30 Hapsford.......C 3
34 Hapton, Lancs....D 6
26 Hapton, Norfolk..F 5
5 Harberton......K 6
5 Harbertonford...K 6
11 Harbledown.....B 10
22 Harborne......D 4
23 Harborough Magna
         D 8
45 Harbottle.......C 7
5 Harbourneford...J 6
23 Harbury.......F 7
32 Harby, Leics....G 5
32 Harby, Notts....C 6
6 Harcombe, Devon H 2
6 Harcombe, Devon G 5
2 Harcourt.......F 5
35 Harden........C 9
15 Hardenhuish....G 12
59 Hardgate, Aber...E 5
43 Hardgate, Kirk...E 9
43 Hardgrove......D 11
9 Hardham.......D 11
34 Hardhorn......C 2
26 Hardingham....E 3
31 Hardings Wood..E 7
23 Hardingstone ...F 11
7 Hardington......A 10
7 Hardington
   Mandeville.....E 8
7 Hardington Marsh E 8
7 Hardisworthy ...D 1
8 Hardley.........F 6
26 Hardley Street....E 7
18 Hardmondsworth..F 1
39 Hardrow.......F 11
32 Hardstoft......D 2
7 Hardway.......C 10
17 Hardwick, Bucks..B 9
25 Hardwick, Cambs..J 5
32 Hardwick, Lincs...C 6
26 Hardwick, Norf...F 5
23 Hardwick, Northants.
         E 11
16 Hardwick, Oxon ..D 5
16 Hardwick, Oxon ..A 7
32 Hardwick Grange .C 4
15 Hardwicke, Glos..B 12
15 Hardwicke, Glos..C 11
21 Hardwicke, Herefs.H 8
19 Hardy's Green....B 9
6 Hare and Hounds Inn
         G 5
19 Hare Green......A 10
17 Hare Hatch......F 9
18 Hare Street, Essex .C 4
18 Hare Street, Herts. A 4
10 Harebeating.....G 5
33 Hareby........D 10
34 Hareden.......B 5
18 Harefield.......E 1
17 Harefield Moor ..E 11
35 Harehills.......D 11
45 Harehope.......A 9
48 Harelaw, Lanark..E 2
47 Harelaw, Renfrew.D 9
49 Harelaw, Rox....G 8
59 Haremuir......K 5
39 Haresceugh.....A 8
15 Harescombe.....C 11
15 Haresfield......C 11
48 Hareshaw......C 1
35 Harewood......C 12
15 Harewood End....B 8
36 Harewood Estate..F 3
4 Harford, Devon...F 7
5 Harford, Devon..K 5
26 Hargate........F 4
31 Hargatewall....C 9
30 Hargrave, Ches...D 3
25 Hargrave, Northants.
         H 1
27 Hargrave Green..J 1
18 Haringey.......E 3
44 Harker........G 2
27 Harkstead......M 5
22 Harlaston......A 5
58 Harlaw House....E 5
32 Harlaxton......C 10
35 Harle Syke......D 7
28 Harlech........G 5
21 Harlescott......A 10
18 Harlesden......F 2

27 Harleston, Norf. . .G 5
27 Harleston, Suffolk .J 3
23 Harlestone......F 10
21 Harley.........B 11
48 Harleyholm......F 2
25 Harlington, Beds..M 1
18 Harlington, Lond..F 1
36 Harlington, Yorks. G 3
62 Harlosh........D 2
18 Harlow........C 5
45 Harlow Hill......F 9
36 Harlthorpe......C 5
25 Harlton........K 5
8 Harman's Cross...H 1
40 Harmby........F 2
18 Harmer Green....B 3
30 Harmerhill......H 3
33 Harmston......D 7
16 Harnhill.......D 2
18 Harold Hill......E 5
12 Haroldston West. .E 2
64 Haroldswick.....A 8
40 Harome........G 6
17 Harpenden.....C 12
49 Harper Ridge....E 11
49 Harpertoun.....E 10
6 Harpford.......G 4
37 Harpham.......A 8
26 Harpley, Norfolk. .C 1
21 Harpley, Worcs...F 12
23 Harpole.......F 10
17 Harpsden......F 8
32 Harpswell......A 6
31 Harpur Hill......C 9
35 Harpurhey......G 7
64 Harra.........B 7
44 Harraby.......H 3
4 Harracott......C 4
62 Harrapool......F 6
52 Harrietfield....D 5
49 Harrietsfield....G 9
11 Harrietsham.....C 7
38 Harrington, Cumb.C 2
33 Harrington, Lincs.C 10
23 Harrington,
   Northants......D 11
23 Harringworth....B 12
31 Harriseahead....E 7
35 Harrogate......B 12
23 Harrold.......F 12
18 Harrow........E 2
27 Harrow Street....L 3
18 Harrow Weald....E 2
3 Harrowbarrow...C 11
3 Harrowbridge...B 9
40 Harrowgate Village C 3
25 Harston, Cambs...K 5
32 Harston, Leics....G 5
36 Harswell.......C 6
40 Hart.........B 5
40 Hart Law......C 10
45 Hartburn......D 9
27 Hartest........K 1
7 Hartfoot Lane ...F 11
30 Hartford, Ches....C 5
25 Hartford, Hunts...H 4
19 Hartford End....B 7
17 Hartfordbridge...H 8
30 Harthill, Cheshire .E 4
31 Harthill, Lanark ..C 2
32 Harthill, Yorks...B 2
31 Hartington......D 9
4 Hartland.......D 1
22 Hartlebury......E 2
40 Hartlepool......B 5
10 Hartley, Kent....A 5
10 Hartley, Kent....E 6
45 Hartley, Northumb.
         E 11
39 Hartley, Yorks...D 10
10 Hartley Green....A 5
17 Hartley Wespall..H 8
17 Hartley Wintney. .H 8
11 Hartlip........B 7
35 Harton, Durham. G 12
21 Harton, Salop....D 10
36 Harton, Yorks....A 5
15 Hartpury......B 11
35 Hartshead......E 10
32 Hartshill.......C 10
31 Hartshorne.....H 11
48 Hartside.......F 2
35 Hartsop........D 6
17 Hartwell, Bucks...C 9
23 Hartwell, Northants.
         H 1
35 Hartwith......A 11
48 Hartwood......C 1
49 Hartwoodburn...C 1
49 Hartwoodmyres..G 7
22 Harvington......G 4
22 Harvington Cross .G 4

16 Harwell.........E 6
27 Harwich........M 6
39 Harwood, Dur...B 10
34 Harwood, Lancs..F 6
45 Harwood, Northumb.
         D 8
41 Harwood Dale...F 9
32 Harworth......A 3
9 Hascombe......D 11
23 Haselbech......D 10
7 Haselbury Plucknett
         E 8
22 Haseley.......E 6
22 Haselor........F 5
15 Hasfield........B 11
12 Hasguard.......F 2
12 Hasguard Cross...F 2
34 Haskayne......F 2
27 Hasketon......K 5
32 Hasland........C 1
9 Haslemere......C 10
34 Haslingden.....E 6
25 Haslingfield....K 5
30 Haslington.....E 6
30 Hassall........D 6
30 Hassall Green...D 6
11 Hassall Street...C 9
49 Hassendean.....G 8
26 Hassingham.....E 6
10 Hassington.....E 10
10 Hassocks.......F 2
31 Hassop........C 10
32 Hastigrow......B 11
11 Hastingleigh.....D 9
11 Hastings.......G 7
11 Hastingwood....C 5
17 Hastoe........C 10
40 Haswell.......A 4
40 Haswell Plough...A 4
48 Haswellsykes....E 5
9 Hatch.........A 8
6 Hatch Beauchamp.D 6
18 Hatch End......E 1
6 Hatch Green....D 6
49 Hatchednize.....E 10
8 Hatchet Gate....F 5
37 Hatcliffe.......G 10
21 Hatfield, Herefs. .F 11
18 Hatfield, Herts...C 2
22 Hatfield, Worcs...G 2
36 Hatfield, Yorks...F 4
18 Hatfield Broad Oak B 5
18 Hatfield Heath....B 5
18 Hatfield Peverel...C 8
36 Hatfield Woodhouse
         F 5
16 Hatford........C 4
8 Hatherden......A 5
4 Hatherleigh.....E 4
32 Hathern.......H 2
16 Hatherop.......D 3
31 Hathersage.....B 10
35 Hathershaw.....G 8
30 Hatherton, Ches..E 5
22 Hatherton, Staffs..A 3
25 Hatley St. George.K 4
3 Hatt.........C 11
9 Hattingley......B 8
58 Hatton, Aberdeen.D 8
30 Hatton, Cheshire..B 4
31 Hatton, Derby...G 10
33 Hatton, Lincs....C 9
18 Hatton, London...F 1
21 Hatton, Salop....C 10
22 Hatton, War.....E 6
58 Hatton Fintray...F 6
30 Hatton Heath....D 3
58 Hattoncrook.....E 6
18 Haultwick......B 3
50 Haunn........C 1
22 Haunton......A 6
45 Hauxley.......C 11
25 Hauxton.......K 5
47 Haugh, Ayr.....G 10
35 Haugh, Lancs...F 8
49 Haugh Head....G 12
58 Haugh of Glass...D 2
43 Haugh of Urr....E 9
33 Haugham......B 10
47 Haughhead.....B 11
27 Haughley......J 3
27 Haughley Green. .J 3
58 Haughs of Clinterty F 6
45 Haughterslaw....A 9
32 Haughton, Notts. .C 4
21 Haughton, Salop. A 5
21 Haughton, Salop. C 12
30 Haughton, Salop. .G 2
31 Haughton, Staffs. .H 7
45 Haughton Castle .F 7
35 Haughton Green .H 8
30 Haughton Moss...E 4
9 Havant........F 8

21 Haven.........G 9
37 Haven Side.....E 10
9 Haven Street.....G 7
36 Havercroft......F 2
12 Haverfordwest ...E 3
25 Haverhill.......L 8
38 Haverigg......G 4
18 Havering.......E 5
18 Havering-atte-Bower
         E 5
18 Havering's Grove .D 6
23 Haversham.....H 11
38 Haverthwaite....G 6
40 Haverton Hill....C 5
29 Hawarden......D 12
19 Hawbush Green..B 8
13 Hawen.........B 7
39 Hawes........F 11
22 Hawford.......F 2
44 Hawick........B 3
31 Hawk Green.....B 8
7 Hawkchurch....F 7
27 Hawkedon......K 1
9 Hawkenbury....D 5
7 Hawkeridge....A 11
22 Hawkes End.....D 6
15 Hawkesbury....F 10
15 Hawkesbury Upton
         F 11
45 Hawkhill.......B 10
10 Hawkhurst.....E 6
9 Hawkley.......C 8
6 Hawkridge.....C 2
34 Hawkshaw Lane ..E 6
38 Hawkshead.....E 6
38 Hawkshead Hill. .E 6
48 Hawksland......E 1
39 Hawkswick .....H 12
32 Hawksworth, Notts.
         F 5
35 Hawksworth, Yorks.
         C 10
19 Hawkwell......E 8
10 Hawley........A 4
17 Hawley........H 9
16 Hawling.......B 2
40 Hawnby.......F 5
35 Haworth.......D 9
27 Hawstead......J 1
40 Hawthorn, Dur....A 4
15 Hawthorn, Wilts. B 11
44 Hawthornside....B 4
24 Hawthorpe......C 2
32 Hawton........E 5
36 Haxby.........A 4
36 Haxey.........G 5
10 Haxted........D 3
21 Hay-on-Wye....H 8
18 Hay Street......A 4
12 Haycastle......D 2
12 Haycastle Cross...D 3
34 Haydock.......G 4
7 Haydon, Dorset..E 11
45 Haydon, Northumb.
         F 7
45 Haydon Bridge ...G 7
16 Haydon Wick....E 2
3 Haye.........C 10
18 Hayes, Kent.....G 4
18 Hayes, London...F 1
31 Hayfield, Derby...B 9
53 Hayfield, Fife....H 7
47 Hayhill........H 9
2 Hayle.........F 3
49 Haymount......F 9
6 Hayne.........F 2
25 Haynes.......L 2
25 Haynes West End .L 2
18 Haysden.......D 4
53 Hayshead........C 11
59 Hayton, Aberdeen.G 7
44 Hayton, Cumb...G 11
44 Hayton, Cumb....G 3
32 Hayton, Notts....B 4
36 Hayton, Yorks....C 6
21 Hayton's Bent...D 10
5 Haytor Vale.....H 6
32 Haywood Oaks...E 3
9 Hazel Grove....B 8
48 Hazelbank......E 1
7 Hazelbury Bryan.E 11
17 Hazeley.......H 8
22 Hazelslade.....A 4
53 Hazelton Walls...E 8
45 Hazlerigg......F 10
16 Hazleton......B 2
31 Hazlewood.....F 11
45 Hazon........C 10
24 Heacham......B 8
8 Headbourne Worthy
         C 6

MAP
21 Headbrook.......G 8
11 Headcorn........D 7
16 Headington........C 6
40 Headlam.........C 2
22 Headless Cross....F 4
9 Headley, Hants....C 9
16 Headley, Hants....H 6
10 Headley, Surrey...C 1
9 Headley Down...B 10
32 Headon..........C 5
47 Heads...........E 12
44 Heads Nook......G 3
32 Heage............E 1
39 Healaugh, N. Riding E 12
36 Healaugh, W. Riding B 3
31 Heald Green......B 7
4 Heale, Devon......A 5
7 Heale, Somerset..B 10
35 Healey, Lancs.....E 7
45 Healey, Northumb.G 8
40 Healey, Yorks.....G 2
45 Healey Cote......C 9
45 Healeyfield.......H 9
37 Healing..........F 10
2 Heamoor.........G 2
32 Heanor...........F 2
4 Heanton Punchardon B 4
32 Heapham.........A 6
48 Hearthstone......G 4
4 Heasley Mill......C 6
62 Heast............F 6
32 Heath............C 2
17 Heath and Reach.A 10
4 Heath Cross......F 7
17 Heath End, Berks. H 7
22 Heath End, Staffs..B 4
9 Heath End, Surrey A 10
22 Heath Hayes......H 3
22 Heath Hill........A 1
7 Heath House......B 7
6 Heath Pault Cross.C 3
22 Heath Town......B 3
31 Heathcote.......D 10
23 Heather..........A 7
62 Heatherfield .....D 4
52 Heatheryhaugh....B 6
43 Heathfield, Cumb.G 12
5 Heathfield, Devon.H 7
47 Heathfield, Ren....C 8
6 Heathfield, Som....D 5
10 Heathfield, Sussex .F 4
43 Heathhall ....D 10
22 Heathton.........C 2
30 Heatley..........A 5
35 Heaton, Lancs....H 7
34 Heaton, Lancs....A 3
31 Heaton, Staffs.....D 8
35 Heaton, Yorks...D 10
34 Heaton's Bridge...F 3
10 Heaverham.......B 4
31 Heaviley.........A 7
6 Heavitree........G 3
45 Hebburn........G 11
35 Hebden..........A 9
35 Hebden Bridge...D 8
30 Hebden Green....D 5
12 Hebron, Carm....D 5
45 Hebron, Northumb. D 10
43 Heck...........D 11
17 Heckfield.........H 8
27 Heckfield Green..H 5
24 Heckington.......A 2
48 Hecklebirnie......F 2
35 Heckmondwike ..E 10
16 Heddington.......G 1
16 Heddington Wick.G 1
4 Heddon..........C 5
45 Heddon on the Wall F 9
26 Hedenham........F 6
5 Hedge Cross......G 4
8 Hedge End ....E 6
17 Hedgerley.......E 10
6 Hedging..........C 6
45 Hedley on the Hill G 9
22 Hednesford.......A 3
37 Hedon..........D 9
17 Hedsor ....E 10
21 Hegdon Hill.....G 11
45 Heiferlaw Bank ..A 10
40 Heighington, Dur..C 3
33 Heighington, Lincs. C 7
56 Heights of Brae...D 1
54 Heights of Kinlochewe C 4
60 Heilam..........B 5
49 Heiton...........F 9
6 Hele, Devon......F 3

MAP
4 Hele, Devon......A 4
5 Hele, Devon......G 2
6 Hele, Somerset....D 5
4 Hele Lane........E 7
47 Helensburgh......A 8
47 Helentongate......F 9
2 Helford..........G 5
2 Helford Passage...G 5
26 Helhoughton .....C 2
25 Helions Bumpstead L 7
3 Helland..........C 8
3 Hellandbridge.....C 8
26 Hellesdon........D 5
23 Hellidon..........F 8
35 Hellifield.........B 7
10 Helling..........G 4
26 Hellington........E 6
45 Helm...........C 10
23 Helmdon ....H 9
27 Helmingham......J 5
40 Helmington Row..B 2
61 Helmsdale.......E 10
34 Helmshore ....E 6
40 Helmsley.........G 6
40 Helperby.........H 5
41 Helperthorpe.....H 9
24 Helpringham......B 2
24 Helpston.........E 2
30 Helsby...........C 3
2 Helston..........G 4
3 Helstone.........B 8
39 Helton...........C 7
39 Helwith Bridge .H 10
17 Hemel Hempstead D 11
36 Hemingbrough....D 4
33 Hemingby........C 9
36 Hemingfield......G 2
25 Hemingford Abbots H 4
25 Hemingford Grey H 4
27 Hemingstone......K 5
32 Hemington, Leics..G 2
25 Hemington, Northants....G 2
7 Hemington, Som. A 10
27 Hemley...........L 6
40 Hemlington.......D 5
37 Hempholme......B 8
26 Hempnall.........F 5
26 Hempnall Green...F 5
25 Hempstead, Essex .L 7
10 Hempstead, Kent..B 6
26 Hempstead, Norf..B 4
15 Hempsted.......C 11
26 Hempton, Norfolk C 2
16 Hempton, Oxon...A 5
26 Hemsby..........D 8
32 Hemswell.........A 6
36 Hemsworth.......F 2
6 Hemyock.........E 5
31 Henbury, Ches....C 7
15 Henbury, Glos....F 9
4 Henderbarrow Corner F 3
18 Hendon, London .E 2
45 Hendon, Dur.....G 12
15 Hendre...........C 8
14 Hendreforgan.....E 3
12 Hendre-wen ......D 3
13 Hendy...........G 9
28 Heneglwys........C 4
12 Hen-feddau.......D 6
15 Henfield, Glos....F 10
10 Henfield, Sussex...F 1
11 Hengherst.........D 8
14 Hengoed, Glam....E 5
21 Hengoed, Rad.....G 8
30 Hengoed, Salop...G 2
27 Hengrave.........H 1
18 Henham..........A 5
45 Henhill..........E 12
21 Heniarth.........B 7
6 Henlade.........D 6
45 Henlaw..........C 11
7 Henley, Dorset...F 10
21 Henley, Salop....D 10
7 Henley, Somerset..C 8
27 Henley, Suffolk ...K 5
9 Henley, Sussex...D 10
22 Henley-in-Arden...E 5
17 Henley-on-Thames.F 8
10 Henley Street......A 5
13 Henllan, Cards....C 7
29 Henllan, Denb.....C 9
12 Henllan Amgoed..E 5
14 Henllys..........E 6
25 Henlow..........L 3
5 Hennock ....H 7
27 Henny Street.......L 2
29 Henryd...........C 7
12 Henry's Moat.....D 4
36 Hensall..........E 4

MAP
44 Henshaw.........G 6
38 Hensingham......D 2
27 Henstead.........G 8
7 Henstridge.......D 10
7 Henstridge Ash..D 10
7 Henstridge Bowden D 10
17 Henton, Oxon....D 8
7 Henton, Som......B 8
7 Hentstridge Marsh D 11
22 Henwick.........G 2
3 Henwood.........B 9
64 Heogan..........D 7
14 Heol Senni.......B 3
13 Heol-las.........G 10
14 Heol-y-Cyw.......F 3
45 Hepburn.........A 9
45 Hepple..........C 8
45 Hepple Whitefield.C 8
45 Hepscott........E 10
35 Hepstonstall......D 8
27 Hepworth, Suff...H 3
35 Hepworth, Yorks. F 10
12 Herbrandston.....F 2
21 Hereford........H 10
22 Hereford & Worcester, Co...F 2
48 Heriot...........D 6
49 Heriot Station....D 7
49 Hermiston.........G 8
16 Hermitage, Berks..G 6
7 Hermitage, Dor...F 10
43 Hermitage, Kirk...E 9
44 Hermitage, Rox....C 3
9 Hermitage, Sussex.F 9
28 Hermon, Anglesey.C 3
13 Hermon, Carm...D 10
12 Hermon, Pemb....D 5
11 Herne...........B 10
11 Herne Bay.......A 10
4 Herner..........C 5
11 Hernhill.........B 9
3 Herodsfoot.......D 9
11 Heronden.......C 11
18 Herongate........E 6
42 Heronsford.......C 2
17 Heronsgate.......E 11
9 Herriard..........B 8
26 Herringfleet.......F 8
25 Herring's Green...L 2
25 Herringswell .....H 8
45 Herrington ....H 11
11 Hersden.........B 10
17 Hersham........H 12
10 Herstmonceux....G 5
8 Herston, Dorset...H 2
64 Herston, Orkney Is.E 2
18 Hertford.........C 3
18 Hertford Heath...C 3
18 Hertfordshire, Co..B 2
18 Hertingfordbury ..C 3
38 Hesket Newmarket A 6
34 Hesketh Bank.....E 3
34 Hesketh Lane......C 5
34 Heskin Green .....F 4
40 Hesleden.........A 4
44 Hesleyside........E 6
36 Heslington.......B 4
36 Hessay..........B 3
3 Hessenford......D 10
27 Hessett...........J 2
47 Hessilhead........D 9
37 Hessle...........E 8
34 Hest Bank.........A 3
18 Heston...........F 1
30 Heswall...........B 1
17 Hethe............A 7
26 Hethersett........E 5
44 Hethersgill........F 3
49 Hethpool.........G 11
40 Hett.............B 3
35 Hetton...........A 8
45 Hetton Downs ..H 11
45 Hetton Law.....C 11
45 Hetton Steads....B 11
45 Hetton-le-Hole ..H 11
45 Heugh...........F 9
58 Heugh-head.......F 1
27 Heveningham.....H 6
10 Hever...........D 4
39 Heversham.......G 7
26 Hevingham.......C 5
15 Hewelsfield ......D 9
15 Hewish, Somerset H 7
7 Hewish, Somerset .E 7
36 Heworth..........B 4
45 Hexham..........G 7
49 Hexpath.........E 9
10 Hextable..........A 4
5 Hexworthy ......H 5
19 Heybridge, Essex..C 8
18 Heybridge, Essex..D 6

MAP
19 Heybridge Basin ..C 8
5 Heybrook Bay....L 4
25 Heydon, Cambs....L 5
26 Heydon, Norfolk..C 4
33 Heydour.........F 7
34 Heysham..........A 3
35 Heyshaw........A 10
9 Heyshott........D 10
8 Heytesbury.......B 1
16 Heythrop.........A 4
35 Heywood, Lancs...F 7
7 Heywood, Wilts..A 12
37 Hibaldstow.......G 7
36 Hickleton........G 3
26 Hickling, Norfolk .C 7
32 Hickling, Notts....G 4
26 Hickling Green....C 7
22 Hidcote Boyce....H 5
32 High Ackworth...E 2
36 High Angerton....E 9
39 High Bankhill.....A 8
18 High Beach.......D 4
39 High Bentham.....H 9
4 High Bickington ..D 5
39 High Birkwith...G 10
47 High Blantyre...D 11
48 High Bonnybridge.B 1
43 High Borgue......F 7
47 High Boydston....E 7
35 High Bradley.....B 9
4 High Bray........C 6
10 High Brooms.....D 5
4 High Bullen.......D 4
40 High Burton......G 2
45 High Buston.....B 10
45 High Callerton...F 10
36 High Catton......B 5
45 High Church.....E 10
47 High Cleughearn .E 11
16 High Cogges......C 5
40 High Coniscliffe ..D 3
47 High Cross, Ayr...E 9
49 High Cross, Ber....E 8
9 High Cross, Hants.C 8
18 High Cross, Herts. B 4
31 High Cross Bank H 11
47 High Duncryne ...A 9
18 High Easter.......B 6
42 High Eldrig.......E 3
40 High Ellington....G 2
40 High Entercommon E 4
21 High Ercall......A 11
40 High Etherley.....B 2
19 High Garrett......A 7
47 High Glengarth...D 8
40 High Grange......B 2
40 High Grantley ...H 3
26 High Green, Norf..E 4
22 High Green, Worcs. H 2
35 High Green, Yorks. G 12
11 High Halden......D 8
10 High Halstow.....A 6
7 High Ham........C 8
38 High Harrington ..C 3
40 High Haswell.....A 4
30 High Hatton .....H 5
41 High Hawsker ...D 9
39 High Hesket......A 7
40 High Hesleden ...A 5
35 High Hoyland ...F 11
37 High Hursley.....D 7
10 High Hurstwood ..E 4
41 High Hutton ......H 8
38 High Ireby........B 5
40 High Kilburn.....G 5
31 High Lane, Ches...B 8
21 High Lane, Herefs. F 12
18 High Laver.......C 5
30 High Legh........B 5
40 High Leven.......D 5
15 High Littleton ....H 9
38 High Lorton......C 4
41 High Marishes....G 8
32 High Marnham...C 5
36 High Melton......G 3
45 High Mickley.....G 9
48 High Mindork ....F 4
41 High Mowthorpe .H 9
38 High Newton.....G 6
45 High Newton by-the-Sea.........E 12
38 High Nibthwaite ..F 5
30 High Offley.......H 6
18 High Ongar.......D 5
22 High Onn........A 2
42 High Pennyvenie ..A 6
18 High Roding......B 6
38 High Row........B 6
34 High Salter.......A 5

MAP
39 High Shaw......F 11
40 High Skelding....H 2
45 High Spen........G 9
40 High Stoop.......A 1
3 High Street, Corn. D 7
27 High St., E. Suff..K 7
27 High St., W. Suff..K 2
27 High Street Green.K 3
40 High Throston ....B 5
33 High Toynton....C 10
45 High Trewhitt.....B 8
48 High Valleyfield...A 3
45 High Warden .....F 7
38 High Wray........E 6
18 High Wych........C 5
17 High Wycombe...E 9
32 Higham, Derby...D 1
27 Higham, E. Suffolk L 3
10 Higham, Kent.....A 6
35 Higham, Lancs....D 7
25 Higham, W. Suff...J 8
45 Higham Dykes....E 9
25 Higham Ferrers ..H 1
25 Higham Gobion..M 2
23 Higham on the Hill C 7
10 Higham Wood....C 5
4 Highampton.......C 6
55 Highbridge, Inver..L 6
6 Highbridge, Som..B 6
10 Highbrook........E 2
35 Highburton.......F 10
7 Highbury....... A 10
44 Highchesters......B 3
16 Highclere.........H 5
8 Highcliffe.........G 4
7 Higher Alham ...B 10
7 Higher Ansty ....F 11
6 Higher Ashton ...H 2
34 Higher Ballam ....D 2
2 Higher Boscaswell .F 1
6 Higher Combe.....C 3
30 Higher Heath.....G 4
29 Higher Kinnerton D 12
7 Higher Nyland...D 10
34 Higher Penwortham D 4
2 Higher Town ......C 2
30 Higher Walton, Ches. B 4
34 Higher Walton, Lancs. D 5
7 Higher Whatcombe F 11
30 Higher Whitley ...B 5
30 Higher Wych ......F 3
47 Highfield, Ayr.....D 8
4 Highfield, Devon..F 6
45 Highfield, Dur.....G 9
32 Highfield, Yorks...B 1
25 Highfields, Cambs. J 5
49 Highfields, Northumb. D 12
18 Highgate, London .E 3
36 Highgate, Yorks...E 4
44 Highgreen Manor .D 6
58 Highlands, Aber...F 6
40 Highlands, Dur....C 2
32 Highlane.........B 1
15 Highleadon.......B 11
9 Highleigh.........F 9
22 Highley...........D 1
17 Highmoor Cross ..F 8
17 Highmoor Hill ....E 8
15 Highnam Green..B 11
4 Highridge........D 6
11 Highsted.........B 8
27 Highstreet Green .M 1
43 Hightae.........D 11
31 Hightown, Ches...D 7
43 Hightown, Dumf. C 11
34 Hightown, Lancs..G 2
43 Hightown of Craigs D 11
2 Highway, Corn....E 4
16 Highway, Wilts....G 2
5 Highweek.........J 7
16 Highworth........E 3
26 Hilborough.......E 1
32 Hilcote..........D 2
16 Hilcott..........H 2
10 Hilden Park......C 4
10 Hildenborough....C 4
25 Hildersham.......K 6
31 Hilderstone ......G 8
37 Hilderthorpe......A 9
6 Hilfarance.......D 5
7 Hilfield..........F 9
24 Hilgay...........F 7
4 Hill, Devon.......C 6
15 Hill, Glos.........E 9
22 Hill, Warwick.....B 5
9 Hill Brow........D 9

MAP
41 Hill Cottages.....E 7
34 Hill Dale.........F 4
33 Hill Dyke.......E 10
39 Hill End, Dur.....B 12
52 Hill End, Fife ....H 5
15 Hill Gate.........B 8
9 Hill Head, Hants..F 7
45 Hill Head, Northumb. F 7
38 Hill Millom ......G 4
12 Hill Mountain.....F 3
52 Hill of Beath......H 6
56 Hill of Fearn......B 4
58 Hill of Maud Crofts B 2
31 Hill Ridware.....H 9
25 Hill Row ....H 5
8 Hill Top, Hants....F 5
35 Hill Top, Yorks. .F 12
8 Hill View.........F 1
36 Hillam...........D 3
39 Hillbeck ....D 10
38 Hillberry.........G 2
11 Hillborough.......A 10
8 Hillbourne.......G 2
58 Hillbrae.........E 5
8 Hillbutts.........F 1
53 Hillcairnie........E 8
6 Hillcommon.......D 5
48 Hillend, Fife.......A 4
48 Hillend, Lanark...E 3
17 Hillersland.......C 9
17 Hillesden..........A 8
15 Hillesley.........E 11
58 Hillhead, Aber.....E 5
47 Hillhead, Ayr ....F 10
47 Hillhead, Ayr.....G 9
5 Hillhead, Devon ..K 8
43 Hillhead, Dumf....B 8
48 Hillhead, Lanark..E 3
45 Hillhead, Northumb. B 9
58 Hillhead of Auchentumb ...B 7
58 Hillhead of Cocklaw C 8
49 Hillhouse........D 7
22 Hilliard's Cross...A 5
18 Hillingdon.......F 1
24 Hillington.......C 8
23 Hillmorton........E 8
59 Hillockhead, Aber. G 1
58 Hillockhead, Aber. F 2
9 Hillpound........D 7
59 Hillside, Angus....L 4
58 Hillside, Banff....A 3
43 Hillside, Dumf...C 12
59 Hillside, Kinc.....H 7
64 Hillside, Shetlands C 7
8 Hillstreet........D 5
64 Hillswick.........C 6
9 Hillway..........G 8
64 Hillwell..........F 7
16 Hilmarton........G 1
15 Hilperton ....H 12
15 Hilperton Marsh.H 11
9 Hilsea...........F 8
37 Hilston.........D 10
25 Hilton............J 4
58 Hilton, Aberdeen .D 7
49 Hilton, Berwick..D 11
31 Hilton, Derby....G 11
7 Hilton, Dorset ...F 11
40 Hilton, Durham...C 2
22 Hilton, Salop......C 1
39 Hilton, Westmor. .C 9
40 Hilton, Yorkshire .D 5
56 Hilton of Cadboll .B 4
22 Himbleton........F 3
22 Himley..........C 2
39 Hincaster........G 7
16 Hinchwick.......A 2
23 Hinckley.........C 7
27 Hinderclay.......H 3
41 Hinderwell.......D 8
30 Hindford.........G 2
9 Hindhead ....C 10
34 Hindley, Lancs....G 5
45 Hindley, Northumb. G 8
34 Hindley Green....G 5
22 Hindlip..........F 2
26 Hindolveston .....C 3
7 Hindon ....C 12
26 Hindringham.....B 3
26 Hingham.........E 3
30 Hinstock.........H 5
27 Hintlesham.......L 4
15 Hinton, Glos.....G 10
8 Hinton, Hants.....G 4
21 Hinton, Herefs....H 9
23 Hinton, Northants.G 8
21 Hinton, Salop....B 9
9 Hinton Ampner...C 7

MAP

7 Hinton Blewett....A 9
15 Hinton Charterhouse H 11
22 Hinton Green....H 4
23 Hinton-in-the-Hedge H 9
9 Hinton Marsh....C 7
8 Hinton Martell....E 2
22 Hinton on the Green H 4
16 Hinton Parva....F 3
7 Hinton St. George.E 7
7 Hinton St. Mary .E 11
16 Hinton Waldrist..D 5
21 Hints, Salop....E 11
22 Hints, Staffs....B 5
23 Hinwick....F 12
11 Hinxhill....D 9
25 Hinxton....L 6
25 Hinxworth....L 3
35 Hipperholme....E 10
40 Hipswell....E 2
12 Hiraeth....E 5
59 Hirn....G 5
29 Hirnant, Mont...H 10
20 Hirnant, Rad.....E 4
45 Hirst....D 11
36 Hirst Courtney..E 4
29 Hirwaen....D 10
14 Hirwaun....D 3
4 Hiscott....C 4
25 Histon....J 5
27 Hitcham....K 3
43 Hitchill....E 12
18 Hitchin....A 2
18 Hither Green....F 4
4 Hittisleigh Cross..F 6
36 Hive....D 6
31 Hixon....H 8
11 Hoaden....B 11
15 Hoaldalbert....B 7
31 Hoar Cross....H 10
15 Hoarwithy....A 8
11 Hoath....B 10
21 Hobarris....E 8
64 Hobbister....D 2
18 Hobbs Cross....D 5
44 Hobkirk....B 4
45 Hobson....G 10
32 Hoby....H 4
26 Hockering....D 4
32 Hockerton....E 4
19 Hockley....E 8
22 Hockley Heath....E 5
17 Hockliffe....A 10
25 Hockwold cum Wilton G 8
6 Hockworthy....D 4
18 Hoddesdon....C 4
34 Hoddlesden....E 6
43 Hoddomcross....D 12
12 Hodgeston....G 4
30 Hodnet....G 5
10 Hodsoll Street....B 5
16 Hodson....F 3
32 Hodthorpe....C 3
9 Hoe, Hampshire..D 7
26 Hoe, Norfolk.....D 3
9 Hoe Gate....E 8
39 Hoff....C 9
17 Hoggeston....B 9
34 Hoghton....E 5
31 Hognaston....E 11
33 Hogsthorpe....C 12
24 Holbeach....C 5
24 Holbeach Bank..C 5
24 Holbeach Clough..C 4
24 Holbeach Drove..D 4
24 Holbeach Hurn....C 5
24 Holbeach St.Johns D 4
24 Holbeach St.Marks C 5
24 Holbeach St. Matthew B 5
32 Holbeck, Notts....C 3
35 Holbeck, Yorks..D 11
22 Holberrow Green..F 4
5 Holbeton....L 5
31 Holbrook, Derby.F 12
27 Holbrook, Suffolk.L 5
8 Holbury....F 6
45 Holburn....B 11
5 Holcombe, Devon.H 8
34 Holcombe, Lancs..E 6
7 Holcombe, Som..A 10
34 Holcombe Brook..F 6
6 Holcombe Rogus .D 4
23 Holcot....E 11
34 Holden....B 6
23 Holdenby....E 10
8 Holdenhurst....G 3
21 Holdgate....C 11
33 Holdingham....E 7
7 Holditch....F 7

MAP

49 Holefield....F 10
47 Holehouse, Ayr ..H 9
47 Holehouse, Ayr....D 8
15 Hole-in-the-Wall ..A 9
43 Holestane....B 9
6 Holford....B 5
38 Holker....G 6
26 Holkham....A 2
4 Hollacombe....F 2
64 Holland, Papa Westray Orkney Is......A 3
64 Holland, Stronsay, Orkney Is......C 4
33 Holland Fen....E 9
19 Holland-on-Sea ..B 11
64 Hollandstoun....A 4
44 Hollee....F 1
27 Hollesley....L 6
11 Hollingbourne....C 7
10 Hollingrove....F 6
31 Hollington,Derby F 10
31 Hollington, Staffs. F 9
10 Hollington, Sussex.G 6
35 Hollingworth....G 8
35 Hollins....F 7
30 Hollins Green....A 5
34 Hollins Lane....B 4
31 Hollinsclough....D 9
21 Hollinswood ....A 12
4 Hollocombe....E 5
22 Hollow Court....F 3
31 Hollow Meadows A 11
31 Holloway....E 11
23 Hollowell....E 10
44 Hollows....E 2
30 Holly Bush, Flint..F 3
15 Holly Bush, Mon..D 5
24 Holly End....E 6
22 Holly Green....H 2
47 Hollybush, Ayr ..H 9
15 Hollybush,Worcs. A 10
31 Hollym....E 11
22 Hollywood....D 4
44 Holm, Dumf....C 1
63 Holm, Ross & Cromarty....D 5
43 Holm St. Cuthbert G 12
4 Holmacott....C 4
35 Holmbridge.....F 10
9 Holmbury St. Mary B 12
3 Holmbush....D 7
31 Holmcroft....H 8
25 Holme, Hunts....G 3
37 Holme, Lincs.....F 7
40 Holme, N. Riding.G 4
32 Holme, Notts....D 5
39 Holme, Westmor. .G 7
35 Holme, W. Riding.F 9
35 Holme Chapel....D 7
26 Holme Hale....E 2
15 Holme Lacy....A 9
21 Holme Marsh....G 9
24 Holme next the Sea A 8
37 Holme on the Wolds C 7
32 Holme Pierrepont .F 3
36 Holm upon Spalding Moor....C 6
21 Holmer....H 10
17 Holmer Green ...D 10
30 Holmes Chapel....C 6
31 Holmesfield....B 11
34 Holmeswood....E 3
32 Holmewood....D 2
35 Holmfirth....F 10
43 Holmfoot....B 9
47 Holmhead....G 10
32 Holmisdal....C 1
37 Holmpton....E 11
38 Holmrook....E 3
45 Holmside....H 10
44 Holmwrangle.....H 4
5 Holne....J 6
4 Holsworthy....F 2
4 Holsworthy Beacon E 2
30 Holt, Denb....E 3
8 Holt, Dorset....F 2
26 Holt, Norfolk....B 4
15 Holt, Wilts....H 11
22 Holt, Worcs....F 2
9 Holt End, Hants..B 8
22 Holt End, Worcs..E 4
22 Holt Heath....F 2
8 Holt Wood....E 2
36 Holtby....B 4
33 Holton, Lincs....B 8
17 Holton, Oxon....G 7
7 Holton, Som....D 10
27 Holton, Suffolk..H 7
8 Holton Heath....G 1

MAP

37 Holton le Clay...G 10
37 Holton le Moor...G 8
27 Holton St. Mary ..L 4
10 Holtye....D 3
7 Holwell, Dorset .E 10
18 Holwell, Herts....A 2
32 Holwell, Leics....H 5
16 Holwell, Oxon....C 3
39 Holwick....C 11
7 Holworth....H 11
22 Holy Cross....D 3
45 Holy Island....B 12
9 Holybourne....B 9
28 Holyhead....B 2
31 Holymoorside....C 11
17 Holyport....F 10
45 Holystone....C 8
47 Holytown....C 12
2 Holywell, Corn....D 5
44 Holywell, Cumb...E 3
7 Holywell, Dorset ..F 9
29 Holywell, Flint...C 1
25 Holywell, Hunts...H 4
45 Holywell, Northumb. F 11
35 Holywell Green ..E 9
6 Holywell Lake ..D 5
25 Holywell Row....H 8
43 Holywood....C 10
15 Hom Green....B 9
49 Homebank....E 10
49 Homebyres....E 9
21 Homer....B 11
27 Homersfield....G 6
8 Homington....D 3
11 Honey Hill....B 10
16 Honey Street.....H 2
27 Honey Tye....L 2
12 Honeyborough....F 3
4 Honeychurch....F 5
22 Honiley....E 6
26 Honing....C 6
26 Honingham....D 4
32 Honington, Lincs. .F 6
27 Honington, Suff...H 2
22 Honington, War..H 6
6 Honiton....F 5
35 Honley....F 10
10 Hoo....A 6
22 Hoobrook....E 2
35 Hood Green....G 11
5 Hooe, Devon....K 4
10 Hooe, Sussex....G 6
10 Hooe Common....G 6
9 Hook, Hants....A 8
18 Hook, London....G 2
12 Hook, Pemb....F 3
16 Hook, Wilts....F 2
36 Hook, Yorks....E 5
10 Hook Green, Kent A 5
10 Hook Green, Kent.D 5
16 Hook Norton....A 4
7 Hooke....F 9
30 Hookgate....G 6
4 Hookway....F 7
10 Hookwood....D 2
30 Hoole....C 3
10 Hooley....B 2
30 Hooton....B 2
32 Hooton Levitt....A 2
36 Hooton Pagnell...F 3
36 Hooton Roberts ..G 3
64 Hoove....D 7
24 Hop Pole ....D 3
31 Hope, Derby....B 10
5 Hope, Devon....M 5
29 Hope, Flint....D 12
21 Hope, Mont....B 8
21 Hope, Salop....B 9
60 Hope, Sutherland .B 5
21 Hope Bagot....E 11
21 Hope Bowdler....C 10
15 Hope Mansell....B 9
21 Hope under Dinmore G 10
56 Hopeman....C 7
21 Hopesay....D 9
36 Hopperton....B 2
31 Hopton, Derby .E 11
30 Hopton, Salop....G 4
31 Hopton, Staffs...H 8
26 Hopton, E. Suffolk.E 8
27 Hopton, W. Suff. .G 3
21 Hopton Cangeford D 11
21 Hopton Castle....E 9
21 Hopton Wafers ..E 11
21 Hoptonheath ....E 9
22 Hopwas....B 5
22 Hopwood....E 4
10 Horam....F 4
24 Horbling....B 2
35 Horbury....E 11

MAP

40 Horden....A 5
21 Horderley....D 9
8 Hordle....F 4
30 Hordley....G 2
5 Hordon....H 4
13 Horeb, Cards....C 7
13 Horeb, Carm....D 8
15 Horfield....F 9
27 Horham....H 5
19 Horkesley Heath..A 9
37 Horkstow....E 7
23 Horley, Oxon....H 7
10 Horley, Surrey....D 2
7 Hornblotton Grn..C 9
39 Hornby, Lancs...H 8
40 Hornby, Yorks...F 2
45 Hornby, Yorks...E 4
33 Horncastle....C 9
18 Hornchurch....E 5
49 Horncliffe....D 11
49 Horndean, Ber...D 11
9 Horndean, Hants..E 8
18 Horndon on the Hill F 6
10 Horne....D 2
6 Horner....B 3
26 Horning....D 6
23 Horninghold....H 1
31 Horninglow....H 10
25 Horningsea....J 6
7 Horningsham....B 11
26 Horningtoft....C 2
3 Horningtops....D 9
4 Horns Cross, Devon D 3
11 Horns Cross, Sussex F 7
44 Hornsby....H 3
58 Hornsea....B 9
37 Hornsea Bridge ..B 9
18 Hornsey....E 3
23 Hornton....H 7
5 Horrabridge....J 4
27 Horringer....J 1
9 Horringford....H 7
9 Horsbridge....C 5
31 Horse Bridge....E 8
8 Horsebridge....C 5
22 Horsebrook....A 2
15 Horsecastle....H 7
21 Horsehay....B 12
25 Horseheath....K 7
39 Horsehouse....G 12
17 Horsell....H 10
30 Horseman's Grn...F 3
17 Horsenden....D 9
26 Horsey....C 8
26 Horsford....D 5
35 Horsforth....C 11
10 Horsham, Sussex..E 1
22 Horsham, Worcs..F 1
26 Horsham St. Faith D 5
33 Horsington, Lincs..C 9
7 Horsington, Som. D 10
32 Horsley, Derby...F 1
15 Horsley, Glos....E 11
45 Horsley, Northumb. C 7
45 Horsley, Northumb. F 9
19 Horsley Cross....A 11
32 Horsley Woodhouse F 1
19 Horsleycross St...A 11
49 Horsleyhill....G 8
6 Horsmonden....D 6
17 Horspath....D 7
26 Horstead....D 5
10 Horsted Keynes...E 3
17 Horton, Bucks...B 10
17 Horton, Bucks....F 11
8 Horton, Dorset...E 2
13 Horton, Glam....H 8
15 Horton, Glos....F 10
23 Horton, Northants. G 11
6 Horton, Somerset .E 6
31 Horton, Staffs...D 8
16 Horton, Wilts...H 2
35 Horton, Yorks...B 7
7 Horton Cross....E 7
30 Horton Green....E 3
8 Horton Heath....D 6
39 Horton in Ribblesdale H 10
10 Horton Kirby....A 4
34 Horwich....F 5
4 Horwood....C 4
44 Hoscote....B 2
32 Hose....G 5
49 Hoselaw....F 10
38 Hoses....F 5
64 Hoswick....E 7

MAP

52 Hotel, Perth....D 1
60 Hotel, Sutherland .E 5
37 Hotham....D 7
11 Hothfield....D 8
32 Hoton....H 3
44 Hott....D 6
64 Houbie....B 8
30 Hough....E 6
30 Hough Green....B 3
32 Hough-on-the-Hill.F 6
32 Hougham....F 6
44 Houghton, Cumb..G 2
8 Houghton, Hants..C 5
25 Houghton, Hunts. H 4
12 Houghton, Pemb. .F 3
9 Houghton, Sussex E 11
25 Houghton Conquest L 2
30 Houghton Green..A 5
17 Houghton Regis .B 11
26 Houghton St. Giles B 2
45 Houghton-le-Spring H 11
23 Houghton on the Hill B 10
41 Houlsyke....D 7
8 Hound....F 6
17 Hound Green....H 8
49 Houndridge....F 10
49 Houndslow....E 9
6 Houndsmoor....D 5
49 Houndwood....C 11
8 Hounsdown....E 5
18 Hounslow....F 2
64 Housay....C 8
59 House of Glenmuick H 1
58 Housieside....E 6
47 Houston....C 9
61 Houstry....D 10
10 Hove....H 2
32 Hoveringham....E 4
26 Hoveton....D 6
41 Hovingham....H 7
44 How....G 3
16 How Caple....A 9
10 How Green....C 4
38 How Head....E 6
35 Howbrook....G 11
49 Howburn....F 10
49 Howden, Rox.....G 9
36 Howden, Yorks...D 5
35 Howden Clough .D 11
40 Howden-le-Wear ..B 2
61 Howe, Caith....B 12
26 Howe, Norfolk....E 6
39 Howe, Westmor...F 7
19 Howe Green....D 2
58 Howe of Teuchar .C 5
19 Howe Street, Essex B 7
25 Howe Street, Essex M 8
33 Howell....F 8
43 Howes....E 12
20 Howey....F 6
48 Howford....F 6
48 Howgate, Lanark..F 2
48 Howgate, Midloth. D 5
45 Howick....A 10
30 Howle....H 5
15 Howle Hill....B 9
25 Howlett End....M 7
6 Howley....E 6
49 Howliston....D 7
49 Hownam....G 10
49 Hownam Mains .G 10
44 Howpasley....F 2
37 Howsham, Lincs. .G 8
36 Howsham, Yorks..A 5
49 Howtel....F 11
64 Howth....D 2
15 Howton, Herefs..A 7
39 Howtown, Westmor. C 7
47 Howwood....C 9
64 Hoxa....E 2
27 Hoxne....G 5
30 Hoylake....A 1
35 Hoyland Nether..G 12
35 Hoyland Swaine .G 11
12 Hubberston....F 2
24 Hubbert's Bridge..A 4
36 Huby, N. Riding..A 3
35 Huby, W. Riding.B 11
15 Hucclecote....C 12
11 Hucking....B 7
32 Hucknall....E 3
35 Huddersfield....E 10
22 Huddington....F 3
40 Hudswell....E 2
36 Huggate....B 6
2 Hugh Town....D 2
17 Hughenden Valley.D 9
21 Hughley....C 11

MAP

4 Huish, Devon....E 4
16 Huish, Wilts....H 2
6 Huish Barton....B 4
6 Huish Champflower C 4
7 Huish Episcopi...D 8
17 Hulcott....B 9
31 Hulland....F 11
17 Hullavington....F 12
19 Hullbridge....D 8
31 Hulme End....D 8
31 Hulme Walfield...D 7
34 Hulton Lane Ends G 6
27 Hulver Street....G 8
8 Hulverstone ....H 5
21 Humber Court...G 11
37 Humberside, Co. ..C 7
37 Humberston....G 10
23 Humberstone....B 10
49 Humbie....C 7
49 Humbleton, Northumb.....G 12
37 Humbleton, Yorkshire.....D 10
49 Hume....E 9
47 Humeston....H 7
45 Humshaugh....F 7
61 Huna....A 12
34 Huncoat....D 6
23 Huncote....B 8
49 Hundalee....G 9
39 Hunderthwaite...C 12
33 Hundleby....D 11
12 Hundleton....G 3
25 Hundon....K 8
9 Hundred Acres...E 7
34 Hundred End....E 3
21 Hundred House...G 7
23 Hungarton....A 10
34 Hunger Hill....F 5
16 Hungerford, Berks. G 4
8 Hungerford, Hants.E 3
16 Hungerford Newtown G 5
32 Hungerton....G 6
62 Hunglader....A 3
35 Hunisish....F 1
41 Hunmanby....G 11
23 Hunningham....E 7
8 Hunny Hill....G 6
18 Hunsdon....C 4
36 Hunsingore....B 2
35 Hunslett Carr....D 11
39 Hunsonby....B 8
61 Hunspow....A 11
24 Hunstanton....B 8
45 Hurstanworth ..H 8
27 Hunston, Suffolk .H 3
9 Hunston, Sussex..F 10
15 Hunstrete....H 9
35 Hunsworth....D 10
9 Hunt End....F 4
41 Hunt Ho....E 7
8 Hunter's Quay...B 7
49 Huntershall....F 10
44 Huntford....B 5
59 Hunthill Lodge ..K 2
25 Huntingdon, Hunts. H 3
22 Huntingdon, Staffs. A 3
25 Huntingdon and Peterborough, Co. H 3
27 Huntingfield....H 6
21 Huntington, Herefs. G 8
21 Huntington, Herefs. H 10
36 Huntington, Yorks. B 4
52 Huntingtower Haugh E 5
15 Huntley, Glos....B 10
31 Huntley, Staffs...F 8
58 Huntly....D 3
49 Huntlywood....E 9
10 Hunton, Kent....C 6
40 Hunton, Yorks....F 2
17 Hunton Bridge...D 11
30 Hunt's Cross....B 3
6 Huntscott....B 3
6 Huntsham....D 3
6 Huntspill....B 6
7 Huntworth....C 7
45 Hunwick....B 2
26 Hunworth....B 4
7 Hurcott....E 7
7 Hurdcott....C 3
17 Hurley, Berks....F 9
22 Hurley, War....C 6
7 Hurlford....F 9
64 Hurliness....E 1
8 Hurn....F 3
31 Hursdfield....C 8

MAP
8 Hursley D 6
17 Hurst, Berks. G 9
35 Hurst, Lancs. G 8
7 Hurst, Somerset D 8
40 Hurst, Yorks. E 1
10 Hurst Green C 3
34 Hurst Green, Lancs. C 6
10 Hurst Green, Sussex E 6
10 Hurst Wickham F 2
8 Hurstbourne Priors A 6
8 Hurstbourne Tarrant A 5
21 Hurstley G 9
10 Hurstpierpoint F 2
21 Hurstway Com. G 8
9 Hurtmore B 11
40 Hurworth D 3
39 Hury C 11
62 Husabost Piers C 1
23 Husbands Bosworth D 10
25 Husborne Crawley L 1
40 Husthwaite H 5
32 Huthwaite D 2
49 Hutlertown G 7
33 Huttoft C 12
49 Hutton, Berwick D 11
39 Hutton, Cumb. C 7
18 Hutton, Essex D 6
34 Hutton, Lancs. D 4
15 Hutton, Somerset H 7
37 Hutton, Yorks. B 8
41 Hutton Buscel G 9
40 Hutton Conyers H 3
39 Hutton End A 7
40 Hutton Hang F 2
40 Hutton Henry B 4
39 Hutton-in-the-Forest B 7
39 Hutton John C 7
41 Hutton-le-Hole F 7
40 Hutton Lowcross D 6
40 Hutton Magna D 2
38 Hutton Roof, Cumb. B 6
39 Hutton Roof, Westmorland G 8
40 Hutton Rudby E 5
40 Hutton Sessay H 5
36 Hutton Wandesley B 3
4 Huxford D 6
6 Huxham F 3
30 Huxley D 4
64 Huxter D 7
30 Huyton A 3
38 Hycemoor F 3
35 Hyde, Cheshire H 8
15 Hyde, Glos. D 12
17 Hyde Heath D 10
31 Hyde Lea H 7
9 Hydestile B 11
38 Hydro F 2
38 Hyndford E 2
21 Hyssington C 8
8 Hythe, Hants. E 5
11 Hythe, Kent E 10
7 Hythe, Somerset A 8
17 Hythe End G 11
58 Hythie C 7
58 Ianstown A 2
7 Ibberton E 11
31 Ible D 11
8 Ibsley E 3
23 Ibstock A 7
17 Ibstone E 8
8 Ibthorpe A 5
9 Ibworth A 7
15 Icelton H 7
26 Ickburgh F 1
18 Ickenham E 1
17 Ickford C 7
11 Ickham B 11
18 Ickleford A 2
25 Ickleton L 6
27 Icklingham H 1
25 Ickwell Green L 3
16 Icomb B 3
16 Idbury B 3
4 Iddesleigh E 4
6 Ide G 2
10 Ide Hill C 4
5 Ideford H 8
11 Iden F 8
10 Iden Green, Kent D 6
11 Iden Green, Kent E 7
35 Idle C 10
22 Idlicote H 6
58 Idoch C 5
13 Idole E 7
31 Idridgehay E 11
62 Idrigil B 3
16 Idstone F 4
53 Idvies B 10
10 Ifield D 1
9 Ifold C 11
10 Iford G 3
15 Ifton E 8
30 Ifton Heath G 2
30 Ightfield F 5
10 Ightham B 5
27 Iken K 7
31 Ilam E 10
7 Ilchester D 8
49 Ilderton G 12
18 Ilford E 4
4 Ilfracombe A 4
32 Ilkeston F 2
27 Ilketshall St. Andrew G 6
27 Ilketshall St. Margaret G 6
35 Ilkley B 9
35 Illingworth D 9
22 Illey D 3
2 Illogan E 4
2 Illogan Highway E 4
23 Illston on the Hill B 10
17 Ilmer D 8
22 Ilmington H 5
7 Ilminster E 7
5 Ilsington H 6
13 Ilston H 9
7 Ilton, Somerset D 7
40 Ilton, Yorkshire G 2
46 Imachar E 4
37 Immingham F 9
37 Immingham Dock E 9
25 Impington J 5
55 Inbhireala or Strathossian Ho. M 8
30 Ince C 3
34 Ince Blundell G 2
34 Ince-In-Makerfield G 5
59 Inch K 4
54 Inchbae Lodge C 8
59 Inchbare L 3
47 Inchbean F 9
58 Inchberry B 1
53 Incheoch B 7
60 Inchina G 2
47 Inchinnan B 9
60 Inchkinloch C 6
55 Inchlaggan J 5
56 Inchlumpie B 1
57 Inchnabobart J 1
59 Inchnacardoch (Hotel) H 7
60 Inchnadamph E 4
57 Inchrory J 7
53 Inchture D 7
54 Inchvuilt F 6
52 Inchyra E 6
2 Indian Queens D 6
4 Indicott B 4
47 Industrial Estate, Dunbarton B 9
48 Industrial Estate, Fife A 4
18 Ingatestone D 6
35 Ingbirchworth G 10
31 Ingestre H 8
32 Ingham, Lincs. B 6
26 Ingham, Norfolk C 7
27 Ingham, Suffolk H 1
24 Ingleborough, Norfolk D 6
39 Ingleborough, Yorks. H 10
31 Ingleby G 12
40 Ingleby Arncliffe E 5
40 Ingleby Cross E 5
40 Ingleby Greenhow E 6
15 Inglesbatch H 10
16 Inglesham D 3
40 Ingleton, Durham C 2
39 Ingleton, Yorks. H 9
34 Inglewhite C 4
45 Ingoe F 8
33 Ingoldmells C 12
33 Ingoldsby G 7
34 Inglewhite C 4
45 Ingoe F 8
33 Ingoldmells C 12
33 Ingoldsby G 7
24 Ingoldsthorpe B 8
45 Ingram A 8
18 Ingrave E 6
35 Ingrow C 9
39 Ings E 7
15 Ingst E 9
26 Ingworth C 5
51 Inistrynich E 8
38 Injebreck G 2
22 Inkberrow F 4
16 Inkpen H 4
61 Inkstack A 11
46 Innellan B 6
48 Innerleithen F 6
53 Innerleven G 8
42 Innermessan E 2
42 Innerwell Fishery G 6
49 Innerwick, E.Loth. B 10
52 Innerwick, Perth B 1
51 Innis Chonain E 8
51 Innischoarach D 12
58 Insch E 4
58 Inschtammack C 2
57 Insh J 4
57 Insh House J 4
51 Inshaig B 7
60 Inshore A 4
34 Inskip C 3
4 Instow C 3
35 Intake Gate C 10
57 Inver, Aberdeen K 8
52 Inver, Perth C 5
56 Inver, Ross & Cromarty B 4
54 Inver Alligin D 2
55 Inver Mallie K 5
55 Inverailort L 1
58 Inverallochy A 8
60 Inveran G 6
57 Inveraray G 8
53 Inverarity C 9
51 Inverarnan F 10
54 Inverasdale A 2
54 Inverbain D 2
51 Inverbeg Hotel H 10
59 Inverbervie K 6
58 Inverboyndie A 4
60 Inverbroom H 3
57 Invercauld House K 7
46 Inverchaolain B 6
46 Inverchapel A 6
51 Invercharnan C 8
54 Inverchoran E 6
51 Invercreran C 7
57 Inverdruie H 5
58 Inverebrie D 7
57 Inveredrie M 7
57 Invereshie House J 4
48 Inveresk B 6
51 Inveresragan D 7
54 Inverewe House B 2
57 Inverey K 6
55 Inverfarigaig G 1
55 Invergarry J 7
52 Invergeldie D 2
55 Invergloy L 6
56 Invergordon C 3
53 Invergowrie D 8
55 Inverguseran J 1
52 Inverhadden A 2
58 Inverharroch D 1
51 Inverherive E 10
55 Inverie J 1
51 Inverinan F 7
55 Inverinate G 3
53 Inverkeilor B 11
48 Inverkeithing A 4
58 Inverkeithny C 4
47 Inverkip B 7
60 Inverkirkaig E 2
60 Inverlael H 3
60 Inverlael Lodge H 3
55 Inverlair L 7
51 Inverlochlarig F 11
51 Inverlochy E 9
59 Invermark Lodge J 2
55 Invermoriston H 8
58 Invernan House F 1
61 Invernaver B 7
56 Inverness E 2
57 Inverness, Co. H 3
58 Invernetie C 8
51 Invernoaden H 8
51 Inveroran Hotel C 10
60 Inverpolly Lodge E 2
58 Inverquhomery C 8
55 Inverroy L 6
50 Inversanda B 7
55 Invershiel H 3
60 Invershin G 6
60 Invershin Station G 6
55 Inverskilavulin L 5
51 Inversnaid Hotel G 10
58 Inverugie, Aber. C 8
56 Inverugie, Moray C 7
51 Inveruglas G 10
57 Inveruglass J 4
58 Inverurie E 5
52 Invervar B 2
59 Invery House H 4
58 Inverythan C 5
4 Inwardleigh F 4
19 Inworth B 8
9 Iping D 10
5 Ipplepen J 7
18 Ippollits A 2
17 Ipsden F 7
31 Ipstones E 8
27 Ipswich L 5
30 Irby B 1
33 Irby in the Marsh D 11
37 Irby upon Humber G 9
23 Irchester E 12
39 Ireby H 9
38 Ireleth G 5
39 Ireshopeburn A 11
55 Irine L 1
34 Irlam H 6
33 Irnham G 7
15 Iron Acton F 10
21 Iron Bridge B 12
22 Iron Cross G 4
43 Ironmacannie D 7
32 Ironville E 2
26 Irstead C 7
23 Irthlingborough E 12
44 Irthington G 3
41 Irton G 10
47 Irvine E 8
44 Irvington F 1
61 Isauld A 9
64 Isbister, Orkney C 2
64 Isbister, Zetland B 7
64 Isbister, Zetland C 8
10 Isfield F 3
23 Isham E 12
50 Ishriff D 4
7 Isle Abbotts D 7
7 Isle Brewers D 7
18 Isle of Dogs F 4
42 Isle of Whithorn H 6
25 Isleham H 7
62 Isleornsay G 6
43 Islesteps D 10
18 Isleworth F 2
32 Isley Walton H 2
18 Islington E 3
25 Islip, Northants. G 1
16 Islip, Oxon C 6
63 Islivig D 1
8 Itchen E 6
9 Itchen Abbas C 7
9 Itchen Stoke C 7
9 Itchingfield C 12
15 Itchington F 10
26 Itteringham C 4
15 Itton Common E 8
38 Ivegill A 6
39 Ivelet E 11
17 Iver F 11
17 Iver Heath F 11
45 Iveston H 9
17 Ivinghoe B 10
17 Ivinghoe Aston B 10
21 Ivington G 10
21 Ivington Green G 10
10 Ivy Hatch C 5
5 Ivybridge K 5
11 Ivychurch E 9
11 Iwade A 7
7 Iwerne Courtney or Shroton E 12
7 Iwerne Minster E 12
27 Ixworth H 2
27 Ixworth Thorpe H 2
35 Jack Hill B 10
32 Jacksdale E 2
58 Jackstown D 5
47 Jackton D 10
2 Jacobstow B 2
4 Jacobstowe F 5
9 Jacobswell A 11
12 Jameston G 4
44 Jamestown, Dumf. C 1
47 Jamestown, Dunb. A 9
54 Jamestown, Ross & Cromarty D 8
61 Janetstown D 11
45 Jarrow F 11
10 Jarvis Brook E 4
10 Jasper's Green A 7
48 Jawcraig B 1
19 Jaywick Sands C 11
17 Jealott's Hill G 9
40 Jeater Houses F 4
49 Jedburgh G 9
12 Jeffreston F 4
56 Jemimaville C 3
13 Jersey Marine H 10
59 Jessiefield G 6
10 Jevington H 4
17 Jockey End C 11
30 Jodrell Bank C 6
35 John O'Gaunts D 12
38 Johnby B 6
10 John's Cross F 6
59 Johnshaven K 6
12 Johnston E 3
44 Johnstone, Dumf. C 1
47 Johnstone, Ren. C 9
43 Johnstonebridge B 11
13 Johnstown, Carm. E 7
29 Johnstown, Denb. F 12
20 Joppa, Cards. F 1
48 Joppa, Midloth. B 6
17 Jordans E 10
12 Jordanston D 3
19 Jordons E 8
35 Jump G 12
8 Jumpers Green G 3
48 Juniper Green B 5
38 Jurby East F 2
38 Jurby West F 2
44 Justicetown G 2
39 Kaber D 10
58 Kaecloch C 4
48 Kaimes C 5
49 Kalemouth G 9
54 Kalnakill D 1
46 Kames, Argyll B 5
50 Kames, Argyll F 5
47 Kames, Argyll G 11
36 Keadby F 6
33 Keal Cotes D 10
34 Kearsley G 6
36 Kearstwick G 8
39 Kearton E 12
60 Kearvaig A 4
39 Keasden H 9
33 Keddington A 10
25 Kedington K 8
31 Kedleston F 11
49 Kedslie E 8
37 Keelby F 9
25 Keeley Green L 1
45 Keepershield F 7
12 Keeston E 3
15 Keevil H 12
32 Kegworth G 2
2 Kehelland F 3
58 Keig F 3
35 Keighley C 9
51 Keil B 7
52 Keilarsbrae H 4
58 Keilhill B 5
46 Keillmore A 2
52 Keillour E 5
7 Keinton Mandeville C 9
52 Keir House G 3
43 Keir Mill B 9
24 Keisby C 1
61 Keiss B 12
58 Keith C 2
58 Keithen C 5
35 Kelbrook C 8
33 Kelby F 7
39 Keld, Westmor. D 8
39 Keld, Yorkshire E 11
41 Keldholme F 7
41 Keldy Castle F 8
36 Kelfield C 4
32 Kelham E 5
43 Kelhead E 12
50 Kellan C 3
53 Kellas, Angus D 9
56 Kellas, Moray D 7
5 Kellaton M 7
16 Kellaways G 1
39 Kelleth E 9
26 Kelling A 4
36 Kellingley E 3
36 Kellington E 3
40 Kelloe B 4
49 Kelloe Mains D 11
5 Kelly H 3
3 Kelly Bray C 10
23 Kelmarsh D 10
16 Kelmscot D 3
27 Kelsale J 7
30 Kelsall C 4
30 Kelsall Hill C 4
25 Kelshall L 4
43 Kelsick F 12
49 Kelso F 10
31 Kelstedge D 11
33 Kelstern A 9
29 Kelsterton C 12
15 Kelston H 10
43 Kelton D 10
43 Kelton Hill F 8
52 Kelty H 6
19 Kelvedon B 8
18 Kelvedon Hatch D 6
2 Kelynack G 1
53 Kemback F 9
22 Kemberton B 1
16 Kemble D 1
22 Kemerton H 3
15 Kemeys Commander D 7
58 Kemnay F 5
10 Kemp Town H 2
60 Kempie B 5
15 Kempley A 10
22 Kempsey G 2
16 Kempsford D 3
9 Kempshott A 7
25 Kempston K 1
25 Kempston Hardwick L 1
25 Kempston West End K 1
21 Kempton D 9
10 Kemsing B 4
11 Kemsley A 8
11 Kenardington E 8
21 Kenchester Sugwas H 10
16 Kencot D 4
39 Kendal F 7
15 Kenderchurch A 7
14 Kenfig F 1
14 Kenfig Hill F 2
22 Kenilworth E 6
51 Kenknock D 11
21 Kenley B 11
51 Kenmore, Argyll G 8
52 Kenmore, Perth C 3
54 Kenmore, Ross & Cromarty D 1
6 Kenn, Devon H 3
15 Kenn, Somerset G 7
63 Kennacley G 3
46 Kennacraig C 3
3 Kennards House A 10
44 Kennedy's Corner E 1
2 Kenneggy Downs G 3
4 Kennerleigh E 7
52 Kennet H 4
43 Kenneth Bank E 10
25 Kennett H 8
6 Kennford G 3
27 Kenninghall G 3
16 Kennington, Berks. D 6
11 Kennington, Kent. D 9
18 Kennington, London F 3
53 Kennoway G 8
47 Kennox E 8
25 Kennyhill G 8
36 Kennythorpe A 6
62 Kensaleyre C 3
18 Kensington F 3
17 Kensworth B 11
17 Kensworth Com. B 11
11 Kent, County C 8
10 Kent Street C 5
51 Kentallen B 7
15 Kentchurch B 7
25 Kentford J 8
6 Kentisbeare E 4
4 Kentisbury B 5
4 Kentisburyford B 5
39 Kentmere E 7
6 Kenton, Devon H 3
18 Kenton, London E 2
27 Kenton, Suffolk J 5
45 Kenton Bank Foot F 10
50 Kentra A 4
38 Kents Bank H 6
15 Kent's Green B 10
8 Kent's Oak D 5
45 Kentstone B 11
30 Kenwick G 3
2 Kenwyn E 5
60 Keoldale A 5
63 Keose E 5
55 Keppoch G 3
46 Keprigan H 2
40 Kepwick F 5
49 Kerchesters F 10
23 Keresley D 7
15 Kerne Bridge B 9
48 Kerrcleuch H 5
31 Kerridge C 8
2 Kerris G 2
54 Kerrowwood F 7
21 Kerry C 7
46 Kerrylamont D 6
15 Kerry's Gate A 7
54 Kerrysdale B 2
46 Kerrytonlia D 6
32 Kersall D 4
6 Kersbrooke H 4
4 Kerscott C 5
47 Kerse D 8
27 Kersey L 3
63 Kershader E 4
44 Kershopefoot E 3
49 Kersmains F 9
22 Kersoe H 3

MAP
6 Kerswell.........F 4
22 Kerswell Green...G 2
27 Kesgrave.........L 5
38 Keskadale........C 4
27 Kessingland......G 8
27 Kessingland Beach.G 8
2 Kestle Mill.......D 5
18 Keston...........G 4
38 Keswick, Cumb...C 5
26 Keswick, Norfolk .B 6
26 Keswick, Norfolk .E 5
21 Ketley...........A 12
49 Kettelshiel.......D 9
23 Kettering.........D 12
26 Ketteringham.....E 5
53 Kettins...........C 7
27 Kettlebaston......K 3
53 Kettlebridge......F 8
22 Kettlebrook.......B 6
27 Kettleburgh.......J 5
53 Kettlehill.........F 8
41 Kettleness........D 8
31 Kettleshulme......B 8
35 Kettlesing........B 11
35 Kettlesing Bottom A 11
26 Kettlestone.......B 3
32 Kettlethorpe......C 6
64 Kettletoft.........B 4
39 Kettlewell ......H 11
24 Ketton............E 1
18 Kew..............F 2
14 Kewstoke........H 6
35 Kexbrough ......F 11
32 Kexby, Lincs......B 6
36 Kexby, Yorks......B 5
31 Key Green........D 7
11 Key Street........B 7
23 Keyham..........B 10
8 Keyhaven ....G 5
37 Keyingham......E 10
10 Keymer..........F 2
15 Keynsham........G 9
33 Key's Toft......D 12
25 Keysoe...........J 2
25 Keysoe Roe.......J 2
25 Keyston..........H 1
32 Keyworth.........G 3
45 Kibblesworth....G 10
23 Kibworth Beauchamp C 10
23 Kibworth Harcourt C 10
18 Kidbrooke........F 4
22 Kiddemore Green .A 2
22 Kidderminster....D 2
16 Kiddington.......B 5
16 Kidlington........C 6
17 Kidmore End.....F 8
30 Kidnall...........E 3
58 Kidrummy........F 2
31 Kidsgrove........E 7
39 Kidstones.......G 11
13 Kidwelly.........F 7
50 Kiel Crofts ......D 6
44 Kielder...........D 4
52 Kilbagie ....H 4
47 Kilbarchan.......C 9
62 Kilbeg ....H 6
46 Kilberry..........C 2
47 Kilbirnie.........D 8
50 Kilbride..........E 6
50 Kilbride, Argyll ..E 6
62 Kilbride, Inver.....F 5
59 Kilburn, Angus....K 1
32 Kilburn, Derby....F 1
40 Kilburn, Yorks....G 5
23 Kilby.............C 9
48 Kilcadzow ....D 2
50 Kilchattan, Arg. .H 1
46 Kilchattan, Bute..D 6
46 Kilchenzie........G 2
50 Kilcheran.........D 5
50 Kilchoan, Argyll ..A 2
50 Kilchoan, Argyll ..F 5
55 Kilchoan, Inver...K 2
51 Kilchrenan.......E 7
53 Kilconquhar......G 9
15 Kilcot............B 10
56 Kilcoy............E 1
47 Kilcreggan........A 7
40 Kildale...........D 6
46 Kildalloig........G 4
46 Kildavanan.......C 5
56 Kildermorie Lodge B 1
46 Kildonan, Arran..G 5
61 Kildonan, Suther..E 9
61 Kildonan Lodge...E 9
42 Kildrochat House .F 2
35 Kildwick.........C 9
46 Kilfinan..........B 4
55 Kilfinnan.........K 6
29 Kilford.........D 10
MAP
12 Kilgetty..........F 5
49 Kilham, Northumb. F 11
37 Kilham, Yorks....A 8
42 Kilkerran.........A 4
4 Kilkhampton.....E 1
32 Killamarsh.......B 2
13 Killay............H 9
50 Killbeg..........C 3
46 Killchianaig......A 1
46 Killean...........E 2
47 Killearn.........A 10
46 Killellan ....H 2
56 Killen............D 2
40 Killerby..........C 2
42 Killern...........F 6
51 Killichonan......B 12
50 Killichronan......C 3
55 Killiechanate.....L 6
52 Killiecrankie.....A 4
57 Killiehuntly.......K 4
50 Killiemor.........D 2
55 Killilan..........G 3
61 Killimster.......B 12
52 Killin............D 1
57 Killin Lodge......J 1
35 Killinghall.......A 11
35 Killington........F 8
49 Killochyett.......E 7
50 Killunaig.........E 2
50 Killundine........C 3
43 Killyleoch........C 9
47 Kilmacolm.......B 8
52 Kilmahog.........F 1
50 Kilmahumaig.....H 5
62 Kilmaluag.........A 4
53 Kilmany...........E 8
62 Kilmarie..........F 5
47 Kilmarnock.......F 9
53 Kilmaron Castle ..E 8
50 Kilmartin.........H 5
47 Kilmaurs.........E 9
50 Kilmelford........F 6
7 Kilmersdon.....A 10
9 Kilmeston.......D 7
46 Kilmichael.......G 2
50 Kilmichael Glassary H 6
46 Kilmichael of Inverlussa......A 3
6 Kilmington, Devon F 6
7 Kilmington, Wilts.C 11
7 Kilmington Street C 11
56 Kilmorack........E 1
50 Kilmore, Argyll...E 6
62 Kilmore, Inver....G 6
50 Kilmory, Argyll...A 3
46 Kilmory, Argyll...B 2
46 Kilmory, Arran...G 4
61 Kilmote...........F 9
62 Kilmuir, Inver.....A 3
62 Kilmuir, Inver.....C 2
56 Kilmuir, Ross & Cromarty.......B 3
56 Kilmuir, Ross & Cromarty.......E 2
46 Kilmun..........A 6
17 Kiln Green.......F 9
44 Kiln Hill ....F 4
45 Kiln Pit Hill.......H 8
10 Kilndown.........E 6
43 Kilness.........D 10
47 Kilnford..........F 8
36 Kilnhurst ....G 2
50 Kilninian.........C 1
50 Kilninver.........E 5
37 Kilnsea.........F 11
39 Kilnsey.........H 12
37 Kilnwick.........B 7
36 Kilnwick Percy....B 6
50 Kiloran..........H 1
46 Kilpatrick........G 4
15 Kilpeck...........A 7
61 Kilphedir.........E 9
36 Kilpin............D 5
36 Kilpin Pike.......D 5
53 Kilrenny........G 10
23 Kilsby...........E 9
53 Kilspindie.......E 7
47 Kilsyth..........B 12
6 Kilton, Somerset ..B 5
41 Kilton, Yorks.....C 7
62 Kilvaxter.........A 3
6 Kilve.............B 5
32 Kilvington........F 5
47 Kilwinning.......E 8
26 Kimberley, Norf...E 4
32 Kimberley, Notts..F 2
17 Kimble Wick.....C 9
45 Kimblesworth....H 11
21 Kimbolton, Herefs. F 10
25 Kimbolton, Hunts. H 2
MAP
23 Kimcote..........C 9
7 Kimmeridge.....H 12
49 Kimmerston......F 12
8 Kimpton, Hants...A 4
18 Kimpton, Herts...B 2
61 Kinbrace.........D 8
55 Kinbreack........K 4
52 Kinbuck..........G 3
47 Kincaidston.......G 8
53 Kincaple.........E 9
59 Kincardine, Co....J 5
52 Kincardine, Fife ..H 4
60 Kincardine, Ross & Cromarty......G 6
59 Kincardine O'Neil.G 3
52 Kinclaven........C 6
59 Kincorth.........G 7
56 Kincorth House ..D 6
57 Kincraig.........J 4
52 Kindallachan .....B 5
56 Kindrummond....F 2
46 Kinerarach.......D 2
16 Kineton, Glos.....B 2
23 Kineton, War.....G 7
52 Kinfauns.........E 6
15 King Stanley ....D 11
50 Kingairloch Ho....B 6
46 Kingarth.........D 6
15 Kingcoed.........D 7
33 Kingerby..........A 7
4 Kingford..........D 5
16 Kingham..........B 3
50 Kingharair........C 2
43 Kingholm Quay..D 10
48 Kinghorn..........A 5
53 Kinglassie........G 7
58 Kingoodie, Aberdeen E 6
53 Kingoodie .Angus.D 8
21 King's Acre.....H 10
31 Kings Bromley....H 9
15 Kings Caple......A 9
24 King's Cliffe......F 1
22 King's Coughton ..F 4
22 Kings Heath......D 4
17 Kings Langley...D 11
24 King's Lynn.....D 7
39 King's Meaburn...C 8
48 Kings Muir.......E 5
23 King's Norton, Leics. B 10
22 King's Norton, War. D 4
4 King's Nympton ..D 6
21 King's Pyon.....G 10
25 Kings Ripton.....H 4
8 King's Samborne..C 5
7 King's Stag......E 10
16 King's Sutton.....A 6
18 King's Walden....B 2
11 Kings Wood......C 7
8 Kings Worth......C 6
3 Kingsand........E 11
53 Kingsbarns.......F 10
5 Kingsbridge, Devon L 6
6 Kingsbridge, Som..C 3
62 Kingsburgh.......C 3
18 Kingsbury, London E 2
22 Kingsbury, War...C 6
7 Kingsbury Episcopi D 8
16 Kingsclere ....H 6
15 Kingscote.......E 11
4 Kingscott........D 4
46 Kingscross.......G 5
7 Kingsdon.........D 8
11 Kingsdown......C 12
52 Kingseat.........H 6
17 Kingsey..........C 8
10 Kingsfold.........D 1
59 Kingsford, Aber...G 6
47 Kingsford, Ayr....E 9
22 Kingsford, Worcs. D 2
27 Kingshall Street....J 2
4 Kingsheanton.....B 4
52 Kingshouse.......E 1
51 Kingshouse Hotel B 10
5 Kingskerswell.....J 7
53 Kingskettle.......F 8
28 Kingsland, Angl...B 2
21 Kingsland, Herefs. F 10
30 Kingsley, Ches....C 4
9 Kingsley, Hants. ..B 9
31 Kingsley, Staffs....F 8
9 Kingsley Green ..C 10
31 Kingsley Holt.....F 9
53 Kingsmuir........B 9
11 Kingsnorth.......D 9
22 Kingstanding.....C 4
5 Kingsteignton ....H 7
15 Kingsthorne......A 8
23 Kingsthorpe.....F 11
MAP
25 Kingston, Cambs..K 4
5 Kingston, Devon..L 5
7 Kingston, Dorset.E 11
8 Kingston, Dorset .H 1
49 Kingston, E. Loth..A 8
8 Kingston, Hants...F 3
8 Kingston, I.o.W...H 6
11 Kingston, Kent ..C 10
58 Kingston, Moray..A 1
9 Kingston, Sussex .F 12
16 Kingston Bagpuize D 5
17 Kingston Blount ..D 8
10 Kingston by Sea...H 1
7 Kingston Deverill C 11
16 Kingston Lisle....E 4
10 Kingston near Lewes G 3
32 Kingston on Soar..G 2
7 Kingston Russell..G 9
6 Kingston St. Mary C 6
15 Kingston Seymour H 7
37 Kingston upon Hull D 8
18 Kingston upon Thames G 2
18 Kingston Vale....G 2
15 Kingstone, Herefs..A 7
7 Kingstone, Som. ..E 7
31 Kingstone, Staffs..G 9
44 Kingstown.......G 2
5 Kingswear........K 7
22 Kingswinford.....C 2
17 Kingswood, Bucks.B 8
15 Kingswood, Glos. E 10
15 Kingswood, Glos. .G 9
21 Kingswood, Mont. B 8
10 Kingswood, Surrey B 1
22 Kingswood, War...E 5
21 Kingswood Com. .G 8
21 Kington, Herefs...G 8
22 Kington, Worcs...G 3
15 Kington Langley .G 12
7 Kington Magna .D 11
15 Kington St. Michael F 12
57 Kingussie.........J 3
7 Kingweston.......C 8
43 Kinharvie.......E 10
52 Kinkell Bridge....E 4
58 Kinknockie, Aber..C 7
58 Kinknockie, Aber..E 7
44 Kinkry Hill.......E 3
22 Kinlet...........D 1
53 Kinloch, Fife.....F 7
62 Kinloch, Inver.....F 6
52 Kinloch, Perth....C 6
53 Kinloch, Perth....C 7
60 Kinloch, Suther. ..D 4
62 Kinloch Castle ...H 3
55 Kinloch Hourn....J 3
57 Kinloch Laggan...K 1
60 Kinloch Lodge....B 6
52 Kinloch Rannoch .A 2
50 Kinlochan........A 5
51 Kinlochard.......G 11
55 Kinlochbeoraid....L 2
60 Kinlochbervie.....B 3
55 Kinlocheil.........L 4
51 Kinlochetive......C 8
54 Kinlochewe ....D 4
51 Kinlochleven......A 9
55 Kinlochmoidart ..M 1
55 Kinlochmorar.....K 2
51 Kinlochmore.....A 9
55 Kinlochnanuagh ..L 1
50 Kinlochspelve.....E 4
55 Kinloid...........L 1
56 Kinloss...........D 6
29 Kinmel Bay.......B 9
58 Kinmuck.........F 6
58 Kinnadie.........C 7
54 Kinnahaird.......D 8
59 Kinnaid Castle....L 4
53 Kinnaird.........D 7
59 Kinneff..........K 6
43 Kinnelhead......B 11
53 Kinnell..........B 10
30 Kinnerley ....H 2
21 Kinnersley, Herefs.G 9
22 Kinnersley, Worcs. H 2
21 Kinnerton.........F 8
52 Kinnesswood.....G 6
40 Kinninvie.........C 1
53 Kinnordy.........B 8
32 Kinoulton.........G 4
57 Kinrara...........J 4
52 Kinross...........G 6
52 Kinross, Co. .....G 6
53 Kinrossie.........D 7
21 Kinsham..........F 9
36 Kinsley ....F 2
8 Kinson............F 2
56 Kinsteary Lodge ..D 5
MAP
63 Kintaravay.......E 3
16 Kintbury.........G 5
56 Kintessack.......D 6
52 Kintillo ....E 6
59 Kintocher........G 3
21 Kinton, Herefs...E 9
30 Kinton, Salop.....H 2
58 Kintore..........F 5
50 Kintra...........F 1
56 Kintrae..........C 7
50 Kintraw..........G 5
50 Kinuachdrach ....H 4
57 Kinveachy ....H 5
22 Kinver...........D 2
36 Kippax...........D 2
52 Kippen ....H 1
43 Kippford or Scaur .F 9
10 Kipping's Cross ..D 5
64 Kirbister.........D 2
38 Kirby ....H 2
26 Kirby Bedon......E 6
32 Kirby Bellars......H 4
26 Kirby Cane.......F 7
19 Kirby Cross .....B 12
41 Kirby Grindalythe.H 9
40 Kirby Hill, Yorks..E 2
40 Kirby Hill, Yorks..H 4
40 Kirby Knowle.....F 5
19 Kirby le Soken...B 12
41 Kirby Misperton ..G 8
23 Kirby Muxloe.....B 8
35 Kirby Overblow..B 12
26 Kirby Row.......F 7
40 Kirby Sigston.....F 4
36 Kirby Underdale..A 6
40 Kirby Wiske......G 4
9 Kirdford........C 11
63 Kirivick..........C 3
61 Kirk.............B 11
36 Kirk Bramwith....F 4
35 Kirk Deighton ...B 12
37 Kirk Ella........D 8
32 Kirk Hallam......F 2
36 Kirk Hammerton..B 3
31 Kirk Ireton......E 11
31 Kirk Langley....F 11
40 Kirk Merrington ..B 3
38 Kirk Michael.....G 1
48 Kirk of Shotts....C 1
36 Kirk Sandall......F 4
36 Kirk Smeaton.....E 3
49 Kirk Yetholm ...G 11
64 Kirkabister.......E 7
43 Kirkandrews......G 7
44 Kirkandrews upon Eden..........G 2
44 Kirkbampton.....G 1
43 Kirkbank.......C 11
43 Kirkbean........F 10
64 Kirkbrae.........A 2
44 Kirkbride, Cumb..G 1
43 Kirkbride, Dumf...C 9
53 Kirkbudd ....C 9
48 Kirkburn, Peeb....F 5
37 Kirkburn, Yorks...B 7
35 Kirkburton ......F 10
34 Kirkby, Lancs.....G 3
33 Kirkby, Lincs......A 8
40 Kirkby, Yorks.....E 5
40 Kirkby Fleetham ..F 3
33 Kirkby Green.....D 8
32 Kirkby in Ashfield.E 2
24 Kirkby le Thorpe .A 2
39 Kirkby Lonsdale..G 8
35 Kirkby Malham....A 7
23 Kirkby Mallory...B 8
40 Kirkby Malzeard .H 2
41 Kirkby Mills......G 7
33 Kirkby on Bain...D 9
39 Kirkby Stephen..D 10
39 Kirkby Thore.....C 9
24 Kirkby UnderwoodC 2
36 Kirkby Wharf......C 3
41 Kirkbymoorside...F 7
53 Kirkcaldy........H 7
44 Kirkcambeck......F 4
43 Kirkcarswell......G 8
42 Kirkcolm..........E 1
47 Kirkconnel ......H 12
43 Kirkconnell, Kirk. E 10
43 Kirkconnell, Kirk..F 7
42 Kirkcowan.......E 4
43 Kirkcudbright.....F 8
43 Kirkcudbright, Co. E 7
30 Kirkdale.........A 2
42 Kirkdale House...F 6
48 Kirkdean.........E 4
48 Kirkfieldbank.....E 1
43 Kirkgunzeon......E 9
34 Kirkham, Lancs...D 3
36 Kirkham, Yorks...A 5
35 Kirkhamgate.....E 11
MAP
45 Kirkharle.........E 8
45 Kirkheaton, Northumb......E 8
35 Kirkheaton, Yorks. E 10
59 Kirkhill, Angus ...L 4
48 Kirkhill, Midloth. .C 5
56 Kirkhill, Ross & Cromarty.......E 1
58 Kirkhill of Kennethmont...E 3
48 Kirkhope.........G 6
48 Kirkhouse........F 6
62 Kirkibost, Inver. ..F 5
63 Kirkibost, Lewis ..C 3
53 Kirkinch..........C 8
42 Kirkinner.........F 5
47 Kirkintilloch.....B 11
39 Kirkland, Cumb...B 9
38 Kirkland, Cumb...C 3
43 Kirkland, Dumf...C 9
43 Kirkland, Dumf...C 11
47 Kirkland, Dumf..H 12
42 Kirkland, Wig.....G 5
43 Kirkland Guards.G 12
43 Kirkland of Gelston F 8
40 Kirkleatham......C 6
40 Kirklevington.....D 4
26 Kirkley...........F 8
45 Kirkley March....E 9
31 Kirkleyditch......B 7
32 Kirklington, Notts.D 4
40 Kirklington, Yorks.G 3
44 Kirklinton........F 3
48 Kirkliston........B 4
42 Kirkmaiden.......H 2
42 Kirkmichael, Ayr..A 4
52 Kirkmichael, Perth A 6
47 Kirkmuirhill......E 12
48 Kirknewton, Midloth. C 4
49 Kirknewton, Northumb.....F 11
58 Kirkney..........D 3
42 Kirkoswald, Ayr...A 3
39 Kirkoswald, Cumb. A 8
43 Kirkpatrick, Dur. .D 8
44 Kirkpatrick-Fleming F 1
38 Kirksanton.......G 4
33 Kirkstead........D 9
58 Kirkstile, Aber....D 3
44 Kirkstile, Dumf. ..D 2
58 Kirkston of Culsalmond....D 4
61 Kirkstyle........A 12
58 Kirkton, Aber....C 6
58 Kirkton, Aber.....E 4
58 Kirkton, Aber.....F 6
58 Kirkton, Aber.....F 4
53 Kirkton, Angus...C 9
59 Kirkton, Angus....J 2
58 Kirkton, Banff....C 4
43 Kirkton, Dumf...C 10
53 Kirkton, Fife.....E 8
56 Kirkton, Inver.....F 2
48 Kirkton, Lanark ..G 2
52 Kirkton, Perth....E 4
56 Kirkton, Ross & Cromarty.......C 3
54 Kirkton, Ross & Cromarty.......F 3
44 Kirkton, Rox......B 4
48 Kirkton Manor...D 5
53 Kirkton of Airlie..B 8
53 Kirkton of Auchterhouse...C 8
56 Kirkton of Barevan E 4
53 Kirkton of Collace.D 7
53 Kirkton of Craig .B 11
59 Kirkton of Durris.H 5
58 Kirkton of Glenbuchat F 1
53 Kirkton of Glenisla A 7
53 Kirkton of Kingoldrum....B 8
53 Kirkton of Largo .G 9
52 Kirkton of Lethendy C 6
58 Kirkton of Logie Buchan.........E 7
59 Kirkton of Menmuir L 3
53 Kirkton of Monikie C 10
58 Kirkton of Oyne ..E 4
59 Kirkton of Skene .G 5
53 Kirkton of Strathmartine...D 8
53 Kirkton of Tealing.C 9
53 Kirktonbarns.....D 9
58 Kirktown.........B 8
58 Kirktown of Alvah.B 4

MAP
58 Kirktown of Auchterless C 5
58 Kirktown of Bourtie E 5
58 Kirktown of Deskford B 2
59 Kirktown of Fetteresso J 6
58 Kirktown of Mortlach D 1
58 Kirktown of Rayne E 4
58 Kirktown of Slains E 8
64 Kirkwall D 2
45 Kirkwhelpington E 8
37 Kirmington F 9
33 Kirmond le Mire A 9
47 Kirn B 7
43 Kirncleuch B 12
53 Kirriemuir B 8
26 Kirstead Green F 6
44 Kirtlebridge F 1
44 Kirtleton E 1
25 Kirtling J 8
25 Kirtling Green K 8
16 Kirtlington B 6
61 Kirtomy B 7
56 Kirton, Inverness D 3
24 Kirton, Lincs. B 4
32 Kirton, Notts. C 4
27 Kirton, Suffolk L 6
24 Kirton End B 4
24 Kirton Holme A 4
37 Kirton in Lindsey G 7
23 Kislingbury F 10
23 Kites Hardwick E 8
6 Kittisford D 4
13 Kittle H 9
31 Kitts Moss B 7
59 Kittybrewster G 7
9 Kitwood C 8
4 Kiverley D 4
15 Kivernoll A 8
32 Kiveton Park B 2
60 Klibreck D 6
60 Klibreck Lodge D 6
32 Knaith B 5
32 Knaith Park B 5
7 Knap Corner D 11
17 Knaphill H 10
53 Knapp, Angus D 7
6 Knapp, Somerset D 6
58 Knaps of Auchlee C 8
26 Knapton, Norfolk B 6
36 Knapton, Yorks. B 3
21 Knapton Green G 10
25 Knapwell J 4
35 Knaresborough A 12
44 Knarsdale H 5
58 Knauchland C 3
40 Knayton F 4
18 Knebworth B 3
36 Knedlington D 5
32 Kneesall D 4
25 Kneesworth L 4
32 Kneeton F 4
13 Knelston H 8
27 Knettishall G 3
4 Knightacott B 5
23 Knightcote G 7
5 Knighton, Devon L 4
7 Knighton, Dorset E 9
23 Knighton, Leics. B 9
21 Knighton, Rad. E 8
30 Knighton, Staffs. F 6
30 Knighton, Staffs. G 6
16 Knighton, Wilts. G 4
22 Knightsfold Bridge G 1
21 Knill F 8
32 Knipton G 5
45 Knitsley H 9
31 Kniveton E 10
50 Knock, Argyll D 3
58 Knock, Banff. B 3
62 Knock, Inverness G 6
63 Knock, Lewis D 6
39 Knock, Westmor. B 9
60 Knockan F 3
56 Knockando E 7
57 Knockandhu G 8
60 Knockanrock F 3
61 Knockarthur F 7
56 Knockbain D 2
62 Knockbreck B 2
43 Knockbrex G 7
61 Knockdee B 11
42 Knockdolian Cas. C 2
42 Knockdon B 5
47 Knockendon D 7
42 Knockenjig H 12
46 Knockenkelly G 5
47 Knockentiber E 9
58 Knockespock Ho. E 3
42 Knockgardner A 4

MAP
42 Knockglass F 1
10 Knockholt B 3
10 Knockholt Pound B 4
55 Knockie Lodge H 8
30 Knockin H 2
47 Knockinlaw E 9
42 Knocklaugh B 3
43 Knocklearn D 8
42 Knocknain E 1
46 Knockrome B 1
53 Knockshannoch A 7
38 Knocksharry G 1
42 Knocksheen C 6
43 Knockvennie D 8
42 Knockycoid D 3
27 Knodishall J 7
7 Knole D 8
15 Knole Park F 9
30 Knolls Green B 6
30 Knolton F 2
8 Knook B 1
23 Knossington A 11
34 Knott End-on-Sea B 2
25 Knotting J 1
25 Knotting Green J 1
36 Knottingley E 3
39 Knotts C 7
30 Knotty Ash A 3
17 Knotty Green E 10
42 Knowe D 4
58 Knowhead, Aber. F 2
43 Knowehead, Kirk. C 7
45 Knowesgate D 8
47 Knoweside H 7
49 Knowetownhead G 8
27 Knowl Green L 1
17 Knowl Hill F 9
6 Knowle, Devon H 4
4 Knowle, Devon F 6
4 Knowle, Devon B 4
15 Knowle, Glos. G 9
7 Knowle, Somerset B 7
22 Knowle, War. D 5
34 Knowle Green C 5
8 Knowlton, Dorset E 2
11 Knowlton, Kent C 11
58 Knowsie B 8
34 Knowsley H 3
4 Knowstone D 7
10 Knox Bridge D 6
21 Knucklas E 8
30 Knutsford B 6
31 Knypersley E 7
2 Kuggar H 4
55 Kyle of Lochalsh G 1
55 Kyleakin G 1
55 Kylechorky Lodge G 8
61 Kyleoag G 7
55 Kylerhea G 2
63 Kyles Scalpay G 3
63 Kyles Stockinish H 2
55 Kylesbeg M 1
55 Kylesknoydart K 2
60 Kylesku D 3
55 Kylesmorar K 2
60 Kylestrome D 4
57 Kyllachy House G 3
15 Kymin C 8
15 Kynaston B 8
21 Kynnersley A 12
21 Kyre Park F 11
63 Labost B 4
37 Laceby F 10
17 Lacey Green D 9
30 Lach Dennis C 5
63 Lackalee H 2
40 Lackenby C 6
27 Lackford H 1
15 Lacock G 12
23 Ladbroke F 7
10 Laddingford C 6
33 Lade Bank E 11
2 Ladock E 6
42 Ladybank, Ayr. A 3
53 Ladybank, Fife F 8
3 Ladycross A 10
49 Ladyflat D 10
49 Ladykirk E 11
58 Ladyleys E 6
58 Ladysford B 6
43 Lag C 9
50 Lagalochan F 6
46 Lagg, Argyll B 1
47 Lagg, Ayr H 7
46 Lagg, Bute G 4
42 Laggan, Ayr C 2
42 Laggan, Ayr C 3
58 Laggan, Banff. D 1
55 Laggan, Inver. K 7
57 Laggan, Inver. K 2
52 Laggan, Perth F 1
42 Lagganmullan F 6

MAP
50 Lagganulva C 2
60 Laid B 5
60 Laide G 1
47 Laigh Braidley E 10
47 Laigh Brocklar G 10
47 Laigh Cleughearn D 11
47 Laigh Fenwick E 9
47 Laigh Smithstone E 8
47 Laighmuir E 9
47 Laighstonehall D 12
43 Laight B 9
19 Laindon E 7
57 Laintachan H 6
54 Lair E 4
60 Lairg F 6
60 Lairg Muir F 6
60 Lairg Station F 6
51 Lairigmor A 8
35 Laisterdyke D 10
39 Laithes B 7
8 Lake B 3
56 Lake of Moy D 6
38 Lake Side F 6
25 Lakenheath G 8
24 Lakes End F 6
17 Laleham G 11
14 Laleston F 2
48 Lamancha D 5
27 Lamarsh L 2
26 Lamas C 5
27 Lamb Corner M 3
64 Lambaness B 4
49 Lambden E 10
10 Lamberhurst D 5
10 Lamberhurst Quarter D 5
18 Lambeth F 3
32 Lambley F 3
44 Lambley G 5
16 Lambourn F 4
18 Lambourne End D 5
10 Lambs Green D 1
12 Lambston E 3
3 Lamellion C 9
5 Lamerton H 3
45 Lamesley G 10
42 Lamford B 6
48 Lamington, Lan. F 3
56 Lamington, Ross & Cromarty B 3
46 Lamlash F 5
42 Lamloch B 6
38 Lamonby B 6
2 Lamorna G 2
2 Lamorran E 6
13 Lampeter B 9
12 Lampeter Velfrey F 5
12 Lamphey G 4
38 Lamplugh C 3
23 Lamport E 11
7 Lamyatt C 10
4 Lana, Devon F 2
4 Lana, Devon E 2
48 Lanark E 2
48 Lanark, Co. E 1
34 Lancashire, Co. E 5
34 Lancaster A 4
45 Lanchester H 10
6 Landacre C 2
25 Landbeach J 6
4 Landcross D 3
59 Landerberry G 5
2 Landewednack H 4
8 Landford D 4
8 Landford Manor D 4
13 Landimore H 8
4 Landkey C 5
13 Landore G 10
3 Landrake, Corn. D 10
6 Landrake, Devon D 3
12 Landshipping F 4
3 Landulph D 11
22 Landywood B 3
2 Lane D 5
17 Lane End, Bucks. E 9
38 Lane End, Cumb. F 3
9 Lane End, Hants. D 7
9 Lane End, Hants. G 8
10 Lane End, Kent A 4
40 Lane Ends B 2
31 Lane Head C 10
34 Lane Head, Lancs. G 5
40 Lane Head, Yorks. D 1
3 Laneast A 9
32 Laneham C 5
44 Lanehead D 6
35 Laneshaw Bridge C 8
32 Langar G 4
47 Langbank B 8
35 Langbar B 9
44 Langburnshiels C 4
35 Langcliffe A 7
41 Langdale End F 9

MAP
61 Langdale Lodge C 7
2 Langdon, Corn. B 2
3 Langdon, Corn. A 10
15 Langdon, Worcs. A 11
39 Langdon Beck B 11
19 Langdon Hills E 7
53 Langdyke G 8
19 Langenhoe B 10
25 Langford, Beds. L 3
6 Langford, Devon F 4
19 Langford, Essex C 8
32 Langford, Notts. D 5
16 Langford, Oxon. D 3
6 Langford Budville D 4
25 Langford End K 3
27 Langham, Essex M 3
26 Langham, Norf. B 3
23 Langham, Rut. A 11
27 Langham, Suffolk H 3
34 Langho D 6
44 Langholm, Dumf. E 2
48 Langholm, Lan. F 3
47 Langlands D 11
49 Langleeford G 12
17 Langley, Bucks. F 11
31 Langley, Ches. C 8
8 Langley, Hants. F 6
18 Langley, Herts. B 2
11 Langley, Kent C 7
44 Langley, Northumb. G 6
6 Langley, Som. C 4
9 Langley, Sussex C 9
22 Langley, War. F 5
15 Langley Burrell G 12
10 Langley Green D 1
11 Langley Heath C 7
25 Langley Lower Green M 5
32 Langley Mill E 2
40 Langley Moor A 3
40 Langley Park A 2
26 Langley Street E 7
25 Langley Upper Green M 5
10 Langney H 5
32 Langold B 3
3 Langore A 10
7 Langport D 7
33 Langrick E 9
15 Langridge G 10
4 Langridge Ford D 4
43 Langrigg G 12
9 Langrish D 8
33 Langriville E 10
35 Langsett G 10
49 Langshaw E 8
47 Langside, Ayr. D 8
52 Langside, Perth F 3
64 Langskaill A 2
9 Langstone F 8
40 Langthorne, N. Riding F 3
40 Langthorpe, N. Riding H 4
39 Langthwaite E 12
24 Langtoft, Lincs. D 2
41 Langtoft, Yorks. H 10
40 Langton, Dur. C 2
33 Langton, Lincs. C 9
33 Langton, Lincs. C 11
41 Langton, Yorks. H 8
33 Langton by Wragby C 8
10 Langton Green D 4
7 Langton Herring H 9
8 Langton Matravers H 2
4 Langtree D 3
39 Langwathby B 8
60 Langwell G 5
61 Langwell Hotel E 10
33 Langworth C 8
3 Lanivet C 7
3 Lank B 8
3 Lanlivery D 8
2 Lanner F 4
3 Lanreath D 9
52 Lanrick Castle G 2
3 Lansallos E 9
16 Lansdown, Glos. B 3
15 Lansdown, Som. G 10
3 Lanteglos Highway D 8
49 Lanton, Northumb. F 11
49 Lanton, Rox. G 9
4 Lapford E 6
22 Lapley A 2
22 Lapworth E 5
50 Larachbeg C 4
48 Larbert A 1
43 Larbreck D 9
58 Largie D 4
46 Largiemore A 4
53 Largo Ward F 9
47 Largs C 7

MAP
46 Largymore G 5
10 Larkfield, Kent B 6
47 Larkfield, Ren. B 7
47 Larkhall D 12
8 Larkhill B 3
26 Larling F 3
51 Laroch B 8
44 Larriston D 4
39 Lartington C 12
59 Lary G 1
9 Lasham B 8
40 Laskill F 6
15 Lassington B 11
52 Lassodie H 6
41 Lastingham F 7
19 Latchingdon & Snoreham D 8
3 Latchley B 11
17 Latchmore Green H 7
34 Lately Common G 5
23 Lathbury H 11
61 Latheron D 11
53 Lathockar F 9
53 Lathones F 9
17 Latimer D 10
38 Latterhead C 4
15 Latteridge F 10
7 Lattiford D 10
16 Latton E 2
58 Lauchintilly F 5
50 Laudale House B 5
49 Lauder E 8
12 Laugharne F 6
32 Laughterton C 5
23 Laughton, Leics. C 10
36 Laughton, Lincs. G 6
10 Laughton, Sussex G 4
32 Laughton en le Morthen A 2
4 Launcells E 1
3 Launceston A 10
7 Launcherley B 9
17 Launton B 7
38 Laurel Bank G 1
59 Laurencekirk K 5
43 Laurieston, Kirk. E 7
48 Laurieston, Stir. A 2
23 Lavendon G 12
27 Lavenham K 2
43 Laverhay B 12
14 Lavernock G 5
8 Laverstock C 3
8 Laverstoke A 6
16 Laverton, Glos. A 2
7 Laverton, Som. A 11
40 Laverton, Yorks. H 2
30 Lavister D 2
48 Law D 1
52 Lawers, Perth. C 2
52 Lawers, Perth. E 3
27 Lawford M 4
3 Lawhitton A 10
39 Lawkland H 10
21 Lawley B 12
31 Lawnhead H 7
12 Lawrenny F 4
27 Lawshall K 2
21 Lawton F 10
63 Laxay E 4
63 Laxdale C 5
38 Laxey G 2
27 Laxfield H 6
64 Laxfirth D 7
60 Laxford Bridge C 4
64 Laxo C 7
64 Laxobigging C 7
24 Laxton, Northants. F 1
32 Laxton, Notts. D 4
36 Laxton, Yorks. E 6
35 Laycock C 9
19 Layer Breton B 9
19 Layer-de-la-Haye B 9
19 Layer Marney B 9
27 Layham L 3
16 Layland's Green G 5
7 Laymore F 7
21 Laysters Pole F 11
36 Laytham C 5
40 Lazenby C 6
39 Lazonby A 8
31 Lea, Derby D 11
15 Lea, Herefs. B 10
32 Lea, Lincs. B 5
21 Lea, Shropshire B 9
21 Lea, Shropshire C 9
15 Lea, Wilts. F 12
22 Lea Marston C 5
34 Lea Town D 4
39 Lea Yeat F 10
32 Leabrooks E 1
55 Leacachan G 3
56 Leachkin E 2
48 Leadburn D 5

MAP
18 Leaden Roding C 6
33 Leadenham E 7
49 Leaderfoot F 8
39 Leadgate, Cumb. A 9
45 Leadgate, Dur. G 9
45 Leadgate, Dur. H 9
48 Leadhills H 2
16 Leafield C 4
17 Leagrave B 11
40 Leake F 4
33 Leake Common Side E 11
33 Leake Hurn's End E 11
41 Lealholm D 8
62 Leatt B 4
23 Leamington E 7
23 Leamington Hasting E 8
22 Leamonsley A 4
45 Leamside H 11
51 Leanach H 7
55 Leanachan L 6
56 Leanaig D 1
46 Leargybreck B 1
39 Leasgill G 7
33 Leasingham E 7
40 Leasingthorne B 3
17 Leatherhead H 12
35 Leathley B 11
43 Leaths E 8
30 Leaton H 3
11 Leaveland C 8
36 Leavening A 5
18 Leaves Green H 4
18 Leavesden Green D 1
45 Leazes G 10
41 Lebberston G 10
16 Lechlade D 3
39 Leck G 9
8 Leckford B 5
61 Leckfurin B 7
16 Leckhampstead, Berks. G 5
23 Leckhampstead, Bucks. H 10
16 Leckhampstead Street F 5
16 Leckhampstead Thicket F 5
15 Leckhampton B 12
54 Leckie C 5
60 Leckmelm G 3
55 Leckroy K 7
14 Leckwith G 5
37 Leconfield C 8
50 Ledaig D 6
17 Ledburn B 10
15 Ledbury A 10
51 Ledcharrie E 12
21 Ledgemoor G 9
54 Ledgowan D 5
21 Ledicot F 9
60 Ledmore F 4
61 Lednagullin B 8
30 Ledsham, Ches. C 2
36 Ledsham, Yorks. D 2
36 Ledston D 2
16 Ledwell A 5
50 Lee, Argyll E 1
4 Lee, Devon A 4
8 Lee, Hampshire D 5
34 Lee, Lancashire B 4
30 Lee, Shropshire G 3
30 Lee Brockhurst G 4
17 Lee Clump D 10
30 Lee Green D 5
5 Lee Mill Bridge K 5
5 Lee Mill Estate K 5
5 Lee Moor J 4
9 Lee-on-the-Solent F 7
21 Leebotwood C 10
38 Leece H 5
11 Leeds, Kent C 7
35 Leeds, Yorks. D 11
2 Leedstown F 3
31 Leek E 8
22 Leek Wootton E 6
40 Leeming F 3
40 Leeming Bar F 3
31 Lees, Derby F 11
35 Lees, Lancashire G 8
44 Lees Hill F 4
29 Leeswood D 12
30 Leftwich Green C 5
33 Legbourne B 10
49 Legerwood E 8
33 Legsby B 8
23 Leicester B 9
23 Leicestershire, Co. B 9
23 Leicester For. East B 8
7 Leigh, Dorset E 9
15 Leigh, Glos. B 11
10 Leigh, Kent C 4

MAP
34 Leigh, Lancs......G 5
21 Leigh, Shropshire..B 9
10 Leigh, Surrey.....C 1
16 Leigh, Wiltshire...E 2
22 Leigh, Worcs......G 1
19 Leigh Beck.......F 8
15 Leigh Delamere..F 12
11 Leigh Green......E 8
19 Leigh-on-Sea......E 8
9 Leigh Park........E 8
22 Leigh Sinton......G 1
7 Leigh upon Mendip.......B 10
6 Leighland Chapel..C 4
15 Leighterton......E 11
21 Leighton, Mont....B 8
21 Leighton, Salop..B 11
7 Leighton, Som....B 10
40 Leighton, Yorks..G 2
25 Leighton Bromswold.....H 2
17 Leighton Buzzard.B 10
59 Leightonhill.......L 4
15 Leighwoods......G 9
21 Leinthall Earls..F 10
21 Leinthall Starkes.E 10
21 Leintwardine......E 9
23 Leire.............C 8
60 Leirinmore.......A 5
54 Leishmore.......F 8
27 Leiston...........J 7
53 Leitfie...........C 7
48 Leith.............B 5
49 Leitholm........E 10
2 Lelant............F 3
37 Lelley...........D 10
22 Lem Hill.........E 1
56 Lemlair..........D 1
45 Lemmington Hall..B 9
49 Lempitlaw.......F 10
63 Lemreway........F 5
18 Lemsford.........C 2
58 Lenabo..........C 8
22 Lenchwick........G 4
42 Lendalfoot.......C 2
51 Lendrick.........G 12
11 Lenham..........C 7
11 Lenham Heath....C 8
49 Lennel..........E 11
42 Lennies.........F 5
47 Lennoxtown.....B 11
17 Lent Rise........F 10
24 Lenton...........C 1
26 Lenwade.........D 4
47 Lenzie..........B 11
58 Leochel-Cushnie...F 3
21 Leominster......F 10
15 Leonard Stanley..D 11
8 Lepe.............F 6
62 Lephin............C 1
51 Lephinchapel.....H 7
51 Lephinmore......H 7
36 Leppington.......A 5
35 Lepton..........F 10
50 Lerags...........E 6
3 Lerryn...........D 8
64 Lerwick.........E 7
45 Lesbury.........B 10
58 Leslie, Aberdeen...E 3
53 Leslie, Fife......G 7
48 Lesmahagow......E 1
2 Lesnewth.........B 2
26 Lessingham.......C 7
44 Lessonhall.......H 1
42 Leswalt..........E 1
18 Letchmore Heath..D 2
25 Letchworth.......M 3
16 Letcombe Bassett..F 5
16 Letcombe Regis...E 5
53 Letham, Angus...B 10
53 Letham, Fife.....F 8
52 Letham, Perth.....E 6
53 Letham Grange..C 11
56 Lethen House.....D 5
57 Lethendryveole...H 5
58 Lethenty.........D 5
27 Letheringham......J 6
26 Letheringsett......B 4
5 Lettaford..........G 6
64 Letten............A 4
54 Letterewe.........C 3
55 Letterfearn.......G 3
55 Letterfinlay.......K 6
55 Lettermorar.......K 1
50 Lettermore.......C 2
60 Letters...........H 3
48 Lettershaws......G 2
12 Letterston........D 3
57 Lettoch, Inver.....H 6
56 Lettoch, Moray...F 6
21 Letton, Herefs...E 9
21 Letton, Herefs.....H 9
18 Letty Green......C 3
MAP
32 Letwell..........B 3
53 Leuchars.........E 9
56 Leuchars House...C 8
63 Leurbost.........D 5
22 Levedale.........A 3
53 Leven, Fife.......G 8
37 Leven, Yorks......C 8
46 Levencorroch.....G 5
39 Levens...........G 7
35 Levenshulme......H 7
64 Levenwick........F 7
63 Leverburgh........H 1
24 Leverington......D 5
16 Leverton, Berks...G 4
33 Leverton, Lincs...E 11
33 Leverton Outgate.E 11
27 Levington........L 5
41 Levisham.........F 8
16 Lew.............D 4
3 Lewannick........B 9
5 Lewdown........G 3
10 Lewes...........G 3
12 Leweston.........E 3
18 Lewisham........G 3
57 Lewiston.........G 1
14 Lewistown........E 3
17 Lewknor.........D 8
4 Leworthy.........B 5
63 Lews Castle......D 5
11 Lewson Street.....B 8
5 Lewtrenchard.....G 3
58 Ley, Aberdeen....F 3
3 Ley, Cornwall.....C 9
10 Leybourne.........B 5
40 Leyburn...........F 1
30 Leycett...........E 6
18 Leygreen.........B 2
17 Leyhill Com.....D 10
34 Leyland...........E 4
58 Leylodge.........F 5
58 Leys.............B 7
56 Leys Castle......F 2
53 Leys of Cossans...B 8
58 Leys of Dummuies.D 3
11 Leysdown-on-Sea..A 9
53 Leysmill.........B 10
18 Leyton...........E 4
18 Leytonstone......E 4
3 Lezant..........B 10
54 Liatrie...........F 6
14 Libanus..........B 3
48 Libberton, Lan....E 3
48 Liberton, Midloth..B 5
22 Lichfield.........A 5
22 Lickey...........E 3
22 Lickey End.......E 3
9 Lickfold.........D 10
50 Liddesdale........B 5
16 Liddington........F 3
25 Lidgate...........J 8
25 Lidlington........L 1
16 Lidstone.........B 4
55 Lienassie.........G 3
53 Liff..............D 8
5 Lifton...........G 3
5 Liftondown.......G 2
23 Lighthorne.......G 7
17 Lightwater......H 10
31 Lightwood.........F 7
23 Lilbourne.........D 9
49 Lilburn Hill.....G 12
45 Lilburn Tower....A 8
22 Lilleshall..........A 1
16 Lilley, Berks......F 5
18 Lilley, Herts.......A 1
49 Lilliesleaf.........G 8
23 Lillingstone Dayrell.......H 10
23 Lillingstone Lovell.......H 10
7 Lillington, Dorset..E 9
23 Lillington, War....E 7
8 Lilliput..........G 2
6 Lilstock..........B 5
47 Lilybank.........B 8
34 Limbrick.........F 5
35 Limefield.........F 7
47 Limekilnburn....D 12
48 Limekilns.........A 3
48 Limerigg.........B 1
8 Limestone........H 6
44 Limestone Brae...H 6
7 Limington........D 8
26 Limpenhoe........E 7
15 Limpley Stoke...H 11
10 Limpsfield........C 3
32 Linby............E 3
9 Linchmere.......C 10
43 Lincluden........D 10
33 Lincoln...........C 7
33 Lincolnshire, Co...D 8
22 Lincomb.........E 2
62 Lincro............B 3
MAP
38 Lindal in Furness.H 5
38 Lindale..........G 6
49 Lindean.........F 7
10 Lindfield.........E 2
9 Lindford.........C 9
53 Lindifferon.......E 8
35 Lindley..........E 10
35 Lindley Green....B 11
53 Lindores.........E 7
21 Lindridge........E 12
18 Lindsell.........A 6
27 Lindsey..........L 3
38 Linefoot..........B 3
19 Linford, Essex.....F 7
8 Linford, Hants....E 3
38 Lingague.........H 1
41 Lingdale.........D 7
21 Lingen...........F 9
10 Lingfield.........D 3
10 Lingfield Com.....D 3
30 Lingley Green.....A 4
26 Lingwood.........E 7
45 Linhope, N'thumb..A 8
44 Linhope, Rox.....C 2
16 Linkenholt........H 5
3 Linkinhorne.....B 10
64 Linklater.........E 2
53 Linktown........H 7
21 Linley Green....G 12
48 Linlithgow.......B 3
48 Linlithgow Bridge.B 3
60 Linneraineach.....F 3
12 Linney............G 2
43 Linns............D 11
63 Linshader ....D 3
45 Linshiels.........B 7
60 Linsidemore......G 6
17 Linslade.........B 10
27 Linstead Parva....G 6
44 Linstock.........G 3
49 Linthaugh.......F 12
22 Linthurst.........E 3
35 Linthwaite.......F 9
49 Lintlaw.........D 11
58 Lintmill..........A 3
25 Linton, Cambs....K 7
22 Linton, Denb.....A 6
35 Linton, Herefs.....B 9
10 Linton, Kent......C 6
49 Linton, Rox......G 10
35 Linton, W. Riding B 12
35 Linton, W. Riding.A 8
36 Linton-on-Ouse...A 3
8 Linwood, Hants...E 3
33 Linwood, Lincs....B 8
47 Linwood, Ren.....C 9
29 Lioc.............C 10
63 Lionel............A 6
9 Liphook.........C 9
6 Liscombe........C 2
3 Liskeard.........C 9
9 Liss.............C 9
9 Liss Forest........C 9
27 Lisset............A 9
33 Lissington........B 8
14 Lisvane...........F 5
15 Liswerry.........F 7
26 Litcham..........D 2
23 Litchborough.....G 9
8 Litchfield.........A 6
34 Litherland........G 2
25 Litlington, Cambs..L 4
10 Litlington, Sussex.H 4
25 Little Abington...K 6
25 Little Addington..H 1
22 Little Alne........F 5
18 Little Amwell......C 3
60 Little Assynt......E 3
22 Little Aston.......B 4
8 Little Atherfield...H 6
64 Little Ayre........E 1
40 Little Ayton......D 6
19 Little Baddow.....C 7
15 Little Badminton.F 11
52 Little Ballinluig...B 4
44 Little Bampton....G 1
25 Little Bardfield...M 8
25 Little Barford.....J 3
26 Little Barningham.B 4
16 Little Barrington..C 3
30 Little Barrow.....C 3
41 Little Barugh.....G 8
45 Little Bavington...E 8
27 Little Bealings....K 5
16 Little Bedwyn.....G 4
42 Little Bennane....C 2
19 Little Bentley....A 11
18 Little Berkhampsted C 3
23 Little Billing.....F 11
15 Little Birch.......A 8
27 Little Blakenham..K 4
39 Little Blencow....B 7
MAP
9 Little Bookham..A 12
23 Little Bowden....C 11
25 Little Bradley.....K 8
21 Little Brampton...D 9
19 Little Braxted.....B 8
59 Little Brechin.....L 3
7 Little Bredy.......G 9
17 Little Brickhill...A 10
23 Little Brington...F 10
19 Little Bromley...A 10
30 Little Budworth...D 5
18 Little Burstead....E 6
24 Little Bytham.....D 1
42 Little Cairnbrock..E 1
33 Little Carlton, Lincs..........B 11
32 Little Carlton, Notts..........D 5
24 Little Casterton...E 1
33 Little Cawthorpe.B 10
17 Little Chalfont...D 11
11 Little Chart.......D 8
7 Little Cheney.....G 9
25 Little Chesterford..L 6
8 Little Cheverell....A 2
25 Little Chishill.....L 5
19 Little Clacton....B 11
38 Little Clifton......B 3
58 Little Colp........C 5
22 Little Comberton..H 3
16 Little Compton...A 4
27 Little Cornard....L 2
21 Little Cowarne...G 11
16 Little Coxwell.....E 4
40 Little Crakehall...F 3
26 Little Cressingham.E 2
34 Little Crosby.....G 2
23 Little Dalby.....A 11
58 Little Dens.......C 8
15 Little Dewchurch..A 8
37 Little Driffield....A 8
26 Little Dunham....D 2
52 Little Dunkeld....C 5
18 Little Dunmow....B 6
18 Little Easton......B 6
31 Little Eaton......F 12
26 Little Ellingham...E 3
7 Little Elm.......B 10
18 Little End........D 5
25 Little Eversden....K 5
27 Little Fakenham..H 2
16 Little Faringdon...D 3
40 Little Fencote.....F 3
36 Little Fenton......D 3
26 Little Fransham...D 2
17 Little Gaddesden.C 11
15 Little Garway.....B 8
25 Little Gidding....G 2
27 Little Glemham...J 6
25 Little Gransden...K 4
7 Little Green.....A 10
33 Little Grimsby...A 10
60 Little Gruinard...G 1
18 Little Hadham....B 4
24 Little Hale.......B 2
18 Little Hallingbury.B 5
17 Little Hampden...D 9
23 Little Harrowden.E 12
17 Little Haseley.....D 7
37 Little Hatfield.....C 9
12 Little Haven......F 2
22 Little Hay........B 5
31 Little Hayfield....A 9
31 Little Haywood...H 8
21 Little Hereford...F 11
27 Little Horkesley..M 2
18 Little Hormead....A 4
10 Little Horsted.....F 3
35 Little Horton....D 10
17 Little Horwood...A 9
23 Little Houghton..F 11
31 Little Hucklow...B 10
34 Little Hulton.....G 1
17 Little Hungerford.G 8
23 Little Irchester...E 12
37 Little Kelk........A 8
17 Little Kimble.....C 9
17 Little Kingshill...D 10
38 Little Langdale....E 5
8 Little Langford....C 2
58 Little Ledikin......E 4
30 Little Leigh.......C 5
19 Little Leighs......B 7
34 Little Lever.......F 6
23 Little Linford....H 11
8 Little London, Hants..........A 5
17 Little London, Hants..........H 7
24 Little London, Lincs...........C 5
10 Little London, Sussex..........F 4
MAP
35 Little London, Yorks.........C 10
31 Little Longstone..C 10
58 Little Lynturk.....F 3
22 Little Malvern....H 1
27 Little Maplestead.M 1
15 Little Marcle.....A 10
17 Little Marlow.....E 9
26 Little Massingham.C 1
26 Little Melton......E 5
12 Little Milford.....F 3
14 Little Mill........D 6
17 Little Milton.....D 7
17 Little Missenden.D 10
30 Little Ness.......H 3
30 Little Neston.....C 2
12 Little Newcastle...D 3
40 Little Newsham...C 1
19 Little Oakley, Essex..........A 12
23 Little Oakley, Northants.....D 12
44 Little Orton......G 2
36 Little Ouseburn...A 2
25 Little Paxton......J 3
2 Little Petherick....B 6
42 Little Pinmore....C 3
26 Little Plumstead...D 6
32 Little Ponton.....G 6
4 Little Potheridge..E 4
25 Little Raveley.....G 4
35 Little Ribson.....B 12
16 Little Rissington...B 3
26 Little Ryburgh....C 3
45 Little Ryle........B 8
39 Little Salkeld.....B 8
8 Little Samborne...C 5
25 Little Sampford...M 7
17 Little Sandhurst...H 9
30 Little Saughall....C 2
27 Little Saxham.....J 1
54 Little Scatwell....D 7
25 Little Shelford.....K 5
4 Little Silver.......F 7
6 Little Silver.......E 3
36 Little Smeaton....E 3
26 Little Snoring.....B 2
15 Little Sodbury....F 10
16 Little Somerford...F 1
40 Little Stainton....C 4
30 Little Stanney.....C 3
25 Little Staughton...J 2
33 Little Steeping...D 11
27 Little Stonham.....J 4
23 Little Stretton, Leics..........B 10
21 Little Stretton, Shropshire.....C 10
39 Little Strickland...C 8
25 Little Stukeley....H 3
45 Little Swinburne...E 8
49 Little Swinton....E 11
16 Little Tew........A 5
25 Little Thetford....H 6
25 Little Thurlow.....K 8
18 Little Thurrock....F 6
42 Little Torhouse....F 5
4 Little Torrington..D 4
45 Little Tosson......C 8
19 Little Totham.....C 9
38 Little Town.......C 5
56 Little Urchany....E 4
38 Little Urswick.....H 5
19 Little Wakering...E 9
27 Little Waldingfield.L 2
26 Little Walsingham.B 2
19 Little Waltham....C 7
18 Little Warley......E 6
37 Little Weighton...D 7
27 Little Welnetham..J 2
21 Little Wenlock...B 12
27 Little Whittingham Green.........H 6
45 Little Whittington.F 8
25 Little Wilbraham..J 6
8 Little Wishford....B 2
22 Little Witley......F 1
16 Little Wittenham..E 6
16 Little Wolford....A 3
23 Little Woolstone.H 12
25 Little Wymington..J 1
18 Little Wymondley.A 2
22 Little Wyrley.....B 4
27 Little Yeldam.....L 1
64 Little-ayre........C 6
41 Littlebeck.........E 9
35 Littleborough, Lancashire......F 8
32 Littleborough, Notts..........B 5
11 Littlebourne.....B 10
25 Littlebury........L 6
34 Littledale.........A 4
MAP
15 Littledean.......C 10
61 Littleferry........G 8
4 Littleham, Devon..D 3
6 Littleham, Devon..H 4
9 Littlehampton....F 11
5 Littlehempston....J 7
45 Littlehoughton...A 10
59 Littlemill, Aber....H 1
47 Littlemill, Ayr.....H 9
56 Littlemill, Nairn...E 5
45 Littlemill, Northumb.....A 10
16 Littlemore........D 6
31 Littleover.......G 11
25 Littleport.........G 7
25 Littleport Bridge..G 7
11 Littlestone-on-Sea.F 9
40 Littlethorpe......H 3
30 Littleton, Ches....D 3
8 Littleton, Hants...C 6
43 Littleton, Kirk.....F 7
53 Littleton, Perth....D 7
7 Littleton, Som.....C 8
9 Littleton, Surrey..A 11
17 Littleton, Surrey.G 11
15 Littleton Drew...F 11
8 Littleton Panell...A 2
15 Littleton upon Severn.........E 9
40 Littletown.........A 4
17 Littlewick Green...F 9
16 Littleworth, Berks..D 4
15 Littleworth, Glos. D 11
22 Littleworth, Staffs..A 4
31 Littleworth, Staffs..H 8
10 Littleworth, Sussex.F 1
22 Littleworth, Worcs.G 2
31 Litton, Denb.....C 10
7 Litton, Som.......A 9
39 Litton, Yorks....H 11
30 Liverpool.........A 2
35 Liversedge.......E 10
5 Liverton, Devon...H 7
41 Liverton, Yorks...D 7
48 Livingston........C 3
48 Livingston Station.C 3
29 Lixwm..........C 11
2 Lizard...........H 4
28 Llaingoch.........B 2
20 Llaithddu........D 6
20 Llan.............B 4
14 Llan-Rumney.....F 5
28 Llanaber.........H 5
28 Llanaelhaearn.....F 3
20 Llanafan.........E 2
20 Llanafan-fawr.....G 5
20 Llanafan-fechan...G 5
28 Llanallgo.........B 4
29 Llanarmon Dyffryn Ceiriog.........G 10
29 Llanarmon-yn-lal.E 11
13 Llanarth, Cards....A 7
15 Llanarth, Mon.....C 7
13 Llanarthney.......E 8
29 Llanasa.........B 10
28 Llanbabo.........B 3
20 Llanbadarn Fawr..D 2
20 Llanbadarn Fynydd E 6
21 Llanbadarn-y-garreg.........G 7
15 Llanbadoc........D 7
28 Llanbadrig.......A 3
15 Llanbeder........E 7
14 Llanbedr, Brec.....B 6
28 Llanbedr, Mer.....H 5
21 Llanbedr, Rad.....H 7
29 Llanbedr-Dyffryn-Clwyd.........D 10
28 Llanbedr-goch....B 4
28 Llanbedrog.......G 3
29 Llanbedr-y-cennin.C 7
28 Llanberis.........D 5
14 Llanbethery.......G 4
20 Llanbister.........E 6
14 Llanblethian.......G 3
12 Llanboidy.........E 5
14 Llanbradach.......E 5
56 Llanbryde.........D 8
20 Llanbrynmair.....B 5
14 Llancadle.........G 4
14 Llancaiach........E 4
14 Llancarfan........G 4
15 Llancayo..........D 7
15 Llancloudy........B 8
21 Llancoch..........E 7
14 Llandaff...........F 5
28 Llandanwg........G 5
13 Llandarcy.........G 10
12 Llandawke........F 6
28 Llanddaniel Fab...C 4
13 Llanddarog........E 8
20 Llanddeiniol......E 1
28 Llanddeiniolen....D 5

MAP
29 Llandderfel......F 9
28 Llanddeusant, Anglesey......B 3
13 Llanddeusant, Carm......E 11
14 Llanddew......A 4
13 Llanddewi......H 8
20 Llanddewi-Brefi..G 2
15 Llanddewi Rhydderch....C 7
12 Llanddewi Velfrey.E 5
20 Llanddewi'r Cwm.G 6
29 Llanddoget......D 7
28 Llanddona......B 5
12 Llanddowror.....F 6
29 Llanddulas......B 8
28 Llanddyfnan....B 4
14 Llandefaelog Fach.A 4
14 Llandefaelog ter-graig....A 4
14 Llandefalle......A 4
28 Llandegai........C 5
28 Llandegfan.......C 5
15 Llandegfedd......E 7
29 Llandegla........E 11
21 Llandegley......F 7
13 Llandeilo.......E 9
20 Llandeilo Graban.H 6
14 Llandeilo'r Fan...A 2
12 Llandeloy......D 2
15 Llandenny......D 7
15 Llandevenny.....F 7
20 Llandewi Ystradenny....E 6
12 Llandilo......D 4
15 Llandinabo......A 8
21 Llandinam......D 6
12 Llandissilio......E 5
15 Llandogo......D 8
14 Llandough, Glam..G 5
14 Llandough, Glam..G 3
13 Llandovery......D 11
14 Llandow......A 4
20 Llandre, Cards...D 2
13 Llandre, Carm...C 10
29 Llandrillo......F 9
29 Llandrillo-yn-Rhos.B 7
20 Llandrindod Wells.F 6
21 Llandrinio......A 8
29 Llandudno......B 7
29 Llandudno Junc..B 7
28 Llandwrog......E 4
13 Llandybie......E 9
13 Llandyfaelog...F 7
13 Llandyfan......E 9
14 Llandyfodwg....F 3
13 Llandyfriog......C 7
28 Llandyfrydog....B 4
12 Llandygwydd....C 6
29 Llandyrnog......D 10
29 Llandysilio......H 12
21 Llandyssil.......C 7
13 Llandyssul......C 7
14 Llanedeyrn......F 5
20 Llaneglwys......H 6
20 Llanegryn......B 2
13 Llanegwad......E 8
28 Llaneilian......A 4
29 Llanelian-yn-Rhos.C 8
21 Llanelidan......E 10
14 Llanelieu......A 5
14 Llanellen......C 6
13 Llanelli, Brec...C 5
13 Llanelli, Carm...G 8
28 Llanelltyd......H 6
20 Llanelwedd......G 6
28 Llanenddwyn....H 5
28 Llanengan......G 2
28 Llanerchymedd...B 4
20 Llanerfyl......A 6
28 Llanfachraeth....B 3
29 Llanfachreth....H 7
28 Llanfaelog......C 3
28 Llanfaelrhys.....G 2
15 Llanfaenor......C 7
28 Llanfaes, Angl...C 5
14 Llanfaes, Brec...B 4
28 Llanfaethlu.....B 3
28 Llanfaglan......D 4
28 Llanfair......G 5
20 Llanfair-Caereinion B 6
20 Llanfair-Clydogau.G 2
29 Llanfair Dyffryn Clwyd......E 10
12 Llanfair Nant-Gwyn....C 5
29 Llanfair Talhaiarn.C 8
21 Llanfair Waterdine.E 8
28 Llanfairfechan...C 6
28 Llanfair-P.G.....C 5
28 Llanfair-y-Cwmmwd......D 4
28 Llanfairynghornwy A 3

MAP
28 Llanfair-yn-Neubwll......C 2
12 Llanfallteg......E 5
12 Llanfallteg West..E 5
20 Llanfaredd......G 6
20 Llanfarian......E 2
29 Llanfechain......H 11
28 Llanfechell......A 3
20 Llanfendigaid.....B 1
29 Llanferres......D 11
28 Llanfflewyn.....A 3
28 Llanfigael......B 3
20 Llanfihangel.....A 6
14 Llanfihangel Crucorney.....B 6
29 Llanfihangel Glyn Myfyr......E 9
14 Llanfihangel Llantarnam.....E 6
14 Llanfihangel Nant Bran......A 3
21 Llanfihangel Rhydithon....F 7
15 Llanfihangel Rogiet F 8
14 Llanfihangel Tal-y-llyn......A 4
13 Llanfihangel ar-arth......C 8
21 Llanfihangel-nant-Melan......G 7
13 Llanfihangel-uwch-Gwili...E 8
20 Llanfihangel-y-Creuddyn....E 2
28 Llanfihangel yn Nhowyn......C 3
20 Llanfihangel-y-Pennant......B 2
28 Llanfihangel-y-pennant......F 5
28 Llanfihangel-y-traethau......G 5
14 Llanfilo......A 4
14 Llanfoist......C 6
28 Llanfor......G 8
14 Llanfrechfa......E 6
28 Llanfrothen......F 5
14 Llanfrynach.....B 4
28 Llanfwrog, Angl...B 2
29 Llanfwrog, Denb. D 10
29 Llanfyllin......H 10
13 Llanfynydd, Carm.D 9
29 Llanfynydd, Flint.E 12
12 Llanfyrnach......D 6
20 Llangadfan......A 6
13 Llangadog, Carm.D 10
13 Llangadog, Carm..F 7
28 Llangadwaladr, Anglesey......C 3
29 Llangadwaladr, Denbigh......G 11
28 Llangaffo......C 4
13 Llangain......E 7
20 Llangammarch Wells......H 5
14 Llangan......G 3
15 Llangarron......B 8
14 Llangasty-Tal-y-llyn......B 5
13 Llangathen......E 9
14 Llangattock......C 5
15 Llangattock Lingoed......B 7
14 Llangattock nigh Usk......C 6
15 Llangattock Vibon-Avel......C 8
29 Llangedwyn......H 11
28 Llangefni......C 4
14 Llangeinor......F 2
28 Llangeinwen.....D 4
20 Llangeitho......F 2
13 Llangeler......C 7
13 Llangendeirne....B 8
13 Llangennech.....G 9
13 Llangennith......H 7
14 Llangenny......C 6
29 Llangernyw......C 8
28 Llangian......G 2
13 Llangiwg......F 10
12 Llangloffan......D 3
14 Llanglydwen.....D 5
28 Llangoed......B 5
12 Llangoedmor.....B 5
29 Llangollen......F 11
12 Llangolman......D 5
14 Llangorse......B 4
15 Llangoven......D 8
29 Llangower......G 8
12 Llangranog......B 6
28 Llangristiolus....C 4
15 Llangrove......B 8

MAP
15 Llangua......B 7
21 Llangunllo......E 7
13 Llangunnor......E 8
29 Llangurig......D 5
14 Llangwm, Denb..F 9
15 Llangwm, Mon...D 7
15 Llangwm, Pemb...F 3
15 Llangwm-isaf...D 7
28 Llangwnnadl......G 2
29 Llangwyfan......D 10
28 Llangwyfanisaf....C 3
28 Llangwyllog......B 4
29 Llangwyryfon....E 2
28 Llangybi, Caer...F 4
20 Llangybi, Cards...G 2
15 Llangybi, Mon....E 7
13 Llangyfelach....G 10
20 Llangynfelyn.....C 2
29 Llangynhafal....D 10
14 Llangynidr......B 5
12 Llangynin......E 6
13 Llangynllo......C 7
13 Llangynog, Carm..E 7
29 Llangynog, Mont..H 9
14 Llangynwyd......E 2
14 Llanhamlach.....B 4
14 Llanharan......F 3
14 Llanharry......F 3
15 Llanhennock.....E 7
14 Llanhilleth......D 5
28 Llaniestyn......G 2
21 Llanigan......H 7
20 Llanilar......E 2
14 Llanilid......F 3
14 Llanilterne......F 4
14 Llanishen, Glam...F 5
15 Llanishen, Mon...D 8
13 Llanllawddog....D 8
13 Llanllechid......C 5
20 Llanllugan......B 6
21 Llanllwchaiarn....C 7
13 Llanllwch......E 7
15 Llanllyfni......E 4
15 Llanllywel......D 7
13 Llanmadoc......H 8
14 Llanmaes......G 3
15 Llanmartin......E 7
21 Llanmerewig.....C 7
14 Llanmihangel....G 3
12 Llanmiloe......F 6
13 Llanmorlais......G 8
15 Llannefydd......C 9
13 Llannon......F 9
28 Llannor......F 3
13 Llanon......F 1
13 Llanpumsaint....D 7
13 Llanreithan......D 2
29 Llanrhaeadr......D 10
29 Llanrhaeadr-ym-Mochnant....H 10
13 Llanrhidian......H 8
29 Llanrhos......B 7
28 Llanrhyddlad.....A 3
29 Llanrhystyd......E 1
12 Llanrian......D 2
28 Llanrug......D 5
29 Llanrwst......D 7
12 Llansadurnen....F 6
28 Llansadwrn, Angl..C 5
13 Llansadwrn, Carm......D 10
13 Llan-saint......C 7
13 Llansamlet......G 10
29 Llansannan......D 8
14 Llansannor......G 3
20 Llansantffraed...B 5
20 Llansantffraed Cwmdeuddwr....F 5
20 Llansantffraed-in-Elvel......G 6
20 Llansantffraid...F 1
29 Llansantffraid Glan Conway......C 7
29 Llansantffraid-ym-Mechain......H 11
13 Llansawel......C 9
29 Llansilin......G 11
13 Llansoy......D 7
14 Llanspyddid......B 3
12 Llanstadwell.....F 3
13 Llanstephan.....F 7
12 Llanteg......F 5
14 Llanthony......A 6
15 Llantilio Crossenny C 7
14 Llantilio Pertholey. C 6
12 Llantood......C 5
15 Llantrisant, Glam..F 4
15 Llantrisant, Mon...E 7
14 Llantrithyd......G 4
14 Llantwit Fardre...F 4
14 Llantwit-Major...G 3
29 Llanuwchllyn....G 8

MAP
15 Llanvaches......E 7
15 Llanvair Discoed..E 8
15 Llanvapley......C 7
15 Llanvetherine....C 7
14 Llanveynoe......A 6
15 Llanvihangel Gobion......C 7
14 Llanvihangel Pontymoel......D 6
15 Llanvihangel Ystern-Llewern......C 7
15 Llanwarne......B 8
29 Llanwddyn......H 9
14 Llanwenarth.....C 6
13 Llanwenog......B 8
15 Llanwern......E 7
12 Llanwinio......D 6
28 Llanwnda, Caernarvon....D 4
12 Llanwnda, Pembroke....C 3
13 Llanwnnen......B 8
20 Llanwnog......C 6
13 Llanwrda......D 10
20 Llanwrin......B 3
20 Llanwrthwl......F 5
20 Llanwrtyd......H 4
20 Llanwrtyd Wells..H 4
20 Llanwyddelan....B 6
30 Llanyblodwel....H 1
13 Llanybri......F 7
13 Llanybyther......C 8
12 Llanycefn......E 4
12 Llanychaer Bridge.C 3
29 Llanymawddwy...H 8
30 Llanymynech....H 1
28 Llanynghenedl....B 3
29 Llanynys......D 10
30 Llan-y-pwll......E 2
14 Llanyre......F 6
28 Llanystumdwy....F 4
14 Llanywern......A 4
14 Llawhaden......E 4
30 Llawnt......G 1
20 Llawr-y-glyn....C 5
14 Llay......E 2
14 Llechfaen......A 4
12 Llechryd, Cards...C 5
14 Llechryd, Mon....C 4
29 Llechrydau......G 11
13 Llethrid......H 8
13 Lledrod......E 2
13 Llidiad-Nenog...C 9
28 Llidiardau, Caer...G 1
29 Llidiardau, Mer...B 8
29 Llidiart-y-parc...F 10
28 Llithfaen......F 3
29 Llong......D 12
21 Llowes......H 7
20 Llundain-fach....G 1
11 Llwydcoed......D 3
13 Llwyn-Celyn.....A 8
13 Llwyn Dafydd...B 7
21 Llwynderw, Mont..B 7
20 Llwynderw, Mont.D 5
12 Llwyn-drain.....D 6
20 Llwyngwril......A 2
13 Llwyn-hendy.....G 9
29 Llwyn-mawr.....G 11
14 Llwyn-on......C 3
20 Llwyn-y-groes....G 2
14 Llwyn-y-pia.....E 3
30 Llynclys......H 1
28 Llynfaes......B 3
20 Llysdinam......F 6
13 Llysfaen......C 8
14 Llyswen......A 4
14 Llysworney......G 3
14 Llys-y-fran......A 2
14 Llywel......A 2
20 Llywernog......D 3
49 Loanend......D 12
47 Loanhead, Ayr...D 9
48 Loanhead, Lan...F 3
48 Loanhead, Midloth.C 5
58 Loanhead of Fedderate......C 6
47 Loans......F 8
45 Loansdean......E 10
4 Lobb......B 3
61 Loch Choire Lodge ......D 7
42 Loch Head......G 4
60 Loch Loyal Lo...C 6
55 Lochailort......L 2
52 Lochaline......F 5
42 Lochans......F 2
43 Locharbriggs...D 10
43 Locharwoods.....E 11
60 Lochassynt Lodge.D 3
51 Lochawe......E 8
50 Lochbuie......E 3
57 Lochcallater......L 7

MAP
54 Lochcarron......F 3
61 Lochdhu Lodge...C 9
51 Lochdochart Ho..E 11
50 Lochdonhead.....D 5
54 Lochdrum......B 6
46 Lochead, Argyll..B 3
46 Lochead, Argyll..A 5
52 Lochearnhead....E 1
53 Lochee......D 8
61 Lochend, Caith...A 11
52 Lochend, Fife....H 6
56 Lochend, Inver...F 2
43 Lochend, Kirk....F 9
43 Locherben......B 10
43 Lochfoot......D 9
50 Lochgair......H 6
47 Lochgarthside....H 1
47 Lochgate......F 11
53 Lochgelly......H 7
46 Lochgilphead....A 4
51 Lochgoilhead....G 9
50 Loch-hill......C 8
56 Lochindorb Lo...F 5
47 Lochingirroch...H 11
60 Lochinver......E 3
48 Lochlycock......F 2
43 Lochmaben......C 11
60 Lochmore Lodge..D 4
52 Lochore......G 6
43 Lochranza......D 4
47 Lochridge......E 9
58 Lochs Crofts......B 1
56 Lochside, Inver...D 4
59 Lochside, Kinc...L 5
61 Lochside, Suther..D 8
60 Lochstack Lodge..C 4
59 Lochstrathy......C 8
59 Lochton......H 5
50 Lochton of Leys..H 4
59 Lochty, Angus...L 3
53 Lochty, Fife....F 10
56 Lochuisge......B 5
43 Lochurr......C 8
47 Lochwinnoch....C 8
43 Lochwood......B 11
55 Lochy Bridge....M 5
44 Lock Hills......H 3
3 Lockengate......D 7
43 Lockerbie......C 12
16 Lockeridge......G 3
8 Lockerley......C 4
15 Locking......H 7
16 Lockinge......E 5
32 Lockington, Leics..G 2
37 Lockington, Yorks.B 7
30 Lockleywood....G 5
8 Lock's Heath......E 6
41 Lockton......F 8
23 Loddington, Leics.B 11
23 Loddington, Northants....D 11
26 Loddon......F 6
25 Lode......J 6
7 Loders......D 8
13 Lodsworth......D 10
35 Lofthouse, W. Riding.....E 12
40 Lofthouse, W. Riding......H 1
41 Loftus......E 9
47 Logan......G 10
42 Logan Mains....G 2
30 Loggerheads.....G 6
53 Logie, Fife......E 7
53 Logie, Fife......E 9
56 Logie Hill......B 3
58 Logie Newton....D 4
59 Logie Pert......L 4
52 Logiealmond Lo..D 4
58 Logierait......B 5
12 Login......E 5
25 Lolworth......J 5
54 Lonbain......D 1
36 Londesborough...C 6
18 London......F 3
3 London Apprentice E 7
18 London Colney...D 2
40 Londonderry.....F 3
33 Londonthorpe....F 7
54 Londubh......B 2
54 Lone......C 4
45 Lonemore......A 5
32 Long Bennington..F 5
7 Long Bredy......G 9
23 Long Buckby.....E 9
7 Long Burton......E 10
32 Long Clawson.....G 4
8 Long Common.....E 6
31 Long Compton, Staffordshire...H 7

MAP
16 Long Compton, Warwickshire....A 4
17 Long Crendon....C 8
8 Long Crichel......E 1
17 Long Ditton.....G 12
36 Long Drax......D 5
32 Long Duckmanton C 2
32 Long Eaton......G 2
30 Long Green......C 3
16 Long Hanborough.C 5
48 Long Hermiston...B 4
23 Long Itchington...F 7
23 Long Lawford....D 8
7 Long Load......D 8
17 Long Marston, Herts......C 9
36 Long Marston, Yorks......B 3
39 Long Marton......C 9
27 Long Melford....K 2
15 Long Newnton...E 12
40 Long Newton.....D 4
35 Long Preston.....A 7
37 Long Riston......C 9
36 Long Sandall.....F 4
25 Long Stanton All Saints......J 5
25 Long Stanton St. Michael.....J 5
26 Long Stratton....F 5
23 Long Street......G 11
9 Long Sutton, Hampshire.....A 9
24 Long Sutton, Lincs.C 5
7 Long Sutton, Somerset......D 8
21 Long Waste......A 11
32 Long Whatton....H 2
41 Long Whins......G 11
16 Long Wittenham...E 6
47 Longbar......D 8
45 Longbenton.....F 11
16 Longborough.....A 3
22 Longbridge, War..D 3
22 Longbridge, War..F 6
7 Longbridge Deverill......B 11
54 Longbridgemuir...E 11
44 Longbyre......F 5
42 Longcastle......G 5
31 Longcliffe......E 10
16 Longcot......E 4
49 Longcroft, Ber...D 8
48 Longcroft, Stir...A 1
17 Longcross......H 10
21 Longden......B 10
22 Longdon......A 4
22 Longdon Green...A 4
21 Longdon upon Tern......A 11
6 Longdown......G 2
2 Longdowns......F 4
45 Longdyke......B 10
10 Longfield......A 5
10 Longfield Hill....A 5
31 Longford, Derby..F 10
15 Longford, Glos...B 11
18 Longford, London. F 1
30 Longford, Salop...G 5
23 Longford, War...D 7
53 Longforgan......D 8
49 Longformacus....D 9
45 Longframlington...C 9
8 Longham, Dorset..F 2
26 Longham, Norf...D 2
58 Longhill......B 7
45 Longhirst......D 10
15 Longhope......B 10
45 Longhorsley......D 9
45 Longhoughton....B 10
38 Longlands......B 5
16 Longlane, Berks...G 6
31 Longlane, Derby..F 11
15 Longlevens......B 11
22 Longley Green....G 1
58 Longmanhill.....A 5
9 Longmoor Camp..C 9
56 Longmorn......D 3
49 Longnewton.....G 8
17 Longney......C 11
49 Longniddry......B 7
31 Longnor......D 9
21 Longnot......B 10
8 Longparish......B 6
34 Longridge, Lancs..D 5
48 Longridge, W. Lothian......C 2
48 Longriggend.....B 1
31 Longsdon......E 8
58 Longside......C 8
30 Longslow......G 5
8 Longstock......B 5
3 Longstone......B 7

MAP
25 Longstowe K 4
24 Longthorpe F 3
34 Longton, Lancs. E 4
31 Longton, Staffs. F 7
44 Longtown, Cumb. F 2
14 Longtown, Herefs. A 6
21 Longville in the Dale C 11
15 Longwell Green G 10
17 Longwick D 8
45 Longwitton D 9
21 Longwood B 11
16 Longworth D 5
49 Longyester C 8
62 Lonmore D 2
10 Loose C 6
17 Loosley Row D 9
58 Lootcherbrae B 3
8 Lopcombe Corner C 4
7 Lopen E 8
30 Loppington G 3
45 Lorbottle B 8
45 Lorbottle Hall B 8
9 Lordington E 9
44 Lordsgate F 3
43 Lorg B 7
32 Loscoe E 2
56 Lossiemouth C 8
30 Lostock Gralam C 5
30 Lostock Green C 5
34 Lostock Junction F 5
3 Lostwithiel D 8
61 Lothbeg F 9
35 Lothersdale C 8
61 Lothmore F 9
7 Lottisham C 9
17 Loudwater E 10
32 Loughborough H 3
13 Loughor G 9
23 Loughton, Bucks. H 11
18 Loughton, Essex D 4
21 Loughton, Salop D 11
24 Lound, Lincs. D 2
32 Lound, Notts. B 4
26 Lound, Suffolk E 8
31 Lount H 12
33 Louth B 10
35 Love Clough D 7
9 Lovedean E 8
4 Loveacott C 4
8 Lover D 4
36 Loversall G 4
18 Loves Green C 6
40 Lovesome Hill E 4
12 Loveston F 4
7 Lovington C 9
42 Low Ardwell G 2
43 Low Barlay F 7
35 Low Bradfield H 11
35 Low Bradley B 9
38 Low Braithwaite A 6
45 Low Brunton F 7
36 Low Burnham G 5
40 Low Burton G 3
45 Low Buston B 10
36 Low Catton B 5
40 Low Coniscliffe D 3
42 Low Craighead A 3
44 Low Cranecleugh D 5
44 Low Crosby G 3
41 Low Dalby F 8
40 Low Dinsdale D 4
36 Low Eggborough E 3
40 Low Etherley B 2
44 Low Geltbridge G 4
47 Low Grange H 8
22 Low Habberley D 2
7 Low Ham C 8
45 Low Hedgeley A 9
39 Low Hesket A 7
45 Low Hesleyhurst C 9
41 Low Hutton H 8
42 Low Knockbrex E 5
31 Low Leighton B 8
38 Low Lorton C 4
42 Low Malzie F 4
41 Low Marishes G 8
32 Low Marnham C 5
41 Low Mill F 7
34 Low Moor C 6
45 Low Moorsley H 11
45 Low Newton-by-the-Sea A 10
44 Low Row, Cumb. G 4
38 Low Row, Cumb. B 6
39 Low Row, Yorks. E 12
42 Low Salchrie E 1
37 Low Santon F 7
47 Low Shawsburn D 12
26 Low Street C 6
26 Low Thurlton E 7
48 Low Torry A 3
45 Low Town C 9

MAP
47 Low Waters D 12
40 Low Worsall D 4
38 Low Wray E 6
39 Lowbridge House E 7
38 Lowca C 2
32 Lowdham F 4
30 Lowe G 4
6 Lower Aisholt C 5
7 Lower Ansty F 11
6 Lower Ashton H 2
17 Lower Assendon F 8
63 Lower Bayble D 6
10 Lower Beeding E 1
39 Lower Bentham H 9
7 Lower Bockhampton G 10
23 Lower Boddington G 8
2 Lower Boscaswell F 1
9 Lower Bourne B 10
22 Lower Brailes H 6
62 Lower Breakish F 6
22 Lower Broadheath F 2
15 Lower Bullingham A 8
25 Lower Caldecote K 3
15 Lower Cam D 10
14 Lower Chapel A 4
8 Lower Chicksgrove C 1
8 Lower Chute A 4
10 Lower Cokeham H 1
31 Lower Crossings B 9
35 Lower Cumberworth F 11
14 Lower Cwm-twrch C 1
34 Lower Darwen E 6
25 Lower Dean H 2
54 Lower Diabaig D 2
10 Lower Dicker G 4
21 Lower Dinchope D 10
61 Lower Dounreay A 9
21 Lower Down D 9
2 Lower Drift G 2
36 Lower Dunsforth A 2
8 Lower Everleigh A 3
15 Lower Failand G 8
9 Lower Farringdon C 8
38 Lower Foxdale G 1
12 Lower Freystrop F 3
9 Lower Froyle B 9
60 Lower Gledfield G 6
10 Lower Green, Kent D 5
26 Lower Green, Norf. B 3
27 Lower Hacheston J 6
62 Lower Halistra B 2
11 Lower Halstow A 7
11 Lower Hardres C 10
56 Lower Hempriggs C 7
21 Lower Hergest G 8
16 Lower Heyford B 6
10 Lower Higham A 6
30 Lower Hordley G 3
10 Lower Horsebridge G 4
51 Lower Kinchrackine E 8
7 Lower Kingcombe F 9
10 Lower Kingswood C 1
30 Lower Kinnerton D 2
15 Lower Langford H 8
53 Lower Largo G 9
31 Lower Leigh G 8
57 Lower Lenie G 1
20 Lower Llanfadog F 5
4 Lower Loxhore B 5
15 Lower Lydbrook C 9
21 Lower Lye F 9
14 Lower Machen E 5
15 Lower Maes-coed A 7
19 Lower Mayland D 9
62 Lower Milovaig C 1
22 Lower Moor G 3
18 Lower Nazeing C 4
52 Lower Oakfield H 6
62 Lower Ollach D 4
14 Lower Penarth G 5
22 Lower Penn C 2
8 Lower Pennington G 5
30 Lower Peover C 6
35 Lower Place F 8
22 Lower Quinton G 5
21 Lower Rochford F 11
34 Lower Salter A 5
16 Lower Seagry F 1
63 Lower Shader A 5
25 Lower Shelton L 1
17 Lower Shiplake F 8
23 Lower Shuckburgh F 8
16 Lower Slaughter B 3
15 Lower Stanton St. Quintin F 12
11 Lower Stoke A 7
26 Lower Street B 6
22 Lower Strensham H 3
17 Lower Sundon A 11
8 Lower Swanwick E 6

MAP
16 Lower Swell B 3
62 Lower Tote B 4
12 Lower Town C 3
23 Lower Tysoe H 7
9 Lower Upham D 7
6 Lower Vexford C 5
34 Lower Walton H 5
7 Lower Waterston G 10
7 Lower Weare A 7
21 Lower Welson G 8
30 Lower Whitley B 5
9 Lower Wield B 8
17 Lower Winchendon C 8
17 Lower Woodend E 9
8 Lower Woodford C 3
22 Lower Wyche H 1
23 Lowesby A 10
26 Lowestoft F 8
26 Lowestoft End F 8
38 Loweswater C 4
10 Lowfield Heath D 2
34 Lowgill, Lancs. A 5
39 Lowgill, Westmor. E 8
25 Lowick, Northants. G 1
45 Lowick, Northum. B 11
38 Lowick Green G 5
14 Lowlands E 6
22 Lowsonford E 5
39 Lowther C 8
37 Lowthorpe A 8
34 Lowton, Lancs. G 5
6 Lowton, Som. D 5
34 Lowton Common G 5
6 Loxbeare E 3
9 Loxhill B 11
4 Loxhore B 5
22 Loxley G 6
7 Loxton A 7
9 Loxwood C 11
60 Lubachoinnich G 5
60 Lubcroy F 4
23 Lubenham C 10
51 Lubnaclach A 11
54 Lubriach B 7
6 Luccombe B 3
9 Luccombe Village H 7
45 Lucker D 11
3 Luckett B 11
15 Luckington F 11
53 Lucklawhill E 9
6 Luckwell Bridge B 2
21 Lucton F 10
37 Ludborough H 10
12 Ludchurch F 5
35 Luddenden E 9
35 Luddenden Foot E 9
10 Luddesdown B 5
36 Luddington, Lincs. E 6
22 Luddington, War. G 5
25 Luddington in the Brook G 2
21 Ludford E 10
33 Ludford Magna A 9
33 Ludford Parva A 9
17 Ludgershall B 7
8 Ludgershall A 4
2 Ludgvan F 2
26 Ludham D 7
21 Ludlow E 10
7 Ludwell D 12
40 Ludworth A 4
4 Luffincott F 2
47 Lugar G 10
49 Lugate E 7
49 Luggate Burn B 8
48 Luggiebank B 12
47 Lugton D 9
21 Lugwardine H 11
62 Luib E 5
51 Luib Hotel E 12
51 Luibeilt A 9
21 Lulham H 9
22 Lullington, Derby. A 6
7 Lullington, Som. A 11
22 Lulsey G 1
15 Lulsgate Bottom H 8
35 Lumb E 9
35 Lumbutts E 8
36 Lumby D 3
47 Lumloch B 11
59 Lumphanan G 3
52 Lumphinnans H 6
49 Lumsdaine B 11
58 Lumsden E 2
53 Lunan B 11
53 Lunanhead B 9
52 Luncarty D 6
37 Lund, E. Riding B 7
36 Lund, E. Riding D 4
51 Lundavra A 8
58 Lunderton C 8
53 Lundie, Angus D 8
55 Lundie, Inverness H 5

MAP
53 Lundin Links G 9
50 Lungar (Hotel) G 5
64 Lunna C 7
64 Lunning C 7
13 Lunnon H 9
10 Lunsford B 6
10 Lunsford's Cross G 6
34 Lunt G 2
21 Luntley G 9
6 Luppitt F 5
35 Lupsett E 11
39 Lupton G 8
9 Lurgashall C 10
56 Lurgmore F 1
33 Lusby C 10
51 Luss H 10
62 Lusta C 2
5 Lustleigh H 6
21 Luston F 10
59 Luthermuir K 4
53 Luthrie E 8
17 Luton, Beds. B 12
5 Luton, Devon H 8
10 Luton, Kent A 6
23 Lutterworth D 9
5 Lutton, Devon K 5
24 Lutton, Lincs. C 5
25 Lutton, Northants. G 2
6 Luxborough B 3
3 Luxulyan D 7
61 Lybster D 11
21 Lydbury North D 9
11 Lydd F 9
11 Lydd-on-Sea F 9
11 Lydden D 11
23 Lyddington B 12
17 Lyde Green H 8
6 Lydeard St. Lawrence C 4
5 Lydford G 4
35 Lydgate E 8
21 Lydham C 9
16 Lydiard Millicent F 2
34 Lydiate G 2
7 Lydlinch E 10
15 Lydney D 9
12 Lydstep G 4
22 Lye D 3
15 Lye Cross H 8
17 Lye Green, Bucks. D 10
10 Lye Green, Sussex E 4
16 Lyford E 5
47 Lylestone, Ayr. E 8
49 Lylestone, Ber. D 8
11 Lymbridge Green D 10
7 Lyme Regis G 7
11 Lyminge D 10
8 Lymington F 4
9 Lyminster F 11
30 Lymm B 5
8 Lymore G 4
11 Lympne E 10
6 Lympsham A 6
6 Lympstone H 3
57 Lynaberack K 3
57 Lynachlaggan J 4
6 Lynch B 3
26 Lynch Green E 4
57 Lynchat J 3
8 Lyndhurst E 4
23 Lyndon B 12
48 Lyne, Peebles E 5
17 Lyne, Surrey G 11
15 Lyne Down A 9
57 Lyne of Gorthleck H 1
58 Lyne of Skene F 5
30 Lyneal G 3
62 Lynedale House C 3
16 Lyneham, Oxon. B 4
16 Lyneham, Wilts. F 1
44 Lyneholmeford F 4
57 Lynemore G 6
45 Lynemouth D 11
64 Lyness E 1
26 Lyng, Norfolk D 4
7 Lyng, Somerset C 7
4 Lynmouth A 6
11 Lynsted B 8
4 Lynton A 6
7 Lyon's Gate F 10
21 Lyonshall G 9
8 Lytchett Matravers G 1
8 Lytchett Minster G 1
61 Lyth B 11
34 Lytham D 3
34 Lytham St. Anne's D 2
41 Lythe D 8
64 Lythes E 3
63 Maaruig F 3
2 Mabe Burnthouse F 5
43 Mabie D 10
33 Mablethorpe B 12
48 Macbiehill D 4

MAP
31 Macclesfield C 7
31 Macclesfield For. C 8
58 Macduff A 4
52 Machany F 4
14 Machen E 5
46 Machrihanish G 1
50 Machrins H 1
20 Machynlleth B 3
31 Mackworth F 11
49 Macmerry B 7
52 Madderty E 4
48 Maddiston B 2
9 Madehurst E 11
21 Madeley, Salop B 12
30 Madeley, Staffs. F 6
30 Madeley Heath F 6
25 Madingley J 5
21 Madley H 9
22 Madresfield G 2
2 Madron F 2
28 Maenaddwyn B 4
12 Maenclochog D 4
14 Maendy G 3
28 Maentwrog F 6
13 Maen-y-groes A 7
30 Maer F 6
13 Maerdy, Carm. D 10
29 Maerdy, Denbigh F 9
14 Maerdy, Glam. D 3
15 Maerdy, Mon. B 7
30 Maesbrook Green H 2
30 Maesbury H 2
30 Maesbury Marsh H 2
12 Maesgwynne E 5
29 Maeshafn D 11
13 Maesllyn C 7
20 Maesmynis H 6
14 Maesteg E 2
13 Maestir B 9
13 Maestwynog C 10
13 Maes-y-bont E 9
13 Maesycrugiau C 8
14 Maes-y-cwmmer E 5
13 Maesymeillion B 7
18 Magdalen Laver C 5
58 Maggieknockater C 1
10 Magham Down G 5
34 Maghull G 3
15 Magor F 7
7 Maiden Bradley B 11
45 Maiden Law H 10
7 Maiden Newton F 9
12 Maiden Wells G 3
5 Maidencombe J 8
48 Maidencots G 2
17 Maidenhead F 10
39 Maidenhill B 7
42 Maidens A 3
17 Maiden's Green G 9
33 Maidenwell B 10
23 Maidford G 9
17 Maids' Moreton A 8
10 Maidstone C 6
23 Maidwell D 10
64 Mail E 7
14 Maindee E 6
47 Mains, Lanark D 11
52 Mains, Perth B 6
61 Mains, Sutherland F 8
42 Mains of Airies E 1
59 Mains of Allardice K 6
59 Mains of Altries H 6
58 Mains of Annochie C 7
53 Mains of Ardestie D 10
58 Mains of Arnage D 7
58 Mains of Auchindachy C 2
58 Mains of Auchmedden A 6
53 Mains of Balgavies B 10
53 Mains of Ballindarg B 9
59 Mains of Balnakettle K 4
58 Mains of Birness D 7
56 Mains of Bunachton F 2
58 Mains of Cairnborrow D 2
58 Mains of Cardno A 7
58 Mains of Crichie C 7
56 Mains of Dalvey F 7
59 Mains of Drum G 5
58 Mains of Drummuir C 2
56 Mains of Drynie E 2
58 Mains of Edingight B 3
58 Mains of Esslemont E 7
59 Mains of Glenfarquhar J 5

MAP
59 Mains of Haulkerton K 5
58 Mains of Inkhorn D 7
58 Mains of Keithfield D 6
58 Mains of Kirkhill F 6
58 Mains of Logie B 8
59 Mains of Melgund L 3
56 Mains of Newhall C 3
43 Mains of Terregles D 10
59 Mains of Thornton K 4
52 Mains of Throsk H 3
56 Mains of Tore D 2
58 Mains of Towie C 5
53 Mains of Usan B 12
40 Mainsforth B 3
43 Mainsriddle F 10
21 Mainstone D 8
15 Maisemore B 11
5 Malborough M 6
18 Malden Rushett H 2
19 Maldon C 8
35 Malham A 8
55 Mallaig K 1
55 Mallaigvaig K 1
48 Malleny Mills C 4
29 Malling G 1
28 Malltraeth Yard C 3
20 Mallwyd A 4
15 Malmesbury F 12
4 Malmsmead A 7
30 Malpas, Cheshire E 3
2 Malpas, Corn. E 5
14 Malpas, Mon. E 6
51 Malt Land F 8
40 Maltby, N. Riding D 5
32 Maltby, W. Riding A 3
33 Maltby le Marsh B 11
11 Maltman's Hill D 8
41 Malton H 8
22 Malvern Link G 1
22 Malvern Wells H 1
21 Mamble E 12
14 Mamhilad D 6
2 Manaccan G 5
21 Manafon B 7
5 Manaton H 6
33 Manby B 11
22 Mancetter C 6
35 Manchester G 7
29 Mancot D 12
24 Manea F 6
42 Maneight A 6
40 Manfield D 2
64 Mangaster C 7
63 Mangersta D 1
44 Mangerton D 3
15 Mangotsfield G 10
12 Manian Fawr B 5
63 Manish H 2
30 Manley C 4
14 Manmoel D 5
16 Manningford Bohune H 2
16 Manningford Bruce H 2
35 Manningham D 10
10 Mannings Heath E 1
8 Mannington F 2
27 Manningtree M 4
59 Mannofield G 6
12 Manorbier G 4
12 Manorbier Newton G 4
49 Manorhill F 9
12 Manorowen C 3
43 Mansefield B 9
13 Manselfield H 9
21 Mansell Gamage H 9
21 Mansell Lacy H 9
39 Mansergh G 8
47 Mansfield, Ayr. H 11
32 Mansfield, Notts. D 3
32 Mansfield Woodhouse D 3
38 Mansriggs G 5
7 Manston, Dorset E 11
11 Manston, Kent B 12
8 Manswood E 2
24 Manthorpe, Lincs. D 2
37 Manthorpe, Lincs. F 6
37 Manton, Lincs. G 7
23 Manton, Rutland B 12
16 Manton, Wilts. G 3
18 Manuden A 5
50 Maolachy F 6
7 Maperton D 10
17 Maple Cross E 11
32 Maplebeck D 4
17 Mapledurham F 7
9 Mapledurwell A 8
10 Maplehurst F 1
10 Maplescombe B 4

MAP
31 Mapleton...E 10
32 Mapperley...F 2
32 Mapperley Park...F 3
7 Mapperton, Dorset...F 12
7 Mapperton, Dorset...F 8
22 Mappleborough Green...E 4
37 Mappleton...C 10
35 Mapplewell...F 12
7 Mappowder...F 10
57 Mar Lodge...K 7
2 Marazion...G 2
30 Marbury...F 4
24 March, Cambs...F 5
48 March, Lan...H 3
16 Marcham...D 5
30 Marchamley...G 4
43 Marchbankwood...B 11
47 Marchburn...H 11
31 Marchington...G 9
31 Marchington Woodlands...G 9
30 Marchwiel...E 2
8 Marchwood...E 5
14 Marcross...G 3
21 Marden, Herefs...H 10
10 Marden, Kent...D 6
16 Marden, Wilts...H 2
10 Marden Beech...D 6
10 Marden Thorn...D 6
14 Mardy...C 6
7 Mare Green...D 7
17 Marefield, Bucks...E 9
23 Marefield, Leics...A 11
33 Mareham le Fen...D 10
33 Mareham on the Hill...C 10
32 Marehey...E 1
10 Maresfield...F 3
37 Marfleet...D 9
30 Marford...E 2
13 Margam...H 11
7 Margaret Marsh...D 11
18 Margaret Roding...C 6
18 Margaretting...D 6
11 Margate...A 12
46 Margnaheglish...F 5
24 Marham...D 8
4 Marhamchurch...F 1
24 Marholm...E 2
28 Marianglas...D 4
4 Mariansleigh...D 6
59 Marionburgh...G 5
62 Marishader...B 4
63 Mariveg...E 5
43 Marjoriebanks...C 11
42 Mark, Ayr...D 2
43 Mark, Kirk...F 7
7 Mark, Somerset...A 7
7 Mark Causeway...B 7
10 Mark Cross...E 5
10 Markbeech...D 4
33 Markby...B 12
23 Market Bosworth...B 7
24 Market Deeping...E 2
30 Market Drayton...G 5
23 Market Harborough...C 10
8 Market Lavington...A 2
23 Market Overton...A 12
33 Market Rasen...A 8
33 Market Stainton...B 9
26 Market Street...C 6
36 Market Weighton...C 6
27 Market Weston...G 3
23 Markfield...A 8
14 Markham...D 5
32 Markham Moor...C 4
53 Markinch...G 8
35 Markington...A 10
49 Markle...B 8
19 Marks Tey...B 9
15 Marksbury...H 10
17 Markyate...C 11
48 Marlage...D 1
16 Marlborough...G 3
21 Marlbrook, Herefs...G 10
22 Marlbrook, Worcs...E 3
22 Marlcliff...G 4
5 Marldon...J 7
27 Marlesford...J 6
30 Marley Green...F 4
45 Marley Hill...G 10
8 Marley Mount...F 4
49 Marleyknowe...F 12
29 Marli...C 9
26 Marlingford...E 4
12 Marloes...F 1
17 Marlow, Bucks...E 9
21 Marlow, Herefs...E 9
MAP
17 Marlow Bottom...E 9
10 Marlpit Hill...C 3
7 Marnhull...D 11
58 Marnoch...C 3
31 Marple...A 8
36 Marr...G 3
61 Marrel...E 9
40 Marrick...E 1
12 Marros...F 5
45 Marsden, Dur...G 12
35 Marsden, Yorks...F 9
39 Marsett...F 11
6 Marsh, Devon...E 6
6 Marsh, Somerset...C 4
16 Marsh Baldon...D 6
16 Marsh Benham...G 5
37 Marsh Chapel...G 11
17 Marsh Gibbon...B 7
6 Marsh Green, Devon...G 4
10 Marsh Green, Kent...D 3
21 Marsh Green, Shropshire...A 11
6 Marsh Street...B 3
18 Marshall's Heath...B 2
26 Marsham...C 5
34 Marshaw...B 5
11 Marshborough...B 11
21 Marshbrook...C 10
15 Marshfield, Glos...G 11
14 Marshfield, Mon...F 6
2 Marshgate...B 2
32 Marshlane...B 1
34 Marshside...E 2
7 Marshwood...F 7
40 Marske...E 1
40 Marske-by-the-Sea...C 6
30 Marston, Ches...C 5
21 Marston, Herefs...G 9
32 Marston, Lincs...F 6
16 Marston, Oxon...C 6
22 Marston, Staffs...A 2
31 Marston, Staffs...G 8
22 Marston, War...C 5
22 Marston, War...G 5
16 Marston, Wilts...H 1
22 Marston Green...D 5
7 Marston Magna...D 9
16 Marston Meysey...D 2
31 Marston Montgomery...F 10
25 Marston Moretaine...L 1
31 Marston on Dove...G 11
23 Marston St. Lawrence...H 8
21 Marston Stannett...G 11
23 Marston Trussell...D 10
15 Marstow...B 9
17 Marsworth...C 10
16 Marten...H 4
30 Marthall...C 6
26 Martham...D 8
8 Martin, Hants...D 2
11 Martin, Kent...C 12
33 Martin, Lincs...D 8
8 Martin Drove End...D 2
22 Martin Hussingtree...F 2
4 Martinhoe...A 5
4 Martinhoe Cross...A 6
30 Martinscroft...A 5
44 Martinshouse...B 3
7 Martinstown...G 10
27 Martlesham...K 6
12 Martletwy...F 4
22 Martley...F 1
7 Martock...D 8
31 Marton, Ches...C 7
37 Marton, E. Riding...C 9
32 Marton, Lincs...B 5
40 Marton, N. Riding...D 5
41 Marton, N. Riding...G 7
21 Marton, Salop...B 8
36 Marton, W. Riding...A 2
23 Marton, War...E 7
40 Marton le Moor...H 4
40 Marton-in-the-Forest...H 6
8 Martyr Worthy...C 6
17 Martyr's Green...H 11
43 Marwhirn...B 8
64 Marwick...C 1
4 Marwood...B 4
4 Marwood Middle...B 4
5 Mary Tavy...H 4
54 Marybank...D 8
56 Maryburgh...D 1
59 Maryculter...G 6
49 Marygold...C 10
58 Maryhill, Aber...C 6
47 Maryhill, Lan...B 10
59 Marykirk...L 4
56 Marypark...F 7
MAP
38 Maryport, Cumb...B 3
42 Maryport, Wig...H 2
53 Maryton, Angus...B 8
53 Maryton, Angus...B 11
59 Marywell, Aber...H 3
53 Marywell, Angus...C 11
59 Marywell, Kinc...G 7
40 Masham...G 2
45 Mason...F 10
32 Mastin Moor...C 2
59 Mastrick...G 6
18 Matching...C 5
18 Matching Green...C 5
18 Matching Tye...C 5
45 Matfen...F 8
10 Matfield...D 5
15 Mathern...E 8
22 Mathon...H 1
12 Mathry...D 2
26 Matlask...B 5
31 Matlock...D 11
31 Matlock Bath...D 11
15 Matson...C 11
38 Matterdale End...C 6
32 Mattersey...A 4
32 Mattersey Thorpe...A 4
17 Mattingley...H 8
26 Mattishall...D 4
26 Mattishall Burgh...D 4
53 Mattocks...C 9
47 Mauchline...G 10
58 Maud...C 7
13 Maudsland...D 7
16 Maugersbury...B 3
38 Maughold...G 3
54 Mauld...F 8
25 Maulden...L 2
39 Maulds Meaburn...D 8
40 Maunby...F 4
21 Maund Bryan...G 11
6 Maundown...C 4
26 Mautby...D 8
22 Mavesyn Ridware...A 4
33 Mavis Enderby...D 10
56 Maviston...D 5
22 Maw Green...B 4
43 Mawbray...G 11
52 Mawcarse...G 6
34 Mawdesley...F 4
14 Mawdlam...F 1
2 Mawgan...G 4
2 Mawla...E 4
2 Mawnan...G 5
2 Mawnan Smith...G 5
24 Maxey...E 2
22 Maxstoke...C 6
11 Maxton, Kent...D 11
49 Maxton, Rox...F 8
49 Maxwellheugh...F 10
42 Maxwellston...B 4
43 Maxwelltown...D 10
5 Maxworthy...G 1
31 May Bank...E 7
3 Mayals...H 9
47 Maybole...H 8
17 Maybury...H 11
31 Mayfield, Staffs...F 10
10 Mayfield, Sussex...E 5
17 Mayford...H 10
19 Mayland...D 9
10 Maynard's Green...F 5
15 Maypole, Mon...C 8
2 Maypole, Is. of Scilly...D 2
26 Maypole Green...F 7
64 Maywick...E 7
4 Mead...D 1
15 Meadgate...H 10
47 Meadowfoot...E 11
21 Meadowtown...B 8
39 Meal Bank...F 8
43 Meals...G 11
38 Mealsgate...A 4
35 Mearbeck...A 7
7 Meare...B 8
6 Meare Green...D 6
47 Mearns...D 10
23 Mears Ashby...E 11
23 Measham...A 7
10 Meath Green...D 2
23 Meathop...G 7
63 Meavag...G 3
5 Meavy...J 4
23 Medbourne...C 11
45 Medburn...F 9
4 Meddon...D 2
17 Medmenham...F 9
45 Medomsley...H 9
9 Medstead...B 8
31 Meerbrook...D 8
33 Meers Bridge...B 12
25 Meesden...M 5
4 Meeth...E 4
MAP
44 Megdale...C 1
48 Meggethead...G 4
12 Meidrim...E 6
21 Meifod...A 7
53 Meigle...C 7
43 Meikle Barncleugh...D 10
43 Meikle Beoch...D 9
47 Meikle Carco...H 12
47 Meikle Earnock...D 12
59 Meikle Fiddes...J 5
52 Meikle Forter...A 6
61 Meikle Gluich...H 7
46 Meikle Grenach...C 6
47 Meikle Hareshaw...E 11
47 Meikle Ittington...E 7
56 Meikle Kildrummie...D 4
49 Meikle Pinkerton...B 9
59 Meikle Strath...K 4
58 Meikle Tarty...E 7
58 Meikle Toux...B 3
58 Meikle Wartle...D 5
43 Meikleholm...C 11
47 Meiklelaught...E 7
52 Meikleour...C 6
58 Meikleton...C 3
28 Meillteyrn...G 2
43 Meinbank...D 12
13 Meinciau...F 8
31 Meirheath...F 8
63 Melbost...D 6
63 Melbost Borve...A 5
25 Melbourn...L 5
31 Melbourne, Derby...H 12
48 Melbourne, Lan...E 4
36 Melbourne, Yorks...C 5
7 Melbury Abbas...D 12
7 Melbury Bubb...F 9
7 Melbury Osmond...E 9
7 Melbury Sampford...F 9
64 Melby...D 6
25 Melchbourne...J 1
7 Melcombe Regis...H 10
5 Meldon, Devon...G 4
45 Meldon, N'thumb...E 9
25 Meldreth...L 5
58 Meldrum House...E 6
50 Melfort...F 5
55 Melgarve...K 8
29 Meliden...B 10
14 Melin Court...D 2
20 Melin-byrhedin...C 4
29 Melin-y-coed...D 7
20 Melin-y-grug...B 6
29 Melin-y-wig...E 9
39 Melkinthorpe...C 8
44 Melkridge...G 5
15 Melksham...H 12
54 Mellangaun...A 2
46 Melldalloch...B 4
39 Melling, Lancs...H 8
34 Melling, Lancs...G 3
34 Melling Mount...G 3
27 Mellis...H 4
60 Mellon Charles...G 1
60 Mellon Udrigle...G 1
31 Mellor, Cheshire...A 8
34 Mellor, Lancs...D 5
34 Mellor Brook...D 5
7 Mells...A 10
39 Melmerby, Cumb...B 8
40 Melmerby, N. Riding...G 4
40 Melmerby, N. Riding...G 1
7 Melplash...F 8
49 Melrose...F 8
64 Melsetter...E 1
40 Melsonby...D 2
35 Meltham...F 9
35 Meltham Mills...F 10
37 Melton, E. Riding...D 7
27 Melton, Suffolk...K 6
26 Melton Constable...B 3
32 Melton Mowbray...H 5
37 Melton Ross...F 8
36 Meltonby...B 6
54 Melvaig...A 1
21 Melverley...A 9
61 Melvich...B 8
6 Membury...F 6
58 Memsie...A 7
59 Memus...L 2
3 Menabilly...E 8
28 Menai Bridge...C 5
27 Mendham...G 6
27 Mendlesham...J 4
27 Mendlesham Green...J 4
3 Menheniot...C 10
43 Mennock...A 9
35 Menston...C 10
MAP
52 Menstrie...G 3
36 Menthorpe...D 5
17 Mentmore...B 10
55 Meoble...L 2
21 Meole Brace...A 10
9 Meonstoke...D 7
10 Meopham...B 5
10 Meopham Green...B 5
10 Meopham Station...A 5
25 Mepal...G 5
25 Meppershall...L 2
21 Merbach...H 8
30 Mere, Cheshire...B 6
7 Mere, Wilts...C 11
34 Mere Brow...E 3
35 Mere Clough...D 7
22 Mere End...E 6
22 Mere Green...B 5
11 Meresborough...B 7
34 Mereside...D 2
30 Meretown...H 6
10 Mereworth...C 5
59 Mergie...H 5
22 Meriden...D 6
62 Merkadale...E 3
43 Merkland...D 8
60 Merkland Lodge...D 5
12 Merlin's Bridge...F 3
30 Merrington...H 3
12 Merrion...G 3
7 Merriot...E 8
5 Merrivale...H 4
9 Merrow...A 11
44 Merrylaw...C 2
3 Merrymeet...C 10
34 Merseyside, Co...H 3
11 Mersham...D 9
10 Merstham...C 2
9 Merston...F 10
8 Merstone...H 6
2 Merther...E 6
13 Merthyr...E 7
14 Merthyr Cynog...A 3
14 Merthyr Mawr...F 2
14 Merthyr Tydfil...D 4
14 Merthyr Vale...D 4
4 Merton, Devon...E 4
18 Merton, London...G 3
26 Merton, Norfolk...F 2
17 Merton, Oxon...B 7
44 Mervinslaw...B 5
4 Meshaw...D 6
19 Messing...B 9
37 Messingham...G 7
27 Metfield...G 6
33 Metheringham...D 8
53 Methil...G 8
28 Methlem...G 1
35 Methley...D 12
58 Methlick...D 6
52 Methven...E 5
24 Methwold...F 8
24 Methwold Hythe...F 8
26 Mettingham...F 6
26 Metton...B 5
3 Mevagissey...E 7
36 Mexborough...G 3
61 Mey...A 12
16 Meysey Hampton...D 2
63 Miavaig...C 2
58 Michael Muir...D 6
15 Michaelchurch...B 8
14 Michaelchurch Escley...A 6
21 Michaelchurch-on-Arrow...G 8
14 Michaelston-le-Pit...G 5
14 Michaelston-super-Ely...G 4
14 Michaelstone-y-Vedw...F 6
3 Michaelstow...B 8
8 Michelmersh...C 5
27 Mickfield...J 4
30 Mickle Trafford...C 3
36 Micklebring...H 3
41 Mickleby...D 8
36 Micklefield...D 2
10 Mickleham...C 1
31 Mickleover...G 11
44 Micklethwaite...H 1
22 Mickleton, Glos...H 5
39 Mickleton, Yorks...C 12
35 Mickletown...D 12
40 Mickley...G 3
45 Mickley Square...G 9
58 Mid Ardlaw...A 7
59 Mid Beltie...G 4
59 Mid Cairncross...J 2
48 Mid Calder...C 3
61 Mid Clyth...D 11
58 Mid Cowbog...B 6
54 Mid Crochail...F 7
MAP
58 Mid Culsh...C 6
47 Mid Drumloch...D 11
14 Mid Glamorgan, Co...E 4
48 Mid Hartwood...C 3
43 Mid Laggan...D 8
9 Mid Lavant...E 10
54 Mid Mains...F 8
46 Mid Sannox...E 5
54 Mid Strom...F 2
46 Mid Thundergay...E 4
64 Mid Yell...B 7
64 Midbea...A 2
17 Middle Assendon...F 8
16 Middle Aston...A 6
16 Middle Barton...B 5
15 Middle Bridge...G 8
7 Middle Chinnock...E 8
59 Middle Drums...L 3
58 Middle Essie...B 8
32 Middle Handley...B 1
17 Middle Claydon...B 8
22 Middle Littleton...G 4
12 Middle Mill...D 2
49 Middle Ord...D 12
33 Middle Rasen...A 8
52 Middle Rigg...F 5
15 Middle Street...D 11
23 Middle Tysoe...H 7
8 Middle Wallop...B 4
8 Middle Winterslow...C 4
8 Middle Woodford...C 3
43 Middlebie...D 12
57 Middlebridge...M 4
49 Middlefield...D 10
43 Middlegill...A 11
40 Middleham...F 2
21 Middlehope...D 10
7 Middlemarsh...E 10
58 Middlemuir...C 6
58 Middlemuir House...E 7
40 Middlesbrough...C 5
43 Middleshaw, Dumfries...D 12
39 Middleshaw, Westmorland...F 8
44 Middlesknowes...B 6
40 Middlesmoor...H 1
40 Middlestone...B 3
40 Middlestone Moor...B 3
35 Middlestown...E 11
49 Middlethird...E 9
58 Middleton, Aber...E 6
47 Middleton, Ayr...E 8
31 Middleton, Derby...E 11
31 Middleton, Derby...D 10
27 Middleton, Essex...L 2
13 Middleton, Glam...H 7
8 Middleton, Hants...B 6
21 Middleton, Herefs...E 11
52 Middleton, Kinr...F 6
34 Middleton, Lancs...A 3
35 Middleton, Lancs...F 7
48 Middleton, Midlothian...D 6
24 Middleton, Norf...D 8
41 Middleton, N. Riding...G 8
25 Middleton, Northants...C 11
45 Middleton, Northumberland...E 9
45 Middleton, Northumb...B 12
52 Middleton, Perth...B 6
21 Middleton, Salop...E 11
30 Middleton, Salop...G 2
15 Middleton, Som...G 8
27 Middleton, Suffolk...H 7
22 Middleton, War...B 5
35 Middleton, W. Riding...D 11
35 Middleton, W. Riding...B 10
23 Middleton Cheney...H 8
31 Middleton Green...G 8
49 Middleton Hall...G 12
39 Middleton in Teesdale...C 11
58 Middleton of Rora...C 8
9 Middleton-on-Sea...F 11
21 Middleton on the Hill...F 11
37 Middleton-on-the-Wolds...B 7
40 Middleton One Row...D 4
21 Middleton Priors...C 11
40 Middleton Quernhow...G 3
40 Middleton St. George...D 4
21 Middleton Scriven...D 12

MAP
16 Middleton Stoney..B 6
40 Middleton Tyas...E 3
21 Middletown......A 8
30 Middlewich.......D 6
27 Middlewood Green J 4
47 Middleyard......F 10
7 Middlezoy........C 7
40 Middridge.......C 3
60 Midfield..........A 6
15 Midford........H 10
34 Midge Hall.......E 4
44 Midgeholme......G 5
35 Midgeley........F 11
16 Midgham........G 6
35 Midgley..........D 9
35 Midhopestones...G 11
9 Midhurst.......D 10
49 Midlem..........G 8
48 Midlock..........G 2
48 Midlothian, Co....C 5
7 Midsomer Norton A 10
60 Midtown.........B 6
54 Midtown Brae.....A 2
59 Midtown of Barras J 6
58 Midtown of
Buchromb......C 1
33 Midville.........E 11
43 Miefield..........F 7
61 Migdale..........G 7
59 Migvie...........G 2
7 Milborne Port...D 10
7 Milborne St. Andrew
F 11
7 Milborne Wick...D 10
45 Milbourne........E 9
50 Milbuie..........H 1
39 Milburn..........B 9
15 Milbury Heath...E 10
40 Milby............H 4
16 Milcombe........A 5
27 Milden..........K 3
25 Mildenhall, Suff...H 8
16 Mildenhall, Wilts..G 3
16 Mile Elm.........G 1
19 Mile End, Essex...A 9
26 Mile End, Suffolk..F 6
21 Milebrook........E 8
26 Mileham..........D 2
15 Miles End........C 9
30 Miles Green.......E 6
21 Miles Hope......F 11
52 Milesmark.......H 5
49 Milfield..........F 12
31 Milford, Derby...F 12
4 Milford, Devon...D 1
31 Milford, Staffs....H 8
9 Milford, Surrey..B 11
8 Milford, Wilts.....C 3
12 Milford Haven....F 4
8 Milford on Sea....G 4
47 Milhall..........D 10
15 Milkwall.........C 9
8 Milkwell..........D 1
35 Mill Bank........E 9
31 Mill Brow........A 8
27 Mill Common....G 7
17 Mill End, Bucks...F 9
17 Mill End, Herts...E 11
25 Mill End, Herts...M 4
25 Mill End, Hunts...G 4
18 Mill Green, Essex.D 6
27 Mill Green, Suffolk L 3
18 Mill Hill..........E 2
39 Mill Houses......H 8
9 Mill Lane.........A 9
58 Mill of Ardo,
Aberdeen.......E 7
58 Mill of Ardo,
Aberdeen.......D 6
58 Mill of Carden....E 4
58 Mill of Culfork....F 2
59 Mill of Gellan....G 3
59 Mill of Mondynes..J 5
59 Mill of Monquich.H 6
58 Mill of Muiresk...C 4
58 Mill of Pot.......C 5
59 Mill of Uras......J 6
26 Mill Street........D 3
38 Millbeck..........C 5
64 Millbounds.......B 3
58 Millbreck........C 7
58 Millbrex..........C 6
9 Millbridge.........B 10
25 Millbrook, Beds....L 1
3 Millbrook, Corn..D 11
4 Millbrook, Devon..C 6
8 Millbrook, Hants..E 5
47 Millburn..........F 9
5 Millcombe........L 7
11 Millcorner........F 7
31 Milldale.........E 10
59 Millden Lodge....J 3
53 Milldens.........B 10

MAP
48 Millerhill.........B 6
31 Miller's Dale.....C 10
31 Millers Green....E 11
59 Millfield.........H 2
30 Millgreen.........G 5
21 Millhalf..........H 8
6 Millhayes.........E 5
47 Millheugh, Lan...D 12
49 Millheugh, Rox....G 9
39 Millholme.........F 8
46 Millhouse, Arg....B 4
38 Millhouse, Cumb..B 6
35 Millhouse, Yorks. G 11
43 Millhousebridge..C 11
32 Millhouses........B 1
43 Milliganton......C 10
47 Millikenpark......C 9
36 Millington........B 6
49 Millknowe........C 9
31 Millmeece........G 7
38 Millom...........G 4
3 Millpool..........C 8
46 Millport..........D 6
43 Millquarter.......C 7
31 Millthorpe.......C 11
39 Millthrop.........F 9
59 Milltimber........G 6
53 Millton..........C 8
57 Millton of
Auchriachan....H 7
58 Milltown, Aber....F 2
58 Milltown, Aber....F 7
59 Milltown, Aber....G 4
58 Milltown, Banff....C 3
32 Milltown, Derby. .D 1
4 Milltown, Devon...B 4
59 Milltown, Kinc....K 5
54 Milltown, Ross &
Cromarty ......D 7
52 Milltown of
Aberdalgie......E 5
58 Milltown of
Auchindown....D 1
59 Milltown of
Campfield......G 4
58 Milltown of
Craigston.......B 5
56 Milltown of
Edinvillie.......F 8
58 Milltown of
Minnes.........E 7
58 Milltown of Towie.F 2
47 Millwell.........D 11
53 Milnacraig........B 7
52 Milnathort.......G 6
43 Milne............B 12
47 Milngavie.......B 10
43 Milnmark........C 7
35 Milnrow..........F 8
39 Milnthorpe.......G 7
21 Milson...........E 11
11 Milstead..........B 7
8 Milston...........B 3
58 Milton, Aber......E 1
59 Milton, Angus.....J 2
42 Milton, Ayr.......B 4
42 Milton, Ayr.......A 3
58 Milton, Banff......A 3
16 Milton, Berks.....E 6
61 Milton, Caith....C 12
25 Milton, Cambs.....J 6
44 Milton, Cumb......G 4
31 Milton, Derby....G 11
43 Milton, Dumf......C 9
47 Milton, Dunb.....B 9
9 Milton, Hants.....F 8
57 Milton, Inver.....H 5
57 Milton, Inver.....G 1
43 Milton, Kirk......D 9
23 Milton,
Northants.....G 10
16 Milton, Oxon......A 5
12 Milton, Pemb.....G 4
52 Milton, Perth......A 6
51 Milton, Perth....G 12
56 Milton, Ross &
Cromarty......D 2
56 Milton, Ross &
Cromarty.......E 1
56 Milton, Ross &
Cromarty.......B 3
54 Milton, Ross &
Cromarty.......E 1
7 Milton, Som.......D 8
14 Milton, Som.......H 6
42 Milton, Wig.......F 3
7 Milton Abbas....F 11
5 Milton Abbot.....H 3
48 Milton Bridge.....C 5
25 Milton Bryan......M 1
7 Milton Clevedon .C 10
58 Milton Coldwells..D 7
4 Milton Damerel...E 3

MAP
16 Milton End.......D 2
25 Milton Ernest.....K 1
30 Milton Green.....D 3
16 Milton Hill.......E 6
23 Milton Keynes...H 12
16 Milton Lilbourne..H 3
58 Milton of
Ardlethen......D 6
59 Milton of
Auchinhove....G 3
53 Milton of Balgonie.G 8
56 Milton of
Braicklaich.....D 3
47 Milton of Campsie B 11
58 Milton of Cushnie .F 3
59 Milton of
Dillavaird.......J 5
56 Milton of Farr....F 2
58 Milton of Fishrie..B 5
58 Milton of Lesmore E 2
59 Milton of Logie...G 2
59 Milton of Murtle..G 6
58 Milton of Noth...E 2
46 Milton of Smerby.G 2
59 Milton of Tullich..H 1
7 Milton on Stour..C 11
11 Milton Regis......B 7
16 Milton under
Wychwood.....B 4
5 Miltoncombe......J 4
56 Miltonduff.......D 7
42 Miltonise.........D 3
6 Milverton.........D 4
31 Milwich..........G 8
51 Minard..........H 7
15 Minchinhampton.D 12
49 Mindrum........F 11
49 Mindrummill.....F 11
6 Minehead........B 3
29 Minera..........E 12
16 Minety...........E 1
28 Minffordd........F 5
50 Mingarrypark.....A 4
33 Miningsby.......D 10
3 Minions..........C 9
47 Minishant........H 8
57 Minmore.........G 7
42 Minnigaff.........E 5
58 Minnonie.........B 5
38 Minorca..........G 2
44 Minsca...........E 1
36 Minskip..........A 2
8 Minstead.........E 4
11 Minster, Kent....B 11
11 Minster, Kent....A 8
16 Minster Lovell....C 4
45 Minsteracres.....G 8
21 Minsterley.......B 9
15 Minsterworth....C 11
7 Minterne Magna .F 10
33 Minting..........C 9
58 Mintlaw..........C 7
49 Minto............G 8
43 Minto Cott.......F 7
21 Minton..........C 9
12 Minwear.........F 4
22 Minworth........C 5
64 Mirbister.........C 1
38 Mirehouse........D 2
61 Mireland........B 12
35 Mirfield.........E 10
15 Miserden........C 12
14 Miskin, Glam.....F 4
14 Miskin, Glam.....D 4
43 Misson..........H 5
36 Misterton,
Nottinghamshire H 5
7 Misterton,
Somerset ...   E 8
23 Misterton,
Warwickshire...D 9
27 Mistley..........M 4
18 Mitcham.........G 3
15 Mitcheldean......B 9
8 Mitcheldever......B 6
15 Mitchel Troy.....C 8
2 Mitchell..........D 6
15 Mitcheltroy Com. .C 8
45 Mitford.........D 10
2 Mithian...........E 4
22 Mitton...........A 2
17 Mixbury.........A 7
31 Mixon...........D 9
53 Moanzie.........E 8
44 Moat Common....F 3
30 Mobberley........B 6
21 Moccas..........H 9
29 Mochdre, Denb....B 7
20 Mochdre, Mont...D 6
42 Mochrum........G 4
10 Mockbeggar.......C 6
10 Mockbegger......A 6
38 Mockerkin........C 3

MAP
5 Modbury.........K 5
31 Moddershall......G 8
61 Modsarie.........B 7
28 Moelfre, Angl.....B 4
29 Moelfre, Denb...G 11
43 Moffat..........A 11
25 Moggerhanger....K 2
60 Moin House......B 6
22 Moira............A 6
11 Molash...........C 9
62 Mol-chlach.......G 4
29 Mold...........D 11
35 Moldgreen.......F 10
18 Molehill Green....A 5
37 Molescroft.......C 8
45 Molesden.........E 9
25 Molesworth......H 2
4 Molland..........C 7
4 Molland Cross....C 6
30 Mollington, Ches...C 2
23 Mollington, Oxon..G 8
47 Mollinsburn.....B 12
19 Molting Green....B 9
13 Monachty........A 8
51 Monachylemore..F 11
46 Monamore Bridge..F 5
21 Monaughty.......F 11
59 Monboddo House.J 5
51 Monevechadan....G 9
27 Moneyden........J 5
52 Moneydie........D 5
43 Moniaive.........C 8
53 Monifieth........D 9
53 Monikie..........C 9
53 Monimail.........F 8
12 Monington.......C 5
35 Monk Bretton....F 12
36 Monk Fryston.....D 3
17 Monk Sherborne..H 7
27 Monk Soham......J 5
45 Monk-
Wearmouth....G 12
21 Monkhide.......H 11
21 Monkhopton....C 11
21 Monkland.......G 10
4 Monkleigh.......D 3
14 Monknash........G 3
4 Monkokehampton.E 5
45 Monkridge.......D 7
27 Monks Eleigh.....K 3
10 Monk's Gate......E 1
31 Monks' Heath.....C 7
23 Monks Kirby.....D 8
17 Monks Risborough D 9
58 Monkshill........D 5
6 Monksilver.......C 4
22 Monkspath Street.D 5
15 Monkswood.......D 7
47 Monkton, Ayr.....G 8
6 Monkton, Devon..F 5
11 Monkton, Kent..B 11
12 Monkton, Pemb...G 3
6 Monkton, Som.....C 6
15 Monkton
Coombe......H 11
7 Monkton Deverill B 11
15 Monkton
Farleigh.......H 11
6 Monkton
Heathfield......D 6
8 Monkton Up
Wimborne......E 2
7 Monkton Wyld....F 7
47 Monktonhill......F 8
9 Monkwood........C 8
15 Monmouth.......C 8
15 Monmouth Cap...B 7
21 Monnington on
Wye...........H 9
53 Monorgan........D 8
42 Monreith.........G 4
42 Monreith Mains...G 4
7 Montacute........E 8
58 Montcoffer House.B 4
21 Montford.........A 9
21 Montford Bridge..A 9
58 Montgarrie.......F 3
21 Montgomery......E 8
47 Montgreenan.....E 8
53 Montrave........F 8
59 Montrose.........L 5
8 Monxton.........B 5
31 Monyash.......D 10
58 Monymusk.......F 4
52 Monzie, Perth.....E 4
57 Monzie, Perth....M 5
47 Moodiesburn....B 11
35 Moor Allerton...C 11
8 Moor Crichel.....E 2
36 Moor Ends.......F 5
36 Moor Monkton....B 3
56 Moor of Granary..D 6
38 Moor Row.......D 3

MAP
11 Moor Street......B 7
33 Moorby.........D 10
8 Moordown.......G 3
30 Moore...........B 4
15 Moorend.........D 10
8 Moorgreen.......E 6
31 Moorhall........C 11
21 Moorhampton....H 9
44 Moorhouse,
Cumb..........G 2
32 Moorhouse, Notts. D 5
7 Moorlinch........C 7
41 Moorsholm.......D 7
5 Moorshop........H 4
35 Moorside, Lancs...F 8
33 Moorside, Lincs...D 9
8 Moortown, Hants..F 3
8 Moortown, I. of
Wight, Hants....H 6
37 Moortown, Lincs..G 8
55 Morar...........K 1
56 Moray, Co........E 7
24 Morborne........F 2
4 Morchard Bishop..E 6
23 Morcott.........B 12
30 Morda...........G 2
7 Morden, Dorset..G 12
18 Morden, London..G 2
15 Mordiford........A 9
49 Mordington
Mains........D 12
40 Mordon..........C 3
21 More............C 9
6 Morebath........D 3
49 Morebattle.......G 10
34 Morecambe.......A 3
7 Morecombelake...G 7
60 Morefield........G 3
39 Moreland........C 8
5 Moreleigh.......K 6
52 Morenish.........D 1
38 Moresby.........C 2
8 Morestead........D 6
30 Moreton, Ches....A 1
7 Moreton, Dorset. G 11
18 Moreton, Essex...C 5
17 Moreton, Oxon....D 8
16 Moreton-in-Marsh.A 3
21 Moreton Jeffries..G 11
22 Moreton Morrell ..F 6
21 Moreton on Lugg H 10
23 Moreton Pinkney..G 9
30 Moreton Say.....G 5
15 Moreton Valence.C 11
5 Moretonhampstead G 6
13 Morfa............F 9
28 Morfa'Bychan.....F 5
14 Morfa Glas.......D 2
28 Morfa-Nefyn......F 2
8 Morgan's Vale....D 4
32 Morley, Derby.....F 1
40 Morley, Dur.......B 2
35 Morley, Yorks...D 11
31 Morley Green.....B 7
26 Morley St. Botolph E 4
26 Morning Thorpe...F 5
48 Morningside, Lan..D 1
48 Morningside,
Midlothian.....B 5
45 Morpeth........D 10
31 Morrey.........H 10
43 Morrington.......C 9
25 Morris Green....M 8
42 Morriston, Ayr....A 3
13 Morriston, Glam. G 10
26 Morston.........A 3
4 Mortehoe........B 3
32 Morthen.........A 2
17 Mortimer Com....H 7
17 Mortimer West
End..........H 7
21 Mortimer's Cross..F 9
18 Mortlake.........F 2
44 Morton, Cumb....H 2
32 Morton, Derby...D 1
15 Morton, Glos.....E 9
24 Morton, Kesteven,
Lincs..........C 2
32 Morton, Lindsey,
Lincs...........A 5
26 Morton, Norf.....D 4
32 Morton, Notts....E 4
30 Morton, Salop....H 2
22 Morton Bagot.....C 4
40 Morton-on-Swale..F 3
40 Morton Tinmouth.C 2
2 Morvah..........F 1
3 Morval...........D 9
55 Morvich.........G 3
61 Morvich Lodge....F 8
21 Morville.........C 12
4 Morwenstow......D 1
32 Mosbrough.......B 2

MAP
47 Moscow, Ayr......E 9
44 Moscow, Cumb....F 4
38 Mosedale.........B 6
35 Moselden Height..F 9
22 Moseley, War.....D 4
22 Moseley, Worcs....F 2
29 Moss, Denb......E 12
50 Moss, Inver.......A 4
36 Moss, Yorks......F 4
34 Moss Bank.......G 4
17 Moss End........G 9
56 Moss of
Barmuckity.....D 8
58 Mossat...........F 2
64 Mossbank........C 7
44 Mossburnford.....A 5
43 Mossdale.........D 7
47 Mossend........C 12
38 Mosser...........C 4
47 Mossgiel.........F 9
49 Mosshouses.......E 8
43 Mosslands.......B 11
31 Mossley, Ches.....D 7
35 Mossley, Lancs....G 8
30 Mossley Hill......B 3
44 Mosspeeble.......D 2
56 Moss-side........D 4
58 Mosstodloch......B 1
7 Mosterton.........F 8
29 Mostyn..........B 11
7 Motcombe.......D 11
5 Mothecombe......L 5
47 Motherwell......D 12
18 Mottingham......G 4
8 Mottisfont.......C 5
8 Mottistone.......H 5
35 Mottram.........H 8
30 Mouldsworth.....C 4
52 Moulin...........A 4
52 Moulinearn.......B 4
17 Moulsford.......F 7
23 Moulsoe........H 12
30 Moulton, Ches....C 5
14 Moulton, Glam....G 4
24 Moulton, Lincs....C 4
26 Moulton, Norf....E 7
23 Moulton,
Northants......E 11
25 Moulton, Suffolk..J 8
40 Moulton, Yorks...E 3
24 Moulton Chapel...D 4
25 Moulton St. Michael
F 5
24 Moulton Seas End.C 4
57 Moulzie..........L 8
44 Mounces.........D 5
58 Mounie Castle....E 5
3 Mount...........C 8
2 Mount Ambrose...E 4
27 Mount Bures.....M 2
2 Mount Hawke....E 4
48 Mount Lothian...D 5
49 Mount Pleasant,
Berwick.......D 10
31 Mount Pleasant,
Derbyshire ....E 11
29 Mount Pleasant,
Flintshire......C 11
14 Mount Pleasant,
Glamorgan.....D 4
8 Mount Pleasant,
Hampshire.......F 4
17 Mount Pleasant,
Hampshire.....H 7
27 Mount Pleasant,
Suffolk.........G 8
22 Mount Pleasant,
Worcestershire..F 3
8 Mount Sorrel.....D 2
35 Mount Tabor.....D 9
45 Mountain.........B 8
14 Mountain Ash....D 4
48 Mountain Cross...E 4
12 Mountain Water..E 3
48 Mountbenger.....G 6
58 Mountblairy......B 4
10 Mountfield........F 6
56 Mountgerald......D 1
2 Mountjoy........D 6
18 Mountnessing.....D 6
15 Mounton.........E 8
58 Mountsolie.......B 7
23 Mountsorrel......A 9
2 Mousehole.......G 2
43 Mouswald.......D 11
31 Mow Cop........D 7
49 Mowhaugh......G 10
23 Mowsley........C 10
59 Mowtie..........H 6
55 Moy, Inverness....L 5
55 Moy, Inverness....L 8
56 Moy, Inverness....F 3
56 Moy Hall........F 3

56 Moy House......D 6
55 Moy Lodge......L 8
56 Moybeg........F 3
55 Moyle.........H 3
8 Moyles Court....E 3
12 Moylgrove.....C 5
46 Muasdale......E 2
15 Much Birch....A 8
21 Much Cowarne..H 11
15 Much Dewchurch.A 8
18 Much Hadham...B 4
34 Much Hoole....A 5
15 Much Marcle...A 10
21 Much Wenlock..B 11
59 Muchalls......H 6
7 Muchelney.....D 8
3 Muchlarnick...D 9
54 Muchrachd.....F 6
56 Muckernich....D 2
42 Muckfoot......C 3
19 Mucking.......F 7
7 Muckleford....G 9
30 Mucklestone...F 6
30 Muckleton....H 4
58 Muckletown...E 3
22 Muckley Corner..B 4
33 Muckton......B 10
60 Mudale.......D 6
4 Muddiford....B 4
10 Muddles Green..G 4
8 Mudeford....G 3
7 Mudford.....D 9
7 Mudgley......B 8
47 Mugdock....B 10
62 Mugeary.....D 4
31 Mugginton....F 11
45 Muggleswick....H 9
61 Muie.......F 7
57 Muir......K 6
54 Muir of Fairburn..D 8
58 Muir of Fowlis..F 3
56 Muir of Ord....E 1
58 Muirden......B 4 7
48 Muirfoot......D 2
53 Muirhead, Angus..D 8
53 Muirhead, Fife..E 9
53 Muirhead, Fife...G 7
59 Muirhead, Kinc...L 5
47 Muirhead, Lan..B 11
47 Muirhouses, Lan. D 11
48 Muirhouses,
    W. Lothian....A 3
47 Muirkirk.......G 11
47 Muirmill......A 12
53 Muirsdrum....C 10
55 Muirshearlich....L 5
47 Muirshield....D 10
59 Muirskie......H 6
58 Muirtack, Aber...C 5
58 Muirtack, Aber...D 7
59 Muirton, Angus..L 4
52 Muirton, Perth..E 6
56 Muirton, Ross &
    Cromarty.....C 3
54 Muirton Mains...D 8
52 Muirton of
    Ardblair....C 6
52 Muirtown......F 4
58 Muiryfold.....C 5
43 Muiryhill.....A 9
39 Muker.......E 11
26 Mulbarton.....E 5
58 Mulben......C 1
41 Mulgrave....D 8
2 Mullion.....H 4
55 Mullochbuie....L 1
13 Mumbles....H 9
33 Mumby......C 12
21 Munderfield Row G 12
21 Munderfield
    Stocks.....G 12
26 Mundesley.....B 6
26 Mundford.....F 1
26 Mundham.....F 6
19 Mundon Hill..D 8
55 Munerigie....J 6
60 Mungasdale....G 2
38 Mungrisdale....B 6
56 Munlochy....D 2
47 Munnoch......D 7
21 Munsley......H 12
21 Munslow....D 10
21 Munslow Aston..D 10
5 Murchington....G 6
17 Murcott......C 7
21 Murkle.......A 11
55 Murlaggan, Inver..K 4
55 Murlaggan, Inver..L 7
48 Murrayfield,
    Midlothian....B 5
52 Murrayfield, Perth.D 5
43 Murraythwaite...D 12
24 Murrow......E 5

17 Mursley.........A 9
59 Murthil.........L 2
52 Murthly........C 6
52 Murthly Castle...C 5
45 Murton, Dur.....H 12
49 Murton,
    Northumb....E 12
39 Murton, Westmor..C 9
36 Murton, Yorks...B 4
40 Murton Grange...F 5
6 Musbury.......G 6
41 Muscoates.....G 7
48 Musselburgh....B 6
32 Muston, Leics....F 5
41 Muston, Yorks...G 11
22 Mustow Green....E 2
43 Mutehill.......G 7
27 Mutford......G 8
52 Muthill.......E 4
6 Mutterton......F 4
21 Muxton......A 12
61 Mybster......B 11
13 Myddfai......D 11
30 Myddle......H 3
13 Mydroilyn....B 8
2 Mylor Bridge.....F 5
12 Mynachlog-ddu....D 5
21 Myndtown......C 9
20 Mynydd-bach,
    Cards......E 8
15 Mynydd-bach,
    Mon........E 8
13 Mynyddygarreg...F 7
28 Mynytho......G 3
58 Myre of Bedlam...C 6
59 Myrebird.....G 5
9 Mytchett......A 10
35 Mytholmroyd....E 9
34 Mythop.......D 2
40 Myton-on-Swale..H 4
36 Naburn......C 4
11 Nackington....C 10
27 Nacton.......L 5
37 Nafferton......A 8
15 Nail Bridge
    Steam Mills....C 9
15 Nailsea.......G 8
23 Nailstone....A 7
15 Nailsworth....D 11
56 Nairn........D 4
56 Nairn, County...E 4
10 Nalderswood....D 1
2 Nancegollan....F 3
2 Nancledra.....F 2
9 Nanhurst......B 11
29 Nannerch.....C 11
32 Nanpantan....H 2
3 Nanpean......D 7
3 Nanstallon....C 7
28 Nant Peris....D 5
14 Nant-ddu......C 3
13 Nanternis.....A 7
13 Nantgaredig....E 8
14 Nantgarw.....F 4
20 Nant-glâs......F 5
29 Nantglyn.....D 9
20 Nantgwyn.....E 5
28 Nantlle......E 4
30 Nantmawr.....H 1
20 Nantmel......E 5
28 Nantmor......F 5
30 Nantwich......E 4
13 Nantybai.....C 11
14 Nant-y-Bwch....C 5
14 Nant-y-cafn....D 2
14 Nant-y-derry....D 6
13 Nant-y-ffin....D 9
14 Nantyffyllon....E 2
14 Nantyglo......C 5
21 Nant-y-
    Meichiaid....A 7
14 Nant-y-moel....E 3
28 Nant-y-pandy....C 6
17 Naphill......D 9
35 Nappa.......B 7
23 Napton on the
    Hill........F 8
12 Narberth......E 4
23 Narborough, Leics.B 8
24 Narborough, Norf..E 1
3 Narkurs......D 10
50 Narrachan......F 6
28 Nasareth......E 4
23 Naseby......D 10
17 Nash, Bucks.....A 8
21 Nash, Herefs....F 8
15 Nash, Mon......F 7
21 Nash, Salop....E 11
24 Nassington.....F 2
18 Nasty.......B 4
4 Natcott......D 2
34 Nateby, Lancs....C 3
39 Nateby, Westmor. D 10

39 Natland......F 7
27 Naughton......K 3
16 Naunton, Glos....B 2
22 Naunton, Worcs...H 2
22 Naunton
    Beauchamp....G 3
54 Naust.......B 2
33 Navenby.......D 7
18 Navestock.....D 5
18 Navestock Side...D 5
61 Navidale......E 10
41 Nawton......G 7
27 Nayland......M 3
19 Naze Park......B 12
18 Nazeing......C 4
8 Neacroft......F 3
64 Neap........D 7
31 Near Cotton....E 9
38 Near Sawrey....F 6
40 Neasham.....D 4
13 Neath.......G 11
13 Neath Abbey....G 10
31 Neather Heage...E 12
26 Neatishead....C 6
18 Nebo, Angl.....A 4
28 Nebo, Anglesey...E 4
26 Nebo, Cards.....F 1
29 Nebo, Denb.....E 7
26 Necton......E 2
60 Nedd.......D 3
27 Nedging......K 3
27 Nedging Tye....K 3
27 Needham......G 5
27 Needham Market..K 4
25 Needingworth....H 4
31 Needlewood....H 10
21 Neen Savage....E 12
21 Neen Sollars....E 12
21 Nenton......D 11
28 Nefyn.......F 3
23 Neithrop......H 8
21 Nelly Andrews
    Green.......A 8
14 Nelson, Glam....E 4
35 Nelson, Lancs....C 7
45 Nelson Village....E 10
48 Nemphlar......E 1
15 Nempnett
    Thrubwell....H 8
39 Nenthall......A 10
39 Nenthead......A 10
49 Nenthorn......F 9
29 Nercwys......D 11
47 Nerston......D 11
35 Nesfield......B 9
49 Nesbit.......F 12
30 Ness.......C 2
30 Nesscliffe....H 3
30 Neston, Ches....B 2
15 Neston, Wilts....G 11
31 Nether Alderley...C 7
49 Nether Blainslie...E 8
31 Nether Booth...B 10
49 Nether
    Brotherstone....D 7
32 Nether Broughton.H 4
39 Nether Burrow...H 8
44 Nether Cassock...C 1
7 Nether Cerne....F 10
59 Nether Contlaw...G 6
43 Nether
    Craigenputtock..C 9
58 Nether Crimond..E 6
48 Nether Dalgliesh..H 5
58 Nether Dallachy...A 1
6 Nether Exe......F 3
48 Nether Fingland..H 2
58 Nether Glasslaw...B 6
43 Nether Gribton...D 10
53 Nether Handwick..C 8
36 Nether Haugh....G 2
23 Nether Heyford...F 10
44 Nether Hindhope..B 6
48 Nether Howcleugh H 3
39 Nether Kellet....H 7
58 Nether Kinmundy..C 8
47 Nether Kirkton...D 9
32 Nether Langwith..C 3
58 Nether Leask.....D 8
47 Nether Newton...E 10
31 Nether Padley....B 11
58 Nether Park.....B 7
59 Nether Pitforthie..J 6
36 Nether Poppleton..B 3
40 Nether Silton....F 5
6 Nether Stowey....F 2
59 Nether Thaneston.K 4
53 Nether Urquhart..F 7
8 Nether Wallop....B 3
22 Nether Whitacre..C 6
48 Nether
    Whitecleuch....G 1
17 Nether Winchendon F 11
16 Nether Worton...A 5

8 Netheravon......A 3
58 Netherbrae......B 5
48 Netherburn......E 1
7 Netherbury......F 8
44 Netherby, Cumb...F 2
35 Netherby, Yorks..C 11
4 Nethercott......B 4
15 Netherend......D 9
10 Netherfield......F 6
8 Netherhampton...C 3
49 Netherhowden....D 7
48 Netherlaw......E 8
59 Netherley......H 6
58 Nethermill, Aber...D 8
43 Nethermill, Dumf..C 10
43 Nethermiln......A 11
58 Nethermuir......C 7
47 Netherplace......D 10
22 Netherseal......A 6
16 Netherstreet......H 1
47 Netherthird, Ayr..G 10
43 Netherthird, Kirk..F 8
35 Netherthong......F 10
47 Netherton......F 11
59 Netherton, Angus..L 3
5 Netherton, Devon.J 8
15 Netherton, Hants..H 5
48 Netherton, Lan....G 2
47 Netherton, Lancs.D 12
34 Netherton, Lancs..G 2
45 Netherton,
    Northumb....B 8
52 Netherton, Perth..B 6
22 Netherton, Staffs...C 3
47 Netherton, Stir...A 10
22 Netherton, Worcs..H 3
35 Netherton, Yorks. F 10
35 Netherton, Yorks. F 11
64 Nethertown,
    Caithness......F 2
38 Nethertown,
    Cumberland...D 23
57 Nethy Bridge....G 6
8 Netley.......E 6
8 Netley Marsh....E 5
17 Nettlebed......E 8
7 Nettlebridge....A 10
7 Nettlecombe,
    Dorset......G 8
9 Nettlecombe I.o.W.H 7
6 Nettlecombe, Som. C 4
17 Nettleden......C 11
33 Nettleham......C 7
10 Nettlestead......C 6
10 Nettlestead Green..C 5
45 Nettlesworth....H 10
37 Nettleton, Lincs...G 9
15 Nettleton, Wilts...F 11
5 Netton, Devon...L 4
8 Netton, Wilts.....B 3
14 Neuadd, Brec.....C 4
20 Neuadd, Mont....B 6
20 Neuadd-ddu......E 5
19 Nevendon......E 7
12 Nevern......C 4
43 New Abbey......E 10
58 New Aberdour....A 6
18 New Addington....H 4
9 New Alresford...C 7
53 New Alyth......B 7
32 New Annesley....E 2
10 New Ash Green....B 5
18 New Barnet......D 3
49 New Belses......G 8
45 New Berwick....A 9
23 New Bilton......E 8
33 New Bolingbroke D 10
23 New Bradwell...H 11
32 New Brampton....C 1
40 New Brancepeth...A 2
43 New Bridge,
    Dumf......D 10
36 New Bridge, Yorks. E 4
30 New Brighton,
    Cheshire.....A 2
29 New Brighton,
    Flintshire.....D 11
32 New Brinsley....E 2
26 New Buckenham..F 4
58 New Byth......B 6
26 New Catton....E 5
10 New Chapel....D 2
32 New Clipstone....D 3
26 New Costessey....E 5
43 New Cowper....G 12
20 New Cross......E 2
39 New Cumnock...H 11
58 New Deer......C 6
45 New Delaval....E 11
17 New Denham....F 11
2 New Downs......E 4

23 New Duston.....F 10
36 New Earswick....B 4
36 New Edlington....G 3
56 New Elgin......D 8
37 New Ellerby.....C 9
22 New End........F 4
30 New Ferry......B 2
36 New Fryston....D 2
43 New Galloway....D 7
2 New Grimsby....D 2
45 New Haggerston..B 11
45 New Hartley....E 11
12 New Hedges....G 5
45 New Herrington..H 11
35 New Hey......F 8
16 New Hinksey....D 6
26 New Holkham....B 2
37 New Holland....E 8
38 New Hotel......E 5
45 New Horton
    Grange......E 10
32 New Houghton,
    Derbyshire.....D 2
26 New Houghton,
    Norfolk......C 1
39 New Houses.....H 10
39 New Hutton......F 8
10 New Hythe......B 6
13 New Inn, Carm....C 8
15 New Inn, Mon....D 8
39 New Inn, Yorks..H 10
21 New Invention....E 8
54 New Kelso......E 3
58 New Kendal.....E 6
45 New Lambton....H 11
48 New Lanark......E 2
34 New Lane......F 3
33 New Leake......D 11
58 New Leeds......B 7
34 New Longton....E 4
42 New Luce......E 3
49 New Mains,
    E. Lothian....A 8
48 New Mains, Lan..F 1
59 New Mains of Ury J 6
18 New Malden......C 4
40 New Marske....C 6
30 New Marton....G 2
59 New Mill, Kinc...J 5
16 New Mill, Wilts..H 3
35 New Mill, Yorks..F 10
2 New Mills, Corn..D 6
31 New Mills, Derby..B 8
20 New Mills, Mont..B 6
8 New Milton......F 4
27 New Mistley....M 4
12 New Moat......D 4
47 New Monkland...C 12
45 New Mousen....C 12
58 New Pitsligo.....B 6
2 New Polzeath....B 6
47 New Prestwick....G 8
13 New Quay......A 7
21 New Radnor....F 7
39 New Rent......B 7
11 New Romney....F 9
36 New Rossington..G 4
20 New Row......E 3
8 New Sarum......C 3
52 New Sauchie....H 4
52 New Scone......E 6
50 New Selma......D 6
63 New Shawbost....B 4
45 New Shoreston..D 12
47 New Stevenston..C 12
8 New Swanage....H 2
63 New Tolsta......B 6
17 New Town, Berks..G 7
8 New Town, Dorset.
    D 2
7 New Town, Dorset.
    D 11
49 New Town,
    E. Lothian....B 7
17 New Town, Hants. H 7
10 New Town, Sussex.F 3
16 New Town, Wilts. G 4
14 New Tredegar....D 5
48 New Trows......F 1
32 New Tupton......D 1
63 New Valley......C 5
37 New Waltham....G 10
25 New Wimpole....K 4
49 New Winton......B 7
16 New Yatt......C 5
33 New York......E 9
45 New York......F 11
64 Newark......A 4
24 Newark......E 3
32 Newark......E 5
47 Newarthill......C 1
48 Newbattle......C 6
39 Newbiggin, Cumb..B 7

44 Newbiggin, Cumb. H 4
39 Newbiggin, Dur...B 11
45 Newbiggin, Dur...H 9
38 Newbiggin, Lancs..H 5
45 Newbiggin,
    Northumb.....G 8
39 Newbiggin,
    Westmorland...B 8
39 Newbiggin, Yorks. F 11
39 Newbiggin, Yorks.G 12
45 Newbiggin-by-the-
    Sea........D 11
39 Newbiggin on Lune E 9
59 Newbigging, Angus K1
49 Newbigging, Ber...D 8
48 Newbigging, Lancs.E 3
32 Newbold, Derby...C 1
32 Newbold, Leics....H 1
23 Newbold on Avon.D 8
22 Newbold on Stour.G 6
22 Newbold Pacey....F 6
23 Newbold Verdon..B 8
28 Newborough, Angl.D 4
24 Newborough,
    Hunts......E 3
31 Newborough,
    Staffordshire...H 10
45 Newbottle, Dur...H 11
23 Newbottle,
    Northants......H 8
27 Newbourn......L 5
2 Newbridge, Corn...F 1
3 Newbridge, Corn. C 10
29 Newbridge, Denb. F 12
8 Newbridge, Hants..E 4
9 Newbridge, I.o.W. G 6
48 Newbridge,
    Midlothian....B 4
14 Newbridge, Mon...E 5
15 Newbridge, Mon...E 7
12 Newbridge, Pemb..D 3
20 Newbridge on Wye F 7
45 Newbrough......F 7
58 Newburgh, Aber..B 7
58 Newburgh, Aber...E 7
53 Newburgh, Fife...E 7
48 Newburgh, Sel...G 6
49 Newburgh Priory..G 5
45 Newburn......E 11
45 Newburn......G 10
16 Newbury......G 5
39 Newby, Westmor..C 8
40 Newby, N. Riding.D 5
41 Newby, N. Riding F 10
39 Newby, W. Riding.H 9
38 Newby Bridge....G 6
44 Newby East......G 3
44 Newby West......H 2
40 Newby Wiske....F 4
15 Newcastle, Mon...C 7
21 Newcastle, Salop...D 8
12 Newcastle Emlyn..C 6
31 Newcastle-under-Lyme
    F 7
45 Newcastle upon Tyne.
    F 10
44 Newcastleton....D 3
12 Newchapel, Pemb..C 6
31 Newchapel, Staffs..E 7
13 Newchurch, Carm. E 7
9 Newchurch, I.o.W.H 7
11 Newchurch, Kent..E 9
35 Newchurch, Lancs. C 7
35 Newchurch, Lancs. E 7
15 Newchurch, Mon...E 8
21 Newchurch, Rad...G 7
31 Newchurch,
    Staffordshire...H 10
6 Newcott......E 6
10 Newdigate......D 1
11 Newell Green....G 9
11 Newenden......E 7
15 Newent......B 10
11 Newerne......D 9
43 Newfield, Dumf...E 12
40 Newfield, Dur....B 2
45 Newfield, Dur....H 10
43 Newfield, Kirk....E 9
56 Newfield, Ross &
    Cromarty......B 3
9 Newfound......A 7
12 Newgale......E 2
36 Newgate......A 3
18 Newgate Street....C 3
64 Newgord......A 8
30 Newhall, Ches....A 8
31 Newhall, Derby...H 11
48 Newhall, Peeb....F 6
56 Newhallpoint....F 4
18 Newham, London .F 4
45 Newham,
    Northumb.....E 12
45 Newham Hall....D 12

MAP

10 Newhaven........H 3
31 Newhaven House.D 10
41 Newholm.........D 8
48 Newhouse........C 1
45 Newhouses.......E 8
10 Newick..........F 3
11 Newingreen......D 10
11 Newington, Kent..B 7
11 Newington, Kent.D 10
32 Newington, Notts.A 4
17 Newington, Oxon..D 7
21 Newington, Salop.D 9
59 Newkirk.........G 2
37 Newland, E. Riding D 7
15 Newland, Glos....C 9
6 Newland, Som....B 2
36 Newland, W. Riding.....E 5
22 Newland, Worcs...G 2
53 Newlandhead.....C 9
47 Newlands, Ayr...G 8
43 Newlands, Dumf..C 10
47 Newlands, Lan...D 11
56 Newlands, Moray..E 8
45 Newlands, Northumb.....G 9
44 Newlands, Rox....D 3
61 Newlands of Geise A 10
2 Newlyn..........G 2
2 Newlyn East.....D 5
58 Newmachar.......F 6
48 Newmains........D 1
63 Newmarket, Ross & Cromarty.....C 5
25 Newmarket, Suff..J 7
58 Newmill, Banff...B 2
2 Newmill, Corn...F 2
44 Newmill, Rox....B 3
59 Newmill of Inshewan.....L 2
35 Newmillerdam....F 12
48 Newmills, Fife...A 3
48 Newmills, Midloth. C 4
15 Newmills, Mon....D 8
56 Newmills, Ross & Cromarty....C 2
58 Newmills of Boyne.B 3
52 Newmiln.........D 6
47 Newmilns.......F 10
15 Newnham, Glos..C 10
9 Newnham, Hants..A 8
25 Newnham, Herts..L 3
11 Newnham, Kent...B 8
23 Newnham, Northants F 9
21 Newnham Bridge.E 11
53 Newpark.........C 9
61 Newport, Caith...E 10
4 Newport, Devon..C 4
25 Newport, Essex..M 6
15 Newport, Glos...E 10
8 Newport, I. o. W..G 6
14 Newport, Mon....F 7
26 Newport, Norfolk.D 8
12 Newport, Pemb...C 4
30 Newport, Salop..H 6
36 Newport, Yorks..D 6
53 Newport-on-Tay..D 9
23 Newport Pagnell.H 12
9 Newpound Com..C 11
2 Newquay.........D 5
52 Newrow..........H 4
35 Newsam Green...D 12
58 Newseat.........D 4
34 Newsham, Lancs..D 4
40 Newsham, N. Riding......D 1
40 Newsham, N. Riding.....G 4
36 Newsholme, E. Riding......D 5
35 Newsholme, W. Riding.....B 7
36 Newsholme, W. Riding.....C 9
45 Newstead, Northumb.....E 12
32 Newstead, Notts...E 2
49 Newstead, Rox...F 8
36 Newthorpe......D 3
58 Newton, Aber.....C 8
61 Newton, Caith...C 12
25 Newton, Cambs..K 5
30 Newton, Ches.....C 3
30 Newton, Ches.....C 3
30 Newton, Ches.....D 4
35 Newton, Ches.....G 8
32 Newton, Derby...D 2
7 Newton, Dorset..E 11
43 Newton, Dumf...B 12
41 Newton, E. Riding H 9
13 Newton, Glam....H 9
14 Newton, Glam....G 2

15 Newton, Herefs...A 7
21 Newton, Herefs...G 10
56 Newton, Inver....E 3
47 Newton, Lan...C 11
48 Newton, Lan.....F 2
34 Newton, Lancs...D 2
34 Newton, Lancs...D 3
38 Newton, Lancs...H 5
39 Newton, Lancs...H 8
24 Newton, Lincs...B 1
56 Newton, Moray...C 7
24 Newton, Norfolk..D 5
26 Newton, Norfolk..D 1
40 Newton, N. Riding D 6
23 Newton, Northants. D 12
45 Newton, Northumb. B 8
45 Newton, Northumb. G 8
32 Newton, Notts....F 4
52 Newton, Perth....D 4
56 Newton, Ross & Cromarty.....C 3
56 Newton, Ross & Cromarty.....E 1
49 Newton, Rox......F 8
6 Newton, Som.....B 5
31 Newton, Staffs...H 9
27 Newton, Suffolk..L 2
60 Newton, Suther...D 4
23 Newton, War......D 8
48 Newton, W. Loth..B 4
34 Newton, W. Riding B 6
36 Newton, W. Riding D 2
8 Newton, Wilts....D 4
5 Newton Abbot...J 7
43 Newton Arlosh...F 12
40 Newton Aycliffe..C 3
40 Newton Bewley...C 5
23 Newton Blossomville G 12
25 Newton Bromshold J 1
23 Newton Burgoland A 7
33 Newton by Toft...B 7
5 Newton Ferrers...L 4
26 Newton Flotman..F 5
23 Newton Harcourt..B 9
58 Newton House....E 4
34 Newton-le-Willows, Lancashire......H 4
40 Newton-le-Willows, Yorkshire......F 2
36 Newton Kyme....C 2
17 Newton Longville..A 9
47 Newton Mearns...D 10
40 Newton Morrell...D 3
41 Newton Mulgrave.D 8
12 Newton Mountain.F 3
50 Newton of Ardtoe.A 4
52 Newton of Balcanquhal....F 6
53 Newton of Falkland F 7
58 Newton of Murcar F 7
60 Newton of Ochtow G 5
52 Newton of Pitcairns F 5
36 Newton-on-Ouse..A 3
41 Newton-on-Rawcliffe F 8
45 Newton-on-the-Moor C 10
32 Newton on Trent..C 5
6 Newton Poppleford G 4
17 Newton Purcell...A 7
22 Newton Regis.....A 6
39 Newton Reigny....B 7
49 Newton St. Boswells F 8
4 Newton St. Cyres..F 7
26 Newton St. Faith..D 5
15 Newton St. Loe..H 10
4 Newton St. Petrock E 3
31 Newton Solney...H 11
8 Newton Stacey...B 6
42 Newton Stewart...E 5
8 Newton Toney....B 4
4 Newton Tracey...C 4
47 Newton upon Ayr.G 8
36 Newton upon Derwent.....B 5
9 Newton Valence...A 10
43 Newtonairds......D 9
58 Newtongarry Croft D 3
48 Newtongrange....C 6
59 Newtonmill......L 3
57 Newtonmore......J 3
31 Newtown, Ches...B 8
30 Newtown, Ches...E 5
2 Newtown, Corn...G 4
44 Newtown, Cumb..G 2
44 Newtown, Cumb..G 3
4 Newtown, Devon..C 6
8 Newtown, Dorset..G 2
15 Newtown, Glos...A 12

15 Newtown, Glos...D 10
8 Newtown, Hants...D 4
9 Newtown, Hants...D 7
8 Newtown, Hants...E 4
9 Newtown, Hants...E 7
16 Newtown, Hants...H 6
21 Newtown, Herefs. G 10
21 Newtown, Herefs. H 11
55 Newtown, Inver...J 7
38 Newtown, I. o. M..H 2
8 Newtown, I. o. W..G 5
34 Newtown, Lancs...E 4
20 Newtown, Mont...C 6
56 Newtown, Moray...C 7
45 Newtown, Northumb......A 8
45 Newtown, Northumb......C 8
49 Newtown, Northumb.....F 12
30 Newtown, Salop...D 7
31 Newtown, Staffs...D 7
31 Newtown, Staffs...D 9
39 Newtown, Westmorland...C 7
7 Newtown, Wilts..C 12
23 Newtown Linfold..A 8
48 Newtown of Covington....E 3
58 Newtown of Melrose......A 5
53 Newtyle.........C 8
12 Neyland.........F 3
15 Nibley..........F 10
6 Nicholashayne...E 5
13 Nicholaston.....H 8
44 Nickie's Hill....F 4
35 Nidd............A 11
59 Nigg, Aber......G 7
56 Nigg, Ross & Cromarty.....C 4
56 Nigg Station.....B 4
6 Nightcott.......D 2
18 Nine Ashes......D 6
48 Nine Mile Burn...D 4
44 Ninebanks.......H 6
10 Ninfield........G 6
8 Ningwood........G 5
49 Nisbet..........G 9
43 Nithside........D 10
8 Niton...........H 8
30 No Man's Heath, Cheshire......E 4
22 No Man's Heath, Warwickshire...A 6
2 No Man's Land, Cornwall......C 6
4 No Man's Land, Devon........E 7
18 Noak Hill.......E 5
48 Noblehall.......E 4
48 Noblehouse......D 5
21 Nobold..........A 10
23 Nobottle........F 10
33 Nocton..........D 8
16 Noke............C 6
12 Nolton..........E 2
12 Nolton Haven....E 2
30 Noneley.........G 3
11 Nonington.......C 11
39 Nook............G 8
30 Norbury, Ches....E 4
31 Norbury, Derby...F 9
21 Norbury, Salop...C 9
30 Norbury, Staffs...H 6
24 Nordelph........E 4
35 Norden.........F 7
8 Norden Heath....H 1
21 Nordley.........C 12
16 Nore Marsh......F 2
26 Norfolk, Co......D 4
49 Norham.........E 11
30 Norley.........C 4
8 Norley Wood....F 5
24 Norman Cross...F 3
33 Normanby, Lincs..A 7
36 Normanby, Lincs..E 6
41 Normanby, Yorks. G 7
37 Normanby le Wold H 9
9 Normandy.......A 10
10 Norman's Bay....G 6
6 Norman's Green..F 4
8 Normansland.....D 4
31 Normanton, Derbyshire...G 11
32 Normanton, Leics. F 5
32 Normanton, Lincs..F 6
32 Normanton, Notts. E 4
36 Normanton, Yorks. E 2
23 Normanton le Heath......A 7
32 Normanton on Soar...........H 2

32 Normanton on the Wolds.........G 3
32 Normanton on Trent..........C 5
34 Normoss.........C 2
9 Norney..........B 10
15 Norrington Com. H 12
31 Norris Hill......H 11
32 North Anston....B 2
34 North Ashton....G 4
16 North Aston.....A 6
58 North Atrochie...D 7
8 North Baddesley..D 5
51 North Ballachulish. B 8
7 North Barrow....C 9
26 North Barsham...B 2
19 North Benfleet...E 7
9 North Bersted...F 10
49 North Berwick...A 8
9 North Boarhunt..E 7
5 North Bovey.....G 6
47 North Brackenridge E 12
7 North Bradley...A 12
5 North Brentor...H 4
7 North Brewham..C 10
7 North Buckland..B 4
26 North Burlingham. D 7
7 North Cadbury...D 9
32 North Carlton, Lincolnshire....B 6
32 North Carlton, Nottinghamshire B 3
46 North Carrine....H 2
36 North Cave......D 6
16 North Cerney....C 1
9 North Chapel....C 11
8 North Charford...D 3
45 North Charlton...A 10
7 North Cheriton...D 10
7 North Chideock...G 8
36 North Cliffe.....C 6
32 North Clifton....C 5
37 North Coates....G 11
33 North Cockerington A 10
7 North Coker.....E 9
32 North Collingham. D 5
10 North Common...F 3
14 North Cornelly...F 2
50 North Corry.....B 5
58 North Cottown...F 5
26 North Cove......F 8
43 North Cowshaw..C 11
40 North Cowton....E 3
44 North Craigs.....E 1
23 North Crawley...H 12
18 North Cray......G 5
26 North Creake....B 2
7 North Curry.....D 7
37 North Dalton....B 7
3 North Darley....B 10
35 North Deighton..B 12
47 North Drumboy...D 10
36 North Duffield...C 5
33 North Elkington..A 10
26 North Elmham....C 3
36 North Elmsall....F 3
7 North End, Bucks..A 9
17 North End, Bucks..E 8
7 North End, Dorset. D 11
18 North End, Essex..B 6
9 North End, Hants..F 8
16 North End, Hants..H 5
34 North End, Lancs. G 2
24 North End, Lincs..B 3
45 North End, Northumb. C 9
6 North End, Som...D 6
15 North End, Som..G 11
15 North End, Som..H 7
9 North End, Sussex E 12
37 North End, Yorks. D10
54 North Erradale...B 1
6 North Esworthy...D 2
19 North Fambridge.D 8
46 North Feorline...F 4
37 North Ferriby....E 7
37 North Frodingham B 8
63 North Galson....A 5
64 North Gluss.....C 7
8 North Gorley....E 3
58 North Gorrachie..B 5
26 North Green.....F 5
44 North Greenhill..F 4
41 North Grimston..H 8
10 North Halling....B 6
14 North Hallington..F 11
47 North Hayling...F 9
45 North Hazelrigg..C 12
9 North Heath....D 12
3 North Hill......B 9

16 North Hinksey....D 6
10 North Holmwood..C 1
56 North Hourat....D 8
5 North Huish.....K 6
32 North Hykeham..D 6
12 North Johnston...F 3
37 North Kelsey....G 8
56 North Kessock...E 2
37 North Killingholme E 9
40 North Kilvington..G 4
23 North Kilworth...D 9
58 North Kinmundy..F 6
58 North Kirkton...C 8
33 North Kyme......E 8
10 North Lancing...G 1
40 North Lees......H 3
23 North Luffenham. B 12
16 North Lopham...G 3
45 North Lyham....C 12
9 North Marden...D 9
17 North Marston...B 8
48 North Middleton, Midlothian....C 6
49 North Middleton, Northumb.....G 12
4 North Molton....C 6
58 North Monkshill..C 5
16 North Moreton...B 5
9 North Mundham..F 10
32 North Muskham..D 5
37 North Newbald...G 4
23 North Newington. H 7
6 North Newton, Somerset......C 6
16 North Newton, Wiltshire......H 2
15 North Nibley....C 9
9 North Oakley....A 7
18 North Ockendon..E 6
40 North Ormesby...C 5
33 North Ormsby...A 10
40 North Otterington. F 4
37 North Owersby...H 8
7 North Perrott....E 8
6 North Petherton..C 6
3 North Petherwin..A 10
26 North Pickenham.E 1
22 North Piddle....G 3
7 North Poorton...F 8
6 North Quarme....C 3
48 North Queensferry. A 4
4 North Radworthy.C 6
33 North Rauceby...F 7
35 North Rigton....B 11
31 North Rode......D 7
64 North Roe......B 7
24 North Runcton...D 7
64 North Sandwick..B 8
38 North Scale.....H 4
32 North Scarle....D 6
45 N. Seaton Colliery D 11
63 North Shawbost..B 4
50 North Shian.....C 6
45 North Shields....F 11
19 North Shoebury..E 9
34 North Shore.....D 2
48 North Shortcleugh H 2
38 North Side, Cumb. B 2
24 North Side, Hunts..E 4
41 North Skelton...D 2
37 North Somercotes G 12
40 North Stainley...G 3
39 North Stainmore. D 10
9 North Stoke.....E 11
15 North Stoke, Oxon. G 10
17 North Stoke, Sussex F 7
17 North Street, Berks. G 7
9 North Street, Hants. C 8
45 North Sunderland D 12
4 North Tamerton..F 2
4 North Tawton...D 5
37 North Thoresby..G 10
8 North Tidworth...A 4
45 North Togston...C 10
63 North Tolsta.....B 6
26 North Tuddenham D 3
45 North Walbottle. F 10
26 North Walsham...C 6
9 North Waltham...B 7
9 North Warnborough A 9
59 North Water Bri..L 4
61 North Watten...B 11
18 North Weald Bassett D 5
32 North Wheatley..B 5
15 North Wick......H 9

5 North Whilborough J 7
33 North Willingham. A 8
32 North Wingfield..D 1
32 North Witham....H 6
7 North Wootton, Dorset.......E 10
24 North Wootton, Norfolk......C 7
7 North Wootton, Somerset......B 9
15 North Wraxall...G 11
16 North Wroughton.F 3
45 North Yardhope..C 7
40 North Yorkshire, Co. F 5
40 Northallerton....F 4
4 Northam, Devon...C 3
8 Northam, Hants...E 6
23 Northampton....F 11
23 Northamptonshire, County.......E 11
18 Northaw.........D 3
24 Northborough Peakirk.......E 3
11 Northbourne.....C 12
8 Northbrook......B 6
17 Northchurch.....C 10
5 Northcott.......G 2
23 Northend.......G 7
59 Northfield, Aber...G 6
49 Northfield, Ber....C 11
22 Northfield, War...D 4
10 Northfleet......A 5
11 Northiam.......F 7
25 Northill........K 3
9 Northington....B 7
33 Northlands......E 10
16 Northleach......C 2
6 Northleigh......G 5
4 Northlew.......F 4
16 Northmoor......D 5
6 Northmoor Green or Moorland......C 6
53 Northmuir......B 8
9 Northney.......F 9
18 Northolt........E 1
29 Northop........C 11
29 Northophall.....C 12
24 Northorpe, Holl...B 3
24 Northorpe, Kest...D 2
37 Northorpe, Lind...G 7
7 Northover, Som...B 8
7 Northover, Som...D 8
35 Northowram.....D 10
8 Northport.......G 1
26 Northrepps......B 5
63 Northton.......H 1
64 Northtown......D 3
45 Northumberland, County.......D 8
15 Northway, Glos...A 12
6 Northway, Som....C 5
30 Northwich......C 5
15 Northwick......F 9
24 Northwold.......F 8
8 Northwood, I. o. W.G 6
18 Northwood, Lond..E 1
30 Northwood, Salop. G 3
25 Northwood End...L 2
15 Northwood Green C 10
30 Norton, Ches....B 4
41 Norton, E. Riding. H 8
15 Norton, Glos....B 11
8 Norton, I. o. W...G 5
15 Norton, Mon....D 8
40 Norton, N. Riding. C 5
23 Norton, Northants. F 9
32 Norton, Notts....C 3
21 Norton, Rad.....F 8
21 Norton, Salop...A 11
22 Norton, Salop...B 1
21 Norton, Salop...D 10
27 Norton, Suffolk..J 3
36 Norton, W. Riding F 3
15 Norton, Wilts...F 12
22 Norton, Worcs...G 2
22 Norton, Worcs...G 4
8 Norton Bavant...B 1
31 Norton Bridge...G 7
22 Norton Canes....A 4
21 Norton Canon...H 9
32 Norton Disney...D 6
22 Norton East.....A 4
7 Norton Ferris...C 11
6 Norton Fitzwarren D 5
23 Norton Green....G 5
15 Norton Hawkfield. H 9
18 Norton Heath....D 6
30 Norton in Gales..F 5
31 Norton in the Moors.........E 7
23 Norton Juxta Twycross......A 7

MAP

40 Norton-le-Clay....H 4
22 Norton Lindsey.....F 6
15 Norton Malreward H 9
7 Norton St. Philip.A 11
7 Norton sub Hamdon
               E 8
26 Norton Subcourse.F 7
32 Norton Woodseats.B 1
32 Norwell..........D 5
32 Norwell Woodhouse
               D 5
26 Norwich...........E 5
64 Norwich...........A 8
32 Norwood..........B 2
10 Norwood Hill.....D 1
23 Noseley.........B 10
5 Noss Mayo........L 4
40 Nosterfield......G 3
55 Nostie...........G 2
16 Notgrove.........B 2
14 Nottage..........F 1
32 Nottingham.......F 3
32 Nottinghamshire,
    County........D 4
15 Notton, Wilts...G 12
35 Notton, Yorks...F 12
19 Nounsley.........C 8
22 Noutard's Green.E 2
56 Novar House......C 2
21 Nox..............A 9
17 Nuffield.........E 7
57 Nuide...........K 3
36 Nun Monkton....A 3
36 Nunburnholme....B 6
32 Nuncargate......E 2
23 Nuneaton........C 7
16 Nuneham Courtenay
               D 6
49 Nunlands....D 12
38 Nunnery Howe...H 2
7 Nunney........B 10
41 Nunnington.....G 7
45 Nunnykirk.....D 9
37 Nunsthorpe.....F 10
40 Nunthorpe......D 5
8 Nunton........C 3
40 Nunwick.......H 3
43 Nunwood....D 10
8 Nursling......D 5
9 Nutbourne.....F 9
9 Nutbourne...D 12
10 Nuthall.......C 2
32 Nuthall.......F 2
25 Nuthampstead....M 5
10 Nuthurst......E 1
9 Nutley, Hants.B 7
10 Nutley, Sussex..E 3
36 Nutwell.......G 4
9 Nyetimber....F 10
9 Nyewood......D 9
4 Nymet Rowland..E 6
4 Nymet Tracey..F 6
15 Nympsfield.....D 11
5 Nynehead.....D 5
7 Nythe.........C 7
9 Nyton........E 10
11 Oad Street....B 7
23 Oadby.........B 9
31 Oakamoor....F 9
48 Oakbank.......C 4
14 Oakdale.......D 5
6 Oake.........D 5
22 Oaken........B 2
34 Oakenclough...B 4
21 Oakengates.....A 12
29 Oakenholt....C 12
40 Oakenshaw, Dur..A 2
35 Oakenshaw, Yorks.
               D 10
8 Oakfield, Hants..C 5
14 Oakfield, Mon....E 6
13 Oakford, Cards...A 8
6 Oakford, Devon..D 3
6 Oakfordbridge....D 3
31 Oakgrove......C 8
23 Oakham........A 12
9 Oakhanger......C 9
7 Oakhill........H 9
25 Oakington......J 5
29 Oaklands.......D 7
15 Oakle Street.....C 10
25 Oakley, Beds...K 1
17 Oakley, Bucks....C 7
8 Oakley, Dorset...F 2
52 Oakley, Fife....H 5
9 Oakley, Hants...A 7
27 Oakley, Suffolk..H 5
17 Oakley Green.....F 10
20 Oakleypark.....D 5
15 Oakleigh Lynch..D 12
16 Oaksey.........E 1
22 Oakthorpe......A 6
40 Oaktree Hill....E 4

MAP

45 Oakwood, Northumb.
               F 8
49 Oakwood, Selkirk.G 7
9 Oakwoodhill......B 12
35 Oakworth.........C 9
11 Oar..............B 9
16 Oare, Berks......G 6
6 Oare, Som........B 2
16 Oare, Wilts......H 3
6 Oareford.........B 2
33 Oasby............F 7
59 Oathlaw..........M 2
50 Oban, Argyll.....E 6
58 Oban, Inverness..K 2
58 Obliston.........B 1
7 Oborne...........D 10
56 Obsdale..........C 2
30 Occleston Green..D 5
27 Occold...........H 5
52 Ochil Hills Hosp..F 6
47 Ochiltree........G 10
52 Ochtermuthill....E 3
52 Ochtrelure.......E 3
32 Ockbrook.........G 2
17 Ockham...........H 11
50 Ockle............A 3
21 Ocle Pychard....H 11
9 Ocley............B 12
41 Octon...........H 10
7 Odcombe..........E 8
15 Odd Down........H 10
39 Oddendale.......D 8
22 Oddingley........F 3
16 Oddington, Glos..B 3
16 Oddington, Oxon..C 6
25 Odell............J 1
64 Odie.............B 4
9 Odiham...........A 9
8 Odstock..........C 3
23 Odstone..........A 7
23 Offchurch........F 7
22 Offenham.........G 4
45 Offerton.........G 11
10 Offham, Kent.....B 5
10 Offham, Sussex...G 3
25 Offord Cluny.....J 3
25 Offord D'Arcy....J 3
27 Offton...........K 4
6 Offwell..........H 5
16 Ogbourne Maizey.G 3
16 Ogbourne St. Andrew
16 Ogbourne St. George
               G 3
45 Ogle............E 9
14 Ogmore..........G 2
14 Ogmore-by-Sea...G 2
14 Ogmore Vale.....E 3
7 Okeford Fitzpaine E 11
4 Okehampton.....F 5
59 Old Aberdeen....G 7
9 Old Alresford....C 7
53 Old Balkello.....C 8
45 Old Berwick......A 9
52 Old Blair........A 4
33 Old Bolingbroke.D 10
35 Old Bramhope....C 11
31 Old Brampton....C 11
43 Old Bridge of Urr..E 8
26 Old Buckenham...F 4
16 Old Burghclere...H 6
40 Old Byland......G 6
37 Old Clee.........F 10
6 Old Cleeve......B 4
43 Old Clouden.....D 9
29 Old Colwyn......B 8
43 Old Craighouse..C 12
42 Old Dailly......B 3
32 Old Dalby.......H 4
58 Old Deer........C 7
60 Old Drumrunie Lo.
               F 3
49 Old Dryburn....E 12
36 Old Edlington...G 3
40 Old Eldon.......B 3
37 Old Ellerby.....C 9
24 Old Fletton.....F 3
36 Old Goole.......E 5
44 Old Graitney....F 2
37 Old Hall........E 10
19 Old Heath.......B 10
10 Old Heathfield..F 5
25 Old Hurst.......H 4
39 Old Hutton......F 8
2 Old Kea.........E 5
47 Old Kilpatrick..B 9
18 Old Knebworth...B 2
26 Old Lakenham....E 5
38 Old Laxey.......G 2
33 Old Leake.......E 11
45 Old Lyham.......C 12
41 Old Malton......H 8
36 Old Micklefield..D 2

MAP

8 Old Milton.......G 4
22 Old Milverton....E 6
47 Old Monkland...C 12
19 Old Montsale....D 10
45 Old Mousen.....C 12
8 Old Netley.......E 6
27 Old Newton......J 4
43 Old Orchardton..F 9
48 Old Philpstoun...B 3
40 Old Quarrington..A 3
32 Old Radford......F 3
21 Old Radnor......F 8
58 Old Rattray.....B 8
58 Old Rayne.......E 4
11 Old Romney......E 9
52 Old Scone.......D 6
36 Old Snydale.....E 2
15 Old Sodbury....F 10
33 Old Somerby.....G 7
23 Old Stratford...H 11
30 Old Swan........A 3
39 Old Tebay.......E 8
40 Old Thirsk......G 4
39 Old Town, Cumb..A 7
2 Old Town, Is. of Scilly
               D 2
45 Old Town, Northumb.
               D 7
39 Old Town, Westmor.
               G 8
35 Old Trafford.....G 7
32 Old Tupton......D 1
25 Old Warden......L 2
36 Old Weston......H 2
17 Old Windsor.....G 10
11 Old Wives Lees...C 9
17 Old Woking......H 11
60 Oldany..........D 3
22 Oldberrow.......F 5
4 Oldborough......A 5
21 Oldbury, Salop..C 12
22 Oldbury, War....C 3
22 Oldbury, War....C 6
15 Oldbury on the Hill
               E 11
15 Oldbury-upon-Severn
               E 9
14 Oldcastle, Brec..B 6
14 Oldcastle, Glam..F 2
32 Oldcotes........A 3
22 Oldfield, Worcs..F 2
35 Oldfield, Yorks..C 8
7 Oldford.........A 11
35 Oldham..........G 8
49 Oldhamstocks...B 10
15 Oldland.........G 10
58 Oldmeldrum.....E 6
58 Oldnoth.........B 3
21 Oldpark.........A 12
33 Oldshore Beg....B 3
60 Oldshore More...B 3
40 Oldstead........G 5
58 Oldtown of Ord..B 4
13 Oldway..........H 9
4 Oldways End.....D 7
58 Oldwhat.........C 6
48 Oliver..........G 4
8 Oliver's Battery.C 6
64 Ollaberry.......C 7
30 Ollerton, Ches..C 6
32 Ollerton, Notts..C 4
30 Ollerton, Salop..H 5
20 Olmarch.........C 7
23 Olney..........G 12
22 Olton...........D 5
15 Olveston........F 9
22 Ombersley.......F 2
32 Ompton..........D 4
38 Onchan..........H 2
31 Onecote.........E 9
15 Onen............C 7
18 Ongar...........D 5
24 Onger Hill......C 7
21 Onibury.........D 10
51 Onich...........A 7
14 Onllwyn.........C 2
30 Onneley.........F 6
9 Onslow Village..A 11
47 Onthank.........E 9
35 Openshaw........G 7
32 Openwoodgate....E 1
54 Opinan, Ross &
    Cromarty......C 1
60 Opinan, Ross &
    Cromarty......G 1
49 Orange Lane.....E 10
62 Orbost..........D 2
33 Orby............C 12
46 Orcadia.........C 6
1 Orchard Hill....C 9
6 Orchard Portman.D 6
8 Orcheston.......B 2
15 Orcop...........B 8

MAP

15 Orcop Hill.......A 8
62 Ord.............G 5
58 Ordens..........B 4
58 Ordhead.........F 4
59 Ordie...........G 2
58 Ordiequish......B 1
32 Ordsall.........B 4
11 Ore.............G 7
21 Oreton, Salop...D 12
21 Oreton, Worcs...F 12
30 Orford, Lancs...A 5
27 Orford, Suffolk..K 7
8 Organ Ford......G 1
64 Orgill..........D 1
22 Orgreave........A 5
11 Orlestone.......E 8
21 Orleton.........F 10
23 Orlingbury......E 12
40 Ormesby.........C 5
26 Ormesby St. Margaret
               E 8
26 Ormesby St. Michael
               D 8
60 Ormiscaig.......G 1
49 Ormiston........B 7
38 Ormley Hall.....F 2
50 Ormsaigbeg......A 2
50 Ormsaigmore.....A 2
46 Ormsary House...B 2
34 Ormskirk........F 3
63 Orosay..........F 5
64 Orphir..........D 2
31 Over Haddon....D 10
43 Over Hazelfield..G 8
39 Over Kellet.....H 7
16 Over Kiddington..B 5
4 Over Norton.....A 4
40 Over Silton.....F 5
6 Over Stowey.....B 5
7 Over Stratton...E 8
30 Over Tabley.....B 6
8 Over Wallop.....B 4
22 Over Whitacre...C 6
49 Over Whitton...G 10
32 Over Woodhouse..C 2
58 Overbister......B 4
22 Overbury........H 3
58 Overhall........C 5
58 Overhill........D 4
7 Overleigh.......C 8
22 Overley Green...F 4
30 Overpool........C 3
22 Overseal........A 6
58 Overside........B 8
11 Overland........B 9
23 Overstone......E 11
26 Overstrand......B 5
62 Osdale..........D 3
6 Ose.............D 2
32 Osgathorpe......H 2
33 Osgodby, Lincs..A 8
36 Osgodby, E. Riding,
               D 4
41 Osgodby, N. Riding,
               G 10
62 Oskaig..........D 5
50 Oskamuil........D 2
31 Osmaston........F 10
7 Osmington......H 10
7 Osmington Mills .H 10
35 Osmondthorpe...D 12
40 Osmotherley.....E 5
11 Ospringe........B 8
35 Ossett..........E 11
32 Ossington.......D 5
19 Ostend..........D 9
40 Oswaldkirk......G 6
34 Oswaldtwistle...D 6
30 Oswestry........G 2
10 Otford..........B 4
11 Otham...........C 7
7 Othery..........C 7
27 Otley, Suffolk..K 5
35 Otley, Yorks....C 10
46 Otter Ferry.....A 4
8 Otterbourne.....D 6
45 Otterburn, Northumb.
               D 7
35 Otterburn, Yorks..A 8
45 Otterburn Camp..C 7
2 Otterham........B 2
6 Otterhampton....B 5
17 Ottershaw......H 11
64 Otterswick......B 7
6 Otterton........H 4
6 Ottery St. Mary..G 5
11 Ottinge.........D 10
37 Ottringham......E 10
39 Oughtershaw....G 11
43 Oughterside....H 12
35 Oughtibridge....H 11
40 Oulston.........H 6
44 Oulton, Cumb....H 1
26 Oulton, Norfolk..C 4

MAP

31 Oulton, Staffs....G 7
26 Oulton, Suffolk..F 8
35 Oulton, Yorks...D 12
26 Oulton Broad....F 8
26 Oulton Street...C 5
25 Oundle..........G 1
39 Ousby...........B 8
61 Ousdale.........E 10
25 Ousden..........J 8
36 Ousefleet.......E 5
45 Ouston, Dur....H 10
45 Ouston, Northumb.F 9
44 Ouston, Northumb.H 6
38 Out Gate........E 6
37 Out Newton.....E 11
34 Out Rawcliffe...C 2
45 Outchester......C 12
64 Outertown.......D 1
39 Outhgill........E 10
35 Outlane.........E 9
24 Outwell.........E 6
8 Outwick.........D 3
10 Outwood, Surrey..D 2
35 Outwood, Yorks..E 12
35 Ovenden.........D 9
49 Ovenscloss......F 7
25 Over, Cambs.....H 5
30 Over, Cheshire..D 5
15 Over, Glos......F 9
43 Over Cleuchbrae.B 11
7 Over Compton....E 9
48 Over Dalgliesh..H 5
31 Over Haddon....D 10
43 Over Hazelfield..G 8
39 Over Kellet.....H 7
16 Over Kiddington..B 5
4 Over Norton.....A 4
40 Over Silton.....F 5
6 Over Stowey.....B 5
7 Over Stratton...E 8
30 Over Tabley.....B 6
8 Over Wallop.....B 4
22 Over Whitacre...C 6
49 Over Whitton...G 10
32 Over Woodhouse..C 2
58 Overbister......B 4
22 Overbury........H 3
58 Overhall........C 5
58 Overhill........D 4
7 Overleigh.......C 8
22 Overley Green...F 4
30 Overpool........C 3
22 Overseal........A 6
58 Overside........B 8
11 Overland........B 9
23 Overstone......E 11
26 Overstrand......B 5
23 Overthorpe......H 8
58 Overton, Aber...F 6
47 Overton, Ayr....D 8
30 Overton, Ches...C 4
22 Overton, Flint..F 2
13 Overton, Glam...H 8
8 Overton, Hants..A 6
43 Overton, Kirk...E 10
48 Overton, Lan....D 1
34 Overton, Lancs...A 3
21 Overton, Salop..E 10
36 Overton, Yorks..B 3
29 Overton Bridge..F 12
30 Overton Green...D 6
58 Overtown, Aber..D 7
48 Overtown, Lan....D 1
39 Overtown, Lancs.H 8
16 Overtown, Wilts..F 3
58 Overtown of Memsie
               B 7
26 Overy Staithe....A 1
17 Oving, Bucks....B 8
9 Oving, Sussex...F 10
10 Ovingdean.......H 2
25 Ovingham........G 9
27 Ovington, Essex..L 1
9 Ovington, Hants...C 7
26 Ovington, Norfolk.E 3
45 Ovington, Northumb.
               G 9
40 Ovington, Yorks..D 2
8 Ower............D 5
7 Owermoigne.....H 11
31 Owler Bar......B 11
32 Owlerton........A 1
17 Owlswick........C 8
33 Owmby, Lincs...A 7
37 Owmby, Lincs...G 8
8 Owslebury.......D 6
23 Owston, Leics...A 11
36 Owston, Yorks...F 3
36 Owston Ferry....G 6
37 Owstwick........D 10
32 Owthorpe........G 4
24 Oxborough......E 8
38 Oxen Park.......F 5

MAP

39 Oxenholme.......F 8
35 Oxenhope........D 9
49 Oxenrig.........E 11
16 Oxenton.........A 1
16 Oxenwood........H 4
25 Oxford..........D 6
4 Oxford Cross....B 8
16 Oxfordshire, Co...C 5
18 Oxhey...........D 1
22 Oxhill..........G 6
22 Oxley...........B 2
19 Oxley Green.....C 9
49 Oxnam..........G 9
17 Oxshott.........H 12
35 Oxspring.......G 11
10 Oxted...........C 3
49 Oxton, Ber......D 7
32 Oxton, Notts....E 3
36 Oxton, Yorks....C 3
13 Oxwich..........H 8
13 Oxwich Green....H 8
60 Oykel Bridge....G 5
58 Oyne............E 4
13 Oystermouth....H 9
7 Packers Hill....E 10
23 Packington.....A 7
22 Packington Park..D 5
53 Padanaram.......B 9
17 Padbury.........A 8
18 Paddington......F 3
11 Paddlesworth...D 10
10 Paddock Wood...D 5
56 Paddockhaugh...D 8
44 Paddockhole....E 1
30 Paddolgreen....G 4
35 Padfield........G 9
30 Padgate.........A 5
35 Padiham........D 7
29 Padog...........E 8
35 Padside.........A 10
2 Padstow.........B 6
17 Padworth........G 7
40 Page Bank......B 3
9 Pagham.........F 10
19 Paglesham......E 9
63 Paible..........G 1
5 Paignton........K 8
23 Pailton.........D 8
11 Painscastle.....H 7
45 Painshawfield...G 9
15 Painswick......C 12
11 Painter's Forstal.B 8
47 Paisley.........C 9
58 Paithnick.......B 2
26 Pakefield.......F 8
27 Pakenham.......J 2
29 Pale...........G 9
10 Palehouse Com..F 4
8 Palestine......B 4
17 Paley Street....G 9
42 Palgowan.......C 5
27 Palgrave........G 4
11 Palmarsh.......E 10
18 Palmers Green...E 3
43 Palnackie......F 9
42 Palnure........E 5
32 Palterton.......C 2
17 Pamber End.....H 7
17 Pamber Green...H 7
17 Pamber Heath...H 7
8 Pamphill.......F 1
25 Pampisford.....K 6
27 Panborough.....B 8
53 Panbride.......D 10
4 Pancrasweek....E 2
29 Pandy, Denb....G 11
20 Pandy, Mer.....B 2
15 Pandy, Mon.....B 7
20 Pandy, Mont....B 5
29 Pandy Tudur....D 8
19 Panfield.......A 7
17 Pangbourne.....F 7
43 Panlands......C 11
35 Pannal.........B 11
59 Pannanich......H 1
30 Pant...........H 1
20 Pant Mawr......D 4
28 Pant-glas, Caer..E 4
21 Pantglas, Salop..C 8
12 Pantgwyn, Cards..B 6
13 Pantgwyn, Carm..D 9
13 Pant-lasau......G 10
33 Panton.........B 9
20 Pant-perthog....B 3
20 Pant-y-dwr.....E 5
21 Pant-y-ffrid....B 7
13 Pantyffynnon....F 9
14 Pantygasseg.....D 5
15 Pant y Goitre...C 7
12 Pantymenyn....D 5
29 Pant-y-mwyr....D 11
14 Pant-yr-awel....E 3
26 Panxworth......D 6

MAP
38 Papcastle........B 3
49 Papple........B 8
32 Papplewick......E 3
25 Papworth Everard.J 4
25 Papworth St. Agnes J 4
3 Par........D 8
7 Parbrook......C 9
29 Parc........G 8
12 Parc-llyn......B 6
38 Pardshaw......C 3
27 Parham......J 6
59 Park, Aberdeen. G 5
50 Park, Argyll....C 6
43 Park, Dumfries .B 10
17 Park Corner, Berks.F 9
17 Park Corner, Oxon.E 8
10 Park Corner, Sussex D 4
45 Park End, Northumb. E 7
40 Park End, Yorks..C 5
9 Park Gate......C 7
44 Park Nook....F 4
58 Parkdargue......C 4
38 Parkend, Cumb..A 5
15 Parkend, Glos..D 9
27 Parkeston......M 5
3 Parkfield......C 10
30 Parkgate, Ches..B 1
43 Parkgate, Dumf..C 11
10 Parkgate, Surrey..D 1
48 Parkgatestone....F 4
4 Parkham......D 3
4 Parkham Ash...D 2
56 Parkhead......F 8
58 Parkhill House...F 6
15 Parkhouse......D 8
8 Parkhurst......G 6
13 Parkmill......H 9
59 Parkneuk......K 5
30 Parkside......E 3
30 Parkstone......G 2
8 Parley Cross....F 2
4 Parracombe......B 5
30 Parrah Green....F 6
12 Parrog......C 4
24 Parson Drove....E 5
19 Parson's Heath...A 10
47 Partick......C 10
34 Partington......H 6
33 Partney......C 11
38 Parton, Cumb...C 2
15 Parton, Glos...B 12
43 Parton, Kirk....E 8
10 Partridge Green..F 1
31 Parwich......E 10
23 Passenham......H 11
9 Passfield......C 9
26 Paston Street....B 6
4 Patchacott......F 3
10 Patcham......G 2
9 Patching......E 12
4 Patchole......B 5
15 Patchway......F 9
35 Pateley Bridge..A 10
19 Paternoster Heath.B 9
52 Path of Condie...F 5
7 Pathe......C 7
53 Pathead, Fife....H 8
48 Pathead, Midlothian C 6
47 Pathhead......H 11
52 Pathstruie......H 8
47 Patna......H 9
16 Patney......H 2
38 Patrick......G 1
40 Patrick Brompton.F 2
34 Patricroft......G 6
37 Patrington......E 10
11 Patrixbourne....C 10
38 Patterdale......D 6
44 Pattieshill......F 3
22 Pattingham......B 2
23 Pattishall......G 10
19 Pattiswick Green..B 8
2 Paul......G 2
23 Paulerspury......G 10
37 Paull......E 9
7 Paulton......A 10
45 Pauperhaugh....C 9
25 Pavenham......K 1
6 Pawlett......B 6
49 Pawston......F 11
22 Paxford......H 5
49 Paxton......D 12
6 Payhembury......F 4
35 Paythorne......B 7
10 Peacehaven......H 3
22 Peachley......F 2
31 Peak Dale......C 9
31 Peak Forest......B 9
58 Peaknowe......B 4
55 Peanmeanach....L 1

59 Pearsie..........L 1
10 Pearsons Green...D 6
10 Pease Pottage.....E 1
7 Peasedown St. John A 10
16 Peasemore......F 5
27 Peasenhall......H 7
9 Peaslake......B 12
34 Peasley Cross....H 4
11 Peasmarsh......F 7
49 Peaston Bank....C 7
53 Peat Inn......F 9
58 Peathill......A 7
23 Peatling Magna..C 9
23 Peatling Parva..C 9
21 Peaton......D 10
27 Pebmarsh......M 2
22 Pebworth......G 5
35 Peckett Well....D 8
30 Peckforton......E 4
18 Peckham......F 3
23 Peckleton......B 8
44 Pedderhill......F 3
11 Pedlinge......E 10
22 Pedmore......D 3
7 Pedwell......C 8
48 Peebles......E 5
48 Peebles, Co.....E 5
38 Peel......G 1
9 Peel Common....F 7
25 Pegsdon......M 2
45 Pegswood......D 10
62 Peinaha......B 4
62 Peinchorran......E 4
62 Peinlick......B 3
62 Peinmore......C 4
12 Pelcomb Cross...E 3
19 Peldon......B 9
22 Pelsall......B 4
45 Pelton......H 10
45 Pelton Fell.....H 10
43 Pelutho......G 12
3 Pelynt......D 9
13 Pemberton, Carm..G 8
34 Pemberton, Lancs..G 4
13 Pembrey......G 7
21 Pembridge......G 9
12 Pembroke......G 3
12 Pembroke Dock...G 3
10 Pembury......D 5
13 Pen Rhiwfawr...F 10
13 Pen-Sarn......E 7
15 Penallt......C 8
12 Penally......G 5
15 Penalt......A 9
3 Penare......F 7
14 Penarth......G 5
20 Pen-bont-rhyd-y-beddau......D 2
12 Penbryn......B 6
13 Pencader......C 8
13 Pen-cae......A 7
28 Pencaenewydd....F 3
28 Pencarnisiog......C 3
13 Pencarreg......G 9
14 Pencelli......B 4
13 Penclawdd......G 9
14 Pencoed, Glam...F 3
15 Pencoed, Herefs..B 8
21 Pencombe......G 11
15 Pencraig, Herefs..B 9
29 Pencraig, Mont..G 9
2 Pendeen......F 1
14 Penderyn......C 3
12 Pendine......F 6
34 Pendlebury......G 6
34 Pendleton, Lancs..C 6
35 Pendleton, Lancs..G 7
15 Pendock......A 11
3 Pendoggett......B 7
7 Pendomer......E 8
14 Pendoylan......G 4
14 Pendre......F 2
20 Penegoes......B 3
12 Penfeidir......D 2
13 Pen-ffordd, Card..C 8
12 Pen-ffordd, Pemb..E 4
14 Pengam......D 5
18 Penge......G 3
3 Pengelly......A 8
14 Pengenffordd....B 5
14 Pengover Green..C 10
14 Pen-groes oped...D 6
2 Penhale......H 4
2 Penhalurick......F 4
16 Penhill......E 2
15 Penhow......E 7
10 Penhurst......F 6
20 Penifiler......B 2
48 Penicuik......C 5
13 Peniel......E 8
62 Penifiler......D 4
46 Peninver......G 4

28 Penisar-waun......D 5
35 Penistone......G 11
30 Penketh......A 4
42 Penkill......B 3
42 Penkiln......G 6
22 Penkridge......A 3
30 Penley......F 3
13 Penllergaer......G 9
28 Pen-llyn, Angl....B 3
29 Pennllyn, Glam...G 3
29 Penmachno......E 7
13 Penmaen......H 8
28 Penmaenan......C 6
28 Penmaenmawr....C 6
28 Penmaenpool......H 6
28 Penmaenrhos......B 8
14 Penmark......G 4
28 Penmon......B 6
50 Penmore Mill....B 1
28 Penmorfa......F 5
28 Penmynydd......C 4
17 Penn......E 10
17 Penn Street......E 10
2 Pennal......B 3
58 Pennan......A 6
13 Pennant, Cards..A 8
29 Pennant, Denb...D 7
29 Pennant, Mer....G 9
20 Pennant, Mont...C 4
29 Pennant-Melangell H 9
21 Pennard......H 9
21 Pennerley......C 9
8 Pennington, Hants.G 4
38 Pennington, Lancs. G 5
14 Pennorth......B 4
15 Pennsylvania Vill..E 8
38 Penny Bridge....G 5
24 Penny Hill......C 5
50 Pennyghael......E 3
47 Pennyglen......H 7
50 Pennygown......C 3
4 Pennymoor......E 7
45 Pennywell......G 11
12 Penparc, Cards..B 5
12 Penparc, Pemb...D 2
20 Penparcau......D 2
14 Penpelleni......D 6
3 Penpillick......D 8
2 Penpol......F 5
14 Penpont, Brec....A 3
43 Penpont, Dumf...B 9
12 Penrherber......C 6
12 Penrhiw......C 6
15 Penrhiwceiber....E 4
13 Penrhiw-goch....E 9
13 Pen-rhiw-llan....C 7
13 Penrhiwpal......B 7
14 Penrhos, Brec....C 1
28 Penrhos, Caer....G 3
28 Penrhos, Mon....C 7
28 Penrhos-garnedd..C 5
28 Penrhyn......A 3
29 Penrhyn Bay....B 7
20 Penrhyn-coch....D 2
28 Penrhyndeudraeth.F 5
29 Penrhynside......B 7
13 Penrice......H 8
12 Penrieth......C 6
39 Penrith......B 7
2 Penrose......C 6
38 Penruddock......B 6
2 Penryn......F 5
29 Pensarn......B 9
22 Pensax......E 1
30 Pensby......B 1
7 Penselwood......C 10
15 Pensford......H 9
2 Penshaw......H 11
10 Penshurst......D 4
3 Pensilva......C 10
28 Pentir......D 5
2 Pentire......D 5
28 Pentireg......B 6
12 Pentlepoir......F 5
27 Pentlow......L 1
24 Pentney......D 8
8 Penton Mewsey...A 5
28 Pentraeth......B 5
29 Pentre, Denb....D 10
29 Pentre, Denb....F 12
14 Pentre, Glam....E 3
21 Pentre, Mont....M 8
21 Pentre, Mont....C 8
21 Pentre, Salop....A 9
29 Pentre Bagillt....C 11
28 Pentre Berw......B 5
20 Pentre Dolau-Honddu H 5
13 Pentre Gwenlais..E 9

28 Pentre Gwyffryn...G 5
29 Pentre Halkyn...C 11
29 Pentre-Isaf......C 8
14 Pentre Meyrick...G 3
29 Pentre Saron......D 9
14 Pentre-bach, Brec..A 2
13 Pentrebach, Cards..B 9
29 Pentre-bach, Denb. G 10
14 Pentrebâch, Glam..D 4
13 Pentrebach, Glam..F 9
21 Pentrebeirdd......A 7
29 Pentre-bont......E 7
13 Pentre-cagal......C 7
29 Pentre-celyn......E 10
13 Pentre-cwrt......C 7
29 Pentre-dwfr......F 11
13 Pentre-dwr......G 10
28 Pentrefelin, Angl...A 4
13 Pentrefelin, Carm..E 9
29 Pentrefoelas......E 8
12 Pentre-galar......D 5
13 Pentregat......B 7
20 Pentre-llwyn-llwyd G 5
14 Pentre-poeth......A 6
14 Pentrer-felin, Brec..A 3
28 Pentre'r felin, Caer. F 5
13 Pentre'r-felin, Cards. B 9
29 Pentre-tafarn-y-fedw D 7
13 Pentre-ty-gwyn...C 11
29 Pentre-uchaf......C 10
8 Pentridge......D 2
14 Pentwyn, Glam...D 4
14 Pen-twyn, Mon...C 8
14 Pentyrch......F 4
14 Penuchadre......G 2
20 Penuwch......A 7
3 Penwithick Stents..D 7
16 Penwood......H 5
14 Penwyllt......C 2
13 Pen-y-banc, Carm..E 9
13 Pen-y-banc, Carm..F 9
29 Pen-y-bont, Denb.H 11
21 Penybont, Rad....F 7
29 Pen-y-bont-fawr..H 10
12 Pen-y-bryn......C 5
14 Pen-y-cae, Brec...C 2
29 Pen-y-cae, Denb..F 12
15 Pen-y-cae-mawr...E 7
15 Pen-y-clawdd....D 7
14 Pen-y-coedcae....F 4
14 Pen-y-cwm......F 2
14 Pen-y-fai......F 2
29 Penyffordd......D 12
21 Pen-y-garnedd...H 10
14 Pen-y-graig......E 3
28 Penygroes, Caer...E 4
13 Pen-y-groes, Carm. F 9
14 Pen-y-groes, Glam. F 5
12 Penygroes, Pemb..C 5
28 Pen-y-Gwryd......E 6
14 Penyrheol......E 5
14 Pen-yr-Heolgerrig. D 4
14 Penyrynys......B 2
28 Penysarn......A 4
29 Pen-y-stryt......E 11
14 Penywaun......D 3
2 Penzance......G 2
22 Peopleton......G 3
30 Peover Heath....C 6
30 Peover Superior...C 6
9 Peper Harow....B 10
30 Peplow......H 5
17 Peppard Common.F 8
45 Peppermoor......B 10
47 Perceton......E 8
58 Percie......H 3
58 Percyhorner......A 7
45 Perkinsville......H 10
32 Perlethorpe......C 4
2 Perranarworthal..F 5
2 Perranporth......D 5
2 Perranuthnoe......G 3
2 Perranwell......D 5
2 Perranwell Station.F 5
2 Perranzabuloe....D 5
25 Perry......J 2
22 Perry Barr......C 4
18 Perry Green......B 4
10 Perry Street......A 5
22 Pershore......G 3
59 Pert......J 2
25 Pertenhall......J 2
52 Perth......E 6
52 Perth, County....C 3
7 Pertwood......C 12
5 Peter Tavy......H 4
24 Peterborough....F 3

54 Peterburn......B 1
21 Peterchurch......H 9
59 Petercutter......G 6
58 Peterhead......C 8
40 Peterlee......A 4
18 Peter's Green......B 2
4 Peters Marland...E 3
9 Petersfield......D 9
14 Peterstone Wentlooge F 6
14 Peterston-super-ElyG 4
15 Peterstow......B 9
2 Petrockstow......E 4
11 Pett......G 7
27 Pettaugh......J 5
9 Petterden......C 9
48 Pettinain......E 2
27 Pettistree......K 6
6 Petton, Devon....D 4
30 Petton, Salop....G 3
18 Petts Wood......G 4
58 Petty......D 5
53 Pettycur......A 5
58 Pettymuck......E 6
9 Petworth......D 11
10 Pevensey......H 5
10 Pevensey Bay....H 5
16 Pewsey......H 3
17 Pheasants......E 9
17 Pheasant's Hill...E 9
2 Phillack......F 3
32 Philleigh......F 6
48 Philpstoun......B 3
15 Phocle Green....B 9
11 Phoenix Green...H 8
57 Phoines......K 3
38 Phurt......F 2
38 Pica......C 3
17 Piccott's End....C 11
36 Pickburn......F 3
41 Pickering......G 8
4 Picket Piece......A 5
8 Picket Post......E 3
40 Pickhill......A 4
21 Picklescott......B 10
53 Pickletillem......E 9
30 Pickmere......C 5
5 Pickney......C 5
4 Pickwell, Devon..B 3
23 Pickwell, Leics...A 11
24 Pickworth, Lincs..B 1
24 Pickworth, Rut...D 1
30 Picton, Cheshire..C 3
40 Picton, Yorks....D 4
10 Piddinghoe......H 3
17 Piddington, Bucks. E 9
23 Piddington, Northants. G 11
17 Piddington, Oxon..E 7
7 Piddlehinton......F 10
7 Piddletrenthide...F 10
25 Pidley......H 4
40 Piercebridge......D 2
64 Pierowall......A 2
7 Pigdon......D 9
31 Pikehall......D 10
18 Pilgrims Hatch...D 6
32 Pilham......A 6
15 Pill......G 8
3 Pillaton......C 10
22 Pillerton Hersey..G 6
22 Pillerton Priors...G 6
21 Pilleth......F 8
9 Pilley, Hants....F 8
35 Pilley, Yorks....G 12
14 Pillgwenlly......F 6
4 Pillhead......C 3
34 Pilling......B 3
34 Pilling Lane......B 3
15 Pillowell......D 11
7 Pilsdon......F 7
31 Pilsbury......D 9
31 Pilsley, Derby...C 11
31 Pilsley, Derby...D 2
25 Pilton, Northants. G 1
23 Pilton, Rutland..B 12
7 Pilton, Somerset..B 9
13 Pilton Green......H 8
7 Pimperne......E 12
24 Pinchbeck......C 3
24 Pinchbeck Bars...C 3
24 Pinchbeck West...C 3
42 Pinclanty......C 3
34 Pinfold......F 3
22 Pinhoe......G 3
17 Pinkneys Green...F 9
22 Pinley Green......E 5
42 Pinminnoch......B 3

42 Pinmore..........B 3
42 Pinmore Mains....C 3
6 Pinn............G 4
18 Pinner..........E 1
22 Pinvin..........E 2
42 Pinwherry........C 3
32 Pinxton..........E 2
21 Pipe and Lyde...H 10
30 Pipe Gate........F 6
22 Pipehill..........A 4
56 Piperhill........E 4
3 Pipers Pool......A 9
23 Pipewell........D 11
4 Pippacott........B 4
14 Pipton..........A 5
12 Pirbright........H 10
49 Pirnie..........G 9
46 Pirnmill........E 4
18 Pirton, Herts....A 2
22 Pirton, Worcs...G 2
17 Pishill..........E 8
28 Pistyll..........F 3
52 Pitagowan........A 3
58 Pitblae..........A 7
53 Pitcairlie Farm...F 7
52 Pitcairn........B 4
52 Pitcairngreen....D 5
58 Pitcaple........E 5
53 Pitcarity........A 8
17 Pitch Green......D 8
9 Pitch Place......A 11
15 Pitchcombe......D 11
17 Pitchcott........B 8
21 Pitchford........B 10
7 Pitcombe........C 10
53 Pitcorthie......F 10
49 Pitcox..........B 9
59 Pitdrichie......J 5
58 Pitfichie........F 4
52 Pitfour Castle....F 7
53 Pitkevy..........G 7
53 Pitlessie........F 8
52 Pitlochry........A 4
58 Pitmachie........E 4
57 Pitmain..........J 3
58 Pitmedden......E 6
6 Pitminster......D 5
53 Pitmuies........B 10
58 Pitmunie........F 4
7 Pitney..........C 8
53 Pitroddie........E 7
53 Pitscottie......F 9
19 Pitsea..........E 7
23 Pitsford........E 11
53 Pitstone........C 10
17 Pitstone Green...C 10
59 Pittarrow........K 5
56 Pittendreich......D 7
61 Pittentraill......F 7
53 Pittenweem......G 10
40 Pittington........A 3
58 Pittodrie........E 4
8 Pitton..........C 4
10 Pittswood........C 5
58 Pittulie........A 7
40 Pity Me, Durham..A 3
45 Pity Me, Northumb. E 7
27 Pixey Green......H 5
10 Pixham..........C 1
21 Pixley..........H 12
58 Plaidy..........B 5
12 Plain Dealings...E 4
48 Plains..........C 1
6 Plainsfield......C 5
21 Plaish..........C 10
9 Plaistow........C 11
10 Plaistow Street...D 3
8 Plaitford........D 4
20 Plas Llysyn......C 5
29 Plas Newydd....F 11
44 Plashetts........D 5
16 Plastow Green...H 6
29 Plas-yn-Cefn....C 9
30 Platt............C 5
34 Platt Bridge....G 5
45 Plawsworth......H 11
10 Plaxtol..........C 5
17 Play Hatch......F 8
11 Playden..........F 8
27 Playford........K 5
2 Playing Place....E 5
15 Playley Green...A 10
21 Plealey..........B 9
52 Plean..........H 3
53 Pleasance........F 7
34 Pleasington......D 5
32 Pleasley........D 2
44 Plenmeller......G 5
18 Pleshey..........B 6
45 Plessey Checks...E 10
54 Plockton........F 2
21 Ploughfield......H 9

MAP		MAP		MAP		MAP		MAP		MAP	
49	Ploughlands....E 10	14	Pontlottyn.......D 4	2	Porthcurno......G 1	7	Powerstock.....G 8	12	Princes Gate.....F 5	23	Quarndon, Leics...A 9
21	Plowden.......D 9	28	Pont-lyfni.......E 4	28	Porthdafarch....B 2	43	Powfoot........E 12	17	Princes Risborough D 9	47	Quarrier's Homes..C 8
21	Ploxgreen........B 9	14	Pontneddfechan..D 2	12	Porthgain.......D 2	53	Powgavie.......E 7	23	Princethorpe.....E 7	24	Quarrington.....A 2
11	Pluckley.......D 8	14	Pontnewydd.....E 6	2	Porthilly.......B 6	22	Powick.........G 2	5	Princetown, Devon.	40	Quarrington Hill..A 4
11	Pluckley Thorne..D 8	20	Pontrhydfendigaid.F 3	14	Porthkerry......H 4	4	Powler's Piece...D 2		H 5	40	Quarry Bank......C 3
43	Plumbland....H 12	13	Pont-rhyd-y-fen..G 11	2	Porthleven......G 3	52	Powmill........G 5	14	Princetown, Glam. C 4	30	Quarrybank.....D 4
30	Plumley........C 6	20	Pont-rhyd-y-groes..E 3	28	Porthmadog.....F 5	20	Powys, Co.....E 6	49	Printonan......E 10	58	Quarryburn.....A 6
10	Plumpton...G 2	14	Pontrhydyrun.....E 6	2	Porthmeor.......F 2	7	Poxwell........H 11	29	Prion.........D 10	56	Quarryhill.......B 3
39	Plumpton Foot...A 7	15	Pontrilas.......B 7	3	Portholland......F 7	17	Poyle.........F 11	21	Priors Frame...H 11	56	Quarrywood.....C 7
10	Plumpton Green...F 2	28	Pont-rug.......D 4	2	Porthoustock.....G 5	10	Poynings.......G 1	23	Priors Hardwick..G 8	47	Quarter.......D 12
39	Plumpton Head...B 7	10	Ponts Green.....F 5	2	Porthowan......E 4	27	Poyntington.....D 10	23	Priors Marston...F 8	6	Quartley.......D 3
39	Plumpton Wall...B 7	13	Pontshaen......B 8	3	Porthpean......E 7	31	Poynton........B 8	21	Priorslee.......A 12	22	Quat.........C 1
26	Plumstead......B 4	15	Pontshill.......B 9	13	Porth-y-rhyd, Carm.	30	Poynton Green...H 4	21	Priory Wood....H 8	22	Quatford.......C 1
32	Plumtree......G 3	14	Pontsticill.......C 4		E 8	27	Poys Street......H 6	15	Priston.......H 10	4	Quebec.......A 2
32	Plungar........G 5	13	Pont-tywely.....C 7	13	Porth-y-rhyd, Carm.	12	Poyston Cross....E 3	19	Prittlewell......E 8	15	Quedgeley......C 11
7	Plush.........F 10	13	Pontyberem.....F 8		C 10	27	Poystreet Green...J 3	27	Privett.........C 8	25	Queen Adelaide..G 7
13	Plwmp.........B 7	29	Pont-y-bodkin...D 12	51	Portincaple.......H 9	51	Praa Sands......G 3	4	Prixford.......B 4	4	Queen Charlton..H 9
5	Plymouth......K 4	29	Pont y Clogwyn...E 8	36	Portington......D 6	62	Prabost........C 3	2	Probus........E 6	4	Queen Dart....D 7
5	Plympton......K 4	14	Pontyclun......F 4	51	Portinnisherrich...F 7	18	Pratt's Bottom...H 5	43	Prospect.......G 12	7	Queen Oak....C 11
5	Plympton St. Maurice	14	Pontycymer......E 2	38	Portinscale......C 5	11	Pratt's Heath....C 7	58	Protstonhill.....A 6	10	Queen Street....D 6
	K 4	12	Pontyglazier.....C 5	15	Portishead......G 8	1	Praze.........F 3	45	Prudhoe.......G 9	11	Queenborough....A 8
5	Plymstock......K 4	14	Pont-y-gwaith....E 3	58	Portknockie......A 2	2	Praze-an-Beeble..F 3	51	Ptarmigan Lodge.G 10	7	Queens Camel...D 9
6	Plymtree........F 4	29	Pont-y-pant......E 7	59	Portlethen......H 7	51	Predannack Manor	51	Pubil.........C 11	30	Queens Head....G 2
40	Pockley........G 6	14	Pontypool......D 6	2	Portloe.........F 6		Farm.......H 4	15	Publow........H 9	30	Queen's Park....E 2
36	Pocklington......B 6	14	Pontypool Road..D 6	61	Portmahomack...H 9	30	Prees.........G 4	18	Puckeridge.....B 4	35	Queensbury.....D 9
24	Pode Hole......C 3	14	Pontypridd......E 4	28	Portmeirion.....F 5	34	Preesall........B 2	30	Puckington......D 7	29	Queensferry, Flint.
7	Podimore.......D 9	12	Pont-yr-hafod....D 3	3	Portmellon......E 7	34	Preesall Park....C 2	15	Pucklechurch....G 10		C 12
23	Podington......F 12	21	Pont-ysgawrhyd...A 7	8	Portmore.......F 5	12	Prendergast.....E 3	30	Puddington, Ches..C 2	48	Queensferry, W. Loth.
30	Podmore.......G 6	14	Pont-y-waun.....E 5	62	Port na Long....E 3	58	Prendwick......B 8	4	Puddington, Devon.		B 4
24	Pointon........B 2	8	Pooksgreen......E 5	63	Portnaguiran.....C 6	13	Pren-gwyn......C 7		E 7	34	Queenstown.....D 2
8	Pokesdown......G 3	2	Pool, Cornwall....E 4	55	Portnaluchaig....K 1	28	Prenteg.......F 5	26	Puddledock......F 4	47	Queenzieburn...B 11
42	Polbae.........D 4	21	Pool, Herefs....H 10	60	Portnancon.....B 5	30	Prenton........B 2	7	Puddletown.....G 10	1	Quemerford.....G 1
60	Polbain........F 2	35	Pool, Yorks.....C 11	51	Portnellan, Perth.E 11	30	Prescot.........A 3	21	Pudlestone......F 11	64	Quendale......F 7
3	Polbathic.......D 10	34	Pool Hay.......F 2	51	Portnellan, Perth..F 11	30	Prescott........H 3	9	Pulborough.....D 12	25	Quendon......M 6
48	Polbeth........C 3	21	Pool Head......G 11	50	Portnocroish.....C 6	30	Pressen.......F 11	35	Puldsey.......D 11	23	Queniborough...A 10
43	Poldean........B 11	52	Pool of Muckart..G 5	48	Portobello......B 6	30	Pressgreen.....G 4	9	Puleston.......H 6	16	Quenington.....D 2
58	Poldullie Bridge...F 1	21	Pool Quay......A 8	8	Porton.........B 3	29	Prestatyn......B 10	30	Puleston........H 6	34	Quernmore.....A 4
35	Pole Moor......E 9	27	Pool Street......L 1	42	Portpatrick......F 1	31	Prestbury, Ches...C 7	30	Pulford........D 2	3	Quethiock......C 10
25	Polebrook......G 2	8	Poole..........G 2	2	Portreath.......E 4	15	Prestbury, Glos...B 12	21	Pulham.......E 10	27	Quidenham......G 3
10	Polegate........G 5	30	Poole Green.....E 5	62	Portree........D 4	21	Presteigne......F 8	27	Pulham Market...G 5	8	Quidhampton, Hants.
30	Polelane Ends....B 5	16	Poole Keynes.....E 1	47	Portrye........D 7	27	Presthope......C 11	27	Pulham St. Margaret		A 6
22	Polesworth......B 6	31	Poolend........D 8	2	Portscatho......F 6	7	Prestleigh......B 9		G 5	8	Quidhampton, Wilts.
60	Polglass.......F 2	54	Poolewe........B 2	9	Portsea.........F 8	49	Preston, Ber.....D 10	25	Pulloxhill......M 2		C 3
3	Polgooth........E 7	39	Pooley Bridge.....C 7	61	Portskerra......A 8	5	Preston, Devon...H 7	48	Pumpherston....B 3	58	Quilquox......D 6
9	Poling.........F 11	15	Poolhill.......A 10	15	Portskewett.....E 8	7	Preston, Dorset..H 10	43	Pumplaburn....B 12	38	Quine's Hill....H 2
9	Poling Corner...E 11	32	Poolsbrook......C 2	10	Portslade, Surrey.G 1	48	Preston, E. Lothian B 6	13	Pumpsaint......C 10	50	Quinish House...B 2
3	Polkerris........D 8	38	Poortown......G 1	10	Portslade, Surrey..G 2	49	Preston, E. Lothian B 8	12	Puncheston.....D 3	23	Quinton.......G 11
60	Polla.........B 5	10	Pootings.......C 3	42	Portslogan......F 1	37	Preston, E. Riding.D 9	7	Puncknoll......G 9	2	Quintrel Downs...D 5
36	Pollington......E 4	17	Popeswood......G 9	9	Portsmouth, Hants.F 8	15	Preston, Glos.....A 10	10	Punnett's Town...F 5	49	Quixwood......C 10
50	Polloch........A 5	9	Popham.........B 7	35	Portsmouth, Yorks.E 7	16	Preston, Glos.....D 2	7	Purbrook.......E 8	9	Quoditch.......F 3
47	Pollockshaws...C 10	18	Poplar.........F 4	58	Portsoy........A 3	18	Preston, Herts...A 2	44	Purdomstone....E 1	52	Quoig.........E 3
47	Pollokshields....C 10	8	Porchfield......G 6	8	Portswood......E 6	11	Preston, Kent....B 9	8	Purewell.......G 3	48	Quothquan......E 3
43	Polmaddie......C 7	2	Porkellis.......F 4	50	Portuairk......A 2	11	Preston, Kent....B 11	18	Purfleet........F 5	14	Quoys.........D 7
54	Polmaily.......F 8	6	Porlock........B 2	63	Portvoller......C 6	34	Preston, Lancs....D 4	7	Puriton........B 7	62	Raasay House (Hotel)
3	Polmassick......E 7	6	Porlock Weir.....B 2	15	Portway, Herefs...A 8	45	Preston, Northumb.	19	Purleigh.......D 8		D 5
48	Polmont........B 2	53	Port Allen......E 7	22	Portway, War.....E 4		E 12	17	Purley, Berks.....H 7	4	Rabscott.......C 7
48	Polmoody......H 4	50	Port Appin......C 6	3	Portwrinkle.....D 10	23	Preston, Rut.....B 12	18	Purley, London...H 3	30	Raby.........B 2
47	Polnessan......H 9	46	Port Bannatyne..C 6	42	Portyerrock......H 5	10	Preston, Sussex...G 2	25	Purls Bridge.....G 6	4	Rackenford.....D 7
55	Polnish.........L 1	44	Port Carlisle....G 1	5	Postbridge......H 5	27	Preston, W. Riding K 2	4	Purse Caundle...D 10	9	Rackham.......E 11
3	Polperro.......E 9	40	Port Clarence....C 5	17	Postcombe......D 8	16	Preston, Wilts....F 1	21	Purslow.......D 9	26	Rackheath Com...D 6
3	Polruan.......E 8	28	Port Dinorwic....C 5	11	Postling........D 10	22	Preston Bagot....E 5	36	Purston Jaglin....E 2	43	Racks.........D 11
7	Polsham........B 8	46	Port Driseach....B 5	27	Postlingford.....K 1	27	Preston Bissett...A 7	7	Purtington......E 7	64	Rackwick, Orkney.D 1
43	Polskeoch......A 8	58	Port Elphinstone...F 5	26	Postwick.......E 6	6	Preston Bowyer...D 5	15	Purton, Glos.....D 10	64	Rackwick, Orkney.A 2
27	Polstead........L 3	38	Port Erin......H 1	59	Potarch........H 3	30	Preston Brockhurst	16	Purton, Wilts.....E 2	31	Radbourne......G 11
6	Poltimore......G 3	58	Port Erroll......D 8	47	Poteath........D 7		H 4	16	Purton Stoke....E 2	34	Radcliffe, Lancs...F 6
48	Polton.........C 5	13	Port Eynon......H 8	44	Potholm........D 2	30	Preston Brook....B 4	49	Purvishaugh.....E 8	45	Radcliffe, Northumb.
49	Polwarth.......D 10	47	Port Glasgow....B 8	17	Potsgrove......A 10	9	Preston Candover..B 7	23	Pury End......H 10		C 11
3	Polyphant......B 9	54	Port Henderson...B 1	24	Pott Row.......C 8	23	Preston Capes....G 9	16	Pusey.........D 4	32	Radcliffe on Soar..G 2
2	Polzeath.......B 6	3	Port Isaac......B 7	31	Pott Shrigley....B 8	17	Preston Crowmarsh	4	Putford.......D 2	32	Radcliffe on Trent.F 4
24	Pondersbridge...F 4	46	Port Lamont.....B 6	17	Potten End.....C 11		E 7	15	Putley.........A 9	17	Radclive.......A 7
9	Pondtail.......A 9	42	Port Logan.....H 2	41	Potter Brompton.G 10	30	Preston Gubbals...H 4	18	Putney.........H 3	16	Radcot........D 4
2	Ponsanooth.....F 5	41	Port Mulgrave...C 8	26	Potter Heigham...D 7	22	Preston on Stour..G 5	4	Putsborough.....B 3	56	Raddery House...D 3
5	Ponsworthy.....H 6	52	Port of Menteith..G 1	18	Potter Street.....C 5	30	Preston on the Hill.B 4	17	Puttenham, Bucks..C 9	23	Radford Semele...F 7
13	Pont-Antwn.....F 8	63	Port of Ness....A 6	33	Potterhanworth...D 7	7	Preston on Wye...H 8	9	Puttenham, Surrey A 10	7	Radipole.......H 10
29	Pont Cyfyng....D 7	3	Port Quin......B 7	33	Potterhanworth	7	Preston Plucknett.E 8	15	Puxton........H 7	18	Radlett........D 2
14	Pont Ebbw......F 6	50	Port Ramsay....C 6		Booths.......C 8	21	Preston upon the	13	Pwll.........G 8	16	Radley........D 6
13	Pont Henry.....F 8	38	Port St. Mary...H 1	16	Potterne........H 1		Weald Moors..A 12	12	Pwllcrochan.....G 3	17	Radnage.......D 8
12	Pont Hirwaun...C 6	51	Port Sonachan...E 7	16	Potterne Wick....H 1	21	Preston Wynne...H 11	28	Pwlldefaid......H 1	7	Radstock......A 10
20	Pont-Llogel.....A 6	30	Port Sunlight....B 2	18	Potters Bar.....D 3	43	Prestonmill......F 10	14	Pwllgloyw......A 3	23	Radstone......H 9
28	Pont Pen-y-benglog D 6	13	Port Talbot.....H 10	22	Potters Cross....B 6	48	Prestonpans......B 6	28	Pwllheli........H 2	31	Radway.......G 7
20	Pont-Robert....A 6	13	Port Tennant...H 10	23	Potterspury.....H 11	40	Preston-under-Scar F 1	15	Pwll-Meyric.....E 8	30	Radway Green...E 6
13	Pont Yates......F 8	42	Port William....G 4	40	Potto.........E 5	35	Prestwich, Lancs..G 7	2	Pwlltrap........E 6	25	Radwell.......J 1
13	Pontamman.....F 9	46	Portachoillan....D 3	25	Potton.........K 3	47	Prestwick, Ayr....G 8	13	Pwll-y-glaw.....H 11	25	Radwinter......L 7
14	Pont ar Hydfer...B 2	46	Port an Eilein....B 5	4	Poughill, Corn....E 1	45	Prestwick, Northumb.	29	Pydew.........B 7	14	Radyr.........F 5
13	Pontardawe....G 10	46	Portavadie......B 4	4	Poughill, Devon...E 7		F 10	32	Pye Bridge......E 2	48	Raecleugh......H 3
13	Pontardulais....G 9	15	Portbury.......G 8	16	Poulshot.......H 1	17	Prestwood......D 9	18	Pye Corner, Herts..C 4	63	Raerinish......D 5
13	Pontargothi.....E 8	9	Portchester.....F 7	30	Poulton, Ches....D 3	14	Price Town......E 3	15	Pye Corner, Mon..F 7	60	Raffin........D 2
13	Pont-ar-llechau..E 10	47	Portencross.....D 7	16	Poulton, Glos....D 2	25	Prickwillow......G 7	22	Pye Green......A 3	56	Rafford.......D 6
13	Pont-ar-Sais....D 8	7	Portesham......H 9	34	Poulton-Le-Fylde..C 2	1	Priddy.........A 8	10	Pyecombe......G 2	53	Ragdale.......H 4
13	Pontblyddyn....D 12	58	Portessie.......A 2	14	Pound.........F 1	39	Priest Hulton.....H 7	14	Pyle, Glam......F 2	53	Ragfield.......F 10
14	Pontbren Llwyd..D 3	38	Port e Vullen....G 3	22	Pound Bank.....E 1	44	Priesthaugh.....C 3	8	Pyle, I.o.W......H 6	15	Raglan........D 7
36	Pontefract......E 2	12	Portfield Gate...E 3	8	Pound Grn, I.o.W.G 5	47	Priesthill.......C 10	7	Pylle.........B 9	32	Ragnall........C 5
45	Ponteland......F 10	5	Portgate.......G 3	10	Pound Grn, Suss..F 4	47	Priestland......F 10	25	Pymore.......G 6	34	Rainford.......G 4
20	Ponterwyd......D 3	58	Portgordon.....A 1	10	Pound Hill......F 2	21	Priestweston....C 8	17	Pyrford........H 11	18	Rainham, Essex..F 5
21	Pontesbury.....B 9	61	Portgower......E 9	42	Poundland, Ayr...C 3	24	Primrose Hill, Cambs.	14	Pyrgad........C 2	11	Rainham, Kent...A 7
21	Pontesford......B 9	14	Porth.........E 4	43	Poundland, Dumf..C 9		F 5	17	Pyrton.........E 8	11	Rainham Mark...A 7
29	Pontfadog......F 11	14	Porth Mellin....H 4	17	Poundon.......B 7	32	Primrose Hill, Notts.	23	Pytchley.......E 12	30	Rainhill........A 4
14	Pont-faen, Brec...A 3	2	Porth Navas.....G 5	10	Poundsbridge....F 4		D 2	9	Pyworthy.......D 2	30	Rainhill Stoops...A 4
12	Pontfaen, Pemb..D 4	3	Porthallow, Corn..D 9	5	Poundsgate.....J 6	49	Primrosehill, Ber..D 10	21	Quabbs.........D 7	31	Rainow........C 8
13	Pontgarreg......B 7	2	Porthallow, Corn..G 5	2	Poundstock......A 2	17	Primrosehill, Herts.	24	Quadring.......B 3	40	Rainton.......H 4
14	Pont-hir.......E 6	14	Porthcawl.......G 1	53	Pourie.........D 9		D 11	17	Quainton.......B 8	37	Rainworth......D 3
13	Pont-llan-fraith..E 5	2	Porthcothan Bay..C 6	45	Powburn.......A 9	49	Primsidemill.....G 10	8	Quarley.........B 4	39	Raisbeck......D 9
13	Pontlliw.........G 9			6	Powderham.....H 3	31	Quarndon, Derby.F 11			44	Raise.........H 5

MAP

36 Raisthorpe.....A 6
53 Rait.....D 7
33 Raithby, Lincs...C 10
33 Raithby, Lincs...B 10
9 Rake.....C 9
11 Ram Lane.....C 8
62 Ramasaig.....D 1
3 Rame, Corn.....E 11
2 Rame, Corn.....F 4
7 Rampisham.....F 9
34 Rampside.....A 1
25 Rampton, Cambs. H 5
32 Rampton, Notts...B 5
35 Ramsbottom.....E 7
16 Ramsbury.....G 4
61 Ramscraigs.....D 10
9 Ramsdean.....D 8
17 Ramsdell.....H 7
16 Ramsden.....C 4
19 Ramsden Bellhouse E 7
19 Ramsden Heath...D 7
27 Ramsey, Essex...M 5
25 Ramsey, Hunts...G 4
38 Ramsey, I.o.M...G 2
19 Ramsey Island...C 9
25 Ramsey St. Mary's G 4
48 Ramseycleuch...H 5
11 Ramsgate.....B 12
26 Ramsgate Street..B 4
40 Ramsgill.....H 1
45 Ramshaw.....H 8
44 Ramshope.....C 6
31 Ramshorn.....F 9
5 Ramsley.....G 5
9 Ramsnest Com...C 11
32 Ranby.....B 4
33 Rand.....A 11
15 Randwick.....D 11
47 Ranfurly.....C 9
31 Rangemore.....H 10
15 Rangeworthy....F 10
47 Rankinston.....H 9
9 Ranmore Com...A 12
34 Rann.....E 6
38 Rannerdale.....C 4
51 Rannoch Station.B 11
55 Ranochan.....L 2
6 Ranscombe.....B 3
32 Ranskill.....A 4
31 Ranton.....H 7
26 Ranworth.....D 7
64 Rapness.....B 3
55 Rarsaidh.....H 2
43 Rascarre.....G 9
58 Rashiereive....E 7
40 Raskelf.....H 5
14 Rassau.....C 5
35 Rastrick.....E 10
55 Ratagan.....H 3
23 Ratby.....B 8
23 Ratcliffe Culey...B 7
23 Ratcliffe on the
   Wreake.....A 9
58 Rathen.....B 7
53 Rathillet.....E 8
35 Rathmell.....A 7
48 Ratho.....B 4
48 Ratho Station..B 4
58 Rathven.....A 2
23 Ratley.....G 7
21 Ratlinghope.....C 9
61 Rattar.....A 11
5 Rattery.....K 6
27 Rattlesden.....J 3
53 Rattray.....C 7
38 Raughton Head...A 6
25 Raunds.....H 1
49 Ravelaw.....D 11
36 Ravenfield.....H 3
38 Ravenglass.....F 3
26 Raveningham....F 7
41 Ravenscar.....E 10
38 Ravensdale.....G 2
25 Ravensden.....K 2
32 Ravenshead.....E 3
30 Ravensmoor.....E 5
23 Ravensthorpe,
   Northants.....E 10
35 Ravensthorpe, Yorks.
     E 10
23 Ravenstone, Bucks.
     G 11
23 Ravenstone, Leics..A 7
39 Ravenstonedale...E 2
48 Ravenstruther...E 2
40 Ravensworth....D 2
41 Raw.....E 9
49 Rawburn.....D 9
36 Rawcliffe, Yorks..E 5
36 Rawcliffe, Yorks..E 5
36 Rawcliffe Bridge..E 5
35 Rawdon.....C 11
36 Rawmarsh.....G 2

MAP

19 Rawreth.....E 8
6 Rawridge.....F 5
47 Raws.....E 9
35 Rawtenstall.....E 7
47 Rawyards.....C 12
58 Raxton.....D 6
27 Raydon.....L 3
19 Rayleigh.....E 8
7 Raymond's Hill...F 7
19 Rayne.....B 7
25 Reach.....J 7
34 Read.....D 6
17 Reading.....G 8
11 Reading Street...E 8
39 Reagill.....C 8
61 Rearquhar.....G 7
23 Rearsby.....A 10
61 Reaster.....A 11
45 Reaveley.....A 8
64 Reawick.....D 6
61 Reay.....B 9
11 Reculver.....A 11
6 Red Ball.....E 4
64 Red Banks.....C 3
44 Red Dial.....H 1
22 Red Hill.....G 2
5 Red Post.....J 7
34 Red Rock.....F 5
12 Red Roses.....F 5
45 Red Row.....C 10
31 Red Street.....E 7
28 Red Wharf.....B 5
12 Redberth.....G 4
17 Redbourn.....C 12
37 Redbourne.....G 7
18 Redbridge.....E 4
30 Redbrook, Flint..F 4
15 Redbrook, Mon...C 8
11 Redbrook Street ..D 8
56 Redburn, Nairn...E 5
44 Redburn, Northumb.
     G 6
56 Redburn, Ross &
   Cromarty.....C 1
40 Redcar.....C 6
53 Redcastle, Angus. B 11
56 Redcastle, Ross &
   Cromarty.....E 1
15 Redcliffe Bay....G 7
47 Redcraig.....G 9
49 Redden.....F 10
48 Redding.....B 2
48 Reddingmuirhead..B 2
35 Reddish.....H 8
22 Redditch.....C 4
47 Reddochbraes....F 12
27 Redenhall.....G 6
44 Redesdale Camp...C 6
45 Redesmouth.....E 7
53 Redford, Angus...C 10
59 Redford, Kinc....K 5
48 Redfordgreen....H 6
52 Redgorton.....D 6
27 Redgrave.....G 3
59 Redheugh.....L 2
58 Redhill, Aber.....D 4
59 Redhill, Aber.....G 5
15 Redhill, Somerset. H 8
10 Redhill, Surrey...C 2
46 Redhouse.....C 2
27 Redisham.....G 7
15 Redland, Glos.....G 9
64 Redland, Orkney...C 2
27 Redlingfield.....H 5
8 Redlynch, Dorset..D 4
7 Redlynch, Som...C 10
38 Redmain.....B 4
15 Redmarley D'Abitot
     A 10
40 Redmarshall.....C 4
32 Redmile.....G 5
40 Redmore.....F 1
3 Redmoor.....D 8
59 Redmyre.....K 5
30 Rednal.....G 2
49 Redpath.....F 8
54 Redpoint.....C 1
2 Redruth.....E 4
48 Redscarhead.....E 5
15 Redwick, Glos.....F 8
15 Redwick, Mon.....F 7
40 Redworth.....C 3
25 Reed.....L 5
26 Reedham.....E 7
36 Reedness.....E 6
49 Reedy Loch....D 11
63 Reef.....C 2
33 Reepham, Lincs...C 7
26 Reepham, Norf....C 4
40 Reeth.....H 1
38 Regaby.....F 2
56 Rehaurie.....E 5
61 Reidhbreac.....G 7

MAP

60 Reiff.....E 2
10 Reigate.....C 1
41 Reighton.....H 11
41 Reighton Gap...G 11
58 Reisque.....E 6
61 Reiss.....B 12
2 Rejerrah.....D 5
2 Releath.....F 4
43 Relief.....D 12
2 Relubbus.....F 3
56 Relugas.....E 5
17 Remenham.....F 8
17 Remenham Hill ..F 9
7 Remony.....C 3
32 Rempstone.....H 3
16 Rendcomb.....C 1
27 Rendham.....J 6
47 Renfrew.....C 10
47 Renfrew, Co.....C 9
32 Renhold.....K 2
32 Renishaw.....B 2
45 Rennington.....A 10
47 Renton.....B 9
39 Renwick.....A 8
26 Repps.....D 7
31 Repton.....G 11
55 Reraig.....G 2
53 Rescobie.....B 10
50 Resipol.....A 4
56 Resolis.....C 2
14 Resolven.....D 2
58 Resourie.....M 2
49 Reston.....C 11
2 Retew.....D 6
2 Rettendon.....D 7
19 Rettendon Place...D 7
2 Retyn.....D 6
50 Reudle.....C 1
33 Revesby.....D 10
8 Rew Street.....G 6
6 Rewe.....F 3
27 Reydon.....G 8
26 Reymerston.....E 3
12 Reynalton.....F 4
13 Reynoldston.....H 8
3 Rezare.....B 10
15 Rhadyr.....D 7
13 Rhandir-mwyn...C 11
20 Rhayader.....F 5
28 Rhegreanoch....E 3
56 Rheindown.....E 1
50 Rhemore.....C 3
60 Rhicarn.....E 2
56 Rhiconich.....B 4
60 Rhidorroch.....C 3
60 Rhidorroch Old Lodge
     G 4
28 Rhid-y-sarn.....F 6
61 Rhifail.....C 7
14 Rhigos.....D 3
60 Rhimichie.....B 4
56 Rhinduie.....E 1
60 Rhiroy.....G 3
28 Rhiw.....G 2
28 Rhiwbryfdir.....F 6
14 Rhiwderyn.....F 6
28 Rhiwlas, Caer.....D 5
28 Rhiwlas, Denb...G 11
29 Rhiwlas, Mer.....F 8
6 Rhode.....C 6
11 Rhodes Minnis ..D 10
32 Rhodesia.....B 3
12 Rhodiad.....D 1
14 Rhoose.....H 4
13 Rhos, Carm.....C 7
13 Rhos, Glam.....G 10
13 Rhos Amman.....F 10
12 Rhos-Hill.....C 5
28 Rhoscolyn.....C 2
12 Rhoscrowther....G 3
29 Rhosesmor.....C 11
12 Rhosfach.....D 5
28 Rhos-fawr.....B 4
28 Rhosgadfan.....D 4
28 Rhosgoch, Angl...A 3
21 Rhos goch, Rad...H 7
28 Rhos-lan.....F 4
28 Rhoslefain.....B 1
29 Rhosllanerchrugog
     F 12
13 Rhosmaen.....E 9
28 Rhos-meirch.....B 4
28 Rhosneigr.....C 3
29 Rhos-on-Sea.....B 8
13 Rhossili.....H 7
12 Rhosson.....D 1
28 Rhostryfan.....D 4
28 Rhostyllen.....E 2
28 Rhosybol.....A 4
29 Rhos-y-gwaliau...G 9

MAP

28 Rhos-y-llan.....F 2
46 Rhu, Argyll.....C 3
47 Rhu, Dunb.....A 7
54 Rhu Noa.....C 4
29 Rhuallt.....C 10
46 Rhubodach.....B 5
30 Rhuddall Heath...D 4
29 Rhuddlan.....B 9
4 Rhude Cross.....E 1
21 Rhulen.....G 7
46 Rhunahaorine....E 2
28 Rhyd, Mer.....F 6
20 Rhyd, Mont.....B 5
28 Rhyd-Ddu.....E 5
13 Rhyd-Lewis.....B 7
29 Rhyd-Lydan.....E 8
13 Rhydargaeau.....D 8
14 Rhydberry.....A 3
13 Rhydcymerau.....D 8
22 Rhydd.....H 2
13 Rhydding.....G 10
13 Rhyddlan.....C 8
29 Rhyd-leos.....G 11
28 Rhydlios.....G 1
29 Rhydlydan.....C 6
13 Rhydowen.....C 8
20 Rhydrosser.....F 1
21 Rhydspence.....H 8
29 Rhydtalog.....E 11
28 Rhydwyn.....A 3
29 Rhyd-y-croesau...G 11
28 Rhydyelafdy.....G 3
14 Rhydyfelin.....E 4
20 Rhyd-y-felin.....D 2
13 Rhyd-y-fro.....F 10
21 Rhyd-y-groes.....B 8
29 Rhydymain.....H 7
14 Rhyd-y-meirch...D 6
29 Rhydymwyn.....D 11
20 Rhyd-yr-onmen...B 2
20 Rhyfud.....F 2
29 Rhyl.....B 9
14 Rhymney.....D 4
53 Rhynd, Fife.....E 9
52 Rhynd, Perth.....E 6
58 Rhynie.....E 2
22 Ribble.....E 1
39 Ribblehead.....G 10
34 Ribbleton.....D 4
34 Ribby.....D 3
34 Ribchester.....D 5
24 Ribygill.....B 6
33 Riseholme.....C 7
25 Riby.....F 9
37 Riby Cross Roads .F 9
36 Riccall.....C 4
47 Riccarton.....F 9
44 Riccarton Junction C 4
21 Richards Castle . E 10
17 Richings Park...F 11
18 Richmond, London F 2
40 Richmond, Yorks. E 2
59 Rickarton.....H 5
31 Rickerscote.....H 7
27 Rickinghall Inferior
     H 3
27 Rickinghall Superior
     H 3
25 Rickling.....M 6
18 Rickling Green...A 5
17 Rickmansworth . E 11
44 Riddings, Cumb...E 3
32 Riddings, Derby...E 2
6 Riddlecombe.....E 5
35 Riddlesden.....C 9
8 Ridge, Dorset.....G 1
8 Ridge, Hants.....D 5
18 Ridge, Herts.....D 2
8 Ridge, Wilts.....C 1
10 Ridge Green.....C 2
22 Ridge Lane.....C 6
20 Ridgebourne.....F 6
15 Ridgehill.....H 8
32 Ridgeway.....B 1
21 Ridgeway Cross..H 12
25 Ridgewell.....L 8
10 Ridgewood.....F 3
25 Ridgmont.....L 1
45 Riding Mill.....G 8
10 Ridley, Kent.....B 5
44 Ridley, Northumb. G 6
26 Ridlington, Norf..B 6
23 Ridlington, Rut..B 11
15 Ridsdale.....E 7
52 Riechip.....B 5
52 Riemore.....B 5
60 Rienachait.....D 2
40 Rievaulx.....G 6
55 Rifern.....K 2
47 Rigfoot.....D 9
44 Rigg.....F 1
47 Riggend.....B 12
47 Righead.....F 10

MAP

56 Righoul.....E 4
39 Rigmaden Park...G 8
33 Rigsby.....C 11
48 Rigside.....F 2
22 Rileyhill.....A 5
3 Rilla Mill.....B 10
41 Rillington.....H 8
35 Rimington.....C 7
7 Rimpton.....D 9
61 Rimsdale.....C 7
37 Rimswell.....D 10
12 Rinaston.....D 3
43 Ringford.....F 8
31 Ringinglow.....B 11
26 Ringland.....D 4
10 Ringles Cross.....F 3
10 Ringmer.....G 3
56 Ringorm.....E 8
24 Ring's End.....E 5
27 Ringsfield.....G 7
27 Ringsfield Corner..G 7
17 Ringshall, Bucks..C 10
27 Ringshall, Suffolk K 3
27 Ringshall Stocks..K 4
24 Ringstead, Norf....B 8
25 Ringstead, Northants.
     H 1
8 Ringwood.....F 3
11 Ringwould.....C 12
58 Rinmore.....F 2
64 Rinnigill.....E 2
2 Rinsey.....G 3
10 Ripe.....G 4
32 Ripley, Derby.....E 1
8 Ripley, Hants.....F 3
17 Ripley, Surrey....H 11
35 Ripley, Yorks....A 11
37 Riplingham.....D 7
40 Ripon.....H 3
24 Rippingale.....C 2
22 Ripple, Kent.....C 12
22 Ripple, Worcs....H 2
35 Ripponden.....E 9
21 Risbury.....G 11
27 Risby, Essex.....J 1
37 Risby, Yorks.....F 7
24 Risegate.....C 3
33 Riseholme.....C 7
25 Riseley, Beds...J 1
17 Riseley, Berks...H 8
27 Rishangles.....H 4
34 Rishton.....D 6
35 Rishworth.....E 9
32 Risley.....G 2
40 Risplith.....H 3
60 Rispond.....A 5
16 Rivar.....H 4
19 Rivenhall End...B 8
25 River Bank.....H 6
10 Riverhead.....B 4
4 Riverton.....C 5
34 Rivington.....F 5
4 Roachill.....D 7
23 Roade.....G 11
44 Roadhead.....F 4
48 Roadmeetings....D 1
47 Roadside, Ayr...H 10
61 Roadside, Caith...B 11
59 Roadside of Catterline
     J 6
59 Roadside of Kinneff
     K 6
6 Roadwater.....B 4
62 Roag.....D 2
42 Roan of Craigoch .A 4
44 Roansgreen.....E 3
14 Roath.....F 5
43 Roberthill.....D 12
32 Roberton, Lan....F 2
44 Roberton, Selkirk..B 3
10 Robertsbridge....F 6
35 Roberttown.....E 10
12 Robeston Cross...F 2
12 Robeston Wathen.E 4
35 Robin Hood.....D 11
31 Robin Hood Inn .C 11
41 Robin Hood's Bay.E 9
4 Roborough.....E 5
30 Roby.....A 3
34 Roby Mill.....F 4
31 Rocester.....F 9
12 Roch.....E 2
12 Roch Gate.....E 2
35 Rochdale.....F 7
3 Roche.....D 7
10 Rochester, Kent...A 6
44 Rochester, Northumb.
     C 6
19 Rochford.....E 8

MAP

2 Rock, Cornwall...B 6
45 Rock, Northumb.A 10
9 Rock, Sussex.....E 12
22 Rock, Worcs.....E 1
30 Rock Ferry.....B 2
22 Rock Hill.....E 3
6 Rockbeare.....G 4
44 Rockcliffe, Cumb..G 2
43 Rockcliffe, Kirk..F 9
15 Rockfield, Mon...C 8
61 Rockfield, Ross &
   Cromarty.....H 9
15 Rockford.....E 3
15 Rockhampton.....E 9
26 Rockheath.....D 6
23 Rockingham.....C 2
26 Rockland All Saints F 3
26 Rockland St. Mary E 6
26 Rockland St. Peter .F 3
16 Rockley.....G 3
17 Rockwell End....E 9
15 Rockwell Green...D 5
15 Rodborough.....D 11
16 Rodbourne, Wilts..F 2
15 Rodbourne, Wilts. F 12
16 Rodbourne Cheney E 2
21 Rodd.....F 8
30 Roddam.....G 12
49 Roddam Rigg....G 12
7 Rodden.....H 9
7 Rode.....A 11
30 Rode Heath.....D 6
31 Rodeheath.....C 7
63 Rodel.....E 2
21 Roden.....A 11
15 Rodley.....C 10
15 Rodmarton.....D 12
10 Rodmell.....G 3
11 Rodmersham.....B 8
7 Rodney Stoke.....A 8
31 Rodsley.....F 10
6 Rodway.....B 6
7 Rodwell.....H 7
35 Roecliffe.....A 12
15 Roehampton.....G 2
64 Roesound.....C 7
10 Roffey.....E 1
61 Rogart.....F 7
9 Rogate.....D 9
14 Rogerstone.....E 4
47 Rogerton.....D 11
15 Rogiet.....E 8
26 Rollesby.....D 7
23 Rolleston, Leics..B 10
32 Rolleston, Notts...E 5
31 Rolleston, Staffs..G 10
37 Rolston.....C 10
11 Rolvenden.....E 7
11 Rolvenden Layne..E 7
39 Romaldkirk.....C 12
26 Roman Hill.....F 8
40 Romanby.....F 4
48 Romannobridge...E 4
6 Romansleigh.....D 6
3 Romesdal.....C 3
18 Romford.....E 5
31 Romiley.....A 8
7 Romsey.....D 5
22 Romsley, Salop...D 1
22 Romsley, Salop...D 3
3 Ronague.....H 1
41 Rookdale.....H 9
39 Rookhope.....A 11
8 Rookley.....H 6
6 Rooks Bridge.....A 7
6 Rook's Nest.....C 4
22 Roos.....D 10
48 Rootpark.....D 2
9 Ropley.....C 8
9 Ropley Dean.....C 7
33 Ropsley.....G 7
58 Rora.....C 8
21 Rorrington.....B 8
2 Rose.....D 5
6 Rose Ash.....D 7
10 Rose Hill.....F 3
10 Roseacre, Kent...C 6
34 Roseacre, Lancs...C 3
48 Rosebank.....D 1
45 Rosebrough.....C 12
2 Rosebush.....D 4
2 Rosecare.....B 8
41 Rosedale Abbey...F 7
45 Roseden.....A 8
60 Rosehall.....F 5
58 Rosehearty.....A 7
35 Rosehill.....G 5
56 Roseisle.....C 7
12 Rosemarket.....F 3
56 Rosemarkie.....D 3

MAP
6 Rosemary Lane...E 5
47 Rosemount, Ayr...F 8
53 Rosemount, Perth..C 7
2 Rosenannon.......C 6
2 Rosewarne........F 3
48 Rosewell.........C 5
40 Roseworth........C 4
2 Roseworthy.......F 3
39 Rosgill..........D 8
55 Roshven..........L 1
62 Roskhill.........D 2
38 Rosley...........A 6
48 Roslin...........C 5
31 Rosliston........H 11
47 Rosneath.........A 7
43 Ross, Kirk.......G 7
45 Ross, Northumb..B 12
54 Ross & Cromarty,
County.........B 6
15 Ross-on-Wye.....B 9
30 Rossett..........D 2
52 Rossie Ochill......F 6
36 Rossington.......G 4
56 Rosskeen.........C 2
47 Rossland.........B 9
61 Roster...........C 11
16 Rostherne........B 6
38 Rosthwaite.......D 5
31 Roston...........F 10
2 Rosudgeon........G 3
48 Rosyth...........A 4
45 Rothbury.........C 9
23 Rotherby.........A 10
10 Rotherfield......E 4
17 Rotherfield Greys..F 8
17 Rotherfield Peppard
F 8
32 Rotherham........A 2
23 Rothersthorpe....F 10
17 Rotherwick.......H 8
56 Rothes...........E 8
46 Rothesay.........C 6
58 Rothiebrisbane....D 5
58 Rothienorman.....D 5
64 Rothiesholm......C 4
45 Rothill..........B 9
23 Rothley..........A 9
58 Rothmaise........D 4
37 Rothwell, Lincs....G 9
23 Rothwell, Northants.
D 11
35 Rothwell, Yorks..D 12
35 Rothwell Haigh..D 12
37 Rotsea...........B 8
59 Rottal...........K 1
10 Rottingdean......H 3
38 Rottington.......D 2
43 Roucan...........D 11
8 Roud.............H 6
31 Rough Close......F 8
11 Rough Common..B 10
31 Rough Hay.......H 10
26 Rougham..........C 1
27 Rougham Green...J 2
27 Roughburn........L 7
35 Roughlee.........C 7
22 Roughley.........B 5
44 Roughsike........E 3
33 Roughton, Lincs...D 9
26 Roughton, Norf...B 5
22 Roughton, Salop..C 1
47 Roughwood.......D 8
17 Round Oak.......H 7
7 Roundham........E 7
35 Roundhay........C 12
43 Roundstonefoot..A 12
9 Roundstreet Com. C 12
19 Roundway........H 1
22 Rous Lench.......G 4
6 Rousdon..........G 6
47 Routdaneburn.....D 7
47 Routenburn.......C 7
37 Routh............C 8
61 Rovie Lodge......F 7
3 Row, Cornwall....B 8
39 Row, Westmor.....F 7
44 Rowanburn........E 2
51 Rowardennan Hotel
H 10
31 Rowarth..........A 8
16 Rowde............H 1
15 Rowden Down...G 12
29 Ro-wen...........C 7
44 Rowfoot..........G 5
19 Rowhedge........B 10
9 Rowhook.........C 12
22 Rowington.......E 5
31 Rowland.........C 10
9 Rowland's Castle..E 9
45 Rowland's Gill...G 10
9 Rowledge.........B 9
21 Rowley, Salop.....B 8
37 Rowley, Yorks....D 7

MAP
22 Rowley Regis.....C 3
15 Rowlstone........B 7
9 Rowly............B 11
22 Rowney Green....E 4
8 Rownhams........D 5
17 Rowsham.........B 9
31 Rowsley..........D 11
33 Rowston..........E 8
30 Rowton, Ches.....D 3
30 Rowton, Salop....H 5
49 Roxburgh.........F 9
49 Roxburgh, Co.....H 9
49 Roxburgh Newtown F 9
37 Roxby, Lincs.....E 7
41 Roxby, Yorks.....D 7
25 Roxton...........K 3
18 Roxwell..........C 6
34 Royal Oak........G 3
55 Roybridge........L 6
25 Roydon, Essex....C 4
27 Roydon, Norfolk..G 4
24 Roydon, Norfolk..C 8
25 Royston, Herts....L 5
35 Royston, Yorks...F 12
35 Royton...........F 8
29 Ruabon...........F 12
2 Ruan High Lanes..F 6
2 Ruan Lanihorne...E 6
2 Ruan Minor.......H 4
15 Ruardean.........C 9
15 Ruardean Woodside
C 9
22 Rubery...........D 3
39 Ruckcroft........A 8
21 Ruckhall Com....H 10
11 Ruckinge.........E 9
33 Ruckland.........B 10
21 Ruckley..........B 10
40 Rudby............D 5
45 Rudchester.......F 9
32 Ruddington.......G 3
15 Rudford..........B 11
7 Rudge............A 11
15 Rudgeway.........F 9
9 Rudgwick.........C 12
15 Rudhall..........B 9
14 Rudry............F 5
41 Rudston..........H 11
31 Rudyard..........D 8
49 Ruecastle........G 8
34 Rufford..........F 3
36 Rufforth.........B 3
45 Ruffside.........H 8
23 Rugby............E 8
31 Rugeley..........H 9
56 Ruilick..........E 1
6 Ruishton.........D 6
18 Ruislip..........E 1
18 Ruislip Common..E 1
44 Ruletownhead.....B 4
49 Rumbletonlaw.....E 9
52 Rumblingbridge...G 5
27 Rumburgh.........G 6
2 Rumford..........C 6
14 Rumney...........F 5
52 Runacraig........F 1
30 Runcorn..........B 4
9 Runcton..........F 10
24 Runcton Holme...E 7
5 Rundlestone......H 4
9 Runfold..........A 10
26 Runhall..........E 4
26 Runham...........D 7
6 Runnington.......D 5
19 Runsell Green....C 8
41 Runswick.........D 8
57 Runtaleave.......M 8
19 Runwell..........D 7
17 Ruscombe.........F 9
56 Rosehaugh House.D 2
19 Rush Green.......B 11
15 Rushall, Herefs....A 9
27 Rushall, Norfolk..G 5
22 Rushall, Staffs....B 4
8 Rushall, Wilts.....A 3
27 Rushbrooke........J 2
21 Rushbury.........C 10
25 Rushden, Herts...M 4
25 Rushden, Northants.
J 1
27 Rushford.........G 2
10 Rushlake Green...F 5
27 Rushmere.........G 8
27 Rushmere St. Andrew
K 5
27 Rushmere Street...K 5
9 Rushmoor, Surrey B 10
8 Rushmore, Wilts...D 1
22 Rushock..........E 2
35 Rusholme.........H 7
30 Rushton, Ches....D 4
23 Rushton, Northants.
D 11

MAP
21 Rushton, Salop...B 11
31 Rushton Spencer..D 8
22 Rushwick.........G 2
40 Rushyford........B 3
52 Ruskie...........G 1
33 Ruskington.......E 8
43 Rusko............F 7
38 Rusland..........F 6
10 Rusper...........D 1
15 Ruspidge.........C 9
10 Russell's Green...G 6
17 Russell's Water....E 8
9 Rustington.......F 11
41 Ruston...........G 9
37 Ruston Parva.....A 8
41 Ruswarp..........D 9
49 Rutherford.......F 9
47 Rutherglen.......C 11
3 Ruthernbridge....C 7
29 Ruthin...........D 10
59 Ruthrieston......G 7
58 Ruthven, Aber....C 3
53 Ruthven, Angus...B 7
49 Ruthven, Ber.....E 10
56 Ruthven, Inver....F 4
57 Ruthven, Inver.....J 3
53 Ruthven House...B 8
2 Ruthvoes.........D 6
43 Ruthwell.........E 11
15 Ruxton Green.....B 8
30 Ruyton Eleven Towns
H 3
45 Ryal.............F 8
7 Ryall............G 7
10 Ryarsh...........B 5
38 Rydal............E 6
9 Ryde.............G 7
4 Rydon............F 2
11 Rye..............F 8
11 Rye Foreign......F 7
11 Rye Harbour......F 8
43 Ryemuir..........D 11
24 Ryhall...........D 1
36 Ryhill, Yorks.....F 2
37 Ryhill, Yorks.....E 10
45 Ryhope..........H 12
33 Ryland...........B 7
35 Rylstone.........A 8
7 Ryme Intrinseca...E 9
49 Ryslaw...........E 10
36 Ryther...........C 3
45 Ryton, Dur.......G 9
15 Ryton, Glos......A 10
21 Ryton, Salop.....B 10
22 Ryton, Salop......B 1
41 Ryton, Yorks......H 8
23 Ryton-on-Dunsmore
E 7
34 Sabden...........C 6
18 Sacombe..........B 3
45 Sacriston........H 10
40 Sadberge.........C 4
46 Saddell..........F 3
23 Saddington......C 10
24 Saddle Bow.......D 7
8 Saddle Heath.....E 3
35 Saddleworth......F 9
39 Sadgill..........E 7
25 Saffron Walden...L 6
12 Sageston.........G 4
26 Saham Hills......E 2
26 Saham Toney......E 2
30 Saighton.........D 3
50 Sailean..........C 6
49 St. Abbs........C 11
2 St. Agnes, Corn....E 4
2 St. Agnes,
Is. of Scilly.....D 2
18 St. Albans.......C 2
2 St. Allen........E 5
53 St. Andrews.....E 10
14 St. Andrews Major G 5
34 St. Anne's.......D 2
43 St. Ann's........B 11
3 St. Ann's Chapel,
Cornwall.......C 11
5 St. Ann's Chapel,
Devon..........L 5
2 St. Anthony......G 5
10 St. Anthony's Hill H 5
15 St. Arvans.......E 8
29 St. Asaph........C 9
14 St. Athan........G 3
3 St. Austell.......D 7
7 St. Bartholomew's
Hill...........D 12
38 St. Bees.........D 2
3 St. Blazey.......D 8
3 St. Blazey Gate...D 7
49 St. Boswells......F 8
3 St. Breock.......C 7
3 St. Breward......B 8
15 St. Briavels......D 9

MAP
12 St. Brides........F 2
14 St. Brides Major..G 2
15 St. Brides
Netherwent.....E 7
14 St. Bride's-super-
Ely............G 4
14 St. Bride's
Wentlooge......F 6
38 St. Bridget
Beckermet.......E 3
5 St. Budeaux......K 3
2 St. Buryan.......G 1
15 St. Catherine...G 11
51 St. Catherines....G 8
12 St. Clears........E 6
3 St. Cleer.........C 9
2 St. Clement......E 5
3 St. Clether.......A 9
46 St. Colmac.......C 5
2 St. Columb Major.C 6
2 St. Columb Minor.C 5
2 St. Columb Porth..C 5
2 St. Columb Road..D 6
58 St. Combs........A 8
27 St. Cross South
Elmham.........G 6
49 St. Cuthberts.....E 11
12 St. David's, Pemb. D 1
52 St. David's, Perth..E 4
2 St. Day..........E 4
6 St. Decumans.....B 4
2 St. Dennis.......D 6
15 St. Devereux......A 7
12 St. Dogmaels.....B 5
12 St. Dogwells......D 3
3 St. Dominick.....C 11
14 St. Donats.......G 3
16 St. Edith's Marsh.H 1
3 St. Endellion.....B 7
2 St. Enoder.......D 6
2 St. Erme........E 5
3 St. Erney........D 10
2 St. Erth.........F 3
2 St. Ervan........C 6
3 St. Ewe..........E 7
14 St. Fagans........F 4
58 St. Fergus.......B 8
52 St. Fillans.......E 2
12 St. Florence......G 4
2 St. Gennys.......B 2
29 St. George.......C 9
14 St. George's, Glam.G 4
15 St. Georges, Som..H 7
3 St. Germans.....D 10
4 St. Giles in the
Wood...........D 4
5 St. Giles on the
Heath..........G 2
20 St. Harmon.......E 5
40 St. Helen Auckland C 2
26 St. Helena.......D 5
9 St. Helens, Hants..G 7
34 St. Helens, Lancs..G 4
2 St. Hilary, Corn...F 3
14 St. Hilary, Glam..G 3
10 Saint Hill........D 3
14 St. Illtyd........D 5
12 St. Ishmael's......F 2
2 St. Issey.........C 6
3 St. Ive..........C 10
2 St. Ives, Corn.....F 2
8 St. Ives, Hants....F 3
25 St. Ives, Hunts...H 4
27 St. James South
Elmham.........G 6
8 St. Joan à Gores
Cross..........A 2
3 St. John........D 11
38 St. John Beckermet D 3
38 St. John's, I. o. M..G 1
22 St. Johns, Worcs..G 2
4 St. John's Chapel,
Devon..........C 4
39 St. John's Chapel,
Durham........A 11
24 St. John's Fen End D 6
24 St. John's Highway D 6
38 St. Judas.........F 2
2 St. Just.........G 1
2 St. Just Lane.....F 6
58 St. Katherines....D 5
2 St. Keverne.......G 5
3 St. Kew..........B 7
3 St. Kew Highway..B 7
3 St. Keyne........D 9
3 St. Lawrence, Corn. C 7
19 St. Lawrence, Essex C 9
9 St. Lawrence,
Hants...........H 7
17 St. Leonards,
Bucks..........C 10
8 St. Leonards,
Hants...........F 3

MAP
11 St. Leonards,
Sussex.........G 7
2 St. Levan........G 1
14 St. Lythans......G 4
3 St. Mabyn........B 7
6 St. Margaret......D 4
27 St. Margaret
South Elmham..G 6
15 St. Margarets,
Herefordshire...A 7
18 St. Margarets,
Hertfordshire...C 4
11 St. Margaret's at
Cliffe.........D 12
64 St. Margaret's
Hope..........E 2
38 St. Mark's.......H 1
3 St. Martin.......D 9
52 St. Martins, Perth .D 6
30 St. Martin's, Salop.G 2
2 St. Martin's Green.G 4
8 St. Mary Bourne..A 6
14 St. Mary Church..G 3
18 St. Mary Cray....G 5
11 St. Mary in the
Marsh..........E 9
18 St. Marylebone....F 3
64 St. Marys.......D 3
11 St. Mary's Bay....E 9
15 St. Mary's Grove..G 8
19 St. Mary's Hoo....F 8
15 St. Maughans.....C 8
2 St. Mawes.......F 5
2 St. Mawgan......C 6
3 St. Mellion......C 11
14 St. Mellons.......F 6
2 St. Merryn.......B 6
3 St. Mewan........E 7
3 St. Michael
Caerhays.......E 7
2 St. Michael
Penkevil.......E 6
27 St. Michael
South Elmham..G 6
11 St. Michaels,
Kent...........E 7
21 St. Michaels,
Worcestershire .F 11
34 St. Michael's on
Wyre...........C 3
3 St. Minver.......B 7
53 St. Monance.....G 10
3 St. Neot.........C 9
25 St. Neots.........J 3
14 St. Nicholas,
Glamorgan ....G 4
12 St. Nicholas, Pemb.C 2
11 St. Nicholas at
Wade..........A 11
52 St. Ninians......H 3
19 St. Osyth.......B 11
15 St. Owen's Cross..B 8
18 St. Pancras.......F 3
18 St. Paul's Cray....G 5
18 St. Paul's Walden..B 2
11 St. Peters.......A 12
12 St. Petrox.......G 3
47 St. Quivox.......G 8
2 St. Stephen......D 6
3 St. Stephens, Corn.A 10
3 St. Stephens, Corn.D 11
3 St. Teath........B 7
3 St. Tudy.........B 8
12 St. Twynnells.....G 3
3 St. Veep.........D 8
53 St. Vigeans......C 11
3 St. Wenn.........C 7
15 St. Weonards.....B 8
22 Saintbury........H 5
51 Salachail........B 8
5 Salcombe.........M 6
6 Salcombe Regis...G 5
19 Salcott..........C 9
35 Sale.............H 7
22 Sale Green.......F 3
33 Saleby...........B 11
10 Salehurst.........F 6
28 Salem, Caer.......E 5
20 Salem, Cards......D 2
13 Salem, Carm......D 9
50 Salen, Argyll......A 4
50 Salen, Mull, Arg...C 3
34 Salesbury........D 5
23 Salford, Beds.....H 12
35 Salford, Lancs....G 17
16 Salford, Oxon.....A 4
22 Salford Priors....G 4
10 Salfords.........C 2
26 Salhouse.........D 6
52 Saline...........H 5
8 Salisbury........C 3
26 Sall.............C 4
51 Sallachan........A 7

MAP
55 Sallachy, Ross &
Cromarty.......G 3
60 Sallachy, Suther...F 6
33 Salmonby........C 10
43 Salmond's Muir..C 10
21 Salop, Co........B 10
16 Salperton........B 2
25 Salph End........K 2
48 Salsburgh........C 1
31 Salt.............G 8
3 Saltash..........D 11
56 Saltburn.........C 3
41 Saltburn-by-the-
Sea............C 7
32 Saltby...........H 6
47 Saltcoats........E 7
35 Salterforth.......C 7
24 Salters Lode......E 7
30 Satterswall.......D 5
33 Saltfleet.........A 11
33 Saltfleetby
St. Clements...A 11
33 Saltfleetby
St. Peter.......A 11
33 Saltfleetby Saints.A 11
15 Saltford.........G 10
37 Salthaugh Grange E 10
26 Salthouse........A 4
36 Saltmarshe.......E 6
30 Saltney..........D 3
41 Salton...........G 7
4 Saltren's.........D 3
45 Saltwick.........E 10
11 Saltwood.........D 10
9 Salvington.......F 12
22 Salwarpe.........F 2
7 Salway Ash.......F 8
22 Sambourne.......F 4
30 Sambrook........H 6
34 Samlesbury.......D 5
34 Samlesbury
Bottoms........D 5
6 Sampford........B 4
6 Sampford Arundel.D 5
4 Sampford
Courtenay.......F 5
6 Sampford Peverell.E 4
5 Sampford Spiney..H 4
19 Samuel's Corner...E 9
49 Samuelston.......B 7
54 Sanachan.........F 2
51 Sanahole.........G 7
2 Sancreed.........G 1
37 Sancton..........C 7
64 Sand.............D 7
36 Sand Hutton......A 5
38 Sand Side........G 5
55 Sandaig, Inver.....J 1
55 Sandaig, Inver.....H 1
35 Sandal Magna...E 12
38 Sandale..........A 5
30 Sandbach........D 6
46 Sandbank.........A 6
8 Sandbanks.......G 2
58 Sandend.........A 3
18 Sanderstead.....H 3
4 Sandford, Devon..F 7
8 Sandford, Dorset..G 1
9 Sandford, Hants...H 7
47 Sandford, Lan....E 12
30 Sandford, Salop...H 2
15 Sandford, Som....H 7
39 Sandford,
Westmorland...D 9
16 Sandford-on-
Thames.........D 6
7 Sandford Orcas...D 9
16 Sandford St. Martin B 5
58 Sandfordhill......C 8
64 Sandgarth........C 3
11 Sandgate........E 10
58 Sandhaven........A 7
42 Sandhead........G 2
47 Sandhill.........H 9
45 Sandhoe..........F 8
44 Sandholm........D 3
24 Sandholme, Lincs..B 4
36 Sandholme, Yorks. D 6
17 Sandhurst, Berks..H 9
15 Sandhurst, Glos...B 11
11 Sandhurst, Kent...E 7
10 Sandhurst Cross...E 6
40 Sandhutton.......G 4
32 Sandiacre........G 2
33 Sandilands.......B 12
30 Sandiway.........C 5
16 Sandleigh........D 6
10 Sandling.........B 6
64 Sandness........D 6
19 Sandon, Essex....C 7
25 Sandon, Herts....M 4
31 Sandon, Staffs....G 8
9 Sandown.........H 7

MAP

3 Sandplace.......D 9
18 Sandridge, Herts...C 2
15 Sandridge,Wilts..H 12
41 Sandsend.......D 8
64 Sandside......D 1
61 Sandside Hotel....A 9
64 Sandsound....D 7
36 Sandtoft......F 5
11 Sandway, Kent...C 7
6 Sandway, Som...C 2
11 Sandwich.......B 12
64 Sandwick,
  Orkney Is.......E 2
63 Sandwick,
  Ross & Crom..D 5
64 Sandwick,
  Shetland Is.....E 7
38 Sandwick, Westmor.C6
38 Sandwith......D 2
25 Sandy........K 3
30 Sandy Bank.....G 4
10 Sandy Cross.....F 5
12 Sandy Haven....F 2
16 Sandy Lane, Wilts.G 1
35 Sandy Lane, Yorks.D 9
29 Sandycroft......D 12
47 Sandyford, Ayr..G 9
43 Sandyford, Dumf. B 12
38 Sandygate......F 2
43 Sandyhills......F 9
34 Sandylands......A 3
4 Sandymoor Cross.F 3
5 Sandypark......G 6
44 Sandysike......F 2
49 Sandystones.....G 8
15 Sandyway......B 8
50 Sanna.........A 2
47 Sanquhar......H 12
38 Santon Bridge....E 4
27 Santon Downham.G 1
23 Sapcote......C 8
21 Sapey Common..F 12
27 Sapiston.......H 2
15 Sapperton, Glos..D 12
33 Sapperton, Lincs..G 7
4 Saracen's Head....C 4
61 Sarclet.......C 12
12 Sardis........F 3
12 Sardis Mountain..F 5
8 Sarisbury......E 6
28 Sarn, Caer......G 2
14 Sarn, Glam......F 2
21 Sarn, Mont......C 7
14 Sarnau, Brec....A 3
12 Sarnau, Cards...B 6
13 Sarnau, Carm...D 8
29 Sarnau, Mer.....F 9
21 Sarnau, Mont....F 9
28 Sarn-back......H 2
21 Sarnesfield.......G 9
28 Saron, Caer.....D 5
13 Saron, Carm.....C 7
13 Saron, Carm.....F 9
17 Sarratt......D 11
11 Sarre........B 11
16 Sarsden......B 4
8 Sarson.......B 4
38 Sartfield......F 2
40 Satley.......A 1
4 Satterleigh......D 5
38 Satterthwaite.....F 6
17 Satwell......F 8
58 Sauchen......F 4
53 Saucher......D 7
59 Sauchieburn.....K 4
47 Sauchrie......H 8
44 Saughtree......C 4
44 Saughtrees......E 3
15 Saul........C 10
32 Saundby......A 5
12 Saundersfoot....F 5
17 Saunderton.....D 9
17 Saunderton Lee..D 9
4 Saunton......B 3
33 Sausthorpe.....C 11
60 Savalmore.....F 6
31 Saverley Green...F 8
50 Savory......C 4
18 Sawbridgeworth..B 5
41 Sawdon......G 9
32 Sawley, Derby...G 2
34 Sawley, Yorks...C 6
25 Sawston......K 6
25 Sawtry......G 5
32 Saxby, Leics....H 5
33 Saxby, Lincs....B 7
37 Saxby All Saints..E 7
32 Saxelby......H 4
32 Saxilby......C 6
26 Saxlingham.....B 3
26 Saxlingham
  Nethergate....F 5
27 Saxmundham....J 7

25 Saxon Street....J 8
32 Saxondale......F 4
27 Saxtead......J 6
27 Saxtead Green...J 6
26 Saxthorpe......C 4
36 Saxton......C 3
10 Sayers Common..F 2
48 Scabcleuch.....H 5
40 Scackleton.....H 6
63 Scadabay......H 3
32 Scaftworth.....A 4
41 Scagglethorpe....H 8
50 Scalasaig......H 1
36 Scalby, E. Riding..D 6
41 Scalby, N. Riding F 10
23 Scaldwell......E 11
44 Scaleby......G 3
44 Scalebyhill......G 3
38 Scales, Cumb....C 6
38 Scales, Lancs....H 5
34 Scales, Lancs....D 3
39 Scales Houses....A 8
32 Scalford......H 5
41 Scaling.......D 7
50 Scallastle......D 4
64 Scalloway......E 7
62 Scalpay House...E 5
55 Scamadale......K 1
55 Scamodale......M 2
41 Scampston......H 8
33 Scampton......B 7
56 Scaniport......F 2
64 Scapa........D 2
64 Scar........A 4
39 Scar End......B 11
63 Scarastavore....H 1
41 Scarborough....F 10
43 Scarbrae......C 9
32 Scarcliffe......C 2
35 Scarcroft......C 12
54 Scardroy......D 6
44 Scare........F 3
61 Scarfskerry....A 11
40 Scargill......D 1
32 Scarrington.....F 4
34 Scarth Hill......F 3
37 Scartho......G 10
64 Scarwell......C 1
56 Scatraig......F 3
64 Scatsta......C 7
37 Scawby......G 7
37 Scawby Brook...F 7
40 Scaynton......G 6
10 Scayne's Hill....F 3
14 Scethrog......B 4
47 Schaw.......G 9
31 Scholar Green....E 7
35 Scholes, W. Riding F 10
35 Scholes, W. Riding F 10
36 Scholes, W. Riding D 2
40 School Aycliffe...C 3
35 Scissett......F 11
12 Scleddau......D 3
26 Sco Ruston.....C 6
27 Scole........G 4
59 Scolly's Cross...J 4
12 Scolton......E 3
62 Sconser......E 4
53 Scoonie......G 8
50 Scoor.......F 2
33 Scopwick......D 8
60 Scoraig......G 2
37 Scorborough.....C 8
47 Scorrieholm....F 12
2 Scorrier......E 4
5 Scorriton......J 6
40 Scorton......E 3
34 Scot Lane End...F 5
44 Scotby......G 3
40 Scotch Corner...E 2
34 Scotforth......A 4
33 Scothern......B 7
45 Scots' Gap.....D 8
33 Scots Hole.....D 8
56 Scotsburn......D 6
61 Scotscalder Sta...B 10
53 Scotscraig......D 9
44 Scotsdike......F 2
59 Scotston, Kinc...K 5
52 Scotston, Perth...C 4
50 Scotstown......A 5
45 Scotswood.....G 10
53 Scottas......J 1
36 Scotter......G 6
36 Scotterthorpe....G 6
37 Scotton, Lincs...G 7
40 Scotton, N. Riding.F 2
35 Scotton, W. Riding
  ....A 12
49 Scoughall......A 8
26 Scoulton......E 3

60 Scourie........C 3
60 Scourie More....C 3
64 Scousburgh.....F 7
61 Scrabster......A 10
49 Scraesburgh....G 9
33 Scrafield......C 10
45 Scrainwood.....B 8
33 Scramblesby....B 10
24 Scrane End.....A 5
23 Scraptoft......D 8
26 Scratby.......D 8
36 Scrayingham....A 5
24 Scredington.....B 4
6 Screedy.......D 4
43 Screel.......F 9
33 Scremby......C 11
49 Scremerston....D 12
32 Screveton......F 4
61 Scriberscross....F 8
33 Scrivelsby......D 9
35 Scriven.......A 12
43 Scroggs......C 12
32 Scrooby......A 4
31 Scropton......G 10
33 Scrub Hill.....E 9
40 Scruton......F 3
37 Sculcoates.....D 8
26 Sculthorpe.....B 2
37 Scunthorpe.....F 7
13 Scurlage......H 8
26 Sea Palling.....C 7
7 Seaborough.....F 8
30 Seacombe......A 2
33 Seacroft, Lincs..D 12
35 Seacroft, Yorks.D 12
47 Seafield, Ayr....G 8
48 Seafield, W. Loth..C 3
10 Seaford......H 4
34 Seaforth......G 2
63 Seaforth Head...E 4
45 Seaham......H 12
45 Seahouses.....D 12
10 Seal........B 4
30 Sealand......C 2
9 Seale........A 10
41 Seamer, N. Riding..E 6
40 Seamer, N. Riding.D 5
47 Seamill......E 7
37 Searby.......G 8
11 Seasalter......B 9
38 Seascale......E 3
33 Seathorne.....D 12
38 Seathwaite, Cumb. D 5
38 Seathwaite, Lancs..F 5
38 Seatoller......D 5
3 Seaton, Corn...D 10
38 Seaton, Cumb...B 3
6 Seaton, Devon...E 6
45 Seaton, Dur....H 12
45 Seaton, Northumb.E 11
23 Seaton, Rut....B 12
37 Seaton, Yorks...B 9
45 Seaton Burn....F 10
45 Seaton Carew...B 5
45 Seaton Delaval..E 11
36 Seaton Ross.....C 6
45 Seaton Sluice...E 11
58 Seatown, Banff..A 3
58 Seatown, Banff...A 2
7 Seatown, Dorset..G 7
40 Seave Green....E 6
9 Seaview......G 8
43 Seaville......F 12
7 Seavington
  St. Mary......E 7
7 Seavington
  St. Michael....E 7
19 Seawick Sands...C 11
14 Sebastopol, Glam..D 5
14 Sebastopol, Mon..E 6
38 Sebergham.....A 6
22 Seckington.....A 6
60 Second Coast...G 1
39 Sedbergh......F 9
15 Sedbury......B 12
39 Sedbusk......F 11
22 Sedgeberow....H 4
15 Sedgebrook.....F 6
40 Sedgefield......B 4
24 Sedgeford......B 8
17 Sedgehill......C 12
22 Sedgley......C 2
39 Sedgwick......F 7
10 Sedlescombe....F 6
10 Sedlescombe St..F 6
15 Seend.......H 12
15 Seende Cleeve...H 12
17 Seer Green.....E 10
26 Seething......F 6
2 Sefton.......G 2
45 Seghill......F 11
31 Seighford......H 7
63 Seilebost......G 2

22 Seisdon........C 2
30 Selattyn......G 1
9 Selborne......C 9
36 Selby.......D 4
9 Selham......D 10
49 Selkirk.......G 7
48 Selkirk, Co......G 6
15 Sellack......B 9
38 Sellafield Station..E 3
64 Sellafirth......B 7
11 Sellindge......D 9
11 Sellindge Lees...D 9
11 Selling......B 9
15 Sells Green.....H 12
22 Selly Oak......D 4
10 Selmeston.....G 4
18 Selsdon......H 4
15 Selsey.......D 11
10 Sellsfield Common.E 2
39 Selside......H 10
11 Selstead......D 10
11 Selston......E 2
6 Selworthy.....B 3
64 Semblister.....D 6
27 Semer........K 3
15 Semington.....H 12
7 Semley.......D 12
9 Send........A 11
9 Sendmarsh.....A 11
14 Senghenydd....E 4
2 Sennen......G 1
2 Sennen Cove...G 1
14 Sennybridge....B 3
43 Senwick Ho....G 7
40 Sessay......H 5
24 Setchey......D 7
8 Setley.......F 5
64 Settascarth.....C 2
64 Setter, Bressay
  Shetland Is....E 7
64 Setter, Zetland
  Shetland Is....D 6
64 Setter, Zetland
  Shetland Is....D 7
35 Settle.......A 7
45 Settlingstones...F 7
41 Settrington.....H 8
6 Seven Ash......C 5
18 Seven Kings....E 4
14 Seven Sisters...C 2
16 Seven Wells....A 2
16 Sevenhampton, Glos.
  ....B 1
16 Sevenhampton, Wilts.
  ....E 3
10 Sevenoaks......C 4
10 Sevenoaks Weald..C 4
15 Severn Beach....F 8
22 Severn Stoke....H 2
11 Sevington, Kent...D 9
15 Sevington, Wilts..F 8
25 Sewards End....L 7
41 Sewerby......H 12
2 Seworgan......G 4
32 Sewstern......H 6
10 Seyning......G 1
17 Shabbington....C 7
23 Shackerstone....A 7
27 Shadingfield....G 7
27 Shackleford....B 10
40 Shadforth.....A 4
11 Shadoxhurst....D 8
27 Shadwell, Norfolk.G 2
35 Shadwell, Yorks..C 12
7 Shaftesbury...D 12
36 Shafton......F 2
16 Shalbourne....H 4
8 Shalcombe.....G 5
9 Shalden......B 8
5 Shaldon......J 8
8 Shalfleet......G 5
19 Shalford, Essex..A 7
9 Shalford, Surrey..A 11
19 Shalford Green...A 7
42 Shallcoch.....B 5
4 Shallowford....B 6
11 Shalmsford Street.C 9
23 Shalstone.....H 9
46 Shalunt......B 5
9 Shamley Green..B 11
43 Shancastle.....C 9
47 Shandon......A 7
56 Shandwick.....B 4
25 Shangton......C 10
45 Shankhouse....E 11
9 Shanklin......H 7
46 Shannochie....G 5
53 Shanzie......B 7
39 Shap........D 8
7 Shapwick, Dorset..F 1
7 Shapwick, Som...B 7
32 Shardlow......G 2
22 Shareshill......B 3

35 Sharlston,
  W. Riding.....E 12
36 Sharlston,
  W. Riding.....E 2
11 Sharnal Street....A 7
25 Sharnbrook.....J 1
23 Sharnford......C 8
23 Sharoe Green...D 4
40 Sharow......H 3
25 Sharpenhoe....M 2
45 Sharperton....C 8
15 Sharpness.....D 10
30 Sharpthorne....E 3
26 Sharrington....B 3
22 Shatterford.....D 1
5 Shaugh Prior...J 4
7 Shave Cross....F 7
30 Shavington.....E 6
16 Shaw, Berks....G 6
34 Shaw, Lancs....F 8
15 Shaw, Wilts....H 12
32 Shawton......E 2
35 Shaw Green....E 4
35 Shaw Mills.....A 11
30 Shawbury......H 4
19 Shawdon Hill...B 9
23 Shawell......D 9
8 Shawford......D 6
35 Shawforth.....E 7
43 Shawhead.....D 9
43 Shawhill......E 12
47 Shawood......G 10
47 Shawton......D 11
7 Shear Cross....B 11
43 Shearington....E 11
23 Shearsby......C 9
4 Shebbear......E 3
31 Shebdon......H 6
61 Shebster......B 9
9 Shedfield.....E 7
31 Sheen.......D 9
21 Sheephouse....H 7
15 Sheepscombe...C 12
5 Sheepstor......J 4
4 Sheepwash, Devon.E 4
4 Sheepwash, Devon.C 7
45 Sheepwash,
  Northumb....D 10
15 Sheepway.....G 8
23 Sheepy Magna..B 7
23 Sheepy Parva...B 7
18 Sheering......C 5
11 Sheerness.....A 8
21 Sheet, Salop...E 10
9 Sheet, Hants...D 9
32 Sheffield......B 1
25 Shefford......L 2
16 Shefford
  Woodlands....G 4
43 Sheillahill......F 8
21 Sheinton......B 11
21 Shelderton.....E 9
6 Sheldon, Devon..E 5
22 Sheldon, War...D 5
11 Sheldwich.....B 9
35 Shelf........D 10
27 Shelfhanger....G 4
22 Shelfield, Staffs..B 4
22 Shelfield, War...F 5
49 Shellacres.....E 11
18 Shelley, Essex...C 5
35 Shelley, Yorks...F 10
16 Shellingford....E 4
18 Shellow Bowells..C 6
22 Shelsley
  Beauchamp....F 1
21 Shelsley Walsh..F 12
32 Shelthorpe.....H 3
26 Shelton, Norfolk..F 5
25 Shelton, Northants.H 1
32 Shelton, Notts...F 5
21 Shelton, Salop...A 10
21 Shelve.......C 9
21 Shelwick......H 10
21 Shelwick Green..H 10
56 Shenachie.....F 4
18 Shenfield......D 6
22 Shenington....H 7
18 Shenley......D 2
17 Shenley Brook End A 9
23 Shenley Church
  End........H 11
15 Shenmore......A 7
22 Shennanton....E 4
22 Shenstone, Staffs..B 4
22 Shenstone, Worcs..E 2
23 Shenton......B 7
57 Shenval......G 8
15 Shepherdine....E 9
24 Shepeu Stow....D 4
18 Shephall......B 3
18 Shepherd's Bush..F 2

17 Shepherd's Green..F 8
11 Shepherdswell...C 11
35 Shepley......F 10
17 Shepperton.....G 11
17 Shepperton Grn..G 11
25 Shepreth......K 5
32 Shepshed......H 2
7 Shepton
  Beauchamp....D 7
7 Shepton Mallet...B 9
7 Shepton MontagueC 10
10 Shepway......C 6
40 Sheraton......B 5
7 Sherborne, Dorset E 10
16 Sherborne, Glos...C 3
9 Sherborne St. John A 8
22 Sherbourne.....F 6
40 Sherburn, Dur....A 3
41 Sherburn, Yorks..G 9
40 Sherburn Hill....A 4
36 Sherburn in Elmet.D 3
9 Shere........A 12
26 Shereford......C 2
8 Sherfield English..D 4
17 Sherfield on
  Loddon......H 7
5 Sherford......L 6
36 Sheriff Hutton...A 3
26 Sheringham....A 4
23 Sherington.....G 12
24 Shernborne....B 8
22 Sherriffhales...A 1
8 Sherrington....B 1
15 Sherston......F 11
4 Sherwood Green..D 4
63 Sheshader.....C 6
47 Shettleston....C 11
34 Shevington....F 4
34 Shevington Moor..F 4
3 Sheviock......D 10
55 Shewglie......G 8
52 Shian........C 3
49 Shidlaw......F 10
43 Shiel, Dumfries...A 8
43 Shiel, Kirk.....D 7
55 Shiel Bridge....H 3
45 Shiel Dykes....B 9
54 Shieldaig......D 2
54 Shieldaig Lodge
  (Hotel)......C 2
43 Shieldhill, Dumf..C 10
43 Shieldhill, Dumf..C 11
48 Shieldhill, Stir...B 2
47 Shieldmuir....D 12
50 Shielfoot......A 4
58 Shielhill, Aber...B 8
59 Shielhill, Angus..L 2
47 Shieloans......F 11
16 Shifford......D 5
21 Shifnal......A 1
45 Shilbottle.....B 10
44 Shilburn Haugh..D 5
40 Shildon......C 3
47 Shillford......D 9
6 Shillingford, Devon D 3
17 Shillingford, Oxon. E 7
6 Shillingford Abbot G 2
6 Shillingford
  St. George....G 2
7 Shillingstone...E 11
25 Shillington....M 2
45 Shillmoor.....B 7
63 Shiltenish.....E 4
16 Shilton, Oxon...C 4
23 Shilton, War....D 7
9 Shilvinghampton.H 9
27 Shimpling, Norf..G 4
27 Shimpling, Suffolk.K 2
27 Shimpling Street..K 2
40 Shincliffe.....A 3
40 Shincliffe Colliery..A 3
45 Shiney Row....H 11
17 Shinfield......G 8
59 Shinfur......J 2
43 Shinninghead...B 8
5 Shinner's Bridge..J 7
10 Shipbourne.....C 5
26 Shipdham......E 3
7 Shipham......A 8
5 Shiphay......J 8
17 Shiplake......D 2
48 Shiplaw......D 5
45 Shipley, Northumb.A 9
22 Shipley, Salop...C 2
9 Shipley, Sussex..D 12
35 Shipley, Yorks...C 10
10 Shipley Bridge...D 2
26 Shipmeadow....F 7
25 Shippea Hill Sta..G 7
16 Shipton, Glos...B 1
21 Shipton, Salop..C 11

MAP

36 Shipton, Yorks....A 3
8 Shipton Bellinger..B 4
7 Shipton Gorge....G 8
9 Shipton Green....F 9
15 Shipton Moyne...E 12
16 Shipton-on-
    Cherwell.....B 6
16 Shipton-under-
    Wychwood....B 4
36 Shiptonthorpe....C 6
17 Shirburn....E 8
34 Shirdley Hill....F 2
22 Shire Oak....B 4
32 Shirebrook....C 3
32 Shiregreen....A 1
15 Shirehampton....F 8
45 Shiremoor....F 11
15 Shirenewton....E 8
32 Shireoaks....B 3
4 Shirewell Cross...B 4
21 Shirl Heath....F 10
32 Shirland....D 1
31 Shirley, Derby..F 10
8 Shirley, Hants...E 5
22 Shirley, War....D 5
9 Shirrell Heath....E 7
4 Shirwell....B 5
46 Shiskine....F 4
21 Shobdon....F 9
4 Shobrooke....F 7
30 Shocklach....E 3
19 Shoeburyness....E 8
11 Sholden....C 12
8 Sholing....E 6
4 Shop, Cornwall...D 1
2 Shop, Cornwall...B 6
27 Shop Street....H 5
44 Shopford....F 4
18 Shoreditch....F 3
10 Shoreham....B 4
10 Shoreham-by-Sea..G 1
56 Shoremill....C 3
49 Shoresdean....E 12
49 Shoreswood....E 12
56 Shoretown....D 2
16 Shorncote....E 1
4 Shorne....A 6
10 Shorne Ridgeway..A 6
22 Short Heath, Leics.A 6
8 Short Heath, Staffs.B 3
22 Short Heath, War..C 4
5 Shortacombe....G 4
10 Shortgate....G 4
2 Shortlanesend....F 5
47 Shortlees....F 9
15 Shortwood....G 10
8 Shorwell....H 6
7 Shoscombe....A 10
30 Shotatton....H 2
26 Shotesham....F 6
19 Shotgate....E 7
45 Shotley Bridge...H 9
27 Shotley Gate....M 5
27 Shotley Street....M 5
45 Shotleyfield....H 9
11 Shottenden....C 9
9 Shottermill....C 10
22 Shottery....G 5
23 Shotteswell....H 8
27 Shottisham....L 6
31 Shottle....E 11
40 Shotton, Durham..A 4
29 Shotton, Flint...C 12
49 Shotton,
    Northumb....F 11
40 Shotton Colliery..A 4
48 Shotts....C 1
30 Shotwick....C 2
38 Shoughlaige-e-
    Caine....G 1
56 Shougle....D 8
24 Shouldham....E 8
24 Shouldham Thorpe E 8
22 Shoulton....F 2
10 Shover's Green...E 5
21 Shrawardine....A 9
22 Shrawley....F 2
17 Shreding Green...F 11
22 Shrewley....E 5
21 Shrewsbury....A 10
8 Shrewton....B 2
9 Shripney....F 10
16 Shrivenham....E 3
26 Shropham....F 3
19 Shrub End....E 7
21 Shucknall....H 11
25 Shudy Camps....L 7
63 Shulishader....C 6
38 Shundraw....C 5
15 Shurdington....B 12
17 Shurlock Row....G 9
61 Shurrery Lodge..B 10
6 Shurton....B 5

22 Shustoke....C 6
22 Shut End....C 2
4 Shute, Devon....F 8
6 Shute, Devon....F 6
23 Shutford....H 7
15 Shuthonger....A 12
23 Shutlanger....G 10
22 Shuttington....B 6
32 Shuttlewood....C 2
43 Sibbaldie....C 12
23 Sibbertoft....D 10
21 Sibdon Carwood..D 9
23 Sibford Ferris....H 7
23 Sibford Gower....H 7
27 Sible Hedingham..M 1
33 Sibsey....E 10
24 Sibson, Hunts....F 2
23 Sibson, Leics....B 7
32 Sibthorpe....F 5
27 Sicklesmere....J 2
35 Sicklinghall....B 12
6 Sid....G 5
6 Sidbury, Devon...G 5
21 Sidbury, Salop...D 12
18 Sidcup....G 5
38 Siddick....B 2
31 Siddington, Ches..C 7
16 Siddington, Glos..D 1
22 Sidemoor....E 3
6 Sidford....G 5
9 Sidlesham....F 10
10 Sidley....G 6
10 Sidlow Bridge....C 1
6 Sidmouth....H 4
5 Sigford....H 6
14 Sigginston....G 3
37 Sigglesthorne....C 9
17 Silchester....H 7
23 Sileby....A 9
38 Silecroft....G 4
20 Silian....G 1
24 Silk Willoughby..A 2
35 Silkstone....G 11
35 Silkstone Com...G 11
44 Silloans....C 6
43 Silloth....F 11
58 Sillyearn....B 3
13 Siloh....C 10
41 Silpho....F 9
35 Silsden....C 9
25 Silsoe....M 2
25 Silver End, Beds..L 2
19 Silver End, Essex..B 8
11 Silver Street....B 7
48 Silverburn....C 5
39 Silverdale, Lancs..H 7
31 Silverdale, Staffs..F 7
23 Silverstone....H 10
6 Silverton, Devon..F 3
47 Silverton, Dunb...B 9
21 Silvington....D 11
45 Simonburn....F 7
6 Simonsbath....B 1
34 Simonstone....D 6
49 Simprim....E 11
23 Simpson, Bucks..H 12
12 Simpson, Pemb...E 2
49 Sinclair's Hill....D 10
47 Sinclairston....H 9
40 Sinderby
    Quernhow....G 4
45 Sinderhope....H 7
17 Sindlesham....G 8
44 Singdean....C 4
17 Singleborough....A 8
34 Singleton, Lancs..C 3
9 Singleton, Sussex..E 10
10 Singlewell or Ifield .A 5
30 Singret....E 2
58 Sinnahard....F 2
41 Sinnington....G 7
22 Sinton....F 2
18 Sipson....F 1
14 Sirhowy....C 5
11 Sissinghurst....D 7
49 Sisterpath....E 10
15 Siston....G 10
2 Sithney....G 3
18 Sittingbourne....B 8
58 Sittyton....E 6
22 Six Ashes....C 2
32 Six Hills....H 4
25 Six Mile Bottom..J 7
31 Six Roads End...G 10
33 Sixhills....B 9
27 Sizewell....J 8
61 Skail....C 7
64 Skaill, Egilsay,
    Orkney Is....B 3
64 Skaill, Mainland,
    Orkney Is....D 3
64 Skaill, Mainland,
    Orkney Is....C 1

47 Skares....H 10
49 Skateraw, E. Loth..B 10
49 Skateraw, Kinc..H 7
62 Skeabost....C 3
40 Skeeby....E 2
37 Skeffington....B 11
37 Skeffling....E 11
32 Skegby....D 2
33 Skegness....D 12
61 Skelbo....G 8
32 Skelbrooke....F 3
24 Skeldyke....B 4
32 Skellingthorpe....C 6
64 Skellister....D 7
36 Skellow....F 3
35 Skelmanthorpe....F 11
40 Skelmersdale....F 4
58 Skelmonae....D 6
47 Skelmorlie....C 7
61 Skelmuir....C 7
61 Skelpick....B 7
39 Skelton, Cumb....B 7
40 Skelton, E. Riding..C 6
36 Skelton, E. Riding..E 5
36 Skelton, N. Riding.B 3
40 Skelton, N. Riding.E 1
40 Skelton, W. Riding H 4
38 Skelwith Bridge...E 6
64 Skelwick....A 3
33 Skendleby....C 11
58 Skene House....F 5
15 Skenfrith....B 8
37 Skerne....B 8
46 Skeroblingarry...G 2
61 Skerray....B 7
61 Skerricha....C 4
34 Skerton....A 4
23 Sketchley....C 7
13 Sketty....H 9
13 Skewen....G 10
40 Skewsby....H 6
26 Skeyton....C 5
60 Skiag Bridge....E 4
61 Skibo Castle....G 7
33 Skidbrooke....A 11
37 Skidby....D 8
63 Skigersta....A 6
5 Skilgate....D 3
32 Skillington....H 6
43 Skinburness....F 12
41 Skinidin....C 1
41 Skinningrove....C 7
46 Skipness....D 4
37 Skipsea....B 9
37 Skipsea Brough...B 9
35 Skipton....B 10
40 Skipton-on-Swale .G 4
36 Skipwith....C 4
24 Skirbeck....A 4
24 Skirbeck Quarter..A 4
48 Skirling....E 3
17 Skirmett....E 8
36 Skirpenbeck....A 5
39 Skirwith, Cumb...B 8
39 Skirwith, Yorks...H 9
21 Skirza....A 12
44 Skitby....F 3
62 Skulamus....F 6
60 Skullomie....B 6
57 Skye of Curr....G 5
35 Slack....D 8
31 Slackhall....B 9
58 Slackhead....A 2
43 Slacks....C 11
58 Slacks of
    Cairnbanno....C 6
15 Slad....D 12
4 Slade....B 4
18 Slade Green....F 5
3 Sladesbridge....C 7
44 Slaggyford....H 5
34 Slaidburn....B 6
59 Slains Park....K 6
49 Slainsfield....E 12
35 Slaithwaite....F 9
45 Slaley....G 8
48 Slamannan....B 1
17 Slapton, Bucks...B 10
5 Slapton, Devon...L 7
23 Slapton, Northants.G 9
54 Slattadale....C 3
35 Slattocks....F 7
10 Slaugham....E 1
30 Slaughter Hill....E 6
3 Slaughterbridge...D 7
15 Slaughterford....G 11
23 Slawston....C 11
9 Sleaford, Hants...F 2
24 Sleaford, Lincs....A 2
39 Sleagill....C 8
21 Sleap....A 11
21 Sleapford....A 11
15 Sledge Green....A 11

37 Sledmere....A 7
44 Sleetbeck....E 3
39 Sleightholme....D 11
41 Sleights....D 8
41 Slepe....G 1
4 Slerra....D 2
61 Slickly....A 12
46 Sliddery....G 4
62 Sligachan....E 4
51 Sligrachan....H 9
15 Slimbridge....D 10
31 Slindon, Staffs...G 7
9 Slindon, Sussex...E 11
9 Slinfold....C 12
28 Sling....D 5
41 Slingsby....H 7
58 Slioch....D 3
17 Slip End, Beds...B 11
25 Slip End, Herts...L 4
26 Slipper's Bottom..D 6
23 Slipton....D 12
31 Slitting Mill....H 9
57 Slochd....M 7
57 Slochnacraig....M 7
50 Slockavullin....H 5
43 Slogarie....E 7
33 Sloothby....C 12
17 Slough....F 10
6 Slough Green....D 6
57 Sluggan....G 4
34 Slyne....A 4
49 Smailholm....F 9
38 Smaithwaite....C 5
10 Small Dole....G 1
11 Small Hythe....E 7
35 Smallbridge....F 8
26 Smallburgh....C 6
58 Smallburn, Aber...D 8
47 Smallburn, Ayr..G 11
32 Smalley....F 1
10 Smallfield....D 2
43 Smallholm....D 11
6 Smallridge....F 6
8 Smannel....A 5
39 Smardale....D 9
11 Smarden....D 7
6 Smeatharpe....E 5
11 Smeeth, Kent....D 9
24 Smeeth, Norfolk...E 6
23 Smeeton Westerby C 10
35 Smelthouses....A 10
61 Smerral....D 11
22 Smethwick....C 4
31 Smisby....H 12
34 Smith Green....B 4
44 Smithfield....F 3
6 Smithincott....E 4
18 Smith's Green....B 6
47 Smithston....H 9
54 Smithstown....E 3
56 Smithtown....E 3
32 Smithy Houses....E 1
45 Snableazes....B 10
43 Snade....C 9
21 Snailbeach....B 8
25 Snailwell....H 7
41 Snainton....G 9
36 Snaith....E 4
31 Snape Inn....A 9
27 Snape, Suffolk....J 7
40 Snape, Yorks....G 3
34 Snape Green....F 3
27 Snape Street....J 7
23 Snarestone....A 7
33 Snarford....B 7
11 Snargate....E 8
11 Snave....E 9
23 Snead....C 8
41 Sneaton....D 9
41 Sneaton Thorpe...E 9
33 Snelland....B 8
31 Snelston....F 10
24 Snettisham....B 8
45 Snitter....C 8
33 Snitterby....A 7
22 Snitterfield....E 5
21 Snitton....E 11
21 Snodhill....H 8
10 Snodland....B 6
11 Snowdown....C 11
16 Snowshill....A 2
14 Soar, Brec....A 3
13 Soar, Carm....D 9
5 Soar, Devon....M 6
9 Soberton....D 7
9 Soberton Heath....E 7
25 Soham....H 7
12 Solbury....F 2
4 Soldon Cross....E 2
9 Soldridge....C 8
10 Sole Street....A 5
11 Solestreet....C 9
22 Solihull....D 5

21 Sollers Dilwyn....G 9
15 Sollers Hope....A 9
34 Sollom....E 3
12 Solva....E 2
44 Solwaybank....E 1
37 Somerby, Leics...A 11
37 Somerby, Lincs....F 8
32 Somercotes....E 2
8 Somerford....G 3
16 Somerford Keynes..E 1
15 Somerley....F 9
26 Somerleyton....F 8
31 Somersal Herbert.G 10
33 Somersby....C 10
6 Somerset, Co....C 6
25 Somersham,
    Hunts....H 5
27 Somersham,
    Suffolk....K 4
16 Somerton, Oxon...A 6
7 Somerton, Som...C 8
27 Somerton, Suffolk .K 1
10 Sompting....G 1
17 Sonning....G 8
17 Sonning Common .F 8
17 Sonning Eye....F 8
59 Sootywells....K 5
8 Sopley....F 3
15 Sopworth....F 11
42 Sorbie, Dumf....D 2
42 Sorbie, Yorks....G 5
44 Sorbietrees....E 3
61 Sordale....B 10
47 Sorn....G 10
47 Sornbeg....F 10
47 Sornfallow....F 2
47 Sornhill....F 10
50 Soroba Farm....E 6
61 Sortat....B 12
33 Sotby....B 9
17 Sotwell....E 8
29 Soughton....D 11
17 Soulbury....A 9
39 Soulby....D 9
16 Souldern....A 6
25 Souldrop....J 1
64 Sound, Zetland,
    Shetland Is....D 7
64 Sound, Zetland,
    Shetland Is....E 7
49 Sourhope....G 11
64 Sourin....B 2
5 Sourton....G 4
38 Soutergate....G 5
26 South Acre....D 1
5 South Allington...M 7
52 South Alloa....H 4
9 South
    Ambersham...D 10
32 South Anston....B 2
17 South Ascot....G 10
8 South Baddesley...F 5
42 South Balloch....B 5
7 South Barrow....C 9
28 South Beach....G 3
48 South Bellsdyke...A 2
19 South Benfleet....E 7
9 South Bersted....F 10
36 South Bramwith...F 4
5 South Brent....K 6
7 South Brewham...C 10
52 South Bridge-end..E 3
45 South Broomhill..C 10
26 South Burlingham .E 7
7 South Cadbury....D 9
42 South Cairn....E 1
33 South Carlton....C 7
46 South Carrine....H 2
37 South Cave....D 7
16 South Cerney....D 2
7 South Chard....F 7
45 South Charlton...A 9
7 South Cheriton...D 10
36 South Cliffe....D 6
32 South Clifton....C 5
33 South
    Cockerington...A 11
32 South
    Collingham....D 5
14 South Cornelly....F 1
27 South Cove....G 8
51 South Creagan....C 7
26 South Creake....B 1
23 South Croxton....A 10
37 South Dalton....C 7
10 South Darenth....A 4
63 South Dell....A 6
58 South Denmore....E 7
46 South Druimachro .E 2
36 South Duffield....D 5
33 South Elkington...A 10
36 South Elmsall....F 3
17 South End, Berks...G 7

17 South End,
    Buckinghamshire B 9
34 South End, Lancs..A 1
37 South End, Lincs...E 9
54 South Erradale....C 1
19 South Fambridge..D 8
16 South Fawley....F 5
46 South Feorline....G 4
37 South Ferriby....E 7
58 South Fornet....F 5
63 South Galson....A 5
46 South Garrochty..D 6
14 South Glamorgan, Co.
    G 4
8 South Gorley....E 3
58 South Gorrachie...B 5
19 South Green,
    Essex....E 7
11 South Green,
    Kent....B 7
46 South Hall....B 5
19 South Hanningfield D 7
9 South Harting....D 9
9 South Hayling....F 8
45 South Hazelrigg..C 11
17 South Heath....D 10
10 South Heighton...H 3
40 South Hetton....A 4
36 South Hiendley....F 2
3 South Hill, Corn..B 10
7 South Hill, Som...D 8
16 South Hinksey....D 6
4 South Hole....D 1
41 South Holme....G 7
10 South Holmwood .D 1
18 South Hornchurch .F 5
47 South Hourat....D 8
32 South Hykeham...D 6
45 South Hylton....G 11
60 South Keanchulish G 3
37 South Killingholme F 9
47 South Kilrusken...D 7
40 South Kilvington..G 4
23 South Kilworth....D 9
36 South Kirkby....F 2
59 South Kirktown...G 5
33 South Kyme....E 9
10 South Lancing....H 1
17 South Leigh....C 5
32 South Leverton....B 5
47 South
    Limmerhaugh..G 11
22 South Littleton....G 4
27 South Lopham....G 3
23 South Luffenham .B 12
53 South Mains....B 11
10 South Malling....G 3
16 South Marston....A 3
49 South Middleton .G 12
36 South Milford....D 3
5 South Milton....L 6
18 South Mimms....D 2
4 South Molton....C 6
16 South Moreton....E 6
9 South Mundham .F 10
32 South Muskham..E 5
37 South Newbald...D 7
45 South Newington..A 5
8 South Newton....C 2
32 South Normanton .E 2
16 South Norwood...G 3
10 South Nutfield....C 2
18 South Ockendon...F 6
33 South Ormsby....C 10
40 South Otterington .F 4
33 South Owersby....A 8
18 South Oxhey....E 1
7 South Perrott....F 8
7 South Petherton...D 8
3 South Petherwin..B 10
26 South Pickenham..E 1
5 South Pool....M 6
4 South Radworthy..C 6
33 South Rauceby....F 7
26 South Raynham...C 2
33 South Reston....B 11
24 South Runcton....E 7
32 South Scarle....D 6
63 South Shawbost...B 3
45 South Shields....F 12
34 South Shore....D 2
37 South Skirlaugh...C 9
33 South Somercotes A 11
35 South Stainley....A 1
18 South Stifford....F 6
17 South Stoke, Oxon. F 7
15 South Stoke, Som.H 10
9 South Stoke,
    Sussex....E 11
11 South Street, Kent.B 9
18 South Street,
    London....H 4

MAP
10 South Street, Sussex F 3
4 South Tawton......F 5
33 South Thoresby..C 11
8 South Tidworth...A 4
9 South Town....B 8
26 South Walsham...D 7
9 S. Warnborough ..A 8
18 South Weald......E 6
17 South Weston....D 8
5 South Wheatley, Corn. G 1
32 South Wheatley, Notts. B 5
7 South Widcombe..A 9
23 South Wigston...B 9
33 South Willingham.B 9
32 South Wingfield..E 1
32 South Witham...H 6
8 South Wonston..B 6
19 South Woodham Ferrers........D 8
24 South Wootton...C 7
15 South Wraxall..H 11
36 South Yorkshire, Co. G 2
4 South Zeal......F 5
18 Southall.......F 1
16 Southam, Glos..B 1
23 Southam, War....F 7
8 Southampton...E 5
10 Southborough...D 4
8 Southbourne, Hants. G 3
9 Southbourne, Sus. E 9
26 Southburgh......B 7
37 Southburn......B 7
19 Southchurch....E 9
4 Southcott, Devon..D 3
16 Southcott, Wilts..H 3
44 Southdean......B 5
10 Southease......G 5
46 Southend, Arg...H 2
16 Southend, Wilts..G 3
19 Southend-on-Sea..E 8
14 Southerndown...G 2
43 Southerness....F 10
49 Southernknowe..G 11
24 Southery......F 7
41 Southfield.....G 7
10 Southfleet.....A 5
13 Southgate, Glam..H 9
18 Southgate, London E 3
24 Southgate, Norfolk B 8
26 Southgate, Norfolk C 4
25 Southill.......L 3
6 Southleigh....G 5
19 Southminster...D 9
45 Southmoor....B 10
25 Southoe.......H 5
27 Southolt......H 5
24 Southorpe.....E 2
35 Southowram....E 10
34 Southport.....E 2
26 Southrepps....B 6
33 Southrey......D 8
16 Southrop......D 3
9 Southrope.....B 8
9 Southsea......F 8
64 Southtown.....E 3
18 Southwark.....F 3
9 Southwater....D 12
7 Southway......B 8
7 Southwell, Dorset.H 7
32 Southwell, Notts..E 4
45 Southwick, Dur..G 12
9 Southwick, Hants..E 8
24 Southwick, Northants.......F 1
10 Southwick, Sussex.G 1
7 Southwick, Wilts..A 11
27 Southwold......H 8
26 Southwood, Norf..E 7
7 Southwood, Som..C 9
49 Soutra Mains...C 7
63 Soval Lodge.....D 4
40 Sowerby, N. Riding G 4
35 Sowerby, W. Riding E 9
35 Sowerby Bridge..E 9
38 Sowerby Row....A 6
6 Sowton.......G 3
44 Spadeadam.....F 4
24 Spalding......C 3
36 Spaldington....D 5
25 Spaldwick.....C 3
53 Spalefield......F 10
32 Spalford......C 5
24 Spanby.......B 2
26 Sparham......D 4
38 Spark Bridge...G 5
7 Sparkford.....D 9
31 Sparklow......B 10
5 Sparkwell.....K 4
31 Sparrowpit.......B 9

MAP
16 Sparsholt, Berks...E 4
8 Sparsholt, Hants...C 6
45 Spartylea......H 7
41 Spaunton......F 7
6 Spaxton.......C 6
55 Spean Bridge...L 6
8 Spearywell.....C 4
43 Speddoch......C 9
16 Speen, Berks...G 5
17 Speen, Bucks...D 9
41 Speeton.......H 11
30 Speke........B 3
10 Speldhurst....D 4
18 Spellbrook......B 5
4 Spelsbury.....B 4
14 Spelter.......E 2
17 Spencers Wood...G 8
40 Spennithorne...F 2
40 Spennymoor....B 3
22 Spetchley.....G 2
7 Spetisbury....F 12
27 Spexhall......G 7
58 Spey Bay......A 1
57 Speybridge....G 6
56 Speyview......E 8
33 Spilsby......D 11
45 Spindlestone...D 11
32 Spinkhill......B 2
23 Spinney Hills...B 9
61 Spinningdale...G 7
61 Spital........B 11
33 Spital in the Street.A 7
33 Spitalford......A 10
10 Spithurst......F 3
49 Spittal, E. Lothian.B 7
42 Spittal, Kirk...E 5
48 Spittal, Lanark..F 3
49 Spittal, Northumb.D 12
12 Spittal, Pemb...E 3
42 Spittal, Wigtown..F 4
36 Spittal, Yorks...B 5
59 Spittal of Glenmuick J 1
57 Spittal of Glenshee M 7
59 Spittalburn.......J 4
52 Spittalfield....C 6
26 Spixworth.....D 5
3 Splatt........A 9
10 Splayne's Green.. F 3
35 Spofforth......B 12
29 Spon Green....D 12
32 Spondon......G 1
26 Spooner Row...F 4
26 Sporle........D 2
49 Spott........B 9
49 Spottiswoode...D 8
23 Spratton......E 10
8 Spreakley.....B 9
4 Spreyton......F 6
33 Spridlington...A 8
38 Spring Valley....H 2
47 Springburn....C 10
44 Springfield, Dumf..F 2
19 Springfield, Essex..C 7
53 Springfield, Fife..F 8
56 Springfield, Moray.G 6
22 Springfield, War..D 4
22 Springhill.....B 3
43 Springholm....E 9
44 Springkell.....E 1
47 Springside.....E 8
32 Springthorpe...A 8
45 Springwell......G 11
37 Sproatley.....D 9
30 Sproston Green..C 6
36 Sprotbrough...G 3
27 Sproughton...L 4
49 Sprouston.....F 10
26 Sprowston....D 6
32 Sproxton, Leics..H 6
40 Sproxton, Yorks..G 6
30 Spurstow.....E 4
57 Sronlairig Lodge...J 1
57 Sronphadruig Lo...L 3
35 Stackhouse....A 7
12 Stackpole.....G 3
35 Stacksteads....E 7
5 Staddiscombe...K 4
36 Staddlethorpe...E 6
17 Staddhampton...D 7
39 Staffield......A 8
62 Staffin.......A 4
31 Stafford......H 8
31 Staffordshire, Co..H 8
49 Stagehall.....E 7
24 Stag's Holt....E 5
25 Stagsden......K 1
25 Stagsden W. End..K 1
31 Stainburn......B 11
32 Stainby.......H 6
35 Staincross.....F 12
17 Staines.......G 11
33 Stainfield, Lind..C 8
24 Stainfield, Kest...C 2

MAP
39 Stainforth, W. Riding.....H 10
36 Stainforth, W. Riding.....F 4
34 Staining.........D 2
35 Stainland......E 9
41 Stainsacre.....D 9
39 Stainton, Cumb...B 7
40 Stainton, Dur...C 1
40 Stainton, N. Rid..D 5
40 Stainton, N. Rid..F 1
39 Stainton, Westmor.G 7
32 Stainton, W. Riding.....A 3
33 Stainton by Langworth.....B 8
37 Stainton le Vale..H 9
38 Stainton with Agarley.....H 5
41 Staintondale.....E 8
47 Stair, Ayr.......G 9
38 Stair, Cumb....C 5
41 Staithes......D 5
34 Stake Pool....B 3
45 Stakeford.....D 11
7 Stalbridge....D 10
7 Stalbridge Weston E 10
26 Stalham......C 7
26 Stalham Green...C 7
11 Stalisfield Green..C 8
39 Stalling Busk...G 11
37 Stallingborough...F 9
34 Stalmine......C 3
35 Stalybridge....G 8
25 Stambourne....L 8
24 Stamford, Lincs..E 1
45 Stamford, Northumb.....A 10
36 Stamford Bridge..B 5
45 Stamfordham...F 9
7 Stanah.......C 6
18 Stanborough...C 2
17 Stanbridge, Beds..B 10
8 Stanbridge, Dorset.F 2
35 Stanbury.....C 9
47 Stand........C 12
48 Standburn.....B 2
22 Standeford....A 3
11 Standen.......D 7
7 Standerwick...A 11
9 Standford.....C 9
34 Standish......F 4
16 Standlake.....D 5
8 Standon, Hants..C 6
18 Standon, Herts..B 4
30 Standon, Staffs..G 6
18 Standon Massey..D 6
27 Standwell Green..H 4
48 Stane........C 2
26 Stanfield......C 2
25 Stanford, Beds...L 3
11 Stanford, Kent...D 10
21 Stanford Bishop..G 12
22 Stanford Bridge..F 1
16 Stanford Dingley..G 6
19 Stanford le Hope..F 7
23 Stanford on Avon.D 9
32 Stanford on Soar..H 3
21 Stanford on Teme F 12
18 Stanford Rivers..D 5
16 Stanford the Vale..E 4
10 Stanford's End...D 3
24 Stanground....F 3
26 Stanhoe......B 6
39 Stanhope.....A 12
23 Stanion......C 12
52 Stank........F 1
32 Stanley, Derby...F 1
45 Stanley, Dur....H 10
52 Stanley, Perth...D 6
31 Stanley, Staffs...E 8
16 Stanley, Wilts...G 1
35 Stanley, Yorks...E 12
32 Stanley Common..F 1
21 Stanley Hill....H 12
35 Stanley Lane Ends E 12
10 Stanmer......G 2
16 Stanmore, Berks..F 6
8 Stanmore, Hants..C 6
18 Stanmore, London E 2
44 Stannersburn....D 5
45 Stannington, Northumb.....E 10
31 Stannington, Yks..A 1
21 Stansbatch....F 9
27 Stansfield.....K 1
31 Stanshope.....E 9
27 Stanstead.....K 1
18 Stanstead Abbots..C 4
27 Stanstead Street..K 1
10 Stansted......B 5
18 Stansted Mountfitchet...A 5

MAP
31 Stanton, Derby...H 11
16 Stanton, Glos....A 2
14 Stanton, Mon...B 6
31 Stanton, Staffs...F 9
27 Stanton, Suffolk..H 3
31 Stanton by Bridge G 12
32 Stanton by Dale...F 2
15 Stanton Drew...H 9
31 Stanton Fitzwarren E 3
16 Stanton Harcourt..D 5
32 Stanton Hill....D 2
31 Stanton in Peak..D 11
21 Stanton Lacy...E 10
21 Stanton Long...C 11
32 Stanton on the Wolds........G 3
15 Stanton Prior...H 10
16 Stanton St. Bernard........H 2
17 Stanton St. John..C 7
15 Stanton St. Quintin.....F 12
27 Stanton Street....J 3
23 Stanton under Bardon......A 8
30 Stanton upon Hine Heath......H 4
15 Stanton Wick...H 9
30 Stanwardine in the Fields.......H 3
19 Stanway, Essex...B 9
16 Stanway, Glos...A 2
17 Stanwell......G 11
17 Stanwell Moor...G 11
25 Stanwick......H 1
41 Stape........F 8
8 Stapehill......F 2
30 Stapeley......E 5
31 Stapenhill.....H 11
11 Staple, Kent...B 11
6 Staple, Somerset..B 4
6 Staple Cross, Devon D 4
10 Staple Cross, Sussex F 6
6 Staple Fitzpaine..D 6
15 Staple Hill.....G 9
10 Staplefield.....E 2
25 Stapleford, Cambs. K 6
18 Stapleford, Herefs..B 3
32 Stapleford, Leics...H 5
32 Stapleford, Lincs...D 6
32 Stapleford, Notts..F 2
18 Stapleford Abbotts D 5
18 Stapleford Tawney D 5
6 Staplegrove...D 6
6 Staplehay.....D 5
10 Staplehurst....D 6
8 Staplers.......G 6
44 Stapleton, Cumb..F 3
21 Stapleton, Herefs..F 9
23 Stapleton, Leics...B 8
21 Stapleton, Salop..B 10
7 Stapleton, Som...D 8
40 Stapleton, Yorks...D 3
44 Stapleton Grange..F 1
6 Stapley.......E 5
25 Staploe.......J 2
25 Staplow.......G 5
27 Starston......G 5
39 Startforth.....D 12
15 Startley......F 12
30 Statham......B 5
7 Stathe........C 7
32 Stathern......G 5
40 Station Town...B 4
25 Staughton Green..J 2
25 Staughton Highway J 2
16 Staunton, Glos...C 9
15 Staunton, Glos...A 11
31 Staunton Harold Hall........H 12
32 Staunton in the Vale........F 5
21 Staunton on Arrow F 9
21 Staunton on Wye..H 9
38 Staveley, Derby...C 2
38 Staveley, Lancs...G 6
39 Staveley, Westmor. E 7
35 Staveley, Yorks...A 12
5 Staverton, Devon..J 7
15 Staverton, Glos...B 12
23 Staverton, Northants.......F 9
15 Staverton, Wilts..H 11

MAP
15 Staverton Bridge..B 12
7 Stawell.......B 7
14 Stawford......G 3
6 Stawley.......D 4
61 Staxigoe......B 12
41 Staxton......G 10
20 Staylittle.....C 4
34 Staynall......C 2
32 Staythorpe....E 5
40 Stean........H 1
6 Stearsby......H 6
6 Steart........B 6
18 Stebbing......B 6
64 Stebbligrind...D 7
45 Stedham......D 10
9 Steel Rigg.....E 8
44 Steele Road....D 4
21 Steen's Bridge...G 11
9 Steep........D 9
19 Steeple, Dorset..H 12
19 Steeple, Essex...D 9
7 Steeple Ashton..A 12
16 Steeple Aston...B 6
16 Steeple Barton...B 5
25 Steeple Bumpstead.L 8
17 Steeple Claydon..A 8
25 Steeple Gidding...G 2
8 Steeple Langford..B 2
25 Steeple Morden...L 4
35 Steeton......C 9
62 Stein........C 2
58 Steinmanhill......C 5
45 Stelling Hall......F 8
11 Stelling Minnis..C 10
3 Stenalees.....D 7
48 Stenhousemuir...A 2
64 Stenness......C 6
62 Stenscholl....A 4
31 Stenson......G 11
64 Stenswall.....D 7
49 Stenton......B 9
12 Stepaside.....F 5
43 Stepends......C 9
18 Stepney......F 4
25 Steppingley...M 1
47 Stepps.......C 11
27 Sternfield.....J 7
16 Stert........H 1
25 Stetchworth...J 7
42 Stevenage.....B 2
47 Stevenston....E 7
16 Steventon, Berks..E 5
8 Steventon, Hants..A 7
25 Stevington....K 1
25 Stewartby.....L 1
46 Stewarton, Argyll.G 2
47 Stewarton, Ayr...E 9
17 Stewkley......B 9
33 Stewton......B 10
12 Steynton......F 4
4 Stibb........E 1
5 Stibb Cross....D 3
16 Stibb Green....H 3
26 Stibbard......C 3
32 Stibbington...F 2
49 Stichill......F 9
33 Sticker......E 7
33 Stickford.....D 10
4 Sticklepath, Devon F 5
6 Sticklepath, Som..E 6
33 Stickney.....D 10
26 Stiffkey......A 3
18 Stifford......F 6
31 Stifford's Bridge..G 1
10 Stile Bridge....C 6
36 Stillingfleet....C 4
40 Stillington, Dur...C 4
40 Stillington, Yorks.H 6
24 Stilton.......F 3
21 Stinchcombe...D 10
16 Stinsford......G 10
21 Stirchley......B 12
61 Stirkoke House...C 12
52 Stirling, Stirling..H 3
58 Stirling, Aber....C 8
16 Stisted.......A 8
16 Stitchcombe...G 3
2 Stithians......F 4
56 Stittenham....B 2
23 Stivichall.....D 7
33 Stixwould.....D 9
3 Stoak........C 3
48 Stobo........F 4
7 Stoborough....H 12
7 Stoborough Grn..H 12
49 Stobswood, Ber..D 9
45 Stobswood, Northumb.....D 10
48 Stobwood.....D 2
19 Stock.........D 7
22 Stock Wood....D 7
58 Stockbridge, Aber..C 8
8 Stockbridge, Hants.C 5

MAP
43 Stockbridgehill...D 12
47 Stockbriggs....F 12
11 Stockbury.....B 7
16 Stockcross....G 5
38 Stockdale Wath...A 6
23 Stockerston...B 11
9 Stockheath....E 8
43 Stockholm....B 11
47 Stockiemuir...A 10
18 Stocking Pelham..A 4
23 Stockingford...C 7
6 Stockland....F 6
6 Stockland Bristol..B 6
4 Stockleigh English.E 7
4 Stockleigh Pomeroy F 7
16 Stockley......G 1
7 Stocklinch....E 7
31 Stockport.....A 7
35 Stocksbridge...G 11
45 Stocksfield....C 8
21 Stockton, Herefs..F 10
26 Stockton, Norfolk.F 7
21 Stockton, Salop...B 8
22 Stockton, Salop...B 1
23 Stockton, War....F 8
8 Stockton, Wilts...B 1
30 Stockton Heath...B 5
40 Stockton on Tees..C 4
22 Stockton on Teme.E 1
36 Stockton-on-the- Forest........B 4
11 Stodmarsh....B 11
26 Stody........B 4
60 Stoer........D 2
7 Stoford, Som...E 9
8 Stoford, Wilts...C 2
6 Stogumber....C 4
6 Stogursey.....B 5
4 Stoke, Devon...D 1
8 Stoke, Hants...A 5
9 Stoke, Hants...F 8
11 Stoke, Kent....A 7
27 Stoke, Suffolk...L 5
7 Stoke Abbott...F 8
23 Stoke Albany...C 11
27 Stoke Ash.....H 4
32 Stoke Bardolph...F 4
21 Stoke Bliss....F 12
23 Stoke Bruerne...G 10
25 Stoke-by-Clare...L 8
27 Stoke-by-Nayland.L 3
6 Stoke Canon...F 3
8 Stoke Charity...B 6
3 Stoke Climsland..B 10
21 Stoke Cross....G 11
17 Stoke D'Abernon.G 1
25 Stoke Doyle....G 1
23 Stoke Dry.....B 12
21 Stoke Edith....H 11
8 Stoke Farthing...D 2
24 Stoke Ferry....E 8
5 Stoke Fleming...L 7
5 Stoke Gabriel...K 7
15 Stoke Gifford...F 9
23 Stoke Golding...B 8
23 Stoke Goldington G 11
17 Stoke Green....F 10
17 Stoke Hammond..A 9
26 Stoke Holy Cross..H 9
21 Stoke Lacy.....G 11
16 Stoke Lyne....A 6
17 Stoke Mandeville..C 9
18 Stoke Newington..E 3
31 Stoke-on-Trent...D 7
15 Stoke Orchard...A 12
6 Stoke Pero....B 2
17 Stoke Poges....F 10
21 Stoke Prior, Herefordshire..G 10
22 Stoke Prior, Worcs. E 3
4 Stoke Rivers...C 5
32 Stoke Rochford...G 6
17 Stoke Row.....F 8
7 Stoke St. Gregory.D 7
6 Stoke St. Mary...D 6
7 Stoke St. Michael.B 10
21 Stoke St. Milborough.D 11
8 Stoke sub Hamdon D 8
17 Stoke Talmage...D 7
7 Stoke Trister...C 10
30 Stoke upon Tern..G 5
7 Stoke Wake....F 11
7 Stokeford......G 12
32 Stokeham.....C 5
5 Stokeinteignhead..J 8
17 Stokenchurch...D 8
5 Stokenham....L 7
21 Stokesay......D 10
26 Stokesby......D 1
40 Stokesley.....D 5
6 Stolford......B 5
7 Ston Easton...A 9

MAP
17 Stone, Bucks......C 8
15 Stone, Glos......E 10
10 Stone, Kent......A 4
11 Stone, Kent......E 8
31 Stone, Staffs......G 7
22 Stone, Worcs......E 2
7 Stone Allerton....A 7
24 Stone Bridge
    Corner........E 4
35 Stone Chair....D 10
4 Stone Cross,
    Devon........C 5
11 Stone Cross, Kent .D 9
10 Stone Cross,
    Sussex........H 5
39 Stone House.....G 10
10 Stone Street......C 4
26 Stonebridge, Norf..B 6
22 Stonebridge, War..D 5
32 Stonebroom......D 1
10 Stonecrouch......E 6
15 Stone-edge Batch .G 8
37 Stoneferry........D 8
47 Stonefield......D 11
46 Stonefield Castle
    Hotel........B 4
44 Stonegarthside.....E 3
10 Stonegate, Sussex..E 5
41 Stonegate, Yorks...D 8
58 Stonegate Crofts..D 8
41 Stonegrave......G 7
44 Stonehaugh......E 6
59 Stonehaven......J 6
5 Stonehouse, Devon.K 3
15 Stonehouse, Glos. D 11
43 Stonehouse, Kirk..E 9
47 Stonehouse, Lan..E 12
44 Stonehouse,
    Northumb......G 5
23 Stoneleigh......E 7
25 Stonely........J 2
19 Stone's Green....A 11
32 Stonesby.......H 5
16 Stonesfield......B 5
38 Stonethwaite.....D 5
8 Stoney Cross......E 4
31 Stoney Middleton C 10
23 Stoney Stanton....C 8
7 Stoney Stoke......C 10
7 Stoney Stratton . .B 10
21 Stoney Stretton . .A 9
48 Stoneyburn,
    Lanark........G 2
48 Stoneyburn,
    W. Lothian......C 2
23 Stoneygate.......B 9
19 Stoneyhills......D 9
42 Stoneykirk......F 2
58 Stoneywood......F 6
27 Stonham Aspal....J 4
17 Stonor.........E 8
23 Stonton Wyville..C 10
4 Stony Cross,
    Devon........C 4
22 Stony Cross,
    Herefordshire...G 1
34 Stony Hill.......C 5
23 Stony Stratford . .H 11
4 Stoodleigh, Devon.C 5
6 Stoodleigh, Devon.D 3
9 Stopham.......D 11
17 Stopsley.......B 12
30 Storeton.......B 2
35 Storiths........B 9
63 Stornoway.......D 5
22 Storridge......G 1
9 Storrington......E 12
39 Storth.........G 7
36 Storwood.......C 5
56 Stotfield.......C 8
25 Stotford.......L 3
21 Stottesdon......D 12
23 Stoughton, Leics..B 9
9 Stoughton, Surrey A 11
9 Stoughton, Sussex .E 9
55 Stoul.........K 1
22 Stoulton.......G 3
7 Stour Provost...D 11
7 Stour Row......D 11
22 Stourbridge......D 2
22 Stourpaine......E 12
22 Stourport-on-
    Severn.......E 2
22 Stourton, Staffs...D 2
22 Stourton, War....H 6
7 Stourton, Wilts...C 11
7 Stourton Caundle.E 10
64 Stove.........B 3
27 Stoven.........G 7
32 Stow, Lincs......D 6
49 Stow, Midlothian..E 7
24 Stow Bardolph....E 7
26 Stow Bedon......F 3

25 Stow cum Quy ....J 6
25 Stow Longa......H 2
19 Stow Maries......D 8
16 Stow-on-the-Wold .B 3
24 Stowbridge......E 7
21 Stowe, Salop.....E 8
31 Stowe, Staffs.....G 8
15 Stowe Green......D 9
7 Stowell.......D 10
27 Stowlangtoft......H 3
27 Stowmarket......J 3
11 Stowting.......D 10
27 Stowupland......J 4
46 Straad.........C 5
57 Straanruie......H 6
59 Strachan.......H 4
51 Strachur.......G 8
27 Stradbroke......H 5
25 Stradishall......K 8
24 Stradsett.......E 8
32 Stragglethorpe....E 6
43 Strahanna......B 7
42 Straid.........C 2
43 Straith.........C 9
42 Straiton.......A 5
58 Straloch, Aber....E 6
52 Straloch, Perth...A 5
31 Stramshall......G 9
59 Stranathro......H 6
48 Strand.........G 2
47 Strandhead......G 9
38 Strands.........E 4
38 Strang.........H 2
41 Stranghow......D 7
59 Stranog.......H 6
42 Stranraer......E 1
20 Strata Florida....C 2
17 Stratfield Mortimer H 7
17 Stratfield Saye....H 8
17 Stratfield Turgis..H 8
18 Stratford.......F 4
27 Stratford
    St. Andrew....J 6
27 Stratford St. Mary M 3
8 Stratford sub
    Castle.......C 3
8 Stratford Tony....C 2
22 Stratford-upon-
    Avon.......G 5
52 Strathallan Castle. F 4
55 Strathan, Inver...K 3
60 Strathan, Suther...E 2
60 Strathan, Suther...A 6
47 Strathaven......E 12
47 Strathblane......B 10
54 Strathcarron......E 3
50 Strathcoil.......D 4
58 Strathdon.......F 1
60 Strathkanaird....F 3
53 Strathkinness.....F 9
57 Strathmashie Ho..K 2
53 Strathmiglo......F 7
61 Strathmore Hotel. C 10
54 Strathpeffer......D 8
54 Strathrannoch....B 8
54 Strathvaich Lo....B 7
61 Strathy........A 8
61 Strathy Inn......A 8
52 Strathyre.......E 1
4 Stratton, Corn....E 1
7 Stratton, Dorset. G 10
16 Stratton, Glos....D 1
17 Stratton Audley...B 7
7 Stratton-on-the-
    Fosse........A 10
16 Stratton
    St. Margaret....E 3
26 Stratton
    St. Michael....F 5
26 Stratton Strawless .C 5
53 Stravithie......F 10
10 Streat.........F 2
18 Streatham......G 3
17 Streatley, Beds....A 11
17 Streatley, Berks...F 7
7 Street, Somerset..C 8
41 Street, Yorks.....E 7
30 Street Dinas.....E 2
11 Street End ,Kent..C 10
9 Street End, Sussex F 10
36 Street Houses.....C 3
57 Street of
    Kincardine....H 5
22 Streethay.......E 2
36 Streethouse......E 2
40 Streetlam......C 3
22 Streetly.......B 4
21 Strefford.......D 10
32 Strelley.......F 2
36 Strensall.......A 4
6 Stretcholt.......B 6
5 Strete.........L 7
35 Stretford.......H 7

25 Strethall........L 6
25 Stretham.......H 6
30 Stretton, Cheshire .B 5
30 Stretton, Cheshire .E 3
32 Stretton, Derby...D 1
23 Stretton, Rut....A 12
22 Stretton, Staffs...A 2
31 Stretton, Staffs...G 11
22 Stretton en le Field A 6
21 Stretton
    Grandison.....H 11
21 Stretton Heath....A 9
23 Stretton-on-
    Dunsmore.....E 7
22 Stretton on Fosse..E 7
21 Stretton Sugwas..H 10
23 Stretton-under-
    Fosse........D 8
58 Strichen.......B 7
6 Stringston......B 5
23 Strixton.......F 12
58 Stroat.........E 9
54 Stromeferry......F 2
54 Stromemore......F 2
54 Stromness......D 1
51 Stronachlachar...F 11
55 Stronchreggan Ho.M 4
43 Strond.........H 1
47 Strone, Arg......A 7
51 Strone, Dunb....H 10
55 Strone, Inver.....L 5
57 Strone, Inver.....G 1
60 Stronechrubie.....E 4
55 Stronenaba......L 6
57 Stronetoper......K 4
51 Stronmilchan.....E 8
50 Strontian.......A 5
50 Strontoiller......E 6
51 Stronuich.......C 12
10 Strood.........A 6
15 Strood Green......C 1
15 Stroud, Glos.....D 11
9 Stroud, Hants....D 8
19 Stroud Green......E 8
17 Stroude........G 11
32 Stroxton.......G 6
62 Struan.........D 3
33 Strubby.......B 11
26 Strumpshaw......E 6
54 Struy.........F 8
58 Stuartfield......C 7
38 Stub Place......F 3
17 Stubbington......F 7
35 Stubbins.......E 7
31 Stubbs Cross......D 8
44 Stubbyknowe.....F 2
8 Stubhampton.....E 1
44 Stublick.......G 6
34 Stubshaw Cross...G 5
32 Stubton.......E 6
46 Stuck.........B 5
51 Stuckgowan......G 10
51 Stuckindroin.....F 10
8 Stuckton.......E 3
27 Stud Green......F 9
45 Studdon.......H 7
39 Studfold.......E 9
32 Studham.......C 11
8 Studland.......H 2
17 Studley, Oxon....C 7
16 Studley, Wilts....G 1
40 Studley Roger....H 3
25 Stump Cross......L 6
25 Stuntney.......G 7
10 Stunts Green.....G 5
31 Sturbridge......G 7
25 Sturmer........L 8
7 Sturminster Com. E 11
8 Sturminster
    Marshall......F 1
7 Sturminster
    Newton.......E 11
11 Sturry.........B 10
37 Sturton.......G 7
32 Sturton by Stow ...B 6
32 Sturton le Steeple. B 5
27 Stuston.......H 4
27 Stutton, Suffolk...M 4
36 Stutton, Yorks....C 3
31 Styal.........B 7
32 Styrrup........A 3
58 Succoth, Aber.....D 2
51 Succoth, Arg.....G 10
9 Suckley.......G 12
25 Sudborough......G 1
27 Sudbourne......K 7
33 Sudbrook, Lincs...F 7
15 Sudbrook, Mon....F 8
33 Sudbrooke......C 7
18 Sudbury, Derby...G 10
18 Sudbury, London..E 2
27 Sudbury, Suffolk ..L 2

56 Suddie.........D 2
15 Sudgrove.......D 12
26 Suffield, Norfolk..B 5
41 Suffield, Yorks....D 9
27 Suffolk, County...J 4
30 Sugnall........G 6
61 Suisgill.........E 9
62 Suisnish.......E 5
38 Sulby.........G 2
23 Sulgrave.......H 9
17 Sulham........G 7
17 Sulhamstead......G 7
17 Sulhamstead
    Abbots.......G 7
62 Sulishaderbeg....D 4
9 Sullington......E 12
64 Sullom........C 7
14 Sully.........G 5
29 Summer Hill.....E 12
35 Summerbridge...A 10
2 Summercourt....D 6
40 Summerhouse....C 2
15 Summerleaze.....F 7
35 Summerseat......F 7
16 Summertown.....C 6
35 Summit, Lancs....F 8
35 Summit, Lancs....E 8
17 Sunbury on
    Thames.......G 11
43 Sundaywell......C 9
38 Sunderland, Cumb. B 4
45 Sunderland, Durham
               G 12
34 Sunderland, Lancs. B 3
40 Sunderland Bridge .A 3
48 Sundhope.......G 6
11 Sundon Park.....B 11
10 Sundridge.......C 4
50 Sunipol........B 1
37 Sunk Island......E 10
17 Sunningdale.....G 10
17 Sunninghill......G 10
16 Sunningwell......D 6
40 Sunniside, Dur...A 2
45 Sunniside, Dur..G 10
38 Sunny Bank......F 5
56 Sunnyhillock.....D 4
52 Sunnylaw.......G 3
10 Sunnyside......D 3
8 Sunton........A 4
49 Sunwick.......D 11
17 Surbiton.......G 11
38 Surby.........H 1
24 Surfleet.......C 3
24 Surfleet Seas End..C 4
26 Surlingham......E 6
10 Surrey, County...C 2
26 Sustead........B 5
36 Susworth.......G 6
64 Sutherland, Co....D 6
26 Suton.........E 4
56 Suters of Cromarty C 4
33 Sutterby.......C 11
24 Sutterton.......B 4
25 Sutton, Beds.....K 3
17 Sutton, Bucks....F 11
25 Sutton, Cambs....G 5
24 Sutton, Hunts....F 2
11 Sutton, Kent....C 12
34 Sutton, Lancs....H 4
18 Sutton, London...H 3
26 Sutton, Norfolk...C 7
32 Sutton, Notts....B 4
32 Sutton, Notts....N 5
16 Sutton, Oxon.....C 5
12 Sutton, Pemb.....E 3
22 Sutton, Salop....C 1
30 Sutton, Salop....G 5
7 Sutton, Som.....C 9
31 Sutton, Staffs....H 6
27 Sutton, Suffolk...K 6
9 Sutton, Surrey...B 12
9 Sutton, Sussex...B 11
36 Sutton, Yorks....F 3
23 Sutton Bassett...C 11
10 Sutton at Hone....A 4
15 Sutton Benger....F 12
32 Sutton Bonington H 2
24 Sutton Bridge....C 6
23 Sutton Cheney....B 7
25 Sutton Coldfield...B 5
16 Sutton Courtenay..E 6
24 Sutton Crosses....C 5
40 Sutton Grange....H 3
9 Sutton Green....A 11
40 Sutton Howgrave..G 3
32 Sutton in Ashfield .D 2
5 Sutton-in-Craven..C 8
23 Sutton in the Elms .C 8
31 Sutton Lane Ends..C 8
21 Sutton Maddock .B 12

7 Sutton Mallet.....C 7
8 Sutton Mandeville. C 1
7 Sutton Montis....D 9
33 Sutton-on-Hull...D 9
33 Sutton on Sea....B 12
36 Sutton-on-the-
    Forest.......A 4
31 Sutton on the Hill G 11
32 Sutton on Trent...D 5
24 Sutton St. Edmund D 5
24 Sutton St. James..D 5
21 Sutton
    St. Michael....H 10
21 Sutton
    St. Nicholas....H 10
22 Sutton Scotney....B 6
22 Sutton-under-
    Brailes.......H 6
40 Sutton-under-
    Whitestonecliffe. G 5
36 Sutton upon
    Derwent......B 5
11 Sutton Valence...C 7
7 Sutton Veny.....B 11
7 Sutton Waldron...E 12
15 Sutton Wick......H 9
33 Swaby.........B 11
31 Swadlincote......H 11
26 Swaffham Bulbeck.E 1
25 Swaffham Prior...J 7
26 Swafield.......B 6
40 Swainby.......E 5
26 Swainsthorpe.....E 5
15 Swainswick......G 10
23 Swalcliffe......H 7
11 Swalecliffe......A 10
37 Swallow.......G 9
8 Swallowcliffe.....C 1
17 Swallowfield......H 8
32 Swallownest......B 2
45 Swalwell.......G 10
30 Swan Green......C 6
8 Swanage.......H 2
64 Swanbister......D 2
17 Swanbourne......A 9
63 Swanibost......A 6
37 Swanland.......D 7
10 Swanley.......A 4
10 Swanley Village...A 4
9 Swanmore.......D 2
23 Swannington, Leics.A 7
26 Swannington, Norf.D 4
10 Swanscombe.....A 5
13 Swansea.......H 10
26 Swanton Abbott...C 6
26 Swanton Morley...D 3
26 Swanton Novers...B 3
32 Swanwick......E 1
24 Swarby.......B 1
26 Swardeston......E 5
31 Swarkestone.....G 12
45 Swarland......C 10
45 Swarland Estate...C 10
9 Swarraton......B 7
24 Swaton........B 2
25 Swavesey.......H 5
8 Sway.........F 4
33 Swayfield.......H 7
8 Swaythling......D 6
21 Sweet Green......F 12
4 Sweetham.......F 7
39 Sweetholme......C 8
49 Sweethope......E 9
3 Sweethouse......C 8
27 Swefling.......J 6
23 Swepstone......A 7
16 Swerford.......A 5
30 Swettenham......C 6
27 Swilland.......K 5
36 Swillington......D 2
30 Swinbridge......C 5
4 Swinbridge
    Newland......C 5
36 Swinbrook......C 4
32 Swinderley......D 6
15 Swindon, Glos....B 12
22 Swindon, Staffs...C 2
16 Swindon, Wilts...F 3
37 Swine.........D 9
36 Swinefleet......E 5
15 Swineford......G 10
25 Swineshead, Beds..J 2
24 Swineshead, Lincs..C 5
24 Swineshead Bridge. A 3
61 Swiney........D 11
16 Swinford, Berks...C 5
23 Swinford, Leics...D 9
49 Swinhoe.......E 12
37 Swinhope.......G 9

40 Swinithwaite......F 1
44 Swinnie.........A 5
31 Swinscoe.......E 9
44 Swinside Hall.....A 5
24 Swinstead......C 1
49 Swinton, Ber.....E 11
34 Swinton, Lancs...G 6
41 Swinton, N. Riding H 7
40 Swinton, N. Riding G 2
36 Swinton, W. Riding G 2
49 Swinton Quarter..E 11
49 Swintonmill......E 10
23 Swithland.......A 9
63 Swordale, Lewis...D 6
56 Swordale, Ross &
    Cromarty......C 1
55 Swordland......K 2
61 Swordly.......B 7
30 Sworton Heath....B 5
20 Swydd-ffynnon....F 3
31 Swynnerton......G 7
7 Swyre.........G 8
20 Sychnant.......E 5
20 Sychtyn.......E 5
15 Syde.........C 12
17 Sydenham......D 8
5 Sydenham Damerel H 3
26 Syderstone......B 1
7 Sydling
    St. Nicholas....F 10
16 Sydmonton......H 6
32 Syerston.......E 5
35 Syke.........F 8
36 Sykehouse......E 4
34 Sykes.........B 5
64 Symbister......D 8
47 Symington, Ayr...F 8
48 Symington, Lan...F 3
15 Symonds Yat.....C 9
7 Symondsbury.....G 8
13 Synod Inn......B 7
49 Synton Parkhead..G 7
61 Syre.........C 7
23 Syresham......H 9
23 Syston, Leics.....A 9
32 Syston, Lincs.....F 6
22 Sytchampton.....F 2
23 Sywell........E 11
54 Taagan.......C 4
47 Tackhouse......E 11
16 Tackley.......B 6
26 Tacolneston......F 4
36 Tadcaster......C 3
31 Taddington......C 10
4 Taddiport......D 4
17 Tadley.........H 7
25 Tadlow.......K 4
23 Tadmarton......H 7
15 Tadwick.......G 10
18 Tadworth......B 1
14 Tafarnau-bach....C 4
29 Tafarn-gelyn.....D 11
12 Tafarn-y-bwlch....D 4
14 Taffs Well......F 5
20 Tafolwern......B 4
29 Tai.........D 7
29 Tai-bach, Denb...G 10
13 Taibach, Glam....H 11
29 Tai-mawr.......F 9
61 Tain, Caithness ..A 11
56 Tain, Ross &
    Cromarty......B 3
29 Tainant.......F 12
13 Tairgwaith......F 10
28 Tai'r-lon.......E 4
18 Takeley.......B 5
18 Takeley Street....B 5
14 Talachddu......A 4
29 Talacre.......B 10
4 Talaton.......F 4
12 Talbenny.......F 2
14 Talbot Green......F 4
8 Talbot Village....G 2
20 Talerddig.......B 5
13 Talgarreg......B 7
14 Talgarth.......A 5
20 Taliesin.......C 2
62 Talisker.......E 3
31 Talke.........E 7
44 Talkin.........G 4
48 Talla Linnfoots...G 4
54 Talladale......C 3
29 Tallard.......G 8
30 Tallarn Green.....F 3
38 Tallentire......B 3
13 Talley.........D 9
28 Tallington......E 2
60 Talmine.......B 6
29 Talog.........D 7
20 Talsarn........G 1
28 Talsarnau......G 5
2 Talskiddy......C 6
28 Talwrn, Angl.....C 4

MAP
29 Talwrn, Denb....E 12
14 Talybont, Brec...B 4
28 Tal-y-bont, Caer...C 5
29 Tal-y-bont, Caer...C 7
20 Talybont, Cards...C 2
28 Tal-y-bont, Mer...H 5
29 Tal-y-cafn......C 7
15 Tal-y-coed......C 7
14 Tal-y-garn......F 4
14 Tal-y-llyn, Brec..B 4
20 Tal-y-llyn, Mer...A 3
28 Tal-y-sarn......C 5
14 Talywain......D 6
20 Tal-y-wern......B 4
40 Tame......D 5
5 Tamerton Foliot..K 3
22 Tamworth......B 5
39 Tan Hill......E 11
12 Tancredston......D 2
11 Tanden......D 8
47 Tandlemuir......C 8
10 Tandridge......C 3
45 Tanfield......G 10
45 Tanfield Lea....H 10
8 Tangley......A 5
9 Tangmere......E 10
64 Tankerness......D 3
35 Tankersley......G 12
28 Tan-lan......F 5
61 Tannach......C 12
59 Tannachie......J 5
59 Tannadice......L 2
27 Tannington......H 5
31 Tansley......D 11
31 Tansley Knoll...D 11
24 Tansor......F 2
45 Tantobie......H 10
40 Tanton......D 5
22 Tanworth in Arden E 5
28 Tan-y-bwlch......F 6
29 Tan-y-fron......D 9
28 Tan-y-graig, Caer..F 3
20 Tan-y-graig, Cards.E 3
28 Tan-y-grisiau......F 6
12 Tan-y-groes......B 6
29 Tan-y-pistyll......G 10
17 Taplow......F 10
46 Tarbert, Argyll...A 1
46 Tarbert, Argyll...C 4
63 Tarbert, Lewis....G 2
51 Tarbet, Dunb...G 10
55 Tarbet, Inver....K 2
60 Tarbet, Suther....C 3
47 Tarbolton......G 9
48 Tarbrax......D 3
30 Tarbuck Green...A 3
44 Tarcoon......E 2
22 Tardebigge......E 3
59 Tarfside......J 2
59 Tarland......G 2
34 Tarleton......F 3
34 Tarlscough......F 3
15 Tarlton......D 12
34 Tarnbrook......B 5
30 Tarporley......D 4
6 Tarr......C 4
8 Tarrant Crawford..F 1
8 Tarrant Gunville..E 1
8 Tarrant Hinton....E 1
8 Tarrant Keyneston.F 1
8 Tarrant Launceston E 1
8 Tarrant Monkton..E 1
8 Tarrant Rawston..E 1
8 Tarrant Rushton..E 1
10 Tarrant Neville...H 3
21 Tarrington......H 11
62 Tarskavaig......G 5
58 Tarves......D 6
54 Tarvie......D 8
30 Tarvin......D 4
26 Tasburgh......F 5
21 Tasley......C 12
16 Taston......B 5
31 Tatenhill......H 10
43 Tath Hill......B 11
39 Tatham......H 8
33 Tathwell......B 10
17 Tatling End......E 11
10 Tatsfield......B 3
30 Tattenhall......D 3
26 Tatterford......C 2
26 Tattersett......C 1
33 Tattershall......D 9
33 Tattershall Bridge.E 9
33 Tattershall Thorpe.D 9
27 Tattingstone......L 4
27 Tattingstone
    Whitehorse.....L 4
6 Tatworth......F 6
58 Tauchers......C 1
6 Taunton......D 6
26 Taverham......D 5
12 Tavernspite......F 5

MAP
5 Tavistock......H 3
4 Taw Green, Devon E 5
4 Taw Green, Devon F 4
4 Tawstock......C 4
31 Taxal......B 8
47 Tayburn......E 10
51 Taychreggan......E 7
46 Tayinloan......E 2
52 Taymouth Castle..C 3
51 Taynafead......F 8
15 Taynton, Glos....B 10
16 Taynton, Oxon...C 3
51 Taynuilt......D 7
53 Tayport......D 9
46 Tayvallich......A 2
33 Tealby......A 8
62 Teangue......G 6
39 Tebay......E 8
17 Tebworth......A 10
4 Teddburn St. Mary.F 7
16 Teddington, Glos..A 11
18 Teddington, London
    G 2
21 Tedstone Delamere
    F 12
21 Tedstone Wafre..F 12
23 Teeton......E 10
8 Teffont Evias.....C 1
8 Teffont Magna....C 2
12 Tegryn......D 6
23 Teigh......A 12
5 Teigngrace......H 7
5 Teignmouth......H 8
44 Teindland......D 8
44 Teindside......B 3
10 Telham......G 6
7 Tellisford......A 11
10 Telscombe......H 3
43 Templand......C 11
3 Temple, Cornwall..B 8
48 Temple, Midloth...D 6
13 Temple Bar, Cards.B 8
13 Temple Bar, Carm.E 9
22 Temple Ballsall....E 5
7 Temple Cloud......A 9
11 Temple Ewell....D 11
22 Temple Grafton...G 5
16 Temple Guiting...A 2
36 Temple Hirst......E 4
32 Temple Normanton
    C 1
39 Temple Sowerby..C 8
7 Templecombe....D 10
53 Templehall......H 7
6 Templeton, Devon. E 2
12 Templeton, Pemb..E 4
4 Templeton Bridge..E 7
25 Tempsford......K 3
24 Ten Mile Bank....F 7
21 Tenbury Wells....F 11
12 Tenby......G 5
19 Tendring......B 7
19 Tendring Green...A 11
64 Tenston......C 1
11 Tenterden......E 7
42 Terally......G 2
19 Terling......B 7
30 Ternhill......G 5
2 Terras......D 6
17 Terrick......C 9
14 Terrington......H 7
24 Terrington St. Clement
    D 6
24 Terrington St. John
    D 6
10 Teston......C 6
8 Testwood......E 2
15 Tetbury......E 12
15 Tetbury Upton...E 12
30 Tetchill......G 3
4 Tetcott......F 2
33 Tetford......C 10
37 Tetney......H 8
37 Tetney Lock......G 11
17 Tetsworth......D 8
30 Tettenhall......B 2
58 Teuchan......D 8
58 Teuchar......C 5
33 Teuchatcroft......B 9
32 Teversal......D 2
25 Teversham......J 6
44 Teviothead......C 2
59 Tewel......J 6
18 Tewin......B 3
15 Tewkesbury......A 12
11 Teynham......B 8
11 Teynham Street...B 8
38 Thackwaite, Cumb.
    C 4
38 Thackthwaite, Cumb.
    C 6
9 Thakeham......D 12

MAP
17 Thame......D 8
17 Thames Ditton...G 12
11 Thanington......B 10
48 Thankerton......F 2
26 Tharston......F 5
16 Thatcham......G 6
34 Thatto Heath......H 4
25 Thaxted......M 7
62 The Aird......C 3
21 The Bage......H 8
43 The Barony, Dumf.
    C 11
64 The Barony, Orkney
    B 1
31 The Beeches......H 9
62 The Braes......E 4
21 The Broad......F 10
15 The Camp......C 12
10 The Chart......C 3
17 The City......D 8
15 The Cleaver......A 8
8 The Common......C 4
21 The Corner......D 10
60 The Craigs......G 5
38 The Cronk......F 2
47 The Den......D 8
24 The Engine......E 4
44 The Fauld......F 2
44 The Flatt......E 4
11 The Forstal......C 7
38 The Green, Lancs. G 4
7 The Green, Wilts..C 12
43 The Grove......D 10
49 The Hardens......D 10
9 The Haven......C 12
27 The Heath......L 2
10 The Hermitage....C 1
46 The Highland Hotel
    A 5
38 The Howe......H 1
19 The Hythe......B 10
43 The Lake......G 7
11 The Leacon......E 8
17 The Lee......D 10
38 The Lhen......F 2
21 The Marsh......C 8
45 The Middles......H 10
10 The Moor......E 6
61 The Mound......G 8
47 The Murray......D 11
64 The Ness......A 8
59 The Neuk......H 5
15 The Oval......H 10
15 The Pill......F 8
58 The Pole of Itlaw..B 4
21 The Pound......E 7
15 The Quarry......D 10
12 The Rhos......F 4
9 The Sands......B 10
16 The Slade......G 6
11 The Stocks......E 8
19 The Stone......C 9
17 The Throat......G 9
2 The Towans......F 3
21 The Vauld......G 10
22 The Wyke......B 1
40 Theakston......G 3
37 Thealby......E 7
17 Theale, Berks....G 7
7 Theale, Somerset.B 8
17 Theale Green......G 7
43 Theapland......H 12
37 Thearne......C 8
27 Theberton......J 7
23 Theddlethorpe......D 10
33 Theddlethorpe
    All Saints.....A 11
33 Theddlethorpe
    St. Helen....A 11
4 Thelbridge Cross..E 7
27 Thelnetham......G 2
30 Thelwall......B 5
26 Themelthorpe......C 4
23 Thenford......H 8
25 Therfield......L 4
27 Thetford......G 2
18 Theydon Bois....D 4
15 Thickwood......G 11
33 Thimbleby, Lincs. C 9
40 Thimbleby, Yorks. F 5
40 Thirkleby......G 5
40 Thirlby......G 5
49 Thirlestane......E 8
38 Thirlspot......C 5
40 Thirn......G 2
40 Thirsk......G 5
38 Thistlebottom......A 5
34 Thistleton, Lancs. C 3
32 Thistleton, Leics..H 6
25 Thistley Green......H 8
36 Thixendale......A 6
45 Thockrington......E 8
24 Tholomas Drove..E 5

MAP
40 Tholthorpe......H 5
12 Thomas Chapel...F 4
39 Thomas Close....A 7
22 Thomas Town......F 4
58 Thomastown......D 3
26 Thompson......F 2
56 Thomshill......D 8
10 Thong......A 5
32 Thonock......A 5
39 Thoralby......F 12
37 Thoresway......G 9
37 Thorganby, Lincs..G 9
36 Thorganby, Yorks. C 5
41 Thorgill......E 7
27 Thorington......H 7
27 Thorington Street..L 3
35 Thorlby......B 8
18 Thorley, Herts....B 5
8 Thorley, I.o.W....G 5
18 Thorley Street, Herts.
    B 5
8 Thorley Street, I.o.W.
    G 5
40 Thormanby......H 5
11 Thorn......F 7
40 Thornaby-on-Tees. C 5
26 Thornage......B 4
17 Thornborough, Bucks.
    A 8
40 Thornborough, Yorks.
    G 3
4 Thornbury, Devon. E 3
15 Thornbury, Glos...E 9
21 Thornbury, Herefs.
    F 11
23 Thornby......E 10
31 Thorncliff......D 8
7 Thorncombe......F 7
9 Thorncombe Street
    B 11
25 Thorncote Green..K 3
8 Thorncross......H 6
27 Thorndon......H 4
4 Thorndon Cross...F 4
6 Thorne, Somerset. D 4
36 Thorne, Yorks....F 5
35 Thorner......C 12
24 Thorney, Hunts...E 4
32 Thorney, Notts....C 6
7 Thorney, Somerset D 7
37 Thorney Crofts....E 9
8 Thorney Hill......F 4
58 Thorneybank......D 4
6 Thornfalcon......D 6
7 Thornford......E 9
44 Thorngrafton......F 6
7 Thorngrove......C 7
37 Thorngumbald......D 9
24 Thornham......A 8
27 Thornham Magna. H 4
27 Thornham Parva. H 4
24 Thornhaugh......E 2
38 Thornhill, Cumb...D 3
31 Thornhill, Derby..B 10
43 Thornhill, Dumf...B 9
14 Thornhill, Glam...F 5
52 Thornhill, Perth...G 2
35 Thornhill, Yorks..E 11
37 Thornholme......A 9
49 Thornielaw......F 8
49 Thornington......F 11
40 Thornley, Dur....A 4
40 Thornley, Dur....B 1
47 Thornliebank......D 10
35 Thorns......K 8
35 Thornseat......H 11
31 Thornsett......D 8
38 Thornthwaite, Cumb.
    C 5
35 Thornthwaite, Yorks.
    A 10
53 Thornton, Angus..C 9
17 Thornton, Bucks...A 8
53 Thornton, Fife....G 7
34 Thornton, Lancs...C 2
34 Thornton, Lancs...C 2
23 Thornton, Leics...A 8
33 Thornton, Lincs...C 9
49 Thornton, Northumb.
    E 12
12 Thornton, Pemb...F 2
36 Thornton, E. Riding
    C 5
40 Thornton, N. Riding
    D 5
35 Thornton, W. Riding
    D 9
37 Thornton Curtis...E 8
18 Thornton Heath...G 3
30 Thornton Hough...B 2
35 Thornton in Craven
    B 8

MAP
39 Thornton in Lonsdale
    H 9
40 Thornton-le-Beans.F 4
36 Thornton-le-Clay..A 5
41 Thornton-le-Dale. G 8
37 Thornton le Moor,
    Lincolnshire....G 8
40 Thornton-le-Moor,
    Yorkshire......F 4
30 Thornton-le-Moors C 3
40 Thornton-le-Street. G 4
49 Thornton Mains..E 12
39 Thornton Rust....F 12
40 Thornton Steward.F 2
40 Thornton Watlass. G 3
47 Thorntonhall......D 10
49 Thorntonloch....B 10
49 Thorntonpark....E 12
18 Thornwood Com...C 5
49 Thornydykes......E 9
32 Thornythwaite....C 6
32 Thoroton......F 5
36 Thorp Arch......C 2
27 Thorp Green......K 2
31 Thorpe, Derby...E 10
33 Thorpe, Lincs...B 12
26 Thorpe, Norf....F 7
32 Thorpe, Notts....E 5
37 Thorpe, E. Riding. B 7
35 Thorpe, W. Riding A 9
17 Thorpe, Surrey...G 11
27 Thorpe Abbots....G 5
32 Thorpe Acre......H 2
32 Thorpe Arnold....H 5
36 Thorpe Audlin....F 3
41 Thorpe Bassett...H 8
19 Thorpe Bay......E 9
23 Thorpe by Water. C 12
22 Thorpe Constantine
    A 6
26 Thorpe End Garden
    Village......D 6
35 Thorpe Hesley...G 12
36 Thorpe in Balne...F 4
32 Thorpe in the Fallows
    B 6
23 Thorpe Langton..C 10
40 Thorpe Larches...C 4
19 Thorpe-le-Soken. B 11
36 Thorpe le Street...C 6
23 Thorpe Malsor...D 11
23 Thorpe Mandeville H 9
26 Thorpe Market....B 5
27 Thorpe Morieux...K 2
32 Thorpe on the Hill. D 6
26 Thorpe St. Andrew D 6
33 Thorpe St. Peter..D 11
32 Thorpe Salvin....B 2
23 Thorpe Satchville. A 10
40 Thorpe Thewles....C 4
36 Thorpe Underwood
    A 3
25 Thorpe Waterville. G 1
36 Thorpe Willoughby
    D 3
27 Thorpeness......J 8
19 Thorrington......B 10
7 Thorverton......F 3
44 Thrandeston......H 4
25 Thrapston......G 1
30 Threapwood......F 3
42 Threave......A 4
10 Three Bridges....D 2
2 Three Burrows....E 4
11 Three Chimneys...D 7
14 Three Cocks......A 5
13 Three Crosses....H 9
10 Three Cups Corner.F 5
7 Three Gates, Dorset
    E 9
40 Three Gates, Dur..B 5
24 Three Holes......E 6
8 Three Legged Cross
    E 3
11 Three Oaks......G 7
24 Threekingham......B 2
34 Threeleg Cross...E 6
31 Threelows......E 9
17 Threemile Cross..G 8
2 Threemilestone....E 5
49 Threepwood......E 8
38 Threlkeld......C 6
35 Threshfield......A 8
26 Thrigby......D 7
39 Thringarth......C 11
32 Thringstone......F 7
40 Thrintoft......F 3
25 Thriplow......K 5
45 Throckenholt......M 4
45 Throckley......F 9
22 Throckmorton......G 3
45 Throphill......D 9

MAP
45 Thropton......C 8
43 Throughgate......C 9
5 Throwleigh......G 5
11 Throwley......C 8
11 Throwley Forstal..C 8
32 Thrumpton......G 2
61 Thrumster......C 12
37 Thrunscoe......F 10
45 Thrunton......B 9
7 Thrupe......B 9
15 Thrupp, Glos....D 11
16 Thrupp, Oxon....C 3
5 Thrushelton......G 3
18 Thrushesbush......C 5
34 Thrushgill......A 5
23 Thrussington......A 10
15 Thruxton, Herefs..A 7
8 Thruxton, Som...B 4
36 Thrybergh......H 3
23 Thurcaston......A 9
32 Thurcroft......A 2
4 Thurdon......E 2
26 Thurgarton, Norf..B 5
32 Thurgarton, Notts. E 4
35 Thurgoland......G 11
23 Thurlaston, Leics..B 8
23 Thurlaston, War...B 8
6 Thurlbear......D 6
24 Thurlby, Lincs...D 2
32 Thurlby, Lincs...D 6
25 Thurleigh......J 2
5 Thurlestone......L 5
6 Thurloxton......C 6
32 Thurlston......G 1
35 Thurlstone......G 11
26 Thurlton......F 7
23 Thurmaston......A 9
23 Thurnby......B 10
26 Thurne......D 7
11 Thurnham, Kent..B 7
34 Thurnham, Lancs..B 3
26 Thurning, Norf....C 4
25 Thurning, Northants.
    G 2
36 Thurnscoe......G 2
44 Thursby......H 2
26 Thursford Green..B 3
9 Thursley......B 10
61 Thurso......A 10
61 Thurso East......A 10
30 Thurstaston......B 1
27 Thurston......J 2
44 Thurstonfield.....G 2
35 Thurstonland......F 10
26 Thurton......E 6
31 Thurvaston......F 11
26 Thuxton......E 3
27 Thwaite, Suffolk..H 4
39 Thwaite, Yorks...E 11
26 Thwaite St. Mary. F 6
41 Thwing......H 1
52 Tibbermore......E 5
43 Tibbers......B 9
15 Tibberton, Glos...B 10
30 Tibberton, Salop..H 5
22 Tibberton, Worcs. F 3
26 Tibenham......F 4
32 Tibshelf......D 2
37 Tibthorpe......B 7
10 Ticehurst......E 6
9 Tichborne......C 7
9 Tichfield......F 7
24 Tickencote......E 1
15 Tickenham......G 8
32 Tickhill......A 3
21 Ticklerton......C 10
31 Ticknall......H 12
37 Tickton......C 8
22 Tidbury Green......E 4
16 Tidcombe......H 4
17 Tiddington, Oxon. D 7
22 Tiddington, War...F 6
10 Tidebrook......E 5
3 Tideford......D 10
3 Tideford Cross....D 10
15 Tidenham......E 9
31 Tideswell......C 10
15 Tidmarsh......G 7
22 Tidmington......H 6
8 Tidpit......D 2
3 Tiers Cross......F 3
23 Tiffield......G 10
58 Tifty......D 5
59 Tigerton......L 3
54 Tighchuig......F 8
52 Tighnablair......E 3
46 Tighnabruaich......B 5
51 Tigh-na-criche......G 8
60 Tighnafiline......G 1
5 Tigley......K 6
25 Tilbrook......H 2
18 Tilbury......F 6
22 Tile Cross......C 5

Map	Place	Ref
17	Tilehurst	G 7
9	Tilford	B 10
10	Tilgale	E 2
58	Tillathrowie	D 2
30	Tilley	G 4
52	Tillicoultry	G 4
19	Tillingham	D 10
21	Tillington, Herefs.	H 10
9	Tillington, Sussex	D 10
21	Tillington Com.	H 10
59	Tillyarblet	L 3
59	Tillybardine	K 2
58	Tillycorthie	E 7
59	Tillydrine House	H 4
58	Tillyfar	E 7
58	Tillyfourie	F 4
58	Tillygrieg	E 6
58	Tillyminnate	D 2
11	Tilmanstone	C 11
24	Tilney All Saints	D 7
24	Tilney High End	D 7
24	Tilney St. Lawrence	D 7
8	Tilshead	A 2
30	Tilstock	F 4
30	Tilston	E 3
30	Tilstone Fearnall	D 4
17	Tilsworth	B 10
23	Tilton on the Hill	B 10
15	Tiltups End	E 11
33	Timberland	D 8
31	Timbersbrook	D 7
6	Timberscombe	B 3
35	Timble	B 10
49	Timpendean	G 9
30	Timperley	A 6
8	Timsbury, Hants.	D 5
15	Timsbury, Som.	H 10
27	Timworth Green	H 2
7	Tincleton	G 11
44	Tindale	G 4
17	Tingewick	G 4
35	Tingley	D 11
25	Tingrith	M 1
5	Tinhay	G 3
48	Tinnis	F 6
35	Tinshill	C 11
3	Tintagel	A 7
15	Tintern Parva	D 8
7	Tintinhull	D 8
35	Tintwistle	G 9
43	Tinwald	C 11
24	Tinwell	E 1
4	Tippacott	A 6
58	Tipperty, Aber.	E 7
58	Tipperty, Banff.	B 4
24	Tipp's End	F 6
8	Tiptoe	F 4
22	Tipton	C 3
6	Tipton St. Johns	G 4
19	Tiptree	B 9
20	Tirabad	H 4
50	Tirghoil	E 1
15	Tirley	A 11
14	Tir-Phil	D 4
39	Tirril	C 7
8	Tisbury	C 1
9	Tisman's Com.	C 12
31	Tissington	E 10
4	Titchberry	C 1
25	Titchmarsh	G 1
26	Titchwell	A 1
32	Tithby	F 4
45	Titlington	B 9
21	Titley	F 9
10	Titsey	C 3
31	Tittensor	F 7
26	Tittleshall	C 2
15	Tittups End	E 11
30	Tiverton, Ches.	D 4
6	Tiverton, Devon.	E 3
6	Tiverton Junction	E 4
27	Tivetshall St. Margaret	G 4
27	Tivetshall St. Mary	G 4
22	Tividale	C 3
6	Tivington	B 3
31	Tixall	H 8
24	Tixover	E 1
64	Toab	D 3
31	Toadmoor	E 12
50	Tobermory	B 2
55	Toberonochy	G 5
63	Tobson	C 2
58	Tocher	D 4
16	Tockenham	F 2
16	Tockenham Wick	F 1
34	Tockholes	E 5
15	Tockington	F 9
36	Tockwith	B 3
7	Todber	D 11
17	Toddington, Beds.	A 11
16	Toddington, Glos.	A 1
22	Todenham	H 6
53	Todhall	E 8
44	Todhills	G 2
35	Todmorden	E 8
49	Todrig	G 7
32	Todwick	B 2
25	Toft, Cambs.	K 5
24	Toft, Lincs.	D 2
40	Toft Hill	B 2
26	Toft Monks	F 7
33	Toft next Newton	A 7
49	Toftbarns	G 8
26	Toftrees	C 2
61	Tofts	A 12
26	Toftwood Com.	D 3
45	Togston	C 10
55	Toigal	K 1
62	Tokavaig	G 5
17	Tokers Green	F 8
36	Toll Bar	F 3
22	Toll End	C 3
58	Toll of Birness	D 7
6	Tolland	C 4
8	Tollard Royal	D 1
7	Toller Fratrum	F 9
7	Toller Porcorum	F 9
32	Tollerton, Notts.	G 3
36	Tollerton, Yorks.	A 3
19	Tollesbury	C 9
19	Tolleshunt D'Arcy	C 9
19	Tolleshunt Major	C 9
56	Tollie	D 1
63	Tolmachan	F 3
64	Tolob	F 7
7	Tolpuddle	G 11
63	Tolstachaolais	C 3
57	Tolvah	J 4
10	Tolworth	B 1
57	Tomatin	G 4
57	Tombain	J 4
56	Tombreck	F 2
55	Tomcrasky	H 6
55	Tomdoun	J 5
56	Tomich, Inver.	E 1
55	Tomich, Inver.	G 7
56	Tomich, Ross & Cromarty	C 3
60	Tomich, Suther.	F 6
57	Tomintoul, Aber.	K 7
57	Tomintoul, Banff.	H 7
57	Tomintoul, Inver.	G 2
58	Tomnaven	D 2
57	Tomnavoulin	G 8
52	Tomphubil	B 3
44	Tomshielburn	E 2
14	Ton	D 6
14	Ton-Pentre	E 3
10	Tonbridge	C 5
14	Tondu	F 2
20	Ton-fanau	B 1
63	Tong, Lewis	C 5
22	Tong, Salop	A 2
35	Tong, Yorks.	D 10
32	Tonge	H 2
9	Tongham	A 10
43	Tongland	F 8
60	Tongue	B 6
60	Tongue House	B 6
14	Tongwynlais	F 5
13	Tonna	G 11
14	Ton-teg	F 4
18	Tonwell	B 3
14	Tonypandy	E 3
14	Tonyrefail	E 3
16	Toot Baldon	D 6
18	Toothill	D 5
35	Top of Hebers	F 7
40	Topcliffe	H 4
26	Topcroft	F 5
26	Topcroft Street	F 5
25	Toppesfield	L 8
34	Toppings	F 7
6	Topsham	G 3
57	Torbain	H 7
59	Torbeg, Aber.	G 1
46	Torbeg, Arran I.	F 4
61	Torboll	F 7
56	Torbreck	F 3
5	Torbryan	J 7
55	Torcastle	H 7
5	Torcross	L 7
57	Torcroy	J 3
55	Torcuileainn	J 2
56	Tore	D 2
55	Torgyle Bridge	H 7
46	Torinturk	C 3
32	Torksey	B 5
55	Torlundy	M 5
15	Tormarton	F 11
42	Tormitchell	B 3
46	Tormore	F 4
56	Tornagrain	E 3
57	Tornahaish	J 8
59	Tornaveen	G 4
57	Torness	G 1
40	Toronto	B 2
41	Torosay Castle	D 4
38	Torpenhow	A 4
48	Torphichen	B 2
59	Torphins	G 4
3	Torpoint	D 11
5	Torquay	J 8
49	Torquhan	E 7
62	Torran, Inver.	C 5
56	Torran, Ross & Cromarty	B 3
47	Torrance	B 11
50	Torraneidhinn	B 3
50	Torrans	E 2
47	Torranyard	E 8
5	Torre, Devon.	J 8
6	Torre, Somerset	B 4
54	Torridon	D 3
54	Torridon House	D 2
62	Torrin	F 5
61	Torrisdale	B 7
34	Torrisholme	A 3
54	Torrlaoighseach	H 3
60	Torroboll	F 6
58	Torry, Aberdeen	D 2
59	Torry, Aberdeen	G 7
48	Torryburn	A 3
58	Torterston	C 8
43	Torthorwald	D 11
9	Tortington	F 11
38	Torver	F 5
48	Torwood	A 1
32	Torworth	B 4
4	Tosberry	D 1
54	Toscaig	F 1
25	Toseland	J 3
34	Tosside	B 6
50	Tostarie	C 1
27	Tostock	J 3
62	Totaig, Inverness	C 1
55	Totaig, Ross & Cromarty	G 2
62	Tote	C 3
61	Totegan	A 8
8	Totland	G 5
31	Totley	B 11
7	Totnell	E 9
5	Totnes	K 7
62	Totscore	B 3
24	Tottenham	E 3
24	Tottenhill	D 7
18	Totteridge	E 2
17	Totternhoe	B 10
34	Tottington	F 6
8	Totton	E 5
17	Touchen-end	F 9
59	Toucks	J 6
6	Toulton	C 5
56	Toulvaddie	B 4
58	Toux	C 7
40	Tow Law	A 1
46	Toward	C 6
46	Toward Quay	C 6
23	Towcester	G 10
2	Towednack	F 2
18	Tower Hamlets	F 4
10	Tower Hill	E 1
17	Towersey	D 8
5	Towie	F 2
58	Towiemore	C 1
39	Town End	G 7
34	Town Green	G 3
10	Town Row	E 4
27	Town Street	G 1
49	Town Yetholm	G 10
43	Townfoot	B 10
42	Townhead, Ayr.	A 3
43	Townhead, Dumf.	C 10
59	Townhead, Kinc.	K 5
43	Townhead, Kirk.	G 8
45	Townhead, Northumb.	F 7
47	Townhead of Aber.	A 9
47	Townhead of Gree.	E 9
43	Townhead of Greenlaw	E 8
52	Townhill	H 6
16	Townsend, Berks.	E 5
7	Townsend, Som.	A 8
2	Townshend	F 3
36	Towthorpe	A 4
36	Towton	C 3
29	Towyn	B 9
33	Toynton All Saints	D 11
33	Toynton Fen Side	D 11
33	Toynton St. Peter	D 11
10	Toy's Hill	C 3
47	Trabboch	G 9
47	Trabboch Mains	G 9
47	Trabbochburn	G 9
2	Traboe	G 4
56	Tradespark	D 4
35	Trafford Park	H 7
55	Traigh House	K 1
43	Traitrow	D 12
14	Trallong	A 3
49	Tranent	B 7
30	Tranmere	A 2
61	Trantlemore	B 8
45	Tranwell	E 10
13	Trapp	E 10
49	Traprain	B 8
48	Traquair	F 6
17	Traveller's Rest	B 10
35	Trawden	C 8
14	Trawscoed	A 4
28	Trawsfynydd	G 6
13	Tre-Herbert	B 9
14	Trealaw	E 3
34	Treales	D 3
28	Trearddur Bay	B 2
62	Treaslane	C 3
3	Trebartha	B 9
3	Trebarwith	A 7
3	Trebetheric	B 6
6	Treborough	C 3
3	Treburley	B 10
3	Trebyan	C 8
14	Trecastle	A 2
14	Trecenydd	F 5
12	Trecwn	D 3
14	Trecynon	D 3
3	Tredaule	B 9
12	Tre-ddiog	D 2
14	Tredegar	C 5
22	Tredington	H 6
2	Tredizzick	B 6
14	Tredomen	A 4
12	Tredrissi	C 4
15	Tredunnock	E 7
14	Tredustan	A 4
2	Treen	G 1
32	Treeton	A 2
12	Trefasser	C 2
28	Trefdraeth	C 3
14	Trefecca	A 5
20	Trefeglwys	E 2
20	Trefenter	E 2
12	Treffgarne	E 3
12	Treffgarne Owen	D 2
28	Treffynnon, Angl.	B 3
12	Treffynnon, Pemb.	D 2
14	Trefil	C 5
14	Trefilan	G 1
29	Trefnant	C 10
30	Trefonen	G 1
28	Trefor	B 3
14	Treforest Industrial Estate	F 4
29	Trefriw	D 7
29	Tref-y-nant	F 12
3	Tregadillett	A 10
28	Tregaian	B 4
15	Tregare	C 7
20	Tregaron	F 2
28	Tregarth	C 5
3	Tregeare	A 9
29	Tregeiriog	G 11
28	Tregele	A 3
2	Tregeseal	F 1
12	Treglemais	D 2
2	Tregonetha	C 6
2	Tregony	E 6
3	Tregoss	D 7
14	Tregoyd	A 5
13	Tre-groes	C 7
2	Tregune	B 2
2	Tregurrian	C 5
20	Tregynon	C 6
14	Trehafod	E 4
14	Treharris	E 4
3	Treherbert	D 3
3	Trekenner	B 10
3	Treknow	A 7
3	Trelash	D 6
2	Trelassick	D 6
29	Trelawnyd	B 10
14	Trelech	D 6
12	Tre-lech-a'r-Betws	D 6
12	Treleddyd fawr	D 1
3	Treligga	A 7
3	Trelights	B 7
3	Trelill	B 7
2	Trelissick	F 5
15	Trelleck	D 8
15	Trelleck Grange	D 8
29	Trelogan	B 10
28	Tremadog	F 5
3	Tremail	A 8
12	Tremain	B 6
3	Tremaine	A 9
3	Tremar	C 9
29	Tremeirchion	C 10
3	Tremore	C 7
2	Trenance, Corn.	C 5
2	Trenance, Corn.	C 6
2	Trenance, Corn.	H 4
3	Trenarren	E 7
21	Trench	A 12
2	Trenear	F 4
3	Treneglos	A 9
2	Trenewan	D 9
7	Trent Nether Compton	D 9
31	Trentham	F 7
4	Trentishoe	A 5
14	Treoes	F 3
14	Treorchy	E 3
3	Trequite	B 7
20	Tre'r-ddol	C 2
3	Trerule Foot	D 10
12	Tresaith	B 6
3	Tresayes	D 7
22	Trescott	B 2
2	Trescowe	G 3
15	Tresham	E 11
12	Tresillian	E 6
12	Tresinwen	C 2
3	Treskinnick Cross	A 2
3	Tresmeer	A 9
2	Tresparrett	B 2
2	Tresparrett Posts	B 2
52	Tressait	B 2
64	Tresta, Zetland	B 8
64	Tresta, Zetland	D 7
32	Treswell	B 5
2	Trethosa	D 6
3	Trethurgy	D 7
12	Tretio	D 1
15	Tretire	B 8
14	Tretower	B 5
29	Treuddyn	D 11
3	Trevadlock	B 9
3	Trevalga	A 8
30	Trevalyn	D 3
3	Trevanson	B 7
3	Trevarren	D 6
2	Trevarrian	C 5
3	Trevarrick	E 7
12	Trevaughan, Carm.	E 5
13	Trevaughan, Carm.	E 7
2	Trevellas	D 4
3	Trevelmond	C 9
2	Treverva	F 5
14	Trevethin	D 6
3	Trevigro	C 10
12	Trevine	D 2
2	Treviscoe	D 6
3	Trevivian	A 9
3	Trevoll	D 5
2	Trevone	B 6
3	Trevor	F 3
3	Trevose	B 6
3	Trewarmett	A 8
3	Trewassa	A 8
3	Trewellard	F 1
3	Trewen	A 9
2	Trewennack	G 4
21	Trewern	A 8
3	Trewerthern	B 7
3	Trewetha	B 7
3	Trewidland	D 9
12	Trewilym	C 5
3	Trewint	B 2
3	Trewithian	F 6
3	Trewoon	D 7
2	Treyarnon Bay	B 5
9	Treyford	D 9
35	Triangle	E 9
8	Trickett's Cross	F 3
44	Triermain	B 4
40	Trimdon	B 4
40	Trimdon Colliery	B 4
40	Trimdon Grange	B 4
26	Trimingham	B 6
27	Trimley	L 6
27	Trimley Heath	L 6
22	Trimpley	D 1
13	Trimsaran	F 8
4	Trimstone	B 4
14	Trinant	D 5
17	Tring	C 10
17	Tring Wharf	C 10
59	Trinity, Angus	L 4
6	Trinity, Devon.	F 3
6	Triscombe	C 5
55	Trislaig	M 5
2	Trispen	E 5
45	Tritlington	D 10
52	Trochrie	C 5
13	Troedyraur	B 7
13	Troed-y-rhiw, Card.	E 8
14	Troedyrhiw, Glam.	D 4
47	Troon, Ayr.	F 8
2	Troon, Cornwall	F 4
43	Troqueer	D 10
51	Trossachs Hotel	G 12
57	Trostan	H 2
10	Trottiscliffe	B 5
9	Trotton	D 9
45	Troughend	D 7
38	Troutbeck, Cumberland	C 6
38	Troutbeck, Westmor.	E 6
38	Troutbeck Bridge	E 6
15	Trow Green	D 9
32	Troway	B 1
15	Trowbridge	H 11
32	Trowell	F 2
15	Trowle Common	H 11
17	Trowley Bottom	C 11
49	Trows	F 9
26	Trowse Newton	E 5
7	Trudoxhill	B 10
6	Trull	D 6
62	Trumpan	B 2
21	Trumpet	H 12
6	Trumpington	K 6
6	Trumps	E 4
26	Trunch	B 6
2	Truro	E 5
3	Truscott	A 10
6	Trusham	H 2
31	Trusley	G 11
33	Trusthorpe	B 12
22	Trysull	C 2
16	Tubney	D 5
5	Tuckenhay	K 7
2	Tuckingmill	F 4
25	Tuddenham, Suff.	H 8
27	Tuddenham, Suff.	K 5
10	Tudeley	D 5
40	Tudhoe	B 3
15	Tudorville	B 9
28	Tudweiliog	G 2
3	Tuesley	B 11
15	Tuffley	C 11
12	Tufton	D 4
21	Tugford	D 11
45	Tughall	E 12
55	Tuirnaig	B 3
57	Tulchan	M 7
52	Tullibody	H 3
7	Tullich, Argyll	F 8
57	Tullich, Inverness	G 2
51	Tullich, Perth	D 12
54	Tullich, Ross & Cromarty	E 3
56	Tullich Muir	B 3
52	Tulliemet	E 3
59	Tullo' of Benholm	K 5
58	Tulloch, Aber.	D 5
55	Tulloch, Inver.	L 7
52	Tullochan	D 1
51	Tullochgorm	H 7
57	Tullochmacarrick	J 8
58	Tullochs	C 2
59	Tullochvenus	G 3
52	Tullybannocher	E 2
53	Tullyfergus	B 7
53	Tullymurdoch	B 7
58	Tullynessle	F 3
13	Tumble	F 9
33	Tumby	D 9
33	Tumby Woodside	D 9
18	Tumford	C 4
52	Tummel Bridge	A 3
10	Tunbridge Wells	D 5
15	Tunley	H 10
45	Tunstall, Dur.	H 12
11	Tunstall, Kent	B 7
39	Tunstall, Lancs.	H 8
31	Tunstall, Staffs.	E 7
27	Tunstall, Suffolk	K 6
37	Tunstall, E.Riding	D 10
40	Tunstall, N. Riding	F 2
27	Tunstall St. Mary	E 7
9	Tunworth	A 8
21	Tupsley	H 10
23	Tur Langton	C 10
17	Turgis Green	H 8
53	Turin	B 10
15	Turleigh Freshford	H 11
15	Turnastone	A 7
42	Turnberry	A 3
31	Turnditch	F 11
10	Turner's Hill	E 2
7	Turners Puddle	G 11

MAP
48 Turnhouse B 4
7 Turnworth E 11
58 Turriff C 5
34 Turton Bottoms F 6
49 Turvelaws F 12
23 Turvey G 12
17 Turville E 8
17 Turville Heath E 8
23 Turweston H 9
48 Tushielaw G 6
31 Tutbury G 10
22 Tutnall E 3
15 Tutshill E 8
26 Tuttington C 5
17 Tutts Clump G 7
3 Tutwell B 11
32 Tuxford C 4
64 Twatt, Orkney Is. C 1
64 Twatt, Shetland Is. D 7
47 Twechar B 11
48 Tweeddaleburn D 5
49 Tweedmouth D 12
48 Tweedshaws H 3
48 Tweedsmuir G 4
2 Twelveheads E 5
30 Twemlow Green C 6
24 Twenty C 3
15 Twerton H 10
44 Twice Brewed F 6
18 Twickenham G 2
15 Twigworth B 11
10 Twineham F 1
15 Twinhoe H 10
27 Twinstead L 2
27 Twinstead Green L 2
4 Twitchen, Devon B 4
4 Twitchen, Devon C 7
21 Twitchen, Salop D 9
5 Two Bridges H 5
31 Two Dales D 11
22 Two Gates B 5
4 Two Pots B 4
23 Twycross B 7
17 Twyford, Berks. G 9
17 Twyford, Bucks. B 7
31 Twyford, Derby. G 11
8 Twyford, Hants. D 6
23 Twyford, Leics. A 10
26 Twyford, Norf. C 3
15 Twyford Com. A 8
13 Twyn Llanan E 11
14 Twyncarno C 4
43 Twynholm F 7
15 Twyning A 12
22 Twyning Green H 3
13 Twyn-mynydd F 10
15 Twyn-y-Sheriff D 7
23 Twywell D 12
28 Ty-Hen G 1
21 Tyberton H 9
28 Ty-croes, Angl. C 3
13 Tycroes, Carm. F 9
29 Tycrwyn H 10
24 Tydd Gote D 5
24 Tydd St. Giles D 5
24 Tydd St. Mary D 5
29 Tyddininco G 9
19 Tye Green, Essex B 7
25 Tye Green, Essex L 7
12 Ty-hen E 6
34 Tyldesley G 6
11 Tyler Hill B 10
17 Tylers Green, Bucks. E 10
10 Tyler's Grn., Surrey C 2
15 Tylorstown E 3
20 Tylwch D 5
29 Ty-nant, Denb. F 9
29 Ty-nant, Mer. H 8
20 Tyncwm D 4
51 Tyndrum E 10
7 Tyneham H 12
45 Tyne & Wear, Co. F 10
48 Tynehead C 6
15 Tynemouth F 11
14 Tynewydd D 3
49 Tyninghame B 8
50 Tynribbie C 6
43 Tynron B 9
20 Tynswydd F 2
29 Ty'n-y-ffridd G 10
28 Ty'n-y-gongl B 4
29 Ty'n-y-groes C 7
28 Tyn-y-pwll B 4
29 Tyn-y-Wern G 10
23 Tyringham G 12
4 Tythecott D 3
14 Tythegston F 2
31 Tytherington, Ches. C 7
15 Tytherington, Glos. E 10
8 Tytherington, Wilts. B 1

MAP
7 Tytherington, Wilts. B 11
7 Tytherleigh F 7
16 Tytherton Lucas G 1
3 Tywardreath D 8
3 Tywardreath Highway D 8
29 Tywyn B 7
20 Tywyn Mer. B 2
54 Uags F 1
54 Uamh on Triall D 1
27 Ubbeston Green H 6
15 Ubley H 8
40 Uckerby E 3
10 Uckfield F 4
15 Uckington B 12
47 Uddingston C 11
48 Uddington F 1
11 Udimore F 7
58 Udny E 6
47 Udston E 12
47 Udstonhead E 12
16 Uffcott F 2
6 Uffculme E 4
16 Uffington, Berks. E 4
24 Uffington, Lincs. E 2
21 Uffington, Salop A 10
24 Ufford, Hunts. E 2
27 Ufford, Suffolk K 6
23 Ufton F 7
17 Ufton Green G 7
17 Ufton Nervet G 7
46 Ugadale F 3
5 Ugborough K 5
27 Uggeshall G 7
41 Ugglebarnby D 9
18 Ugley A 5
41 Ugthorpe D 8
63 Uig, Lewis D 2
62 Uig, Skye C 1
62 Uig, Skye B 3
62 Uigshader D 4
50 Uisken F 1
61 Ulbster C 12
33 Ulceby, Lincs. C 11
37 Ulceby, Lincs. F 8
33 Ulceby Cross C 11
37 Ulceby Skitter F 9
11 Ulcombe C 7
38 Uldale B 5
39 Uldale House F 9
15 Uley D 11
45 Ulgham D 10
60 Ullapool G 3
22 Ullenhall E 5
15 Ullenwood C 12
36 Ulleskelf C 3
23 Ullesthorpe C 8
32 Ulley B 2
21 Ullingswick G 11
62 Ullinish D 2
38 Ullock C 3
8 Ullwell H 2
38 Ulpha F 4
37 Ulrome B 9
64 Ulsta C 7
49 Ulston G 9
50 Ulva House D 2
38 Ulverston G 5
43 Ulzieside A 8
62 Umachan C 5
4 Umberleigh D 5
60 Unapool D 4
44 Under Burnmouth E 3
10 Under River C 4
39 Underbarrow F 7
35 Undercliffe D 10
47 Underhills F 9
64 Underhoull A 8
32 Underwood E 2
15 Undy F 7
64 Unifirth D 6
59 Union Croft H 6
38 Union Mills H 2
32 Unstone C 1
32 Unstone Green C 1
35 Unsworth F 7
44 Unthank, Cumb. H 2
39 Unthank, Cumb. A 8
39 Unthank, Cumb. B 7
49 Unthank, Northumb. E 12
39 Unthank End B 7
7 Up Cerne F 10
6 Up Exe F 3
15 Up Hatherley B 12
34 Up Holland G 4
9 Up Marden E 9
9 Up Nately A 8
8 Up Somborne C 5
7 Up Sydling F 9
8 Upavon A 3
11 Upchurch A 7

MAP
4 Upcott, Devon E 4
21 Upcott, Herefs. G 8
6 Upcott, Somerset D 3
17 Updown Hill H 10
48 Uphall B 3
48 Uphall Station B 3
4 Upham, Devon E 7
9 Upham, Hants. D 7
21 Uphampton, Herefs. F 9
22 Uphampton, Worcs. F 2
14 Uphill H 6
47 Uplawmoor D 9
15 Upleadon B 10
40 Upleatham C 6
11 Uplees B 8
7 Uploders G 8
6 Uplowman E 4
6 Uplyme G 6
18 Upminster E 6
6 Upottery E 5
71 Uppat F 8
21 Upper Affcott D 10
60 Upper Ardchronie G 6
22 Upper Arley D 1
17 Upper Arncott B 7
23 Upper Astrop H 8
42 Upper Barr E 5
63 Upper Barvas B 5
17 Upper Basildon F 7
63 Upper Bayble D 6
10 Upper Beeding G 1
24 Upper Benefield F 1
22 Upper Bentley E 3
58 Upper Boddam E 4
23 Upper Boddington G 8
20 Upper Borth D 2
9 Upper Bourne B 9
58 Upper Boyndie A 6
22 Upper Brailes H 6
62 Upper Breakish F 6
21 Upper Breinton H 10
32 Upper Broughton H 4
16 Upper Bucklebury G 6
8 Upper Burgate D 3
59 Upper Burnhaugh H 6
58 Upper Cairnargot D 2
25 Upper Caldecote L 3
8 Upper Canterton E 4
23 Upper Catesby F 8
20 Upper Chapel H 6
6 Upper Cheddon C 6
8 Upper Chicksgrove C 1
14 Upper Church Village F 4
8 Upper Chute A 4
8 Upper Clatford B 5
43 Upper Clifton F 10
28 Upper Clynnog F 4
63 Upper Coll C 5
20 Upper Corris B 3
42 Upper Craigenbay D 6
35 Upper Cumberworth F 10
14 Upper Cwmbran E 6
13 Upper Cwm-twrch F 11
58 Upper Dallachy A 1
43 Upper Dalveen A 9
25 Upper Dean H 1
35 Upper Denby F 11
44 Upper Denton G 4
56 Upper Derraid F 6
54 Upper Diabaig D 2
58 Upper Dicker G 4
61 Upper Dounreay A 9
50 Upper Druimfin B 2
31 Upper Elkstone D 9
31 Upper End C 9
56 Upper Ethie C 3
15 Upper Framilode C 10
22 Upper Gornal C 3
25 Upper Gravenhurst L 2
16 Upper Green H 5
15 Upper Grove Com. B 9
9 Upper Hale A 10
62 Upper Halistra B 2
17 Upper Halliford G 11
10 Upper Halling B 6
23 Upper Hambleton A 12
11 Upper Hardress Court C 10
10 Upper Hartfield E 3
36 Upper Haugh G 2
21 Upper Heath D 11
26 Upper Hellesdon D 5
36 Upper Helmsley A 5
21 Upper Hergest G 8
23 Upper Heyford, Northants. F 10
16 Upper Heyford, Oxon. B 6
21 Upper Hill G 10
44 Upper Hindhope B 6

MAP
35 Upper Hopton E 10
10 Upper Horsebridge G 5
31 Upper Hulme D 8
16 Upper Inglesham D 3
57 Upper Inverbrough G 4
58 Upper Ironside B 6
53 Upper Kenley F 10
13 Upper Killay H 9
58 Upper Kinkell E 5
19 Upper Kirby B 11
58 Upper Knaven C 6
56 Upper Knockando E 7
16 Upper Lambourn F 4
15 Upper Langford H 8
32 Upper Langwith C 2
31 Upper Leigh F 8
59 Upper Lochton H 4
22 Upper Longdon A 4
61 Upper Lybster D 11
15 Upper Lydbrook C 9
21 Upper Lye F 9
62 Upper Milovaig C 1
16 Upper Minety E 1
35 Upper Moor Side D 11
15 Upper Morton E 9
58 Upper Mulben B 1
44 Upper Mumble E 2
49 Upper Nisbet G 9
17 Upper North Dean D 9
52 Upper Obney C 5
62 Upper Ollach E 4
22 Upper Penn C 3
36 Upper Poppleton B 3
21 Upper Pulley B 10
22 Upper Quinton G 5
8 Upper Ratley D 5
21 Upper Rochford F 11
42 Upper Rusko E 6
55 Upper Sandaig H 2
21 Upper Sapey F 12
46 Upper Scoulag C 6
16 Upper Seagry F 1
63 Upper Shader B 5
23 Upper Shelton L 1
26 Upper Sheringham A 4
48 Upper Side D 6
47 Upper Skelmorlie C 7
16 Upper Slaughter B 3
51 Upper Sonachan E 8
15 Upper Soudley C 10
15 Upper Stanton Drew H 9
25 Upper Stondon M 3
22 Upper Stonnall B 4
23 Upper Stowe F 10
8 Upper Street, Hants. D 3
26 Upper Street, Norf. D 7
22 Upper Strensham H 3
17 Upper Sundon A 11
16 Upper Swell B 3
26 Upper Tasburgh F 5
31 Upper Tean F 8
52 Upper Tillyrie F 6
62 Upper Tote B 4
21 Upper Town, Herefs. G 11
15 Upper Town, Som. H 8
23 Upper Tysoe H 7
16 Upper Upham F 3
10 Upper Upnor A 6
23 Upper Wardington G 8
23 Upper Weald H 11
23 Upper Weedon F 9
17 Upper Winchendon C 8
8 Upper Woodford B 3
58 Upper Woodhead F 4
9 Upper Wootton A 7
22 Upper Wyche H 1
44 Upperby H 2
58 Uppertack of Gressiehill B 6
35 Upperthong F 10
59 Upperton, Kinc. K 5
9 Upperton, Sussex D 11
64 Uppertown F 2
21 Uppington A 11
40 Upsall F 5
18 Upshire D 4
11 Upstreet B 11
16 Upton, Berks. E 6
17 Upton, Berks. F 10
30 Upton, Cheshire C 3
30 Upton, Cheshire A 1
4 Upton, Cornwall E 1
6 Upton, Devon F 4
8 Upton, Dorset G 1
7 Upton, Dorset H 11
8 Upton, Hants. D 5
24 Upton, Hunts. E 2

MAP
25 Upton, Hunts. G 3
32 Upton, Lincs. B 6
26 Upton, Norfolk D 7
23 Upton, Northants. F 10
32 Upton, Notts. C 5
32 Upton, Notts. E 4
8 Upton, Notts. A 5
6 Upton, Somerset C 3
7 Upton, Somerset D 8
22 Upton, War. F 5
36 Upton, Yorkshire F 3
15 Upton Bishop B 9
15 Upton Cheyney G 10
21 Upton Cressett C 12
9 Upton Grey A 8
4 Upton Hellions F 7
8 Upton Lovell B 1
21 Upton Magna A 11
7 Upton Noble B 10
6 Upton Pyne F 3
15 Upton St. Leonards C 11
7 Upton Scudamore A 12
22 Upton Snodsbury G 3
22 Upton upon Severn H 2
22 Upton Warren E 3
9 Upwaltham E 10
25 Upware H 6
24 Upwell E 6
7 Upwey H 10
25 Upwood G 4
64 Urafirth C 6
56 Urchal E 3
56 Urchany E 4
16 Urchfont H 2
63 Urgha Beag G 3
40 Urlay Nook D 4
34 Urmston H 6
56 Urquhart, Moray C 8
56 Urquhart, Ross & Cromarty D 1
40 Urra E 6
56 Urray D 1
40 Ushaw Moor A 3
15 Usk D 7
37 Usselby H 8
56 Ussie D 1
64 Ustaness D 7
45 Usworth G 11
35 Utley C 9
4 Uton F 7
37 Utterby H 10
31 Uttoxeter G 9
28 Uwchmynydd H 1
18 Uxbridge F 1
64 Uyeasound B 8
12 Uzmaston F 3
12 Vachelich D 1
28 Valley B 2
3 Valley Truckle A 8
64 Valsgarth A 8
62 Valtos, Skye B 4
63 Valtos, Lewis C 2
20 Van D 5
19 Vange E 7
14 Varteg Hill D 6
62 Vatten D 2
14 Vaynor C 4
14 Velindre, Brec. A 5
13 Velindre, Carm. C 7
12 Velindre, Pemb. C 4
6 Vellow B 4
64 Vementry D 6
64 Veness B 3
6 Venn Ottery G 4
21 Vennington A 9
4 Venny Tedburn F 7
9 Ventnor H 7
16 Vernham Dean H 4
16 Vernham Street H 4
12 Verwig B 5
8 Verwood E 2
2 Veryan F 6
6 Vicarage G 5
38 Vickerstown H 4
3 Victoria, Corn. D 7
14 Victoria, Mon. D 5
64 Vidlin C 7
10 Vinehall Street F 6
10 Vine's Cross F 5
15 Viney Hill D 9
17 Virginia Water G 10
5 Virginstow G 3
7 Vobster A 10
64 Voe C 7
15 Vowchurch A 7
64 Voxter C 7
64 Voy C 1
40 Wackerfield C 2
26 Wacton F 5
22 Wadborough G 3
17 Waddesdon B 8
37 Waddingham G 7

MAP
33 Waddington, Lincs. D 7
34 Waddington, Yorks. C 6
3 Wadebridge B 7
6 Wadeford E 6
25 Wadenhoe G 1
18 Wadesmill B 4
10 Wadhurst E 5
31 Wadshelf C 11
31 Wadsley A 11
32 Wadsley Bridge A 1
15 Wadswick G 11
36 Wadworth G 3
29 Waen D 11
29 Waen Fach H 11
61 Wag E 9
33 Wainfleet All Saints D 12
33 Wainfleet Bank D 11
45 Wainfordrigg C 7
32 Waingroves E 1
2 Wainhouse Corner B 2
10 Wainscott A 6
35 Wainstalls D 9
39 Waitby D 10
35 Wakefield E 12
24 Wakerley F 1
19 Wakes Colne A 9
29 Wal-Wen C 11
27 Walberswick H 8
9 Walberton E 11
45 Walbottle F 10
24 Walcot, Kest. B 2
33 Walcot, Lincs. E 8
21 Walcot, Salop A 11
21 Walcot, Salop D 9
22 Walcot, War. F 5
16 Walcot, Wilts. F 3
23 Walcote D 9
26 Walcott B 7
39 Walden Head G 12
36 Walden Stubbs E 3
10 Walderslade B 6
9 Walderton E 9
7 Walditch G 8
31 Waldley F 9
45 Waldridge H 10
27 Waldringfield L 6
10 Waldron F 4
32 Wales B 2
33 Walesby, Lincs. A 8
32 Walesby, Notts. C 4
15 Walford, Herefs. B 9
21 Walford, Herefs. E 9
30 Walford, Salop H 3
30 Walford Heath H 3
30 Walgherton E 5
23 Walgrave E 11
8 Walhampton F 5
35 Walk Mill D 7
34 Walkden G 6
45 Walker G 11
34 Walker Fold C 5
48 Walkerburn F 6
32 Walkeringham A 5
32 Walkerith A 5
18 Walkern A 3
21 Walker's Green H 10
53 Walkerton G 7
8 Walkford G 4
5 Walkhampton J 4
37 Walkington C 8
32 Walkley A 1
45 Wall, Northumb. F 7
22 Wall, Staffs. B 4
44 Wall Bowers G 4
21 Wall under Heywood C 10
43 Wallaceton C 9
42 Wallacetown, Ayr. A 4
47 Wallacetown, Ayr. G 8
30 Wallasey A 2
19 Wallend, Kent F 8
38 Wallend, Lancs. G 5
17 Wallingford E 7
9 Wallington, Hants. E 7
25 Wallington, Herts. M 4
18 Wallington, London H 3
9 Walliswood B 12
64 Walls D 6
45 Wallsend F 11
38 Wallthwaite C 6
48 Wallyford B 6
11 Walmer C 12
34 Walmer Bridge E 3
35 Walmersley F 7
22 Walmley C 5
27 Walpole H 7
24 Walpole Crosskeys D 6
24 Walpole Highway D 6
24 Walpole Island D 6
24 Walpole St. Andrew D6

24 Walpole St. Peter..D 6
22 Walsall.........B 4
22 Walsall Wood......B 4
35 Walsden.........E 8
23 Walsgrave on Sowe D 7
27 Walsham le Willows H 3
34 Walshaw......F 6
35 Walshford....B 12
48 Walston.......E 3
18 Walsworth......A 2
17 Walter's Ash...D 9
14 Walterston......G 4
15 Walterstone.....B 7
11 Waltham, Kent...C 9
37 Waltham, Lincs..G 10
18 Waltham Abbey...D 4
9 Waltham Chase...E 7
18 Waltham Cross...D 4
18 Waltham Forest...E 4
32 Waltham on the Wolds H 5
17 Waltham St. Lawrence F 9
18 Walthamstow.....E 3
23 Walton, Bucks..H 12
44 Walton, Cumb...G 3
32 Walton, Derby...C 1
24 Walton, Hunts....E 3
23 Walton, Leics...C 9
21 Walton, Rad.....F 8
30 Walton, Salop...H 4
7 Walton, Som....C 8
27 Walton, Suffolk..L 6
22 Walton, War.....G 6
36 Walton, Yorks...B 2
35 Walton, Yorks..E 12
15 Walton Cardiff..A 12
7 Walton Elm...D 11
12 Walton East.....E 4
15 Walton-in-Gordano G 7
34 Walton Le Dale...D 4
17 Walton-on-Thames G 12
34 Walton on the Hill, Lancashire.....H 3
31 Walton-on-the-Hill, Staffordshire..H 8
10 Walton on the Hill, Surrey......C 1
19 Walton on the Naze B 12
32 Walton on the Wolds H 3
15 Walton Park.....G 7
31 Walton upon Trent H 10
12 Walton West....F 2
45 Walwick......F 7
45 Walwick Grange..F 7
40 Walworth......C 3
12 Walwyn's Castle..F 2
6 Wambrook.....E 6
43 Wamphraygate..B 12
9 Wanborough, Surrey A 10
16 Wanborough, Wilts. F 3
48 Wandel.......G 2
45 Wandon......C 11
18 Wandsworth....F 3
45 Wandylaw.....A 9
27 Wangford.....G 8
23 Wanlip.......A 9
48 Wanlockhead...H 2
10 Wannock......H 4
24 Wansford, Hunts..F 2
37 Wansford, Yorks..B 8
18 Wanstead......E 4
7 Wanstrow.....B 10
9 Wanswell Green..D 10
16 Wantage......E 5
23 Wappenbury....E 7
23 Wappenham....H 9
39 Warcop.......D 9
10 Warbleton.....F 5
9 Warblington....E 8
17 Warborough....E 7
25 Warboys......G 4
34 Warbreck......C 2
2 Warbstow.....B 2
30 Warburton....A 5
27 Ward Green....J 4
11 Warden......A 9
31 Wardgate......E 11
23 Wardington....G 8
47 Wardlaw, Ayr...E 4
48 Wardlaw, Sel...H 5
30 Wardle, Ches....E 5
35 Wardle, Lancs...E 8
35 Wardley......B 11
31 Wardlow......C 10

45 Wardon........F 7
25 Wardy Hill......G 6
18 Ware, Herts.....C 4
11 Ware, Kent.....B 11
8 Wareham......G 1
11 Warehorne.....E 8
45 Waren Mill.....C 12
45 Warenford.....C 12
45 Warenton.....C 12
18 Wareside......B 4
25 Waresley, Hunts...K 3
22 Waresley, Worcs..E 2
17 Warfield.......G 9
5 Warfleet......L 7
24 Wargate......C 3
17 Wargrave......F 9
26 Warham All Saints A 3
26 Warham St. Mary A 2
45 Wark, Northumb..E 7
49 Wark, Northumb. E 11
4 Warkleigh.....D 5
23 Warkton........D 12
23 Warkwork......H 8
45 Warkworth.....B 10
40 Warlaby.......F 4
35 Warland.......E 8
22 Warleggan.....C 8
22 Warley.......C 3
10 Warlingham....B 2
35 Warmfield.....E 12
30 Warmingham....D 5
24 Warmington, Hunts. F 2
23 Warmington, War. G 7
7 Warminster....B 11
11 Warmlake......C 7
15 Warmley......G 10
15 Warmley Tower..G 10
36 Warmsworth....G 3
7 Warmwell......H 11
22 Warndon.......F 2
9 Warnford.....D 8
10 Warnham......E 1
9 Warningcamp...E 11
10 Warninglid.....E 1
31 Warren, Ches....C 7
12 Warren, Pemb....G 3
5 Warren House Inn.H 5
17 Warren Row.....F 9
11 Warren Street....C 8
23 Warrington, Bucks. G 12
30 Warrington, Lancs. A 5
8 Warsash.......E 6
31 Warslow.......D 9
32 Warsop.......C 3
36 Warter.......B 6
40 Warthermarske..G 2
33 Warthill.......B 4
10 Wartling......G 5
32 Wartnaby......H 4
24 Warton, Lancs....D 3
39 Warton, Lancs...H 7
45 Warton, Northumb. C 8
22 Warton, War....B 6
44 Warwick, Cumb..G 3
22 Warwick, War....F 6
44 Warwick Bridge..G 3
22 Warwickshire, Co. F 6
44 Warwicksland....E 3
64 Wasbister......B 2
38 Wasdale Head....D 4
16 Wash Common...H 5
3 Washaway......C 7
5 Washbourne....K 7
31 Washerwall.....E 8
6 Washfield......E 3
40 Washfold......E 1
6 Washford......B 4
4 Washford Pyne...E 7
33 Washingborough..C 7
45 Washington, Dur. G 11
9 Washington, Sussex E 12
17 Wasing.......H 7
40 Waskerley......A 1
22 Wasperton.....F 6
40 Wass.........G 6
6 Watchet.......B 4
16 Watchfield, Berks. E 3
7 Watchfield, Som...B 7
39 Watchgate.....E 8
43 Watchill.....G 12
38 Watendlath....D 5
5 Water, Devon...H 6
35 Water, Lancs....E 7
18 Water End, Herts..C 2
36 Water End, Yorks..C 6
24 Water Newton....F 2
22 Water Orton.....C 5
17 Water Stratford..A 7
14 Water Street.....F 1

38 Water Yeat.......F 5
25 Waterbeach......J 6
44 Waterbeck......E 1
26 Waterden.......B 2
17 Waterend......C 11
31 Waterfall......E 9
45 Waterfoot, Lan..D 10
35 Waterfoot, Lancs..E 7
8 Waterford, Hants..G 5
18 Waterford, Herts..B 3
47 Waterhead, Ayr..H 10
43 Waterhead, Dumf.B 12
43 Waterhead, Dumf..C 8
38 Waterhead, Westmor. E 6
48 Waterheads......D 5
40 Waterhouses, Dur..A 2
31 Waterhouses, Staffs. E 9
33 Watering Dyke Houses B 7
10 Wateringbury... C 6
64 Waterhouse.....E 2
15 Waterlane.....D 12
32 Waterloo, Derby...D 1
8 Waterloo, Dorset..G 2
48 Waterloo, Lan....D 1
34 Waterloo, Lancs...G 2
26 Waterloo, Norf...D 5
12 Waterloo, Pemb...G 3
52 Waterloo, Perth...C 5
62 Waterloo, Skye...F 6
6 Waterloo Cross...E 4
9 Waterlooville.....E 8
48 Watermeetings...H 2
17 Waterperry......C 7
6 Waterrow......D 4
30 Waters Upton....H 5
9 Watersfield......E 11
58 Waterside, Aber...E 7
42 Waterside, Ayr....A 5
47 Waterside, Ayr...E 9
44 Waterside, Cumb..H 1
43 Waterside, Dumf. D 12
47 Waterside, Dunb..B 11
17 Waterstock.....D 7
12 Waterston......F 3
18 Watford, Herts....D 1
23 Watford, Northants. E 9
40 Wath, N. Riding .G 3
40 Wath, W. Riding .H 2
38 Wath Brow......D 3
36 Wath upon Dearne G 2
15 Watley's End.....F 9
24 Watlington, Norf..D 7
17 Watlington, Oxon..E 8
32 Watnall Chaworth.F 2
61 Watten........B 11
27 Wattisfield......H 3
27 Wattisham......K 3
26 Watton, Norf.....E 2
37 Watton, Yorks....B 8
18 Watton-at-Stone..B 3
47 Wattston......B 12
14 Wattstown......E 3
55 Wauchan......L 3
37 Wauldby......D 7
20 Waun Fawr......D 2
13 Waunarlwydd....G 9
13 Waun-deg......D 7
28 Waunfawr......D 5
14 Waunlwyd......D 5
23 Wavendon......H 12
44 Waverbridge....H 1
30 Waverton, Ches...D 3
44 Waverton, Cumb..H 1
37 Wawne........C 8
26 Waxham......C 7
37 Waxholme.....D 11
6 Way Village.....E 3
10 Wayfield......B 6
7 Wayford.......F 7
7 Waytown.......F 8
6 Weacombe......B 5
18 Wealdstone......E 2
35 Weardley......C 11
7 Weare.........A 7
4 Weare Gifford....D 3
39 Wearhead......A 11
39 Weasdale......E 9
26 Weasenham All Saints C 1
26 Weasenham St. Peter C 1
30 Weaverham......C 5
41 Weaverthorpe....H 9
22 Webheath......A 4
15 Webton........A 7
58 Wedderlairs......D 6
49 Wedderlie......D 9
23 Weddington......C 7
16 Wedhampton....H 2

7 Wedmore........A 8
22 Wednesbury......C 3
22 Wednesfield......B 3
17 Weedon.........B 9
23 Weedon Bec......F 9
23 Weedon Lois....G 9
22 Weeford.......B 5
34 Weeton, Lancs....D 3
35 Weeton, Yorks....B 1
49 Weetwoodhill....F 12
35 Weir..........E 7
15 Weirend.......B 9
32 Welbeck Abbey...C 3
32 Welbeck Colliery..C 3
33 Welbourn......E 7
41 Welburn, Yorks...G 7
41 Welburn, Yorks...H 7
40 Welbury.......E 4
33 Welby.........F 7
25 Welches Dam.....G 6
6 Welcombe......D 1
23 Weldon........C 12
23 Weldon Bridge...C 9
16 Welford, Berks...G 5
23 Welford, Northants. D 9
22 Welford-on-Avon..G 5
23 Welham........C 11
18 Welhamgreen....C 2
9 Well, Hants......A 9
33 Well, Lincs......C 11
40 Well, Yorks......G 3
7 Well Bottom....E 12
17 Well End.......E 9
16 Well Hill.......B 4
6 Well Town......E 3
22 Welland.......H 2
53 Wellbank......C 9
43 Welldale......E 12
22 Wellesbourne Hastings G 6
22 Wellesbourne Mountford.....G 6
41 Wellfields......A 4
59 Wellford......L 2
18 Welling.......F 5
23 Wellingborough..E 12
26 Wellingham....C 2
33 Wellingore......E 7
38 Wellington, Cumb..E 3
21 Wellington, Herefs. H 10
21 Wellington, Salop A 12
6 Wellington, Som...D 5
21 Wellington Heath H 12
21 Wellington Marsh H 10
6 Wellow, I.o.W....G 5
32 Wellow, Notts....D 4
15 Wellow, Som....H 10
7 Wells.........B 9
26 Wells-next-the-Sea A 2
58 Wells of Ytham...D 4
23 Wellsborough....B 7
5 Wellswood......J 8
52 Wellwood......H 6
14 Welney........F 6
4 Welsford......D 1
15 Welsh Bicknor...C 9
30 Welsh Frankton..G 2
12 Welsh Hook.....D 3
15 Welsh Newton....B 8
14 Welsh St. Donats. G 4
30 Welshampton....G 3
21 Welshpool......B 8
38 Welton, Cumb....A 6
33 Welton, Lincs....B 7
23 Welton, Northants. E 9
7 Welton, Som....A 10
37 Welton, Yorks....D 7
33 Welton le Marsh .C 11
33 Welton le Wold...B 10
37 Welwick.......E 11
15 Welwyn.......A 7
18 Welwyn Garden City C 2
30 Wem..........G 4
6 Wembdon......C 6
18 Wembley......E 2

5 Wembury........L 4
4 Wembworthy.....E 5
47 Wemyss Bay.....B 7
25 Wendens Ambo..L 6
16 Wendlebury.....B 6
26 Wendling......D 2
17 Wendover......C 9
2 Wendron......G 4
25 Wendy........K 4
27 Wenhaston......H 7
25 Wennington, Hunts. G 3
39 Wennington, Lancs. H 8
18 Wennington, London F 5
31 Wensley, Derby...D 11
40 Wensley, Yorks....F 1
36 Wentbridge......E 3
21 Wentnor.......C 9
25 Wentworth, Cambs. G 6
35 Wentworth, Yorks. G 12
14 Wenvoe.......G 4
21 Weobley.......G 9
21 Weobley Marsh...G 9
24 Wereham......E 8
22 Wergs........B 2
14 Wern.........C 4
13 Wernffrwd......H 8
15 Wernyrheolydd...C 7
3 Werrington, Corn.A 10
24 Werrington, Hunts. E 3
31 Werrington, Staffs..E 8
30 Wervin........C 3
34 Wesham.......D 3
32 Wessington....D 1
26 West Acre......D 1
16 West Adderbury...A 5
6 West Adsborough..C 6
22 West Allerdean . E 12
45 West Allotment ..F 11
5 West Alvington...L 6
8 West Amesbury...B 3
4 West Anstey.....C 7
4 West Ash.......D 2
33 West Ashby.....C 9
9 West Ashling.....E 9
7 West Ashton....A 12
40 West Auckland....C 2
41 West Ayton......C 9
59 West Balhagarty...K 5
6 West Bagborough..C 5
33 West Barkwith....B 8
41 West Barnby.....D 8
49 West Barns......B 9
42 West Barr......G 4
7 West Bay.......G 8
26 West Beckham....B 4
17 West Bedfont....G 11
45 West Benridge...D 10
19 West Bergholt....A 9
7 West Bexington...H 9
24 West Bilney.....D 8
49 West Blackadder .D 11
10 West Blatchington. G 2
48 West Bold......F 6
45 West Boldon....G 11
43 West Bowhill....D 12
35 West Bowling....D 10
26 West Bradenham..E 2
34 West Bradford...C 6
7 West Bradley....C 9
59 West Braidieston..K 5
35 West Bretton....F 11
32 West Bridgford...G 3
22 West Bromwich...C 4
47 West Browncastle E 11
4 West Buckland...C 5
6 West Buckland...D 5
64 West Burrafirth...D 6
7 West Burton, Sussex E 11
39 West Burton, Yorks. F 12
40 West Butsfield...A 1
36 West Butterwick..G 8
17 West Byfleet....H 11
49 West Byres......C 7
26 West Caister....D 8
48 West Calder.....C 3
7 West Camel.....D 9
58 West Cannahars..C 7
47 West Carberth...B 10
36 West Carr.......F 5
47 West Cauldcoats..E 11
7 West Chaldon...H 11
16 West Challow....E 4
7 West Chelborough.F 8
45 West Chevington. C 10
9 West Chiltington. D 12

9 West Chiltington Common......D 12
8 West Chinnock...E 8
8 West Chisenbury..A 3
9 West Clandon...A 11
11 West Cliffe.....D 12
61 West Clyth.....D 11
7 West Coker.....E 8
7 West Compton, Dorset.......G 9
7 West Compton, Somerset......B 9
36 West Cowick....E 4
7 West Cranmore..B 10
27 West Creeting Grn. J 4
13 West Cross......H 9
44 West Curthwaite..H 2
8 West Dean, Hants. C 4
9 West Dean, Sus...E 10
24 West Deeping....E 2
30 West Derby......A 3
24 West Dereham....E 7
45 West Ditchburn..A 9
4 West Down......B 4
18 West Drayton, London F 1
32 West Drayton, Notts. C 4
45 West Edington...E 9
37 West Ella......D 8
17 West End, Berks. H 10
28 West End, Caer...G 3
8 West End, Hants...E 6
18 West End, Herts...C 3
48 West End, Lan...E 2
37 West End, Lincs..G 11
26 West End, Norf...D 8
15 West End, Som...G 8
17 West End, Surrey..G 9
8 West End, Wilts..D 1
37 West End, Yorks..D 7
45 West Fallodon...A 10
10 West Farleigh....C 6
30 West Felton.....H 2
10 West Firle......G 3
36 West Garforth...D 2
13 West Glamorgan, Co. G 10
16 West Grafton....H 3
17 West Green.....H 8
8 West Grimstead...D 4
16 West Gringe.....E 5
10 West Grinstead...F 1
36 West Haddlesey...D 3
23 West Haddon....E 9
16 West Hagbourne ..E 6
22 West Hagley.....D 3
44 West Hall......F 4
32 West Hallam.....F 2
37 West Halton.....E 7
18 West Ham.......F 4
16 West Hanney....E 5
19 West Hanningfield.D 7
36 West Hardwick...E 2
8 West Harnham...C 3
7 West Harptree...A 9
45 West Harrington. H 11
40 West Hartlepool...B 5
6 West Hatch.....D 6
15 West Hay.......H 8
24 West Head......E 7
17 West Heath.....H 9
61 West Helmsdale..E 9
16 West Hendred....E 5
41 West Heslerton..H 9
6 West Hill, Devon..G 4
15 West Hill, Som...G 8
10 West Hoathly....E 2
7 West Holme.....H 12
49 West Hopes.....C 8
18 West Horndon....E 6
7 West Horrington..A 9
9 West Horsley....A 12
45 West Horton....C 11
11 West Hougham .D 11
10 West Humble....C 1
6 West Huntspill...B 6
17 West Hyde......E 11
11 West Hythe.....E 10
16 West Ilsley.....F 6
9 West Itchenor...F 9
33 West Keal......D 10
16 West Kennett....G 2
47 West Kilbride....E 7
10 West Kingsdown..B 5
15 West Kington....F 11
58 West Kinharrachie D 7
58 West Kinnernie...F 5
30 West Kirby......B 1
41 West Knapton...H 9
7 West Knighton..G 10
7 West Knoyle....C 11

MAP
45 West Kyloe......B 11
7 West Lambrook...D 7
11 West Langdon....C 11
61 West Langwell....F 7
9 West Lavington,
   Sussex........D 10
8 West Lavington,
   Wiltshire........A 2
40 West Layton.....D 2
32 West Leake.......G 3
49 West Learmouth..F 11
26 West Lexham....D 1
36 West Lilling.....A 4
45 West Linkhall...A 10
48 West Linton....D 4
9 West Liss.......C 9
15 West Littleton...G 11
3 West Looe......D 9
48 West Lothian, Co..B 3
6 West Luccombe...B 2
7 West Lulworth...H 11
41 West Lutton.....H 9
45 West Lydford....C 9
45 West Lyham....C 12
7 West Lyng......C 7
24 West Lynn......D 7
47 West Mains, Ayr..D 8
48 West Mains, Lan..D 2
45 West Mains,
   Northumb.....B 12
10 West Malling....B 5
22 West Malvern.....G 1
9 West Marden.....E 9
32 West Markham....C 4
37 West Marsh......F 10
35 West Marton.....B 8
9 West Meon......D 8
19 West Mersea, Co..C 10
22 West Midlands, Co.
            C 4
7 West Milton.....G 8
11 West Minster.....A 8
17 West Molesey...G 12
8 West Moors.....F 2
7 West Morden....G 12
49 West Morrison....E 8
41 West Ness......G 7
24 West Newton, Norfolk
            C 8
37 West Newton, Yorks.
            C 9
5 West Ogwell.....J 7
7 West Orchard....E 10
16 West Overton.....G 2
59 West Park......H 5
8 West Parley.....F 2
5 West Panson....G 2
49 West Peaston.....C 7
10 West Peckham....C 5
45 West Pelton.....H 10
7 West Pennard....B 9
2 West Pentire.....D 5
6 West Porlock....B 2
4 West Putford.....D 2
6 West Quantoxhead B 5
45 West Rainton..H 11
33 West Rasen......A 8
26 West Raynham....C 2
40 West Rounton.....E 4
25 West Row.......H 8
26 West Rudham....C 1
26 West Runton....A 5
49 West Saltoun.....C 7
4 West Sandford....F 7
64 West Sandwick...B 7
40 West Scrafton.....G 1
48 West Sidewood...D 3
43 West Skelston....C 9
45 West Sleekburn..E 11
26 West Somerton...D 7
7 West Stafford....G 10
36 West Stockwith...H 6
9 West Stoke......B 3
39 West Stonesdale..E 11
7 West Stoughton...A 7
7 West Stour.....D 11
11 West Stourmouth.B 11
27 West Stow......H 1
16 West Stowell.....H 2
60 West Strathan....B 6
8 West Stratton....B 6
11 West Street......B 11
40 West Summer Side.G 2
10 West Sussex, Co...E 1
40 West Tanfield....C 8
3 West Taphouse....C 8
46 West Tarbert....C 3
49 West Third...F 9
45 West Thirston..C 10
9 West Thorney....F 9
18 West Thurrock...F 6
9 West Tisted.....C 8
52 West Tofts......D 6

MAP
33 West Torrington...B 8
9 West Town, Hants.F 8
21 West Town, Herefs.
           F 10
15 West Town, Som. G 8
15 West Town, Som. H 8
8 West Tytherley...C 4
24 West Walton.....D 6
24 West Walton
   Highway.......D 6
4 West Warlington..E 6
53 West Wemyss....H 8
15 West Wick......H 7
25 West Wickham,
   Cambs........K 7
18 West Wickham,
   London.......G 4
12 West Williamston..F 4
8 West Willow.....D 4
24 West Winch.....D 7
8 West Winterslow...C 4
9 West Wittering....F 9
40 West Witton.....F 1
45 West Woodburn...D 7
16 West Woodhay...H 5
7 West Woodlands.B 11
9 West Worldham...B 9
25 West Wratting....K 7
17 West Wycombe...E 9
64 West Yell......C 7
35 West Yorkshire, Co.
           D 10
4 Westacott.....C 5
11 Westbere......B 10
32 Westborough....F 6
8 Westbourne, Hants.
           G 2
27 Westbourne, Suff..K 5
9 Westbourne, Sussex
           E 9
16 Westbrook......G 5
17 Westbury, Bucks...A 7
21 Westbury, Salop...A 9
7 Westbury, Wilts...A 12
7 Westbury Leigh..A 12
15 Westbury on Trym G 9
15 Westbury-on-Severn
           C 10
7 Westbury-sub-Mendip
           A 8
34 Westby........D 3
9 Westcatt.....A 12
19 Westcliff on Sea...E 8
7 Westcombe......B 10
16 Westcote......B 3
17 Westcott, Bucks...B 8
6 Westcott, Devon..F 4
16 Westcott Barton..B 5
10 Westdean......H 4
57 Wester Aviemore..H 4
52 Wester Balgedie..G 6
48 Wester Causewayend
           C 3
52 Wester Clunie....A 4
49 Wester Essenside..G 2
58 Wester Fintray....F 6
57 Wester Fodderletter
           G 7
60 Wester Greenyards G 6
48 Wester Happrew...E 4
49 Wester Housebyres F 8
56 Wester Lamington.B 3
56 Wester Milton....D 5
53 Wester Newburn..G 9
48 Wester Ochiltree..B 3
49 Wester Pencaitland C 7
64 Wester Quarff....E 7
56 Wester Rarichie...B 4
57 Wester Shennach..G 7
54 Wester Slumbay...F 3
56 Wester Teaninich..C 2
61 Westerdale, Caith.C 10
41 Westerdale, Yorks..E 5
27 Westerfield......K 5
9 Westergate.....F 10
34 Westerham...C 3
45 Westerhope.....F 10
15 Westerleigh......F 10
44 Westermill......E 3
58 Westerton, Aber...C 3
53 Westerton, Angus B 11
40 Westerton, Dur....B 3
41 Westerton, Sussex E 10
58 Westertown.......C 3
58 Westfield, Aber....E 7
61 Westfield, Caith...B 10
38 Westfield, Cumb..B 2
21 Westfield, Herefs..G 1
26 Westfield, Norf...D 3
45 Westfield, Northumb.
           D 12
11 Westfield, Sussex.J 7
7 Westfields......F 10

MAP
52 Westfields of Rattray
           C 6
39 Westgate, Dur.....A 11
36 Westgate, Lincs....F 5
26 Westgate, Norf....B 3
11 Westgate on Sea..A 11
44 Westgillsyke......F 2
27 Westhall......A 11
7 Westham, Dorset. H 10
7 Westham, Som....B 7
10 Westham, Sussex..H 5
9 Westhampnett.....E 10
58 Westhaugh......E 4
7 Westhay......B 7
34 Westhead......F 3
21 Westhide......H 11
59 Westhill.......G 4
21 Westhope, Herefs.G 10
21 Westhope, Salop .D 10
24 Westhorpe, Lincs..B 3
27 Westhorpe, Suff...H 3
34 Westhoughton....G 5
39 Westhouse.....A 9
32 Westhouses......D 2
4 Westleigh, Devon..C 3
6 Westleigh, Devon..D 4
34 Westleigh, Lancs..G 5
27 Westleton......H 7
21 Westley, Salop....B 9
27 Westley, Suffolk...J 1
25 Westley Waterless.K 7
17 Westlington......C 2
44 Westlinton......G 2
11 Westmarsh......B 11
10 Westmeston......G 2
18 Westmill......A 4
18 Westminster.....F 3
53 Westmuir......K 5
64 Westness...B 2
43 Westnewton, Cumb.
           G 12
49 Westnewton,
   Northumb.....F 11
16 Weston, Berks.....G 5
30 Weston, Ches.....E 6
30 Weston, Ches.....B 4
6 Weston, Devon....F 5
6 Weston, Devon....G 5
7 Weston, Dorset...H 7
9 Weston, Hants....D 8
18 Weston, Herts.....A 3
48 Weston, Lan......E 3
24 Weston, Lincs.....C 4
23 Weston, Northants.G 9
32 Weston, Notts.....C 5
21 Weston, Salop...C 11
21 Weston, Salop....E 9
30 Weston, Salop....G 4
15 Weston, Som.....H 10
31 Weston, Staffs....G 8
35 Weston, Yorks...B 10
7 Weston Bampfylde D 9
21 Weston Beggard..H 11
15 Weston Birt......E 11
23 Weston by Welland
           C 11
25 Weston Colville...K 7
31 Weston Coyney....G 7
23 Weston Favell...F 11
25 Weston Green....K 7
22 Weston Heath....A 1
24 Weston Hills.....C 4
15 Weston-in-Gordano
           G 8
30 Weston Jones.....H 6
26 Weston Longville..D 4
30 Weston Lullingfields
           H 3
22 Weston-on-Avon...G 5
16 Weston-on-the-Grn.B 6
9 Weston Patrick....B 8
30 Weston Rhyn.....G 1
15 Weston Road.....H 2
22 Weston Sudedge..H 5
14 Weston-super-Mare
           H 6
17 Weston Turville...C 9
15 Weston under Penyard
           B 9
23 Weston under
   Wetherley......E 7
23 Weston Underwood,
   Bucks........G 12
31 Weston Underwood,
   Derbyshire.....F 11
32 Weston upon Trent G 1
22 Weston-under-Lizard
           A 2
25 Westoning.......M 1
7 Westonzoyland....C 7
36 Westow........A 5
46 Westport, Arg....G 2
7 Westport, Som....D 7

MAP
16 Westridge Green...F 6
48 Westrigg........C 2
49 Westruther.....D 9
24 Westry.......F 5
32 Westville......E 2
38 Westward......A 5
4 Westward Ho...C 3
44 Westwater.....E 1
11 Westwell, Kent...C 8
16 Westwell, Oxon...C 3
11 Westwell Leacon..C 8
25 Westwick, Cambs..J 5
40 Westwick, Dur....D 1
6 Westwood, Devon..F 4
45 Westwood, Dur...G 9
47 Westwood, Lan...D 11
15 Westwood, Wilts. H 11
36 Westwoodside.....G 5
40 Wether Cote.....F 6
44 Wetheral......H 3
27 Wetherby......B 12
27 Wetherden......J 3
27 Wetheringsett....J 4
25 Wethersfield....M 8
64 Wethersta......C 7
27 Wetherup Street...J 4
30 Wetley Rocks.....E 8
30 Wettenhall......D 5
31 Wetton......E 9
24 Wetwang......A 7
30 Wetwood......G 6
16 Wexcombe......H 4
17 Wexham Street...F 10
26 Weybourne.....A 4
27 Weybread......G 5
7 Weybridge......H 11
6 Weycroft......F 6
61 Weydale......A 10
8 Weyhill......B 5
7 Weymouth......G 7
17 Whaddon, Bucks...A 9
15 Whaddon, Cambs..K 4
15 Whaddon, Glos...C 11
15 Whaddon, Wilts...C 3
39 Whale......C 7
32 Whaley......C 2
31 Whaley Bridge....B 8
31 Whaley Thorns....C 3
34 Whalley......D 6
45 Whalton.....E 9
34 Wham......A 6
24 Whaplode......C 4
24 Whaplode Drove..D 4
24 Whaplode
   St. Catherine...D 4
39 Wharfe......H 10
34 Wharles......D 3
45 Wharmley.....F 7
35 Wharncliffe Side..H 11
24 Wharram-le-Street.A 6
30 Wharton, Ches....D 5
21 Wharton, Herefs..G 10
30 Whashton......E 2
39 Whasset......G 7
22 Whatcote......H 6
22 Whateley......B 6
27 Whatfield......K 3
10 Whatlington.....F 6
31 Whatstandwell...E 11
32 Whatton......F 5
42 Whauphill......G 5
32 Wheatacre......F 8
18 Wheathampstead..C 2
9 Wheatley, Hants...B 9
17 Wheatley, Oxon...D 7
40 Wheatley Hill...A 4
35 Wheatley Lane...C 7
22 Wheaton Aston...A 2
58 Wheedlemont.....E 2
17 Wheeler's Green...B 8
21 Wheelerstreet....B 11
30 Wheelock......D 6
30 Wheelock Heath..D 6
34 Wheelton......E 5
59 Wheen......K 1
6 Wheddon Cross...B 3
24 Wheldrake......C 4
16 Whelford......D 3
45 Whelpo......A 5
40 Whenby......H 6
27 Whepstead......J 1
27 Wherstead......L 5
8 Wherwell......B 5
31 Wheston......C 10
10 Whetsted......C 5
32 Whetstone......B 9
16 Whichford......A 4
45 Whicham, Cumb..G 4
45 Whickham, Dur...G 10
5 Whiddon Down...G 6
53 Whigstreet......C 9
41 Whilton......F 9
4 Whimble......F 2

MAP
6 Whimple........F 4
26 Whimpwell Green .C 7
26 Whinburgh......E 3
49 Whinkerstones....E 10
43 Whinnie Liggate...F 8
58 Whinnyfold......D 8
8 Whippingham.....G 6
17 Whipsnade......B 11
6 Whipton......G 3
23 Whissendine.....A 11
26 Whissonsett......C 2
17 Whistley Green...G 9
30 Whiston, Lancs...A 3
23 Whiston, Northants.
           F 11
22 Whiston, Staffs...A 2
31 Whiston, Staffs...F 9
32 Whiston, Yorks...A 2
30 Whiston Lane Ends A 3
38 Whitbeck......G 3
21 Whitbourne.....G 12
22 Whitbourne Ford..F 1
45 Whitburn, Dur...G 12
48 Whitburn, W. Loth.C 2
45 Whitburn Colliery G 12
30 Whitby, Cheshire..C 3
41 Whitby, Yorks...D 9
15 Whitchurch, Bucks.B 9
17 Whitchurch, Devon.
           H 4
14 Whitchurch, Glam..F 5
8 Whitchurch, Hants.A 6
15 Whitchurch, Herefs.
           C 8
17 Whitchurch, Oxon..F 7
12 Whitchurch, Pemb.D 2
30 Whitchurch, Salop.F 4
15 Whitchurch, Som..G 9
17 Whitchurch Hill...F 7
17 Whitcombe.....C 9
21 Whitcott Keysett...D 8
34 White Chapel.....C 4
34 White Coppice.....E 5
6 White Cross, Devon.
           G 4
7 White Cross, Som..A 9
7 White Lackington F 10
22 White Ladies Aston
           G 3
13 White Mill......E 8
19 White Notley.....B 8
33 White Pit......B 11
18 White Roding.....C 5
21 White Stone.....H 11
17 White Waltham...F 9
56 Whiteacen......E 8
22 Whiteacre Heath...C 5
55 Whitebridge.....H 8
15 Whitebrook......D 8
49 Whiteburn.....E 8
42 Whitecairn.....F 3
58 Whitecairns.....F 7
48 Whitecastle.....E 3
7 Whitechurch
   Canonicorum...G 7
48 Whitecraig......B 6
15 Whitecroft.....D 9
42 Whitecrook......F 3
3 Whitecross, Corn..B 7
48 Whitecross, Stir...B 2
61 Whiteface.....G 7
46 Whitefarland......E 4
42 Whitefaulds.....A 4
35 Whitefield, Lan...G 7
52 Whitefield, Perth...D 6
6 Whitefield, Som...C 4
58 Whiteford......E 5
6 Whitehall, Devon..E 5
64 Whitehall, Orkney.B 4
44 Whitehaugh......B 3
38 Whitehaven......C 2
47 Whitehill, Ayr...D 7
58 Whitehill, Banff...B 3
9 Whitehill, Hants...C 9
58 Whitehills, Banff..A 4
47 Whitehills, Ren...D 11
58 Whitehouse, Aber..F 4
46 Whitehouse, Arg...C 3
49 Whitekirk......A 8
59 Whiteknowes.....G 3
7 Whitelackington...E 7
49 Whitelaw......D 11
49 Whitelee......F 8
36 Whitely......E 3
9 Whiteley Bank...H 7
31 Whiteley Green..B 8
17 Whiteley Village..H 11
10 Whitemans Green..E 2
56 Whitemire.....D 5
3 Whitemoor......D 7
31 Whitemore......D 7

MAP
8 Whitenap........D 5
8 Whiteparish......D 4
58 Whiterashes......E 6
15 Whiteshill......D 11
44 Whiteside, Northumb.
           F 5
48 Whiteside, W. Loth.
           C 2
10 Whitesmith......G 4
6 Whitestaunton....E 6
59 Whitestone, Aber..H 4
4 Whitestone, Devon.A 4
4 Whitestone, Devon.F 7
58 Whitestones......B 6
15 Whiteway......C 12
6 Whiteway House..H 2
34 Whitewell......B 5
5 Whiteworks......J 5
56 Whitewreath.....D 8
15 Whitfield, Glos...E 10
11 Whitfield, Kent..D 11
23 Whitfield, Northants.
           H 9
44 Whitfield, Northumb.
           G 6
48 Whitfield, Peeb....D 4
6 Whitford, Devon..G 6
29 Whitford, Flint...B 10
36 Whitgift........E 6
31 Whitgreave......G 7
42 Whithorn......G 5
46 Whiting Bay.....G 5
24 Whittington......E 8
12 Whitland......E 5
44 Whitlaw......B 3
47 Whitletts......G 8
17 Whitley, Berks....G 8
15 Whitley, Wilts...H 12
45 Whitley Bay.....F 11
45 Whitley Chapel...G 7
35 Whitley Lower....E 11
22 Whitlock's End...D 4
15 Whitminster.....D 11
31 Whitmore......F 7
6 Whitnage......E 4
21 Whitney......H 8
38 Whitrigg, Cumb...A 4
44 Whitrigg, Cumb..G 1
44 Whitriggs......B 4
8 Whitsbury......D 3
4 Whitsleigh Barton.D 4
49 Whitsome......D 11
49 Whitsomehill....D 11
15 Whitson......F 7
15 Whitson Common .F 7
11 Whitstable.....A 9
4 Whitstone......F 1
45 Whittingham....B 9
21 Whittingslow.....D 9
32 Whittington, Derby.C 1
16 Whittington, Glos..B 1
39 Whittington, Lancs.
           H 8
30 Whittington, Salop G 2
22 Whittington, Staffs.A 5
22 Whittington, Worcs.
           D 2
22 Whittington, Worcs.
           G 2
34 Whittle-le-Woods..E 5
23 Whittlebury.....H 10
24 Whittlesey......F 4
25 Whittlesford....K 6
34 Whittlestone Head.C 4
40 Whitton, Dur....C 8
37 Whitton, Lincs...E 7
45 Whitton, Northumb.
           C 9
21 Whitton, Rad.....F 8
49 Whitton, Rox....G 10
21 Whitton, Salop...E 11
27 Whitton, Suffolk..K 4
16 Whittonditch....G 4
45 Whittonstall......G 9
16 Whitway......H 6
32 Whitwell, Derby...C 3
18 Whitwell, Herts...B 2
9 Whitwell, I.o.W....H 7
23 Whitwell, Rut....A 12
40 Whitwell, Yorks...E 3
41 Whitwell-on-the-
   Hill..........H 7
23 Whitwick......A 8
36 Whitwood......E 2
35 Whitworth......E 7
30 Whixall......G 4
36 Whixley......A 2
22 Whoberly......D 6
40 Whorlton, Dur...D 1
40 Whorlton, Yorks...E 5
44 Whygate......E 6
9 Whyle......F 11
10 Whyteleafe......B 2

MAP
15 Wibdon E 9
23 Wibtoft C 8
11 Wichling B 8
61 Wick, Caith. C 12
14 Wick, Glam. G 3
5 Wick, Glos. G 10
8 Wick, Hants. G 3
6 Wick, Som. B 5
7 Wick, Som. D 7
9 Wick, Sussex F 11
8 Wick, Wilts. D 3
22 Wick, Worcs. H 3
17 Wick Hill H 9
16 Wick Rissington B 3
15 Wick St. Lawrence H 7
25 Wicken, Cambs. H 7
23 Wicken, Northants. H 10
25 Wicken Bonhunt M 6
33 Wickenby B 8
22 Wichenford F 1
32 Wickersley A 2
19 Wickford E 7
16 Wickham, Berks. G 5
9 Wickham, Hants. E 7
19 Wickham Bishops C 8
16 Wickham Heath G 5
27 Wickham Market K 6
27 Wickham St. Paul L 1
27 Wickham Skeith H 4
27 Wickham Street, Suffolk H 4
27 Wickham Street, Suffolk K 1
11 Wickhambreaux B 10
25 Wickhambrook K 8
22 Wickhamford H 4
26 Wickhampton E 7
26 Wicklewood E 4
26 Wickmere B 5
10 Wickstreet G 4
15 Wickwar E 10
25 Widdington M 6
45 Widdrington C 10
45 Widdrington Sta. D 10
45 Wide Open F 10
5 Widecombe in the Moor H 6
3 Widegates D 10
2 Widemouth A 2
64 Widewall E 2
19 Widford, Essex C 7
18 Widford, Herefs. B 4
17 Widmere E 9
17 Widmer End D 9
32 Widmerpool G 4
30 Widnes B 4
6 Widworthy F 5
9 Wield B 7
34 Wigan F 5
8 Wigbeth E 2
6 Wiggaton G 5
24 Wiggenhall St. Germans D 7
24 Wiggenhall St. Mary Magdalen D 7
24 Wiggenhall St. Mary the Virgin D 7
36 Wiggington A 4
17 Wigginton, Herts. C 10
16 Wigginton, Oxon. A 5
22 Wigginton, Staffs. A 6
35 Wigglesworth A 7
44 Wiggonby H 1
9 Wiggonholt D 11
36 Wighill B 3
8 Wight, Isle of, Co. G 6
26 Wighton B 2
8 Wigley D 5
21 Wigmore, Herefs. E 9
11 Wigmore, Kent B 7
32 Wigsley C 6
25 Wigsthorpe G 1
23 Wigston Magna B 9
24 Wigtoft B 4
44 Wigton H 1
42 Wigtown F 5
42 Wigtown, County E 3
35 Wigtwizzle G 11
35 Wike C 12
23 Wilbarston C 11
36 Wilberfoss B 5
25 Wilburton H 6
26 Wilby, Norfolk F 3
23 Wilby, Northants. E 12
27 Wilby, Suffolk H 5
16 Wilcot H 2
30 Wilcott H 2
15 Wilcrick E 7
31 Wildboarclough C 8
25 Wilden K 2
8 Wildhern A 5
36 Wildsworth G 6

MAP
32 Wilford F 3
30 Wilkesley F 5
61 Wilkhaven H 9
48 Wilkieston C 4
18 Wilkin's Green C 2
6 Willand E 4
18 Willaston, Ches. B 2
30 Willaston, Ches. E 5
23 Willen H 12
22 Willenhall, Staffs. B 3
23 Willenhall, War. E 7
37 Willerby, Yorks. D 8
41 Willerby, Yorks. G 10
22 Willersey H 4
21 Willersley H 8
11 Willesborough D 9
18 Willesden E 2
4 Willesleigh C 5
23 Willey, Leics. D 8
21 Willey, Salop C 12
9 Willey Green A 11
23 Williamscot H 8
18 Willian A 2
18 Willingale C 6
4 Willingcott B 4
10 Willingdon H 5
25 Willingham, Cambs. H 5
32 Willingham, Lincs. B 6
25 Willington, Beds. K 2
31 Willington, Derby. G 11
40 Willington, Dur. B 2
22 Willington, War. H 6
30 Willington Corner D 4
36 Willitoft D 5
6 Williton B 4
44 Willmontswick G 6
33 Willoughby, Lincs. C 11
23 Willoughby, War. E 8
32 Willoughby on the Wolds H 4
23 Willoughby Waterleys C 9
32 Willoughton A 6
19 Willows Green B 7
15 Willsbridge G 10
5 Willsworthy H 4
22 Wilmcote F 5
6 Wilmington, Devon. F 5
10 Wilmington, Kent A 4
10 Wilmington, Sussex H 4
31 Wilmslow B 7
22 Wilnecote B 6
34 Wilpshire D 5
35 Wilsden D 9
33 Wilsford, Lincs. F 7
8 Wilsford, Wilts. B 3
8 Wilsford, Wilts. H 2
25 Wilshamstead L 2
35 Wilsill A 10
30 Wilsley Pound D 6
15 Wilson, Herefs. B 9
32 Wilson, Leics. H 1
48 Wilsontown D 2
24 Wilsthorpe D 2
17 Wilstone C 10
38 Wilton, Cumb. D 3
16 Wilton, Hants. H 4
15 Wilton, Herefs. B 9
44 Wilton, Rox. B 3
8 Wilton, Wilts. C 3
40 Wilton, Yorks. C 6
41 Wilton, Yorks. G 8
16 Wiltshire, Co. G 2
25 Wimbish L 7
25 Wimbish Green M 7
18 Wimbledon G 2
24 Wimblington F 5
8 Wimborne Minster F 1
8 Wimborne St. Giles E 2
24 Wimbotsham E 7
25 Wimpole Lodge K 4
22 Wimpstone G 5
7 Wincanton C 10
9 Winchfield A 9
30 Wincham C 5
48 Winchburgh B 4
16 Winchcombe C 6
11 Winchelsea F 8
11 Winchelsea Beach F 8
8 Winchester C 6
10 Winchet Hill D 6
17 Winchmore Hill E 10
31 Wincle D 8
38 Windermere E 6
23 Winderton H 7
17 Windlesham H 10
31 Windley F 11
31 Windmill B 10

MAP
6 Windmill Hill, Som. E 6
10 Windmill Hill, Sussex G 5
16 Windrush C 3
44 Windshielknowe C 4
17 Windsor G 10
15 Windsoredge D 11
47 Windy Yet D 9
59 Windyedge H 6
53 Windygates G 8
49 Windywalls F 10
10 Wineham F 1
37 Winestead E 10
35 Winewall C 8
27 Winfarthing G 4
9 Winford, I.o.W. H 7
15 Winford, Som. H 8
21 Winforton H 8
7 Winfrith Newburgh H 11
17 Wing, Bucks. B 9
23 Wing, Rut. B 12
40 Wingate A 4
34 Wingates, Lancs. F 5
45 Wingates, Northumb. D 9
32 Wingerworth C 1
17 Wingfield, Beds. B 11
27 Wingfield, Suffolk H 5
7 Wingfield, Wilts. A 11
11 Wingham B 11
11 Wingmore C 10
17 Wingrave B 9
32 Winkburn D 4
17 Winkfield G 9
17 Winkfield Row G 10
17 Winkfield Street G 10
31 Winkhill E 9
9 Winklebury A 7
4 Winkleigh E 5
40 Winksley H 3
8 Winkton F 3
45 Winlaton G 10
45 Winlaton Mill G 10
61 Winless B 12
34 Winmarleigh B 3
8 Winnall, Hants. C 6
15 Winnall, Herefs. A 7
2 Winnard's Perch C 6
17 Winnersh G 8
38 Winscales C 3
15 Winscombe H 7
30 Winsford, Ches. D 5
6 Winsford, Som. C 3
7 Winsham F 7
31 Winshill H 11
13 Winsh-wen G 10
39 Winskill B 8
9 Winslade A 8
35 Winsley H 11
17 Winslow A 8
16 Winson C 2
8 Winsor E 5
31 Winster, Derby. D 11
38 Winster, Westmor. F 6
40 Winston, Dur. D 2
27 Winston, Suff. J 5
15 Winstone C 12
4 Winswell E 4
44 Winter Shields F 4
7 Winterborne Clenston F 11
7 Winterborne Herringston G 10
7 Winterborne Houghton F 11
7 Winterborne Kingston F 11
7 Winterborne Monkton G 10
7 Winterborne Stickland F 11
7 Winterborne Whitechurch F 11
7 Winterborne Zelston F 12
16 Winterbourne, Berks. G 5
15 Winterbourne, Glos. F 9
7 Winterbourne Abbas G 9
16 Winterbourne Bassett G 2
8 Winterbourne Dauntsey C 3
15 Winterbourne Down F 10
8 Winterbourne Earls C 3
8 Winterbourne Gunner C 3

MAP
16 Winterbourne Monkton G 2
7 Winterbourne Steepleton G 9
8 Winterbourne Stoke B 2
35 Winterburn A 8
48 Wintercleugh H 2
37 Winteringham E 7
30 Winterley E 6
35 Wintersett F 12
8 Winterslow C 4
37 Winterton E 7
26 Winterton-on-Sea D 8
33 Winthorpe, Lincs. D 12
32 Winthorpe, Notts. E 5
8 Winton, Hants. G 2
39 Winton, Westmor. D 10
40 Winton, Yorks. F 4
41 Wintringham H 9
25 Winwick, Hunts. G 2
34 Winwick, Lancs. H 5
23 Winwick, Northants. E 9
31 Wirksworth E 11
30 Wirswall F 4
24 Wisbech E 6
24 Wisbech St. Mary E 5
9 Wisborough Green C 11
47 Wishaw, Lan. D 12
22 Wishaw, War. C 5
17 Wisley H 11
33 Wispington C 9
27 Wissett G 6
21 Wistanstow D 10
30 Wistanswick G 5
30 Wistaston E 5
30 Wistaston Green E 5
48 Wiston, Lan. F 2
12 Wiston, Pemb. E 4
25 Wistow, Hunts. G 4
36 Wistow, Yorks. D 4
34 Wiswell C 6
25 Witcham G 6
8 Witchampton E 1
25 Witchford G 6
19 Witham B 8
7 Witham Friary B 11
24 Witham on the Hill D 2
33 Withcall B 10
10 Witherenden Hill E 5
4 Witheridge E 7
23 Witherley B 7
33 Withern B 11
37 Withernsea D 11
37 Withernwick C 9
27 Withersdale Street G 6
25 Withersfield K 7
39 Witherslack G 7
3 Withiel C 7
6 Withiel Florey C 3
16 Withington, Glos. C 1
21 Withington, Herefs. H 11
35 Withington, Lancs. H 7
21 Withington, Salop A 11
31 Withington, Staffs. G 9
30 Withington Green C 6
21 Withington Marsh H 11
6 Withleigh E 3
34 Withnell E 5
23 Withybrook D 8
6 Withycombe B 3
6 Withycombe Raleigh H 4
10 Withyham E 4
6 Withypool C 2
9 Witley B 11
27 Witnesham K 5
16 Witney C 5
24 Wittering E 2
11 Wittersham E 7
59 Witton, Angus K 3
22 Witton, Worcs. F 2
45 Witton Gilbert H 10
40 Witton le Wear B 2
40 Witton Park B 2
6 Wiveliscombe C 4
9 Wivelrod B 8
10 Wivelsfield F 2
10 Wivelsfield Green F 2
19 Wivenhoe B 10
19 Wivenhoe Cross B 10
26 Wiveton A 3
19 Wix A 11
22 Wixford G 4
25 Wixoe L 8
17 Woburn A 10
23 Woburn Sands H 12
17 Woking H 11

MAP
17 Wokingham G 9
5 Wolborough J 7
37 Wold Newton, Lincs. G 10
41 Wold Newton, Yorks. H 10
10 Woldingham C 3
48 Wolfclyde F 3
24 Wolferton C 7
52 Wolfhill D 6
12 Wolf's Castle D 3
12 Wolfsdale E 3
49 Woll G 7
23 Wollaston, Northants. F 12
21 Wollaston, Salop A 9
30 Wollerton G 5
31 Wolseley H 9
40 Wolsingham A 1
31 Wolstanton E 7
23 Wolston E 7
16 Wolvercote C 6
22 Wolverhampton B 2
30 Wolverley, Salop G 3
22 Wolverley, Worcs. D 2
23 Wolverton, Bucks. H 11
16 Wolverton, Hants. H 6
22 Wolverton, War. F 5
16 Wolverton Com. H 6
15 Wolvesnewton D 8
23 Wolvey C 8
40 Wolviston C 5
41 Wombleton G 7
22 Wombourn C 2
36 Wombwell G 2
11 Womenswold C 11
36 Womersley E 3
9 Wonersh B 11
5 Wonsan G 5
17 Wooburn E 10
17 Wooburn Green E 10
17 Wooburn Moor E 10
26 Wood Dalling C 4
25 Wood End, Beds. K 1
25 Wood End, Beds. K 2
18 Wood End, Herts. A 3
22 Wood End, War. B 6
22 Wood End, War. E 4
33 Wood Enderby D 10
18 Wood Green E 3
22 Wood Hayes B 3
26 Wood Norton C 3
25 Wood Walton G 3
4 Woodacott E 3
39 Woodale G 12
32 Woodall B 2
26 Woodbastwick D 6
32 Woodbeck B 5
7 Woodbridge, Dorset. E 10
27 Woodbridge, Suff. K 6
32 Woodborough, Notts. E 3
16 Woodborough, Wilts. H 2
6 Woodbury, Devon. G 4
7 Woodbury, Som. B 9
6 Woodbury Salterton G 4
15 Woodchester D 11
11 Woodchurch E 8
6 Woodcombe B 3
17 Woodcote, Oxon. F 7
22 Woodcote, Salop A 1
8 Woodcott A 6
15 Woodcroft E 8
8 Woodcutts D 1
25 Woodditton J 8
16 Woodeaton C 6
59 Woodend, Aber. H 3
38 Woodend, Cumb. F 4
48 Woodend, Lan. F 2
23 Woodend, Northants. G 9
8 Woodfalls D 3
47 Woodfield, Ayr. G 8
44 Woodfield, Dumf. F 1
10 Woodfield, Surrey B 1
31 Woodford, Ches. B 7
4 Woodford, Corn. E 1
15 Woodford, Glos. E 10
18 Woodford, London E 4
25 Woodford, Northants. H 1
7 Woodford, Som. B 9
23 Woodford Halse G 9
26 Woodgate, Norf. D 3
9 Woodgate, Sussex F 10
22 Woodgate, Worcs. E 3
8 Woodgreen D 3
49 Woodhall, E. Loth. B 9
45 Woodhall, Northumb. B 9

MAP
39 Woodhall, Yorks. F 12
33 Woodhall Spa D 9
17 Woodham H 11
19 Woodham Ferrers D 8
19 Woodham Mortimer C 8
19 Woodham Walter C 8
53 Woodhaven D 9
58 Woodhead, Aber. D 5
35 Woodhead, Derby. G 9
58 Woodhead House C 5
49 Woodheads E 8
22 Woodhill, Salop D 1
15 Woodhill, Som. G 8
56 Woodholme D 2
45 Woodhorn D 11
45 Woodhorn Demesne D 11
32 Woodhouse, Derby. B 1
23 Woodhouse, Leics. A 9
35 Woodhouse, Yorks. D 11
23 Woodhouse Eaves A 8
5 Woodhuish K 8
25 Woodhurst H 4
10 Woodingdean G 2
58 Woodland, Aber. E 6
58 Woodland, Aber. F 6
5 Woodland, Devon. J 7
40 Woodland, Dur. C 1
8 Woodlands, Dorset. E 2
43 Woodlands, Dumf. D 11
8 Woodlands, Hants. E 4
59 Woodlands, Kinc. H 5
56 Woodlands, Ross & Cromarty D 1
17 Woodlands Park F 9
16 Woodlands St. Mary G 4
31 Woodlane H 10
43 Woodlea C 8
5 Woodleigh L 6
35 Woodlesford D 12
17 Woodley, Berks. G 8
35 Woodley, Lancs. H 8
16 Woodmancote, Glos. A 1
16 Woodmancote, Glos. C 1
9 Woodmancote, Sussex E 9
9 Woodmancott B 7
37 Woodmansey C 8
9 Woodmansgreen C 10
10 Woodmansterne B 2
8 Woodminton D 2
11 Woodnesborough B 11
24 Woodnewton F 1
34 Woodplumpton D 4
26 Woodrising E 3
10 Wood's Green E 5
30 Woodseaves, Salop G 5
30 Woodseaves, Staffs. H 6
16 Woodsend F 3
32 Woodsetts B 3
7 Woodsford G 11
59 Woodside, Aber. G 7
17 Woodside, Berks. G 10
43 Woodside, Dumf. D 11
53 Woodside, Fife F 9
49 Woodside, Northants. E 12
53 Woodside, Perth. C 7
59 Woodside of Arbeadie H 5
44 Woodslee F 2
16 Woodstock B 5
12 Woodstock Cross D 4
12 Woodstock Slop D 4
32 Woodthorpe, Derby. C 2
32 Woodthorpe, Leics. H 3
26 Woodton F 6
4 Woodtown, Devon. C 4
4 Woodtown, Devon. D 3
59 Woodtown, Kinc. K 3
34 Woodvale F 2
31 Woodville H 11
8 Woodyates D 2
21 Woofferton F 10
7 Wookey B 8
7 Wookey Hole A 9
7 Wool H 11
4 Woolacombe B 3
11 Woolage Green C 11
15 Woolard H 9
15 Woolaston D 9
7 Woolavington B 7

MAP

9 Woolbeding.....D 10
6 Woolbrook.......G 5
6 Woolcotts.......C 3
35 Wooldale......F 10
49 Wooler.........G 12
4 Woolfardisworthy .E 7
48 Woolfords Cotts..D 3
8 Woolgarston....H 2
17 Woolhampton....G 7
15 Woolhope.......A 9
7 Woolland......F 11
4 Woollaton.......E 3
4 Woolley, Corn....D 1
25 Woolley, Hunts..H 3
15 Woolley, Som...G 10
35 Woolley, Yorks..F 11
18 Woolmer Green..B 3
22 Woolmere Green..F 3
27 Woolpit.........J 3
27 Woolpit Green....J 3
23 Woolscott.......E 8
4 Woolsey........D 2
21 Woolstaston.....C 10
32 Woolsthorpe, Lincs.
                G 5
32 Woolsthorpe, Lincs.
                H 6
5 Woolston, Devon..L 6
8 Woolston, Hants..E 6
30 Woolston, Lancs..A 5
21 Woolston, Salop..D 9
30 Woolston, Salop..H 2
5 Woolston Green..J 6
16 Woolstone.......E 4
30 Woolton........B 3
16 Woolton Hill.....H 5
27 Woolverstone...L 5
7 Woolverton....A 11
18 Woolwich.......F 4
21 Woonton.......G 9
45 Wooperton.....A 8
49 Wooplaw.....E 7
30 Woore.........F 6
25 Wootton, Beds..L 1
16 Wootton, Berks..D 6
8 Wootton, Hants..F 4
11 Wootton, Kent..C 11
37 Wootton, Lincs..E 8
23 Wootton, Northants.
                F 11
16 Wootton, Oxon..B 5
21 Wootton, Salop..E 10
31 Wootton, Staffs..F 9
31 Wootton, Staffs..G 7
16 Wootton Bassett..F 2
9 Wootton Bridge..G 7
9 Wootton Com.....G 7
6 Wootton Courtenay
                B 3
7 Wootton Fitzpaine G 7
16 Wootton Rivers...H 3

MAP

9 Wootton St. Lawrence
                A 7
22 Wootton Wawen..F 5
22 Worcester.......G 2
22 Wordsley.......C 2
22 Worfield........C 1
64 Work...........C 3
38 Workington......B 2
32 Worksop........B 3
37 Worlaby........F 8
16 World's End, Berks.
                F 6
9 Worlds End, Hants.
                E 8
15 Worle..........H 7
30 Worleston.......E 5
26 Worlingham......F 7
25 Worlington......H 8
27 Worlingworth....H 5
35 Wormald Green..A 11
15 Wormbridge.....A 7
24 Wormegay......D 8
15 Wormelow Tump..A 8
31 Wormhill........C 9
53 Wormiehills.....C 11
27 Wormingford....M 2
17 Worminghall.....C 7
16 Wormington.....A 1
7 Worminster......B 9
48 Wormiston......E 5
53 Wormit.........E 9
23 Wormleighton....G 8
18 Wormley,
     Hertfordshire...C 4
9 Wormley, Surrey.B 10
11 Wormshill.......B 7
21 Wormsley.......H 9
9 Worplesdon....A 11
35 Worrall........H 11
35 Worsbrough....G 12
34 Worsley........G 6
26 Worstead......C 6
25 Worsted Lodge..K 6
35 Worsthorne.....D 7
34 Worston........C 6
5 Worswell......L 4
11 Worth, Kent...C 12
10 Worth, Sussex....D 2
8 Worth Matravers..H 1
27 Wortham.......H 4
21 Worthen........B 9
30 Worthenbury....F 3
26 Worthing, Norf...D 3
9 Worthing, Sussex.F 12
32 Worthington......H 1
6 Worthy.........A 2
9 Worting........A 7
35 Wortley, Yorks..D 11
35 Wortley, Yorks..G 11
16 Worton.........H 1
27 Wortwell........G 6

MAP

5 Wotter.........J 4
9 Wotton........A 12
15 Wotton-under-Edge
                E 11
17 Wotton Underwood
                C 8
23 Woughton on the
     Green.......H 12
10 Wouldham......B 6
27 Wrabness......M 5
58 Wraes.........D 3
4 Wrafton.......C 4
33 Wragby, Lincs..B 8
36 Wragby, Yorks..E 2
37 Wragholme.....G 11
26 Wramplingham..E 4
36 Wrangbrook....F 3
58 Wrangham, Aberdeen
                D 4
49 Wrangham,
     Northumb....F 12
33 Wrangle.......E 11
33 Wrangle Com...E 11
33 Wrangle Lowgate.E 11
6 Wrangway.....D 5
6 Wrantage......D 6
37 Wrawby........F 8
7 Wraxall, Dorset..F 9
15 Wraxall, Som...G 8
7 Wraxhall, Som...C 9
39 Wray..........H 8
5 Wrayland......H 7
17 Wraysbury.....G 11
34 Wrea Green....D 3
39 Wreay, Cumb....C 7
44 Wreay, Cumb....H 3
9 Wrecclesham...B 9
45 Wrekenton.....G 11
41 Wrelton........F 8
30 Wrenbury......E 4
26 Wreningham....F 4
27 Wrentham......G 8
35 Wrenthorpe....E 11
21 Wrentnall......B 9
36 Wressle........D 5
26 Wrestlingworth..K 4
24 Wretton........E 8
30 Wrexham......E 2
30 Wrexham Industrial
     Estate.......E 2
22 Wribbenhall....E 2
34 Wrightlington Bar.F 4
30 Wrinehill.......E 6
15 Wrington......H 8
7 Writhlington...A 10
19 Writtle.........C 7
21 Wrockwardine..A 11
30 Wroot.........G 5
10 Wrotham.......B 5
10 Wrotham Heath..B 5
16 Wroughton.....F 3

MAP

22 Wroxall........E 6
21 Wroxeter......B 11
9 Wroxhall......H 7
26 Wroxham......D 6
23 Wroxton.......H 7
31 Wyaston......F 10
24 Wyberton......B 4
25 Wyboston......K 3
30 Wybunbury....E 5
10 Wych Cross....E 3
22 Wychbold......F 3
22 Wychnor......A 5
22 Wychnor Bridges..A 5
9 Wyck.........B 9
40 Wycliffe.......D 1
17 Wycombe Marsh.E 10
25 Wyddial.......M 5
11 Wye..........C 9
27 Wyerstone.....H 3
27 Wyerstone Street..H 3
15 Wyesham......C 8
7 Wyke, Dorset...D 11
21 Wyke, Salop...B 12
9 Wyke, Surrey...A 10
35 Wyke, Yorks....D 10
7 Wyke Champflower
                C 10
7 Wyke Regis....H 7
41 Wykeham, Yorks. G 9
41 Wykeham, Yorks..H 8
30 Wykey.........H 2
45 Wylam........G 9
22 Wylde Green....C 5
14 Wyllie.........E 5
8 Wylye.........B 2
9 Wymering......E 8
32 Wymeswold....H 3
25 Wymington....J 1
32 Wymondham, Leics.
                H 6
26 Wymondham, Norf.
                E 4
14 Wyndham......E 3
7 Wynford Eagle...G 9
40 Wynyard Forest..C 4
22 Wyre Piddle....G 3
32 Wysall........G 3
22 Wythall.......E 4
16 Wytham.......C 6
38 Wythburn......D 6
31 Wythenshawe...A 7
25 Wyton........H 4
32 Wyville........G 6
54 Wyvis Lodge....B 8
36 Yaddlethorpe...F 6
8 Yafford.......H 6
40 Yafforth.......F 4
5 Yalberton......K 7
10 Yalding........C 6
16 Yanworth......C 2
36 Yapham.......B 6

MAP

9 Yapton........F 11
33 Yarburgh......A 10
6 Yarcombe......E 6
4 Yard..........D 6
4 Yard Gate......C 6
22 Yardley.......D 5
23 Yardley Gobion..H 11
23 Yardley Hastings .F 12
21 Yardro........F 8
21 Yarkhill.......H 11
31 Yarlet.........G 7
7 Yarlington.....C 10
40 Yarm..........D 4
8 Yarmouth......G 5
8 Yarmouth......G 5
4 Yarnacott......C 5
7 Yarnbrook....A 12
31 Yarnfield......C 2
4 Yarnscombe....D 4
16 Yarnton.......C 6
21 Yarpole.......F 10
24 Yarwell........F 2
15 Yate..........F 10
16 Yatesbury.....G 2
16 Yattendon......G 6
15 Yatton, Herefs..A 9
21 Yatton, Herefs...F 9
15 Yatton, Som....H 7
15 Yatton Keynell..G 12
9 Yaverland......H 7
26 Yaxham.......D 3
24 Yaxley, Hunts...F 3
27 Yaxley, Suffolk..H 4
21 Yazor.........H 9
24 Yarwell........F 2
35 Yeadon.......C 10
39 Yealand Conyers..H 7
39 Yealand Redmayne
                H 7
5 Yealmpton.....K 4
40 Yearby........C 6
44 Yearsley.......H 6
30 Yeaton.......H 3
31 Yeaveley......F 10
49 Yeavering....F 12
16 Yelford.......D 4
25 Yelling........J 4
18 Yelsted.......B 7
23 Yelvertoft.....E 9
5 Yelverton, Devon. J 4
26 Yelverton, Norfolk
                E 6
7 Yenston.......D 10
4 Yeo Mill......C 7
4 Yeoford.......F 6
3 Yeolmbridge...A 10
7 Yeovil.........D 9
7 Yeovil Marsh...D 9
7 Yeovilton......D 9

MAP

12 Yerbeston.......F 4
12 Yerbeston Mountain
                F 4
64 Yesnaby........C 1
49 Yetholm Mains...F 11
45 Yetlington......B 8
7 Yetminster......E 9
47 Yett, Ayr......G 9
47 Yett, Lanark....C 12
6 Yettington......H 4
52 Yetts of Muckart..G 5
25 Yielden........J 1
48 Yieldshields....D 2
18 Yiewsley........F 1
20 Ynys..........F 2
20 Ynys Tachwedd..C 2
14 Ynys-boeth.....E 4
14 Ynysbwl.......E 4
14 Ynysddu.......E 5
14 Ynyshir........E 4
13 Ynystawe......G 10
39 Yockenthwaite..G 11
21 Yockleton......A 9
36 Yokefleet......E 6
47 Yoker.........C 10
58 Yonder Bognie...C 3
36 York..........B 3
17 York Town......H 9
11 Yorkletts.......B 9
15 Yorkley........D 9
48 Yorkston......D 6
4 Youldonmoor Cross
                E 2
31 Youlgreaves....D 10
36 Youlthorpe.....B 5
36 Youlton.......A 3
19 Young's End....B 7
31 Yoxall........H 10
27 Yoxford.......H 7
29 Ysbyty Ifan....E 8
20 Ysbyty Ystwyth..E 3
29 Ysceifiog......C 10
13 Yspitty........G 9
20 Yspytty Cynfyn...B 3
13 Ystalyfera.....F 11
14 Ystrad........E 3
13 Ystrad Aeron...A 8
20 Ystrad Meurig...F 3
14 Ystradfellte.....C 3
13 Ystrad-ffin.....B 11
14 Ystradgynlais...C 1
14 Ystrad-mynach...E 5
13 Ystradowen, Carm.F10
14 Ystradowen, Glam.G 3
20 Ystumtuen.....D 3
58 Ythsie........D 6
4 Zeal Monachorum .F 6
7 Zeals.........C 11
2 Zelah.........D 5
2 Zennor........F 2
64 Zetland, Co.....D 7

PRINTED IN GREAT BRITAIN BY GEORGE PHILIP PRINTERS LTD., LONDON.

INDEX TO LONDON MAPS

ABBREVIATIONS

App. – *Approach*
Av. – *Avenue*
Bdy. – *Broadway*
Bldg. – *Building(s)*
Br. – *British*
Bri. – *Bridge*
Ch. – *Church*
Cin. – *Cinema*
Cl. – *Close*
Cnr. – *Corner*
Coll. – *College*
Con. – *Convent*
Cres. – *Crescent*
Ct. – *Court*
Dri. – *Drive*
Ex. – *Exchange*
Gdns. – *Gardens*
Gro. – *Grove*
Gt. – *Great*
Ho. – *House*
Hosp. – *Hospital*
Hot. – *Hotel*
Inst. – *Institute*
La. – *Lane*
Lit. – *Little*
Min. – *Ministry*
Mkt. – *Market*
Mt. – *Mount*
Mus. – *Museum*
Nat. – *National*
Nth. – *North*
Pal. – *Palace*
Pk. – *Park*
Pl. – *Place*
Pol. – *Police*
Poly – *Polytechnic*
Pr. – *Prince*
R.C. – *Roman Catholic*
Rd. – *Road*
Sanct. – *Sanctuary*
Sch. – *School*
Soc. – *Society*
Sq. – *Square*
St. – *Street, Saint*
Sta. – *Station*
Sth. – *South*
Ter. – *Terrace*
Th. – *Theatre*
Wk. – *Walk*
Yd. – *Yard*

The normal abbreviations for the London Postal Districts have been used throughout, e.g., NW10. For the Postal Districts outside the London Central area, the following abbreviations have been used:—

Bark. – *Barking*
Bec. – *Beckenham*
Belv. – *Belvedere*
Bex. – *Bexley*
Bex'h. – *Bexley Heath*
Brent. – *Brentford*
Brom. – *Bromley*
Ches. – *Chessington*
Chisl. – *Chislehurst*
Cro. – *Croydon*
Dag. – *Dagenham*
E. Mol. – *East Molesey*
Edgw. – *Edgware*
Eps. – *Epsom*
Esh. – *Esher*
Gnfd. – *Greenford*
Ham. – *Hampton*
Har. – *Harrow*
Houn. – *Hounslow*
Ilf. – *Ilford*
Isle. – *Isleworth*
K'gst. – *Kingston*
Mitch. – *Mitcham*
Mord. – *Morden*
New M. – *New Malden*
Orp. – *Orpington*
Rich. – *Richmond*
Rom. – *Romford*
Sid. – *Sidcup*
S'hall. – *Southall*
Stan. – *Stanmore*
Surb. – *Surbiton*
Sut. – *Sutton*
Ted. – *Teddington*
T. Hth. – *Thornton Heath*
Twick. – *Twickenham*
Wal. – *Wallington*
Wem. – *Wembley*
W. Wick. – *West Wickham*
Wfd. Gn. – *Woodford Green*
Wor. Pk. – *Worcester Park*

MAP
79 Abbeville Rd. . . . . . H 9
73 Abbey Av. . . . . G 3
81 Abbey Gdns. . . . . . C 4
76 Abbey La. . . . . G 4
87 Abbey Orchard St. D 7
76 Abbey Rd. E15. . . . F 5
76 Abbey Rd. E15. . . . G 5
74 Abbey Rd. NW6 & NW8. . . . . F 4
81 Abbey Rd. NW8. . B 4
73 Abbey Rd. NW10. G 5
88 Abbey St. . . . . D 5
67 Abbey Wood. . . . G 12
73 Abbeydale Rd. . . . . F 4
79 Abbeyfield Rd. . . . C 16
73 Abbots Dri. . . . . . . C 2
88 Abbots La. . . . . B 4
79 Abbots Pk. . . . . J 11
78 Abbotsbury Rd. . . . A 3
80 Abbotshall Rd. . . . K 4
79 Abbotswood Rd. . . K 9
76 Abbott Rd. . . . . J 4
76 Abbott's Pk. Rd. . . A 4
68 Abbs Cross La. . . . D 3
84 Abchurch La. . . . . H 3
78 Abdale Rd. W12. . A 1
76 Aberavon Rd. . . . . H 2
81 Abercorn Mews South C 4
81 Abercorn Pl. . . . . . . C 3
74 Aberdare Gdns. . . . F 5
75 Aberdeen Pk. . . . D 12
81 Aberdeen Pl. . . . . . . E 5
75 Aberdeen Rd. . . . . D 12
88 Aberdour St. . . . . . . E 3
76 Aberfeldy St. . . . . . J 4
80 Abergeldie Rd. . . . . H 7
85 Abingdon Rd. . . . . . D 1
87 Abingdon St. . . . . . . D 8
85 Abingdon Villas. . . D 1
80 Abinger Gro. . . . . . . D 2
77 Abinger Rd. . . . . . . B 7
79 Ablett St. . . . . C 16
73 Aboyne Rd. NW10 C 7
78 Aboyne Rd. SW17. L 5
67 Abridge Rd. . . . . . A 12
79 Acacia Gro. . . . . . K 13
81 Acacia Pl. . . . . B 5
76 Acacia Rd. E11. . . C 6
76 Acacia Rd. E17. . . A 2
81 Acacia Rd. NW8. . B 5
73 Acacia Rd. W3. . . K 6
67 Academy Rd. . . . . H 11
74 Achilles Rd. . . . . . . D 4
78 Ackmar Rd. . . . . . . E 4
80 Ackroyd Rd. . . . . . . J 1
79 Acland Cres. . . . . . G 13
77 Acol Rd. . . . . F 4
79 Acre La. SW2. . . . G 10
70 Acre La. Wal. . . . . . E 5
78 Acris St. . . . . H 5
73 Acton. . . . . L 6
77 Acton Central Station. . . . . A 6
77 Acton Green. . . . . . C 6
77 Acton Hosp. . . . . A 5
73 Acton La. NW10. . G 7
77 Acton La. W3. . . . . . A 6
77 Acton La. W4. . . . . . B 6
73 Acton Sta. . . . . J 7
73 Acton (Main Line) Sta. . . . . K 6
83 Acton St. . . . . D 9
77 Acton Town Sta. . . B 5
78 Acuba Rd. . . . . K 4
76 Ada Gdns. . . . . J 4
75 Ada St. . . . . F 15
74 Adair Rd. . . . . H 3
83 Adam St. . . . . J 9

MAP
85 Adam & Eve Mews D 2
82 Adams Row. . . . . . J 4
74 Adamson Rd. NW3 E 6
71 Addington, Cro . . . F 8
71 Addington Court GC. . . . . F 8
71 Addington G.C. . . . F 8
71 Addington Palace G.C. . . . . F 8
76 Addington Rd. E3. G 3
71 Addington Rd., Sanderstead. . . . . G 7
71 Addington Rd., W. Wick. . . . . E 9
88 Addington Sq. . . . . . J 2
87 Addington St. . . . . C 10
71 Addington Village Rd. . . . . F 8
71 Addiscombe. . . . . . E 7
71 Addiscombe Rd. . . E 7
71 Addiscombe Sta. . . E 7
78 Addison Av. . . . . . . A 2
78 Addison Cres. . . . . . B 3
78 Addison Gdns. . . . . B 2
76 Addison Rd. E11. . A 6
77 Addison Rd. W4. . B 7
78 Addison Rd. W14. A 3
69 Addlestone. . . . . . . F 4
80 Adelaide Av. . . . . . . G 2
73 Adelaide Gro. . . . . . L 8
76 Adelaide Rd. E10. . C 4
74 Adelaide Rd. NW3 F 6
83 Adelaide St. . . . . . . J 8
75 Adelina Gro. . . . . J 16
83 Adelphi Ter. . . . . . . J 9
83 Adelphi Th. . . . . . . J 9
75 Aden Gro. . . . . . . D 13
78 Adeney St. . . . . D 2
84 Adler St. . . . . G 6
80 Admiral St. . . . . E 3
87 Admiralty. . . . . B 8
75 Adolphus Rd. . . . B 12
80 Adolphus St. . . . . . D 2
87 Adpar St. . . . . F 5
79 Ady's Rd. . . . . F 15
80 Africa Rd. . . . . G 1
74 Agamemnon Rd. . . D 3
75 Agar Gro. . . . . F 9
83 Agar St. . . . . J 8
78 Agate Rd. . . . . B 1
83 Agdon St. . . . . E 12
77 Agincourt Rd. . . . . . D 7
77 Agnes Rd. . . . . A 7
79 Agnew Rd. . . . . J 1
78 Aide Rd. . . . . B 1
76 Ailsa St. . . . . J 4
74 Ainger Rd. . . . . F 7
73 Ainsdale Rd. . . . . . . H 3
75 Ainsworth Rd. . . . F 16
73 Aintree Rd. . . . . G 1
87 Air Ministry. . . . . . . B 8
82 Air St. . . . . J 6
77 Airedale Av. . . . . . . C 7
78 Airedale Rd. SW12 J 7
77 Airedale Rd. W5. . B 2
85 Airways Terminal B.E.A. . . . . E 3
86 Airways Terminal B.O.A.C. . . . . F 4
80 Aislibie Rd. . . . . . . G 5
74 Ajax Rd. . . . . D 3
77 Akehurst St. . . . . . . H 8
74 Akenside Rd. . . . . . E 6
79 Akerman Rd. . . . . . E 12
88 Akers St. . . . . F 3
87 Alaska St. . . . . B 11
74 Alba Gdns. . . . . A 3
80 Albacore Cres. . . . . H 3
71 Albany Park Sta. . C 12

MAP
76 Albany Rd. E10. . . A 3
75 Albany Rd. N4. . . A 11
88 Albany Rd. SE5. . . H 3
77 Albany Road, Brent. . . . . D 3
82 Albany St. . . . . C 5
82 Albemarle St. . . . . . J 5
86 Albert Bri. . . . . J 1
78 Albert Bri. Rd. . . . . E 7
78 Albert Dri. . . . . K 3
87 Albert Embankment. . . . . F 9
85 Albert Pl. . . . . D 3
76 Albert Rd. E10. . . . B 4
67 Albert Rd. E16. . . G 11
75 Albert Rd. N4. . . B 11
74 Albert Rd. NW6. . G 3
73 Albert Rd. W5. . . . H 1
77 Albert Rd., Rich. . . G 3
76 Albert Sq. E15. . . . E 5
79 Albert Sq. SW8. . . E 10
82 Albert St. . . . . B 5
82 Albert Ter. NW1. . . A 3
79 Albert Ter. SW8. . E 10
82 Albert Terrace Mews. . . . . A 3
87 Alberta St. . . . . G 12
79 Albion Av. . . . . F 9
81 Albion Cl. . . . . H 6
75 Albion Dri. . . . . F 15
81 Albion Mews. . . . . H 6
75 Albion Rd. . . . . D 13
79 Albion St. SE16. . A 16
81 Albion St. W2. . . . . H 6
79 Albion Villas Rd. . K 16
80 Albion Way. . . . . . G 4
79 Albrighton Rd. . . . . F 14
80 Albyn Rd. . . . . E 3
67 Aldborough Hatch . . . . C 12
67 Aldborough Rd. . . C 12
73 Aldbourne Rd. . . . . L 8
88 Aldbridge St. . . . . . G 4
78 Aldebrook Rd. . . . . . H 8
65 Aldenham Rd., Bushey. . . . . A 5
66 Aldenham Rd., Watford. . . . . A 2
82 Aldenham St. . . . . . . C 7
78 Aldensley Rd. . . . . . B 1
73 Alder Gro. . . . . C 8
84 Aldermanbury. . . . . G 2
88 Alderminster Rd. . . F 6
76 Alderney Rd. . . . . . . H 1
86 Alderney St. . . . . . . F 5
76 Aldersbrook. . . . . . . C 6
76 Aldersbrook Rd. . . C 8
83 Aldersgate Sta. . . . F 13
83 Aldersgate St. . . . . F 13
86 Aldford St. . . . . A 4
84 Aldgate. . . . . H 5
84 Aldgate High St. . G 5
74 Aldridge Rd. Villas J 3
83 Aldwych. . . . . H 10
83 Aldwych Th. . . . . . . H 9
65 Alexander Av., Har. . . . . D 6
85 Alexander Pl. . . . . . E 6
65 Alexander Rd. . . . C 10
85 Alexander Sq. . . . . . E 6
71 Alexander St. . . . . . G 2
85 Alexandra Gro. . . B 12
86 Alexandra Palace. . C 6
76 Alexandra Park. . . C 6
66 Alexandra Pk. Rd. . C 6
76 Alexandra Rd. E10 C 4
76 Alexandra Rd. E17 A 2
77 Alexandra Rd. W4. E 6

MAP
77 Alexandra Rd., Rich. . . . . F 4
77 Alexandra Rd., Twick. . . . . H 2
88 Alexis St. . . . . E 6
82 Alfred Mews. . . . . . F 7
82 Alfred Pl. . . . . F 7
81 Alfred Rd. W2. . . . F 1
77 Alfred Rd. W3. . . . A 6
76 Alfred St. . . . . G 2
67 Alfreds Way. . . . . . F 11
78 Alfriston Rd. . . . . . G 7
80 Algernon Rd. . . . . . G 3
80 Algiers Rd. . . . . G 3
88 Alice St. . . . . E 3
84 Alie St. . . . . G 6
75 Alkham Rd. . . . . . . C 15
70 All England Lawn Tennis Club . . . . C 4
77 All Saints Rd. W3. B 5
70 All Saint's Rd., Sut. . . . . E 4
83 All Saints St. . . . . . B 9
73 All Souls Av. . . . . . . G 9
75 Allas St. . . . . H 16
79 Allen Edwards Dri. . . . . E 10
75 Allen Rd. . . . . D 14
85 Allen St. . . . . D 1
73 Allen Way. . . . . J 6
80 Allenby Rd. . . . . . . K 1
75 Allerton Rd. . . . . . B 13
79 Alleyn Pk. . . . . K 14
79 Alleyn Rd. . . . . K 13
78 Allfarthing La. . . . . H 5
84 Allhallows La. . . . . J 2
73 Alliance Rd. . . . . . . H 5
83 Allingham St. . . . . B 13
73 Allington Cres. . . . . B 6
86 Allington St. . . . . . D 5
79 Allison Gro. . . . . . J 14
73 Allison Rd. . . . . K 6
81 Allitsen Rd. . . . . . . B 6
80 Alloa Rd. . . . . C 1
82 Allsop Pl. . . . . E 3
66 Allum La. . . . . A 2
88 Alma Gro. . . . . F 6
78 Alma Rd. . . . . G 5
81 Alma Sq. . . . . C 4
74 Alma St. . . . . E 8
77 Almond Av. . . . . B 3
75 Almorah Rd. . . . . F 13
76 Alnwick Rd. E16. . K 8
80 Alnwick Rd. SE12. J 7
73 Alperton. . . . . F 3
73 Alperton La. . . . . . . G 2
73 Alperton Sta. . . . . . F 3
80 Alpha Gro. . . . . A 3
86 Alpha Pl. . . . . H 1
80 Alpha Rd. . . . . E 2
79 Alphia St. . . . . E 15
73 Alric Av. . . . . F 6
75 Alroy Rd. . . . . A 11
88 Alsace St. . . . . G 4
88 Alscot Rd. . . . . E 5
75 Alsen Rd. . . . . C 11
77 Altenburg Av. . . . . B 1
78 Altenburg Gdns. . . G 7
78 Althea St. . . . . F 5
78 Althorp Rd. . . . . J 7
77 Alton Rd. . . . . J 8
76 Alton St. . . . . J 3
78 Alverstone Av. . . . . K 4
74 Alverstone Rd. . . . . F 1
80 Alverton St. . . . . . . D 2
75 Alvington Crescent. . . . . . D 15
80 Alwood Cres. . . . . . H 7
77 Alwood Rd. . . . . B 9

MAP
77 Alwyn Av. . . . . C 6
75 Alwyne Pl. . . . . E 12
75 Alwyne Rd. . . . . . . F 12
75 Alwyne Sq. . . . . E 12
75 Alwyne Villas. . . . E 12
83 Ambassadors Theatre H 8
87 Ambergate St. . . . . G 12
76 Amberley Rd. E10. . . . . A 3
81 Amberley Rd. W9. E 2
70 Amberwood Rise. . E 3
75 Ambler Rd. . . . . C 12
86 Ambrosden Av. . . . . E 6
74 Ambrose Av. . . . . . . A 3
79 Ambrose St. . . . . . . C 15
87 Amelia St. . . . . F 13
78 Amerland Rd. . . . . . H 3
80 Amersham Gro. . . . D 2
80 Amersham Rd. . . . . E 2
80 Amersham Vale. . . D 2
79 Amesbury Av. . . . K 10
73 Amherst Av. . . . . . . K 2
73 Amherst Rd. . . . . . . K 2
75 Amhurst Pk. . . . . . A 14
75 Amhurst Rd. . . . . . D 15
79 Amott Rd. . . . . F 15
82 Ampthill Sq. . . . . . . C 6
83 Ampton St. . . . . . . D 10
83 Amwell St. . . . . . . D 11
80 Amyruth Rd. . . . . . . H 3
74 Anatole Rd. . . . . . . C 8
80 Anchor & Hope La. B 7
79 Anchor St. . . . . C 16
73 Ancona Rd. . . . . G 8
86 Anderson St. . . . . . . F 2
81 Andover Pl. . . . . C 2
75 Andover Rd. . . . . . . C 11
75 Andre St. . . . . D 15
75 Andrews Rd. . . . . . G 15
71 Anerley Rd. . . . . C 7
71 Anerley Sta. . . . . D 7
83 Angel Cin. . . . . C 11
76 Angel La. . . . . E 5
67 Angel Rd. . . . . B 8
67 Angel Rd. Station B8
79 Angell Park Gdns. F 11
79 Agnell Rd. . . . . F 11
84 Anglesea St. E7
80 Angus St. . . . . D 2
78 Anhalt Rd. . . . . D 6
76 Anmis Rd. . . . . E 1
80 Annandale Rd. . . . . C 6
85 Anne La. . . . . J 5
74 Annes Rd. . . . . L 2
75 Annette Rd. . . . . . . D 11
84 Anning St. . . . . E 4
79 Ansdell Rd. . . . . . . F 16
85 Ansdell St. . . . . D 3
85 Ansdel Ter. . . . . D 2
85 Anselm Rd. . . . . H 1
76 Ansittart Rd. . . . . . D 6
75 Anson Rd. N7. . . . . D 9
74 Anson Rd. NW2. . D 1
79 Anstey Rd. . . . . F 15
75 Anthony St. . . . . . K 16
76 Antill Rd. . . . . G 2
74 Antrim Rd. . . . . E 7
77 Antrobus Rd. . . . . . B 6
76 Apostle Rd. . . . . J 2
79 Appach Rd. . . . . . . H 11
86 Apple Tree Yd. . . . A 7
76 Appleby La. . . . . . . K 6
84 Appleby St. . . . . B 5
84 Appold St. . . . . F 4
75 Approach Rd. . . . . G 16

MAP
73 Approach, The. . . . J 7
86 Apsley Ho. . . . . C 4
75 Apsley St. . . . . J 16
86 Apsley Way. . . . . . . C 4
81 Aquila St. . . . . B 5
87 Aquinas St. . . . . . . B 11
80 Arabin Rd. . . . . G 2
76 Arbery Rd. . . . . G 1
76 Arbour Sq. . . . . J 1
80 Arbuthnot Rd. . . . . . F 1
75 Arbutus St. . . . . . . F 14
87 Arch St. . . . . E 13
87 Archbishop's Park D 10
78 Archel Rd. . . . . D 3
82 Archer St. . . . . H 7
82 Archery Cl. . . . . H 2
76 Archibald St. . . . . . H 3
74 Archway Rd. . . . . . . A 8
75 Archway Sta. . . . . . C 9
77 Archway St. . . . . . . F 7
75 Arcola St. . . . . D 15
79 Ardberg Rd. . . . . . H 13
79 Arden St. . . . . D 9
80 Ardfillan Rd. . . . . . K 5
80 Ardgowan Rd. . . . . J 5
68 Ardleigh Green. . . . C 3
68 Ardleigh Green La. C 3
75 Ardleigh Rd. . . . . . E 13
79 Ardlui Rd. . . . . K 12
80 Ardoch Rd. . . . . K 5
76 Argall Av. . . . . B 1
66 Argyle Rd. W13. . . F 1
83 Argyle Sq. . . . . D 9
76 Argyle St. E11. . . . C 5
83 Argyle St. WC1. . . D 9
85 Argyll Rd. . . . . D 1
82 Argyll St. . . . . H 6
79 Aristotle Rd. . . . . . G 10
66 Arkley. . . . . A 4
80 Arklow Rd. . . . . D 2
74 Arkwright Rd. . . . . . E 5
79 Arlesford Rd. . . . . F 10
79 Arlingford Rd. . . . H 11
84 Arlington Av. . . . . . . B 2
77 Arlington Gdns. . . . C 5
82 Arlington Rd. NW1 B 5
73 Arlington Rd. W3. K 11
77 Arlington Rd. Twick. H 2
84 Arlington Sq. . . . . . B 2
86 Arlington St. . . . . . . B 6
83 Arlington Way. . . C 11
77 Arlton Rd. . . . . B 6
80 Armada St. . . . . D 3
85 Armadale Rd. . . . . . J 1
74 Armitage Rd. NW11 B 3
80 Armitage Rd. SE10. C 6
78 Armoury Way. . . . . G 4
73 Armstrong Rd. . . . . L 7
83 Arne St. . . . . H 9
80 Arngask Rd. . . . . . . J 4
84 Arnold Circus. . . . . D 5
76 Arnold Rd. . . . . H 3
72 Arnolds La. . . . . C 3
66 Arnos Gro. Sta. . . . B 6
88 Arnside St. . . . . H 2
79 Arodene Rd. . . . . . H 11
80 Arran Rd. . . . . K 4
76 Arrow Rd. . . . . H 3
75 Arsenal F.C. . . . . . D 12
75 Arsenal Sta. . . . . . C 11
81 Artesian Rd. . . . . . . H 1
76 Arthugworth St. . . F 5
48 Arthur St. . . . . J 3
80 Arthurdon Rd. . . . . H 3
84 Artillery Ground. . E 2

MAP
84 Artillery La. F 4
86 Artillery Row D 7
83 Arts Th. H 8
75 Arundel Gro. D 14
75 Arundel Pl. E 11
83 Arundel St. H 10
78 Ascalyon St. E 9
77 Ascot Av. A 3
72 Ash F 5
75 Ash Gro. E8 G 16
74 Ash Gro.NW2 D2
77 Ash Gro. W5 B 3
76 Ash Road D 5
79 Ashbourne Gro. SE22 G 14
77 Ashbourne Gro. W4 C 7
73 Ashbourne Rd. H 4
76 Ashbridge Rd. A 6
81 Ashbridge St. E 6
75 Ashbrock Rd. B 9
85 Ashburn Gdns. E 3
85 Ashburn Mews E 3
85 Ashburn Pl. F 3
80 Ashburnham Gro. E 4
80 Ashburnham Pl. E 4
74 Ashburnham Rd. NW10 G 1
78 Ashburnham Rd. SW10 D 5
77 Ashburnham Rd., Rich. L 2
75 Ashburton Gro. D 11
78 Ashbury Rd. F 7
80 Ashby Rd. F 2
83 Ashby St. D 12
77 Ashchurch Gro. B 8
77 Ashchurch Pk. Villas B 8
73 Ashcombe Pk. C 7
76 Ashcroft Rd. H 1
80 Ashdale Rd. J 7
78 Ashen Gro. K 4
76 Ashenden Rd. D 1
73 Ashfield Rd. K 7
75 Ashfield St. J 16
69 Ashford C 4
69 Ashford Manor G.C. C 3
74 Ashford Rd. NW2 D 2
69 Ashford Rd., Feltham C 4
69 Ashford Rd., Staines D 3
82 Ashland Pl. F 3
77 Ashleigh Rd. F 7
77 Ashley Gdns. K 2
69 Ashley Park E 4
86 Ashley Pl. E 6
75 Ashley Rd. N19 B 10
70 Ashley Rd., Epsom G 3
69 Ashley Rd., Walton E 4
76 Ashlin Rd. D 5
78 Ashlone Rd. F 2
80 Ashmead Rd. F 3
81 Ashmill St. F 6
87 Ashmole Pl. J 10
87 Ashmole St. J 10
74 Ashmore Rd. H 3
75 Ashmount Rd. B 9
70 Ashtead H 2
70 Ashtead Common G 1
70 Ashtead Park H 2
75 Ashtead Rd. A 15
70 Ashtead Sta. H 1
80 Ashwater Rd. K 7
81 Ashworth Rd. D 3
77 Askew Cres. A 8
77 Askew Rd. A 8
78 Aslett St. J 5
74 Asmara Rd. D 3
79 Aspian St. D 13
80 Aspinall Rd. F 1
79 Astbury Rd. E 16
86 Astell St. G 1
65 Aston Rd. B 4
76 Aston St. J 1
78 Astonville St. J 4
82 Astoria Cin. G 7
85 Astwood Mews F 3
79 Asylum Rd. E 16
78 Atheldene Rd. J 5
80 Athelney St. K 3
80 Athenlay Rd. H 1
75 Atherden Rd. D 16
79 Atherfold Rd. F 10
85 Atherstone Mews E 4
76 Atherton Rd. E 6
79 Athlone Rd. J 11

MAP
74 Athlone St. E 8
79 Atkins Rd. J 9
79 Atlantic Rd. G 11
73 Atlas Rd. H 7
78 Atney Rd. G 3
87 Atterbury St. F 8
78 Attewood Av. C 7
83 Attneave St. D 11
77 Atwood Av. F 4
75 Aubert Park D 12
78 Aubrey Rd. A 3
78 Aubrey Walk A 3
77 Aubyn Sq. G 8
76 Auckland Rd. C 3
87 Auckland St. G 9
73 Audley Rd. J 4
76 Augustia St. J 3
78 Augustus Rd. J 2
82 Augustus St. C 5
78 Auriol Rd. C 2
84 Austin Friars G 3
84 Austin St. D 5
87 Austral St. E 12
73 Australia Rd. K 9
83 Ave Maria La. H 12
84 Avebury St. A 3
68 Aveley G 4
68 Aveley Rd. E 4
87 Aveline St. G 10
75 Avenell Rd. C 12
84 Avenue, The, EC3 H 4
74 Avenue, The, NW6 F 2
78 Avenue, The, SW4 H 8
77 Avenue, The, W4 B 7
77 Avenue, The, Rich. F 4
69 Avenue, The, Sunbury D 5
77 Avenue, The, Twick. H 2
73 Avenue, The, Wem. B 4
82 Avenue Cl. B 1
77 Avenue Cres. A 5
77 Avenue Gdns. A 5
79 Avenue Pk. Rd. K 12
76 Avenue Rd. E11 D 5
75 Avenue Rd. N6 A 9
66 Avenue Rd. N14 A 6
81 Avenue Rd. NW8 B 6
77 Avenue Rd. W3 A 5
68 Avenue Rd., Bex. H 1
71 Avenue Rd., Bex. A 12
77 Avenue Rd., Brent. C 2
71 Avery Hill Rd. B 11
82 Avery Row H 5
80 Avingnon Rd. F 1
88 Avon Pl. C 2
80 Avon Rd. F 3
73 Avondale Av. C 7
74 Avondale Pk. Rd. K 2
79 Avondale Rise F 14
76 Avondale Rd. E16 J 5
76 Avondale Rd. E17 A 2
88 Avondale Sq. G 6
79 Avonley Rd. SE14 D 16
80 Avonley Rd. D 1
78 Avonmore Rd. B 3
87 Avonmouth St. D 13
75 Axminster Rd. C 10
82 Aybrook St. F 3
73 Aycliffe Rd. L 8
88 Aylesbury Rd. G 3
83 Aylesbury St. EC1 E 12
73 Aylesbury St. NW10 C 6
86 Aylesford St. G 7
66 Aylmer Rd. N2 D 5
77 Aylmer Rd. W12 B 7
74 Aylstone Av. F 2
80 Aylward Rd. K 1
78 Aynhoe Rd. B 2
77 Aynscombe La. F 6
88 Ayres St. C 1
75 Ayrsome Rd. C 14
79 Aysgarth Rd. H 13
80 Azof St. C 5
75 Baalbec Rd. E 12
84 Baches St. D 3
84 Back Church La. H 6
83 Back Hill E 11
68 Back Lane, Aveley G5
77 Back La., Rich. K 2
85 Bacon Gro. E 5
84 Bacon St. E 6
72 Badger's Mount G 1
78 Badminton Rd. H 8
78 Bagleys La. E 5
88 Bagshot St. G 4
83 Bainbridge St. G 8
79 Baizdon Rd. F 5
82 Baker St. F 3
75 Bakers Hill B 16

MAP
82 Baker's Mews G 3
76 Bakers Row E15 G 5
83 Baker's Row EC1 E 11
76 Balaam St. H 7
88 Balaclava Rd. F 6
82 Balcombe St. E 2
75 Balcorne St. F 16
80 Balder Rise K 7
82 Balderton St. H 4
79 Baldwin Cres. E 12
84 Baldwin St. D 2
83 Baldwin Ter. B 13
83 Baldwin's Gdns. F 11
65 Baldwin's La. A 4
83 Balfe St. C 9
75 Balfour Rd. D 12
88 Balfour St. E 2
68 Balgores La. C 3
78 Balham J 8
78 Balham Gro. J 8
78 Balham Hill J 8
78 Balham High Rd. K 8
78 Balham New Rd. J 8
78 Balham Pk. Rd. J 7
78 Balham Sta. J 8
78 Balham & Upper Tooting Sta. J 8
80 Ballamore Rd. L 6
76 Ballance Rd. E 1
66 Ballards La. C 5
73 Ballards Rd. C 8
79 Ballater Rd. G 10
80 Ballina St. H 1
80 Balloch St. K 5
75 Balls Pond Rd. E 14
75 Balmes Rd. F 13
76 Balmoral Rd. E7 D 8
73 Balmoral Rd. NW2 E 9
84 Baltic St. E 1
78 Balvernie Gro. J 3
73 Bamford Av. G 4
80 Bamton Rd. K 1
76 Banbury Rd. F 1
76 Bancroft Rd. E1 H 1
78 Bangalore St. F 2
80 Banim St. B 1
77 Bank La. H 7
84 Bank of England G 3
88 Bankend A 2
80 Bankhurst Rd. J 2
83 Bankruptcy Ct. H 10
87 Bankside A 13
84 Banner St. E 2
80 Banning St. C 5
70 Banstead Downs & G.C. G 4
70 Banstead Rd. G 3
70 Banstead Rd. Sth. F 5
70 Banstead Sta. G 4
79 Banstead St. F 16
79 Banyard Rd. B 16
75 Barbara St. E 11
75 Barbauld Rd. C 14
79 Barbers Alley G 7
76 Barbers Rd. G 3
78 Barchester St. J 3
76 Barclay Rd. E11 B 6
78 Barclay Rd. SW6 E 4
79 Barcombe Av. K 10
80 Bardsley La. D 4
75 Bardwells St. E 10
83 Barford St. B 11
79 Barforth Rd. G 16
87 Barge Ho. St. A 11
80 Barger Rd. K 4
73 Barham Pk. E 2
80 Baring Rd. K 6
84 Baring St. A 2
81 Bark Pl. J 2
67 Barking E 11
76 Barking Rd. H 7
67 Barking Sta. E 11
67 Barkingside C 11
85 Barkston Gdns. F 2
79 Barkworth Rd. C 16
80 Barlborough St. D 1
74 Barlby Rd. J 2
83 Barlett Ct. G 11
67 Barley La. D 12
73 Barlow Rd. L 5
88 Barlow St. F 3
80 Barmeston Rd. K 3
78 Barmouth Rd. H 5
78 Barn Elms Park E 1
72 Barn End La. C 2
73 Barn Hill B 5
73 Barn Hill Pk. B 4
73 Barn Way B 4
76 Barnabas Rd. E 1
82 Barnby St. C 6
72 Barnehurst A 1

MAP
77 Barnes F 8
77 Barnes Av. D 8
77 Barnes Bri. F 7
77 Barnes Bri. Sta. F 7
77 Barnes High St. E 7
77 Barnes Sta. F 8
76 Barnes St. J 1
77 Barnes Ter. F 7
66 Barnet By-Pass A 3
66 Barnet Gate A 3
84 Barnet Gro. D 6
66 Barnet La. N20 A 4
66 Barnet La. Elstree A 2
66 Barnet Rd. A 4
66 Barnet Way A 3
70 Barnetwood La. H 1
73 Barnfield Rd. H 2
88 Barnham St. C 4
75 Barnsbury Gro. E 11
75 Barnsbury Pk. F 11
83 Barnsbury Rd. B 11
75 Barnsbury Sq. F 11
75 Barnsbury St. F 11
74 Barnsdale Rd. H 3
79 Barnwell Rd. G 11
76 Baron Rd. J 6
83 Baron St. C 11
84 Baroness Rd. C 5
77 Barons, The H 1
78 Barons Court Rd. C 3
78 Barons Court Sta. C 3
87 Baron's Pl. C 11
77 Baronsmede B 4
73 Barrets Green Rd. G 6
82 Barrett St. H 4
75 Barretts Gro. D 14
76 Barrie St. H 4
80 Barriedale F 2
79 Barrington Rd. F 12
81 Barrow Hill Rd. C 6
67 Barrowell Green B 7
77 Barrowgate Rd. C 6
79 Barry Rd. SE22 H 15
79 Barset Rd. F 16
83 Barter St. G 9
83 Bartholomew Cl. F 13
84 Bartholomew La. G 3
75 Bartholomew Rd. E 9
88 Bartholomew St. E 3
73 Bashley Rd. H 6
86 Basil St. D 2
74 Basing Hill, NW11 B 3
73 Basing Hill, Wem. B 4
74 Basing Hill Pk. B 3
84 Basing Pl. C 4
79 Basingdon Way G 13
84 Basinghall Ave. G 2
84 Basinghall St. G 2
75 Basire St. F 12
78 Baskerville Rd. J 6
79 Bassand St. G 14
77 Bassein Pk. Rd. B 8
74 Bassett Rd. J 2
78 Bassingham Rd. SW18 J 5
73 Bassingham Rd. Wem. E 2
71 Baston Rd. E 9
84 Bastwick St. E 1
78 Basuto Rd. E 4
83 Batchelor St. B 11
65 Batchworth B 3
65 Batchworth Heath B 4
65 Batchworth Heath Hill B 3
82 Bateman St. H 7
84 Bateman's Row D 4
77 Bath Rd. W4 B 7
69 Bath Rd. Houn. A 11
84 Bath St. D 2
88 Bath Ter. D 1
78 Bathgate Rd. L 2
74 Bathurst Gdns. G 1
81 Bathurst Mews H 5
81 Bathurst St. H 5
78 Batoum Gdns. B 1
80 Battersby Rd. K 5
78 Battersea E 7
85 Battersea Bri. J 5
78 Battersea Bri. Rd. E 6
78 Battersea Ch. Rd. E 6
78 Battersea High St. E 6
78 Battersea Park E 7
86 Battersea Park J 2
78 Battersea Pk. Rd. SW11 E 7
78 Battersea Pk. Sta. E 8
78 Battersea Rise G 6
88 Battle Bri. La. B 3
83 Battle Bri. Rd. B 8

MAP
75 Battledean Rd. D 12
84 Batty St. G 7
80 Baudwin Rd. K 5
75 Bavaria Rd. C 10
79 Bavent Rd. F 13
79 Bawdale Rd. H 14
79 Baxall Rd. J 13
84 Baxendale St. C 6
76 Baxter Rd. E16 J 8
75 Baxter Rd. N1 E 13
82 Bayham St. B 6
82 Bayley St. F 7
87 Baylis Rd. C 11
78 Bayonne Rd. D 2
75 Bayston Rd. C 14
74 Bayswater K 5
81 Bayswater Rd. J 4
76 Baythorne St. J 2
79 Baytree Rd. G 11
76 Bazeley St. K 4
76 Beachcroft Rd. E11 C 5
78 Beachcroft Rd. SW17 K 6
76 Beachy Rd. F 3
75 Beacon Hill Rd. D 10
80 Beacon Rd. H 5
76 Beaconsfield Rd. E16 H 6
80 Beaconsfield Rd. SE3 D 6
77 Beaconsfield Rd. W4 B 6
77 Beaconsfield Rd. W5 A 2
68 Beacontree Heath D 1
76 Beacontree Rd. B 6
80 Beadnell Rd. J 1
78 Beadon Rd. C 1
82 Beak St. H 6
76 Beale Rd. G 2
72 Bean C 4
88 Bear Gdns. A 1
87 Bear La. B 12
83 Bear St. J 7
80 Bearsted Rise H 2
79 Beatrice Rd. C 15
75 Beatty Rd. D 14
82 Beatty St. B 6
86 Beauchamp Pl. D 2
78 Beauchamp Rd. G 7
83 Beauchamp St. F 11
86 Beaufort Gdns. D 2
73 Beaufort Rd. J 4
85 Beaufort St. H 5
77 Beaumont Av. Rich. G 3
73 Beaumont Av. Wem. D 2
82 Beaumont Mews F 4
82 Beaumont Pl. E 6
76 Beaumont Rd. E10 B 3
76 Beaumont Rd. E13 H 7
78 Beaumont Rd. SW19 J 2
77 Beaumont Rd. W4 B 6
76 Beaumont Sq. J 1
82 Beaumont St. F 44
79 Beauval Rd. H 1
77 Beavor La. C 8
75 Beck Rd. F 16
71 Beckenham D 8
71 Beckenham Hill Rd. C 8
71 Beckenham Hill Sta. C 8
71 Beckenham Junction Sta. D 8
71 Beckenham Place G.C. C 9
71 Beckenham Rd. D 8
77 Becklow Rd. A 8
67 Beckton F 11
79 Beckwith Rd. H 13
68 Becontree E 1
67 Becontree Av. E 12
67 Becontree Sta. E 12
76 Bective Rd. E7 D 7
78 Bective Rd. SW15 G 3
88 Bedale St. B 2
70 Beddington F 6
70 Beddington Corner E 5
70 Beddington La. E 6
70 Beddington La. Sta. E 5
71 Beddlestead La. H 9
69 Bedfont Rd. Feltham C 4
69 Bedfont Rd. Stanwell B 3
83 Bedford Av. G 7

MAP
82 Bedford Coll. E 3
85 Bedford Gdns. B 1
78 Bedford Hill K 8
83 Bedford Pl. F 8
79 Bedford Rd. SW4 G 10
77 Bedford Rd. W4 B 6
83 Bedford Row F 10
83 Bedford Sq. F 7
83 Bedford St. J 8
75 Bedford Ter. C 11
83 Bedford Way E 8
83 Bedfordbury J 8
80 Bedivere Rd. L 6
68 Bedonwell Rd. H 1
77 Beech Av. D 1
71 Beech Farm Rd. H 9
77 Beech Gdns. B 3
84 Beech St. F 1
77 Beechcroft Av. A 3
73 Beechcroft Gdns. C 4
79 Beechdale Rd. H 11
72 Beechenlea La. D 2
78 Beeches Rd. L 7
75 Beechfield Rd. N4 A 13
80 Beechfield Rd. SE6 J 2
77 Beechwood Av. E 4
75 Beechwood Rd. E 14
80 Beecroft Rd. G 2
71 Beehive Sta. B 11
74 Beethoven St. G 3
80 Begbie Rd. E 8
75 Belgrade Rd. D 14
86 Belgrave Mews Nth. D 3
86 Belgrave Mews W. D 3
86 Belgrave Pl. D 4
76 Belgrave Rd. E11 B 6
76 Belgrave Rd. E13 H 7
86 Belgrave Rd. SW1 F 6
86 Belgrave Sq. D 4
76 Belgrave St. J 1
78 Belgravia B 8
83 Belgrove St. C 8
79 Belham St. E 13
75 Belitha Villas F 11
84 Bell La. G 5
81 Bell St. F 6
83 Bell Yd. H 11
84 Bell Wharf La. J 2
78 Bellamy St. J 8
71 Belle Grove Rd. A 11
78 Belle Vue Rd. J 7
79 Bellefields Rd. F 11
79 Bellenden Rd. F 14 & E 15
78 Belleville Rd. H 7
79 Bellfort Rd. E 16
80 Bellingham L 3
80 Bellingham Rd. K 4
80 Bellingham Sta. L 3
80 Bellot St. C 5
79 Bells Gdn. Rd. E 15
66 Belmont C 1
66 Belmont G.C. C 1
80 Belmont Hill F 4
80 Belmont Pk. G 5
76 Belmont Pk. Rd. A 4
70 Belmont Rise F 4
76 Belmont Rd. E15 H 5
77 Belmont Rd. W4 C 6
74 Belmont St. E 8
66 Belmont Sta. C 1
70 Belmont Sta. Sut. F 4
75 Belsham St. E 16
74 Belsize Av. NW3 E 6
77 Belsize Av W13 B 1
74 Belsize Gro. E 6
74 Belsize La. E 6
74 Belsize Pk. Sta. E 6
74 Belsize Pk. E 6
74 Belsize Pk. Gdns. E 6
74 Belsize Rd. F 5
74 Belsize Sq. E 6
73 Belton Rd. E 8
68 Belvedere G 2
76 Belvedere Rd. E10 B 2
87 Belvedere Rd. SE1 B 10
79 Belvoir Rd. J 15
83 Bemerton St. A 9
76 Ben Jonson Rd. J 1
78 Benbow Rd. B 1
80 Benbow St. D 3
78 Bendon Valley J 4
79 Bengeworth Rd. F 12
70 Benhill Av. E 4
79 Benhill Rd. SE5 E 13
70 Benhill Rd. Sut. E 5
80 Benin St. J 5
83 Benjamin St. F 12
78 Bennerley Rd. G 7
67 Bennet Castle La. E 12

Map	Name	Ref
80	Bennett Pk.	F 6
79	Benson Rd.	J 16
75	Benthal Rd.	C 15
76	Bentham Rd.	E 1
82	Bentinck St.	G 4
73	Bentworth Rd.	K 8
75	Benwell Rd.	D 11
68	Beredens La.	C 5
77	Beresford Av. Twick.	H 2
73	Beresford Av. Wem.	F 4
75	Beresford Rd.	E 13
86	Berkeley Hotel	B 5
82	Berkeley Mews	G 3
77	Berkeley Rd.	E 8
82	Berkeley Sq.	J 5
86	Berkeley St.	A 5
73	Berkhamsted Av.	E 4
76	Berkshire Rd.	E 2
73	Bermans Way	D 7
79	Bermondsey	B 14
88	Bermondsey St.	C 4
88	Bermondsey Wall E.	C 7
88	Bermondsey Wall W.	C 6
77	Bernard Av.	B 1
83	Bernard St.	E 8
82	Berners Mews	G 6
82	Berners Pl.	G 6
83	Berners Rd.	B 12
82	Berners St.	G 6
83	Berry St.	E 12
87	Berryfield Rd.	G 13
70	Berrylands Sta.	D 2
77	Berrymead Gdns.	A 6
71	Berry's Green Rd.	H 11
71	Berry's Hill	G 11
73	Bertie Rd.	E 8
73	Bertram Rd.	A 8
68	Berwick Pond Rd.	E 3
76	Berwick Rd.	K 7
82	Berwick St.	H 7
77	Berwyn Rd.	G 5
78	Beryl Rd.	C 2
74	Besant Rd.	D 2
87	Bessborough Gdns.	G 8
87	Bessborough Pl.	G 7
87	Bessborough Rd.	J 8
86	Bessborough St.	G 7
79	Bessemer Rd.	F 13
80	Besson St.	E 1
76	Bethnal Green	G 1
84	Bethnal Green Rd.	D 6
84	Bethnal Green Sta.	H 16
75	Bethune Rd. N16.	A 13
73	Bethune Rd. NW10	H 6
87	Bethwin Rd.	J 13
72	Betsham	C 5
83	Betterton St.	G 9
78	Bettran Rd.	F 4
78	Bettridge Rd.	F 3
71	Beulah Hill	C 7
84	Bevan St.	B 1
84	Bevenden St.	C 3
77	Beverley Bri.	K 7
73	Beverley Gdns.	B 4
77	Beverley Rd. SW13.	F 8
77	Beverley Rd. W4.	C 7
75	Beversbrook Rd.	C 9
74	Bevington Rd.	J 3
88	Bevington St.	D 7
84	Bevis Marks	G 4
75	Bewdley St.	F 11
80	Bexhill Rd.	H 2
71	Bexley	B 12
72	Bexley Hosp.	C 1
71	Bexley La.	C 2
71	Bexley Rd. SE9.	B 11
68	Bexley Rd. Erith.	H 2
71	Bexley Heath G.C.	B 12
72	Bexleyheath	B 1
88	Bianca Rd.	H 6
87	Bicester Rd.	F 5
82	Bickenhall St.	F 3
74	Bickerton Rd.	A 9
71	Bickley	D 10
76	Bickley Rd.	A 3
83	Bidborough St.	D 8
71	Biddestone Rd.	D 11
81	Biddulph Rd.	D 2
75	Big Hill	B 16
71	Biggin Hill	H 10
75	Bigland St.	K 16
76	Bignold Rd.	D 7
67	Billet Rd. E17.	C 8
67	Billet Rd. Ilf.	C 12
85	Billing Pl.	J 3
85	Billing Rd.	J 3
85	Billing St.	J 3
84	Billingsgate Mkt.	J 3
80	Billington Rd.	E 1
84	Billiter St.	H 4
80	Billson St.	C 4
73	Bilton Rd.	F 2
85	Bina Gdns.	F 3
77	Binden Rd.	B 8
79	Binfield Rd.	E 10
75	Bingfield St.	F 10
82	Bingham Pl.	F 3
71	Bingham Rd. Sta.	E 7
76	Bingley Rd.	J 8
82	Binney St.	H 4
77	Binns Rd.	C 7
80	Birch Gro. SE12.	J 6
73	Birch Gro. W3.	K 4
76	Birchdale Rd.	E 8
73	Birchen Gro.	C 6
84	Birchin La.	H 3
78	Birchlands Av.	J 7
72	Birchwood Rd.	C 1
79	Bird in Bush Rd.	D 15
68	Bird La.	C 4
82	Bird St.	H 4
80	Birdbrook Rd.	G 8
86	Birdcage Walk	C 7
82	Birkbeck Coll.	E 7
77	Birkbeck Gro.	A 6
79	Birkbeck Hill	K 12
77	Birkbeck Rd.	A 6
71	Birkbeck Sta.	D 8
73	Birkdale Rd.	H 3
83	Birkenhead St.	C 9
80	Birkhall Rd.	K 5
75	Birnam Rd.	C 11
78	Biscay Rd.	C 2
74	Bishops Av. The.	A 6
78	Bishops Av. SW6.	F 2
81	Bishop's Bri. Rd.	G 4
74	Bishops Gro.	A 6
78	Bishops Pk. Rd.	E 2
74	Bishop's Rd. N6	A 8
78	Bishops Rd. SW6	E 3
87	Bishop's Ter.	E 11
75	Bishops Way	G 16
70	Bishopsford Rd.	E 4
84	Bishopsgate	G 4
74	Bishopswood Rd.	A 7
73	Bispham Rd.	H 4
76	Bisson Rd.	G 4
69	Bittams La.	E 2
67	Black Horse La.	C 8
67	Black Horse Rd. Sta.	C 8
77	Black Lion La.	C 8
87	Black Prince Rd.	F 10
84	Blackall St.	E 3
73	Blackbird Hill	C 6
82	Blackburnes Mews.	J 3
71	Blackfen	B 11
71	Blackfen Rd.	B 11
83	Blackfriars Bridge	J 12
83	Blackfriars La.	H 12
87	Blackfriars Rd.	C 12
83	Blackfrairs Sta.	H 12
80	Blackheath	F 6
80	Blackheath Gro.	F 6
80	Blackheath Hill.	E 4
80	Blackheath Pk.	F 6
80	Blackheath Rise.	F 4
80	Blackheath Rd.	E 3
71	Blackheath Royal GC	B 10
80	Blackheath Sta.	F 5
80	Blackheath Village.	F 6
80	Blackhorse Rd.	C 2
86	Blacklands Ter.	F 2
79	Blackpool Rd.	F 15
80	Blackstock Rd.	C 12
74	Blackstone Rd.	D 2
76	Blackwall	K 5
80	Blackwall La.	B 5
80	Blackwall Tunnel	A 4
76	Blackwall Way	K 4
88	Blackwood St.	G 2
80	Blagdon Rd.	H 3
76	Blair St.	J 4
79	Blairderry Rd.	K 10
78	Blake Hall Cres.	B 7
76	Blake Hall Rd.	B 7
88	Blake's Rd.	J 4
73	Blakesley Av.	J 2
76	Blanche St.	H 6
79	Blanchedowne	G 13
78	Blandfield Rd.	J 8
82	Blandford Estate	F 1
82	Blandford Pl.	B 3
77	Blandford Rd. W4.	B 7
77	Blandford Rd. W5.	A 3
82	Blandford Sq.	E 1
82	Blandford St.	G 3
85	Blantyre St.	J 4
80	Blashford St.	J 5
71	Blendon Rd.	B 12
88	Blendon Row	F 2
74	Blenheim Cres.	K 3
74	Blenheim Gdns. NW2	E 1
73	Blenheim Gdns. Wem.	C 3
81	Blenheim Rd. NW8	B 4
79	Blenheim Rd. SE15.	F 15
77	Blenheim Rd. W4.	B 7
81	Blenheim Ter.	B 3
78	Blenkarne Rd.	H 7
80	Blessington Rd.	G 5
84	Bletchley St.	C 2
85	Blissett St.	E 4
85	Blithfield St.	E 2
79	Blockhouse St.	D 16
73	Blockley Rd.	C 2
73	Bloemfontein Rd.	K 8
81	Blomfield Rd.	F 3
84	Blomfield St.	G 3
81	Blomfield Villas.	F 3
77	Blondin Av.	B 2
86	Bloomfield Ter.	F 4
75	Bloomsbury	H 10
83	Bloomsbury Sq.	F 9
83	Bloomsbury St.	G 8
83	Bloomsbury Way	G 8
84	Blossom St.	E 4
76	Blount St.	J 2
76	Bloxhall Rd.	B 2
79	Blue Anchor La.	B 15
69	Blundell La.	G 6
81	Blundell St.	E 10
76	Blyth Rd. E17.	B 2
80	Blythe Hill	J 2
80	Blythe Hill Fields.	J 2
80	Blythe Hill La.	J 2
78	Blythe Rd.	B 2
75	Blythe St.	G 15
80	Blythe Vale.	K 2
75	Blythwood Rd.	A 10
80	Boadicea St.	B 9
69	Board Lane	C 6
78	Bodmin St.	K 4
77	Bodney Rd.	D 15
77	Boileau Rd. SW13.	D 8
73	Boileau Rd. W5.	J 4
76	Boleyn Rd. E7.	F 7
75	Boleyn Rd. N16.	E 14
78	Bolingbroke Gro.	H 6
78	Bolingbroke Rd.	B 2
77	Bollo Bridge Rd.	B 5
77	Bollo La.	B 5
82	Bolsover St.	F 5
70	Bolters La.	G 4
87	Bolton Cres.	J 12
85	Bolton Gdns.	F 3
76	Bolton Rd. E15.	E 6
77	Bolton Rd. W4.	E 6
86	Bolton St.	B 5
85	Boltons, The.	G 3
87	Bolwell St.	F 10
76	Bomore Rd.	K 2
73	Bond St.	K 2
87	Bondway	H 9
80	Bonfield Way	G 4
79	Bonham Rd.	H 10
84	Bonhill St.	E 3
75	Bonner Rd.	G 16
75	Bonner St.	G 16
87	Bonnington Sq.	H 9
80	Boone St.	G 5
80	Boord St.	B 5
84	Boot St.	D 3
75	Boothby Rd.	B 9
67	Borders La.	A 11
76	Boreham Rd.	K 6
66	Borehamwood	A 3
79	Borland Rd.	G 16
73	Borne Way	F 5
72	Borough Green	H 5
88	Borough High St.	C 2
87	Borough Rd.	D 12
87	Borrett Rd.	G 13
76	Borthwick Rd.	D 5
74	Boscastle Rd.	C 8
80	Boscobel St.	E 5
77	Boscombe Rd.	A 8
88	Boss St.	C 2
67	Bostall Hill Rd.	G 12
77	Boston Manor Pk.	C 1
77	Boston Manor Rd.	C 1
66	Boston Manor Sta.	G 1
77	Boston Pk. Rd.	C 2
82	Boston Pl.	E 2
76	Boston Rd. E17.	A 3
66	Boston Rd. W7.	G 1
83	Boswell St.	F 9
80	Bosworth Rd.	A 1
86	Botanic Gdns.	H 2
76	Botha Rd.	J 7
76	Botley Rd.	H 3
66	Botleys	E 1
84	Botolph La.	J 3
76	Botolph Rd.	H 3
66	Bounces Rd.	B 8
78	Boundaries Rd.	K 7
76	Boundary Rd. E13.	G 8
76	Boundary Rd. E17.	A 2
74	Boundary Rd. NW8	F 5
71	Boundary Rd. Fickleshole	G 9
87	Boundary Row	C 12
84	Boundary St.	D 5
80	Boundfield Rd.	K 5
66	Bounds Green Rd.	C 6
76	Bourdon St.	J 5
82	Bourlet Cl.	F 6
66	Bourne, The.	B 6
66	Bourne Hill.	B 6
86	Bourne St.	F 3
81	Bourne Ter.	F 2 & F 3
68	Bournebridge La.	A 2
79	Bournemouth Rd.	F 15
80	Bourneville Rd.	J 3
80	Bousfield Rd.	F 1
75	Bouverie Rd.	B 14
83	Bouverie St.	H 11
80	Boveney Rd.	J 1
80	Bovill Rd.	J 1
73	Bovingdon Av.	E 5
75	Bow	G 2
76	Bow Common La.	H 2
84	Bow La.	H 2
76	Bow Rd.	H 2
83	Bow St.	H 9
76	Bowdon Rd.	A 3
80	Bowen Dri.	L 14
73	Bowes Rd.	K 7
66	Bowes Park Sta.	C 6
80	Bowland Rd.	G 9
88	Bowles Rd.	H 6
83	Bowling Green La.	E 11
87	Bowling Green St.	H 11
84	Bowling Green Walk	D 3
76	Bowman La.	K 6
80	Bowness Rd.	J 4
73	Bowrons Av.	F 3
79	Bowyer St.	D 12
73	Boycroft Av.	A 6
84	Boyd St.	H 6
87	Boyfield St.	C 12
73	Boyle St.	J 5
80	Boyne Rd.	F 4
79	Brabourn Gro.	F 16
74	Bracken Av.	H 8
77	Brackenbury Rd.	B 9
84	Brackley St.	F 1
84	Bracknell Gdns.	D 4
87	Brad St.	B 11
81	Braden St.	E 2
80	Bradfield Rd.	A 7
80	Bradgate Rd.	H 3
79	Brading Rd.	J 11
73	Bradley Gdns.	K 1
76	Bradwell St.	H 1
75	Brady St.	H 16
73	Braemar Av. NW10	C 6
78	Braemar Av. SW19	K 4
73	Braemar Av. Wem.	F 3
76	Braemar Rd. E13	H 6
74	Braemar Rd. Brent.	D 3
87	Braganza St.	G 12
84	Braham St.	G 5
84	Braidwood Rd.	J 4
88	Braidwood St.	B 4
79	Brailsford Rd.	H 11
78	Braintree St.	H 16
79	Bramah Rd.	E 11
78	Bramber Rd.	D 3
84	Bramble La.	E 4
79	Bramcote Gro.	C 16
78	Bramcote Rd.	G 1
84	Bramdean Cres.	K 6
85	Bramerton St.	H 6
78	Bramfield Rd.	H 7
78	Bramford Rd.	D 3
82	Bramham Gdns.	F 2
80	Bramhope La.	D 7
77	Bramley Rd. W5.	B 2
74	Bramley Rd. W10.	K 2
66	Bramley Rd. Southgate	A 6
73	Brampton Gro.	B 4
71	Brampton Rd.	A 12
74	Bramshill Gdns.	C 8
73	Bramshill Rd.	G 7
78	Bramston Rd.	G 8
78	Bramwell St.	F 9
74	Branch Hill	C 5
74	Branch Rd.	A 3
80	Brand St.	E 4
75	Brandon Rd.	E 10
88	Brandon St.	F 2
80	Brandram Rd.	G 5
72	Brands Hatch	F 4
79	Branksome Rd.	G 10
79	Brantwood Rd.	G 12
73	Brassie Av.	J 7
71	Brasted Hill.	H 12
71	Brasted La.	H 12
78	Brathway Rd.	J 4
74	Bravington Rd.	H 3
80	Braxfield Rd.	G 2
86	Bray Pl.	F 2
85	Brechin Pl.	F 4
75	Brecknock Rd.	D 9
74	Bredgar Rd.	A 9
78	Breer St.	F 4
79	Brenchley Gdns.	H 16
73	Brenda Rd.	K 7
82	Brendon St.	G 1
73	Brent Cres.	G 4
74	Brent Sta.	A 2
66	Brent St.	C 4
73	Brent Way.	E 5
73	Brentfield Rd.	E 9
77	Brentford	C 3
77	Brentford Cen, Sta.	D 2
73	Brentham Halt Rd.	H 3
73	Brentham Way.	H 2
75	Brenthouse Rd.	E 16
73	Brenthurst Rd.	E 7
73	Brentmead Gdns.	G 4
73	Brentvale Av.	G 4
77	Brentwick Gdns.	C 3
68	Brentwood	B 6
68	Brentwood & Warley Sta.	B 5
68	Brentwood By-Pass	B 5
68	Brentwood Rd.	D 3
86	Bressenden Pl.	D 5
69	Bretlands	E 2
82	Brewer St.	H 7
75	Brewery Rd.	E 10
74	Brewster Gdns.	J 1
76	Brewster Rd.	B 1
80	Briant St.	E 1
77	Briar Wk.	G 9
74	Briardale Gdns.	C 4
79	Briarwood Rd.	G 9
84	Brick La.	E 5
86	Brick St.	B 4
76	Brickfield Rd.	H 3
83	Bride La.	H 12
75	Bride St.	E 11
83	Bridewell Pl.	H 12
82	Bridford Mews.	F 5
76	Bridge Rd. E15.	F 5
76	Bridge Rd. E17.	A 2
73	Bridge Rd. NW10.	E 7
69	Bridge Rd. Chertsey	E 3
70	Bridge Rd. Ches.	F 2
69	Bridge Rd. Esh.	D 6
73	Bridge Rd. Wem.	C 5
69	Bridge St. Walton.	E 4
73	Bridge Way.	F 3
87	Bridgefoot	G 9
76	Bridgeland Rd.	K 7
81	Bridgeman St.	C 6
78	Bridgend Rd.	G 5
73	Bridgewater Rd.	F 2
82	Bridgeway St.	C 7
82	Bridle La.	H 6
65	Bridle Rd.	D 5
84	Bridport Pl.	B 3
67	Bridport Rd.	B 7
81	Bridstow Pl.	G 1
76	Brierley Rd.	D 5
76	Bright St.	J 4
80	Brightfield Rd.	G 6
80	Brightling Rd.	H 2
75	Brighton Rd. N16.	D 14
70	Brighton Rd. Cro.	G 6
70	Brighton Rd. Sut.	F 4
79	Brighton Ter.	G 11
80	Brightside Rd.	H 5
70	Brigstock Rd.	D 6
67	Brimsdown Sta.	A 8
76	Brisbane Rd.	C 3
79	Brisbane St.	E 13
83	Briset St.	F 12
78	Bristol Gdns. SW15	J 1
81	Bristol Gdns. W9.	F 3
81	Bristol Mews.	E 3
75	Britannia Row.	F 12
83	Britannia St.	C 9
76	Britannia Wk.	C 2
83	British Mus.	F 8
76	British St.	H 2
79	Britten St.	G 6
83	Britton St.	F 12
79	Brixton Hill.	J 10
76	Brixton Rd. SW2.	F 11
87	Brixton Rd. SW9.	J 11
79	Brixton Sta.	G 11
79	Brixton Water La.	H 11
80	Broadfield Rd.	J 5
67	Broad La. N15.	C 8
72	Broad La. Dartford	C 2
67	Broad Mead Rd.	C 10
87	Broad Sanctuary.	D 8
84	Broad St. EC.	F 3
80	Broad Way.	E 3
65	Broadcasting Ho.	G 5
78	Broadhinton Rd.	F 8
74	Broadhurst Gdns.	E 4
79	Broadlands Av.	K 10
74	Broadlands Rd.	A 7
81	Broadley St.	F 6
82	Broadley Ter.	E 1
80	Broadmead	L 3
82	Broadstone Pl.	G 3
76	Broadway E15.	E 5
80	Broadway, SW1.	D 7
73	Broadway, W5.	K 3
78	Broadway, W6.	C 1
71	Broadway, Bexleyheath	B 12
73	Broadway, The, NW 9	A 8
70	Broadway, The, SW19	C 4
65	Broadway, The, S'hall	G 5
75	Broadway Mkt.	F 15
82	Broadwick St.	H 6
76	Brock Rd.	J 7
88	Brockham St.	D 2
80	Brocklebank Rd.	J 5
80	Brocklehurst St.	D 1
80	Brockley	G 2
80	Brockill Cres.	G 1
80	Brockley Gro.	H 2
66	Brockley Hill.	B 2
80	Brockley Pk.	J 1
80	Brockley Rise.	J 1
80	Brockley Rd.	G 2
80	Brockley Sta.	F 2
80	Brockley View.	J 2
80	Brockley Way.	H 1
79	Brockwell Pk.	H 12
80	Brockwell Pk. Gdns.	J 12
78	Brodrick Rd.	K 6
75	Broke Rd.	F 15
84	Broken Wharf.	H 1
79	Brokesley St.	H 2
79	Bromar Rd.	F 14
79	Bromells Rd.	G 9
83	Bromfield St.	B 11
79	Bromfelde Rd.	F 10
71	Bromley	D 9
76	Bromley	H 3
71	Bromley Comm.	E 10
76	Bromley High St.	G 3
71	Bromley Hill.	C 2
76	Bromley Nth. Sta.	D 9
76	Bromley Rd. E10.	A 3
76	Bromley Rd. SE6.	C 9
71	Bromley Rd. Bec.	D 9
71	Bromley Rd. Chisl.	D 11
71	Bromley Sth. Sta.	D 9
76	Bromley St.	J 1
78	Brompton	B 7

MAP
85 Brompton Hosp...F 5
85 Brompton Oratory. E 6
86 Brompton Pl.....D 2
85 Brompton Rd.....D 6
85 Brompton Sq.....D 6
74 Bromwich Av.....C 8
73 Bromyard Av.....K 7
74 Brondesbury......E 2
74 Brondesbury Pk...F 2
74 Brondesbury Pk. Sta.
　F 2
74 Brondesbury Rd...G 3
74 Brondesbury Sta....E 2
74 Brondesbury Villas.G 3
78 Bronsart Rd......E 2
88 Bronti Cl.......G 2
73 Brook Av......C 4
80 Brook Dale......H 3
87 Brook Dri......E 12
71 Brook Fever Hosp.
　A 10
78 Brook Green......B 2
77 Brook La......C 2
81 Brook Mews Nth..H 4
73 Brook Rd......C 8
77 Brook Rd.,Sth.....D 3
82 Brook St. W1.....H 4
81 Brook St. W2.....H 5
68 Brook St. Brent..B 4
80 Brook Way.......G 6
80 Brookbank Rd....F 3
75 Brooke Rd.....C 15
83 Brooke St......F 11
80 Brookehowse Rd...K 3
74 Brookfield Pk....C 8
76 Brookfield Rd. E9. E 2
77 Brookfield Rd. W4.B 6
78 Brookhouse Rd....F 4
73 Brooklands Dri....G 2
80 Brooklands L.C.C.
　Estate.......F 7
80 Brooklands Pk....F 6
69 Brooklands Rd....G 3
80 Brookmill Rd......E 3
82 Brook's Mews.....H 5
75 Brooksby St......F 11
76 Brooksby's Wk...D 1
66 Brookshill......B 1
74 Brookside Rd.....A 3
78 Brookwood Rd...G 3
70 Broom Rd.......C 1
77 Broomfield Rd....E 4
76 Broomfield St......J 3
78 Broomhill Rd....H 4
72 Broomsleigh.....H 2
78 Broomwood Rd...H 7
79 Brough Rd......E 10
75 Brougham Rd...F 15
78 Broughton Rd. SW6
　E 4
73 Broughton Rd. W13
　K 1
78 Broughton St......F 8
77 Brouncker Rd....A 5
82 Brown St......G 2
82 Brown Hart Gdns..H 4
80 Brownhill Rd......J 4
76 Browning Rd......B 6
88 Browning St......F 2
75 Brownlow Rd. E8. F 15
73 Brownlow Rd. NW10
　F 7
83 Brownlow St....F 10
75 Brownswood Rd..C 12
69 Brox.........F 2
78 Broxash Rd......H 7
68 Broxhill.........B 2
79 Broxholm Rd....L 11
67 Bruce Gro. Sta.....C 7
76 Bruce Rd. E3.....H 3
37 Bruce Rd. NW10..F 6
84 Brune St.........F 5
81 Brunel Estate...F 1
79 Brunel Rd. SE16..A 16
73 Brunel Rd. W3....J 7
73 Brunner Rd......H 2
88 Brunswick Ct.....C 4
73 Brunswick Gdns. W5
　H 3
85 Brunswick Gdns. W8
　B 2
66 Brunswick Pk. N11.B 5
79 Brunswick Pk. SE5
　E 13
84 Brunswick Pl......D 3
76 Brunswick Rd. E14. J 4
73 Brunswick Rd. W5.H 3
83 Brunswick Sq.....E 9
82 Bruton La......J 5
82 Bruton Pl......J 5
82 Bruton St......J 5

74 Bryan Av........F 1
82 Bryanston Mews E. G 2
82 Bryanston Mews W.
　G 2
82 Bryanston Pl.....G 2
82 Bryanston Sq.....G 2
82 Bryanston St......H 3
68 Bryant Av........C 3
75 Bryantwood Rd...D 11
88 Brymer Rd......H 5
74 Brynmaer Rd......E 7
73 Bryony Rd......K 8
79 Buchan Rd......F 16
74 Buchanan Gdns...G 1
84 Buckfast St......D 6
78 Buckhold Rd......H 4
67 Buckhurst Hill....B 10
71 Buckhurst Rd...H 11
86 Buckingham Gate .D 6
86 Buckingham Pal...C 5
86 Buckingham Pal.
　Gdns...........C 5
86 Buckingham Pal. Rd.
　E 5
86 Buckingham Pl....D 6
76 Buckingham Rd. E10
　C 3
76 Buckingham Rd. E15
　D 6
75 Buckingham Rd. N1
　E 14
73 Buckingham Rd.
　NW10........G 8
77 Buckingham Rd. Rich.
　K 2
87 Buckingham St....A 9
74 Buckland Cres.....E 6
76 Buckland Rd......B 4
84 Buckland St......C 3
84 Buckle St......G 6
84 Bucklersbury......H 2
74 Buckley Rd......F 3
83 Bucknall St......G 8
76 Buckthorne Rd....H 1
71 Bug Hill........H 8
87 Bulinga St......F 8
68 Bull La........D 2
76 Bull Rd........G 6
82 Bulstrode St......G 4
76 Bulwer Rd......B 4
84 Bunhill Fields....E 2
84 Bunhill Row......E 2
72 Bunkers Hill La...F 5
79 Burbage Rd......H 13
76 Burcham St......J 4
67 Burchell Rd. E10. B 3
79 Burchell Rd. SE15
　E 16
78 Burcote Rd......J 6
75 Burder Rd......E 14
76 Burdett Rd......H 2
87 Burdett St......D 11
80 Burford Rd. SE6..K 2
77 Burford Rd. Brent. C 3
78 Burgess Av......A 6
74 Burgess Hill......D 3
76 Burgess Rd......D 5
76 Burgess St......J 2
70 Burgh Heath.....H 4
70 Burgh Heath Rd...G 3
83 Burgh St......B 13
74 Burghley Rd......D 8
75 Burgoyne Rd....A 12
76 Burhill G.C......F 4
76 Burke Rd......J 6
71 Burling La......H 11
76 Burlington Arcade. J 6
77 Burlington Av....E 4
82 Burlington Gdns. W1
　J 6
77 Burlington Gdns. W4
　C 6
86 Burlington Ho....A 6
77 Burlington La....D 6
77 Burlington Rd....C 5
82 Burlington St......J 6
83 Burleigh St......H 9
75 Burma Rd......D 13
76 Burnaby Gdns....D 5
78 Burnaby St......E 5
79 Burnbury Rd......J 9
81 Burne St......F 6
87 Burnett St......G 9
80 Burney St......D 4
78 Burnfoot Av......E 3
73 Burnley Rd......D 8
73 Burns Rd. NW10..F 7
78 Burns Rd. SW11...H 7
73 Burns Rd. Wem....G 3
86 Burnsall St......G 1
73 Burnside Rd......F 2

80 Burnt Ash Hill....J 7
71 Burnt Ash La.....C 9
80 Burnt Ash Rd.....H 6
66 Burnt Oak......C 3
78 Burnthwaite Rd...E 3
78 Burntwood La. SW17
　K 5
71 Burntwood La.
　Coulsdon.......H 7
78 Burr Rd........J 4
76 Burrard Rd. E16...J 7
74 Burrard Rd. NW3.D 4
87 Burrell St......B 12
74 Burrows Rd......G 1
78 Burstock Rd......G 2
86 Burton Ct......G 3
88 Burton Gro......G 3
79 Burton Rd......E 11
83 Burton St......D 8
69 Burtons Rd......C 6
76 Burwell Rd......B 1
81 Burwood Pl......G 6
69 Burwood Rd......F 4
84 Bury Ct........G 4
83 Bury Pl........G 8
84 Bury St. EC3......G 4
67 Bury St. N9......A 7
86 Bury St. SW1.....B 6
79 Bury St. SE15....D 16
65 Bury St. Ruislip..D 4
85 Bury Wk........F 6
75 Busby Pl......E 9
84 Busby St......E 6
73 Bush Gro......A 6
67 Bush Hill......A 7
67 Bush Hill G.C.....A 7
67 Bush Hill Park
　Station......A 7
83 Bush Ho........H 10
84 Bush La........H 2
76 Bush Rd. E11.....B 6
80 Bush Rd. SE8.....C 1
77 Bush Rd. Rich....D 4
76 Bush Wood......B 6
76 Bushberry Rd......E 2
65 Bushey.........
65 Bushey & Oxhey Sta.
　A 5
65 Bushey Hall G.C...A 5
66 Bushey Heath....A 1
79 Bushey Hill Rd...E 14
76 Bushey Rd. E13...G 8
70 Bushey Rd. SW20.D 3
84 Bushfield St......F 4
67 Bushill Pk......A 7
78 Bushnell Rd......K 8
76 Bushwood......B 6
77 Bushwood Rd....D 4
84 Busk St......B 6
76 Butcher Row.....K 1
76 Butcher's Rd.....J 7
78 Bute Gdns......C 2
85 Bute St......F 5
78 Buttermere Dri...H 3
84 Buttesland St.....D 3
72 Button St......D 2
77 Butts, The......D 2
68 Butts La......D 3
73 Buxton Gdns.....K 5
71 Buxton La......H 7
76 Buxton Rd......D 5
84 Buxton St......E 6
78 Byam St......F 5
78 Byam St......F 5
69 Byfleet......G 3
69 Byfleet Rd......G 4
69 Byfleet & New Haw
　Sta......F 3
76 Bygrove St......J 3
82 Byng Pl......E 7
80 Byng St......A 3
78 Byrne Rd......K 8
76 Byron Rd. E10....B 3
73 Byron Rd. Wem...C 2
76 Byron St......J 2
84 Byward St......J 4
86 Bywater St......G 2
81 Cabbell St......G 6
84 Cable St......H 6
78 Cabul Rd......H 6
71 Cackets La......G 11
88 Cadbury Rd......E 6
74 Caddington Rd....B 3
78 Cader Rd......H 5
80 Cadet St......C 5
88 Cadiz St......G 2
86 Cadogan Gdns....E 3
86 Cadogan Gate....E 3
86 Cadogan La......E 3
86 Cadogan Pl......E 3
86 Cadogan Sq......E 2
86 Cadogan St......F 2

76 Cadogan Ter......E 2
84 Caesar St......C 4
80 Cahir St......C 3
77 Cairn Av......A 2
73 Cairnfield Av......C 7
78 Cairns Rd......G 6
76 Caistor Pk. Rd....F 6
78 Caistor Rd......J 8
78 Caithness Rd......B 2
75 Calabria St......E 12
78 Calais St......E 12
78 Calbourne Rd.....J 7
73 Caldbury Av......E 5
76 Caldecot Rd......F 13
79 Caldervale Rd....H 9
79 Caldew St......J 2
79 Caldwell St......E 11
85 Cale St......F 6
83 Caledonia St......C 9
83 Caledonian Rd. N1 B 9
75 Caledonian Rd. Sta.
　E 10
75 Caledonian Rd. &
　Barnsbury Sta..F 11
80 Callander Rd......K 4
74 Callicott Rd......F 3
74 Callow St......H 4
83 Calmington Rd....H 4
83 Calshot St......B 9
83 Calthorpe St......E 10
79 Calton Av......H 14
75 Calverley Gro....B 9
84 Calvert Av......D 4
84 Calvert Rd......C 6
84 Calvin St......E 5
78 Cambalt Rd......G 2
79 Camberwell......E 13
79 Camberwell Ch. St.
　E 13
79 Camberwell Grn...E 13
79 Camberwell Gro. E 13
87 Camberwell New Rd.
　J 11
88 Camberwell Rd....J 2
79 Camberwell Sta. Rd.
　E 12
79 Cambria Rd......F 12
79 Cambray Rd......J 9
77 Cambrian Rd......H 4
74 Cambridge Av......G 4
83 Cambridge Circus.H 8
74 Cambridge Gdns...J 2
75 Cambridge Heath Rd.
　H 16
75 Cambridge Heath Sta.
　G 16
76 Cambridge Pk. E11.A 6
70 Cambridge Pk. Twick.
　B 1
77 Cambridge Pk. Twick.
　H 2
81 Cambridge Pl. NW6
　C 1
85 Cambridge Pl. W8 .D 3
76 Cambridge Rd. E11
　A 6
76 Cambridge Rd. E17
　A 2
81 Cambridge Rd. NW6
　C 1
80 Cambridge Rd. SE12
　H 6
78 Cambridge Rd. SW11
　E 7
70 Cambridge Rd. K'gst.
　D 2
77 Cambridge Rd. Twick.
　H 2
81 Cambridge Sq......G 6
86 Cambridge St......F 5
76 Cambus Rd......J 7
82 Camden High St...B 6
75 Camden Mews....E 9
75 Camden Pk. Rd...E 9
75 Camden Rd......E 9
75 Camden Rd. Sta...E 9
82 Camden Sq......E 9
82 Camden St......B 6
82 Camden Town......E 9
74 Camden Town Sta..F 8
83 Camden Wk......B 12
76 Camera Pl......H 4
84 Camlet St......D 5
83 Camley St......B 8
79 Camomile St......G 4
79 Camoulla St......C 15
78 Campana Rd......E 4
76 Campbell Rd. E3..H 3

75 Campbell Rd. N16
　E 14
81 Campbell St......E 4
75 Campdale Rd......C 9
73 Campden Cres....C 2
85 Campden Gro.....C 1
76 Campden Hill....A 3
85 Campden Hill Rd..C 1
85 Campden St......B 1
78 Campion Rd......G 1
80 Camplin St......D 1
80 Campshill Rd....H 4
66 Camrose Av......C 2
73 Canada Cres......J 5
73 Canada Rd......J 5
73 Canada Way......K 9
80 Canadian Av......J 3
76 Canal Rd......H 2
88 Canal St......H 3
79 Cancell Rd......E 11
78 Candahar Rd......F 6
70 Cane Hill Hosp...H 5
74 Canfield Gdns....F 5
77 Canham Rd......A 7
76 Cann Hall......C 5
76 Cann Hall Rd......D 5
85 Canning Pl......D 3
76 Canning Rd. E15..G 5
75 Canning Rd. N5..C 12
76 Canning Town......J 7
76 Canning Town Sta..J 5
79 Canobie Rd......J 16
79 Canon St......A 1
79 Canonbie Rd......H 16
75 Canonbury......E 12
75 Canonbury Gro...F 12
75 Canonbury Pk. Nth.
　E 12
75 Canonbury Pk. Sth.
　E 12
75 Canonbury Pl......E 12
75 Canonbury Rd......E 12
75 Canonbury Sq.....E 12
75 Canonbury Sta....E 13
75 Canonbury Villas. F 12
66 Canons Pk......B 2
75 Canrobert St......G 15
79 Canterbury Cres...F 11
76 Canterbury Rd. E10
　A 4
74 Canterbury Rd. NW6
　G 4
75 Cantlowes Rd.....E 9
76 Canton St......K 3
76 Cantrell Rd......H 2
76 Capel Rd......D 7
81 Capland St......E 5
82 Capper St......E 6
76 Capworth St......B 3
77 Carberry Rd......A 4
82 Carburton St......F 5
79 Carden Rd......G 16
76 Cardigan Rd. E3..G 2
81 Cardigan Rd. NW6 D 1
77 Cardigan Rd.
　Richmond......H 3
82 Cardington St......D 6
75 Cardozo Rd......D 10
77 Cardross St......B 9
77 Carew Rd......A 2
84 Carey La......G 1
83 Carey St......G 10
78 Cargill Rd......J 5
80 Carholme Rd......K 7
75 Carleton Rd......D 9
84 Carlisle Av. EC3...H 5
73 Carlisle Av. W3...J 7
87 Carlisle La......D 10
81 Carlisle Mews....F 5
86 Carlisle Pl......E 6
76 Carlisle Rd. E10...B 3
74 Carlisle Rd. NW6..F 3
82 Carlisle St......G 7
82 Carlos Pl......J 4
82 Carlow St......B 6
73 Carlton Av. E......B 3
73 Carlton Av. W......C 2
78 Carlton Dri......H 2
86 Carlton Gdns. SW1 B 7
73 Carlton Gdns. W5. K 2
79 Carlton Gro......E 16
81 Carlton Hill......B 3

87 Carlton Ho. Ter.....B 7
77 Carlton Rd. SW14.G 5
73 Carlton Rd. W5...K 2
82 Carlton Th......J 7
81 Carlton Vale......C 1
74 Carltoun Rd......E 8
77 Carlyle Rd......C 2
85 Carlyle Sq......G 5
85 Carlyle's Ho......H 6
73 Carlyon Rd......G 3
83 Carmelite St......H 11
78 Carminia Rd......K 8
82 Carnaby St......H 6
74 Carnarvon Rd......E 6
83 Carnegie St......B 10
78 Carnwath Rd......F 4
81 Caroline Pl......J 2
86 Caroline Ter......F 3
65 Carpenters Pk.....B 5
84 Carpenters Rd.....E 3
76 Carr St......J 2
86 Carriage Rd., The...J 2
77 Carrington Rd.....G 4
87 Carroun Rd......J 10
70 Carshalton......E 5
70 Carshalton Beeches
　Sta......F 5
70 Carshalton Ho.....F 5
70 Carshalton on the Hill
　F 5
70 Carshalton Rd.
　W'dmansterne...G 5
72 Carslake Rd......H 1
76 Carson Rd. E16...J 7
79 Carson Rd. SE21.K 13
83 Carter La......H 11
88 Carter Pl......G 1
87 Carter St......G 13
86 Carteret St......D 7
77 Carthew Rd......B 9
83 Carthusian St.....F 13
83 Carting La......J 9
82 Carton St......G 3
83 Cartwright Gdns..D 8
84 Cartwright St......J 6
79 Carver Rd......H 12
77 Carville Cres......C 3
76 Cary Rd......D 5
80 Casella Rd......E 1
75 Carysfort Rd......D 13
73 Cashmir Rd......C 6
79 Casino Av......G 13
84 Casket St......D 5
80 Casslee Rd......J 2
84 Casson St......F 6
81 Castellain Rd......E 3
78 Castello Av......H 1
77 Castelnau......E 8
80 Castillon Rd......K 5
66 Castle Bar Pk. Sta..F 1
86 Castle La......D 6
74 Castle Rd......E 8
73 Castlebar Hill.....J 2
73 Castlebar Mews...J 2
73 Castlebar Pk......J 2
73 Castlebar Rd......J 2
74 Castlehaven Rd....E 8
73 Castleton Av......D 3
78 Castletown Rd.....C 3
80 Castlewood Rd....A 15
66 Cat Hill........A 5
80 Caterham Rd......F 4
83 Catesby St......F 3
80 Catford........J 4
80 Catford Bri. Sta...J 3
80 Catford Bdy......J 3
80 Catford Hill......K 2
80 Catford Rd......J 3
80 Cathall Rd......C 5
74 Cathcart Hill......A 9
85 Cathcart Rd......H 3
85 Catherine Pl......D 6
83 Catherine St......H 9
78 Cathles Rd......H 8
78 Cathnor Rd......A 8
79 Catlin St......C 15
79 Cato Rd......G 10
84 Cato St......G 1
69 Catos Hill......E 6
79 Caulfield Rd......E 16
78 Causeway, The...G 4
87 Causton St......F 7
79 Cautley Av......H 9
85 Cavaye Pl......G 4
76 Cave Rd......G 7

MAP

83 Cave St.........B 10
75 Cavell St.........J 16
81 Cavendish Av.....C 5
81 Cavendish Cl.....C 5
76 Cavendish Dri.....B 4
82 Cavendish Pl.....G 5
74 Cavendish Rd. NW6
               F 3
78 Cavendish Rd. SW12
               J 8
77 Cavendish Rd. W4.E 6
82 Cavendish Sq.....G 5
84 Cavendish St.....C 2
75 Caversham Rd.....E 9
86 Caversham St.....H 2
86 Caxton St.........D 7
84 Cayton St.........D 2
75 Cazenove Rd.....B 15
73 Cecil Av.........E 2
76 Cecil Rd. E11.....C 5
76 Cecil Rd. E13.....F 7
73 Cecil Rd. NW10...G 7
73 Cecil Rd. W3.....J 6
75 Cecile Pk.........A 10
75 Cecilia Rd.......D 15
77 Cedar Gro.........B 3
74 Cedar Rd.........D 2
73 Cedar Way.......K 7
80 Cedarhurst Rd....H 8
76 Cedars Rd. E15...E 5
78 Cedars Rd. SW4...G 8
77 Cedars Rd. W4...D 6
76 Cemetery Rd.....D 6
87 Cenotaph.........C 8
87 Centaur St. .....D 10
77 Central Acton Pk. A 6
83 Central Criminal Ct.
              G 12
71 Central Hill.......C 7
73 Cen. Middx. Hosp. G 5
70 Central Rd.......D 4
83 Central St.......D 13
76 Centre Rd.........C 7
75 Cephas Av.......H 16
75 Cephas St.......H 16
79 Cerise Rd.........E 15
78 Ceylon Rd.........B 2
67 Chadwell Heath .D 12
67 Chadwell Hth. La.D 12
83 Chadwell St.......C 11
76 Chadwick Rd. E11.A 5
79 Chadwick Rd. SE15
              F 14
86 Chadwick St.....E 7
76 Chadwin Rd.......J 7
82 Chagford St.......E 2
74 Chalcot Cres.....F 7
74 Chalcot Rd.......F 7
80 Chalcroft Rd.....H 5
78 Chaldon Rd.......D 3
79 Chale Rd.........H 10
73 Chalfont Av.......E 5
65 Chalfont Common. B 1
65 Chalfont St. Peter..C 1
74 Chalk Farm Rd....F 8
74 Chalk Farm Sta...F 7
71 Chalky Hill.......G 11
77 Challis Rd.........C 2
78 Chalmers St.......F 9
80 Chalsey Rd.......G 2
82 Chalton St.......C 7
84 Chamber St.......H 6
74 Chamberlayne Rd..F 1
74 Chambers La.......F 1
88 Chambers St.......C 6
84 Chambord St.....D 5
79 Champion Hill....F 13
79 Champion Pk.....F 13
87 Chancel St.......B 12
79 Chancellor Gro...K 13
78 Chancellors Rd....C 1
83 Chancery La.....G 10
77 Chandos Av.......B 2
83 Chandos Pl.......J 8
76 Chandos Rd. E15.D 5
74 Chandos Rd. NW2.E 1
73 Chandos Rd.NW10 H 7
82 Chandos St.......G 5
76 Chant St.........F 5
83 Chantry St.......B 13
88 Chapel Ct.........C 2
67 Chapel End.......C 9
80 Chapel House St...C 3
65 Chapel La.........F 4
81 Chapel Side.......J 2
81 Chapel St. NW1...F 6
86 Chapel St. SW1...D 4
79 Clapham Rd.......E 8
73 Chaplin Rd. NW2.E 8
73 Chaplin Rd. Wem..E 2
75 Chapman St.....K 16

73 Chapter Rd. NW2. E 8
87 Chapter Rd. SE17.G 13
86 Chapter St.........F 7
75 Chardmore Rd.. .B 15
76 Chargeable La.....H 6
76 Chargeable St.....H 6
78 Charing Cross Hosp.
              C 2
83 Charing Cross Rd..H 8
87 Charing Cross Sta.. A 8
81 Charlbert St.......B 6
73 Charlbury Gro.....J 2
81 Charles La.........E 8
86 Charles II St.......A 7
84 Charles Sq.........D 3
77 Charles St. SW13..F 7
86 Charles St. W1....B 4
88 Charleston St.......F 2
78 Charleville Rd....C 3
82 Charlotte Mews...F 6
84 Charlotte Rd.......D 4
82 Charlotte St.......F 6
83 Charlotte Ter.....B 10
80 Charlton.........D 8
80 Charlton Ch. La...C 8
80 Charlton Dene....D 8
69 Charlton La.......D 4
83 Charlton Pl.......B 12
73 Charlton Rd. NW10
              F 7
80 Charlton Rd. SE3 &
    SE7.........D 7
69 Charlton Rd.
    Shepperton.....D 4
73 Charlton Rd. Wem.B 4
80 Charlton Sta......C 8
80 Charlton Way.....E 6
86 Charlwood Pl......F 6
78 Charlwood Rd.....G 2
86 Charlwood St.....G 6
71 Charmwood La...F 12
82 Charrington St...B 7
84 Chart St.........D 3
83 Charterhouse.....F 13
73 Charterhouse Av...D 2
83 Charterhouse Sq. F 12
83 Charterhouse St...F 12
75 Charteris Rd. N4. B 11
74 Charteris Rd. NW6 F 3
78 Chartfield Av.....H 1
73 Chartley Av.......C 7
78 Chase, The.......G 8
66 Chase Rd. N14....A 6
73 Chase Rd. NW10..H 6
66 Chase Side........A 6
75 Chatham Pl......E 16
78 Chatham Rd.......H 7
88 Chatham St.......E 3
79 Chantrey Rd......F 11
73 Chatsworth Gdns..K 5
76 Chatsworth Rd. E5.D 1
74 Chatsworth Rd. NW2
              E 2
77 Chatsworth Rd. W4
              D 6
73 Chatsworth Rd. W5
              H 4
79 Chatsworth Way .K 12
75 Chatterton Rd....C 12
78 Chatto Rd.........H 7
77 Chaucer Av.......F 5
76 Chaucer Rd. E7...E 7
79 Chaucer Rd. SE24 H 12
73 Chaucer Rd. W3..L 6
70 Cheam...........F 4
70 Cheam Rd.........F 3
70 Cheam Sta.........F 4
84 Cheapside........H 2
76 Chelmer Rd.......D 1
76 Chelmsford Rd.E11 B 5
74 Chelmsford Sq....F 1
78 Chelmsford St....D 2
78 Chelsea.........D 6
86 Chelsea Bri.......H 4
86 Chelsea Bri. Rd...G 4
86 Chelsea Embankment
              H 3
85 Chelsea Manor Gdns.
              G 6
86 Chelsea Manor St..H 1
85 Chelsea Manor St..G 6
85 Chelsea Pk. Gdns..H 5
85 Chelsea Sq.........G 5
71 Chelsfield Hill ...F 12
72 Chelsfield La. Orp. F 1
71 Chelsfield La. Orp.
              E 12
71 Chelsfield Rd....E 12
71 Chelsfield Sta....F 12
71 Chelsfield Village F 12
71 Chelsham.........H 8

71 Chelsham Court Rd.
              H 9
79 Chelsham Rd.....F 10
76 Cheltenham Rd. E10
              A 4
79 Cheltenham Rd. SE15
              G 16
86 Cheltenham Ter....F 2
78 Chelverton Rd.....G 2
85 Chelwood Gdns...F 5
83 Cheney Rd.........C 8
76 Cheneys Rd.......C 5
82 Chenies Mews.....E 7
82 Chenies St.........F 7
85 Cheniston Gdns....D 2
86 Chepstow Cres....H 1
81 Chepstow Pl......H 1
81 Chepstow Rd......G 1
81 Chepstow Villas..H 1
84 Chequer St........E 2
84 Cherbury St.......C 3
80 Cheriton Sq........K 8
79 Cherry Gdns.....A 15
65 Cherry La.........G 4
69 Chertsey.........E 2
69 Chertsey G.C.....D 2
69 Chertsey La.......D 2
69 Chertsey Rd. Byfleet
              G 3
69 Chertsey Rd. Feltham
              C 4
69 Chertsey Rd.
    Shepperton.....E 3
86 Chesham Mews...D 3
86 Chesham Pl.......D 3
73 Chesham St. NW10
              D 6
86 Chesham St. SW1..E 3
84 Cheshire St.......E 6
78 Chesilton Rd.......E 3
70 Chessington.......F 2
78 Chipstead St......E 4
70 Chessington Nth. Sta.
              F 2
70 Chessington Rd. Eps.
              G 2
70 Chessington Rd. Ewell
              F 2
70 Chessington Sth. Sta.
              F 2
78 Chesson Rd.......D 3
81 Chest Clinic......G 2
77 Chester Av.........H 4
77 Chester Cl.........D 4
82 Chester Gate......D 5
86 Chester Mews.....D 4
86 Chester Pl.........C 5
76 Chester Rd. E11...A 7
76 Chester Rd. E16...H 5
74 Chester Rd. N19..C 8
82 Chester Rd. NW1.D 4
86 Chester Row.......F 4
86 Chester Sq.........E 4
86 Chester St.........D 4
82 Chester Ter.......D 5
82 Chester Ter. Mews.D 5
87 Chester Way......F 11
74 Chesterfield Gdns..D 5
79 Chesterfield Gro..G 14
86 Chesterfield Hill.. A 4
76 Chesterfield Rd. E10
              A 4
77 Chesterfield Rd. W4
              D 6
86 Chesterfield St....E 8
76 Chesterton Rd. E13
              G 6
74 Chesterton Rd. W10
              J 2
76 Chesterton Ter....G 6
77 Chestnut Av. E7...D 7
66 Chestnut Av. Brent.C 3
78 Chestnut Gro. SW12
              J 8
77 Chestnut Gro. W5.B 3
76 Chestnut Rd. E11..A 6
79 Chestnut Rd. SE27
              L 12
74 Chetwynd Rd.....D 8
85 Cheval Pl.........D 8
71 Chevening Pk.....H 12
74 Chevening Rd. NW6
              F 2
80 Chevening Rd. SE10
              C 6
75 Cheverton Rd.....B 9
76 Chevet St.........E 1
74 Cheviot Gdns.....C 2
86 Cheyne Gdns......H 1
85 Cheyne Hosp.....H 6
85 Cheyne Row......H 6
85 Cheyne Wk. J 5 & H 6

74 Chichele Rd.......D 2
87 Chicheley St......C 10
76 Chichester Rd. E11.
              C 5
74 Chichester Rd. NW6
              G 4
86 Chichester St......G 6
81 Chichester Ter.....F 3
84 Chicksand St......F 6
67 Chigwell.........B 11
67 Chigwell La.......A 11
67 Chigwell Rd.......C 10
67 Chigwell Rise.....B 11
67 Chigwell Row.....B 12
78 Childebert Rd......K 8
68 Childerditch La...D 6
80 Childeric Rd.......D 1
80 Childers St.........D 2
74 Child's Hill.......C 3
74 Childs Hill Pk.....B 3
85 Child's Pl.........F 2
85 Child's St.........F 2
75 Chillingworth St..E 11
70 Chiltern Rd.......F 4
82 Chiltern St.........F 3
77 Chilton Rd.........F 4
84 Chilton St.........E 6
81 Chilworth Mews..H 4
81 Chilworth St......H 4
80 Chinbrook Rd.....L 7
67 Chingford.........B 9
67 Chingford Hatch..B 9
67 Chingford La.....B 9
67 Chingford Mount Rd.
              B 9
67 Chingford Rd.....C 9
81 Chippenham Gdns.D 1
81 Chippenham Mews.E 1
81 Chippenham Rd...E 1
70 Chipstead.........H 5
78 Chipstead St......E 4
70 Chipstead Valley Rd.
              H 5
76 Chisenhale Rd.....G 1
77 Chisholm Rd......H 4
71 Chislehurst.......C 10
71 Chislehurst G.C...C 10
71 Chislehurst Station
              D 10
71 Chislehurst Rd. Brom.
              D 10
71 Chislehurst Rd. Orp.
              E 11
71 Chislehurst West.C 10
84 Chiswell St.......F 2
77 Chiswick.........C 7
77 Chiswick Bri......F 6
77 Chiswick Common C 6
77 Chiswick Common
    Rd.........C 6
77 Chiswick High Rd.C 4
66 Chiswick Ho......H 3
77 Chiswick La.......C 7
77 Chiswick Mall.....D 7
77 Chiswick Pk. Sta..C 6
77 Chiswick Sta......C 6
77 Chiswick Village..D 5
78 Chivalry Rd.......H 1
76 Chobham Rd.....D 5
74 Cholmeley Cres....A 7
74 Cholmeley Pk.....B 8
65 Chorleywood Rd...A 3
79 Choumert Gro....E 15
79 Choumert Rd......F 14
76 Chrisp St.........J 3
77 Christ Church Rd..C 5
74 Christchurch Av.
    NW6.........F 2
66 Christchurch Av.
    Har.........C 1
74 Christchurch Rd. NW3
              C 5
79 Christchurch Rd. SW2
              J 11
86 Christchurch St....G 2
80 Christchurch Way.C 5
84 Christian St.......H 7
76 Christie Rd.......E 1
84 Christina St.......E 4
84 Christopher St.....F 3
80 Chudleigh Rd.....H 3
88 Chumleigh St.....H 4
77 Church Av.........G 6
74 Church Cres......F 1
73 Church Dri.......B 6
68 Church Elm La....E 2
66 Church End.......C 4
77 Church Gdns......A 2
72 Church Hill, Dartford
              C 2

67 Church Hill,
    Loughton......A 10
69 Church Hill, Pyrford
              H 2
66 Church Hill Rd....A 5
76 Church La. E11...B 5
73 Church La. NW9..A 6
71 Church La. Chelsham
              G 9
77 Church Path......B 6
80 Church Rise......K 1
76 Church Rd. E10...B 3
74 Church Rd. N6....A 7
73 Church Rd. NW10. F 7
71 Church Rd. SE19..D 16
77 Church Rd. SW13.E 8
70 Church Rd. SW19.C 4
77 Church Rd. W3...A 5
69 Church Rd.,
    Addlestone.....F 2
69 Church Rd. Ashford
              C 3
69 Church Rd. Byfleet.G 3
71 Church Rd. Chelsfield
              F 12
65 Church Rd. Northolt
              E 5
77 Church Rd. Rich...G 3
72 Church Rd. Sutton-at-
    Hone.........C 3
69 Church Rd. Ted...C 6
74 Church Row......D 5
81 Church St. NW8...F 5
80 Church St. SE13...G 6
77 Church St. W4....D 7
67 Church St.,
    Edmonton......A 7
67 Church St. Enfield.A 7
70 Church St. Eps....G 3
69 Church St. Walton
              E 4
80 Church Ter.......F 5
80 Church Vale......K 1
74 Church Wk.......C 3
80 Churchbury Rd....J 8
73 Churchfield Rd. W3
              L 6
77 Churchfield Rd.W13A 2
73 Churchill Gdns....K 5
86 Churchill Gdns. Rd.
              G 5
76 Churchill Rd. E16.
              J 8
73 Churchill Rd. NW2
              E 9
74 Churchill Rd. NW5
              D 8
75 Churchill Wk.....D 16
76 Churchston Av....F 7
83 Churchway.......D 7
87 Churchyard Row. E 12
87 Churton St.......F 6
80 Cibber Rd.........K 1
78 Cicada Rd.........H 5
79 Cicely Rd.........E 15
73 Circle, The.......C 7
88 Circular Rd.......D 2
80 Circus, The.......D 4
81 Circus Rd.........C 5
75 Citizen Rd.......D 11
72 City...........J 13
85 City & Guild's Coll.
              D 5
83 City Garden Row.C 13
83 City Hall.........J 8
84 City of London Club
              G 3
83 City Rd. EC1.....C 12
84 City Rd. EC1.....D 2
78 Clabon Mews.....E 2
81 Clancarty Rd......F 4
81 Clanricarde Gdns..J 2
78 Clapham.........G 9
78 Clapham Common G 7
78 Clapham Common,
    Nth. Side.......G 8
78 Clapham Common,
    Sth. Side......H 8
79 Clapham Common
    Sta.........G 9
78 Clapham Common,
    W. Side.......G 7
79 Clapham High St..G 9
78 Clapham Junc. Sta. G 6
79 Clapham Manor St.
              F 9
79 Clapham Pk. Rd...G 9
78 Clapham Sth. Sta. H 8
79 Clapham Sta......F 9
75 Clapton Common B 15
75 Clapton Sq.......D 16

75 Clapton Way....D 15
77 Clare Lawn Av....H 6
83 Claremont Cl.....C 11
76 Claremont Rd. E7.E 7
74 Claremont Rd. N6.A 9
74 Claremont Rd. NW2
              B 2
83 Claremont Sq....C 11
79 Clarence Av.......H 9
79 Clarence Cres.....H 9
82 Clarence Gdns....D 5
86 Clarence Ho.......B 6
77 Clarence La.......H 7
75 Clarence Pl.......D 16
75 Clarence Rd. E5..D 16
76 Clarence Rd. E16..J 5
78 Clarendon Dri....G 1
81 Clarendon Gdns. W9
              E 4
73 Clarendon Gdns.
    Wem.........D 3
81 Clarendon Gate..H 6
82 Clarendon Gro....C 7
81 Clarendon Pl......H 6
80 Clarendon Rise....G 4
76 Clarendon Rd. E11.B 5
73 Clarendon Rd. W5.H 3
74 Clarendon Rd. W11
              K 3
86 Clarendon St.....G 5
80 Clarens St.........K 2
85 Clareville Gro.....F 4
85 Clareville St.......F 4
86 Clarges Mews.....B 5
86 Clarges St.........B 5
79 Claribel Rd.......E 12
82 Claridge's Hotel...H 4
75 Clarissa St.......K 14
75 Clark St.........J 16
76 Claude Rd. E10...B 4
76 Claude Rd. E13...F 7
79 Claude Rd. SE15. F 15
80 Claude St.........B 3
79 Claverdale Rd....J 11
86 Claverton St.......G 6
78 Claxton Gro.......C 2
82 Clay St.........F 3
67 Claybury Hosp...C 11
70 Claygate.........F 1
67 Clayhall.........C 11
67 Clayhall Av.......C 11
87 Claylands Rd.....J 10
65 Claypit La.........B 4
77 Claypond La.......C 3
77 Clayponds Av.....C 3
76 Clays La.........D 4
73 Clayton Av.......F 3
77 Clayton Cres......C 2
79 Clayton Rd. SE15.E 15
70 Clayton Rd.
    Surbiton.......F 1
87 Clayton St.......H 11
87 Cleaver Sq.......G 11
87 Cleaver St.......G 11
73 Clematis St.......K 8
76 Clemence St.......J 2
72 Clement St.......C 2
76 Clementina Rd....B 2
84 Clement's La......H 3
79 Clement's Rd......B 15
87 Cleopatra's Needle.A 9
75 Clephane Rd......E 13
84 Clere Pl.........E 3
84 Clere St.........E 3
75 Clerkenwell......H 11
83 Clerkenwell Cl....E 11
83 Clerkenwell Grn..E 12
83 Clerkenwell Rd...E 12
74 Cleve Rd.........F 4
77 Clevedon Rd......H 2
77 Cleveland Av......C 7
74 Cleveland Gdns. NW2
              C 2
77 Cleveland Gdns. SW13
              F 7
81 Cleveland Gdns. W2
              H 3
75 Cleveland Rd. N1 F 13
77 Cleveland Rd. SW13
              F 7
86 Cleveland Row....B 6
81 Cleveland Sq......H 3
82 Cleveland St.......F 6
81 Cleveland Ter.....G 4
75 Cleveland Way....H 16
73 Cleveley Cres.....G 3
75 Cleveleys Rd......C 16
76 Clifden Rd. E5....D 1
76 Cliff St.........J 6
77 Clifford Av.......F 5
74 Clifford Gdns.....G 1

MAP
76 Clifford Rd. E16...H 6
77 Clifford Rd. Rich..K 3
73 Clifford Rd. Wem..F 2
82 Clifford St........J 5
73 Clifford Way.....D 7
80 Cliffview Rd......G 3
84 Clift St..........B 3
73 Clifton Av........E 4
79 Clifton Cres.....D 16
81 Clifton Gdns.....E 3
81 Clifton Hill......B 3
81 Clifton Pl........H 5
80 Clifton Rise......D 2
76 Clifton Rd. E16...J 5
81 Clifton Rd. W9....E 4
84 Clifton St........E 3
75 Clifton Ter......B 11
81 Clifton Villas....H 7
79 Clifton Way.....E 16
88 Clink St..........A 2
76 Clinton Rd. E3...H 7
76 Clinton Rd. E7...D 7
82 Clipstone St......F 5
75 Clissold Cres....D 13
75 Clissold Pk......C 13
75 Clissold Rd......C 13
77 Clitherow Rd.....C 2
74 Clitterhouse Rd...B 1
79 Clive Rd.........L 13
86 Cliveden Pl......F 3
84 Cloak La.........H 2
71 Clock House Sta...D 8
69 Clockhouse La....C 3
74 Cloister Rd. NW2.C 3
73 Cloister Rd. W3..J 6
78 Clonmel Rd.......E 3
78 Cloncurry St.....E 2
78 Clonmore St.....K 3
74 Clorane Gdns....C 4
73 Close, The.......E 3
83 Cloth Fair.......F 13
84 Clothworkers Halt.H 4
83 Cloudesley Pl....B 11
83 Cloudesley Rd....B 11
83 Cloudesley Sq...A 11
83 Cloudesley St....B 11
76 Clova Rd.........E 6
77 Clovelly Rd. W4..B 6
77 Clovelly Rd. W5..A 2
80 Clowders Rd......K 2
84 Club Row.........D 5
80 Clyde St.........D 2
78 Coalecroft Rd....G 1
84 Coate St.........B 7
84 Cobb St..........G 5
76 Cobbold Rd. E11..C 6
73 Cobbold Rd. NW10
              E 7
77 Cobbold Rd. W12.A 7
76 Cobden Rd.......C 5
76 Cobden St........J 4
69 Cobham..........G 4
69 Cobham Rd.......H 6
69 Cobham Sta......H 5
72 Cobham Ter. Rd..B 4
76 Coborn Rd........G 2
76 Coborn St........G 2
88 Cobourg Rd......G 5
84 Cock Hill........G 4
83 Cock La.........G 12
66 Cockfosters......A 5
66 Cockfosters Sta...A 6
81 Cochrane St......C 5
87 Cockspur St......A 8
84 Code St..........E 6
87 Codrington Hill...J 1
87 Coin St.........B 11
85 Colbeck Mews....F 3
75 Colberg Pl......B 14
76 Colchester Rd. E10.A 4
68 Colchester Rd. Rom.
              C 3
86 Colchester St......G 6
80 Cold Bath St......B 3
80 Cold Blow La.....D 1
72 Coldblow.........B 1
79 Coldharbour La. SE5
              F 12
79 Coldharbour La. SW9
              G 11
65 Coldharbour La.
    Hayes.........G 5
70 Cole Pk.........B 1
88 Cole St..........D 2
75 Colebert Av......H 16
76 Colebrooke Dri. ..A 7
83 Colebrooke Row B 12
79 Colegrove Rd....D 15
85 Coleherne Mews...G 2
85 Coleherne Rd.....G 2

MAP
78 Colehill La........E 3
75 Coleman Fields...F 12
84 Coleman St.......G 2
88 Coleman Rd.......J 4
80 Coleraine Rd......D 6
75 Coleridge Rd......A 9
73 Coles Green Rd....C 9
78 Colet Gdns........C 2
75 Coley St.........E 10
80 Colfe Rd.........K 1
65 Colham Green....F 4
73 Colin Deep La....C 3
73 Colin Rd.........C 8
66 Colindale.........C 3
66 Colindale Av......C 3
66 Colindale Sta.....C 3
78 Colinette Rd......G 1
78 Coliseum Th......J 8
78 Collamore Av......K 6
82 College Pl........A 6
84 College Hill......H 2
74 College Rd. NW10.G 1
79 College Rd. SE21. J 14
71 College Rd. Brom..D 9
72 College Rd. Dfrd...D 1
70 College Rd. Eps...G 3
73 College Rd. Wem..B 3
84 College St. EC4...H 2
75 College St. N1...F 12
78 College Row......E 1
80 Collerston Rd......C 6
68 Collier Rd.........C 2
68 Collier Row.......C 2
68 Collier Row Lane C 2
83 Collier St........C 10
70 Collier's Wood....C 5
85 Collingham Gdns...F 3
85 Collingham Pl.....F 2
85 Collingham Rd....F 3
75 Collingwood Rd...A 2
75 Collingwood St...H 16
75 Collins Rd.......D 13
83 Collinson St......C 13
79 Colls Rd.........E 16
84 Colman Rd........J 8
78 Colne Rd.........D 1
65 Colney Butts......A 5
66 Colney Hatch.....B 5
66 Colney Hatch La...C 6
78 Cologne Rd.......G 6
80 Colombo St.......B 12
83 Colonnade........E 9
83 Columbia Cin....H 7
84 Columbia Rd. E2..D 5
76 Columbia Rd. E13 H 6
75 Colvestone Cres...E 14
85 Colville Pl........F 7
76 Colville Rd. E11...C 4
74 Colville Ter......K 3
74 Colworth Rd......A 5
72 Colyers La.......A 1
79 Colyton Rd......H 16
80 Combedale Rd....C 6
78 Combemartin Rd..J 3
79 Comber Gro.....E 12
79 Combermere Rd..F 11
75 Comberton Rd...C 16
78 Comeragh Rd....C 3
78 Comerford Rd....G 2
73 Common, The...K 3
77 Common Rd......F 8
74 Commerce Rd....D 2
84 Commercial Rd. E1 G 6
84 Commercial St....F 5
77 Commercial Way. E 14
76 Commodore St....H 1
72 Common La.....C 2
66 Common Rd......B 1
83 Commondale......F 1
70 Commonside E...D 5
70 Commonside W...D 5
73 Commonwealth Av.
              K 9
80 Como Rd........K 1
74 Compayne Gdns...E 4
74 Compton Av......A 6
75 Compton Cres...D 6
75 Compton Rd. E. E 12
83 Compton St.....E 12
76 Comyn Rd.......G 10
79 Concanon Rd....G 10
79 Condell Rd.......E 9
75 Conder St........J 1
81 Conduit Mews....H 4
81 Conduit Pl........H 5
82 Conduit St........H 5
73 Conduit Way.....F 5

MAP
75 Conewood St.....C 12
88 Congreve St......F 4
78 Coniger St........F 4
77 Coningham Rd....A 8
80 Conington Rd......F 4
80 Conisborough
   Crescent.........L 4
73 Coniston Av......G 2
77 Connaught Av.....G 5
82 Connaught Pl.....H 2
76 Connaught Rd. E11
              B 5
76 Connaught Rd. E16
              K 8
75 Connaught Rd. N4
              A 11
73 Connaught Rd. NW10
              G 7
82 Connaught Sq.....H 2
81 Connaught St.....H 6
73 Connell Cres......H 2
77 Conningsby Rd....A 2
87 Cons St..........C 11
79 Consort Rd......E 15
74 Constantine Rd....D 7
86 Constitution Hill ..C 5
88 Content St........F 2
77 Convent Gdns....C 2
69 Convent Rd.......C 4
82 Conway St.......F 5
76 Cooks Rd. E15... G 3
87 Cooks Rd. SE17..H 12
75 Coolhurst Av......A 9
75 Coolhurst Rd......A 9
70 Coombe Hill G.C..C 2
70 Coombe La.......D 2
70 Coombe Rd. K'gst.D 2
70 Coombe Rd. New M.
              D 3
71 Coombe Rd. Sta...E 7
70 Coombe Wood G.C.
              C 2
83 Coomb's St......C 12
73 Cooper Rd.......E 8
80 Coopers La. E10..B 4
80 Cooper's La. SE12.K 7
88 Cooper's St......G 5
76 Coopersale Rd....D 1
85 Cope Pl..........D 1
79 Copeland Rd.....F 15
83 Copenhagen St...A 10
73 Copland Av.......E 2
79 Copleston Rd....F 14
76 Copley St........J 1
80 Copperas St......D 3
76 Copperfield Rd...J 2
87 Copperfield St....C 13
76 Coppice Dri......H 8
70 Copse Hill.......D 3
69 Copsem La.......F 6
83 Coptic St........G 8
87 Coral St........C 11
83 Coram St........E 8
85 Corbet Pl........F 5
68 Corbets Tey.....E 4
68 Corbets Tey Rd...E 4
75 Corbyn Rd.......B 10
75 Cordelia St........J 3
75 Cordwell St......H 16
73 Corfton Rd........J 3
75 Corinne Rd......D 9
79 Cormont Rd.....E 12
77 Corney Rd.......D 7
78 Cornford Gro.....K 8
84 Cornhill.........H 3
75 Cornthwaite Rd...C 16
74 Cornwall Cres.....K 3
85 Cornwall Gdns....E 3
75 Cornwallis Rd....C 10
87 Cornwall Rd. SE1.
              B 11
86 Cornwall St......G 6
75 Cornwall Rd. N4.A 11
80 Corona Rd........J 7
76 Coronation Rd. E13
              H 8
73 Coronation Rd. NW10
              H 4
84 Coronet St........D 3
76 Corporation St. E15
              G 5
75 Corporation St. N7
              E 10
79 Corrance Rd.....G 10
74 Corringham Rd.
   NW11.........A 4
73 Craven Pk.......F 6

MAP
73 Corringham Rd. Wem.
              C 4
73 Corringway.......J 4
84 Corsham St.......D 3
75 Corsica St.......E 12
78 Cortis Rd.........H 1
79 Cosser St........D 11
79 Costa St.........F 15
81 Cosway St........F 6
82 Cotall St.........J 3
75 Cotesbach Rd.....C 16
81 Cotham St........F 2
89 Cottage Gro.....F 10
83 Cottage La.......C 12
85 Cottage Pl........D 6
86 Cottage Wk.......D 3
70 Cottenham Pk....D 3
70 Cottenham Pk. Rd.D 3
85 Cottesmore Gdns..D 3
87 Cottington St.....F 12
76 Cotton St.........K 4
74 Cottrill Rd.......E 15
70 Coulsdon.........H 6
70 Coulsdon Ct. G.C.G 6
70 Coulsdon La......H 5
70 Coulsdon North. Sta.
              G 6
70 Coulsdon Rd......H 6
86 Coulson St.......F 2
80 Coulter Rd........B 1
79 County Gro......E 12
87 County Hall......C 9
77 County Pk. Sch....A 4
88 County St........E 2
79 Courland Gro....E 10
73 Court Way.......J 6
74 Courtenay Av.....A 6
75 Courtenay St....G 10
85 Courtfield Gdns...F 3
85 Courtfield Rd......F 3
80 Courthill Rd......G 4
74 Courthope Rd....D 7
77 Courtlands.......G 4
80 Courtlands Av.....G 7
80 Couthurst Rd.....D 7
76 Coutts Rd........J 2
82 Coval Rd.........G 5
83 Covent Garden...H 9
82 Coventry St......J 7
74 Coverdale Rd.....F 2
88 Cowan St........H 4
83 Cowcross St.....F 12
79 Cowper Rd......D 14
84 Cowper St........D 3
65 Cowley..........F 3
77 Cowley Rd. SW9..H 2
77 Cowley Rd. SW14..F 7
87 Cowley St........D 8
79 Crabtree Av......G 3
78 Crabtree La.......D 2
83 Crinan St.........B 9
70 Cradocks Av......H 2
79 Craignair Rd.....J 11
88 Crail Row........F 3
82 Cramer St........F 4
79 Crampton St.....F 13
83 Cranbourn St....H 8
80 Cranbrook Rd. SE8
              D 1
77 Cranbrook Rd. W4 C 7
67 Cranbrook Rd. Ilf.
              D 1
78 Cranbury Rd......F 4
80 Cranfield Rd......F 2
65 Cranford.........H 4
65 Cranford La......H 5
68 Cranham.........D 5
74 Cranham Rd.....C 16
74 Cranhurst Rd.....E 1
76 Cranmer Rd. E7...D 7
79 Cranmer Rd. SW9
              D 11
82 Cranleigh St.......C 6
85 Cranley Gdns.....G 4
85 Cranley Mews....G 4
85 Cranley Pl........F 5
80 Cranston Rd......K 1
79 Cranswick Rd...C 16
80 Crantock Rd......K 4
84 Cranwich Rd.....A 13
84 Cranwood St.....D 3
79 Cranworth Gardens
              E 11
79 Craster Rd......J 11
80 Crathie Rd......A 10
82 Craven Av.......K 2
81 Craven Hill......H 4
81 Craven Hill Gardens
              H 3
73 Craven Pk.......F 6

MAP
75 Craven Pk. Rd. N15
              A 15
73 Craven Pk. Rd. NW10
              F 7
81 Craven Rd. W2...H 4
87 Craven St.........A 8
81 Craven Ter.......H 4
75 Craven Wk.......A 15
73 Crawford Av......E 2
82 Crawford Pl.......G 1
79 Crawford Rd.....E 13
82 Crawford St......F 2
82 Crawley Mews....C 6
79 Crawshay Rd....E 12
79 Crawthew Gro...G 15
72 Crayford..........A 2
75 Crayford Rd. N7. D 10
72 Crayford Rd. Dartford
              B 2
79 Crebor St........H 15
74 Crediton Hill......E 4
74 Credition Rd......G 2
76 Credon Rd. E13...G 8
79 Credon Rd. SE16.C 16
84 Creechurch La....G 4
83 Creed La.........H 12
80 Creek Rd.........D 3
67 Creekmouth......F 12
80 Creekside.........D 3
73 Creffield Rd......K 4
84 Cremer St........C 5
77 Crescent, The.....E 8
79 Crescent Gro.....G 9
79 Crescent La.......G 9
85 Crescent Pl.......E 6
79 Crescent Rd......A 9
80 Crescent Way....F 3
79 Crescent Wood Rd.
              L 15
75 Cresset Rd.......E 16
75 Cressida Rd.......B 9
80 Cressingham Rd...F 4
85 Cresswell Gdns...F 3
85 Cresswell Pl......G 4
77 Cresswell Rd......H 2
73 Crest Rd.........C 8
83 Crestfield St......C 9
77 Crestway........H 8
73 Creswick Rd......K 5
80 Crew St.........B 3
79 Crewdson Rd....D 11
74 Crewys Rd........E 2
75 Cricketfield Rd...D 16
79 Cricklade Av.....K 10
74 Cricklewood.....D 1
74 Cricklewood Bdy. D 2
74 Cricklewood La....C 3
74 Cricklewood Sta...D 2
78 Crieff Rd.........H 5
79 Criffel Av........K 9
88 Crimscott St......E 4
83 Crinan St.........B 9
86 Cringle St........J 6
78 Crisp Rd.........C 1
82 Crietrion Th......J 7
72 Crockenhill......E 1
78 Crockerton Rd....K 7
73 Croft, The.......D 2
74 Croftdown Rd....C 8
80 Crofton Pk. Rd...H 2
80 Crofton Pk. Sta...H 2
76 Crofton Rd. E13..H 7
79 Crofton Rd. SE5. E 16
71 Crofton Rd. Orp. E 11
71 Croham Hurst G.C.
              F 7
71 Croham Rd.......F 7
83 Cromer St........D 9
78 Cromford Rd......G 3
81 Crompton St......E 4
74 Cromwell Av......B 8
85 Cromwell Cres....F 1
85 Cromwell Gdns...E 5
78 Cromwell Gro....B 1
85 Cromwell Mews...E 5
85 Cromwell Pl......E 5
76 Cromwell Rd. E7..F 8
85 Cromwell Rd. SW5 &
   SW7.........E 5
69 Cromwell Rd. Houn.
              B 6
78 Crondace Rd......E 4
84 Crondall St........C 3
88 Cronin Rd.........J 5
80 Crooke Rd.......C 1
80 Crooms Hill......D 4
84 Cropley St........B 3
76 Crosby Rd........E 6
88 Crosby Row......C 3
84 Crosby Sq........G 4
87 Crosier St........D 10

MAP
76 Cross St. E15.....F 5
75 Cross St. N1......F 12
70 Crossdeep........C 1
74 Crossfield Rd......E 6
74 Crossland Rd......E 8
79 Crossthwaite Av..G 13
84 Crosswall.........H 4
75 Crossway.........E 14
73 Crossways, The...B 4
75 Crouch End.......A 10
75 Crouch End Hill..A 10
75 Crouch Hall Rd...A 9
75 Crouch Hill.......A 10
75 Crouch Hill Sta...B 10
75 Crouch Rd........E 6
68 Crow La..........D 2
79 Crowhurst Rd....F 11
70 Crown Dale.......C 6
70 Crown La.........C 6
83 Crown Office Row H 11
76 Crown Rd........H 1
88 Crown St. SE5....J 2
77 Crown St. W3....A 5
82 Crowndale Rd.....B 6
76 Crownfield Rd....D 4
73 Crownhill Rd......F 7
79 Crownstone Rd...H 11
77 Crowther Av......C 3
65 Croxley Green Sta.A 4
73 Croxley Rd........H 4
65 Croxley Sta.......A 4
65 Croxleygreen.....A 3
79 Croxted Rd.......J 13
70 Croydon.........E 7
70 Croydon La.......G 4
76 Croydon Rd. E13. H 6
70 Croydon Rd. SE20.D 7
71 Croydon Rd. Bec..D 8
71 Croydon Rd. Brom.
              E 10
71 Croydon Rd.
   Chelsham.......H 9
70 Croydon Rd. Cro..E 6
70 Croydon Rd. Mitch.
              D 5
70 Croydon Rd.
   Wallington.....E 5
88 Crucifix La.......C 4
83 Cruden St.......B 12
83 Cruikshank St...C 10
84 Crutched Friars...H 4
80 Crutchley Rd.....K 5
71 Crystal Pal. Park..C 7
79 Crystal Pal. Rd...H 15
70 Crystal Pal. Sta...C 7
80 Cuba St..........A 3
83 Cubitt St.........D 10
80 Cuddington G.C...E 4
71 Cudham.........G 11
71 Cudham La......G 11
71 Cudham Rd......G 11
75 Cudworth St.....H 16
86 Culford Gdns.....F 2
75 Culford Rd......F 14
79 Culling Rd.......B 16
73 Cullingworth Rd...D 8
77 Cullum St........H 4
77 Culmington Rd...A 2
79 Culmore Rd......E 16
80 Culmstock Rd....H 7
83 Culpeper St......B 11
82 Culross St........J 3
80 Culverden Rd.....K 9
80 Culverley Rd......J 4
78 Culvert Rd.......E 7
77 Culworth St......C 6
73 Cumberland Av...H 5
82 Cumberland Gate .H 2
82 Cumberland Mkt..D 5
73 Cumberland Pk...K 6
76 Cumberland Rd. E13
              J 7
77 Cumberland Rd. SW13
              E 8
73 Cumberland Rd. W3
              K 6
77 Cumberland Rd. Rich.
              E 4
86 Cumberland St....G 5
82 Cumberland Ter...C 5
83 Cumbrian Gdns...C 2
83 Cummings St.....C 10
73 Cunard Rd........H 6
81 Cunard St........H 3
86 Cundy St.........F 4
81 Cunningham Pl...E 5
77 Cunnington St....B 6
80 Cupley St.........J 4
87 Cureton St.......F 8
88 Curlew St........C 5
83 Cursitor St.......G 11

MAP
84 Curtain Rd.:.....E 4
88 Curtis St. ....E 5
73 Curve, The.......K 8
77 Curwen Rd.......A 8
73 Curzon Cres.....F 7
73 Curzon Rd.......H 1
86 Curzon St........B 4
76 Custom House
   Station......K 7
87 Cut, The......C 11
79 Cutcombe Rd....F 13
79 Cuthill Rd......E 13
84 Cutler St........G 4
80 Cyclops Pl......B 3
83 Cynthia St......C 10
75 Cyprus St.......G 16
79 Cyrena Rd......H 15
83 Cyrus St.......D 12
80 Dacca St........C 2
76 Dace Rd........F 3
80 Dacre Pk.......G 5
76 Dacre Rd. E7...F 7
76 Dacre Rd. E11..B 6
86 Dacre St........D 7
80 Dacres Rd......K 1
73 Daffodil St......K 8
78 Dafforne Rd.....L 7
68 Dagenham......E 2
68 Dagenham Av...E 1
68 Dagenham Dock Sta.
             F 1
68 Dagenham E. Sta..E 2
68 Dagenham Heathway
   Sta.........E 1
68 Dagenham Rd...E 2
73 Dagmar Av.....D 4
75 Dagmar Rd. N4..A 11
79 Dagmar Rd. SE5.E 14
78 Dagnal St.......E 7
78 Dagnan Rd......J 8
78 Daisy La........F 4
79 Dalberg Rd.....G 11
78 Dalebury Rd....K 7
76 Dalecage Rd....J 5
74 Daleham Gdns...E 6
75 Daleview Rd....A 14
74 Dalgarno Gdns...J 1
74 Dalgarno Way...H 1
79 Dalkeith Rd.....J 13
77 Dalling Rd......B 9
80 Dallinger Rd....H 6
83 Dallington St....E 12
80 Dalmain Rd......J 1
75 Dalmeny Av.....D 10
73 Dalmeny Cl......E 2
75 Dalmeny Rd.....D 9
79 Dalmore Rd.....K 13
80 Dalrymple Rd....G 2
75 Dalston........E 14
75 Dalston La......E 15
72 Daltons Rd......F 1
79 Dalyell Rd......F 11
79 Dalwood St.....E 14
83 Dame St........B 13
76 Dames Rd......C 6
83 Danbury St......B 12
79 Danby St........F 14
77 Dancer Rd......F 4
83 Dane St.........F 9
77 Danebury Av....J 8
80 Daneby Rd......K 4
79 Danecroft Rd....G 13
78 Danehurst St....E 3
78 Danemere St....F 1
76 Danesdale Rd....E 1
80 Daneswood Av..L 4
73 Danethorpe Rd...E 2
79 Daneville Rd....E 13
76 Dangan Rd......A 6
79 Daniel's Rd.....F 16
87 Danson Rd. SE17 G 13
71 Danson Rd. Bex'h B 12
87 Dante Rd.......F 12
85 Danvers St......H 5
82 D'Arblay St......H 6
84 Darby St........J 6
77 Darell Rd.......F 4
72 Darenth........C 3
75 Darenth Rd. N16.B 14
72 Darenth Rd.
   Dartford.....B 3
80 Darfield Rd.....H 2
78 Darley Rd.......H 7
80 Darling Rd......F 3
75 Darling Row....H 16
75 Darnley Rd.....E 16
79 Darrell Rd......H 15
72 Dartford........B 2
72 Dartford G.C....B 2
72 Dartford Rd.
   Dartford.....B 2

MAP
72 Dartford Rd. Hextable
             C 2
80 Dartmouth Hill...E 4
74 Dartmouth Pk. Av. C 8
74 Dartmouth Pk. Hill
             C 8
74 Dartmouth Pk. Rd. C 8
76 Dartmouth Rd. E16 J 6
74 Dartmouth Rd. NW2
             E 2
73 Dartmouth Rd. NW4
             A 8
79 Dartmouth Rd. SE23
   & SE26....K 16
86 Dartmouth St....D 7
88 Dartnell Rd......H 4
78 Darvall Sq.......G 5
75 Darville Rd......C 14
77 Darwin Rd.......C 2
88 Darwin St.......F 3
80 Datchet Rd......K 2
88 Date St.........G 2
76 Daubeney Rd....D 1
78 Dault Rd.......H 5
84 Davenant St.....F 6
80 Davenport Rd....H 4
81 Daventry St.....F 6
88 Davey St.......H 5
76 David St........E 5
79 David's Rd......K 16
71 Davidson Rd.....E 7
76 Davies La.......B 6
82 Davies Mews....H 4
82 Davies St.......H 4
77 Davis Rd........A 7
76 Davis St........G 7
77 Davisville Rd.....A 8
78 Dawes Rd.......D 3
88 Dawes St.......G 3
65 Dawley Rd......A 4
76 Dawlish Rd......B 4
78 Dawnay Rd......K 5
73 Dawpool Rd.....C 7
67 Daws Hill.......A 9
81 Dawson Pl......H 1
74 Dawson Rd......D 1
77 Daylesford Av...G 8
71 Days La........B 11
79 Daysbrook Rd...K 10
79 Dayton Gro.....E 16
75 De Beauvoir Rd..F 14
75 De Beauvoir Sq..F 14
79 De Crespigny Pk..F 13
87 De Laune St.....G 12
79 De Montfort Rd..K 10
85 De Vere Gdns....D 3
82 De Waldon St....F 4
73 Deacon Rd......E 8
88 Deacon St.......E 1
84 Deal St.........F 6
78 Dealtry Rd......G 1
87 Dean Bradley St...E 8
73 Dean Ct........C 2
86 Dean Farrar St...D 7
74 Dean Rd........E 1
87 Dean Ryle St....E 8
87 Dean Stanley St...E 8
82 Dean St........H 7
76 Deanery Rd.....E 5
86 Deanery St......B 4
77 Deanhill Rd.....G 5
88 Dean's Bldgs....F 3
83 Dean's Ct.......H 13
66 Dean's La.......B 3
87 Dean's Yd.......D 8
66 Deansbrook Rd...B 3
73 Deanscroft Av....B 6
67 Debden Sta......A 11
88 Decima St.......D 4
77 Dee Rd.........G 4
76 Dee St.........J 4
79 Deepdene Rd....G 13
87 Deer Pk........K 6
79 Deerbrook Rd....J 12
87 Defence, Min. of..B 8
77 Defoe Av.......F 5
75 Defoe Rd.......C 14
79 Dekker Rd......H 14
80 Delafield Rd....C 7
79 Delaford Rd. SE16 C 16
78 Delaford Rd. SW6.D 3
78 Delaforte Sq.....G 5
81 Delamere Cres...F 3
77 Delamere Rd.....A 3
81 Delamere Ter....F 3
82 Delancey St.....E 5
81 Delaware Rd.....E 2
83 Delhi St........A 9
78 Delvino Rd......E 4
77 Denbigh Gdns....H 4
86 Denbigh Pl......F 6

MAP
73 Denbigh Rd. W13.K 1
86 Denbigh St......F 6
78 Dendy St........J 7
74 Dene, The......D 3
74 Denehurst Gdns...A 1
74 Denewood Rd....A 7
65 Denham........D 2
74 Denison Rd.....H 2
79 Denman Rd......E 14
82 Denman St......J 7
83 Denmark Gro....B 11
79 Denmark Hill....E 13
79 Denmark Hill Sta. F 13
74 Denmark Rd. NW6
             G 3
79 Denmark Rd. SE5 E 12
73 Denmark Rd. W13.K 1
76 Denmark St. E13..H 7
83 Denmark St. WC2.G 8
84 Denne Ter.......A 5
79 Dennett's Rd....E 16
70 Denning Av......F 6
79 Dennington Pk. Rd.
             E 4
68 Dennises La......C 1
87 Denny Cres.....F 11
87 Denny St.......F 11
77 Denton Rd......H 2
78 Dents Rd.......H 7
75 Denver Rd......A 14
86 Denyer St.......F 2
73 Denzil Rd.......E 7
78 Deodar Rd......G 3
88 Depot St.......G 2
80 Deptford.......E 3
80 Deptford Bri.....E 3
80 Deptford Ch St...D 3
80 Deptford Ferry Rd. C 3
80 Deptford Grn....D 3
80 Deptford High St..D 3
80 Deptford Pk.....C 1
79 Derby Hill......K 16
77 Derby Rd.......G 5
85 Derby St........D 2
84 Derbyshire St....D 7
84 Dereham Pl......D 4
84 Derek Av.......F 5
82 Dering St.......H 5
80 Dermody Rd.....G 4
74 Deronda Rd......J 12
71 Derry Downs.....E 12
85 Derry St........G 2
79 Derwent Gro.....G 14
79 Desenfans Rd....H 14
76 Desford Rd......H 5
78 Desmond Av.....E 4
76 Devas Rd.......H 4
88 Deverell St......E 2
86 Devereux Ct.....H 7
73 Devon Cl.......F 2
79 Devon St.......D 16
80 Devonia Rd......B 12
78 Devonport Rd....A 1
75 Devonport St....K 16
76 Devons Rd......H 3
87 Devonshire Cl....F 5
80 Devonshire Dri...E 3
77 Devonshire Gdns..E 5
76 Devonshire Mews Sth.
             F 4
82 Devonshire Mews W.
             F 4
80 Devonshire Rd. SE23
             J 1
77 Devonshire Rd. W4
             C 7
77 Devonshire Rd. W5
             B 2
84 Devonshire Row...G 4
84 Devonshire Sq....G 4
83 Devonshire St....F 4
81 Devonshire Ter...H 4
76 Dewberry St.....J 4
82 Dewey Rd.......B 11
73 Dewsbury Rd....D 8
79 Deynsford Rd....E 13
82 Diana Pl.......E 5
75 Dibden St.......F 12
75 Dibdin Rd......A 14
88 Dickens Sq......D 2
78 Dickens St......F 8
75 Dickenson Rd....A 10
75 Digby Cres......C 12
76 Digby Rd.......E 1
75 Digby St........H 16
73 Dighton Rd......G 5
83 Dignum St......B 11
86 Dilke St........H 2

MAP
73 Dimsdale Dri.....B 6
84 Dingley Pl......D 2
84 Dingley Rd......D 1
80 Dinsdale St......D 6
78 Dinsmore Rd.....J 8
76 Disraeli Rd. E7....E 6
73 Disraeli Rd. NW10
             G 6
78 Disraeli Rd. SW15.G 2
77 Disraeli Rd. W5...A 2
84 Diss St.........C 5
84 Distaff La.......H 1
77 Distillery Rd.....D 3
87 Distin St.......F 11
87 Ditton Hill......E 1
70 Ditton Rd.......E 2
76 Dixon St........J 2
70 Dobree Av......F 9
88 Dockhead.......C 6
76 Dock Rd. E16....K 6
77 Dock Rd. Brent...D 3
84 Dock St........J 6
88 Dockley Rd......E 6
76 Dod St.........J 2
87 Doddington Gro..G 12
87 Dodson St......D 11
79 Dog Kennel Hill..F 14
80 Doggett Rd......J 3
87 Dolben St.......B 12
73 Dollis Hill......D 8
73 Dollis Hill Av....C 9
73 Dollis Hill La....C 8
73 Dollis Hill Sta....E 8
86 Dolphin Sq......G 7
83 Dombey St......F 9
84 Dominion St.....F 3
83 Dominion Th.....G 7
88 Domville Gro....G 5
76 Donald Rd......F 7
74 Donaldson Rd....G 3
83 Donegal St......C 10
78 Doneraile St.....E 2
86 Donne Pl.......E 1
73 Donnington Rd...F 9
87 Doon St........B 10
77 Dordrecht Rd....A 7
73 Doreen Av......B 6
82 Doric Way......D 7
73 Doris Cl........B 6
80 Dorlking Rd......D 2
78 Dorncote Rd.....J 6
78 Doroton Rd......K 8
73 Dorothy Av......F 3
78 Dorothy Rd......F 7
83 Dorsington St....F 11
82 Dorset Cl.......F 2
86 Dorset Mews....D 4
86 Dorset Pl.......F 7
83 Dorset Rise.....H 12
76 Dorset Rd. E7....F 8
87 Dorset Rd. SW8...J 9
70 Dorset Rd. SW19..D 4
77 Dorset Rd. W5...B 2
82 Dorset Sq......E 2
82 Dorset St.......F 3
80 Dorville Rd......H 6
83 Doughty Mews...E 10
83 Doughty St.....E 10
73 Douglas Av......E 3
76 Douglas Rd. E16..J 6
75 Douglas Rd. N1..E 13
86 Douglas St......F 7
80 Douglas Way....D 2
85 Douro Pl.......D 3
85 Dove Mews.....F 4
75 Dove Rd........E 13
84 Dove Row.......B 6
79 Dovedale Rd.....H 16
85 Dovehouse St....G 6
77 Dover Ho. Rd....G 8
76 Dover Rd.......B 8
82 Dover St........J 5
79 Dovercourt Rd...H 14
79 Doverfield Rd....H 10
84 Dowgate Hill....H 2
79 Dowlass St......D 14
80 Dowlass Rd......D 14
86 Down St........D 5
71 Downe.........G 10
71 Downham Estate..C 9
87 Downham Rd....F 13
71 Downham Way...C 9
87 Downing St......C 8
80 Downs Pk. Rd....D 15
75 Downs Rd. E5....D 15
70 Downs Rd., Epsom
             G 3

MAP
70 Downs Rd.
   Sutton.......F 4
72 Downs Rd.
   Swanscombe....C 6
76 Downsell Rd.....D 4
76 Downsfield Rd....A 2
74 Downshire Hill...D 6
69 Downside.......H 11
74 Downside Crescent
             E 7
69 Downside Rd....H 5
79 Downton Av.....K 10
77 Doyle Gdns......G 9
86 D'Oyley St......E 3
87 Draco St.......H 13
80 Dragor Rd......H 6
80 Drake Rd.......F 3
80 Drakefell Rd.....F 1
76 Drakefield Rd....K 8
84 Drant St........F 5
87 Draper St.......E 12
76 Drapers Rd......D 4
88 Drappers Rd.....E 7
76 Draycot Rd......A 7
86 Draycott Av.....F 1
86 Draycott Pl......F 2
86 Draycott Ter.....F 2
85 Drayson Mews...C 2
66 Drayton Green...F 1
75 Drayton Pk.....D 11
79 Drayton Pk. Sta..D 11
76 Drayton Rd. E11..B 5
73 Drayton Rd. NW10
             F 7
75 Dresden Rd......B 9
79 Drewstead Rd....K 9
80 Driffield Rd......G 1
67 Drive, The, Ilf....D 11
73 Drive, The, Wem...C 5
80 Droop St.......H 2
74 Druce Rd.......H 14
88 Druid St........C 5
79 Drummond Cres..C 7
79 Drummond Rd...B 15
82 Drummond St....D 6
83 Drury La.......H 9
78 Dryburgh Rd.....G 1
82 Dryden St......H 9
84 Drysdale St......D 4
73 Du Cane Rd......K 8
73 Duchess St......F 5
83 Duchess Th......H 9
85 Duchess of Bedford's
   Wk.........C 1
87 Duchy St.......B 11
79 Ducie St........G 10
76 Ducket St.......J 1
65 Ducks Hill.......C 4
65 Ducks Hill Rd....C 4
65 Ducks Island.....A 4
66 Dudden Hill La...D 7
77 Dudley Gdns.....A 1
84 Dufferin St......E 2
88 Duffield St......F 6
77 Duke Rd........C 6
86 Duke St., St. James's,
   SW1........A 6
82 Duke St. W1.....H 4
88 Duke St. Hill....B 3
86 Duke of York St..A 6
83 Duke of York's
   Theatre......J 8
66 Dukes Av.......C 6
85 Duke's La.......C 2
84 Duke's Pl......H 4
73 Dukes Rd. W3....H 4
85 Duke's Rd. WC1..D 7
79 Dulwich Common K 14
78 Dulwich Fields Sta..K 14
79 Dulwich Court La.
            H 14
79 Dulwich Pk......J 14
79 Dulwich Rd......H 12
79 Dulwich Village..H 13
71 Dulwich Wood Park
            C 7
79 Dumbarton Rd....H 10
79 Dumont Rd......C 14
76 Dunbar Rd......E 7
84 Dunbridge St....E 7
83 Duncan St......B 12
83 Duncan Ter.....B 12
83 Duncannon St....J 8
80 Duncombe Hill...J 1
75 Duncombe Rd....B 9
80 Duncrievie Rd....H 5
80 Dundalk Rd......F 1
79 Dundas Rd......E 16
76 Dundee Rd......G 7
74 Dundonald Rd....G 2

MAP
76 Dunedin Rd......C 4
84 Dunk St........F 6
74 Dunlace Rd......D 1
84 Dunloe St.......C 5
88 Dunlop Pl.......E 6
74 Dunmow Rd.....D 5
68 Dunning's La....D 6
79 Dunoon Rd......J 16
84 Dunraven Rd.....K 8
82 Dunraven St.....H 3
75 Dunsmure Rd....B 14
76 Dunstan Rd......B 3
70 Dunstans Hill....F 4
79 Dunstan's Rd....H 15
73 Dunster Dri......B 6
74 Dunster Gdns....F 3
84 Dunston Rd......A 5
72 Dunton Green...H 2
76 Dunton Rd. E10..A 3
88 Dunton Rd. SE1..F 5
80 Duplex Ride.....C 3
80 Dupree Rd......C 7
79 Durand Gdns.....E 11
84 Durant St.......C 5
75 Durham Rd. N7..C 11
70 Durham Rd. SW20 D 3
77 Durham Rd. W5..B 2
87 Durham St......G 10
81 Durham Ter......G 2
75 Durley Rd.......A 14
76 Durlston Rd......C 15
78 Durnsford Av....K 4
66 Durnsford Rd. N11
             C 6
78 Durnsford Rd. SW19
             K 4
76 Durrington Rd....D 1
80 Dursley Cl.......E 8
80 Dursley Rd......F 7
75 Durward St......J 15
84 Duval St........F 5
76 Dyers Hall Rd....B 5
79 Dylways........G 13
78 Dymock St......F 4
74 Dyne Rd.......F 3
75 Dynevor Rd. N16.C 13
77 Dynevor Rd. Rich. G 3
74 Dynham Rd......F 4
83 Dyott St........G 8
84 Dysart St.......E 3
76 Dyson Rd.......A 5
73 Eade Rd........A 13
77 Eagle Rd.......F 3
83 Eagle St........F 9
84 Eagle Wharf Rd..B 2
80 Ealdham Sq......G 8
73 Ealing.........K 2
73 Ealing Common...K 3
73 Ealing Common Sta.
             L 4
66 Ealing G.C......F 1
77 Ealing Pk. Gdns..C 2
77 Ealing Rd. Brent..C 3
65 Ealing Rd. Grnfd..E 6
73 Ealing Rd. Wem...F 3
81 Eamont St......B 6
85 Eardley Cres.....G 1
88 Earl Rd........F 5
84 Earl St........F 3
76 Earlham Gro.....E 6
83 Earlham St......H 8
85 Earl's Ct.......G 1
85 Earl's Ct. Gdns...F 2
85 Earl's Ct. Rd....F 2
85 Earl's Ct. Sq.....G 2
85 Earl's Ct. Sta....F 2
67 Earl's Path......A 10
85 Earl's Wk.......E 1
78 Earlsfield......K 5
78 Earlsfield Sta....K 5
78 Earlsfield Rd....J 5
83 Earlstoke St.....D 12
80 Earlswood Rd....C 5
83 Earnshaw St.....G 8
73 East Acton......K 7
73 East Acton La....K 7
75 East Bank......A 14
66 East Barnet.....A 5
69 East Bedfont....B 10
79 East Brixton Sta..G 12
73 East Ct.........C 2
71 East Croydon Sta..E 7
79 East Dulwich....H 14
79 East Dulwich Gro.G 14
79 East Dulwich Rd..G 15
79 East Dulwich Sta..G 14
66 East End Rd.....C 5
70 East Ewell......F 4
80 East Ferry Rd....B 4
66 East Finchley....C 5
66 East Finchley Sta..C 5

MAP
71 East Hall Rd. E 12
67 East Ham & Barking By-Pass F 10
74 East Heath Rd. C 5
78 East Hill, SW18 H 5
72 East Hill, Dartford B 3
73 East Hill, Wem. B 4
76 East India Dock Rd. K 3
73 East La. Wem. C 2
69 East Molesey D 6
75 East Mount St. J 16
78 East Putney Sta. G 3
84 East Rd. D 3
71 E. Rochester Way B 11
74 East Row H 3
77 East Sheen G 5
77 East Sheen Av. G 6
84 East Smithfield J 6
88 East St. SE17 F 3
70 East St. Eps. G 3
88 East Surrey Gro. J 5
84 East Tenter St. H 6
71 East Wickham A 11
73 Eastbourne Av. K 6
81 Eastbourne Mews G 4
76 Eastbourne Rd. E15 F 5
75 Eastbourne Rd. N15 A 14
77 Eastbourne Rd. W4 D 6
77 Eastbourne Rd. Brent C 2
81 Eastbourne Ter. G 4
80 Eastbrook Rd. E 7
65 Eastbury B 4
77 Eastbury Gro. C 3
82 Eastcastle St. G 6
84 Eastcheap H 3
80 Eastcombe Av. D 7
65 Eastcote D 5
65 Eastcote La. E 5
65 Eastcote Rd. D 5
80 Eastdown Pk. G 5
67 Eastern Av. D 10
68 Eastern Av. East C 2
68 Eastern Av. West C 1
75 Eastern Hosp. D 16
76 Eastern Rd. G 7
73 Eastfield Rd. J 5
78 Easthall La. F 3
67 Eastham Manor Way F 11
79 Eastlake Rd. F 12
79 Eastlands Cres. H 14
79 Eastmearn Rd. K 13
80 Eastney C 5
83 Easton St. D 11
76 Eastway E 2
83 Eastwick St. E 13
69 Eastworth E 3
69 Eastworth Rd. E 2
86 Eaton Gate E 3
86 Eaton La. D 5
86 Eaton Mews Nth. E 3
86 Eaton Mews Sth. E 4
86 Eaton Mews W. E 4
86 Eaton Pl. E 3
73 Eaton Rise J 2
74 Eaton Rd. E 7
86 Eaton Row D 4
86 Eaton Sq. E 4
86 Eaton Ter. F 4
78 Eatonville Rd. K 7
87 Ebbisham Dri. H 9
84 Ebenezer St. D 2
84 Ebor St. E 5
75 Eburne Rd. C 10
86 Ebury Bri. F 4
86 Ebury Bri. Rd. G 4
86 Ebury Mews E 4
86 Ebury Mews E. E 4
86 Ebury Sq. F 4
86 Ebury St. E 4
78 Eccles Rd. G 7
75 Ecclesbourne Rd. F 13
86 Eccleston Bri. E 5
86 Eccleston Pl. E 5
86 Eccleston Sq. F 5
86 Eccleston St. E 4
86 Eccleston St. Mews F 5
80 Ector Rd. K 5
81 Edbrooke Rd. E 1
73 Eden Cl. G 2
75 Eden Gro. D 11
78 Edenhurst Av. F 3
77 Edensor Rd. D 7
73 Edge Hill Rd. W13. J 2
70 Edge Hill Rd. Beddington F 6
MAP
85 Edge St. B 1
79 Edgeley Rd. F 9
80 Edgeworth Rd. G 8
66 Edgware B 3
74 Edgware Rd. NW2 C 1
66 Edgware Rd. NW9 C 3
81 Edgware Rd. W2 F 5
76 Edinburgh Rd. G 7
85 Edith Gro. J 4
76 Edith Rd. E15 D 5
78 Edith Rd. W14 C 2
85 Edith Ter. J 4
67 Edmonton B 8
88 Edmund St. J 3
78 Edna St. E 6
80 Edric Rd. D 1
80 Edward Pl. D 2
76 Edward Rd. E 2
80 Edward St. D 2
78 Edwardes Sq. B 3
78 Eel Brook Common E 4
80 Effingham Rd. H 6
79 Effra Parade H 11
79 Effra Rd. G 11
85 Egerton Cres. E 6
80 Egerton Dri. E 3
85 Egerton Gdns. E 6
85 Egerton Pl. E 6
75 Egerton Rd. N16 A 15
73 Egerton Rd. Wem. F 4
85 Egerton Ter. E 6
69 Egham C 1
76 Egham Rd. J 7
78 Eglantine Rd. H 5
78 Egliston Rd. F1
80 Egmont Rd. E 1
79 Elam St. F 12
78 Eland Rd. F 7
88 Elba Pl. E 2
78 Elbe St. E 5
78 Elborough St. J 4
84 Elder St. E 5
77 Elderberry Rd. B 3
76 Elderfield Rd. D 1
85 Eldon Rd. D 3
84 Eldon St. F 3
75 Eleanor Rd. E8 F 16
76 Eleanor Rd. E15 E 6
76 Eleanor Rd. H 3
87 Elephant & Castle Sta. E 13
87 Elephant Rd. E 13
77 Elers Rd. A 2
79 Elfindale Rd. H 13
75 Elfort Rd. D 12
77 Elgar Av. A 3
80 Elgar St. B 2
81 Elgin Av. D 2
74 Elgin Cres. K 3
83 Elia St. C 12
79 Eliot Bank K 16
80 Eliot Hill F 4
80 Eliot Pk. F 4
80 Eliot Pl. F 5
80 Eliot Vale F 5
75 Elizabeth Av. F 13
86 Elizabeth Bri. F 5
86 Elizabeth St. F 4
76 Elkington Rd. H 7
84 Ellen St. H 6
78 Ellerby St. E 2
74 Ellerdale Rd. D 5
80 Ellerdale St. G 3
77 Ellerker Gdns. H 3
76 Ellerman St. J 3
78 Ellerton Rd. J 6
76 Ellesmere Rd. E3 G 1
73 Ellesmere Rd. NW10 D 8
77 Ellesmere Rd. W4 D 6
77 Ellesmere Rd. Twick. H 2
76 Ellesmere St. J 3
76 Ellingham Rd. D 5
75 Ellington St. E 11
79 Elliot Rd. SW9 E 12
77 Elliot Rd. W4 C 7
87 Elliott's Row E 12
86 Ellis St. E 3
80 Elliscombe Rd. D 8
75 Ellsworth St. G 16
77 Elm Av. W5 A 3
65 Elm Av. Ruislip D 5
77 Elm Bank Gdns. F 7
77 Elm Cres. A 3
75 Elm Gro. N8 A 10
74 Elm Gro. NW2 D 2
79 Elm Gro. SE15 E 15
77 Elm Gro. Rd. E 8
80 Elm La. K 2
MAP
79 Elm Pk. SW2 H 11
68 Elm Pk. Hornchurch D 3
85 Elm Pk. Gdns. G 5
85 Elm Pk. La. G 4
85 Elm Pk. Rd. H 5
85 Elm Pl. G 5
76 Elm Rd. E7 E 6
76 Elm Rd. E11 C 4
77 Elm Rd. SW14 G 6
83 Elm St. E 10
81 Elm Tree Rd. C 5
78 Elmbourne Rd. L 8
79 Elmcourt Rd. K 12
74 Elmcroft Av. A 3
74 Elmcroft Cres. A 2
75 Elmcroft St. D 16
80 Elmer Rd. J 4
71 Elmers End D 8
78 Elmfield Rd. K 8
77 Elmgrove Rd. A 3
76 Elmhurst Rd. F 7
79 Elmington Rd. E 13
80 Elmira St. F 4
75 Elmore St. F 13
65 Elmpark Rd. C 5
79 Elms Cres. H 9
81 Elms Mews J 4
79 Elms Rd. H 9
77 Elmshaw Rd. G 8
71 Elmstead C 10
73 Elmstead Av. B 3
71 Elmstead La. C 10
69 Elmwood Av. C 5
79 Elmwood Rd. SE24 H 13
77 Elmwood Rd. W4 D 5
81 Elnathan Mews E 2
75 Elsdale St. E 16
78 Elsenham St. K 3
76 Elsham Rd. E11 D 5
78 Elsham Rd. W14 B 2
79 Elsie Rd. G 14
80 Elsiemaud Rd. H 2
80 Elsinore Rd. K 2
78 Elsley Rd. F 7
78 Elspeth Rd. G 7
88 Elsted St. F 3
66 Elstree A 2
66 Elstree & Borehamwood Sta. A 2
66 Elstree Hill Sth. A 2
66 Elstree Rd. Bushey A 1
66 Elstree Rd. Stan. B 2
74 Elsworthy Rd. F 6
78 Elsynge Rd. G 6
71 Eltham B 10
71 Eltham By-Pass C 10
80 Eltham Green G 8
71 Eltham Hill B 10
80 Eltham Pal. Rd. H 8
71 Eltham Pk. Sta. B 10
80 Eltham Rd. H 7
71 Eltham (Well Hall) Sta. B 10
88 Eltham St. F 2
71 Eltham Warren G.C. B 11
66 Elthorne Heights F 1
75 Elthorne Rd. N19 B 9
73 Elthorne Rd. NW9 A 6
73 Elthorne Way A 6
80 Elthruda Rd. H 5
73 Elton Av. D 1
75 Elton Rd. D 14
85 Elvaston Mews D 4
85 Elvaston Pl. D 4
73 Elveden Pl. G 4
73 Elveden Rd. G 4
70 Elvers Way H 3
86 Elverton St. E 7
84 Elwin St. C 6
75 Elwood St. C 12
83 Ely Pl. F 11
76 Ely Rd. A 4
86 Elystan Pl. F 2
85 Elystan St. F 6
73 Emanuel Av. K 6
78 Embankment F 2
86 Embankment Gdns. H 3
69 Ember La. E 6
80 Embleton Rd. G 3
78 Emden St. E 5
83 Emerald St. F 10
68 Emerson Pk. D 3
87 Emerson St. A 13
86 Emery Hill St. E 6
77 Emlyn Rd. B 7
76 Emma Rd. G 6
79 Emmanuel Rd. K 9
MAP
76 Emmett St. K 2
74 Emmott Cl. A 5
76 Emmott St. J 1
85 Emperor's Gate E 3
83 Empire Cin. C 12
73 Empire Rd. F 2
83 Empire Th. J 7
73 Empire Way D 4
76 Empress Av. C 8
76 Empson St. H 4
79 Emsworth St. K 10
83 Endell St. H 8
67 Endlebury Rd. B 9
78 Endlesham Rd. J 7
82 Endsleigh Gdns. D 7
83 Endsleigh Pl. E 7
83 Endsleigh St. D 7
80 Endwell Rd. F 2
75 Endymion Rd. N4 A 12
79 Endymion Rd. SW2 H 11
67 Enfield A 7
67 Enfield Chase Sta. A 7
67 Enfield G.C. A 7
77 Enfield Rd. W3 B 5
77 Enfield Rd. Brent. C 2
66 Enfield Rd. Enfield A 6
67 Enfield Town Sta. A 7
82 Enford St. F 2
78 Engadine St. J 3
73 Engineers Way D 4
74 Englands La. E 7
75 Englefield Rd. E 13
80 Engleheart Rd. J 4
78 Englewood Rd. H 8
88 English Grounds B 4
88 Enid St. D 6
77 Enmore Gdns. G 6
78 Enmore Rd. G 1
77 Ennerdale Rd. F 4
80 Ennersdale Rd. H 4
75 Ennis Rd. B 11
85 Ennismore Gdns. D 6
85 Ennismore Gdns. Mews D 5
85 Ennismore Mews D 6
85 Ennismore Pl. D 6
85 Ennismore St. D 6
84 Ensign St. J 6
79 Ephraim Rd. K 10
78 Epirus Rd. D 3
67 Epping Forest A 10
67 Epping New Rd. A 10
78 Epple Rd. E 3
70 Epsom G 2
70 Epsom Common G 2
70 Epsom Downs Sta. G 3
70 Epsom G.C. G 3
70 Epsom La. H 3
76 Epsom Rd. E10 A 4
70 Epsom Rd. Cro. E 6
70 Epsom Rd. Eps. G 2
70 Epsom Rd. Ewell G 3
70 Epsom Rd. Leatherhead H 1
70 Epsom Rd. Mord. E 4
84 Epworth St. E 3
87 Erasmus St. F 8
73 Erconwald St. J 7
76 Eric St. H 2
68 Erith H 2
72 Erith Rd. A 1
80 Erlanger Rd. E 1
80 Ermine Rd. G 3
76 Ernest Rd. H 6
76 Ernest St. H 1
78 Erpingham Rd. F 1
84 Errol St. E 2
69 Esher F 6
69 Esher Common F 6
69 Esher La. E 6
69 Esher Rd. F 5
69 Esher Sta. E 6
88 Esmeralda Rd. F 6
77 Esmond Rd. B 6
81 Essendine Rd. D 1
77 Essex Pk. Mews A 7
76 Essex Rd. E10 A 4
75 Essex Rd. N1 F 12
73 Essex Rd. NW10 E 7
73 Essex Rd. W3 K 5
75 Essex Rd. Sta. F 12
76 Essex St. E7 D 6
83 Essex St. WC2 H 10
85 Essex Villas D 1
78 Este Rd. F 6
74 Estelle Rd. D 7
76 Esther Rd. A 5
79 Etherow St. H 15
MAP
79 Ethnard Rd. D 15
74 Eton Av. NW3 E 6
73 Eton Av. Wem. D 2
74 Eton College Rd. E 7
74 Eton Rd. NW3 E 7
74 Eton Villas E 7
76 Etropol Rd. D 1
80 Etta St. D 2
76 Ettrick St. J 4
80 Eugenia Rd. C 1
85 Eustace Rd. J 1
82 Euston Rd. E 6
82 Euston Sq. D 7
82 Euston Sta. D 7
82 Euston Sta. Colonnade D 7
82 Euston St. D 6
79 Evandale Rd. E 12
80 Evans Rd. K 5
76 Eve Rd. G 5
79 Evelina Rd. F 16
85 Evelyn Gdns. G 4
80 Evelyn St. C 2
83 Everilda St. A 10
75 Evering Rd. E5 C 15
75 Evering Rd. N16 C 15
73 Everitt Rd. H 6
75 Eversholt Rd. B 11
82 Eversholt St. C 6
78 Eversleigh Rd. F 7
73 Eversley Av. C 4
80 Eversley Rd. D 7
80 Ewart Rd. J 1
70 Ewell F 3
70 Ewell By-Pass F 3
70 Ewell W. Sta. F 3
79 Ewelme Rd. J 16
87 Ewer St. B 13
80 Ewhurst Rd. H 2
80 Exbury Rd. K 2
74 Exeter Rd. NW2 E 2
83 Exeter St. H 9
80 Exford Gdns. K 7
80 Exford Rd. J 7
85 Exhibition Rd. D 5
74 Exmoor St. J 1
83 Exmouth Mkt. D 12
76 Exning Rd. H 6
88 Exon St. F 4
87 Exton St. B 11
83 Eye Hosp. G 8
79 Eynella Rd. J 14
74 Eynham Rd. J 1
72 Eynsford E 3
83 Eyre St. Hill E 11
79 Eythorne Rd. E 12
84 Ezra St. C 6
69 Faggs Rd. B 4
88 Fair St. C 5
79 Fairbairn Rd. E 11
75 Fairbridge C 9
80 Fairby Rd. G 7
84 Fairchild St. E 4
71 Fairchildes Rd. G 9
84 Fairclough St. H 6
74 Fairfax Pl. F 5
74 Fairfax Rd. NW6 F 5
77 Fairfax Rd. W4 B 7
73 Fairfield Dri. G 2
76 Fairfield Rd. G 3
78 Fairfield St G 4
76 Fairfoot Rd. H 3
74 Fairhazel Gdns. F 5
75 Fairholt Rd. B 13
76 Fairland Rd. E 6
77 Fairlawn Gro. B 6
79 Fairlie Gdns. J 16
76 Fairlop Rd. B 5
67 Fairlop Sta. C 11
67 Fairmead Rd. A 10
69 Fairmile G 5
69 Fairmile La. G 5
79 Fairmount Rd. H 11
70 Fairoak La. G 1
72 Fairseat G 5
73 Fairview Av. E 2
73 Fairway, The, W3. J 7
73 Fairway, The, Wem. C 1
78 Falcon Rd. F 6
76 Falcon St. H 6
71 Falconwood Station B 11
74 Falkland Rd. A 9
84 Falkirk St. C 4
65 Falling La. F 3
88 Falmouth Rd. E 2
84 Fann St. E 1
84 Fanshaw St. C 4
74 Faraday Rd. J 2
88 Faraday St. G 3
71 Farleigh G 8
MAP
71 Farleigh Ct. Rd. G 8
75 Farleigh Rd. D 14
80 Farley Rd. SE6 H 4
71 Farley Rd. Cro. F 7
74 Farm Av. NW2 C 3
73 Farm Av. Wem. E 2
85 Farm La. SW6 J 1
70 Farm La. Eps. H 2
82 Farm St. J 4
80 Farmcote Rd. J 7
76 Farmer Rd. B 3
85 Farmer St. B 1
76 Farmilo Rd. A 2
71 Farnborough F 10
71 Farnborough By Pass F 11
71 Farnborough Common E 10
88 Farncombe St. D 7
87 Farnham Pl. B 13
87 Farnham Royal G 10
72 Farningham E 3
72 Farningham Rd. D 3
72 Farningham Rd. Sta. D 3
78 Faroe Rd. B 2
76 Farrance St. J 2
80 Farren Rd. K 1
83 Farringdon Rd. E 11
83 Farringdon Sta. F 12
83 Farringdon St. G 12
76 Farringford Rd. F 5
84 Fashion St. F 5
77 Fauconberg Rd. D 5
87 Faunce St. G 12
78 Favart Rd. E 4
80 Faversham Rd. J 2
85 Fawcett St. H 3
78 Fawe Pk. Rd. G 3
72 Fawkham Green E 4
74 Fawley Rd. E 4
76 Fawn Rd. G 8
79 Fawnbrake Av. G 12
79 Faygate Rd. K 11
80 Fearon St. C 6
71 Featherbed La. F 8
84 Featherstone St. E 2
73 Federal Rd. G 2
80 Felday Rd. H 3
78 Felden St. E 3
79 Fellbrigg Rd. H 15
74 Fellows Rd. F 6
78 Felsham Rd. F 2
76 Felstead Rd. A 7
76 Felstead St. E 2
69 Feltham C 4
69 Feltham Rd. C 4
69 Felthamhill C 4
69 Felthamhill Rd. Ashford C 4
69 Felthamhill Rd. Hanworth C 11
68 Fen La. E 5
67 Fencepiece Rd. B 11
84 Fenchurch Av. H 4
84 Fenchurch Bldgs. H 4
84 Fenchurch St. H 4
84 Fenchurch St Sta. H 4
88 Fendall St. D 4
79 Fenham Rd. E 15
87 Fentiman Rd. J 9
79 Fenwick Rd. F15
74 Ferdinand St. E 8
80 Fermor Rd. K 2
74 Fermoy Rd. H 3
76 Fern St. H 3
80 Fernbrook Rd. H 5
75 Ferncliff Rd. D 15
74 Ferncroft Av. D 4
76 Ferndale Rd. E7 F 7
76 Ferndale Rd. E11 B 6
79 Ferndale Rd. SW4 G 10
79 Ferndene Rd. G 13
74 Fernhead Rd. H 3
80 Fernholme Rd. G 1
78 Fernlea Rd. K 8
83 Fernsbury St. D 11
85 Fernshaw Rd. J 3
78 Fernside Rd. J 7
75 Ferntower Rd. D 13
78 Ferrier St. G 4
67 Ferry La. N17 C 8
77 Ferry La. Brent. D 3
77 Ferry La. Rich. D 4
77 Ferry Rd. E 8
80 Ferry St. C 4
78 Festing Rd. F 2
86 Festival Pleasure Gdns. J 1
83 Fetter La. G 11

MAP		MAP		MAP		MAP		MAP		MAP	
71	Fickleshole.......G 9	76	Follett St........K 4	77	Fraser St........C 7	78	Garratt La. SW18.J 5	73	Gladstone Pk......D 8	74	Golders Manor Dri.
65	Field End Rd.....D 5	78	Fontenoy Rd.....K 8	84	Frazier St.......C 11	84	Garrett St........E 1	73	Gladstone Pk. Gdns.		A 2
77	Field La........D 2	75	Fonthill Rd......B 11	88	Frean St........D 6	74	Garrick Av........A 3		C 9	77	Goldhawk Rd.....B 8
83	Field Pl........C 11	71	Foots Cray.....C 12	75	Frederica St.....F 10	83	Garrick St........H 8	87	Gladstone St.....D 12	78	Goldhawk Rd. Station
76	Field Rd. E7......D 6	71	Foots Cray La....C 12	79	Frederick Cres...E 12	83	Garrick Th........J 8	78	Gladstone Ter.....E 8		A 1
78	Field Rd. W6.....C 2	71	Foots Cray Rd...B 10	83	Frederick St......D 10	74	Garth Rd. NW2...C 3	75	Gladwell Rd......A 10	74	Goldhurst Ter.....F 5
84	Fieldgate St......G 6	84	Forbes St........H 6	75	Freegrove Rd....D 10	70	Garth Rd. Mord...E 3	75	Glamis Rd.......K 16	75	Golding St.......K 15
79	Fieldhouse Rd....J 9	75	Forburg Rd......B 15	88	Freeland Rd......K 4	80	Garthorne Rd.....J 1	78	Glasgow Rd.......J 8	82	Goldington Cres...B 7
77	Fielding Rd......B 6	69	Ford Bri. Rd......C 3	88	Freemantle St.....F 4	78	Gartmoor Gdns....K 3	87	Glass Hill St......C 13	82	Goldington St.....B 7
78	Fieldview.......K 6	76	Ford Rd.........G 2	73	Freemasons Rd....J 7	78	Garvan Rd........D 2	82	Glasshouse St.....J 6	81	Goldney Rd.......E 1
76	Fife Rd. E16......J 6	75	Ford Sq.........J 16	69	French St.........D 5	81	Garway Rd........H 2	87	Glasshouse Wk....G 9	73	Goldsmith Av.....K 6
77	Fife Rd. SW14....H 5	76	Ford St.........G 2	80	Frendsbury Rd....G 1	84	Gascoigne Pl......D 5	83	Glasshouse Yd....E 13	76	Goldsmith Rd. E10.B 3
74	Fifth Av........H 2	69	Fordbridge Rd....D 4	77	Frensham Dri.....K 8	74	Gascony Av.......F 4	76	Glaucus St........J 3	79	Goldsmith Rd. SE15,
75	Filey Av........B 15	80	Fordel Rd........J 4	88	Frensham St......H 6	76	Gascoyne Rd.....E 1	85	Glebe, The.......F 5		E 15
76	Fillebrook Rd.....B 5	73	Fordhook Av.....K 4	78	Frewin Rd........J 6	87	Gasholder Pl......G 10	85	Glebe Pl.........H 6	84	Goldsmiths Row...B 7
78	Filmer Rd........E 3	80	Fordmill Rd......K 3	77	Friars La.........G 2	78	Gaskarth Rd......H 8	73	Glebe Rd. NW10...E 6	75	Gomm Rd........B 16
82	Filston La........G 1	76	Fords Pk. Rd.....J 6	77	Friars Place La....K 6	69	Gastonbridge Rd...E 4	78	Glebe Rd. SW13...F 8	74	Gondar Gdns.....D 3
75	Finborough Rd....H 3	74	Fordwych Rd.....D 3	77	Friars Stile Rd....H 3	73	Gate Rd..........F 7	77	Glebe St.........C 7	83	Goodge Pl........F 6
84	Finch La. EC3.....H 3	80	Fordyce Rd.......H 4	73	Friars Way.......K 6	83	Gate St..........G 9	85	Gledhow Gdns.....F 3	82	Goodge St........F 6
65	Finch La. Bushey..A 6	84	Fore St. EC2......F 2	78	Friary Rd. SE15..D 15	81	Gateforth St......E 6	73	Glen Albyn Rd....K 2	73	Goodhall St.......H 7
66	Finchley........C 5	67	Fore St. N18......B 8	73	Friary Rd. W3.....J 6	79	Gateley Rd......F 11	76	Glen Rd..........H 7	75	Gooding Rd......E 10
66	Finchley Cen. Sta..C 5	65	Fore St. Ruislip...C 4	83	Friend St.........C 12	88	Gateway........H 2	76	Glenarm Rd......D 1	84	Goodman St......H 6
66	Finchley G.C......B 5	87	Foreign Office....C 8	79	Friendly St.......E 3	86	Gatliff Rd........G 4	73	Glenburnie Rd....L 7	84	Goodmans Yd.....H 5
74	Finchley Rd. NW3.D 4	79	Foreign St.......F 12	82	Friends' Ho.......D 7	79	Gauden Rd.......F 9	73	Glencairn Dri.....H 2	67	Goodmayes......D 12
81	Finchley Rd. NW8.B 4	76	Forest Dri. E......A 5	66	Friern Barnet.....B 5	87	Gaunt St.........D 13	73	Glendale Gdns....B 3	67	Goodmayes La...D 12
74	Finchley Rd.&	76	Forest Dri. W......A 4	75	Friern Rd........H 15	79	Gautrey Rd.......E 16	80	Glenelg Rd.......G 10	79	Goodrich Rd.....H 14
	Frognall Sta.....E 5	76	Forest Gate.......E 7	76	Frith Rd.........D 4	80	Gavestone Cres....J 7	80	Glenfarg Rd......J 4	83	Goods Way......B 8
77	Findon Rd.......A 8	76	Forest Gate Hosp.D 6	82	Frith St.........H 7	75	Gawber St.......G 16	79	Glenfield Rd.....J 9	77	Goodwin Rd......A 8
80	Fingal St........C 6	76	Forest Gate Sta...D 7	78	Frithville Gdns....A 1	87	Gayfere St........E 8	80	Glenfinlas Way...J 12	80	Goodwood Rd.....E 1
87	Fink St.........D 10	76	Forest Glade......A 5	80	Frogmore Rd.....G 4	77	Gayford Rd.......A 8	80	Glenforth St......C 6	84	Gopsall St.......B 3
80	Finland Rd.......G 1	79	Forest Hill Rd....H 16	74	Frognal.........D 5	75	Gayhurst Rd......F 15	80	Glengall Gro......B 3	74	Gordon Ho. Rd....D 8
78	Finlay St........E 3	79	Forest Hill Sta....K 17	74	Frognal Gdns.....D 5	80	Gaynesford Rd....K 1	73	Glengall Rd. NW6.F 3	85	Gordon Pl........C 2
75	Finsbury........H 12	67	Forest Hosp......A 10	74	Frognal La.......D 4	74	Gayton Rd.......D 5	88	Glengall Rd. SE15.H 6	76	Gordon Rd. E11...A 6
84	Finsbury Circus....F 3	76	Forest La.........E 6	74	Frognal Way.....D 5	78	Gayville Rd.......H 7	88	Glengall Ter......H 5	79	Gordon Rd. SE15.F 16
75	Finsbury Pk......H 11	75	Forest Rd. E8....E 14	78	Frome St.........B 13	87	Gaywood St......E 12	79	Glengarnock Av...C 4	77	Gordon Rd. W4...D 5
75	Finsbury Pk. Rd..C 12	76	Forest Rd. E11....A 5	73	Fryent Gro.......A 7	87	Gaza St.........G 12	79	Glengarry Rd.....G 14	73	Gordon Rd. W5 &
75	Finsbury Pk. Sta..C 11	67	Forest Rd. Ilf.....C 12	73	Fryent Way.......A 5	73	Geary Rd.........D 8				W13........K 2
84	Finsbury Pavement.F 3	70	Forest Rd. Rich...D 4	78	Fulham..........E 3	83	Gee St..........E 13	80	Glensdale Rd......F 2	80	Gordon Sq.......E 7
84	Finsbury Sq......F 3	70	Forest Rd. Sut....E 4	78	Fulham Bdy.......D 4	84	Geffrye Mus......C 4	80	Glentham Rd......D 8	82	Gordon Sq. WC1...E 7
84	Finsbury Sq......F 2	67	Forest Side.......A 10	78	Fulham High St....F 3	84	Geffrye St........B 5	78	Glenthorn Rd.....C 1	80	Gordonbrook Rd...H 3
79	Finsen Rd........F 13	76	Forest St.........D 6	78	Fulham Palace Rd.	75	Geldeston Rd.....C 15	82	Glentworth St.....E 2	72	Gore Hill.........C 3
78	Fircroft Rd.......K 7	79	Forester Rd......G 16		D 2	80	Gellatly Rd.......F 1	73	Glenville Gro......E 2	85	Gore St..........D 4
80	Firhill Rd........L 3	81	Formosa St.......E 3	78	Fulham Pk. Gdns..F 3	83	GPO.............G 13	73	Glenwood Av.....B 6	67	Goresbrook Rd...E 12
67	Firs La..........B 7	82	Forset St.........G 2	78	Fulham Pk. Rd....F 3	79	Geneva Rd.......G 12	73	Glenwood Gro....B 5	72	Gorse Rd.........E 1
75	Firsby Rd........B 15	80	Forster Mem. Pk..L 4	78	Fulham Rd. SW6...E 3	78	Genoa Av........H 1	80	Glenwood Rd......J 2	73	Gorst Rd. NW10...H 6
76	First Av. E13......H 7	76	Forster Rd. E17...A 1	85	Fulham Rd. SW10.G 5	80	Geoffrey Rd......F 2	75	Globe Rd........H 16	78	Gorst Rd. SW11...H 7
77	First Av. SW14....F 7	79	Forster Rd. SW2.J 10	78	Fuller St.........D 6	85	Geological Mus....E 5	88	Globe St.........D 2	84	Gorsuch St.......C 5
73	First Av. W3.....L 7	84	Forston St........B 2	78	Fullerton Rd......G 5	73	Geology Rd......G 3	87	Globe Th. SE1.....E 3	78	Gosberton Rd.....J 7
74	First Av. W10....H 3	87	Forsyth Gdns.....H 12	69	Fulwell G.C.......C 6	65	George V Av......C 6	82	Globe Th. W1......H 7	82	Gosfield St.......F 5
73	First Av. Wem.....B 3	88	Fort Rd..........F 6	69	Fulwell Sta.......C 6	80	George La........H 4	82	Globe Yd.........H 5	79	Gosling Way.....E 11
86	First St.........E 1	84	Fort St. E1.......F 4	73	Fulwood Av......G 3	88	George Row......C 6	76	Gloucester Av.....F 8	74	Gospel Oak Sta....D 8
73	First Way.......D 5	75	Fortescue Av.....F 16	79	Furley Rd........E 15	82	George St. W1....G 2	76	Gerald Rd. E16...H 6	84	Gosset St........D 6
70	Firtree Rd.......G 3	74	Fortess Rd.......D 8	75	Furlong Rd.......E 11	77	George St. Rich...G 2	86	Gerald Rd. SW1...F 4	80	Gosterwood St....D 2
84	Fish St. Hill......J 3	88	Forthbridge Rd...G 8	73	Furness Rd. NW10.	82	George Yd........H 4	87	G.M. Harmsworth Pk.	83	Goswell Rd......D 12
76	Fisher St. E16.....J 6	66	Fortis Green Rd....C 5		G 8	73	Georgian Ct......E 5		E 11	83	Goswell Ter......D 12
83	Fisher St. WC1....F 9	73	Fortune Gate Rd..F 7	78	Furness Rd. SW6..F 4	76	Gerald Rd. E16...H 5	75	Gloucester Dri....B 12	76	Gough Gro.......K 3
81	Fisherton St......E 5	74	Fortune Green Rd.	83	Furnival St.......G 11	87	Geraldine St......E 12	80	Gloucester Circus.D 4	83	Gough Sq.......G 11
87	Fitzalan St.......E 10		D 4	80	Further Green Rd..J 5	77	Gerard Rd........E 7	74	Gloucester Cres...F 8	83	Gough St........E 10
82	Fitzhardinge St....G 3	84	Fortune St.......E 2	80	Furze Field Rd....D 7	68	Gerpins La.......E 4	82	Gloucester Gate...B 4	84	Goulston St......G 5
74	Fitzjohns Av......E 5	73	Forty Av........C 4	78	Furze Hill........H 4	83	Gerrard Rd.......B 12	82	Gloucester Gdns..A 3	75	Goulton Rd......D 16
86	Fitzmaurice Pl.....A 5	73	Forty La.........C 5	76	Furze St.........J 3	83	Gerrard St.......H 7	82	Gloucester Gate...B 4	78	Gowan Av.......E 2
73	Fitzneal St.......J 7	80	Fossil Rd........G 3	66	Furzehill Rd......A 3	65	Gerrards Cross....D 1	81	Gloucester Mews..H 4	82	Gower Mews......F 7
74	Fitzroy Pk.......B 7	77	Foster La.........G 1	80	Fyncs St.........E 7	87	Gerridge St......D 11	81	Gloucester Mews W.	82	Gower Pl........E 7
82	Fitzroy Pl.......E 5	77	Foster Rd.......C 6	80	Gabriel St........J 1	85	Gertrude St......H 4		H 4	76	Gower Rd.......E 7
74	Fitzroy Rd.......F 7	82	Foubert's Pl......H 6	75	Gainford St.......F 11	79	Gervase St.......D 16	82	Gloucester Pl......F 2	82	Gower St........E 7
82	Fitzroy Sq.......E 6	75	Foulden Rd......D 14	76	Gainsborough Rd. E11	80	Ghent St.........K 3	82	Gloucester Pl. Mews	84	Gower's Wk.......H 6
82	Fitzroy St........E 6	84	Fountain St.......D 5		A 5	76	Gibbins Rd.......F 4		G 3	79	Gowlett Rd......G 15
75	Fitzwarren Gdns..B 9	84	Fountayne Rd....C 15	76	Gainsborough Rd. E15	79	Gibbon Rd. SE15..F 16	85	Gloucester Rd. SW7	78	Gowrie Rd.......G 8
76	Fladgate Rd......A 5	84	Fournier St.......F 5	77	Gainsborough Rd.	73	Gibbon Rd. W3....K 7		D 4	76	Grace St.........H 3
73	Flamsted Av......E 4	74	Fourth Av........H 3		Rich...........F 4	73	Gibbons Rd.......E 6	77	Gloucester Rd. W5.B 2	84	Gracechurch St....H 3
77	Flanchford Rd.....B 8	73	Fourth Way.......D 5	88	Gainsford St......C 5	75	Gibson Sq.......F 12	77	Gloucester Rd. Rich.	79	Graces Rd.,......E 14
77	Flanders Rd......B 7	73	Fowlers Wk.......H 2	74	Gaisford St.......E 8	68	Gidea Pk........C 3		D 4	77	Graemesdyke Av...G 4
74	Flask Wk........D 5	73	Fox Ct..........F 11	76	Gale St. E3.......J 3	80	Giffin St.........D 3	81	Gloucester Sq.....H 5	82	Grafton Mews.....E 6
79	Flaxman Rd......F 12	69	Fox Hill Rd.......F 1	66	Gale St. Dag......J 3	75	Gifford St........F 10	86	Gloucester St......G 6	82	Grafton Pl.......D 7
83	Flaxman Ter......D 8	66	Fox La...........B 6	79	Gallery Rd.......J 13	83	Gilbert Pl........G 8	81	Gloucester Ter.....G 3	74	Grafton Rd. NW5.E 8
83	Fleet La.........G 12	80	Foxberry Rd......G 2	72	Galley Hill.......B 5	87	Gilbert Rd........F 11	85	Gloucester Wk....C 1	73	Grafton Rd. W3...K 6
74	Fleet Rd.........D 7	80	Foxbourne Rd....K 8	84	Galley La........A 4	82	Gilbert St........H 4	83	Gloucester Way...D 11	79	Grafton Sq.......F 9
83	Fleet St.........H 11	80	Foxes Dale.......F 6	79	Galleywall Rd....C 16	75	Gilda Cres.......B 15	78	Glycena Rd.......F 7	82	Grafton St.......J 5
73	Fleetwood Rd.....D 8	71	Foxgrove G.C.....C 9	67	Galliard Rd.......A 8	72	Gildenhill Rd.....D 2	76	Glyn Rd..........D 1	82	Grafton Way......E 6
87	Fleming Rd......H 12	79	Foxham Rd......C 9	80	Galloway Rd......L 8	87	Gilbert Pl........G 8	87	Glyn St..........G 9	75	Graham Rd. E8...E 15
76	Flempton Rd.....B 2	79	Foxley Rd........D 12	74	Galsworthy Rd....D 3	82	Giltspur St.......H 4	78	Goda St..........F 10	77	Graham Rd. W4...B 5
77	Fletcher Rd......B 6	69	Foxoak Hill......F 4	78	Galveston Rd......G 3	75	Gilda Cres.......B 15	76	Godbold Rd.......H 5	83	Graham St.......C 13
75	Fletching Rd.....C 16	80	Fox's La.........E 16	84	Galway St.......C 12	79	Gilkes Cres......H 14	86	Godfrey St.......G 1	86	Graham Ter......F 4
84	Fleur-de-Lis St....E 4	80	Foyle Rd........D 6	87	Gambia St.......B 12	80	Gill St..........K 2	79	Goding St........G 9	87	Granada Cin......F 11
88	Flint St.........F 3	76	Gamuel Rd.......A 2	75	Gillespie Rd......C 12	83	Giltspur St.......G 12	78	Godley Rd........J 6	78	Granard Av.......H 9
88	Flinton St.......F 4	70	Gander Green La..E 4	74	Gillies St........E 8	71	Gipsy Hill Sta....C 7	83	Godliman St......H 13	78	Granard Rd......J 7
79	Flodden Rd......E 12	82	Ganton St.......H 6	80	Gillingham St.....E 6	77	Gipsy La.........G 8	87	Godman Rd......F 15	84	Granby St........D 6
86	Flood St.........H 2	67	Gants Hill Sta....D 11	80	Gilmore Rd.......G 4	76	Giraud St........J 3	77	Godolphin Rd.....A 9	82	Granby Ter......C 6
86	Flood Wk........G 1	82	Garbutt Pl.......F 4	77	Gilpin Av........G 6	84	Garlick Hill......H 2	83	Godson St.......B 11	73	Grand Av........E 4
83	Floral St.........H 8	78	Franche Ct. Rd....L 5	77	Gilpin Rd........D 1	80	Garlies Rd........K 1	80	Godstone Rd......G 6	70	Grand Dri.......D 3
76	Florence Rd. E11..C 5	76	Francis Rd. E10...B 4	81	Garden Rd........C 4	77	Gilpin Av........G 6	76	Godwin Rd.......D 7	70	Grand Stand Rd...H 3
75	Florence Rd. N4..B 11	73	Francis Rd. Gnfd..G 2	87	Garden Row......D 12	85	Gilston Rd........F 3	80	Goffers Rd.......E 5	78	Grandison Rd.....G 7
80	Florence Rd. SE14.B 4	86	Francis St........E 6	84	Garden Wk.......D 4	83	Giltspur St.......G 12	80	Golborne Rd.......J 3	88	Grange, The......B 4
73	Florence Rd. W5..K 3	79	Franconia Rd.....H 9	79	Gardens, The....G 15	71	Gipsy Hill Sta....C 7	84	Golden La.......E 1	75	Grange Gro......E 12
76	Florence St. E16..H 6	79	Frank Dixon Cl...J 14	76	Gardner Rd.......H 7	77	Gipsy La.........G 8	82	Golden Sq.......H 6	67	Grange Hill......B 11
75	Florence St. N1...E 12	79	Frank Dixon Way J 14	82	Garford St.......K 2	76	Giraud St........J 3	74	Golders Green....A 3	79	Grange La.......K 14
84	Florida St........D 7	77	Frankfurt Rd.....H 13	84	Garlick Hill......H 2	74	Girdle's Rd.......B 2	74	Golders Green	77	Grange Pk. W5...A 3
84	Flower & Dean St..F 5	75	Franklin St.......A 14	80	Garlies Rd.......K 1	74	Girdlestone Rd....A 9		Cres...........B 3	73	Grange Pk. W5...L 3
80	Floyd Rd........C 8	86	Franklin's Row....G 3	83	Garnault Pl.......D 11	74	Girdwood Rd......J 3	74	Golders Green Rd..A 3	76	Grange Rd. E13...B 2
82	Foley St.........F 6	73	Franklyn Rd......E 7	75	Garnet St........K 16	75	Gladsmuir Rd....B 9	74	Golders Green Sta..B 4	67	Grange Pk. Sta....A 7
84	Folgate St.......F 4	73	Fraser Rd........G 2	70	Garratt La. SW17.C 5	75	Gladstone Rd.....B 9	74	Golders Hill Pk....B 4	76	Grange Rd. E10...B 3

MAP
76 Grange Rd. E13...H 6
74 Grange Rd. N6....A 7
88 Grange Rd. SE1...E 5
71 Grange Rd. SE25..D 7
77 Grange Rd. SW13.E 8
73 Grange Rd. W5...L 3
84 Grange St........B 3
88 Grange Wk.......D 4
88 Grange Yd.......E 5
80 Grangemill Rd....K 3
80 Grangemill Way...K 3
71 Grangewood.......D 7
76 Granleigh Rd......C 5
83 Grant St.........B 11
83 Grantbridge St....B 12
79 Grantham Rd. SW9 F 10
77 Grantham Rd. W4.D 7
76 Grantley St.......H 1
81 Grantully Rd......D 2
80 Granville Pk.......F 4
82 Granville Pl.......H 3
76 Granville Rd. E16. J 6
75 Granville Rd. N4 & N8...........A 11
74 Granville Rd. NW2 C 3
81 Granville Rd.NW6 C 1
78 Granville Rd. SW18 J 3
83 Granville Sq......D 10
83 Grape St..........G 8
73 Grasmere Ave.....K 6
72 Gravel Hill.......B 1
84 Gravel La. E1.....G 5
67 Gravel La. Abridge A 12
72 Gravesend G.C....C 6
75 Grayling Rd......B 13
83 Grays Inn.........F 10
83 Grays Inn Gdns...F 10
83 Grays Inn Rd......E 10
71 Grays Rd..........H 11
68 Grays Thurrock...H 6
75 Grazebrook Rd...C 13
67 Gt. Cambridge Rd..B 7
82 Gt. Castle St......G 5
82 Gt. Central St......F 2
82 Gt. Chapel St.....G 7
77 Gt. Chertsey Rd...E 6
87 Gt. College St.....D 8
82 Gt. Cumberland Pl. H 2
88 Gt. Dover St.......D 2
76 Gt. Eastern Rd....E 5
84 Gt. Eastern St.....E 4
82 Gt. George St......C 8
87 Gt. Guildford St..B 13
83 Gt. James St.....F 10
82 Gt. Marlborough St. H 6
66 Gt. North Way....C 4
83 Gt. Ormond St....F 9
83 Gt. Percy St......C 10
87 Gt. Peter St.......D 8
82 Gt. Portland St....F 5
82 Gt. Pulteney St....H 6
83 Gt. Queen St......G 9
83 Gt. Russell St.....G 8
84 Gt. St. Helen's....G 4
87 Gt. Scotland Yd...B 8
87 Gt. Smith St......D 8
69 Gt. South West Rd. B 4
87 Gt. Suffolk St....C 13
83 Gt. Sutton St.....E 12
84 Gt. Swan Alley....G 3
70 Gt. Tattenhams...H 3
82 Gt. Titchfield St...G 6
84 Gt. Tower St.......J 4
68 Gt. Warley........C 5
77 Gt. W. Rd. W6 ... C 8
77 Gt. W. Rd. Brent.. C 3
66 Gt. W. Rd. Isle. & Brent..........H 1
74 Gt. Western Rd....J 3
84 Gt. Winchester St..G 3
82 Gt. Windmill St....J 7
72 Greatness.........H 2
84 Greatorex St.......F 6
83 Greek St..........H 7
76 Green, The, E11 ..A 7
77 Green, The, SW14. F 6
73 Green, The, W3 ...J 7
65 Green, The, S'hall .G 5
77 Green Av..........B 1
79 Green Bank.......A 16
72 Green Court.......E 1
79 Green Dale.......G 13
67 Green Dragon La..A 7
74 Green Hill.........D 6
79 Green Hundred Rd. D 15
71 Green La. SE9...C 11
70 Green La. SW16...D 6
69 Green La. Hatton .A 5
67 Green Lane, Ilf....D 11
70 Green La. Mord....E 4
65 Green La. Northwood B 4
69 Green La. Shepperton D 4
75 Green Lanes, N4 & N16..........C 13
86 Green Pk.........C 5
72 Green Rd.........C 4
76 Green St. E7 & E13 E 7
82 Green St. W1......H 3
67 Green St. Enfield..A 8
69 Green St. Sunbury D 4
72 Green Street Green, Dartford........C 4
71 Green Street Green, Farnborough...F 11
83 Green Ter.........D 11
70 Green Wrythe La..E 5
74 Greenaway Gdns..D 4
81 Greenberry St.....C 6
86 Greencoat Pl......E 6
86 Greencoat Row....E 6
74 Greencroft Gdns...F 5
77 Greenend Rd......A 7
74 Greenfield Gdns...C 3
84 Greenfield Rd......G 7
66 Greenford.........F 1
66 Greenford Av......F 1
66 Greenford Green...E 1
66 Greenford Rd......E 1
66 Greenford Sta......E 1
76 Greengate St......G 7
66 Greenhill ....D 1
73 Greenhill Pk.......G 7
73 Greenhill Way.....B 5
72 Greenhithe........B 4
75 Greenman St......F 12
77 Greenside.........G 2
77 Greenside Rd......B 8
82 Greenwell St......E 5
80 Greenwich.........D 4
80 Greenwich High Rd. E 3
80 Greenwich Pk......E 5
80 Greenwich Sth. St..E 4
80 Greenwich Sta.....D 4
75 Greenwood Rd. E8 E 15
77 Greet Rd..........C 3
87 Greet St..........B 11
77 Grena Gdn........G 4
77 Grena Rd..........G 4
76 Grenade St........K 2
73 Grendon Gardens........C 4
85 Grenville Pl.......E 3
75 Grenville Rd......B 10
83 Grenville St.......E 9
74 Gresham Gardens........B 3
73 Gresham Rd. NW10 E 6
79 Gresham Rd. SW9 F 11
84 Gresham St........G 2
82 Gresse St..........G 7
78 Gressenhall Rd....H 3
74 Greville Pl.........G 4
74 Greville Rd. NW6.G 4
77 Greville Rd. Rich..H 4
83 Greville St........F 11
86 Greycoat Pl.......E 7
86 Greycoat St.......E 7
84 Greyeagle St.......E 5
78 Greyhound Rd....D 2
80 Grierson Rd.......H 1
76 Griggs Rd.........A 4
84 Grimsby St........E 6
79 Grimworth Rd.....E 9
80 Grinstead Rd......C 1
73 Grittleton Av......E 5
81 Grittleton Rd......E 1
80 Groom Pl..........D 4
76 Groombridge Rd...F 1
75 Grosvenor Av. N5 E 13
77 Grosvenor Av. SW14 F 7
86 Grosvenor Bri.....H 5
86 Grosvenor Cres....C 4
86 Grosvenor Cres. Mews C 3
86 Grosvenor Gdns...D 5
82 Grosvenor Hill....J 5
82 Grosvenor Ho.....J 3
87 Grosvenor Pk.....J 13
86 Grosvenor Pl......D 4
76 Grosvenor Rd. E7. E 7
86 Grosvenor Rd. SW1 H 6
77 Grosvenor Rd. W4. C 5
77 Grosvenor Rd. Rich. H 3
82 Grosvenor Sq.....H 5
82 Grosvenor St......H 5
87 Grosvenor Ter....J 13
76 Grove, The, E15...E 5
74 Grove, The, NW3. B 7
74 Grove, The, NW3. C 5
74 Grove, The, NW11. A 3
73 Grove, The, W5...K 3
81 Grove End Rd......C 4
76 Grove Green Rd...C 4
79 Grove Hill Rd.....F 14
73 Grove La..........E 13
78 Grove Mews.......B 1
79 Grove Pk. SE5....F 14
71 Grove Pk. SE12...C 10
77 Grove Pk. Gdns...D 5
80 Grove Pk. Hosp...K 7
77 Grove Pk. Rd......D 5
77 Grove Pk. Ter.....D 5
73 Grove Pl..........K 3
76 Grove Rd. E2......G 1
76 Grove Rd. E11....B 6
67 Grove Rd. E18...C 10
77 Grove Rd. SW13...F 7
77 Grove Rd. W3.....A 6
70 Grove Rd. Mitch...D 5
77 Grove Rd. Rich....H 4
67 Grove Rd. Rom...D 12
80 Grove St..........C 2
79 Grove Vale.......G 14
75 Grove Wk.........D 14
73 Grove Way........D 5
75 Grovedale Rd......B 9
79 Groveway.........E 11
86 Guards' Club......A 4
68 Gubbins La........C 4
79 Gubyon Av......H 12
79 Guernsey Gro....J 12
80 Guibal Rd..........J 7
80 Guildford Gro.....E 3
79 Guildford Rd. SW8 E 10
69 Guildford Rd. Ottershaw......F 2
84 Guildhall, EC2...G 2
87 Guildhall, SW1...C 8
86 Guildhouse St.....F 6
83 Guilford St........E 9
80 Gulliver St........B 2
87 Gundulf St.......F 11
77 Gunnersbury......C 5
77 Gunnersbury Av...B 4
77 Gunnersbury Cres..A 4
77 Gunnersbury Dri. B 4
77 Gunnersbury Gdns. A 4
77 Gunnersbury La...A 5
77 Gunnersbury Pk...B 4
77 Gunnersbury Station.........C 5
85 Gunter Gro.......J 3
78 Gunterstone Rd....C 3
75 Gunton Rd.......C 16
80 Gurdon Rd.......C 7
76 Gurney Rd.........D 5
88 Guy St............C 3
88 Guys' Hosp........B 3
78 Gwendolen Av....G 2
76 Gwendoline Av....F 7
78 Gwynne Rd........F 6
87 Gye St............G 9
84 Haberdasher St....C 3
84 Haberdasher's Hall G 1
70 Hackbridge........E 5
79 Hackford Rd......E 11
75 Hackney..........E 16
75 Hackney Downs..D 15
75 Hackney Downs Sta. E 15
84 Hackney Rd.......C 5
76 Hackney Wick.....E 2
76 Hacton La.........E 4
88 Hadden Hall St....E 3
77 Hadley Gdns......C 6
74 Hadley St.........E 8
77 Hadyn Pk. Rd......A 8
80 Hafton Rd.........K 5
75 Haggerston.......G 15
75 Haggerston Rd....F 14
75 Hague St........H 15
76 Haig Rd..........G 8
79 Hailsham Av......K 11
67 Hainault.........C 12
67 Hainault Estate...B 12
76 Hainault Rd. E11..B 4
67 Hainault Rd. Rom. C 12
67 Hainault Rd. Wfd. Gn. B 11
84 Halcomb St.......A 4
75 Halcrow St.......J 16
78 Haldane Rd.......D 3
78 Haldon Rd........H 3
67 Hale End.........B 9
73 Hale Gdns........L 4
76 Hale St...........K 3
80 Halesworth Rd....F 3
77 Half Acre.........D 2
83 Half Moon Cres..B 10
79 Half Moon La.....H 12
86 Half Moon St......B 5
85 Halford Rd. SW6..H 1
77 Halford Rd. Richmond H 3
71 Halfway St.......B 11
75 Halidon St.......D 16
70 Haling Pk. Rd.....F 6
86 Halkin Pl..........D 3
86 Halkin St..........C 4
67 Hall La. E4........B 9
68 Hall La. Brent....D 6
68 Hall La. Hornchurch D 4
81 Hall Pl............F 5
76 Hall Rd. E11.......D 6
81 Hall Rd. NW8.....D 4
83 Hall St...........C 12
82 Hallam St.........F 5
76 Halley Rd.........E 8
69 Halliford Rd......D 4
75 Halliford St......F 13
75 Halse St..........E 10
86 Halsey St..........E 2
79 Halsmere Rd......E 12
72 Halstead..........G 1
80 Halstow Rd........C 6
75 Halton Rd.......F 12
70 Ham..............C 2
77 Ham, The.........E 2
70 Ham Common.....C 2
76 Ham Pk. Rd.......F 6
77 Ham St............K 2
79 Hambalt Rd.......H 9
78 Hamble St.........F 5
78 Hambledon Rd....J 3
81 Hamilton Cl.......D 4
81 Hamilton Gdns....C 4
75 Hamilton Pk.....D 12
86 Hamilton Pl........B 4
76 Hamilton Rd. E15.H 5
73 Hamilton Rd. NW10 D 8
73 Hamilton Rd. W5.K 3
77 Hamilton Rd. Brent D 2
81 Hamilton Ter......C 3
76 Hamlets Way......H 2
76 Hammersley Av....J 6
78 Hammersmith......B 1
78 Hammersmith Bri..C 1
78 Hammersmith Bri. Rd. C 1
78 Hammersmith Gro. B 1
73 Hammersmith Hosp. J 8
78 Hammersmith Rd..C 2
78 Hammersmith Sta..C 1
81 Hampden Cres.....F 2
66 Hampden Way.....B 6
65 Hampermill La....A 5
74 Hampstead.......D 5
74 Hampstead Gro....C 5
74 Hampstead Heath .C 6
74 Hampstead Heath Sta. D 6
74 Hampstead Hill Gdns. D 6
74 Hampstead La.....B 6
82 Hampstead Rd.....C 6
74 Hampstead Sta....D 5
74 Hampstead Way...B 5
70 Hampton Ct. Bri...D 1
70 Hampton Ct. G.C..D 1
70 Hampton Ct. Pal...D 1
69 Hampton Ct. Rd...D 6
69 Hampton Ct. Way. E 6
76 Hampton Rd. E7 .D 7
69 Hampton Rd. Feltham C 5
69 Hampton Rd. Twick. C 6
81 Hampton St. NW6. D 1
88 Hampton St. SE17.F 1
70 Hampton Wick.....D 1
71 Hamsey Green....G 8
77 Hanbury Rd.......B 5
84 Hanbury St.......F 6
83 Handel St.........E 8
80 Handen Rd.......H 6
75 Handley Rd......F 16
69 Hangar Hill.......F 4
73 Hanger La.........J 4
73 Hanger La. Sta....H 3
73 Hanger Vale La....J 4
88 Hankey Pl.........D 3
75 Hanley Rd.......B 10
75 Hannibal Rd......J 16
87 Hanover Gdns.....J 10
79 Hanover Pk......E 15
74 Hanover Rd.......F 1
82 Hanover Sq.......H 5
82 Hanover St........H 5
82 Hanover Ter......D 2
82 Hanover Ter. Mews D 2
86 Hans Cres.........D 2
86 Hans Pl...........D 2
86 Hans Rd...........D 2
86 Hans St...........D 2
79 Hansler Rd......G 14
82 Hanson St.........F 6
82 Hanway Pl.........G 7
82 Hanway St.........G 7
66 Hanwell...........G 1
69 Hanworth.........C 5
69 Hanworth Park, Hanworth......C 5
69 Hanworth Rd. Hanworth......C 5
69 Hanworth Rd. Hounslow.......B 6
69 Hanworth Rd. Twick. C 5
74 Harben Rd.........F 5
75 Harberton Rd......B 9
81 Harbet Rd.........F 5
80 Harbinger Rd......C 2
78 Harbord St.........E 3
78 Harbut Rd.........G 5
75 Harcombe Rd... C 14
76 Harcourt Rd. E15.G 6
80 Harcourt Rd. SE4.G 2
82 Harcourt St.......F 1
85 Harcourt Ter......G 3
77 Hardbridge Av....J 8
79 Harders Rd......E 15
83 Harding St.......G 11
74 Hardinge Rd......G 1
75 Hardinge St......K 16
69 Hardwick La......E 2
83 Hardwick St......D 11
80 Hardy Rd.........D 6
80 Hare & Billet Rd..E 5
69 Hare Hill..........F 2
69 Hare La...........F 6
68 Hare St...........C 3
84 Hare Wk..........B 4
65 Harefield.........C 3
80 Harefield Rd. SE4. F 2
65 Harefield Rd. Rickmansworth.....B 3
82 Harewood Av......E 1
68 Harewood Hall La. E 4
82 Harewood Pl......H 5
82 Harewood Row...F 2
76 Harford St........H 1
80 Hargood Rd.......E 8
75 Hargrave Rd......C 9
74 Hargreave Pk.....A 9
79 Hargwyne St.....F 10
80 Harland Rd.......J 6
80 Harlescott Rd.....G 1
73 Harlesden.........G 7
73 Harlesden Gdns....F 7
73 Harlesden Rd......F 8
73 Harlesden Sta.....G 6
85 Harley Gdns.......G 4
76 Harley Gro........G 2
82 Harley Pl.........G 4
74 Harley Rd. NW3 F 6
73 Harley Rd. NW10.G 7
82 Harley St..........F 4
87 Harleyford Rd.....H 9
87 Harleyford St.....H 11
65 Harlington........H 4
65 Harlington Rd.....F 3
69 Harlington Rd. E..B 11
65 Harmondsworth...H 3
65 Harmondsworth La. H 3
74 Harmood St.......E 8
87 Harmsworth St...G 12
68 Harold Hill........B 3
87 Harold Pl.........G 10
76 Harold Rd. E11...B 5
76 Harold Rd. E13...F 7
73 Harold Rd. NW10.H 6
68 Harold Wood.....C 4
84 Harp La..........J 4
76 Harpenden Rd. E12 B 8
79 Harpenden Rd. SE27 K 12
88 Harper Rd........D 2
83 Harpur St.........F 9
80 Harraden Rd......E 8
86 Harriet Wk........D 3
75 Harringay Pk.....A 10
75 Harringay Stad...A 12
75 Harringay W. Sta. A 12
85 Harrington Gdns..F 3
76 Harrington Rd. E11 B 5
85 Harrington Rd. SW7 E 5
82 Harrington Sq.....B 6
82 Harrington St.....C 6
76 Harris St. E17.....B 2
79 Harris St. SE5....D 13
83 Harrison St.......D 9
66 Harrow...........D 1
66 Harrow & Wealdstone Sta........C 1
66 Harrow on the Hill D 1
84 Harrow Pl.........G 4
76 Harrow Rd. E11...C 6
73 Harrow Rd. NW10 F 5 & G 9
74 Harrow Rd. W2...J 5
74 Harrow Rd. W9 & W10...........H 3
71 Harrow Rd. Chelsham G 8
73 Harrow Rd. Wem. E 2 & E 4
73 Harrow View Rd...H 1
66 Harrow Weald.....C 1
82 Harrowby St......G 2
73 Harrowdene Rd....D 2
76 Harrowgate Rd....E 1
77 Hart Gro..........A 4
84 Hart St...........H 4
75 Hartham Rd......E 10
76 Hartland Rd. E15.F 6
74 Hartland Rd. NW1 F 8
74 Hartland Rd. NW6 G 3
72 Hartley...........E 5
76 Hartley Rd........B 6
75 Hartley St.......G 16
79 Hartington Rd. SW8 E 10
77 Hartington Rd. W4 E 5
80 Harts La..........E 1
65 Hartsbourne G.C..B 6
77 Hartswood Rd.....B 7
80 Harvard Rd. SE13 H 4
77 Harvard Rd. W4..C 5
80 Harvey Gdns......C 8
76 Harvey Rd. E11...B 6
79 Harvey Rd. SE5..E 13
84 Harvey St.........A 3
65 Harvil Rd.........D 3
75 Harvist Rd. N7...D 11
74 Harvist Rd. NW6..G 2
78 Harwood Rd.......E 4
67 Haselbury Rd......B 7
79 Haselrigge Rd....G 10
86 Hasker St.........E 2
78 Haslemere Av.....K 4
75 Haslemere Rd.....A 10
80 Hassenden Rd.....D 7
76 Hassett Rd........E 1
74 Hassop Rd........D 2
65 Haste Hill........C 4
65 Haste Hill G.C....C 4
73 Hastings Rd.......K 1
83 Hastings St.......D 8
66 Hatch End........C 1
65 Hatch End Sta.....C 6
67 Hatch La. E4......B 9
65 Hatch La. Harmondsworth.H 3
80 Hatcham Pk. Rd...E 1
79 Hatcham Rd......D 16
69 Hatchord Pk......H 10
77 Hatfield Rd. W4...A 6

MAP
84 Hatfield St.......E 1
87 Hatfields.......B 12
81 Hatherley Gro....G 2
69 Hatton.........B 4
83 Hatton Gdn......F 11
69 Hatton Rd......B 4
81 Hatton St.......E 5
83 Hatton Wall.....F 11
80 Havannah St.....A 3
83 Havelock St......A 9
73 Haven Green....K 2
74 Haven Rd. .....E 8
79 Haverhill Rd....J 9
68 Havering-atte-Bower B 2
68 Havering Pk......B 2
68 Havering Rd......B 2
74 Haverstock Hill...E 7
83 Haverstock St....C 13
79 Havil St.......E 14
79 Hawarden Gro....J 12
75 Hawes St.......F 12
76 Hawgood St.......J 3
80 Hawkesfield Rd....K 2
80 Hawkslade Rd....G 1
75 Hawksley Rd.....C 14
72 Hawley.........C 2
74 Hawley Rd. NW1..F 8
72 Hawley Rd. Dartford C 3
80 Hawstead Rd.....H 3
71 Hawsted Rd.....F 12
79 Hawstone Rd.....B 16
77 Hawthorn Rd....E 1
76 Hay Currie St....J 4
82 Hay Hill........J 5
73 Haycroft Gdns...G 8
76 Hayday Rd......J 6
70 Haydon's Rd. Sta..C 4
65 Hayes.........G 4
71 Hayes, Brom....E 10
65 Hayes & Harlington Sta.......G 4
65 Hayes End.......F 4
71 Hayes La. Bec...D 9
71 Hayes La. Brom...E 9
70 Hayes La. Coulsdon H 6
82 Hayes Pl........E 1
65 Hayes Rd........G 5
87 Hayles St........E 12
65 Hayling Rd.......B 5
82 Haymarket.......J 7
82 Haymarket Th......J 7
88 Haymerle Rd.....H 6
83 Hayne St........F 13
86 Hay's Mews.....A 4
79 Haytor Rd......G 10
83 Hayward's Pl.....E 12
78 Haywood Gdns...H 1
77 Hazel Cl.......D 1
77 Hazel La........K 3
74 Hazel Rd.......H 1
71 Hazel Wood.....G 11
80 Hazelbank Rd....K 5
78 Hazelbourne Rd..H 8
78 Hazelbury Rd....F 4
80 Hazeldon Rd.....H 2
75 Hazellville Rd....B 9
73 Hazelmere Av....A 2
74 Hazelmere Rd....G 3
74 Hazlewell Rd.....G 1
76 Head St.......J 1
86 Headfort Pl.......D 4
78 Headington Rd....K 5
79 Headlam Rd......H 9
75 Headlam St......H 16
70 Headley Rd......H 2
66 Headstone.......C 1
66 Headstone Dri....C 1
65 Headstone La....C 6
66 Headstone La. Sta..C 1
84 Hearn St........E 4
74 Heath Cl.......B 4
74 Heath Dri.......D 4
80 Heath La. SE3....F 5
72 Heath La. Dartford B 2
68 Heath Pk........D 3
68 Heath Pk. Rd.....D 3
78 Heath Rise......H 2
78 Heath Rd. SW8....F 8
69 Heath Rd. Houn..B 6
69 Heath Row......F 3
74 Heath St.......D 5
98 Heath Way......E 1
66 Heathbourn Rd....B 1
77 Heathcote Rd....H 1
83 Heathcote St.....D 9
73 Heathcroft.......H 4
73 Heather Pk. Dri...F 4

73 Heather Rd. NW2..C 7
80 Heather Rd. SE12..K 7
77 Heathfield Av......A 5
74 Heathfield Gdns. NW11.......A 2
77 Heathfield Gdns. W4 C 6
78 Heathfield Rd.....H 5
77 Heathfield Ter.....C 6
74 Heathgate.......A 4
75 Heathland Rd....B 13
69 Heathrow Airport, London......A 3
73 Heathstan Rd....K 8
74 Heathurst Rd.....D 6
78 Heathview Gdns...J 1
75 Heathville Rd....B 10
76 Heaton Pl........E 4
79 Heaton Rd......F 15
72 Heaverham.......H 4
74 Heber Rd. NW2...D 2
79 Heber Rd. SE22..H 14
76 Heckford St......K 1
82 Heddon St.......J 6
67 Hedge La........B 7
68 Hedgemans Rd...E 1
80 Hedgley St......G 6
80 Heights, The.....C 8
87 Heiron St.......H 13
80 Helder Gro......J 6
76 Helena Rd. E13...G 6
73 Helena Rd. NW10. D 9
74 Helenslea Av.....B 3
79 Helix Rd........H 11
84 Helmet Row......D 1
75 Hemingford Rd...F 11
73 Hemlock Rd......K 8
84 Hemming St......E 7
88 Hemp Row.......F 3
74 Hemstal Rd......F 4
84 Hemsworth St.....D 4
85 Hemus Pl........G 6
73 Henchman St......J 7
76 Henderson Rd. E7. E 8
78 Henderson Rd. SW18 J 6
78 Hendham Rd.....K 7
66 Hendon........C 4
66 Hendon Cent Sta..D 4
66 Hendon G.C......C 4
73 Hendon Sta......A 8
74 Hendon Way......H 2
66 Hendon Wood La..A 3
88 Hendre Rd.......F 4
84 Heneage La......G 4
84 Heneage St......F 6
80 Hengist Rd......J 7
80 Hengrave Rd.....J 1
85 Henniker Mews...H 4
78 Henning St......E 6
82 Henrietta Pl......G 5
83 Henrietta St......J 9
84 Henriques St......H 7
75 Henry Rd.......B 12
80 Henryson Rd.....H 2
88 Henshaw St......E 3
79 Henslowe Rd......H 15
86 Her Majesty's Th..A 7
83 Herbal Hill......E 11
73 Herbert Gdns....G 8
76 Herbert Rd......B 2
76 Herbert St.......G 7
83 Herbrand St......E 8
87 Hercules Rd......D 10
75 Hercules St......C 10
81 Hereford Rd. W2..G 1
73 Hereford Rd. W3..K 5
85 Hereford Sq......F 4
84 Hereford St......D 6
83 Hermes St.......C 10
76 Hermit Rd.......H 6
83 Hermit St.......C 12
74 Hermitage La.....C 4
75 Hermitage Rd.....A 12
81 Hermitage St.....F 5
88 Hermitage Wall...B 7
79 Herne Hill.......H 12
79 Herne Hill Rd.....F 12
79 Herne Hill Sta....H 12
79 Herne Pl........H 12
78 Herondale Av.....K 4
76 Herongate Rd....B 8
75 Herrick Rd......C 12
87 Herrick St.......F 8
74 Herrie St.......H 3
88 Herring St.......H 4
80 Herringham Rd....B 8
69 Hersham........F 5
77 Hersham Cl......J 8
69 Hersham Rd......E 5

69 Hersham Sta......E 5
86 Hertford Av......G 7
75 Hertford Rd. N1..F 14
67 Hertford Rd. Enfield.......E 7
86 Hertford St......B 4
78 Hertslet Rd......D 10
71 Heseirs Hill......H 9
71 Heseirs Rd.......H 9
78 Heslop Rd.......J 7
85 Hesper Mews.....F 2
80 Hesperus Cres....C 3
78 Hester Rd.......D 6
65 Heston.........H 6
65 Heston Rd.......H 6
74 Hetley Rd.......A 9
84 Hewett St.......E 4
71 Hewitts Rd.......F 12
76 Hewlett Rd......G 2
80 Hexel Rd.......K 5
79 Hexham Rd......K 12
72 Hextable........D 2
78 Heyford Av......J 9
78 Heythorp St......K 3
75 Heyworth Rd....D 15
86 Hide Pl........F 7
66 High Barnet Sta...A 4
71 High Elms.......F 11
83 High Holborn....G 9
77 High Pk. Rd......E 4
76 High Rd. E10......A 4
76 High Rd. E11.....C 5
66 High Rd. N2......C 5
67 High Rd. N17.....C 7
66 High Rd. N20.....A 5
73 High Rd. NW10...E 7
69 High Rd. Byfleet..G 3
67 High Rd. Chigwell B 11
65 High Rd. Eastcote. D 5
72 High Rd. Dartford.C 2
67 High Rd. Ilf......D 12
76 High Rd. Leyton..C 4
67 High Rd. Loughton A 10
71 High Rd. Orp.....E 11
67 High Rd. Rom....D 3
73 High Rd. Wem....E 3
67 High Rd. Wfd. Gn. B 10
76 High Stone......A 6
67 High St. E11......D 10
76 High St. E13......G 7
76 High St. E15......G 4
66 High St. N8......C 6
74 High St. NW3....D 5
73 High St. NW10...G 8
80 High St. SE13....G 4
70 High St. SW19....C 4
77 High St. W3......A 5
73 High St. W5......K 2
68 High St. Aveley...G 4
70 High St. Banstead G 4
71 High St. Bec......D 8
71 High St. Bex'h...A 12
77 High St. Brent...D 3
65 High St. Bushey...A 6
70 High St. Carshalton F 5
71 High St. Cro......E 7
70 High St. Eps......G 2
69 High St. Feltham..C 4
65 High St. Harlington G 4
66 High St. Har......C 1
68 High St. Hornchurch D 3
69 High St. Houn...A 6
67 High St. Ponders End A 8
65 High St. Rickmansworth......A 3
69 High St. Shepperton E 4
71 High St. Sid......C 12
69 High St. Stanwell..B 3
70 High St. Sut......E 4
70 High St. Ted......C 1
69 High St. Walton...A 4
65 High St. Watford..A 5
71 High St. W. Wick..E 8
67 High St. Nth......E 11
67 High St. Sth......F 11
79 High Trees......J 11
67 Higham Hill......C 8
67 Highams Pk......B 9
75 Highbury.......D 12
75 Highbury & Islington Sta.........E 12
75 Highbury Cres....E 12
75 Highbury Grange. D 12

75 Highbury Gro....D 12
75 Highbury Hill....D 12
75 Highbury New Pk.D 13
75 Highbury Pk......D 12
75 Highbury Pl......E 12
75 Highbury Quad...C 12
75 Highbury Sta. Rd.E 11
77 Highcliffe.......H 8
80 Highcombe......D 7
73 Highcroft Av......F 4
74 Highcroft Gdns...A 3
74 Highfield Av......A 2
74 Highfield Gdns....A 2
73 Highfield Rd......J 5
74 Highgate.......B 8
74 Highgate Av......A 7
74 Highgate G.C.....A 6
74 Highgate Hill.....B 8
74 Highgate Hill St...B 8
74 Highgate Hosp....B 8
74 Highgate Rd......D 8
74 Highgate Sta.....A 8
74 Highgate W. Hill..C 7
73 Highmead Gdns...F 4
79 Highshore Rd....E 15
75 Highway, The....K 16
66 Highwood Hill...B 3
73 Hilary Rd.......K 7
76 Hilda Rd.......H 5
85 Hildyard Rd......H 1
74 Hiley Rd.......G 1
66 Hilfield La......A 1
74 Hilgrove Rd......F 5
65 Hill End.......B 3
65 Hill End Rd......C 3
73 Hill Dri........B 5
77 Hill Rise.......H 3
81 Hill Rd.......C 4
86 Hill St. W1......A 4
77 Hill St. Rich.....H 3
74 Hill Way.......C 8
75 Hillborough Rd...F 14
78 Hillbury Rd......L 8
79 Hillcourt Rd......H 15
77 Hillcrest Rd. W3..A 5
73 Hillcrest Rd. W5...J 3
73 Hillcroft Cres. W5. J 3
73 Hillcroft Cres. Wem. D 4
75 Hilldrop Cres.....D 9
75 Hilldrop Rd......D 9
88 Hillery Rd.......F 3
73 Hillfield Av......F 3
74 Hillfield Rd......D 4
85 Hillgate Pl......B 1
85 Hillgate St......B 1
78 Hillier Rd.......H 7
65 Hillingdon......F 3
65 Hillingdon G.C....F 3
65 Hillingdon Heath..F 4
65 Hillingdon Hill...F 3
65 Hillingdon Rd.....E 3
65 Hillingdon Sta....E 4
87 Hillingdon St.....H 13
75 Hillmarton Rd....D 10
79 Hillreach.......G 10
79 Hillsborough Rd..H 14
73 Hillside........F 6
75 Hillside Rd. N15.A 14
79 Hillside Rd. SW2.K 11
73 Hillside Rd. W5...J 3
79 Hillworth Rd.....J 11
79 Hillyard St......E 11
80 Hilly Fields......G 3
80 Hilly Fields Cres..G 3
86 Hilton Hot.......B 4
70 Hinchley Wood...E 1
76 Hind St........J 3
82 Hinde St.......G 4
79 Hindmans Rd.....H 15
79 Hinton Rd.......G 12
76 Hitcham Rd......B 2
80 Hither Green.....J 4
80 Hither Green Hosp.H 4
80 Hither Green Sta..H 5
79 Hitherfield Rd....K 11
79 Hoadly Rd.......K 9
86 Hobart Pl.......D 4
87 Hobson St.......F 13
85 Hockey Rd.......H 1
84 Hocker St.......D 5
74 Hocroft Av......C 3
74 Hocroft Rd......D 3
74 Hodford Rd......B 3
76 Hoe La........A 12
67 Hoe St........C 9
77 Hogarth La......D 7
85 Hogarth Rd......F 2
66 Hogarth's Ho....H 3

71 Hogtrough Hill...H 11
86 Holbeach Rd......J 3
86 Holbein Mews....F 3
86 Holbein Pl.......F 3
83 Holborn.........G 11
83 Holborn Circus...G 11
76 Holborn Rd......J 7
83 Holborn Viaduct.G 12
83 Holborn Viaduct Sta. G 11
76 Holbrook Rd......G 6
80 Holburne Rd.....E 8
87 Holcroft Rd......F 16
73 Holden Av.......B 6
80 Holdenby Rd......H 2
80 Holders Hill.....C 4
66 Holders Hill Rd...C 4
83 Holford Gdns....C 10
78 Holland Gro......D 11
78 Holland Pk.......A 3
78 Holland Pk Av....A 3
78 Holland Pk. Gdns. A 3
78 Holland Pk. Mews. A 3
78 Holland Pk. Rd....B 3
73 Holland Rd. NW10 G 8
78 Holland Rd. W14..B 2
73 Holland Rd. Wem..E 2
85 Holland St.......C 2
78 Holland Villas Rd..A 3
82 Hollen St.......G 7
82 Holles St.......G 5
79 Hollingbourne Rd. H 13
76 Holloway Rd. E11.C 5
75 Holloway Rd. N7 & N19.........D 11
78 Holloway Rd. Sta.D 11
84 Holloway St......G 6
79 Holly Gro.......E 15
86 Holly Hill.......D 5
70 Holly La. Banstead.H 4
74 Holly Lodge Gdns. B 7
79 Holly Rd. E11.....A 6
77 Holly Rd. W4.....C 6
75 Hollybush Gdns...G 16
76 Hollybush St.....G 7
74 Hollycroft Av.....C 4
79 Hollydale Rd.....E 16
85 Hollywood Rd....H 3
76 Holmbrook St.....E 1
75 Holmbury View..B 16
75 Holmbush Rd.....H 2
75 Holmdale Rd. N15 A 14
74 Holmdale Rd. NW6 E 4
79 Holmdene Av....H 13
80 Holme Lacey Rd...H 6
74 Holmes Rd......E 8
74 Holmesdale Rd...A 7
78 Holmesley Rd....H 1
79 Holmewood Gdns. J 11
79 Holmewood Rd...J 10
80 Holmleigh Rd....B 14
84 Holms St.......B 6
78 Holmside Rd.....H 8
84 Holroyd Rd......G 1
73 Holt Rd........C 2
77 Holybourne Av...J 8
80 Holyoake Rd......F 12
73 Holyoake Wk......H 2
88 Holyrood St......B 4
84 Holywell La......E 4
84 Holywell Row....E 3
87 Home Office......C 8
72 Home Rd. Dartford C 2
77 Homefield Rd....C 7
80 Homeleigh.......G 1
82 Homer Row......F 1
82 Homer St.......F 1
76 Homerton......E 1
76 Homerton Gro....D 1
76 Homerton High St. E 1
76 Homerton Rd.....D 2
76 Homerton Row....E 16
79 Homestall Rd.....G 16
87 Hone Parade.....E 10
86 Honeybourne Rd..E 4
78 Honeybrook Rd...J 9
76 Honeypot La......C 2
78 Honeywell Rd.....H 2
80 Honley Rd.......J 4
79 Honor Oak Pk.....H 1
79 Honor Oak Rd....J 16
70 Hook.........E 2
76 Hook Green......E 6
72 Hook Green.....C 5
72 Hook Green Rd...C 2
71 Hook La. Bex'h...B 11

68 Hook La. Stapleford Abbotts......A 2
70 Hook Rise.......E 2
70 Hook Rd. Ches. & Surb.........E 2
70 Hook Rd. Eps....G 2
71 Hook Wood Rd..G 12
79 Hooks Rd.......E 16
74 Hoop La.......A 4
84 Hooper St.......H 6
80 Hopedale Rd......D 7
84 Hopetown St......F 6
82 Hopkins St......H 7
87 Hopton St.......A 12
76 Horace Rd.......D 7
84 Horatio St.......C 6
78 Horder La.......E 3
74 Hormead Rd......H 3
80 Horn La. SE10....C 6
73 Horn La. W3.....K 5
80 Horn Pk. Rd......H 7
77 Hornbeam Cres...D 1
80 Horncastle Rd....J 7
68 Hornchurch......D 3
68 Hornchurch Rd....D 3
68 Hornchurch Stadium......E 4
78 Horne Way......F 1
79 Horniman Dri....J 16
79 Horniman Mus...K 16
71 Horns Green.....H 11
67 Horns Rd. ....D 11
75 Hornsey La.......B 9
75 Hornsey La. Gdns. B 9
75 Hornsey Rise....D 10
75 Hornsey Rd......C 10
67 Hornsey Sta......C 7
79 Hornshay St......D 16
85 Hornton Pl.......C 2
85 Hornton St......C 1
80 Horsa Rd.......J 7
87 Horse Guards.....B 8
87 Horse Guards Av..B 8
87 Horseferry Rd.....E 8
75 Horsell Rd.......E 11
88 Horselydown La...C 5
79 Horsford Rd.....H 10
88 Horsley St.......H 2
85 Hortensia Rd......J 3
70 Horton, Ewell....F 2
69 Horton, Staines...A 1
74 Horton Av.......D 3
70 Horton Hosp.....D 3
72 Horton Kirby.....D 3
70 Horton La.......G 2
75 Horton Rd. E8...E 15
69 Horton Rd.......A 1
78 Hosack Rd.......K 7
83 Hosier La.......G 12
80 Hoskins St......C 5
69 Hospital Bri. Rd...B 6
82 Hosp. for Nervous Diseases......G 4
83 Hosp. for Sick Children......E 9
81 Hosp. of St. John..C 5
78 Hotham Rd.......G 1
76 Hotham St.......F 5
77 Houblon Rd......G 3
82 Houghton Pl......C 6
83 Houghton St......H 10
84 Houndsditch......G 4
69 Hounslow.......A 6
69 Hounslow Central Sta. A 6
69 Hounslow E. Sta...A 6
69 Hounslow Sta.....B 6
69 Hounslow W. Sta..A 5
87 Houses of Parliament D 9
80 Houston Rd......K 2
74 Hoveden Rd......D 2
73 Howard Cl.......J 5
76 Howard Rd. E11..C 5
75 Howard Rd. N15. A 14
75 Howard Rd. N16.D 13
74 Howard Rd. NW2.D 2
83 Howard St.......H 10
78 Howards La......G 1
76 Howards Rd......G 6
79 Howbury Rd......F 16
75 Howden St.......F 15
70 Howell Hill.......F 3
86 Howick Pl.......E 6
74 Howitt Rd.......H 1
82 Howland St......F 6
81 Howley Pl.......F 4
84 How's St........E 6
77 Howsman Rd.....D 8
80 Howson Rd......G 2
75 Hoxton.........G 13

MAP

84 Hoxton Sq........D 4
84 Hoxton St........C 4
73 Hoylake Rd.......J 7
79 Hubert Gro.......F 10
76 Humberstone Rd..H 8
76 Huddart St........J 2
75 Huddleston Rd....D 9
76 Huddlestone Rd...D 6
86 Hugh Mews.....F 5
86 Hugh St.........F 5
78 Hugon Rd.......F 4
78 Huguenot Pl......G 5
84 Hull St..........D 1
73 Humber Rd. NW2.C 9
80 Humber Rd. SE3..D 6
78 Humboldt Rd.....D 3
75 Hungerford Rd...E 10
80 Hunsdon Rd.....D 1
83 Hunter St........E 9
75 Huntingdon St....F 11
77 Huntingfield Rd...G 8
82 Huntley St.......E 7
84 Hunton St.......E 6
79 Hunts Slip Rd...K 14
78 Huntsmoor Rd...G 5
82 Huntsworth Mews.E 2
87 Hurlbutt Pl......F 13
78 Hurlingham Ho...F 4
78 Hurlingham Pk...F 3
78 Hurlingham Rd...F 3
78 Huron Rd........K 8
69 Hurst Rd. E. & W.
   Mol.........D 5
71 Hurst Rd. Sid. & Bex.
   B 12
79 Hurst St........H 12
80 Hurstbourne Rd..K 2
73 Huxley Gdns.....G 4
76 Huxley Rd.......C 4
66 Hyde, The.......C 3
85 Hyde Pk.........A 6
86 Hyde Pk. Corner..C 4
81 Hyde Pk. Cres....H 6
81 Hyde Pk. Gdns...H 5
81 Hyde Pk. Gdns. Mews
   H 5
85 Hyde Pk. Gate...D 4
86 Hyde Pk. Hot....C 2
81 Hyde Pk. Sq.....H 6
81 Hyde Pk. St......H 6
80 Hyde Vale.......E 4
79 Hydethorpe Rd...J 9
69 Hythe...........C 2
69 Hythe End.......C 1
77 Ibsley Gdns......J 8
75 Ickburgh Rd....C 15
65 Ickenham.......D 4
76 Idmiston Rd. E15..D 6
79 Idmiston Rd. SE27
   K 12
84 Idol La..........J 4
80 Idonia St........D 2
78 Iffley Rd........B 1
85 Ifield Rd........H 3
72 Ightham........H 5
74 Ilbert St........H 2
81 Ilchester Gdns...H 2
78 Ilchester Pl......H 3
79 Ilderton Rd., SE15
   D 16
79 Ilderton Rd. SE16.
   C 16
73 Ilex Rd.........E 7
67 Ilford G.C......D 11
67 Ilford La.......E 11
87 Iliffe St........F 13
84 Imber St........B 2
85 Imperial Coll....D 4
85 Imperial Coll. of
   Science.......E 5
65 Imperial Dri....D 6
85 Imperial Inst. Rd. D 5
78 Imperial Rd.....E 5
87 Imperial War Mus.
   E 11
80 Inchmery Rd....K 4
84 India St.........H 5
73 India Way.......K 9
80 Indus Rd........D 8
76 Ingatestone Rd..B 7
78 Ingelow Rd......F 8
82 Ingestre Pl......H 7
83 Inglebert St....C 11
80 Inglemere Rd....L 1
78 Inglethorpe St....E 2
74 Inglewood Rd....E 4
73 Inglis Rd........K 4
74 Ingram Av.......A 5
74 Ingram Rd.......D 4
68 Ingrave.........B 6
68 Ingrave Green.....B 6

MAP

74 Inkerman Rd......E 8
73 Inman Rd. NW10.
   F 7
78 Inman Rd. SW18..J 5
82 Inner Circle.....D 3
78 Inner Pk. Rd....K 2
76 Inniskilling Rd....G 8
85 International Hot..E 2
80 Inverine Rd......C 7
81 Inverness Pl.....H 3
81 Inverness Ter.....H 3
80 Inverton Rd......G 1
88 Inville St........G 3
78 Irene Rd........E 4
75 Ireton St........C 9
84 Ironmonger Pas..D 1
84 Ironmonger Row..D 1
84 Ironmonger St....D 2
83 Irving St........J 8
87 Isabella St.....B 12
78 Isis St..........K 5
80 Isle of Dogs.....B 3
75 Isledon Rd......C 11
66 Isleworth........H 1
66 Isleworth Sta.....H 1
75 Islington........E 11
83 Islington Green...B 12
83 Islington High Street
   B 12
75 Islington Park Street
   F 12
75 Islip St.........E 9
87 Italian Wk......G 9
79 Ivanhoe Rd......F 14
73 Iveagh Av.......G 4
66 Iveagh Bequest
   (Kenwood).....D 5
78 Iveley Rd........F 9
78 Iver............F 2
65 Iver Heath......E 2
65 Iver La.........F 3
65 Iver Sta........G 2
85 Iverna Ct.......D 2
85 Iverna Gdns.....D 2
74 Iverson Rd......E 4
86 Ives St.........E 1
82 Ivor Pl.........E 2
77 Ivy Cres........B 5
74 Ivy Rd. NW2....D 1
80 Ivy Rd. SE4.....G 2
84 Ivy St..........B 4
80 Ivydale Rd......G 1
72 Ivyhouse La.....H 1
85 Ixworth Pl......F 6
71 Jackass La......F 10
75 Jackman St......F 15
75 Jackson Rd.....D 11
74 Jackson's La.....A 8
88 Jacob St........C 6
71 Jail La.........G 10
88 Jamaica Rd......D 6
75 Jamaica St......J 16
76 James La........A 4
82 James St. W1....H 4
83 James St. WC2...G 1
80 James's St......E 2
85 Jameson St......B 1
74 Jamestown Rd....F 8
80 Janet St........B 3
76 Janson Rd......D 5
75 Japan Cres.....B 11
88 Jardin St........H 4
85 Jay Mews.......D 4
79 Jebb Av........H 10
79 Jedburgh Rd.....G 8
77 Jeddo Rd........A 7
79 Jeffreys Rd.....F 10
79 Jelf Rd.........G 11
76 Jenkins Rd......H 7
75 Jenner Rd......C 15
79 Jennings Rd.....H 14
76 Jephson Rd......F 8
78 Jephtha Rd......H 4
86 Jermyn St......A 6
80 Jerningham Rd...F 1
84 Jerome St.......F 5
76 Jersey Rd. E10...B 4
66 Jersey Rd., Hounslow
   H 1
75 Jessam Av.....B 15
78 Jessica Rd......H 5
80 Jevington Way...K 7
84 Jewry St........H 5
78 Jews Row.......G 5
74 Jeymer Av......E 1
84 Joan St........B 12
77 Jocelyn Rd......F 3
83 Jockey's Fields..F 10
65 Joel St.........C 5
83 John Adam St....J 9

MAP

83 John Carpenter St.
   H 12
84 John Fisher St....J 6
87 John Islip St ....F 8
80 John Penn St.....E 3
82 John Princes St...G 5
87 John Ruskin St..H 13
83 John St.........E 10
83 John's Mews....E 10
75 Johnson St.....K 16
87 Jonathan St.....F 10
73 Jordan Rd.......F 2
75 Joseph St.......E 6
79 Josephine Av...H 11
79 Jowett St......D 15
72 Joyce Green La...A 3
86 Jubilee Pl.......G 1
75 Jubilee St.......J 16
83 Judd St.........D 8
75 Jude St........E 14
80 Judkin St........B 4
78 Juer St.........E 6
73 Julian Av.......K 5
77 Julian Rd.......B 2
75 Junction Mews...G 6
75 Junction Rd. N19.C 9
77 Junction Rd. W5..C 2
75 Juniper St......K 16
76 Jupps Rd.......H 1
85 Justice Wk......H 6
73 Jutland Rd......J 4
87 Juxon St.......E 10
76 Katherine Rd....E 8
73 Kathleen Av......F 3
79 Kay Rd........F 10
84 Kay St..........B 6
83 Kean St........H 9
74 Keats Gro......D 6
83 Keeley St.......G 9
88 Keesey St.......H 3
74 Kelfield Gdns.....J 2
80 Kellerton Rd.....G 5
79 Kellett Rd.....G 11
78 Kelly St........E 8
78 Kelmscott Rd....H 7
75 Kelross Rd.....D 12
85 Kelso Pl........D 2
78 Kelvedon Rd.....E 3
75 Kelvin Rd......D 12
80 Kelvington Rd....H 1
80 Kemble Rd......K 1
83 Kemble St.......H 9
79 Kemerton Rd....F 13
74 Kempe Rd.......G 2
85 Kempsford Gdns..G 2
79 Kempsford Rd...F 12
88 Kempshead Rd...H 4
72 Kemsing.......H 3
74 Ken Wood.......D 5
73 Kendal Av.......J 5
73 Kendal Rd.......D 8
81 Kendal St.......H 6
82 Kendall Pl......G 3
79 Kender St......E 16
76 Kenilworth Rd. E3.G 1
74 Kenilworth Rd. NW6
   F 3
77 Kenilworth Rd.W5 A 3
71 Kenley.........H 7
74 Kenley St.......K 2
73 Kenmere Gdns...F 4
74 Kenneth Cres....E 1
75 Kenninghall Rd..C 15
87 Kennings Way...G 11
79 Kennington.....D 11
87 Kennington Gro..H 10
87 Kennington La...G 10
87 Kennington Oval.H 10
87 Kennington Pk...H 11
87 Kennington Pk. Gdns.
   H 12
87 Kennington Pk. Pl.
   H 12
87 Kennington Pk. Rd.
   G 12
87 Kennington Rd...F 11
82 Kenrick Pl.......F 3
74 Kensal Green....G 1
74 Kensal Green Sta..H 1
74 Kensal Rise......G 2
74 Kensal Rd.......H 3
85 Kensington......B 4
85 Kensington Ct....C 3
85 Kensington Ct. Pl..D 3
85 Kensington Ch. St..B 1
85 Kensington Gate..D 4
85 Kensington Gdns..B 3
81 Kensington Gdns. Sq.
   H 2
85 Kensington Gore..C 4
85 Kensington High St.D 1

MAP

85 Kensington Mall..B 1
85 Kensington Pal...B 3
85 Kensington Pal. Gdns.
   B 2
85 Kensington Pal. Green
   C 2
74 Kensington Pk. Gdns.
   K 3
74 Kensington Pk. Rd. K 3
85 Kensington Pl....B 1
85 Kensington Rd...C 3
85 Kensington Sq....D 2
78 Kensington (Olympia)
   Sta..........B 3
73 Kent Gdns......J 1
71 Kent Ho. Sta.....D 8
77 Kent Rd........B 6
84 Kent St.........B 5
82 Kent Ter........D 2
74 Kentish Town....E 8
74 Kentish Town Rd..E 8
74 Kentish Town Sta..E 8
66 Kenton.........D 2
66 Kenton La.......C 2
76 Kenton Rd. E9...E 1
66 Kenton Rd. Har...C 2
83 Kenton St.......E 8
80 Kenward Rd.....H 8
85 Kenway Rd......F 2
76 Kenworthy Rd...E 1
73 Kenwyn Dri.....C 7
78 Kenyon St.......C 8
76 Keogh Rd.......E 5
79 Kepler Rd......G 10
77 Kerrison Rd......A 3
80 Kerry Rd........D 2
78 Kersfield Rd.....H 2
78 Kersley St.......E 7
78 Keslake Rd......G 2
71 Keston.........F 10
71 Keston Mark....E 10
79 Keston Rd......G 15
79 Kestrel Av......G 12
78 Keswick Rd......H 3
74 Kettlebaston Rd...B 2
76 Kettleby Way....D 2
79 Kew............E 4
77 Kew Bri........D 4
77 Kew Bri. Rd.....D 4
77 Kew Bri. Sta.....C 4
77 Kew Foot Rd....G 3
77 Kew Gdns. Rd...E 4
77 Kew Gdns. Sta...E 4
77 Kew Green......D 4
77 Kew Rd.........F 3
74 Keyes Rd.......D 2
88 Keyse Rd.......E 5
83 Keystone Cres....C 9
87 Keyworth St....D 12
76 Khartoum Rd....H 7
80 Kidbrooke Gdns..E 6
80 Kidbrooke Green..F 8
80 Kidbrooke Gro...E 7
80 Kidbrooke Pk. Rd.G 7
80 Kidbrooke Sta....F 7
74 Kidderpore Av...D 4
74 Kilburn.........F 3
74 Kilburn La.......H 2
74 Kilburn Grange Pk.
   F 3
74 Kilburn High Rd...F 3
74 Kilburn High Rd. Sta.
   G 4
81 Kilburn Pk. Rd...D 1
74 Kilburn Priory...G 4
74 Kilburn Sta......E 3
76 Kildare Rd......J 6
81 Kildare Ter......G 2
79 Kildovan Rd....G 10
80 Kilgour Rd......H 1
78 Kilkie St........F 5
80 Killearn Rd......J 4
83 Killick St.......C 9
79 Killieser Av.....K 10
79 Killyon Rd......F 9
77 Kilmington Rd...D 8
80 Kilmorie Rd.....K 1
79 Kilner St........J 2
78 Kimber Rd......J 4
76 Kimberley Av...F 16
76 Kimberley Rd. E16.H 6
79 Kimberley Rd. SW9
   F 10
79 Kimpton Rd.....E 13
80 Kinburn St......H 1
88 King & Queen St..F 2
87 King Charles St...C 8
73 King Edward VII Pk.
   D 3
83 King Edward St...G 13
87 King Edward Wk.D 11

MAP

77 King Edward's Gdns.
   A 4
76 King George Av...J 8
80 King George St...D 4
78 King George's Pk..H 4
68 King Harolds Way H 1
75 King Henry St....D 14
74 King Henry's Rd..F 6
75 King Henry's Wk. E 14
84 King James St....D 12
84 King John's Ct....E 4
83 King Sq.........D 13
84 King St. EC 2....G 2
86 King St. SW1.....B 6
86 King St. WC2....H 8
77 King St. W6......C 8
77 King St. Rich.....G 2
83 King William St...H 3
80 King William Wk..D 4
84 King's Arms Yd...G 2
79 King's Av. SW4...H 10
73 King's Av. W5....J 3
77 King's Bench St...C 12
83 King's Bench Wk..H 11
77 King's Bri. Av....A 4
83 King's Coll......H 10
87 King's Coll. Hosp.F 13
83 King's Cross Rd..D 10
83 King's Cross Sta...C 8
73 King's Dri.......C 5
77 King's Farm Av...G 4
79 King's Gro......E 16
67 King's Head Hill..A 9
88 King's Head Yd...B 3
76 King's Mead Way .D 2
83 King's Mews....F 10
88 King's Pl........D 1
76 King's Rd. E11...A 5
73 King's Rd. NW10.F 9
86 King's Rd. SW1...E 4
86 King's Rd. SW3...G 2
85 King's Rd. SW10..J 4
77 King's Rd. SW14..F 6
73 King's Rd. W5....J 3
77 King's Rd. Rich...H 4
86 King's Scholars'
   Passage......E 6
82 King's Ter.......B 6
66 Kingsbury Green D 3
66 Kingsbury Rd. NW9
   D 3
75 Kingsbury Sta....D 2
75 Kingsbury Ter....E 14
77 Kingscote Rd.....B 6
79 Kingscourt Rd...L 10
72 Kingsdown.......F 4
77 Kingsdown Av....A 1
76 Kingsdown Rd. E11
   C 5
75 Kingsdown Rd. N19
   C 10
74 Kingsgate Rd.....C 4
65 Kingshill Av......F 5
80 Kingshurst Rd....F 2
75 Kingsland High St.E 14
84 Kingsland Rd. E2..C 4
81 Kingsland Rd. E13.H 8
66 Kingsley Rd......H 1
78 Kingsley St......F 7
76 Kingsmead Rd...K 11
78 Kingsmere Pk....B 5
78 Kingsmere Rd....K 2
81 Kingsmill Ter.....B 5
70 Kingston Bri....D 1
70 Kingston By-Pass..D 3
70 Kingston Hill....D 2
76 Kingston Rd. E11.D 5
77 Kingston Rd. SW15
   K 8
70 Kingston Rd. SW20
   D 4
69 Kingston Rd. Staines
   C 3
70 Kingston Rd.
   Leatherhead....H 1
70 Kingston Rd. New M.
   D 2
70 Kingston Rd. Ted..C 1
70 Kingston Rd. Tol...E 2
70 Kingston-upon-
   Thames.......D 2

MAP

70 Kingston Vale.....C 3
74 Kingstown St.....F 7
77 Kingsway SW14...F 5
83 Kingsway, WC2...G 9
73 Kingsway, Wem...D 3
74 Kingswood Av....G 3
79 Kingswood Rd...H 10
70 Kingswood Sta....H 4
84 Kingward St.....F 6
78 Kingwood Rd.....E 2
73 Kinloch Dri......A 6
77 Kinnard Av......E 5
86 Kinnerton St.....D 3
79 Kinsdale Rd.....F 15
88 Kintore St.......E 5
88 Kipling St.......C 3
73 Kirby Gro.......C 3
83 Kirby St........F 11
83 Kirk St.........E 10
79 Kirkdale.......K 16
76 Kirkdale Rd......B 5
80 Kirkside Rd......D 6
79 Kirkstall Rd.....J 10
79 Kirkwood Rd....F 16
86 Kirtling St......J 6
76 Kirton Rd.......G 8
87 Kirwyn Way....J 13
76 Kitchener Rd....E 7
88 Kitson Rd.......J 2
80 Kitto Rd.........F 1
78 Klea Av.........H 9
80 Knapmill Rd.....K 3
76 Knapp Rd.......H 3
85 Knaresborough Pl..F 2
76 Knatchbull Rd....E 12
70 Knight's Hill.....C 6
76 Knighton Rd......D 7
80 Knights Rd......A 2
86 Knightsbridge....C 2
75 Knightsland Rd...B 16
69 Knipp Hill......G 5
85 Knivet Rd.......J 1
71 Knockholt.......H 12
71 Knockholt Main Rd.
   H 11
72 Knockholt Pound.G 1
71 Knockholt Rd....G 12
71 Knockholt Sta....F 12
79 Knollys Rd......L 11
75 Knottisford St...H 16
80 Knotts Green Rd..A 4
69 Knowle Green....C 2
69 Knowsley Rd.....F 7
82 Knox Rd.........E 6
82 Knox St.........F 2
85 Kynance Mews...E 3
85 Kynance Pl......E 3
75 Kynaston Rd....C 14
78 Kyrle Rd........H 7
75 Kyverdale Rd....C 15
84 Laburnum St.....B 5
84 Lackington St....F 3
74 Lacy Rd........G 2
74 Ladbroke Gro....J 2
74 Ladbroke Rd.....K 3
74 Ladbroke Sq.....K 3
75 Lady Margaret Rd.
   NW1.........D 9
65 Lady Margaret Rd.
   S'hall........F 6
74 Lady Somerset Rd. D 8
76 Ladysmith Rd....H 6
80 Ladywell Lodge..H 3
80 Ladywell Rd.....G 3
80 Ladywell Sta.....G 3
88 Lafone St.......C 5
78 Laitwood Rd.....J 8
76 Lake Ho. Rd.....C 6
78 Lakeside Gdns....B 2
73 Lakeside Way....D 4
69 Laleham........D 3
80 Laleham Rd. SE6..J 4
69 Laleham Rd.Shep. D 3
69 Laleham Rd. Staines
   C 2
75 Lamb La........F 16
84 Lamb St........F 5
88 Lamb Wk........C 4
77 Lambert Av......C 3
79 Lambert Rd. SW2.H10
79 Lambeth........B 11
87 Lambeth Bri.....E 9
87 Lambeth High St...E 9
87 Lambeth Hosp...F 12
87 Lambeth Pal.....E 9
87 Lambeth Pal. Rd..D 10
87 Lambeth Rd......E 10
84 Lambeth St......H 6
87 Lambeth Wk.....E 10
74 Lamble St.......D 7
74 Lambolle Rd.....E 6

MAP
78 Lambourn Rd.....F 8
83 Lamb's Conduit St.
F 9
84 Lamb's Passage...E 2
75 Lambton Rd....B 10
69 Lammas La.......F 6
77 Lammas Pk.......B 2
77 Lammas Pk. Rd...A 2
77 Lammas Rd.......A 2
85 Lamont Rd.......J 4
75 Lampard Gro...B 14
80 Lampmead Rd....G 6
69 Lampton.........A 6
69 Lampton Rd.....A 6
81 Lanark Pl.......E 4
81 Lanark Rd.......D 3
79 Lancaster Av....K 12
81 Lancaster Gate...J 4
74 Lancaster Gro....E 6
81 Lancaster Pk.....H 3
83 Lancaster Pl.......J 9
76 Lancaster Rd. E11.C 6
75 Lancaster Rd. N4.
A 11
73 Lancaster Rd. NW10
D 8
74 Lancaster Rd. W11.K 2
87 Lancaster St.....D 12
81 Lancaster Ter.....H 5
74 Lancefield St.....G 3
73 Lancelot Cres....D 2
86 Lancelot Pl.......D 2
73 Lancelot Rd......D 3
82 Lancing St.......D 7
79 Landcroft Rd....H 14
79 Landells Rd....H 15
78 Landford Rd.....G 1
79 Landor Rd......F 10
75 Landseer Rd....C 10
79 Lanercost Rd...K 11
87 Lanfranc St.....D 11
74 Langbourne Av...C 8
73 Langdon Dri.....B 5
74 Langdon Pk. Rd...A 8
81 Langford Pl.......B 4
78 Langford Rd......E 5
73 Langham Gdns....C 2
82 Langham Pl......G 5
82 Langham St......F 5
74 Langler Rd......G 2
65 Langley.........G 1
76 Langley Cres....A 7
76 Langley Dri.....A 7
87 Langley La......H 9
83 Langley St.......H 8
71 Langley Pk. G.C...E 9
70 Langley Vale.....H 3
77 Langside Av....G 8
76 Langthorne Rd....C 4
78 Langthorne St. SW6
E 2
83 Langton Cl.....D 10
79 Langton Rise....J 16
79 Langton Rd.....E 12
85 Langton St.......J 4
80 Langton Way....E 6
81 Lanhill Rd.......E 1
76 Lansdown Rd......H 1
86 Lansdowne Club...A 5
74 Lansdowne Cres..K 3
75 Lansdowne Dri...F 15
79 Lansdowne Gdns..E 10
79 Lansdowne Hill..L 12
76 Lansdowne Rd. E11 C 6
67 Lansdowne Rd. N17
C 8
74 Lansdowne Rd. W11
K 3
83 Lansdowne Ter....E 9
74 Lansdowne Wk....K 3
79 Lansdowne Way...E 10
88 Lant St........C 1
74 Larch Rd. NW2...D 2
81 Larch Rd. SW12...K 8
88 Larcom St.......F 2
77 Larden Rd.......A 7
79 Larkhall La.....E 10
79 Larkhall Rise...F 9
78 Larpent Av......G 1
80 Lassell St......C 5
78 Latchmere Gro...F 7
78 Latchmere Rd....F 7
77 Lateward Rd.....D 3
76 Latham St......J 3
76 Latimer Rd. E7...D 7
74 Latimer Rd. W10 .K 2
88 Latona Rd......H 6
87 Laud St........H 6
87 Lauderdale Dri...K 3
81 Lauderdale Rd....D 2

73 Launceston Gardens
F 2
85 Launceston Pl....D 3
73 Launceston Rd....F 2
68 Launders La......F 3
77 Laurel Rd.......F 8
84 Laurence Pountney La.
J 3
74 Laurier Rd......C 8
76 Lauriston Rd.....F 1
79 Lausanne Rd....E 16
79 Lavanor Rd.....F 16
73 Lavender Av.....B 6
78 Lavender Gdns....G 7
75 Lavender Gro.....F 15
78 Lavender Hill....F 7
78 Lavender Sweep...C 7
79 Lavengrove Rd...K 12
78 Lavenham Rd.....G 3
75 Lavers Rd.....C 14
77 Laverstoke Gardens
J 8
85 Laverton Pl.......F 2
77 Lavington Rd......A 1
87 Lavington St.....B 13
83 Lavinia Gro......B 9
88 Law St..........D 3
76 Lawes St.......H 3
76 Lawford Rd......E 9
78 Lawn, The.......A 1
74 Lawn Av........A 7
74 Lawn Cres.......E 4
87 Lawn La........H 9
74 Lawn Rd.......E 7
80 Lawn Ter.......F 5
76 Lawrence Rd. E3..G 2
77 Lawrence Rd. W5.B 2
66 Lawrence St. NW7.B 4
83 Lawrence St. SW3.H 6
79 Layard Rd......B 16
79 Laycock St.....E 11
73 Layer Gdns......K 4
73 Layfield Cres....A 9
73 Layhams Rd......F 9
83 Laystall St.....E 10
77 Layton Rd......C 2
76 Lea Bri. Rd......B 2
76 Lea Bri. Sta.....B 1
76 Lea Hall Rd.....B 3
80 Lea Rd.........G 6
67 Lea Valley Rd....A 9
75 Leabourne Rd...A 15
75 Leacroft Av.....J 7
75 Leadale Rd.....A 15
84 Leadenhall Mkt...H 3
84 Leadenhall St....H 4
76 Leahurst Rd.....H 5
87 Leake St.......C 10
74 Leamington Rd. Villas
J 3
76 Leamouth Rd.....K 5
79 Leander Rd.....H 11
76 Leas Rd........H 8
75 Leaside Rd.....B 16
76 Leasowes Rd.....B 3
76 Leather La......F 11
76 Leatherdale St....H 1
70 Leatherhead By-Pass
H 1
70 Leatherhead Common
H 1
70 Leatherhead G.C..G 1
70 Leatherhead Rd...G 1
70 Leatherhead Rd.
Chess'ton.....F 1
88 Leathermarket St..C 3
78 Leathwaite Rd....G 7
75 Leaves Green....G 10
78 Lebanon Gdns....H 4
74 Lechmere Rd.....E 1
76 Leckford Rd.....K 5
75 Leconfield Rd....D 13
74 Ledbury Rd......J 3
79 Ledbury St.....D 15
71 Ledgers Rd......H 8
80 Lee ....H 6
76 Lee Conservancy Rd.
E 2
80 Lee High Rd.....G 5
76 Lee Pk.........G 6
73 Lee Rd.........F 2
80 Lee Sta.........H 6
78 Lee St..........F 14
80 Lee Ter.........F 5
83 Leeke St.......C 9
82 Lees Pl.........H 4
71 Lecsons Rd.....D 11
76 Lefevre Rd......F 2
83 Leghorn Rd......G 8
83 Leicester Sq.......J 7
83 Leicester Sq. Th..J 7

74 Leigh Gdns.......G 1
88 Leigh Hunt St....C 1
76 Leigh Rd. E10....A 4
75 Leigh Rd. N5....D 12
83 Leigh St.........D 8
79 Leigham Av.....L 10
79 Leigham Court Rd.
K 10
79 LeighamVale.....K 11
74 Leighton Gdns.....G 1
75 Leighton Gro......D 9
75 Leighton Rd......E 9
77 Leinster Av......G 5
81 Leinster Gdns....H 13
81 Leinster Mews.....J 4
81 Leinster Rd......C 1
81 Leinster Sq.......H 2
73 Leith Cl.........B 6
84 Leman St.......H 6
80 Lemay Av.......K 7
76 Lemma Rd......B 5
78 Lena Gdns.......B 1
80 Lenham Rd......G 6
73 Lennox Gdns. NW10
D 7
86 Lennox Gdns.SW1 E 2
86 Lennox Gdns. Mews
E 2
75 Lennox Rd......B 11
80 Lenthorp Rd.....C 6
79 Leo St.........D 16
76 Leonard Rd......D 6
84 Leonard St......E 3
73 Leopold Rd......F 7
76 Leopold St.......J 2
87 Leopold Wk......G 9
79 Leppoc Rd......H 9
74 Leroy Rd.......A 7
88 Leroy St.......E 4
75 Lesbia Rd......D 16
76 Leslie Rd. E11....D 4
76 Leslie Rd. E16....D 4
75 Lesly St........E 11
76 Lessada St.......G 1
78 Lessar Av.......H 9
80 Lessing St.......H 1
75 Lindley Rd......J 16
76 Lester Av.......H 5
75 Leswin Rd.....C 14
76 Leswin Rd.....C 14
76 Leven Rd.......J 4
80 Levendale Rd.....K 2
83 Lever St.......D 13
74 Leverton St......A 9
75 Leweston Pl.....B 14
74 Lewis St.......E 8
80 Lewisham.......G 3
80 Lewisham High St..H 4
80 Lewisham Hosp...H 3
80 Lewisham Pk.....H 4
80 Lewisham Rd.....H 4
88 Lewisham Sta.....F 4
87 Lewisham St.....C 7
80 Lewisham Way....E 2
73 Lexden Rd......K 5
85 Lexham Gdns....E 2
85 Lexham Mews....E 1
82 Lexington St.....H 6
79 Lexton Gdns....J 10
67 Ley St.........D 11
77 Leyborne Av.....A 2
77 Leyborne Pk.....E 4
76 Leybourne Rd. E11 B 6
74 Leybourne Rd. NW1
F 8
84 Leyden St.......G 5
76 Leyes Rd.......K 8
73 Leyfield Rd......A 9
80 Leyland Rd......H 6
80 Leylang Rd......D 1
76 Leyspring Rd.....B 6
77 Leythe Rd......A 6
76 Leyton..........J 2
76 Leyton Green Rd..A 4
76 Leyton Midland Rd.
Sta.........H 1
76 Leyton Pk. Rd....C 4
76 Leyton Rd......E 4
76 Leytonstone.....B 5
76 Leytonstone High Rd.
Sta..........B 5
76 Leytonstone Rd...D 5
76 Leytonstone Sta..B 5
76 Lichfield Rd. E3..G 2
76 Lichfield Rd. NW2 D 2
77 Lichfield Rd. Rich..E 4
74 Liddell Gdns. ....G 1

76 Liddington Rd....F 6
83 Lidiard St.......K 5
85 Lido, The.......B 6
84 Ligonier St......D 5
77 Lilac Gdns.......B 3
75 Lilac St........K 8
79 Lilford Rd......F 12
77 Lillian Av......B 4
77 Lillian Rd......D 8
78 Lillie Rd.......D 3
78 Lillieshall Rd....F 8
86 Lillington St.....F 6
73 Lily Gdns.......G 2
76 Lily Rd.........A 3
84 Limburg Rd......G 7
78 Lime Gro.......A 1
84 Lime St.......H 4
76 Limehouse.......K 2
76 Limehouse Causeway
K 2
85 Limerston St.....H 4
74 Limes Av.......A 3
80 Limes Gro.......G 4
80 Limesford Rd.....G 1
78 Limpsfield Av.....K 2
78 Limpsfield Rd.....G 7
74 Linacre Rd......E 1
80 Linchmere Rd.....J 6
83 Lincoln's Inn....G 10
80 Lincoln's Inn Fields
G 10
76 Lincoln Rd. E13...H 7
73 Lincoln Rd. Wem..E 3
86 Lincoln St. E11...C 5
86 Lincoln St. SW3...F 2
74 Linden Av. NW10.G 2
88 Linden Av. Wem..D 4
81 Linden Gdns. W2..J 1
77 Linden Gdns. W4..C 7
79 Linden Gro.....F 16
74 Lindfield Gdns....D 5
73 Lindfield Rd......H 2
73 Lindfield St......J 3
76 Lindley Rd......B 4
75 Lindley St......J 16
73 Lindsey St......F 13
76 Ling Rd.........J 6
79 Lingham St......F 10
76 Lingwell Rd......L 6
75 Lingwood Rd....A 15
73 Link, The.......J 5
73 Links Rd. NW2...C 7
73 Link's Rd. W3....J 4
73 Linnell Dri......A 4
79 Linnell Rd......E 14
88 Linsey St.......E 6
75 Linthorpe Av.....E 2
75 Linthorpe Rd....A 14
84 Linton St.......B 1
76 Linver Rd.......B 7
77 Lion Gate Gardens
F 4
77 Lionel Rd......C 3
79 Liphook Cres....J 16
80 Liskeard Gdns....E 6
83 Lisle St........H 7
79 Lissenden Gdns...D 8
81 Lisson Gro......E 6
76 Lister Rd.......B 6
75 Listria Pk.....B 14
73 Litchfield Gardens
E 8
82 Little Albany St.
D 5
85 Lit. Boltons, The..G 3
75 Lit. Bushey La....A 6
86 Lit. Chester St....D 4
77 Lit. Ealing La....B 2
82 Lit. Edward St....C 5
68 Lit. Gaynes La....E 4
87 Lit. George St....C 8
83 Lit. Green La.....A 4
82 Lit. Marlborough St.
H 6
83 Lit. New St.....G 11
65 Lit. Oxhey La.....B 5
82 Lit Portland St....G 6
83 Lit. Russell St....G 8
86 Lit. St. James's St..B 6
84 Lit. Trinity La....H 1
70 Lit. Woodmansterne
La..........G 5
74 Lit. Wormwood Scrubs
J 1
69 Littleton.......D 3

69 Littleton La......E 3
78 Littleton St......K 5
75 Livermere Rd....F 14
88 Liverpool Gro.....G 2
84 Liverpool St.....G 4
84 Liverpool St. Sta..F 4
76 Liverpool Rd. E16. J 5
75 Liverpool Rd. N7 &
N1.......E 11
77 Liverpool Rd. W5 A 3
76 Livingstone Rd. E15
G 4
82 Livonia St......H 6
84 Lizard St.......D 2
80 Lizban St.......D 7
74 Llavanor Rd......C 3
73 Llanover Rd......D 3
83 Lloyd Baker St...D 10
83 Lloyd Sq.......D 10
83 Lloyd St.......C 10
84 Lloyd's Av......H 4
84 Lloyd's Bldgs....H 4
80 Lloyd's Pl.......F 5
83 Lloyd's Row....D 12
75 Londesborough Rd.
D 14
84 London Bri......J 3
84 London Bri. Sta...B 3
88 London Bri. St....B 3
82 London Clinic....E 4
75 London Fields....F 15
75 London Fields E. Side
F 15
75 London Fields Sta.
F 15
75 London Fields W. Side
F 15
75 London La......F 16
82 London Pavilion...J 7
82 London Planetarium
E 3
76 London Rd. E13...G 6
87 London Rd. SE1.D 12
79 London Rd. SE23.K 16
68 London Rd. Aveley
65 London Rd.
Batchworth.....B 3
70 London Rd. Cheam
E 3
72 London Rd. Dartford
B 3
72 London Rd. Dunton
Grn..........H 1
67 London Rd. Enfield
A 7
70 London Rd.
Hackbridge.....E 5
70 London Rd. K'gst.D 2
70 London Rd. Mitch.
D 5
70 London Rd. Mord..D 4
70 London Rd. Norbury
C 3
68 London Rd. Rom..D 2
68 London Rd. Shenfield
A 6
69 London Rd. Staines
C 3
66 London Rd. Stan..B 2
72 London Rd.
Swanscombe....B 4

73 London Rd. Wembley
E 3
83 London Sch. of
Economics.....H 10
69 London St.......E 2
84 London St. EC3...H 4
81 London St. W2...G 5
84 London Wall.....H 5
83 Long Acre......H 8
70 Long Ditton.....E 1
73 Long Dri........J 7
66 Long Elmes......C 1
70 Long Gro. Hosp...F 2
70 Long Gro. Rd.....F 2
83 Long La. EC1....F 13
88 Long La. SE1.....D 3
88 Long La. Bex'h...H 1
71 Long La. Cro.....D 8
69 Long La. Staines..B 3
65 Long La. Uxbridge.E 4
70 Long Pond Rd....E 5
78 Long Rd.........G 9
84 Long St.........C 5
38 Long Wk.........D 4
67 Longbridge Rd....E 11
80 Longbridge Way...H 5
80 Longcroft Rd.....H 4
70 Longdown La. Nth.
G 3
76 Longfellow Rd. E3.H 1
76 Longfellow Rd. E17
A 2
72 Longfield........D 5
73 Longfield Av......K 2
77 Longfield Dri.....G 5
72 Longfield Hill....D 6
73 Longfield Rd. W5.K 2
72 Longfield Rd.
Longfield......D 5
78 Longfield St.......J 4
65 Longford.......H 3
82 Longford St......E 5
80 Longhill Rd......K 5
80 Longhurst Rd.....H 5
74 Longland Gdns...D 5
71 Longlands......C 11
67 Longleigh La....H 12
73 Longley Av......G 4
88 Longley St.......F 6
66 Longmore Av.....A 5
86 Longmore St......F 6
76 Longnor Rd......H 1
85 Longridge Rd.....E 1
84 Longstafford Cres..H 4
73 Longstone Av.....F 8
77 Longwood Dri....H 8
67 Longwood Gdns..C 11
73 Lonsdale Av......E 3
74 Lonsdale Rd. NW6 G 3
77 Lonsdale Rd. SW13
E 7
74 Lonsdale Rd. W11.K 3
75 Lonsdale Sq......F 11
81 Lord Hill's Rd....F 2
87 Lord North St.....E 8
81 Lord's Cricket Grnd.
D 5
67 Lordship La. N17..C 7
79 Lordship La. SE22
J 15
75 Lordship Pk......B 13
75 Lordship Rd......B 13
75 Lordship Ter.....C 13
83 Lorenzo St......C 10
79 Lorn Rd........E 11
76 Lorne Rd. E7.....D 7
75 Lorne Rd. N4....B 11
75 Lorraine Rd......D 11
87 Lorrimore Sq....H 13
87 Lorrimore Rd....H 13
75 Lothair Rd. Nth..A 12
72 Lothair Rd. Sth..A 12
84 Lothbury.......G 3
79 Lothian Rd......E 12
73 Lothrop St......H 3
78 Lots Rd........E 5
84 Loudoun Rd.....B 4
65 Loudwater La.....A 3
79 Loughborough Junc.
Sta.........F 12
79 Loughborough Pk.
G 12
79 Loughborough Rd.
F 12
87 Loughborough St.G 10
67 Loughton........A 11
67 Loughton Way...A 10
76 Louise Rd......E 5
78 Louisville Rd.....H 5
76 Lovat La........J 3
76 Love La. E1......K 1

MAP
84 Love La. E.C.2....G 2
70 Love La. Mord...E 4
79 Love Wk.......F 13
77 Loveday Rd......A 1
88 Lovegrove St.....G 7
79 Lovelace Rd....K 12
79 Lovelinch St.....D 16
74 Loveridge Rd...E 3
79 Lowden Rd.....G 12
71 Lower Addiscombe
   Rd.........E 7
70 Lower Ashtead...H 2
68 Lower Bedford Rd.C 2
86 Lower Belgrave St.E 5
75 Lower Clapton...D 16
75 Lower Clapton Rd.
   D 16
78 Lower Common Sth.
   F 1
67 Lower Edmonton..B 8
69 Lower Feltham....C 5
69 Lower Green.....E 6
69 Lower Green Rd...E 6
86 Lower Grosvenor Pl.
   D 5
75 Lower Holloway..D 10
80 Lower Kid.......G 7
87 Lower Marsh ...C 11
74 Lower Merton Rise
   F 6
70 Lower Morden La. E 4
77 Lower Mortlake Rd.
   G 3
77 Lower Richmond Rd.
   F 5
80 Lower Rd.......B 1
86 Lower Sloane St..F 3
69 Lower Sunbury Rd.
   D 5
71 Lower Sydenham..C 8
74 Lower Ter.......C 5
84 Lower Thames St. J 3
73 Lowfield Rd......J 5
72 Lowfield St......B 3
76 Lowhall La.......A 2
66 Lowlands Rd....D 1
75 Lowman Rd....D 11
86 Lowndes Pl......D 3
86 Lowndes Sq......D 3
86 Lowndes St......D 3
79 Lowth Rd......E 13
80 Lowther Hill.....J 1
77 Lowther Rd......E 8
78 Loxley Rd.......J 6
80 Loxton Rd.......K 1
85 Lucan Pl........F 6
76 Lucas Av.......F 7
80 Lucas St........E 2
75 Lucerne Rd......D 12
88 Lucey Rd........E 6
78 Lucien Rd.......K 4
83 Ludgate Circus..H 12
83 Ludgate Hill....H 12
73 Ludlow Rd.......H 2
80 Luffman Rd......L 7
79 Lugard Rd. E 16
84 Luke St.........E 4
74 Lukes Rd. ...J 3
75 Lukin St........K 16
72 Lullingstone Cas. F 2
72 Lullingstone Pk...F 1
74 Lulot St........C 8
82 Lumley St.......H 4
85 Luna St.........J 4
71 Lunghurst Rd....H 8
86 Lupus St........G 6
78 Lurline Gdns.....E 8
76 Lurton Rd.......D 1
87 Luscombe Way...J 8
73 Lushington Rd....G 8
71 Lusted La.......H 10
76 Luton Rd.......H 6
81 Luton St........E 5
78 Luttrell Av......G 1
80 Lutwyche Rd.....K 2
82 Luxborough St...F 3
78 Luxemburg Gdns. B 2
71 Luxted Rd.......G 10
76 Lyal Rd.........G 2
86 Lyall St.........E 3
83 Lyceum Th.......H 9
78 Lydden Gro......J 4
78 Lydden Rd......J 4
74 Lydford Rd......H 3
79 Lydhurst Av.....K 11
78 Lydon Rd.......F 9
78 Lyford Rd.......J 6
80 Lyme Farm Rd...G 7
75 Lyme St.........F 9
74 Lymington Rd....E 4
74 Lyncroft Gdns....D 4

MAP
74 Lyndale Av.......C 3
76 Lyndhurst Dri....A 4
74 Lyndhurst Gdns...E 6
79 Lyndhurst Gro....F 14
74 Lyndhurst Rd....D 6
79 Lyndhurst Way...E 14
78 Lynette Av......H 8
73 Lynmouth Gdns...F 1
75 Lynmouth Rd. N16
   B 14
73 Lynmouth Rd. Gnfd.
   F 1
78 Lynn Rd.........J 8
88 Lynton Rd. SE1...F 6
79 Lynton Rd. SE17.C 15
73 Lynton Rd. W3...K 5
73 Lynwood Rd......H 3
73 Lyon Pk. Av.....E 3
81 Lyons Pl........E 5
77 Lyric Rd........E 7
82 Lyric Th.........J 7
78 Lysia St........D 2
78 Lysias Rd.......H 8
79 Lytham Rd.....H 10
88 Lytham St.......G 3
66 Lyttelton Rd.....C 5
76 Lyttleton Rd.....C 4
78 Lytton Gro......H 2
76 Lytton Rd.......A 5
80 Lyveden Rd......D 7
83 Mabledon Pl......D 8
76 Mabley St.......E 1
78 Macaulay Rd.....G 8
83 Macclesfield Rd..D 13
79 McDermott Rd...F 15
76 Macdonald Rd....D 6
79 McDowall Rd....E 12
79 Mace St.........G 1
81 Mackennal St....B 6
75 Mackenzie Rd....E 11
79 McKerrell Rd....E 15
83 Macklin St......G 9
88 Macks Rd.......E 6
80 Maclean Rd......H 1
88 Macleod St......G 2
85 McLeod's Mews...E 3
79 McNeil Rd......F 14
73 Madaley Rd......K 3
82 Mme. Tussaud's..E 3
82 Maddox St.......H 5
75 Madras Pl.......E 11
77 Madrid Rd.......E 8
88 Madron St.......F 4
77 Mafeking Av.....D 3
79 Magdalen Hosp..K 10
78 Magdalen Rd.....J 5
88 Magdalen St......B 4
87 Magee St.......H 11
81 Maida Av.......F 4
81 Maida Vale......C 3
83 Maiden La.......J 9
76 Maiden Rd......E 5
80 Maidenstone Hill..E 4
72 Maidstone Rd....D 1
84 Maidstone St.....B 6
71 Main Rd........H 10
71 Main Rd. Sid....C 11
72 Main Rd. Sutton-at-
   Hone........C 3
68 Main Rd. Wennington
   F 3
74 Maitland Pk.....E 7
74 Maitland Pk. Rd...E 7
79 Major Rd. SE16..B 15
74 Makepeace Av....C 8
86 Makins St......F 1
75 Malbrook Rd.....G 1
75 Malcolm Rd.....H 16
70 Malden.........E 3
76 Malden Rd. NW5.E 7
70 Malden Rd. Cheam
   D 3
70 Malden Rd. New M.
   D 3
70 Malden Rushett..D 1
70 Malden Way.....D 3
73 Maldon Rd......K 6
82 Malet Pl.........E 7
83 Malet St........F 7
80 Malham Rd......J 1
78 Mall Rd.........C 1
86 Mall, The, SW1...B 7
77 Mall, The, SW14..H 5
73 Mall, The, W5...K 3
73 Mallard Way.....A 4
76 Mallinson Rd.....G 6
85 Mallord St.......H 5
84 Mallow St.......E 2
76 Malmesbury Rd. E3
   G 2

MAP
76 Malmesbury Rd. E16
   J 5
80 Malpas Rd.......F 2
88 Malt St.........H 6
88 Malta Rd........B 3
83 Malta St........D 12
78 Maltby St.......D 5
78 Malvard St......H 4
81 Malvern Mews...D 1
75 Malvern Rd. E8..F 15
76 Malvern Rd. E11..C 6
81 Malvern Rd. NW6.D 1
76 Malwood Rd.....H 8
80 Malyons Rd......H 3
79 Manaton Rd.....F 15
76 Manbey Gro.....E 5
76 Manbey Pk......E 5
76 Manbey St.......E 5
80 Manchester Gro...C 4
86 Manchester Rd....B 4
82 Manchester Sq....G 4
82 Manchester St....G 3
78 Manchuria Rd....H 7
88 Manciple St......D 3
82 Mandeville Pl.....G 4
75 Mandeville St....C 1
78 Mandrake Rd....K 7
83 Manette St......H 7
76 Manilla St.......A 3
76 Manisty St.......K 4
88 Mann St.........G 3
80 Manor Av.......F 2
73 Manor Dri.......D 4
73 Manor Farm Rd..G 2
79 Manor Gro.SE15.D 16
77 Manor Gro. Rich..G 4
75 Manor Gdns.....C 10
70 Manor Hosp......G 2
74 Manor Ho. Dri...F 2
75 Manor Ho. Sta...B 12
80 Manor La........H 5
80 Manor La. Ter...G 5
79 Manor Mount....J 6
67 Manor Pk.......E 11
80 Manor Pk. SE13..G 5
73 Manor Pk. Rd....G 7
87 Manor Pl.......G 13
67 Manor Rd. E4...A 10
76 Manor Rd. E10...B 3
76 Manor Rd. E15...G 5
75 Manor Rd. N16..B 14
77 Manor Rd. Mitch..D 5
77 Manor Rd. Rich..G 4
70 Manor Rd. Wal..F 5
67 Manor Rd. Wfd. Gn.
   B 11
70 Manor Rd. Nth...E 1
70 Manor Sta.......E 3
80 Manor Way.....G 6
78 Manville Rd......K 8
85 Manresa Rd......G 6
75 Manse Rd.......D 15
77 Mansell Rd......A 6
88 Mansell St.......H 5
67 Mansfield Hill....A 9
76 Mansfield Rd. E11.A 7
76 Mansfield Rd. NW3 D 7
73 Mansfield Rd. W3.H 5
82 Mansfield St......F 5
84 Mansford St.....C 7
84 Mansion Ho......H 2
84 Mansion Ho. Pl...H 2
71 Mansion, The....B 12
85 Manson Pl......F 4
83 Mantell St.......B 11
83 Mantus Rd......H 16
80 Manwood Rd....H 2
75 Mape St.........H 15
76 Mapesbury Rd....D 1
73 Maple Gro. NW9.A 6
77 Maple Gro. W5...B 3
76 Maple Rd.......A 5
82 Maple St.........F 6
72 Maplescombe.....F 3
76 Maplin St.......H 2
82 Marble Arch.....H 2
77 Marble Hill......J 2
77 Marble Hill Pk...J 2
83 Marchmont St....E 8
77 Marchmont Rd...H 4
72 Marchwind Cres..J 2
88 Marcia Rd.......F 4
75 Marcon Pl......E 15
79 Marden Rd......B 16
75 Mare St........F 16
74 Maresfield Gdns...E 5
82 Margaret St......G 6
80 Margarets Rd....G 2
75 Margaret's Gro...E 14
85 Margaretta Ter...H 6

MAP
79 Margate Rd......G 10
76 Margery Rd......E 6
83 Margery St......D 11
78 Margravine Gdns..C 2
78 Margravine Rd...D 2
80 Maria St........B 3
73 Marian Way.....F 7
79 Marigold St......A 15
80 Marischal Rd....G 4
78 Marius Rd.......K 7
84 Mark La........H 2
76 Mark St. E15....F 5
84 Mark St. EC2....E 3
86 Market Mews....B 4
82 Market Pl.......G 6
75 Market Rd......G 10
86 Markham Sq.....G 2
86 Markham St.....G 2
76 Markhouse Rd...A 2
76 Markmanor Av...A 2
68 Marks Gate.....C 1
68 Marks Gate Rd...C 1
77 Marksbury Av....F 4
78 Marl St.........G 5
75 Marlborough Av..F 15
77 Marlborough Cres..B 6
88 Marlborough Gro..G 6
81 Marlborough Hill..B 4
86 Marlborough Ho...B 6
80 Marlborough La...D 8
81 Marlborough Pl....B 4
76 Marlborough Rd.E7
   E 8
75 Marlborough Rd. N19
   C 10
86 Marlborough Rd. SW1
   B 6
77 Marlborough Rd. W4
   C 5
77 Marlborough Rd. W5
   A 3
77 Marlborough Rd.
   Rich........H 3
85 Marlborough St...F 6
80 Marler Rd.......K 2
85 Marloes Rd......E 2
76 Marlow Rd......E 1
70 Marlpit La......H 6
78 Marmion Rd.....G 8
79 Marmont Rd....E 15
79 Marmora Rd....H 16
74 Marne St.......H 3
76 Maroon St.......J 1
75 Marquess Rd....E 13
73 Marquis Cl......F 4
75 Marquis Rd. NW1 E 10
75 Marquis Rd. N4..B 11
75 Marriot Rd......B 11
80 Marsala Rd......G 3
79 Marsden Rd....G 14
74 Marsden St......E 7
76 Marsh Hill......E 1
76 Marsh La. E10...B 3
66 Marsh La. Stan...B 2
65 Marsh Rd.......C 5
67 Marsh Side......B 8
82 Marshall St......H 6
88 Marshalsea Rd...C 2
87 Marsham St.....E 8
80 Marshfield St.....B 4
76 Marshgate La....G 4
87 Marsland Rd....G 13
83 Mart St.........H 9
84 Martin La......J 3
79 Martell Rd......L 13
75 Martello St......F 16
75 Martha St.......K 16
84 Martin La.......J 3
70 Martin Way.....D 4
77 Martindale......G 5
69 Martindale Rd....B 5
80 Marvels La......K 7
76 Marville Rd......E 3
74 Mary Pl.........K 2
84 Mary St. N1.....A 2
76 Maryland Pk.....E 5
76 Maryland Rd....E 5
76 Maryland Sta....E 5
81 Marylands Rd....E 1
82 Marylebone High St.
   F 4
82 Marylebone La...G 4
82 Marylebone Mews.G 4
82 Marylebone Rd...F 1
82 Marylebone Sta...E 2
87 Marylee Way....F 10
78 Masbro Rd......B 2
68 Mascalls La......B 5

MAP
80 Mascalls Rd......D 7
86 Mason St........E 3
71 Masons Hill.....D 9
88 Massinger St.....F 4
80 Mast House Ter...C 3
76 Matcham Rd....C 5
78 Matheson Rd....C 3
76 Matilda St......A 10
76 Matlock Rd......A 4
87 Matthew Parker St.
   D 8
75 Matthias Rd.....D 13
73 Mattock La......K 2
76 Maud Rd. E10...C 4
76 Maud Rd. E13...G 6
79 Maude Rd......E 14
76 Maudslay Hosp..F 13
79 Mauleverer Rd...H 10
86 Maunsel St......E 7
76 Mauritius Rd....C 5
75 Maury Rd.......C 15
88 Mawbey Pl......G 6
86 Mawbey St......E 10
68 Mawney Rd.....C 2
88 Mawson St......E 14
74 Maxilla Gdns....J 2
74 Maxted Rd......F 15
73 May Gdns.......E 8
78 May St..........C 3
79 Mayall Rd......G 12
69 Maybury........H 1
73 Maybury Gdns...E 8
76 Maybury Rd.....H 8
74 Mayfair.........K 8
86 Mayfair Hot.....A 5
86 Mayfair Pl......B 5
77 Mayfield Av.....C 7
74 Mayfield Gdns....A 2
79 Mayfields........C 5
79 Mayflower Rd....F 10
78 Mayford Rd......J 7
83 Maygood St.....B 10
74 Maygrove Rd....E 3
80 Mayhill Rd......D 7
80 Mayo Rd........K 2
75 Mayola Rd......D 16
72 Maypole........B 1
71 Maypole Rd.....F 12
66 Mays La ....A 4
78 Maysoule Rd....G 5
79 Mayton St......C 11
76 Mayville Rd.....C 5
80 Maze Hill.......D 5
88 Maze Pond......B 3
75 Mead Pl........E 16
87 Mead Row......D 11
87 Meadcroft Rd...H 12
87 Meadlands Dri...K 2
73 Meadow Bank Rd. A 6
87 Meadow Rd......J 9
87 Meadow Row....E 13
73 Meadow Way....D 3
73 Meadowside Rd...G 8
73 Meadvale Rd.....H 2
74 Meadway.......A 4
74 Meard St.......H 7
76 Meath Rd.......G 6
83 Mecklenburgh Pl..E 9
83 Mecklenburgh Sq..E 9
82 Medburn St.....B 7
77 Medfield St......J 8
77 Medhurst Rd.....G 1
75 Median Rd......D 16
75 Medina Rd......C 11
79 Medlar St.......E 13
79 Medora Rd......H 11
80 Medusa Rd......H 3
86 Medway St......E 7
75 Medwin St......G 10
78 Meek St........D 5
76 Meeson St......D 1
75 Meetinghouse La..E 15
75 Mehetabel Rd....E 16
79 Melbourne Gro...G 14
83 Melbourne Pl....II 10
76 Melbourne Rd....A 3
79 Melbourne Sq....E 11
76 Melbury Rd......B 3
82 Melbury Ter......E 2
82 Melcombe Pl.....F 2
82 Melcombe St.....E 2
76 Melford Rd. E11..C 5
76 Melford Rd. SE22.J 15
70 Melfort Rd......D 6
75 Melgund Rd.....E 11
81 Melina Pl.......D 4
79 Melina Rd......A 8
88 Melior St........C 3
80 Meliot Rd.......K 5
75 Mellish Rd......B 3
73 Mellitus St......J 7
78 Melody Rd......H 5

MAP
74 Melrose Av. NW2.D 1
78 Melrose Av. SW19.K 3
78 Melrose Gdns....B 1
78 Melrose Rd......H 3
82 Melton St.......D 7
77 Melville Rd. SW13.E 8
76 Memorial Av....G 5
76 Menelik Rd......D 3
75 Mentmore St....F 16
77 Meon Rd.......A 6
72 Meopham.......E 6
72 Meopham Green..E 6
72 Meopham Sta....D 6
87 Mepham St.....B 10
80 Mercator Rd.....G 5
83 Mercer St.......H 8
75 Mercers Rd......C 10
76 Merchant St.....H 2
84 Merchant Taylor's
   Hall.........H 3
78 Mercier Rd......H 2
83 Meredith St. EC1.D 12
83 Merlin St........D 11
88 Mermaid Ct.....C 2
83 Mermaid Th.....H 12
88 Merrick Sq......D 2
80 Merriman Rd....E 8
80 Merritt Rd......G 2
88 Merrow St......G 3
65 Merry Hill......B 6
65 Merryhill Rd....A 6
70 Merton.........D 4
77 Merton Av......C 7
74 Merton La......B 7
70 Merton Park Sta..E 4
78 Merton Rd. SW18.H 4
70 Merton Rd. SW19.C 4
80 Merttins Rd......G 1
79 Mervan Rd.....G 11
73 Messaline Av.....K 6
74 Messina Av......F 4
87 Methley St......G 11
78 Mexfield Rd......G 3
87 Meymott St.....B 12
74 Meynell Cres....F 1
76 Meynell Rd......F 1
84 Micawber St....C 1
76 Michael Rd. E11..B 6
78 Michael Rd. SW6..E 5
80 Micheldever Rd...A 4
85 Micklethwaite Rd..H 1
74 Middle Row.....H 2
83 Middle St.......F 13
83 Middle Temple La.
   H 11
82 Middlesex Hosp...F 6
84 Middlesex St.....G 5
75 Middleton Rd. E8.F 15
74 Middleton Rd. NW11
   A 4
75 Middleton St....G 16
71 Midfield Way....D 11
73 Midholm........B 5
74 Midland Brent Ter.C 2
83 Midland Rd......C 8
76 Midlothian Rd....J 2
79 Midmoor Rd....J 9
85 Milborne Gro....G 4
80 Milborough Cres...J 5
69 Milbourne La....F 5
75 Mildenhall Rd....C 16
75 Mildmay Gro....E 8
84 Mildmay Miss. Hosp.
   D 5
75 Mildmay Pk.....E 14
75 Mildmay Rd.....D 13
75 Mildmay St......E 13
76 Mile End Rd.....H 1
76 Mile End Sta....H 2
69 Miles La........G 5
87 Miles St........H 8
73 Milford Ct......D 2
83 Milford La......H 10
84 Milk St.........G 2
79 Milkwood Rd....G 12
66 Mill Hill........B 3
66 Mill Hill (Bdy.) Sta.
   B 3
66 Mill Hill E. Sta...C 4
66 Mill Hill G.C....A 5
77 Mill Hill Gro....A 5
77 Mill Hill Rd. SW13
78 Mill Hill Rd. W3..A 5
74 Mill La. NW6....E 3
69 Mill La. Chertsey..D 2
68 Mill La. Dag.....G 4
80 Mill Rd. E16....A 7
84 Mill Row.......A 2
88 Mill St. SE1.....C 6
82 Mill St. W1.....H 5

MAP
76 Millais Rd........D 4
87 Millbank.........E 8
67 Millers La.........B 12
74 Millfield La........C 7
76 Millfields Rd. E5..C 1
75 Millfields Rd. E5.D 16
83 Millman St.........E 9
80 Millmark Gro......F 2
76 Mills Gro..........J 4
80 Millwall...........B 3
74 Milman Rd.........G 2
85 Milman's St........J 5
76 Milner Rd..........H 5
75 Milner Sq..........F 12
86 Milner St...........E 2
77 Milnthorpe Rd......D 6
78 Milson Rd..........B 2
74 Milton Av. N6......A 9
73 Milton Av. NW10 F 6
75 Milton Gro.........D 13
74 Milton Pk...........A 9
79 Milton Rd. SE24.H 12
77 Milton Rd. SW14.G 6
73 Milton Rd. W3.....L 6
84 Milton St...........F 2
74 Milverton Rd.......F 2
87 Milverton St.......G 11
88 Mina Rd............G 4
80 Minard Rd..........J 5
84 Mincing La.........H 4
86 Minerva Mews......E 4
73 Minerva Rd.........H 6
73 Minet Av............G 7
79 Minet Rd............F 12
78 Minford Gdns......A 2
76 Ming St.............K 3
88 Minnow St..........F 4
84 Minories............H 5
77 Minstead Gdns.....H 7
74 Minster Rd.........D 3
88 Mint St..............C 1
84 Mintern St..........B 3
75 Miranda Rd.........B 9
70 Mitcham.............D 5
70 Mitcham Common.D 5
70 Mitcham G.C........D 5
70 Mitcham Junc.......D 5
70 Mitcham La.........C 5
70 Mitcham Rd. SW17 C 5
70 Mitcham Rd. Cro..E 6
70 Mitcham Sta........D 5
81 Mitcham St..........E 6
84 Mitchell St..........D 1
73 Mitchell Way.......E 6
75 Mitchison Rd......E 13
76 Mitchley Av........G 7
71 Mitchley Hill.......G 7
87 Mitre Rd............C 11
84 Mitre St.............H 4
69 Molesey Rd.........E 5
80 Molesworth St......F 4
82 Molyneux St........G 1
87 Monck St............E 7
79 Moncrieff St........E 15
76 Monega Rd..........E 8
76 Moness St...........J 5
76 Monier Rd...........F 3
76 Monk St..............K 6
73 Monks Dri...........J 4
73 Monks Pk............E 5
87 Monkton St.........E 11
81 Monmouth Rd......H 2
83 Monmouth St.......H 8
75 Monnery Rd.........C 9
88 Monnow Rd.........F 6
77 Monroe Dri..........G 5
75 Monsell Rd.........C 12
73 Monson Rd. NW10 G 8
80 Monson Rd. SE14.D 1
86 Montacute Rd.......J 2
82 MontaguMansions F 3
82 Montagu Mews Nth. F 2
82 Montagu Mews S..G 2
82 Montagu Mews W..G 2
82 Montagu Pl..........G 2
73 Montagu Rd.........A 8
82 Montagu Row.......F 3
82 Montagu Sq.........G 2
82 Montagu St..........G 2
80 Montague Av.......G 2
88 Montague Cl........B 2
73 Montague Gdns....K 4
83 Montague Pl........F 8
75 Montague Rd. E8..E 15
76 Montague Rd. E11.C 6
67 Montague Rd. N18.B 8
73 Montague Rd. W13 J 1
77 Montague Rd. Rich. H 3
83 Montague St........F 8
84 Montclare St........D 5
80 Montem Rd..........J 2
87 Montford Pl.........G 10
78 Montholme Rd.....H 7
75 Montpelier Gro.....D 9
85 Montpelier Pl.......D 6
73 Montpelier Rise....B 2
74 Montpelier Rd. NW11 A 2
79 Montpelier Rd. SE15 E 16
73 Montpelier Rd. W5 J 2
80 Montpelier Row, SE3 F 6
77 Montpelier Row, Twick..........J 2
86 Montpelier Sq.......D 1
86 Montpelier St.......D 1
85 Montpelier Wk......D 6
79 Montrell Rd.........J 10
74 Montrose Av. NW6 G 3
66 Montrose Av. Hendon C 3
86 Montrose Pl.........D 4
78 Montserrat Rd......G 2
84 Monument St.......J 3
76 Moody St............H 1
84 Moor La. EC2.......F 2
68 Moor La. Hornchurch C 5
70 Moor La. Surb......F 2
65 Moor La. Rickmansworth..........B 3
65 Moor Pk. G.C.......B 4
65 Moot Pk. Sta........B 4
78 Moore Pk. Rd.......E 4
86 Moore St.............E 2
84 Moorfields...........F 3
84 Moorfields Eye Hosp. D 2
65 Moorfields Rd......D 3
84 Moorgate.............G 2
81 Moorhouse Rd......G 1
74 Mora Rd.............D 1
84 Mora St..............D 2
76 Morant St............K 3
72 Morants Ct. Rd.....H 1
79 Morat St.............E 11
75 Moray Rd............B 11
73 Mordaunt Rd........G 6
79 Mordaunt St.........F 11
70 Morden...............D 4
70 Morden G.C.........D 4
70 Morden Hall Rd....D 4
80 Morden Hill.........F 4
80 Morden La...........E 4
70 Morden Pk...........E 4
80 Morden Rd. SE3...F 6
70 Morden Rd. Merton D 4
70 Morden Rd. Mitcham.........D 5
70 Morden Rd. Halt...D 4
80 Morden Rd. Mews.F 6
70 Morden Sta..........D 4
88 Morecambe St......F 2
83 Moreland St.........C 13
78 Morella Rd...........J 7
75 Moresby Rd.........B 16
86 Moreton Pl...........G 6
86 Moreton St...........F 7
86 Moreton Ter.........G 6
76 Morgan St............H 2
88 Morgan's La.........B 4
76 Morieux Rd..........B 2
71 Morland Rd..........E 7
76 Morley Rd. E10....B 4
76 Morley Rd. E15....G 6
80 Morley Rd. SE13..G 4
77 Morley Rd. Twick..H 2
87 Morley St............D 11
75 Morning La.........E 16
82 Mornington Cres...B 6
76 Mornington Gro...H 3
76 Mornington Rd....B 6
82 Mornington St......B 5
82 Mornington Ter....B 5
88 Morocco St..........C 4
76 Morpeth Rd..........F 1
76 Morpeth St...........H 1
86 Morpeth Ter.........E 6
76 Morris Rd............J 3
79 Morrish Rd..........J 10
78 Morrison St..........F 7
81 Morshead Rd........D 2
79 Morten Cl.............H 9
74 Mortimer Cres.......G 4
74 Mortimer Rd. NW10 G 1
73 Mortimer Rd. W13. J 2
82 Mortimer St..........G 6
77 Mortlake..............F 6
77 Mortlake High St..F 6
76 Mortlake Rd. E16. J 7
77 Mortlake Rd. Rich. E 5
77 Mortlake Sta........F 6
87 Morton Pl............D 11
75 Morton Rd...........F 13
79 Morval Rd...........H 11
76 Morville St..........G 3
82 Morwell St...........G 7
81 Moscow Rd..........H 2
86 Mossop St............E 1
73 Mostyn Av............D 4
73 Mostyn Gro..........G 2
79 Mostyn Rd. SW9.E 11
70 Mostyn Rd. Morden..........D 4
86 Motcomb St..........D 3
78 Motley St.............F 9
70 Motspur Pk..........D 3
71 Mottingham.........C 10
71 Mottingham La. SE9 B 10
80 Mottingham La. SE12 J 8
71 Mottingham Rd...C 10
75 Moundfield Rd....A 15
73 Mount, The..........C 5
79 Mt. Adon Pk........J 15
77 Mt. Ararat Rd......H 3
79 Mt. Ash Rd..........L 16
73 Mount Av.............J 2
73 Mount Dri............C 5
79 Mt. Ephraim La.....L 9
79 Mt. Ephraim Rd..K 10
79 Mt. Nod Rd.........K 11
73 Mount Pk. Cres.....J 3
73 Mount Pk. Rd.......J 2
65 Mount Pleasant....F 6
83 Mt. Pleasant, WC1 E 10
73 Mt. Pleasant, Wem. F 3
75 Mt. Pleasant Hill.C 16
75 Mt. Pleasant La...B 16
74 Mt. Pleasant Rd. NW10..........F 1
80 Mt. Pleasant Rd. SE13..........H 4
73 Mt. Pleasant Rd. W5 H 2
75 Mt. Pleasant Villas A 10
73 Mount Rd. NW4...A 8
78 Mount Rd. SW19..K 4
72 Mount Rd. Swanscombe....B 4
82 Mount Row..........J 4
82 Mount St.............J 4
65 Mt. Vernon Hosp..B 4
75 Mt. View Rd........A 10
79 Mountearl Gdns...K 10
75 Mountgrove Rd...C 12
80 Mountsfields Pk...J 4
80 Mounts Pond Rd...F 5
74 Mowbray Rd........F 3
79 Mowll St.............E 11
82 Moxon Pl.............F 4
84 Moye St...............B 6
73 Moyne Pl.............G 4
80 Muirkirk Rd.........K 4
84 Mulberry St..........G 6
85 Mulberry Wk........H 5
73 Mulgrave Rd. NW10 D 8
73 Mulgrave Rd. W5.H 3
70 Mulgrave Rd. Sut..F 4
75 Mulkern Rd.........B 10
81 Mulready St.........E 6
78 Multon Rd............J 6
78 Muncaster Rd.......G 7
79 Mundania Rd.......H 16
76 Munday Rd..........K 6
78 Munster Rd..........E 3
82 Munster Sq..........D 5
88 Munton Rd...........E 2
76 Murchison Rd.......B 4
83 Muriel St.............B 10
80 Murillo Rd...........G 5
87 Murphy St...........D 11
84 Murray Gro..........C 2
73 Murray Rd. W5....C 2
77 Murray Rd. Rich..K 2
75 Murray St............E 9
78 Musard Rd...........D 3
79 Muschamp Rd.......F 15
83 Museum St...........G 8
78 Musgrave Cres.....E 4
80 Musgrove Rd........E 1
66 Muswell Hill.........C 6
66 Muswell Hill G.C..C 6
66 Muswell Hill Rd...C 6
79 Myatt Rd.............E 12
79 Myatt's Fields......E 12
80 Mycenæ Rd..........D 6
83 Myddelton Pass....C 11
83 Myddelton Sq......C 11
83 Myddelton St......D 11
76 Myrtle Rd............A 2
84 Myrtle St.............C 4
78 Mysore Rd...........G 7
80 Nadine St.............C 8
68 Nags Head La.......C 4
67 Nags Head Rd......A 8
76 Nailour St...........E 10
76 Nairn St..............J 4
78 Nansen Rd...........G 8
74 Nant Rd..............C 3
78 Napier Av............F 3
84 Napier Gro...........B 2
76 Napier Rd. E15.....G 5
73 Napier Rd. Wem...E 3
80 Napier St.............D 2
78 Narbonne Av........H 9
74 Narcissus Rd.......E 4
75 Narford Rd.........C 15
76 Narrow St............K 1
71 Nash...................F 9
80 Nash Rd..............G 1
72 Nash St...............D 6
77 Nasmyth St..........B 9
77 Nassau Rd............E 7
82 Nassau St.............F 6
74 Nassington Rd......D 7
73 Nathans Rd..........B 2
82 Nat. Dent. Hosp...F 5
87 National Film Th.B 10
83 National Gallery...J 8
82 Nat. Heart. Hosp..F 4
85 Nat. History Mus..E 5
83 National Hosp......E 9
83 Nat. Portrait Gallery J 8
82 Nat. Temp. Hosp..D 6
76 Naval Row...........K 4
75 Navarino Rd.........E 15
84 Navarre St............D 5
79 Navy St...............F 9
79 Naylor Rd............D 15
83 Neal St................H 8
79 Nealden St...........H 8
73 Neasden..............C 7
73 Neasden Hosp.......E 6
73 Neasden La..........C 6
73 Neasden Sta.........D 7
88 Neate St..............H 4
88 Neckinger............D 5
81 Needham Rd.........H 1
80 Nelgarde Rd.........J 3
84 Nelson Gdns.........C 7
83 Nelson Pl............C 12
80 Nelson Rd. SE10..D 4
69 Nelson Rd. Twick..B 6
87 Nelson Sq............C 12
75 Nelson St.............J 16
83 Nelson Ter...........C 12
79 Nelson's Row........G 9
77 Nepean St.............H 8
66 Nether St..............C 4
77 Netheravon Rd.......C 7
79 Netherby Rd.........J 16
79 Netherford Rd.......F 9
74 Netherhall Gdns....E 5
66 Netherland Rd.......A 5
85 Netherton Gro......H 4
78 Netherwood Rd.....B 2
74 Netherwood St......E 4
73 Nettleden Av.........E 4
80 Nettleton Rd.........E 1
77 Netley Rd.............D 3
82 Netley St..............D 6
80 Neuchatel Rd........K 2
85 Nevern Pl.............F 1
85 Nevern Rd............F 1
85 Nevern Sq............F 1
75 Nevill Rd..C 14 & D 14
74 Neville Dri............A 5
76 Neville Rd. E7.....F 7
73 Neville Rd. W5....H 2
85 Neville St.............F 5
78 Nevis Rd..............K 7
71 New Addington.....F 9
72 New Barn............C 5
71 New Barn La. Cudham H 11
72 New Barn La. Swanley Village..........D 1
76 New Barn St.........H 7
66 New Barnet..........A 5
71 New Beckenham....C 8
82 New Bond St.........H 5
83 New Bri. St..........H 12
84 New Broad St.......G 3
73 New Broadway.....K 2
82 New Burlington St. H 6
82 New Cavendish St..F 5
84 New Change..........H 1
83 New Charles St....C 12
88 New Church Rd....J 3
76 New City Rd.........H 8
83 New Compton St..H 8
80 New Cross............E 2
80 New Cross Gate Sta. E 1
80 New Cross Rd.......E 1
80 New Cross Stadium D 1
80 New Cross Sta......E 2
72 New Cut..............H 1
65 New Denham.........E 3
71 New Eltham..........C 11
74 New End..............D 5
83 New Fetter La.......G 11
69 New Haw.............F 3
69 New Haw Rd.........F 3
84 New Inn St............E 4
84 New Inn Yd...........E 4
88 New Kent Rd........E 2
80 New King St..........D 3
78 New King's Rd......F 3
70 New Malden..........D 2
70 New Malden G.C...D 3
84 New Nth. Pl..........E 4
84 New Nth. Rd. N1..B 2
67 New Nth. Rd. Hainault..........B 12
83 New Nth. St..........F 9
83 New Oxford St......G 8
87 New Palace Yd......C 8
79 New Pk. Rd..........J 10
76 New Plaistow Rd...F 5
82 New Quebec St.....H 3
85 New Ride..............C 5
75 New Rd. E1.........J 15
67 New Rd. E4..........B 9
80 New Rd. SE16.......C 1
77 New Rd. Brent......C 3
65 New Rd. Croxleygreen A 3
68 New Road, Dag....F 2
69 New Rd. Littleton.D 1
69 New Rd. W. Molesey D 6
83 New Row..............J 8
87 New Scotland Yd..C 8
66 New Southgate......B 6
83 New Sq................G 10
84 New St.................G 4
83 New St. Sq...........G 11
83 New Th................J 8
83 New Wharf Rd.......B 9
65 New Years Grn. La D 3
71 New Years La.......G 11
73 Newark Cres.........H 6
69 Newark La...........H 2
75 Newark St............J 16
82 Newburgh St........H 6
87 Newburn St..........G 10
67 Newbury Pk.........D 11
83 Newbury St.........F 13
76 Newby Pl..............K 4
81 Newcastle Mews...F 5
85 Newcombe St........B 1
88 Newcomen St........C 2
81 Newcourt St..........C 6
83 Newgate St...........G 13
76 Newham Way.......J 7
88 Newhams Row......D 4
75 Newick Rd...........C 16
79 Newington...........B 13
87 Newington Butts..F 12
87 Newington Causeway D 13
87 Newington Cres...F 12
75 Newington Green.D 13
75 Newington Green Rd. E 13
82 Newman St...........G 6
83 Newport Pl...........H 8
76 Newport Rd...........B 4
87 Newport St...........F 10
80 Newquay Rd.........K 4
80 Newstead Rd.........J 6
77 Newton Av............A 6
75 Newton Cl.............A 13
84 Newton Gro. N1...B 3
81 Newton Rd. W2....G 2
77 Newton Gro. W4..B 7
73 Newton Rd. Wem..F 4
83 Newton St............G 9
77 Niagara Av...........B 2
84 Nicholas La..........H 3
75 Nicholas Rd.........H 16
75 Nicholay Rd..........B 9
87 Nicholson St.........B 12
73 Nicoll Rd..............G 7
78 Nicosia Rd............J 6
70 Nigel Hill..............E 4
76 Nigel Rd. E7.........E 8
77 Nigel Rd. SE15....F 15
80 Nightingale Gro....H 5
78 Nightingale La......J 7
73 Nightingale Rd. NW10 G 8
67 Nightingale Rd. Edmonton........A 8
70 Nightingale Rd. Wal. E 5
78 Nightingale Wk.....H 8
84 Nile St..................C 2
88 Nile Ter................G 5
86 Nine Elms La........J 6
77 Niton Rd..............F 4
78 Niton St...............D 2
68 Noak Hill..............B 3
68 Noak Hill Rd........B 3
87 Noar St................B 13
84 Noble St...............G 1
67 Noel Pk................C 7
83 Noel Rd. N1.........B 12
73 Noel Rd. W3........J 5
82 Noel St.................H 6
84 Norah St...............D 7
70 Norbiton...............D 2
73 Norbrook St..........K 7
70 Norbury...............D 6
70 Norbury Cres........D 6
70 Norbury Hill.........C 6
75 Norcott Rd...........C 15
75 Norfolk Av...........A 14
81 Norfolk Cres.........G 6
81 Norfolk Pl............G 5
81 Norfolk Rd...........A 5
87 Norfolk Row........E 10
81 Norfolk Sq...........G 5
83 Norfolk St...........H 10
78 Norland St...........A 3
76 Norlington Rd......B 4
76 Norman Gro.........G 2
76 Norman Rd. E11..C 5
80 Norman Rd. SE10 D 3
81 Norman St...........D 1
73 Norman Way........J 5
73 Normanby Rd.......D 8
78 Normand Rd.........D 3
79 Normandy Rd.......E 11
84 Norman's Building D 1
78 Normanton Av......K 4
78 Norroy Rd............G 2
73 North Acton Rd....G 6
73 North Acton Sta....J 6
82 North Audley St....H 3
81 North Bank...........D 6
76 North Birkbeck Rd. C 5
70 North Cheam.........E 4
73 North Circular Rd. NW2..........C 7
73 North Circular Rd. NW10..........F 5
74 North Circular Rd. NW11..........A 2
67 North Circular Rd. Wood Grn.......B 7
73 North Common Rd. K 3
71 North Cray...........C 12
71 North Cray Rd....C 12
82 North Cres...........F 7
79 North Cross Rd..G 15
83 North Down St.....C 9
79 North Dulwich Sta. H 13
72 North End............A 2
74 North End, NW3..B 5
71 North End, Cro....E 7
71 North End La.......F 10
74 North End Rd. NW11 B 4
78 North End Rd. W14 C 3
73 North End Rd. Wem. C 5
74 North End Way....C 5
66 North Finchley.....B 5
82 North Gower St....D 6
74 North Gro............B 7
65 North Harrow Sta..D 6

MAP		MAP		MAP		MAP		MAP		MAP	
74 North Hill	A 7	65 Norwood Green	G 6	85 Old Brompton Rd	F 4	73 Orchid St	K 8	65 Oxhey Dri	B 5	79 Park Hall Rd	K 13
65 North Hyde	G 5	79 Norwood Rd. SE27	K 12	82 Old Burlington St	J 6	83 Orde Hall St	F 9	65 Oxhey La	A 5	79 Park Hill, SW4	G 10
65 North Hyde La	G 5	65 Norwood Rd. S'hall.	G 6	84 Old Castle St	G 5	76 Ordell Rd	G 2	69 Oxshott	G 6	73 Park Hill, W5	J 3
83 North Mews	E 10	85 Notting Hill Gate	A 1	82 Old Cavendish St	G 5	80 Ordnance Av	A 5	69 Oyster La	A 5	77 Park Hill, Rich	H 4
66 Nth. Middlesex G.C.	B 5	76 Nottingham Av	J 8	84 Old Change	H 1	81 Ordnance Hill	B 5	76 Pacific Rd	J 6	74 Park Hill Rd. NW3	E 7
67 Nth. Middlesex Hosp.	B 7	82 Nottingham Pl	F 3	73 Old Church La	C 6	76 Ordnance Rd	J 6	83 Packington St	A 13	71 Park Hill Rd. Bex.	B 12
68 North Ockendon	E 5	76 Nottingham Rd	A 4	67 Old Church Rd. E4.	B 9	76 Oriel Rd	E 1	77 Paddenswick Rd	B 8	86 Park Ho. Gdns	H 2
65 North Orbital Rd	C 2	82 Nottingham St	F 3	68 Old Church Rd. Rom.	D 2	87 Orient St	E 12	74 Paddington	J 5	86 Park La. W1	B 4
84 North Pl	E 6	78 Novello St	E 4	85 Old Church St	H 5	76 Oriental St	K 3	81 Paddington Green	F 5	70 Park La. Ashtead	H 2
74 North Pole Rd	J 1	77 Nowell Rd	D 8	82 Old Compton St	H 7	87 Orlando Rd	F 9	81 Paddington Sta	G 4	73 Park La. Rich	G 3
81 North Ride	J 6	81 Noyna Rd	K 7	70 Old Coulsdon	H 6	77 Orleans Pk	J 1	82 Paddington St	F 3	67 Park La. Tott.	C 8
75 North Rd. N7	E 10	81 Nugent Ter	C 4	85 Old Court Pl	C 2	77 Orleans Rd	J 2	73 Paddock Rd	C 8	73 Park La. Wem	D 3
77 North Rd. W5	B 3	79 Nunhead	F 16	77 Old Deer Pk	F 2	81 Orleston Rd	E 11	67 Paddocks, The	B 15	86 Park La. Hot	B 5
77 North Rd. Brent	D 3	79 Nunhead Gro	F 16	77 Old Deer Pk. Gdns.	F 3	81 Orme Ct	J 2	67 Padnall Cnr	C 12	73 Park Parade	G 8
68 North Rd. Purfleet	G 4	79 Nunhead La	F 16	78 Old Devonshire Rd.	J 8	81 Orme La	J 2	87 Page St	E 8	84 Park Pl	B 6
77 North Rd. Rich	F 4	79 Nursery Rd. SW9	G 11	80 Old Dover Rd	D 7	81 Orme Sq	J 2	88 Page's Wk	E 4	81 Park Pl. Villas	F 4
68 North Rd. Rom	B 2	81 Nursery Rd. Sunb.	D 4	71 Old Farleigh Rd	G 8	78 Ormeley Rd	J 8	75 Paget Rd	B 13	80 Park Rise Rd	J 2
82 North Row	H 3	88 Nursery Row	F 2	76 Old Ford	F 2	80 Ormiston Rd	C 6	83 Paget St	C 12	76 Park Rd. E10	B 3
77 North Sheen	F 4	79 Nutbrook St	F 15	76 Old Ford Rd	F 2	81 Ormond Rd	H 3	77 Pagoda Av	F 4	75 Park Rd. E12	B 7
77 North Sheen Sta	G 4	79 Nutcroft Rd	D 15	83 Old Gloucester St	F 9	86 Ormond Yd	A 6	75 Paignton Rd	A 14	82 Park Rd. NW1	D 1
76 North St. E6	G 7	73 Nutfield Rd	C 8	88 Old Jamaica Rd	D 6	86 Ormonde Gate	G 2	67 Painters Rd	C 12	73 Park Rd. NW4	A 8
78 North St. SW4	F 9	82 Nutford Pl	G 2	84 Old Jewry	H 2	76 Ormonde Rd	G 5	83 Pakenham St	D 10	73 Park Rd. NW10	F 7
68 North St. Rom	C 2	74 Nutley Ter	E 5	88 Old Kent Rd	G 5	82 Ormonde Ter	B 2	81 Palace Ct	J 2	77 Park Rd. W4	D 6
70 North Sugden Rd	E 1	84 Nuttall St	B 4	69 Old La	K 7	84 Ormsby St	B 5	85 Palace Gdns. Mews	B 2	70 Park Rd. Banstead	G 4
84 North Tenter St	H 5	77 Nylands Av	C 4	81 Old Marylebone Rd.	G 6	73 Ormston Gro	L 8	85 Palace Gdns. Ter	B 2	71 Park Rd. Fickleshole	G 9
85 North Ter	E 6	80 Nynehead St	D 1	84 Old Montague St	F 6	74 Ornan Rd	E 6	85 Palace Gate	D 3	77 Park Rd. Isle	F 1
75 North Villas	E 9	80 Nyon Gro	K 2	84 Old Nichol St	E 5	75 Orpingley Rd	C 11	85 Palace Green	B 2	77 Park Rd. Rich	H 3
81 North Wharf Rd	G 5	80 Oak Av	C 5	73 Old Oak Common	J 7	71 Orpington	E 12	71 Palace Parade	C 7	69 Park Rd. Stanwell	B 3
70 North Wood Rd	D 6	74 Oak Gro	D 2	73 Old Oak Com. La.	J 7	71 Orpington-By-Pass	D 12	79 Palace Rd	J 11	73 Park Rd. Wem	E 3
67 North Woolwich	G 10	76 Oak Hall Rd	A 7	73 Old Oak La	H 7	71 Orpington Rd	D 11	86 Palace St	D 6	70 Park Rd. Ted	C 1
80 Nth. Woolwich Rd.	A 7	74 Oak Tree Rd	D 5	77 Old Pal. Yd	J 7	81 Orsett Mews	G 3	83 Palace Th	H 7	77 Park Rd. Twick	H 2
77 North Worple Way	F 6	78 Oakbury Rd	F 4	87 Old Paradise St	E 10	87 Orsett St	G 10	76 Palamos Rd	B 3	69 Park Rd. Twick	C 6
75 Northam St	G 16	80 Oakcroft Rd	F 4	78 Old Pk. Dri	H 8	81 Orsett Ter	G 3	77 Palatine Rd	D 14	77 Park Rd. E	A 5
75 Northampton Pl	E 13	80 Oakdale Rd. E7	F 7	86 Old Pk. La	B 4	84 Orsman Rd	A 4	73 Palermo Rd	G 8	80 Park Row	D 5
83 Northampton Rd	E 11	76 Oakdale Rd. E11	C 4	86 Old Pye St	D 7	76 Orwell Rd	G 8	77 Palewell Common	H 6	73 Park Royal	G 4
83 Northampton Sq	D 12	87 Oakden St	E 11	82 Old Quebec St	H 3	75 Osbaldeston Rd	B 15	77 Palewell Com. Dri.	G 6	73 Park Royal Rd	H 6
70 Northborough Rd	D 6	69 Oaken La	F 6	87 Old Queen St	C 7	80 Osberton Rd	H 6	77 Palewell Pk	G 6	73 Park Royal Stad	G 5
80 Northbrook Rd	G 5	74 Oakeshott Av	C 8	65 Old Redding	B 6	84 Osborn St	G 6	79 Palfrey Pl	D 11	73 Park Royal Sta	H 4
83 Northburgh St	E 12	72 Oakfield La	C 2	80 Old Rd. SE13	G 5	76 Osborne Rd. E7	D 7	84 Palgrave Rd	B 7	73 Park Side NW2	D 8
75 Northchurch Rd	F 13	75 Oakfield Rd. N4	A 11	72 Old Rd. Bex'h	B 1	76 Osborne Rd. E9	E 2	84 Palissy St	D 5	70 Park Side SW19	C 3
78 Northcote Rd	G 7	74 Oakhill Av	D 4	67 Old Royal Observa-tory	H 9	75 Osborne Rd. N4	B 11	86 Pall Mall	B 7	82 Park Sq. E	E 5
76 Northern Rd	G 7	74 Oakhill Pk	D 5	84 Old St	D 3	69 Oseney Cres	E 9	87 Pall Mall E	A 7	82 Park Sq. W	E 4
76 Northey St	K 2	78 Oakhill Rd	G 3	83 Old Seacoal La	G 12	66 Osidge La	B 6	82 Palladium	H 6	88 Park St. SE1	B 2
77 Northfield Av	B 1	74 Oakhill Way	D 5	87 Old Vic, Nat. Th	C 11	78 Osiers Rd	G 4	76 Palmer Rd	H 7	82 Park St. W1	J 3
75 Northfield Rd. N16	A 14	79 Oakhurst Gro	G 15	79 Old Town	G 9	82 Osnaburgh St	E 5	86 Palmer St	D 7	73 Park View, W3	J 6
73 Northfield Rd. NW10	J 5	73 Oakington Av	C 4	69 Old Woking Rd	G 2	74 Ospringe Rd	A 9	66 Palmers Green	B 6	73 Park View, Wem	D 5
78 Northfields	G 4	73 Oakington Manor Dri.	E 4	80 Old Woolwich Rd	C 5	75 Ossian Rd	A 11	67 Palmerston Rd. E4	B 10	73 Park View Rd. NW10	D 8
77 Northfields Sta	B 2	81 Oakington Rd	E 1	73 Oldborough Rd	C 2	82 Ossington St	J 2	76 Palmerston Rd. E7.	E 7	73 Park View Rd. W5	J 3
72 Northfleet	B 6	74 Oaklands Rd	D 2	72 Oldbury	H 4	83 Ossory Rd	H 6	77 Palmerston Rd. SW14	G 6	82 Park Village E	B 5
83 Northington St	E 10	66 Oakleigh Pk	A 5	82 Oldbury Pl	F 4	83 Ossulston St	C 7	77 Palmerston Rd. W3	B 5	80 Park Vista	D 5
75 Northolme Rd	D 12	66 Oakleigh Pk. Sth	B 5	80 Oldfield Gro	C 1	79 Osten Mews	E 3	70 Pampisford Rd	F 6	85 Park Wk	H 4
65 Northolt	E 5	73 Oakley Av	K 4	66 Oldfield La	F 1	66 Osterley	H 1	84 Pancras La	H 2	81 Park W. Pl	G 6
65 Northolt Aerodrome	E 4	83 Oakley Cres	C 12	75 Oldfield Rd. N16	C 14	66 Osterley La	G 1	83 Pancras Rd	C 8	80 Parkcroft Rd	J 6
65 Northolt Pk	E 6	86 Oakley Gdns	H 1	73 Oldfield Rd. NW10	F 7	65 Osterley Park House	G 6	80 Pandora Rd	E 4	77 Parke Rd	E 8
65 Northolt Rd	E 6	88 Oakley Pl	G 5	70 Oldfield Rd. Mord	E 4	76 Oswald St	C 1	74 Pangbourne Av	J 2	88 Parker's Row	D 6
65 Northolt Pk. Sta	E 6	75 Oakley Rd	F 13	75 Oldhill St	B 15	87 Oswin St	E 12	79 Panmure Rd	L 16	77 Parkfield Av	G 7
71 Northover Rd	C 9	82 Oakley Sq	B 6	78 Oldridge Rd	J 8	80 Otford Cres	H 2	82 Panton St	J 7	83 Parkfield St	B 11
84 Northport St	B 3	85 Oakley St	H 6	76 Olga St	G 1	72 Otford La	G 1	86 Parade, The	J 3	73 Parkfields Av	B 6
84 Northumberland Alley	H 4	78 Oakmead Rd	K 8	74 Olinda Rd	A 14	76 Otley Rd	J 8	77 Paradise Rd	G 3	78 Parkgate Rd	E 6
76 Northumberland Av. E12	B 8	84 Oakwood Ct	B 3	74 Oliphant St	H 2	69 Ottershaw	F 2	85 Paradise St	A 16	75 Parkholme Rd	E 15
87 Northumberland Av. WC2	B 8	67 Oakwood Hill	A 11	76 Olive Rd. E13	H 8	78 Ottways La	H 1	86 Paradise Wk	H 2	88 Parkhouse St	J 3
68 Northumberland Heath	H 2	66 Oakwood Sta	A 6	69 Olive Rd. NW2	D 1	78 Ouseley Rd	J 7	80 Paragon, The	E 6	75 Parkhurst Rd	D 10
81 Northumberland Pl.	G 1	74 Oakworth Rd	J 2	77 Olive Rd. W5	B 3	82 Outer Circle	B 2	86 Paragon Pl	F 6	71 Parklangley	D 9
67 Northumberland Pk. Sta	C 8	84 Oat Lane	G 1	76 Oliver Rd	C 3	74 Outram St	A 9	75 Paragon Rd	E 16	84 Parkmead	H 9
76 Northumberland Rd.	A 3	69 Oatlands Av	F 4	80 Olmar St	H 6	70 Outwood La	H 4	80 Parbury Rd	H 1	77 Parkshot	G 3
87 Northumberland St.	A 8	69 Oatlands Chase	E 4	88 Olney Rd	H 1	87 Oval, The	H 10	80 Parch Rd	D 6	77 Parkstead Rd	H 8
65 Northview	D 5	69 Oatlands Dri	E 4	78 Olympia	B 3	74 Oval Rd	F 8	88 Pardoner St	D 3	79 Parkthorne Rd	J 9
79 Northway Rd	F 13	69 Oatlands Pk	E 4	73 Olympic Way	C 4	87 Oval Way	G 10	84 Parfett St	G 7	82 Parkway	A 5
73 Northwick Rd	G 3	80 Oareboro Rd	D 1	74 Oman Av	D 1	71 Ovenden Rd	H 12	87 Parfitt Rd	C 16	65 Parkway, The	G 5
75 Northwold Rd	C 15	76 Oban St	J 5	78 Ondine Rd	G 14	76 Overbury St	D 1	87 Paris Gdns	B 12	77 Parma Cres	G 7
65 Northwood	B 4	77 Observatory Rd	G 5	79 One Tree Hill	H 16	80 Overcliffe Rd	F 3	83 Parker St	G 9	76 Parnell Rd	F 2
65 Northwood G.C	C 4	77 Occupation La	C 3	78 Ongar Rd	H 1	77 Overdale Rd	B 2	74 Parliament Hill	C 7	75 Parolles Rd	B 9
74 Northwood Rd. N6	A 8	87 Occupation Rd	G 3	76 Onra Rd	A 3	79 Overhill Rd	J 15	87 Parliament Sq	C 8	84 Parr St	B 2
80 Northwood Rd. SE23	K 2	75 Ockendon Rd. N1	E 13	77 Onslow Av	H 3	75 Overlea Rd	A 15	87 Parliament St	C 8	87 Parry St	H 9
65 Northwood Rd. Ruislip	C 3	68 Ockendon Rd. Dag.	E 4	85 Onslow Gdns	F 4	78 Overstone Rd	B 1	78 Park, The, NW11	B 4	74 Parsifal Rd	D 4
81 Northwick Cl	E 5	69 Ockham Common	H 4	77 Onslow Rd	H 3	79 Overton Dri	A 7	77 Park, The, W5	A 3	66 Parson St	C 4
81 Northwick Ter	E 4	69 Ockham La	H 3	85 Onslow Sq	F 5	76 Overton Rd. E10	B 1	73 Park Av. NW10	G 4	80 Parsonage St	C 4
84 Norton Folgate	F 4	78 Octavia St	E 6	87 Ontario St	D 13	79 Overton Rd. SW9	F 12	74 Park Av. NW11	B 4	78 Parson's Green	F 4
76 Norton Rd. E10	B 2	80 Octavus St	D 2	87 Opal St	F 12	85 Ovington Gardens	D 6	77 Park Av. SW14	G 6	78 Parson's Green La	E 4
73 Norton Rd. Wem	E 2	88 Odell St	G 5	82 Open Air Th	D 3	85 Ovington Sq	E 7	67 Park Av. Enfield	A 7	69 Parvis Rd	G 3
73 Norval Rd	B 2	83 Odeon, Leic. Sq	J 8	75 Openview	K 5	86 Ovington St	E 2	65 Park Av. Watford	A 5	82 Pascal St	J 8
76 Norwich Rd. E7	E 6	76 Odessa Rd	D 6	74 Oppidans Rd	F 7	82 Oxendon St	J 7	73 Park Av. Nth	E 9	87 Pasley Rd	G 13
84 Norwich Rd. E8	A 7	80 Odessa St	B 2	83 Orange St	J 7	82 Oxford Circus	G 5	73 Park Chase	D 4	86 Passmore St	F 3
83 Norwich St	G 11	87 Offley Rd	J 11	88 Orb St	F 2	77 Oxford Gdns. W4	C 5	82 Park Cres	E 5	87 Paston Cres	J 7
71 Norwood	C 7	75 Offord Rd	F 11	78 Orbel St	E 6	74 Oxford Gdns. W10	J 2	82 Park Cres. Mews E.	E 5	80 Pasture Rd	J 6
73 Norwood Av	G 4	79 Oglander Rd	G 14	77 Orchard, The	B 6	74 Oxford Rd. NW6	G 4	82 Park Cres. Mews W.	E 4	85 Pater St	D 1
		82 Ogle St	F 6	76 Orchard Gate	E 1	78 Oxford Rd. SW15	G 3	74 Park Dri NW11	B 4	83 Paternoster Sq	G 13
		76 Ohio Rd	H 6	76 Orchard Pl	K 5	77 Oxford Rd. W4	C 5	77 Park Dri. SW14	G 6	79 Patmore St	E 9
		67 Okehampton Cres.	H 12	77 Orchard Rise	G 5	73 Oxford Rd. W5	K 3	77 Park Dri. W3	B 4	79 Patmos Rd	E 12
		74 Okehampton Rd	F 2	77 Orchard Rd	D 2	65 Oxford Rd. Gerrard's Cross	D 1	68 Park Farm Rd	E 4	84 Paton St	D 1
		83 Old Bailey	G 12	87 Orchard St	H 3	81 Oxford Sq	H 6	80 Park Gate	F 6	76 Patrick Rd	H 8
		75 Old Bethnal Green Rd.	G 15	81 Orchardson St	E 5	82 Oxford St	G 5	76 Park Gro. E11	C 5	75 Patshull Rd	E 9
		86 Old Bond St	A 6			74 Oxgate Gdns	C 1	76 Park Gro. E15	F 6	74 Patten Rd	J 6
		84 Old Broad St	G 3			73 Oxgate La	C 9			74 Pattison Rd	C 4
						65 Oxhey	A 5			84 Paul St. EC2	E 3
										79 Paulet Rd	E 12

MAP
85 Paultons Sq. H 5
85 Paultons St. H 5
79 Pavement, The G 9
86 Pavilion Rd. E 2
73 Paxford Rd. C 2
77 Paxton Rd. D 7
80 Payne St. D 2
68 Pea La. E 5
86 Peabody Av. G 5
84 Peace St. E 7
87 Peacock St. F 13
83 Pear Tree Ct. E 11
83 Pear Tree St. D 13
76 Pearcroft Rd. C 4
80 Pearfield Rd. K 1
87 Pearman St. D 11
69 Pears Rd. A 6
78 Pearscroft Rd. E 4
84 Pearson St. B 5
79 Peckham F 15
79 Peckham High St. E 15
79 Peckham Hill St. E 15
79 Peckham Pk. Rd. D 15
79 Peckham Rd. E 14
79 Peckham Rye G 15
79 Peckham Rye Common G 15
79 Peckham Rye Pk. G 16
79 Peckham Rye Sta. F 15
84 Pedley St. E 6
73 Peel Rd. C 2
85 Peel St. B 1
84 Peerless St. D 2
77 Peldon Av. G 4
85 Pelham Cres. F 6
85 Pelham Pl. F 5
85 Pelham St. E 5
88 Pelier St. H 1
80 Pelinore Rd. K 5
84 Pell St. H 7
79 Pellatt Rd. H 14
76 Pelly Rd. F 7
84 Pelter St. C 5
80 Pelton Rd. C 5
74 Pember Rd. H 2
75 Pemberton Gdns. C 9
75 Pemberton Ter. C 9
74 Pembridge Cres. K 3
81 Pembridge Gardens J 1
81 Pembridge Pl. H 1
81 Pembridge Rd. J 1
81 Pembridge Sq. J 1
81 Pembridge Villas H 1
86 Pembroke Cl. C 4
78 Pembroke Gdns. B 3
85 Pembroke Pl. D 1
85 Pembroke Rd. W8 E 1
65 Pembroke Rd. Ruislip D 4
73 Pembroke Rd. Wem. C 3
85 Pembroke Sq. E 1
85 Pembroke Villas, W8 E 1
77 Pembroke Villas, Rich. G 2
75 Pembury Gro. D 16
75 Pembury Rd. D 16
79 Penarth Rd. D 16
80 Penberth Rd. K 4
76 Penda Rd. D 1
80 Penderry Rise K 4
80 Pendragon Rd. L 6
80 Pendrell Rd. F 1
80 Penerley Rd. K 4
81 Penfold Pl. F 5
81 Penfold St. E 5
79 Penford St. E 12
71 Penge C 7
76 Penge Rd. F 7
71 Penhill Rd. B 12
80 Penhall St. B 8
75 Penn Rd. D 10
84 Penn St. A 3
88 Pennack Rd. H 5
85 Pennant Mews E 2
78 Pennard Rd. A 1
74 Pennine Dri. C 1
84 Pennington St. J 7
76 Pennyfields K 3
77 Penrhyn Cres. G 6
87 Penrose Gro. G 13
87 Penrose St. G 13
82 Penryn St. B 7
77 Pensford Av. F 4
76 Penshurst Rd. F 1
78 Pentlow St. F 1
78 Pentney Rd. J 9
87 Penton Pl. G 13
83 Penton Rise C 10
83 Penton St. B 10
75 Pentonville G 11
83 Pentonville Rd. C 10
78 Penwith Rd. K 4
85 Penywern Rd. F 2
88 Pepler Rd. G 5
74 Peploe Rd. G 2
80 Pepys Rd. SE14 E 1
70 Pepys Rd. SW20 D 3
84 Pepys St. H 4
83 Percival St. D 12
83 Percy Circus C 10
76 Percy Rd. E11 A 5
76 Percy Rd. E16 J 5
81 Percy Rd. NW6 C 1
77 Percy Rd. W12 A 8
69 Percy Rd. Hampton C 6
69 Percy Rd. Twick. B 6
82 Percy St. G 7
78 Perham Rd. C 3
73 Perimeade Rd. G 2
73 Perivale H 1
86 Perkins Rents D 7
73 Perpyn Rd. K 6
80 Perry Hill K 2
80 Perry Rise L 1
71 Perry St. C 11
80 Perry Vale K 1
78 Perrymead St. E 4
80 Persant Rd. K 5
76 Perth Rd. E10 B 2
75 Perth Rd. N4 B 11
73 Peter Av. F 9
82 Peter St. W1 H 7
76 Peterborough Rd. E10 A 5
78 Peterborough Rd. SW6 F 4
83 Peters La. F 12
77 Petersfield Rd. A 6
77 Petersham K 2
77 Petersham Common J 3
77 Petersham Meadow J 3
85 Petersham Mews E 4
77 Petersham Pk. K 3
85 Petersham Pl. D 4
77 Petersham Rd. H 3
75 Petherton Rd. D 13
78 Petley Rd. D 2
82 Peto Pl. E 5
84 Petticoat Sq. G 5
71 Petts Wood D 11
71 Petts Wood Rd. D 11
86 Petty France D 7
78 Petworth St. E 7
86 Petyward F 1
76 Pevensey Rd. D 6
88 Phelp St. H 2
85 Phene St. H 6
85 Philbeach Gdns. F 1
67 Philip La. C 7
79 Philip Rd. F 15
81 Philip Ter. F 2
74 Phillimore Gdns. NW10 F 1
85 Phillimore Gdns. W8 D 1
85 Phillimore Pl. C 1
85 Phillimore Wk. D 1
84 Phillipp St. B 4
84 Philpot La. H 3
75 Philpot St. J 16
84 Phipp St. E 4
83 Phoenix Pl. E 10
82 Phoenix Rd. C 7
83 Phoenix St. H 8
83 Phoenix Th. H 8
83 Piccadilly B 5
82 Piccadilly Circus J 7
82 Piccadilly Hot. J 6
82 Piccadilly Th. J 7
83 Pickard St. C 13
75 Pickering St. F 12
68 Pickford La. H 1
71 Pickhurst La. E 9
79 Pickwick Rd. J 13
82 Picton Pl. G 4
79 Picton St. D 13
80 Pier St. B 4
73 Pierrepoint Rd. K 5
76 Pigott St. K 2
68 Pike La. E 5
83 Pilgrim St. H 12
88 Pilgrimage St. D 2
68 Pilgrims Hatch A 4
71 Pilgrims Way, Knockholt H 12
72 Pilgrims Way, Otford H 2
73 Pilgrims Way, Wem. B 5
79 Pimlico C 9
86 Pimlico Gdn. H 7
86 Pimlico Rd. F 4
84 Pinchin St. H 6
84 Pindar St. F 4
81 Pindock Mews E 3
74 Pine Rd. D 2
83 Pine St. E 11
66 Pinkham Way C 6
65 Pinner C 5
65 Pinner Green C 5
65 Pinner Hill G.C. C 5
65 Pinner Hill Rd. C 5
66 Pinner Rd. D 1
78 Pirbright Rd. J 3
76 Pitchford St. F 5
84 Pitfield St. B 3
80 Pitfold Rd. H 6
87 Pitman St. J 13
73 Pitshanger La. H 2
73 Pitshanger Pk. H 1
85 Pitt St. C 1
86 Pitts Hd. Mews B 4
76 Plaistow G 7
76 Plaistow Gro. F 6
71 Plaistow La. C 10
76 Plaistow Rd. G 6
76 Plashet Rd. F 7
80 Plassy Rd. J 3
79 Plato Rd. G 10
72 Platt H 6
78 Platt, The F 2
82 Platt St. B 7
74 Platts La. C 4
86 Plaza Cin. A 7
77 Pleasance, The G 8
77 Pleasance Rd. G 8
75 Pleasant Pl. F 12
73 Pleasant Way G 2
82 Plender Pl. B 6
82 Plender St. B 6
75 Pleshey Rd. D 9
80 Plevna St. B 4
75 Plimsoll Rd. C 12
69 Plough La. H 5
78 Plough Rd. G 6
80 Plough Way B 1
84 Ploughyard E 4
76 Plover St. E 2
83 Plum Tree Ct. G 12
84 Plumbers Row G 6
67 Plumstead G 11
67 Plumstead Common Rd. H 11
67 Plumstead High St. G 12
67 Plumstead Rd. G 11
76 Plymouth Rd. J 6
74 Plympton Rd. F 3
81 Plympton St. E 6
87 Pocock St. C 12
78 Podmore Rd. G 5
75 Poets Rd. D 13
80 Point Hill E 4
78 Point Pleasant G 4
69 Pointers Rd. H 4
72 Pol Hill G 1
82 Poland St. H 6
66 Police College C 3
84 Pollard Row D 7
88 Pollock Rd. E 2
80 Polstead Rd. J 2
82 Polygon Rd. C 7
79 Pomeroy St. E 16
85 Pond Pl. F 6
76 Pond Rd. E15 G 5
80 Pond Rd. SE3 F 6
74 Pond St. D 6
75 Ponder St. E 11
67 Ponders End A 8
87 Ponsonby Pl. F 8
87 Ponsonby Ter. G 8
86 Pont St. E 2
76 Poole Rd. E 1
84 Poole St. B 2
88 Pope St. D 4
77 Popes La. B 3
75 Popham Rd. F 12
76 Poplar K 3
78 Poplar Gro. B 1
76 Poplar High St. K 3
81 Poplar Pl. J 2
79 Poplar Wk. G 12
79 Poplar Wk. Rd. G 12
76 Poplars Rd. A 3
76 Poppleton Rd. A 5
81 Porchester Gardens H 3
81 Porchester Pl. H 6
81 Porchester Rd. G 2
81 Porchester Sq. G 3
81 Porchester Sq. Mews G 3
81 Porchester Ter. H 3
81 Porchester Ter. Nth. G 3
79 Porden Rd. G 11
88 Porlock St. C 3
76 Portelet Rd. H 1
67 Porters Av. E 12
81 Porteus Rd. F 4
78 Portinscale Rd. H 3
75 Portland Av. B 14
82 Portland Pl. F 5
75 Portland Rise B 12
74 Portland Rd. W11 K 3
71 Portland Rd. Croydon D 7
88 Portland St. G 3
77 Portland Ter. G 3
77 Portman Av. G 6
82 Portman Cl. G 3
82 Portman Mews South H 3
75 Portman Pl. H 16
82 Portman Sq. G 3
82 Portman St. H 3
69 Portmore Pk. Rd. E 3
74 Portnall Rd. H 3
70 Portnalls Rd. H 5
74 Portobello Rd. J 3
83 Portpool La. F 11
76 Portree St. J 5
82 Portsea Pl. H 2
79 Portslade Rd. F 9
69 Portsmouth Rd. Esh. F 6
70 Portsmouth Rd. Thames Ditton E 1
83 Portsmouth St. G 10
84 Portsoken St. H 5
83 Portugal St. G 10
76 Portway F 6
88 Potier St. F 3
65 Potter St. C 5
88 Potter's Fields B 4
65 Potterstreet Hill B 5
77 Pottery Rd. D 3
84 Poultry H 2
73 Pound La. NW10 E 8
71 Pound La. Knockholt G 12
69 Powdermill La. B 6
75 Powell Rd. C 16
77 Power Rd. C 5
75 Powerscroft Rd. D 16
84 Pownall Rd. A 6
69 Poyle A 2
79 Poynders Rd. J 9
74 Poynter St. L 2
81 Praed St. G 5
76 Pragel St. G 7
80 Pragnell Rd K 7
78 Prairie St. F 8
82 Pratt Mews A 6
82 Pratt St. A 6
87 Pratt Wk. E 10
71 Pratt's Bottom F 12
74 Prayle Gro. B 2
77 Prebend Gdns. B 7
84 Prebend St. A 1
76 Presburg St. C 1
84 Prescot St. H 6
73 Press Rd. C 6
76 Prestbury Rd. F 8
73 Preston Pk. B 2
76 Preston Rd. E11 A 5
73 Preston Rd. Wem. B 3
76 Preston's Rd. E14 K 4
85 Prestwick Rd. B 5
76 Pretoria Rd. B 5
87 Price's St. B 12
83 Prideaux Pl. D 10
80 Priestfield Rd. L 2
87 Prima Rd. J 11
74 Primrose Gardens E 6
74 Primrose Hill F 7
83 Primrose Hill, EC4 H 11
74 Primrose Hill Rd. F 7
74 Primrose Hill Sta. F 7
76 Primrose Rd. B 3
84 Primrose St. F 4
73 Primrose Way G 2
73 Primula St. K 8
82 Pr. Albert Rd. B 2
74 Pr. Arthur Rd. D 5
80 Pr. Charles Rd. E 6
83 Pr. Charles Th. H 8
85 Pr. Consort Rd. D 4
75 Pr. George Rd. D 14
78 Pr. of Wales Dri. E 7
76 Pr. of Wales Rd. E16 K 8
74 Pr. of Wales Rd. NW5 E 8
80 Pr. of Wales Rd. SE3 E 6
82 Pr. of Wales Th. J 7
76 Pr. Regent's La. H 7
80 Prince St. D 2
74 Princedale Rd. L 3
84 Princelet St. F 5
73 Princes Ct. D 3
85 Prince's Gdns. SW7 D 5
73 Princes Gdns. W3 J 4
73 Princes Gdns. W5 H 2
85 Prince's Gate C 5
85 Prince's Gate Mews D 5
81 Princes Mews H 2
80 Princes Rise F 4
72 Princes Rd. Dartford B 2
77 Princes Rd. Rich. G 3
81 Prince's Sq. H 2
84 Princes St. EC2 H 2
82 Princes St. W1 H 5
77 Princes St. Rich. E 4
78 Prince's Way J 2
77 Princess Av. B 5
85 Princess Beatrice Hosp. G 2
75 Princess May Rd. D 14
74 Princess Rd. NW1 F 8
81 Princess Rd. NW6 C 1
87 Princess St. E 12
83 Princeton St. F 10
80 Priolo Rd. C 7
80 Prior St. E 4
88 Prioress St. E 3
77 Priory, The G 7
74 Priory Gdns. A 8
77 Priory La. H 7
80 Priory Pk. G 6
74 Priory Pk. Rd. F 3
66 Priory Rd. N8 C 6
74 Priory Rd. NW6 F 4
77 Priory Rd W4 B 7
77 Priory Rd. W4 B 6
77 Priory Rd. Rich. D 4
74 Priory Ter. F 4
85 Priory Wk. G 4
84 Pritchard's Rd. B 7
88 Priter Rd. D 6
83 Procter St. F 9
77 Promenade, The E 7
77 Promenade App. Rd. D 7
78 Protheroe Rd. D 3
73 Prout Gro. D 7
75 Prout Rd. C 16
84 Provost St. C 2
84 Pudding La. EC3 J 3
67 Pudding La. Chigwell A 12
76 Pudding Mill La. G 4
83 Puddle Dock H 12
72 Puddledock La. C 2
78 Pulborough Rd. J 3
78 Pullman Gdns. H 1
79 Pulross Rd. F 11
88 Purbrook St. D 4
87 Purcell Room B 10
84 Purcell St. B 4
82 Purchese St. C 7
76 Purdy St. H 3
68 Purfleet G 4
68 Purfleet By-Pass G 4
68 Purfleet Rd. G 4
70 Purley G 6
74 Purley Av. C 3
71 Purley Downs G.C. G 7
71 Purley Downs Rd. G 7
71 Purley Oaks Sta. F 7
70 Purley Way E 6
74 Purves Rd. G 1
78 Putney G 2
78 Putney Bri. F 2
78 Putney Bri. App. F 3
78 Putney Bri. Rd. G 3
78 Putney Bri. Sta. F 3
78 Putney Heath J 1
78 Putney Heath La. H 2
78 Putney High St. G 2
78 Putney Hill H 2
78 Putney Hosp. F 1
77 Putney Pk. Av. G 8
78 Putney Sta. G 2
69 Pyrcroft E 2
69 Pyrford H 2
69 Pyrford Common Rd. H 2
69 Pyrford Rd. G 2
75 Pyrland Rd. N5 D 13
77 Pyrland Rd. Richmond H 4
79 Pytchley Rd. F 14
77 Quadrangle, The G 3
73 Quainton St. C 6
84 Quaker St. E 5
78 Quarrendon St. E 4
78 Quarry Rd. H 5
87 Q. Alexandra Military Hosp. F 8
82 Queen Anne Mews G 5
76 Queen Anne Rd. E 1
82 Queen Anne St. G 4
77 QueenAnne'sGdns. B 7
86 Queen Anne's Gate C 7
77 Queen Anne's Gro. W4 B 7
77 Queen Anne's Gro. W5 A 3
78 Queen Caroline St. C 1
85 Queen Elizabeth Coll. C 1
87 Queen Elizabeth Hall B 10
70 Queen Elizabeth Hosp. H 5
88 Queen Elizabeth St. C 5
75 Queen Elizabeth's Wk. B 13
77 Queen Mary's (Roehampton Hosp.) H 8
82 Queen Mary's Gdns. D 3
71 Queen Mary's Hosp. C 12
70 Queen Mary's Hosp. for Children F 5
83 Queen Sq. F 9
76 Queen St. E15 E 5
84 Queen St. EC4 H 2
86 Queen St. W1 B 5
84 Queen St. Pl. J 2
83 Queen Victoria St. H 13
78 Queens Circus E 8
78 Queens Club Gardens D 3
82 Queen's Coll. G 4
80 Queens Court D 3
74 Queens Cres. E 7
75 Queen's Dri. N4 C 12
73 Queens Dri. W3 J 4
81 Queen's Gdns. W2 H 4
73 Queen's Gdns. W5 H 2
85 Queen's Gate D 4
85 Queen's Gate Gdns. E 4
85 Queen's Gate Mews D 4
85 Queen's Gate Pl. E 4
85 Queen's Gate Pl. Mews E 4
85 Queen's Gate Ter. D 4
81 Queen's Gro. B 5
83 Queen's Head St. A 13
81 Queen's Mews H 2
74 Queens Pk. G 2
74 Queens Pk. Sta. G 3
77 Queen's Ride F 8
76 Queens Rd. E11 B 5
76 Queens Rd. E13 G 7
76 Queens Rd. E17 A 2
79 Queens Rd. SE15 E 16
77 Queen's Rd. SW14 F 6
77 Queens Rd. Rich. H 4
70 Queens Rd. Ted. C 1
69 Queens Rd. Weybridge F 4
79 Queen's Rd. Sta. SE15 E 16
78 Queens Rd. Sta. SW8 E 8
88 Queen's Row H 2
81 Queen's Ter. B 5
82 Queens Th. H 7
73 Queens Wk. NW9 B 6
73 Queen's Wk. W5 J 2
85 Queensberry Pl. E 4
85 Queensberry Way E 5
81 Queensborough Ter. H 3
84 Queensbridge Rd. B 6
66 Queensbury C 2
73 Queensbury Rd. NW9 B 6
73 Queensbury Rd. Wem. G 4

MAP
66 Queensbury Sta....C 2
78 Queensdale Rd....A 2
75 Queensland Rd...D 11
78 Queensmere Rd...K 2
78 Queensmill Rd....E 2
75 Queenstown Rd. E5
　　　　　　　　D16
78 Queenstown Rd. SW8
　　　　　　　　F 8
79 Queensville Rd...J 9
81 Queensway, W2..H 3
80 Quentin St......F 5
75 Quernmore Rd...A 11
74 Quex Rd.........F 4
77 Quick Rd........C 7
83 Quick St........C 12
88 Quilp St.........C 2
84 Quilter St.......C 6
78 Quinton St.......K 5
76 Quixley Rd......K 4
79 Quorn Rd.......G 14
74 Rackholm St......J 2
85 Racton Rd.......H 1
79 Radbourne Rd....J 9
80 Radford Rd......H 4
78 Radipole Rd.....E 3
76 Radland Rd......J 6
85 Radley Mews....E 2
76 Radlix Rd.......B 3
81 Radnor Mews....H 5
81 Radnor Pl.......H 6
79 Radnor Rd......D 15
84 Radnor St.......D 2
87 Radnor Ter......J 9
86 Radnor Wk......G 2
79 Raeburn St......G 10
71 Rag Hill.........H 10
79 Railton Rd......G 12
88 Railway App.....B 3
80 Railway Gro.....E 2
83 Railway St. N1...C 9
77 Railway St. SW13.A 7
88 Rainbow St......J 4
68 Rainham........F 3
74 Rainham Rd. NW10
　　　　　　　　H 2
68 Rainham Rd. Dag..E 2
68 Rainham Rd. South
　　　　　　　　E 2
73 Rainsford Rd.....G 5
81 Rainsford St......G 6
78 Rainville Rd......D 1
77 Raleigh Rd.......F 4
83 Raleigh St.......B 13
88 Ralph St.........D 2
82 Ramillies Pl......H 6
77 Ramillies Rd......B 6
82 Ramillies St......H 6
86 Rampayne St.....F 7
76 Ramsay Rd......D 5
78 Ramsden Rd.....J 8
84 Ramsey St.......E 7
73 Randall Av.......C 7
87 Randall Rd.......F 9
87 Randall Row.....F 9
70 Randalls Rd......H 1
75 Randell's Rd.....F 10
80 Randlesdown Rd..L 3
81 Randolph Av.....D 3
81 Randolph Cres....E 3
81 Randolph Gdns...C 2
81 Randolph Mews...E 4
76 Randolph Rd....E 16
81 Randolph Rd. W9.E 4
77 Ranelagh Av.....F 8
81 Ranelagh Dri......G 3
77 Ranelagh Dri.....G 2
86 Ranelagh Gdns. SW3
　　　　　　　　G 4
78 Ranelagh Gdns. SW6
　　　　　　　　F 3
86 Ranelagh Gro....F 4
76 Ranelagh Rd. E11.D 5
76 Ranelagh Rd. E15.G 5
77 Ranelagh Rd. W5..A 3
73 Ranelagh Rd. Wem.
　　　　　　　　E 3
67 Rangers Rd.....A 10
78 Rannoch Rd.....D 2
81 Ranston St.......F 6
74 Ranulf Rd.......D 3
86 Raphael St.......C 2
79 Rastell Av.......K 9
76 Ratcliff Rd.......E 7
82 Rathbone Pl......G 7
82 Rathbone St. W1.G 6
80 Rathfern Rd......K 2
77 Rathgar Av......A 1
80 Rathmore Rd....C 7
79 Rattray Rd.......G 11
75 Raven Row......J 16

MAP
76 Ravenhill Rd.....G 8
78 Ravenna Rd......G 2
78 Ravens Lea Rd....J 7
80 Ravens Way......G 6
80 Ravensbourne Pk.. J 2
80 Ravensbourne Pk.
　　　　Cres.........J 2
80 Ravensbourne Rd.
　　　　SE6..........J 2
77 Ravensbourne Rd.
　　　　Twick.........H 2
71 Ravensbourne Sta..D 9
78 Ravensbury Rd....K 4
77 Ravenscourt Gdns..B 8
77 Ravenscourt Pk. Sta.
　　　　　　　　C 8
77 Ravenscourt Rd....B 8
77 Ravenscourt Sq....B 8
74 Ravenscroft Av....A 3
84 Ravenscroft St....C 5
75 Ravensdale Rd....A 15
87 Ravensdon St....G 11
74 Ravenshaw St.....E 3
78 Ravenswood Rd...J 8
84 Ravey St.........E 4
86 Rawlings St......F 2
83 Rawstorne St....D 12
83 Ray St..........E 11
74 Raydon St........C 8
80 Rayford Av.......J 6
76 Raymond Rd.....F 8
79 Raymouth Rd...C 16
65 Rayners La......D 5
78 Rayner's Rd......H 2
70 Raynes Pk.......D 3
70 Raynes Pk. Sta...D 3
77 Rayston Rd.......H 3
79 Reardon Path...A 16
75 Reardon St......K 16
77 Reckitt Rd.......C 7
84 Rector St.........A 1
79 Rectory Gro......F 9
69 Rectory La. Byfleet G 3
67 Rectory La. Loughton
　　　　　　　　A 11
70 Rectory La. Mitch.
　　　　　　　　C 5
70 Rectory La. Sut...D 5
75 Rectory Rd. N16.C 15
77 Rectory Rd. SW13. F 8
75 Rectory Rd. Sta...C 15
80 Reculver Rd......C 1
88 Red Lion Row...H 2
83 Red Lion Sq......F 9
83 Red Lion St. WC1 F 10
77 Red Lion St. Rich..H 3
71 Red Lodge Rd....E 9
82 Red Pl..........H 3
79 Red Post Hill...G 13
81 Redan Pl........H 2
78 Redan St........B 2
67 Redbridge La....D 10
76 Redbridge La. W...A 7
67 Redbridge Sta...D 10
86 Redburn St......G 2
84 Redchurch St.....E 5
85 Redcliffe Gdns...H 3
85 Redcliffe Mews...G 3
85 Redcliffe Pl......H 3
76 Redcliffe Rd. E6..F 8
85 Redcliffe Rd. SW10
　　　　　　　　H 4
85 Redcliffe Sq......H 3
85 Redcliffe St......H 3
88 Redcross Way....C 2
86 Redesdale St......G 2
73 Redfern Rd......F 7
85 Redfield La......E 2
69 Redhill Rd.......G 4
82 Redhill St.......C 5
74 Redington Rd....C 4
70 Redlane.........F 1
75 Redmans Rd.....J 16
88 Redmead La......B 7
80 Redriff Rd.......B 1
76 Redwald Rd......D 1
85 Reece Mews......F 4
68 Reede Rd.........E 2
87 Reedworth St....F 11
84 Rees St..........A 2
73 Reeves Av.......A 6
82 Reeves Mews.....J 4
76 Reeves Rd.......H 3
78 Reform St........E 7
82 Regal La........A 4
84 Regan Way......C 4
86 Regency St......F 7
79 Regent Rd......H 12
83 Regent Sq......D 9
82 Regent St. W1....H 6

MAP
77 Regent St. W4....C 4
82 Regent's Pk......C 3
66 Regent's Pk. Rd. N3
　　　　　　　　C 4
74 Regent's Pk. Rd. NW1
　　　　　　　　F 7
84 Regents Row.....A 6
75 Regina Rd......B 11
76 Reginald Rd. E7...E 6
80 Reginald Rd. SE8..E 3
70 Reigate Av.......E 4
80 Reigate Rd. Bromley
　　　　　　　　K 6
70 Reigate Rd. Ewell .G 3
75 Reighton Rd.....C 15
79 Relf Rd.........F 15
83 Remington St.....C 12
83 Remnant St......G 9
75 Rendlesham Rd...C 15
87 Renfrew Rd.....F 12
84 Rennie St........A 12
74 Renters Av.......A 1
88 Rephidim St......E 3
78 Replingham Rd....J 3
78 Reporton Rd.....E 3
73 Repton Av.......D 2
85 Reston Pl.........D 3
74 Retcar St.........C 8
82 Retreat Pl......E 16
76 Revelon Rd......G 1
78 Revelstoke Rd....K 4
87 Reverdy Rd......F 6
73 Review Rd.......C 7
86 Rex Pl..........A 4
83 Rheidol Ter......B 13
79 Rhodesia Rd.....F 10
76 Rhodeswell Rd....J 2
76 Rhondda Gro....H 2
82 Rialto Cin.......J 7
76 Ricardo St.......J 3
75 Richard St.......K 15
84 Richard's Pl......E 1
87 Richborne Ter....J 9
76 Richford Rd......F 6
78 Richford St......B 1
65 Richings Pk......G 2
77 Richmond.......G 3
77 Richmond Av....F 11
75 Richmond Bri....H 2
75 Richmond Cres...F 11
77 Richmond Green..G 2
77 Richmond Hill...H 3
82 Richmond Mews..H 7
77 Richmond Pk....J 5
77 Richmond Pk. Rd..G 6
75 Richmond Rd. E8.E 15
76 Richmond Rd. E11.C 4
87 Richmond Rd. E17.A 2
75 Richmond Rd. N15
　　　　　　　　A 14
70 Richmond Rd. K'gst.
　　　　　　　　C 2
77 Richmond Rd. Twick.
　　　　　　　　H 2
77 Richmond Sta....G 3
77 Richmond Ter....E 7
76 Richmond Way, E11
　　　　　　　　B 6
78 Richmond Way, W14
　　　　　　　　B 2
85 Rickett St........H 1
71 Ricketts Hill Rd..H 10
65 Rickmansworth...A 3
65 Rickmansworth Rd.
　　　　　　　　A 4
65 Rickmansworth Rd.
　　　　Harefield......C 3
76 Riddlesdown Rd...G 6
71 Riddlesdown Sta..G 7
77 Ride, The........C 2
74 Ridge Av........A 7
74 Ridge Hill.......B 3
75 Ridge Rd. N8...A 11
74 Ridge Rd. NW2...C 3
70 Ridge Rd. Mord...E 4
80 Ridgebrook Rd...G 8
74 Ridgeway, The, E4.B 9
74 Ridgeway, The,
　　　　NW11......B 3
74 Ridgeway, The,W3 B 4
82 Ridgmount Gdns..F 7
82 Ridgmount St.....F 7
77 Riding Ho. St....F 6
73 Ridings, The.....H 4
76 Ridley Rd. E7....D 7
76 Ridley Rd. E8 ..E 14
76 Ridley Rd. NW10.G 8
74 Riffel Rd........E 1
78 Rigault Rd.......F 3
79 Rignold Rd......F 14

MAP
85 Riley St..........J 5
81 Ring, The........H 6
78 Ringford Rd......H 3
78 Ringmer Av.....E 3
79 Ringmore Rise...J 16
80 Ringstead Rd.....J 4
69 Ripley.........H 3
76 Ripley Rd.......J 8
67 Ripple Rd......E 11
75 Ripplevale Gro...F 11
73 Rise, The........D 6
83 Riseldine Rd.....H 1
87 Rita Rd.........J 9
83 Ritchie St.......B 11
78 Ritherdon Rd....K 8
83 Ritz Cin........J 7
86 Ritz Hot........B 6
77 River La........J 3
77 River Rd........C 8
83 River St........C 11
80 River Way.......K 4
77 Riverdale Gdns...H 2
77 Riverdale Rd.....H 2
75 Riversdale Rd....C 12
73 Riverside, NW4..A 8
80 Riverside, SE7...B 7
77 Riverside, Rich...H 1
77 Riverside Dri. W4.E 7
77 Riverside Dri Rich.
　　　　　　　　K 2
77 Riverview Gro...D 5
84 Rivington St.....D 4
76 Roach Rd........F 3
80 Roan St.........D 4
82 Robert Adam St...G 3
82 Robert St........D 5
84 Roberta St.......D 6
78 Robertson St.....F 8
76 Robeson St......J 2
74 Robin Gro.......C 7
76 Robin Hood La...K 4
70 Robin Hood Way..C 3
75 Robinson Rd....G 16
79 Robsart St......F 11
73 Robson Av......F 8
79 Robson Rd......L 12
76 Rochdale Rd.....A 3
84 Rochelle St......D 5
74 Rochester Pl.....E 9
74 Rochester Rd.....E 9
86 Rochester Row...E 7
86 Rochester St.....E 7
80 Rochester Way, SE3
　　　　　　　　F 8
71 Rochester Way, SE9
　　　　　　　　A 10
76 Rock Rd.........D 1
80 Rockbourne Rd...J 1
87 Rockingham St...E 13
78 Rockley Rd.......A 2
77 Rocks La........F 8
83 Rocliffe St......C 12
74 Rodborough Rd...B 3
84 Rodd La.........H 4
75 Roden St........C 11
79 Rodenhurst Rd...H 9
74 Roderick Rd.....D 7
67 Roding La. E18..C 10
67 Roding La. Buckhurst
　　　　Hill..........B 11
67 Roding La. Sth...C 10
76 Roding Rd.......D 1
82 Rodmarton St....G 3
88 Rodney Pl.......E 2
88 Rodney Rd.......F 2
83 Rodney St.......B 10
77 Rodway Rd......J 8
79 Rodwell Rd.....H 14
76 Roedean Cres....H 7
78 Roehampton.....J 1
77 Roehampton Cl...G 8
77 Roehampton Club.G 7
77 Roehampton High St.
　　　　　　　　J 8
77 Roehampton La...J 8
77 Roehampton Vale.K 7
80 Roffey St........B 4
83 Roger St........E 10
76 Rogers Rd.......J 6
76 Rokeby Rd. E15...F 5
80 Rokeby Rd. SE4..E 2
85 Roland Gdns.....G 4
85 Roland Way......G 4
75 Rollins St.......D 16
88 Rolls Rd.........G 6
79 Rollscourt Av...G 12
76 Roman Rd.......G 16
72 Roman Villa Rd...C 3
75 Roman Way.....E 11
80 Romborough Way.H 4
80 Romer Av.......G 3

MAP
79 Romeyn Rd......L 11
68 Romford........D 2
68 Romford G.C....D 3
76 Romford Rd. E7...E 6
68 Romford Rd. Aveley
67 Romford Rd. Hainault
　　　　　　　　B 12
67 Romford Rd. Ilf..E 11
75 Romilly Rd......C 12
83 Romilly St.......H 7
80 Romney Rd......D 4
72 Romney St., Kent.G 3
80 Romney St. SW1..E 8
79 Romola Rd......J 12
76 Rona Rd.........D 7
78 Ronald Av.......H 5
75 Ronalds Rd......E 11
80 Ronver Rd.......J 6
78 Rookery Rd......G 9
76 Rookwood Rd...A 15
84 Ropemaker St.....F 2
76 Ropery St.......H 2
78 Ropley St........C 6
78 Rosaline Rd......D 3
85 Rosary Gdns.....F 4
84 Roscoe St.......E 2
73 Rosdale Dri......B 5
88 Rose Alley.......A 1
78 Rose Gdns.......B 3
70 Rose Hill.......E 4
68 Rose La.........C 1
83 Rosebery Av....D 11
79 Rosebery Rd....H 10
78 Rosebury Rd.....F 5
74 Rosecroft Av.....C 4
76 Rosedale Rd.....E 8
79 Rosedene Av....L 11
73 Rosehill Rd......H 5
77 Rosemont Rd. W3.K 5
77 Rosemont Rd. Rich.
　　　　　　　　H 3
86 Rosemoor St.....F 2
78 Rosenau Rd......E 7
79 Rosendale Rd....J 12
78 Roseneath Rd....H 7
80 Rosenthal Rd....H 4
80 Rosenthorpe Rd...G 1
79 Roseway.......H 13
73 Rosoman St......D 11
75 Rossall Cres......H 4
75 Rossington St....C 15
78 Rossiter Rd......J 8
76 Rosslyn Av......F 7
73 Rosslyn Cres.....D 3
74 Rosslyn Hill.....D 6
74 Rosslyn Rd......H 2
82 Rossmore Rd.....E 1
82 Rosswell Rd......E 8
75 Rostrevor Av....A 14
78 Rostrevor Rd.....E 3
87 Rotary St.......D 12
75 Rotherfield St....F 13
75 Rotherhithe......A 1
79 Rotherhithe New Rd.
　　　　　　　　C 16
79 Rotherhithe Sta..A 16
80 Rotherhithe St....A 2
73 Rotherwick Hill..H 4
76 Rotherwick Rd...A 4
78 Rotherwood Rd...F 2
77 Rothesay Av.....G 4
86 Rothsay Rd......E 8
88 Rothsay St......D 3
77 Rothschild Rd....B 6
77 Rott St.........E 6
85 Rotten Row......C 6
88 Rouel Rd........E 6
78 Round Hill.....K 16
70 Roundshaw......K 6
78 Roundtable Rd....L 6
67 Roundway, The...C 7
73 Roundwood Pk...F 8
73 Roundwood Rd...F 7
76 Rounton Rd......H 3
87 Roupell St......B 11
65 Rousebarn La....A 4
78 Roustock Gdns...E 10
84 Routh Rd........J 6
78 Rowan Rd. W6...C 2
77 Rowan Rd. Brent..C 5
70 Rowan Rd., Mitch.D 6
88 Rowcross St......G 5
73 Rowden Av......F 9
78 Rowditch Lane....F 7
78 Rowfant Rd......K 7
84 Rowland St......F 7
78 Rowley Bank.....A 3

MAP
73 Rowley Cl.......F 4
66 Rowley La.......A 3
76 Rowsell St........J 2
66 Roxeth..........D 1
66 Roxeth Green Av..D 1
82 Royal Acad. of Arts J 6
82 Royal Academy of
　　　　Dramatic Art...F 7
82 Royal Academy of
　　　　Music.........E 4
66 Royal Air Force
　　　　Museum......C 2
85 Royal Albert Hall.D 4
86 Royal Automobile
　　　　Club........B 7
86 Royal Av........G 2
77 Royal Botanic Gdns.
　　　　　　　　E 3
85 Royal Cancer Hosp.
　　　　　　　　F 5
85 Royal Coll. of Art.D 5
85 Royal Coll. of Music
　　　　　　　　D 4
83 Royal Coll. of
　　　　Surgeons......G 10
82 Royal College St...B 7
83 Royal Cts. of Justice
　　　　　　　　H 10
79 Royal Circus....L 12
78 Royal Cres......A 2
82 Royal Ear Hosp...E 7
87 Royal Eye Hosp..D 12
84 Royal Ex........H 3
87 Royal Festival Hall
　　　　　　　　B 10
83 Royal Free Hosp. N1
　　　　　　　　A 11
74 Royal Free Hosp.
　　　　NW3.........D 6
83 Royal Free Hosp. WC1
　　　　　　　　D 10
85 Royal Geog. Soc..C 5
80 Royal Hill.......D 4
86 Royal Hosp......G 3
86 Royal Hosp. Rd...G 3
82 Royal Inst. of Br.
　　　　Arch.........F 5
86 Royal Mews, The..D 5
77 Royal Mid-Surrey
　　　　G.C..........F 2
84 Royal Mint......J 5
84 Royal Mint St.....J 5
80 Royal Naval Coll..D 4
80 Royal Observatory.D 5
83 Royal Opera Ho...H 9
76 Royal Rd. E16...K 8
87 Royal Rd. SE17..H 12
82 Royal Soc.......J 6
87 Royal St........D 10
82 Royal Vet. Coll...A 7
87 Royal Waterloo Hosp.
　　　　　　　　B 10
70 Royal Wimbledon
　　　　G.C..........C 3
65 Royston Pk......B 6
78 Rozel Rd........F 9
78 Ruckholt Rd.....D 3
73 Rucklidge Av....G 8
78 Rudloe Rd.......J 9
76 Rudolph Rd. E13..G 6
81 Rudolph Rd. NW6.C 2
84 Rufus St.........D 4
84 Rugby Av.......D 2
83 Rugby St.......F 9
65 Ruislip.........D 4
65 Ruislip Common..C 4
65 Ruislip Gdns. Sta. E 5
65 Ruislip G.C......D 4
65 Ruislip Lido.....D 4
65 Ruislip Manor Sta..D 5
65 Ruislip Rd......F 5
78 Rumbold Rd.....E 4
81 Rundell Rd......E 4
88 Runham St......G 3
75 Rupert Rd. N19..C 9
77 Rupert Rd. W4...B 7
82 Rupert St........H 7
76 Ruscoe Rd.......J 6
68 Rush Green......D 2
68 Rush Green Rd...D 2
78 Rusham Rd......H 7
79 Rushcroft Rd...G 11
70 Rushett La......G 1
80 Rushey Green....J 3
78 Rushford Rd.....H 2
71 Rushmore Hill Rd.
　　　　　　　　G 12
76 Rushmore Rd....D 1
78 Rusholme Rd....H 2
84 Rushton St......B 3
87 Rushworth St....C 12

MAP

79 Ruskin Pk......G 13
79 Ruskin Wk.......H 12
66 Russell La........B 5
76 Russel Rd. E16...J 7
78 Russell Rd. W14...B 3
83 Russell Sq.......F 8
83 Russell St. WC2..H 9
75 Russia La........G 16
88 Rust Sq..........J 2
77 Rusthall Av......B 6
76 Ruston St........F 2
86 Rutherford St.....E 7
85 Rutland Gdns....C 6
85 Rutland Gate....C 6
85 Rutland Mews....D 6
74 Rutland Pk........E 1
76 Rutland Rd.......F 1
85 Rutland St........D 6
80 Rutland Wk......K 2
87 Rutley Cl. .....H 12
69 Ruxbury Rd.......E 2
70 Ruxley La........F 2
73 Rydal Cres........G 1
69 Rydens Rd.......E 5
81 Ryder's Ter.......B 3
79 Rye Hill Pk......G 16
79 Rye La..........E 15
80 Rye Rd..........G 1
80 Ryecroft Rd......G 4
79 Ryedale.........H 16
86 Ryder St.........B 6
78 Ryfold Rd........L 4
77 Rylett Cres.......B 7
77 Rylett Rd........B 5
78 Rylston Rd.......D 3
77 Sabine Rd........F 7
75 Sach Rd.........B 16
82 Sackville St........J 6
83 Sadler's Wells Th..C 11
83 Saffron Hill......F 11
83 Saffron St.......F 11
87 Sall St..........E 10
78 Sainfoin Rd.......K 8
87 St. Agnes Pl.....H 12
79 St. Aidan's Rd. SE22
       H 15
77 St. Aidan's Rd. W13
       A 1
77 St. Alban's Av......B 6
85 St. Alban's Gro....D 3
74 St. Alban's Rd. NW5
       C 8
73 St. Alban's Rd. NW10
       F 7
82 St. Alban's St......J 7
84 St. Alphage Gdn..F 2
79 St. Alphonsus Rd..G 9
83 St. Andrew St....G 11
83 St. Andrew's Gdns.
       E 10
75 St. Andrew's Gro..B 13
83 St. Andrew's Hill .H 12
73 St. Andrew's Hosp. C 8
76 St. Andrew's Rd. E13
       H 7
73 St. Andrew's Rd. W3
       K 7
78 St. Ann's Cres......H 5
73 St. Anne's Gdns...G 4
78 St. Ann's Hill.....H 5
67 St. Ann's Rd. N15.D 7
69 St. Ann's Rd. Chertsey
       E 2
87 St. Ann's St........D 7
81 St. Ann's Ter.......B 5
76 St. Antony's Rd...F 7
80 St. Asaph Rd......F 1
73 St. Augustine's Av..C 3
75 St. Augustine's Rd..E 9
80 St. Austell Rd......F 4
76 St. Barnabas Rd....A 3
86 St. Barnabas St....F 4
83 St. Bartholomew the
     Great Ch......F 13
83 St. Bartholomew's
     Hosp........G 12
66 St. Bernard's Hosp. G 1
84 St. Botolph St.... G 5
83 St. Bride St......G 12
83 St. Chad's Pl......C 9
83 St. Chad's St.....C 9
74 St. Charles' Sq....J 2
84 St. Clare St......H 5
83 St. Clement Dane's
     Ch........H 10
75 St. Clement St....E 11
83 St. Clement's La..H 10
83 St. Cross St......F 11
78 St. Dionis Rd......E 3
80 St. Donatt's Rd....E 2
73 St. Dunstan's Av..K 6

84 St. Dunstan's Hill..J 4
78 St. Dunstan's Rd...C 2
82 St. Edmund's Ter..B 2
71 St. Elder Rd.......C 7
77 St. Elmo Rd.......A 8
74 St. Ervan's Rd.....J 3
79 St. Faith's Rd.....K 12
80 St. Fillans Rd.....J 4
79 St. Francis Hosp..G 14
87 St. Gabriel St......E 12
74 St. Gabriel's Rd....E 2
76 St. George's Av.E7. F 7
75 St. George's Av. N7 D 9
69 St. George's Av.
   Weybridge.......F 4
87 St. George's Circ..D 12
86 St. George's Dri....F 6
83 St. George's Gdns..D 9
69 St. George's Hill G.C.
       F 4
86 St. George's Hosp..C 4
76 St. George's Rd. E7
       E 7
76 St. George's Rd. E10
       C 4
87 St. George's Rd. SE1
       E 12
77 St. George's Rd.
   Twick.........H 1
76 St. George's Sq. E7.E 7
86 St. George's Sq. SW1
       G 7
82 St. George St.....H 5
88 St. George's Way..H 4
80 St. German' Pls...E 6
80 St. German's Rd...J 2
83 St. Giles High St...G 8
79 St. Giles Rd......E 13
80 St. Helena Rd....C 1
81 St. Helena St.....D 11
84 St. Helen's Ct......G 4
84 St. Helen's Pl......G 4
70 St. Helier.........E 4
70 St. Helier Av......E 4
70 St. Helier Hosp.. E 4
76 St. James Rd. E15.D 6
75 St. James's Av....G 16
86 St. James's Ch.....A 6
86 St. James's Club...B 5
79 St. James's Cres...F 12
78 St. James's Dri.....J 7
82 St. James's Gdns. NW1
       D 6
74 St. James's Gdns. W11
       L 2
73 St. James Gdns. Wem.
       F 3
86 St. James's Pal....B 6
76 St. James Pk. E17..A 1
86 St. James's Pk. SW1
       C 7
86 St. James's Pl......B 6
88 St. James's Rd. SE16
       E 16
71 St. James's Rd.Cro E 7
83 St. James's Row..E 12
86 St. James's Sq.....B 7
86 St. James's St......B 6
67 St. James's St. Sta..D 8
82 St. James's Ter. Mews
       B 2
83 St. James's Wk....E 12
83 St. John St......D 12
73 St. John's Av. NW10
       F 7
78 St. John's Av. SW15
       G 2
79 St. John's Cres....F 11
74 St. John's Gdns...K 3
83 St. John's Gate...E 12
75 St. John's Gro.....C 9
78 St. John's Hill.....G 6
78 St. John's Hill Gro.
       G 6
83 St. John's La.....F 12
80 St. John's Pk.....E 6
75 St. John's Rd. N15
       A 14
75 St. John's Rd. N19. B 9
74 St. John's Rd. NW11
       A 3
78 St. John's Rd. SW11
       G 6
77 St. John's Rd. Rich.
       G 3
73 St. John's Rd. Wem.
       D 3
83 St. John's Sq......E 12
80 St. John's Sta......F 3
80 St. John's Vale....F 3
75 St. John's Villas...C 9

81 St. John's Wood High
   St.............C 6
81 St. John's Wood Pk.
       A 5
81 St. John's Wood Rd.
       D 5
81 St. John's Wood Ter.
       B 6
75 St. Jude's Rd.....G 16
88 St. Katharine's Way
       B 6
75 St. Kilda's Rd.....B 13
79 St. Lawrence Rd...E 11
74 St. Lawrence Ter...J 3
84 St. Leonard's Hosp.B 4
76 St. Leonard's Rd. E14
       J 4
73 St. Leonard's Rd.
   NW10.........H 6
77 St. Leonard's Rd.
   SW14.........F 5
73 St. Leonard's Rd. W13
       K 2
86 St. Leonard's Ter..G 2
86 St. Loo Av.......H 2
79 St. Luke's Av......G 9
85 St. Luke's Hosp....G 6
85 St. Luke's St.......G 6
70 St. Margarets......B 1
77 St. Margaret's Dri..G 1
76 St. Margaret's Rd...G 4
77 St. Margaret's Sta..H 1
87 St. Margaret's St...D 8
84 St. Mark St.......H 4
83 St. Mark's Hosp..C 13
75 St. Mark's Rise...E 14
74 St. Mark's Rd.....J 2
83 St. Martin's La....J 8
83 St. Martin's Pl.....J 8
79 St. Martin's Rd....F 11
83 St. Martin's St.....J 8
83 St. Martin's Th...H 8
83 St. Martins-in-the-
   Fields Ch......J 8
83 St. Martin's le Grand
       G 13
85 St. Mary Abbots
   Hosp...........E 2
84 St. Mary-at-Hill...J 3
84 St. Mary Axe.....G 4
79 St. Mary Ch. St...A 16
71 St. Mary Cray....D 12
74 St. Mary Islington
   Hosp.........B 8
84 St. Mary-le-Bow Ch.
       H 2
74 St. Marylebone....H 7
76 St. Mary's Av......J 2
87 St. Mary's Gdns...E 11
75 St. Mary's Gro. N1E 12
77 St. Mary's Gro. SW13
       F 9
77 St. Mary's Gro. W4D 5
81 St. Mary's Hosp. W2
       G 5
81 St. Mary's Hosp. W9
       F 1
68 St. Mary's La......D 4
76 St. Mary's Rd. E10.C 4
76 St. Mary's Rd. E13
       H 7
73 St. Mary's Rd. NW10
       F 7
79 St. Mary's Rd. SE15
       E 16
77 St. Mary's Rd. W5. A 2
70 St. Mary's Rd. Surb.
       E 1
81 St. Mary's Ter......F 4
87 St. Mary's Wk.....E 11
86 St. Matthew St....D 7
79 St. Matthew's Rd.H 11
84 St. Matthew's Row.D 6
78 St. Maur Rd......E 3
74 St. Michael's Av. NW2
       D 1
73 St. Michael's Av.
   Wem.........E 5
79 St. Michael's Rd..E 11
81 St. Michael's St....G 5
80 St. Mildred's Rd...J 6
80 St. Norbert Rd.....G 1
78 St. Olaf's Rd......E 3
87 St. Oswald Pl.....G 10
74 St. Pancras........F 8
82 St. Pancras Gdns...B 7
82 St. Pancras Hospital
       B 7
83 St. Pancras Sta....C 8
82 St. Pancras Way...A 7
84 St. Paul St........A 1

74 St. Paul's Av......E 1
83 St. Paul's Cathedral
       H 13
83 St. Paul's Churchyard
       H 13
71 St. Paul's Cray...D 12
71 St. Paul's Cray Rd.
       D 11
75 St. Paul's Cres....F 9
75 St. Paul's Rd. N5. E 12
77 St. Paul's Rd. Rich. F 4
87 St. Paul's Ter......H 12
76 St. Paul's Way....J 2
71 St. Paul's Wood Hill
       D 11
84 St. Peter's Av......C 7
84 St. Peter's Cl......C 7
77 St. Peter's Rd......G 1
77 St. Peter's Sq......C 8
83 St. Peter's St......B 13
81 St. Petersburgh Mews
       J 2
81 St. Petersburgh Pl..J 2
78 St. Philip St......F 8
84 St. Philip Way......A 2
75 St. Philip's Rd....E 15
74 St. Quintin Av....J 2
73 St. Raphael's Way.E 6
78 St. Rule St........F 9
78 St. Simon's Av.....G 2
77 St. Stephen's Av...A 9
81 St. Stephen's Gdns.
   W9...........G 1
77 St. Stephen's Gdns.
   Twick.........H 2
85 St. Stephen's Hosp.
       H 4
76 St. Stephen's Rd. E3
       G 2
76 St. Stephen's Rd. E6
       F 8
73 St. Stephen's Rd. W13
       J 2
79 St. Stephen's Ter..E 10
84 St. Swithin's La...H 3
65 St. Thomas Dri....C 5
88 St. Thomas St......B 3
87 St. Thomas's Hosp.
       D 9
75 St. Thomas's Rd..C 12
82 St. Vincent St......G 4
87 Salamanca St......F 9
76 Salcombe Rd......A 2
78 Salcott Rd........H 6
81 Sale Pl..........G 6
80 Salehurst Rd......H 2
81 Salem Rd........H 2
79 Salford Rd.......K 9
83 Salisbury Ct......H 12
82 Salisbury Pl......F 2
76 Salisbury Rd......E 6
88 Salisbury Row....F 3
81 Salisbury St......E 6
76 Salmen Rd.......G 6
76 Salmon La........J 1
73 Salmon St........B 5
71 Salmons La.......H 7
75 Salterton Rd......C 10
79 Saltoun Rd.......G 11
74 Saltram Cres.......G 3
76 Saltwell St........K 3
74 Salusbury Rd......G 3
81 Samford St.......E 5
76 Samson St. E13...G 7
79 Samson St. SE5...E 13
87 Sancroft St.......F 10
88 Sanctuary St......C 2
73 Sandal Cl........H 3
76 Sandal St........F 5
73 Sandall Rd.......H 3
80 Sandbourne Rd....F 1
75 Sandbrook Rd...C 14
71 Sanderstead......G 7
74 Sanderstead Av...C 2
71 Sanderstead Hill..G 7
76 Sanderstead Rd. E10
       B 2
71 Sanderstead Rd. Cro.
       F 7
71 Sanderstead Sta....F 7
88 Sandford Row.....G 3
80 Sandhurst Rd.....J 5
78 Sandilands Rd.....E 4
83 Sandland St......F 10
79 Sandmere Rd.....G 10
80 Sandock Rd.......F 3
88 Sandover Rd......G 4
76 Sandringham Rd. E7
       E 8
75 Sandringham Rd. E8

76 Sandringham Rd. E10
       A 5
73 Sandringham Rd.
   NW2..........E 8
80 Sandrock Rd......F 3
80 Sandtoft Rd.......D 7
83 Sandwich St......D 8
74 Sandy Heath......B 5
68 Sandy La. Dag....F 4
69 Sandy La. Esh....G 5
77 Sandy La. Rich...K 2
70 Sandy La. Twick..D 1
76 Sandy La. Sth....F 5
65 Sandy Lodge G.C..B 4
65 Sandy Lodge La...B 4
65 Sandy Lodge Rd...B 4
84 Sandy Row.......F 4
77 Sandycombe Rd. Rich.
       F 4
77 Sandycombe Rd.
   Twick..........H 2
79 Sandgate St......D 15
80 Sanford St........D 1
75 Sanford Ter......C 14
80 Sangley Rd.:......J 4
83 Sans Wk.........E 12
79 Santley St........G 10
83 Santos Rd........G 4
83 Sardinia St........G 9
74 Sarre Rd.........D 3
84 Sarsfeld Rd.......K 7
73 Sarsfield Rd.......G 2
80 Saunders Ness Rd..C 4
76 Saunders St......E 10
86 Savage Club......B 7
84 Savage Gdns.....H 4
77 Savernake Rd.....D 7
84 Savile Club......H 4
82 Savile Row.......J 6
76 Saviours Rd......H 10
83 Savoy Hill.......J 9
83 Savoy Hot.......J 9
83 Savoy Pl.........J 9
83 Savoy St.........J 9
83 Savoy Th.........J 9
73 Sawley Rd........K 8
87 Sawyer St........C 13
73 Saxon Dri........J 5
76 Saxon Rd.........G 2
87 Sayer St.........E 13
82 Scala St.........F 6
84 Scarborough Rd..B 5
84 Scarborough St....H 5
73 Scarle Rd........E 3
80 Scarlet Rd.......K 5
80 Scarsdale Rd.....H 4
85 Scarsdale Villas...E 1
80 Scawen Rd.......C 1
78 Scholars Rd.......J 9
76 Scholefield Rd.....B 9
69 School La........F 2
73 School Rd.......H 6
76 Schubert Rd......G 3
85 Science Mus......E 5
84 Sclater St........E 5
87 Scoresby St......B 12
80 Scotsdale Rd.....H 7
75 Scott St. E1.....H 15
81 Scott Ellis Gardens.D 4
88 Scott Lidgett Crescent
       D 6
71 Scotts La........D 9
71 Scott's Lodge.....H 11
76 Scotts Rd. E10....B 4
78 Scotts Rd. W12...A 1
71 Scottshall La......W 3
87 Scovell Rd.......D 13
73 Scrubs La........H 8
84 Scrutton St.......E 3
72 Scudders Hill.....D 4
79 Scutari Rd........H 16
79 Scylla Rd........F 15
83 Seacoal La.......G 12
83 Seaford St.......D 9
76 Seagrave Rd......H 1
72 Seal............H 3
88 Searles Rd.......E 3
88 Sears St.........J 2
85 Seaton St........J 4
75 Sebastian St......D 12
75 Sebbon St........F 12
76 Sebert Rd........D 7
83 Secker St........B 11
76 Second Av. E13....G 6
77 Second Av. SW14..F 7
74 Second Av. W3....A 7
74 Second Av. W10...H 3
73 Second Av. Wembley
       B 3

73 Second Way......D 5
88 Secretan Rd.......H 4
86 Sedding St........F 3
73 Sedgeford Rd......K 8
79 Sedgmoor Pl.....E 14
76 Sedgwick Rd......C 4
85 Sedlescombe Rd...H 1
84 Seething La.......J 4
78 Sefton St.........F 1
83 Sekforde St.......E 12
79 Selborne Rd.......E 13
76 Selby Rd. E11.....C 5
76 Selby Rd. E13.....J 7
73 Selby Rd. W5.....H 2
84 Selby St..........E 7
80 Selcroft Rd.......C 6
71 Selhurst..........D 7
71 Selhurst Rd.......D 7
87 Sellon Mews......F 10
73 Sellons Av........F 7
82 Selous St.........A 6
71 Selsdon Pk. G.C...G 7
71 Selsdon Pk. Rd....F 8
76 Selsdon Rd. E11...A 6
76 Selsdon Rd. E13...G 8
73 Selsdon Rd. NW2..C 8
71 Selsdon Rd. Croydon
       F 7
71 Selsdon Sta.......F 7
76 Selsey St.........J 2
85 Selwood Pl........G 5
85 Selwood Ter.......G 5
80 Selworthy Rd......L 2
77 Selwyn Av........G 3
76 Selwyn Rd. E3....G 2
76 Selwyn Rd. E13...F 7
86 Semley Pl........F 4
83 Senate Ho........F 8
81 Senior St.........F 2
80 Senlac Rd........K 7
83 Serle St.........G 10
86 Serpentine Rd.....B 2
88 Setchell Rd.......E 5
84 Settles St.........G 7
78 Settrington Rd.....F 4
83 Seven Dials......H 8
67 Seven Kings......D 12
75 Seven Sisters Rd..B 12
67 Seven Sisters Sta..D 7
80 Sevenoaks Rd. SE4
       H 2
71 Sevenoaks Rd. Orp.
       F 12
69 Severn Hills Rd...G 4
86 Seville St.........C 3
81 Sevington St......E 2
83 Seward St........D 13
75 Sewardstone Rd...G 16
67 Sewardstone Rd...A 9
67 Sewardstonebury...A 9
76 Sewdley St........D 1
82 Seymour Mews....G 3
82 Seymour Pl.......G 2
76 Seymour Rd. E10..B 2
78 Seymour Rd. SW18
       H 3
78 Seymour Rd. SW19
       K 2
82 Seymour St.......H 2
85 Seymour Wk.......H 4
80 Seyssel St........K 6
73 Shaa Rd.........K 6
75 Shacklewell La...D 15
88 Shad Thames......C 5
75 Shadwell.........K 16
83 Shaftesbury Av...H 8
76 Shaftesbury Rd.E7.F 8
75 Shaftesbury Rd. N19
       B 10
84 Shaftesbury St....B 2
83 Shaftesbury Th....G 8
79 Shakespeare Rd. SE24
       G 12
73 Shakespeare Rd. W3
       K 6
75 Shakespeare Wk..D 13
85 Shalcomb St......H 4
77 Shalstone Rd......F 5
88 Shand St.........C 4
79 Shandon Rd......H 9
76 Shandy St........J 1
80 Shardeloes Rd.....F 2
79 Sharratt St.......D 16
87 Sharsted St......G 12
71 Shaw La.........H 7
79 Shawbury Rd.....G 15
86 Shawfield St......G 2
77 Shearwater Rd....G 2
77 Sheen Common...H 5
77 Sheen Common Dri.
       G 5

MAP

77 Sheen Ct. Rd......G 4
77 Sheen Gate Gardens
                     G 6
77 Sheen La.........G 6
77 Sheen Pk........G 3
77 Sheen Rd........G 3
75 Sheep La.......F 15
85 Sheffield Ter......B 1
79 Shelbury Rd....H 16
74 Sheldon Av.....A 6
74 Sheldon Rd......D 2
85 Sheldrake Pl......C 1
78 Shelgate Rd......G 7
80 Shell Rd.........G 3
73 Shelley Gdns.....C 2
71 Shelleys Hill....H 11
75 Shellgrove Rd...D 14
78 Shellwood Rd....F 7
83 Shelton St.......H 8
68 Shenfield........A 5
79 Shenley Rd. SE5. E 14
66 Shenley Rd.
    Borehamwood...A 2
86 Shepherds.......B 4
86 Shepherd Mkt....B 5
84 Shepherdess Wk...C 2
78 Shepherd's Bush...A 1
78 Shepherd's Bush Rd.
                     B 2
74 Shepherds Hill....A 8
74 Shepherd's Wk....D 6
76 Sheppard St......H 6
69 Shepperton.......E 4
75 Shepperton Rd. N1
                   F 13
69 Shepperton Rd.
    Staines.........D 3
82 Sheraton St......H 7
73 Serbourne Gdns...J 1
84 Sherborne La.....H 3
75 Sherborne St.....F 13
78 Sherbrook Rd....E 3
77 Sherefield Gdns...H 7
75 Sheringham Rd...E 11
80 Sherington Rd....D 7
74 Sherlock Rd......D 7
76 Sherrard Rd......E 8
73 Sherrick Green Rd.E 9
74 Sherriff Rd......D 2
80 Sherwin Rd......E 1
71 Sherwood Rd.....D 11
71 Sherwood Park Av.
                   B 12
78 Shillington St......F 6
71 Ship Hill........H 10
77 Ship La. SW14....F 6
68 Ship La. Aveley...G 4
72 Ship La. Dartford..D 3
76 Shipman Rd. E16. K 7
80 Shipman Rd. SE23.K 1
84 Shipton St.......C 6
76 Shirbutt St.......K 3
71 Shire La.........F 10
74 Shirehall La......A 2
74 Shirehall Pk......A 2
72 Shirehall Rd.....C 2
81 Shirland Rd......E 2
71 Shirley.........E 8
71 Shirley Pk. G.C...E 7
71 Shirley Rd.......E 7
76 Shirley St.......J 6
83 Shoe La.........G 11
74 Shoot-up-Hill....E 3
71 Shooter's Hill...A 11
71 Shooter's Hill G.C.
                   A 11
80 Shooters Hill Rd..E 5
75 Shore Pl.........F 16
75 Shore Rd........F 16
75 Shoreditch......G 14
84 Shoreditch High St.
                   E 4
72 Shoreham.......G 1
88 Shorncliffe Rd....G 5
80 Shorndean St.....J 4
78 Shorrolds Rd.....D 3
76 Short Rd........C 5
87 Short St........C 11
71 Shortlands......D 9
71 Shortlands G.C...D 9
76 Shortlands Rd. E10
                   A 3
71 Shortlands Rd. Brom.
                   D 9
71 Shortlands Sta...D 9
83 Short's Gdns.....H 8
78 Shottendane Rd...E 4
82 Shouldham St.....G 2
81 Shrewsbury Mews.G 1
81 Shrewsbury Rd. W9
                   G 1

80 Shroffold Rd.....L 6
81 Shroton St.......F 6
75 Shrubland Rd....F 15
78 Shuttleworth Rd...E 6
79 Sibella Rd.......F 9
71 Sidcup..........C 12
71 Sidcup By-Pass...C 11
71 Sidcup G.C......B 12
71 Sidcup Hill......C 12
80 Sidcup Rd. SE12..J 8
71 Sidcup Rd. Sid...C 11
82 Siddons La.......E 2
80 Siddons Rd......K 1
87 Sidford Pl......E 10
76 Sidmouth Rd. E10.C 4
74 Sidmouth Rd. NW2
                   F 1
83 Sidmouth St......D 9
77 Sidmouth Wood...J 4
79 Sidney Rd.......F 11
75 Sidney St.......J 16
87 Silex St.........C 12
77 Silver Cres.......C 5
73 Silver Jubilee Park
                   A 6
67 Silver St. N18....B 7
79 Silverlock St......C 16
78 Silverthorne Rd...F 8
80 Silvertown.......A 8
76 Silvertown Way...J 6
79 Silvester Rd.....H 15
79 Silwood St......C 16
78 Simpson St.......F 6
88 Simms Rd........F 6
74 Sinclair Gro......A 2
74 Sinclair Rd......B 2
86 South Eaton Pl....F 4
84 Singer St........D 3
71 Single St........G 10
65 Sipson..........H 4
65 Sipson La........G 4
69 Sipson Rd........A 3
74 Sirdar Rd.......K 2
80 Sirthorpe Rd.....J 7
78 Sispara Gdns.....H 3
78 Sisters Av.......G 7
78 Sistova Rd.......J 8
74 Sixth Av........H 2
69 Sixth Cross Rd...C 6
78 Skeena Hill......J 3
72 Skeet Hill La.....E 1
76 Skelton Rd......E 7
76 Skelton's La......A 4
71 Skibbs La.......E 12
83 Skinner St......D 11
84 Skinners La......H 2
87 Skipton St.......D 12
72 Slade Green......A 2
67 Slades Hill......A 7
85 Slaidburn St......J 4
80 Slaithwaite Rd....G 4
71 Slines New Rd....H 8
71 Slines Oak Rd....H 8
83 Slingsby Pl......H 8
86 Sloane Av.......F 1
86 Sloane Ct. E......G 3
86 Sloane Ct. W.....G 3
86 Sloane Gdns......F 3
86 Sloane Sq.......F 3
86 Sloane St.......E 3
86 Sloane Ter.......E 3
73 Slough La.......A 6
75 Smalley Rd......C 14
78 Smeaton Rd......J 4
76 Smeed Rd........F 3
87 Smith Sq........E 8
86 Smith St........G 2
86 Smith Ter.......G 2
70 Smitham Sta.....G 6
83 Smithfield St.....G 12
83 Smithfield Market
                   F 12
75 Smithy St.......J 16
88 Smyrk's Rd.......G 4
67 Snaresbrook.....D 10
67 Snaresbrook Rd...C 9
74 Sneath Av.......A 3
74 Sneyd Rd........D 1
83 Snow Hill........G 12
84 Snowden St......F 4
88 Snow's Fields....C 3
75 Soho............K 9
82 Soho Sq.........G 7
82 Soho St.........G 7
76 Solebay St.......H 1
74 Solent Rd.......E 4
79 Solon Rd........G 10
90 Solway Rd.......G 15
74 Somali Rd.......D 3
75 Somerfield Rd...D 15
75 Somerford St.....H 16
79 Somerleyton Rd...G 12

81 Somers Cres.....H 6
81 Somers Mews....G 6
79 Somers Rd......H 11
75 Somers Town....G 9
83 Somerset Ho.....J 10
77 Somerset Rd. W4..B 6
83 Somerset Rd. W13.A 1
77 Somerset Rd. Brent.
                   D 2
77 Somerton Av.....F 5
74 Somerton Rd.....C 2
79 Somertrees Av....K 7
79 Somerville Rd....E 17
88 Sondes St........H 3
73 Sonia Gdns......D 7
79 Sonning St.......E 11
76 Sophia Rd.......B 3
75 Sotheby Rd......D 12
74 South Acton Sta...B 5
74 South Africa Rd...K 1
86 South Audley St...A 4
79 South Bermondsey Sta.
                   C 16
76 South Birkbeck Rd.
                   C 5
85 South Bolton Gdns.G 3
82 South Cres.......F 7
79 South Croxted Rd.
                   L 13
70 South Croydon....F 6
71 South Croydon Sta.
                   F 7
72 South Darenth....D 3
78 South Ealing Rd...B 2
77 South Ealing Sta...B 2
86 South Eaton Pl....F 4
71 South Eden Pk....D 8
71 South End SE9....B 11
85 South End W8....D 2
71 South End Croydon
                   F 7
74 South End Rd. NW3
                   D 6
68 South End Rd. Dag.
                   E 3
85 South End Row...D2
76 South Esk Rd.....E 8
66 South Greenford Halt
                   F 1
74 South Gro.......B 8
74 South Hampstead Sta.
                   F 5
65 South Harrow....D 6
66 South Herts G.C...A 5
74 South Hill Pk. Gdns.
                   D 6
68 South Hornchurch. E 3
79 South Island Pl...E 11
73 South Kenton Sta..B 2
87 South Lambeth Rd.
                   H 9
70 South La.........E 3
70 South Merton Sta..D 6
82 South Molton La...H 4
82 South Molton St...H 4
71 South Norwood...D 7
71 South Norwood Hill
                   D 7
68 South Ockendon...F 5
65 South Oxhey......B 5
85 South Parade,SW3 G 5
77 South Parade, W4.B 6
78 South Pk........H 6
80 South Pk. Cres....J 6
67 South Pk. Dri....E 12
84 South Pl.........F 3
80 South Row.......E 6
80 South Rd. SE23...K 1
77 South W5.......B 3
81 South Wharf Rd...G 5
67 South Woodford Sta.
                   C 10
77 South Worple Way.A 1
65 Southall.........G 5
65 Southall Green....G 5
65 Southall La.......G 5

83 Southampton Bldgs.
                   G 10
83 Southampton Pl...G 9
74 Southampton Rd...D 7
83 Southampton Row.F 9
83 Southampton St...J 9
79 Southampton Way,
                   D 13
71 Southborough, Brom.
                   D 10
70 Southborough, Surb
                   E 1
71 Southborough La. D10
76 Southborough Rd. E 9
71 Southborough Rd.
    Brom..........D 10
76 Southbrook Rd....H 6
67 Southbury Rd.....A 7
70 Southcroft Rd.....C 5
78 Southdean Gdns...K 3
71 Southend........C 9
67 Southend Rd. E18.C 10
68 Southend Rd. Rom.
                   C 4
76 Southern Gro.....H 2
76 Southern Rd......G 7
74 Southern Row....H 2
83 Southern St......B 9
78 Southerton Rd....B 1
79 Southesk St......F 10
79 Southey Rd......E 11
77 Southfield Rd.....A 6
78 Southfields......J 3
72 Southfleet.......C 5
66 Southgate.......A 6
75 Southgate Rd.....F 13
78 Southmead Rd....J 2
73 Southview Av.....D 7
79 Southwark.......B 12
84 Southwark Bri....J 2
87 Southwark Bri. Rd.
                   C 13
88 Southwark Cath...B 2
79 Southwark Pk....B 16
88 Southwark Pk. Rd.
                   E 6
87 Southwark St.....B 13
85 Southwell Gdns...E 3
76 Southwell Gro. Rd. C 5
79 Southwell Rd.....F 12
75 Southwold Rd....C 16
81 Southwick Mews..G 5
81 Southwick Pl......H 6
81 Southwick St......H 6
75 Southwood Rd....C 16
74 Southwood Av....A 7
74 Southwood La....A 7
74 Southwood Rd....A 7
71 Spa Hill.........D 7
88 Spa Rd..........E 5
74 Spaniards Rd.....B 5
82 Spanish Pl.......G 4
77 Spankers Hill Wood
                   K 6
66 Sparrowsherne....A 1
75 Sparsholt Rd.....B 10
85 Spear Mews......F 2
75 Spears Rd.......B 10
75 Speldhurst.......F 16
76 Speldhurst Rd. E9. F 1
77 Speldhurst Rd. W4.B 6
84 Spelman St......F 6
75 Spencer Gro.....D 14
78 Spencer Pk......H 6
74 Spencer Rd. NW5.D 8
75 Spencer Rd. SW18.G 6
73 Spencer Rd. W3...K 6
77 Spencer Rd. W4...E 6
73 Spencer Rd. Wem..B 2
83 Spencer St......D 12
79 Spenser Rd......H 12
86 Spenser St......D 6
69 Spinney Hill......F 2
68 Spital La........B 5
84 Spital Sq........F 4
84 Spital St........F 6
84 Spitalfields Mkt...F 5
80 Sportsbank St....J 4
86 Sprimont Pl......F 2
87 Spring Gdns......B 8
66 Spring Gro......H 1
77 Spring Gro. Rd....G 4
76 Spring Hill......A 15
74 Spring Pl.........E 8
81 Spring St.......H 5
80 Springbank Rd...H 5
75 Springdale Rd....D 13
75 Springfield......B 15
75 Springfield Gdns. E5

78 Springfield Hosp..K 6
75 Springfield Pk...B 15
81 Springfield Rd....A 3
80 Springrice Rd.....H 4
73 Springwell Av....G 8
76 Sprowston Rd.....E 6
80 Sprules Rd.......F 1
71 Spur Rd.........E 11
88 Spurgeon St......D 2
75 Spurstowe Rd....E 15
69 Squires Bri. Rd....D 3
68 Squirrels Heath...C 3
68 Squirrels Heath Rd. C 4
84 Squirries St......D 7
83 Stacey St.......H 8
73 Stadium Way......D 4
84 Staff St.........D 3
76 Staffa Rd........B 1
81 Stafford Mews....D 1
86 Stafford Pl......D 6
76 Stafford Rd. E3...G 2
81 Stafford Rd. NW6.C 1
70 Stafford Rd.
    Beddington.....F 6
81 Stafford Ter......D 1
66 Stag La. NW9....C 3
77 Stag La. SW15....K 8
86 Stag Pl.........D 6
69 Staines..........C 2
69 Staines La.......D 2
69 Staines Rd. E.....D 5
69 Staines Rd. Houn..B 5
69 Staines Rd. Laleham
                   D 2
69 Staines Rd. Twick..C 6
69 Staines Rd. W....C 4
69 Staines Cent. Sta...C 2
69 Staines W. Sta....C 2
78 Stainforth Rd.....F 7
80 Stainton Rd......J 4
81 Stalham St.......F 2
77 Stamford Brook Av.
                   B 8
77 Stamford Brook Rd.
                   B 7
77 Stamford Brook Sta.
                   C 8
75 Stamford Hill....B 14
75 Stamford Rd.....E 14
87 Stamford St......B 11
85 Stamford Bri. Stadium
                   J 2
73 Standard Rd......H 6
78 Standen Rd......J 3
77 Standish Rd......C 8
85 Stanford Rd......D 3
87 Stangate........D 9
74 Stanhope Gdns. N6
                   A 8
85 Stanhope Gdns. SW7
                   E 4
85 Stanhope Mews E..E 4
85 Stanhope Mews W..E 4
82 Stanhope Pl......H 2
75 Stanhope Rd......A 9
86 Stanhope Row....B 4
82 Stanhope St......D 6
81 Stanhope Ter.....H 5
78 Stanlake Rd......A 1
73 Stanley Av.......F 3
74 Stanley Cres......K 3
78 Stanley Gdns.....A 7
78 Stanley Gro......F 8
73 Stanley Pk. Dri...F 4
76 Stanley Pk. Rd....F 5
83 Stanley Passage...C 8
77 Stanley Rd. SW14.G 5
69 Stanley Rd. Twick..C 6
80 Stanley St.......E 2
66 Stanmore........B 2
77 Stanmore Gdns...F 4
66 Stanmore Hill....B 1
76 Stanmore Rd. E11.B 6
77 Stanmore Rd. Rich.F 4
75 Stanmore St......F 10
87 Stannary St......G 11
79 Stansfield Rd.....F 11
80 Stanstead Rd.....J 1
72 Stansted........F 4
80 Stanton Rd.......F 7
73 Stanway Gdns....K 4
84 Stanway St.......C 4
69 Stanwell........B 3
69 Stanwell Rd......B 3
69 Stanwell Rd. Staines
                   C 3
69 Stanwell Moor Rd. A 2
88 Stanwellmoor.....B 2
88 Staple St........D 3
68 Stapleford Abbotts.A 2
75 Stapleton Hall Rd.A 11

78 Stapleton Rd.....L 7
76 Star La.........H 5
78 Star Rd.........C 3
81 Star St.........G 5
77 Star and Garter Hill J 3
72 Star Hill Rd......H 1
77 Starch Green.....A 8
82 Starcross St......D 6
77 Starfield Rd......A 8
77 Station App. Rich..E 4
73 Station App. Wem..E 1
69 Station Av.......E 4
69 Station Gro......E 3
68 Station La.......D 3
76 Station Rd. E4....A 9
76 Station Rd. E7....D 6
76 Station Rd. E10...C 4
76 Station Rd. E15...E 4
73 Station Rd. NW4..A 8
74 Station Rd. NW10.G 2
73 Station Rd. NW10.G 7
77 Station Rd. SW13. F 8
69 Station Rd.
    Addlestone.....F 3
66 Station Rd. Har...C 1
65 Station Rd. Hayes.G 4
66 Station Rd. New
    Barnet........A 5
71 Station Rd. Orp...E 11
71 Station Rd. Sid...C 11
80 Staunton St......D 2
77 Staveley Gdns....E 6
77 Staveley Rd......D 6
74 Staverton Rd.....F 1
75 Stavordale Rd....D 12
88 Stead St........F 2
71 Stean St........F 14
80 Stebondale St.....C 4
87 Steedman St......F 13
76 Steele Rd. E11....D 5
73 Steele Rd. NW10..G 6
74 Steele's Rd......E 7
69 Steels La........G 6
82 Stephen St.......G 7
78 Stephendale Rd...F 5
76 Stephen's Rd.....C 3
76 Stephenson St. E16.H 5
73 Stephenson St. NW10
                   H 7
82 Stephenson Way..D 6
76 Stepney.........K 1
76 Stepney Causeway.K 1
76 Stepney E. Sta....K 1
76 Stepney Green....J 1
76 Stepney Green Sta.H 1
76 Stepney High St...J 1
76 Stepney Way.....J 1
85 Sterling St.......D 6
78 Sterndale Rd.....B 2
79 Sternhold Av.....K 9
88 Sterry St.......C 2
78 Stevenage Rd.....E 2
73 Steventon Rd.....K 8
84 Steward St.......F 4
76 Stewart Rd......D 4
80 Stewart St.......B 4
78 Stewart's Gro.....F 5
78 Stewarts Rd.....E 9
73 Steyne Rd.......L 5
68 Stifford.........G 6
68 Stifford Rd.......G 4
77 Stile Hall Gdns....C 4
77 Stillingfleet Rd....D 8
80 Stillness Rd......H 2
76 Stirling Rd. E13...G 7
79 Stirling Rd. SW9..F 10
77 Stirling Rd. W3...B 5
84 Stock Ex........G 3
75 Stock Orchard Cres.
                   D 11
76 Stock St........G 6
79 Stockfield Rd....K 11
65 Stockley Rd......G 4
75 Stockmar Rd.....E 16
79 Stockwell........F 10
79 Stockwell Rd.....F 11
79 Stockwell Sta....E 10
79 Stockwell Pk. Cres.
                   E 11
79 Stockwell Pk. Rd..E 11
69 Stoke D'Abernon..E 4
75 Stoke Newington. C 13
75 Stoke Newington Ch.
                   C 13
75 Stoke Newington High
    St...........C 14
75 Stoke Newington Rd.
                   D 14
75 Stoke Newington Sta.
                   B 14

MAP
69 Stoke Rd.........G 5
80 Stondon Pk........H 1
72 Stone.............B 4
83 Stone Bldgs......G 10
66 Stone Gro........B 2
73 Stonebridge Pk...F 6
70 Stonecot Hill.....E 4
75 Stonefield St.....F 11
77 Stonehill Rd. SW14
               H 6
69 Stonehill Rd.
    Ottershaw......F 1
71 Stonehouse La. Orp.
              F 12
68 Stonehouse La. W.
    Thurrock......G 4
79 Stonehouse St....F 9
88 Stones End St.....D 1
84 Stoney La.........G 4
88 Stoney St.........B 2
72 Stony Cnr.........D 6
76 Stopford Rd. E13..F 7
87 Stopford Rd. SE17
              G 13
76 Store St. E15......E 5
82 Store St. WC1.....F 7
87 Storey's Gate......C 8
76 Stork Rd..........E 6
88 Storks Rd.........D 7
74 Stormont Rd. N6..A 7
78 Stormont Rd. SW11
              G 7
76 Stour Rd..........F 3
82 Stourcliffe St......G 2
80 Stowage, The.....D 3
77 Stowe Rd..........A 9
76 Stracey Rd.........D 7
79 Stradella Rd.......H 12
80 Strafford St........A 3
76 Strahan Rd.........G 2
68 Straight Rd.........B 3
80 Straightsmouth....D 4
83 Strand.............J 9
77 Strand on-the-Green
              D 4
83 Strand Th.........H 9
74 Stratford..........F 4
78 Stratford Gro......E 2
76 Stratford New Town
              D 5
82 Stratford Pl.......H 4
76 Stratford Rd. E6..G 6
85 Stratford Rd. W8..E 2
76 Stratford Sta......E 4
80 Strathaven Rd.....H 7
78 Strathblaine Rd...G 6
73 Strathcona Rd.....C 2
81 Strathearn Pl.....H 5
80 Stratheden Rd.....E 6
79 Strathleven Rd....G 10
88 Strathnairn St.....F 7
78 Strathville Rd.....K 4
86 Stratton St........B 5
70 Strawberry Vale...C 1
69 Strawberry Hill G.C.
              C 6
69 Strawberry Hill Sta.
              C 6
66 Streatfield Rd.....C 2
70 Streatham.........C 6
70 Streatham Common
    Nth............C 6
70 Streatham High Rd.
              C 6
79 Streatham Hill....K 10
79 Streatham Pl.....J 10
70 Streatham Rd.....D 5
70 Streatham Sta.....C 6
83 Streatham St......G 8
70 Streatham Vale...C 6
78 Streathbourne Rd..K 8
74 Streatley Rd.......F 3
70 Street, The........H 2
77 Stretton Rd.......K 2
80 Strickland St......E 3
76 Strode Rd. E7....D 7
73 Strode Rd. NW10..E 8
76 Strone Rd.........E 8
77 Stroud Cres.......L 8
75 Stroud Green Rd..B 11
78 Stroud Rd.........K 4
69 Stroude...........D 1
86 Strutton Ground..D 7
84 Strype St.........G 5
73 Stuart Av. NW9...B 8
77 Stuart Av. W5....A 4
79 Stuart Rd. SE15 G 16
78 Stuart Rd. SW19..K 4
81 Stuart Rd. W9....D 1
77 Stuart Rd. Rich...K 2
68 Stubbers La.......E 4

MAP
78 Studdridge St.....F 4
79 Studholme Rd....D 16
76 Studley Rd. E7...E 7
79 Studley Rd. SW4..E 10
76 Stukeley Rd........F 7
83 Stukeley St.......G 9
87 Sturgeon Rd.....G 13
73 Sturgess Av.......A 9
84 Stutfield St........H 7
79 Sudbourne Rd....G 10
77 Sudbrook La.......K 3
77 Sudbrook Pk.......K 3
78 Sudbrooke Rd....H 7
73 Sudbury..........E 2
73 Sudbury Av.......D 2
66 Sudbury Hill &
    Harrow Sta.....E 1
66 Sudbury Sta.......E 1
73 Sudbury Town Sta.E 1
83 Sudeley St........C 12
78 Sudlow Rd.........G 4
87 Sudrey St........C 13
84 Suffolk La.........J 2
84 Suffolk Rd. E8....A 7
77 Suffolk Rd. SW13.E 8
76 Suffolk St. E7.....D 6
87 Suffolk St. SW1...A 7
76 Sugar Ho. La......G 4
78 Sugden Rd........G 7
78 Sulgrave Rd.......B 1
79 Sulina Rd........J 10
78 Sulivan Rd........F 4
88 Sultan St..........J 1
74 Sumatra Rd.......E 4
70 Summer Rd........D 1
80 Summerfield St....J 6
78 Summerley St.....K 5
66 Summers La.......C 5
85 Sumner Pl.........F 5
79 Sumner Rd.......D 14
87 Sumner St........B 13
84 Sun St............F 3
73 Sunbeam Rd......H 6
69 Sunbury..........D 4
77 Sunbury Av.......G 6
80 Sunderland Rd....K 1
81 Sunderland Ter....G 2
73 Sundew Av........K 8
80 Sundorne Rd......C 7
71 Sundridge Hill Rd.
              H 12
71 Sundridge Pk. G.C.
              C 10
71 Sundridge Pk. Sta..D 9
72 Sundridge Rd......H 1
73 Sunleigh Rd.......F 3
80 Sunnymead Rd....B 9
73 Sunnymead Rd. NW9
              A 6
77 Sunnymead Rd. SW15
              H 9
76 Sunnyside Rd. E10 B 3
75 Sunnyside Rd. N19.B 9
77 Sunnyside Rd. W5.A 2
79 Sunray Av.......G 13
79 Sunset Rd........G 13
79 Sunwell St.......E 16
70 Surbiton..........E 2
70 Surbiton G.C......E 1
81 Surrendale Pl......E 2
78 Surrey La.........E 6
80 Surrey Rd.........G 1
87 Surrey Row......C 12
88 Surrey Sq.........F 4
83 Surrey St.........H 10
88 Surrey Ter.........F 4
81 Sussex Gdns......G 6
82 Sussex Pl. NW1...G 1
81 Sussex Pl. W2....H 5
79 Sussex Rd........G 12
81 Sussex Sq.........H 5
86 Sussex St.........G 5
75 Sussex Way......C 10
80 Sutcliffe Pk.......G 7
81 Sutherland Av.....E 2
78 Sutherland Gro...J 3
81 Sutherland Pl......G 1
76 Sutherland Rd.....G 2
88 Sutherland Sq.....G 1
86 Sutherland St.....G 5
88 Sutherland Wk....G 2
80 Sutlej Rd..........D 8
70 Sutton............F 4
72 Sutton at Hone....D 3
72 Sutton at Hone Rd.
              C 2
68 Sutton Av.........D 3
76 Sutton Ct. Rd. E13 H 8
77 Sutton Ct. Rd. W4.D 6
70 Sutton Com. Rd...E 4
77 Sutton La. W4....C 5

MAP
69 Sutton La. Houn..A 5
70 Sutton La. Sut....G 4
76 Sutton Rd.........H 6
82 Sutton Row.......G 7
70 Sutton Sta........F 4
75 Sutton St........K 16
74 Sutton Way.......J 1
78 Swaby Rd.........K 5
76 Swaffield Rd.......J 5
74 Swain's La........C 8
65 Swakeleys........E 4
82 Swallow St........J 6
80 Swallowfield Rd...C 7
88 Swan Mead.......E 4
79 Swan Rd.........A 16
88 Swan St..........D 2
86 Swan Wk.........H 2
78 Swanage Rd......H 5
84 Swanfield St......D 5
72 Swanley...........D 2
72 Swanley La........D 2
72 Swanley Vill. Rd..D 2
77 Swanscombe.....B 5
76 Swanwick Cl......J 7
76 Swaton Rd........H 3
88 Sweeney Cres.....D 5
76 Swete St..........G 7
74 Swinbrook Rd....J 3
77 Swinburne Rd....G 8
73 Swinderby Rd.....E 3
76 Swinnerton St.....E 1
83 Swinton St.........D 9
74 Swiss Cottage Sta..F 5
77 Swyncombe Av....C 1
76 Sybourn St........B 2
78 Sycamore Gdns...B 1
85 Sydner Rd........D 14
76 Sydney Pl.........F 5
76 Sydney Rd. E7....G 6
79 Sydney Rd. Rich..G 3
85 Sydney St.........G 6
77 Sydenham.........G 2
79 Sydenham Hill...K 15
71 Sydenham Hill Sta..C 7
79 Sydenham Pk....L 16
79 Sydenham Rise...K 16
71 Sydenham Rd......C 8
71 Sydenham Sta.....C 8
79 Sylvan Gro.......D 16
73 Sylvester Rd.......D 2
86 Sylvia Gdns........F 5
86 Symons St.........F 3
77 Syon Ho..........E 2
66 Syon La...........H 1
78 Syon Pk...........E 2
88 Tabard St.........D 3
84 Tabernacle St......E 3
75 Tabley Rd........D 10
78 Tabor Rd..........B 1
78 Tachbrook St......F 6
78 Tadema Rd.......D 5
78 Tadmor St........A 2
73 Tadworth Rd......C 8
78 Talacre Rd........E 8
76 Talbot Rd. E7....D 6
74 Talbot Rd. N6....A 7
81 Talbot Rd. W2....G 1
73 Talbot Rd. Wem..E 2
81 Talbot Sq.........H 5
88 Talbot Yd.........B 2
79 Talfourd Rd.......E 14
78 Talgarth Rd........C 2
78 Tallack Rd.........B 2
80 Tallis Gro.........D 7
83 Tallis St..........H 11
82 Talma Rd........G 11
76 Talwin St.........H 3
85 Tamworth St......H 1
77 Tanfield Av.......C 7
77 Tangier Rd.......G 5
78 Tangley Gro......H 8
68 Tank La..........G 4
88 Tanner St.........C 4
80 Tanner's Hill......E 2
81 Tantallon Rd......J 7
74 Tanza Rd.........D 7
80 Taplow St.........D 11
79 Tappesfield Rd....F 16
79 Tarbert Rd........G 14
76 Tarling Rd.........K 6
87 Tarver Rd.........G 13
74 Tasker Rd.........E 7
74 Tasman St........F 10
78 Tasso Rd.........D 8
87 Tate Gallery......F 2
65 Tatling End.......D 1
80 Tatnell Rd.........H 1
71 Tatsfield..........H 10
71 Tatsfield La.......H 10
70 Tattenham Cnr. Rd.
              H 3

MAP
70 Tattenham Cnr. Sta.
              H 3
70 Tattenham Way...H 4
88 Tatum St..........F 3
82 Taunton Pl........E 2
80 Taunton Rd.......H 6
74 Tavistock Cres.....J 3
73 Tavistock Pl.......E 8
76 Tavistock Rd. E15.E 6
74 Tavistock Rd. W11.J 3
83 Tavistock Sq.......E 8
83 Tavistock St......H 9
75 Tavistock Ter.....C 10
73 Taviton St.........E 7
78 Taybridge Rd......G 8
77 Taylor Av.........F 5
76 Taymount Rise...K 16
84 Teale St..........B 7
70 Teddington........C 1
86 Tedworth Sq......G 2
75 Teesdale St.......G 15
74 Teignmouth Rd....E 2
70 Telegraph Rd.....J 1
79 Telferscot Rd......J 9
79 Telford Av.........K 9
74 Telford Rd........J 2
73 Telford Way.......J 7
75 Templar Rd.......D 16
79 Templar St.......E 12
83 Temple, The......H 11
83 Temple Av........H 11
83 Temple Bar.......H 11
74 Temple Fortune La.
              A 4
83 Temple Gdns......H 11
83 Temple La.........H 11
76 Temple Mill La....D 3
83 Temple Pl........H 10
74 Temple Rd. Eps...G 2
70 Temple Rd. Eps...G 2
77 Temple Rd. Rich..F 4
77 Temple Sheen Rd.G 5
75 Temple St.........G 15
85 Templeton Pl......F 1
74 Templewood Av...C 4
65 Ten Tellow La.....G 6
79 Tench St..........A 15
79 Tenham Av........K 9
88 Tennis St.........C 2
76 Tennyson Av......A 7
74 Tennyson Rd. NW6
              F 3
75 Tent St..........H 15
86 Terminus Pl.......E 5
77 Terrace Gdns......H 3
76 Terrace Rd. E13...G 7
69 Terrace Rd. Walton
              E 5
78 Terrapin Rd.......K 8
76 Teviot St..........J 4
79 Tewkesbury Av...J 16
78 Thackeray Rd......F 8
85 Thackeray St......D 2
70 Thames Bank.....F 6
70 Thames Ditton....E 1
77 Thames Rd........D 5
80 Thames St. SE10..D 4
69 Thames St. Weybridge
              E 4
75 Thane Villas......C 11
83 Thanet St.........D 8
83 Thavies Inn......G 11
82 Thayer St.........G 4
83 Theatre Royal....H 9
87 Theed St.........B 11
76 Theobald Rd......A 2
66 Theobald St.......A 2
83 Theobald's Rd....F 10
79 Therapia Rd......H 16
80 Thermopylae Gate C 3
79 Thessaly Rd.......E 9
75 Theydon Rd.......B 16
76 Theydon St........A 2
76 Third Av. E13....G 7
77 Third Av. W3.....A 7
74 Third Av. W10...H 3
73 Third Av. Wem...B 2
73 Third Way........D 5
86 Thirleby Rd.......E 6
78 Thirsk Rd.........G 7
69 Thistlecroft......F 5
75 Thistlewaite Rd...C 16
87 Thomas Doyle St.D 12
88 Thomas More La..A 6
76 Thomas Rd........J 2
77 Thompson Av.....F 5
88 Thorburn Sq......F 6
84 Thoresby St.......C 1

MAP
79 Thornbury Rd....H 10
79 Thornby Rd......C 16
68 Thorndon G.C.....C 6
79 Thorne Rd........E 10
77 Thorne St.........F 7
87 Thorney Hedge Rd.C 5
65 Thorney La........F 2
87 Thornbury St......E 8
78 Thornfield Rd......A 1
80 Thornford Rd......H 4
81 Thorngate Rd.....E 1
76 Thorngrove Rd....F 7
83 Thornhaugh St....F 8
75 Thornhill Cres....F 11
76 Thornhill Rd. E10.C 3
75 Thornhill Rd. N1..F 11
75 Thornhill Sq......F 11
80 Thornsbeach Rd...K 4
79 Thornton Av. SW2
              K 10
77 Thornton Av. W4.C 7
70 Thornton Heath..D 6
82 Thornton Pl.......F 2
76 Thornton Rd. E11.B 5
79 Thornton Rd. SW12
              J 9
70 Thornton Rd. Cro.D 6
80 Thornwood Rd....H 5
79 Thorparch Rd.....E 9
69 Thorpe...........D 2
76 Thorpe Rd. E7....D 6
69 Thorpe Rd. Chertsey
              D 2
69 Thorpe Rd. Staines.C 2
73 Thorpebank Rd...L 8
75 Thorpedale Rd....B 10
76 Thorpewood Av...K 16
76 Thoydon Rd......G 1
87 Thrale St........B 14
84 Thrawl St.........G 5
84 Threadneedle St...H 3
76 Three Colt St......K 2
76 Three Colts La...K 16
82 Three Kings Yd...H 4
76 Three Oak La.....H 4
84 Three Oak La.....C 5
84 Throgmorton Av...G 3
84 Throgmorton St...G 3
88 Thrush St.........G 13
88 Thurland Rd......D 6
73 Thurlby Rd........E 3
78 Thurleigh Rd......H 7
85 Thurloe Pl........E 5
85 Thurloe Sq........E 5
85 Thurloe St........E 5
73 Thurlow Gdns....E 3
79 Thurlow Hill......K 12
76 Thurlow Pk. Rd..K 12
74 Thurlow Rd.......D 6
88 Thurlow St.......G 3
78 Thursley Gdns....K 2
80 Thurston Rd......F 3
84 Thurtle Rd........B 5
80 Ticehurst Rd......K 2
78 Tideswell Rd......G 2
76 Tidey St...........J 3
76 Tidworth Rd.......H 3
79 Tierney Rd......J 10
80 Tilbrook Rd.......G 8
72 Tilbury..........A 6
78 Tildesley Rd.......H 1
78 Tilehurst Rd.......J 6
78 Tilford Gdns......K 2
80 Tiller Rd..........B 3
76 Tilney St.........B 4
86 Tilney St.........B 4
79 Tindal St.........E 12
79 Tintern St.......G 10
77 Tinworth St.......F 9
88 Tisdall Pl.........F 3
81 Titchborne Row...H 6
82 Titchfield Rd......B 2
78 Titchwell Rd.......J 6
88 Tite St...........H 2
75 Tiverton Rd. N15.A 13
74 Tiverton Rd. NW10
              F 2
87 Tiverton St.......D 13
84 Tokenhouse Yd...G 3
73 Tokyngton Av....E 4
77 Toland Sq.........H 8
76 Tollet St..........H 1
75 Tollington Pk......B 11
75 Tollington Pl......B 10
75 Tollington Way...C 10
82 Tolmer's Sq.......D 6
65 Tolpits La.........A 4
70 Tolworth..........E 2
70 Tolworth Rise.....E 2
70 Tolworth Rd.......E 2

MAP
76 Tomlins Ter.......J 2
83 Tompion St.......D 12
67 Tomswood Hill...C 11
83 Tonbridge St......D 8
75 Tonsley Hill.......G 5
78 Tonsley Rd.........G 5
80 Tooke St..........A 3
78 Tooley St..........B 4
79 Tooting Bec Com..L 5
70 Tooting Bec Rd...C 5
78 Tooting Bec Sta...K 7
70 Tooting Graveney.C 5
70 Tooting High St...C 5
83 Topaz St.........E 10
85 Tor Gdns.........C 1
76 Torbay Rd.........F 3
78 Toronto St.........D 5
81 Torquay St........F 2
75 Torrens St........C 12
75 Torriano Av.......E 9
80 Torridon Rd.......J 5
73 Torrington Gdns..F 2
82 Torrington Pl......F 7
73 Torrington Rd.....F 2
83 Torrington Sq.....E 7
87 Tothill St.........D 7
76 Totnes Rd.........J 7
67 Tottenham.........C 7
82 Tottenham Ct. Rd..F 7
67 Tottenham Hale...C 8
67 Tottenham Hale Sta.
              C 8
66 Tottenham La.....D 6
75 Tottenham Rd....E 14
78 Tottenham Rd.....F 6
66 Totteridge........A 4
66 Totteridge &
    Whetstone Sta..B 5
66 Totteridge La.....B 4
76 Totty St..........G 1
87 Toulmin St.......C 13
78 Tournay Rd.......D 3
79 Tovey Gdns......C 8
84 Tower, The.......J 5
88 Tower Bri........B 5
84 Tower Bri. App...J 5
88 Tower Bri. Sta....B 5
76 Tower Hamlets Rd.D 6
84 Tower Hill........J 5
73 Tower Rd.........F 8
83 Tower St..........H 8
69 Town La..........B 3
79 Townley Rd. SE22
              H 14
71 Townley Rd. Bex.B 12
78 Townmead Rd.....F 5
73 Townsend La......A 6
88 Townsend St......F 3
81 Townshend Rd. NW8
              B 6
77 Townshend Rd. Rich.
              G 4
77 Townshend Ter...G 4
79 Towton Rd.......K 15
84 Toynbee St.......G 2
88 Trafalgar Av......G 5
80 Trafalgar Rd......C 5
87 Trafalgar Sq......A 8
88 Trafalgar St......G 2
78 Tranmere Rd......K 5
80 Tranquil Vale.....F 5
81 Transept St.......F 6
88 Tranton Rd........D 7
67 Traps Hill........A 11
70 Traps La..........D 3
86 Travellers' Club...B 7
74 Treadgold St......K 2
87 Treasury..........C 8
83 Treaty St.........B 9
85 Trebovir Rd.......F 1
76 Tredegar Rd.......E 2
76 Tredegar Sq.......H 2
75 Trederwen Rd....F 15
76 Tree Rd...........J 8
77 Treen Av.........F 7
75 Tregaron Av.....A 10
85 Tregunter Rd......G 3
79 Treherne Rd......E 11
76 Trehurst St........D 1
76 Trelawn Rd. E10..C 4
79 Trelawn Rd. SW2.H 11
76 Tremadoc Rd....G 10
73 Trenmar Gdns....E 8
79 Trent Rd.........H 10
78 Trentham St......J 4
76 Tredegar Rd.......E 2
79 Tresco Rd........G 16
75 Tresham Av......D 16
80 Tressillian Cres...F 3
80 Tressillian Rd.....F 3
87 Treveris St.......B 12

MAP

86 Trevor Pl.........D 1
86 Trevor Sq.........D 2
86 Trevor St.........C 2
79 Triangle Pl.......G 9
87 Trigon Rd.........J 10
80 Trilby Rd.........K 1
77 Tring Av..........A 4
88 Trinity Church Sq.D 2
78 Trinity Cres......K 7
79 Trinity Gdns.....G 11
79 Trinity Rise......J 12
78 Trinity Rd........J 6
84 Trinity Sq........J 4
76 Trinity St. E11...C 5
88 Trinity St. SE1...D 2
73 Trinity Way......K 7
82 Triton Sq.........E 5
79 Trossachs Rd.....G 14
88 Trothy Rd.........F 6
72 Trottiscliffe......G 6
80 Troughton Rd.....C 7
80 Troutbeck Rd.....E 1
79 Trouville St.......H 9
75 Truman's Rd.....D 14
76 Trumpington Rd...D 6
80 Trundley's Rd.....C 1
86 Tryon St..........F 2
71 Tubbenden La....E 11
73 Tubbs Rd.........G 8
73 Tudor Cl..........C 6
73 Tudor Ct. Nth....E 5
73 Tudor Ct. Sth....E 5
70 Tudor Dri.........E 4
73 Tudor Gdns. NW9.C 6
73 Tudor Gdns. W3..J 4
75 Tudor Gro........F 16
82 Tudor Pl..........G 7
76 Tudor Rd. E6.....G 8
75 Tudor Rd. E9....F 16
69 Tudor Rd.
    Twickenham....C 6
83 Tudor St..........H 11
77 Tudor Way.......A 4
75 Tufnell Pk. Rd....D 9
75 Tufnell Pk. Sta....D 9
87 Tufton St.........E 8
84 Tuilerie St........B 6
79 Tulse Hill.........H 11
79 Tulse Hill Sta....K 12
75 Tulsmere Rd.....K 13
78 Tunis Rd..........A 1
73 Tunley Rd. NW10.F 7
78 Tunley Rd. SW17..K 7
76 Tunmarsh La.....H 8
76 Tunnel App.......K 1
80 Tunnel Av........B 5
79 Tunstall Rd......G 11
86 Turf Club.........B 5
84 Turin St..........D 6
86 Turk's Row.......G 3
75 Turle Rd..........B 10
74 Turner Dri.........A 4
75 Turner St.........J 15
76 Turners Rd........J 2
79 Turney Rd........J 13
77 Turnham Green...C 6
77 Turnham Grn. Ter.C 7
80 Turnham Rd.....G 1
83 Turnmill St......F 12
67 Turnpike La......C 7
78 Turret Gro.......F 9
80 Tuskar St........C 5
79 Tustin St.........D 16
79 Tweed St.........D 9
76 Tweedrith Rd....G 7
69 Twickenham.....B 6
77 Twickenham Bri..G 2
70 Twickenham Pk...B 1
70 Twickenham Rd...C 1
76 Twickenham Rd. E11
              C 4
77 Twickenham Rd. Rich.
              G 2
69 Twickenham Rd.
    Twick..........C 5
78 Twilley St.........J 4
74 Twisden Rd.......D 8
73 Twybridge Way...F 6
73 Twyford Abbey Rd.
              G 4
73 Twyford Av.......K 4
73 Twyford Cres.....L 4
75 Twyford St.......F 10
76 Tyas Rd..........H 6
82 Tyburn Way......H 2
88 Tyers Gate.......C 4
87 Tyers St.........G 9
87 Tyers Ter........G 10
76 Tylney Rd........D 7
78 Tyneham Rd......F 8
79 Tyrrell Rd........G 15

80 Tyrwhitt Rd......F 3
79 Tyson Rd.........J 16
83 Tysoe St.........D 11
75 Tyssen St........E 14
75 Tytherton Rd.....C 9
76 Uamvar St........J 4
86 Udall St..........F 6
73 Uffington Rd......F 9
87 Ufford St........C 12
75 Ufton Rd.........F 13
77 Ullswater Rd......D 8
80 Ulundi Rd........D 5
79 Ulverscroft Rd....H 15
75 Umfreville St......A 12
80 Undercliff Rd......F 3
66 Underhill.........A 4
79 Underhill Rd......H 15
84 Underwood Rd....E 6
84 Underwood St....C 2
79 Union Gro........F 9
76 Union Rd. E17....A 2
79 Union Rd. SW4...F 9
73 Union Rd. Wem...E 3
84 Union Sq.........B 1
76 Union St. E15.....F 4
87 Union St. SE1....B 13
84 Union Wk.........C 4
82 University Coll....E 7
82 Univ. Coll. Hosp..E 7
83 Univ. of London..F 8
82 University St......E 6
81 Unwin Pl.........F 5
88 Unwin Rd.........H 6
81 Upbrook Mews...H 4
78 Upcern Rd.......E 5
79 Upcot St.........D 16
79 Upland Rd.......H 15
68 Upminster........D 4
68 Upminster Bri. Sta.
              D 4
68 Upminster G.C...D 4
68 Upminster Rd.....D 4
68 Upminster Rd.
    Rainham........F 3
67 Upney...........E 12
67 Upney La........E 12
78 Upper Addison Gdns.
              A 2
86 Upper Belgrave St..D 4
82 Upper Berkeley St..G 2
80 Upper Brockley Rd.
              F 2
82 Upper Brook St...J 3
77 Upper Butts......D 2
85 Upper Cheyne Row
              H 6
75 Upper Clapton....B 15
75 Upper Clapton Rd.
              C 16
67 Upper Edmonton..B 8
71 Upper Elmers End.E 8
82 Upper Grosvenor St.
              J 3
87 Upper Ground....A 11
69 Upper Halliford Rd.
              D 4
82 Upper Harley St...E 4
75 Upper Holloway...C 9
77 Upper Mall........D 2
87 Upper Marsh.....D 10
82 Upper Montagu St.
              F 2
76 Upper Nth. St....J 3
70 Upper Norwood...C 6
74 Upper Pk. Rd.....E 7
85 Upper Phillimore
    Gdns..........C 1
68 Upper Rainham
    Rd............D 2
77 Upper Richmond Rd.
    SW14..........G 6
78 Upper Richmond Rd.
    West SW15.....G 2
76 Upper Rd.........G 8
83 Upper St. Martin's La.
              H 8
71 Upper Selsdon Rd..F 7
83 Upper St.........B 12
69 Upper Sunbury Rd.
              D 5
71 Upper Sydenham..C 7
84 Upper Thames St..H 1
75 Upper Tollington Pk.
              B 11
78 Upper Tooting Pk..K 7
70 Upper Tooting Rd..C 7
79 Upper Tulse Hill..J 11
67 Upper Walthamstow
              C 9
71 Upper Warlingham
    Sta...........H 7

71 Upper Wickham La.
              A 12
82 Upper Wimpole St. F 4
83 Upper Woburn Pl..D 7
76 Upperton Rd......H 8
79 Upstall St........E 12
76 Upton............F 7
76 Upton Av........F 7
76 Upton La.........E 7
76 Upton Pk. Rd....F 7
76 Upton Pk. Sta....F 7
71 Upton Rd.........B 12
74 Upton St.........A 9
80 Upwood Rd......H 6
88 Urlwin St........H 1
78 Ursula St........E 6
76 Urswick Rd......D 16
78 Usk Rd..........G 5
76 Usk St..........G 1
80 Uvedale Rd......D 5
65 Uxbridge........E 3
73 Uxbridge Rd. W3..K 4
73 Uxbridge Rd. W5..K 2
77 Uxbridge Rd. W12.A 8
69 Uxbridge Rd. Feltham
              C 5
69 Uxbridge Rd. Ham C 6
66 Uxbridge Rd. Hanwell
              E 3
65 Uxbridge Rd. Hayes'
    End............F 4
65 Uxbridge Rd. Pinner
              C 5
65 Uxbridge Rd.
    Rickmansworth .B 2
65 Uxbridge Rd.S'hall F 5
85 Uxbridge St......B 1
74 Vale, The, NW11..B 3
77 Vale, The, W3....A 7
74 Vale of Health....C 5
81 Vale Cl..........D 3
76 Vale Rd. E7.......E 7
75 Vale Rd. N4......A 13
67 Valence Av.......D 12
87 Valentine Pl......C 12
76 Valentine Rd......E 1
76 Valetta Gro.......G 6
77 Valetta Rd........A 7
84 Vallance Rd.......E 7
80 Valley Gro........C 8
80 Vanbrugh Fields..D 6
80 Vanbrugh Hill....D 6
80 Vanbrugh Pk......D 6
80 Vanbrugh Pk. Rd..D 6
80 Vanbrugh Pk. Rd. W.
              D 6
77 Vanbrugh Rd......B 6
80 Vanbrugh Ter.....E 6
80 Vancouver Rd....K 2
78 Vanderbilt Rd.....J 5
86 Vandon St........D 6
84 Vandy St.........E 3
85 Vanguard St......J 1
85 Vanston Pl.......J 1
79 Varcoe Rd........C 16
75 Varden St........J 16
78 Vardens Rd........G 6
76 Varley Rd.........J 7
80 Varna Rd.........D 3
82 Varndell St........D 6
75 Vartry Rd........A 14
79 Vassall Rd.......E 11
88 Vauban St........E 5
83 Vaudeville Th.....J 9
76 Vaughan Rd......E 6
79 Vauxhall.........C 11
87 Vauxhall Bri......G 8
86 Vauxhall Bri. Rd..F 7
87 Vauxhall Gro......H 9
87 Vauxhall Pk......H 9
87 Vauxhall Sta......G 10
87 Vauxhall St......G 9
87 Vauxhall Wk......G 9
80 Veda Rd.........G 3
81 Venables St......F 5
79 Venetian Rd......F 13
79 Venn St..........G 9
80 Ventnor Rd......D 1
76 Venue St.........J 4
80 Vera Rd..........E 3
80 Verdant La.......J 5
77 Verdun Rd.......D 8
78 Vere St..........H 4
78 Vereker Rd.......C 3
79 Verney Rd.......C 15
79 Verney St........G 9
83 Vernon Rise......C 10
76 Vernon Rd. E3....G 2
76 Vernon Rd. E11...B 5
76 Vernon Rd. E15...F 5
77 Vernon Rd. SW14.F 6

78 Veronica Rd......K 8
83 Verulam St.......F 11
77 Vespan Rd........A 8
80 Vesta Rd.........F 1
80 Vestris Rd........K 1
76 Vestry Rd........E 14
84 Vestry St........C 3
78 Vicarage Cres.....E 6
76 Vicarage Farm Rd..H 5
85 Vicarage Gate....B 2
79 Vicarage Gro.....E 13
76 Vicarage La. E15..F 6
67 Vicarage La. Chigwell
              B 11
68 Vicarage La. South
    Weald..........B 4
76 Vicarage Rd. E10..B 3
76 Vicarage Rd. E15..F 6
73 Vicarage Rd. NW4.A 8
73 Vicarage Rd. NW10
              E 7
77 Vicarage Rd. SW14 G6
69 Vicarage Rd. Feltham
              C 4
80 Vicar's Hill.......G 3
74 Vicar's Rd........D 7
85 Vicat St..........J 4
75 Victor Rd........C 11
85 Victoria & Albert Mus.
              E 5
73 Victoria Av.......E 5
86 Victoria Coach Sta..E 4
76 Victoria Dock Rd..K 6
78 Victoria Dri.......J 2
87 Victoria Embankment
              A 9
87 Victoria Embankment
    Gdns. SW1....B 9
87 Victoria Embankment
    Gdns. WC2.....A 9
85 Victoria Gro......D 3
86 Victoria Hosp.....H 2
86 Victoria Pal. Th...E 5
76 Victoria Pk.......F 1
76 Victoria Pk. Rd...F 1
75 Victoria Pk. Sq...G 16
78 Victoria Rise......E 8
76 Victoria Rd. E11..D 5
76 Victoria Rd. N16 D 14
74 Victoria Rd. NW6 G 3
73 Victoria Rd. NW10 &
    W3..............H 7
75 Victoria Rd. W4..B 11
85 Victoria Rd. W8...D 3
68 Victoria Rd. Rom..D 2
65 Victoria Rd. Ruislip
              D 5
86 Victoria Sq.......D 5
86 Victoria Sta......E 5
76 Victoria St. E15...F 5
86 Victoria St. SW1..D 7
87 Victoria Tower Gdns.
              D 9
80 Victoria Way......C 7
75 Victorian Gro.....C 14
88 Victory Pl........E 2
88 Victory Sq.......J 3
74 View Rd.........A 7
78 Viewfield Rd......H 3
82 Vigo St..........J 6
79 Villa Rd.........F 11
80 Village, The......D 8
73 Village Way, NW10
              D 6
79 Village Way, SE21
              H 13
67 Village Way, Enfield
              A 7
65 Village Way, Harrow
              D 5
73 Villiers Rd........E 8
87 Villiers St........A 9
84 Vince St.........D 3
73 Vincent Gdns.....C 8
86 Vincent Sq.......E 7
76 Vincent St. E16...J 6
87 Vincent St. SW1..G 1
83 Vincent Ter......B 12
83 Vine Hill........E 11
88 Vine La..........B 4
77 Vine Rd.........F 8
84 Vine St..........H 5
65 Vine St. Sta......E 3
80 Viney Rd.........F 3
77 Vineyard, The....H 3
81 Violet Hill.......C 4
76 Violet Rd........H 3
87 Virgil St........D 10
84 Virginia Rd.......D 3
69 Virginia Water Sta..D 1
73 Vivian Av........E 5

76 Vivian Rd........G 1
79 Voltaire Rd.......F 9
80 Vulcan Rd.......F 2
73 Vyner Rd.........K 6
75 Vyner St........G 16
88 Wadding St......F 2
70 Waddington......H 6
70 Waddington St....E 5
70 Waddon..........E 6
76 Wade St.........K 3
75 Wadeson St......G 16
74 Wadham Gdns....F 6
67 Wadham Rd. E17. C 9
78 Wadham Rd. SW15
              G 3
76 Wadley Rd........A 5
76 Wadsworth Rd....G 2
76 Wager St.........H 2
76 Waghorn Rd......G 7
75 Waghorn St......F 15
80 Waite Davies Rd..J 6
88 Waite St.........H 5
76 Wakefield St......D 9
78 Wakehurst Rd....H 7
74 Wakeman Rd.....H 2
84 Walbrook.........H 2
87 Walcot Sq........E 11
76 Waldeck Rd. W4..D 4
73 Waldeck Rd. W13.K 1
70 Waldegrave Rd....C 1
78 Waldemar Av. SW6
              E 3
77 Waldemar Av. W13
              A 2
75 Walden St.........J 16
73 Waldo Rd.........H 8
80 Waldram Park Rd
              K 1
78 Waldron Rd.......K 5
76 Walerand Rd......F 4
73 Wales Farm Rd...J 6
75 Walford Rd.......D 14
76 Walham Green....E 4
85 Walham Gro......J 1
75 Wall St..........E 13
76 Wall Wood Rd....B 5
82 Wallace Collection G 3
75 Wallace Rd......E 13
75 Wallbutton Rd....F 1
74 Wallcote Av.......B 2
67 Wallend..........E 11
81 Waller Rd........E 1
85 Wallgrave Rd.....F 2
70 Wallington.......F 5
76 Wallwood St......J 2
74 Walm La.........E 2
76 Walmer Rd.......E 5
83 Walmsley St......D 12
80 Walnut Tree Rd...C 5
87 Walnut Tree Wk..E 11
80 Walpole Pk.......A 2
80 Walpole Rd.......E 2
86 Walpole St.......G 2
83 Walmsley St......D 12
76 Walter St.........H 1
75 Waltersville Rd....A 10
74 Walterton Rd.....H 3
67 Walthamstow Av..C 9
67 Walthamstow Central
    Sta...........C 9
67 Walthamstow Queen's
    Rd. Sta........D 9
69 Walton Bri........E 4
80 Walton Pl........D 2
69 Walton Rd........D 5
76 Walton Rd. E13...G 8
86 Walton St.........E 1
73 Walton Way......J 5
69 Walton upon Thames
              E 11
79 Walworth........C 12
88 Walworth Pl......G 2
88 Walworth Rd......F 1
78 Wandle Rd.......K 6
76 Wandsworth......G 5
87 Wandsworth Bri..D 3
78 Wandsworth Bri. Rd.
              F 4
78 Wandsworth Common
              H 5
78 Wandsworth Common,
    Nth. Side......G 5
78 Wandsworth Common
    Sta............J 7
78 Wandsworth High St.
              H 4
78 Wandsworth Pk...G 3
87 Wandsworth Rd..H 8
79 Wandsworth Rd. Sta.
              F 9

78 Wandsworth Town
    Sta...........G 5
76 Wanlip Rd........H 7
88 Wansey St........F 1
76 Wanstead........H 7
67 Wanstead G.C....D 10
76 Wanstead Pk. Sta..D 7
76 Wanstead Sta.....A 7
80 Wantage Rd......H 6
79 Wapping.........A 15
88 Wapping High St..B 7
75 Wapping La......K 16
79 Wapping Sta.....A 16
75 Wapping Wall....K 16
78 Warbeck Rd.......A 1
74 Warden Rd.......E 8
80 Wardo Av........E 2
82 Wardour St.......H 7
70 Warham Rd.......F 6
87 Warham St.......J 12
68 Warley Rd........C 4
76 Warley St.........H 1
71 Warlingham.......H 8
74 Warlock Rd.......H 3
75 Warlters Rd.......D 10
83 Warner Cin.......H 8
84 Warner Pl........C 6
79 Warner Rd.......E 12
83 Warner St.......E 11
78 Warple Rd........G 4
77 Warple Way......A 7
68 Warren La.
    W. Thurrock....G 5
69 Warren La. Woking
              H 2
76 Warren Rd. E10...C 4
76 Warren Rd. E11...A 7
73 Warren Rd. NW2.C 7
71 Warren Rd. Orp..F 11
82 Warren St........E 6
78 Warriner Gdns....E 7
81 Warrington Cres..E 3
79 Warrior Rd.......D 12
81 Warwick Av......E 3
81 Warwick Cres.....F 3
78 Warwick Gdns....B 3
75 Warwick Gro.....B 16
87 Warwick Ho. St...B 7
83 Warwick La. EC4.G 12
68 Warwick La. Rainham
              F 4
81 Warwick Pl.......F 3
76 Warwick Rd. E15..E 6
85 Warwick Rd. SW5.G 1
77 Warwick Rd. W5..A 3
86 Warwick Row......D 5
86 Warwick Sq......F 6
82 Warwick St.......J 6
86 Warwick Way......F 7
80 Warwickshire St...D 2
80 Wat Tyler Rd......E 4
76 Water La. E15....E 5
84 Water La. EC3....J 4
67 Water La. Ilf.....D 12
73 Water Rd.........G 4
76 Waterden Rd......E 5
78 Waterford Rd.....E 4
83 Watergate.......H 12
80 Watergate St.....D 3
70 Waterhouse La...H 4
87 Waterloo Bri......A 10
86 Waterloo Pl.......B 7
76 Waterloo Rd. E10.B 3
73 Waterloo Rd. NW2
              B 8
87 Waterloo Rd. SE1.B 10
87 Waterloo Sta.....C 10
74 Waterlow Pk......B 8
74 Waterlow Rd......A 9
80 Waters Rd........K 5
84 Waterson St......E 2
69 Watersplash Rd...D 9
65 Watford..........A 5
66 Watford By-Pass..A 1
65 Watford Heath....A 5
65 Watford (High St.) Sta.
              A 5
66 Watford Rd. Har..D 1
65 Watford Rd.
    Rickmansworth.A 3
65 Watford Sta......A 4
66 Watford Way......B 3
66 Watling Av.......C 3
84 Watling St. EC4...H 1
72 Watling St.
    Swanscombe...C 6
77 Watney Rd........F 5
75 Watney St.......K 16
80 Watson St........E 2
76 Watts Gro........J 3

MAP

71 Watts La.......D 11
75 Watts St.......L 16
75 Wattsfield Rd...C 16
71 Wash Pond Rd...H 9
77 Washington Rd...D 8
77 Wavendon Av...C 6
79 Waveney Av...G 16
73 Waverley Av....E 4
81 Waverley Pl....B 4
81 Waverley Wk....F 1
86 Waverton St....A 4
79 Wavertree Rd...K 10
73 Waxlow Rd......G 6
87 Waxwell Ter...D 10
78 Wayfoot St.....F 6
75 Wayland Av...E 15
78 Waynflete St....K 5
74 Wayside.......B 3
66 Wealdstone.....C 1
80 Wearside Rd....G 4
84 Weaver St......E 6
88 Weaver's La....B 4
88 Webb St. SE1....C 4
87 Webber Row....D 11
87 Webber St......C 12
78 Webbs Rd......H 7
77 Webster Gdns...A 3
74 Wedderburn Rd...E 6
75 Wedmore St.....C 10
80 Weigall Rd......G 7
82 Weighhouse St...H 4
79 Weir Hosp......J 9
79 Weir Rd........J 9
83 Weirs Pass......D 8
78 Weiss Rd.......F 2
82 Welbeck St......G 4
82 Welbeck Way....G 4
76 Welfare Rd......F 5
71 Well Hall La....B 10
72 Well Hill.......F 1
77 Well La........G 5
74 Well Rd........C 5
75 Well St........E 16
76 Well St. Common..F 1
74 Well Wk........H 8
82 Wellcome Institute.D 7
84 Wellclose Sq.....H 6
88 Weller St.......C 4
76 Wellesley Rd. E17.A 3
77 Wellesley Rd. W4..C 5
76 Wellesley St......J 1
84 Wellesley Ter....C 2
74 Wellgarth Rd.....B 4
71 Welling.......A 12
71 Welling Way....A 11
80 Wellington Gdns...C 8
81 Wellington Pl.....C 5
76 Wellington Rd. E10
          B 1
81 Wellington Rd. NW8
          C 5
77 Wellington Rd. W5.B 2
69 Wellington Rd. S..B 5
84 Wellington Row...D 6
86 Wellington Sq....G 2
83 Wellington St.....H 9
76 Wellington Way...H 4
80 Wellmeadow Rd...H 5
73 Wells Dri.......B 6
73 Wells Ho. Rd.....J 7
82 Wells Mews.....G 6
82 Wells Rise......B 2
82 Wells St........G 6
88 Wells Way......J 3
88 Welsford St......F 6
75 Welshpool St... F 15
77 Weltje Rd......C 8
73 Wembley.......D 3
73 Wembley Central Sta.
          E 3
73 Wembley Hill Rd..D 4
73 Wembley Hill Sta..D 4
73 Wembley Pk. Dri..C 4
73 Wembley Pk. Sta..C 4
73 Wembley Stadium.D 4
73 Wembley Way....E 5
80 Wemyss Rd.....F 6
77 Wendell Rd......B 7
76 Wendon St......F 2
73 Wenlock Rd......G 7
84 Wenlock Rd......C 1
84 Wenlock St......C 2
68 Wennington.....F 3
76 Wennington Rd...G 1
80 Wentland Rd....K 5
74 Wentworth Rd....A 3
84 Wentworth St....G 5
82 Werrington St....B 6
78 Werter Rd.......G 2
73 Wesley Av......G 6
76 Wesley Rd......B 4

MAP

74 Wessex Gdns.....B 3
75 Wessex St.......H 16
73 West Acton Sta...J 4
75 West Bank.......A 14
69 West Bedfont....B 3
78 West Bri. Rd.....E 6
69 West Byfleet....G 2
69 West Byfleet G.C..G 2
69 West Byfleet Sta...G 2
83 West Central St...G 8
73 West Cl.........B 4
71 West Common Rd..E 9
85 West Cromwell Rd.F 1
71 West Croydon Sta..E 7
65 West Drayton....G 3
65 West Drayton &
     Yewsley Sta....G 3
65 West Drayton Rd..F 4
79 West Dulwich Sta. K 13
73 West Ealing Sta...J 4
86 West Eaton Pl....E 3
73 West Ella Rd.....F 7
69 West End, Esher...F 6
69 West End, S'hall...F 5
74 West End La.....E 4
65 West End Rd.....E 5
70 West Ewell......F 3
80 West Ferry Rd....A 3
66 West Finchley Sta..B 5
67 West Green......C 7
67 West Green Rd....C 7
69 West Gro.......F 5
86 West Halkin St...D 3
77 West Hall St.....E 5
78 West Hill Rd.....H 3
76 West Ham.......F 6
76 West Ham La.....F 5
76 West Ham Pk.....F 6
74 West Hampstead Sta.
          E 4
66 West Harrow.....C 16
67 West Heath, SE2.H 12
74 West Heath Av....H 8
74 West Heath Cl....C 4
74 West Heath Rd. NW3
          C 5
74 West Heath Rd. NW11
          B 4
78 West Hill, SW18..H 2
72 West Hill, Dartford B 2
68 West Horndon Sta.D 6
76 West India Dock Rd.
          K 2
78 West Kensington Sta.
          C 3
71 West Kent G.C...G 11
79 West La........A 16
77 West Lodge Rd....A 4
85 West Mall.......A 1
66 West Middlesex G.C.
          F 1
69 West Molesey....D 12
71 West Norwood....C 7
70 West Norwood Sta.
          C 6
77 West Pk. Av......E 5
70 West Pk. Hosp....G 2
77 West Pk. Rd......E 4
76 West Rd. E15.....F 6
86 West Rd. SW3....G 3
79 West Rd. SW4...G 10
74 West Row.......H 2
65 West Ruislip Sta..D 4
83 West Smithfield...F 12
68 West Thurrock....G 5
87 West Sq........E 12
76 West St. E11......C 5
83 West St. WC2....H 8
70 West Sutton Sta...C 4
77 West Temple Sheen G 5
84 West Tenter St....H 5
71 West Wickham....E 9
71 West Wood La...B 11
74 Westbere Rd.....D 3
81 Westbourne Cres..H 4
80 Westbourne Dri...K 1
81 Westbourne Gdns..G 2
81 Westbourne Gro...H 1
81 Westbourne Pk. Rd.
     W2..........G 1
74 Westbourne Pk. Rd.
     W11..........J 3
74 Westbourne Pk. Sta.
          J 3
81 Westbourne Pk. Villas
          G 2
75 Westbourne St....E 11
81 Westbourne St....H 5
81 Westbourne Ter...E 2

MAP

81 Westbourne Ter...G 4
81 Westbourne Ter. Rd.
          F 3
67 Westbury Av.....C 7
76 Westbury Rd. E7..E 7
81 Westbury Rd. W2.F 2
81 Westbury Ter.....F 2
80 Westcombe Hill...D 7
80 Westcombe Pk. Rd.
          D 6
80 Westcombe Park
     Sta..........C 6
87 Westcott Rd.....H 12
80 Westdean Av.....K 7
76 Westdown Rd. E15.D 4
80 Westdown Rd. SE6.J 3
69 Westend La......F 5
76 Westerham Rd....A 3
74 Western Av. NW11 A 2
73 Western Av. W5...H 2
66 Western Av. Bushey
          A 1
65 Western Av. Uxbridge
          E 4
73 Western Gdns.....K 4
85 Western Hosp.....E 2
76 Western Rd. E13..G 7
73 Western Rd. W5...K 3
70 Western Rd. Mitch.
          D 5
65 Western Rd. Southall
          G 5
73 Westfields Rd.....J 5
75 Westgate St......F 16
85 Westgate Ter.....G 3
80 Westgrove La.....E 4
71 Westhall Rd......H 7
71 Westhorne Av. SE9
          B 10
80 Westhorne Av. SE12
          H 7
79 Westlake Rd......C 16
84 Westland Pl......D 2
78 Westleigh Av.....H 1
77 Westmead.......H 8
70 Westmead Rd....E 5
79 Westminster......A 9
87 Westminster Abbey D 8
87 Westminster Bri...C 9
87 Westminster Bri. Rd.
          D 11
86 Westminster
     Cathedral......E 6
87 Westminster Hall..D 8
87 Westminster Hosp. E 8
86 Westminster Th....D 5
86 Westmoreland Pl...G 5
77 Westmoreland Rd.
     SW13.........E 8
88 Westmoreland Rd.
     SE 17.........H 2
71 Westmoreland Rd.
     Brom.........D 9
82 Westmoreland St...F 4
86 Westmoreland Ter.
          G 5
70 Weston Green....E 1
69 Weston Green Rd.
          E 6
88 Weston Pl.......C 3
83 Weston Rise.....C 10
88 Weston St.......C 3
77 Westons Ms......B 5
78 Westover Rd.....H 5
72 Westport St......J 1
77 Westville Rd.....B 8
81 Westway.......F 3
71 Westwood.......C 4
71 Westwood Hill...C 7
79 Westwood Pk....J 16
77 Westwood Rd.....F 7
79 Wetherby Gdns...F 3
85 Wetherby Pl......F 4
85 Wetherden St....A 2
76 Wetherell Rd.....F 1
78 Wexford Rd......J 7
69 Weybridge.......E 4
69 Weybridge Rd....E 3
69 Weybridge Sta....F 3
80 Weyman Rd......E 8
77 Weymouth Av....B 2
82 Weymouth Mews..F 5
82 Weymouth St.....F 4
84 Weymouth Ter....B 5
68 Whalebone La....C 1
68 Whalebone La. Sth.
          D 1
83 Wharf Rd. N1....B 8
83 Wharf Rd. N1....C 13
83 Wharfdale Rd.....H 5
83 Wharton St......D 10

MAP

79 Whateley Rd.....H 14
80 Whatman Rd.....J 1
75 Wheelwright St...E 11
84 Wheler St.......E 5
66 Whetstone.......B 5
83 Whetstone Pk....G 15
80 Whetstone Rd....E 8
83 Whidborne St....D 8
76 Whipps Cross Hosp.
          A 5
76 Whipps Cross Rd..A 6
83 Whiskin St......D 11
84 Whiston Rd......B 6
80 Whitbread Rd....G 2
80 Whitburn Rd.....G 4
73 Whitby Av.......G 5
84 Whitby St.......E 5
76 Whitchurch La....C 2
83 Whitcomb St.....J 7
84 White Church La..G 6
74 White City Rd....K 1
74 White City Stadium
          K 1
74 White City Sta....L 1
83 White Conduit St.
          C 7
77 White Hart La. N17
          C 7
67 White Hart La. SW13
          F 7
67 White Hart La. Sta.
          C 7
88 White Hart Yd....B 2
65 White Hill.......B 4
72 White Hill La....F 6
71 White Horse Hill.C 10
76 White Horse La....J 1
76 White Horse Rd...J 1
86 White Horse St....B 5
84 White Kennett St..G 4
83 White Lion St....C 11
75 Whitechapel.....J 15
84 Whitechapel High St.
          G 5
84 Whitechapel Rd...G 6
75 Whitechapel Sta..J 16
84 Whitecross St....F 2
74 Whitefield Av.....B 1
71 Whitefoot La.....C 9
80 Whitefoot Ter....L 5
87 Whitefriars St.....H 11
87 Whitehall.......B 8
87 Whitehall Ct......B 8
87 Whitehall Gdns. SW1
          B 8
77 Whitehall Gdns. W3
          A 4
75 Whitehall Pk......B 9
87 Whitehall Pl......B 8
67 Whitehall Rd.....D 7
87 Whitehall Th......B 8
86 Whiteheads Gro...F 2
71 Whitehorse Rd....D 7
69 Whiteley Village..F 4
86 White's Club......B 6
84 White's Grounds...C 4
84 White's Row......F 5
77 Whitestile Rd.....C 2
82 Whitfield Pl......E 6
82 Whitfield St......F 6
87 Whitgift St......F 9
74 Whitmore Gdns...G 1
84 Whitmore Rd.....A 3
76 Whitney Rd......A 3
86 Whittaker St.....F 3
87 Whittlesey St.....B 11
69 Whitton........B 6
73 Whitton Av......E 1
69 Whitton Rd......B 6
79 Whorlton Rd.....F 15
71 Whyteleafe......H 7
71 Whyteleafe Rd....H 7
71 Whyteleafe Sth. Sta.
          H 7
76 Whyteville Rd.....E 7
76 Wick La.........F 2
67 Wickham La.....H 12
80 Wickham Rd. SE4.F 2
71 Wickham Rd. Bec..D 8
71 Wickham Rd. Cro..B 8
87 Wickham St......G 10
71 Wickham Way....D 9
83 Wicklow St......C 9
75 Widdenham Rd...D 11
84 Widegate St......F 4
81 Widley Rd.......D 1
71 Widmore Rd. D 10
73 Wigginton Av....E 5
67 Wightman Rd....C 7
82 Wigmore Hall....G 4
82 Wigmore Pl......G 5

MAP

82 Wigmore St.......G 4
76 Wigston Rd.......H 7
75 Wilberforce Rd...C 12
86 Wilbraham Pl.....E 3
67 Wilbury Way.....B 7
79 Wilcox Rd........D 10
83 Wild Ct..........G 9
83 Wild St..........H 9
74 Wild Hatch......A 4
80 Wildfell Rd.......J 3
88 Wild's Rents.....D 3
74 Wildwood Rd.....A 5
86 Wilfred St.......D 6
84 Wilkes St.......F 5
74 Wilkin St.......E 8
79 Wilkinson St.....E 10
77 Willcott Rd......A 5
71 Willersley Av....B 11
74 Willes Rd.......E 8
73 Willesden.......E 8
74 Willesden Green..E 1
73 Willesden Junc. Sta.
          G 8
74 Willesden La.....F 3
83 William IV St.....J 8
86 William Mews....C 3
82 William Rd......D 6
76 William St. E10...A 4
86 William St. SW1...C 3
77 Williams La......F 5
79 Willington Rd....F 10
88 Willis St.........J 4
67 Willoughby La....B 8
71 Willow Gro.
   Chislehurst....C 10
86 Willow Pl.......E 6
74 Willow Rd. NW3..D 6
77 Willow Rd. W5...B 3
88 Willow St.......D 3
73 Willow Vale.....L 8
88 Willow Wk......E 5
65 Willowbank......E 3
75 Willowbridge Rd..E 12
88 Willowbrook Rd...J 5
84 Wilmer Gdns....B 4
70 Wilmerhatch La...H 2
84 Wilmington Av...D 6
83 Wilmington Sq...D 11
76 Wilmot Rd.......C 3
75 Wilmot St.......H 16
78 Wilna Rd........J 5
74 Wilsham St......K 2
79 Wilson Gro......A 15
86 Wilson Rd.......E 13
84 Wilson St.......F 3
86 Wilton Cres.....D 3
86 Wilton Mews....D 4
86 Wilton Pl.......C 3
86 Wilton Rd.......E 6
86 Wilton Row......C 3
84 Wilton Sq........A 2
75 Wilton St.......F 13
86 Wilton Ter.......D 3
75 Wilton Way.....E 15
79 Wiltshire Rd.....F 11
84 Wiltshire Row....A 3
70 Wimbledon......C 4
70 Wimbledon Chase Sta.
          C 3
70 Wimbledon Common
          C 3
70 Wimbledon Hill Rd.
          C 4
70 Wimbledon Pk....C 4
70 Wimbledon Pk. G.C.
          C 4
78 Wimbledon Pk. Rd.
          K 3
78 Wimbledon Pk. Side
          K 2
70 Wimbledon Sta...C 4
84 Wimbolt St......C 6
82 Wimborne Gdns...J 1
84 Wimbourne St....B 2
78 Wincanton Rd....J 3
76 Winchelsea Rd. E7.D 6
73 Winchelsea Rd. NW10
          G 6
74 Winchester Rd. NW3
          F 6
74 Winchester Rd. NW6
          F 3
86 Winchester St. SW1
          G 5
77 Winchester St. W3.A 6
88 Winchester Wk....B 2
88 Winchmore Hill..A 7
87 Wincott St.......F 11

MAP

77 Windermere Rd...B 2
78 Winders Rd......F 6
77 Windham Rd.....F 4
78 Windmill Dri.....H 8
76 Windmill La. E15..E 5
66 Windmill La. Brent.
          G 1
78 Windmill Rd. SW18
          H 6
78 Windmill Rd. SW19
          K 1
77 Windmill Rd. W5..B 2
77 Windmill Rd. Brent.
          D 2
82 Windmill St......F 7
82 Windmill Th......H 7
87 Windmill Wk.....C 11
76 Windsor Rd. E7...E 7
76 Windsor Rd. E10..C 3
76 Windsor Rd. N7...C 10
73 Windsor Rd. NW2.E 9
73 Windsor Rd. W5..K 3
77 Windsor Rd. Rich..F 4
84 Windsor Ter......C 2
79 Windsor Wk......F 13
75 Windus Rd......B 14
78 Winfrith Rd......J 5
77 Wingate Rd......B 8
76 Wingfield Rd.....D 5
76 Wingfield St. E15..D 5
79 Wingfield St. SE15
          F 15
79 Wingford Rd......H 10
68 Wingletye La.....D 4
70 Winkworth Rd....G 4
80 Winn Rd........J 7
74 Winnington Rd...A 5
73 Winscombe Cres...B 3
80 Winsford Rd......K 2
78 Winsham Gro....H 7
81 Winsland Mews...G 5
81 Winsland St......G 5
82 Winsley St.......G 6
75 Winston Rd......D 13
82 Winterbrook Rd..H 13
69 Wisley.........G 3
69 Wisley Common..H 3
69 Wisley La.......G 3
80 Wisteria Rd......G 4
75 Witherington Rd..D 11
79 Wivenhoe Rd....F 15
78 Wix's La........G 8
69 Woburn Hill......E 3
83 Woburn Pl......E 8
83 Woburn Sq......E 8
69 Woking.........H 1
71 Woldingham Rd...H 8
78 Wolseley Av......K 4
77 Wolseley Gdns...D 5
83 Wolseley St......C 6
75 Wolsey Rd......E 13
65 Wolsey Way......B 4
75 Womersley Rd...A 10
78 Wontner Rd......K 7
66 Wood End, Gnfd..E 1
65 Wood End, Hayes..F 4
67 Wood Green......C 7
66 Wood Green Sta...C 6
73 Wood Hayes Rd...E 6
73 Wood La. NW9....B 6
74 Wood La. W12....K 1
68 Wood La. Dag.....E 3
67 Wood La. Ilf.....E 12
66 Wood La. Stan....B 2
80 Wood Rd........G 1
67 Wood St. E17.....C 9
84 Wood St. EC2....G 2
66 Wood St. Barnet...A 4
67 Wood St. Sta.....C 9
79 Wood Vale......J 15
75 Woodberry Down B 13
75 Woodberry Gro...A 12
77 Woodborough Rd..G 9
83 Woodbridge St....E 12
81 Woodchester Sq...F 2
74 Woodchurch Rd...F 4
79 Woodcombe Cres. J 16
70 Woodcote Gro. Rd.
          G 6
70 Woodcote La......G 6
70 Woodcote Pk. G.C.G5
70 Woodcote Pk. G.C.
   (R.A.C.)......H 2
76 Woodcote Rd. E11.A 6
70 Woodcote Rd. Sutton
          F 5
79 Woodfarrs.......G 13
86 Woodfall St......G 2
79 Woodfield Av. SW16
          L 9

MAP

73 Woodfield Av. W5.H 2
73 Woodfield Av. Wem. D 2
73 Woodfield Cres....H 2
70 Woodfield La.....H 2
73 Woodfield Pk.....B 7
74 Woodfield Rd. W9. J 3
67 Woodford........C 10
67 Woodford Av....C 10
67 Woodford Bri....B 10
67 Woodford Green.B 10
67 Woodford New Rd.C 9
76 Woodford Rd....D 7
67 Woodford Wells..B 10
69 Woodham........G 2
69 Woodham La.....G 2
80 Woodham Rd....L 4
76 Woodhouse Rd...C 6
73 Woodhurst Rd....K 6
75 Woodland St.....E 14
72 Woodlands.......G 3
80 Woodlands, The...J 5
76 Woodlands Av...B 7
69 Woodlands La....H 5
80 Woodlands Pk. Rd. D 5
77 Woodlands Rd....F 7
80 Woodlands St.....J 5
78 Woodlawn Rd....E 2
70 Woodmansterne...G 5
70 Woodmansterne La. G 4
70 Woodmansterne Rd. F 5

MAP

80 Woodpecker Rd...D 1
79 Woodquest Av...H 12
65 Woodridings......C 6
76 Woodriffe Rd......A 5
82 Woods Mews.....H 3
79 Woods Rd.......E 16
84 Woodseer St.......F 6
71 Woodside........E 7
66 Woodside Av. N6.C 5
73 Woodside Av. Wem. F 3
73 Woodside Ct......F 3
73 Woodside End....F 3
66 Woodside Park Sta. B 5
65 Woodsland G.C....F 2
74 Woodsome Rd....C 8
78 Woodspring Rd...K 3
74 Woodstock Av....A 3
70 Woodstock La.....E 1
76 Woodstock Rd. E7. F 8
75 Woodstock Rd. N4
74 Woodstock Rd. NW11 B 3
77 Woodstock Rd. W4 B 7
73 Woodstock Rd. Wem. F 4
82 Woodstock St.....H 5
76 Woodstock Ter....K 3
69 Woodthorpe Rd....C 3
73 Woodville Gdns...J 3
76 Woodville Rd. E11 B 6

MAP

75 Woodville Rd. N16 D 14
74 Woodville Rd. NW11 A 2
77 Woodville Rd. Rich. K 2
67 Woodward Rd....E 12
79 Woodwarde Rd...H 14
80 Woodyates Rd. SE12 H 6
80 Woodyates Rd. SE12 J 7
80 Woolacombe Rd...E 7
88 Wooler St........G 3
80 Woolstone Rd....K 2
67 Woolwich.......G 11
67 Woolwich Ch. St. G 10
80 Woolwich Rd. SE10 C 6
68 Woolwich Rd. W. Heath........G 1
67 Woolwich Arsenal Sta. G 11
67 Woolwich Dockyard Sta............G 11
87 Wootton St.....B 11
70 Worcester Pk.....E 3
75 Wordsworth Rd..D 14
78 Worfield St......E 6
87 Worgan St.......G 9
87 Worlingham Rd...G 15
73 Wormholt Pk....K 8
73 Wormholt Rd....K 8
84 Wormwood St....G 4

MAP

73 Wormwood Scrubs.J 8
74 Wornington Rd....J 3
81 Woronzow Rd.....B 6
70 Worple Rd. SW19.D 3
69 Worple Rd. Staines.D 2
77 Worple Way......G 3
84 Worship St.......E 3
76 Worsley Rd. E11..D 5
74 Worsley Rd. NW3 D 6
79 Worsopp Dri.....G 9
74 Wotton Rd. NW2..C 1
76 Wragby Rd.......C 5
75 Wray Cres.......B 10
69 Wraysbury.......B 1
74 Wren Av.........D 1
83 Wren St........E 10
74 Wrentham Av.....G 2
76 Wrexham Rd......G 3
80 Wricklemarsh Rd..E 8
88 Wright's Bldgs....E 4
85 Wright's La.......D 2
76 Wrights Rd......G 2
72 Wrotham.........H 5
72 Wrotham Heath..H 6
72 Wrotham Heath G.C. H 6
75 Wrotham Rd. NW1 F 9
72 Wrotham Rd. Northfleet......D 6
73 Wrottesley Rd....G 6
78 Wroughton Rd...H 7
70 Wrythe, The......E 5
70 Wrythe La.......E 4

MAP

73 Wulfstan St......J 7
79 Wyatt Pk. Rd....K 10
76 Wyatt Rd. E7.....E 7
75 Wyatt Rd. N5....C 12
83 Wyclif St........D 12
76 Wycliffe Rd. E15..D 4
78 Wye St.........F 8
78 Wyfold Rd.......E 3
66 Wyke Green G.C..G 1
76 Wyke Rd.........F 3
73 Wyld Way........E 5
80 Wyleu St.........H 1
81 Wymering Rd....D 2
80 Wyndcliff Rd.....D 7
82 Wyndham Mews...F 2
82 Wyndham Pl.....F 2
79 Wyndham Rd.....E 12
82 Wyndham St......F 2
83 Wyndham's Th....J 8
80 Wynell Rd.......K 1
83 Wynford Rd......B 10
85 Wynnstay Gardens D 1
78 Wynter St........G 5
83 Wynyatt St......D 12
82 Wythburn Pl.....G 8
87 Wyvil Rd........J 2
87 Wyvil St.........J 9
76 Wyvis St.........J 4
88 Yalding Rd.......E 6
76 Yattan St........J 4
75 Yeate St.........F 13
74 Yeatman Rd.....A 7

MAP

78 Yeldham Rd......C 2
76 Yeo St...........J 3
85 Yeoman's Row....E 6
69 Yeoveney Sta.....B 2
73 Yewfield Rd......E 7
73 Yewtree Rd......K 8
75 Yoakley Rd......C 14
75 Yonge Pk........C 11
77 York Av.........G 6
80 York Bldgs.......J 9
82 York Bri.........E 3
82 York Gate.......E 3
79 York Gro........E 16
79 York Hill.......K 12
85 York Ho. Pl......C 2
74 York Rise........C 8
76 York Rd. E7......E 6
76 York Rd. E10.....C 4
87 York Rd. SE1...C 10
78 York Rd. SW11...G 5
73 York Rd. W3.....J 6
77 York Rd. Brent....C 2
84 York Row.......B 4
82 York St.........F 2
82 York Ter.........E 3
83 York Way.......B 9
84 Yorkton St.......B 6
85 Young St........C 8
78 Yukon Rd........J 2
65 Zealand Rd......G 1
78 Zennor Rd.......J 8
76 Zetland Rd.......J 4
82 Zoological Gdns...B 3

PRINTED IN GREAT BRITAIN BY GEORGE PHILIP AND SON LIMITED, LONDON